the ultimate
book of
gardening

the ultimate book of gardening

ANTONY ATHA

JANE COURTIER

MARGARET CROWTHER
& SUE HOOK

DAVID SQUIRE

p

This is a Parragon Publishing Book
This edition published in 2003

Parragon Publishing
Queen Street House
4 Queen Street
Bath BA1 1HE, UK

Created and produced for Parragon Publishing by
The Bridgewater Book Company Ltd.

Illustrations Vanessa Luff, Barry Robson, Anne Winterbotham
Line artwork Coral Mula
Photography and Picture Research Liz Eddison

ISBN: 0-75259-097-9

Printed in China

NOTE
For growing and harvesting, calendar information applies
only to the Northern Hemisphere (US zones 5–9).

contents

container gardening

the small garden

gardening through the year

garden design

introduction

Gardening is a life-long passion and with this comprehensive and abundantly illustrated book by your side you will need no other advice about planning and developing a brand new garden, revitalizing an established one, or adding special features to enhance your garden and give it a distinctive and individualistic nature. This detailed and imaginative book also gives thoroughly practical advice about the gardening year, such as when to sow seeds, buy and put in plants, prune shrubs, and trees and maintain lawns, as well as other vital information gardeners need to have at their finger tips.

Nowadays, few houses have large gardens and therefore part of this book seeks to show both novice and experienced gardeners how to make the best use of a restricted area. Problems created by small gardens include those closely encircled by other houses and with little natural privacy. Also, awkwardly shaped gardens, perhaps narrow, short or with an irregular outline, create design problems, as well as areas that are dark or buffeted by wind. Additionally, in areas around newly constructed houses the soil may be an unenviable muddle of builders' debris, much of which needs to be sorted and removed. Predominantly light and sandy or sticky and wet soils cause difficulties. Clay soil— with its nature of sticking to boots and remaining wet and greasy in winter and, conversely, becoming bone-dry and cracked in summer— can be improved over several years by the installation of drains and mixing in bulky, well decomposed compost. These problems may appear to conspire against the creation of an attractive garden as an outdoor living area for the whole family, but they need not be insurmountable drawbacks.

Privacy can be quickly and easily created by constructing free-standing trellises, perhaps 90cm/3ft from a boundary to insure that climbing plants do not eventually trespass on a neighbor's property; while rose or

◄ *A restful area in a seashore garden is a pleasant contrast to the sand and pebbles beyond the fence.*

laburnum arches, when straddling a wide path, form an eye-catching way both to block off a line of vision and to produce an attractive and unique feature. Summerhouses and gazebos also play a role in creating a private garden. Decorative boundaries, perhaps constructed of screen-block walling, wattle fencing panels for cottage gardens, and more formal close-boarded types for modern sites can also be used to create privacy.

Getting the soil right

In a small area the nature of the soil inherited with the garden is not such a problem as in a large plot. Raised beds filled with specially prepared soil eliminate problems with extremely acid or alkaline soils, while boggy gardens also benefit from these raised areas. In a big garden improving a large area of soil requires systematic treatment over many years. However, where the soil is constantly wet the installation of land drains soon produces a better tempered garden.

The styles of gardening, whether formal or with a rustic and informal nature, are many and imaginative and provide a wide range of opportunities to please all gardeners and families. Apart from strictly formal gardens, with plants in attractive and regimented designs, and cottage gardens which are steeped in the traditions of earlier years when plants of many differing

▲ *Rhododendrons are among the plants that are particular as to soil pH. They should be planted in acid soil in order to thrive.*

types grew together in the same border, this stunningly illustrated book reveals the secrets of creating meadow and shade gardens, as well as scented, night, and Zen gardens which engender an aura of tranquillity and peace.

Plants and colors for all seasons

Color is the main inspiration for most gardeners and to help in the selection of plants with a particular color chapters are devoted to color-themed borders such as pink-and-red, blue-and-purple, yellow-and-gold, and white-and-silver. Additionally, there are mixed flower color borders, as well as those with variegated foliage.

Seasonal color interests some gardeners and, apart from color-themed designs, plants for creating spring, summer, fall, and winter are described. Trees with attractive bark and colored stems are included as, throughout the year, they continually brighten gardens.

Container gardening

Gardening in containers on patios, in courtyards, and on terraces is ideal in small gardens and on hard-surfaced areas in larger gardens. Gardening in this way is carefully explained within these pages, together with copious illustrations.

Many gardeners specialize in container gardening and have refined it to an art where plants bring color and scent during summer, those with an "architectural" shape and strong impact provide focal points, and spring-flowering bulbs and other plants introduce vitality after the dull winter months. Roof-top gardens are a facet of container gardening and, in this world of diminishing space, enable plants to be grown in places not earlier conceived to be suitable.

Apart from being decorative, gardens are often sources of food, from vegetables and soft fruits such as lettuce, strawberries, and raspberries to tree fruits like apples and pears. Many of these can be successfully grown in a small garden, especially if suitable varieties are selected. Techniques such as growing strawberries in barrels and tomatoes

▲ *Tranquillity combined with the sight and sound of moving water, provides a captivating garden feature.*

and lettuces in growing-bags make the production of food possible in any garden.

Culinary herbs can also be grown in containers on a patio, as well as in borders specially devoted to them. And for extra interest try growing herbs in a cartwheel or chessboard design, or in windowboxes, planters, and growing-bags.

Tranquil yet exciting water gardens

Water is introduced into many gardens, where it creates a restful ambience yet one that is continually active through the repetitious nature of water splashing on a pond's surface or running over a waterfall. Some ponds are constructed on patios or terraces, thereby enabling chairs and tables to be positioned close to them. The water's surface can be level with the surrounding paving, or the edges of the pond raised 30–45cm/1–1½ft so that the fish and plants can be more easily seen.

Alternatively, water gardens are often integrated with rock gardens, with a series of waterfalls throughout the feature. Wildlife ponds are ideal for attracting native insects and animals into a garden, while bog gardens at the edges of informal ponds enable moisture-loving plants to be grown.

There is, of course, the danger of young children falling into the water, but miniponds in large, wooden tubs on a patio or terrace reduce this risk.

Also, pebble ponds are generally considered safe for toddlers.

Changing patterns

Within the life of every garden there arrives a time to change its nature, perhaps replacing earlier play areas for children with a bed of scented flowers, an informal pond, or a rock garden. Many ideas for changing gardens are featured in this comprehensive book, together with inspirational plans and illustrations on their adoption and construction. Where families are still young and the garden is new, there are suggestions for creating children's activity gardens.

Gardening is a year-through pastime and there are tasks and planning to be pursued at all times. Winter, of course, is a season more for planning than doing, but it is a time for clearing up and, especially, for digging the soil in preparation for the following year. Vegetable plots, annual beds, and herbaceous borders that are to be planted in late spring or early summer all benefit from having their soil dug in fall or early winter. This enables wind, frost, snow, and ice to break the surface soil into a fine tilth by the time planting or seed sowing arrives. It also helps to prevent the growth of weeds and to eliminate some soil pests. This is just one element of gardening that is described in this comprehensive account of lawn care, growing

ornamental plants, producing fruit and vegetables, and looking after plants in a greenhouse. The seasons are conveniently separated into spring, summer, fall, and winter, with each further divided into early, mid- and late parts. This enables gardeners wherever they may be—in the warmer climates or cooler states—to judge when the time is right to use the invaluable instructions in this detailed book.

Choosing the right plants

As well as the features described in this all-color book, suitable plants are described and recommended for planting in them. These plants range from annuals and herbaceous perennials to shrubs, trees, climbers, rock garden plants, bulbs, corms, and tubers, and those suitable for planting in a water garden. Their heights and spreads are indicated, as well as the soil and conditions they require. Each of the four parts contain comprehensive plant directories.

The inevitable presence of pests and diseases is recognized and garden-friendly ways to control them are suggested, as well as environmentally-friendly methods to

▲ *Floriferous herbaceous borders, with their relaxed and informal nature, have been a traditional part of English gardens.*

dispose of unwanted garden chemicals. And to guide you through garden terminology there is a glossary with terms ranging from "acid" and "alkaline" to "wildlife pond" and "windbreak."

With this ultimate gardening book by your elbow, gardening becomes a friendly and familiar hobby for the entire family, and one that will enthral you throughout each year and for decades into the future.

container
gardening

containers in
the garden

Containers are used in different ways in different gardens. In a traditional garden, containers can be filled with special plants. In a small patio garden all the gardening has to be done in containers. Plants have to be bought, planted, fed, and watered through the year. This book shows you how.

the importance of planning

The first thing you have to do when planning a garden is to measure the available space accurately. This is particularly important when planning a small patio garden, because the smaller the space, the more care is needed to insure that every part of the garden is used to the very best advantage.

What is the garden used for?

Once you have measured and assessed the garden, you need to think how it can be used by the family. Space is the key. In a very small garden there may only be room for a table and chairs, somewhere to eat outside in summer. In such a restricted space the gardener may have to be content with just a few containers filled with herbs for the kitchen, or summer annuals and flowering climbers to brighten up the walls.

The larger the garden though, the more possibilities there are and the more problems that might occur. First, think

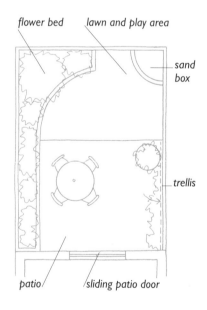

▲ *A small garden at the rear of a town house. The trellis and tree on the right help to break up the space.*

◄ *A well-designed patio with a splendid hosta in a container. The bright orange and yellow flowers of the nasturtiums complement the green foliage.*

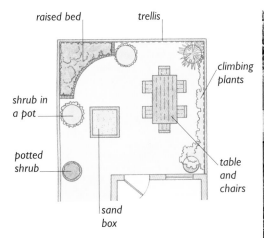

raised bed   trellis

climbing plants

shrub in a pot

potted shrub

table and chairs

sand box

▲ *A smaller version of the design on page 20 for a town house with a side passage. The sand box can be seen from the kitchen. The containers provide accent points around the edges.*

▶ *A sophisticated patio where the main feature is the square pool surrounded by ferns. The balls of clipped box soften the right angles of the pool.*

about the family. Many boys fancy themselves as young soccer stars but ball games and plants do not mix, and hydrangeas do not make good goal posts. Girls are usually quieter, but all children are likely to want an area to ride their bikes and very young children appreciate a small sand box, which can often be included even in a small patio garden. (If you include one make sure it can be covered against the unwelcome attentions of neighborhood cats.)

The vital questions It is a good idea to draw up a series of questions. Is the garden for eating outside in the summer? Is it an extra room? Does the family sit there? How much competition for the space is there between the gardening and

nongardening members of the family? When you have answered these questions you can answer some of the specific gardening queries. Which direction does the garden face? How much sun does it get, or is it totally shaded? Once these questions have been answered you can decide, for example, whether there is room for a raised bed around a patio area, the type of containers that you need to buy, and the type of plants that you want to grow. Raised beds have many advantages—they are more easily reached by the elderly and disabled, they provide sufficient space for more permanent trees and shrubs, and they give a container garden more substance. If you are planning to build a raised bed, do allow space between it and the walls

of the house, otherwise the damp course will get blocked and become damaged.

Essential rules Whether the space is large or small, certain rules apply. All the elements of a container garden must be easily reachable, and there must be a clear plan to the area. This may seem obvious and unnecessary but it guarantees essential factors, such as space to walk out of the back door. It also makes sure that you can reach all the containers to water them properly, and that you can reach permanent plants to train or prune them as necessary. Don't forget you will need easy access to any outside faucet for watering purposes, and make sure that kitchen windows will not end up covered with foliage that blocks out the light.

21

containers as focal points

Nothing is more challenging to the garden designer than an ordinary narrow rectangular garden, open to view, revealing everything. This is not what gardening should be. All gardens, even the smallest, need secrets, and the judicial use of containers can help the designer add many little extras.

A small formal garden using containers

Formal gardens are laid out in geometric patterns and have developed from the Elizabethan knot gardens of the late 16th century. Squares, rectangles and circles are the easiest shapes to use, and they can look very good in a small space. Faced with a fairly narrow rectangle the garden designer could start by narrowing the shape even further. Plant a dark green yew hedge around the garden or, if there is not room, train dark ivy up all the walls. Then, build a brick or flagged path right down the center of the garden leading to a striking container at the end to draw the eye down the path, through the garden. Next, divide the garden more or less into four equal parts by creating a circle in the center. This gives you four equal borders with a quadrant cut out of each in the center. Edge each quadrant with box, *Buxus sempervirens*, to create the outlines. At the corners of each segment place matching containers. Plant these with the gold-leaved, *B. s.* 'Marginata' that can be clipped into balls. Because the balls are in containers they will appear higher than the low-growing box hedge, and give the garden vertical interest. Also, because they are evergreen, they will give the garden shape and form during winter. Planting the four borders depends on their size and your personal preference. Keep the planting as symmetrical as possible, and use plants of differing heights.

◄ *A rustic summerhouse in a formal garden, flanked by standard wisterias and tubs of lilies and auricula primulas. Euphorbias frame the steps up from the herbal knot garden.*

An informal town garden Another approach to the same basic shape involves informal curved lines, using plants and containers to alter the perspective of the garden. Map out the garden on a piece of graph paper and then make a series of curves around the edge. These will be the flower borders. Put lawn in the center of the garden and then position a slightly winding path of stepping stones through the middle leading to a circular area where you can stand a striking container or sundial. Then place small containers where each curve joins the next. Some will not be visible from the house, or they will be partially obscured, and will therefore provide the garden with a series of secret spaces, each one highlighted by a container. Such a garden can be framed by planting one or two trees or large shrubs that initially draw the eye away from the shape of the beds, giving the whole garden an added air of mystery.

Planting a garden should vary with the seasons. Smaller spring bulbs, such as crocuses and chionodoxa, look lovely early in the year. In the early summer, colorful garden perennials, such as aquilegia and corydalis, are very useful and attractive. And, depending on the space available, do not forget smaller roses to provide color throughout the summer, while the containers can be filled with bright summer annuals.

▶ *A monumental antique jar in a formal garden surrounded by neat low hedges of clipped box. Any unusual container or garden statue helps to draw the eye and makes a good focal point.*

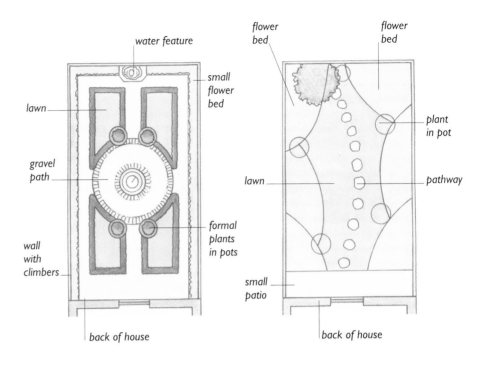

▲ *Formal and informal designs for a long town garden. The planting in the formal garden (left) can be varied with the seasons. The informal design (right) can contain a variety of plants.*

2 3

creating rooms and features

One of the best ways to use containers is to divide one area of the garden from another. This applies just as much to large, formal gardens in the country as to small town gardens. They are an easy way to create a barrier, and if you change your mind after a season, they can always be moved.

Using containers in a small town garden

A typical small town garden has a paved area outside the back door that leads to a lawn flanked by flower beds. Two design ideas for this type of garden have been suggested on pages 22–23, but if you have a particularly long and narrow garden that you want to separate into two or three divisions, then why not go even further and divide it crosswise?

To make the first division, range an even number of fairly formal containers along the edge of the patio. They do not have to block the patio from the lawn but they do create the illusion of a division, and if they are planted with colorful annuals in summer, such as petunias and lobelias, they will attract more attention. (They will also attract butterflies and bees during the hot weather.) These plants in turn make a stronger visual statement.

If there is room you could think about making a slightly raised bed at the end of the first division. Build a small retaining wall, say two or three bricks in

height, with a single step in the middle, and position four containers in front of it, two at each end, and two flanking the center step. You can complete this design by positioning a garden seat right at the end of the garden, flanking it with a further two containers to provide a slightly formal focal point.

Containers for paths The same idea lies behind containers placed at regular intervals down a garden path, flanking the walkway rather like soldiers. This idea requires quite a large garden because, ideally, any formal path should be wide enough for two people to walk down it side by side, or for the gardener to push a loaded wheelbarrow down its length.

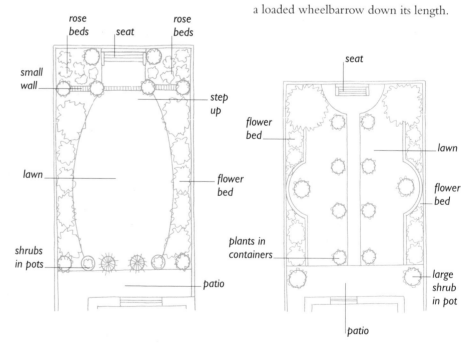

▲ *A most effective design for a larger town garden dividing the space into three "rooms" using containers and varying levels.*

▲ *A formal garden that relies on symmetry for its effect. Matching containers flank the path down the center of the lawn.*

◀ *Rough sketches of different areas show the number and type of container you will need. Here the gardener plans to surround a seating area with scented plants.*

❶ *Lilium* Golden Splendor

❷ *Nicotiana* Domino Mixed

❸ *Phlox* Palona Mixed

❹ *Nicotiana* Domino Mixed

Planting containers for emphasis and accent The beauty of using containers in this way is the variety that they bring to planting schemes, and the color accents that they provide. In the summer, bright red and white pelargoniums can be planted together, or in separate containers. Blue lobelias can also be included for a red, white, and blue effect.

Another approach is to use the softer colors of mixed petunias in lilac, pink, and white. Gray-colored stone, concrete, or fiberglass containers are an ideal foil for these paler colors, for the neutral color of the container will blend in with the plants. Beware of using colored containers in such positions though, because they may produce an unpleasantly jarring color contrast.

▶ *A particularly striking and unusual display, showing sunflowers and ceanothus. Late daffodils will achieve the same color contrast.*

the importance of background

Plants never appear in isolation—colored flowers are softened by green foliage, trees are silhouetted against the sky, and white clematis growing up a trellis will appear differently from one rambling up the wall. Always remember your garden background, and make sure that you use it well.

◀ *Any number of variegated grasses can be used to recreate this startling design. Secure the polystyrene foam with nylon netting.*

Easy backgrounds

Some backgrounds are simple. The easiest is the classic hedge of dark green, evergreen yew, *Taxus*, against which all colors will appear brighter and stronger. White plants in matching containers are particularly effective. Lacking a yew hedge, a similar color effect can be obtained by covering a wall with ivy, *Hedera*. If you are growing ivy as a background to other plants, then choose one of the dark green varieties. If you want the wall itself to appear more interesting there are many forms of ivy available with variegated gold or white-splashed leaves. They look more attractive on their own, but are not so successful as a background, because the variegated leaves tend to detract from the color of the plants.

Brick backgrounds

Many backgrounds in small gardens are the plain brick of the house or the

Contrasting containers are a clever idea against a neutral fence. Here blue meets green.

Terracotta looks best against a brick wall. All plants look well in classically designed pots.

Avoid a color clash with a strong background color with both the plants and containers.

garden wall. In fact most bricks are red or yellowish, although this can also depend on the age of the structure. If you have a brick background then you may be tempted to paint it white, but do not. The predominant color of plants is green, which goes well with the red, orange, and dusky yellow color of most brickwork. Also, plants grow quite quickly and the leaves will soon cover the new paint. Before that stage, the white really makes too bright a background and drains color away from the plants. And white also excludes a wide range of excellent white or pale cream climbers. You cannot grow a white plant effectively against a white wall.

Using smaller containers against informal backgrounds Most plants grow in front of other plants. The standard design rule of tallest at the back, shortest at the front, is as applicable to plants in containers as in any herbaceous border. Many containers are made from terracotta and

this forms a pleasant background suitable for most plants. If you have new pots they can always be aged by applying a coating of sour milk and yogurt to dull the new clay and help algae form on the surface.

Also, take care to balance the color of the leaves with the color of the pots, and the pots against their background. The only area where there may be some difficulty is on a roof garden. Erecting a trellis around the edge of a roof garden will enable you to enclose the space with green-leaved climbers, but the best and cheapest solution when it comes to containers for roof gardens is to use fiberglass or plastic. These are lighter than clay, stone, or wood and, if wanted, they can be painted in a variety of colors. However a roof garden is probably the one case where it is best to have uniform white containers, and let the planting provide the color.

▶ *Madonna and regal lilies are good scented plants for containers. Unless they are grown in a very sheltered site they require staking.*

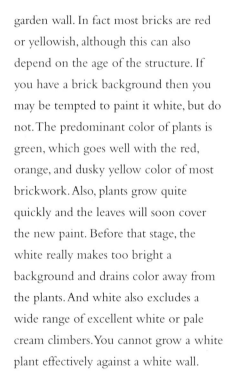

containers in doors and arches

Doorways and arches are the most important points in any house or garden. The front door of a house announces the style you are aiming for. Similarly, an archway in a garden makes a statement about what is to come. It follows that any containers used need to emphasize your design.

◀ *A delightful garden with containers of hostas and dicentras and an archway of honeysuckle. Cut this back hard to keep it within bounds.*

Framing formal doorways

A much used, ever popular theme for the formal front door of a Georgian town house is two Versailles tubs, each planted with a standard bay tree, *Laurus nobilis*, clipped into a mophead. It is unnecessary to add anything else, although the trees can be mulched with stones or gray gravel to highlight the planting. Clipped box, *Buxus*, in antique terracotta pots, or spiral-shaped standards are equally good alternatives. If you want to add some color then substitute a standard marguerite daisy, *Argyranthemum*, for its gray leaves and white flowers.

Creating a colorful welcome

In less formal surroundings with more room, you can contrive a very different effect, whether your house has a front garden or a paved area for a number of containers. In a cottage garden you can plant a climbing rose, such as the climbing form of 'Iceberg', which you can train over the door: its nodding white flowers are even more delicate when viewed from below. The rose can be surrounded by any number of containers planted with blue and white flowers, such as *Geranium* 'Johnson's Blue', *Lavandula angustifolia* 'Hidcote' with its dark blue flowers, complemented by white petunias or *Penstemon* 'White Bedder'. Planted in weathered terracotta pots against a matching background of brick, plants such as these provide an immediate welcome.

Formal arches

One of the most striking aspects of any garden is an archway in a formal evergreen hedge, flanked by terracotta or stone urns filled with plants of a single color. In such cases it is almost impossible to improve on a pure white scheme, for the dark green complements the white so well, although white and blue is also very effective. Make sure that the containers suit the hedge: if you have a formal yew hedge, for example, then grand terracotta pots always look stylish.

framing a doorway

1 Measure the space around the door and then erect the trellis using battens and Rawlplugs. If you wish you can train wires instead of trellis.

Planting care If you have decided to plant matching bay trees, or any formal evergreens, in pots, then you must insure that the plants are properly pruned to shape, watered, and fed. Annuals can be

2 Choose matching containers for the climbing plants and stand them on blocks to keep the containers off the ground to allow free drainage.

changed every year and cost relatively little, but a trained standard tree is a hefty capital investment that, with care, can provide enjoyment for many years. Alternative suggestions include conifers

3 *Clematis* 'Jackmanii Superba' and *Rosa* 'Zéphirine Drouhin', the thornless rose, are good choices for a front door. They provide color in the summer.

or even an olive tree, *Olea europaea*, which is planted in formal tubs. The latter often needs protection in the winter, and should be placed under glass during cold weather to protect it from frost.

KEEPING DOORWAY DESIGNS IN PROPORTION

One thing not to forget, when you frame the front door of a house, is the height of the door itself. Keep the container in proportion with the doorway, tall enough to make a statement, but not so tall that it is out of proportion. Try out the container, and then add the height of an imaginary plant to see what sort of effect you have achieved. Also be certain that the style of the container matches the house. Weathered terracotta pots suit old brick cottages but formal town houses look best flanked by Versailles tubs or classical urns and planters.

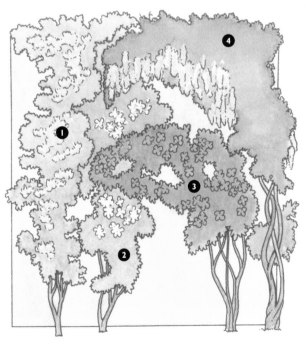

◀ *There are a number of climbers that can be used to frame doorways. Honeysuckle smells lovely but is rather untidy.* Clematis montana *is very vigorous. Wisteria is best planted in the ground and needs careful pruning.*

1 Honeysuckle (*lonicera*)
2 *Clematis montana*
3 *C. 'Jackmanii Superba'*
4 *Wisteria sinensis*

containers on steps and paths

The most dramatic use of containers is to flank formal flights of steps. Steps may lead from the semibasement of a house to the garden or, where the garden is on several levels, they can link one area with another. Containers in these situations make a bold statement.

Matching the containers to the garden design

The first thing to consider is the style of the staircase. A narrow rustic flight built out of old bricks or wooden railroad ties in a cottage garden demands small intimate containers planted to match the surroundings. A black iron fire escape or balustrade in a town garden can be brightened with red pelargoniums in terracotta pots. Informal steps leading into the house can also be decorated using climbing plants, such as clematis, planted in containers at the foot. The climbers can be tied in to the banisters, which often helps to soften what can be a harsh feature. Large stairways in grand formal gardens demand classic containers filled with matching plants, such as white hydrangeas. They draw attention to the steps and lead the walker to the next level. This is particularly true in town houses where steps lead up to the garden from a semibasement.

▶ *Bricks make good paths, flanked here by beds with roses, foxgloves, and heucheras. The container and statue add an air of mystery.*

Making use of limited space

There are many gardens where space is limited, but excellent use can be made of any steps or pathways, such as a flight of steps outside a kitchen. Culinary herbs are an excellent choice for such a position, and many will flourish in shade or partial shade. The cook has only to walk from the kitchen armed with a pair of scissors to have fresh herbs for the pot.

► *In the summer, ordinary staircases can be disguised by containers of colorful annuals: pelargonium, petunias, and verbenas are all good choices.*

① *Pelargonium Horizon Series*

② *Verbena × hybrida*

③ *Pelargonium Horizon Series*

④ *Pelargonium Horizon Series*

⑤ *Pelargonium Horizon Series*

If you want to brighten a dull passage-way, for example a side passage next to a town house, then this too is possible, but if you are growing flowering plants that need sun, make sure that you rotate the containers so that the plants regularly get bright light. If you just use a few sun-loving plants as accents the task need not be too onerous.

Containers along passageways

Remember that there is likely to be more light in a passageway the higher up the wall you go. The maximum shade is usually at ground level. There may well be a case for using wall pots positioned on the wall, especially if it catches some sun. Another advantage is that space can be left for pedestrians, bicycles, and children's toys. There must also be room to walk down flights of stairs easily, especially fire escapes, and you can only place containers on steps or walkways if they leave excellent access.

Aspect—sun and shade

When you are planning and planting your containers you must always remember the aspect. Containers placed in south-facing positions that are in the sun a lot can get very hot. Grow plants that will flourish in hot dry conditions: any plant, such as lavender or rosemary, that comes from the Mediterranean will do well. Similarly, north-facing and shaded areas need plants that will survive in shade with low light levels. Suitable plants are listed on pages 254–257.

▲ *A wrought-iron spiral staircase looks good in a small garden with different levels: lupins, foxgloves and lilies add color in the summer.*

▲ *Cactus plants can be put outside in the summer months. The blue-gray leaves make a good background for the scarlet pelargoniums.*

31

containers
for gardens

There are very few gardens that cannot be improved by containers. As a general rule, the smaller the garden, the more important containers become, and in very small gardens they may be the only way to accommodate both plants and people in a restricted outside space.

planning and design

When you look at a new garden you have to think of the practical family aspects. How is the garden going to be used? Is there space for tables and chairs? A basketball area, or a sand box? And all the gardening factors. Especially, what is the soil like and which direction does the garden face?

Soil and its implications

If the whole garden consists entirely of containers, then the type of soil does not really matter. It is under your control. You can choose various composts—acid, alkaline, or neutral—to suit the plants you wish to grow. However, if there is space for a small raised bed around the edge of a patio, and you plan to use existing soil, then you should check its relative acidity or alkalinity. This is done by measuring the pH of the soil, and anyone can do this very easily using a small inexpensive test kit available from garden centers or nurseries. It is very, very important and can save a great deal of heartache and money.

Plant requirements Different plants have different requirements. Some plants, such as camellias and blueberries, will only grow in acid soil, that is soil with a pH below 6.5. If you try to grow them in alkaline soil the leaves will turn yellow, developing chlorosis, and the plants will eventually die. Quite a number of common plants, notably soft fruit, strawberries and raspberries, prefer soil that is slightly acid. Conversely a number of plants, such as brassicas and aquilegias, grow best in alkaline soils and will not flourish when the soil is acid.

Aspect—the unalterable factor

Aspect is all important and you must look to see how much sun the garden gets, not just through the summer, but in the winter as well. Some plants prefer shade and do best when they are sheltered from the sun—the common primrose, *Primula vulgaris,* is a good example—while others need several hours sun each day to flower properly. Some varieties of roses, for instance, will grow happily on a north wall, but others

▲ *The delicately scented wild primrose, Primula vulgaris, prefers partial shade and moist soil. It will not flourish in a dry position.*

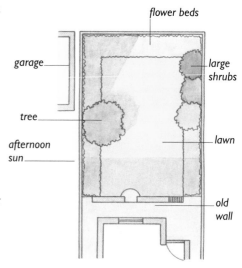

▲ *A north-facing town garden may be in shade for much of the day. It will also be shaded in the evening as shown in the diagram above.*

▲ *A sunny patio is a good place to grow colorful annuals and also a variety of vegetables, such as tomatoes and bell peppers.*

1. Sunflowers
2. Sunflowers
3. Clipped bay tree
4. Petunia

5. Pansies
6. Marigold
7. Lavender
8. Roses

9. California poppies
10. Apple tree
11. Pole beans
12. Tomato 'Tumbler'

prefer to be in sun. If you take care at the planning stage you will not make the mistake of buying plants that do not suit your garden. Check the Plant Lists on pages 254–261 to make sure you buy plants that will grow properly in the conditions which you offer.

The best starting points

Check the garden area and measure the whole garden exactly. Plot out the garden to scale on graph paper. Decide what you can achieve within the limitations of the space available, check the aspect and also whether the garden is shaded by surrounding buildings for any significant part of the day. Town gardens surrounded by tall houses may not receive that much sun, even when they face south. Carefully examine the Plant Directory and Plant Lists on pages 224–261 and decide which plants are suitable for your garden, and then buy them from a local garden center or a specialist supplier. Finally, cultivate patience as well as your garden. Gardening is a long-term occupation.

▶ *Measure the garden carefully, especially when planning any major reconstruction. This applies particularly to overgrown and neglected plots.*

Shrubs, trees, and perennials take time to mature. Most new gardens will need several years before they start to reach their full potential.

the vertical dimension

Just think how dull a garden would be without variations in height. There are any number of small trees that can be grown in pots or barrels in small gardens, and even if there is not enough room for a tree, walls and fences can be used to grow climbing plants and shrubs adding color and interest.

Small trees for the container garden

If you want to consider planting small trees then miniature fruit trees are an excellent choice, as are conifers, especially if you have room for two or three containers and choose trees with different colored foliage. Or consider a weeping birch, good varieties are *Betula pendula* 'Purpurea' with purple-tinged bark and dark purple leaves, and *B. p.* 'Youngii' with silvery white bark. Both eventually will outgrow their allotted space but they take time to mature. Small varieties of Japanese maple, *Acer palmatum*, are also very suitable. They really need acid soil and will provide brilliant fall color, making them a real focal point in a small garden.

Planning climbers and wall plants for a container garden

As in all gardening you have to ask yourself a series of questions before you choose the correct plant. Do you want the wall or fence to be covered all year— or just in the summer? If you want permanent cover, then you have to choose an evergreen but how much space have you got? Some climbers are extremely vigorous even when grown in a container, and are unsuitable for small gardens. Is your garden sheltered and warm, or in a cold part of the country? In this case avoid climbers which are not totally hardy. Do you want a brilliant

◀ Cordyline australis 'Variegata' makes a spectacular plant in a large container. Half hardy, they will only flourish in mild areas.

evergreen climbers for year-round interest

1 If you have space then the evergreen clematis, *C. armandii*, is a good choice. It is vigorous, with large leathery leaves and fragrant white flowers in spring.

2 The variegated ivy, *Hedera colchica* 'Sulphur Heart', known as 'Paddy's Pride', has yellow-edged leaves. Confederate jasmine is scented.

3 Pyracanthus tolerate most situations and have white flowers in spring followed by clusters of red to yellow berries, depending on the variety grown.

flash of colour in the fall? If yes, then choose a climber that has vividly colored leaves, such as a Boston ivy, *Parthenocissus tricuspidata*, but beware, they do need a bit of space and need to be cut back each year to prevent them getting under roof tiles. And are you covering north- or south-facing walls? Make sure you choose climbers and wall plants suitable for these conditions. Once you have asked and answered these questions, you can make a more informed choice.

Evergreen climbers for north- and east-facing walls The coral plant, *Berberidopsis corallina*, is one: it is not fully hardy and prefers acid soil, but it has lovely red flowers. It can be rather difficult to get going. Also consider *Clematis armandii* which is very vigorous, again not fully

hardy, but with wonderful long, pointy, green leathery leaves and a sweet scent from the white flowers early in the year. Only grow it if you have quite a bit of room. Common ivy, *Hedera helix,* may sound a bit dull but there are dozens of varieties with variegated foliage.

Evergreen climbers for south- and west-facing walls The slightly tender Canary Island ivy, *Hedera canariensis* and its varieties, offer white or cream-splashed leaves. Other possibilities include: Confederate jasmine, *Trachelospermum jasminoides*, which needs acid soil; or the potato vine, *Solanum jasminoides*, and its relation, the Chilean potato vine,

▶ *Group pots so that there is a variety of heights. Here a tall "chimney" pot is emphasized by the variegated foliage of the pelargoniums.*

S. crispum—'Glasnevin' is the variety grown most and it has lovely purple flowers, but it is a semievergreen and may well lose its leaves in frosty winters. A firethorn, *Pyracantha*, is another good choice for color throughout the fall.

container-only gardens

It goes without saying that all plants in very small gardens or roof gardens, have to be grown in containers. But if the space is large enough then build a permanent raised bed in the center of the garden, or around the walls. Do this if possible for it extends the range of plants that can be grown.

◀ *Climbing hydrangea, H. petiolaris, is a good climber that will flower on north-facing walls. It needs to be controlled.*

Arranging containers in a small space

First you have to buy a number of containers that fit neatly into your garden and do not clash with the surrounding walls. Buying and choosing containers is covered on pages 84–91. Containers should be grouped for the best advantage. Draw the garden to scale on a piece of graph paper, marking in all the essential features such as doors, windows, walls, fences, and faucets. Then transfer this design on to the ground, marking out the areas you have chosen for the containers in chalk on the patio, or use wastepaper baskets to give you an idea of the look. Put them in position and see whether this makes sense. Walk round them and, if necessary, change their position. It is always possible to move containers around, although this should be done before they have been filled with compost. Note that containers work best in groups, in odd numbers,

different sizes, and heights. Also note that it is even more important to mark out the space taken by a permanent raised bed before building it.

Making a framework of plants

Every garden needs a framework of plants, and if possible you should plan to plant a number of trees or shrubs that will form the permanent features. Although relatively expensive, fruit trees grafted on dwarfing rootstock are an excellent idea for a small container garden. They require care and attention but will provide spring blossom and fresh fruit in the fall.

Deciduous climbers and wall shrubs

If you can do without permanent color on the walls throughout the year, there are many excellent deciduous plants to choose from. Suitable climbers that will grow in containers include clematis, Virginia creeper, *Parthenocissus*, and common jasmine, *Jasminum officinale*, usually semievergreen in mild climates, but it does require some cutting back after flowering each year to keep it within its allotted bounds.

The best wall shrubs include climbing roses that can provide repeat color and scent throughout the summer and often well into the fall—the climbing form of 'Iceberg' is often still in flower in midwinter given a relatively mild fall. Some roses will also grow on north-facing walls, although they will usually only flower once a year. An excellent wall shrub that really does cover the wall is climbing hydrangea, *Hydrangea petiolaris*. It has clusters of white flowers in summer and dark green leaves that turn yellow in the fall.

Color and form Whatever your priorities, it is important to think of the balance of color and form in a container garden. Choose attractive containers and a selection of leaf colors for maximum variety. You need two or three evergreen foliage plants that give

color in the winter, tall plants or shrubs to break up the shape, for instance bay trees in tubs, and herbs with gold and purple-leaved varieties. Group them to provide interesting contrasts.

▲ Containers of tall plants arranged in rows on walls or staging create a colorful hedge that allows people to see through into the garden beyond. Here a vertical planting of verbascum is complemented by pinks, hostas, veronicas, euphorbias, and irises.

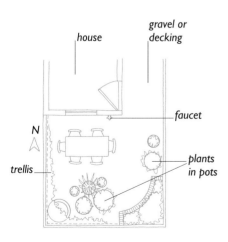

▲ A garden plan showing containers in groups with a small raised bed in the left-hand corner. Access to the table must be a priority here.

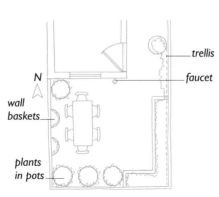

▲ An L-shaped raised bed allows more room in a town garden. Wall pots filled with annuals add height and color in the summer.

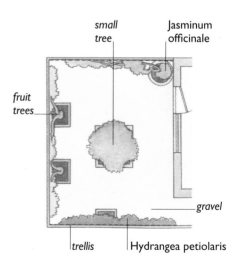

▲ Even a small raised bed placed in the center of the garden allows you to plant a tree, such as a Japanese maple, as a focal point

planting and arranging

When the trees, wall shrubs and climbing plants—the main elements of the container garden—are in place, you have to decide on the remainder of your planting. How much time have you got for gardening? Herbs, fruit, even vegetables can all be grown in containers with a little care.

Do you only use the garden in summer, and if so do you just need colorful summer annuals? Do you want to include spring bulbs in any of the containers, or plant some colorful perennials? Do you want to grow herbs, fruit, and vegetables? Do you want to grow containers of scented plants, or hang pots on the walls with colorful annuals? All of these things are possible options.

Another question that you need to answer before you buy any plants is how long do you want the garden to stay colorful and interesting? It is much easier to fill containers with summer annuals, and then forget about them when the first frosts arrive and the annuals die.

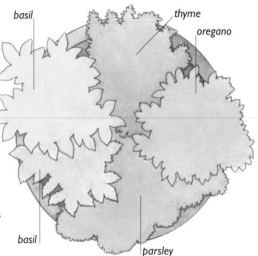

basil

thyme

oregano

basil

parsley

However, summer annuals can be replaced by winter-flowering ones, and with a little care and attention any patio garden can provide interest and color throughout the year. Further ideas for fall and winter color can be found on pages 188–191 and 200–203.

◀ *Pots of semitender herbs make excellent container plants. The small shrubs, thyme and oregano, will both survive the winter out of doors but may need some shelter in severe frosts.*

Planning a container of herbs

Many gardeners use containers to grow herbs, and all patio gardeners should include at least one container of herbs for use in the kitchen. Many herbs, such as mint, are actually better grown in a pot because they are too invasive in the ground; some are also tender and can be brought indoors in the winter, or sheltered from frosts by covering the containers with a horticultural fleece.

Initially, concentrate on the easy herbs that are available throughout the summer—parsley, thyme, basil, and oregano can all be grown in the average container garden, as can various mints such as applemint, spearmint, the larger peppermint, eau de cologne or lemon mint, and Bowles' mint, which is the best for new potatoes. Chives are another decorative herb to give flavor to summer soups, and small shrubs, such as

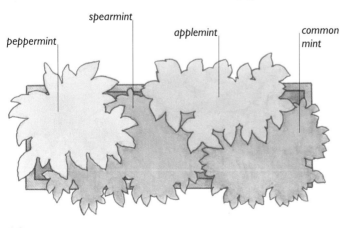

peppermint

spearmint

applemint

common mint

◀ *A mixed container of various mints is much appreciated in the kitchen. They have very different leaf shapes and varying colors.*

◄ *Chives have a delicate onion-like flavor and are good herbs to grow in containers. The flowers are edible and can be used for decoration. Sow parsley in succession through the summer so there is always some available.*

grow raspberries because they need space to spread. Cultivated berries, such as tayberries or blackberries, are a better choice and are excellent grown against a wall, while blueberries should be grown in containers of ericaceous compost. The other easily grown fruit is strawberries, and there are several special planters readily available. The best thing to use is the traditional strawberry barrel, but tower pots add height and variety to the patio design and can be used imaginatively to grow pyramids of strawberry plants that drip with fruit.

rosemary and bay, add a more permanent touch. If you want to be more ambitious try a container or two of scented herbs such as the sun-loving thyme, oregano, marjoram, rosemary, and sage with its many varieties and leaves in contrasting colors of green and purple.

Growing vegetables

You can grow some vegetables even if your patio is quite small. Peas and pole beans can be grown in pots, training them up pyramids of sticks or stakes. This adds height to the garden, and varieties

of pole beans also have yellow or purple pods. Lettuces with their varied colored leaves are also excellent plants for the container garden, and there are now a number of miniature vegetables available, specifically designed for containers.

Fruit can also be grown in containers, but do not try to

▶ *Pole beans can be planted around the edge of a container and trained up a wigwam of stakes. These always provide a good crop.*

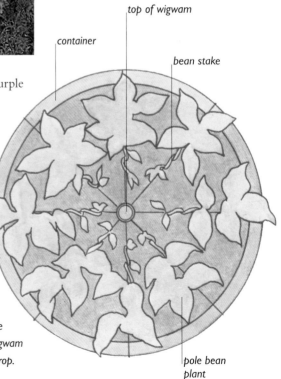

top of wigwam

container

bean stake

pole bean plant

4 1

Grouping containers in a small garden

One of the advantages of gardening with containers is that you can move them about constantly, creating new color combinations. You can also take say three identical plants, such as trailing lobelia or petunias, and plant them in containers of varying heights to give a different look to each flower. Furthermore, many flowers look quite different when you look up at them in wall pots, instead of looking down on them.

If the garden has a number of containers then some can be positioned on staging so that the plants appear in rows, broadening the band of color. In fact you can use this technique to divide the garden into sections. Some gardeners group a number of containers with vegetables together, while you can also construct a bank of trailing plants to give the impression of a floral waterfall. It is even possible to make a containerized hedge, dividing the garden into rooms

using pots placed on pedestals each with fragrant small shrubs, such as the favorite choice of scented lavender.

Follow the principles of flower arranging

Two basic principles of flower arranging are variation of height and grouping colors to make a harmonious picture. A container gardener can achieve the same

▲ *Trailing nasturtiums are extremely popular annuals and here look as if they were the fire and smoke issuing from the mouth of an ancient cannon. They can be eaten in salads and are excellent companion plants deterring a number of garden pests.*

effect on a grander, bolder scale. Do not make the mistake of trying to achieve height difference with plants, as the traditional gardener would do in a herbaceous border. Let the size of the container dictate the height of the

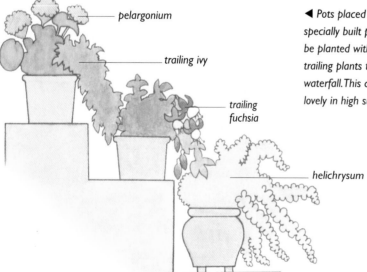

pelargonium

trailing ivy

trailing fuchsia

helichrysum

◀ *Pots placed on steps or on specially built pedestals can be planted with a variety of trailing plants to make a floral waterfall. This can look very lovely in high summer.*

TRAILING PLANTS

Many plants hang down naturally, covering walls and steps, and others have been bred for planting in tubs and baskets. Choose some of these to create a floral waterfall. Small-leaved ivies, such as *Hedera helix* 'Glacier', dark green with white edges, or *H.h.* 'Green Ripple', dark green pointed leaves, are good evergreens. Annuals include: trailing petunias—the Super Cascade hybrids or Surfinia are good choices—trailing fuchsias, and verbenas.

arrangement, using everything from miniature pots to Ali Baba jars. Make groups with odd numbers of containers because they are more effective than even numbers. And make sure that the containers blend together. Brightly painted buckets and large cans are a good idea in the right place, and they can add a dramatic touch of eccentricity, for instance on a town windowsill, but they do not blend well with weathered terracotta or stone troughs placed against old brick or stone walls.

Let the garden develop

However much planning you do, and however carefully you choose the plants and containers for your garden, you will find that your ideas change over the years as the garden matures. It has already been stressed that gardening is an activity that requires patient application, and that plants take time to grow. Only experience will reveal which plants will grow well and which plants do not like your garden. Concentrate on these: the garden will be the better for it.

One of the best phrases to describe certain town gardens is that they suffer from "shrinking lawn syndrome." The gardener just wants to grow more and more plants, the flower beds get larger and larger and the lawn smaller. The same is often true of container gardens. The desire is often to cram in more containers to grow more plants.

▶ *Lavender makes a good small shrub growing in a container. It prefers a warm sheltered position. It should be pruned hard in the spring.*

containers with themes

All enterprising gardeners seek ways of developing interest in their gardens. One good way is to plan various stories, or themes, that can be varied from one container to another. This adds that touch of mystery, an element that is found in all the best gardens.

Ideas for scented containers

One of the best themes to develop in a summer container garden is scent. There are many scented plants, ranging from climbers to annuals, and you can include many of the most fragrant plants in any container garden scheme.

Good scented climbers include *Clematis armandii* and *Wisteria sinensis*, but only grow them if you have a good deal of room. Also note that newly planted wisterias require careful, exact pruning.

Scented climbing roses include 'Golden Showers', yellow; 'Maigold', bronze-yellow; and 'Zéphirine Drouhin', pink—all suitable for a north wall and poor aspect; 'Compassion', pinkish-yellow; 'Climbing Ophelia', blush-pink; 'Constance Spry', deeper pink; and 'Sympathier', deep crimson; while both 'Climbing Iceberg' and 'White Cockade' are lovely, small, white, climbing roses, very suitable for a small town garden, but not so fragrant as the others.

Fragrant shrubs include the floribunda roses—'Margaret Merril', white; and 'English Miss', pink; lavender, blue-purple or pale lavender flowers with narrow gray leaves; *Daphne odora*, evergreen with deep purple to white flowers in late winter and early spring; sweet box, *Sarcococca hookeriana*, which needs acid soil, as do the scented rhododendrons, such as *R. luteum* with its fragrant yellow flowers; *Viburnum carlesii* with its pink buds and white flowers smells very sweetly; and rosemary, *Rosmarinus officinalis*, has fragrant leaves and purple-blue flowers in the spring.

Suitable perennials include scented pinks, such as the old-fashioned *Dianthus*,

◄ *Scented plants can be grouped together even though they flower at different times of the year. Leave the containers in place as permanent features or shift them around.*

❶ Rose 'English Miss'	❻ *Daphne odora*
❷ *Viburnum carlesii*	❼ Heliotrope
❸ Rosemary	❽ Pinks
❹ Rose 'Margaret Merril	❾ Lily-of-the-valley
❺ Pinks	❿ Wisteria

▶ *Herbal and vegetable themes also work well in containers, the varying shades of green contrasting well with each other.*

'Mrs Sinkins', with its feathery white flowers, but many modern pinks, available in a range of colors, have a distinct scent of cloves. Lily-of-the-valley, *Convallaria*, is also heavily scented.

For a really striking display of bulbs, plant the white-flowered regal lily, *Lilium regale*. They will need staking, but they perfume the whole garden when the flowers emerge in midsummer.

Scented annuals Many annuals are strongly scented, and top of any list should be tobacco plants, *Nicotiana*; marigolds, phlox, and sweet-scented stocks, *Matthiola*. They all smell delicious when they are in flower in summer. Good scented herbs include: heliotrope, *Heliotropium arborescens*; sweet rocket, *Hesperis matronalis*; hyssop, *Hysoppus officinalis*; bergamot, *Monarda* spp. with its scarlet flowers; sweet cicely, *Myrrhis odorata*; and scented pelargoniums. Flowering medicinal herbs include calamint, *Calamintha grandiflora*;

▶ *A group of fragrant flowering herbs and useful vegetables.*

California poppies, *Eschscholzia;* cornflowers, *Centaurea cyanus*; and thrift, *Armeria maritima*. All these medicinal herbs will flower in the summer months.

Gray- and silver-leaved plants should also be included in most garden schemes. Among the best are lamb's ears, *Stachys byzantina*; lavender; mugwort, *Artemisia* spp.—there are a number of good silvery varieties; and *Senecio*, now known as *Brachyglottis*. These look good planted in contrast to other colors.

A MINIATURE KITCHEN GARDEN

Vegetables are the ultimate theme for a container garden. It is surprisingly easy to grow many vegetables in containers, and the best ones are described on pages 216–221. Do not think that vegetables are visually dull. Many have delicately colored green leaves, and some have variegated leaves of various colors. A container of vegetables topped by miniature bright red cherry tomatoes can make a real talking point.

① California poppy
② Thrift
③ Scented pelargonium
④ Ruby Swiss chard
⑤ Chives
⑥ Variegated mint
⑦ Heliotrope
⑧ Bergamot
⑨ Sweet rocket
⑩ Cornflower
⑪ Lamb's ears
⑫ Artemisia
⑬ Sweet cicely
⑭ Pelargonium
⑮ Beet
⑯ Thrift

containers for patios
and patio gardens

Patios are different from patio gardens. Patio gardens are small, paved with brick or stone, enclosed between walls. Patios are convenient seating areas or margins separating the house from the garden. They are a place to grow herbs, or are filled with decorative pots with colorful annuals.

planning and design

The first consideration is space. Measure the size of the patio and draw it to scale on a piece of graph paper. Then mark in the tables and chairs, positioning them so that you can get in and out of the doorway easily. If you have outdoor tables put them in position and check they fit properly.

Once you have established the position of the main furniture, you can consider how you would like to decorate the remainder of the patio. Again space is the key. It is no good filling a patio so full of containers and plants that you cannot walk round it easily, carrying trays, plates, and glasses. It is a question of priorities. What is the main purpose of the patio—a miniature garden, or a seating area? And if the answer to the question is a seating area then that must take priority in the organization and design.

Compatible plants

It is pleasant to decorate the patio with containers full of plants that complement the surroundings and make a colorful outside room, but there are one or two do's and don'ts when you choose the plants. Don't plant roses, euphorbias, or rue where they can be rubbed against. Roses have thorns while euphorbias, and

◀ *Shrub roses and lady's mantle planted in a modern container make a pleasing contrast on a well-designed patio with a raised bed.*

a number of other plants, have irritant properties that can cause a skin rash if they are brushed against, especially when the sun is shining. Check with a nursery before buying. On the other hand, a number of plants release their scent as you brush against the leaves. The scented-leaved pelargonium is a good example, lemon verbena, another. Scented-leaved plants make it even more pleasant to sit outside in the summer sun.

Creating a barrier

If the patio is large enough, you can make a containerized hedge to separate the patio from the lawn and garden beyond. A line of miniature evergreen conifers will work quite well but they can be a bit dull in summer. They are also expensive plants to purchase. Brightly coloured pelargoniums with trailing ivy and trailing lobelia make a perfect summer barrier, and the containers can be formal or informal.

Some designers might plant a more permanent screen using an arch or a trellis, framed by containers or even a small hedge. This is another excellent idea, and the ideal plants for a miniature hedge are box or lavender that smells so lovely and can be trimmed after flowering. Do not plant a high hedge. Not only would it take light away from the house, but it is essential in all gardens to allow glimpses of what lies beyond.

▶ *A mixed container garden designed for a flower show with aquilegias, French lavender, foxgloves and alliums all in flower together.*

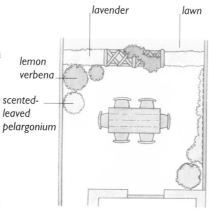

▲ *This table has been positioned so that there is room around the table unlike the example on the right where the plants are closer.*

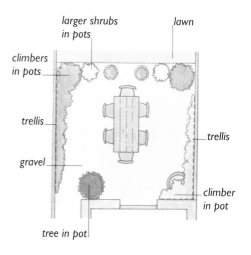

▲ *In a small garden you may only just have room for a standard table. Consider using a circular one as this will take up less room.*

planning a patio garden

Patio gardens need to be planned with extra care. In a small back yard there may not be room for more than a few containers outside the back door. It is a question of measuring and deciding what is possible, what might be attempted, and then trying to put the plan into practice.

Using containers to make rooms

If there is space then you can consider changing the shape of the garden, cutting it in two, positioning groups of containers so that some corners become round, introducing curved lines and containers of different heights to add more interest and visual variety.

Splitting very small gardens in two Many terraced houses in towns have a passageway leading down the side of the house. If the line of the house is taken down to the end of the garden using containers, or a dividing line of trellis, it automatically splits it into two. If the garden gets enough sun then you might be able to grow colorful sun-loving plants in one half and shade-loving plants in the other. Another idea would be to divide the garden by a "hedge" of pots placed on staging, or use a series of taller containers. You could grow flowers in one group and herbs, many of which will flourish in shade, in the other. The exact division will depend on the size and shape of the patio and the aspect.

Rounding off the corners

If this is not possible then you can change the shape of the garden by placing containers in curved lines around the boundaries, varying the height. If you put very tall containers opposite the door, and then smaller and smaller ones on either side, the garden will appear wider and be more interesting. Exercise your imagination. A small water feature added in one corner, partly hidden by two containers of hostas, could also transform a tiny space. And containers of individual plants can be placed alongside larger troughs planted with contrasting light green and red-leaved lettuces, or a group of sages, so useful in the kitchen, have lovely varied-colored leaves, especially *Salvia officinalis* 'Purpurascens' and *S. o.* 'Tricolor'.

An oriental touch Individual pots can be planted with evergreen grasses that will

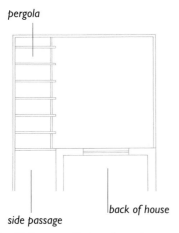

pergola

side passage

back of house

▲ *The side passage of a town house is continued down the garden under a pergola.*

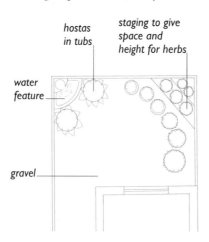

hostas in tubs

staging to give space and height for herbs

water feature

gravel

▲ *Pots placed in a curve create a secret area in the garden. Allow space to walk behind them.*

provide interest all through the year. More importantly, they also add movement when the stems stir in the breeze. Patio gardens in a town may be very sheltered, and any movement of plant or water makes a great difference, particularly in the summer months when the air can be heavy and still.

Covering the wall In the smallest space you may not have room for large containers, but you can cover the walls if you plant a series of wall shrubs, each in a separate container. They can be grown as a hedge or you can grow ivy in containers. This will cover the wall and make an evergreen background for any flowering plants that you have.

Developing a theme

The best gardens, even when very constricted, are those that develop a theme, and this can be achieved in a container garden by planting individual plants in separate containers. If you use annuals you might try a color theme, grading shades of red through rose pink to pale pink and then white or, in the spring, plant containers with bulbs that flower in varying shades of yellow.

You could grade plants by size, taking care to have a number of varieties that flower at the same time, each in an individual pot, or you could tell a story by planting a selection of medieval medicinal herbs. The cook can have containers of miniature vegetables, and you could add a series of scented plants to perfume the air in the evening. All these plantings will create a garden full of interest whatever its size and prove that, with a little imagination, the good gardener is not confined by small boundaries and lack of space.

▲ Chimney pots filled with petunias surround a cordyline in a small town garden.

▼ The color scheme of this garden is nicely restrained with the candelabra primulas, stone edging, and white gravel and seats.

containers on paved areas

Almost every garden has some paved areas that can be decorated with containers filled with plants. As opposed to patio gardens, these areas are part of the garden design and containers and plantings have to fit in with the overall plan. These areas include steps, back yards and garden pools.

Back-door paved areas

Many gardens have a paved area outside the back door, that often leads on into the garden itself. Very often this area is ignored by the gardener and this is a mistake, for there are many uses to which it can be put. The simplest is to plant two or three containers of herbs. Fresh herbs are therefore readily available for the cook, who does not have to go down to the bottom of the garden to cut fresh parsley. It is best if this space is in the sun so the tender herbs that originate from the Mediterranean can easily be grown there. Another practical use is to put house plants, such as small citrus trees or clivias, outside during the summer months. This can benefit them greatly.

If there is a substantial paved area in this position, use containers to divide it off from the rest of the garden to create the impression of an additional room. A line of containers can be planted with evergreens, if you wish, or brightly colored bedding plants, such as winter-flowering pansies in winter, and summer annuals, such as dazzling colored pelargoniums in summer. These cheer up the view from the kitchen window.

Planting beside a pool

Swimming pools and water features can also have containers beside them filled in summer with colorful annuals, such as petunias or pelargoniums. If you are planting containers beside swimming pools, they must be set back out of the way and you have to make sure that they do not contain any plants that

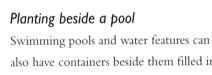
◄ *A specially designed water feature on a paved area surrounded by garden seats. The planting is imaginative and attractive.*

might cause rashes when brushed against by an enthusiastic swimmer.

Special water features often have custom-made beds beside them as part of the overall design, as shown in the photograph on page 52. Here a water trough leads down a silvery chute into a zinc container, and the sides of the chute are designed and planted as mini herbaceous borders with stachys, miniature roses, hostas, and sedums among the plants. Such a plan is immensely stylish and turns an ordinary paved area into something colorful.

Decorating steps and stairways

Often gardens are on different levels. This is a great opportunity for the gardener to decorate plain steps with containers of bright annuals in summer that can match in with the planting in the rest of the garden. If some evergreen plants are included, such as trailing ivy, then they will retain some interest during the winter when the annuals have died

down. It is even possible to erect small pieces of trellis beside many steps of this type and grow climbers, such as ivies and clematis, up the walls. Brick steps beside old houses can be decorated with terracotta pots, each containing a single plant. Match the containers and the plants to the surroundings.

Using neglected areas

Some parts of the garden are often completely ignored: in particular side alleys in town houses. These get little light or sun but they can be used to grow plants in containers that prefer shade, and they give serious gardeners the opportunity to expand their repertoire of plants. Plants for this type of position include ferns, hostas, pulmonarias, and periwinkles.

▲ *In any garden feature it is important that everything matches. Here modern steps are matched by purpose-built containers.*

▼ *A paved area for herbs used to harden off tender plants in summer. Group the containers for a pleasing arrangement.*

HERBS AS COSMETICS

During the 13th and 14th centuries, herbs were mainly employed by monks for medicinal uses. However, they were also used as charms to beautify the skin and hair of courtly ladies. Many herbs were used to clear the skin of freckles and spots; sowbread, *Cyclamen europaeum*, and watercress were applied to the hair to make it grow and chamomile was put on fair hair to lighten it. Hungary water—rosemary tops steeped in alcohol—was the first beauty lotion and made Queen Isabella of Hungary so beautiful in old age that the King of Poland proposed to her.

containers in courtyards

When courtyards are mentioned one visual image could be of grand palaces in Spain, a vast expanse of immaculate gravel, and rows of trees in formal lines interspersed with containers of flowers or smaller shrubs. With a little planning, you can realize this vision—and many more.

The cloistered courtyard

The effect is cool and peaceful, the main point of attraction being a statue or fountain in the center. The sight and sound of water add to the peaceful setting. Few gardens have the space for this type of design, but many gardens with formal areas can incorporate walkways under arches or pergolas with green climbing plants, such as the golden hop, *Humulus lupulus* 'Aureus', and a formal sundial or small fountain in the center. To create this effect position matching containers at the foot of each leg of the arch, plant the chosen climbers in suitable compost, and train them up. Keep the scheme cool and green, with white as the accent color, and remember that the hard lines of the posts are soon softened as the plants grow.

The formal courtyard

In a formal courtyard the emphasis is on the division of space. As in the knot garden of Elizabethan times, the effect of this type of garden relies on precise geometric patterns and the exact positioning of all the elements within the walls. If the courtyard acts as an entrance, then access must be easy and unimpaired. The dividing lines of the trees and containers should then create the illusion of rooms, for example one large "reception" room being in the center and smaller "anterooms" on either side. This is done by positioning lines of formal evergreens, such as bay trees, *Laurus nobilis*, or conifers, interspersed with containers that can be filled with brightly colored accent plants to complement the scheme and add interest

◀ *A formal courtyard profusely planted with shrubs and flowering plants. The statue of Aphrodite complements the design beautifully.*

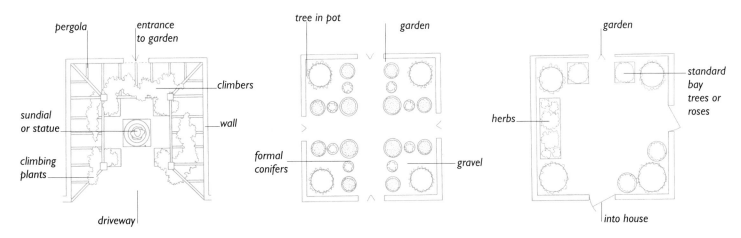

▲ A small courtyard covered by a pergola with a statue or sundial in the center. This design emulates the quiet of a cathedral cloister.

▲ Lines of conifers in matching containers divide the courtyard into a series of smaller rooms. This design works best in a large space.

▲ An outdoor room decorated with containers of trees and shrubs. The entrance to the garden beyond is flanked by matching containers

to the design. These plants can be changed throughout the year, and design of the courtyard will subtly alter.

If you want to try and achieve this effect, plot the elements on paper first, and then simulate the design, using kitchen chairs or any matching pieces of furniture that you have available. Half-close your eyes, and imagine that the chairs are trees or containers filled with plants. This will help you to see whether the design works as a mock-up, before embarking on the expense of buying matching containers, half-barrels or large terracotta pots, and the necessary evergreen trees or shrubs.

The inner courtyard

The third courtyard design can be much more informal. By definition, this is another room in the house that just

happens to be outside. The decoration can be planned to match the inside of the home, with containers placed in the corners filled with bright plants to give color throughout the year. If the courtyard leads on into the garden then the arch or doorway at the end can be flanked by containers, or small borders

can be filled with herbs for the kitchen, and containers can be used as accent points to provide color in the summer.

Adopt a planting theme. Marigolds and nasturtiums are vividly colored annuals that are also well-known culinary plants. Many medicinal herbs are very colorful when in flower.

▶ A formal knot garden with low-growing box hedges, classical urns, and topiary box spirals. Jasmine has been carefully trained up the arch.

containers for
a roof garden

This is the ultimate container garden: all the plants, the soil mix, every pot and trough has to be carried up, through the building, and placed into position. Roof gardens are usually found in towns and cities: the best are quite extraordinary both in design and execution.

practical considerations

The first thing any roof gardener has to do is to get the roof checked by a structural engineer. Containers and plants are fairly heavy, especially when they have been watered, and it is essential that the roof is strong enough to bear their weight. Some roofs may have to be strengthened.

Screens and seclusion

Roof gardens are exposed and you may want to erect screens to provide shelter and seclusion—it is generally best to get professional help to do this to make sure everything is safe. Both screens and plants must be absolutely secure so that there is no risk that they might blow away in a high wind and fall off the roof, injuring pedestrians in the street below.

Flooring

Roof gardens will require flooring. It is a good idea to keep this as light as possible to avoid increasing the weight on the roof. Special light tiles, wooden decking, and gravel are worth considering, and the choice will depend on the type of garden you plan and the number of uses to which it will be put. Gravel is aesthetically pleasing if you are trying to create a cottage garden effect.

Watering

Another extremely important aspect for all roof gardeners is watering. Containers, especially containers on roofs, need to be watered every day in summer and during dry periods. Every roof garden must have a supply of water that is easily accessible, and there is a strong case for installing an automatic watering system. At the very least install an outside faucet for on-site watering.

◄ *Ornamental onions match the color of the painted chair. This is a good idea on a roof garden; the bay tree provides vertical interest.*

One of the most important things when planning and creating a roof garden is not to interfere with the drainage of the roof in any way. Even the flattest of flat roofs will be canted so that rainwater drains away, and the fall of the roof must never be interrupted or problems will build up in the roof itself.

Choosing containers

The first thing to think about is access to the roof. Is there room to carry large containers on to the roof, or is the only access up a narrow flight of attic steps? If the access from the house is restricted then the containers have to be fairly small, or if your design demands a large container, it may have to be built outside, carrying the wood and tools up separately. Keep the containers as light as possible and choose lightweight materials such as fiberglass and tufa, rather than stone and terracotta. Remember though that roof gardens are often miniature in scale, and every element is subject to close inspection; take care to make everything as attractive as possible.

Aspect Finally look at the aspect of the roof garden. As with any garden, this is the most important feature, and the one that is unalterable. Many roof gardens are sunny and open, but some may be overshadowed by taller buildings or the walls of the house. Before you decide on the garden you want and the plants you plan to grow, check that there is plenty of sun—there may be less than you think. If not, plan to grow plants that will flourish in shade.

◄ *A group of modern containers based on classical designs. All containers acquire the patina of age outside in the garden.*

▶ *A large balcony surrounded by walls that is in shade for most of the day. Choose climbers that flourish without the sun.*

▲ *A collection of ornamental grasses with broad-leaved hostas for contrast. The blue stars could be replaced by painted rocks or tufa.*

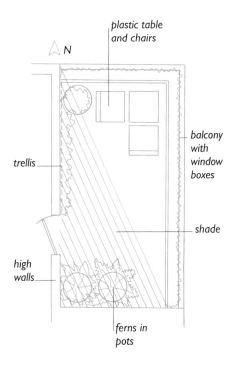

plastic table and chairs

N

trellis

balcony with window boxes

shade

high walls

ferns in pots

Planning the space—the outdoor room

Large roof gardens present a number of opportunities. They can be planned as one large open space or, more effectively, as a series of rooms, each one contributing something different. If the roof can be divided in two, then one half can be used as a seating and eating area with tables and chairs, surrounded by containers of flowers or scented plants. This can be separated from the second half of the garden which may be more formal, with containers of roses or small shrubs, or be used as a miniature kitchen garden with vegetables and herbs.

When there is space, roof gardens can be divided in a number of ways. The division may be just a line of containers separating one area from another, or more formal. Fixed divisions can be made by erecting trellises, by planting a screen of trees in tubs or creating a line of miniature espaliered fruit trees. Roof

▲ *A row of lavenders in containers make a small hedge. This idea can be copied on roof gardens using lightweight materials.*

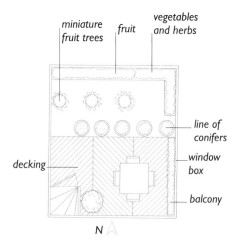

miniature fruit trees / fruit / vegetables and herbs / line of conifers / window box / balcony / decking

N

▲ *A large roof garden divided into two by a line of conifers. The containers around the sides are used for growing vegetables and herbs.*

gardens do allow the gardener to grow freestanding trees, and pyramid fruit trees, such as apple and plum, can be grown without training them against a wall. A line of evergreen conifers planted in containers would make another division, while some gardeners use pots, placed at different levels, planted with small shrubs, such as lavender, to make a sweetly scented, eye-level hedge.

All this requires careful planning and you may well need to construct special containers on site, to make the best use of the space available.

The small roof garden

More often than not roof gardens are restricted in space. If this is the case aim for originality and charm. Use unusual containers, such as metal buckets, and

paint them in matching colors, and also choose plants that look attractive, and be prepared to alter the planting scheme throughout the year. If there is room for just a few plants and containers choose plants with calm, pale colors rather than brilliant red and dark blue that have more impact. You do not want to overwhelm a small space with very bright colors which in any case make small areas appear even smaller. Pale colors, such as white, pale pink, lavender, and gray recede and make a small roof garden appear a bit larger. Sometimes the roof garden may be more formal, for example a large balcony outside a bedroom which is accessible through French windows. The planting here should complement and embellish the space and the most effective schemes are simple, perhaps just one plant in a special container, such as a white hydrangea, or a passionflower, *Passiflora* spp., climbing up a miniature trellis.

Watching the details The most successful roof gardens need to be planned extremely carefully. Every detail must be as perfect as possible. Make sure that any trellis fits in with the surroundings, and that matching trellises are exactly the same design. Also check that the containers are grouped properly, and that all the plants blend together so that plants and containers decorate the garden to the best advantage. For example, if you plan to use growing bags on a roof garden to raise tomatoes, sweet peppers, or beans, make sure that the bags are hidden in specially constructed troughs to conceal the brightly colored plastic. Finally, be as ambitious as you can. Some roof gardens are urban oases of quiet, overhung by mature trees, with fruit and shrubs, white painted trellises and walkways wandering through areas of containers filled with plants of many colors, each with a different tone of green leaf. Such roof gardens always evolve over time, but an ambitious plan never did any harm.

▶ Fruit trees grafted on to dwarfing rootstocks are good plants for containers and provide both fruit and the lovely blossom of spring.

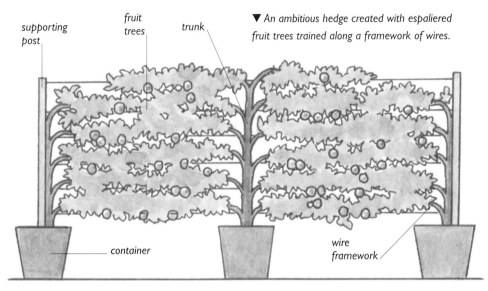

supporting post | fruit trees | trunk

▼ An ambitious hedge created with espaliered fruit trees trained along a framework of wires.

container | wire framework

practical planting

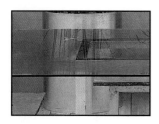

The first practical consideration is size and the second is aspect. How big is the garden, do you need to erect screens, is the garden totally open or is it bounded by walls on one or two sides? You may need professional help erecting screens: anything on a roof must be absolutely secure.

Plants for screens

If you have erected screens or trellises to hide the garden from view, then you need to plant climbers that will cover the screens. Ivy is often the most suitable evergreen climber, and the Confederate jasmine, *Trachelospermum jasminoides*, is excellent but it prefers the shelter of a sunny wall. Ivies cling on with their suckers, and may need tying in and encouragement of a plank or two to get them going up a trellis.

The choice of deciduous climbers is larger and all clematis are suitable, except perhaps the evergreen *C. armandii*. It is very rampant and also needs shelter. Winter jasmine, *Jasminum nudiflorum*, and weeping forsythia, *Forsythia suspensa*, both need tying in and pruning after flowering, but you can also plant one of the climbing roses to be trained along a trellis or against a wall (roses and clematis mix well together). Virginia creepers, *Parthenocissus* spp. and honeysuckles are too rampant, but one of the ornamental grape vines, *Vitis vinifera* 'Purpurea', or the hop, *Humulus lupulus*, are suitable.

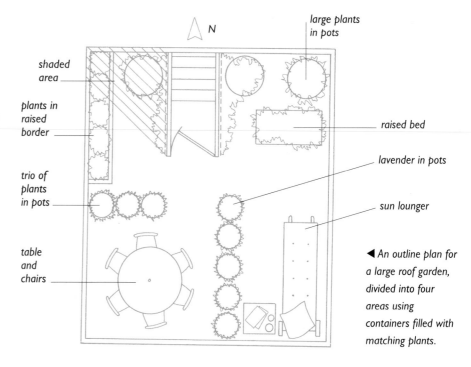

An outline plan for a large roof garden, divided into four areas using containers filled with matching plants.

Annual climbers, such as morning glory, or nasturtium can also be used.

Making internal divisions

If the roof garden is large, you may want to divide it into two or three rooms. These divisions may be formal physical barriers or just a line of pots containing identical plants to suggest separate spaces. There are a number of small or large hedging plants that are suitable.

For a small dividing hedge lavender is ideal. It is evergreen, smells delicious and has lovely blue or white flowers in summer. Lavender hedges need to be planted in fairly tall containers to achieve this effect. The same goes for box, although it can be used as a low edging plant in closely positioned containers to emphasize a formal division.

A line of matching evergreen conifers makes another excellent

◄ *A mature roof garden of the most ambitious kind shows what can be achieved over time. Evergreen shrubs, dwarf conifers, and the weeping birch insure that the garden remains interesting even during the winter months.*

▼ *A minimalist garden design using aluminum containers and a glass table top. The plant element is restricted to a few bamboos.*

dividing line. Try *Juniperus communis* 'Compressa', slow-growing, vertical, and suitable for containers, or try *J. c.* 'Hibernica' or *J. scopulorum* 'Skyrocket'. These two have a similar, upright shape but grow more quickly. *Picea glauca* 'Albertiana Conica' is another good small slow-growing conifer with smoky blue foliage. In a mild climate the evergreen or semievergreen *Abelia* x *grandiflora* makes a good flowering hedge, and is ideal for a sunny or partially shaded position. There is also a dwarf form. It will need fairly hard clipping in spring, as does lavender and box.

You can achieve the same effect with fruit trees which can be trained to make an excellent dividing barrier. They will need a framework of wires to which the branches can be tied, but it is quite easy to tie them in correctly. They have lovely blossom in late spring and fruit in the fall. Trees grafted on to suitable miniature rootstocks are available from most nurseries. Do check their pollination requirements. Some fruit trees may need two or even three varieties growing nearby to achieve pollination, and some are what are called self-fertile and don't need this.

The importance of height

Make sure that the plants vary in height. Use clipped bay trees, *Laurus nobilis*, planted in individual containers, or grow matching standard roses in tubs. Also note that you can place containers on stands, and pole beans and peppers can be trained up stakes. There are a number of suitable climbing plants that will grow in shade, even roses. Hide the parapet walls with ivy planted in containers all along it, or try the climbing *Hydrangea petiolaris* or the similar deciduous climber, *Schizophragma hydrangeoides*—both have clumps of white flowers in summer.

containers for balconies

There are three approaches to gardening on a balcony. If the balcony is small then you may be restricted to one or two formal plants in matching containers, or you can cram in as many plants as possible to create a riot of color. The third approach is to treat the balcony as a small herb garden.

Aspect—colorful annuals in the sun

The style of planting and the type of plant you can grow greatly depends on the situation. If the balcony is in the sun for much of the day then you can grow colorful annuals that love the sun. Everyone has an image of a Swiss chalet with wooden balconies filled to the brim with red and white alpine pelargoniums, with ivy or lobelia trailing over the edge. This style of planting may not be to everybody's taste, but if you want to copy this effect then, above all, you need a balcony that faces south. You also need special containers designed to fit exactly along its length. You should rotate the plants throughout the year, changing the summer bedding plants for winter-flowering pansies. You may find it a help to include a few permanent evergreen plants, such as trailing ivy, to provide a framework. Finally, note that all containers need to be watered at least

DOING YOUR OWN THING

The essential in this type of gardening is to please yourself, experiment, try out various plants, and as in all gardening on a small scale, be ruthless when a plant does not live up to your expectations or grows too large for its place. One of the beauties of container gardening is that when a plant does outgrow its welcome it can be uprooted easily, thrown away and the container refilled with compost and another, smaller version planted for the next few years. Be ruthless about this. Nothing is worse than seeing a small garden dominated by one tree or shrub that has outgrown its space, however attractive it may be.

◄ *Petunias mixed with alpine pelargoniums smother a balcony in summer. Massed plantings using one color are most effective.*

once every day because the compost will dry out quickly in the sun. Annuals also need to be deadheaded regularly.

The informal balcony

Where there is room, pack in as many containers and plants as possible. As in all gardening some planning is essential. Place the chairs, benches, and tables and then add the containers. They can be filled with a variety of evergreen, perennial and annual plants, and the small scale will provide its own interest. Try to include some climbers.

If the balcony is large and almost a roof garden, you can grow any of the plants listed in that section. Another climber you might consider is the deciduous *Actinidia kolomikta* that has green leaves that quickly turn pink and white with age. It is a bit rampant and may require some restricting. It also has fragrant white flowers in summer. If this is not possible then include some hanging baskets filled with colorful annuals to provide the vertical dimension. Include pots of spring, summer, and fall bulbs. Regal lily, *Lilium regale*, is a wonderful plant for a container with an overpowering scent, and agapanthus lilies are beautiful in late summer. Smaller containers should be included with miniature plants, such as houseleeks, *Sempervivum* spp., or cactuses placed outdoors for the summer months.

▶ *A really beautifully designed balcony planted to make a cool impression in summer using mainly white and yellow flowers.* ·

the small formal balcony

A typical balcony is small with wrought iron outside the large window of a town house. Here space is severely limited and the planting must be restrained to match the style of the house. The best idea is to include two matching containers and plants to frame the window.

▶ *A design for a formal balcony with the doorway or French windows flanked by matching evergreen trees. If there is room then you can add a trellis and a climber, such as ivy or winter jasmine.*

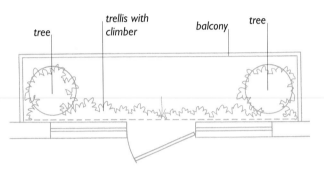

tree   trellis with climber   balcony   tree

Good formal small trees for this situation would be the evergreen bay, or camellias (if the balcony is shaded). Camellias can be pruned quite hard to maintain their shape, and this is best done after flowering is over in late spring. An alternative is clipped box, trained into a ball or spiral. It is worthwhile buying trained shrubs from a specialist supplier for this type of planting because you are aiming for an instant effect, and it takes a number of years to train box properly. The box can be complemented in

ESSENTIAL ASPECT

Some balconies face north and are in the shade for most of the day, even in high summer. You need to choose plants that will provide some color in this type of situation because the sun-lovers will end up long and lanky if they get too much shade, and produce few flowers. See panel on page 67 for plants that are suitable for any balcony that is in shade for much of the day.

◀ *Containers of different heights grouped in a roof garden. The cordyline palm adds height and red-striped phormium gives fall color.*

summer with low containers filled with white daisies or petunias, and possibly one or two blue trailing lobelias. This is not the place to indulge in flashy colors and take care, also, to choose containers that blend with the style of the house.

A kitchen garden balcony

Balconies that face the sun can support a number of vegetables, planted in growing bags or special containers—pole beans, tomatoes, and sweet peppers are all favorite choices. They need regular watering and care throughout the summer. It is best to concentrate on vegetables that mature relatively quickly, and provide some bright color and interesting form in a small space.

Herbs on balconies

Herbs that originated from the hot climate of the Mediterranean like dry, sunny conditions and will flourish if your balcony receives plenty of sun throughout the day. If you do have a sunny balcony and want to produce fresh herbs then you can include rosemary, with its light blue to purple flowers in spring, sage, thyme, chives, basil, and dill.

If you live on the other side of the building then herbs that will flourish in shade include parsley (although it can also be grown in sun), chervil, most mints, and oregano. Stick to the rules to start with but also experiment, you may well be surprised at the result. All sites are different, and there are an infinite variety of microclimates, especially to be found in towns and town gardens.

▲ *A kitchen garden balcony of vegetables and herbs can look attractive with different colors.*

1 Pole beans
2 Carrots
3 Tomato 'Tumbler'
4 Tomato 'Tornado'
5 Applemint
6 Mint
7 Basil
8 Parsley
9 Thyme

SUITABLE PLANTS FOR SHADED BALCONIES

Climbers and wall shrubs

Coral plant, *Berberidopsis corallina*—prefers moist acid soil. Not fully hardy.

Clematis—many large-flowered clematis, such as 'Hagley Hybrid', 'Jackmanii Superba', 'Nelly Moser', 'Comtesse de Bouchaud', and 'Guernsey Cream', will grow on a north wall, as will all *alpina* and *macropetala* varieties.

Weeping forsythia, *Forsythia suspensa*

Climbing hydrangea, *Hydrangea petiolaris*

Winter jasmine, *Jasminum nudiflorum*

Roses—'Königin von Dänemark' ('Queen of Denmark'), 'Madame Legras de Saint Germain', 'Maigold'

Schizophragma hydrangeoides

Tropaeolum—the annual climbing nasturtium.

Shrubs

Box, *Buxus sempervirens*

Camellias

Ivy, *Hedera*

Hydrangeas

Calico bush, *Kalmia latifolia*—'Elf' is a small variety with white flowers; all need moist acid soil.

Bay, *Laurus nobilis*

Rhododendrons—several small varieties are suitable for a container.

Skimmia japonica 'Rubella'

Perennials and annuals

Lady's mantle, *Alchemilla mollis*

Begonia rex hybrids

Ferns—most are suitable.

Fuchsias

Hostas

Busy Lizzy, *Impatiens*, New Guinea Group

Primrose, *Primulas*

Violas

walls and trellises

The container gardener with limited room has to seize every opportunity to make the best use of the available space. The most obvious extension to a small garden is extending the walls upward by erecting a trellis. Climbers can be grown up the trellis to give the garden more seclusion.

How plants climb

Climbing plants operate in three main ways. The serious climbers—ivy, Boston ivy, or Virginia creeper and climbing hydrangea, *Hydrangea petiolaris*—all cling to the wall by suction pads or aerial roots. Pull any away from the wall and you will see the small spots left by the pads. These climbers prefer a flat surface and do best grown against a wall. They need no support. The next group are the clingers—clematis, everlasting pea, *Lathyrus* spp., passionflower, and vines, *Vitis* spp. These wind their leaf tendrils or, in the case of peas, passionflowers, and vines, special climbing tendrils, around anything they find on their way up. They need something to hold on to whether it be netting, trellis, wire, or pea sticks. The last group are the twiners—wisteria, pole (stick) beans, and summer jasmine—that wind their stems around poles or trellis, whatever is to hand.

▶ *Colored trellis can look very striking, especially if a climber with bright flowers is trained up it: purple looks good with blue.*

There are also a number of climbers that need help on their way up. These plants, such as bougainvillea, *Solanum crispum*, roses, and winter jasmine, *Jasminium nudiflorum*, throw out long shoots that need to be tied in. There are also rambling roses that climb using their thorns to hold on to their host trees. Ramblers are vigorous and are unsuitable for growing in a container garden.

planting a climber in a container

1 Put broken crocks in the base to prevent the compost being washed away when the container is watered. Add more stones or gravel to aid drainage.

2 Fix a small purpose-built trellis to the wall behind the container and then fill the container with suitable compost and firm the plant in position. Water well.

3 Tie in the shoots of any climber, here some variegated ivy, to get the climber started. As the plant grows tie the shoots until the suckers take hold.

Using trellis to the best advantage

Ordinary trellis is ideal for any of these climbers and can even accommodate ivy and Virginia creeper with some judicious help. If you plan to grow climbers against a garden or house wall, and you do not wish to cover it with ivy, then you will need to erect a frame of trellis against it, either to tie in the shoots or to let the plant use it as a climbing frame. The best way to do this is to secure wooden battens against the wall so that the trellis is not fastened to the wall itself. This also allows air to circulate behind the plant. If you then fix the bottom of the trellis to the battens with hinges and secure it to the top with hooks and eyes, you can unhook it and lower the whole trellis to the ground, including the plant, when you need to repaint or repair the wall. It is worth doing this properly.

The best containers for climbers

If you are planning to grow a climber as a permanent feature in the garden you should try to give it as large a container as possible. No one wants to try pulling a climber away from the trellis every two years so that it can be potted on.

Ideally climbers should be grown in permanent containers or trenches around the walls, and if you want to grow dense permanent climbers, such as ivy or a climbing hydrangea, this is absolutely essential. Even some of the smaller climbers, such as clematis, need their roots to be cool and moist if they are to grow properly and this is best achieved in a large container mulched with stones. Half-barrels are ideal for growing clematis in because they are not subject to such extremes of temperature as terracotta or stone are in winter months.

▲ *The blue flowers of the ceanothus are lovely in early summer. They can be tied against a wall on a suitable trellis arrangement.*

planting tips for climbers

If you are growing a small climber you can buy specially made trellis panels that have two legs at the bottom designed to fit into a container. These can be used with ordinary terracotta pots, and the trellis can be bedded in with the compost. Tie the climber to the trellis when you have planted it.

If you want to grow a climber standing on its own on a terrace or patio, choose one of the lower growing varieties of clematis and plant it in a half-barrel.

Secure some lengths of pipe vertically around the inside of the barrel, and then push long canes into the pipes. Secure them at the top to make a wigwam.

Plant the clematis deeply and tie in the shoots to individual canes. Use a rich compost and make sure that there is adequate drainage for the roots.

▶ *Hops are good, vigorous climbers that will quickly cover a pergola. Cut them right down in the fall. Only the female plants have flowers.*

▼ *Pyracanthus make excellent evergreen wall shrubs and their colored berries last all winter. They need careful pruning in spring.*

◀ Chaenomeles, *usually called just japonica, is another good wall shrub. The flowers usually emerge on bare branches before the leaves.*

A brief guide to climbers

A surprising number of climbers can be grown against a north-facing wall although not all are suitable for growing in containers. They include: the chocolate vine, *Akebia quinata*; the coral plant, *Berberidopsis corallina*; some, but not all, kinds of ivy; the crimson glory vine, *Vitis coignetiae*; and the perennial flame creeper, *Tropaeolum speciosum*.

Evergreen climbers include: ivy; the coral plant, *Berberidopsis corallina*; *Clematis armandii*; *Clerodendrum splendens★*; *C. thomsoniae★*; *Eccremocarpus scaber* (usually grown as an annual in temperate climates); blue passionflower, *Passiflora caerulea*; *Stephanotis floribunda★*, and *Trachelospermum jasminoides*. A good number of evergreen climbers come from tropical or semitropical climates

and need some form of protection over the winter. The climbers marked ★ are not hardy and should either be brought inside, or at the least given the shelter of a warm south-facing wall. Check the precise requirements of each plant before purchasing and planting.

A number of climbers provide superb fall color. The main climbers grown for their foliage are the Virginia creepers, *Parthenocissus* spp., and the decorative kinds of vine, *Vitis* spp. The best foliage climbers include: *Actinidia kolomikta*, pink, white, and green leaves; the golden hop, *Humulus lupulus* 'Aureus', golden-yellow leaves; Boston ivy, *Parthenocissus tricuspidata*, red to purple leaves in the fall; and *Vitis coignetiae* and *V. vinifera*, both of which have leaves that turn dark red, then purple in the fall.

OTHER WALL PLANTS

If you have room, then you can consider the merits of some of the wall shrubs that can be planted in containers and trained against a wall. One of the best is firethorn, *Pyracantha*, evergreen with clumps of white flowers in spring followed by bright red, yellow, or orange berries in the fall, depending on the species. They respond well to hard pruning and are easy to shape against a wall. Their only disadvantage is the long sharp thorns on the branches. Japonica or Japanese quince, *Chaenomeles*, is another common shrub often trained against a wall. It is deciduous and flowers early in the year, generally in pink or red, although some white varieties are available. These are followed by edible fruits. Fruit trees are also excellent plants to grow against a wall and if you can offer a warm, south-facing position you can grow some of the tender kinds such as peaches or nectarines. Finally, all gardens are brightened by climbing roses. They have to be tied in to any trellis or wire frame, but the scent and flowers they provide are one of the highlights of the summer.

Not all climbers are suitable for growing in containers: among the most suitable are: bougainvillea, that needs a hot climate; *Clematis alpina* and *C. macropetala*; many different kinds of ivy; common jasmine, *Jasminum officinale;* Chilean bellflower, *Lapageria rosea*; and the passionflower, *Passiflora caerulea*. Climbing annuals that give instant effect include: *Eccremocarpus scaber*; morning glory, *Ipomea tricolor*; and black-eyed Susan, *Thunbergia alata*.

window boxes

Attractive window boxes can be marvels of ingenuity, both in design and color. Successful window box gardening takes thought, time, and care. Each one is rather like a semipermanent flower arrangement and many of the rules that apply to flower arranging also apply to window box gardening.

Practical aspects

There are a number of practical things to consider. First, the window box must fit on or beneath a window and it must be securely fastened in place. It will be fairly heavy when full of plants and compost, and anyone planning a window box overhanging a street must be certain that it is retained securely in position. This is usually done by securing metal brackets to the wall. (If you are not an expert get

professional help.) In this type of position make certain that the window box has safety chains which can be secured to the wall or the window frame.

Window boxes must also blend in with the building. Normally they are made of wood or plastic, and can be painted to match the color of the paintwork around the window. They must also be able to drain freely. The bottom must have a number of drainage holes and if it is placed flat on a windowsill, it should be supported on and raised by wood battens to facilitate good drainage. If this is not done then the plants will suffer as they become waterlogged, and the base of the window box will rot if it is made of wood.

Window boxes, indeed all containers, need watering frequently and they need feeding at least once a fortnight. They do not contain a large amount of soil mix, and therefore the plants will need additional encouragement if they are to grow properly. This is particularly true when you are growing vegetables and fruit.

▲ *This window box includes variegated ivy, small tobacco plants, verbena, helichrysum, and pansies in a carefully controlled design.*

MAKING A WINDOW BOX

If you cannot buy a window box that will fit your windowsill, the solution is to build your own. This is not difficult as long as you have some basic carpentry skills and the right tools. The most important thing is to measure the window space and wood accurately. There is nothing more aggravating than finding the window box is a bit too long, and it is quite easy to do this if you forget to add the thickness of the wood on both sides.

Secure the sides and the bottom firmly using battens to hold them in place. Use good screws and do not just nail one piece of wood to another. Treat all the timber with wood preservative before you start (using proper preservative that will not damage the plants) and drill drainage holes in the bottom. Then, when the box is complete, line it with polyethylene, holding this in place with staples (use a staple gun). Finally, cut out matching holes in the liner to marry up with the drainage holes, and the box is ready for planting. A window box treated in this way should give good service for many years.

▶ *Careful planning has created this brilliant yellow window box using broom (genista), ivy, and chrysanthemums.*

assembling the window box

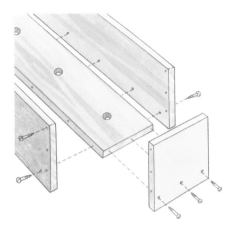

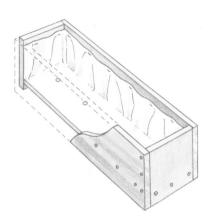

1 Measure the space and cut all the timber to size. Drill holes for the screws or, preferably, use battens to hold the sides and bottom in place.

2 When you have screwed the window box firmly together, line it with heavy-duty polyethylene to prevent the timber rotting. Staple the lining in place.

3 If the window box is freestanding fix it to the wall with brackets as shown. Make sure these are really secure and attach safety chains to the sides.

a variety of window boxes

Window boxes can be used in many ways. Most are planted with colorful annuals, but there are many other schemes that can be adopted. Some of the most effective window boxes are planted to give color during the cold, gray months of winter when few flowers are in bloom.

A colorful window box for winter

Many people imagine that gardens come to a full stop at the end of the fall but this certainly is not true of window boxes. There are plants that will provide color in the winter months, and they can be used to enliven the darkest days of the year. There are two main groups of plants that flower in winter and are suitable for window boxes. The first is the winter-

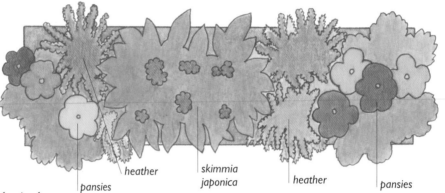

heather   *skimmia japonica*   *heather*   *pansies*   *pansies*

◀ *A simple design for a window box that will give color through the winter. Make certain that this container is filled with ericaceous compost otherwise the heathers will die.*

flowering heathers, *Erica carnea*, and the second the winter-flowering pansies, varieties of *Viola* x *wittrockiana*. Another colorful addition for a winter box are the bright red berries of the small evergreen

Skimmia japonica reevesiana. These are a wonderful scarlet that remain on the plant for many months. Heathers, too, are evergreen, although their leaves are a bit insignificant and the flowers are mainly pink or white.

If you are planting violas in a container with heathers for the winter, it is probably best to choose a white heather, such as *E. carnea* 'Springwood White', *E.* x *darleyensis* 'White Glow', or the slightly larger *E.* x *d.* 'White Perfection'. They will not clash with any brightly colored violas. 'Springwood White' also has the advantage of a

◀ *Erica x darleyensis 'Ghost Hills' has a mass of lovely pink flowers that last from the winter to early spring. They need acid soil.*

slightly trailing habit, so it hangs down and helps to soften the edge of the window box. Although some heathers will tolerate alkaline conditions most really prefer acid soil, and you need to insure that the window box is filled with ericaceous soil to guarantee success.

Window boxes of spring bulbs

There are a number of bulbs that grow well in window boxes but that favorite spring bulb, the snowdrop, *Galanthus* spp., is not really one of them. Snowdrops like to naturalize under trees and in grassy places, and they do best when they are planted "in the green," i.e. dug up, split, and replanted at the end of their flowering period. You cannot plant

snowdrop bulbs in the fall and expect them to do very well, and no self-respecting window box gardener can afford the straggly foliage that takes some time to die down. Crocuses, on the other hand, work well. Plant them in the container in the fall and they will flower the following year at the end of winter. They like a sunny position, and are a welcome sight when they open their petals wide in the spring.

Miniature kinds of daffodil, *Narcissus* spp. also flower well in containers. You can plant a number of crocuses and daffodils in the same container with the narcissus bulbs below the level of the crocuses, and then one will flower after the other. If you add some good

▲ *A formal balcony in spring planted with daffodils and forget-me-nots, with ivy trailing over the front to soften the railings.*

evergreens, such as trailing ivy to provide contrasting foliage, the arrangement can be most successful. Other bulbs that will succeed, providing you plant them deep enough, are small tulips, the low-growing cultivars from Division 1 called Single Early Tulips, and those from Division 14, the Greigii Group. Choose ones with good contrasting colors.

Finally, buy the bulbs from a specialist supplier with an extensive catalog, and never buy a cheap mixed group of daffodils from a supermarket or garden center. They will flower at different times and look dreadful.

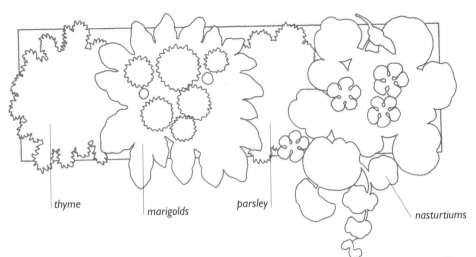

thyme   marigolds   parsley   nasturtiums

◄ *A plan for a small window box filled with an edible mixture of flowering annuals and herbs. Raise the parsley in separate pots and insert these into the window box, for the seeds take a long time to germinate. Use the marigolds for tea and food coloring and the nasturtiums in salads.*

Window boxes full of summer annuals

It is inevitable that the finest and most colorful window boxes are planted with annuals in the summer. Annuals are wonderful plants for all containers, and they are especially effective when they are planted in a small space giving concentrated color. You should also match the color of the window box with the arrangement. White works well with all colors, while a neutral shade of green provides a quiet foil for most plants and their blooms.

Alternatively, paint the window boxes a bright color, in which case a white, or a varied tonal planting would look best. If possible plant the boxes with flowers in bloom because few gardeners are so expert that they can judge matching color tones exactly, before the flowers begin to emerge.

The planting principle is the same as in flower arranging. Plant blocks of color like reds and pinks, or lilac, blues, and white. Use strong colors sparingly in quiet arrangements, or unreservedly fill the window box with brilliant tones. Add taller plants for height and trailing plants to hang over the edge. The choice is entirely personal. For a choice of summer annuals see pages 260–261.

The edible window box —herbs and flowers

Many people use their window boxes to grow herbs for the kitchen, and even gardeners with large vegetable plots often have a window box near the kitchen door, ready for a quick supply of ingredients. Before planning a window box of herbs you need to check which way it faces because some herbs do best in the sun and some in shade. A number of attractive plants can be included and the planting need not just be varying

◄ *A window box of tomato plants, lettuces, carrots, strawberries, and mini-cauliflowers makes a talking point on a town windowsill.*

◀ Blue and white arrangements make a cool statement in summer. Petunias, white daisies, and variegated ivy are the main ingredients.

shades of green. Try some flowering herbs, especially the trailing nasturtium, *Tropaeolum*, that can be used in salads and can be planted with a few marigolds (the flowers can be used as a food coloring and the leaves can be made into tea). Chives have attractive light purple flowers but there might be a bit of a color clash if they are planted with the orange and yellow flowers of the first two plants. And purple-leaved basil, sage, variegated mint, and the curly-leaved parsley can all be included in a small herbal window box.

A window box of miniature vegetables
Miniature vegetables are a good idea. These are now readily available, and a variety can be planted in a vegetable-only window box. Beets, carrots, cauliflowers, leeks, lettuce, onions, corn, turnips, and zucchini are just some of the mini-vegetables available, and many have contrasting leaf colors and shapes. The seed can be sown in patches and the seedlings thinned to produce the most attractive effect. The good thing about mini-vegetables is that they mature more quickly than larger ones, and in less

than three months you should be able to visit your window box and cut plenty of lettuce and scallions for salads, and pull beets and carrots as well.

Mixed window boxes of fruit and vegetables If you want to add variety and colour to the vegetable window box include one or two plants of the small tomatoes that have been developed for the container gardener. 'Tumbler' and 'Patio' are both good varieties and they can even be grown in a hanging basket. You can also include the dwarf sweet pepper 'Jingle Bells' or a miniature cucumber, although this will not provide the flash of brilliant red color.

Add one or two strawberry plants if you want; there are varieties specially bred for the container gardener that flower and fruit over a long period, or if you prefer old-fashioned plants, grow a few wild strawberries. The small berries are most enticing and you won't be able to buy them in the stores either.

beets   scallions   lettuces   carrots   corn

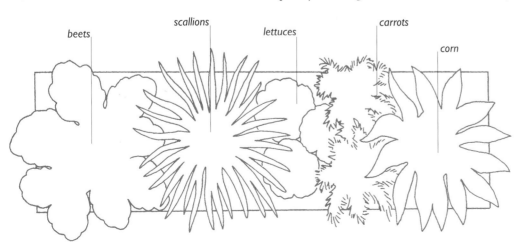

◀ Mini-vegetables have been developed for window boxes and containers. They enable the gardener to provide fresh organic crops for some special meals in season, and are well worth the effort of planting and harvesting.

hanging baskets

Hanging baskets are one of the glories of summer and brighten porches, city streets, and balconies. They are not all that difficult to manage and maintain, but you do have to take care when choosing the plants if you want to achieve the best effect.

A blue, red, and white basket

For a 40cm/16in diameter hanging basket you will need: six trailing plants such as…

Helichrysum petiolare—trailing variety, heart-shaped leaves, densely gray-wooly above, lighter underneath. Off-white flower heads.

Hedera helix (ivy)—use small-leaved variegated varieties such as 'Adam', 'Asterisk', or 'Glacier'.

Plectranthus forsteri 'Marginatus'—trailing, variegated green and white leaves, and *P. australis*—small bright green leaves; or

P. oertendahlii—white-veined leaves with rosy-purple undersides.

Also use…

3–6 trailing *Pelargonium* 'Roulette', with crimson and white striped flowers.

1–2 *Pelargonium* 'Pulsar Scarlet' for the top of the basket, or red dwarf plants from the 'Video Mixed' Series.

6–9 *Petunia grandiflora*—a white variety.

6 *Lobelia* 'Sapphire'—violet blue with a white eye or 'Crystal Palace'—blue.

Larger or smaller baskets may require more or fewer plants, bearing in mind that it is best to overcrowd the basket for maximum effect. Plant the trailing foliage plants around the rim of the basket to trail down the sides, and plant the colored plants in bands. They will grow through the trailing green-leaved ivy, *Hedera*, and make an increasing impact throughout the summer.

A yellow and orange hanging basket for maximum impact

For a 40cm/16in diameter hanging basket you will need…

6–9 trailing *Tropaeolum majus* (nasturtium), either Double Gleam Hybrids or Alaska Mixed.

6 *Lysimachia congestiflora* (loosestrife)— clumps of yellow tubular flowers with red centers.

6 *Bidens ferulifolia*—small yellow star-shaped flowers that cascade down the sides of the basket.

6 *Tagetes* (marigold)—French or signet marigolds are best for baskets—look for Disco Series and Gem Series in shades of orange, gold, and yellow. 'Naughty Marietta' has yellow flowers with maroon markings.

▶ *This is another red, white, and blue design using ageratum and begonias for a blue and red effect. Start planting at the base of the basket and push the plants through the wire from inside to the outside. Keep the plant as intact as possible.*

❶ Begonia (red)
❷ Ageratum (blue)
❸ Petunia (white)
❹ Lobelia (blue)
❺ Ivy

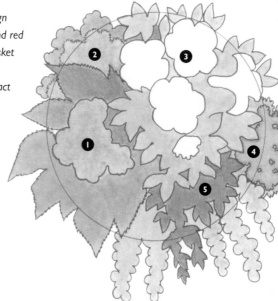

▲ *Hanging baskets can be used as part of the overall garden design. The main plants used in this fragrant garden are scented geraniums.*

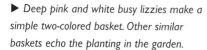

▶ *Deep pink and white busy lizzies make a simple two-colored basket. Other similar baskets echo the planting in the garden.*

A hanging basket for the winter months

Almost all hanging baskets are planted for summer display, but you can contrive an attractive mixture of plants that will give color throughout the winter provided you can keep the basket in a relatively frost-free environment. The basis for a winter basket is hardy evergreen plants that provide a green backdrop. The plants to include are…
Hedera helix 'Glacier' or *H. h.* 'Pin Oak' (both ivies)—if the basket is in an exposed position make sure you choose varieties that are fully hardy.
Polypodium vulgare—an evergreen fern.

Vinca minor, lesser periwinkle— evergreen, with trailing shoots and flowers from early in spring to the fall. *Viola x wittrockiana*, winter pansy—either choose mixed colors or plain blue or white varieties. They provide color for months over the winter.

Simple baskets for summer color

Some of the most effective hanging baskets are those where only one plant is used, often in a variety of colors. The best annual for a tonal basket is the petunia. There are three types: grandiflora, the one with the largest flowers up to 12.5cm/5in across;

multiflora, with each plant carrying many flowers, single or double up to 7.5cm/3in across; and milliflora, smaller plants carrying many flowers. Most petunias are in shades of red, pink, purple, and white. Plants from the Celebrity Mixed Series, the Celebrity Bunting Series (darker colors), and Celebrity Pastel Mixed Series, produce matching displays with a random variety of color. Single color petunias, such as 'Sonata' in white and Supercascade in rose-pink, are also good. The grandiflora petunias in the Picotee Series and Razzle Dazzle Series produce flowers in vivid colors, often bicolored, with ruffled margins.

tonal baskets

Some gardeners prefer to create quieter displays with varying shades. There are an infinite number of plants and color schemes that can be used in this way. Concentrate on one color, such as pink or pale blue, or plant a variety of complementary colors in the paler shades of the color circle.

A pink and purple hanging basket

Use lavender, *Lavandula* 'Munstead', deep purple, or the pink, *Dianthus* 'London Delight', light rose with a deeper eye. Use some of the half-hardy fuchsias, such as, 'Auntie Jinks', white and purple; 'Micky Gault', white with cerise pink centers; or 'Leonora', soft pink; the bright pink busy lizzie, *Impatiens* New Guinea Hybrid, for the center of the basket. Include some gray-green trailing foliage, *Hedera helix* 'Glacier' or *Helichrysum*

petiolare 'Roundabout', to hold the elements together.

A blue, purple, and silver basket

A similar color scheme, but even quieter, could be obtained using purple-blue pansies from the *Viola* x *wittrockiana* range as the main accent, with purple-flowered *Salvia officinalis* 'Aurea' that is small enough for a hanging basket, with *Hedera helix* 'Glacier', helichrysum, and gray-leaved *Senecio cineraria* 'Silver Dust'.

A hanging basket of vegetables

This is an unusual idea but it can work well and provides a talking point. Make sure that all vegetables are fed regularly, at least once a week, during their growing period. This is particularly important for the trailing tomatoes that form the highlight of any display.

Salvia officinalis

Senecio cineraria 'Silver Dus[t]'

Helichrysum petiolare 'Roundabout'

Hedera helix

Viola x wittrockiana

▲ *A blue and white basket is always effective and creates a calm atmosphere. Always use water-retaining granules when planting baskets.*

Lettuce—choose a selection of the loose-leaf varieties, such as 'Red Fox' with red and green leaves; 'Lollo Biondo' with pale green leaves; 'Lollo Rosso' with red frilled leaves; and 'Red and Green Salad Bowl'. Plant them in the sides of the baskets with the darker colored leaves at the bottom, and the light green 'Lollo

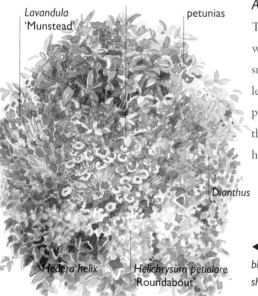

Fuchsia

Lavandula 'Munstead'

petunias

Dianthus

Hedera helix

Helichrysum petiolare 'Roundabout'

◀ *A basket of pink flowers contrasted with the blue lavender. Lavenders need careful placing to show the flowers properly.*

A HERBAL HANGING BASKET

Plant a smaller hanging basket with herbs because they are attractive and useful in the kitchen. Herbs do not produce the vibrant colors of annuals but they have attractive variegated leaves. Also use nasturtium, *tropaeolum*, as trailing plants because they are attractive and edible. The leaves add bite to any salad and the flowers add decoration. The main choice should include…

Thyme—*Thymas herba-barona*, the herb traditionally served with roast beef, will hang down; *T. vulgaris* 'Aureus' and 'Silver Posie' have gold and silver-edged leaves.

Sage—*Salvia officinalis* 'Icterina' has variegated yellow and green leaves; *S. o.* 'Purpurascens' has red-purple young leaves; other varieties are available with different colored leaves.

Chives—delightful lilac flowers.

Parsley—the curly leaved form.

Finally add a few yellow marigolds, the French marigold *Tagetes patula* 'Lemon Drop' is excellent, or the old medieval "pot" herb, the orange marigold, *Calendula officinalis*.

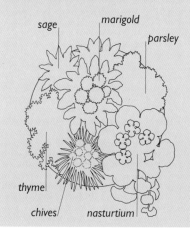

sage | marigold | parsley

thyme | chives | nasturtium

Biondo' around the rim to give a good contrast between the different greens. Then add three plants of the cherry tomato 'Tumbler', that has been specially bred for growing in hanging baskets, and add one or two basil or oregano plants to give a herbal touch if there is room.

▲ *Strawberries and parsley go well together with their contrasting leaf shapes and green colors fringed with white alyssum.*

practical considerations

Container gardening is much the same as any other form of gardening. Seed is sown, plants grow, mature, flower, set seed, and die. The main thing to remember is that the plant roots are more restricted, and therefore they need feeding more often than plants in open ground.

large containers for impact

The choice of container is not something to be rushed. Really large containers made from terracotta or reconstituted stone are extremely expensive, and antique containers even more so. Large containers can be used as accent points, drawing the eye, for plants of special interest.

Using tall pots

Very often the choice of container is dictated either by the height of the plant you wish to grow or the overall garden design. In a garden that is full of containers you will need varying heights. The tallest, the large Ali Baba type jars, may well be difficult to find and are expensive. Sometimes a search around antique or junk shops reveals some surprising treasures that are cheaper and more interesting than those available in garden centers. Take time to find the right one that suits your garden. Very often you find old Victorian pots used for indoor plants or umbrella stands that look perfect in a container garden.

Care in planting One of the things to watch out for when planting large containers is the shape of the neck. Old chimney pots are both popular and decorative, as are Ali Baba jars, but they, and all other containers with narrow necks, are unsuitable for any permanent planting. The problem is that when you plant a shrub in a container the roots expand over time. The only way you can then pot on the shrub into a larger container is to break the top of the jar. Always put permanent plants in an open container where they can be removed relatively easily.

ivy

ornamental grass

◀ Large pots grouped together to give different heights and shapes. Trailing ivy, the decorative grass, Hakonechloa, and thyme would be good plants to include in this type of arrangement.

▼ Large containers and brightly colored pots make their own statement in a garden. Plan with care or they may overwhelm the plants.

blue-glazed pot

square planter   *ornamental urn*

Terracotta pots

The most common material for garden containers is terracotta (which means "cooked or baked earth"). The beauty of terracotta is the large variety of styles and shapes that are available. You can form attractive groups of terracotta containers, either using pots of the same basic design in a variety of sizes, or using a number of

how to age a terracotta pot

1 Modern terracotta pots are often brightly colored and look garish and out of place in the garden. They can easily be aged so that they blend in.

2 Paint the surface of the pot with yogurt, or a mixture of yogurt and sour milk. This attracts algae that will discolor the pot.

3 After a few weeks the pot will be covered with algae and will look as if it is several years old. Leave the inside of the pot unpainted.

different shapes such as egg pots, half-pots, third-pots, and various shapes and styles of seed pans. They can be interspersed by some "long Toms" that are both taller and narrower.

Many designs now on the market are copies of older-style pots that were available in the 19th century, and some of the more elaborate urns are based on classical designs. To give new pots an ancient look, either paint them in softer colors or age them by applying yogurt or sour milk. This attracts algae and the pot soon looks suitably aged. Another alternative is to buy the colored terracotta pots that are now available in a range of soft, muted shades.

▶ *A classical container filled with a mound of sempervivums. Some varieties have red leaves and carry upright flowers in summer.*

other types of container

Many different types of container can be used and the garden designer should not be confined to standard pots available at garden centers. Old tin baths, kitchen sinks, stone troughs, all make excellent containers and add interest to a container garden. Insure that all plants can drain freely.

Troughs

The most expensive and heaviest troughs are made from lead, and they definitely are not suitable for roof gardens. Copies of traditional lead troughs are now made from fiberglass, and traditional stone troughs are available made from reconstituted stone or hypertufa. Be absolutely certain where you are going to position any trough in the garden before buying it though, and put any large container in position first before filling it with compost and planting. Containers are much easier to move around when they are empty. This particularly applies when you are arranging a group of containers in a container-only garden. Place them all in position and move them around until you are completely satisfied with the arrangement. Leave the pots in position overnight and check the grouping again in the morning before finally filling them with compost and plants.

Strawberry planters

One of the favorite containers for the patio is the strawberry planter, and many gardeners have visions of ripe fruit dripping down the sides of the pot. They are readily available in all garden centers but in truth it is difficult to cultivate a huge crop using them, and the greatest

◀ *Strawberries ripening in a traditional strawberry planter. These need to be turned each week to give the plants equal sun.*

care needs to be taken if you are to succeed. The first and most important thing is to buy a perforated central plastic pipe. Put this in position because it enables you to water the bottom of the container as well as the top. Add some stones or pot shards to hold the pipe upright and provide additional drainage. Then fill the strawberry planter with a well fertilized, loam-based soil mix—strawberries are greedy plants and need all the encouragement they can get. Plant the strawberries as you fill up the container, pushing the plants through from the inside—choose a variety especially developed for growing in pots. Firm in all the roots and then water well. If you really want to be successful with strawberries you should pick off the flowers in the first year to build up the strength of the plant.

Keep the planter watered throughout the summer and turn it every week so that all the sides get an

equal amount of sun. Feed the plants with liquid fertilizer every two weeks after the flowers appear in the spring. Protect from birds if necessary.

Versailles tubs

These were traditionally used for clipped bay, *Laurus nobilis*, and orange or lemon trees in conservatories. They have a pleasing shape but are only suitable where there is space to design a fairly formal garden. They can be made from wood or plastic, and while the wooden ones are more decorative they require a plastic liner to prevent the wood rotting over the years. They are also heavier and much more expensive, but look the part.

▲ *Proper lead containers are both heavy and expensive. Fiberglass copies of classical designs look just as good. Line them with polyethylene.*

Unusual containers

A number of unusual containers can be used and there is plenty of choice. Old sinks and tin baths are good contenders but check that they fit in with the garden design and are suitable for your planting. Sinks, in particular, are often used for low-growing alpine plants. Old cattle troughs are another idea if you have room, as are smaller discarded water cisterns. They do weigh quite a lot though, so don't fill them before you have to move them and be sure that you can make drainage holes in the base before putting in rubble and compost.

Versailles tub

zinc bucket

wire basket

▲ *Many different containers can be used in gardens, both formal and informal. Punch holes in the bottom of buckets to allow drainage.*

smaller containers

The smaller the space the more care has to be taken to choose containers that fit the garden design and match the plants. Often the small containers in a grouping get ignored; take care to see they blend with the others. Wall pots, too, are most important and can extend the garden upward.

Small containers for small spaces

When it comes to choosing small containers there is a considerable choice, and with a little imagination the gardener can achieve great effects in a tiny space. Often in small gardens there is only room for a few plants, and each can be matched individually to the container. Small pots can be grouped together with small plants, such as primroses, *Primula* spp. or violas, while larger flat-bottomed bowls can be filled with rosette-shaped *Sempervivum*s that rejoice in the common name of houseleek.

The important point is to focus on your favorite plants—small lavender bushes, spring bulbs, herbs, and colorful annuals. Then collect a number of similar terracotta pots in varying sizes, plant them up and arrange them to suit the space. There may even be room for one or two climbing plants, such as a clematis, that can be trained up the wall of the house if a larger pot can be found to accommodate their root systems. Clematis like their roots to be cool, so shade the pots of clematis from the sun if

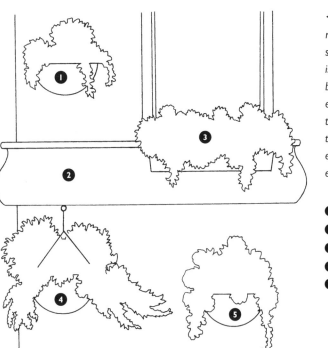

◀ *When the gardener is restricted to a small space such as a balcony then there is often scope to add hanging baskets and window boxes to extend the number of plants that can be grown. Make sure that these plantings match each other in style or the effect may be incongruous.*

❶ Wall pot
❷ Balcony outside window
❸ Window box
❹ Hanging basket
❺ Wall pot

ANTIQUE WALL POTS

Plain wall pots are most suitable for many situations but there are a number of shapes available, either copied from classical designs or from ancient civilizations such as the Aztecs and Mayans. These can look very good on old walls in the right surroundings. They include shell wall pots, masks, lattice designs, honeypots, and gourds. All wall pots dry out quickly in summer so it is essential to include water-retaining granules when planting and to water them at least once a day, if not more.

▶ *Ordinary terracotta pots secured to a garden fence with wire rings, planted with bright busy lizzies to make everyone sit up and notice.*

you can. Even if you do not have a lot of space many lovely effects can be created with a bit of imagination.

Wall pots and hanging baskets

Container-only gardeners should always be aware of the vertical dimension. There is enormous scope to extend a garden upward, given a suitable wall, or even some firm trellis, using a variety of wall pots. These are half-pots with flat backs that fit against a wall and hold plants that trail over the edge. If you fill these half-pots with colorful annuals they make a series of vivid splashes. Used with imagination, the keen gardener can paint a series of abstract pictures using the flowers and plants.

There are many kinds of wall pots, including honeypots, decorated and plain shells, and fluted and rounded terracotta, emulating the styles of full pots. If you have a number of terracotta pots in the garden of varying shapes and designs, try to match the half-pots to the full ones, integrating the design. Also make sure that they are firmly secured to the wall, and that you can reach them easily with a hose extension for watering. Being that much more in the sun they will require watering as frequently as hanging baskets. Finally, when planting wall pots insure, as far as possible, that the plants will flower at the same time. That way you will obtain the maximum effect.

Hanging baskets

Most hanging baskets are plain, made from wire, and the two most common sizes are 40cm/16in and 30cm/12in diameter. You can buy ornate filigree metal baskets if you want but the plain ones are generally better as the metalwork is soon obscured by the plants. Make sure that the hook and beam on which the basket hangs is strong and secure. Hanging baskets weigh a surprising amount when they are in full growth and have been watered. For care and planting details see pages 102–103.

Both wall pots and hanging baskets are especially useful for balconies. Unless the balcony is very large, it is unlikely that there will be room enough for large containers or a raised bed big enough to accommodate climbers. In this situation, carefully positioned wall pots and hanging baskets provide color and interest.

containers for large plants

It stands to reason that large plants need large containers, especially if they are going to grow successfully. Much thought should be given to purchasing larger containers, as they are often expensive, and it is important that they fit into the style that you have decided on for your garden.

Containers for large plants

If you want to grow large plants, you have got to think big. In fact all large plants, trees, fruit, and shrubs will need as

◄ *Canna lilies contribute to a garden planned to give the feeling of a tropical forest. Heat and sun are necessary for success.*

large a container as you can provide if they are to flourish and attain anything like their potential proportions. They are best grown in raised beds or in special large containers to match the overall design of the patio, roof garden, or terrace. All containers need good drainage at the bottom, and an automatic watering system is a great help.

The next key factor is style—you have to think carefully about how a large expensive container will fit into the garden, and how the container will relate to the type and shape of the plant. Trees or shrubs with a spreading habit look best in wide-brimmed pots, and formal clipped topiarized trees need formal containers to look their best. Very often large containers are made from terracotta, but other materials, such as stone or glazed earthenware, are also suitable provided they can accommodate the root system of the plant. Also, keep

the containers and their contents in proportion. It is always possible to pot on a tree into a larger container as it grows, while a small plant alone in a large pot will look bare and isolated. It is best to fill the space around the main plant with low-growing herbs or annuals to keep the planting in proportion.

Half-barrels

Half-barrels make good containers and can accommodate quite large trees. They look natural and suit almost any surrounding. You may be able to find old barrels in a junkyard, but good copies are now made specifically as plant containers. If you are lucky enough to get some barrels they need to be cut in half. Do this carefully with a saw, marking the circumference with a chalk line to guide you. Then fill the barrel with water and leave it overnight so that the wood swells. You may have to soak the barrel for even longer if the wood has become extremely dry. Then make drainage holes in the bottom and line the barrel with a thick plastic liner, holding it in place

with staples. Make holes in the liner at
the bottom to fit the drainage holes.
Trim the plastic neatly before filling the
barrel with hardcore and compost.

Positioning tall pots to the best advantage

Tall pots make excellent features on a
patio garden and hardly need any plants
to make them attractive. Ali Baba pots, in
particular, are very decorative on their
own but be careful if you are planning to
plant up a very tall pot. There are few
plants that work well and you should aim
for some trailing nasturtium, *Tropaeolum*,
or something equally simple.

Very large containers need to be
placed carefully in the garden, and care
has to be taken over the color of the
pot and the background that it is against.
The design of a garden is composed of
many things and background color
and planting are often overlooked.

The shape of the container often dictates the type of plant. Trees suit Versailles tubs while trailing nasturtiums fit Ali Baba jars.

DRAINAGE FEET

Although it does not matter in every case it
can be very important to keep the base of the
container off the ground. This particularly
applies to window boxes and any container
made from wood or MDF. Raise them using
wooden battens or tiles. Special feet are
available for most terracotta pots and they
should be placed underneath to let the water
drain away freely. Half-barrels should always be
placed on bricks.

▶ *Foliage plants look good in spectacular
containers. Here the blue-gray leaves of the
agave tone in with the color of the jars, and
the spiky leaves contrast well.*

building raised beds

Raised beds are an excellent idea in all container gardens where there is sufficient room. They enable the gardener to create a permanent display and increase the range of plants that can be grown. They are also extremely useful for disabled gardeners who cannot reach beds at soil level.

Planning and measuring

Begin by making sure that there is enough space around the edges of the bed to allow adequate access. Plan out the size of the bed on paper and then calculate the amount of material needed. Raised beds can be built from bricks, stone slabs, decorative blocks, or cinder blocks, whichever you prefer. Cinder or concrete blocks are the cheapest, but they will need rendering and painting if they are going to look satisfactory. Stone and stone slabs are rather difficult to handle, and decorative blocks are not really satisfactory. Bricks, old or new, are probably best and fit in with most designs, but there will be a number of gardens in parts of the country where stone is the predominant building material. Any raised bed there would have to be built from stone because brick would look quite inappropriate.

Having decided on the material you then have to mark out the area accurately with string, making sure that all the corners are square—assuming you are building a square bed. Then dig out a trench, 30cm/12in wide and 30cm/12in deep, for the footing that supports the walls. Fill this with concrete, make sure that it is quite level and leave overnight. If you are building your raised bed on a solid foundation, such as a patio, you then need to break up the base to allow the water to drain through properly into the subsoil. If you do not do this all you will do is create a miniature swimming pool filled with earth or compost, and all the plants will eventually rot and die. Do

◄ *A simple wooden trough is the easiest form of raised bed, here devoted to vegetables and herbs. The leaves make a pleasing contrast.*

making a raised bed

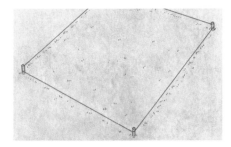

1 Measure the area and mark it out with pegs and string. Make sure that the corners are at right angles. Break up the base to allow free drainage.

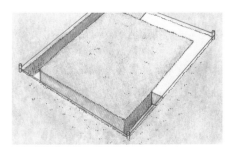

2 Dig out a trench around the sides of the raised bed 30cm/12in high and 30cm/12in deep. Tamp down some hardcore in the bottom and then fill the trench with cement.

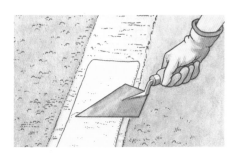

3 Leave the cement overnight to dry. Protect in wet or frosty weather. Start by building an inner wall of cinder blocks. Lay these on a bed of mortar at least 12mm/½in thick.

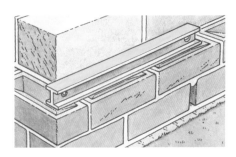

4 Check the levels with string and a level and insert wall ties at intervals to give the walls extra strength. It is best to build from the corners outward.

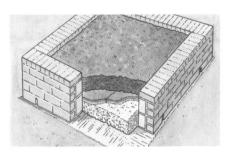

5 Finish off the walls by laying bricks across the cinder blocks and brick walls as shown to make a neat finish. Fill the bed with compost and allow this to settle before planting.

this part properly so that the container can drain freely and well. And take particular care, if you are doing this on a patio, not to obstruct or damage any of the main services or drains.

If you are constructing a traditional brick bed, now build an inner wall using cinder blocks. Lay each block on a 12mm/½in-layer of mortar with one end butted against the next side of the bed using a dab of the mortar. When the inner walls have been completed, check that they are level and then build the outer wall using bricks. Build the outer wall out from each corner, and then set a string guideline between the corners and infill the corners with bricks insuring that they are totally level. Insert some metal wall ties at intervals to add to the strength of the wall. When the walls are finished lay a final course of bricks lengthwise across the inner and the outer wall as shown in the picture on the left. Add a good layer of rubble or stones to the base to assist drainage, and then fill the bed with good soil mix or good quality garden soil.

▲ *An extremely glamorous patio designed in the style of Charles Rennie Mackintosh with raised beds that complement the colors used.*

building permanent trenches

A raised trench in any container garden is wonderful for all elderly or disabled gardeners confined to a wheelchair; special long-handled tools are available that enable anyone to reach the center of the bed. They also allow anyone to grow a selection of more permanent plants.

A number of patio gardens can be improved if there are permanent trenches or beds positioned around the side or sides of the garden. The principles of building a trench around the perimeter of a small garden are exactly the same as building a raised bed in the center, but there are one or two extra questions that you should ask yourself, and one or two additional factors to be taken into account. The first question is width. There is no point in building a permanent bed around the walls of your garden if you cannot reach the back easily to prune and tie in any plants and shrubs growing there.

You then have to decide on the height. Should it be relatively high, the same height as a raised bed accessible from a wheelchair, or just one or two bricks high, holding a small bed in place around the edge of the garden? And which way does the garden face? A raised bed in the center of the garden is relatively unaffected by aspect, but a bed against a south- or southwest-facing wall is very different from one against a north-facing wall. For example, a south-facing wall will support a number of fruit trees from peaches to pears that can be trained against it on a framework of wires. On a north-facing wall, if you are lucky, you may be able to grow a Morello cherry, but they make large trees and grow too big for the normal container garden.

If you do plan to use an old garden wall as the back of the raised trench, is it in good enough condition to stand the additional weight, or are the bricks and mortar old, crumbly and unable to cope

◄ *A raised trench enables the gardener to grow a good selection of more permanent plants, such as larger shrubs and trees.*

making a permanent trench

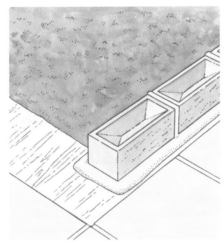

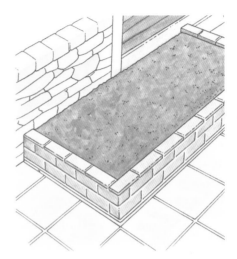

1 Measure the space for a permanent trench and then remove enough topsoil around the walls to lay the cement footing for the walls.

2 Lay the bricks once the footing is dry. If the trench is built against a freestanding wall, as shown, you need only build three walls.

3 Always leave a small gap if the trench is built against the wall of the house so that there is no chance of damaging the damp course.

with damp earth and winter frosts? If the wall is in really poor condition then you may need to rebuild it before starting. Alternatively, you may have to build a retaining wall in front of it, leaving a gap for the air to circulate. This also applies to the walls of the house or apartment. Never, ever, build a garden trench right

up against the house walls because it will interfere with the damp course and cause problems. Always leave a good gap.

Design

Now check the design and plan everything before you start. Two small beds may look better than one large one. There may even be room for small free-standing beds in the middle of a terrace or roof garden. They should be made

from wood or plastic because bricks would normally be too heavy. Natural materials, wood, and brick always look attractive, but all surfaces can be painted and this may work better.

Work out the size of the bed and the number of bricks and slabs you need. But remember, however easy it may look, bricklaying is quite a skilled profession. Call for an expert if you have any doubt in your ability to do a good job.

PLANTS FOR RAISED TRENCHES

The main benefit of making a raised trench or bed in or around the patio is the increased range of plants that this allows you to grow. Fruit trees trained on a framework of wire make excellent use of wall space and small climbing roses are another excellent wall-covering plant in a small garden, and they can be used as ladders by large-flowered clematis in summer.

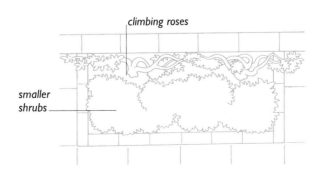

climbing roses

smaller shrubs

◄ *Choose suitable climbing plants for the back of a raised trench and then place smaller shrubs in front. Climbing roses are excellent but evergreen climbers and shrubs are available for color over winter.*

paths, steps, and trellises

The design of the patio or garden must be considered as a whole. This entails looking at the flooring, the seating areas, steps, trellises, and pergolas. Any reasonably confident handyman can build any of these features, but it is best to consult a specialist manual before starting.

Flooring—paving stones, blocks, and bricks

There are many attractive flooring materials available for any patio. Natural stone crazy paving is one of the best, but it is very expensive and difficult for the amateur to lay correctly. It may be better to consider one of the modern concrete look-alikes. They mimic the qualities of natural stone but are more regular, easier to lay and provide an attractive surface.

Another good flooring material that looks most attractive and is extremely flexible is brick. It can be laid in various patterns including herringbone, circles, and quadrants. In fact different patterns can be used to delineate and highlight particular areas of the patio.

There are a large variety of brick and paving blocks available at various prices that can be used. Anyone wanting to relay the surface of a patio or garden is advised to consult a specialist manual and follow the instructions carefully. It is essential that there is a really good foundation of hardcore and sand, and that adequate allowance is made for good drainage. All external flooring must also allow rainwater to drain away from the walls of the house, and if you are laying or relaying a patio butting on to the lawn, it is advisable to dig out a soakaway at the edge of the patio that can be returfed when the patio is complete. If you do not do this the edge of the lawn will be extremely damp and sodden whenever it rains.

◀ An old brick path in a small garden that blends with the terracotta container. Note how closely the bricks have been laid together.

laying a brick path

1 Brick paths are best laid on a sand base. Spread the sand evenly and make sure that the surface is level before putting the bricks in place.

2 Brick paths are more interesting if the bricks are set out in a variety of patterns. Make sure that they are placed close together and check the level.

3 When the path has been laid brush a weak mixture of sand and cement lightly over the bricks and then water it in. Keep the bricks as clean as possible.

Gravel paths and walkways

Gravel and cobblestones are two other materials for patterning the surface of the patio. Gravel can be used as a garden surface in a small town garden where a grass lawn would be inappropriate. If you want to make a gravel garden just lay 25mm/1in of gravel directly on top of the soil; you can plant directly into the soil beneath. Apply a simazine-based weedkiller to the gravel areas in the summer to stop any weeds germinating. When laying a gravel path it needs to be excavated more deeply, and depending on the amount of traffic, you may need to put down a layer of hardcore before

▶ Old railroad ties have been used to surround a novel water feature, flanked by painted wooden decking.

spreading the gravel on top. Cobble-stones can be used as decoration.

Wooden decking If the shape and design of the garden allows, consider putting down wooden decking as a sitting or walking area. Wood is a most sympathetic material, and timbered flooring on a

balcony or raised terrace always looks exactly right. Although not quite as permanent as paving, good quality timber that has been properly treated with preservative will last for a long time. The same applies to trellises, archways, and pergolas. They can all add interest to the design of a patio garden.

using extraordinary containers

In any formal garden odd and unusual containers look out of place. Elegant balconies and balustrades need formal terracotta and stoneware pots. In a small private garden you can let your imagination run riot, and any number of unusual containers and vessels can be pressed into use.

Found containers

If buying new containers is too expensive look out for all kinds of pots, baskets, and buckets in out-of-the-way places. Most can be painted, and all they need is adequate drainage holes. Tin baths; discarded sinks; troughs used for animal feed, and old buckets that can be painted to fit in with the design and color of the garden, are all useful.

Another good idea is old car or tractor tires. They may not be hugely elegant but they are extremely useful, and many professional potato growers produce record yields by adding tire upon tire,

▲ *Old chimney pots can be found in junkyards. They allow the container gardener to present brilliant annuals in a new way.*

◄ *The dark green leaves and bright orange fruit of the calamondin make a glorious contrast with the polished steel bucket.*

topping up the compost as the potato plant grows. If they are painted white, grouped together and sensitively covered with some trailing plants they will not look too outrageous.

Temporary containers

Try to find containers that will last for a good length of time, but if that is not possible several objects can be used for a while and then discarded when something better turns up. Wooden boxes can hold soil mix and plants for a period even if they will eventually rot away. Plastic crates are another idea: cover them with plants, or paint them to match your garden color scheme. Garbage cans, tin or plastic, can also be used, preferably brightened with a coat of paint. Catering-sized food cans, if you can get hold of them, are another good idea.

Smaller containers

When you come to smaller plants and containers there is more scope. China and pottery are tricky. One of the essential things with all containers is adequate drainage and this means making holes in the base. It is very difficult to make a series of holes in the base of jam jars or mustard pots although they can be used for some plants for short periods. Great care has to be taken to make sure that any plant grown in this type of container does not become waterlogged, for inevitably the roots will rot and the plant will die.

Among the best small containers are cans of various shapes and sizes. Holes

can easily be punched in the bottom and they can be painted to disguise their origin; any number of small plants can be grown in them. Another good idea is to use wicker baskets of varying sizes lined with polyethylene. These do look attractive in an informal setting, but they should be used with care for, however meticulous you are when planting and watering, inevitably some water will get on to the wickerwork and it will eventually rot—move them inside when it rains.

▲ *A galvanized garbage can is used here to present foxgloves with clematis and grasses. The wild garden effect contrasts sharply with the materials used as containers and background.*

USING YOUR IMAGINATION

The great thing with all container gardening is to use your imagination. Lovely gardens can be made using the most unpromising receptacles and if painted the effect can be extremely exciting and unusual.

tufa and hypertufa

Tufa is porous limestone rock, light in weight, that can be used for growing small plants, and it is most often used in an alpine garden. Tufa can be used in a bed on its own, or positioned in groups in troughs. Not only does tufa look attractive but it retains water well.

Using tufa

Buy some tufa rocks and then chisel out holes in them about 2.5cm/1in diameter and 7.5cm/3in deep. Make the holes about 10cm/4in apart. Put some sharp sand in the bottom of each hole and then insert small alpine plants or rooted cuttings. Then fill in any gaps with compost, firming around the plants gently with a pencil or small dibble. Wedge some pieces of rock in the hole to keep the plant in place, and keep watering the tufa well until the plants have become established. It is important that at least half to one-third of the tufa rock is buried below the surface of the soil, and that holes are made at a variety of angles so that plants grow down all the sides of the rock.

Hypertufa can be used to make realistic troughs that can also be used as window boxes. Alternatively, with suitable molds, it can be fashioned into rocks and stones.

Hypertufa is made by mixing 2 parts peat, 1 part cement, and 3 parts coarse sand. Mix as you would cement. Check the color and add paint if you want the mixture to be a certain hue.

It is possible to make all types of shapes using hypertufa. To do this it is probably easiest to make papier mâché molds. Put strips of wire over the molds to give them some strength and then cover with hypertufa, adding it bit

HYPERTUFA ROCKS

If you have fashioned a number of hypertufa rocks they can be placed in an alpine garden. See that they are firmly embedded in the soil or compost. Chisel away some holes in the rocks and then fill them with compost. Keep the compost topped up through the year because it will tend to shrink away. Plant small alpines or trailing plants in these holes and they will soon cover the rocks.

◄ *The pink flowers of the winter-flowering heather* Erica carnea *'Springwood Pink' are most welcome in the winter months.*

making a hypertufa trough

1 To make a trough you now need two boxes, one smaller than the other. Cut squares of wire netting to fit the sides of the smaller box. Coat the boxes with oil to stop the hypertufa sticking.

2 Put a layer of hypertufa in the bottom of the large box, add the wire and a sandwich layer of hypertufa, repeat around the sides. Press a sawn up broom handle into the base to make drainage holes.

3 Cover and then leave for about one week for the hypertufa to set properly. Finally, remove the boxes. Roughen the surface and then paint with liquid manure to encourage algae.

by bit until you have achieved the effect you wish. Hypertufa can also be used to cover up old troughs and even glazed surfaces, although it is best to score them with a tile- or glass-cutter first to help the hypertufa stick.

▶ *The finished hypertufa trough planted with heathers and mulched with gravel. This is light enough to be moved easily around the garden and looks perfectly natural.*

hanging baskets

Most hanging baskets are filled with bright annuals that make a glorious impact in summer. Practically all hanging baskets have to appear against a strongly colored background, such as a brick wall, and they have to compete. The background for a hanging basket is not a muted green.

Planting a hanging basket

Choose the biggest basket you can because they work best when they are fairly large. Place the basket on top of a large bucket to hold it level when planting. Traditionally the basket was lined with sphagnum moss, but preformed liners are much more environmentally friendly although they do not look so attractive. Fill the liner with multipurpose mix, adding water-retaining granules to help the basket stay moist during the summer, and slow-release fertilizer. Now make slits in the liner at regular intervals. Water the plants well and then push them through the basket from the inside. Plant the bottom row of annuals on their sides so that they hang down as they grow. Continue in this way until you reach the top of the basket, and then plant around the rim so

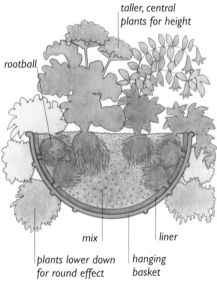

taller, central plants for height

rootball

mix   liner

plants lower down for round effect   hanging basket

▲ *Cross-section of a small hanging basket showing the plants in full growth. Cut slits in the liner when planting.*

◄ *A delicate hanging basket that relies for its effect on the lemon-yellow petunias surrounded by brachyscome, sutera, and lysimachia.*

that the plants will hide the edge. Finally, put some upright plants in the middle. Add more mix as required, water the basket well and mulch with moss to minimize moisture loss. The plants will soon fill out the basket and will quickly hide the liner.

Keep the basket in a frost-free place, such as a conservatory or porch, until you can put it outside safely. You can buy self-watering baskets that have a reservoir of water at the base, and they are useful if you do not have the time to water the basket more than once a day.

General points for hanging baskets Use soilless multipurpose mix. This is the best for annuals and bedding plants that are only grown for one season. Put the mix on the compost heap or throw it away at the end of the summer when the baskets are dismantled.

Plant all baskets thickly. Aim for the maximum color impact and fill in any gaps that may appear in the summer. Water the plants and the container when planting is finished, and never let the container dry out. It is essential that hanging baskets are watered every day, and they should be watered twice a day in very hot weather in summer. If they do dry out it can be difficult to resurrect them. Try putting the basket in a large bowl of water, or the bath, and leave it there for several hours.

Feed the hanging basket regularly with a liquid fertilizer and add slow-release fertilizer granules to the mix when planting; you can also add foliar

feed to the water with advantage. This helps to keep the plants healthy.

Deadhead the flowers regularly—this applies to all annuals and all containers, and never let the plants set seed because if they do they think their work is done. Check the baskets for disease, spray when

necessary, and mist the plants regularly when the weather is hot to prevent the spread of spider mites.

▼ *A vivid hanging basket of trailing nasturtiums topped by begonias. The canna lilies extend the line of color along the garden.*

WATERING

It is worth repeating that hanging baskets need constant watering during the summer when the soil mix can dry out very quickly. Rather than climb long ladders, have the basket on a pulley system or use a long-armed attachment to make the job easier.

growing bags

One of the most useful (and most hideous!) containers in the small garden is the growing bag. Growing bags really are excellent. They are simple to use, contain the right type of soil mix for plants such as tomatoes and cucumbers, and can be used to grow other shallow-rooted vegetables.

◀ *Tomatoes in a growing bag trained up a fence, with a few pot marigolds planted in front to deter butterflies and aphids.*

Concealing growing bags

There are two ways of hiding growing bags. The first is to make a special container the same shape as the bag and put the growing bag inside it. The second method that is useful on a patio is to leave a special space in the floor of the patio so that the growing bag can be put in, level with the patio itself. This does not necessarily conceal the growing bag to start with, but when the plants grow it becomes much less noticeable. Another idea is to make small pockets of soil in the patio when it is laid out. Plant ground-covering plants, such as creeping thyme, around the growing bag trench and then train them over the surface.

Stake supports

It is now possible to buy special wire holders that go with growing bags into which three stakes can be inserted. They hold the stakes in exactly the right place

▶ Tomatoes and bell peppers in growing bags against a south-facing wall. With careful feeding these can produce prolific crops.

and make tying in the plants much easier. The holders are extremely neat and helpful, especially if the bag is positioned away from a wall.

Plants for growing bags

The traditional plants for growing bags are tomatoes. Depending on the climate, these will grow well outside: 'First Lady', 'Oregon Spring', and 'Celebrity'. 'Taxi' has good yellow fruits while 'Whipper-snapper', 'Sun Cherry', and 'Sun Gold' are popular cherry tomatoes. Many gardeners like to grow peppers and cucumbers, and they and eggplants can be grown provided the patio gets the sun. 'Ace' bell pepper ripens to green in 50 days and to red in 70. The eggplant 'Little Finger' can also be grown while, of the outdoor cucumbers, 'Little Leaf' or 'Jazzer' are good.

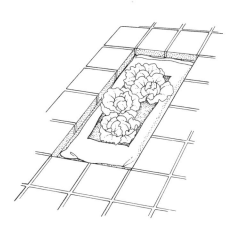

▲ To conceal growing bags make a shallow trench in the patio the same dimensions as the bag. The plants will soon cover the edges.

▲ Low-growing plants, such as thyme or Campanula carpatica, can be planted around the bag and trained over the surface.

GROWING PLANTS IN GROWING BAGS

The beauty of using bags is that they initially save the gardener a lot of time. That is because they contain a nutrient-enriched soil mix, originally peat based, now more often peat substitute, such as coir. There are adequate nutrients in the mix to establish all the plants. As they mature, these nutrients need replenishing and it is necessary to feed all plants with a liquid food, such as tomato fertilizer, every week or 10 days. The other essential is watering. The bags need to be watered every day like most containers, particularly in hot weather. Make sure that you buy one of the special pipe and water holders now available. They allow the bag to be watered along the whole of its length and make sure an even distribution of nutrients when the plants are fed.

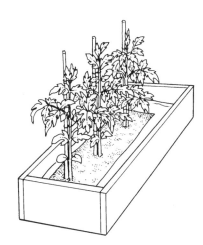

▲ Growing bags can be hidden in containers. This is a good idea on roof gardens and small patios to keep them looking neat and tidy.

gardening basics

All gardening depends on three things—the soil or growing medium, light, and water. Soil is essential, and is acid, neutral, or alkaline. Some plants grow best in one type of soil, some in another. The light or aspect is almost as important, and for the same reason. Some plants only grow well in full sun, others only grow well in shade or partial shade. See which way your garden faces and plant accordingly. As for water, all normal plants in temperate zones need a drink, so see that they get it.

soil and soil mixes

It is a good idea to use proper potting mix for all containers; this has a number of advantages. It is clean, sterile, and contains the nutrients necessary for plant growth. It is also light, easy to handle, and has no unwanted weed seeds (at least to start with). It is, however, quite expensive.

Using topsoil

A cheaper growing medium is topsoil. Sterilized topsoil can be bought from garden suppliers or specialists. Any specialist firm will advise you on the amount you will require, given the cubic volume of the containers you are going to fill. One of the difficulties about using topsoil though is that it usually arrives by truck, and if you live in a row house in a town, you have to be on hand to barrow it up and take it through the house. You also have to clean up the street properly afterward otherwise the neighbors may complain. Technically there should not be much difference between topsoil and soil mix. Topsoil, even when sterilized, will contain the seeds of some weeds but these are pretty unimportant. What you must do though is test the topsoil to establish whether it is acid, alkaline, or neutral. This is easy to do using a simple chemistry kit which is available from all gardening centers and nurseries. You can also test for the nutrients at the same time if you wish, but this is not so important.

Testing your soil The basic soil test will establish the pH of the soil. Neutral soil, suitable for growing most plants, has a pH of between 6.5–7, acid soils have a lower pH and alkaline soils a higher one.

TESTING YOUR SOIL

It is vital that you test your soil to see what kind you have in your garden. This is particularly important to do before you start planning your planting and buying expensive plants. Both of these kits are very easy to use and will tell you what kind of soil you have in a matter of minutes. It is always possible to make alkaline soil more acid, or acid soil more alkaline, so don't despair if your soil is strongly one or the other. The first pH-testing meter consists of a probe, which you push into the ground, and a display that tells you what kind of soil you have. To use the other kit, you must mix a sample of your soil with the chemicals provided to find out the type.

1 Testing the acidity or alkalinity of soil is easy with a pH-testing meter. This device is essential for gardeners who are red/green color blind.

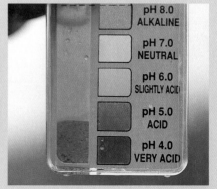

2 Lime-testing kits, in which a soil sample is mixed with water and chemicals, are inexpensive and easy to use. Check the color indicator against a color chart.

▲ Lime can be added to acid soil for alkalinity.

▲ Peat soils are generally acid, for acid-loving plants.

▲ Vermiculite is often added for better drainage.

▲ Multipurpose mix can be bought everywhere.

▲ Use bulb-fiber mix for indoor bulbs.

Some plants prefer acid soil, such as camellias or rhododendrons. You can always make acid soil more alkaline by adding lime over the winter (sprinkle it on the surface and let the rain and weather wash it in) or, conversely, alkaline soil more acid by adding peat, sulfur chips or sulfur powder (flowers of sulfur).

Types of soil mixes

There are three main types of soil mix and the beginner is often confused over when and how they should be used.

Seed starting mix—this is specifically for growing seeds. Seed mixes may be loam-based (i.e. with soil) or be peat (or peat-substitute) based. They are very fine so that the medium is in direct contact with the small seeds, and they contain few nutrients, because small plants do not require many. If seedlings are kept in the original seed mix for any length of time after germination though, they will need feeding as the original nutrients will soon be exhausted.

Universal or multipurpose mix—these are the most popular mixes and can be used to germinate seeds and grow most plants. They contain rather fewer nutrients than potting mixes, and the plants should be fed rather more frequently than those grown in them, but this is really a minor consideration. They are probably the best medium for general gardening, but they should not be used for containers where you plan to grow large permanent plants.

Potting mixes—these are loam-based or peat- (or peat-substitute) based. Loam-based soil mixes are based on the John Innes formulae developed by the John

▲ Low-growing azaleas make good container plants, although most will eventually outgrow their position. A number are sweet-smelling.

◀ Rhododendrons make spectacular plants early in the summer. They need acid soil. Take care when watering them in hard-water areas.

109

Innes Horticultural Institute in the 1930s. This is not a trade name but a recipe. The number refers to the amount of nutrients present in the soil. For example, John Innes No. 3 has three times the amount of nutrients of John Innes No. 1. Loam-based mixes retain water and nutrients better than any peat-based mixes, and therefore are more suitable for any permanent plants in containers such as fruit trees, wall shrubs and any permanent climbers. They are not suitable for acid-loving plants, such as camellias or rhododendrons, for these

▲ *A grouping of formal containers topped by a lacecap hydrangea. Hydrangeas need a good supply of water during the summer.*

◄ *An ambitious evergreen arrangement in a blue-glazed pot using* Fatsia japonica *and ivy. This is suitable for a shady garden.*

▶ *Healthy strawberry plants in a planter with the young fruit forming after the flowers. Strawberries are greedy plants and require regular feeding throughout the summer.*

need special ericaceous mix. Loam-based mixes are rather more difficult to find than peat-based ones and more difficult to handle. Peat-based potting mixes are lighter, easier to use, cleaner, and more satisfactory for general gardening. They are ideal for small and medium-sized containers.

Special mixes—besides the three basic types of mix described above, there are a number of other mixes. They include ericaceous mix for acid-loving plants such as rhododendrons; orchid mix for growing orchids indoors; alpine and cacti mix; bulb fiber (specifically formulated for forcing bulbs to flower indoors in the winter; and hanging basket mix that includes water-retaining granules to help the baskets retain moisture during the summer. In addition, you can always make your own mix using sterilized soil or potting mix, adding grit and vermiculite to improve the drainage, and slow-release fertilizer granules to supply the nutrients necessary.

Standard potting mix is made using 7 parts sterilized loam, 3 parts peat or peat substitute and 1 part washed sharp sand, with some balanced fertilizer as required. Mixes for cuttings need to be free draining and is best made using equal quantities of peat substitute and sand, with some slow-release fertilizer granules added to provide the necessary nutrients that the cuttings need.

TOOLS FOR THE CONTAINER GARDENER

The container gardener has one major advantage over the ordinary gardener—the range of tools required is very limited: no spade, fork, lawnmower, hedge trimmer or shears for edging the lawn. What you will need though is a hand fork, two trowels (one wide one and one narrow mainly for transplanting young plants), a hand rake, a good pair of pruners (the "parrot-beak" type are the best), a watering can with a long arm to reach over the bed, a sprayer (you will not usually require a very large one), and a garden basket or trug and possibly a garden sheet to make collecting garden waste much easier. You will also need a hammer, masonry drill, vine eyes, tensioning bolts, ring eyes, screws, various nails and Rawlplugs if you plan to construct a wire frame around the walls to train fruit trees or tie in roses and other climbing plants. Nonessential items include a pair of hand shears, a pruning saw, a garden knife, a sieve and one or two pairs of gardening gloves. Heavy duty gloves are essential if you need to prune roses except the climber Zéphirine Drouhin, which has no thorns.

watering can

atomizer spray

fork

trowel

small trowel

pruners

aspect and position

Look at your garden and see exactly how much sun it gets each day. Does it face north or south, east or west? South and west are best but many successful gardens face north or east. Which direction do the walls face—a south-facing wall enables you to grow a number of trees and tender shrubs.

Check on the sun

In an urban garden it may not be enough to see which way the garden faces. You may well be surrounded by office or apartment blocks, terraces, and tall buildings that shade the garden even when it should be in sun. And then how much sun does it get in the winter? Most roses, for example, need at least three hours sunshine a day for six months of the year if they are to repeat flower. That

said there are a number that will flower in poor conditions, and even some that can be grown against a north-facing wall. You just have to check which plants will grow best in your situation.

Check the orientation

If a garden or street has been built running north–west or south–east, the gardener will feel that the garden actually faces north or south and plant

accordingly. This can be a great mistake. In fact the side wall is the best spot and should be treated as a south wall because it will receive more sun during the day. Once you are aware of this you can plant shade-loving plants such as primroses on the opposite side of the garden, and they will flourish in the partial shade.

Temperature and shelter

Almost as important as the aspect is the temperature in the garden, especially in the winter and early spring, and the amount of shelter it provides. A small town garden may be an unlikely candidate for a frost pocket but if you are unlucky then the whole garden, or just parts of it, may be liable to frosts in the winter and early spring, when all around is frost free. Before the middle of winter frosts often have little or no effect because most plants are dying back, and have reached their dormant stage. It is only in the spring, especially after an unaccustomed mild spell early in the year has started plants and shrubs into premature growth, that a sudden hard

roses and lavender   N

pots with pelargoniums   N

patio

climbers on trellis

patio

sunny area

clematis on trellis

shaded area

ferns

water butt   shaded area

hedge to hide shed

pergola for shade

sunny area pots

camellias

small tree   'Maigold' roses

▲ *South-facing walls enable the gardener to grow a number of climbers and trees that relish the sun, such as peaches and lavender.*

▲ *When the main part of the garden is in shade, choose plants with care. Camellias in tubs are good plants for shady areas.*

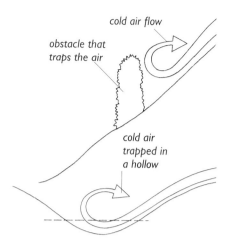

cold air flow

obstacle that
traps the air

cold air
trapped in
a hollow

▲ *Frost pockets occur when cold air flows
downhill and becomes trapped in a hollow or by
an obstacle such as a dense hedge. Frost pockets
seldom occur in gardens on convex slopes.*

frost matters, and then it can do major
damage if they are left unprotected.

    If your garden is seriously bothered
by late frosts then you must take care to
avoid semitender plants. The most likely
candidates are a number of early
flowering trees or shrubs, such as
camellias or the beautifully fragrant,
half-hardy wintersweet, *Chimonanthus
praecox*. Fruit blossom too, especially on
early flowering peach and apricot trees,
can suffer badly. If this is a rare
occurrence you may be able to cover the
plants when a late frost is forecast, but if
it is a common occurrence, only grow
plants that are fully hardy. Otherwise you
will be doomed to disappointment.
Strong, cold winds are another factor.
These can be a problem on roof gardens,
and you need to supply adequate shelter.

▶ *Containers of lavender and pelargoniums for
a hot, sunny position in a rustic garden. The white
daisies help to emphasize the bright colors.*

choosing and buying plants

Do not buy all the plants for your garden in one go. Since garden centers tend to stock plants flowering at that particular time, you need to visit on a regular basis, right through the year, to make sure your garden will have a continuous succession of flowers.

Ordering plants from specialist nurseries

The best plan of action is to make a list of the plants that you plan to grow and check if there are any specialist suppliers near you. Garden centers really only sell a very small selection. For example, if you want to grow a climbing rose against a north wall, then it is unlikely that a garden center will stock a suitable variety. If there is a specialist nursery near you, they will provide a good choice, if

not buy one by mail order. Specialist nurseries are used to sending plants through the mail, and they nearly always arrive in good condition.

Bare-root plants Always plant at the right time of the year, and this particularly applies to trees and shrubs. Generally they are best planted in the fall when their growth is dying down but there is enough warmth and moisture in the soil to let the root system establish

itself. Also, roses and fruit trees are best bought as bare-root and not container-grown plants. This may sound a strange piece of advice especially if they are to be grown in a container, but plants raised in containers inevitably have a restricted root system and the bare-root kind, planted at the right time of the year, do better in the end. No reputable supplier would send out bare-root plants at the wrong time of the year. If you cannot plant trees or shrubs as soon as they

▲ *Always soak bare-root roses for a good half an hour before planting.*

▶ *A container-grown shrub for repotting. If the roots are congested, tease them out gently to allow the plant to establish more quickly.*

HEELING IN PLANTS

If you are unable to plant bare-root plants when you receive them, heel them in. Dig a trench with a sloping side, lay the plants in the trench as shown and then firm soil over the roots. These can wait until you have time to plant them.

▲ *Garden centers are fun to look around and the plants in flower may well give you some new ideas. Check out each plant before buying it.*

▼ *The climbing form of the rose 'Iceberg' makes a graceful nodding plant. The honeysuckle helps to make a scented screen.*

arrive, dig a small trench in one container, lay the plants in it at an angle of 45° and cover firmly with soil until you do have time to complete the job properly. They are unlikely to come to any harm if they are not left for too long. But do not let them dry out.

Checking the plants If you plan to buy the plants at a garden center or nursery, there are a number of things to look for. Check the leaves for signs of pests or disease, avoid plants that have moss growing on the surface of their container because they have been in it for too long, check that few roots have grown out of the holes at the bottom for the same reason, and make sure that the plant is healthy with a good shape and equally spaced branches. It is worth taking time over each purchase to get what you want.

planting—potting and repotting

Don't be put off by technical planting terms. Potting up means transferring a young seedling into its first pot; repotting means taking the plant out of the container and then replanting it in the same container with new soil mix; and potting on means transferring a plant to a larger container.

The general principles of planting

All plants must be planted in containers large enough to accommodate their root systems. The container should be 5cm/2in larger than the rootball of the plant. To plant a shrub remove it from the original container and gently tease out the roots if they have become congested, and trim off any damaged roots. Put a good layer of pot shards, broken tiles, or stones at the bottom of the new container to provide adequate drainage, and then add a layer of soil mix. Put the plant in the container, making certain that the soil level is the same in the new container as it was in the old. Check the soil mark on the plant to do this accurately. Add the mix around the sides of the pot making sure that it is pressed firmly against the roots. Firm the soil with your hands or a dibble, but do not ram the mix down too tightly. Lift the container, if you can, and rap it down

◀ *When a plant outgrows its container, pot it on into a container that is approximately 5cm/2in larger than the present one.*

repotting a plant

1 Put a handful of pot shards or small stones in the bottom of any container. This prevents the soil mix draining away when the plant is watered.

2 Remove the plant carefully from the old container. Check the soil level. The plant should be replanted at the same depth in the new container.

3 Tease out the roots if they have become congested and trim away any that are damaged. This helps them to spread out into the new mix.

on a hard surface two or three times to shake out any air pockets. Finally, water thoroughly and top up the level with soil mix as it settles. To save moving a heavy pot into position, site it where you need it before starting.

◀ *Agapanthus lilies make good container plants with a color range from white to deep blue. They usually need staking.*

Potting on Young plants need to be transferred from small pots to larger pots, depending on their rate of growth. This should be done carefully. Transfer a growing plant to a pot just larger than the existing one, say by about 5cm/2in. This helps to keep the plant growing at a steady rate—if you potted on into a much larger pot, the roots would spread out too quickly, upsetting the growth balance. If a plant is slow growing the roots will not fill the large container quickly enough, while quick-growing plants tend to produce too much foliage and not enough flowers and fruit.

REPOTTING

Large raised beds, especially when they contain permanent trees or shrubs, cannot easily be emptied. What you must do in these cases is remove as much of the topsoil as possible and replace it with fresh mix and add a balanced granular fertilizer. In smaller containers the soil should be emptied and replaced every other year, or every year when the plant is growing well. Remove the plant from the container and shake the root system clear of old soil, put the plant in a bucket of water for an hour or more, then follow the planting steps above. When repotting you can tease out the root system and trim away any damaged roots.

planting—general tips

As a general rule planting in container gardens can be done at almost any time of the year. Fall is still preferred but if you do repot in high summer, make sure that the plant is kept really moist to start with so that the roots have the best chance to grow into the new potting mix.

Planting bare-root trees and shrubs

There are some plants that do better, even in containers, if they are planted as bare-root specimens in the fall. This particularly applies to roses and fruit trees. Order your roses for fall delivery from a reputable rose grower and plant them out when you receive them. They make better plants than container-grown roses bought and planted in the spring. The same goes for fruit trees. Try and choose a specialist nursery that is used to sending larger horticultural specimens through the mail. It is best to buy one-year-old trees as bare-root plants, or at a pinch two-year-old trees (the latter take time to become established and are more difficult to train).

▶ *Small apple trees can be grown quite happily in containers. Use an appropriate soil mix from a garden center and feed them regularly.*

PLANTING BULBS

Bulbs absorb their strength through their foliage so never cut it off after flowering—let it yellow and fade naturally. Although this may mean untidy containers, you will get better flowering results in the long run. One solution to the straggly leaves, if cost be no object, is to throw them all away and plant new bulbs each year. If you only have room for one container of bulbs, try planting a number of different ones in layers, one below the other. All bulbs should be planted two and a half times their depth—plant the largest daffodil, *Narcissus*, bulbs at the bottom of the container with smaller crocuses and chionodoxa on top. The bulbs will grow up through each layer and flower one after the other.

planting bulbs

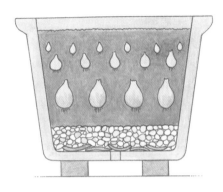

1 Put a good layer of gravel in the bottom of the container to aid drainage before starting to plant the bulbs. Use specially prepared bulb fiber.

2 Plant the largest bulbs first. Space them out evenly but put them closer together than you would if you were planting them in open ground.

3 Plant them in layers as shown above. After flowering, any bulbs grown in containers can be planted out in the garden for the following year.

Planting vines

Vines can be grown in containers, and bare-root specimens should be planted in winter when they are dormant. Add a good quantity of granular fertilizer and make sure that the vine is well watered during the initial growing period. Vines bought as container-grown specimens can be potted on from one container to another at any time before growth starts. Be sure that you have erected a suitable framework of wires and posts up which the vines can be trained.

Planting annuals and small bedding plants

When planting small annuals take care that the roots are not damaged. Make sure the young plants are well watered, ease the plants out of the seed tray, and then firm the soil mix gently around their roots in their new container. When you have finished planting out summer annuals, water them lightly with a weak solution of liquid fertilizer.

▲ *Planting a container with pansies. Position the plants at regular intervals around the rim and firm the plants in with your fingers.*

PRICKING OUT SEEDLINGS

If you have sown your own seeds, you need to prick out the seedlings into larger containers when they have germinated. Wait until they have two pairs of leaves and then ease them out of the seed tray using a small knife or a pencil. Always hold the seedlings by the first pair of leaves (the seed leaves), and not by the stalk. Handling them in this way does not damage the plant. Harden off the seedlings by placing them outside for part of the day when they are large enough, and plant out when there are no more frosts.

how to prune

Nothing in gardening causes as much bother as pruning. In fact pruning is not difficult. The elementary principles are easy to learn, and once you understand them, the whole subject loses its mystique. The most important thing is to try and prune each plant at the correct time of the year.

Pruning principles

The two basic pruning principles are: first, that some plants flower and fruit on wood produced in the current year, while others flower on last year's growth. Second, pruning stimulates growth; cutting a single branch back to a bud (usually) means that two branches will grow from the cut. The purpose of pruning is to stimulate the correct growth to produce the optimum amount of flowers and fruit.

The basic pruning steps for most plants that you are likely to grow in a container garden are listed below.

Climbing roses—if you are growing roses against a wall in a container garden the best ones to plant are some of the modern climbers with hybrid tea-shaped flowers that grow fairly slowly. Other suitable roses include climbing varieties of some hybrid tea and floribunda roses, such as the climbing variety of the very popular 'Iceberg' or 'Climbing Ophelia'. Most of these roses are repeat flowering.

On planting, trim away any damaged roots, then train in the shoots, cut back any damaged growth and cut out weak sideshoots. The following summer tie in the sideshoots as growth develops, and train the shoots into a fan. Deadhead the roses after flowering. Early in spring or late winter the following year, cut back all the flowering laterals (side-shoots) to 15cm/6in from the main branches, and tie in any shoots to form a framework. Repeat this on an annual basis. As the main shoots become exhausted they can be removed, one at a time, to within

◀ *Box needs to be clipped two or three times a year to preserve its shape. Take care pruning rosemary: it will not regenerate from old wood.*

▶ *Vigorous climbers, such as the golden hop and ornamental vines, should be cut back hard in late winter and as needed in the summer.*

5cm/2in of the ground. This stimulates new growth from the base that should always be tied in as it develops.

Summer-flowering jasmine is a vigorous plant and may have to be cut back to keep it within bounds. It is not wholly suitable for container gardens but it is widely grown. It should be cut back after flowering. Thin any old weak wood, and cut out up to one-third of the shoots if necessary. Tie in new growth as it develops—if it is too long it will need to be shortened. Be fairly ruthless.

Winter jasmine, *Jasminum nudiflorum*, should be pruned after flowering in early spring. Cut back all the shoots that have flowered by one third. Cut out completely any shoots that appear weak, damaged, or dead. Tie in the shoots.

Hop, *Humulus*, is a vigorous climber. Cut back hard in the spring to within 60–90cm/2–3ft of the ground if it needs to be kept within bounds. Ivy, *Hedera*; the climbing hydrangea, *Hydrangea petiolaris*; and all forms of Virginia creeper, *Parthenocissus*—are all climbers that adhere to the wall by suckers. None of them requires specific pruning. Clip the ivy and the climbing hydrangea to keep them within bounds after flowering. Cut back the Virginia creeper or Boston ivy hard in the spring before growth has started, especially if it threatens to get into gutters or under roof tiles. This should be avoided at all costs for the shoots will pull away tiles and damage any roof. It is quite easy to pull the old shoots away from the wall by hand.

▲ *Summer prune all roses by removing dead heads before they develop into hips. This helps to build up the strength of the plant.*

▲ *On an upright rose remove weak and crossing branches and tie in shoots as they develop. Cut back flowered laterals as shown.*

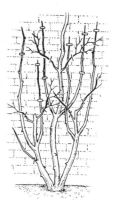

▲ *On new climbing roses tie in laterals as they develop. Remove crossing branches. Cut back flowered laterals to 3–4 eyes, about 15cm/6in.*

Pruning clematis and vines

Clematis—it is probably more difficult for the amateur gardener to prune a clematis correctly than any other group of plants. The problem is not one of pruning, but identification. There are three groups for pruning and they should be treated in different ways.

Group 1—this group flowers on wood made the previous year. In an ideal world this group should not be pruned at all, but as the plants need to be confined within their allotted space they have to be thinned after flowering. Cut out any old and dead stems, and cut back all growth. This will probably mean that

there are fewer flowers next year but that cannot be helped in this case.

Clematis that need to be treated in this way are all the *alpina* and *macropetala* kinds; all *montana*s (if you cannot identify any of these you will have to ask a knowledgeable neighbor, but as a rule all these clematis flower in late spring and early summer and have small flowers); some small-flowered hybrids and species (as a general rule those that flower early in the year or in winter); a few large-flowered varieties (those that flower before midsummer); and almost all double and semidouble large-flowered varieties. If you do not know

▲ *Clematis montana is difficult to prune successfully. Cut it back after flowering to keep it within its allotted bounds.*

the name and type of your clematis, and cannot obtain any information from anyone, then you should leave the clematis unpruned for a year and make a note of the month in which the first flowers start to appear.

Group 2—these varieties can be left unpruned, but it is best to cut out old and dead wood in late winter and then cut the remaining stems down to a strong pair of buds. Do not be seduced by mild weather early in the year and do

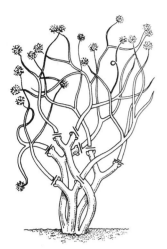

▲ *Group 1 clematis, those that flower on the new season's growth, should be cut back hard in spring to a pair of buds.*

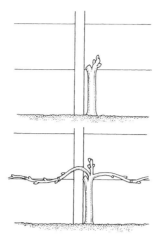

▲ *The first and second years of a newly planted vine. Cut back the leader to three buds in winter and tie in the shoots. Trim the sideshoots.*

three buds will produce three shoots and they should be tied in vertically as they grow. Pinch out any other side-shoots. That winter train the two lowest shoots horizontally on to a wire, cutting each one back to about 90cm/3ft or 12 buds. Cut the central shoot back to three buds. The horizontal shoots will produce laterals that are then trained up the wall, or over the top of a pergola as they grow, and the three shoots from the main stem are tied in vertically as before. When summer is over cut away the horizontal laterals that have born fruit, and repeat the process the following year.

this too soon, which may result in damage by late frosts. Clematis that should be pruned in this way include some large-flowered varieties, and some small-flowered hybrids and species (those that flower from midsummer onward). *Group 3*—these clematis flower on new wood produced in the current year and they should be cut back to 25–50cm/10–20in from the ground in late winter or early spring. Cut the plants back to a strong pair of buds.

Clematis that should be treated in this way include a number of the large-flowered varieties (those that flower first after midsummer); almost all the herbaceous, semiherbaceous and sub-shrubs; all the *viticellas*; a good number of the small-flowered hybrids and species (again the ones that first come into flower after midsummer). Rest assured that if you do not prune clematis they will still flower perfectly well. The only

trouble with most of them is that the base of the plant will become bare and the flowers will appear amidst a straggly and unsightly tangle of foliage at the top. **Vine, *Vitis***—these are popular plants to grow on patios and are frequently trained over pergolas to form shady arches in summer. Ornamental vines, such as *Vitis* 'Brandt' or *V. coignetiae* should be pruned in midwinter to make sure that they remain within their allotted space. Formal pruning is not required, but do prune when the plant is dormant otherwise they bleed sap excessively.

Grape vines are best pruned on what is called the Double Guyot system. This may sound frightfully technical, but it just means cutting the main stem right down to three buds. The first year these

▶ *A mature vine in a container trained over a pergola. Reduce the number of leaves in the summer to allow the sun to ripen the grapes. Protect from birds.*

Pruning shrubs and fruit trees

Herbs and shrubs—trim all shrubby herbs, such as thyme, sage, and marjoram, to keep them neat in their container in early spring, otherwise they do not need specific pruning. The same applies to the winter-flowering heathers, *Erica carnea* and *E.* x *darleyensis*. Clip them over when flowering has finished in spring to keep them neat and tidy.

Rosemary should have any misplaced shoots cut back in the spring, but beware, rosemary will not regenerate if it is cut back into the hard wood. Trim new growth lightly. If a branch dies, cut it back to the joint or base, whichever is appropriate. Prune lavender hard in mid-spring each year to keep the bushes within bounds and stimulate new growth. Cut all flowering shoots right

back including at least 2.5cm/1in of last year's wood. Do not prune after flowering because this only stimulates fresh growth that may be damaged in a hard winter. Lavender may regenerate from old wood, and if you have a very old and unsightly plant it is worth trying cutting it back really hard in spring just to see what happens.

Apples and pears—in a container garden they should be trained as cordons or grown as espaliers against a wall.

Cordons are generally single-stem trees, although double or even triple cordons can be created. Apple and pear cordons are generally planted at an angle of 45° and trained to a height of 1.8m/6ft. This produces a stem 2.4m/8ft long. All cordons should be pruned in the summer (little winter pruning is necessary). Cut back all laterals to three buds beyond the basal cluster (the cluster of leaves nearest the main stem). Tie in the leader but do not prune it until it has reached 1.8m/6ft in height. Mature cordons may need some of the fruiting spurs thinned in the course of time.

Espaliers are trees with branches radiating horizontally from a main stem. Before planting the tree erect a horizontal wire framework with each wire 38–45cm/15–18in apart. To create an

◀ *Low-growing shrubs in containers may have to be clipped after flowering to keep them looking neat and tidy.*

CREATING A FAN-TRAINED PLUM TREE

Buy a feathered maiden (a whip with side-shoots), and plant it in the fall. In late spring cut back the central stem to the uppermost of two strong laterals growing on opposite sides of the stem. Train these horizontally against the wall, the top side-shoots should be about 60cm/2ft above the ground. Tie these shoots in and then cut them back by one half to an upward-facing bud. They form the first ribs. During the summer select two new shoots from each branch growing upward and one shoot growing downward, spaced evenly along the rib. Tie these in and pinch back any other side-shoots to 1–2 leaves. Rub out any shoots growing inward toward the wall or outward. The following spring cut back the new ribs by between one half and one-third, and during the summer select three new shoots from each of these. Continue this process on an annual basis until the tree has taken up its allotted space.

espalier, plant a whip (a young single-stem tree) in the fall. In the spring cut back the stem to a bud about 60cm/2ft above the ground, making sure that there are two further buds below the top one. The tree will produce three shoots in the summer. Tie in the top one vertically and the two side-shoots at an angle of 45° to stakes attached to the wires. In the summer prune any other shoots that emerge to three leaves from the basal cluster.

The second year cut back the leader again to three good buds in the spring and take down the first two side-shoots from 45° to the horizontal. Tie these shoots on to stakes attached to the wires. Then repeat this process each year until

creating an espalier

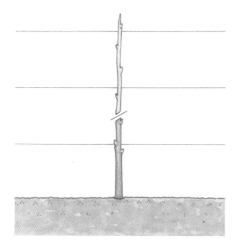
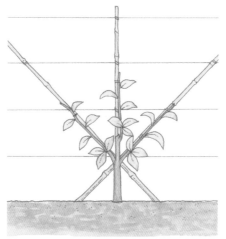
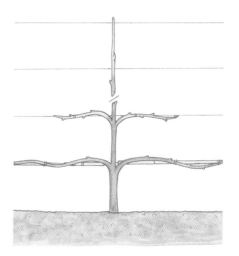

1 Plant an unfeathered maiden and cut it back to about 45cm/18in from the ground. Make sure it has three good buds with the lower two facing each other.

2 As the shoots grow during the summer, tie in the three shoots. Keep the leader vertical and tie in the two main sideshoots at 45°. Secure to stakes.

3 In early winter, lower the sideshoots to the horizontal. Tie them in and cut them back by one-third. Cut the main leader to 45cm/18in and repeat 1 and 2.

the tree has reached the height and spread that you wish, at which point the extension leaders should then be stopped and the lateral shoots treated as if they were cordons.

▲ *Trim shrubby herbs to keep them neat in their allotted containers.*

▶ *This unusual pear is 'Mrs Seddon' with dark purple fruit. Pears can be grown against a wall.*

staking and supporting

Many plants need support during their growing periods, and a number need a permanent framework of wire or trellis to make sure that they grow well and can be trained to best advantage. Always put permanent supports, such as a wire frame, in place before planting any tree.

Erecting a wire framework

If you have a wall and can grow plants up it, you may want to erect a wire framework to which you can tie in espaliered apples or pears, or other trained trees that make a container garden so satisfying. First of all check the condition of the wall. See that it is sound, that the bricks are properly bedded in, and that the wall needs neither repointing nor rebuilding. Both are fairly expensive tasks but do not attempt to put up a wire frame on an unsound wall, for tensioning bolts put quite a strain on the wire and the bricks may well pull out of the wall.

You will need a mortar drill, plastic Rawlplugs, screw eyes, a hammer, screwdriver and tensioning bolts, as well as strong 3mm/⅛in wire. Check where you want the framework to go. Allow 38–45cm/15–18in between the rows of horizontal wires, then drill proper holes in the bricks and tap in the Rawlplugs so

securing a wire framework

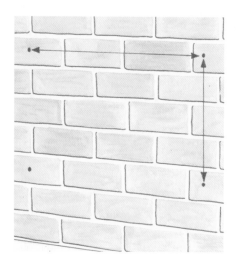

1 Mark out the area of the wall you want to cover with the frame. Allow 45cm/18in between the rows. Use sturdy 2mm wire for the main strands.

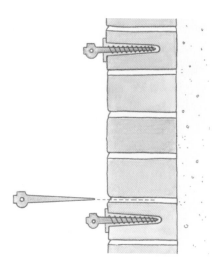

2 Drill holes in the brick and insert plastic Rawlplugs. You will need a proper masonry drill for this. Insert the retaining screws so that they are vertical.

3 Alternatively, hammer vine eyes into the mortar. This is not so secure a method. Secure the wires to tensioning bolts and tighten. Tie stakes to the wires.

erecting a trellis

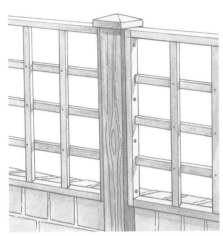

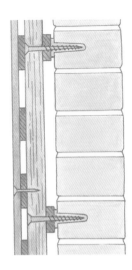

1 Measure the height of the trellis and then secure uprights to the wall with Rawlplugs and screws. Check them with a level to insure they are vertical.

2 Fix each length of trellis to the upright. This can be done with screws or metal brackets. Check they are level and fix a cap to the post to prevent rot.

3 When fixing a trellis, use battens to insure good air circulation. Fix the bottom of the trellis to one with hinges, and then the trellis can be lowered.

that they are level with the brickwork. Screw in the screw eyes. Position them about 60cm/2ft apart. Thread the wire through the screw eyes and secure it firmly at one end. Attach the tensioning bolt at the other end, attach the wire to the bolt, and then twist it until the slack has been taken up and the wire is taut.

Erecting a trellis

If the garden wall is not very tall you may want to erect a trellis around it to give more vertical gardening space. It is worth doing this job properly or it might get damaged in a high wind. If you are able to dig a hole, or series of holes, in

▶ A trompe l'oeil trellis used to create the illusion of space in a small town garden. This can be combined with outdoor mirrors.

the ground around the wall you can either cement in the posts or, much better, cement in small preformed concrete foundation posts with holes so you can screw the wooden posts in position behind them. Although tempting, it is not really a good idea to set a wooden post in concrete in the ground. However carefully you shape the concrete to allow the water to run off, and however well you treat the timber, eventually it rots and you are left with a concrete plug that is difficult to remove.

If you cannot cement concrete foundation posts into the ground it is better to fix the timber posts directly to the wall. This can be done with large screws and plastic Rawlplugs. Decide on the height you want your trellis to be. Check the length of the wall and the number of pieces of trellis that you will need, then buy all the materials—upright posts, trellis, and long screws. Drill three or four holes in the uprights at intervals. Put the posts against the wall and check that they are vertical. Then tap a long nail or screw through the holes to mark the wall behind the post. Drill holes in the wall using a mortar drill and tap in the Rawlplugs. Match up the holes in the post with those in the wall: hopefully they will fit exactly. Secure each post in place using long screws. Attach the trellis to the post using special fitments or screw them in place if you prefer. If you are securing a trellis against a wall, make sure that you leave a gap between the wall and the trellis to allow air to circulate behind the plant and let you tie in shoots properly. Never, ever, however tempting it may be, secure a shoot by pushing it through the trellis, or behind a wire. It will always need pulling out and retraining which is often impossible after a year or two.

Staking trees and standards

It is essential to stake all trees and standards when they are planted, even if they are growing in containers. Insert a stake before planting and make sure it is upright. When the tree has been planted, secure the trunk to the stake using proper tree ties that do not damage the bark. If you need to secure larger trees do this is by using guy ropes attached to ring bolts inserted in the patio floor. Again make sure that they are firm, and protect the trunk of the tree from chafing by running the wires through a length of old hosepipe or a rubber protective tube.

Supporting perennials Perennials can be supported in a number of ways. The best method is to position a ring stake above each plant early in the year, letting the

◄ *Sweet peas trained up a wigwam of specially constructed wickerwork. The more flowers you cut, the more the plant produces.*

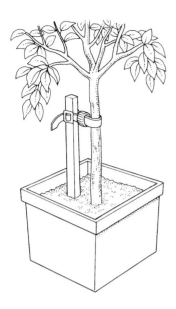

▲ *On a windy patio or roof garden even the small trees are better staked. Secure the stake to the side of the container before planting.*

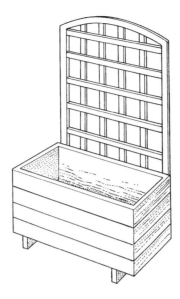

▲ *Special small trellises are available that can be secured to the back of wooden troughs and containers. These are suitable for small climbers.*

▲ *Bulbs, such as agapanthus, can be secured by inserting short bamboo stakes around the pot and joining these with circles of garden twine.*

plant grow upward through the mesh at the top. Another method is to surround the plant with stakes and make rings of garden twine to contain the plant as it grows. Pea sticks or twigs are the third method and they are pretty unobtrusive.

Staking container-grown plants

A number of plants that are regularly grown in containers need supporting as a matter of course. Among these are regal lilies, *Lilium regale*, and agapanthus. The best method is to insert a ring of small stakes around the rim of the container and then tie garden twine in rings around them. The plants will then be confined within the circumference of the string circle and will not flop over.

Supporting climbers All climbers except those that climb by suckers need support. Climbing roses in a container

need to be tied to a framework of wire, and pillar roses can be tied to pergolas to give height and color to the garden. Clematis need a trellis through which they can twine and annual climbers, such as sweet pea, *Lathyrus odoratus*, need a frame of netting or wire that they can cling to with their tendrils. Vines in particular need a permanent frame in place before planting, and in a small patio garden in a mild climate that attracts sufficient sun, they can be trained over a pergola to great effect. If you are growing a small climber in a wooden container you can attach a small piece of wooden trellis to the back to make an effective frame. These can be bought from garden centers. Otherwise you have to make certain that containers of all climbers are positioned close to the wall so that they can easily reach the wall or trellis in order to climb up it.

Don't forget that climbing plants, such as ivy, need a surface to cling to. They will not climb up a wire fence and the solution is to tie planks of wood to the fence to allow the ivy purchase.

SECURING CONTAINERS ON A ROOF GARDEN

One of the problems with containers is that they may blow over in high winds, especially if they are on an exposed roof garden and are top-heavy with trees or shrubs. To avoid this it is most important to insure that all containers are supported securely, and this equally applies to any screen or trellis put up around a roof garden for shelter and screening. Common sense must be the guide. If you have a really large tree in a container, it may be necessary to secure the container with guy ropes or wire fastened to ring bolts on the roof or walls of the garden. If you are not confident in your ability to do this yourself, you must get professional help.

watering

Watering is all important for the container gardener. All plants need water, and containers dry out extremely quickly, especially on hot summer days. This is particularly true of terracotta pots and tubs where the porous clay allows water to evaporate more quickly than through plastic or stone.

In the summer, in hot sunny weather, a large container may lose up to 5 litres/1.3 gallons a day through transpiration (water evaporating from the leaves of the plants) and evaporation through the sides of the container. Evaporation from a terracotta container can be restricted if you take the trouble to line the insides of the container with plastic sheeting when it is planted.

Hanging baskets and wall pots are subject to an even greater degree of water loss, and in the case of wall pots this can be exacerbated by the heat generated by the sun on the wall itself. Touch the south wall of your house on a hot sunny afternoon and see just how hot it feels. The baskets also contain relatively little soil mix and dry out all the sooner. It follows that you have to water a

container garden at least once a day during the summer, and hanging baskets and wall pots may require watering twice a day. If you cannot do this, then there is little point in trying to create a successful container garden. That does not mean to say that you have to water *every* single day. When the weather is dull and rainy additional watering is unnecessary, but if you go away on holiday when there is a hot dry spell and you have not arranged for the plants to be watered, do not be surprised if most of them are dead when you return from your trip.

Making watering as easy as possible

If you do not want to install an automatic watering system then you can take certain steps to make the chore of watering much easier. If you are going to water by hand install an outside faucet—this is essential on a roof garden when you do not want to traipse through the house carrying heavy watering cans. Buy a proper watering can with a long arm that will easily reach to the back of any bed. Use it to water specific containers

▲ *Water hanging baskets with a special long-armed hose attachment.*

▲ *A rose attachment to a garden hose speeds up watering in summer.*

▲ *Delicate plants can be watered with a watering can and a fine rose.*

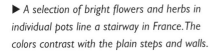
▲ A lilac-colored pergola with matching containers contrasts with the bright orange nasturtiums and canna lilies.

▶ A selection of bright flowers and herbs in individual pots line a stairway in France. The colors contrast with the plain steps and walls.

and plants at times when general watering may not be required. Also buy a hose attachment for the faucet, a reinforced plastic hosepipe that will last longer and a range of nozzles. Watering using a hose is far quicker and easier than filling a watering can time after time. If you have a number of hanging baskets get a long-arm attachment for the hose that enables you to reach all the baskets and wall pots in the garden. And finally, invest in a feeder attachment. They allow you to supply the plants with diluted foliar feed when you water.

How to water Make sure that each container is watered thoroughly, but do not overwater or the plant will become waterlogged, and may even start to rot. Fill it to the brim and let the water drain down through the soil. You should check on the condition of the soil mix as well as the plants before you start, for if the plants are wilting they may be lacking in nutrients, or the soil mix may even be waterlogged. Feel the soil about 2.5cm/1in below the surface, and if it is dry to the touch then the container should be watered. Water regularly but do not overwater.

Watering systems If you have a large container garden, or you know that you are unable to water the garden regularly in the summer, then consider investing in a computer-controlled automatic watering system. They operate on a 24-hour time clock and are installed with a time switch to turn them on and off. The most sophisticated systems can be attached to sensors that switch on when the soil is too dry. If you install one of these then all your problems are solved. There are three main systems—overhead sprinklers, trickle hoses, and the capillary system. Each system has its advantages and disadvantages.

Overhead systems are probably the cheapest to install. They have a series of small sprinklers that can be directed on to the plants. However, they use the most water and much of it may evaporate quickly in hot dry weather. Watering systems are so sophisticated now that you can even get special systems to water hanging baskets, and minisystems are available to water window boxes. It is worth investigating them thoroughly because they are enormously helpful. And do not forget to incorporate some water-retaining granules in the soil mix you use for hanging baskets, wall pots and window boxes because this cuts

down on the amount of water that the soil mix needs, and helps to prevent it from drying out during very hot weather in the summer months.

Trickle hoses are often more expensive than overhead sprinklers, but they are more effective because they allow water to seep into the soil where it reaches the roots of the plants directly. And they do not use so much water. There are even very small trickle hose systems for window boxes and containers on balconies.

▼ *A greenhouse full of half-hardy flowering plants ready for placing outside in the summer. Hanging baskets benefit from this treatment.*

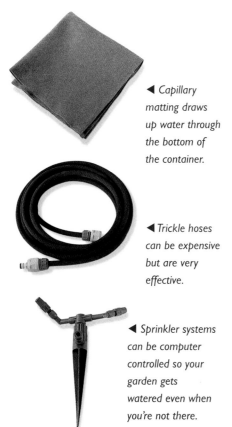

◀ *Capillary matting draws up water through the bottom of the container.*

◀ *Trickle hoses can be expensive but are very effective.*

◀ *Sprinkler systems can be computer controlled so your garden gets watered even when you're not there.*

▲ *Hanging baskets need plenty of water during the summer months to stop them drying out. Use a long-handled device to reach the basket.*

Capillary systems draw up water through the bottom of the container. They are mainly used by nurseries and in greenhouses. The amateur gardener can go some way to imitating a capillary system by placing containers full of plants in a larger bowl, and then filling the base with gravel. If this gravel container is filled with water the plant will draw up the water it needs in a gradual manner and the soil will not become waterlogged.

A warning If you live in a hard water area and want to grow a number of acid-loving plants, such as camellias, heathers, *pieris sarcococa*, or rhododendrons, in ericaceous soil mix, you need to take some precautions when you water to alleviate the effect of the lime in the water. The best solution, that is not always possible, is to install a water butt so that you can water the plants with rainwater taken directly from the roof.

If you cannot do this then add some flowers of sulfur or sulfur chips or some sequestered iron to the container to help acidify the soil and keep the pH at the correct level.

It is important to test the soil at intervals to check its acidity, which can change. Acid-loving plants that grow in a mix that is too alkaline soon develop chlorosis, where the leaves turn yellow, and if this is not corrected then the plants will soon die.

REVIVING PLANTS

If a plant appears totally dead and dried out, then it is worth plunging the pot in a bucket of water and leaving it there until the soil has reabsorbed the water. Sometimes the plant will revive. This is certainly worth trying with small plants in small containers that can be moved about easily.

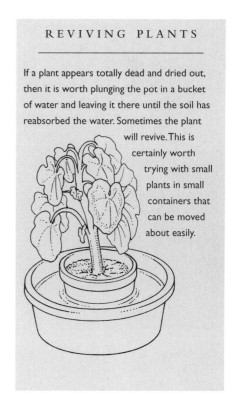

feeding and maintenance

All plants require nutrients to thrive and grow. In a garden these are present naturally in the soil, but in a container this is different. Not only is the volume of the growing medium far less, but frequent watering washes the nutrients away. They need to be replaced.

▲ *An ambitious fruit and vegetable garden with a traditional strawberry pot and a raised bed. The contrasting leaf colors are most attractive.*

The basic nutrients

There are three main nutrients in all soils that are needed by all plants. Each has a different function. They are nitrogen (N), phosphorus (P), and potassium (K). Nitrogen promotes good leafy growth, phosphorus enables the plant to develop a good root system, and potassium helps the plant to produce flowers and fruit. In addition to the main nutrients there are a number of other nutrients or trace elements required by plants, such as magnesium (Mg), calcium (Ca), and manganese (Mn), but they are only required in tiny amounts and can safely be ignored by container gardeners.

Organic versus inorganic It has to be said that it is very much easier for the container gardener to use inorganic fertilizers than to rely on organic alternatives. There are two main reasons for this, availability and bulk. In a standard garden there is always room for a compost heap, and if there is a lawn, grass clippings provide the essential ingredients for organic compost.

A container gardener has neither of these things, although a small wormery might be a possibility, feeding the worms on suitable kitchen waste.

Compost, in a garden, has two functions. It provides much of the nutrients necessary for healthy growth, but more importantly it gives any soil bulk and helps to improve the structure. Containers, filled with prepared compost, do not require such help and do not have room for the additional bulk. Inorganic alternatives are available in compact pelleted form or in bottles of liquid fertilizer. Both can be applied easily when required. The organic alternatives of bonemeal or fish, blood and bone are perfectly satisfactory but may attract unwelcome predators.

Basic steps

When putting a permanent plant in a container you should incorporate a general fertilizer. The easiest to use is in granular form: an inorganic balanced NPK formula, 7:7:7, that contains equal proportions of nitrogen,

feeding a plant correctly

1 When planting a shrub or tree add some bonemeal or general fertilizer to the soil mix. Follow the manufacturer's instructions on the packet.

2 Slow-release fertilizers can be added in spring in pellet form. There are various types that work in different ways. One application lasts through summer.

3 Liquid fertilizers and foliar feeds can be added when plants are watered. These should be used when the plant is in growth, and then every 2 or 3 weeks.

phosphorus, and potassium and provides all the plant's requirements. Do not use the organic alternatives of bonemeal or fish, blood, and bone if you live where there are urban foxes. They will arrive

each night and dig up your plants time after time, looking for bones and old fish.

Vegetables, such as tomatoes, peppers, or eggplants, all need high nitrogen feeds to start them into growth, followed by a

high potassium (potash) feed when the plants are bearing fruit. Tomato feed is high in potash and is excellent for all plants as well as tomatoes.

General feeding It is a good idea to apply slow-release fertilizer granules or pellets to all permanent containers at the start of each year. Follow the manufacturer's instructions. Very often plants in containers will require no additional feeding, but if the plants do show signs of wilting, they can be watered using a foliar feed absorbed through the leaves of the plant, or be given liquid fertilizer. Foliar feeds are extremely economical and effective. When using all liquid and foliar feeds be sure to follow the manufacturer's instructions carefully or you may damage the plant.

HOW TO BUILD A WORMERY

You can buy a ready-made wormery or make your own using a plastic garbage bin with a faucet to drain off excess moisture or drainage holes and collection tray. Drill air holes around the top and make sure the lid can be fastened securely. Fill the bin with 10cm/4in gravel and then put a divider (old carpet is good) on top. Add 10cm/4in of multipurpose soil mix and shredded newspaper, then at least 100 red brandling worms (from angling shops). Add kitchen waste in thin layers, about 5cm/2in. Cover with damp newspaper. When the food scraps are full of worms you can add more.

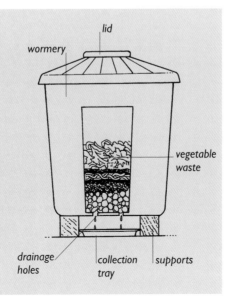

lid

wormery

vegetable waste

drainage holes

collection tray

supports

basic pests and diseases

Pests and diseases are inevitable. The best cure is constant vigilance and what is known as good garden hygiene. If you walk around your garden every evening you will soon spot any unwelcome pests, and if they are sprayed straight away the infestation is much easier to control.

Start by creating as healthy an environment as possible. As a first rule try to insure adequate ventilation. If you have a large number of plants in an enclosed space then diseases will flourish. It is difficult to do this if you are growing a number of plants in a small space (a balcony or patio). Make sure though that the center of each plant is open, and that air can circulate. This applies to fruit trees and shrubs.

Common pests

Ants—they cause more damage than is commonly realized. They feed on the honeydew excreted by aphids and will carry them from plant to plant. They cause damage to the roots of plants by tunneling underground and will eat newly sown seeds. If you find a nest destroy it immediately by pouring boiling water over it. Then dust affected areas with a recommended insecticide, or apply a residual product that forms a lasting barrier.

Aphids—there are many kinds of aphids but they all suck the sap from the plant and weaken it. Some plants such as roses, *Philadelphus*, and broad beans are particularly prone to infestation. Pinch off all the infected plant parts and spray with a contact or systemic insecticide, or organically with a solution of dishwashing liquid. This may not be so effective as nonorganic kinds.

Birds—particularly troublesome when it comes to fruit or vegetables, although they are unlikely to cause so much damage in a container garden as they do in a traditional kitchen garden. The only thing that really works is to net everything at risk and to keep the plants netted.

Caterpillars—companion planting will go a long way to avoiding these pests. If you grow vegetables that do become

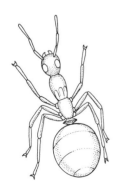

Ant

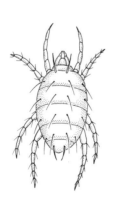

Spider mite

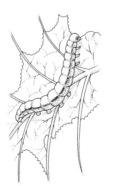

Aphid

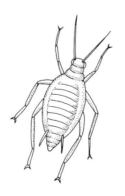

Caterpillar

Pigeon

▶ *Tomatoes make good companion plants as they help to deter cabbage white butterflies from laying their eggs on brassicas.*

infested with caterpillars, pick them off by hand and spray with a suitable pesticide. Sadly, this may be too late.

Leafminers—these are small insect larvae that feed inside the leaves of plants. Eventually the whole leaves will be destroyed. Pick off infested leaves and spray with a suitable pesticide as soon as you see any signs appearing. Spraying may have to be repeated every two weeks if the infestation is bad.

Japanese beetle—these shiny green beetles are about ⅓in long and chew the leaves and flowers of many plants. The larvae are grayish white with a dark brown head and feed on roots and tubers. Pick them off by hand whenever you see them, dropping the beetles into a jar of water and detergents; then spray the plants weekly with neem until the beetles are under control.

Spider mite—tiny creatures the size of a pin head, with several species. They are serious pests and do considerable damage to plants such as tomatoes, grapes, chrysanthemums, and house plants. Spray the plants with water to keep the atmosphere moist. Outdoors, spray infested plants with a strong jet of water to knock mites off leaves. Repeat daily for three days. Many species are resistant to pesticides.

Sawfly—they cause serious damage to fruit, including apples, pears, and cherries. Spray with an insecticide.

Slugs and snails—these well-known creatures can be a major problem, especially in moist, damp areas. There are various methods of control. Trap them under an upturned half grapefruit skin, or sink a shallow pot half filled with sweet liquid in the soil into which they will fall and drown. Deter them by cutting up plastic bottles and putting collars of plastic around young plants, or surround the plants with a circle of grit—this will work because slugs do not like to slide over sharp surfaces.

Squirrels—birds, especially pigeons, may be bad but squirrels are far worse. There are two ways to deal with squirrels. One is to erect a permanent wire barrier over everything that matters, because netting simply is not strong enough to keep them out. The other is to obtain a humane squirrel trap.

Whitefly—the nymphs of these small creatures attack plants out of doors, but they also attack house plants. They are easily seen hanging off the flowers and foliage off the plant they have decided to attack. Spray with an insecticide.

SPRAYING—ORGANIC OR NON-ORGANIC

This is a vexed question and the approach you take to spraying and pest control depends entirely on how strictly you adhere to organic principles. There are organic alternatives to most normal garden pesticides but you have to decide whether they are sufficiently effective for the extra work they may involve.

Remember that tomatoes and marigold, *Tagetes*, will deter many butterflies from laying their eggs, particularly on brassicas, and if you grow them together you may avoid infestation by their caterpillars. This is known as companion planting.

Common diseases

Black spot—common on roses. Spray weekly with garden sulfur before the disease appears.

Canker—shrunken scars that appear on the shoots of woody plants especially apple, pear, and plum trees in summer. Cut off the infected branches immediately and dispose of them, and paint the wound with fungicide paint.

Damping off—a fungal disease of seedlings that makes them collapse and die. It is usually caused by damp soil that is too cold, or overcrowding. To control, water the seedlings regularly with a suitable fungicide, throw away any trays of seedlings that are affected and disinfect all your seed trays.

Botrytis—caused by cold, damp conditions and affects fruit such as

◀ *Crowded plum trees can sometimes be prone to botrytis. Thin out the crop to prevent overcrowding. Remove infected fruit immediately.*

Powdery mildew affects many plants. Spray with garden sulfur.

Whitefly affects indoor and outdoor plants. Spray with insecticide.

Canker affects fruit trees. Cut off and destroy affected shoots.

Black spot is prevalent on roses. Spray with garden sulfur.

▶ *Organic sprays are available for most garden pests and diseases, and it is up to the individual gardener to find out which one works best.*

strawberries. Spray susceptible plants early in spring with garden sulfur, and keep plants as dry and well ventilated as possible; removing infected leaves will help prevent the disease spreading.

Fungal diseases—they cause mold, mildew, and wilt, and thrive in humid conditions. All fungal diseases are difficult to control and improved ventilation is the best prevention. The same applies to leaf spot.

Downy mildew—caused by various species of fungi but they are not the ones that produce powdery mildew. They are more prevalent in damp weather and cause white growths to appear on the underside of the leaves and blotches on the surface. It can affect many bulbs, garden perennials, and vegetables such as lettuce and onions. Once present the

disease is difficult to control. Make sure that all plants are properly watered, and avoid overcrowding and overhead watering where possible. Spray affected plants with copper sulfate early in the morning on a bright, dry day.

Powdery mildew—a common fungal disease that can affect many garden plants. The symptoms are a white powdery coating that appears on the leaves and the stems of plants. The white coating later thickens, turns brown, and small black dots appear on the surface. Spray susceptible plants with garden sulfur before the disease appears, and avoid watering leaves.

Viruses—there are several kinds that affect many plants, but they all show roughly the same symptoms. The leaves become mottled and distorted, and they may also develop yellow or brown

blotches. If you are certain that your plants are suffering from a viral disease, then you should pull them up and destroy them straight away. There is no effective chemical control for this problem but some plants are sold certified virus-free. Keeping aphids under control helps because the disease is spread through the sap of the plant which the aphids feed on. Advice may be available from professional organizations.

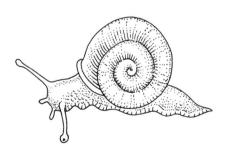

Slugs and snails can be trapped or controlled with slug pellets.

DEFICIENCIES

As if the gardener's life was not complicated enough, many soil deficiencies, such as chlorosis and nitrogen deficiency, cause plants to behave in much the same way as if they had some disease. The container gardener can be thankful that soil deficiencies are unlikely to affect plants in containers.

overwintering

Containers get too hot and dry in summer, and in winter they get colder than the surrounding garden. Plants in containers may therefore need special protection in hard weather: containers on roof gardens can be a particular problem for they are more likely to be buffeted by stormy winds.

Growing and protecting tender plants

If you have room you can grow tender plants in containers provided you can give them shelter indoors in the winter. Most plants require a cool light area free of central heating. A north-facing room that is unused and can be kept reasonably cool is ideal, or failing that use a cool porch, but remember that some plants do not like drafts. If you want to grow semitender plants in containers and have the facilities to winter them indoors, consult a specialist plant encyclopedia. This should provide accurate information about the minimum temperature they require and the conditions they prefer. A number of attractive flowering shrubs and climbers suitable for containers that will need protection include lemon tree, *Citrus limon*, *Abutilon* 'Nabob' or *A.* 'Souvenir de Bonn', and the many varieties of *Hibiscus rosa-sinensis* or even one of the bougainvilleas, although all bougainvilleas will eventually outgrow their allotted space. There are also a number of smaller plants, such as streptocarpus and cyclamen, that will flower out of doors in mild climates in summer if they are kept in a sheltered spot.

Protecting plants out of doors

If you do not have the facilities to keep containers inside then tender plants need

◀ *Grasses and bamboo covered in snow in midwinter. Shake any heavy snow off the branches of fir trees or they may break.*

▶ Spring crocuses surrounded by old fallen chestnut leaves after a slight frost. Such a frost is unlikely to do much damage in the garden.

protection outside. Traditionally they were wrapped in straw or bracken and covered with burlap. Tender perennials can be protected by a good layer of straw or bracken that is removed in the spring. Secure some netting over the top to prevent it blowing away.

Wrapping plants in garden fleece is also excellent because it allows light and moisture to penetrate, although it is flimsy and liable to tear if subjected to strong winds and sharp corners. And being fairly thin it will not provide complete protection for tender plants in a really hard frost. Another idea is to wrap the plants in bubble wrap. This gives excellent insulation and allows some light to penetrate, but it should not be kept on any longer than is strictly necessary because it does not allow the

plant to breathe and can lead to disease. A surprising amount of protection can also be obtained by wrapping plants in netting, and this is most suitable if you want to protect a half-hardy fruit tree, such as a peach or nectarine, growing against a wall. Two or three layers of netting will generally give perfectly adequate protection when late frosts threaten the emerging blossom in early spring. There are two other things worth

remembering when it comes to protection. The frosts that occur in spring and hit the new young growth do the real damage. Frost before Christmas seldom kills anything. And second, cold strong winds, especially from the east, can do just as much damage as frosts. This is where netting really helps because it filters the wind, reduces its speed and often prevents damage to the leaves. It is particularly important on roof gardens.

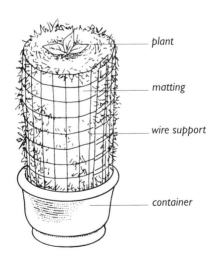

plant

matting

wire support

container

▲ Plants in circular containers can be covered with matting or straw held in place by a wire frame. Alternatively, wind fleece around the plant.

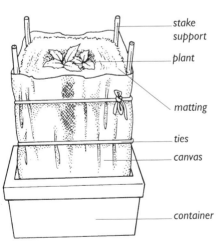

stake support

plant

matting

ties

canvas

container

▲ Plants in square containers can be protected as shown. Do not leave covering, such as plastic sheets, on plants for longer than necessary.

LOOKING AFTER CONTAINERS

Plants are not the only things that require protection. Terracotta pots may well crumble and crack if they are subjected to extremes of frost and rain. They can be wrapped in plastic bubble wrap. Cracking can often be prevented by securing the top of the pot with wire under the rim and twisting it tight.

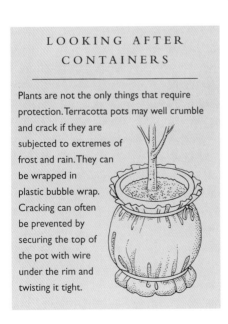

raising plants

The container gardener may well not have sufficient room to contemplate raising plants. Even the simplest form of propagation, sowing seeds, requires a certain amount of space, or, at the least, some vacant window ledges. It can be very easy to get carried away.

◄ *It is much cheaper to raise your own bedding plants for the summer by sowing seed in spring. Nicotianas and petunias are easy to grow.*

Sowing seed—general advice

Before you start consider how many plants you actually can use, how many varieties you want to raise, and how much time you are prepared to give to raising and tending seedlings. If you have room then this can save a good deal of money, for a packet of seeds costs very little and produces more plants than you need. Don't be too ambitious.

Scarification and stratification

Some plants have specific requirements before their seed will germinate properly. This involves two processes, scarification and stratification. Scarification applies to certain large kinds of seed with a hard outer coating. In the wild it would remain in the ground over winter and the outer coating of the seed would gradually rot, allowing the seed to absorb water and start into growth. Without this process the seed needs to have its outer

propagating seeds

1 Cover drainage holes with crocks and fill tray with seed mix. Water it and let the moisture drain off. Seeds like warm, damp conditions.

2 Seeds should be sown thinly over the seed mix surface. With fine seed, it is helpful to use a sheet of white paper as shown to scatter the seeds thinly.

3 Seed trays with plastic tops and ventilation holes help to keep moisture at the right level. If using plastic wrap, remove once the seeds germinate.

coating chipped or weakened to allow growth to take place. This is usually done by rubbing the seeds with sandpaper or by chipping them with a knife. You can do this with both stick and pole beans to accelerate their germination but it is not strictly necessary.

SOWING SEED

At its simplest sowing seed merely involves buying seed trays and seed starting mix, and spreading the mix evenly in the tray. Water it so that it is reasonably moist and then sprinkle the seed over the surface, covering the tray with a sheet of glass or clear plastic, and then leave it somewhere light and warm until the seed germinates. Read the instructions on each packet carefully because these basic requirements often vary from plant to plant.

Stratification is when the seed germinates better after a period of either hot or cold. The gardener with space and time can usually overcome this, but two good very ordinary examples from the vegetable garden are parsnips, where seed should be sown very early in the year when the ground is still extremely cold, and parsley, a notoriously slow germinator, where success can be virtually guaranteed if you pour boiling water on to the seed mix before you sow in the spring.

You can achieve both these effects artificially by either keeping the seed in a plastic bag mixed with peat substitute and sand in a heated closet, if the seed needs a period of warmth, or in the refrigerator if it needs cold. Few kinds of seed need either treatment.

Light and darkness

Some seed requires light to germinate, in other words it germinates on the surface of the compost. The sprouts of alfalfa and mung beans are good examples, but some kinds of seed need to be kept in the dark and covered with soil mix. Read the instructions on the seed packet.

Once the seed has germinated it needs to be kept in good light on a windowsill, out of direct sunlight. Keep the soil moist and turn the seed tray every day to stop the seedlings growing at one angle toward the light. The first leaves that appear are the seed leaves, which are followed by the true leaves, and when there are two pairs of them the seedlings can be pricked out into a larger container filled with general purpose or potting mix.

sowing seed—handy tips

Fine seeds should be sown as thinly as possible. Take care and time when sowing to achieve this. There isn't any point in filling a seed tray with a large number of seeds, for when they all germinate, the tray is too congested, the seedlings don't grow properly, and it is difficult to prick them out.

Sowing larger seeds

They are much easier to sow and generally include vegetables, i.e. peas and beans, although clivias have lovely dark brown seeds that in two year's time make excellent and unusual presents.

If you plan to grow vegetables in your container garden then it is a good idea to sow them separately, and you should plan to operate on the two-for-one principle. Sow peas and beans, for example, in degradable cardboard pots or modules, two seeds at a time and discard one if both germinate. Then plant the pot or module directly into the container in early summer when all danger of frost has passed. The plants will then grow without suffering any check.

Watering Try to water seed pans and small seedlings from below, rather than from above. It is very difficult to get a fine enough rose spray, and the heavy drops of water damage the seedlings and can even wash out the roots. Stand the trays in a tray of water and the seed mix will absorb sufficient water to keep the seeds moist and the small plants growing.

Temperature

Every seed has a temperature at which it will germinate, and it is particularly important to stick to this. It will be stated on the seed packet. Nearly all vegetables require a soil temperature of above 7°C/45°F for a week before they germinate, and a number of annuals require temperatures from 13°C–21°C/55°–70°F. Read the instructions carefully on the packet before you sow anything.

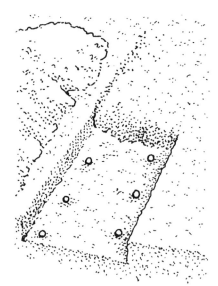

▲ *Larger seeds, such as peas and beans, can be sown in shallow double trenches. Space them out according to packet instructions.*

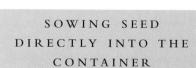

SOWING SEED DIRECTLY INTO THE CONTAINER

Some plants are difficult to handle when they are small and should be sown directly where they are to grow, even in a container. This applies to a number of vegetables such as carrots, beets, and chives. Thin the seedlings when they appear. Hardy annuals are often sown in this way in the kitchen garden, and if you have a container devoted to hardy annuals you can follow this practice. Draw shapes on the surface of the container, and then sow individual plants in each section. Sow the seed thinly. Borage, flax, California poppy, *Eschscholzia,* and poached-egg plant, *Limnanthes,* can all be sown in this way for a summer display.

Aftercare

The worst thing that can happen to a tray of seedlings is the fungal disease called "damping off." This usually happens when seedlings are too crowded within the seed tray, or when the soil itself is too cold and too wet.

Spray the seedlings from time to time with a fungicide as a prevention, and take care to keep all containers that you use as clean as you possibly can. And do not forget to turn the seed trays on windowsills every day or the plants will grow lopsided toward the light. Put them outside as soon as possible, shade them from direct sunlight to start with, and water them with a diluted liquid fertilizer every week.

▲ Growing peas in a container is most satisfying; train the plants up a wigwam of stakes. Choose a snow pea variety.

▼ It is a help when raising annuals from seed to stick to one color, as this can then be matched with other plants in beds and pots.

propagation—taking cuttings

There is something very satisfying about taking cuttings and propagating your own plants. It is actually very simple and the principle is invariably the same—cut off a portion of the parent plant, dip the cutting in hormone rooting powder, and replant it in moist cutting mix.

Softwood cuttings

They are taken in the spring when the new shoots are fully formed and are just starting to harden. They are usually taken from the tips of new shoots but with some plants the cuttings are taken from new basal shoots, growing from the base of the plant. Make the cut just below a node (a leaf joint), and then reduce the number of leaves and the leaf area by cutting some of the leaves in half. Cuttings require some leaf growth but find it difficult to support a large leaf system. Dip the cutting in hormone rooting powder and push the cutting into moist cutting mix. It is important to keep softwood cuttings in a moist environment, preferably a propagating frame because they lose moisture quickly.

Semiripe cuttings

They are taken in late summer from new wood produced in the current year.

▶ *Pelargoniums are easily raised from cuttings and can be overwintered on windowsills or in a cool greenhouse. This is a great money saver!*

▶ *Osteospermums are easily raised from softwood cuttings taken early in the year. The variety 'Whirligig' has wheel-like petals.*

Choose a nonflowering shoot if available. Cuttings 5–10cm/2–4in long are about the normal length. Trim them just below a leaf joint and remove the lower leaves. Remove the top leaves to reduce moisture loss. Dip the cutting in rooting powder and insert it gently into the cutting mix.

Some shrubs and herbs root best from semiripe cuttings taken with a "heel" of the old wood. Pull the shoot

VARIOUS SORTS OF CUTTINGS

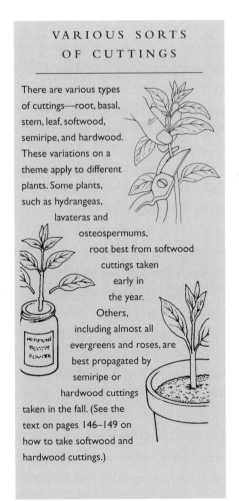

There are various types of cuttings—root, basal, stem, leaf, softwood, semiripe, and hardwood. These variations on a theme apply to different plants. Some plants, such as hydrangeas, lavateras and osteospermums, root best from softwood cuttings taken early in the year. Others, including almost all evergreens and roses, are best propagated by semiripe or hardwood cuttings taken in the fall. (See the text on pages 146–149 on how to take softwood and hardwood cuttings.)

away from the plant in a downward direction and it will come away with a heel of wood. Trim this if necessary.

Stem cuttings

Most hardwood and semiripe cuttings are stem cuttings taken from a straight length of shoot. The normal length is around 5–12cm/2–5in. Trim each stem to length just below a node, and strip away the lower leaves to allow the shoot to be inserted in the soil. Also remove all flowering shoots and buds because they reduce the effect of the root-producing

hormones that cuttings rely on. Pelargoniums, *pelargoniums*, are normally propagated from stem cuttings, as are a number of other plants. In fact, pelargoniums are a good example of those plants that need to be left in the open air overnight to form a pad at the foot of the stem. In some plants this helps rooting, in others it helps to prevent the cuttings rotting. If you have difficulty in getting pelargoniums to root then this is worth trying. Dip all the cuttings in hormone rooting powder, or a hormone rooting solution.

taking cuttings and division

Division Many plants, especially perennials that have spreading rootstocks, can easily be propagated by division in spring. This is something that all gardeners should practice because some plants, such as delphiniums, form large clumps of roots where the center dies away. Such plants should be split and only the healthy outer sections of the roots replanted. Primroses, hostas, irises, and pulmonarias should all be divided in this way. There are two schools of thought about how this should be done. Some plants, such as primroses, can simply be pulled apart and the various portions replanted. Other fibrous-rooted plants have to be split by cutting through the rootball with a spade, or pulling the plant apart, using two forks back to back. This is hardly something that the everyday container gardener will have to do, but if the case does arise, it is best to split the rootball cleanly with a spade or a sharp knife.

Leaf cuttings

This is the simplest form of propagation and is normally used for house plants, such as streptocarpus and African violet, *Saintpaulia*. Some plants root best when a whole leaf is used, pinned out flat on the soil, with a few small cuts or nicks made in the veins on the underside of the leaf. This encourages the plants to form calluses and the roots spring from them (begonias are often propagated in this way). Another common house plant

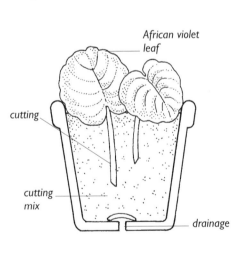

▲ *African violets are easy to propagate by leaf cuttings. Pull off a number of leaves and insert them in the mix around the edge of the pot.*

◄ *Make sure the base of the leaf is touching the surface of the cutting mix. New leaves will show in a few weeks.*

dividing plants successfully

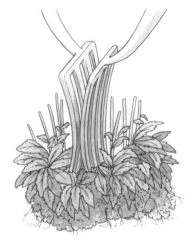

1 Some smaller plants, such as primroses and pulmonarias, can be divided easily by hand. Dig up the plant when flowering is over and pull it apart.

2 Large perennials can be divided with two forks, as shown. Put the forks in back to back and lever the plant apart. Or, just cut the plant in two with a spade.

3 Irises can be divided, cutting the new rhizomes away from the old clump. Dust with fungicide powder and cut back the leaves by two-thirds before replanting.

propagated by leaf cuttings is the African violet. Pull off whole leaves including the stalk and push them into cutting mix around the rim of a pot. Some of these may not take but others will. Streptocarpus is best propagated by cutting the leaf into strips and then planting them in the mix, edge down.

Layering This occurs naturally in many plants, and the method can be used to propagate a number of plants that are difficult to raise from cuttings, such as rhododendrons. Strawberries propagate themselves by sending out runners that root. They can then be severed from the parent plant and potted up separately. Blackberries propagate themselves by tip-layering where the tips of shoots bury themselves in the ground and

develop roots. This is the principle behind layering. Peg a branch of a plant or shrub down, burying part of it in the ground. You can nick the stem lightly to promote rooting if you wish. Serpentine layering is where a long branch is pegged down in waves with the crests above ground. This can produce several plants from one stem.

General points when taking cuttings

Choose shoots without flowers or flowering buds if possible: nonflowering shoots produce roots more quickly. Use a sharp knife and make your cuts cleanly between or just below a node. Keep all cuttings moist and use a propagating frame for softwood cuttings. Leave hardwood cuttings in the ground for one year. They are generally slow to take.

HARDWOOD CUTTINGS

They are taken in the fall from new shoots that have completed their first year of growth. Cut the shoots into lengths 25–30cm/10–12in long. Trim them at the top above a pair of buds and at the foot below a pair of buds. Remove a sliver of wood from the base of the cutting. Insert the cuttings in a trench with coarse sand or grit in the bottom to aid drainage, 7.5–10cm/3–4in apart, to at least half their depth. They may take a long time to develop—leave them undisturbed for one year unless they have obviously failed.

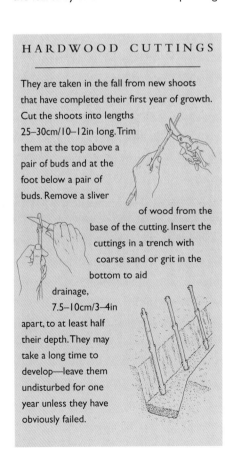

training and topiary

Topiary is important for the container gardener. In formal gardens clipped shapes complement the garden design. In patios and on roof gardens topiary shapes can be used to divide the garden into different areas, and give height to the garden.

There are not all that many plants that are suitable for topiary. The most impressive is yew, *Taxus baccata*, but it requires a good deal of space to show off its best attributes and only flourishes in large formal gardens where fantastic tortured shapes can be created over the years. This kind of skill and patience is usually outside the scope of the normal gardener. Box, *Buxus sempervirens,* and bay trees, *Laurus nobilis*, are the plants most commonly used, and a number of pleasing shapes can be contrived with a little care and some patience.

Training box

This is easier to train than bay, and it can be clipped into balls, cones, and spirals. The principle behind all topiary is to place a frame in position on or around the plant, and then clip away all shoots as they poke out of the confines of the frame. The simplest shape, much used for box, is the cone that is easily constructed from three stakes placed in a tripod around the plant. Trim to shape and a cone soon forms. For more complex shapes it is best to buy ready-made frames, balls, spirals, and pyramids, though you can construct your own frame using chicken wire. Tie in some branches to the frame to help the plant make a shape.

Clipping

Once the topiary form has become established the plant needs to be clipped regularly throughout the summer to maintain the required shape. Stop clipping as fall advances, for young shoots produced in late fall might not survive a hard winter.

Other suitable plants

While box and bay are the most common, good topiary shapes can also be made from privet, *Ligustrum ovalifolium*, although being semievergreen it is not so satisfactory. Ivy, *Hedera*, can be trained to grow into various shapes, and makes useful evergreen topiary in a small space. If you want to use ivy, first design the shape you require using chicken wire, and then sandwich some moss between another layer of wire. When the shape is satisfactory put it over a container filled with soil mix, and then set ivy plants around the edge and train them up the shape as they grow. Once they have reached the top they can be pruned back to keep them in shape.

TRAINING BAY TREES

One of the simplest plants to train into a ball or a mophead shape is bay, *Laurus nobilis*. Once the plant has reached the height you require, you can stop it and cut off all the side-shoots that you do not want, leaving the trunk bare. Then cut the head of the tree into shape. It is probably easiest to clip bay trees by eye and it is surprising how good an effect can be achieved, even on large trees that have been allowed to grow wild in a garden. It is even possible to cut the head right off and new shoots will sprout that can then be trimmed into the shape you want. Do not worry if the shape is uneven to start with. When the new growth starts you can let it grow out to cover any imperfections while keeping the remainder in trim.

training ivy into a cone shape

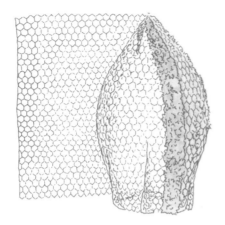  

1 Make the basic shape from chicken wire and then cover it with a good layer of sphagnum moss, sandwiching it in place with a second layer of wire.

2 Put the wire shape on the container and then surround the rim with small plants, like ivy. These can be tied in to start with until they cling by themselves.

3 Cut away any shoots that grow too long or in the wrong direction. Ivy will soon cover the surface but keep turning the container to even the growth.

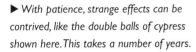

▲ *Clipping box into shape. Some topiary can be clipped by eye but complicated shapes may require guides to keep the training even.*

▶ *With patience, strange effects can be contrived, like the double balls of cypress shown here. This takes a number of years.*

plants for containers— planting schemes

The smaller the garden, the more important the choice of plants. Plants will be seen close up, and the colors and form need to be considered carefully so that they complement the house and patio. Each container is a small and impermanent painting, decorating the space it inhabits.

creating a color scheme

Most garden color schemes work reasonably well. The green leaves help to give an overall balance and white and pale flowers link the stronger shades. But rather than leaving everything to chance, it is better to plan definite color schemes. This is especially important in a small container garden.

The color wheel

Color theory is based on the color wheel. An understanding of how this works explains the relationship between colors, and helps the gardener to achieve balanced plantings.

Primary colors The three primary colors are red, yellow, and blue. They cannot be obtained, in a painter's palette, by mixing other colors together. Mixtures of the primary colors,

▲ *A color wheel composed of plants, showing the primary and secondary colors. Check to see which color combination you prefer.*

together with black and white, produce virtually all the other colors available. In gardening terms the primary colors fit together quite nicely. For example you could plant a spring container with forget-me-not, *Myosotis*, primrose, *Primula vulgaris* and a few early tulips, such as 'Brilliant Star', scarlet-vermilion, or 'Mme. Le Fefeber', fire-red. They would all flower together in early to mid-spring, and the effect would be bright and cheerful. If you wanted a quieter scheme you could leave out the tulips and just have the blue and yellow of the forget-me-nots and primroses. The forget-me-nots are important because they provide the groundcover necessary for this type of planting.

Later in the year beds or containers based on the primary colors might contain red and yellow celosias with blue cornflower, *Centaurea cyanus*—the variety 'Dwarf Blue' only reaches 30cm/12in and is suitable for containers. You might find these colors too strong in midsummer because the shades are deeper than the spring planting, and

colors appear brighter in the summer months than they do earlier in the year. when the sun is lower in the sky. The effect would be vivid rather than restful.

Secondary and complementary colors

If you mix any two primary colors in varying quantities you will obtain a secondary color. Red and blue make purple, red and yellow make orange, and blue and yellow make green.

Complementary colors are those that lie opposite one another on the color wheel, and in theory if you mix two of them you should obtain a pale gray, although if you try this with paint the pigments are seldom pure enough for this to happen. If you add white to a colour this produces a tint, and if you add black this produces a shade.

Adding combinations of both black and white produces a number of tonal values. These tonal values are most important for the gardener and the planning of planting schemes, and the best combination of plants is where there is a tonal harmony in the planting.

◀
A red, yellow, and orange scheme for the fall can be created with a variety of dahlias and daylilies with low-growing scarlet begonias in front and taller red crocosmia plants at the rear. This produces a good blend of strong but not overvibrant colors.

❶ *Crocosmia* 'Lucifer'

❷ *Dahlia* 'Bishop of Llandaff'

❸ *Begonia* 'Barcos'

❹ *Dahlia* Unwins Dwarf Group

❺ *Hemerocallis* 'Bertie Ferris'

❻ *Hemerocallis* 'Lusty Lealand'

❼ *Dahlia* 'Preston Park'

❽ *Dahlia* Unwins Dwarf Group

❾ *Dahlia* 'Jeanette Carter'

The effect of various plantings

Plantings based on the hot colors, red, yellow, and orange, are vivid and striking while the cooler colors are more restful. The same goes for the various shades. Pale colors blend softly together and are easy to live with.

All plant groupings in a small container garden need to be planned so that they fit in with the house and its surroundings. The walls of the house and garden may well be built of brick in various colors. New red bricks may not make the best background for plants. One solution might be to paint the inside of the garden walls white, but a longer term plan might be to grow ivy in a container to cover it. Green foliage is often the best foil for flowers.

▶ *Plantings of primary colors, such as red and yellow, certainly catch the eye, but the general effect can be a bit hot and restless.*

hot planting schemes

Brightly colored plants from the hot section of the color wheel achieve instant effect whether in a border or a container. Hot schemes need to be planned with care because the effect can be unsettling unless the color is controlled. Such plantings can be softened with white or pale flowers.

Hot schemes with red and yellow bulbs

The most important red and yellow bulbs are tulips and daffodils, *Narcissus*. They do not really flower at the same time with the daffodils coming first. If you want to try to achieve simultaneous flowering, you need to read the catalogs carefully and choose tulips from Division 1—Single Early Group, Division 12—Kaufmanniana Group or Division 14—the Greigii Group. These groups all flower relatively early in spring. Tulips have a complicated classification and there are 15 divisions in all. Daffodils are almost equally complicated and have 11 divisions. Those that flower latest are varieties from Division 5—Triandrus, Division 7—Jonquilla and Division 9—Poeticus. In general gardening terms most people refer to flowers from all these groups as *Narcissus*. In fact dwarf narcissus are very suitable for containers and there are

▲ *An attractive spring container of red, blue, and yellow flowers. Choose small tulips from the Kaufmanniana or Greigii groups.*

many good varieties. *N.* 'February Gold', *N.* 'Jumblie', and *N.* 'Hawera' are all clear yellow, while *N.* 'Shining Light' is a typical narcissus, with yellow petals and a strong orange-colored cup.

There are many red, yellow, and orange tulips. Among the best for the container gardener are the smaller varieties, such as *Tulipa praestans* 'Fusilier', 'Red Riding Hood', and 'Unicum', all red; *T. linifolia* Batalinii Group 'Bright Gem' and 'Yellow Gem', yellow; and *T.* 'Orange Monarch' and 'Shakespeare', orange. If you want to combine two hot colors in one flower, *T. clusiana* var. *chrysantha* is red and yellow, and 'Keizerskroon' is red with yellow on the petal margins.

◀ *A brilliant hot arrangement of annuals. The whole effect is softened by the white petunias that emphasize the startling reds and purples.*

You can plan a most effective hot planting scheme using different varieties of tulips, each in its own container. Choose tulips from the same division to insure, as far as possible, that they flower at the same time to make the most impact. And if you do not want just red and yellow then you can choose any number of color combinations.

Hot-colored bulbs and tubers for summer schemes

Other red bulbs or corms you might consider for the container garden include *Crocosmia* 'Lucifer', red, and *C.* 'Golden Fleece', yellow, although crocosmia reach 1–1.2m/3–4ft in height and will probably need staking. Daylilies, *Hemerocallis*, are more suitable for they are smaller. The varieties 'Red Joy', 'Red Rum', and 'Stafford' are red; 'Golden Chimes', 'Little Rainbow', and 'Nova' are yellow; and 'Francis Joiner' and *H. fulva* 'Flore Pleno' are orange. Daylilies flower in midsummer; some varieties are evergreen and continue to add interest during the months of winter.

A hot scheme of dahlias

The other excellent tuber for the dedicated container gardener is the dahlia. Dahlias should be lifted when the first frosts arrive in the fall, and be stored in a frost-free environment over winter. They are ideal plants to alternate with tulips if you want to produce a hot color scheme in late spring, and again in late summer in the same container. Lift the tulips when flowering is over and keep

them in a spare container until the foliage has died down, then store and replant the bulbs in the fall. Plant out the dahlia tubers in late spring or early summer after the tulips are over. Hot-colored dahlias include 'Bishop of Llandaff', 'Christopher Taylor', and 'Rothesay Superb', all red; 'Sunny Yellow', 'Lady Sunshine', and 'Ruskin Diane', all yellow; and 'Gateshead Festival' and 'Wiggles', both orange, but there are many thousands of varieties to choose from. Some of those mentioned will reach 1–1.2m/3–4ft high and require staking. Dwarf bedding dahlias are usually grown as annuals.

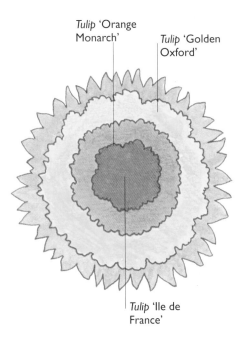

Tulip 'Orange Monarch'
Tulip 'Golden Oxford'
Tulip 'Ile de France'

▲ *A hot color wheel of tulips looks spectacular but it has to be planned and planted with care. The trouble with tulips is that there are a number of divisions, many with different shaped flower-heads, different heights, and all flowering at different times.*

Hot schemes for midsummer containers—climbers and perennials

Red and orange flowers in containers in the summer must inevitably revolve around annuals and bedding plants. Red geraniums would be a popular first choice, closely followed by busy lizzie, *Impatiens*. However, larger containers can support larger plants, and when planning a planting scheme in a container garden it is a good idea to use some of these as visually stunning highlights.

Climbers for the container garden

The favourite climber is the rose—if you can, plant a climbing rose and train it against a wall. Most will flourish perfectly well in containers provided they are fed

properly. There are two things to look out for but first check how much sun it will receive, and then how much room have you got. Do not choose a rose, such as an old-fashioned rambler, because it will rapidly outgrow the confines of the container garden, and you need to make sure you have room to walk around it. Also only the pink rose 'Zéphirine Drouhin' is completely thornless. Climbing roses for a hot color scheme include 'Climbing Ena Harkness', scarlet; 'Paul's Scarlet Climber' and 'Parkdirektor Riggers', deep crimson; 'Golden Showers', golden-yellow and suitable for a north wall; 'Maigold', yellow-orange and suitable for a north wall; 'Gloire de Dijon', buff yellow; and 'Paul's Lemon Pillar', paler yellow.

◀ *'Paul's Lemon Pillar' is a popular climbing rose that is often trained up pergolas. The flowers are double, white, with a lemon scent.*

Red and yellow clematis

If you want to grow a climber but do not want to plant a rose try a clematis. There are not that many with red and yellow flowers because most are white or varying shades of blue and violet, but of the larger-flowered varieties there are 'Guernsey Cream', creamy yellow, and 'Rouge Cardinal', 'Niobe', 'Mme. Edouard André', 'Ville de Lyon', and 'Vino', differing shades of red. These all flower from midsummer onward. Of the smaller-flowered varieties there are *C. alpina* 'Constance', red; *C. macropetala* 'Rosy O'Grady', deep pink; and *C. viticella* 'Mme. Julia Correvon', wine-red. The best yellow clematis are *C. orientalis* and *C. tangutica*. The last two flower from late summer into the fall.

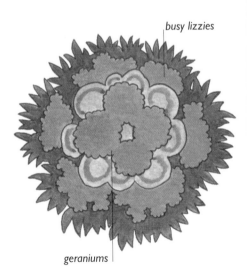

busy lizzies

geraniums

▲ *Red geraniums can be surrounded by busy lizzies but schemes of this type can be softened by including white and pink varieties.*

Two yellow wall shrubs

If you have large enough containers and want a background for a hot color scheme, there are two rather unusual yellow wall shrubs that you might consider: *Fremontodendron* 'Californian Glory' and pineapple broom, *Cytisus battandieri*. Both need a south or south-west wall and a good deal of sun. Otherwise, to vary the color schemes during the seasons, a firethorn, *Pyracantha*, could be planted in a raised bed and trained against a wall. It is prickly and evergreen, and a good guard against intruders. It has white flowers in late spring but the chief glory is the clusters of bright red, or red and orange berries that follow in the fall. They last the whole winter untouched by the birds.

Japonica, *Chaenomeles speciosa*, and its varieties also have thorny stems: they carry red flowers on bare branches in early spring, while *Abutilon megapotamicum* is evergreen and bears drooping red and yellow flowers through the summer.

Once you have decided on the climber or wall shrub that you want, you can consider the rest of the planting scheme. It would be a mistake to plant the hot-colored red-hot poker, *Kniphofia*, in a container. It takes up too much room and spreads endlessly. Also avoid the brilliant red poppies for they last such a short time in flower, but *Rudbeckia laciniata* 'Goldquelle' is reasonably compact with clear yellow daisy-like, multipetaled flowerheads, and there is no red in the garden like *Salvia splendens*, which is a must.

Rose 'Golden Showers'

Rose 'Ena Harkness'

▼ The clematis 'Mme. Julia Correvon' flowers from midsummer to late fall. The wine-red flowers are single with yellow stamens.

▲ If you have room plant two climbing roses together. 'Golden Showers' is a free-flowering yellow rose, 'Climbing Ena Harkness' is red.

cool planting schemes

Blue and white are the colors for cool planting schemes, and they can be complemented by adding gray and silver-leaved plants. They help to make any garden a calm and restful place in summer. Pale color schemes can be used to link stronger schemes and look best against a dark background.

Using blue and white plants

Blue plants can be used in a number of ways. In a traditional garden border, blue flowers, such as anchusas or dark blue delphiniums, can be used to contrast with the vivid red poppies, *Papaver*. In late spring red tulips might be planted amongst a bed of grape hyacinths, *Muscari*. These contrasting primary colors are very effective, but a garden full of such color contrasts would not be a restful place. In the confines of a container garden space is at a premium so avoid such luxuries.

In the early months of the year blue and white schemes are easy to create using bulbs. For example, a container planted with alternate blue and white hyacinths, *Hyacinthus*, looks and smells wonderful, but they will probably need some form of staking to keep them upright. Or include some other plants.

Winter-flowering heathers, *Erica carnea* and *E.* x *darleyensis*, have a number of white forms, and white *Erica* can be planted in containers with blue and purple crocuses, such as *Crocus chrysanthus* 'Blue Pearl', *C. c.* 'Ladykiller', *C. tommasinianus,* and *C. vernus* 'Pickwick' —all flower at the time when winter seems never-ending and are doubly welcome. If you do not want to go to the trouble of filling a container with ericaceous mix, necessary if *Erica* is to flower at its best, then other blue and white bulb combinations could include glory-of-the-snow, *Chionodoxa luciliae* Gigantea Group—*C. gigantea* is blue with white stripes, and *C. g. alba* is white.

If you have a larger container and would like to expand the range of plants to cover a larger canvas, then you can add some small conifers, such as *Chamaecyparis lawsoniana* 'Barry's Silver', green with silvery-white tips on the new

Erica x *darleyensis* 'White Perfection'

Crocus 'Blue Pearl'

Crocus 'Pickwick'

Viola x *wittrockiana* 'True Blue'

Viola 'Joker Light Blue'

Iris 'Joyce'

Erica x *darleyensis* 'White Glow'

◀ *A charming mixture of spring-flowering plants. For interest and variety try V. 'Freckles' or the black 'Molly Sanderson'.*

shoots in summer; *Picea glauca* 'Alberta Blue', smoky gray-blue; or *Juniperus communis* 'Compressa', green and found in many a rock garden. They all provide permanent color and form. Miniature daffodils, *Narcissus*, such as 'Jumblie', which is a yellow variety, add a touch of sunlight and can be planted in small groups with similar narcissus with contrasting colors that will flower at the same time. 'Jack Snipe' has white petals and bright yellow trumpets, while 'Jenny is almost pure white.

Blue-flowering bulbs that flower at roughly the same time include glory-of-the-snow, *Chionodoxa*, and *Scilla sibirica*. Grape hyacinths, *Muscari*, flower slightly later. Alternatively plant some of the bulbous *Reticulata* irises that flower in late winter and early spring—'Harmony' and 'Joyce' have striking blue flowers with a splash of yellow.

Clumps of *Alyssum spinosum* and *Iberis saxatilis* continue the white theme into early summer, and can be intermingled with the brilliant blue of aubretia, *Aubrieta*, planted so that it falls over the front of the container. The only problem with such an arrangement is the straggly foliage when the flowering is over. Since bulbs absorb their strength from the foliage as it dies down you either have to live with this or, more extravagantly, dig up the bulbs and replant with new ones in the fall.

▶ *A deep purple, pale yellow, cream, white, green, and silver grouping of annuals frames an old chimney in a small garden.*

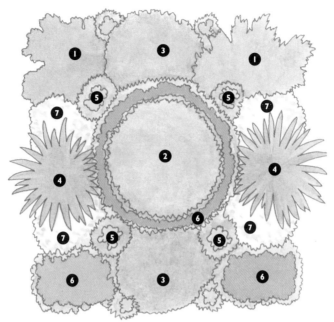

◀ *Conifers are the basis of this green. blue, and yellow arrangement that looks good all year.*

1 *Cedrus deodora* 'Feelin' Blue'
2 *Chamaecyparis lawsoniana*
3 *Picea pungens* 'Globosa'
4 *Thuja orientalis* 'Raffles'
5 *Narcissus* 'Jumblie'
6 *Muscari armeniacum*
7 *Iberis saxatilis*

blue and white schemes

Blue and white planting schemes, often mixed with yellow, are most successful in the spring before the annuals come into flower. All container gardeners should try one. Similar herbaceous border schemes later in the year include blue delphiniums or hardy geraniums grown against a background of the honey-scented, billowing white of the 2.1m/7ft high *Crambe cordifolia*, blue and white irises that complement each other and, as summer comes to an end, blue, purple, and white Michaelmas daisies, *Aster novi-belgii*, to provide a restraining influence on the golden colours of the fall. The container gardener, however, will have difficulty growing such plants effectively because they either take up too much room or have too large roots, and in almost all cases such attempts are doomed to failure.

Using African lilies

There are, nevertheless, a number of ideas that are worth considering. If you have a sunny garden or patio and a mild climate, consider planting a container with  *Agapanthus*, African blue lily. They are ideal container plants, although they require staking. The best and hardiest are the Headbourne Hybrids that are widely available. 'Bressingham Blue', another popular hybrid, is a deep violet color. Surround the agapanthus with two matching containers, lower in height, and plant one of the lovely white rock roses, *Cistus*, in each. *Cistus* x *cyprius* is justifiably popular, each petal marked with a maroon blotch in the center, while *Cistus* x *corbariensis* has clear white petals and yellow stamens. Rock roses will flower before agapanthus, through early to late summer.

◄ *Mauve petunias, verbena, and salvias are emphasized by white daisies. Take care when placing flowers against a dark background.*

▶ *Agapanthus make good container plants. Headbourne Hybrids are popular blue forms, 'Bressingham White' is white.*

Consider hardy geraniums

Another colourful scheme would be to take a selection of the smaller hardy geraniums and group them together. Cranesbills, *Geranium*, are a large genus and some are quite unsuitable for the container gardener because they grow too tall and are too vigorous, but some of the smaller ones are among the most charming and rewarding plants in any garden, flowering for months on end. The main difficulty is trying to group those that flower at the same time because they have rather different time clocks. *Geranium wallichianum* 'Buxton's Variety' is deservedly popular, its petals sky-blue on the outside and white veined within. However it can be difficult to find in ordinary nurseries, and it flowers rather late in the year from late summer into early fall. *Geranium clarkei* 'Kashmir Blue' has soft pale-blue flowers and *G. c.* 'Kashmir White' is white with

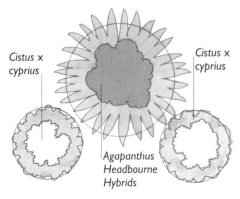

Cistus x cyprius

Cistus x cyprius

Agapanthus Headbourne Hybrids

▲ *An easy way to group colors is to grow one variety of plant in each container. Move them around until you have the right color balance.*

thin pink veins on the petals. Neither is too vigorous and they flower early in the summer months.

Other suitable white geraniums for containers include *G. sanguineum* 'Album', white flowers throughout the summer; *G. renardii*, white to pale-lavender flowers with strong violet veins on the petals in early summer; and *G. pratense* 'Striatum', somewhat larger, with white flowers streaked with blue in midsummer. These white varieties can all be mixed with any of the lovely violet-blue forms, such as *G.* 'Johnson's Blue', the most popular geranium of all. The whole design can be further warmed by the addition of one of the wonderful pink varieties, such as *G. c.* 'Kashmir Pink'.

A blue and white scheme in summer can be mixed with climbers. White climbing roses suitable for a small space include the slow-growing 'White Cockade', delicately scented with small, perfect tea-shaped flowers, or 'Mme Plantier', a vigorous white noisette-flowered climbing rose.

Large-flowered white clematis that flower from midsummer onward include *C.* 'Henryi', 'Gillian Blades', and 'John Huxtable', and attractive blue forms include 'General Sikorski', 'H.F. Young', and the ever-popular 'Jackmanii Superba', although there are many other kinds available. They can create a cool space in a summer garden and make it both restful and pleasurable.

pale pink and red schemes

Hot and cool schemes may look well in isolation and garden designers can achieve spectacular effects with them, but a mixture of shades is still the most popular plan for ordinary gardeners. The secret is to combine plants to provide constant color and a changing emphasis throughout the year.

▲ *A pink and red spring mixture of pansies, heather, and ranunculus. The clipped box provides a pleasing green background.*

The effect of white flowers

There are two points to bear in mind. The first is the blending effect that white plants have on other colors. Red, blue, and yellow plants all work well together if there are white plants in between, and the use of white also strengthens the other colors and makes them more effective. The other main point is to try and include one plant with a stronger color impact, for instance a group of pale pink flowers might look slightly anaemic, a dark red rose in the middle gives the whole design more purpose.

Various color combinations work particularly well especially those from the same quarter of the color wheel— blue, pink, and white are one good combination and you can add some yellow plants for contrast provided that the yellow is not too strong and it matches the tones of the blues. Cream and pale orange flowers are equally effective. Another good color combination includes various shades of red through to pink, and another green, white, and yellow. The main points are to match the general tone of each plant.

Certain color combinations are easier to achieve at different times of the year. Blue and yellow flowers are easy to find during the early months of the year but there are very few pink and red flowers in bloom. In the summer, pink, mauve, red, and white flowers often predominate and are easy to group together. The container gardener is also limited by the suitability of the various plants and this has to be born in mind.

A pink, white, and red scheme for the spring garden

One of the best small trees to grow in a container is a camellia, and one of the pink, white, or red varieties can be the starting point for a pink-based spring planting scheme. Camellias prefer a shady site, and their shiny dark green leaves remain attractive when the flowers have faded and fallen. Although some varieties will tolerate lime in the soil, the majority need acid soil, and therefore if you would like to grow a camellia and you have alkaline soil, a container filled with ericaceous mix is the only way you will achieve success. Ideally you should also try to collect and use rainwater because tap water may well contain lime. Alternatively sprinkle the soil with sulfur powder or add sulfur chips to keep the mix at the right pH level.

There are large numbers of suitable camellias and they come from two main groups, the *japonica* hybrids and the x *williamsii* hybrids. Eventually plants from both groups will grow too large for a container, but they are slow-growing shrubs and can be pruned back quite hard when they threaten to outgrow their surrounds. Pink camellias include 'Akashigata' ('Lady Clare'), 'Brigadoon', 'Helen's Ballerina', 'Ave Maria', 'Lady Loch', 'Lasca Beauty', and 'Spring Festival'. White varieties include 'Lovelight', 'Janet Waterhouse', 'White Nun', and 'Charlie Bettes'. The red ones include 'Adolphe Audusson', 'R. L. Wheeler', 'Coquetii', and 'Royal Velvet'. A pleasant scheme for the early spring might include three camellias in separate containers underplanted with white *Anemone blanda* 'White Splendour', or the pink form *A. b.* 'Charmer'. Other low-growing plants include varieties of *Primula allionii*. They vary in color from white to pink to reddish-purple; *P. vulgaris* 'Cottage White' is white, and the long-flowering *P.* 'Wanda' is a wonderful deep red.

▶ *A most imaginative arrangement of white and mauve busy lizzies against a background of white astilbes growing in a raised bed.*

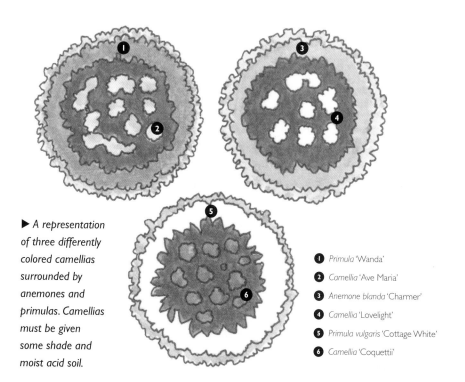

▶ *A representation of three differently colored camellias surrounded by anemones and primulas. Camellias must be given some shade and moist acid soil.*

1 *Primula* 'Wanda'
2 *Camellia* 'Ave Maria'
3 *Anemone blanda* 'Charmer'
4 *Camellia* 'Lovelight'
5 *Primula vulgaris* 'Cottage White'
6 *Camellia* 'Coquettii'

a scheme for a large container

If your garden gets a good amount of sun then you can create the equivalent of a summer border with a variety of colors. The only thing to watch out for is size but, with care, you can contrive many excellent effects. Any number of plants can be grouped together.

One idea would be to grow sweet peas, *Lathyrus odoratus*, up a trellis or wigwam of poles at the back of the container. Make sure that you can cut the flowers because regular snipping produces more buds. The fairly low-growing pink geranium *G. macrorrhizum*, can be placed in the middle, backed by the silver-leaved lamb's ears, *Stachys byzantina*, with some pinks, *Dianthus*, planted in the front. For this scheme use scented pinks, such as 'Mrs Sinkins', an old cottage-garden favorite, white with feathery petals and an unrivaled scent. 'Doris' and 'Little Jock' are two good modern pinks, both scented, pale pink on the outside, with darker markings in the center. If the container is large enough then you can plant two penstemons to add a darker shade of red and give the scheme more emphasis. The best choice would be *P.* 'Andenken an Friedrich Hahn' that used to be called 'Garnet', with deep red flowers through summer into fall, unless winter happens to arrive very early.

A varied container of pink, red, and white miniature roses

One of the easiest containers to design is composed of small roses that are available in a number of colors, red, white, and pink. Small roses come in three groups, patio roses that grow to 45–60cm/ 1½–2ft, dwarf polyantha roses that are about the same size, and miniature roses that are generally slightly smaller.

To design an effective display start by planting one of the smaller cluster-flowered bush or floribunda roses to act as a centerpiece. The bright red 'Evelyn Fison' would be a good choice but, if you want a quieter display, 'English Miss', pink, or 'Margaret Merril', white with pink buds, are both lovely roses and exceptionally fragrant. All these floribundas will grow to 75–90cm/ 2½–3ft or slightly more. Then surround

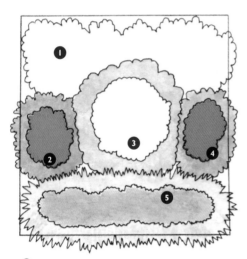

① *Stachys byzantina*
② *Lathyrus odoratus*
③ *Geranium macrorrhizum*
④ *Penstemon* 'Andenken an Friedrich Hahn'
⑤ *Dianthus*

▲ *A good pink, red, and white scheme for a container in summer. The pinks and sweet peas smell delicious, which adds to the attraction.*

▲ *Patio roses such as the white 'Bianco' carry a mass of small shapely flowers in summer. They repeat flower throughout the year.*

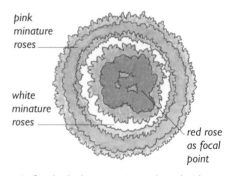

pink miniature roses

white miniature roses

red rose as focal point

▲ *Circular beds or containers planted with roses always catch the eye in summer. Include scented roses if possible, and feed them too.*

the center rose with red, pink, or white miniature roses. The two schemes that you could choose are pink roses on the inside surrounded by white on the outside, and white surrounded by pink, both of which look most attractive; a container of each on a patio would look marvelously fresh.

Since most patio roses have a spread of 45cm/1½ft you need to allow this distance between each plant. If you use miniature roses you halve that distance. 'Bianco' and 'White Pet' are both white patio roses, 'Innocence' is a white miniature rose and 'Katharina Zeimet' and 'Yvonne Rabier' are both attractive dwarf white polyanthas. Suitable pink roses include the patio roses 'Bedazzled', 'Queen Mother', and 'Hugs 'n Kisses'; 'Queen Margrethe' and 'Gracie Allen' are both white with pink hearts.

All these roses need to be fed. The ideal feed is well-rotted manure or compost but this may not be possible if you are growing roses in a container. Feed with bonemeal (unless your garden is frequented by urban foxes) in the fall and then add a balanced fertilizer in the spring. The roses should be pruned hard when they are dormant in late winter or early spring to keep them within bounds, and to encourage new growth. Cut them back to a half or a quarter of the original height, removing any dead or damaged wood completely. Thin them as appropriate.

▶ A wigwam planted with sweet peas and nasturtiums makes an unusual focal point in a small garden in summer.

foliage plants

Very often container gardens are small and shady places where the sun seldom reaches. Such gardens are often unsuitable for colorful plants, and the answer is to use a variety of foliage plants. There are several attractive combinations that can create wonderful effects in containers.

The importance of background

The first thing to think about in a small shady garden is the background, and a background of ivy, *Hedera*, that remains green throughout the year is suitable and easy. Common ivy, *Hedera helix,* will grow almost anywhere and is still a good choice. However there are many varieties, both green and variegated, that are more interesting. Try *H. h.* 'Dragon Claw' that has a medium-sized soft green leaf, if you have a shady garden, or the variegated form *H. h.* 'Goldheart' with its gold-splashed leaves to give a touch of color. Like all variegated ivies, this prefers some sun and shelter.

A container of ferns

Ferns are wonderful: soft, green, tolerant of deep shade, requiring little attention. A container of ferns is easy to plan and plant and if it is to be really successful it needs a story and focal point. The best fern to use for this is Wallich's wood fern, *Dryopteris wallichiana*. This is a striking plant. It is deciduous and carries erect strong, dark green fronds that are almost yellow when they first emerge in spring. The fronds are covered with dark brown or black scales. It can reach 1.8.m/6 ft in height, although it is unlikely to grow quite so tall in a container. This can be surrounded by the evergreen Japanese holly fern, *Cyrtomium falcatum*, and the smaller evergreen Hart's tongue fern, *Asplenium scolopendrium,*— the variety 'Crispum' with its wavy mid-green fronds is more attractive than the species plant which is rather plain.

There are two choices to plant at the edge of the container. The small rusty-back fern, *Asplenium ceterach*, evergreen, with attractive fronds, only grows to 20cm/8in in height. This is a most useful plant for growing in walls or in cracks in paving. The other choice for a small fern is the common polypody, *Polypodium vulgare*, that reaches 30cm/12in and is also evergreen. This container gives differing heights, leaf shapes, and colors throughout the year, and in the spring the grandest fern will rise up from the underworld and unfurl its leaves.

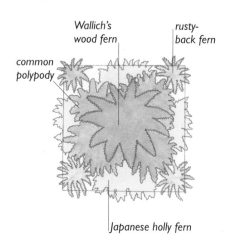

▲ *A container of ferns of different colors and leaf shapes can bring a cool shady garden to life in summer. There are a number to choose from.*

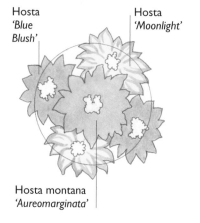

▲ *A container of hostas always looks attractive in a shady garden. Choose the varieties carefully to achieve the right balance of height and color.*

◀ *A polypody fern is the center of a green courtyard, including fatsia and a Japanese maple. The water feature is a soothing addition.*

▼ *Hostas grow well in containers for they prefer some shade and are less prone to slugs. Varieties of* H. undulata *have centrally marked leaves.*

A *container of hostas*

Many gardeners will not attempt to grow hostas because they are loved by slugs and snails who cheerfully demolish plants wherever they are grown. They flourish much better in containers where the approach of the slug can be more readily repelled and, because they prefer shade to sun, they make ideal plants for a shady patio garden. The beauty of hostas is the enormous variety of leaf color although they do carry spires of white to violet-blue flowers in summer. If you choose some of the smaller varieties, you can grow three or four hostas in a circular container 90cm/3ft in diameter. Good varieties to choose include: 'Moonlight' that reaches 50cm/20in high, light green leaves that merge into yellow during the summer, with thin white margins around the edge; *H. montana* 'Aureomarginata', dark green leaves with splashed yellow margins; 'Blue Blush' and 'Hadspen Blue', both with a height and spread of 25cm/10in x 60cm/24in, blue-gray leaves, while those of 'Hadspen Blue' are larger; 'Blue Moon' is another, smaller, blue-gray hosta; and *H. fortunei* 'Albomarginata', a bit larger, dull-green leaves with irregular cream margins.

evergreens for lasting interest

Evergreens should be present in every garden. They add interest, color, and shape, especially during the dull months of winter and many, particularly conifers, change in color in spring and summer. This provides varying color tones at different times of the year.

◄ *A gravel forecourt can be used to arrange the plants symmetrically. The use of evergreen emphasizes the formal nature of the planting.*

Evergreen trees and shrubs for permanent containers

There are more evergreen trees suitable for growing in containers than might, at first, be apparent. The main container-grown small tree is the sweet bay tree, *Laurus nobilis*, found clipped into shape at the front of many town houses. These can be bought ready-shaped from nurseries, or they can be raised from semiripe cuttings taken in late summer. They grow fairly slowly and take time to develop. They have the added advantage that the leaves are useful for flavoring food.

Another excellent small tree for the container garden is the camellia. There are many varieties and they need shade, moisture, and acid soil mix to flourish, but they have unrivaled flowers in early spring, mainly in white, pink, or red although there are a few yellow varieties, and some, such as 'Tricolor', have white, pink, and red variegated petals.

▶ *The red berries of a standard holly tree brighten the fall, complemented by the vivid Virginia creeper trained along the fence.*

The other tree or small shrub that shares similar requirements with camellias is the rhododendron, another excellent container plant. There are more varieties of rhododendron than any other garden plant so any choice is particularly invidious. They have a laxer habit than camellias, and it is not so easy to underplant them with early spring bulbs, but the flowers are lovely and come in many different colors, some are scented, and there are many evergreen varieties that keep their interest when the flowering period is over.

Grow rhododendrons and camellias in suitably large individual containers, unless you have a large raised bed that has room for more than one. Suitable rhododendrons that are evergreen and do not usually reach more than 1.5m/5ft in height and spread include 'Azuma-kagami', pink; 'Blue Diamond', violet-blue; 'Doc', rose-pink with deeper colored margins and spots; 'Fabia', orange-red; 'Hatsugiri', crimson-purple; 'Hello Dolly', apricot-orange; 'Hydon Dawn', pale pink to white; 'Kirin', deep pink; 'Mrs Furnival', light rose-pink; 'Percy Wiseman', peach-cream; 'President Roosevelt', red with variegated leaves; 'Ptarmigan', white; 'Purple Gem', light purple; 'Rose Bud', rose-pink; 'Scarlet Wonder', bright red; 'Kure-no-yuki' ('Snowflake'), semi-dwarf white; and *R. russatum*, red to purple.

Holly trees may not seem an ideal choice for the container garden. Common English holly, *Ilex aquifolium*, and its varieties have prickly leaves—not ideal in a confined space, male and female plants are needed to produce berries, and most grow too large for containers. Nevertheless they are worth considering growing in a larger, formal, garden, for they can be trimmed hard to make neat low-growing hedges and none of them grows very quickly. The varieties *I. a.* 'Argentea Marginata' and 'Silver Queen' have gold and white-edged leaves respectively that provide an added touch of color. The other evergreen holly for the smaller garden is the Japanese holly, *I. crenata*, and its varieties.

GRAY-LEAVED EVERGREENS

There are two other small trees that can be grown in containers, and both provide gray foliage throughout the winter. The first is the Australian cider gum tree, *Eucalyptus gunnii*. This is an excellent tree for a container because it can be treated as a shrub and cut back hard to the ground each spring. It will then throw up a number of young shoots throughout the summer with pale gray leaves that remain on the branches throughout the winter. The other small evergreen tree being grown more in containers, especially as the winters are generally rather milder, is the olive tree, *Olea europaea*. Olives are very slow growing and will not outgrow their situation too quickly, and eventually develop a rounded head with gray-green leaves with silvery gray undersides that flicker in the breeze.

conifers and grasses

Conifers are popular in all gardens but they have a special part to play in container gardens. They can be used in two ways: planted in individual containers to act as accent points, drawing the eye to that part of the garden, or they can be used more subtly to create an illusion of space.

Conifers on a roof garden— an illusion of space

Roof gardens are best planned as a series of rooms. Sometimes, however, such a plan is not possible and in this case the containers or Versailles tubs will march down each side of the roof space. Conifers graded in height with the tallest in the nearest container and the smallest in the farthest will extend the length of

the garden, even though this is an optical illusion. It is the same principle as changing a square or rectangular lawn in a small town garden into an irregularly curved oval, with the far end considerably narrower than the end nearest the house. The garden instantly appears longer and more spacious.

Winter color with various varieties

Conifers have the added bonus that they provide interest throughout the winter and, when teamed with the evergreen hedging box, *Buxus sempervirens*, the effect is doubled. This may be difficult to achieve in an informal patio garden with many different containers of varying shapes, but it is possible to design and plant such a scheme in a low-level raised bed on a formal patio. Plant box hedging around the edge of the bed to make a frame and, if there is room, it can be divided into a variety of geometric patterns with the conifers planted as accent points within this formal scheme. The effect, especially when there is snow or frost on the ground, can be

spectacular. Choose conifers in contrasting colors with an upright habit that will not grow too fast. Among those worth considering are *Chamaecyparis lawsoniana* 'Barry's Silver', green with silvery white tips in summer; *C. thyoides* 'Rubicon', bronze-green in summer turning purple-red in winter; *Juniperus communis* 'Compressa', green; *J.* 'Gold Coast', yellow; *J. c.* 'Hibernica', gray-green, very upright; *Picea glauca* 'Alberta Blue', blue-gray; and *Thuja orientalis* 'Aurea Nana', gold and green.

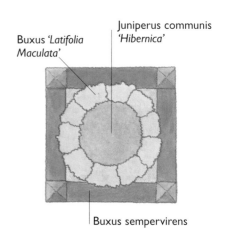

Buxus 'Latifolia Maculata'

Juniperus communis 'Hibernica'

Buxus sempervirens

▲ *Conifers can be positioned in a square container surrounded by an evergreen box hedge, with a contrasting leaved box inside.*

▲ Picea glauca *var.* albertiana *'Conica', a variety of the white spruce, has blue-green leaves and a neat shape. It may grown 2–4m/6–12ft high.*

Ornamental grasses and rushes

One way of making a container patio garden unusual is to plant some grasses or rushes in individual pots and then move them around, changing their position throughout the year. This alters the perspective and decoration of the garden and insures that it has continuing interest. In a small space it is best to choose grasses that will not grow too tall, and there are a number to choose from with attractive foliage. Zebra grass, *Miscanthus sinensis* 'Zebrinus', is one. It grows to about 1.2m/4ft and the upright leaves have creamy white bands. It is a perennial and dies back in the winter months. Pheasant-tail grass, *Stipa arundinacea*, is evergreen and turns orange-brown in winter. Since it is not totally hardy and has a tendency to flop down, a raised container is best. For the small garden *Hakonechloa macra* 'Aureola' would be a good choice. It grows to 40cm/16in and the leaves are green, striped with yellow in the summer turning reddish-brown in winter.

1 *Festuca glauca* 'Blaufuchs'

2 *Stipa arundinacea*

3 *Miscanthus sinensis* 'Zebrinus'

4 *Hakonechloa macra* 'Aureola'

▼ Grasses are excellent for displaying in container gardens where their individual colors and forms can be appreciated.

TALL PLANTS

The principle of planting one fairly tall-growing plant in an individual container can be extended to include flowering plants such as lupins, delphiniums, foxgloves, or hollyhocks, although these perennials will only provide form and color over a relatively short period.

▶ Elymus magellanicus, *wild rye, has intense blue leaves and comes from South America. It is one of the most striking of the grasses.*

bedding plants

Bedding plants are the stand-by of the container garden. Many are annuals, some biennials, and others can be planted out as garden perennials once their flowering season is over. As their name implies, annuals grow, flower, and die within one year. The majority are plants of the summer.

Bedding schemes for the winter and early spring

The stand-by bedding plants for all spring and winter containers are the colored primulas, daisies, and violas that have been bred to produce their brightly colored flowers during the months of winter and early spring. They are best planted in separate containers rather than being grouped together for the varying habits and foliage do not mix very well. They are available in many colors.

Primulas

Winter and early spring-flowering primulas belong to the primula-polyanthus group. Those called polyanthus have longer flower stalks than primulas, and are grown as biennials. The

seed is sown in the summer and the young plants come into flower in late winter and early spring the following year. Unless you are a real enthusiast, and want to raise your own plants from seed, it is best to buy plants from the local nursery when they become available in winter and then plant them out. Many are very brightly colored and the gardener can use them to experiment with schemes of primary colors, in red, yellow, and blue, either planting the colors in sequence or in small blocks. As a general rule these bright colors look best if they are planted singly, one color block succeeding another.

Daisies

When you look at the red, pink, and white balls held aloft on 5cm/2in stalks rather like miniature dahlias, it is difficult to believe that the common daisy found on so many imperfect lawns is the ancestor of such highly developed plants. Those daisies sold as bedding plants have all been bred from the *Bellis perennis* of gardens, and the most common ones are from the Pomponette, Roggli, and Tasso series. They are all reared as biennials, in the same way as the brightly colored primulas, with the seed sown in the summer and the plants flowering early the following spring in full sun or partial shade. As the color range is limited a pleasant design can be created in any

◀ *Heathers, polyanthus, pansies, and the red buttercup make a good arrangement in colors varying from deep red to pale pink.*

▶ *The brilliant yellow-orange flowers of* Primula forrestii *surround the golden-yellow foliage of a small cypress tree.*

circular container with red plants in the center, surrounded by rings of pink and then white flowers. Another very pleasant combination is to fill three similar small containers with each color and place them together.

Violas

Without any shadow of doubt, cultivated varieties (cultivars) of *Viola x wittrockiana* are the most valuable plants for any garden with containers, and they surpass all others for winter and early spring bedding schemes. Many kinds of viola have been developed over the years, each with different characteristics, but they all flower for a long period and provide a real winter treat. Winter-flowering violas, bought and planted in mid-fall, will still be flowering in spring and early summer the following year, over six or even nine

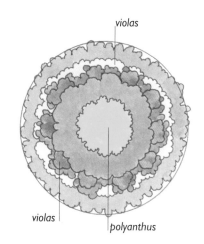

violas

violas | polyanthus

▲ *A diagram of a blue and yellow winter/early spring bedding scheme that can be designed using winter pansies or varieties of polyanthus.*

months later. As with primulas and daisies, violas are usually grown as biennials. They are either single-colored, or have the traditional pansy-type markings in two colors with a darker "face" in the center of the bloom. How they are planted must be a matter of personal choice, but groups of single-colored varieties, either in separate containers or planted together in a large container, are extremely effective. This follows one of the first rules of gardening—plant in blocks of color for the maximum impact. White flowers planted with those of a clear blue enliven the winter months, and this is a simple and most effective planting scheme. It is best to confine violas to containers because in garden beds their bright colors only draw attention to the bare drab stalks of the other plants in winter.

◀ Petunias and marigolds go well together. Note the green foliage prevents this planting from becoming too garish.

Pelargoniums, are a must, the trailing forms that hang down over the edge of the container are most useful for hiding a wall, and the scheme should include lobelias, busy lizzies, many pelargoniums, schizanthus, and fuchsias. This gives a bright glorious mixture.

If such a bright scheme is too strong and you prefer quieter colors, you can follow the same idea but concentrate on paler flowers. Mixed sweet pea, *Lathyrus odoratus*, can be grown in containers against a wall, and the wall pots above it can be filled with petunias from one of the softer mixed series, such as Milleflora Fantasy Mixed or Daddy Mixed. Even here a number of white plants, such as the petunia Supercascade White, will help the scheme to work and some of the soft-colored fuchsias can be added.

There are so many summer annuals that a gardener might spend months each winter devising different plantings and color schemes. Annuals are best used in three ways: as fringe plants to frame a border in summer, to fill any gaps, or to fill in a specific area and make a color statement. The best example of the latter is the park bedding schemes that can be seen in many towns and cities in the summer months.

In a container garden they can be used in all ways. If you have a large raised bed, then you can add white or red pelargoniums in summer. White is a good color because it links all the other colors together in the bed.

Red, white, and blue

Individual containers can be used for individual plants and color schemes, and the effect you achieve depends entirely on your choice of plants. Very often you can be too bold. The red, white, and blue effect using violet-blue lobelias, the scarlet *Salvia splendens*, and white pelargoniums can be a bit glaring, especially in a confined space. Leave out the blue or red and the two colors work better together. There are a number of white and red annuals that you can plant, such as reddish-orange mimulus, red and pink busy lizzie, *Impatiens*, red *Amaranthus caudatus*, red and white forms of *Begonia semperflorens*, and white petunias.

Color against a wall

Annuals are ideal for planting in wall pots. Here you should aim for a mass of mixed colors, mainly red and pink, but blue, purple, even orange, shades will not look out of place provided there are sufficient white plants to bind the scheme together. Geraniums,

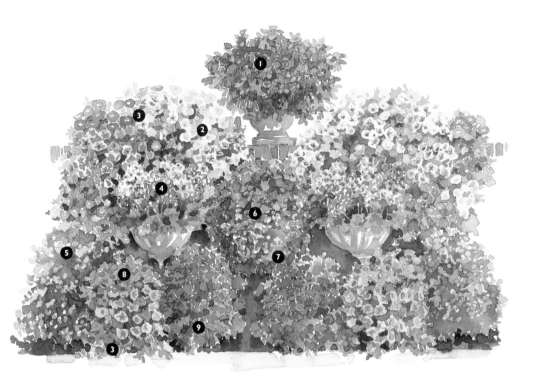

❶ *Fuchsia* 'Gartenmeister Bonstedt'

❷ *Petunia* 'Lemon Plume'

❸ *Petunia* 'Carpet Mixed'

❹ *Schizanthus* 'Gay Pansies'

❺ Million Bells 'Terracotta'

❻ *Impatiens* 'Coral Bells'

❼ *Lobelia* 'Sapphire'

❽ *Tagetes* 'Safari Tangerine'

❾ *Pelargonium* 'Gillian'

Orange annuals for the fall

Orange can be a difficult color to blend with other plants but an individual container of orange, yellow, and lemon marigold, *Tagetes* Marvel Mixed, planted with some nasturtium, *Tropaeolum*, gives a lift to fall days. A very pretty arrangement is to have the leaves of the nasturtium hang down over the container's edge, and the marigolds can stand in the center.

You can substitute pot marigold, *Calendula officinalis*, for the African marigold, *Tagetes,* and achieve almost the same effect, although the flowers are smaller and less opulent. Add the leaves of both to late summer salads, and the petals of the pot marigold can be used for food coloring.

▶ *Nasturtiums, red geraniums, and the red lily 'Fire King' make a brilliant red and orange corner on a patio in high summer.*

creating an alpine garden

The small size of alpines makes them most suitable for growing in a container as they are neat attractive plants. Their only disadvantage is that so many flower in late spring and early summer, and if you want the bed to be colorful for the remainder of the year you have to choose with care.

Soil and site

The majority of alpines need a sunny open site, preferably facing south or south-west. If you want to create an alpine bed and cannot offer such a position in your garden, you can concentrate on those alpines that come from woodland areas and like moist soil and dappled shade. There are a number of these, and they are best grown in a peat bed. Many gardeners make special raised beds for alpines, and this is most effective when the bed is constructed from natural stone, with cracks and crevices, in which many alpine plants flourish. If you are building a raised bed from bricks or stone and are using mortar to bind the material together, leave some gaps between the courses that can be filled with soil. Many alpines flourish in these situations.

It is essential that any growing medium should be free draining. The best mix to use is a mixture of two parts good quality loam topsoil (if available), mixed with one part of coarse grit and one part peat or peat substitute. Add some slow-release fertilizer if you use topsoil. Make sure that there is a good layer of hardcore in the bottom of the container, that there are plenty of drainage holes if you are planning to plant alpines in a trough or window box, and finally, when planted, cover the surface with a 1cm/½in layer of stone chippings or gravel. The chippings not

◀ *Low stone troughs or old sinks are ideal containers for a bed of alpines. These must have free drainage. Check the requirements of the ones you choose: most alpines prefer a sunny open site.*

1. *Aubrieta 'Greencourt Purple'*
2. *Saxifraga Moss Varieties Mixed*
3. *Fritillaria meleagris*
4. *Geranium dalmaticum*
5. *Gentiana aucalis*
6. *Armeria maritima*
7. *Pulsatilla rubra*
8. *Campanula carpatica 'Bressingham White'*
9. *Gypsophila repens 'Dorothy Teacher'*

planting an alpine garden

1 Prepare the mix of 2 parts loam to 1 part coarse grit and peat substitute, or buy specialized mix. Space the plants out on the surface of your container.

2 Firm all the plants in position, allow more room than you think between them, and then put as many decorative rocks on the container as you wish.

3 Cover the surface of the container with a mulch of stone chippings. These help to retain the moisture in the soil mix and suppress weeds.

only mulch the plants, retaining moisture during dry periods in the summer, but also help to smother weeds. Even though they are small do not plant alpines too close together. It is surprising how quickly a number of them spread.

Some popular alpines

Stone cress, *Aethionema*—evergreen or semievergreen subshrubs with clumps

of pink flowers from late spring onward. The most common are *A. armenum*, *A. grandiflorum* and *A.* 'Warley Rose'.

Alyssum and **Aurinia**—two closely related groups of clump-forming plants with evergreen leaves and yellow or white fragrant flowers. *Alyssum spinosum* has white flowers, and *Aurinia saxatile* yellow.

Rock jasmine, *Androsace*—these plants make dense cushions with single or clustered flowers. *A. lanuginosa* has soft pink flowers, *A. pyrenaica*, white flowers.

Rock cress, *Arabis*—mat- or cushion-forming plants suitable for growing in crevices. *A. caucasica* has white and pale pink flowers. *A. c.* 'Flore Pleno' has pure white double flowers.

Sea thrift, *Armeria maritima*—cushion-forming plants whose pink flowers are familiar to everybody who visits the

seaside. There are a number of species and cultivars in deeper colors.

Aubrieta—this is the favorite plant for all cottage garden walls with evergreen gray-green leaves and violet and purple flowers that hang down in long tresses, which cover the plant throughout the early summer months.

Bellflower, *Campanula*—there are a number of small alpine bellflowers. They include: fairy's thimble, *C. cochleariifolia* with white to lavender flowers; *C. carpatica*, white and blue flowers that spread quickly; and Dalmatian bellflower, *C. portenschlagiana*, that has deep purple flowers in late summer.

New Zealand daisy, *Celmisia*—evergreen with white daisy-like heads with a pronounced yellow center. *C. spectabilis* is particularly striking.

Sowbread, *Cyclamen*—most attractive tuberous-rooted plants, generally with pink or white flowers. Varieties of *C. coum* flower in late winter and early spring. *C. hederifolium*, better known as *C. neapolitanum*, flowers in the fall.

Fleabane or wall daisy, *Erigeron karvinskianus*—small evergreen perennial, often grown down and in walls, with daisy-like flowers that open white and then turn from pink to red.

Fairy foxglove, *Erinus alpinus*—a tufted perennial, evergreen in mild winters, that has a mass of white, pink, or purple flowers. The plants usually self-seed.

Fritillaria—some of the small fritillaries look lovely in an alpine garden when they flower in late spring. The lovely snake's head fritillary, *F. meleagris*, only reaches 30cm/12in in height, while the yellow fritillary, *F. pontica*, is only half this size.

Gentians, *Gentiana*—one of the most popular alpine plants, gentians are grown for their vivid blue, trumpet-shaped flowers. *G. alpina* and *G. aucalis* flower in late spring to early summer, and *G. sino-ornata* flowers in the fall.

Cranesbills, *Geranium*—only the smallest cranesbills qualify as suitable alpine plants. They include the evergreen *G. cinereum* with white or pale pink flowers, *G. c.* ssp. *subcaulescens* with vivid magenta flowers and black centers, and *G. dalmaticum*, usually evergreen, with bright pink flowers.

Alpine gypsophila, *Gypsophila repens*—a spreading, mat-forming plant with white through to rose-pink flowers. The best variety is 'Dorothy Teacher', which has delicate pale pink flowers.

Rock rose, *Helianthemum nummularium*—a dwarf evergreen shrub with bright yellow flowers in summer.

Flax, *Linum*—*Linum arboreum* is a dwarf evergreen shrub with yellow flowers in late spring, and *L. suffruticosum* ssp. *salsoloides* is a cushion-forming perennial with white flowers, with pink or violet veins in summer.

Lithodora diffusa—small evergreen shrub with striking blue flowers in late spring.

Penstemons—*Penstemon* are better known as herbaceous perennials but there are some small mat-forming species that come from alpine regions. They include *P. newberryi* with deep pink flowers in early summer, and rock penstemon, *P. rupicola*, with pale flowers in late spring.

Phlox—there are many small alpine phloxes. They include moss phlox, *P. subulata*, with purple to white flowers in late spring, creeping phlox, *P. stolonifera*,

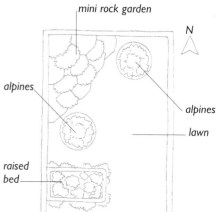

▲ *A complete area of the garden can be devoted to alpines in containers and this can be complemented by a mini rock garden in the sun.*

◄ *The saxifrage is a must for any alpine container gardener. These form springy mats of flowers in white, pink, purple, and yellow.*

▶ *Alpines look at their best in a raised trough. The white clouds of* Iberis sempervirens *contrast with the deep pink of the sea thrift.*

with purple flowers in early summer, *P. adsurgens* with pink flowers and *P. douglasii* with mauve to crimson flowers.

Milkwort, *Polygala calcarea*—mat-forming evergreen perennial with trailing stems of bright blue flowers in early summer.

Primrose, *Primula*—ideal plants for a shaded alpine garden because they will not flourish in full sun. There are many colored varieties available.

Pasque flowers, *Pulsatilla*—popular clump-forming flowers whose foliage is among the finest in the alpine garden. The most popular are varieties of *P. vulgaris*, with purple flowers, f. *alba* has pure white flowers with deep yellow centers and *P. rubra* has red-violet flowers.

Rock soapwort, *Saponaria ocymoides*—the epitome of an alpine plant, it carries pale pink flowers from late spring through the summer. The variety 'Alba' has white flowers.

Saxifrage, *Saxifraga*—an important group for the alpine gardener. The majority form compact cushions with flowers ranging from white through to pink, purple, and yellow. Among the most popular are *S. burseriana*, with white flowers, *S. exarata*, with yellow flowers throughout the summer and *S. x irvingii* 'Jenkinsiae', which is dark-centered with pale pink flowers in early spring.

Stonecrop, *Sedum*—small sedums are good succulent plants for the alpine garden. Golden carpet, *S. acre*, has yellow flowers throughout the summer, *S. sieboldii* has colored leaves and pink flowers, and the variety *S. s.* 'Mediovariegatum' has amazing yellow, blue, and red leaves, and pink flowers.

Houseleek, *Sempervivum*—large group of succulent plants notable for their extraordinary rosettes of leaves topped with pink flowers in summer. The most spectacular are cobweb houseleek, *S. arachnoidum*, and common houseleek, *S. tectorum*, hens and chicks, with red leaves.

Prostrate speedwell, *Veronica prostrata*—mat-forming perennial with blue flowers and a number of good varieties.

▼ *A diagrammatic plan of an alpine garden with a color scheme that could be achieved by several different plants.*

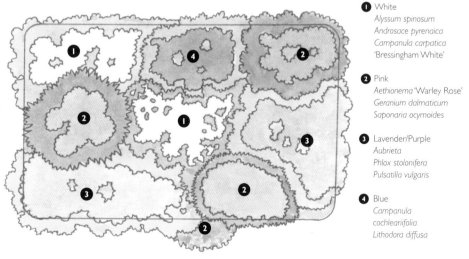

❶ White
Alyssum spinosum
Androsace pyrenaica
Campanula carpatica
'Bressingham White'

❷ Pink
Aethionema 'Warley Rose'
Geranium dalmaticum
Saponaria ocymoides

❸ Lavender/Purple
Aubrieta
Phlox stolonifera
Pulsatilla vulgaris

❹ Blue
Campanula cochleariifolia
Lithodora diffusa

water gardens and features

Water is one of the most attractive features in any garden, and running water can create a great sense of peace. In fact there are more opportunities to make a water container garden than you might think, and with some imagination wonderful effects can be contrived.

◀ *A miniature water garden in a container adds interest in any garden. Choose plants carefully and check the depth of water they prefer.*

The complete water garden

A patio garden can be transformed into a cool oasis if you build a central bed in the middle of the garden but, instead of filling it with hardcore and soil, add a liner and then turn it into a raised pond. The best design has troughs running around the edges of the pond under water that can be filled with earth and then planted with marginal aquatic plants, or shelves for planting on. Always let the water settle for several days after filling the pool because this will give any sediment time to sink to the bottom.

To make such a pond you must excavate the area. Line it with thick plastic sheeting then lay concrete over wire mesh for the floor, and do the same for the walls putting shuttering in place to hold the wet concrete in position. If you do not feel that you have the necessary expertise to construct such a pond this can always be done by a

creating a water garden

1 Fill up any drainage holes in the container and insure it is watertight. Silicon plugs are available that can be held in place with waterproof cement.

2 Choose the plants you wish from a specialist supplier and check the depth they prefer. Put bricks in the bottom to raise the level of each plant.

3 Fill the container with water and make sure there is a good gravel mulch around each plant. This stops soil leaking and sinks the plant.

professional. If you match the materials used for the patio floor with the surrounds of the pool then the whole design looks infinitely more harmonious. Do allow ample wall space around the pond, which can be used for seating, and in the summer guests can sit and gaze at the water and the plants.

Introducing fish If there is sufficient water you can even include a goldfish or two, assuming you are not troubled by herons. And if you plan to have some fish in your pond make sure that the pond is well established, that there are plenty of oxygenating plants, and that the fish are introduced gradually. If you have bought them in a plastic bag filled with water and oxygen, float this on the surface of the pool until the temperatures are even

and then introduce some of the pond water little by little. Never put fish directly into pond water and never renew the water all at one time. Leave any pump switched on overnight to help to oxygenate the water.

Water features

Fountains in a small container garden might be too much to ask for but water spouts can be included in almost all small gardens and miniature fountains can be contrived by small pumps placed in the center of any garden pond. These can be set at various heights. In any garden with a wall a water spout can be inserted in the wall and then connected up to a pump. Get a professional to connect the electrics for you unless you know exactly what you are doing. The water will

tumble down into a trough from which it is then recirculated. Such a feature can be flanked by matching containers of foliage plants such as hostas, or one of the delicate grasses, such as Bowles' golden sedge, *Carex elata* 'Aurea'.

Even if you cannot install a waterspout you can make the smallest water garden by filling a waterproof tub or tin bath with water and planting it with some floating aquatics or miniature waterlilies. Paint the inside of any container of this type with a suitable sealant, because the metal may be harmful to the plants.

All waterlilies need some depth of water in order to grow properly. Check the depth of water in your pond to make sure it is suitable and the requirements of each plant before buying and planting.

plants for a water garden

Plants for a pond can be divided into four main groups—marginal plants, plants that will grow in shallow water, deep-water plants such as waterlilies, which require a considerable depth of water if they are to flourish, oxygenating plants, and floating aquatics that exist floating on the surface.

Deep-water plants

The pride of all aquatic plants is the waterlily. Small waterlilies require a water depth of 30–45cm/12–18in, large ones, 45–60cm/18–24in. Young plants should be planted in containers using special aquatic soil or garden soil provided it does not contain any fertilizer. Plant the new root in a planting basket or an ordinary container, with the tip of the rhizome at surface level. Cover the soil with washed pea gravel and then sink the container in the pool. The container should start off in shallower water and gradually be lowered into deeper water as the plant becomes established. Anyone wanting to grow waterlilies should visit a specialist nursery and choose one of the many hybrids available in a number of colors, white, yellow, red, and pink. Another possible deep-water plant is Cape pondweed, *Aponogeton distachyos*, but it is not as spectacular as the waterlily either in leaf or flower.

Oxygenating plants Oxygenating plants are essential to any pool, particularly if you are planning to keep fish. They compete with algae for the dissolved nutrients in the water and eventually starve the algae to death. The best known are water thyme, *Lagarosiphon crispa*, still known as *Elodea crispa*, which looks rather like a lot of curled snakes; milfoil, *Myriophyllum aquaticum*; and curled pondweed, *Potamogeton crispus*, the best oxygenator for polluted water.

◄ *An old zinc bath makes a good water feature surrounded by ferns. A number of water plants only flourish in standing water.*

▶ A water feature surrounded by giant cowslips, hostas, and knautia. The sleeping nymph lies unawakened beneath a cover of lichen.

Floating aquatics They also help to reduce algae in a pool but they do so by cutting down the amount of light that penetrates the water surface. Most of them spread fairly rapidly and need to be controlled. They include fairy moss, *Azolla filiculoides*; frogbit, *Hydrocharis morsus-ranae*, which has attractive white flowers; and water chestnut, *Trapa natans*, which has very pretty leaves and white flowers during the summer.

Marginal plants

This is the largest group of plants suitable for a pond or water garden, and the number and type you grow depends on the size of your pond and the depth of the marginal shelf around the edge. Some marginals grow in fairly shallow water, up to 15cm/6in deep, while others require twice this depth of water to flourish. Be warned, a number of the best known are extremely vigorous and need to be carefully controlled if they are not to take over the pond completely.

Shallow marginal plants include kingcup or marsh marigold, *Caltha palustris* var. *alba*, with white flowers, while 'Flore Pleno' has double yellow flowers and is less vigorous than the species; *Houttuynia cordata*, with attractive blotched leaves with red margins; *Iris laevigata*, blue flowers in summer (many varieties to choose from); water mint, *Mentha aquatica*, with lilac flowers in

summer; water forget-me-not, *Myosotis scorpioides*, with bright blue flowers in early summer; and the small bulrush, *Typha minima*, but do not plant the common bulrush *T. latifolia* in a small space.

Deep-water marginals include the water plantain, *Alisma plantago-aquatica*, with attractive foliage and very small white flowers; water violet, *Hottonia palustris*, with violet, lilac, or white flowers in spring; pickerel weed, *Pontederia cordata*, with blue flowers in late summer; and possibly the spectacular arum lily, *Zantedeschia aethiopica*.

◀ A grouping of aquatic plants around a garden pool, with a ledge running round the side for marginal plants.

1 *Typha minima*
2 *Iris laevigata*
3 *Caltha palustris* 'Flore Pleno'
4 *Lagarosiphon crispa*
5 *Houttuynia cordata*
6 *Nymphaea* 'Indiana'
7 *Hydrocharis morsus-ranae*
8 *Azolla filiculoides*
9 *Myriophyllum aquatica*
10 *Trapa natans*

seasonal ideas

The best gardens provide interest for twelve months of the year. In the summer, gardens are full of color with bedding plants, roses in bloom, and many perennials in flower. The colors of the fall are gold and orange, while the spring provides the bright yellow and blue of daffodils and bluebells. Winter, too, has its attractions, and with a little planning any container garden can provide color and variety, even in the bleakest months of the year.

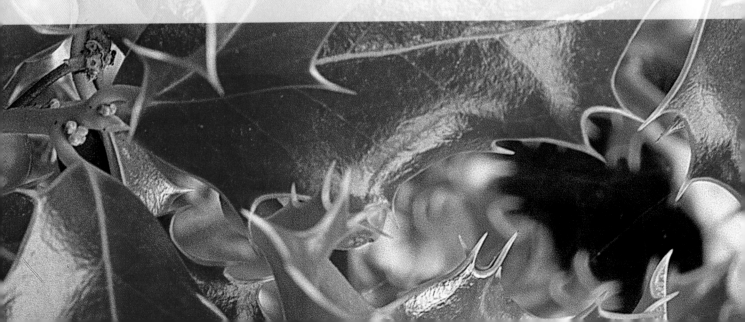

a container garden in winter

Many plants are suitable for a container garden in winter: evergreens, shrubs with berries, winter-flowering shrubs, early spring bulbs, and most importantly, winter-flowering annuals or biennials. It is best to confine them to one or two containers, leaving room for the plants of spring and summer.

Evergreens for the winter garden—conifers

The most popular, and most suitable, evergreen trees for containers are conifers. They offer a choice of colors,

▲ *Conifers are among the best plants for the winter. There are yellow, blue, and green varieties, and many change color throughout the year.*

blue-gray, green, and yellow-green, and many are dwarf, only reaching a height of 1.8m/6ft or less over a period of years. However, if you are particularly fond of the coloring of other conifers, it is worth checking on their growth rate with a reputable conifer nursery. While many are scheduled to reach a height of 12–15m/40–50ft in optimum conditions in open gardens, they can grow very slowly and will only reach 3m/10ft after 10 years. If they grow too large too fast, then they can always be removed. This applies to the lovely blue conifers *Picea pungens* 'Koster' and *Chamaecyparis lawsoniana* 'Pembury Blue', both popular choices in a number of gardens. Playing safe, the following dwarf conifers are worth considering: Upright conical trees—*Juniperus communis* 'Compressa', green; *J. c.* 'Gold Cone', and 'Golden Showers', golden yellow; and *J. c.* 'Hibernica', gray-green. Low-growing spreading trees—*J. x media* 'Golden Saucer', yellow; *J. x m.* 'Pfitzeriana', green; and *J. horizontalis* 'Douglasii', blue-gray.

Rounded conical trees—*Chamaecyparis lawsoniana* 'Barry's Silver', silver-gray; *C. l.* 'Minima', green; *Taxus baccata* 'Aurea', and *Thuja occidentalis* 'Rheingold', both golden yellow.

Evergreen and winter-flowering shrubs

There are a number of these, including: *Camellia japonica* and *C. x williamsii* hybrids. Attractive evergreen small trees or shrubs, camellias have glossy evergreen leaves and gorgeous multipetaled flowers, generally red, pink, or white. They are slow growing, and can be pruned back quite hard when they threaten to outgrow their space (you do lose some flowers). They need at least semishade and acid soil to flourish. Pink camellias include 'Akashigata' ('Lady Clare'), 'Brigadoon', 'Helen's Ballerina', 'Ave Maria', 'Lady Loch', 'Lasca Beauty', and 'Spring Festival'. White varieties include 'Lovelight', 'Janet Waterhouse', 'White Nun', and 'Charlie Bettes'. And red ones include 'Adolphe Audusson' and 'R. L. Wheeler'.

Daphne: this is a group of deciduous and evergreen shrubs that are noted for their heavily scented flowers. The following are worth considering—*Daphne cneorum*, evergreen with rose-pink flowers in late spring; *D. mezereum*, deciduous, with heavily scented pink to purple flowers in late winter and early spring; and *D. odora*, evergreen, with very fragrant flowers in winter and early spring but it is not fully hardy.

Elaeagnus x *ebbingei* and its cultivars are evergreen and grown for their yellow and green-splashed leaves. They have small white, rather insignificant flowers in the fall. Eventually they will grow too large for a container garden and have to be replaced, although this will take some time.

Erica carnea and *E.* x *darleyensis*. The winter-flowering heathers are great stand-bys for the winter container gardener. They prefer acid soil, although there are some varieties that tolerate alkaline soil provided it is not too limy. The colors range from white through pink to a deep purple-pink. The varieties *E. c.* 'Springwood Pink' and 'Springwood White' both trail and are suitable for covering the fronts of window boxes.

Firethorns, *Pyracantha*, make excellent evergreen wall shrubs whose only disadvantage is the long spikes that grow on the branches. Their chief glory is the berries, red, orange, and yellow,

▶ *Some dwarf conifers are very small indeed and grow remarkably slowly. They are suitable for small containers.*

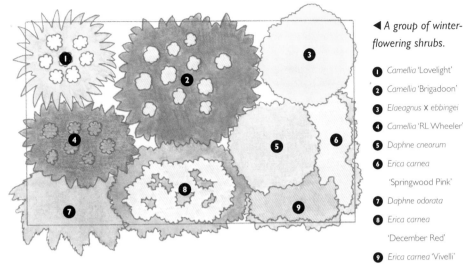

◀ *A group of winter-flowering shrubs.*

❶ *Camellia 'Lovelight'*

❷ *Camellia 'Brigadoon'*

❸ *Elaeagnus* x *ebbingei*

❹ *Camellia 'RL Wheeler'*

❺ *Daphne cneorum*

❻ *Erica carnea* 'Springwood Pink'

❼ *Daphne odorata*

❽ *Erica carnea* 'December Red'

❾ *Erica carnea* 'Vivelli'

according to the variety grown, that stay on the plants throughout the winter. In the spring they carry white flowers.

Skimmia japonica is another evergreen shrub, and the variety 'Bowles' Dwarf' is

small and compact (male and female plants are needed to produce flowers and fruit). 'Rubella' is a compact male clone. Skimmias have bright red berries that last throughout the winter.

◄ Helleborus lividus *has beautiful green flowers early in the year. All hellebores are poisonous and should be handled with care.*

being grown, and the flowers are often marked with spots and veins on the inside. They like a degree of shade and some, such as stinking hellebore, *H. foetidus*, will flourish in deep shade.

Iris unguicularis is the winter-flowering rhizomatous iris that produces blue-purple flowers on short stalks early in the year. The sedge-like leaves are evergreen. It is a good plant for a single container because otherwise it spreads too freely. After 3–5 years split and replant the rhizomes, discarding the portions from the center.

Early bulbs

Early snowdrop, *Galanthus* spp., will flower at the beginning of the New Year, with the main flowering period being the following month. (In the northern hemisphere their common name used to be Fair Maids of February.) Lovely as

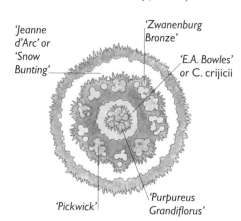

▲ *You can make a color wheel of crocuses, varying the colors according to your taste. Plant them thickly for maximum impact.*

Clematis cirrhosa is an evergreen climber with green leaves, bronze underneath. Small cup-shaped cream flowers appear in late winter and early spring. The variety *balearica* has fragrant cream flowers with red speckles inside, and 'Freckles' has creamy pink flowers that are similarly heavily speckled.

Ivy, *Hedera*, creates a permanent background in a container garden, and the best ivies to grow are varieties of Canary Island ivy, *H. canariensis*, although they may suffer in hard winters, or common ivy, *H. helix*; *H. c.* 'Gloire de Marengo' has gold-splashed leaves, *H. h.* 'Anne Marie' has leaves with white margins, and *H. h.* 'Atropurpurea' has bronzy leaves. Many other varieties are available in varying shades of green.

Winter jasmine, *Jasminum nudiflorum*, is an excellent wall shrub that does not climb, cling, or twine and therefore needs to be tied in. It is grown for the long pendent green shoots and the bright yellow flowers that appear before the leaves in late winter and early spring. Cut out dead wood, and shorten flowering shoots by a third after flowering.

Winter flowering plants

The Christmas rose, *Helleborus niger*, and the Lenten rose, *H. orientalis*, are both slightly misnamed because they seldom appear exactly when the name suggests. Putting that quibble aside, they are wonderful winter plants with bold clumps of flowers, white, pink, creamy yellow, or green, according to the kind

▶ A grouping of climbers and containers that will give flowers in the early part of the year. Winter jasmine flowers on bare branches and needs to be pruned after flowering.

1 *Clematis cirrhosa* 'Freckles'

2 *Jasminum nudiflorum*

3 *Hellebore argutifolius*

4 *Crocus* 'Queen of the Blues'

5 *Iris unguicularis*

6 *Hedera helix* 'Anne Marie'

7 *Crocus vernus*

they are it is doubtful whether they are really suitable for a container garden because they should have been planted when they were in leaf the previous year, and then left through the summer for the leaves to die down until they spring to life again in the middle of winter. If you want to grow snowdrops, plant them quite deeply in a container with small groups of crocus bulbs.

Crocuses are much easier than snowdrops, and can be planted early in the fall to flower the following spring. Some of the best are varieties of Dutch crocus, *C. vernus*. Look out for 'Pickwick', lilac-striped; 'Jeanne d'Arc', white and purple; 'Vanguard', pale lilac; and *C. chrysanthus* hybrids such as 'E.A. Bowles', gold and bronze; 'Snow

Bunting', white; and 'Gipsy Girl', yellow and purple. There are many available.

Winter aconite, *Eranthis hyemalis*, is a tuberous perennial that will make large clumps in alkaline soil, so do not grow it in any container with acid soil mix. The yellow flowers open just after the first snowdrops, and when they flower together they make a lovely picture, signifying the approach of spring.

Finally, there are the winter annuals. The best flowers are provided by a number of the winter-flowering primulas that appear in so many bright colors, and the winter-flowering pansy, *Viola* x *wittrockiana*. Every garden should have some containers planted with them because they flower from early fall right through the winter into the spring.

▼ A number of the smaller irises make excellent plants in a container in early spring. This vigorous variety is I. histrioides 'Major' with beautiful deep-blue flowers.

spring

Spring is one of the loveliest times of the year in the garden but the container gardener needs to plan carefully. Space is often limited and containers that will be filled with summer annuals or vegetables need to be empty and prepared to receive the summer plants.

Spring-flowering bulbs

Most people associate spring with bulbs. Daffodils and narcissus are everybody's favorite but there are many other bulbs that are suitable for the container garden. They include tulips, scillas, grape hyacinth, *Muscari*, hyacinth, *Hyacinthus*, glory-of-the-snow, *Chionodoxa*, and dog-toothed violet, *Erythronium*. With a little trouble you can create a considerable display of spring bulbs in a small container by taking advantage of the differing sizes of the bulbs. The container needs to have been planted early in the fall the previous year, and planned with care. Plant the largest bulbs, the daffodils, at the bottom, and then plant other bulbs in layers with the smallest at the top. All bulbs should be covered at least two and a half times their height with soil. The large bulbs will grow between the smaller ones, and the container will

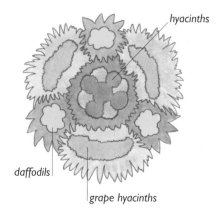

hyacinths

daffodils

grape hyacinths

▲ *An arrangement of primary colors for late spring. This type of selection can be brightened by adding white and orange narcissi.*

◄ *The deep, deep purple of these 'Black Swan' tulips recalls the tulipomania of the 18th century. 'Queen of the Night' is also deep purple.*

◄ Narcissus 'Tête-à-Tête' is a popular bulb for containers and makes a good display indoors. Plant in the fall for early spring flowering.

although not all are suitable for growing in containers, a number are. Plan carefully because much depends on how much room is available, and what you intend growing in the summer.

Some of the best flowering shrubs are those that flower early in the year, notably camellias and pieris. They both require acid soil with camellias needing partial shade, and pieris full sun or partial shade. The attraction of pieris is the new red leaves and bunches of white flowers. The most commonly grown are varieties of *Pieris japonica*. Both pieris and camellias grow slowly enough to be included in a container garden.

Another lovely spring-flowering shrub that does not grow too quickly is the pearl bush, *Exochorda* x *macrantha* 'The Bride'. It prefers neutral or slightly acid soil, and has waterfalls of white flowers that hang from the branches.

produce a succession of flowers. It may be difficult to plan for them all to flower together. There are many varieties of daffodils and tulips, all with different flowering periods. Broadly speaking the daffodils flower before the tulips, the scillas and chionodoxa flower at roughly the same time, just after the crocuses and before the daffodils, while grape hyacinths, hyacinths, and dog-toothed violets flower a few weeks later.

1. *Scilla siberica*
2. *Muscari armeniaca*
3. *Chionodoxa luciliae*
4. *Narcissus*
5. *Hyacinthus* 'Pink Pearl', 'Innocence'
6. *Tulip kaufmanniana*
7. *Erythronium* 'Pagoda'
8. *Erythronium revolutum*

► Containers of spring bulbs that will come into flower one after another. They can include tulips, grape hyacinths, and daffodils.

Spring-flowering shrubs

When confronted with the question 'What should I plant to flower in spring?', many a gardener finds it difficult to come up with anything beyond spring bulbs and forsythia. However, there are many shrubs that flower in spring and

◄ Clematis macropetala 'Jan Lindmark' has more purple flowers than the species plant. The single flowers appear early in the year.

There are many rhododendrons (some scented) that can be grown in containers that flower in late spring and early summer. Again, they need acid soil. Suitable small varieties include 'Blue Diamond', violet-blue; *R. calostratum*, rose-pink; 'Cilpinense', pale pink; 'Doc', rose-pink; 'Greeting', orange-red; *R. kiusianum*, pink to purple; 'Moerheim', violet-blue; 'Patty Bee', lemon-yellow; 'Kure-no-yuki', pure white; and 'Vida Brown', rose-pink.

Other good shrubs for the spring include *Spiraea japonica* 'Goldflame', bronze-red young leaves, and some of the viburnums. Eventually most viburnums grow too large for a normal container garden, but the lovely *V. plicatum* 'Mariesii' does not gallop away, and *V. p.* 'Roseumi' is a reasonably compact example with leaves that turn dark red before the fall.

Early-flowering clematis

The most popular spring-flowering climber is the clematis. *C. armandii* is evergreen with heavily scented white flowers in early spring, but it is not totally hardy and is extremely vigorous. You do need plenty of room to grow it. A better choice for the container gardener would be one of the *alpina* and *macropetala* varieties that flower from mid-spring into early summer. They are totally hardy, although they will not tolerate wet soil. They are quite small, usually only reaching 3m/10ft in height and are exactly right for growing in containers. They should be pruned lightly when flowering is over in midsummer, and only cut back hard if they have outgrown their allotted space. Alpinas have single bell-shaped flowers and include 'Frances Rivis', lantern-like mid-blue flowers; 'Pink Flamingo', pale

pink; 'Ruby', red with white stamens; and 'White Columbine', white. *Macropetala* varieties are very similar to *alpina*s but look as if they have double flowers because they have inner stamens shaped like petals. The best known include 'Blue Bird', 'Markham's Pink', 'Rosy O'Grady', and 'White Swan'.

The fruit blossom of spring

In Japan they have a festival of spring, devoted to the blossom of the cherry tree. There are few container gardens with the room to grow individual ornamental cherry trees, and even the upright *Prunus* 'Amanogawa' will eventually grow too tall and large, but fruit trees trained against a wall or fence are possible. The blossom they carry in

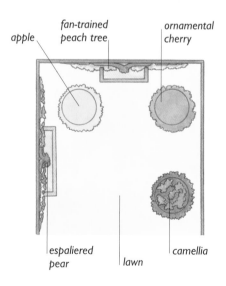

▲ A small garden can take fruit trees in containers, as shown in this plan. Make sure there is plenty of room for growth.

► *Small fruit trees can produce surprisingly good crops when grown in containers. They should be fan-trained, espaliered, or minarette.*

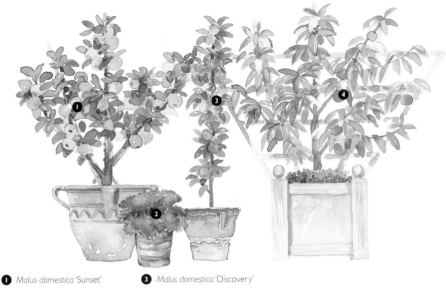

1 *Malus domestica 'Sunset'*

2 *Lettuce*

3 *Malus domestica 'Discovery'*

4 *Prunns persica 'Peregine'*

spring is one of the real bonuses. The earliest fruit trees to flower are the peach and apricots, followed by pears, then apples. Peach and apricot flower on bare branches early in spring before the leaves appear. The flowers are single, pink or red, and it is essential to protect them whenever any late frost threatens. Pears have clusters of white flowers just as the trees are starting to come into leaf. The blossom arrives earlier than on the apple trees and covers the trees with white flowers. Plums have white blossom about the same time as the pear trees, that also emerges just as the trees are starting to come into leaf. It is not so spectacular as pear blossom.

Apples have probably the loveliest blossom of all, and it is something that no keen gardener should be without. The pink-tinged white flowers open from pink buds later in the spring. Some of the crabapple varieties have blossom in many colors, which range from pure white to deep rose-pink.

Spring-flowering perennials

There are not all that many perennials that flower in spring, and the container gardener with only a small amount of space is, perhaps, better to concentrate

► *Apple blossom is probably the loveliest of all with its pink-edged petals. You need at least two varieties of apple trees for pollination.*

on spring bulbs, which are reliable and always lovely to look at. If you have got room though, probably the best spring perennial is lungwort, *Pulmonaria*. There are different kinds (many with spotted leaves), which look a bit like the inside of

the lung, hence their name. They are one of the sights of spring and have erect sprays of pink, white, red, blue, and purple flowers that last for several weeks. They prefer shade and will spread quite freely, providing good cover.

summer

Summertime is when gardens look at their best. The trees are in new leaf and many plants are in flower. The favorite garden flowers for containers in summer are the summer annuals. But for any gardener who wants to be different there is a multitude of choices, some unusual, some well known.

Summer-flowering bulbs

When people think of bulbs they inevitably think of spring bulbs but there are many that flower in summer. They should not be ignored because they are quite easy to grow, and many are ideal in containers. They include Peruvian lilies, *Alstroemeria* Ligtu Hybrids, in a multitude of pastel shades in late summer; *Galtonia candicans* and *G. viridiflora*, with white lily-like flowers that need some protection in hard winters; *Gladiolus*, extremely popular corms, available in

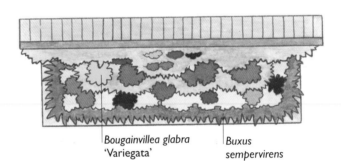

Bougainvillea glabra 'Variegata'

Buxus sempervirens

◀ *Climbers and shrubs in shades of red, pink, and purple can be grouped in a sunny sheltered position. Add some white flowers to highlight the colors.*

many sizes and colors; Jacobean lily, *Sprekelia formosissima*, with beautiful red flowers in early summer, but needing a warm south wall and winter protection; and the peacock flower, *Tigridia pavonia*, a most exotic looking flower rather like an orchid with an inner spotted face—the flowers range in color from yellow through orange to red.

Lilies

Lilies are a huge genus with over 100 species and countless hybrids. There are six divisions. They need to be staked in advance so that the stems of the plants

◀ *Lilium 'Sun Ray' is quite a small lily with bright yellow flowers, lightly dotted with brown. Although a good container plant, it is not scented.*

are held upright as they grow. Otherwise they will flop over. Grown in a container the bulbs should be planted in deep pots in fertile soil mix made up with equal parts of loam, peat substitute, and leaf mold, and the addition of some well-rotted manure or slow-release fertilizer. Cover the bulbs with at least 7.5cm/3in of soil. Among the best are the Asiatic Mixed hybrids, smaller than the trumpet lilies, but very suitable for a large container, and the showy trumpet lilies. The latter includes *L. speciosum* var. *rubrum* with pink flowers and red spots, regal lily, *L. regale*, with wonderfully scented white inner flowers, striped purple-violet on the outside, and *L. r.* var. *album* with almost pure white flowers. There are also yellow or orange ones.

planting summer bulbs

1 It is easiest to plant the bulbs and fill the container at the same time. As a general rule, plant bulbs deeply, at least 2½ times the height of the bulb.

2 In a raised bed or open ground a bulb planter is a helpful tool. Most have various depths marked on the sides and are hinged so you can remove the soil.

3 Some bulbs have to be planted just below or on the surface. These include amaryllis and hyacinths grown in containers for flowering indoors.

Summer-flowering shrubs and climbers

The temptation to rely on annuals entirely in the summer garden should be resisted. All gardens look better for varied planting, with shrubs and climbers adding color at different height levels.

Climbers that flower in summer include the coral plant, *Berberidopsis corallina*, that needs shade, acid soil, and protection in hard winters. It is evergreen and carries dark red ball-like flowers on long stalks that hang down the length of the branches. *Bougainvillea glabra* is a strong-growing evergreen climber that can be grown in containers, provided

that it is pruned hard to keep it within bounds. It is suitable for gardens free of winter frost. The flowers are normally brilliant shades of purple and red.

Summer is also a good time for the large-flowered clematis. They can be

trained along a trellis and up a wall. The most attractive are 'Comtesse de Bouchaud', pink; 'Jackmanii Superba', violet; 'Henryi', creamy white; 'Marie Boisselot', white; 'Lasurstern', lavender-blue; and 'Nelly Moser', pinkish-mauve.

▶ Bougainvillea grows quite happily in containers provided it is kept free from frost and placed in a warm sunny position.

Like the climbing hydrangea which it resembles, *Schizophragma hydrangeoides* clings by aerial roots. It has fragrant, tiny white flowers in summer that are surrounded by creamy white bracts. The effect is quite striking and it looks good against a colored plain background. It needs a bit of space and in a container garden is most suited to a permanent bed against a wall. Plant 60cm/2ft away from the bricks, and tie the plant to a support until it becomes established.

The Confederate jasmine, *Trachelospermum jasminoides*, is another evergreen climber that grows in partial shade, and does best in neutral to slightly acid soil. The leaves turn bronze-red in winter. It is not fully hardy and does not tolerate strong winds. The flowers appear in mid to late summer and are pure white with five flat petals, rather like a miniature catherine wheel.

Flame creeper, *Tropaeolum speciosum*, is another unusual climber but it can be maddeningly difficult to get established, and may need shelter in hard winters. It requires a deep container, neutral to acid soil, and the roots need to be cool at all times but with the flowers in the sun. Once established it will scramble up other plants or a trellis and has trails of brilliant, bright red flowers from midsummer onward. It looks at its best when it is allowed to peep out prettily through a wall shrub.

◀ *Summer jasmine is an attractive climber, semievergreen in mild climates, with scented white flowers in summer. It needs controlling.*

Flowering shrubs for the summer garden

There are a number that can be considered. Flowering maple, *Abutilon*, is frequently trained against a south-facing wall because it needs sun and warmth. 'Boule de Neige' is evergreen with bell-shaped white flowers from spring through the summer, *A.* x *suntense* is deciduous with violet-blue flowers, 'Gorer's White' has white flowers, and *A. vitifolium* 'Veronica Tennant' has pink to mauve flowers.

Pineapple broom, *Cytisus battandieri*, is another shrub usually grown against a south-facing wall because it needs sun and warmth. In late summer it carries large clusters of fragrant bright yellow flowers that look a bit like miniature pineapples and have a pineapple scent. *Deutzia* is one of the more unusual shrubs that carries fragrant white to pink flowers in clusters from the middle of spring through to midsummer. Two of the best kinds are *D.* x *elegantissima* 'Rosealind' with pink flowers and the pink *D.* 'Mont Rose' with violet-streaked petals. Both can be accommodated in a medium-sized container.

The flannel bush, *Fremontodendron* 'California Glory', is another evergreen wall shrub that should be trained against a south-facing wall. It will usually tolerate occasional low temperatures. It has beautiful large yellow flowers throughout the summer from late spring onwards. *Hebe* is a large genus of evergreen shrubs, many of which have spikes of blue, white, pink, and lilac

▶ *Hostas come in a wide variety of leaf colors, yellow to smoky blue, with pale white to violet flowers held on spikes in summer.*

flowers, although there is a great variety of flower color and form. Some make large shrubs, and other species, such as *H. cupressoides* 'Boughton Dome', are suitable for growing in alpine gardens. Two smallish popular shrubs suitable for containers are *H.* 'Bowles Hybrid' that has lavender-blue flowers and *H. pinguifolia* 'Pagei', pure white.

Summer perennials There is a great tendency to ignore perennials in a summer container garden. This should be resisted as they can be very attractive and are good for filling bare spaces. They are best used in two ways. If you have the room you can make a careful plan to create a small herbaceous border using specially bred miniature varieties of common herbaceous flowering plants, such as lupins, hollyhocks, and delphiniums; some of the smaller varieties of hardy geraniums, phlox, penstemons, pinks, or scabious are also suitable for such a plan.

The second approach that can be extremely effective, and is better where room is constricted, is to choose some of your favourite perennials and plant them in individual containers where they can be grouped with other plants. Hostas are ideal, as are some of the lower-growing plants, such as the pincushion flower, *Scabiosa caucasica*, or the blue balloon flower, *Platycodon grandiflorus* 'Mariesii'.

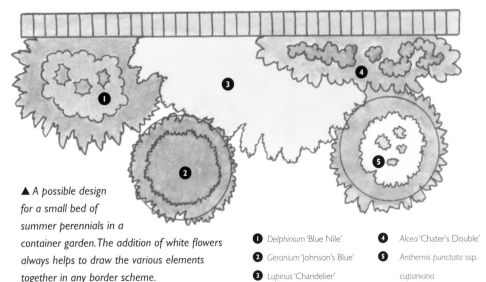

▲ *A possible design for a small bed of summer perennials in a container garden. The addition of white flowers always helps to draw the various elements together in any border scheme.*

❶ *Delphinium* 'Blue Nile'
❷ *Geranium* 'Johnson's Blue'
❸ *Lupinus* 'Chandelier'
❹ *Alcea* 'Chater's Double'
❺ *Anthemis punctata* ssp. *cupaniana*

fall

For many people, fall is the loveliest time of the year. The season is over, the crops have ripened, the leaves on the trees turn yellow and gold and then fall to the ground, slowly at first but with increasing speed as the first frosts or equinoctial gales shorten their lives.

The importance of fall color

Fall color does not last for ever and depends very much on the weather, rain or sun, frost or warm wet winds, but it is something to be treasured and every garden, however big or small, should contain some plants that look their best at this time of year. Among the most popular are the Japanese maples, varieties of *Acer palmatum*, that are generally slow growing, making mounded shrubs, although eventually they become too big for the average container. They have mid-green leaves in the summer, but in the fall these change to varied shades of orange, yellow, red, and gold.

The varieties 'Burgundy Lace', 'Butterfly', 'Garnet', and 'Red Pygmy' are all good and widely available. They prefer sun or partial shade and slightly acid soil.

Another shrub that does not grow too quickly and that provides sensational fall color is *Fothergilla major*. It prefers neutral to acid soil and has small, white, bottlebrush flowers in late spring and early summer. In the fall the leaves turn from yellow through orange to red, blue, and black before falling. They stand out like the brightest flower in the garden in high summer.

Fall berries

Many of the best berries are much appreciated by birds and squirrels, and do not remain long on the trees. Rowan berries, for example, hardly last any time at all. Small crabapples are not so popular and can be grown for their bright red and yellow fruit, as well as the

◀ *The brilliant red berries and bronze leaves of cotoneaster 'Cornubia' are spectacular in the fall. It is a large shrub and needs space.*

► 'Lucifer' is a dwarf canna lily that stays in flower from midsummer until fall. They need a warm site and water in dry spells.

lovely apple blossom in spring. They are good for a container garden, provided there is room to grow them as pyramids —*Malus* 'John Downie' has red fruit, and 'Golden Dream' bright yellow. Both have the advantage of being self-fertile, and if they are grafted on to a dwarfing rootstock they will not grow too large.

Snowberry, *Symphoricarpos* x *doorenbosii*, is another possibility. Grow it in its own container because it spreads if unconfined. The fall berries are slightly poisonous to humans and are not appreciated by birds so they may remain on the bushes for months during the winter. The best-known varieties are 'White Hedge' with clusters of white berries, and 'Mother of Pearl', which has pinkish berries.

Firethorn, *Pyracantha*, is well-known for its clusters of berries, as is hawthorn, *Crataegus*. Hawthorns are too large for a container garden, but smaller shrubs include shallon, *Gaultheria shallon*, and varieties of *G. mucronata*. Like the snowberry, they are suckering shrubs and need to be confined in a single container. They were formerly known as *pernettya* and must be grown in acid soil. They have prominent round berries in colors ranging from white to magenta, depending on the variety grown.

The other excellent shrub for fall and winter color is *Skimmia japonica*. The many forms have bright red berries and small varieties fit well into window boxes where they brighten the winter months. The only drawback if you wish to grow them as permanent shrubs in a container garden, is that both male and female plants are necessary if they are to flower and bear fruit.

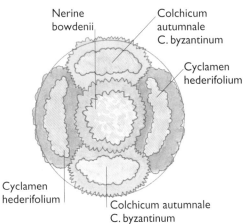

▲ Fall bulbs are at their best either growing in drifts in grassland or, in the case of nerines, given the shelter of a warm wall.

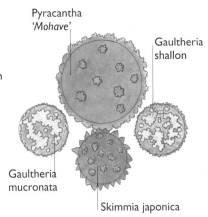

▲ Always consider whether any shrub in the garden has colored berries in fall. This is a bonus for birds as well as gardeners.

The most spectacular climber of the fall is Virginia creeper. The best one to grow is Boston ivy, *Parthenocissus tricuspidata* and its varieties. The true Virginia creeper is *P. quinquefolia*, that used to be known by the charming Latin name of *Vitis inconstans*; this provides a brief show of fall glory before the leaves drop. A number of the oriental vines also provide brilliant color, *Vitis coignetiae* and *V. vinifera* 'Purpurea' are the two most commonly grown. Golden hop, *Humulus lupulus* 'Aureus', is another climber whose leaves turn golden yellow in the fall. One climber that gives fall flowers and color is the small-flowered *Clematis tangutica* and its varieties that have nodding yellow flowers, followed by attractive silver seedheads.

Fall bulbs

Fall bulbs are dominated by the fall crocus, *Colchicum*, that flowers from late summer through the fall into winter, depending on the species grown. The most common is meadow saffron, *C. autumnale*, which has pink flowers. It has a number of varieties, 'Alboplenum' is white and 'Pleniflorum' has rounded pink flowers. Other popular species are *C. byzantinum*, with pinkish-lilac flowers, and *C. speciosum* with flowers of a deeper pink. The variety *C. s.* 'Album' has pure white flowers shaped like wine goblets. The flowers of autumn crocuses emerge before the leaves giving them their other common name, naked ladies. A number will naturalize in the wild but all can be grown in containers. Plant them in a deep container in well-drained soil in late summer.

There are two other notable autumn-flowering bulbs or corms that grow well in containers. Guernsey lily, *Nerine bowdenii*, is one. It prefers to be pot-bound and needs a warm sunny position. It produces sprays of pink flowers that last for several weeks. The second is the autumn cyclamen, varieties of *C. hederifolium*, that you may still find sold under its former name of *C.*

◄ *The leaves of the ornamental vine,* Vitis vinifera *'Purpurea', turn deep purple in the fall. The grapes it produces are not really edible.*

▶ *Smaller dahlias can be grown in small spaces in containers. Some of the dwarf mixtures available, which grow to 60cm/2ft, are ideal.*

neapolitanum. They have charming little flowers in shades of pink to white held aloft on stalks. They are also suitable plants for an alpine garden.

Dahlias

Dahlias are *the* fall flower. No other plant is so easy to cultivate or provides such spectacular blooms, and you have a choice of over 20,000 varieties. Dahlias are divided into 11 groups depending on the shape of their flowerheads. These vary from single through pompom to orchid and peony. Some are enormous with flowerheads over 25cm/10in in diameter, but many are much neater with flowerheads under 10cm/4in across. The colors range from pink, red, yellow through orange, and white. Anyone who wants to cultivate dahlias should consult a specialist catalog to choose specimens of the type, size, and color that will suit

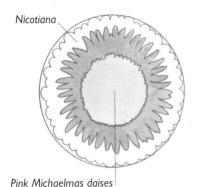

Nicotiana

Pink Michaelmas daises

▲ *Plant a container with* Aster novae-belgii *'Apple Blossom' and surround it with tobacco plants, such as* Nicotiana *'Domino White'.*

their garden. Plant the tubers in mid to late spring when all danger of frost has passed. The plants need to be staked, and this is best done at planting to avoid damaging the tubers. Plant them at least 10cm/4in deep in fertile soil mix, and add a phosphate-based fertilizer (bonemeal is the easiest). Protect the young shoots from slugs.

Fall-flowering perennials

The most popular fall-flowering perennials are Michaelmas daisies, *Aster novi-belgii*, and their twin the New England aster, *A. novae-angliae*; both come into bloom when almost all other flowers have finished flowering. They carry clumps of daisy-like flowers in varying colors from blue and lilac, to pink and white, and a number have the typical yellow centers of the daisy family. They are quite tall plants and generally reach about 1.2m/4ft and do require staking at this height. They are not particularly suitable for a small container garden. *A. n-b.* 'Apple Blossom' is pure pink and 'Marie Ballard' a delicate light blue. Another good fall perennial is *Ceratostigma willmottianum*. This has leaves that turn red in the fall, and attractive pale blue flowers shaped like those of the periwinkle.

the productive
container garden

It is surprising how much fruit and vegetables can be grown in a small container garden. You will never be able to keep the household in onions or potatoes for a year, but you can plan a succession of vegetables that will taste a great deal better than anything you can buy in the local supermarket.

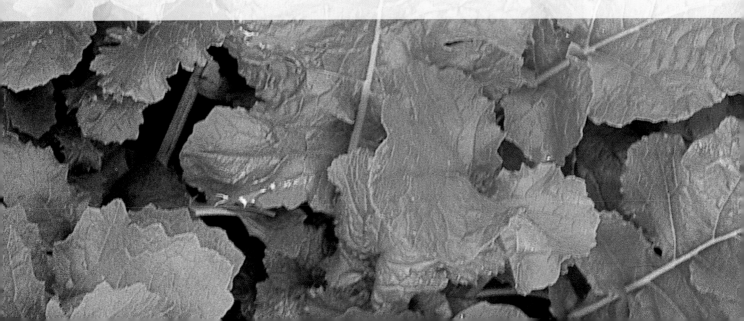

planning and planting

Growing vegetables and fruit in a small space means careful planning. Decide how much space you have available and how it can best be used. Fruit trees can be grown against a wall, and give blossom in the spring and fruit in the fall, and "mini" vegetables can be grown in window boxes.

The essence is careful planning. There is little point in sowing a whole packet of lettuce seeds at the same time for this just produces a hundred or so plants at once and most of them will be wasted.

The first thing therefore is to decide how much space you can devote to vegetables and fruit. Do you have room for just one container of vegetables, or can you spread them around the garden?

Which direction does your patio wall face and can you train a fruit tree against it? How many growing bags do you want in the garden or on the patio? Do you just want to grow tomatoes, or some peppers or cucumbers? Is there room for pots of peas or pole beans trained up a small trellis or a wigwam of poles, or a special container of herbs?

Once these questions have been answered you then have to decide exactly what you want to eat and grow. Many gardeners like to grow containers of herbs or create separate strawberry planters. Containers of vegetables need to be planned to see which kinds can be grown together at the same time, or whether the planting can be staggered throughout the year.

The key to planning successful vegetable growing in a container garden is the amount of time that every vegetable takes to mature. Parsnips, for

◀ *A really ambitious container vegetable garden with perpetual strawberries, tomatoes, and fennel all growing in galvanized containers.*

◀ *Vegetables and herbs can make a colorful display on a patio in summer, although they will not all flower at the same time.*

1 Pole beans
2 Globe artichoke
3 French beans
4 Thyme
5 Tomato 'Tumbler'
6 Purple pod beans
7 Mint
8 Parsley
9 Sugar Snap peas
10 Basil
11 'Oregon' snow peas
12 Nasturtiums
13 Marigolds
14 Lollo Rosso

example, really need to be sown very early in the year and are seldom harvested before late fall. Although their foliage is an attractive green in summer, they may well be in the ground for 10 or 11 months, occupying valuable space. This is fine in the traditional kitchen garden or allotment where there is plenty of room, but you cannot afford

artichokes

▲ *Jerusalem artichokes grow well in containers. They require staking but their upright foliage adds height to the garden in summer.*

this luxury in a container garden where every plant has to earn its keep, both in looks and on the table.

Also remember to plant any vegetables closer together than is recommended and to concentrate on quick-maturing crops, such as lettuces, to make the best use of the available space. Check the dimensions of each plant and feed them more than you would normally since they will be hungrier than usual for nutrients.

Lastly, think about the appearance of the containers. Plan the vegetables to display contrasting colors of foliage and form. Consider how they look as they mature—onions look straggly and floppy as they ripen, and a worn-out broccoli plant is not a thing of any great beauty. These are the kind of vegetables best avoided where space is limited.

The vertical dimension

A number of vegetables can be grown to add height to a container garden. Among them are Jerusalem artichokes, which can be planted in a container by themselves. They remain in the ground until the fall when they are harvested, but they are tall and stately and if confined in one place cannot spread all over the garden as they do in open ground; they make delicious soup. Peas and pole beans are two other favorite vegetables that add height. Peas can be trained up sticks or a small trellis, and take well to containers. The snap pea varieties, such as Sugar Snap, are particularly delicious, but the variety grown is a matter of personal taste. Pole beans make another excellent container crop, and their red, or red and white, flowers are most attractive when they are grown in a container.

herbs

A study of herbs is one of the most interesting aspects of gardening. Most people think of herbs as plants used in the kitchen, but herbs are the original medicines of humans and lists of them have been found on Sumerian tablets written 5,000 years ago at the dawn of civilization.

Many gardeners use containers to grow herbs, whether they have a large garden or not. This has many advantages: the containers can be positioned on the patio or terrace outside the kitchen door, so that they are easily available to the cook; many herbs, such as mint, are invasive in the ground and are better confined within a pot; a number of herbs are tender and the containers can be brought indoors in the winter, or they can be sheltered by the walls of the house or covered with protective fabric.

Herbs are fascinating plants, for if you have room, you can pick out different aspects of herb gardening and grow scented, medicinal, or culinary herbs from different parts of the world. A container of flowering medicinal herbs could include calamint, *Calamintha*, California poppies, *Eschscholzia*, cornflowers, *Centaurea*, arnica, *Arnica*, and sweet woodruff, *Galium*, grown as a ground-cover plant. A container of

▶ Thyme is a decorative herb and many garden varieties are grown as rock plants. It grows wild on mountainsides in the Mediterranean.

scented herbs might include heliotrope, *Heliotropium*, sweet rocket, *Hesperis*, hyssop, *Hyssopus*, bergamot, *Monarda*, sweet cicely, *Myrrhis*, and the scented geranium, *Pelargonium*, with sweet violets, *Viola odorata*, planted in the front.

Containers of kitchen herbs can be devoted to one herb, such as mint, or herbs from one part of the world, perhaps the Mediterranean. This is particularly suitable if you have a sunny open patio and can grow the herbs that love the heat, such as thyme, oregano, marjoram, sage, and rosemary. Sages, in particular, come in many varieties with attractive leaves in contrasting colors of green and purple.

Common kitchen herbs

Chives—can be grown as decorative edging in containers, and both the flowers and leaves are used in the kitchen as a strong and tasty flavoring. Surplus leaves can be frozen for use in the winter when the foliage has completely died down. Sow in seed trays indoors in spring, and then plant out in groups of three or four seedlings. Established groups can be divided every three or four years in the spring or fall. They look particularly attractive in pots.

◀ Differing leaf colors of the common sage look good in a herb garden. The varieties are Salvia officinalis 'Pupurascens' and 'Icterina'.

Mint—the most common mints grown for the kitchen are spearmint and peppermint. Spearmint is considered by many as the best for making mint sauce and for flavoring mint drinks in summer.

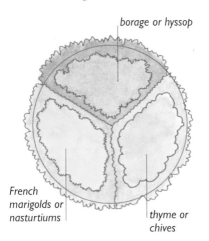

borage or hyssop

French marigolds or nasturtiums

thyme or chives

▲ There are many different colored herbs, both medicinal and culinary. With careful planning you could make a color wheel in a round bed.

Other favored mints are apple mint, there is a variegated kind with attractive white and green leaves, and Bowles' mint, a popular mint and the best for flavoring new potatoes.

Buy mint from a reputable nursery and never attempt to grow mint from seed because the varieties are unlikely to breed true. Propagate by division. Also note that mints have hairy leaves which can cause skin irritations and rashes. Handle with care. Similarly mint tea should not be drunk continuously over a long period of time.

Oregano—a favourite Mediterranean herb used to flavor stews and pasta dishes, oregano is a bushy rhizomatous perennial with flowers on upright stalks. They attract bees and insects, and emerge

◄ Origanum vulgare 'Aureum' is a cultivated form of oregano, often called wild marjoram. Sweet marjoram, O. majorana, tastes different.

directly in the kitchen garden. The densely ruffled leaves can be used to flavor soups, stews, and other dishes.

Rosemary—can be grown easily in any container herb garden given a sheltered position, for although it comes from the Mediterranean it will tolerate some frost and cold weather. It flowers early in the year at the end of winter. In the kitchen it is the traditional accompaniment for roast lamb and has many other uses. It is a slightly untidy plant but it will not regenerate from old wood so care must be taken not to go overboard when trimming it back. To propagate take semiripe cuttings in summer.

Common sage—Salvia officinalis has been a culinary herb for centuries. The leaves are often dried and stored for use. Sage and onion stuffing is the traditional accompaniment for roast poultry. Sow seeds in a cold frame in spring, take semiripe cuttings in summer. There are a number of colored-leaved varieties that are welcome in a container herb garden.

Common thyme—a number of thymes can be used in the kitchen including caraway-scented thyme, which was traditionally used to flavor a baron of beef. Sow seeds in spring in a cold frame, and take semiripe cuttings in summer.

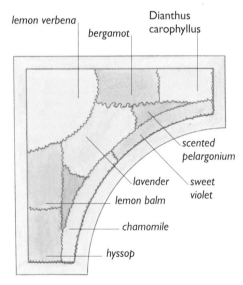

lemon verbena
bergamot
Dianthus carophyllus
scented pelargonium
lavender
sweet violet
lemon balm
chamomile
hyssop

▲ A small raised bed in a sunny corner is an ideal place to grow a number of culinary herbs. Many have the added bonus of scented foliage.

pinkish-white from deep red bracts although there are several color variations. Varieties that have been bred for the herb garden include 'Aureum' (gold leaves), 'Aureum Crispum' (curly gold leaves) and 'Compactum' (smaller in habit). 'Heiderose' is more upright with pink flowers. Oregano self-seeds and can be divided in the spring.

Parsley—a biennial that is best grown as an annual. It is difficult to germinate and requires a high temperature. Some people delay sowing until the summer, but it is a help to soak the seed in hot water overnight and pour boiling water on the soil if parsley is to be sown

▶ Low-growing rosemary plants can sometimes be trimmed into hedges along the front of containers. It prefers a sheltered site.

GOOD HERBS FOR CONTAINERS

Scented herbs

Anise hyssop, *Agastache foeniculum*
Lemon verbena, *Aloysia triphylla*
Garden calamint, *Calamintha grandiflora*
Lawn chamomile, *Chamaemelum nobile*
Clove pink, *Dianthus caryophyllus*
Sweet woodruff, *Galium odoratum*
Heliotrope, *Heliotropium arborescens*
Sweet rocket, *Hesperis matronalis*
Hyssop, *Hyssopus officinalis*
Jasmine, *Jasminum officinale*
Lavender, *Lavandula*
Lemon balm, *Melissa officinalis*
Bergamot, *Monarda didyma*
Scented geranium, *Pelargonium*
Hedgehog rose, *Rosa rugosa*
Sweet violet, *Viola odorata*

Extra herbs for the kitchen

Anise hyssop, *Agastache foeniculum*
Dill, *Anethum graveolens*
Chervil, *Anthriscus cerefolium*
French tarragon, *Artemesia dracunculus*
Borage, *Borago officinalis*
Caraway, *Carum carvi*
Coriander, *Coriandrum sativum*
Bay, *Laurus nobilis*
Sweet basil, *Ocimum basilicum*
Sweet marjoram, *Origanum majorana*
Nasturtium, *Tropaeolum majus*

Medicinal herbs

Arnica, *Arnica montana*
Borage, *Borago officinalis*
English marigold, *Calendula officinalis*
Lady's smock, *Cardamine pratensis*
Purple coneflower, *Echinacea purpurea*
Viper's bugloss, *Echium vulgare*
Meadowsweet, *Filipendula ulmaria*
Herb robert, *Geranium robertianum*
Hyssop, *Hyssopus officinalis*
Ox-eye daisy, *Leucanthemum vulgare*
Pennyroyal, *Mentha pulegium*
Sweet cicely, *Myrrhis odorata*
Parsley, *Petroselinum crispum*
Common sage, *Salvia officinalis*
Feverfew, *Tanacetum parthenium*
Tansy, *Tanacetum vulgare*

Good flowering herbs

Yarrow, *Achillea millefolium*
Thrift, *Armeria maritima*
Daisy, *Bellis perennis*
Borage, bugloss, *Borago officinalis*
English marigold, *Calendula officinalis*
Cornflower, *Centaurea cyanus*
Clove pink, *Dianthus caryophyllus*
Jasmine, *Jasminum officinale*
Bee balm, bergamot, *Monarda didyma*
Scented geranium, *Pelargonium*
French marigold, *Tagetes patula*
Sweet violet, *Viola odorata*

fruit

Fruit grown in containers needs to be trained against a wall. The only exceptions are fruit trees on a roof garden that can be grown as free-standing pyramids, or strawberries grown in individual pots or strawberry planters. The possibilities vary according to the size of your garden.

Note that if you want to grow fruit in a window box your choice is limited to some alpine strawberries grown among other herbs and vegetables. On a balcony or a patio, any fruit you grow will really be decided by the aspect and amount of space you have. Roof gardens may attract the sun all day, but they may lack the warm walls necessary for tender fruits.

Limited options

If you cannot offer a warm wall and your patio faces east or north, then the options are limited. Morello cherries like a north wall. Some of the hardier apples that resist late frosts may well fruit on walls with an easterly aspect, although they are unlikely to yield as much as in a sunnier position. Pears flower earlier than apples and are less resistant to late frosts, and at the least will need a southeasterly wall. A number of plums, though, particularly the favorite 'Victoria', will yield good fruit without too much sun if they can be sheltered in early spring from late frosts.

In colder areas some of the hybrid berries or currant bushes that can be trained against a wall are more likely to succeed than stoned fruit. But if you do try to grow fruit on a very shady patio, do not persist if the tree or bush fails to flower and produce within three years. It is better to start again with an alternative.

Growing tender fruit outdoors

Container fruit trees need not just be confined to fruit that remains outside all year. Many a patio is brightened by small

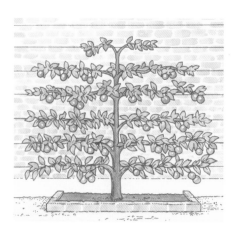

▲ *An apple tree in a small bed trained as an espalier against a wall. The steps for training these are shown on pages 124–125.*

▲ *When potting on a small fruit tree choose a pot slightly bigger than the original. Fill in the sides; insure the soil level stays the same.*

▲ *A small bush fruit tree such as lemon or orange can be taken indoors in winter and then placed outside for the summer.*

pruning a bush fruit tree

1 To make a bush, cut back a maiden in the first winter to the required height. The aim is to create 4 strong branches. Fruit will take 4–5 years.

2 Remove the leader and select 4 good branches growing at angles. Cut away any others and then reduce the main branches by half to two-thirds.

3 By the end of the second year, secondary branches will have formed. Select 8 of these and cut as above. Cut back inner branches to four buds.

trees of citrus fruits, and oranges and lemons can be put outside in the summer and brought inside in winter where they can be treated as house plants. The most suitable varieties are the x *Citrofortunella* varieties of small oranges and lemons, or some of the small lemon trees. They need a minimum winter temperature of 10°C/50°F, and can be put outside in the summer after a period of acclimatisation.

Hints and tips for growing fruit trees

The four keys to success begin with space and training. Cordon-trained trees occupy the least space, about 1.8m/6ft by 1.2m/4ft while fan-trained trees might require three times this amount depending on the rootstock used. Measure how much wall space you have

and plan accordingly. Second, consider minarette trees. If you want a free-standing tree, try planting one or more of the modern minarette fruit trees in a large container and use them as standard accent points in the container garden. Minarette trees grow upright on a single stem and will eventually reach a height of 1.8–2.4m/6–8ft. They can be planted as closely as 60cm/2ft apart, and therefore two or three trees can be grown together in a big container. Third, check the rootstock on which the fruit tree has been grafted. You need to be sure that your tree is grafted on to a dwarfing or semidwarfing rootstock, otherwise it

▶ *A vine grown in a container and trained over a pergola to make an arch. This transforms this small garden into a series of rooms.*

will grow too big for the container. And, finally, check the pollination requirements. Many fruit trees are not self-fertile, and you need to grow at least two varieties if you want fruit.

unusual fruit in containers

Don't be put off growing fruit just because the space in your garden is limited. Even if there is insufficient room for apples or pears many container gardens can support currants, or one of the unusual berries. These take up little space and are seldom found in the shops.

There are a number of excellent fruits that the container gardener can consider. *Fig*—a good tree to grow in a container because if planted unchecked in the garden the roots spread with abandon and the tree grows bigger and bigger, seldom fruiting. The common fig can be grown out of doors in any reasonably warm situation. It will ripen best in areas that do not suffer from severe winter frosts, and in cooler areas will do better grown in a greenhouse. Figs need to be pruned properly if they are to provide fruit. Consult a pruning manual for detailed instructions. The embryo fruits need protection over the winter.

Plums and damsons—plums are a good choice to grow on a sheltered patio because they flower early in the year, although plum blossom often needs protection against the unwelcome frosts of late spring. Choose varieties grafted on to Pixy (dwarfing) rootstocks. In some years the trees may bear an overload of fruit. If so, the fruit should be thinned because otherwise the branches may break under the weight of the crop. If you only have room for one tree, choose one of the luscious dessert plums and train it as a fan against a warm wall.

Sweet and acid cherries—the development of the Giessen rootstock means that a fan-trained cherry can be planted in a container and only require a wall space of 1.8m/6ft high by 3.6m/12ft wide. A number of self-fertile varieties have also been developed. The

◀ *Fig trees will fruit on warm walls. Confine their roots when planting and study the pruning requirements in a specialist manual.*

pruning and training a hybrid berry

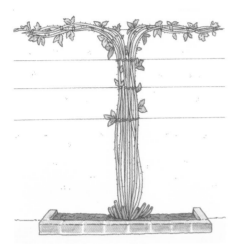

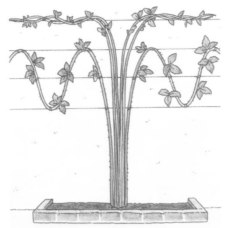

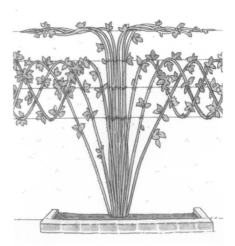

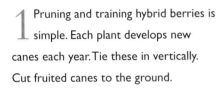

1 Pruning and training hybrid berries is simple. Each plant develops new canes each year. Tie these in vertically. Cut fruited canes to the ground.

2 Choose 6 good canes and weave them along a wire frame. The finished result will look like the bottom half of illustration 3.

3 The fruit as it looks at the end of the year when the berries have ripened. New canes are tied vertically and the old canes cut away completely as stage 1.

favourite acid cherry 'Morello', which can be grown on a north wall, needs about the same size space. Grown against a wall, a net can be placed over the ripening fruit of any cherry to protect it from hungry birds. If you don't do this they may well take the whole crop.

Peach—peaches can quite easily be grown outdoors in temperate zones, but there is no point in pretending that the cultivation of peach trees is a simple matter. Anyone who wants to grow a peach tree on a patio is advised to study their requirements carefully before starting. If you plan to grow a fan-trained peach on a patio four things are essential: you need a wall, 1.8m/6ft x 3.6m/12ft; you need a firm framework of wires on which you can tie canes to secure the branches; you need the time and

patience to establish the fan properly; and you have to remember that peaches produce fruit on wood of the previous year, and then study the pruning requirements to achieve this. Finally you must remember to spray in winter to protect against the damaging diseases that often affect them.

Soft fruit

Currants—they grow well in cool temperate climates and make a good alternative for the patio gardener who lives in a colder climate. Black, red, and white currants can all be grown in containers against a wall, and can be trained as cordons or espaliers.

Hybrid berries—some of the hybrid berries, thornless blackberries, tayberries, and loganberries can be grown in a

container against a wall. They do need a framework of wire but they are easy to train, and are a satisfactory substitute for raspberries, which are unsuitable for growing in containers because they are too spreading and vigorous.

Strawberry—the favorite fruit for the patio gardener. Strawberries are especially attractive grown in special planters or tubs, with white flowers in late spring and delicious red fruits ripening in summer. They can also be grown in growing bags, planted in late summer to bear fruit the following year. It is possible to retain strawberry plants in growing bags for two years but it is probably best if they are replaced annually. Since they are a greedy crop make sure you add slow-release fertilizer when you plant them.

215

vegetables

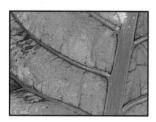

In the limited space of a container garden it is best to concentrate on your favorite vegetables: they will taste far better than anything you can buy in the shops. Grow quick-maturing crops, the "mini" vegetables that have been developed for containers, and special vegetables for special occasions.

There are many reasons for growing vegetables in containers: they can be picked fresh and eaten immediately; they taste considerably better than any vegetable you can buy; you know exactly how they have been grown and the fertilizers that have been used; and you have the satisfaction of personal achievement, of producing your own food for your own family.

Containers devoted to vegetables need very careful planning. Space is extremely limited and there will only be

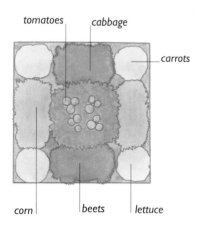

tomatoes   cabbage
carrots
corn   beets   lettuce

▲ *A variety of vegetables that could be grown in a container. Choose some of the "mini" vegetables now available, which taste as good.*

room to raise a few plants of each vegetable. Check on the amount or room that each variety requires, and try to get seed of the smaller varieties or grow the special "mini" vegetables designed for container gardens. Also grow those that will give you the greatest yield in the smallest space.

Beets—a delicious vegetable, and when eaten fresh with butter and garlic it is a culinary delight. The leaves are most decorative and beets grown in a container look attractive on a patio garden. Sow outdoors from mid-spring onward when the soil has warmed up. Soak the seed overnight before sowing and it will germinate in 10–14 days.

Cabbage—a cabbage might not be everyone's choice for growing in the limited space available in a container garden, but it is considerably more compact than most brassicas, and a number of the red and savoy cabbages are attractive plants. Most cabbages are grown to mature in the fall, but spring cabbages are also a possibility for the keen gardener and provide fresh

vegetables early in the year. Sow summer, fall, and winter cabbages thinly in succession between early spring and early summer; you will only have room for a few. Sow spring cabbages in late summer.

Carrot—if you are growing vegetables in containers you need to concentrate on those carrot varieties that are short and dumpy, rather than the larger winter carrots that take longer to mature. Also give the carrots as much depth as possible because they will not grow very well in a shallow growing bag. The attractive green foliage makes a pleasing contrast to other vegetables when they

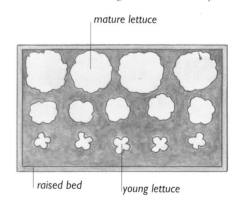

mature lettuce
raised bed   young lettuce

▲ *Grow lettuces in succession to insure a fresh supply in summer. There are a number of varieties such as 'Salad Bowl' and 'Lollo Rosso'.*

► Peas look very attractive growing in a container, and they will yield a surprising crop! This is a variety called 'Feltam First', which will grow well in a large tub.

are grouped in a trough or planter, and of all vegetables, except possibly peas, a fresh carrot tastes far better than anything you can buy. Seed should be sown very thinly *in situ*. If you like you can sow seed in modules and then plant them out in position. If you have room sow them at two-weekly intervals to produce a succession of crops.

Cucumber—outdoor or ridge cucumbers used to be practically unheard of, and when they were grown, they only produced small, rather bitter, misshapen fruits. Modern varieties, however, have changed all this as plant breeders have developed long, smooth cucumbers suitable for growing out of doors, that are tolerant of lower temperatures. Put the seeds on their edge in pots, or better still directly into the soil outside or sow in degradable pots: cucumbers do not like being transplanted. Seeds germinate at 20°C/68°F.

Eggplant—the eggplant is a vegetable that needs warmth and protection to grow well, but there is no reason why it should not flourish outside, provided that you can give it a warm sheltered position in full sun. It is a useful vegetable to start off in a container indoors and then move outside as summer advances. Ideally it

► Swiss chard or rhubarb chard is grown for its brightly colored leaves that can be cooked and eaten as spinach.

should have a minimum day and night temperature of 16–18°C/60–64°F for growth to continue unchecked. Eggplants have deep roots and should be grown in large containers in fertile soil. They should be allowed to develop without forcing, and require regular watering during the growing period. Sow seed indoors in spring at a temperature of 21–30°C/70–86°F.

Lettuce—a good stand-by for the container gardener. Lettuces mature quickly, take little room and can be grown easily in between other vegetables, and can be planted to take the place of crops that have already been harvested. The container gardener is unlikely to fall into the common trap of growing too many lettuces at one time. Sowings should be planned carefully to

insure that you have as long a supply as possible. Rather than sow directly into the ground the container gardener should sow two seeds in a small degradable pot, using as many small pots as necessary. If both germinate discard the weakest seedling. Harden the plants off by putting them outside before planting out in position. There are four types of lettuce: butterhead, crisphead, looseleaf, and romaine.

Salad greens—dark green, extra tender leaves add a piquant flavor to sandwiches and salads. Just a few leaves of argula, mache/corn salad, or upland cress will lend a tasty, distinctive, peppery sharpness. Sow from mid-spring onward for a continuous harvest.

For even more variety, mesclun is a mixture of young salad leaves. The seed

comes already mixed to be sown at two-weekly intervals for a continuous supply of tender leaves. Growth is rapid with the first harvest beginning in about three weeks from sowing.

Peas—peas are one of the commonest and most loved garden vegetables, but they can be maddeningly difficult to grow because they are popular with birds and mice. They can also be difficult to germinate because they do not relish cold soils, and conversely they are a cool-weather crop and dislike open hot positions. They can be grown successfully in containers, and should be grown as a feature plant in pots up a decorative trellis. If you plan to do this check the height of the variety you choose before planting, this can vary from 45cm–1.5m/1½–5ft. If your patio or roof

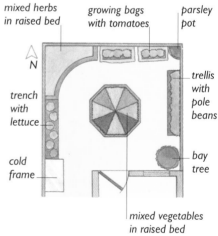

mixed herbs in raised bed

growing bags with tomatoes

parsley pot

N

trench with lettuce

trellis with pole beans

cold frame

bay tree

mixed vegetables in raised bed

▲ A patio garden laid out to grow vegetables in the summer. In winter the central bed could be filled with winter-flowering pansies for color.

◄ 'Salad Bowl' lettuce makes a brave splash of color. It is advisable to grow just a few lettuces at any one time as they will be wasted.

staking and tying tomatoes in pots

1 Standard tomatoes growing in pots trained up 1.2m/4ft stakes. If possible, run a wire along the wall behind and tie the stakes to this for security.

2 As the tomato plants grow, tie in the leading growth and pinch out the sideshoots that emerge at the joint of the branches and main stem. Water well.

3 When the tomato has set 4 trusses of fruit, or reached the top of its stake, nip out the growing point two leaves above the top truss. Feed well.

garden is exposed they may require shelter, both from the wind and birds. When ripe, peas should be cooked immediately after picking as the sugar starts to turn to starch once the pod has been picked. If you have room for more than one container, sow seed in succession from spring to early summer. *Bell pepper*—new varieties of this tropical fruit have been developed that flourish in more temperate climates; they are good plants to grow outside on a warm patio. They are popular as a vegetable in salads, and when roasted or served stuffed. They are similar in habit to tomatoes and are grown in the same way either inside, in a

▶ *Eggplants are rather unusual plants that can be grown in containers on a sunny patio. They should be treated like bell peppers.*

◄ *'Lollo rosso' lettuce can be picked a leaf at a time. They add color and interest to any vegetable container.*

▼ *New varieties of cucumber produce sweet-tasting fruit and can be grown outside.*

POLE OR STICK BEANS

Pole beans are relatively simple to grow, and the plants can be trained up canes against a wall to form a colorful backdrop with their bright red, or red and white flowers, and succulent pods. Dwarf forms are available that grow about 45cm/18in high and are suitable for troughs and window boxes. For best results pole beans need to be grown on very fertile soil, and they must be picked continually when the pods start to form. For container-grown plants, plant two seeds in a 7.5cm/3in pot of seed and cutting mix, and discard one if both germinate. Plant out when all danger of frost has passed.

greenhouse, or outside. Sow them in mid-spring under cover at 21°C/70°F. The seeds will germinate in 14–21 days.

Radish—one of the easiest of all vegetables to grow, radishes are the best way to introduce children to the delights of gardening. They germinate easily, and mature quickly, in about a month. Gardeners with large vegetable gardens often use them as a marker crop between rows of vegetables that take longer to germinate, and for the adventurous there are several winter-maturing radishes and the giant Japanese mooli radishes.

For the container gardener, the ordinary globe-shaped summer radish is a good companion plant to grow in pots with lettuces or chard, or it can be used

as a useful filler among brassicas.

Tomato—outdoor tomatoes are quite easy to grow and are among the best vegetables for the container gardener. They are attractive plants in flower and fruit, but they do best in a relatively warm climate and are difficult to grow outside unless they can be offered the protection of a south-facing wall and a sheltered position.

Tomatoes can be divided into two types: bush and cordon. The cordon varieties are the most common, and to be successful they need to be trained up a stake or tied in to wires. Tie the plants in at regular intervals using a loose knot and garden string or raffia. And pinch out all the sideshoots where the leaf stalks join the stem. This leaves you with one straight stem and a number of trusses of fruit. When the fourth truss has small tomatoes the growing tip should be pinched out, or "stopped" at two leaves above the truss. This allows the tomatoes to develop properly and ripen well.

If by any chance the summer ends rather earlier than it should, and you are left with a large number of green tomatoes, they can be picked and brought inside the house to ripen. Alternatively use them to make green tomato chutney, a delicious relish prized above many others.

Bush tomatoes are simpler. They grow either as small bushes, as the name implies, or trailing along the ground. They do not require training or stopping, but you do have to cover the ground to keep the fruit off the soil. Dwarf tomatoes, plants that grow little more than 20cm/8in high, are very suitable for growing in window boxes and small pots, but the yield is not large. Sow two seeds in a small pot and discard the weaker if both germinate.

Zucchini—another member of the cucumber family, zucchini are widely grown and are a favorite summer vegetable. The yellow-skin varieties are also very visually pleasing.

The ones grown in the garden are far better to eat than any bought in a store. The best zucchini to grow are the compact bush varieties and, provided the fruits are harvested regularly, they will continue to produce fruit over a long period. Sow in the same way as cucumbers and the seeds will germinate at 15°C/59°F. Generally zucchini are raised in pots first, and then planted out when the soil has warmed up and all danger of frost is past.

Plants grown in pots should be hardened off by putting them outside during the day before they are finally planted in position in the container. They generally do best if they are grown in a rich soil mix.

▶ *A splendid frame used for tomatoes that have been immaculately grown and cared for. All tomatoes need plenty of sunshine.*

plant directory

All the plants included in this directory are suitable for growing in containers. The lists are by no means comprehensive but provide ideas for a wide range of interesting plants. So much depends on the site of each garden, the aspect, and climate. Choose carefully and, if necessary, consult a comprehensive encyclopedia that gives greater details about growing requirements.

Trees

FRUIT TREES
Malus domestica
Apple

Height 1.8m/6ft

Spread 1.8m/6ft

These are grown most successfully in containers as cordons or espaliers trained against a wall, and are a popular choice on roof gardens, where they can be used to divide up the space. Grafted on an M9 dwarfing rootstock, they occupy 1.8m/6ft and 3m/10ft of wall space respectively, both 1.8m/6ft high, so make sure this amount of space is available. Columnar trees, single standards, can be grown as freestanding trees in containers and reach 1.8–2.4m/6–8ft. Most apples need a pollinator, so two varieties need to be grown, unless a neighboring garden has apple trees. Check with the nursery before buying as some varieties will not pollinate others. Suggested dessert varieties include: 'Gravenstein', 'Fiesta', 'North Pole', 'Golden Sentinel', and 'William's Pride'.

Pyrus communis
Pear

Height 1.8m/6ft

Spread 1.8m/6ft

Pears are grown in the same way as apples but they are trickier for the blossom flowers earlier in the year and is thus more liable to damage by late frosts. However, the beauty of the blossom makes this worthwhile. They prefer a south- or southwest-facing wall. In a container garden they should be grafted on a semi-dwarf rootstock. As with apples you need to grow two compatible varieties at the same time for they are not reliably self-fertile. Check with the nursery when buying the trees. Favorite pears include: 'Highland', 'Conference', 'Comice', 'Warren', and 'Harrow Delight'.

Prunus domestica
Plum

Height 1.8.m/6ft

Spread 3.7m/12ft fan-trained

In a container garden plums should be grafted on to Pixy rootstock and trained as a fan. Fan-training is more difficult than training an espalier, and a good pruning manual will provide instructions. Columnar trees are also available. It is best in limited space to grow one of the self-fertile varieties, such as, 'Italian Prune', 'Golden Transparent Gage', 'Cambridge Gage', 'Santa Rosa', or the old favorite 'Victoria'. This last one will grow quite well in a certain amount of shade.

ORNAMENTAL TREES
Acer palmatum var. *dissectum*
Japanese maple

Height 1.8m/6ft

Spread 3m/10ft (after some years)

Japanese maples are ideal container plants. They create an Oriental feel in a small garden. They hug the ground and the long, feathery, deeply divided leaves hang down most attractively. Their chief glory is the wonderful shades of red, yellow, and purple that the leaves turn in the fall. If you cannot find *A. p.* var. *dissectum*, choose one of the slow-growing varieties, such as, *A. p.* Dissectum Atropurpureum Group.

Pyrus communis 'Conference'

Prunus domestica

Acer palmatum var. dissectum

Ilex aquifolium

green leaves and white scented flowers in spring followed by orange or yellow fruit. Lemon trees have pale green leaves and exceptionally fragrant flowers followed by lemons. The variety 'Meyer' is the one most usually grown for it has a more compact habit than the species. Both of these small trees make an excellent focal point in a container garden in the summer, especially if planted in a grand terracotta urn.

Ilex aquifolium
Holly

Height 3m/10ft
Spread 2m/6ft

Hollies should be grown in containers more often than they are for they grow very slowly and have good evergreen foliage and lovely red berries in the winter that can be cut for Christmas decoration. They can also be clipped and trained as low-growing hedges. The male variety 'Silver Queen' has white-edged leaves and the female 'J. C. van Tol' has dark green leaves. Both male and female plants are needed to produce berries.

Camellia 'Donation'
Camellia

Height 5m/16ft
Spread 2.5m/8ft

Camellias can either be classified as a small tree or shrub. Eventually, growing in the wild under favorable conditions, they reach considerable proportions. But they are slow-growing and tolerant of pruning, so can be confined satisfactorily in containers for many years. They make ideal formal small trees with their neat pointed evergreen leaves and perfect flowers in early spring. They need both shade and acid soil to flourish. There are many varieties. Most camellias are pink, white, or red. *C.* 'Donation' is widely grown in container gardens and has pink semidouble blooms. It prefers deep shade.

× *Citrofortunella microcarpa/*
Citrus limon
Calamondin, Panama
orange/lemon tree, citrus tree

Height and spread 45–60cm/18–24in

Citrus trees grown indoors as pot plants in temperate climates are good small decorative trees to put out on patios in the summer, provided these are sheltered and sunny. The calamondin orange has dark

Camellia 'Leonard Messel'

Laurus nobilis
Bay tree, sweet bay

Height 12m/40ft

Spread 9m/30ft

Growing in the wild in good conditions the evergreen bay tree can become quite large. However it is justifiably one of the most popular trees for all container gardeners for it does not resent being confined in a pot, it grows pretty slowly, and it can be clipped to shape to make balls, mopheads, and cones. Grown and trained as a standard it is a dignified tree that is welcome in many small gardens and on patios and balconies. The leaves are dark green and pointed and are used to flavor marinades and sauces in the kitchen. Bay trees have small white, insignificant flowers in spring, followed by tiny black fruits.

Olea europaea
Olive

Height and spread: 6m/20ft or more.

The slow-growing olive from the Mediterranean is increasingly grown in containers in temperate climates. Winters are getting milder and small trees can always be given some shelter in very hard weather. Olives are evergreen with pointed leaves, gray-green above and silvery-gray beneath. The trees form a rounded head. They need a good fertile compost and feeding with liquid fertilizer every month in the growing season. The small white flowers are fragrant and the fruit starts green, turning black as it ripens.

Conifers

Conifers are one of the mainstays of the container and alpine garden. The varieties described are all slow growing and have different-colored foliage. Grouped together they provide contrast of shape and color.

Cedrus deodara 'Feelin' Blue'
Deodar cedar

Height 30cm/12in

Spread 90cm/3ft

Most cedars are large trees that require a good deal of room but a number of new varieties have been developed as dwarf forms that can be grown in container gardens and in alpine beds where space is limited. This deodar cedar has a weeping habit with attractive blue-green leaves and branches that hang down. Like all cedars it prefers well-drained moist soil and full sun. Other small cedars include *C. deodara* 'Golden Horizon', slightly larger, the leaves will be darker and bluer if grown in shade; and *C. d.* 'Aurea', golden foliage.

Chamaecyparis lawsoniana 'Barry's Silver'
False cypress

Height 1.5m/5ft

Spread 75cm/30in

There are a number of false cypresses with varying foliage colors. 'Barry's Silver' is a comparatively recent introduction that originated in New Zealand. It is quite slow growing and in the summer the tips of the new leaves appear silvery white, changing to green. It has an upright habit. It is best planted in a sheltered position in full sun where the soil does not dry out. Other varieties include 'Little Spire', blue-green, and 'Stardust', yellow.

Laurus nobilis

Juniperus communis 'Compressa'

Buxus sempervirens

Juniperus communis 'Compressa'
Common juniper

Height 30cm/12in

Spread 9cm/4in

Probably the most popular conifer for the small garden, *J. c.* 'Compressa' makes a slender compact column, bright green with silver-backed foliage. It is extremely slow growing and is most unlikely to outgrow its allotted station in the garden. It is suitable for planting in window boxes if needs be to add some vertical interest, and looks well in an alpine garden. *J. c.* 'Depressa Aurea' is another good small juniper with golden yellow leaves in summer, turning bronze-green in winter. It will eventually reach 30cm–1. 5m/2–5ft.

Picea glauca 'Alberta Blue'
White spruce

Height and spread: 45–60cm/18–24in

A lovely conical dwarf conifer with intense silvery-blue new shoots in early summer that gradually darken as summer progresses. This is another dwarf conifer that looks ideal in alpine gardens and all forms of container. It prefers sun or light shade and well-drained soil. *P. abies* 'Ohlendorffii' is another slow-growing spruce suitable for the container garden that has dark green foliage, and is definitely ball-shaped. It might eventually reach 3m/10ft in height.

Thuja orientalis 'Raffles'
Red cedar

Height 30–45cm/12–18in

Spread 30cm/12in

One of the bonuses in growing red cedars is the changing colors of the foliage throughout the year. The variety 'Raffles' has yellowish-green leaves in spring but these turn to reddish-bronze as the cold winds of fall come at the end of the year. It is small and slow-growing with a conical habit and very suitable for a container of conifers. The plant is poisonous and the leaves are harmful if eaten.

Shrubs

Buxus sempervirens
Common box

Height (grown as a tree): 5m/16ft

Spread 5m/16ft

Box is actually a tree, but it is virtually always grown as a small shrub, used for formal edging and topiary in many gardens throughout the world. Box is an essential ingredient in all knot gardens and a neat, clipped low-growing box hedge conveys an instant impression of professional competence. In containers box is very often found trained into various topiary shapes, for the small leaves lend themselves to clipping to shape. A number of good

Fatsia japonica

varieties have been developed: 'Aureovariegata' has variegated gold-splashed leaves; 'Elegantissima' is very dense; and 'Suffruticosa' is compact and slow growing.

Exochorda × *macrantha* 'The Bride'
Pearlbush

Height 1.2m/4ft

Spread 1.5m/5ft

This is a slow-growing shrub very suitable for any container or small garden. It flowers in late spring or early summer and flourishes in sun or partial shade. In flower it is one of the most beautiful shrubs in the garden with cascades of pure white flowers hanging down the pendent branches. It deserves to be better known. The flowers are born on the previous year's growth and it is better if left unpruned. Exochordas flourish in most garden soils but do best in neutral soil. Some species dislike lime.

Fatsia japonica
Japanese aralia

Height and spread: 1.5m/5ft

This is an architectural shrub grown entirely for its shape and large sculptural evergreen leaves. It does have small clumps of white flowers in late summer that appear on long stalks, which look a bit like a space station from a sci-fi movie, but they are very insignificant, as are the black berries that follow them. The plants are not fully hardy but they tolerate shade and pollution and make excellent container plants in a town garden for their large leaves are very striking. There are a number of varieties.

× *Halimiocistus wintonensis*

Height 60cm/2ft

Spread 90cm/3ft

Another small shrub that deserves to be a great deal better known than it is, and it is a good addition to any container garden. The genus is a cross between *Cistus* and *Halimium*, the rock roses, and has many of the qualities of the parents. All are excellent shrubs to include in an open sunny position and look well with other rock roses in an alpine garden. The shrubs are evergreen with gray-green leaves and the flowers are a beautiful white saucer shape with yellow stamens in the center surrounded by a dark maroon band.

Hebe 'Rosie'
Hebe

Height 30cm/1ft

Spread 60cm/2ft

Hebes are a large genus with over 100 species of evergreen shrubs of varying sizes, ranging from 2.5m/8ft to dwarf species suitable for rock and scree gardens. They vary in hardiness. They are grown for their

conical spikes of flowers, often blue, white, or purple, that emerge in midsummer and last for a long time. 'Rosie' is a comparatively new, dwarf variety, very suitable for containers and alpine gardens that has lovely darkish-pink flowers that last for several months. It is very hardy.

Hydrangea macrophylla
Common hydrangea

Height 1.2m/5ft

Spread 1.8m/6ft

Hydrangeas make good container plants and create an instant and colorful effect in any garden. They should be planted on their own. The most striking is the hortensia division of *H. macrophylla*. These shrubs carry large heads of flowers, pink, white, blue, and lilac, depending on the variety grown and the acidity of the soil. 'Générale Vicomtesse de Vibraye' is one of the best to grow. It makes a good container plant and can also be raised as an indoor plant when young. The flowers are either pale blue, if grown in acid soil, or varying shades of pink.

Kolkwitzia amabilis 'Pink Cloud'
Beautybush

Height 3m/10ft

Spread 4m/13ft

This is another shrub that is seldom grown and deserves to be better known and used in all gardens, not just the container garden. In fact, it should be confined to its own container for it has a suckering habit. It is fairly slow growing and takes a long time to reach its full size. It needs fertile soil and prefers sun or partial shade. The glory of the shrub is the cascades of pink flowers that appear in late spring and hang down on the branches. The variety is preferred to the species plant as the flowers are a deeper pink. It is deciduous and the young leaves may become damaged by late frosts, so it may need some protection.

Lavandula angustifolia 'Hidcote'
Lavender

Height and spread 45cm–90cm/18in–3ft

Lavender is one of the very best shrubs to grow in a container garden, provided that it has a warm and sunny position, for it originally comes from the Mediterranean and like all shrubs from that region prefers sun and warmth. The leaves and flowers are both wonderfully fragrant, and it is good used as a dried flower to stuff scented pillows. The variety 'Hidcote' has dark purple flowers and is commonly grown. 'Munstead' has deep blue-purple flowers and 'Loddon Pink' has pink flowers. The other main lavenders grown are *L.* × *intermedia*, English lavender, and *L. stoechas*, French lavender. Prune all lavenders hard in the spring to keep them in shape.

Hydrangea macrophylla

Pieris formosa

Pieris formosa var. *forrestii*
Pieris

Height 4m/13ft

Spread 3.5m/11ft

Don't be put off growing a pieris by the eventual size that it might attain. They grow quite slowly and only achieve their maximum dimensions in optimum conditions. They are lovely shrubs for a spring container garden, as the young leaves appear bright red, changing to light green as summer progresses, and the white flowers emerge from dark pink buds. They must be grown in acid soil and partial shade and dislike cold winds in spring. Varieties of *P. formosa* are fairly upright, 'Wakehurst' is very popular, those of *P. japonica* are more rounded in form.

Spiraea japonica 'Goldflame'
Spiraea

Height 1.8m/6ft

Spread 1.5m/5ft

Spiraeas are deciduous shrubs and a number are very suitable for containers and small gardens, for they hug the ground

Lavandula angustifolia 'Hidcote'

Spiraea japonica 'Goldflame'

forming low clumps. *S. j.* 'Goldflame' is one of the commonest and is largely grown for its golden, bronze to red, young leaves that emerge in spring, turning green as the year progresses, and again to gold with the onset of fall. It also has spires of deep pink flowers from midsummer onward. It prefers full sun and most fertile soils.

Small roses

Small roses belong to one of three groups: miniature roses, the smallest, that usually only reach 30cm/12in in height; patio roses that reach 45cm/18in; and dwarf polyantha roses that may reach 60–90cm/2–3ft.

'Pretty Polly'
Miniature rose

Height 25cm/10in

Spread 45cm/18in

An excellent miniature rose with masses of small rose-pink, fully double flowers. As with all miniature roses this is a good flowering plant for a very small patio garden or even a window box: some gardeners grow them as flowering hedges around beds or containers. In interesting contrast, 'Black Jade' has deep red, almost black, flowers from spring to fall. 'Little White Pet' blooms for the same long period. Red buds open to sprays of white.

'Stars 'n' Stripes'
Miniature rose

Height 30cm/12in

Spread 60cm/24in

Miniature roses are attractive bushy plants with tiny flowers. They are extremely useful in a container garden where there is little room, and can even be grown in window boxes. In large gardens they can be grown as a small hedge. 'Stars 'n' Stripes' was developed on the west coast of America and has white flowers, blotched and striped with red, like a miniature of the old rose *R. gallica* 'Versicolor'. Other miniature roses include; 'The Fairy', pale pink moss-like flowers, and 'Innocence', creamy white flowers.

'Singin' in the the Rain'
Patio rose

Height and spread 60cm/2ft

This is one of the best patio roses for it has a mass of dark green foliage and the flowers are an apricot-peach color held upright like many-petaled cups. It is slightly fragrant. Patio roses are just a bit larger than miniature roses and they repeat flower well. 'George Burns' has yellow, red, pink, and cream striped flowers while 'Gracie Allen' has white flowers with a pink heart. If you prefer stronger colors, 'Europeana' is velvety dark red, 'Sun Flare', yellow, and 'Judy Garland', chrome yellow blushing to hot orange and scarlet.

'Katharina Zeimet'
Dwarf polyantha

Height and spread 30–90cm/1–3ft

There are two types of dwarf polyantha roses: those whose flowers resemble rambler roses, which are close-packed and held in large sprays, and the roses whose flowers are shaped like small miniature hybrid tea roses. Both are appealing. 'Katharina Zeimet' is one of the best of the rambler types with white, fragrant flowers; pink-flowered roses of this type include 'Coral Cluster' and 'Nathalie Nypels'. 'Cécile Brünner', the 'Sweetheart Rose', is the best known of the hybrid tea forms. The flowers are blush pink; 'Perle d'Or' is similar with apricot flowers.

Climbing roses

Climbing roses need to be differentiated from ramblers. Climbers have larger flowers and most repeat flowerings. Most modern climbers repeat throughout the summer. Ramblers are often very vigorous—too vigorous, in fact, for any container garden, however wonderful they look growing through an old tree.

'Blairii Number 2'
Bourbon

Height 4.5m/15ft

Spread 1.8m/6ft

A Bourbon rose, a class of rose that mostly dates from the latter part of the 19th century, 'Blairii Number 2' has retained its popularity as a climber for 150 years. It has beautiful, pink many-petaled, fragrant flowers, darker in the center and pale toward the edges. It really only flowers once in summer, although there is a small second flowering. The young leaves are reddish green when they emerge, changing to mid-green as the summer progresses. It is sometimes prone to attacks of mildew.

'Compassion'
Modern climber

Height 3m/10ft

Spread 2.5m/8ft

One of the very best and most popular of the modern climbers, 'Compassion' has large tea-shaped flowers, paleish pink on the outside and apricot-yellow on the inside. They are substantial blooms and deliciously fragrant, giving the lie to anyone who says that modern roses have no perfume. It repeat flowers throughout

Rosa 'Sweet Dream'

Rosa 'Compassion'

the summer and has a strong bushy growth with dark green leaves. It looks its best when grown as a focal point on a southfacing wall where the blooms make the most impact.

'Constance Spry'
English rose

Height 3.5m/12ft
Spread 3.5m/12ft

This is one of the first English roses bred by David Austin. It can be grown as a shrub but makes an excellent climber when the lax shoots are given support and tied in to a frame The flowers are huge, clear pink, with the most pronounced myrrh fragrance. It makes a definite statement in any garden. Its only disadvantage is that unlike so many of the English roses it only flowers once, but those who grow it think the advantages far outweigh this.

'Copenhagen'
Modern climber

Height 2.5m/8ft
Spread 2.5m/8ft

This is another modern climber with flowers of superb fragrance. They are medium-sized, hybrid tea-shaped and deep scarlet. The rose will repeat flower throughout the summer and looks exceptional if it is grown in company with a large-flowered white clematis, such as 'Gillian Blades'. Another modern climber with deep red flowers that can be grown as an alternative is 'Crimson Cascade'. This rose is similar in size but has larger flowers. It is extremely vigorous and disease resistant.

'Golden Showers'
Modern climber

Height 3m/10ft
Spread 3m/10ft

One of the very best and most amenable of all the climbing roses, 'Golden Showers' has double, clear yellow flowers that fade to a paler cream as they age. It repeat flowers throughout the summer and the flowers have a pleasing fragrance. Its main advantage is that it will flourish happily on a north wall, making it invaluable for any garden denied the benefit of walls with better aspects. 'Danse du Feu' is another climber that will grow against a north wall. This rose has orange-scarlet flowers.

'Climbing Iceberg'
Floribunda

Height 3m/10ft
Spread 2.5m/8ft

The climbing form of the ever-popular 'Iceberg' is an excellent rose to grow against a wall and forms an admirable background to all other plants. The foliage is light green and the white flowers, sometimes tinged with pale pink, are held in delicate sprays. Its only disadvantage is that it has little or no scent. 'Iceberg' remains in flower longer than almost any other rose in the garden and it is not unusual to be able to gather sprays in midwinter, on Christmas Day.

'Maigold'
Climber

Height 3.5m/12ft
Spread 3m/10ft

Like 'Golden Showers', 'Maigold' has some supreme advantages over other climbing roses as it is one of the toughest roses around, and be grown almost anywhere. It has superb bronze-yellow, semidouble flowers, which are produced in abundance. The flowers are extremely fragrant. It has a mass of dark glossy leaves and is generally disease-free but, alas, it only flowers once during the summer. It is probably the best rose to grow in poor conditions against a north-facing wall and should be considered by anyone who wants to grow a climbing rose and can only offer these conditions.

Rosa 'Constance Spry'

Rosa 'Copenhagen'

'New Dawn'
Modern climber

Height 3m/10ft

Spread 2.5m/8ft

A deservedly popular climbing rose was one of the first modern climbers. It is very vigorous, has lovely, glossy, light- to mid-green leaves, and delicate silvery pink flowers with a slightly deeper color in the center. The flowers are born in clusters and repeat throughout the summer. They have a light delicate fragrance. 'New Dawn' is not prone to disease and tolerates a partially shaded site although it should not be planted against a north-facing wall.

'Paul's Lemon Pillar'
Hybrid tea

Height 6m/20ft

Spread 3m/10ft

The classic pillar rose that is found in many gardens growing up pergolas or old tree stumps. It can be grown in containers at the foot of an arch and trained over a pergola. The rose has large, creamy lemon, tea-shaped, fully double flowers with petals

Rosa 'New Dawn'

that curl back at the edges. The flowers are very fragrant. The leaves are dark green. It is a strong, hardy, vigorous rose that should be tied in to make a columnar shape.

'A Shropshire Lad'
English rose

Height 2.5m/8ft

Spread 1.8m/6ft

This is another English rose that makes an excellent climber planted against a warm wall. It is a rose well worth growing for the flowers are large, of the typical cupped-rosette form found on many English roses and deliciously fragrant. The color is a beautiful peachy pink, fading slightly as the flowers age. Although it will grow best as a climber against a south wall, it can be planted in any position in the garden.

Climbers and wall plants

Abutilon × suntense 'Violetta'
Flowering maple, Indian mallow

Height 5m/16ft

Spread 3m/10ft

Some abutilons are evergreen, some deciduous, and none are fully hardy, but varieties of the deciduous *A. × suntense* are among the easiest to grow if they can be provided with a sheltered south-facing wall. They make excellent plants for containers. Flowers of the species are large and saucer-shaped. The variety 'Violetta' has intense violet flowers that appear in late spring. Any frost-damaged shoots should be cut back to sound wood in spring.

Clematis alpina 'Frances Rivis'
Clematis

Height 4m/13ft

Spread 1.8m/6ft

The alpina varieties of clematis are very suitable for growing in containers for they are relatively small in size and far less vigorous than montanas. They flower in spring. The flowers are single, and bell-shaped, like narrow pixies' caps with pointed petals. 'Frances Rivis' is the largest of the alpinas and has lovely dark blue flowers followed by fluffy seedheads. The alpinas are very hardy and will survive planted in the most unpromising positions, but they will not tolerate water-logged soil.

Clematis tangutica
Clematis

Height 4. 5m/15ft

Spread 1. 8m/6ft

One of the latest flowering of the clematis that brightens the autumn, *C. tangutica* carries funny, solitary, bright yellow flowers, bell-shaped but whose ends often appear as if they are crimped together.

Rosa 'Paul's Lemon Pillar'

They have striking seedheads that remain on the plant over the winter. The variety 'Helios' is shorter in growth and particularly suitable for a small container garden and there are a number of other hybrids. It is fully hardy.

Fremontodendron 'California Glory'
Flannel bush

Height 3m/10ft

Spread 3m/10ft

Fremontodendrons must be grown against a wall. They need tying in and are not considered particularly hardy although they will survive surprisingly cold winters given adequate protection. They are evergreen with rather sparse dark green leaves, up to 7.5cm/3in long. They are grown for the large deep buttercup-yellow flowers that appear in late spring and continue throughout the summer. The flowers are a shallow saucer shape. They prefer deep soil, so plant in a large container and see that there is good drainage. Cut back any frost-damaged shoots to good wood in spring.

Hydrangea petiolaris syn. *H. anomala* ssp. *petiolaris*

Clematis tangutica

Hedera helix 'Glacier'
Common ivy, English ivy

Height 1.8m/6ft or more

Spread 1.8m/6ft

Hedera helix, the common English ivy, has given rise to a large number of varieties. These can be grown against a wall to provide evergreen cover throughout the year, used as groundcover, or grown indoors as a house plant. The variety 'Glacier' is excellent for all these purposes. It has dark gray-green leaves with variegated margins marked silver and cream. When grown outside, it needs a sunny position to show its best color.

Hydrangea petiolaris syn. *H. anomala* ssp. *petiolaris*
Climbing hydrangea

Height 10m/33ft

Spread 10m/33ft

This is one of the best shrubs to cover a wall for it is not fussy over situation or aspect, and grows well in extremely shaded town gardens. It is a vigorous shrub but it can be cut back hard each spring. It clings to the wall by aerial roots and the bright green leaves turn yellow in the fall before they drop. In the summer it is covered with clusters of white flowers surrounded by prominent sterile flowers.

233

Jasminum officinale
Common jasmine, summer jasmine

Height and spread 12m/40ft

This is another vigorous climber often found growing in containers that will quickly cover a wall or trellis with its long trailing dark green shoots. Jasmine needs a frame to wind itself around. The flowers are white and emerge in summer, lasting into the early fall. They are very fragrant. It is best to prune jasmine after flowering is over, when it will often need to be cut back quite hard to keep it within its allotted space. It does not grow well in cold exposed sites.

Lapageria rosea
Chilean bellflower

Height and spread: 5m/16ft

A twining climber that will need support and protection in cold winters and will only flourish with the aid of a warm shady wall, as it comes from the forests of Chile and does not like full sun. It also needs acid soil. However if you can provide suitable

Jasminum officinale

conditions it is a most attractive plant, evergreen with long dark green leaves, and long flowers, pink or rose-pink in color, and shaped a bit like narrow trumpets. These first appear in midsummer and last until the fall.

Pyracantha 'Orange Glow'
Firethorn

Height and spread: 3m/10ft

These are tough evergreen shrubs that can easily be trained against a wall and will grow in any situation from full sun to full shade. The less sun the plants get the fewer flowers and fruit they will bear. When grown against a wall they should be cut back hard in spring and trained to wires and then again in summer to remove shoots growing outward and reveal the clusters of berries. They have white flowers in spring followed by orange, red, or yellow berries that last through the winter.

Solanum crispum 'Glasnevin'
Chilean potato vine

Height and spread: 6m/20ft

There are two members of the potato family that are popular climbers, *S. crispum* and *S. jasminoides*. Both are evergreen or semievergreen, and both are only partly hardy. The variety 'Glasnevin' is the one most popularly grown in temperate climates and has proved it can survive quite severe winters, given the protection of a warm wall. They are all scrambling climbers and the young shoots generally need to be tied in to a trellis or some other support. 'Glasnevin' has lovely purple-blue flowers that last from summer into the fall.

Perennials

Container gardeners concentrate more on annuals and climbers than they do on perennials. Nevertheless there are a number that should be considered as permanent features in the garden.

Agapanthus Headbourne hybrids
African blue lily

Height 90cm/3ft

Spread 45cm/18in

In spite of their common name agapanthus are herbaceous perennials that are popular plants for containers where they flourish. They are grown largely for their dramatic clusters of flowers that emerge in late summer and resemble huge balls of bluebells held aloft on a large thick stalk. They like a sunny position and have thick roots that store water in dry periods. *Agapanthus* are not fully hardy and may need some protection in hard winters, but the Headbourne Hybrids, and a number of the named varieties, such as 'Blue Giant' and 'Alice Gloucester' are generally hardier than the species.

Pyracantha 'Orange Glow'

Aponogeton distachyos
Cape pondweed, water hawthorn

Spread 1.2m/4ft

A rhizomatous perennial, the water hawthorn comes from South Africa, and has large deep green oval leaves that float on the surface of the water, like those of a water lily. The plants carry small white hawthorn-scented flowers in spring, and again in the fall, that are held aloft on forked flowering branches about 5cm/2in above the water. It prefers full sun but will tolerate partial shade. The water hawthorn is a good plant to grow to restrict the spread of algae in a pond or water garden.

Aquilegia vulgaris
Granny's bonnets, columbine

Height 90cm/3ft
Spread 45cm/18in

A favorite cottage garden perennial that flowers in late spring and early summer and is suitable for growing in any container, either on its own, or in company with other flowers. Granny's bonnets have dark

blue-violet flowers, and a number of the varieties have flowers varying from white, through pale shades of blue, to pink and yellow. They are the most attractive flowers, rising on long stalks above pools of green leaves. They self-seed freely and when they are grown in a confined space need to be controlled ruthlessly.

Aster novi-belgii
Michaelmas daisies

Height 90–120cm/3–4ft
Spread 60–90cm/2–3ft

Michaelmas daisies are one of the most colorful plants to be found in the container garden, and they flower in the late summer and early fall. They are usually found in varying shades of pink, violet, purple, and white and most of them have the typical yellow center of the daisy family. Among the most attractive are 'Marie Ballard', pale blue; 'Jenny' and 'Royal Ruby', deep pink; 'Lassie', pale pink; and 'Kristina', white. They like well-drained soil and will flourish in partial shade. They require staking when grown in containers.

Dicentra formosa
Bleeding heart

Height 45cm/18in
Spread 60cm/2ft

D. spectabilis, bleeding heart or Dutchman's trousers, is a favorite spring border perennial. However it is probably too large for the average container garden and a better choice for a confined space is D. formosa, that spreads quite freely and has charming small purple flowers held up rather like branches of purple heather above silvery gray leaves. The variety 'Stuart Boothman' is very similar, slightly larger, and f. *alba* has white flowers and is less vigorous. They all flower in late spring and early summer and prefer some shade and neutral soil. Propagate by division.

Euphorbia amygdaloides
Wood spurge, milkweed

Height 75cm/30in
Spread 30cm/12in

There are over 2,000 species of euphorbia and they range in size from trees to tiny succulents. Probably the best-known garden euphorbia is E. *characias* ssp. *wulfenii*, which is a huge spectacular border plant. This, however, is not suitable for the average container garden. The wood spurge, E. *amygdaloides*, is much more suited as it is a small ground-covering plant that flourishes in shade. It has dark green leaves and green-yellow flowers that are held aloft on stalks. The variety 'Purpurea' has reddish-purple leaves and yellow flowers, and var. *robbiae*, 'Mrs Robb's bonnet', has much broader leaves. This variety may become invasive, so keep an eye on it.

Solanum crispum 'Glasnevin'

Aster novi-belgii

Geranium farreri

Geranium farreri
Cranesbill, hardy geranium

Height 10–15cm/4–6in

Spread 15cm/6in

Few garden plants provide as much pleasure to the gardener as the cranesbills. They flower throughout the summer and range in size from the spectacular *G. psilostemon*, to the tiny *G. farreri*, beloved by alpine gardeners. This small plant has flowers in an enchanting pale pink with conspicuous black anthers. Other favored cranesbills that are suitable for a container garden include *G. wallichianum* 'Buxton's Variety', sky-blue with white veins and

dark anthers in the center, and *G. clarkei* 'Kashmir White', which is white with deeper pink veins.

Helianthus × *multiflorus*
'Loddon Gold'
Perennial sunflower

Height 1.5m/5ft

Spread 90cm/3ft

Most sunflowers are grown as annuals and afford great amusement on the principle that "I can grow a bigger one than you can." The perennial sunflower, too, is quite a large plant but it can make a dynamic impact in a container garden if you have

room to accommodate it. It has great bushy flowerheads of bright yellow and does not really require staking. There are a number of other varieties including, 'Capenoch Star', single yellow flowerheads, and 'Soleil d'Or', double yellow flowerheads. They need to grow in full sun.

Helleborus orientalis
Hellebore, Lenten rose

Height 45cm/18in

Spread 45cm/18in

Lenten roses flower early in the year shortly after the Christmas rose, *H. niger*. The flowers are saucer-shaped and hang down from their stems. There are a number of colors and shades of mauve, pink, white, and red are common. The flowers are attractively marked on the inside and remain on the plant for several weeks, at a time of the year when there is little else in flower. In mild climates the leaves are evergreen. There are many named varieties: Millet hybrids are popular. They need some shade and prefer to be sheltered from rain and wind if possible.

Helleborus orientalis

Hosta 'Blue Moon'
Plantain lily

Height 10cm/4in

Spread 30cm/12in

Hostas grow better in containers than they do in borders where, in damp conditions, slugs devour them with an unbelievable relish. Slugs are not so prone to climb the sides of containers and the area is easier to control. Hostas are grown chiefly for their wonderful foliage, blue-gray, green, yellow-green, and variegated white that, when grown together, can make such an impact in a shady garden where they flourish best. 'Blue Moon' is a small hosta with blue-gray foliage, 'Aureomarginata' has white-edged green leaves, and 'Gold Standard' has yellow leaves, edged with green.

Lobelia cardinalis
Cardinal flower

Height 90cm/3ft

Spread 30cm/1ft

The cardinal flower is a short-lived rhizomatous perennial with dark red stems and bright green, bronze-tinted leaves. It is grown for its brilliant scarlet flowers that emerge in late summer and early fall. Few garden plants have such vivid coloring. The flowers can form the basis for a hot color scheme in late summer. Cardinal flowers prefer deep, moist soil in full sun although they will tolerate partial shade. *L. erinus* varieties are low-growing trailing perennials usually grown as annuals.

Lupinus Gallery Hybrids
Lupins

Height 50cm/20in

Spread 20cm/8in

Many lupins, including the popular Russell Hybrids, are rather large for the average container garden, reaching 1.2m/4ft, but if you are seeking to create a cottage garden effect in a small space, then the smaller Gallery Hybrids, developed as a dwarf strain, are well worth considering. The colors are rather paler than the Russell Hybrids but there is a good choice of the traditional pale pink, yellow, blue, red, purple, and lavender available. The flowers are more compact than in the larger varieties. Like with all lupins they prefer a sunny position. Lulu Series and Dwarf Russell Mixed are two more small series.

Nymphaea 'Gonnère'
Waterlily

Spread 90–120cm/3–4ft

Waterlilies have to be chosen with care, and the ones that you can grow depend entirely on the depth of water and the size of your pool. 'Gonnère' is one of the most beautiful white waterlilies, with many-petaled flowers, fragrant, with a clear yellow center. It needs a pool about 90cm/3ft deep to flourish and its spread is less than many of the larger lilies. All waterlilies grow best in full sun and they will not grow in running water, although some will tolerate very gentle movement.

Penstemon 'Andenken an Friedrich Hahn'
Penstemon

Height 75cm/30in

Spread 60cm/24in

Penstemons are rather underrated as garden perennials, which is a pity. They make outstanding plants, evergreen or semievergreen, with long tubes of flowers from midsummer through into the fall. They are easy to raise from cuttings taken in summer, or division in spring. They make excellent plants in a container garden if you do not want to include too many annuals. There are many excellent named varieties; three of the best known are: 'Andenken an Friedrich Hahn', deep red; 'Apple Blossom', a charming pink; and 'Maurice Gibbs', red with white centers.

Lobelia cardinalis

Lupinus

Phlox paniculata
Perennial phlox

Height 1.2m/4ft

Spread 60–90cm/2–3ft

Another glorious summer-flowering perennial that lasts in flower for weeks from the middle of summer into the fall. There are many varieties in varying shades of pink, red, purple, lilac, blue, and white. The glory of phloxes is their mop-headed flowers that look a bit like a colorful cloche hat on the top of the flower stalk. Among the most popular varieties are: 'Amethyst', violet; 'Eva Cullum', deep pink; 'Fujiyama', white; 'Le Mahdi', blue-purple; 'Mother of Pearl', white tinged with pink; and 'Prince of Orange', orange-red.

Primula vulgaris
Primrose

Height 20cm/8in

Spread 30cm/12in

Primulas are a large genus with over 400 species and thousands of varieties. In spite of this the common primrose, *P. vulgaris*, has remained the firm favorite for many gardeners. The flowers are a delicate pale yellow, with a darker yellow center. They are fragrant, and they have a charming modesty, as if apologizing for rising above their green leaves. They are also extremely easy to grow and propagate through division when flowering is over. They prefer growing in some shade and will not flourish in hot, dry conditions.

Pulmonaria saccharata
Lungwort

Height 30cm/12in

Spread 60cm/24in

Pulmonarias are one of the loveliest sights in spring when the flowers emerge on stalks held above the blotched and spotted leaves that give the flower its common name. They are good plants to grow in a container, for they spread freely in open ground and if the container is raised the flowers can be inspected at eye level. Generally the flowers are blue or pink with some white varieties, and a number open pink and turn blue after some days. Blue and pink flowers are often present on the same flower stalk. There are a number of named varieties; Argentea Group has silvery leaves with red flowers turning violet, and 'Mrs Moon' has pink buds, opening to lilac-blue flowers.

Scabiosa caucasica 'Clive Greaves'
Scabious, pincushion flower

Height 60cm/2ft

Spread 60cm/2ft

Wild small scabious, *S. columbaria*, is a common and lovely wildflower, but the genus is quite large and there are over 80 species. The cultivated varieties retain much of the charm of the parent and many have the lovely blue and lilac coloring, although various shades are available ranging from purple to white. Scabious is a flower of the late summer when many others are over and should be planted to continue the flowering interest in the garden. 'Clive Greaves' has lavender-blue flowers, 'Perfecta Alba' has white, as does 'Mrs Willmott'.

Stachys byzantina
Lambs' ears

Height 45cm/18in

Spread 60cm/24in

Certainly one of the best-known gray foliage plants in the garden, Lambs' ears can be grown anywhere as a foil for the green foliage of so many garden plants. It makes a dense mat of silvery white, wooly, felted leaves topped in summer by purple lavender flowers held aloft on spikes. They prefer full sun and will tolerate most soils provided they are well drained. There are a number of varieties: 'Big Ears' has green

Phlox paniculata

Primula vulgaris

leaves with a gray bloom, and 'Silver Carpet' has silver leaves. This variety is grown as groundcover, for it does flower.

Annuals and bedding plants

These are the mainstay of the container gardener and different displays and color schemes can be contrived from year to year, Some of the plants are perennials but they are normally grown as bedding plants.

Ageratum houstonianum
Floss flower

Height 15–30cm/6–12in

Spread 15–30cm/6–12in

Low-growing, half-hardy annuals that are native to Mexico. Blue, pink, or white varieties can all be found although the most common color is blue. The mounds of small flowers are held just above the foliage. There are a number of named varieties: those most commonly grown are the Hawaii Series; the dwarf 'Swing Pink', pink-red; 'Blue Danube', a soft powder blue. Sow seed in spring at 16°C/60°F.

Pulmonaria saccharata

Amaranthus caudatus
Love-lies-bleeding, tassel flower

Height 75cm/30in

Spread 45cm/18in

A hardy annual that has extraordinary crimson tassels that droop down. On some varieties the flower tassels are upright. It is rather larger than many annuals. Varieties of *A. tricolor* are bushy with vividly colored leaves. Sow seeds in spring at 20°C/68°F.

Antirrhinum majus
Snapdragons

Height 30–45cm/12–18in

Spread 30cm/12in

These are half-hardy perennials that are normally grown as half-hardy annuals. They are a favorite flower of children who love popping the flowerheads open, hence the common name. The flowers come in all shades of brilliant colors: red, yellow, orange, and white. There are a number of series: Rocket Series is the tallest, Sonnet Series flowers early and is intermediate in size, and both Tahiti Series and 'Floral Showers' are dwarfing.

Aubrieta × cultorum
Aubrieta

Height 5cm/2in

Spread 60cm/2ft

Aubrieta is a hardy perennial that can be propagated by seed sown indoors in early spring or outdoors in early summer. It forms trailing mats of blue flowers and is grown in cracks of walls. It needs to be clipped back after flowering. The flowers are nearly always purple-blue in color, 'Hartswood Purple' and 'Joy' are popular.

Begonia
Begonias

Height 25cm/10in

Spread 30cm/12in

There are many different types of begonias but the ones usually grown in the summer garden are varieties of *B. tuberosa*, the tuberous begonias that have colorful large flowers, or *B. semperflorens*, which carry a mass of small flowers often with bronze foliage. Both should be treated as half-hardy annuals. There are an enormous variety of flower shapes and colors. Cocktail Series is a good *semperflorens* variety, the tuberous 'Can-Can' has huge yellow flowers with red-picotee margins.

Bellis perennis
Daisy

Height 15–20cm/6–8in

Spread 15cm/6in

Ornamental daisies are another hardy perennial usually treated as an annual. The flowers are held aloft on large pompoms and are red, pink, or white in color. They can be overwintered but most gardeners

Antirrhinum majus

replant them each year. Sow seed indoors at 10°C/50°F in early spring. The best known are the Pomponette, Roggli, and Tasso Series, although there are many others that are available.

Brachyscome iberidifolia
Swan River daisy

Height 30cm/12in

Spread 30cm/12in

Popular small annuals that form clumps of flowers that appear as massed daisies, the colors are usually white, lilac-pink, or purple. The Splendour Series is the one most commonly grown. Dwarf Bravo Mixed is a bit smaller and Summer Skies has flowers in attractively varied shades of blue, pink, and white.

Calceolaria Herbeohybrida Group
Slipper flower, pouch flower, slipperwort

Height 25cm/10in

Spread 15cm/6in

These are half-hardy biennials normally grown as summer-flowering container

Calceolaria integrefolia

plants. They look like large bunches of small lozenges and are often a striking yellow or orange in color. Sometimes the yellow varieties also have attractive orange drops in the center. 'Bright Bikinis' has yellow, orange, and red flowers, Anytime Series is compact and comes into flower very quickly. Sow seeds at 18°C/64°F in late summer or early spring.

Calendula officinalis
English marigold, pot marigold

Height 30–45cm/12–18in

Spread 30cm/12in

Extremely popular annuals that have been cultivated for many centuries. They are yellow and orange in color and look rather like miniature chrysanthemums. They are hardy annuals so seed can be sown outside in spring or fall where they are to flower. The Pacific Beauty Series is the most popular. *C. officinalis*, the traditional pot marigold, has single flowers.

Callistephus chinensis
China aster

Height 20–45cm/8–18in

Spread 20–45cm/8–18in

Half-hardy annuals that quickly make good bushy plants with flowers that are like miniature chrysanthemums in a multitude of colors: pink, yellow, red, mauve, and white. Some of the more open varieties resemble Michaelmas daisies. There are many series. Among the best known are Ostrich Plume, Comet, Milady Mixed, and Thousand Wonder. Sow seed at 15°C/60°F in early spring or outside later where the plants are to flower.

Campanula carpatica
Bellflower

Height 30cm/12in

Spread 30–60cm/12–24in

There are many bellflowers, aptly named for their glorious bell-like flowers usually found in various shades of blue, purple, and white. *Carpatica* are clump-forming, hardy perennials that make excellent edging plants for beds or pathways. They are extremely vigorous and may need to be controlled. The most popular varieties are 'Jewel', deep purple; 'Blue Clips', blue; and 'Bressingham White'. In the spring, sow seed *in situ* or divide established plants.

Catananche caerulea
Cupid's dart, blue cupidone

Height 75cm/30in

Spread 30cm/12in

An attractive clump-forming, short-lived perennial with gray-green grass-like leaves in summer, that produces large numbers of single flowers on upright stalks, dark to pale blue, throughout the summer. It is sometimes grown as an annual. There are a

Calendula officinalis

number of named varieties. 'Bicolor' has white petals with a purple center, 'Major' has lilac flowers with a dark center, and 'Perry's White' has white flowers with a creamy center. The varieties need to be raised by division or root cuttings for they will not come true from seed.

Celosia argentea
Cockscomb

Height 20–50cm/8–20in

Spread 15–45cm/6–18in

There are two types of celosia: the Plumosa Group has open, feathery, pyramidal flowerheads, while the Cristata Group has crested, tightly clustered flowerheads. The Plumosa Group are those used in summer bedding schemes in many parks and gardens. They appear in very bright colors of yellow, pink, orange, and red and simply cannot be missed. Varieties from the Century Series are the most commonly grown, the Kimono Series is smaller and more suited to a container garden scheme. Sow seed at 18°C/64°F from early spring onward.

Chrysanthemum parthenium 'Aureum'

Campanula carpatica 'Blue Gem'

Centaurea cyanus
Cornflower, batchelor's buttons

Height 25–90cm/9–36in

Spread 15–25cm/6–10in

Cornflowers are hardy annuals available in blue, claret, red, or pink. However, the traditional color of the cornflower is deep blue and many gardeners prefer to grow this color and no other. There are a number of series, including the Boy Series, which includes the bright blue 'Blue Boy', but individual varieties are available, such as 'Jubilee Gem', 'Pinkie', and 'Florence Blue'. Sow seed *in situ* in spring or in the fall the previous year.

Chrysanthemum parthenium syn. Tanacetum parthenium
Feverfew

Height 45–60cm/18–24in

Spread 30cm/12in

This short-lived perennial is another plant that has had its name changed and you may also find it listed under *Tanacetum parthenium*. The border varieties have yellow or white flowers and some have yellow leaves. The best are the double forms, such as 'Plenum' and 'Snowball', both white. Sow seed in late winter or early spring at 10°C/50°F; take softwood cuttings in spring.

Cineraria maritima
syn. *Senecio cineraria*

Height 20–30cm/8–12in

Spread 23–30cm/9–12in

The 'correct' name for this plant is now *Senecio cineraria* but you are far more likely to find it listed under its old name. It is the classic foliage bedding plant with silvery-white leaves that make an excellent foil to all colorful annuals. The best-known varieties are 'Silver Dust' and 'Cirrus'. Sow seed in spring at 20°C/68°F. If you can overwinter them you can take semiripe cuttings at the end of the summer.

Clarkia amoena
Satin flower

Height 75cm/30in

Spread 30cm/12in

Most attractive annuals with fluted flowers, sometimes with a marked center. They can also be found listed as *Godetia amoena* and *G. grandiflora*. The flowers are usually pink, white, or a deep lavender. The Satin Series is smaller. *C. unguiculata*, also sold as *C. elegans*, is larger with erect spikes of flowers,

Consolida ajacis

which in the Royal Bouquet Series look like small hollyhocks. Sow seed *in situ* in early spring, do not transplant. They make good dried flowers.

Consolida ajacis
Larkspur

Height 30–50cm/12–20in

Spread 15–25cm/6–10in

Attractive annuals grown for their erect spikes of flowers usually in soothing pastel colors of white, pale blue, and pink, although some are deep violet. The smaller varieties are the ones most usually grown; Dwarf Hyacinth Series and Dwarf Rocket Series are both popular. They are strong plants and withstand wind well. The Giant Imperial Series is much larger, reaching 90cm/3ft, and should be planted at the back of a container or border. Hardy annual seed should be sown outside *in situ* in spring or the previous fall. The plants are poisonous to humans.

Convolvulus tricolor
Bindweed

Height 30–40cm/12–16in

Spread 23–30cm/9–12in

Common bindweed is one of the most pernicious garden weeds but its cultivated relations are charming plants and range from shrubs to annuals. *C. tricolor* is grown as a hardy annual. The series Flagship Mixed appears in a variety of colours: red, deep blue, light blue, white, and pink. The trumpet-shaped flowers have strongly marked white and yellow centers. *C. sabatius* is a lovely blue hardy perennial normally grown in rock or scree gardens.

It may need some protection in hard winters. Sow seed *in situ* in mid-spring. Take cuttings of perennials.

Coreopsis tinctoria
Tickseed

Height 30cm/12in

Spread 15cm/6in

The smaller tickseeds are varieties of *C. tinctoria*. The ones most usually grown are Dwarf Mixed or the variety 'Mahogany Midget'. The latter has bronze-red flowers with a yellow center that are carried in profusion from midsummer until the autumn. *C. grandiflora* and its varieties are hardy perennials, sometimes grown as annuals, and usually have yellow flowers. 'Early Sunrise' and 'Tiger Flower' are two good varieties. Sow seed *in situ* in spring.

Dianthus chinensis
China pink, Indian pink

Height 15–25cm/6–10in

Spread 10–15cm/4–6in

Dianthus is a large genus with many different types of pinks and carnations that

Eschscholzia californica

are grown both indoors and out. The common border pinks are those grown as half-hardy annuals where the seed is sown in spring at 16°C/60°F and the plants flower in late summer of that year. A number of series have been cultivated, and there are a number of named varieties. The Baby Doll and Carpet Series both have single flowers that range from red to white, but are mainly pink. The striking 'Raspberry Tart' has pink flowers with deep red centers. 'Dad's Favorite' has white flowers with a red margin and purple center.

Erigeron karvinskianus
Midsummer daisy, Mexican daisy, fleabane

Height 15–30cm/6–12in

Spread to 90cm/3ft

This is an excellent plant to grow hanging down a wall, in a hanging basket or balcony container. Small daisy-like flowers emerge white in midsummer and then gradually turn through pink to red. If grown in a basket or window box it should be treated as a hardy annual; if grown down

Fuchsia 'Tennessee Waltz'

a wall it can be treated as a hardy perennial although it is very vigorous and may well need controlling. 'Profusion' is the variety most often grown. Sow seed in a cold frame in spring.

Eschscholzia californica
California poppy

Height 15–30cm/4–12in

Spread 15cm/6in

California poppies are one of the easiest of all plants to grow for the seed will take root anywhere, even in a gravel border. The plants self-seed vigorously and need to be controlled. They have single erect flowers on stalks in attractive colors, mainly yellow and orange, but some varieties are red, pink, and white. The most spectacular is the Thai Silk Series that has semidouble flowers in a variety of colors. Sow seed *in situ* in spring.

Fuchsia
Fuchsia

Height (small varieties): 45–60cm/18–24in

Spread 30–60cm/12–24in

Fuchsias are mainly half-hardy shrubs, although there are some hardy varieties that will survive temperatures down to -5°C/23°F. They have pendent flowers, mostly in attractive pastel shades of pink, and many are bicolored. They make excellent shrubs for hanging baskets and containers and can be brought indoors over winter where circumstances permit. Good varieties include: 'Margaret Brown', two-toned pink flowers; 'La Campanella', white and purple; and 'Swingtime', white double flowers with red outer petals.

Gazania

Height 20cm/8in

Spread 25cm/10in

Half-hardy perennials that are grown as half-hardy annuals. They are members of the daisy family and the flowers are daisy-like with rather broader petals. There are a number of series normally grown. The Chansonette Series has flowers in a mixture of colors: yellow, pink, red, and orange. The Mini-star Series is smaller and has a wider range of colors. Sow seed in early spring at 18–20°C/64–68°F.

Heliotropium arborescens
Heliotrope, cherry pie

Height 30–45cm/12–18in

Spread 30–35cm/12–14in

Many varieties of *H. arborescens* make good sized shrubs, but the smaller varieties are usually grown as half-hardy annuals. 'Marine' is the most popular variety and has the characteristic smell of cherries that gives the plant its common name. 'Mini Marine' is a bit smaller and more compact. The flowers are violet blue and they make

Gazania

Lavatera trimestris 'Silver Cup'

a wide variety of colors: pink, cerise, red, white, some bicolored, held above light green and bronze leaves, some of which can be variegated. They prefer to grow in partial shade and will even provide color in complete shade, making them invaluable for gardeners with shady gardens. Many other series are available. Sow seed in spring at 16°C/60°F. You can take cuttings in summer to overwinter indoors.

Lavatera trimestris
Annual mallow

Height 60–90cm/2–3ft

Spread 30–45cm/12–18in

These are extremely attractive annuals, although some are a bit larger than most. They have that lovely mallow-shaped flower which is like a shallow trumpet. 'Pink Beauty' is white with pink veins on the petals and a darker center; 'Silver Cup' is a deeper pink; 'Mont Blanc' is almost pure white; 'Ruby Regis' has deep reddish-pink flowers. Sow seed out of doors where the plants are to flower from mid-spring onward.

excellent plants for containers in the summer. Seed can be sown in spring at 16°C/60°F but named varieties are best propagated by tip cuttings taken in summer, for they may not come true from seed.

Iberis umbellata
Globe candytuft

Height 15–30cm/6–12in

Spread 20cm/8in

Another extremely popular hardy annual that should be sown out of doors where it is to flower in fall or early spring. The two most popular series are Fairy Series, clusters of pale pink, lavender, and white flowers,

and Flash Series, stronger colors of pink, purple, or red. The flowers are made up of many small petals shaped like a shallow dome and completely cover the plant, giving rise to its common name, which is very descriptive.

Impatiens New Guinea Group
Busy Lizzie, balsam

Height 35cm/14in

Spread 30cm/12in

Almost the most popular summer bedding plant, busy lizzies are half-hardy perennials although they are almost always grown as annuals. The New Guinea Group come in

Impatiens New Guinea Group

Limnanthes douglasii
Poached-egg plant

Height 15cm/6in

Spread 15cm/6in

An aptly named, low-growing annual, that has saucer-shaped flowers, white on the margin with deep yellow centers. It also has lovely bright green leaves. The flowers are attractive to bees and flower throughout the summer. It is easy to grow and seed should be sown *in situ* in spring or fall for earlier flowering the next year. Fall sowings need to be protected from frosts during the winter.

Linum grandiflorum
Flowering flax

Height 45–60cm/18–24in

Spread 15cm/6in

Flax flowers are supposed to be blue, and most perennial flaxes are, but the species plant of the annual flowering flax has rose-pink flowers. Of the named varieties 'Bright Eyes' is white, 'Caeruleum', blue, 'Magic Circles', red and white, and 'Rubrum', red. They are among the easiest

of all hardy annuals to cultivate. Sow seed *in situ* outdoors in spring. Annual flax is best grown in blocks of color so that it achieves its maximum effect.

Lobelia erinus
Trailing lobelia

Height 10–15cm/4–6in

Spread 15cm/6in

These are low-growing bushy perennials that are grown as annuals. They are the mainstay of hanging baskets throughout the world where the small flowers, generally blue with pale marked centers, hang down the sides. If grown in a rock garden they will fall over rocks and they look their best grown in a blue and white border with silver *Cineraria* (*Senecio*) and the white variety 'White Cascade'. The Cascade Series has pink, red, blue, and white flowers, Palace Series is mainly blue or white. There are border-edging and taller kinds available.

Matthiola incana
Sweet-scented stock

Height 20–45cm/8–18in

Spread 25–30cm/10–12in

Stocks are upright perennials or sub-shrubs but they are usually grown as half-hardy annuals. They are sometimes called "ten-week stocks" for they achieve maturity quite quickly. They have upright spikes of flowers, usually white, red, pink, and purple, and are very sweet-smelling. The Virginia stock, *Malcolmia maritima*, belongs to another genus. There are a number of series available. Brompton Series is grown as a biennial, Ten-Week Mixed has mostly double flowers and Sentinel Series is taller.

Mesembryanthemum criniflorum
Livingstone daisy

Height 8cm/3in

Spread 15cm/6in

Livingstone daisies are a popular half-hardy annual and flourish in dry conditions, but need sun to be at their best. The massed, typical daisy-like flowerheads are pink, white, cerise, and yellow, with paler shades in between. They make good groundcover. Sow indoors in early spring at 16°C/60°F.

Mimulus × hybridus
Monkey flower

Height 12–30cm/5–12in

Spread 30cm/12in

Tender perennials that are usually grown as annuals. There are a number of series: Calypso, Magic, and Mystic are the ones usually grown. They have open trumpet-shaped flowers usually yellow or orange but creamy white, red, and pink flowers are also found. They are often spotted in the center. They prefer slightly damp soil. Sow seed indoors in spring at a temperature of 7°C/45°F or over.

Lobelia erinus

Matthiola incana

Nemesia strumosa
Nemesia
Height 20–30cm/8–12in

Spread 10–15cm/4–6in

Popular half-hardy annuals for the rock and scree garden, nemesias have charming, rather informal flowers that open into two halves and are often bicolored. 'KLM' is blue and white, 'National Ensign' and 'Danish Flag' are both red and white. 'Blue Gem' is sapphire blue with white eyes and plants from the Carnival Series are smaller. Sow seed in spring at 15°C/59°F, or sow in the fall for early flowering the following year. Water the plants well when they come into flower and protect them from frost if they are to be overwintered.

Nicotiana × sanderae
Tobacco plant
Height 30–60cm/12–24in

Spread 20–45cm/8–18in

These are rather smaller than the traditional tobacco plant and the flowers are open during the day, not just in the evening. However they are not so fragrant.

'Lime Green' is a popular variety with green flowers. There are a number of series available, notably Domino and Havana, while Merlin was bred for containers. They should be grown as half-hardy annuals. Sow seed in spring at 18°C/64°F.

Petunia
Height 20–30cm/8–12in

Spread 30–90cm/12–36in.

Undoubtedly the most popular and widely grown of all summer bedding plants, petunias are half-hardy perennials that are almost always grown as annuals. They are divided into two groups: the Grandiflora varieties with large single flowers, and the Multiflora varieties that are bushier and produce a greater quantity of smaller flowers. The range of colors available is immense: single colors, double colors, and many have variegated center markings, either darker or in a second color. The Supercascade Series is extremely popular for planting in hanging baskets, Carpet Series is an excellent bedding plant and the Picotee Series has white ruffled margins.

Sow seed outdoors in spring and deadhead flowering plants regularly through the summer to keep them flowering.

Pelargonium
Geranium
Height 12–60cm/5–24in

Spread 20–30cm/8–12in

A large genus of plants with six divisions. Those most commonly grown in borders are the Zonal geraniums and they have seven further subdivisions, depending on the flower shape. Trailing geraniums are excellent for window boxes on balconies, and also work well in hanging basket schemes. The flowers range from brilliant red, through all the varying shades of pink and purple, to white. Plants from the Horizon Series are compact and bushy—and good for containers—while those from the Orbit Series flower early. There are large numbers of named varieties. Geraniums can be raised from seed sown in spring at 16°C/60°F, but they are best propagated from softwood cuttings. These can be taken throughout the year.

Nicotiana x sanderae

Petunia

Sidalcea malviflora

Phlox drummondii
Annual phlox

Height 10–45cm/4–18in

Spread 20cm/8in

A pretty half-hardy annual that is grown for its attractive clusters of flowers that are slightly reminiscent of a small hydrangea. The flowers are generally white, purple, lavender, pink, and red and the shades are very similar to many petunias. There are several series and they vary in size. Among the most popular are Twinkle Star Mixed with star-shaped petals. Fantasy Series is scented with clear colors and Palona Series is dwarf with bushy plants. Sow seed at 16°C/60°F early in spring, sow outdoors early in summer.

Salvia splendens
Scarlet sage

Height 30–40cm/12–16in

Spread 15–20cm/6–8in

Salvias are a large and varied genus but those grown as annual bedding plants have been developed from *S. splendens* that has such vivid red upright flowers in summer.

Tropaeolum majus

They are among the most popular bedding plants for the summer garden, and work well in a container. Several series have been developed. These include Sizzler, which can be found in eight colours, including salmon, deep pink, pale yellow, lavender, red, and purple, and the dwarf 'Firecracker'. There are also many named varieties. Sow seed at 16°C/60°F in mid-spring.

Schizanthus pinnatus
Butterfly flower, poor man's orchid

Height 20–50cm/8–20in

Spread 20–30cm/8–12in

These are popular house plants when grown in a cool greenhouse but they can also be grown outside as hardy annuals, provided you have a warm sheltered border, and they can also be sown under glass over winter. They have attractive open tubular flowers held in clusters, which are generally white, yellow, pink, red, and purple, and they have prominent yellow, or yellow-red central markings. 'Hit Parade' and 'Star Parade' are the ones most commonly grown. Sow seed at 16°C/60°F in spring or in late summer for plants to flower indoors during the winter.

Sidalcea malviflora
False mallow, prairie mallow

Height 30–90cm/12in–3ft

Spread 10–45cm/4–18in

Sidalceas are perennials that, in the wild, flourish in the grasslands, woodland glades, and by the rivers and streams of the north and west. They grow in almost any soil except when it is waterlogged, and they

prefer full sun. The best small varieties for a container garden are probably the compact 'Loveliness' with pale pink flowers, 'Puck', which has deeper pink flowers in mid-summer, or some of the special bedding mixtures available. As might be imagined from their common name the flowers are open and saucer-shaped, and held upright on stalks above a rosette of basal leaves.

Tropaeolum majus
Nasturtium, Indian cress

Height 30cm/12in

Spread 45cm/18in

Popular climbing plants that are easy to grow in almost any soil and can be sown out of doors from late spring onward. They do prefer a sunny position. There are a large number of varieties and these can be grown as bushy annuals or as semitrailing plants in hanging baskets. They all have yellow and orange flowers in varying shades. The Whirlybird Series is popular as are the Gleam Mixed hybrids that have double flowers

Verbena × hybrida
Verbena

Height 30cm/12in

Spread 25cm/10in

Shrubby perennials that are grown as annual bedding plants. A number of series have been developed in a wide variety of colors from deep violet to blue, red, pink, peach, and white. The flowers appear in clusters and each flowerhead is a bit like a very small primrose. Often they have a strongly marked center. Some series are erect, others are trailing or spreading in habit, which makes them very suitable for hanging baskets and containers. Good series include Sandy and Romance, both erect in habit. The Romance Series, and the varieties 'Peaches and Cream' and 'Imagination' are all spreading.

Viola × *wittrockiana*
Winter-flowering pansies

Height 20–30cm/8–12in

Spread 20–30cm/8–12in

The development of winter-flowering pansy has transformed gardens in the winter. They can be planted out in the fall and will continue in flower for months on end. They are hardy perennials but should be treated as half-hardy annuals and fresh stock planted each year. Grow them in containers to provide individual bright spots in the garden. A huge number of series have been developed over the years, mostly multicolored, or bicolored, but single-colored varieties are available. The colours run from deep violet and yellow, to purple, blue, and white. Most varieties have the typical "pansy" face with its strong

Chionodoxa luciliae syn. gigantea

central marking. The Fama, Regal, and Ultima Series are all good winter-flowering plants; many other series flower in the summer.

Spring bulbs

Chionodoxa luciliae
Glory of the snow

Height 15cm/6in

Spread 5cm/2in

Chionodoxa are less well known than many of the early spring bulbs but they are extremely attractive and deserve to be more widely grown. They have small, six-petaled, star-shaped flowers, in varying shades of blue, often with a pronounced white center. Once established they self-seed readily. They prefer full sun. There are a number of varieties but the botanical names have become muddled. You will usually find them sold as *C. gigantea*, blue with white center; *C. g.* 'Alba', white; *C. luciliae*, pale blue with white center, *C. l.* 'Pink Cloud', pink, or *C. sardensis*, blue.

Fritillaria meleagris

Crocus chrysanthus
Spring-flowering crocus

Height 5cm/2in

Spread 5cm/2in

Crocuses flower both in the fall and early spring, but it is the ones that flower early in the year that attract the most attention. The best known are varieties of *C. chrysanthus* and *C. tommasinius*. The majority are yellow, orange, purple to pale lilac, and white in color. They are easy to grow given a certain amount of sun and well-drained soil. When the flowers open in spring they are a charming sight on a sunny day with the petals spread wide apart to catch the rays of the sun.

Cyclamen coum
Hardy cyclamen

Height 5cm/2in

Spread 10cm/4in

The hardy cyclamen that flower in spring are varieties of *C. coum*. *C. hederifolium* and its varieties look exactly the same but flower in the fall. Both species have attractive small white, pink, purple, and red flowers held aloft on short stalks, a bit like upside-down small butterflies. They prefer soil that does not dry out but they need protection from excessive moisture and grow best in the shelter of trees or spreading shrubs. Mulch in the winter to protect the leaves from frost.

Narcissus
Daffodils, narcissus

Height 30–60cm/1–2ft

There are thousands of different daffodils available and a glance through the catalog of any reputable bulb supplier gives some idea of the variety. There are 12 divisions. The best ones for the small container garden are varieties of *N. cyclamineus*, Division 6, which, in general gardening terms, would be called small narcissi. 'Little Witch' is pure yellow, 'Jack Snipe', white with yellow center, 'Foundling', white with orange center, and 'Jenny', white with white to pale yellow center. Other good small varieties are those from Division 7, Jonquilla.

Erythronium dens-canis
Dog's tooth violet, trout lily

Height 10–15cm / 4–6in

Spread 10cm / 4in

The dog's tooth violet is another charming spring bulb that flowers slightly later than most spring bulbs. It needs moist, shady conditions and well-drained soil that does not dry out. It is grown for its attractive spotted foliage, which gives it the name of trout lily, as well the flowers that are held aloft on stalks with widely spaced, swept-back petals and long anthers. The best

Narcissus

known are 'Pink Perfection'; 'Lilac Wonder', rich purple; 'Snowflake', white with pink markings. There are a number of other varieties available.

Fritillaria meleagris
Snake's head fritillary

Height 30cm / 12in

Spread 5–7.5cm / 2–3in

The snake's head fritillary is a popular bulb that will happily naturalize in grassland. It is also a good bulb to include in an alpine garden, for here its charms can be appreciated at close quarters. The bulbs need full sun to flourish. *F. meleagris* is

widely available with spotted purple flowers and there is a white form, *F. m. alba*. Other taller and interesting species that can be grown in the alpine garden include; *F. acmopetala*, green bell-shaped flowers flushed pink, and *F. camschatcensis*, black-purple flowers with yellow centers.

Hyacinthus orientalis
Hyacinth

Height 30cm / 12in

Spread 7.5cm / 3in

Hyacinths make excellent container-grown bulbs and are equally welcome planted in

Hyacinthus orientalis 'Pink Pearl'

the fall in prepared bulb fiber to flower indoors in the early months of the year, or grown in a container outside. The flowers are held on long spikes and are extremely fragrant. Plant hyacinths in groups of two or three colors: white, lilac-blue, and pink are the most common and the most effective. White hyacinths include, 'Carnegie' and 'Innocence'. 'Lady Derby' and 'Pink Pearl' are pink, and 'Blue Jacket' and 'Delft Blue' are soft blue. Make sure to stake the plants as they are liable to topple over. Bulb suppliers sell special hyacinth stakes for this purpose.

Iris reticulata and *I. unguicularis*
Early-flowering iris

Height 7.5–15cm and 3–6in/30cm/12in
Spread 2.5–5cm/1–2in and
30–45cm/12–18in

The bulbous irises known as reticulata are the ones that flower early in the year along with the rhizomatous *I. unguicularis* and its varieties, which were formerly called *I. stylosa*. They nearly all have lovely blue, violet, and yellow flowers with attractive

Iris reticulata

markings, although 'Natasha' is virtually white. *I. danfordiae* has yellow flowers, 'Cantab', rich blue with a yellow stripe, 'Harmony', deep velvet blue. *I. unguicularis* is pale blue to violet with a yellow band on the fall; good varieties are 'Mary Barnard', violet, and 'Walter Butt', a paler lavender.

Muscari armeniacum
Grape hyacinth

Height 20cm/8in
Spread 5cm/2in

Grape hyacinths are obliging plants for they flower when many of the early spring bulbs are over and they are easy to grow and undemanding in their needs. The flowers are usually differing shades of blue, although violet-pink and white forms are available. The most popular are varieties of *M. armeniacum*, all of which have bright blue flowers. They do colonize freely and may require controlling when they are grown in a restricted space.

Tulipa
Tulip

Height 15–65cm/5–26in
Spread 5–7.5cm/2–3in

There are so many different tulips of varying colors and sizes that any container gardener has to choose carefully according to the color scheme of the garden and the space available. There are 14 divisions that all flower at slightly different times, so if you want a display all flowering together, it is advisable to choose bulbs from the same division. The colors range from yellow, orange, pink and red, to deep purple, almost black, back to white. There are a

number of striped and double colored varieties. Sturdy mid-season tulips (Triumph, Group 3) include 'Don Quichotte', pink; 'Margot Fonteyn', cardinal red, yellow margins; 'Shirley', white, purple margins; and 'Palestrina', pink.

Summer- and
fall-flowering bulbs

Bulbs are not confined to the spring. There are many lovely bulbs that flower in the summer and fall and a number of these are definitely worth considering for the container garden.

Allium
Ornamental onions

Height 60–150cm/2–5ft
Spread 5–15cm/2–6in

Many ornamental onions flower in late spring and early summer but there are some that flower in late summer and into the fall, and the smaller varieties can add much welcome color to an alpine garden

Tulipa

Trees

FRUIT TREES

Malus domestica
Apple

Height 1.8m/6ft

Spread 1.8m/6ft

These are grown most successfully in containers as cordons or espaliers trained against a wall, and are a popular choice on roof gardens, where they can be used to divide up the space. Grafted on an M9 dwarfing rootstock, they occupy 1.8m/6ft and 3m/10ft of wall space respectively, both 1.8m/6ft high, so make sure this amount of space is available. Columnar trees, single standards, can be grown as freestanding trees in containers and reach 1.8–2.4m/6–8ft. Most apples need a pollinator, so two varieties need to be grown, unless a neighboring garden has apple trees. Check with the nursery before buying as some varieties will not pollinate others. Suggested dessert varieties include: 'Gravenstein', 'Fiesta', 'North Pole', 'Golden

Sentinel', and 'William's Pride'.

Pyrus communis
Pear

Height 1.8m/6ft

Spread 1.8m/6ft

Pears are grown in the same way as apples but they are trickier for the blossom flowers earlier in the year and is thus more liable to damage by late frosts. However, the beauty of the blossom makes this worthwhile. They prefer a south- or southwest-facing wall. In a container garden they should be grafted on a semi-dwarf rootstock. As with apples you need to grow two compatible varieties at the same time for they are not reliably self-fertile. Check with the nursery when buying the trees. Favorite pears include: 'Highland', 'Conference', 'Comice', 'Warren', and 'Harrow Delight'.

Prunus domestica
Plum

Height 1.8.m/6ft

Spread 3.7m/12ft fan-trained

In a container garden plums should be grafted on to Pixy rootstock and trained as a fan. Fan-training is more difficult than training an espalier, and a good pruning manual will provide instructions. Columnar trees are also available. It is best in limited space to grow one of the self-fertile varieties, such as, 'Italian Prune', 'Golden Transparent Gage', 'Cambridge Gage', 'Santa Rosa', or the old favorite 'Victoria'. This last one will grow quite well in a certain amount of shade.

ORNAMENTAL TREES

Acer palmatum var. *dissectum*
Japanese maple

Height 1.8m/6ft

Spread 3m/10ft (after some years)

Japanese maples are ideal container plants. They create an Oriental feel in a small garden. They hug the ground and the long, feathery, deeply divided leaves hang down most attractively. Their chief glory is the wonderful shades of red, yellow, and purple that the leaves turn in the fall. If you cannot find *A. p.* var. *dissectum*, choose one of the slow-growing varieties, such as, *A. p.* Dissectum Atropurpureum Group.

Camellia 'Donation'
Camellia

Height 5m/16ft

Spread 2.5m/8ft

Camellias can either be classified as a small tree or shrub. Eventually, growing in the wild under favorable conditions, they reach considerable proportions. But they are slow-growing and tolerant of pruning, so can be confined satisfactorily in containers for many years. They make ideal formal small trees with their neat pointed

Alstromeria Ligtu hybrids

Colchicum

Galtonia candicans

hang in much the same manner. They prefer to grow in good, fertile moist soil that does not dry out, in full sun. They are not totally hardy and containers of bulbs should be brought indoors in very hard winters. Two species are commonly grown: *G. candicans* and *G. viridiflora*. The flowers of the latter have a greenish tinge and they have a more upright habit.

Lilium
Lily
Height 90–150cm/3–5ft
Spread 25cm/10in

Lilies form a huge genus that has been divided into 9 main divisions and 11 sub-divisions. They make wonderful container plants; a large container filled with one variety can be a most effective focal point. All the large lilies need staking when they are planted. A number of them are exceptionally fragrant. Among the most popular are: *L. regale*, the regal lily, *L. candidum*, Madonna lily, *L.* 'Casa Blanca', white, *L.* 'Citronella', yellow, and *L. martagon*, the turkscap lily, purple.

below the surface in moist rich soil. It prefers partial shade and will not flourish in direct sun. Take offsets from the main bulb after flowering.

Cyclamen hederifolium X
neapolitanum
Baby cyclamen
Height 15cm/6in
Spread 20cm/8in

This is the autumn-flowering form of the hardy cyclamen. It is a tuberous perennial. The flowers appear from a corm before the leaves and are usually varying shades of pink; there are also white forms. They

flourish in dry shade and grow well beneath trees. The leaves, as the Latin name implies, are marked like ivy. The flowers self-seed freely in good conditions and eventually they form large colonies.

Galtonia candicans
Summer hyacinth
Height 90–120cm/3–4ft
Spread 10cm/4in

This is a large summer bulb that has beautiful spires of white flowers that hang down when the flowers finally emerge in late summer. The individual flowers are shaped rather like large snowdrops and

Lilium 'Sunray'

Nerine bowdenii
Nerine

Height 35cm/15in

Spread 7.5cm/3in

Nerines used to be thought of as very tender and were only grown in greenhouses. However they are perfectly hardy in mild areas, as long as you can give them the shelter of a south- or southwest-facing wall. They have lovely pink trumpet-shaped flowers born in clumps in early fall. The flowers last for quite a long time. The form *alba* has white, flushed pale pink flowers. 'Mark Fenwick' has deep pink flowers on dark stalks. They need to be left undisturbed after planting for they grow best when they are pot-bound.

Sparaxis
Harlequin flower

Height 10–25cm/4–10in

Spread 7.5cm/3in

These are cormous perennials that come from South Africa. There are 6 species but they are most commonly sold under the label Mixed Varieties. They are the most

attractive small summer plants, flowering from midsummer onward in varying shades of white through pink to red, each flower having a prominently marked central ring at the base of the petals with a yellow center. A bowl full of them makes a wonderful display. They need full sun and are only suitable for growing in mild districts in temperate climates. They need protection in winter if grown out of doors.

Sprekelia formosissima
Aztec lily, Jacobean lily

Height 15–35cm/6–14in

Spread 15cm/6in

There is only one species of this lily but it is well worth growing as a house plant in temperate climates, although it flourishes out of doors when the temperature does not drop below 7°C/45°F. It has striking scarlet red flowers that give the impression that it is sticking out its tongue. When grown as a pot plant indoors, it needs full light and requires watering and feeding when in growth. It flowers in late spring or early summer. Keep dry when it is dormant.

Tigridia pavonia
Peacock flower, tiger flower

Height 40cm/16in

Spread 10cm/4in

Another unusual summer bulb that comes from Mexico and Guatemala where it grows in dry grassland, sand and occasionally among rocks. In temperate climates they should either be grown as pot plants and brought indoors in the winter, or in mild districts, planted out in a sunny border, lifted in the fall and brought indoors for the winter. They can also be grown permanently as container plants in a cool greenhouse or conservatory. They prefer well-drained, sandy, fertile soil. *T. pavonia* is a bulbous perennial with lance-shaped leaves. They are the most exotic looking plants—the flowers resemble orchids with their three large, white, pink, yellow, and soft red outer petals, tiny inner petals, and contrasting central markings of vivid red and yellow spots. Sow seed at 13–18°C/55–64°F in spring. Separate offsets when dormant, avoiding plants affected by viruses.

Nerine bowdenii

Sparaxis Mixed Varieties

Tigridia pavonia

Anchusa azurea 'Loddon Royalist'

Osteospermum

Phormium 'Pink Panther'

Plant Lists

These lists are a guide to those plants that are suitable for growing in varying parts of a garden or have special requirements. Many of the plants, particularly those where only the genus name is given, e.g. *Rhododendron*, have a number of different species and cultivated varieties (cultivars) available, for instance there are literally thousands of different rhododendrons. Always check in a good encyclopedia or with the garden center how suitable that plant is for growing in containers before you buy a specific plant. You don't want to buy something that grows too big, too quickly.

Plants for sunny places

Most plants flourish in sun or partial shade. The following plants not only need full sun to show their best, but will survive in dry conditions

PERENNIALS
- *Acantholimon glumaceum*
  Prickly thrift
- *Acanthus spinosus*
  Acanthus, Bear's breeches
- *Achillea filipendulina*
  Yarrow
- *Aethionema grandiflorum*
  Stone cress
- *Agapanthus* Headbourne
  Hybrids
  African blue lily
- *Anchusa azurea*
  Alkanet
- *Anthemis tinctoria*
  Ox-eye chamomile
- *Artemesia absinthium*
  Absinth, Wormwood
- *Aster novi-belgii*
  Michaelmas daisy
- *Campanula carpatica*
  Bellflower
- *Carex elata* 'Aurea'
  Bowles' golden sedge
- *Catananche caerulea*
  Cupid's dart
- *Dianthus*
  Pinks

- *Echinops bannaticus*
  Globe thistle
- *Eryngium bourgatii*
  Sea holly
- *Gypsophila paniculata*
  Baby's breath
- × *Halimiocistus wintonensis*
- *Helianthemum*
  Rock rose, Sun rose
- *Helichrysum italicum* ssp.
  serotinum
  Curry plant
- *Hibiscus syriacus*
  Hibiscus
- *Hypericum olympicum*
  St John's wort
- *Iris germanica*
  Iris
- *Liriope muscari*
  Lilyturf
- *Lithodora diffusa*
- *Lychnis chalcedonica*
  Jerusalem Cross,
  Maltese Cross
- *Lysimachia punctata*
  Loosestrife
- *Nepeta racemosa*
  Catmint
- *Oenothera biennis*
  Evening primrose
- *Osteospermum*
  Osteospermum
- *Papaver*
  Poppy
- *Pelargonium*
  Geranium

- *Penstemon*
  Penstemon
- *Perovskia atriplicifolia*
  Russian sage
- *Phlox paniculata*
  Perennial phlox
- *Phormium tenax*
  New Zealand flax
- *Ruta graveolens*
  Common rue
- *Salvia officinalis*
  Common sage
- *Saponaria ocymoides*
  Rock soapwort
- *Senecio (Brachyglottis)*
  Dunedin Hybrids
- *Sisyrinchium striatum*
- *Stachys byzantina*
  Lambs' ears
- *Stipa arundinacea*
  Pheasant's tail grass
- *Thymus vulgaris*
  Common thyme
- *Veronica prostrata*
  Prostrate speedwell
- *Yucca filamentosa*
  Yucca
- *Zauschneria californica*
  California fuchsia

SHRUBS AND TREES
- *Abelia* × *grandiflora*
  Abelia
- *Buxus sempervirens*
  Box
- *Carpenteria californica*
- *Caryopteris* × *clandonensis*

- *Ceratostigma willmottianum*
  Chinese plumbago
- *Cistus* × *cyprius*
  Sun rose, rock rose
- *Convolvulus ceonorum*
  Bindweed, silverbush
- *Cotoneaster horizontalis*
  Cotoneaster
- *Cytisus battandieri*
  Pineapple broom
- *Cytisus kewensis*
  Broom
- *Escallonia*
  Escallonia
- *Eucalyptus gunnii*
  Cider gum
- *Euonymus fortunei*
  Wintercreeper
- *Fremontodendron*
  'California Glory'
  Flannel bush
- *Hebe pinguifolia* 'Pagei'
  Hebe
- *Ilex aquifolium*
  Holly
- *Indigofera heterantha*
- *Lavandula*
  Lavender
- *Myrtus communis*
  Myrtle
- *Olearia* × *haastii*
  Daisy bush
- *Philadelphus* vars.
  Mock orange
- *Phlomis fruticosa*
  Jerusalem sage
- *Potentilla fruticosa*
  Shrubby cinquefoil
- *Rosmarinus officinalis*
  Rosemary
- *Santolina chamaecyparissus*
  Lavender cotton
- *Spiraea japonica*
- *Teucrium fruticans*
  Shrubby germander

CLIMBERS
- *Campsis radicans*
  Trumpet creeper

- *Clematis tangutica*
  Russian virgin's bower
- *Eccremocarpus scaber*
  Chilean glory flower
- *Ipomoea hederacea*
  Morning glory
- *Parthenocissus tricuspidata*
  Boston ivy
- *Passiflora caerulea*
  Blue passionflower
- *Vitis coignetiae*
  Crimson glory vine

Plants for shade

- *Aconitum napellus*
  Aconite, monkshood
- *Adiantum pedatum*
  American maidenhair fern
- *Ajuga reptans*
  Bugle
- *Alchemilla mollis*
  Lady's mantle
- *Begonia rex* hybrids
  King begonia, Painted
  leaf begonia
- *Brunnera macrophylla*
  Siberian bugloss
- *Carex elata* 'Aurea'
  Bowles' golden sedge
- *Dicentra formosa*
  Bleeding heart
- *Digitalis purpurea*
  Foxglove
- *Dodecatheon pulchellum*
  Shooting stars
- *Dryopteris filix-mas*
  Male fern
- *Epimedium grandiflorum*
  Bishop's hat, barrenwort
- *Euphorbia amygdaloides*
  Wood spurge
- *Galium odoratum*
  Sweet woodruff
- *Gentiana asclepiadea*
  Willow gentian
- *Geranium* vars.
  Cranesbill, Hardy
  geranium

- *Helleborus orientalis*
  Christmas rose
- *Hepatica nobilis*
  Hepatica
- *Hosta* vars.
  Plantain lily
- *Houttuynia cordata*
- *Hypericum calycinum*
  Aaron's beard
- *Oxalis acetosella*
  Shamrock, Sorrel
- *Paeonia lactiflora* vars.
  Peony
- *Polypodium vulgare*
  Wall fern
- *Pulmonaria saccharata*
  Bethlehem sage
- *Smilacina racemosa*
  False Solomon's seal
- *Thalictrum aquilegiifolium*
  Meadow rue
- *Tradescantia* vars.
- *Trillium grandiflorum*
  Trinity flower, Wakerobin
- *Trollius europaeus*
  Common European
  Globe flower
- *Viola riviana*
  Purpurea Group
  Dog violet

SHRUBS AND
TREES FOR SHADE
- *Acer palmatum*
  Japanese maple
- *Buxus sempervirens*
  Box
- *Camellia*
  Camellia
- *Choisya ternata*
  Mexican orange blossom
- *Clethra delavayi*
  Summersweet
- *Cotoneaster horizontalis*
  Cotoneaster
- *Elaeagnus* × *ebbingei*
  Elaeagnus

Euonymus fortunei 'Harlequin'

Passiflora caerulea

Choisya ternata 'Sundance'

Kerria japonica

Camellia williamsii 'Debbie'

Erica carnea 'Golden Starlet'

- *Fatsia japonica*
  Japanese aralia
- *Fuchsia*
  Fuchsia
- *Gaultheria mucronata*
- *Kalmia latifolia*
  Calico bush
- *Leucothoe fontanesiana*
  Drooping leucothoe
- *Rhododendron*
  Rhododendron
- *Skimmia japonica*
- *Symphoricarpos × doorenbosii*
  Snowberry

CLIMBERS FOR SHADE
- *Berberidopsis corallina*
  Coral plant
- *Clematis*
  Clematis
- *Forsythia suspensa*
  Weeping forsythia
- *Hedera helix*
  Ivy
- *Hydrangea petiolaris* syn.
  H. anomala ssp. *petiolaris*
  Climbing hydrangea
- *Kerria japonica*
- *Parthenocissus*
  Virginia creeper
- *Pyracantha*
  Firethorn
- *Rosa* (some varieties
  including)
  Rose
  R. alba
  R. 'Gloire de Dijon'
  R. 'Golden Showers'
  R. 'Maigold'
- *Schizophragma hydrangeoides*
  Japanese hydrangea vine
- *Tropaeolum speciosum*
  Scottish flame flower

Unlike most annuals both *Impatiens* (busy lizzies) and *Meconopsis cambrica* (Welsh poppy) will flower in shady conditions.

Evergreens

Plants marked (s) are semievergreen and will lose their leaves in cold winters

TREES AND SHRUBS
- *Abelia × grandiflora* (s)
  Abelia
- *Abies* (small varieties)
  Silver fir
- *Andromeda polifolia*
  Bog rosemary
- *Arbutus unedo* 'Elfin King'
  Strawberry tree
- *Arctostaphylos uva-ursi*
  Bearberry
- *Aucuba japonica*
  Japanese laurel
- *Buxus sempervirens*
  Box
- *Calluna vulgaris*
  Heather
- *Camellia*
  Camellia
- *Chamaecyparis*
  (small varieties)
  Cypress
- *Choisya ternata*
  Mexican orange blossom
- *Cistus*
  Rock rose
- *Cotoneaster*
  Cotoneaster
- *Cryptomeria japonica*
  Japanese cedar
- *Cupressus*
  Cypress
- *Daboecia cantabrica*
  Cantabrian heath,
  Irish heath
- *Daphne odora*
  Daphne
- *Elaeagnus × ebbingei*
  Elaeagnus
- *Embothrium coccineum*
  Chilean fire bush,
  flame flower

- *Erica carnea*
  Winter-flowering heather
- *Escallonia*
  Escallonia
- *Eucalyptus gunnii*
  Cider gum
- *Euonymus fortunei*
  Wintercreeper
- *Fatsia japonica*
  Japanese aralia
- *Grevillea alpina*
- *Hebe*
  Veronica
- *Hypericum*
  St John's wort
- *Ilex*
  Holly
- *Juniperus communis*
  Common juniper
- *Kalmia latifolia*
  Calico bush,
  Mountain laurel
- *Laurus nobilis*
  Bay tree
- *Lavandula*
  Lavender
- *Ligustrum ovalifolium* (s)
  Privet
- *Myrtus communis*
  Myrtle
- *Olearia haastii*
  Daisy bush
- *Picea* (small varieties)
  Spruce
- *Pinus* (small varieties)
  Pine
- *Pittosporum tenuifolium*
  (small varieties)
  Kohuhu
- *Prunus laurocerasus*
  'Otto Luyken'
  Cherry laurel
- *Rhododendron*
  Rhododendron
- *Rosmarinus officinalis*
  Rosemary
- *Santolina chamaecyparissus*
  Lavender cotton

- *Skimmia japonica*
  Skimmia
- *Taxus baccata*
  Yew
- *Vaccinium*
  Blueberry
- *Viburnum tinus*
- *Laurustinus*
- *Vinca major*
  Periwinkle
  V. minor
- *Yucca filamentosa*
  Yucca

**CLIMBERS AND
WALL SHRUBS**
- *Carpentaria californica*
- *Ceanothus*
  California lilac
- *Garrya elliptica*
  Silk-tassel bush
- *Hedera*
  Ivy
- *Pyracantha*
  Firethorn

Scented plants

TREES AND SHRUBS
- *Chimonanthus praecox*
  Wintersweet
- *Clethra arborea*
  Lily of the
  valley tree
- *Cytisus battandieri*
  Pineapple broom
- *Daphne odora*
  Daphne
- *Hamamelis mollis*
  Witch hazel
- *Lonicera fragrantissima*
  Winter honeysuckle
- *Magnolia stellata*
  Star magnolia
- *Osmanthus delavayi*
- *Philadelphus*
  Mock orange
- *Pittosporum tenuifolium*
  Kohuhu

- *Robinia pseudoacacia*
  Black locust
- *Rosa* (many varieties)
  Rose
- *Stephanotis floribunda*
  Floradora,
  Madagascar jasmine
- *Trachelospermum jasminoides*
  Confederate jasmine,
  Star jasmine

PERENNIALS
- *Convallaria majalis*
  Lily-of-the-valley
- *Dianthus*
  Pinks
- *Hosta plantaginea*
  Hosta
- *Iris unguicularis*
  Iris
- *Primula veris*
  Cowslip
- *P. vulgaris*
  Primrose

ANNUALS AND BIENNIALS
- *Centaurea moschata*
  Sweet sultan
- *Erysimum cheiri*
  Wallflower
- *Exacum affine*
  Persian violet
- *Lathyrus grandiflorus*
  Everlasting pea
- *Matthiola incana*
  Stock
- *Scabiosa atropurpurea*
  Pincushion flower
- *Viola odorata*
  Sweet violet

CLIMBING PLANTS
- *Clematis*
  Clematis
- *Jasminum officinale*
  Summer jasmine
- *Lonicera*
  Honeysuckle

- *Rosa* (climbing varieties)
  Rose
- *Stephanotis floribunda*
  Floradora,
  Madagascar jasmine

BULBS AND CORMS
- *Crinum bulbispermum*
- *Crocus angustifolius*
  Cloth-of-gold crocus
- *Crocus longiflorus*
- *Cyclamen purpurascens*
  Sowbread
- *Lilium*
  Lily
- *Narcissus*
  Daffodil

Plants that prefer acid soil

All the plants listed prefer neutral or acid soil. For a number an ericaceous soil mix is essential. Check in a detailed plant encyclopedia if you are not certain. Plants that will only grow in an ericaceous soil mix will be marked as lime-haters.

TREES AND SHRUBS
- *Abies* (small varieties)
  Silver fir
- *Acer palmatum*
  Japanese maple
- *Arbutus unedo* 'Elfin King'
  Strawberry tree
- *Arctostaphylos uva-ursi*
  Bearberry
- *Berberis*
  Barberry
- *Calluna vulgaris*
  Heather
- *Camellia*
  Camellia
- *Cassiope*
- *Ceanothus*
  California lilac

Ilex aurea marginata

Viburnum tinus 'Eve Price'

Ceanothus 'Concha'

Cotinus obovatus

Mahonia japonica 'Bealei'

Centranthus ruber

- *Choisya ternata*
  Mexican orange blossom
- *Cotinus coggygria*
  Smoke tree
- *Disanthus cercidifolius*
- *Enkianthus campanulatus*
  Redvein enkianthus
- *Erica carnea*
  Winter-flowering heather
- *Eucryphia × nymansensis*
- *Euonymus fortunei*
  Wintercreeper
- *Fothergilla major*
- *Gaultheria mucronata*
- *Indigofera heterantha*
- *Kalmia latifolia*
  Calico bush
- *Lavatera* 'Barnsley'
  Mallow
- *Lithodora diffusa*
- *Mahonia*
  Oregon grapeholly
- *Menziesia ciliicalyx*
- *Osmanthus delavayi*
- *Picea* (small varieties)
  Spruce
- *Pieris*
  Pieris
- *Pinus* (small varieties)
  Pine
- *Rhododendron*
  Rhododendron
- *Sarcococca humilis*
  Christmas box, Sweet box
- *Styrax americanus*
  American snowbell
- *Vaccinium*
  Blueberry

CLIMBERS
- *Berberidopsis corallina*
  Coral plant
- *Forsythia suspensa*
  Weeping forsythia
- *Tropaeolum speciosum*
  Scottish flame flower

PERENNIALS
- *Aconitum napellus*
  Monkshood
- *Alchemilla mollis*
  Lady's mantle
- *Astrantia major*
  Masterwort
- *Campanula*
  Bellflower
- *Centranthus ruber*
  Jupiter's beard, red valerian
- *Ceratostigma willmottianum*
  Chinese plumbago
- *Corydalis cashmeriana*
- *Cypripedium reginae*
  Showy lady's slipper orchid
- *Epimedium grandiflorum*
  Bishop's hat, barrenwort
- *Filipendula palmata*
  Meadowsweet
- *Galium odoratum*
  Sweet woodruff,
  lady's bedstraw
- *Gentiana sino-ornata*
  Gentian
- *Lapageria rosea*
  Chilean bellflower
- *Lupinus luteus*
  Lupin
- *Meconopsis betonicifolia*
  Himalayan poppy
- *Myosotis sylvestris*
  Forget-me-not
- *Ourisia*
- *Phlomis fruticosa*
  Jerusalem sage
- *Santolina chamaecyparissus*
  Lavender cotton
- *Sarracenia purpurea*
  Pitcher plant,
  Huntsman's cup
- *Tradescantia*
- *Trillium grandiflorum*
  Trinity flower, Wakerobin
- *Veronica prostrata*
  Speedwell
- *Vinca minor*
  Periwinkle

- *Viola*
  Viola, pansy

Plants for fall and winter flowers and color

TREES AND SHRUBS
- *Acer palmatum*
  Japanese maple
- *Calluna vulgaris*
  Heather, Ling
- *Ceratostigma willmottianum*
- *Cotinus coggygria*
  Smoke tree
- *Daboecia cantabrica*
  Cantabrian heath,
  Irish heath
- *Disanthus cercidifolius*
- *Enkianthus campanulatus*
  Redvein enkianthus
- *Erica carnea*
  Winter-flowering heather
- *Euonymus fortunei*
  'Emerald 'n' Gold'
  Wintercreeper
- *Fothergilla major*
- *Hamamelis mollis*
  Witch hazel
- *Lagerstroemeria indica*
  Crape myrtle
- *Spiraea japonica* 'Goldflame'
- *Symphoricarpos × doorenbosii*
  Snowberry
- *Thuja occidentalis*
  White cedar
- *Viburnum opulus*
  Guelder rose
- *V. tinus*
  Laurustinus

CLIMBERS AND WALL SHRUBS
- *Celastrus orbicularis*
  Oriental bittersweet,
  Staff vine
- *Dregea sinensis*
- *Humulus lupulus* 'Aureus'
  Golden hop

- *Jasminum nudiflorum*
  Winter jasmine
- *Parthenocissus quinquefolia*
  Virginia creeper
- *Pyracantha*
  Firethorn
- *Vitis coignetiae*
  Crimson glory vine
  V. vinifera
  Purpleleaf grape

PERENNIALS AND BULBS
- *Chiastophyllum oppositifolium*
- *Chionodoxa luciliae*
  Glory-of-the-snow
- *Crocus*
  Crocus
- *Epimedium grandiflorum*
  Bishop's hat, barrenwort
- *Eranthis hyemalis*
  Winter aconite
- *Festuca glauca*
  Blue fescue
- *Galanthus*
  Snowdrop
- *Helleborus niger*
  Christmas rose
- *Iris unguicularis*
  Winter iris
- *Narcissus*
  Daffodil
- *Persicaria affinis*
  Himalayan knotweed
- *Primula*
  Winter-flowering primrose
- *Scilla sibirica*
  Siberian squill
- *Viola × wittrockiana*
  Winter-flowering pansy

Plants for an alpine garden

- *Acantholimon glumaceum*
- *Aethionema grandiflorum*
  Persian stone cress
- *Androsace lanuginosa*
  Rock jasmine

- *Anemone blanda*
  Windflower
- *Antirrhinum molle*
  Snapdragon
- *Aquilegia flabellata*
  Fan columbine
- *Arabis caucasica*
  Rock cress
- *Armeria maritima*
  Sea thrift
- *Aubrieta deltoidea*
  Aubretia
- *Aurinia saxatile* syn.
  Alyssum saxatile
  Basket of gold, Gold dust
- *Campanula cochleariifolia*
  Fairies' thimbles
- *Celmisia coriacea*
  New Zealand daisy
- *Chiastophyllum oppositifolium*
- *Corydalis flexuosa*
  C. solida
- *Cyclamen hederifolium*
  Baby cyclamen
- *Dianthus alpinus*
  Alpine pink
  D. deltoides
  Maiden pink
- *Draba aizoides*
  Yellow Whitlow grass
- *Erigeron karvinskianus*
  Fleabane
- *Erinus alpinus*
  Fairy foxglove,
  alpine liverwort
- *Erodium petraeum*
  Heron's bill, Stork's bill
- *Gentiana aucalis*
  Trumpet gentian
- *Geranium dalmaticum*
  Dalamatian cranesbill
- *Gypsophila repens*
  Baby's breath
- *Haberlea rhodopensis*
- *Hacquetia epipactis*
- *Horminum pyrenaicum*
  Dragon's mouth

- *Incarvillea mairei*
  Garden gloxinia
- *Leontopodium alpinum*
  Edelweiss
- *Lewisia* Cotyledon Hybrids
- *Linum arboreum*
  Flax
- *Lychnis alpina*
  Alpine catchfly
- *Meconopsis cambrica*
  Welsh poppy
- *Oenothera biennis*
  Evening primrose
- *Onosma alborosea*
- *Papaver alpinum*
  Alpine poppy
- *Penstemon newberryi*
- *Phlox subulata*
  Moss phlox
- *Platycodon grandiflorus*
  Balloon flower
- *Polemonium pulcherrimum*
  Skunkleaf, Jacob's ladder
- *Polygala calcarea*
  Milkwort
- *Polygonatum hirtum*
  Solomon's seal
- *Primula*
  Primrose
- *Pterocephalus perennis*
- *Pulsatilla vulgaris*
  Pasque flower
- *Ramonda myconi*
- *Saponaria ocymoides*
  Rock soapwort
- *Saxifraga*
  Saxifrage
- *Sedum*
  Stonecrop
- *Sempervivum arachnoideum*
  Cobweb houseleek
- *Silene maritima*
  Sea campion
- *Soldanella montana*
  Snowbell
- *Tropaeolum polyphyllum*
  Nasturtium
- *Veronica prostrata*
  Speedwell

Calluna vulgaris 'Peter Sparkes'

Vibernum opulus

Sedum hispanicum 'Minor Glaucum'

Rhododendron

Diascia

Papaver 'Patty's Plum'

• *Viola*
  Pansy, viola

**ALPINE SHRUBS
AND CONIFERS**

• *Abies balsamea* 'Nana'
  Balsam fir
• *Chamaecyparis lawsoniana*
  'Gnome'
  Cypress
• *Clematis alpina*
  Alpine clematis
• *Cytisus ardoinii*
  Broom
• *Daphne*
  Daphne
• *Dryas octopetala*
  Mountain avens
• *Erinacea anthyllis*
  Hedgehog broom
• *Genista delphinensis*
  Broom
• *Helianthemum nummularium*
  Rock rose
• *Hypericum balearicum*
  St John's wort
• *Iberis sempervirens*
  Candytuft
• *Juniperus communis*
  'Compressa'
  Juniper
• *Lithodora diffusa*
• *Origanum rotundifolium*
  Oregano
• *Picea mariana* 'Nana'
  Spruce
• *Pinus mugo* 'Humpy'
  Pine
• *Rhododendron* 'Dwarf'
  Rhododendron
• *Salix reticulata*
  Willow
• *Taxus baccata* 'Dwarf White'
  Yew
• *Thuja orientalis* 'Aurea
  Nana'
  Red cedar
• *Verbascum dumulosum*
  Mullein

Annuals and bedding plants

Many annuals are listed in seed catalogs under their common name rather than their Latin name. The list here lists the plants in the order that you will find them with the alternative, either the Latin or the common name, given where appropriate. Plants marked (p) are perennials frequently used as bedding plants.

• Agastache (p)
• Ageratum
• Alyssum (annual and
  perennial)
• Amaranthus
  Love-lies-bleeding
• Antirrhinum
  Snapdragon
• Aubretia (p)
• Balsam
  Busy Lizzie
• *Begonia semperflorens*
  B. tuberosa
  B. rex
• *Bellis perennis* (p)
  English daisy
• Bells of Ireland
  Moluccella laevis
• Bidens
• Brachyscome
  Swan River daisy
• *Calendula officinalis*
  Pot marigold
• *Campanula* (p)
• Candytuft
  Iberis
• Carnation
  Dianthus
• Catananche (p)
  Cupid's dart
• Celosia
  Cockscomb
• Cerinthe

• Chinese lanterns
  Physalis
• Chrysanthemum
  (annual varieties)
• Cineraria
• Cornflower (p)
  Centaurea
• Clarkia
• Clary
  Salvia horminum
• Cleome
  Spider flower
• Coreopsis (p)
  Tickseed
• Cosmea
  Cosmos
• Cynoglossum
  Hound's tongue
• Dahlia (dwarf varieties)
• Diascia
• Dianthus
  Pinks
• Echinacea (p)
  Coneflower
• Echium
• Erigeron
  Fleabane
• Eschscholzia
  California poppy
• Gazania
• Geranium
  Pelargonium
• Godetia
• Helianthemum (p)
  Rock rose
• Helichrysum
  Strawflower
• Heliotrope
• Larkspur
  Consolida
• Lavatera
  Mallow
• Limnanthes
  Poached-egg plant
• Lobelia
• Impatiens
  Busy Lizzie
• Malcolmia
  Virginian stock

- Marigold
  Tagetes
- Mesembryanthemum
  Livingstone daisy
- Ipomoea
  Morning glory
- Nasturtium
  Tropaeolum
- Nemesia
- Nicotiana
  Tobacco plant
- Nigella
  Love-in-a-mist
- Pansy
  Viola
- Petunia
- Phacelia
- Phlox drummondii
- Poppy
  Papaver
- Polyanthus
  Primula
- Rudbeckia
  Coneflower
- Salvia
  Sage
- Saxifrage (p)
  Saxifraga
- Scabiosa
  Scabious
- Silene
  Catchfly
- Stock
  Matthiola
- Sunflower
  Helianthus
- Sweet William
  Dianthus barbatus
- Sweet pea
  Lathyrus odoratus
- Thunbergia alata
  Black-eyed Susan
- Tithonia
  Mexican sunflower
- Verbena
- Veronica (p)
- Viola
  Pansy
- Zinnia

Cerinthe major purpurescens

the small
garden

introduction

Gardening is a lifelong hobby, and you do not need a big space to do it. Even a small garden can be designed and planted in thousands of different ways. Besides the satisfaction of seeing plants grow and flower, there is the added opportunity of creating an oasis of tranquillity and peace that is so necessary in a world of increasing stress.

Many garden features, from arbors to courtyards, are good for creating seclusion and privacy, while some also have a therapeutic quality. Such features include scented plants with their wide range of memorable fragrances, and comforting sounds produced by wind chimes, rustling leaves, and garden birds.

Inspirational yet practical

This all-color, information-packed book has been created to help novice and experienced gardeners create a beautiful garden in a small area. The aim of the first chapter is to inspire. It makes a visual exploration of the many different styles of gardening that can be featured in a small area, and gives advice on tackling difficult soils, adverse terrain, and severe conditions such as deep shade and intense sunlight.

Chapter 2 is thoroughly practical and leads gardeners through the complexities of a wide, varied spectrum of tasks that range from assessing the acidity or alkalinity of soil to laying paving slabs and constructing a compost pile. Chapter 3 explains how best to use plants in small gardens. This covers borders saturated in a medley of colors, and color-themed beds where flowers of a specific color are grown. These single-color features range from pink and red borders to those with white and silver flowers or foliage. In addition there is advice on creating distinctive displays throughout the year, especially on planning spring, summer, fall, and winter displays. Producing displays in window boxes, hanging baskets, tubs, pots, and sink gardens on a patio or a terrace is also explained, with tips on scented borders, a flower-arranger's garden, and growing roses.

Chapter 4 has information on more than 100 plants, including hardy annuals, herbaceous perennials, shrubs, trees and

▲ A border can become awash with colorful flowers and attractive leaves. There are plants for all places, sunny and shady.

HEIGHTS AND SPREADS

The heights and spreads given for shrubs and trees in Chapter 4 relate to 15–20-year-old specimens growing in good conditions. Eventually, these plants may grow even larger.

climbers, including detailed explanations of how best to grow them. In addition, there is information about garden and greenhouse pests and diseases, including their identification and control. The identification and eradication of garden weeds is another key feature. The book ends with a detailed glossary.

This thoroughly practical section of *The Ultimate Book of Gardening* will help you enrich a small garden with beautiful plants and attractive garden structures, such as paths, fences, patios, and terraces.

▶ Achillea *is an ideal herbaceous perennial for growing in a dry, sunny border. Its flowers are ideal for cutting and displaying indoors.*

▼ *Plants with variegated leaves create color all summer long, and evergreens keep their color through the year.*

design
inspirations

soils, contours, shapes, and aspects

Beautiful gardens can be created in all types of soil, and in shade and full sun. Do not be alarmed if your garden has heavy clay soil or well-drained sandy ground, because such extremes are not an insurmountable problem. Solutions range from improving the soil to creating raised beds and growing plants in containers. Even steep slopes can be turned to your advantage using some inspired design tips.

making the best of your soil

Soil can be slowly improved by adding well-decayed manure or garden compost, but more instant ways to create a colorful garden are to select plants that survive the conditions in the garden being planted. It is inevitable, however, that gardeners will wish to grow other kinds of plants.

Raised beds

Where the ground is continually moist and drainage is difficult, or if the soil is exceptionally chalky or acid, construct a raised bed 12–18in/30–45cm high and fill it with good soil. This enables a wide range of plants to grow. Use cascading plants at the sides to cloak the edges.

Preparing planting areas

Where the soil is exceptionally dry or of poor quality, small areas can be improved to enable climbers and other plants to be grown. Dig out the soil from an area about 2ft/60cm square and deep, and fill the lower 4in/10cm with rubble. Top up with good topsoil, and firm it. Put in the plant and water the area regularly until it is established. Do not plant climbers less than 1ft/30cm from a wall, because the soil is always fairly dry close to a wall.

Growing acid-loving plants

Most soils are only slightly acid and can be improved by dusting the surface with hydrated lime or ground limestone each winter (see pages 316–317). It is better to grow acid-loving plants such as callunas and heathers on soils that are strongly acid and formed mainly of peat. There are many varieties of these plants. Some have attractive foliage and others are grown for their flowers. Many varieties flower through cold winter months. Azaleas can be planted in lightly shaded

◀ *When there is a problem with the soil, a raised bed is an ideal solution. It also enables plants to be seen and reached easily.*

areas with slightly acid soils to create a spectacular spring display.

Growing chalk-loving plants

It is more difficult to correct chalky soils than acid types. Acidic fertilizers, such as sulfate of ammonia, can be used with additions of peat, but if the underlying soil is alkaline it is better to grow only chalk-loving plants. A raised bed is the best solution for gardeners with acid soil and an irrepressible desire to grow chalk-loving plants.

Wet and boggy areas

Many soils with a high water level can be drained, enabling a wide range of plants to be grown. However, if the area is naturally wet, difficult to drain, and perhaps close to a stream, it is better to plant moisture-loving plants. They include *Lysichiton americanus* (skunk cabbage) with bright yellow, arum-like flower heads in spring and its near relative *Lysichiton camtschatcensis*, with pure white flowers. Along the sides of streams plant shrubs such as *Cornus stolonifera* 'Flaviramea' and *C. alba* 'Sibirica' for their colored winter stems.

Hot, dry soils

Gardening successfully on hot, dry soils depends on three factors: mixing in bulky materials such as well-rotted manure and garden compost annually, to aid water retention; regular watering; and adding a mulch each spring. Selecting plants that survive in hot, dry soils is also important (see pages 322–323).

Pots, tubs, and other containers

Some soils are so inhospitable that plants cannot be grown easily. This problem is best solve by planting a wide range of plants in containers. They range from pots and tubs to window boxes, hanging baskets, troughs, and wall baskets. Buying, planting and looking after plants in containers is more expensive and involves more work than caring for plants in borders and beds. However, it does provide you with the opportunity to change and recreate your garden as often as you wish, which can be a great advantage and very rewarding.

▲ To bring color through the year, plant large pots with dwarf or slow-growing conifers and position them along the edges of a path.

▼ Cloak the sides of a natural stone wall in plants. They may grow in the wall or be planted at its foot. Planted pots are an alternative.

gardening on slopes

Sloping ground offers an opportunity to create an unusual garden, but it will be more expensive to develop than a flat site. A number of paved, terraced areas around a house make an attractive feature when the ground slopes downward from the house.

▲ *A paved area halfway up a slope creates an exciting yet practical leisure area, especially when it features a pond and a fountain.*

Terraced gardens

A garden may be terraced in formal or informal style, depending partly on the style of the house. Formal terraces connected by flights of steps usually suit modern houses. Cottages demand an informal style. A slope dotted with fruit trees is an attractive feature.

Paved areas

When a house stands at the bottom of a facing slope, a flat, paved area can usually be laid at the base of the slope. An alternative is to create a paved area about one-third of the way up the slope to break up the degree of incline. Where possible, position the area so that it is easily visible from the ground floor of the house, so that people do not have to look sharply up to see it.

Where the ground falls away from the house, lay a flat, paved area as near to the house as possible. Meandering paths can be laid to lead downward from it, perhaps criss-crossing the slope to make them appear less steep and easier to use. These paved areas need not be central but off to one side, which particularly suits informal gardens. Where the end of a garden rises, lay a paved area and erect a summerhouse on top. Check that the neighbors will not think it an intrusion on their privacy.

Retaining walls

These are invariably constructed across slopes to retain banks of soil up to 4ft/1.2m high. Some walls are formal, perhaps built from bricks or blocks, while others are made of natural stone. These are particularly suitable for planting *Aurinia saxatilis* (still better known as *Alyssum saxatile*) and aubretia. By positioning wide paths along the base of informal retaining walls the plants can be admired without being damaged. Formal retaining walls, especially when made of brick, do not need a wide path alongside them. However, if a lawn is positioned close to them, construct a mowing strip at the base to enable a lawn mower to cut as close to the wall as possible.

Sloping woodland and wild gardens

Old railroad ties are ideal for retaining soil on steep slopes in rustic areas. Secure the ties in position, using strong wooden posts or metal spikes. Beds of heathers and deciduous azaleas create superb displays on slopes. Peat blocks can also be used to restrain soil and to form areas to grow acid-loving plants. Where the peat is likely to become dry and crumbly, use a combination of railroad ties to form the main soil-retention edging, with peat blocks behind them.

Lawn banks

Traditionally, especially on large country estates, slopes were terraced and grassed, with 45° slopes separating level areas 10–12ft/3–3.6m wide. These dramatic features can easily be replicated on a smaller scale in formal gardens. The key is to keep it all in proportion.

▲ *Flights of steps create visually exciting features in gardens. Insure that they are soundly constructed and have all-weather surfaces.*

◄ *Slopes are ideal places for a series of waterfalls. If these cover a large area, a reservoir tank may be needed at the top.*

the long and short of gardens

Few small gardens have a perfect shape. They may be long and narrow, short and wide, or with a tapering outline that makes planning difficult. Fortunately, beautiful gardens can be created on the most improbably shaped piece of land, and there are many excellent ways to disguise a garden's true shape.

Shortening gardens

When a plot of land is long and narrow the easiest way to create the impression of a shorter garden is to split it into several smaller units. Either create a long path down the center or one that alternates from one side to the other as it progresses through the garden areas. If a path is constructed down the center of a garden, passing through separate areas, insure that a focal point such as a large urn or a fountain is at the end, and not just a blank fence or wall. Hedges and freestanding trellises play an important role in dividing gardens.

Broadening gardens

Shortening a garden by bringing the far boundary closer to the house will give the impression of a wider and a shorter garden, but take care not to overdo it; this will only confuse the eye. A free-standing trellis makes an ideal boundary with a central feature such as a sundial or an armillary sphere.

Narrowing gardens

It is easier to create the impression of narrowness in a large garden than in a small one. Free-standing trellises, pillar roses, narrow conifers, and hedges can be used to section off the central area. Alternatively, position a summerhouse in one corner and perhaps a paved area in the other.

Informal gardens

An informal area can even be created within the formal outline imposed by a square or rectangular area, by introducing flower beds and lawns with serpentine outlines. An informal pond—made with a flexible liner—can be designed to any shape or size, and integrated into casually shaped borders and lawns. Rustic trellis and arches over paths are useful features because they add height and informality.

▲ *Meandering paths make interesting features in gardens and often enable secluded areas to be created, hidden from immediate view.*

▲ *An attractive feature at the end of a short,*
square garden makes a focal point, which brings
interest to a small area.

aspect, light, and shade

The range of trees, shrubs, herbaceous perennials, annuals, and other garden plants is wide, and there are types for all aspects and intensities of light or shade. Some of these extremes can be lessened by planting or cutting down trees, but it is usually a matter of learning to live with your garden.

The lottery of aspect

A garden's aspect is not usually the first consideration when buying a house. Rather, it is one of the lotteries of gardening. Cold, searing wind is a problem for some plants, while strong, intense sunlight causes difficulties for many. All gardens have possibilities and limitations, and there are plants for even the most inhospitable places. This book explores many ideas that will make growing plants easy. For example, pages 322–323 suggest plants for hot, sunny areas and advise on growing them, and shade-loving plants are on pages 324–325.

Coastal considerations

Coastal gardens are at risk from several factors. Cold, strong, buffeting winds may deform trees and shrubs, especially in winter, and the salt-laden wind will damage leaves and flowers. It is essential to create windbreaks and hedges to filter

◀ *A shady border can bloom as brightly as a sunny border. Plants with colorful flowers and attractive leaves will grow in all garden areas.*

the wind and reduce its speed, especially in gardens close to the sea. A range of plants that thrive in coastal areas is given on pages 326–327.

Winter wonderlands

In some areas, winter weather is so harsh that the likelihood of growing flowers is dramatically reduced. However, several hardy trees flower during winter and they include *Hamamelis mollis* (Chinese witch hazel) and *Cornus mas* (Cornelian cherry). Bear in mind that frost forms attractive patterns on leaves, while a light dusting of snow can be attractive.

In exceptionally cold areas, a layer of snow helps insulate bulbs against low temperatures, but where possible remove snow carefully from the leaves of evergreen shrubs before it weighs them down and disfigures the branches.

▲ *Steps strongly constructed and recessed in a retaining wall are attractive, and give ready access to the border behind.*

▼ *An ornamental pond needs to be positioned in good light and where leaves will not litter the water through the fall.*

gardening styles

The most exciting part of gardening is deciding which style you want. There is a big choice, from traditional cottage gardens with flowers, fruit trees, rich colors, and scented flowers, to smart formal designs with special bedding schemes for spring and summer, using tulips and all kinds of annuals. You can be as nostalgic or as modern as you want. You can even try Mediterranean gardening with brightly colored pots and drought-tolerant plants, or elegant Japanese gardens with calm stretches of gravel and water.

English flower gardens

Few gardening styles are as relaxed and informal as an English country garden. Herbaceous borders are packed with plants that mostly die down to soil level in the fall, and develop fresh shoots and leaves in spring. Mixed borders are a medley of plants, including shrubs and bulbs.

▲ *The fleshy-rooted border perennial* agapanthus *creates a mass of large, umbrella-shaped flower heads mainly during mid- and late summer.*

Herbaceous borders

During the late 1800s the Irish garden writer William Robinson (1838–1935) published *The English Flower Garden*, in which he enthused about herbaceous perennials. He claimed that the English cottage had for many years been a repository for herbaceous plants. His writings came at a time when there was a general hunger for information about plants, and a popularization of gardening books and magazines. However, Gertrude Jekyll (1843–1932) is the best-known advocate of herbaceous plants. Her first book about these plants, *Wood and Garden*, appeared in 1899, followed by others that included ideas about single-color borders. Pages 434–447 explain color-themed borders, including pink and red, blue and mauve, yellow and gold, and white and silver plants.

Mixed borders

Few small gardens can have more than a corner devoted to a color-themed border, so tend to display a mixture of herbaceous perennials, bulbs, annuals, shrubs, and trees producing a rich array of colors, sizes, and shapes. Such borders create a good opportunity to have all the plants you like.

Hardy and half-hardy annuals are excellent space fillers during the early years of a mixed border. The half-hardy

annuals are planted in gaps in early summer, as soon as all risk of frost has passed, while hardy annuals can be sown earlier. Always sow the seeds of hardy annuals thinly.

Bulbs provide extra color and include lilies that delight in soil shaded and cooled by other plants. Clumps of trumpet-type daffodils are very welcome in early spring and, although they leave a legacy of untidy leaves during early summer, they are rich in color.

Hardy annual borders

If you have a passion for bright colors which you can change each year, think of planting a border of hardy annuals. A few packets of seeds will produce glorious displays of color. Sowing and looking after hardy annuals is discussed on pages 384–385. Be careful not to sow seeds too early in the year. They will not germinate if the soil is not warm enough, and they may start to decay if conditions are too wet.

In windy areas, select moderately tall hardy annuals, and support them with twiggy sticks. A few annuals have special appeal to children, particularly *Helianthus annuus*, the sunflower, which has large flowers often as wide as 12in/30cm wide. Some grow as high as 10ft/3m, although others are much shorter, and these varieties are ideal for windy sites. Sunflowers are easy to grow in a sunny position and look especially attractive against a white wall that highlights the yellow petals and brown or purple centers.

▲ Use relatively low-growing and lax flowering plants to create bright edges to paths, especially where informality is desired.

◄ Floriferous herbaceous borders, with their relaxed and informal nature, have been a traditional part of English gardens.

HARDY ANNUALS FOR ROCK GARDENS

Even in a small garden hardy annuals have a useful role, especially in rock gardens where they fill bare areas and add extra color. There are several plants to choose from, including:
Adonis annua (pheasant's eye)—10in/25cm high with deep crimson flowers with black centers.
* *Limnanthes douglasii* (Poached-egg plant)— 6in/15cm high with bright white flowers with yellow centers.

informal gardens

Informal gardens appeal to many gardeners because they have a more restful atmosphere than more regimented gardens with plants in straight lines and borders in geometric shapes. Cottage gardens are the epitome of informality because plants of many types grow together in a relaxed way.

Cottage gardens

To many gardeners, the key features of cottage gardens are secluded bowers, rustic trellises with scented climbers and beds patchworked with flowers, fruit, and vegetables. There is even space for topiary birds and animals trained in *Taxus* (yew) and *Ligustrum* (privet). Armillary spheres,

with their circular arrangement of rings showing the relative positions of celestial bodies, are less formal than sundials, and add to the relaxed atmosphere.

To insure an authentic cottage garden, you can also grow apple varieties with wonderful flavors. They include 'McIntosh', 'Gold Rush', 'Rome',

'Newtown Pippin', and 'Spartan'. Good pear varieties include 'Comice', 'Harrow Delight', 'Harvest Queen', and 'Stark Honeysweet'. Pole beans (*Phaseolus vulgaris*) on tripods in borders add height and create a background for other plants.

Wild gardens

Wild gardens are not a contradiction in terms but a way of bringing a hint of the wild landscape into a small, controlled environment. A light, overhead canopy of trees helps to create shade for plants from *Hyacinthoides* (bluebell) to azaleas. If you have inherited a garden with deeper shade you can alleviate the conditions by thinning branches, but in any case stick to shade-loving plants (see pages 324–325). Other features to include are meandering rustic paths linking garden areas, and alpine "meadows" with low-growing bulbous plants in short grass. These are lovely in full sun, especially on a slope.

◀ *Benches and other seats are an essential feature in a garden, since they create places from which it can be admired.*

Wild flowers are also necessary to attract a wide range of insects. Many seed companies sell special mixtures of wild flowers and they are best sown in the spring. Most will reseed themselves during the following year and, although not all gardeners will wish to create such informal areas, they constitute an environmentally friendly way of keeping a healthy garden.

Soothing sounds

Most gardens have colorful flowers and attractive foliage, but why not add comforting sounds as a new dimension? These can range from the rustling of leaves to the reassuring pitter-patter of water splashing and tumbling from fountains or bubbling along in streams. Some plants are especially known for

their ability to create sound in even the slightest breeze. Grasses and bamboos rustle, as do the leaves of some trees, and a gravel path with bamboos on either side is a joy throughout the year. Encourage birds and birdsong with a bird bath or a feeding area well out of the reach of cats. Continue feeding the birds in winter, but go not leave whole peanuts, hard fat, or too much bread in early spring when there may be young in the nests.

WIND CHIMES

Wind chimes suspended from trees close to a house add a gentle and comforting sound to the garden. However, do not put them where they may cause irritation through being repeatedly knocked.

▲ *A stream meandering through a wild flower garden is a captivating feature. A bench is a resting point from which plants may be admired.*

▼ *Wild flower gardens are easily created and mixtures of wild flower seeds are available from seed companies. Always sow the seeds thinly.*

formal gardens

Formally designed gardens appeal to many gardeners. They provide a neat appearance and a better opportunity than informal types to change arrangements of plants from spring to summer, as well as from one year to another. Small front gardens often have a formal design.

Carpet bedding

During the mid-1800s many low-growing, subtropical plants were introduced into gardens, and by the 1870s they were grown to form carpets of color in borders. Most were planted in geometric patterns, but some formed monograms, especially in large estates.

The art of carpet bedding spread to botanical and municipal gardens, and

▲ *Formal gardens have a clinical nature that suits many small areas. Ponds, either round or square, create attractive features.*

towns competed to create the most original and attractive display. Some designs of carpet bedding were even used as advertisements, as commemorative notices, and to depict the names of towns. Carpet bedding is still widely practiced in formal parks, the centers of large cities, and in popular coastal resorts.

Home gardeners pursue this type of gardening by growing half-hardy annuals in summer, and bulbs and biennials in spring and the fall.

Summer displays

Plant summer bedding displays in late spring or early summer, as soon as all risk of damage from frost has passed. The plants are raised from seeds sown in late winter or early spring in gentle warmth in greenhouses, and are later acclimatized to outdoor conditions. As well as half-hardy annuals, plants with attractive foliage are also used and they range from *Bassia scoparia trichophylla* better known as *Kochia trichophylla* (burning bush, summer cypress) and *Euphorbia marginata* 'Snow on the mountain' to *Abutilon pictum*

'Thompsonii'. They are often used as "dot" plants to create height in an otherwise low display.

Plants traditionally used in formal bedding displays include *Lobularia maritima,* still known as *Alyssum maritimum* (sweet alyssum), bushy forms of *Lobelia erinus* in colors including blue, white, and red, and the many forms of *Tagetes* (marigold).

Spring displays

Early bedding displays usually contain a medley of biennials and spring-flowering bulbs, especially tulips. Biennials are sown in nursery beds in late spring or early summer, and are planted in borders in late summer or early fall. Bulbs such as tulips are planted at the same time.

Spring displays can be a rich mix of colors, shapes, and heights and include biennials such as *Bellis perennis* (English daisy), wallflowers, *Dianthus barbatus* (sweet william) and *Myosotis sylvatica* (forget-me-not). In late spring or early summer, after their display has finished, the plants are pulled up. The soil is then forked over, lightly firmed by shuffling over it, and planted with summer-flowering displays.

Knot gardens

The knot garden was once an expression of the unchanging, endless nature of life. By the mid-1600s "knot garden" had become a term to describe a flower garden surrounded by and interwoven with paths. Today, it is associated with miniature hedges of *Buxus sempervirens* 'Suffruticosa' (edging boxwood) surrounding small flower beds. These intricate shapes are ideal in small gardens.

Formal ponds

Round ponds are simple but distinctive, especially when they feature a fountain. They need a formal setting, perhaps in a wide lawn surrounded, at a distance, by a formal hedge of *Taxus baccata* (English yew). Alternatively, lay wide paths around the pond and divide the surrounding space into four separate garden areas planted with summer-flowering bedding plants. Use dot plants to create height.

FORMAL TOPIARY

Unlike topiary animals and birds, which are traditional in cottage gardens, topiary cones, pyramids, and squares may be more suited to formal areas. These can be grouped, perhaps toward the end of a formal lawn, or dotted around a garden.

▶ *Miniature hedges grown from edging boxwood are ideal for encircling a border. They create formality without dominating the garden.*

Mediterranean gardens

Clear blue skies, warm breezes, and little rain epitomize the Mediterranean, especially to visitors who know the region and its multicolored gardens only through summer visits. Yet the gardens change through the year, reflecting a dramatic swing from hot, dry summers to cooler, wetter winters.

Mediterranean plants

Spring-flowering bulbs and tuberous-rooted plants soon burst into flower as the cool of winter is replaced by spring warmth, while annuals burgeon into growth ready for later flowering. Native plants include rosemary, myrtle, *Cistus* (rock rose), laurel, olives, figs and dwarf palms. Best known is *Cupressus sempervirens* (Italian or Mediterranean cypress), particularly the narrow forms. They are often seen in small clusters in Mediterranean gardens.

Silver-leaved plants are better able to survive hot, dry conditions than plants with green leaves. They include shrubby and herbaceous *Artemisias*. Plants with hairy leaves are also equipped for hot regions and perhaps one of the best known is *Stachys byzantina* (lamb's ears). It has oval leaves densely covered with white, silvery hairs. *Cistus* (rock rose) has leaves that emit resinous scents and it also thrives in warm areas.

◀ *Bright surfaces, colored tiles, and plants with variegated, daggerlike leaves, such as* Agave americana 'Marginata', *create a vibrant setting.*

Warm terraces

Wide terraces with ornate stone balustrades are ideal areas for enjoying outdoor life. These areas are also perfect for plants in a wide range of containers. Where possible, position them in partial shade, which helps prevent the compost becoming too hot, and reduces the amount and frequency of watering.

Shade is as important for people as plants, and a tall tree with a climber such as *Clematis montana* 'Elizabeth'—or another mountain clematis—clambering through its branches makes a spectacular feature when flowering in late spring and early summer. It also gives shade in summer and so is splendid for creating a cool outdoor living area. If it becomes too large, cut it back as soon as the flowers fade. Other climbers create shade, and where there is a large pergola, a wisteria can be planted to clamber over it, although it needs more pruning than the clematis, and it will not create such a dense canopy of shade.

Brightening steps

Wide flights of steps that link terraces with lower levels need not be solely functional. Position clusters of plants in containers at the top and bottom, especially if the lower area is wider. Narrow steps, perhaps positioned to one side of a terrace and connecting to a lower garden, can have their sides clothed in trailing plants. If the sides have a dry stone wall, plant the yellow-flowered *Aurinia saxatilis* (still better known as *Alyssum saxatile*) and the contrasting *Aubrieta deltoidea* (aubretia) for a wealth of purple to rose-lilac flowers in late spring and early summer.

TEMPERATE PALM

A few palms are sufficiently hardy to survive temperate areas and they include the Chinese *Trachycarpus fortunei*. Plant it in well-drained but moisture-retentive soil in a warm, sunny, sheltered position. Placed near a terrace it will provide shade. It takes about 15 years to grow to 10ft/3m high and has large, pleated leaves up to 3ft/90cm wide, and a trunk covered decoratively in wiry black fiber.

▲ Even the smallest paved area can have Mediterranean plantings. Color-washed walls and metal-framed furniture complete the design.

◀ Colorful pots with low-growing and slightly bushy plants are ideal for positioning along the edges of steps. Insure that they are secure.

Japanese gardens

The traditional gardens of Japan exude serenity and peace. They are simple, uncluttered, and well-defined, engendering an atmosphere of tranquillity and contemplation. The design of early Japanese gardens was influenced in the seventh century by a Japanese ambassador returning from China.

Gravel gardening

Few features in Japanese gardens are as restful to the eye as a gravel garden, perhaps composed of a large, level area of gravel and well-spaced groupings of two, three or five large rocks that assume the appearance of small islands. The gravel is raked to create the impression of shallow waves. Large areas of gravel can be given extra interest by laying a stepping stone path across them, but avoid splitting up the area and producing two seas of gravel. If laying a second path, use smaller stone to make the feature less dominant.

Paths and rivers

In slightly less formal areas—and where there is a gentle slope—use pebbles instead of gravel and create two or three paths and rivers. Using large, irregular-shaped stepping stones and surrounding them with colored shale will create the impression of a stream. Where the area is moderately steep, stones and shale may be used to form a narrow stream; in flatter areas this may be made wider to give a more natural, harmonious outline.

Water and bridges

Moving water is an essential element in some Japanese gardens. Tumbling and splashing water can be achieved with a small pump and this creates an exciting feature throughout the year. Japanese wooden bridges are distinctive and often have a misleading appearance of frailty. Where just a simple bridge is needed

◄ *Japanese gardens have a serenity unmatched by any other style of gardening. Large rocks, gravel, and bamboos are the main features of many gardens.*

over a narrow stream, thick planks of wood or long slabs of stone are attractive and easy to use. Where the stream is wide and the current is slow, several pieces of stone or wood can be linked. Large stepping stones also look attractive and may occasionally be located down the center of a stream.

TEA GARDENS

Tea gardens are the traditional, tranquil setting for the tea ceremony. Those taking part first assemble in the garden to cast off worldly cares before drinking tea. Gravel and stepping stones are prime features. Others are trees, shrubs, and ferns, with their timeless and contemplative character. Ephemeral flowers, do not feature because they reveal the changing seasons and the passing of time.

Shrubs and bamboos

Bamboos are a characteristic plant in Japanese gardens and many grow well beside streams. Some varieties also grow easily in a large tub or a square, wooden container. Bamboos are described in more detail on pages 476–477.

Two small trees typical of Japanese gardens, and which are ideal in tubs, are the Japanese maples, *Acer palmatum dissectum* and *Acer palmatum d. atropurpurea*, the former with deeply cut green leaves and the latter with bronze-red foliage. They are both deciduous and have a wide, dome-like outline. The evergreen *Fatsia japonica* can also be planted in a large container. Its large, rich glossy green leaves with seven to nine lobes provide a good structural contrast.

▲ Small trees with finely divided green or bronze-purple leaves are instantly associated with Japanese gardens.

▼ Meandering streams, simple bridges, and gravel paths bordered with low-growing plants create a restful ambience.

surfaces, walls, and trellises

The key part of a garden that hardly ever changes is the structure, and that includes walls, paths, and arbors. They are all extremely important because they have two functions. They divide and shape the garden, creating outdoor rooms, passages, and places to sit, lending atmosphere to the garden, and they add distinctive, attractive features. But before deciding to put up a trellis, think how and where it is to be used, and what you are going to grow it on. These pages look at the wide range of possibilities to be encountered, and the many exciting new materials to use.

paths for all gardens

Paths should not just be ribbon-like features providing quick access from one part of a garden to another, they should be attractive in their own right, with surfaces that harmonize with the rest of the garden. These pages explore the many different construction materials available for paths.

Why have a path?

Paths are essential in many parts of a garden. An all-weather surface right around a house is especially necessary to link it with a garage, fuel store, and sheds. But even these domestic demands do not mean that a path need be featureless and unimaginative. Areas around cottages can have gray, ribbed-surfaced paving stones spaced 4in/10cm apart in a sea of gravel, or a natural stone path with spaces for low plants. Modern houses need a more formal style, which may be provided by a wide range of plain or mixed surfaces. It is, fortunately, no longer necessary to lay a path alongside a clothes line, thanks to the introduction of compact clothes lines which rotate on a single pole.

Constraints and opportunities

The choice of materials for the construction of a path is influenced by the garden's topography and shape.

▶ *Crazy-paving paths are right for flat and for sloping gardens because they can hug closely to the most twisting and undulating contours.*

Materials such as square or rectangular paving slabs are ideal for straight paths, whereas crazy paving is more adaptable and can be used for straight and for curved paths. Grass paths, with or without stepping stones running down the center, may be curved or straight, while informal paths of thyme look particularly eye-catching when in flower.

A garden that is undulating or markedly sloped has a strong influence on the selection of materials. Crazy paving is perfectly suited to ground that slopes in several directions, whereas formal paths are best where the ground slopes in one direction. Gravel paths should be reserved for flat areas because the gravel inevitably migrates slowly downhill.

Materials used to construct a path should be in proportion to its width. A path formed of a combination of small, rectangular and square paving slabs looks out of proportion if over 2ft/60cm wide. For a wider path use larger paving slabs. Conversely, narrow paths of crazy paving appear confusing, but look better when wider and irregularly shaped.

Medley paths

Paths can be formed of several different materials. Those for informal areas could include cross-slices of tree trunks positioned as stepping stones in a sea of coarse gravel, or six-sided concrete slabs with pebbles, while railroad ties spaced 3–4in/7.5–10cm apart in cobbles or gravel also work well. In wild gardens, make gravel or grass paths edged with logs, and in rural gardens where borders are wide, use sections of logs as stepping stones to give access to the entire area.

For formal gardens, the range of materials is much wider. Make patterns from paving slabs of different shapes but similar texture and color, with gaps left for cobbles, but remember that this may make the path very uneven. Bricks and flexible pavers can also be laid in attractive patterns.

WINTER WARNING

Where plants are positioned in gaps between paving slabs, do not use salt to remove ice, or use a shovel or spade to scrape away snow. Instead, leave these winter hazards alone and let them melt naturally.

▲ Informal paths formed of a well-drained but firm base covered with shredded bark and with a low, woven edging are ideal for rustic gardens.

▼ Concrete pavers are right for straight paths in formal gardens. The pavers can be laid in straight lines or in complex patterns.

walls and fences

Most gardens have a wall or a fence to define boundaries, create privacy, deflect noise, and screen unpleasant views. The main constructional difference is that a wall needs strong foundations along its entire length, whereas a fence requires support only for the concrete or wooden posts.

◀ *Walls of all types, formal or informal, create secluded and cloistered spots which may have small paved areas for garden furniture.*

Fence or wall?

Brick walls are much more expensive to construct than fences. A wall 6ft/1.8m high needs to be 9in/23cm thick, with strengthening piers every 6ft/1.8m. Even screen-block walling (blocks 12in/30cm square and 4in/10cm thick, with a latticework design) needs strong foundations and piers every 10ft/3m, and supports at the ends. Screen-block walling can be combined attractively with a traditional brick wall or with bricks of reconstituted stone.

Fences range from white picket fencing to close-boarding. The framework of a close-boarded fence is built from 4–6in/10–15cm wide pales (strips of wood) nailed to arris rails. Such fences are usually 4ft/1.2m to 6ft/1.8m high. Always select a fence to harmonize with the garden. For example, a picket fence is ideal for the front boundary of a

cottage garden, whereas wattle fencing and chestnut paling are better suited for the back area. Panel fencing, with 6ft/1.8m long panels from 4ft/1.2m to 6ft/1.8m high, is popular and somewhat cheaper than close-boarding.

Low-slung post and chain fencing is ideal for marking a boundary, but it will not keep people out. The chain is now usually made of strong plastic and needs no maintenance. Ranch-style fencing, with planks of wood 6–8ft/1.8–2.4m long and 6–8in/15–20cm wide nailed to posts, has a modern, open feel. Gaps of about 4in/10cm are left between the planks, but to stop people looking through, nail planks on alternate sides of the supporting posts which are concreted into the ground. These fences can be 3ft/90cm to 6ft/1.8m high.

Cast-iron fencing is ideal for surrounding the front gardens of Victorian, Georgian, and other period town houses. This kind of fence is usually 3–6ft/90cm–1.8m high and painted black. The fences are very attractive and can be used as features on their own, or underplanted with a range of colorful flowers and leafy plants.

Gates for all gardens

Walls and fences in front gardens are not complete without a complementary gate. White picket fences need rustic wooden gates while an old, weathered brick wall with an arch requires a wrought-iron gate with a round top.

The range of decorative patterns in wrought-iron gates is wide, and this is usually reflected in the cost. Wooden gates vary in style, and apart from the paling type there are overlapping board gates and those with diamond-slatted cladding.

▼ *Choose a fence that suits your garden. Wattle fencing panels secured to stout posts are informal and rustic, and right for a cottage garden style.*

THIEF-PROOF GATES

Wrought-iron gates are usually hung on peg hinges and can be stolen quickly and easily. To prevent this happening, secure the lower hinge to the post, and with the peg upward, hang the gate and secure the top hinge with the peg downward. Now the gate cannot be lifted off. Wooden gates are usually more secure because the hinge is screwed to the gate and the supporting post.

decking

Decking is increasingly popular and creates all-weather leisure areas above ground level. Decking was traditionally laid along one side of a house, often forming a veranda complete with a balustrade. Nowadays it is also built along boundaries or as a free-standing feature.

◀ *Combining decking with a fountain and a pond creates an attractive feature. Large-leaved, evergreen plants make an ideal background.*

Constructing decking

The basic construction of a deck is of planks of Western red cedar or another softwood which has been pressure-impregnated with a wood preservative. The planks are attached by galvanized nails to a supporting timber frame, with a ¼–½in/6–12mm space between each pair of planks.

The timber framework supporting the decking is secured to sturdy uprights mounted on metal plates, which are bolted to concrete foundation pads. This allows for sloping ground and demands careful construction and levelling.

Decking can be built from wood bought from a timber yard, but partly constructed units are now available from large home improvement outlets. There are also many companies that specialize in decking and will customize a deck to your specific needs, building the deck and also installing it.

Economy decking

A deck is expensive and time-consuming to build. Multilevel designs are especially costly. An alternative to decking is to use cinder blocks and fence posts. The blocks need to be half-buried in the ground with their surfaces level, and the fence posts (available up to 3m/10ft long) positioned on top. Pressure-treated gravel boards (normally used for close-board fencing) are then nailed to the fence posts.

Encircling mature trees

People often want to build a deck in an area where an established tree is growing. This need not be a problem because you can arrange the decking around the tree. Begin by cutting off low-growing branches and then build a square brick plinth around it. This will need strong foundations. Extend the plinth upward until the top is about 15in/38cm above the planned level of the decking. The last stage is to construct the decking around the plinth and to put a capping 6–8in/15–20cm wide on top of the wall, which can serve as a very useful seat.

WOODEN TILES

These look like decking when laid, but are formed of 2ft/60cm square units. They are easily laid. The first stage is to level the ground. Insure the roots of perennial weeds are dug up, and then spread and rake level a layer of horticultural sand 2in/5cm-thick. Place the wooden tiles on top, with the slatted surface in a criss-cross pattern. Lay the tiles so they abut closely, and use stout pegs around the outside to prevent them being knocked out of position.

◀ *Steps formed of decking and edged with leafy plants are a practical and attractive means of leading from one level to another.*

▼ *Old railroad ties laid with their surfaces flush with the soil's surface, and with gravel between them, make an attractively uneven surface.*

steps for all gardens

Handsome flights of steps that harmonize with the rest of the garden become enduring features of interest. They must, of course, be functional, but there is no reason why they cannot also be attractive. Here is a range of steps that will enhance your garden, whatever its style or size.

Informal steps

Log steps are essential for wild gardens on slopes. Thick logs or old railroad ties can be used to form the risers. They have a relaxing appearance and can be enhanced by daffodils naturalized in the grass beside them. Instead of forming narrow ribbons of daffodils, plant them in wide groups, about one-third the width of the steps.

Where peat beds are constructed next to a path and near a flight of steps, use railroad ties rather than logs, especially when the peat needs to be hemmed in.

Consider planting trees on either side of narrow, informal steps set in a steep bank. This will create a light canopy of branches and leaves. Grass steps look good in informal and semiformal gardens. Log steps with grass forming the treads are also informal, but they are not all-weather surfaces. For long flights of steps, a strimmer is essential for cutting the grass, whereas in small areas a pair of hedging shears is sufficient. Semiformal grass steps use bricks at the edges of the treads, with grass behind them.

Formal steps

Large, wide flights of steps, especially those with wide areas at the top and base, make dominant features. Narrow steps can also be attractive in small gardens, especially when built with unusual materials. Bricks with a chamfered edge can be used as part of the tread, with other bricks as the risers.

▲ *A flight of garden steps, especially when constructed from attractive natural materials, creates a pleasing feature.*

Steps with a semicircular design and a full circle of bricks at the top, are very attractive and always capture attention. The inner parts of the treads can be formed using colored gravels, bricks or grass. Semicircular steps work well as a link between patio or terrace and grass lawn, and between different levels of

grass, but do not attempt to form large flights of these steps; usually, three steps on a slight slope is sufficient.

▼ *Wrought-iron spiral staircases create unusual features, either in basement gardens or, when shortened, as steps to a different level.*

RECYCLING SPIRAL STAIRCASES

Old spiral staircases are very decorative and can be used in basement gardens as a feature. They look good when cloaked in small-leaved *Hedera* (ivy), with supporting pots and small hanging baskets.

shady patios

We owe the term "patio" to the Spanish, who used it to describe an inner courtyard, surrounded by a dwelling and open to the sky. Patios are an integral part of the house, providing shade and shelter throughout the day, and they were traditionally planted with leafy plants and colorful flowers.

◀ *A secluded patio, shaded from strong sunlight, is an oasis of calm. Tables and benches are essential for outdoor living.*

Publicizing patios

The concept of patios spread from Spain to the southern United States and then westward to California, where they were ideally suited to the climate. Later, the term migrated to the temperate regions of Europe, where it is often now used instead of the word terrace.

The L-shaped patio

Many houses have an L-shaped area outside a rear entrance, and it can be partly enclosed by a fence. An alternative is to use a free-standing trellis, erected about 18in/45cm from the boundary, and with one end forming an L-shape, to create an even more cloistered area. To make an evergreen screen of foliage, erect a trellis and plant a large-leaved variegated ivy such as *Hedera colchica* 'Sulphur Heart' or *H. c.* 'Dentata Variegata'. Both have variegated leaves. For summer foliage the herbaceous climber *Humulus lupulus* 'Aureus' (Hops) creates a handsome screen of leaves. Where a flowering screen is desired, plant *Clematis montana*.

Surfacing patios

An attractive, well-drained surface is essential. It need not be consistent across the entire patio because you can leave spaces for shrubs and small trees. Other areas can be laid with cobbles, with large containers standing on top.

Paving slabs with raised patterns, brick-like slabs positioned together to create a pattern, and granite setts can all be used, but do avoid smooth, highly colored and checkerboard surfaces.

Healing nature

Part of the enchantment of a patio is the opportunity to have cool, refreshing water splashing from a fountain into a central pond. Repetitive but irregular gentle sound has a therapeutic effect that helps to reduce stress. Also, an enclosed

patio stops the scent of plants from being blown away. *Helichrysum serotinum* (curry plant) may well trigger memories of a visit to Asia, while the unforgettable perfume of lilac may conjure up thoughts of a wedding bouquet. Many fragrances are more personal. A mistress

of the novelist H. G. Wells claimed that his body emitted a honey-like fragrance. She could have recaptured this with the honey-scented bulbs *Crocus chrysanthus* or *Iris danfordiae*. Both can be grown beside paths and also in containers such as pots and window boxes.

▶ *An ornamental pond has calming, therapeutic qualities which help to reduce stress, making it a perfect feature for a patio.*

sunny terraces

A terrace is an open and usually paved area connecting a house with its garden. It usually has a balustrade or a low wall, especially if raised above the level of the garden. Many houses and bungalows have a flat, all-weather surface like a terrace at the back which may be used to create an outdoor leisure area.

Ancient heritage

Terraced landscapes with superb views were known in Thebes, Egypt, in about 1500 BCE. This style of gardening progressed westward to Italy, where terraces were created as status and power symbols, while giving views over the surrounding countryside. During the Middle Ages the viewing equivalent of a terrace was constructed on castle walls, while in 13th-century Spain the gardens on the hill slopes of the Alhambra had similar constructions. The English landscape designer Humphry Repton (1752–1818) was very keen on terracing, and in 18th-century England a variation known as the terrace walk became popular, with a surface of grass rather than paving. Such terraces were often long and especially sited to give views of the surrounding landscape. Grassed terraces were either straight or gently curved.

Versatile terraces

Most paved areas in temperate climates are terraces. They are usually adjacent to a house, open to the sky and, where possible, positioned to gain the maximum sun (unlike patios, which are features of hot countries where shade is essential). The surface of terraces varies from natural stone paving, ideal for areas around cottages, to paving slabs that suit modern demands. Natural stone paving can be made even more informal by planting prostrate plants between the irregular-sized slabs. For formal terraces that dominate a garden, choose brightly colored, smooth-surfaced slabs perhaps laid in a checkerboard fashion. For other formal areas where plants are cherished as much as they are on the patio, use less dramatically colored slabs, perhaps with a ribbed surface.

Large terraces are still sometimes built and include raised beds. Plant them

◀ *South-facing terraces bask in sun through the summer. A garden pond with a fountain give eye-catching movement and cool the air on hot days.*

with shrubs and small trees to provide some shade. Tubs, ornamental stone sinks, pots, window boxes, and troughs are other worthwhile features.

Balustrades and walls

In Classical times, terraces had carved stone balustrades. Today, these can be superb features around the edge of a terrace, giving it a hint of Classical style. This type of feature is most appropriate for more formal architecture. Balustrades in this style are totally unsuited to a modern, brightly colored area, for which a wall partly formed of screen blocks with a concrete capping is much more

appropriate. Bear in mind that safety is a priority along the edge of a terrace on a steep slope, especially when young children are likely to use the area. A wall about 2½ft/75cm high is essential.

Wooden balustrades are seldom seen, although a form of ranch-style fencing about 2½ft/75cm high suits terraces surfaced with brightly colored, smooth-surfaced paving slabs. They can be painted white, and built even higher if privacy from prying eyes is an important consideration.

▲ Where sunlight is strong throughout summer, attach canopies to the top of patio windows. Insure that they can be taken down in the fall.

▼ All-weather surfaces for terraces are essential. They should slope away from the house a little so torrential rain can drain away.

courtyards

Courtyards have a history that extends back more than 1,000 years. They have long been a key functional area in forts and castles, and they were built into the palaces of the Moslem rulers of Arabia, North Africa, and Spain, where they provided pleasant relief from the heat of the sun.

Shady and secluded

Today, courtyards in town gardens are usually small, secluded and protected from strong wind, although where gates are on the north side there is a risk of cold winter winds searing the foliage of evergreen plants. Courtyards always have shady areas but this need not be a problem as many plants, including ferns, grow in shade and moist soil (see pages 324–325). You can also grow almost anything, from small trees to bulbs in containers placed to catch the sun.

Seclusion and shade appeal to many gardeners, especially in towns where privacy is hard to find. Shade from strong sun is welcome during the day, but in the late evening the gloom may make the area too dark to use. One solution is to have spotlights and concealed lighting fitted by a qualified electrician.

Basement apartments sometimes have cloistered areas. These can be

treated as courtyards, and decorated with plants in containers. If they have stone steps connecting them with ground level, these can be made more attractive by planting trailing plants such as variegated forms of *Vinca minor* (lesser periwinkle), beside them. Plant it toward the top of the steps, so it can trail freely downward. The prostrate *Lysimachia nummularia* (creeping jenny) will also brighten the edges of steps, and grows

well in partial shade. For extra color choose the form 'Aurea' with yellow leaves. However, this variety does not thrive in deep shade.

Flooring a courtyard

A wide variety of paving materials is suitable for terraces. Large, aged, well-worn flagstones are ideal, but they can be difficult to obtain and are usually expensive. Alternatives are brick pavers,

▶ *Courtyards have a secluded and often partly shaded nature. Use plants in pots and tubs and select those that thrive in shaded areas.*

granite setts, and reconstituted flagstones. Cobbles are another possibility but they are difficult to walk on.

Furniture and gates for courtyards

Wrought-iron or aluminum furniture with an aged, ornate appearance suits a cloistered, shady courtyard. Besides harmonizing with the walls, nonferrous metal furniture does not deteriorate, although it is usually necessary to scrub off lichen and moss in spring. Wooden

furniture, such as conjoined benches and tables, are always much in demand. In late fall stand each leg on a brick, and cover the entire table with a plastic sheet tied down securely to protect it from winter weather. Collapsible, slatted furniture has the advantage that it can be taken indoors and stored. Ornate wrought-iron gates make ideal entrances to courtyard gardens. They are not as dominant as wooden doors and allow the outside world to be seen at a glance.

▲ *Courtyards are not complete without furniture; wrought iron is ideal for these small areas because it takes up little space and can often be folded for storage.*

EARLY MOTELS

In the Near and Far East caravanserais, or caravansary, have been known for many centuries. These were caravan hostels for merchants and travelers built around a large courtyard. They provided a secure and peaceful temporary resting place.

pergolas, arches, and trellises

Structures like pergolas were known in warm countries from the earliest times. In Egypt they were probably used to support vines and create shade. The Italians took up the idea and came up with the term "pergola," meaning an arbor, bower, or a walk of bowers covered mainly with vines.

Pergolas for all places

Pergolas can be informal, formal, or even oriental. Those constructed from rustic poles, often astride paths, are ideal for giving support to leafy climbers such as *Vitis vinifera*. The leaf shapes look more informal than the leaves of the ordinary vine. If an informal flowering and highly fragrant climber is desired, choose *Lonicera periclymenum* 'Belgica' (early Dutch honeysuckle) or *L. p.* 'Serotina' (late Dutch honeysuckle). *Lonicera japonica* (Japanese honeysuckle) also has a free-flowing show of flowers.

Formal pergolas formed of planed timber, with square-cut uprights and crossbeams, make ideal supports for wisteria. Although wisteria can be grown against a house wall, it is better where the large bunches of flowers can hang freely. It is a vigorous climber, so it soon drains the border soil around a house of any moisture, which can be detrimental to the house and to other plants growing alongside it.

An oriental look can be given to formal pergolas by cutting the underside edges and ends of the crossbeams at a sloping angle. Lean-to pergolas are another variation and can be made to look like an arbor if climbing plants are trained around uprights and crossbeams. Proprietary brackets are available for securing the crossbeams to a wall, with wooden uprights on the other side.

◄ *Most pergolas are straight and straddle paths, but an alternative use is to enclose a rounded area, perhaps devoted to growing bush roses.*

Arches

At their simplest, arches are just inverted hoops over a path covered in climbers, from roses to the leafy herbaceous climber *Humulus lupulus* 'Aureus' (Hops). However, the ingenuity of gardeners has resulted in arches of all shapes and sizes, including four-way arches at the junctions of paths.

Use arches to create height and focal points, as well as to grow climbers. Metal arches are increasingly used to grow roses over paths and as features on lawns, where, covered in leafy plants, they take on the role of an arbor. Indeed, metal and wooden arches against a wall or a fence will create an attractive and romantic arbor.

Trellises

Trellises were traditionally secured to walls, but are increasingly used as a free-standing feature to provide privacy and to create smaller areas, each with a different atmosphere. They are also ideal for screening garbage cans.

Rose enthusiasts welcome free-standing trellis as an opportunity to grow more climbers. At the end of a broad lawn erect a line of trellis panels, with shorter panels at right-angles to them. This produces features resembling stalls for horses. Pillar roses, where both climbing and rambling-type roses are grown up rustic poles or tripods of sawn timber, can be integrated into the display to create a variety of shapes.

▲ *Plants that reveal their flowers at eye-level create exciting gardens, with flowers and scent where they can be readily appreciated.*

▼ *Trellises attached to a wall make ideal homes for climbing roses, as well as for other climbers that require a supporting framework.*

arbors and tunnels

Arbors and tunnels come in all shapes and sizes, and are mainly admired for their romantic, cloistered leafiness. Arbors are usually smothered in flowering and leafy climbers, while tunnels often have flowering or fruiting trees trained over a wooden or a metal structure.

▲ *Laburnum trained over metal arches is awash with long, pendulous clusters of yellow flowers during late spring and early summer.*

Arbors for all gardens

There are arbors for all gardens. There are many suitable for small areas, where they fit into corners or alongside walls. Arbor units are increasingly sold either fully constructed or flat-packed, and are ready to erect, complete with a bench-style seat. Informal types are made of rustic poles, and formal ones of sawn timber. Some are made of wrought iron and have a delicate, aged look that suits roses and less vigorous climbers, such as *Clematis orientalis* (Oriental clematis), *C. tangutica* and *C. macropetala*.

An arbor in the center of a garden is a eye-catching feature. It needs a firm, paved base to provide an area for seats and chairs, and perhaps a small, low table. Some arbors are constructed on a base raised slightly above the surrounding area. This arrangement may suit a more formal garden. An informal arbor with a floor of natural stone paving, may look better if level with the ground. Crazy paving has a semiformal appearance and is also most suitable for an arbor at ground level.

Tunnels

Tunnels are ideal for channeling people from one part of a garden to another, and if a sundial, an ornamental well or a seat is positioned at the far end of the tunnel, it creates an attractive focal point. A tunnel may have a decorative quality, especially when clothed in laburnum or climbing roses. Apples and pears may also be planted to clothe a series of metal hoops reminiscent of arches. Brambles were traditionally used to make fruiting tunnels. Nut walks were once also popular, but they did not rely for support on large wire hoops. Instead, the branches were pruned to form a kind of tunnel over a rustic path.

Do not make a tunnel long in a short garden, because its length will draw attention to the garden's lack of length. Because they are symmetrical, tunnels are often located in a central position. Where a garden is divided by a crosswise free-standing trellis, bisecting it with a tunnel divides the garden and leads the eye toward another part of it. Feature a herb garden at the end of a fruit tunnel. Alternatively, position a sundial or a seat as a focal point, with a circular gravel path around it with beds for the herbs.

▲ A wrought-iron framed gazebo is an open structure, perfect for climbing roses and for climbers with pendulous flowers.

▲ Cloistered corners, heavily canopied with leafy and flowering climbers, can become secluded and romantic areas in gardens.

◄ A small gazebo is a striking structure, especially when positioned on a firm surface and nestling among shrubs and border plants.

309

porches and entrances

Porches prevent rain saturating people on arrival at a door. Large and ornate porches are often built around a front door, while less decorative and more functional types are at the rear. Rustic or formal arches can also be secured to walls around doors.

Brightening porches

A bare area around a front door gives an impression of lack of imagination, or neglect, but when a porch or a structure like a porch is fitted, it brightens the house and garden, especially when covered in leafy plants or flowers. Where a permanent brick-built structure is not possible, an arch may serve. Some may be bought for home assembly. Fit rustic arches around cottage doors and formal styles for more modern houses. Where extra weather protection is needed, secure an unobtrusive piece of wood to the top, to form a flat roof or one with a pitch. This will eventually be covered by the climber. Always secure the arch to the wall and insure that the four posts are concreted into the ground, so that they remain firm. The weight of climbers can be deceptively heavy, and winter winds may loosen weak fixtures.

The insides of large porches can be decorated with hanging baskets with drip trays in their base, and a bright show of tender plants. In summer they can range from *Campanula isophylla* (Star of Bethlehem) to *Chlorophytum comosum* 'Variegatum' (spider plant) and tradescantias. And in summer, the outside can be festooned with hanging baskets

◀ *Climbing plants enrich the outsides of entrances, creating a warm and friendly ambience in the garden and the house.*

suspended from brackets. Take care not to put them where the basket will be knocked, or where water will drip on to plants below. At ground level, hardy plants in containers can be left outside all year. They include narrow conifers, clipped box, and half-standard bay trees planted in tubs.

Not only can flowers and leafy plants make a porch more attractive inside an out but they can keep it colorful through the year. If you have a built porch, secure pieces of narrow trellis to the wall on either side of the door. Position each piece about 9in/ 23cm from the outer edge of the porch and plant variegated evergreens or plants that flower at different times of year to cover them.

Brightening gates and entrances

Front gardens bordered by a hedge such as a common privet or yew can be given a fresh identity by training branches to form an arch over a path. The training takes several years and is best performed on a tall hedge. Where paths are long, consider a metal or a wooden arch over the path, positioned about two-thirds of the way along it. Climbing roses clustered over metal arches are suitable for formal and informal areas. Arches constructed from rustic poles are strictly for cottage gardens and are ideal for supporting honeysuckle or jasmine.

Where there is not room for an arch, one or two pillar roses on either side of a path will introduce height to a garden.

▲ Small porches make a useful and attractive shelter from wind and rain. Linking them with a boundary fence creates a unified feature.

▼ Wrought-iron gates and rustic entrances are especially attractive when roses or honeysuckle are trained over an arch.

creating your garden

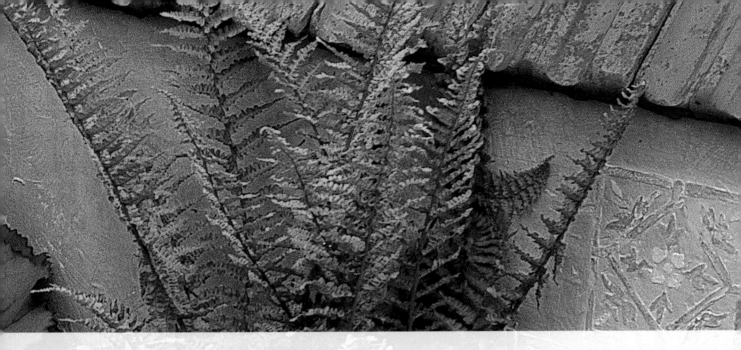

special conditions

Making the most of your garden means knowing how to pick the right plant for the right place. Some plants demand full sun, others need shade, and some can be grown in quite a few different settings. If you have a garden by the shore, for example, you will need to know which plants can survive and even thrive in wind and salt spray. And anyone with a slope will need handy hints on gardening in the apparently difficult conditions it brings. While these important aspects of your garden might be out of your control, there is much you can do to produce a creative show of plants in your garden.

living with your soil

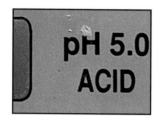

All gardeners want an ideal plot of land: one that is well drained, fertile, free from weeds and soil pests, retaining moisture in summer, with a slight southward slope to encourage rapid growth in spring, and sheltered from cold winds. Unfortunately, few gardens have all these qualities.

Assessing soil

In broad terms, soil is either light, medium, or heavy, and making an assessment is one of the first things you have to do when taking over a new garden. If the soil sticks to your boots in lumps, it contains clay. Other ways of assessing soil include holding a handful and rubbing some of it between thumb and forefinger. If it forms a smooth,

slippery, greasy surface, the soil contains clay, but if it remains gritty between your fingers it is predominantly sandy.

A more scientific assessment may be made by half-filling a screw-top jar with soil, then filling it three-fourths full with water. Shake the jar vigorously and allow one hour for it to settle. Stones will fall to the bottom, and coarse sand, light sand, silt, and clay will settle on top of them. Organic material floats on the surface. The proportions of these layers give a good idea of the soil's composition.

Improving clay soil

This mainly involves improving drainage and encouraging better aeration. If water remains on the surface, install land drains (see pages 348–349) and, during winter, dig in copious amounts of bulky material, like well-decomposed manure and garden compost. Small areas can be improved by adding horticultural sand,

but this is expensive in large gardens. Dust the surface of the soil in winter with hydrated lime or ground limestone to encourage clay particles to stick together, thereby improving drainage. However, do not add fertilizers at the same time, and always check the soil's acidity first to assess the quantity of lime

Improving sandy soil

Sandy soils are easy to cultivate, they warm up early in spring and do not become waterlogged. Unfortunately, because water rapidly drains through them, plants quickly become deprived of moisture and nutrients. Improve the soil

◄ *A simple method of assessing soil is by mixing soil and water together and allowing it to settle. Its composition can then be seen.*

CORRECTING ACIDITY

Soil	Hydrated lime	Ground limestone
Clay	18oz/sq yd 610g/sq m	24oz/sq yd 810g/sq m
Loam	12oz/sq yd 410g/sq m	16oz/sq yd 540g/sq m
Sand	6oz/sq yd 200g/sq m	8oz/sq yd 270g/sq m

by digging in quantities of manure and garden compost. Other moisture retention methods include maintaining a mulch 3in/7.5cm thick over the soil all summer through to impede evaporation, and installing water sprinklers

Judging a soil's acidity

The acidity or alkalinity of soil is measured on a pH scale, which ranges from 0–14 with 7.0 as neutral. Figures falling below 7.0 indicate increasing acidity, while those above signify greater alkalinity. The amount of lime needed to make soil less acid depends on its nature (see below), and the type of lime applied.

Assessing soil to see if it is acid or alkaline is quite easy using readily available lime-testing kits. You simply mix some of the soil with water and chemicals and check its resultant color against a color chart. Also available are pH-testing meters which are ideal for gardeners who are red/green color blind.

If your soil is alkaline, dig in plenty of garden compost or manure, and use acid fertilizers such as sulfate of ammonia. Alternatively, grow plants in neutral soil in raised beds, or plant only lime-loving plants. If your soil is acid, apply lime immediately after winter digging. The amount needed depends on the degree of acidity. The quantities indicated left are for every 1.0 pH. Aim for a pH of 6.5.

▶ *Add well-decomposed garden compost or manure to the soil just prior to digging in late fall or winter.*

assessing acidity or alkalinity

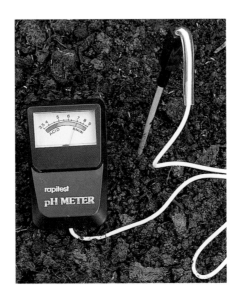

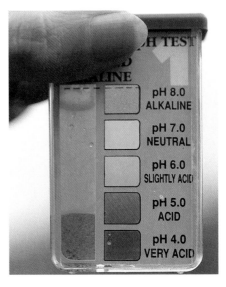

1 Testing the acidity or alkalinity of soil is easy with a pH–testing meter. This device is essential for gardeners who are red/green color blind. When not in use, store the meter in a dry cupboard.

2 Lime-testing kits, in which a soil sample is mixed with water and chemicals, are inexpensive and easy to use. Check the resultant color indicator against a color chart to identify the acid or alkaline levels.

the ups and downs of gardens

A level garden has many advantages, especially where easy-access paths are needed for wheelchairs and play areas for young children, but slopes do provide opportunities to create greater visual excitement and mystery. So do not be dismayed if your garden has a slope or steep banks.

Practical thoughts

Instead of working against nature and the natural contours of a garden, harness them to your advantage. Moving and leveling vast areas of soil is hard work and time consuming, even when machinery is hired. And there is always the risk of burying topsoil (the upper 1ft/30cm of earth, which is best for plant growth) underneath subsoil. Furthermore, when soil is dug up it initially increases in volume, and fitting it all into a new area may be a problem until it resettles. The natural drainage of the soil may also be destroyed.

MOVING SOIL UPHILL

Moving large quantities of soil uphill is tiring. Ease the problem by tying a rope to the front of the wheelbarrow so that it can also be pulled by a companion. And, where possible, lay down boards so that the wheel does not dig into the soil.

▶ *On steep slopes construct long flights of steps that cross the area, rather than going straight up, and create resting places at intervals.*

Paths on slopes

Where sloping ground has been terraced into separate areas, flights of steps are usually built to link them. In addition, try to incorporate a gently sloping path, perhaps as an inconspicuous side feature,

so that a wheelbarrow can be moved easily through the garden. Stepping stones may be laid in a grass path, but if you do a great deal of gardening, the grass will suffer. When laying paths on a particularly steep slope, make the surface

firm for winter and use a material that does not become slippery in wet weather. Instead of terracing an entire garden you can build an interesting feature by laying meandering paths around a slope, rather than directly over it. It is always essential to make firm foundations for all paths.

Steeply sloping banks

A grassy bank is a more economical alternative to a retaining wall. The slope of the bank should be no steeper than 45°. Use a small hover-type mower to trim the grass. Round off the top of the slope slightly to reduce the risk of the mower's blades scalping the grass. Use turf to form the surface because seed may be washed to the base of the slope before it germinates. In formal areas, separate these grassy slopes with a flight of paved or brick steps. In relaxed and informal areas a flight of log steps is cheaper and much quicker to install.

Retaining walls

Besides containing the soil and separating one level from another, retaining walls offer opportunities to grow rock-garden plants. A drystone wall may be covered in flowers, with bushy and bulbous plants along the top, and trailing plants ones lower down. Do not make the walls more than 4ft/1.2m high,

and fill the rear side with coarse drainage material to prevent the pressure of water pushing it over. Also install weep-holes every 4ft/1.2m along the base of the wall so that water can escape freely.

Another technique for preventing a retaining wall from falling over is to build it so it leans slightly backward. Make certain that its base is firm.

Sunken gardens

A sunken garden must be in a part of the garden that is low and well-drained. If it is low but badly drained you can install drains to channel the water to a nearby soakaway. This is particularly important if water from the rest of your garden, or from a neighbor's garden, soaks into the area. Most sunken gardens are fairly

formal, with a lawn surrounded by a dry-stone wall about 3ft/90cm high. Do not forget to incorporate access for a lawn mower into your sunken garden.

Constructing a retaining wall

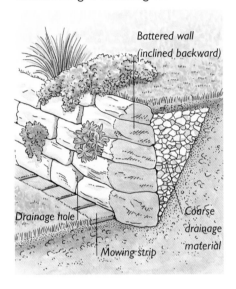

Battered wall (inclined backward)

Drainage hole

Mowing strip

Coarse drainage material

▼ Sunken gardens can be enhanced by installing garden ponds. However, insure that the area is well drained to prevent flooding and fish escaping.

Juniperis communis 'Compressa'

Slightly raised ponds

Aubrieta deltoidea (aubretia)

Aubrieta deltoidea (aubretia)

319

shapely gardens

Whatever the shape of a plot of land—long, narrow, wide, square or even triangular—it can make an attractive garden. Indeed, areas that at first sight appear to have impossible shapes often produce the most interesting gardens.

Shaping up

A garden can be as formal or informal as you want, no matter what its shape. For a relaxed atmosphere, consider a lawn with serpentine edges, with a spring-flowering cherry tree and paths that meander. If a formal design is wanted, the lawn might be square or rectangular, and surrounded by flower beds. Clearly, these are just two basic, contrasting examples, and we will look at many more. Other important factors to bear in mind are that trees and shrubs, which form the main garden structure, will eventually mature and may need to be thinned or removed, while the needs of a family usually progress from grassed areas for children to more elaborate, intricate features.

Creating privacy

As the gardens of newly built houses become smaller, privacy is increasingly difficult to achieve. The problem is that when houses are built close together, the upstairs windows will overlook the gardens. Free-standing trellises drenched with roses and other climbers, tunnels of fruit trees and laburnum, pergolas covered by wisterias, and hedges can all be used to screen your garden. Gazebos also lend privacy.

◀ *Scree beds can be fitted into most gardens but well-drained soil is essential. Add a few small conifers to create height and color.*

Positioning a summerhouse with its back to a boundary wall or a fence and its windows looking out over the garden, is another good way to create privacy, especially if a pergola is linked to it.

Long, narrow gardens

These are typically town gardens and provide an opportunity to create a series of small, individual areas, each linked but separate. Evergreen hedges can be grown using dark green *Taxus baccata* (English yew), or bright green Monterey cypress, (*Cupressus macrocarpa*) creating year-round seclusion and privacy, and parts of them can be trained and clipped to form arches. Free-standing trellises and arches make an excellent support for climbing

CHANGES IN SHAPE

Depending on where you stand, the shape of a circular pond appears to change. When seen from a bedroom window at a short distance, a round pond looks circular. But at ground level, and seen from a distance, it appears to be a more interesting oval shape.

roses and other deciduous climbers, which also create summer privacy. And the bright yellow leaved herbaceous climber *Humulus lupulus* 'Aureus' (Hops) gives a superb summer display. Unless a central vista to the end of the garden is desired—and only then if a feature such as a statue can be seen clearly through several arches—change the position of the path within each area. This also adds variety to the garden.

Short and wide shapes

These need careful design to avoid making the area look exceptionally wide in relation to its depth. The absence of a focal point will confuse the eye. Use a decorative screen so that a central or off-central area meets the eye. Other features should not be so immediately apparent.

Pergolas and trellises give essential privacy from nearby houses overlooking a small garden. In a more open situation, consider installing a sundial or an armillary sphere on a low plinth, encircled by a lawn and rose beds. A summerhouse may also be placed to create a central background feature, with a lawn in front for children to play on.

A freestanding trellis with square or diamond patterning makes a formal screen and can be erected quickly. A rustic pergola entwined with honeysuckle is best in a rural garden. *Clematis montana* is a climber for formal and informal trellis.

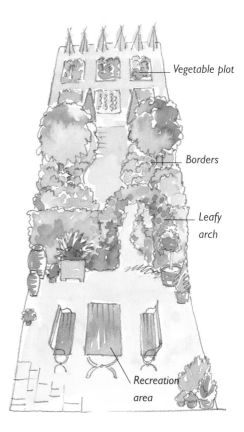

▶ *Design the garden so that it cannot be seen at a single glance. Hedges and leafy screens are decorative ways to separate garden areas.*

▼ *Securely constructed arches clothed in leafy climbers help to separate parts of the garden without segregating them completely.*

gardening in full sun

Many plants, including hardy annuals, herbaceous perennials, and shrubs, grow well in strong sunlight. Unfortunately, hot sunshine inevitably means dry soil, but this is not an unsurmountable problem. A surprisingly large number of plants grow in these conditions.

Living with dry, hot soils

Full sun invariably means dry, impoverished soil unless provisions are made to improve it. These include digging in plenty of well-decayed garden compost or manure to increase the soil's ability to retain moisture. Also, watering the soil thoroughly and then adding a mulch 3in/7.5cm thick mulch improves moisture retention and keeps the soil cool. In a rock garden or on a scree bed, a mulch of pea gravel or stone chippings will keep the soil cool and moist.

Hardy annuals for full sun

A few hardy annuals grow well in sun or partial shade, but some are especially at home in full sun. Adding well-decayed garden compost or manure to the soil in winter, followed by regular watering through the summer, are aids to success, particularly in hot, dry places. Sun-loving hardy annuals include the following:

▶ Achillea *(yarrow) flourishes in strong sunlight and contrasts well with hollyhock, a hardy perennial usually grown as a biennial.*

- *Agrostemma githago* 'Milas' (corn-cockle)
- *Argemone mexicana* (prickly poppy)
- *Asperula orientalis* (woodruff)
- *Calendula officinalis* (pot marigold)
- *Carthamus tinctorius* (safflower)
- *Centaurea cyanus* (cornflower)
- *Eschscholzia californica* (California poppy)
- *Godetia amoena* (satin flower)
- *Gypsophila elegans* (baby's breath)
- *Helichrysum bracteatum* (strawflower)
- *Iberis amara* (rocket candytuft)
- *Limnanthes douglasii* (poached-egg flower)
- *Malope trifida* (annual mallow)
- *Nicandra physaloides* (shoo-fly)
- *Nigella damascena* (love-in-a-mist)
- *Phacelia campanularia* (California bluebell)
- *Scabiosa atropurpurea* (pincushion flower)

Herbaceous plants for sunny borders

Because herbaceous perennials produce fresh leaves, stems, and flowers each year, they need to grow rapidly and without restriction from spring to fall. Many plants native to the Mediterranean region can survive in full sun with dry soil, especially those with silver leaves. Herbaceous perennials that survive in full sun and dry soil include

- *Achillea millefolium* (yarrow)
- *Alstroemeria ligtu* 'Hybrids' (Peruvian lily)
- *Anaphalis margaritacea* (pearly everlasting)
- *Asphodeline lutea*
- *Baptisia australis* (plains false indigo)
- *Buphthalmum salicifolium*
- *Catananche caerulea* (Cupid's dart)
- *Centaurea macrocephala*
- *Echinops ritro* (small globe thistle)
- *Eryngium* (sea holly)
- *Gypsophila paniculata* (baby's breath)
- *Heliopsis helianthoides scabra*
- *Limonium latifolium* (sea lavender)
- *Nepeta* × *faassenii* (catmint)
- *Solidago* (goldenrod)
- *Stachys byzantina* (lamb's ears).

Shrubs for dry, sunny borders

Thorough soil preparation is essential before planting shrubs for dry, sunny border. First-rate shrubs for full sun and dry soil include:

- *Artemisia abrotanum* (lad's love, southernwood)
- *Artemisia absinthium* (common wormwood)

▲ Achillea *is an ideal herbaceous perennial for growing in a dry, sunny border. Its flowers are perfect for cutting and displaying indoors.*

- *Brachyglottis* 'Sunshine' (better known as *Senecio* 'Sunshine')
- *Buddleja davidii* (butterfly bush)
- *Caryopteris* × *clandonensis*
- *Ceratostigma willmottianum* (Chinese plumbago)

CONTAINER GARDENING

Container gardening is popular in hot, sunny countries and a wide range of sun-loving plants can be grown in pots, tubs, and window boxes. If pots and tubs are put in groups, perhaps to one side of a patio, they can be watered more easily. Grouping containers in this way also helps keep them cooler than they would be if positioned separately. If pots and tubs at the back are difficult to reach for watering, tie a stiff bamboo cane, 4ft/1.2m long to the end length of hose pipe so that you can hold it out.

- *Choisya ternata* (Mexican orange blossom)
- *Cistus* (rock rose)
- *Cytisus* × *praecox* 'Warminster' (Warminster broom)
- *Genista aetnensis* (Mount Etna broom)
- *Hebe speciosa* (shrubby veronica)
- *Helichrysum serotinum* (curry plant)
- *Kolkwitzia amabilis* (Beauty bush)
- *Lavandula angustifolia* (lavender)
- *Lavatera* 'Rosea' (tree mallow)
- *Romneya coulteri* (tree poppy)
- *Rosmarinus officinalis* (rosemary)
- *Salvia officinalis* (common sage)—several colored leaf forms
- *Spartium junceum* (Spanish broom)

gardening in shade

Most gardens have a shady area, perhaps beside a house, a large tree, a fence or a hedge. Such places can be a problem, but they also create opportunities to grow a wider range of plants. In fact, once established, many plants grow in shade, in dry and moist soil.

Getting plants established

Plants in dry, shady areas are more difficult to establish than those in moisture-retentive soil. Dig dry areas thoroughly and mix in plenty of well-decayed garden compost or manure.

▲ *Many leafy plants thrive in shade. In this moist area, Fatsia japonica forms a perfect corner feature in a border and alongside a path.*

If the soil is impoverished, perhaps under trees or around the bases of shrubs, it will need a dusting of fertilizer. However, take care not to boost the growth of existing plants. Instead, add bonemeal to the planting hole, and a couple of times during the first year fork in a general fertilizer around the stem. Whatever happens, water plants regularly until they are established. Also lay a mulch, 3in/ 7.5cm thick around plants every spring. In moist, shady areas make sure that the soil is adequately drained by adding horticultural sand. The danger is that the plant roots may rot and die.

Plants for dry shade

Many highly attractive shrubs are sufficiently resilient to survive these conditions, and they include *Mahonia aquifolium* (Oregon grapeholly), which has leathery, glossy green leaves and fragrant, rich yellow flowers in spring. *Ruscus aculeatus* (butcher's broom) is another tough shrub. *Symphoricarpos* (snowberry) and osmanthus are other suitable shrubs. Good herbaceous

perennials include *Anaphalis margaritacea*, with gray-green leaves and pearly white flowers in late summer. Its near relative, *Anaphalis triplinervis*, also grows in dry shade. For a taller and more dominant display, plant *Crambe cordifolia* (colewort), which grows 5–6ft/1.5–1.8m high. It has branching stems with white flowers in early summer. Epimediums grow about 12in/30cm high and will cover the soil with colorful leaves and flowers. *Persicaria affinis* (still better known as *Polygonum affine*) also makes good ground cover.

Plants for moist shade

Several shrubs flourish in moist soil and shade, including camellias, whose blooms herald the approach of spring, *Elaeagnus angustifolia*, *Gaultheria shallon*, *Gaultheria procumbens* and *Fatsia japonica*, with its distinctively large, glossy green leaves. Herbaceous perennials include *Aruncus dioicus* (goatsbeard), *Brunnera macrophylla*, *Cimicifuga racemosa* (bugbane), the popular hostas, *Lysimachia nummularia* (creeping Jenny), *Pulmonaria angustifolia* (lungwort) and *Rodgersia pinnata*.

Climbers and shrubs for a shady wall

It is inevitable that one side of a wall will be in shade. Fortunately, there are climbers that grow well, even on the northern, less congenial side of a wall.

Garrya elliptica is an evergreen wall shrub that grows on both sunny and shady sides of walls, but it flowers best on the brighter side. *Hydrangea anomala petiolaris* (climbing hydrangea) is a vigorous climber that does well on a north or north-east wall. Its creamy white flowers appear during early summer. *Jasminum nudiflorum* (winter jasmine) also grows well on an almost sunless, north-facing wall, and produces yellow flowers during winter. Several pyracanthas with attractive berries will grow against both sunny and shady walls.

Shade-loving ferns

Most ferns grow in shade, in damp soil although some will thrive in dry areas that are fully shaded. Visit a specialist nursery and you will find a wide range of plants that are easy to grow and make a very useful addition to the shaded border. Ferns for moisture-retentive soil include *Asplenium scolopendrium* (hart's-tongue fern) (also known as *Phyllitis scolopendrium* or *Scolopendrium vulgare*), *Matteuccia struthiopteris* (ostrich fern); *Onoclea sensibilis* (sensitive fern) and *Osmunda regalis* (royal fern). Ferns for dry soil, as well as modestly moist soil, include the widely grown *Dryopteris filix-mas* (male fern), *Athyrium filix-femina* (lady fern) and *Polypodium vulgare* (the wall polypody).

GROUND-COVER PLANTS IN SHADE

There are many suitable plants, but first take the opportunity to improve the soil (see pages 316–317). Plants include

- *Ajuga reptans* (bugleweed)
- *Alchemilla mollis* (lady's mantle)
- *Bergenia* (elephant's ears)
- *Epimedium* (barrenwort)
- *Hedera* (ivy)
- *Hypericum calycinum* (rose of sharon)
- *Lamium maculatum* (dead nettle)
- *Pachysandra terminalis*
- *Tellima grandiflora*
- *Tiarella cordifolia*
- *Vinca* (periwinkle)

▼ *Many ferns thrive in shade and moist soil, although some do well in dry soil. Here is a superb example of a fern with* **Fatsia japonica**.

coastal gardening

Strong winds and salt-laden sea spray that blows a long way inland are the two main problems encountered by gardeners on the coasts. Fortunately, many plants grow in these conditions, from conifers, shrubs, and herbaceous plants to bulbs and corms—with the help of a resilient boundary hedge.

Windbreaks and hedges

In small gardens you may have to rely on existing plants to reduce the wind's speed, but where a new boundary is possible, plant a windbreak formed by the conifer *Cupressus macrocarpa* (Monterey cypress). It eventually forms a hedge at least 30 ft/6m high. The hybrid × *Cupressocyparis leylandii* is sometimes recommended, but is far too vigorous for a small or even a medium-size garden. If you do grow it, be sure to clip it regularly.

Shrubs for coastal gardens

The range of shrubs tolerant of salt spray is remarkably large and includes the fast-growing hybrid *Elaeagnus × ebbingei*, which takes about 12 years to grow to a height of 10–15ft/3–4.5m. Its evergreen, silvery gray leaves form an all-year background for other plants. *Griselinia littoralis* is slower growing and ideal as a hedge or as a specimen shrub in a border. It is evergreen, with thick, lustrous, apple-green leaves, but is often seen in one of its variegated forms such as 'Dixon's Cream', with leaves splashed creamy white.

If you seek a hardy, deciduous shrub with the bonus of bright orange berries from fall to late winter, choose *Hippophae rhamnoides* (sea buckthorn). It can also be planted to create a hedge. The berries are shunned by birds. The New Zealand shrub *Olearia macrodonta* (daisy bush) is evergreen, with leaves like holly leaves and masses of small, white, daisy-like flowers during midsummer, but it is slightly tender and best grown in warm areas. *Olearia × haastii* is a hardier form for cooler gardens.

▲ *Many plants help to soften the edges of paths, including the soft and silver-leaved lamb's ears (Stachys byzantina).*

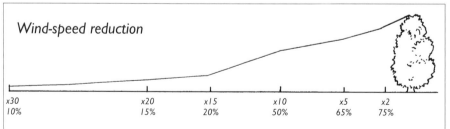

Wind-speed reduction

| x30 | x20 | x15 | x10 | x5 | x2 |
| 10% | 15% | 20% | 50% | 65% | 75% |

This simplified diagram shows how the benefit of a hedge or a windbreak can be felt up to a distance of 30 times the height of the hedge or shelter belt, although most of the protection is in the first one-third of this distance.

The hardy deciduous shrub *Tamarix tetrandra* (tamarisk) has an appealing wispy look. It grows 10–12ft/3–3.6m high. During late spring it bears bright pink flowers. Because it does not present a solid screen of foliage it often thrives close to the sea, but note that it dislikes chalky soil. If you need something to cover large areas, the suckering, thicket-forming, deciduous shrub *Symphoricarpos albus* (snowberry) has few rivals. It will soon cover a large bank, with the bonus of white berries from early fall to the first frosts. There are one or two superb varieties, including 'White Hedge'. If yellow flowers delight you, plant the deciduous shrub *Spartium junceum* (Spanish broom). Its rush-like green stems make it look evergreen, but it is the tiny bright yellow, fragrant flowers which bloom from early to late summer that have most appeal.

Pittosporum tenuifolium is not fully hardy in temperate climates but it is ideal if you want to create a hedge in a mild

coastal garden. It is known for its pale-green leaves with wavy edges, which are borne on almost black stems.

Herbaceous perennials for coastal areas

Once a wind-filtering hedge has been established, many herbaceous plants survive in coastal gardens. The wide range includes plants with attractive flowers, such as *Aster amellus* (Italian aster) and kniphofia hybrids (red-hot poker), and plants with attractive foliage. These include *Stachys byzantina* (lamb's ears) with silver-gray leaves. Other choice herbaceous perennials include:

• *Anemone × hybrida*
• *Centaurea macrocephala*
• *Crambe cordifolia*
• *Cynara scolymus* (globe artichoke)
• *Dierama pulcherrimum* (angel's fishing rod)
• *Eryngium alpinum* (alpine sea holly)
• *Eryngium varifolium* (Moroccan sea holly)
• *Kniphofia* hybrids
• *Phlomis russeliana*
• *Salvia superba*
• *Sedum spectabile*
• *Veronica spicata*.

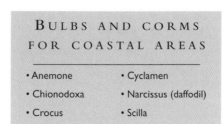

▲ Screens formed of laths nailed to a supporting framework will make an artificial windbreak while plants are established.

BULBS AND CORMS FOR COASTAL AREAS

• Anemone	• Cyclamen
• Chionodoxa	• Narcissus (daffodil)
• Crocus	• Scilla

▲ Kniphofias (red-hot pokers) are ideal herbaceous perennials for planting in coastal areas. There are many hybrids to choose from.

constructing paths, steps, and trellises

Many garden features, including paths, steps, and wall and freestanding trellises, can be constructed easily. The following pages explain how to lay paths made from many different materials, from paving slabs laid on mortar, which look best in formal gardens, to more versatile and less formal crazy paving, and gravel paths, which need side restraints to confine the gravel. They show how to build steps, from easy-to-construct log steps to paved steps for formal gardens, and erect trellises.

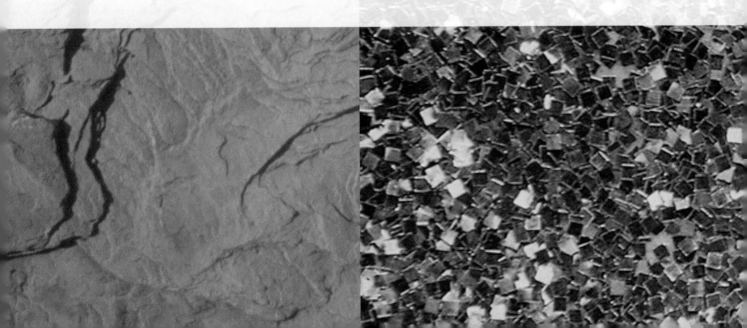

laying gravel paths and drives

Gravel paths and drives have an informal nature that blends with many plants and gardening styles. They are quick and relatively inexpensive to construct, and also act as a good alarm system—you can hear anyone coming by the crunch of their feet.

Basic construction

Paths and small drives are best made with ¼in/6mm pea gravel. Larger gravel is better suited to drives because it is less likely to spread sideways, and is not so easily picked up on shoes or scattered by the tires of automobiles.

Pea gravel and larger gravel settle in time, so be prepared after a few years to top up with another load. Weeds can be a problem, although weedkillers can be used. Do not use sodium chlorate if there are plants growing nearby because when the soil is constantly wet there is a risk that the sodium will spread through the soil and kill them. Instead, use a specific, non-residual path-clearing weedkiller.

Constructing a path

You will need to edge the path with a restraint to hold and contain the gravel. In rustic areas you can use stout logs pegged into the soil, while straight paths in formal settings need concrete or wood edgings. Use concrete edging slabs 3ft/90cm long, 6in/15cm deep, and 1¾in/42mm thick, and with rounded

tops. Alternative, you can use rough-cut planks, 6ft/1.8m long, 6in/15cm deep and 1in/2.5cm thick, coated with a wood preservative.

Dig out the line of the path, 3–4ft/90cm–1.2m wide and 6in/15cm deep. Place topsoil on shrub borders, but dispose of the subsoil. Put the side edging restraints in place and check that their tops are slightly above the level of the surrounding soil or grass. Use a level to check that the parallel edging is level. Then cement the concrete edging into place, or use stout wooden pegs to secure the wood. Line the base with clean rubble, to about 3in/7.5cm below the tops of the side restraints, and top up with pea gravel to about 1in/2.5cm below the rim.

Constructing a gravel drive

Check that the area drains freely (see pages 348–349) and, if necessary, install drains. Mark out the area of the drive by using a garden hose and view it from all angles to make sure that it is right. Dig out the area to about 8in/20cm deep,

removing perennial weed roots. The depth of the base depends on the weight and usage. If it is a standing area, a depth of 6in/15cm is sufficient.

Strong side restraints will prevent the gravel spreading. Concrete in place a row of bricks, with their tops about ¾in/18mm above the surface of the gravel. Bricks with one side beveled will cause least damage to car tires.

Fill the base with a 3in/7.5cm thick layer of clean, compacted rubble, then top up with gravel.

▶ *Gravel paths can be made more interesting with an attractive pattern of all-weather bricks or paving slabs. Lay these on concrete pads.*

laying a shingle path

1 Dig out the area of the path 3–4ft/ 90cm–1.2m wide and 6in/15cm deep. Place topsoil on shrub borders, but dispose of heavy, sticky clay. Make certain that all perennial weeds are dug out.

2 Install strong side restraints formed of concrete edging slabs 3ft/90cm long, and cement them into place. Alternatively, install strong planks of wood, each about 6ft/1.8m long.

3 Spread clean rubble over the base to 3in/7.5cm below the top of the side restraints. If all perennial weeds have been removed, add gravel immediately. If weeds remain, use a water-permeable membrane.

4 Spread gravel to within 1in/2.5cm of the top of the side restraints, smoothing to even the surface. Gravel will settle eventually, so be prepared to add more later.

laying paving slabs

Paving slabs can be used to create all-weather, firm-surface paths as well as patios. They are widely available, and look good on their own or when attractively combined with bricks and pebbles. Have a look at neighboring gardens for design ideas.

Wide range of slabs

Precast paving slabs are available in a wide range of colors, textures, shapes and sizes. Their thickness may also vary, but is usually 1¾–2in/42–50mm. While the most common size is 18in/45cm square, quarter- and half-sizes are available. Other sizes include 24in/60cm square and 30in/75cm long and 24in/60cm wide, but these are difficult for one

▲ *Paving slabs make all-weather surfaces for patios and terraces, helping to create a practical and attractive outdoor living area.*

person to handle. Hexagonal slabs are also available. Note that riven surfaces produce slipproof areas, and that smooth, brightly colored slabs may be used for formal paved areas, perhaps around a pool, but not in informal settings.

If the slabs arrive weeks before you can lay them, do not leave them in a pile. Instead, position two stout boards about 12in/30cm apart on a firm, level surface and at a rightangle to a wall. Position a slab near the wall, leaning against it, and place a piece of wood between the slab and the wall. Continue, with the other slabs, standing each one on its edge.

Laying a path

Use a garden line to mark out the width and length of the path. Its width should blend with the garden. A path that is too narrow in a wide garden will look like a ribbon. The path needs to be broad enough for two people to walk side by side, but ideally, there should be room for a wheelchair with someone walking alongside it. A path should also be an attractive, eye-catching feature.

Laying a patio

The preparation for laying a patio is exactly the same as for a path, but on a larger scale. Checking that it is absolutely level is vital. Where a patio adjoins a building it is essential that its surface is at least 6in/15cm below the damp course; this is usually seen as a continuous line of moisture-proof membrane or slate. If this is not possible, leave a 4in/10cm-wide and 6in/15cm-deep space between the slabs and the building and fill the gap with pea gravel to allow drainage.

CHECK LEVELS

Where levels need to be checked over a long distance, use a hose pipe filled with water and with a piece of clear plastic tubing inserted in each end. On each piece of plastic tubing, make a mark 3in/7.5cm from the end. Tie one end of the hose pipe to a stout stick, positioning the mark on the plastic at the desired level. Check that the level of water in the hose pipe reaches the marks on the plastic. The unsecured end can then be moved down the garden to check the levels.

laying paving slabs

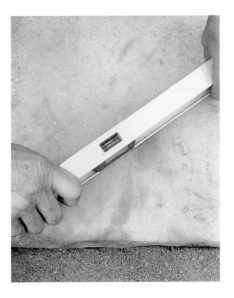

1 Make a 4in/10cm thick base of compacted clean rubble, then spread a layer of horticultural sand 2in/5cm thick. Use a garden rake to spread it evenly to create a firm, level surface.

2 Use the five-blob method to lay each slab: one in each corner and one in the center. This enables easy leveling of the slab and is a good way for beginners to lay slabs. Always wear gloves when cementing.

3 Check that each slab is level by using a level on one of its narrow edges. Next, check carefully that each slab is level with its neighbors by laying a level across each pair of paving slabs.

4 Carefully fill the gaps between slabs, using a stiff, dry mortar mix. Avoid spreading the mortar all over the slabs and clean off any loose mortar immediately as it stains permanently.

▲ *A strong, firm base is essential for all leisure surfaces, especially where edges overlap water features.*

laying crazy paving

Crazy paving paths, drives, and patios are traditionally formed from broken paving slabs, usually with a smooth surface and plain coloring. Increasingly, however, pieces of colored paving are being added to make the surface brighter and more attractive.

Constructing a crazy paving path

Side restraints are essential to prevent horticultural sand at the base from spilling out. Use wood 6in/15cm wide, 6ft/1.8m long and ¾in/18mm thick, and thinner flexible wood for a serpentine outline.

▲ *Crazy paving is a good material for where a twisting path is needed or where the contours of the ground vary in several directions.*

Begin by securing the side restraints with supporting pegs on the outer edge; this allows the edging to be removed at a later date, should a lawn abut the path. Spread out the crazy paving so that each piece can be seen clearly. Pieces with straight edges should be positioned along the sides. Then dig out the area of the path to about 6in/15cm deep, and install a compact layer of clean rubble 2in/25cm thick. Spread a similar thickness of horticultural sand over this, and rake it level, then lay an ¾in/18mm-thick layer of mortar over it. It is best to tackle long paths in several sections, each about 6ft/1.8m long. This insures that the mortar does not dry before each piece of crazy paving is laid on top.

Place the large, straight-edged pieces of crazy paving along the sides. Fill the gaps between them with smaller pieces, fitting them in like a jigsaw. It is essential that the surface is level, even though it may slope in several directions. Each piece of crazy paving must be laid on a firm bed of mortar. When the path is complete, fill any gaps between the

pieces of paving with mortar, taking care not to smear it on the surface of the slab. Work it between the slabs until level with the surface, but with the center slightly lower to allow rain to drain away freely.

Laying a natural stone path

Of all surfacing materials, natural stone paving creates the most informal effect, especially when plants are grown between the slabs. If natural stone is too expensive. use reconstituted stone. Because of its uneven thickness, natural stone paving is more difficult to lay than crazy paving and unless sawn (when it loses some of its charm) it has an irregular outline. Where plants are to be grown between them, the

---

A CRAZY PAVING DRIVEWAY

A slightly thicker base of compacted rubble to a depth of about 4in/10cm is needed for a driveway to allow for the weight of vehicles. Also, a base layer of concrete laid over the sand and compacted rubble is advisable if traffic is extra heavy. The crazy paving is laid on a bed of mortar on top of this.

laying crazy paving

1 Use strong side restraints (concrete slabs or wood) and dig out the area of the path to 6in/15cm deep. Lay clean rubble 2in/5cm thick, and firm it.

2 Spread a layer of horticultural sand, 2in/5cm thick over the rubble. Leave a 2in/5cm space between the top of the side-restraints and the sand.

3 Spread a layer of mortar over the sand and position large, straight-sided pieces of broken paving along the edges. Check that the edges are level.

slabs can be laid on a 2in/5cm-thick layer of horticultural sand placed directly on firm soil. Alternatively, if a more functional path is desired, it can be laid in a similar way to crazy paving.

When laying a decorative natural stone path, first use strings to mark the edges of the path, then remove soil to about 3in/7.5cm deep. Firm the base, then lay horticultural sand 2in/5cm thick. Each slab is bedded onto the sand to hold it firm, but for extra rigidity lay each slab on five blobs of mortar. Fill the cracks where plants are not being used.

▶ *The relaxed appearance of crazy-paving paths suits informal gardens. Position plants along the sides to cloak the edges*

4 Lay smaller pieces of broken paving in the center of the path and fill the gaps between the stones with mortar to just below the surface.

laying concrete pavers

Concrete pavers or paving blocks may be used to construct hardwearing surfaces for paths and drives. They are sometimes called flexible pavers, because they are laid on a bed of horticultural sand and, if necessary, they can be lifted and relaid. Their popularity has increased in recent years.

Range of pavers

Pavers come in a wide range of colors and textures. They are usually 8in/20cm long, 4in/10cm wide, and 2in/5cm thick, although some come in 1½–2⅓in thickness. The edges on the upper side of some pavers are beveled. While most are straight-edged, they differ from house bricks in that they do not have recesses on the face side. Some pavers have wavy edges. These are known as fishtails—each brick closely interlocks with its neighbors to produce an extremely strong surface.

Laying a path

Side restraints are essential to retain the foundations and pavers. Select the type of bond (see below), then form the pattern on a piece of flat ground and measure its width. This will indicate the distance between the two side restraints, which will be concrete, brick, or wood edgings. Dig out the path to the length and width you want it, and to a depth of 6in/15cm, then position the side restraints. Then lay clean, compacted rubble 3in/7.5 cm deep over the dug out area, and spread a layer of horticultural sand over the rubble. This layer should be the thickness of the paver less ⅜in/9mm below the top of the side restraints. This can be achieved by using a piece of wood 5in/13cm deep and a little wider than the path. Measure the

width of the path and cut the ends of the board so that its center, when scraped along the sand inside the restraints, leaves the surface of the sand at the right depth. Do not compress the sand at this stage.

The pavers can then be positioned on the sand in the desired pattern. Their surfaces will protrude slightly above the top of the side restraints, and to compact them use a motorized plate-compactor (also known as a plate vibrator), which can be hired, or a thick, flat piece of wood laid on the surface and repeatedly tapped with a club hammer. This hand method is usually adequate for laying a path. When the pavers have been laid, cover the surface of the path with dry horticultural sand and brush it over the entire area. This is best done several times. Finish by watering the surface lightly.

▲ *Brick paths have a cottage garden informality. Staggering the joints creates a stronger surface than if bricks are laid with joints aligned.*

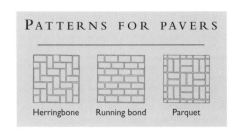

PATTERNS FOR PAVERS

Herringbone   Running bond   Parquet

Patterns for pavers

Pavers can be laid in several patterns, some of which are illustrated on page 336. Some patterns are complex and laying them requires expertise and skill, but the following are fairly simple to achieve:

❀ Running bond—easy to create and needs only a few half-pavers at the ends to complete the pattern (they can be cut with a hacksaw if a hydraulic stone splitter is not available). Bricks are laid lengthwise, with staggered joints.

❀ Cane-weave bond—creates an attractive surface, and is a pattern that does not require pavers to be cut. It is strong enough for paths, but not for drives. It is formed of rows of three parallel pavers with another paver positioned between and crossing them.

❀ Herringbone pattern—popular for paths and especially suitable for drives, since it forms a strong surface. It involves cutting a large number of pavers.

❀ Basketweave pattern—easy to lay, with two parallel bricks laid at a right-angles to two others. It is ideal for paths, but not for drives.

❀ Squared design—good for rectangular and square areas, for drives with light traffic, and for paths. Whole pavers are laid to form a square, with a half-brick in the center. This pattern requires a great deal of cutting, and a hydraulic stone splitter will be needed if you intend to pave a large area.

❀ Fishtail weave—forms a strong surface and is especially suitable for informal garden areas.

laying concrete pavers

1 Dig out the area of the path to 6in/15cm deep and install strong side restraints. Compact a layer of clean rubble 3in/7.5cm thick in the base. The rubble needs to be broken up evenly.

2 Spread horticultural sand loosely over the rubble, so that its surface is the same thickness as the paver less ⅜in/9mm below the top of the side restraints. Lay the pavers on top of the sand.

3 Compact the pavers by using a motorized plate-compactor (also known as a plate vibrator) or a thick piece of wood laid on the surface and hit with a club hammer repeatedly.

4 When the surface of the pavers is level with the side restraints, cover them with dry horticultural sand. Brush the sand over the surface. Repeat this once, and then water the entire area.

choosing and installing edgings

Edgings should be both functional and attractive, marking the edges of borders, lawns, paths, and drives, and harmonizing with their surroundings. Edgings range from corrugated plastic strips to bricks, concrete, and logs, and some are quickly installed while others need to be mortared in place.

Bricks and paving blocks

Frost-resistant bricks and concrete pavers create attractive edgings alongside flower beds and gravel drives and paths. They are placed upright and concreted into position, and because they are only 4in/ 10cm wide they can be used around curved as well as straight edges. Bricks make an informal edging if they are placed at an angle of 45°, with one brick leaning against another. Between half and one-third of each brick is buried in the soil, and this keeps the edging in position without any need for mortar.

Tiles

Glazed and unglazed tiles, usually 9in/23cm long and 6in/15cm deep make decorative edgings. Placed directly in the soil they do not need mortar.

Strips

These are varied, ranging from shaped concrete edging to plastic strips. Concrete edgings are usually 3ft/90cm long, 6in/ 15cm deep, and 1¾in/42mm thick, with rounded or crenated (notched) tops. They are ideal for edging straight gravel paths and drives, and must be concreted into place. Corrugated green plastic edging strips, bought in rolls and in several depths, are best used to edge borders. Their corrugated shape prevents the edges of lawns from being cut straight.

▲ *Log rolls create attractive edgings for informal borders. They are easily installed and can be bought in several heights.*

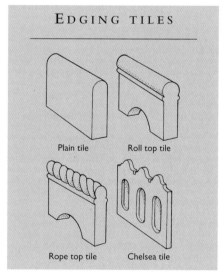

EDGING TILES

Plain tile

Roll top tile

Rope top tile

Chelsea tile

installing edging tiles

1 When installing an edging for a straight border, first stretch a garden line along the edge. Dig out a narrow trench 3–4in/7.5–10cm deep.

2 Position the tiles so that two-thirds will be buried when the job is complete. Check that each tile is upright and extends uniformly above the border.

3 Draw soil around the base of each tile and firm it to the level of the surrounding soil. Take care not to push the tiles out of line.

Wooden edgings

These range from log rolls, which blend with informal areas, to planks of wood, used to edge straight paths. To insure these planks have a long life, use a wood preservative.

Log rolls make an attractive edging especially for meandering paths in informal and rustic gardens. They are made by securing one-third to half-sections of logs to galvanized wires, They are available in 3½ft/1m lengths and in several heights, including 6in/15cm, 12in/30cm, and 18in/45cm. These rolls are installed very simply by inserting the log roll into a narrow trench to about half the depth of the edging, and firming the soil around it.

Whole logs make attractive edgings for straight and meandering paths in informal gardens. Select logs about 4in/10cm thick. Make a shallow depression at the side of the path to be edged, put the logs in position along it, and firm the soil. Secure the logs with wooden pegs.

GRAVEL GULLEYS

Gulleys, often seen around bowling greens, may be dug around a lawn and filled with pea gravel. A gulley 6–12in/15–30cm wide makes an attractive edge and improves a lawn's ability to drain freely. Where there is a risk of the lawn edge being trodden on and crumbling, install planks of wood with their surfaces level with the lawn. Then fill the gulley with pea gravel to within 2in/5cm of the lawn's surface.

▲ *Bricks placed at a shallow angle make attractive edging in an informal garden. They do not need to be cemented into position.*

constructing garden steps

Garden steps can be more than just a safe and convenient way of getting from one level to another. They should form attractive features, with proportions and style that unify them with the rest of the garden, and materials that harmonize with their surroundings.

The structure of steps

To be sure that steps are easy to walk on they must have the right proportions. Steps have their own technical vocabulary:

⚙ Base stone—the stone at the bottom of a flight of steps. It is essential where steps lead directly onto a lawn.

⚙ Flight—the complete run of steps.

⚙ Landing—an extra wide area of tread, often used as a resting area on a long flight of steps.

⚙ Overhang (also known as the "nosing") the distance by which the edge of a tread overhangs the riser. An overhang gives steps a professional appearance.

⚙ Riser—the distance between the tread on one step and the tread of the one above. Usually, 4–7in/10–18cm.

⚙ Tread—the surface which is walked on. A tread is usually 12–18in/30–45cm deep, with a slight slope from back to front so that water drains away freely.

⚙ Width of steps—for two people to use the steps side by side, steps need to be at least 4½ft/1.3m wide. For one person, 3ft/75cm is sufficient.

Types of steps

There is a wide range of styles to choose from for garden steps, from formal to rustic, and they may be made in many different materials.

⚙ Cut-in steps—built into slopes and made easily from paving slabs and bricks. The shape of the steps has to be cut in, allowing slightly more depth for strong foundations. The paving slabs form the treads, with bricks as the risers.

⚙ Free-standing steps—required where a bank is almost vertical, and the steps are built on a level surface but with the top step abutting and level with the top of the bank. Paving slabs and bricks are the easiest materials to use. These steps need more foundation material and concrete than cut-in types, so take longer to make.

⚙ Log steps—ideal for rustic gardens, and used mainly on gentle slopes. The level areas between the steps can be formed of grass, but for all-year use a thin coating of gravel is better. The steps (risers) are formed of logs 4–6in/10–15cm thick, or stout, roughly cut pieces of wood coated in plant-friendly wood preservative.

Start from the base of the slope and bed the first log slightly into the soil to give it greater stability. Secure it in position with two stout pegs. Place gravel behind the log, compact it, level the surface, and secure another log. Shredded bark can be used instead of gravel, but birds often scatter it and bark can be slippery in wet weather and on a steep slope.

MEASURING STEPS

To make steps comfortable to use, it is essential that the depth of the tread and the riser are right. Before deciding on these distances, try walking up and down steps in gardens belonging to friends. Take the measurements and use them to build your steps.

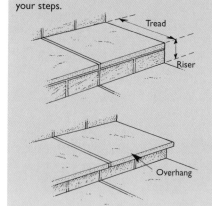

making cut-in steps

1 Start at the base of the flight of steps and dig out the soil to a depth of about 6in/15cm. Lay clean rubble 2–3in/5–7.5cm thick evenly over the entire area, and firm it.

2 Spread a layer of horticultural sand 2in/5cm deep over the rubble. Firm it and rake level, using a level. Set paving slabs on top, each one on a layer of mortar.

3 When the mortar has set, use bricks to form the riser which will support the next step. Check that they are level. Dig out and prepare the base for the next level.

▲ *A flight of steps built of frost-resistant bricks makes an attractive yet practical feature in a cottage garden or an informal area.*

4 Lay and firm clean rubble at the bottom, then lay and firm a layer of horticultural sand. Use a long, straight-edged piece of wood to check that the surface is level.

erecting trellis

Trellis has several roles in a garden. It provides a good opportunity to grow more climbers, and a freestanding trellis erected near a boundary creates privacy. It can also be used inside a garden to form an arbor and as a screen, separating one garden area from another.

Erecting a wall trellis

Direct your attention to the wall before securing the trellis. Check that it is sound and will hold wall-fixings when drilled. Repaint the wall if necessary. Measure it and buy trellis to fit the area, and make sure that the eventual spread of the climbers you intend to plant will equal the dimensions of the trellis. A vigorous climber on an inadequate trellis is a recipe for disaster.

The trellis needs to be positioned against the wall so that its base is 9–12in/23–30cm above the soil. Use a level to get its positioning right, and when you are satisfied that it is level, mark the positions of the corners of the trellis on the wall and the spots where the holes need to be drilled, so it can be returned to the same place. Remove the trellis and drill the holes, countersinking them to make certain that the head of each screw will be flush with the surface of the wood. Reposition the trellis against the wall, insert a screw into each hole, and tap each one gently to mark its position.

Remove the trellis and use a masonry drill to make each hole, then insert a wall-fixing. Put the trellis back in position and screw it into place. Tighten each screw just partially at first, then when all screws are in position, tighten them fully. Always use galvanized screws to secure trellis.

Plants with a scrambling habit are best grown on a trellis fixed to battens that position it 1in/2.5cm from the wall. The stems can then entangle with the trellis.

Constructing freestanding trellis

Square- and diamond-shaped trellis panels may be used for a freestanding trellis, but they must have wooden battens, secured to upright posts, 4–5in/10–15cm square, cemented at least 18in/45cm into the ground. To create a screen 6ft/1.8m high, posts measuring 8ft/2.4m long are needed, with trellis panels 6ft/1.8m long and 5ft/1.5m high. Use a garden line to indicate the position of the trellis and mark 12in/30cm square holes every 6ft/1.8m apart for the posts. Dig holes 18in/45cm deep.

▲ *Trellis is an attractive feature when covered with plants. It is easy to attach trellis to a wall and to build a freestanding trellis structure.*

ON SLOPING GROUND

Where ground slopes it is usually necessary to step the trellis panels. The top of the post on the lower end needs to be 1in/2.5cm above the top of the trellis. Each piece of trellis needs to be level and aligned with its neighbors.

The easiest way to begin erecting a free-standing trellis is to lay two posts on the ground and secure the trellis to it, using galvanized nails, so that its top is about 1in/2.5cm below the top of each post. Then, with the help of two people, lift the trellis and position each post in a hole. Use a level to check that the posts are upright and the trellis is level. Wedge each post upright with pieces of wood.

Prepare the next panel by nailing it to a post. Put the post in a hole and secure the trellis to the post erected just before it. Continue erecting the trellis in this way. Recheck the alignment of trellis and posts with a level, then mix some concrete and pour it into the holes around the posts. Finally, about a week later, nail a cap to the top of each post. This helps to prevent water entering the end grain of the wood and rotting it.

erecting a wall trellis

1 First, check that the trellis fits the area of the wall and is not too large. Position the trellis and mark the drilling holes on it, then take the trellis down and drill the holes.

2 Position the trellis on the wall, level it, and mark the positions of the drilling holes on the wall, using a pencil, a bradawl. or just the tip of the drill.

▲ *The range of ornamental trellis is wide and includes patterns with diamond-shaped squares, as well as the traditional pattern of squares.*

3 Drill each hold marked on the wall and insert a wall fixing, tapping it gently into position. The fixing must be the same size as the screws that will be used to secure the trellis to the wall.

4 Screw the trellis to the wall, using a normal screwdriver or a drill that can double as a screwdriver. When the screws are in place, do not tighten them excessively since this can damage the trellis.

getting the
basics right

You do not need many gardening skills to create a good garden, but it helps if you know how to improve the soil and plant trees to give them an excellent start. Here is a guide to the best way to garden, with ideas on digging and draining, making compost piles, and staking tall plants. You will also find tips on assessing the soil, lighting up the garden, knowing when you might need to apply lime, and how to stock your shed with all the right equipment for your needs. In short, everything you need to know that will get your garden off to a good start.

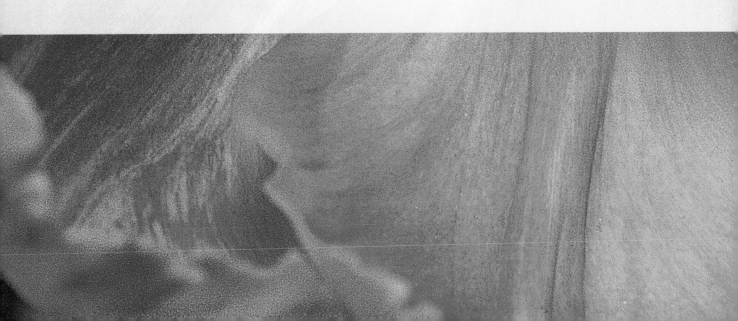

the tools you will need

Garden tools should be a pleasure to use, as well as being functional. Buy the best quality that you can afford and, if possible, always handle pieces of garden equipment before buying them to check that their weight and size suit you. Looking after your tools will insure that they last for many years.

Digging and forking tools

❁ Garden spades—in several sizes, with blades about 11in/27cm long and 7½in/19cm wide; border spades have blades 9in/23cm long and 5½in/14cm wide. Some spades have blades with tread-like ledges that enable more pressure to be applied by foot to force the blade into the soil. Most spades have handles 28in/72cm long (the distance between the top of the handle and the top of the blade). Some are longer at 32in/82cm.

❁ Garden forks—for heavy digging and for breaking down large clods of soil in spring. Also for shallow digging between shrubs and herbaceous plants. There are several sizes: digging forks have four tines (prongs), each 11in/27cm long, while the tines on border forks are 9in/23cm long. Potato forks have flat-sectioned tines about 11in/27cm long.

Hoeing tools

❁ Draw hoes—a handle of plastic or wood, 5–6ft/1.5–1.8m long is attached through a swan-like neck to a sharp-edged cutting blade. Have several uses, including forming shallow drills into which seeds can be sown, and severing annual weeds at ground level.

❁ Weeding hoes—wood or plastic handle 5–6ft/1.5–1.8cm long is attached to a forward-pointing blade used to sever weeds and to create a fine tilth. When using a weeding hoe, walk backward.

❁ Onion hoes—resemble draw hoes, but are only 12–15in/30–38cm long and are used to sever weeds around young plants.

Raking

❁ Metal rakes—sometimes called iron rakes, are used for leveling soil. They have heads 10–12in/25–30cm wide, each with 10–14 teeth 2½–3in/6–7.5cm long. The wood or plastic handle is 5–6ft/1.5–1.8m in length.

❁ Landscape rakes—used to level large areas. They have a wooden head, 28in/72cm wide with 3in/7.5cm long tines spaced 1½in/36mm apart.

Planting tools

❁ Hand trowels— a metal scoop attached to handle 6–12in/15–30cm long.

❁ Dibbles—range in size and are used to make planting holes for cabbages and other brassicas in vegetable plots, and small holes for seedlings in seed trays.

❁ Bulb planters—are for planting bulbs in grass, they remove a core of turf.

◀ *Garden spades and forks have multiple uses, including digging the soil in winter, in preparation for sowing and planting in spring.*

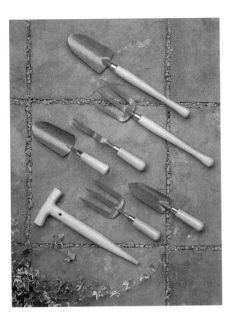

▲ *Trowels, hand forks and large dibbles are used to plant small, ornamental plants and cabbages, cauliflowers, and Brussels sprouts.*

Cutting and sawing

⊛ Pruners—these are designed to cut stems and they have two cutting actions: the anvil type has a blade that cuts against a firm, flat surface, while the bypass pruner has two parrot-shaped blades that cross each other.

⊛ Saws—range from Grecian saws (with a curved blade and teeth that cut on the pull stroke) to large saws for cutting thick wood.

Lawn tools

⊛ Rakes—are used to rake debris. Range from spring-tined types to rubber and plastic-tined models.

⊛ Half-moon edging irons—used to cut lawn edges, so need to be kept sharp.

⊛ Edging shears—used to cut long grass at the edges of lawns. They have strong handles usually 32in/82cm long and shears about 8in/20cm long.

⊛ Hand shears—used to cut hedges as well as long grass.

▲ *Essential tools for pruning and clipping are the long-handled saw (top), garden shears (center), and hand saw (bottom).*

◄ *Weeding and draw hoes are used for weeding and digging seed drills, while edging irons are for straightening lawn edges.*

draining soil

If soil is constantly saturated with water, the roots of many cultivated plants will decay. Some plants thrive in moisture-saturated soil and they can be grown in bog gardens, but most garden plants need soil that is well-drained to a depth of 2ft/60cm through most of the year.

The need for drains

If water is continually seen on the soil surface, drains are needed. Rushes and reeds growing in an area are also signs of excess water. The need for drains can also be established by digging a hole 4ft/ 1.2m deep, in the fall, and monitoring the level of water in it through the winter. If the water remains within 9in/23cm of the surface, land drains are required.

Drainage options

There are choices between rubble drains, clay pipes, and perforated plastic tubing.
❀ Rubble drains—relatively cheap to install if you have sufficient rubble available. Only one main drain is usually needed, with minor drains feeding into it, leading to a soakaway or a ditch. The spacings between side drains depend on the soil: 12–15ft/3.6–4.5m for clay soils and 40ft/12m for sandy ones. Dig the trenches 12–18in/30–45cm wide and 2–2½ft/60–75cm deep, with a minimum slope of 1 in 90 toward the outlet. Fill the trenches about half-full with rubble, and place thick polyethylene over it to

prevent the soil clogging it up. Add soil until level with the surface, then firm it.
❀ Clay pipe drains—a traditional way of draining soil. Use unglazed clay pipes 12in/30cm long and 5in/13cm wide to form main drains, with 4in/10cm-wide pipes as side drains. Like rubble drains they are laid in trenches Lay gravel 3in/7.5cm thick in each trench. Place the pipes on top and cover the joints with pieces of broken tiles or sheets of double-thick polyethylene. Over this lay shingle 4in/10cm thick, and strong polyethylene sheeting, and add a layer of well-drained soil. Clay pipes are now difficult to find and plastic tubing may have to be substituted.
❀ Perforated plastic tubing—quicker to install than pipe drains, this is corrugated for extra strength and bought in 82ft/25m rolls with a 4in/10cm or 3in/7.5cm bore.

Soakaways or ditches

It is essential to direct surplus water into a soakaway or a ditch. If you are fortunate enough to have a ditch, allow the end of the pipe to extend into the ditch and

cover it with netting to keep out vermin. However, most gardeners have to construct a soakaway at the lowest point. Dig a hole about 4ft/1.2m square and deep; its base must be 12in/30cm below the lowest part of the trench. Fill to half its depth with clean rubble, then to within 12in/30cm of the surface with gravel. Cover this with double-thick polyethylene and fill up with soil.

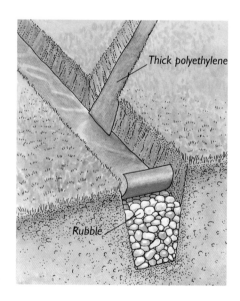

Thick polyethylene

Rubble

▲ *Rubble drains are relatively inexpensive, especially in a new garden and where a builder has left a mass of clean rubble.*

installing plastic drains

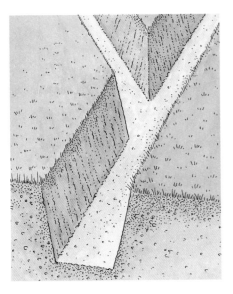

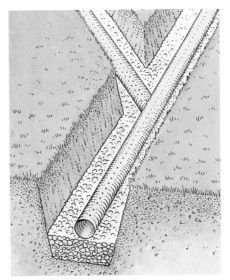

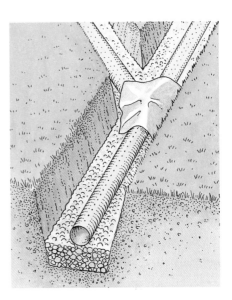

1 Use string to indicate the width and position of the main and side drains. Dig out the drain trenches, making a slight slope toward a drainage ditch or a sump. Take care not to break the edges of the trenches.

2 Spread a layer of clean gravel 3in/7.5cm deep in each trench and lay the plastic pipe in the center. Where each side drain meets the main pipe, cut its end at an angle so they fit together snugly.

3 Spread a double thickness of strong polyethylene over the joints to prevent soil entering the pipes and blocking them. Use a little gravel to hold the polyethylene in place while the other joints are covered.

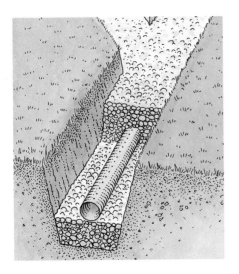

4 Cover all the pipes with a layer of gravel 3in/7.5cm deep. Over this position a layer of strong polyethylene and then top up with well-drained soil. Mound the soil a little to allow for settlement.

▲ *Well-drained soil is essential for most garden plants. If their roots are perpetually in water, they will decay and will eventually die.*

preparing the soil

Digging is a traditional part of gardening and is mainly performed in late fall or early winter to prepare the soil for crops during the following year. Single-digging (to the depth of a spade's blade) is the normal way to prepare soil for planting.

Why dig?

Apart from making a garden neat and tidy, digging has several other benefits. It enables air and water to penetrate the top 10in/25cm of soil, and drains excess water into the subsoil. However, if lower layers are impervious, water may remain on the surface. If this happens, install drains (see pages 348–349).

When the topsoil is broken up, roots are better able to penetrate the soil. Also, annual weeds become buried and perennial weeds can be removed. Digging also allows garden compost and well-decayed manure to be mixed with the soil. The process of digging usually leaves large lumps of soil on the surface, and winter weather will break them down to a fine tilth by spring. Digging may also leave soil pests such as the larvae of craneflies and cockchafers on or near the surface for birds to pick off.

Single digging

Digging is a systematic activity, and one you will soon master. Do not dig too quickly, or for too long at a time. As you

progress, you will find your own rhythm and the work can becomes satisfying and less strenuous.

Rotating crops

If vegetables of a similar type are grown continuously on the same piece of land, it depletes the soil of the plant foods necessary for the healthy growth of those vegetables, while encouraging the build up of pests and diseases. Rhubarb and asparagus are permanent crops and are left in the same place, but for other types of vegetables the plot needs to be divided into three and the different groups of vegetables in the following order.

❀ Root crops—when preparing the soil, do not add lime or manure. Instead, rake in a general fertilizer a couple of weeks before planting or sowing. Root vegetables include beetroot, carrots, Jerusalem artichokes, parsnips, potatoes, salsify, and scorzonera.

❀ Brassicas—dig in well-decayed manure or garden compost if the soil lacks humus. If it is acid, apply lime in late winter and a general fertilizer prior to

sowing or planting. Brassicas include broccoli, Brussels sprouts, cabbages, cauliflowers, radishes, rutabagas, and turnips.

❀ Other crops—dig in well-decayed manure or garden compost. If the soil is acid, dust it with lime in late winter and rake in a general fertilizer before sowing or planting. Vegetables include eggplants, beans, bell peppers, celery, leeks, salad vegetables, marrows, onions, peas, corn, and tomatoes.

NO-DIGGING PHILOSOPHY

This has many advocates but is successful only where the soil is light, well drained and aerated, and free from perennial weeds. Crops are grown on top of compost laid regularly on the surface of the soil. However, it can be expensive to buy compost each year. Where soils have a high percentage of clay there is no alternative but to dig, and to mix in well-decomposed compost or manure.

▶ *Digging flower and vegetable beds in winter improves the soil, and makes the entire garden look tidier during the winter months.*

single digging

1 The first step is to dig a trench 10–12in/25–30cm deep and 12in/30cm wide across one end of the plot of land. Move the soil to the other side of the plot.

2 Skim off weeds and grass from the adjacent strip of soil and place them in the trench. Add well-decomposed manure or garden compost to the trench.

3 Insert the blade of the spade into the soil, at right-angles to the trench and the width of the blade. This will enable a block of soil to be removed easily.

4 Push the blade into the soil and parallel to the trench, lift out the block of soil, and place it upside down in the trench. Repeat this action all along the trench.

351

compost piles

Digging in garden compost made from kitchen waste and soft, non-woody parts of garden plants is an inexpensive and environmentally friendly way to feed and aerate the soil and aid moisture retention. Compost can be dug into the soil in winter, or be used as a mulch in spring and summer.

Making garden compost

Garden and kitchen waste can just be placed in a pile on the ground and left to decay, but this is not the best way to make compost. Instead, place it in layers in compost bins. It is best to have three bins: one being filled; another that was filled months before and whose contents are rotting down; and a third holding decayed compost that is being emptied and used currently in the garden.

Compost bins that measure 3–4½ft/1–1.3m high and are square—allowing air to enter the compost without rapidly drying it out—are best. Proprietary types are available, while home-made bins built from planks of wood 6–9in/15–20cm wide with 2in/5cm-wide gaps between them, work extremely well. Wire-netting bins can be used, but they need to be lined with punctured black polyethylene sheets to prevent rapid drying.

Filling a compost bin

Place a compost bin on a well-drained piece of soil and put a thick layer of coarse material such as straw, 9–12in/23–30cm thick, at the bottom. Tread it firm, then add vegetable waste such as grass cuttings, spent annuals, weeds, and soft parts of plants, in a layer 6in/15cm thick. When using only grass cuttings, make each layer thinner because thick layers become compacted, excluding air.

The next stage is to lay garden soil 2in/5cm thick on top. Finally, water it thoroughly and dust it with sulfate of ammonia at 2oz/14g per 1sq yd/1sq m. Alternatively, you can buy proprietary compost activators and use as instructed.

◄ *Circular compost bins made of wire netting are easily made. Line the sides with punctured polyethylene to keep the compost moist.*

Continue building up the layers and, when the heap reaches the top of the bin, water the contents thoroughly and cover with 1–2in/2.5–5cm of soil. Place a plastic sheet over the top and secure it to prevent the compost from becoming too wet or dry. After about six months in winter (less in summer) the compost will be ready to be used.

Medley of waste

In addition to soft garden plants, other materials can be added to a compost heap, including newspapers (but not glossy magazines), crushed eggshells, pea pods, potato peelings, and tea bags. Do not use grass cuttings if the lawn has been treated recently with a hormone weedkiller. Do not add perennial weeds to the compost.

Mix up the waste as it is put into a compost bin because thick layers of the same material can prevent air from entering the mixture.

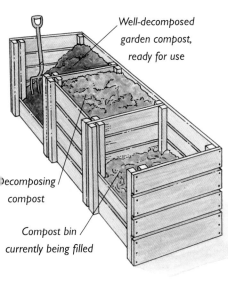

Well-decomposed garden compost, ready for use

Decomposing compost

Compost bin currently being filled

▲ *Use three compost bins in a sequence to insure a regular supply of well-decomposed garden compost.*

LEAF MOLD

The leaves of deciduous shrubs and trees can be collected in the fall and placed in layers 6–9in/15–23cm thick in a compost bin, with a sprinkling of sulfate of ammonia between them. Leaves from evergreen shrubs and trees are unsuitable, while leaves from poplar, plane, and sycamore take longer to decompose than those from beech and oak.

Leaves can also be encouraged to decay by putting them in perforated bags of black polyethylene (a good way to decompose leaves in small gardens). Add a sprinkling of sulfate of ammonia between the layers, and, when the bag is full, add water and seal the top. About six months later the leaf mold can be used as a mulch or dug into the soil. It is an excellent reconditioning treatment for soil.

▲ *The range of proprietary composters is wide and includes this green design which is attractive yet practical for a small garden.*

staking and supporting plants

Many plants, from hardy annuals to fruit trees, need support. Those used to support ornamental plants must be unobtrusive, whereas for fruit trees they need to be strong, functional, and durable. Here is a good range of ways to support plants in your garden.

Hardy annuals

Each year these plants grow from seed and create spectacular summer displays. Many of them benefit from support.
⊛ Twiggy supports—also called pea sticks, these are cut from beech, hornbeam, or birch trees and are needed in several sizes, from 12in/30cm to 4ft/1.2m long. Insert them among young plants immediately after their final thinning. Push them firmly into the soil, and use pruners to trim their tops to just below the expected height of the fully grown plants.

Herbaceous perennials

These are plants that die down to soil level in the fall and develop fresh shoots in the spring. Not all herbaceous plants need support but when they do, try:
⊛ Twiggy sticks—like those used for annuals, but usually stronger and longer. Insert them around young plants in spring and early summer. Many herbaceous perennials are self-supporting but others, especially those with a multitude of stems, require support.
⊛ Stakes and string—a good way to support dahlias. Push three stakes, 4ft/ 1.2m long about 9in/23cm into the soil to form a triangle around a plant. Then encircle the plant with several tiers of string looped tightly around each stake.
⊛ Metal supports—several proprietary types are available, one of the most popular having two halves, each with a curved top to form a circle, which encloses the stems.

▲ *Support sweet peas on a framework of sticks tied together with garden string, or with a twiggy stick. Pole beans also need support.*

Herbaceous supports

Sticks and string

Twiggy sticks

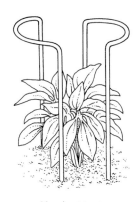

Metal supports

Trees

Strong supports are essential to prevent wind breaking branches and trunks. Choose from the following:

⚜ Vertical supports—the easiest way to support ornamental and fruit bearing trees. Use a stake of stout ash, spruce, or chestnut, which, when knocked about 12in/30cm into the soil will have its top slightly below the lowest branch. Knock the stake into the hole before the tree is planted. Position the stake on the windward side, using proprietary ties to secure the trunk and prevent it rubbing against the stake. This is the best way to support an ornamental tree in a lawn, allowing grass to be cut neatly close to the tree and its support.

⚜ Oblique supports—this involves inserting a stake at a 45° angle into the soil, with its top slightly below the lowest branch. The top of the stake must face into the prevailing wind. This is often used to replace a broken stake.

⚜ H-stakes—used after a tree has been planted. Knock two stakes into the soil, one on each side of the trunk, and secure a cross-stake to each of them, a little below the lowest branch. Secure the cross-stake to the trunk.

Vegetables

Supports for vegetables need to remain strong through summer. Some vegetables need support into the fall as well.

⚜ Pole beans—use bean poles 8–9ft/ 2.4–2.7m long inserted about 12in/30cm apart, in two rows 18–24in/45–60cm apart, with their tops inclined toward each other and crossed, making an inverted V-shape. Position a horizontal pole along the top and tie it in place. An alternative method is to use three or four poles to form a wigwam up which plants can clamber.

⚜ Peas—use twiggy sticks or large-mesh wire netting, 3ft/90cm to 4ft/1.2m high, held upright by canes.

⚜ Fava beans—insert a stout stake at the ends of the row, and encircle the plants with strong string tied to it.

▶ *Herbaceous perennials with masses of stems can be supported with twiggy sticks pushed into the ground when plants are young.*

Tree supports

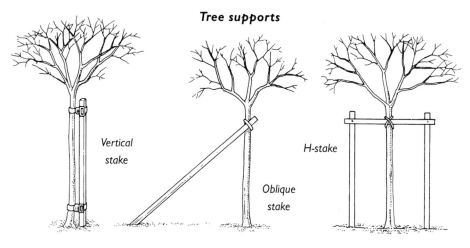

Vertical stake

Oblique stake

H-stake

SUPPORTING HEAVILY LADEN FRUIT BRANCHES

Sometimes, branches of fruit trees become so heavily laden with fruit that they bow downward. Where this happens use Y-shaped pieces of wood knocked into the soil beneath a laden branch to give it support. Alternatively, drive a stake 10ft/3m long into the soil near the trunk, from which branches can be supported by stout strings.

355

choosing and erecting a shed

A dry, vermin-proof shed is essential in a garden to store gardening tools and a wide range of other equipment. Always buy the largest shed you can. The average size is about 8ft/2.4m by 6ft/1.8m. Before erecting or installing it, level the site it is to stand on, and firm the ground.

Range of sheds

Sheds come in many shapes and sizes, some with a traditional apex roof (the ridge along the center), others with a roof that slopes from front to back. A few have a combination of a back-sloping roof and a greenhouse area at one end. There are also summerhouses that combine garden room with storage space. When choosing a shed, its style should suit the style of your garden, even if it is to be sited at the far end of your garden (if gasolene or kerosene is to be stored in your shed, do not locate it close to your house). Put your shed on a patch of poor soil or position it to hide unsightly features. You could camouflage an unattractive shed by putting a freestanding trellis in front of it. You will need an all-weather path to connect the shed to the house.

Most sheds are made of wood. Rigid PVC is an alternative, but it is not always considered attractive. Wooden sheds are made of a timber frame and clad with overlapping or tongue-and-grooved planks of wood. The type of wood influences the price of the shed and its longevity. Softwood (usually deal and often fir or pine) must be pressure-treated with a preservative, while more costly timber such as western red cedar has greater resistance to water but still needs to be coated regularly with cedar oil.

Erecting a shed

A firm, level base is essential. First, clear the area of vegetation and overhanging branches. A shed can be erected directly on timber bearers, usually 2–2½in/5–6.5cm square, pressure-treated with a wood preservative, and laid directly on soil. However, it is better to lay paving slabs. Mark out on the ground an accurately square area for the shed. Use a level to check its horizontal alignment. Then use flat paving slabs, 18in/45cm square or 2ft/60cm-square to form a

base. Space the slabs 12–18in/30–45cm apart, and in three rows. The timber bearers are laid on top, and at right angles to the timbers that secure the floor of the shed.

If the shed is made of softwood, coat all surfaces and edges thoroughly with a wood preservative. Then position the flow and recheck the levels. Two or three people will be needed to build the shed quickly and easily. Screw or bolt the sides into position, holding each piece in place until it is secure, then position the roof and secure it. Cover the roof in roofing felt and to stick the edges of the felt together with adhesive. The windows will need glazing. Non-opening window panes can be secured by glazing sprigs (or panel pins). Windows that open are more securely bedded in a layer of putty.

GAZEBOS

These are distinctive features which, by definition, let people gaze out onto a garden. They have a long history. In early Persian gardens they evolved from dovecotes which were located close to each corner. Gazebos make beautiful focal points when positioned toward the end of a large, broad lawn. Alternatively, position the gazebo in a corner from where there is a wide view of the garden. A gazebo generally has a wooden frame, with wooden latticework at the back, and an ornate roof. Simple ones can be made from four stout, upright posts supporting a pitched roof. The back and roof are clad in latticework painted white.

◄ *Plant shrubs and climbers and tall biennials, around a shed to blend it into the garden and harmonize with the plants growing there.*

erecting a shed

1 The base of a shed can be laid directly on strong timber bearers. However, laying paving slabs first and then laying the bearers on top makes a more substantial and frostproof base.

2 Ask a couple of friends to help you put the sides and ends of the shed into position. These may be screwed or bolted together. The finished construction must be square and upright.

3 When the ends and sides are in position, put the roof in place. Lodge the ends of the roof firmly in their sockets, and check all round the shed to insure that it overhangs evenly around the sides.

4 Place the roofing felt in position: it can be laid longitudinally or across the ridge. Use galvanized, large-headed nails to secure it, and coat the overlaps with a roofing adhesive.

electricity in a garden

Electric power in a garden means you can use a wide range of equipment, including heated propagation units in greenhouses, lights in sheds, fountains, ponds, and decorative lights on a patio. But the wiring must be installed correctly and safely by a qualified professional electrician.

Lights on a patio

Warm summer evenings provide the perfect opportunity to linger on patios, especially if lighting is installed. Lights are also a good way of deterring burglars, especially if an infrared detector is

Types of lighting installation

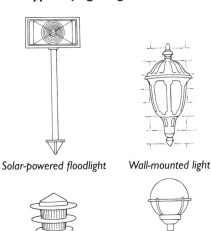

Solar-powered floodlight   Wall-mounted light

Tiered light   Globe light

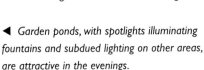

◀ *Garden ponds, with spotlights illuminating fountains and subdued lighting on other areas, are attractive in the evenings.*

attached. This works when it is dark. It responds to body heat by turning on the light. It can also be fitted to a spotlight circuit at the front of a house to light a drive or a path, but it should not be activated by people walking on a nearby sidewalk, or it may be turning on and off all night. The range of patio lights is wide and includes low-level spotlights and lights mounted on the top, at the sides, and at the base of a walls. Some can be placed among the plants in patio borders.

Pond power

In ponds there are two choices of power: mains electricity or low-voltage power. In most areas in a garden, from patios to greenhouses and garden sheds, mains electricity is best because it provides strong lighting and power, but in or near ponds many gardeners prefer the safer lower voltage supply (a transformer reduces the power) for lights and a small fountain. If you need power to run several fountains, a waterfall, and strong lighting, you will need mains electricity, but note that it is far more expensive to install a mains supply than a low voltage system. You can also buy solar-powered water fountains. These are easy to install, but your garden will need regular sunshine if you want a fountain running on solar power to work constantly.

Greenhouse power

Mains electricity is useful in a greenhouse, especially if electrical tubular heaters are installed. Fan heaters and propagation units also need this power. Small mist-

propagation units are now available for amateur greenhouses, and they too require mains electricity.

Have the power installed by a qualified electrician, with a mains board fitted near the door and at least 4ft/1.2m above the ground. Tack a loose sheet of plastic over it to keep off water droplets, but maintain good air circulation around it. In addition, have a Ground-Fault-Interrupter (GFI) fitted into the circuit to cut off the power if a fault occurs.

Power in sheds

This is not essential but it makes life easier, especially in winter when lawn mowers and other equipment need to be serviced. Have a mains board fitted, so that the power supply can be isolated from the main house supply.

▲ *Lights at ground level and flush with the surface are ideal for illuminating plants around paved areas. Containers can be placed on top.*

SAFETY IN GARDENS

The top five tips are:

⊛ Consult a specialist when installing electricity in a garden. Do not take short cuts or use inferior materials.

⊛ Where cables are buried, keep a record of their position. Have all buried cables installed in a conduit. If you sell your property, inform the new owner about the position of underground cables.

⊛ Have all equipment checked each year. Equipment must be specified as being designed for outdoor use.

⊛ Never use mains electricity without a Ground-Fault-Interrupter fitted into the circuit. This especially applies when using mains operated lawn and hedge cutters.

lawns and their care

Lawns are too often taken for granted, yet in most gardens they are the biggest, most eye-catching feature. Lawns provide essential places to play, sit, and eat, areas that link different sections of a garden, and foils for a wide range of plants. Looking after them is not difficult, but you have to know what to do. Here are some essential tips on feeding and watering, and on repairing holes, hollows, and bumps, along with ideas on creating chamomile lawns to give a stylish look.

creating a lawn from seed

In temperate regions there are two main ways to create lawns: sowing seed or laying turfs. There are other methods, however. In warm climates, dibbling tufts of grass about 3in/7.5cm apart is successful. In a tropical climate, spreading a mud plaster of chopped grass, water, and soil works well.

Preparing the site

Whether you create a lawn from seed or by laying turfs, preparation of the soil is the same. First, check that the ground is well drained (pages 348–349) and, if necessary, install drains. In winter, dig the soil (pages 350–351), removing perennial weeds. A few weeks before sowing seeds, rake the area level or with a slight slope. Firm the soil by shuffling sideways over

the whole area, so that it is uniformly firm. Do not use a roller. Rake the soil to create a fine tilth.

Sowing lawn seed

About a week before sowing lawn seed (usually in late spring, or from late summer to early fall), scatter a general fertilizer evenly over the area at 1½oz per sq yd/50g per sq m. Use a metal rake to mix it lightly into the surface. Wait for a day when the surface soil is dry, and use string to section the area into strips 3½ft/1m wide. Then use a couple of bamboo canes 4ft/1.2m long to form a 1m/3½ft square at one end of the strip.

Into this area sow lawn seed at the rate of 1½oz per sq yd/50g per sq m. Sowing less than this amount results in a thin, sparse lawn, while too much produces masses of tightly bunched seedlings susceptible to disease.

Next, move one of the canes to form another square and sow with more seed, continuing in this way until the whole area has been covered. Then, standing on a plank of wood, rake the seed lightly and

ADVANTAGES OF SOWING SEEDS

- Cheaper than laying turfs.
- Lighter work than laying turfs.
- Easier to create intricately shaped areas.
- There is lawn seed for almost every part of the garden, from sunny sites to shady areas, and from play areas to ornamental lawns.

DISADVANTAGES OF SOWING SEEDS

- It takes from 3–4 months before a lawn can be used.
- Cats often disturb the sown surface, and dogs and toddlers may tread on it.
- Perennial weeds can be a problem if the area has not been prepared thoroughly.

HINTS AND TIPS

Always buy a little more seed than you will need. Small bare areas often occur and it is useful to have the same type and batch of seed handy to resow them.

evenly into the surface. It is important that you do not walk on newly sown areas of lawn because this depresses the soil and seed may stick to your shoes. If the weather forecast indicates a dry period, water the soil lightly but thoroughly. Also provide protection from hungry birds by stretching black thread about 6in/15cm above the surface and 6in/20cm apart. An alternative method which is unlikely to harm birds is to lay large sheets of black polyethylene on the sown surface to give protection and retain moisture. However, the sheets must be removed immediately once the grass seeds have germinated.

▶ *Lawns provide a natural foil that shows off plants to perfection. Grass paths may also be sown to connect parts of a garden.*

lawns from seed

1 Level the soil and remove any large stones. Work in a general fertilizer at 1½ oz per sq yd/50g per sq m using a garden rake or a metal-tined lawn rake.

2 Stretch two garden lines across the area to be sown, a yard apart. Then, place two garden canes 4ft/1.2m long to form a square yard.

3 Scatter seed evenly into each square at the rate of 1½ oz per sq yd/50g per sq m. Take care to sow each part of the square, not just the center.

4 When the square has been sown, move one of the canes to form another square. Then repeat the sowing until the row is complete. Use a garden or lawn rake to work the seed lightly into the surface.

creating lawns from turfs

Lawns made of turfs are thought to be instant features, but be warned, you will have to wait at least four weeks before they are established and can be used. Soil preparation is exactly the same as when creating lawns from seed (pages 362–363).

Laying turfs

Turfs can be laid from spring to fall, although early fall is the most popular period because the soil is warm and usually moist. After preparing the soil thoroughly, use a metal rake to level the surface and, about one week before laying turfs, scatter a general fertilizer at 2oz per sq yd/70g per sq m. Rake it lightly into the surface.

Mark out the area to be laid and stretch a garden line down one edge. As an insurance against dry weather and damage to the edges, make the area about 3in/7.5cm wider than required. Should the edges become dry the lawn will not be spoiled because it can be cut back to the desired size.

Start laying the lawn by positioning a row of turfs along the garden line, closely abutting their ends. Then, place a plank of wood 8in/20cm wide and 8–10ft/2.4–3m long on top of the turfs. Stand on this plank (moving it as necessary) to lay another row of turfs. Stagger the joints. Again, move the plank and lay another row, continuing until the whole area is covered.

Always insure that each turf is in close contact with the soil by using a firming device made from a thick piece of wood, 18in/45cm square, attached at its center to a vertical handle, usually a thick, 5ft/1.5m-long pole. Gaps will inevitably occur between the turfs, at their ends and their sides. Trickle a mixture of equal parts of sieved soil and fine peat into the gaps. When the area has been turfed, use a sprinkler.

Types of turf

Two main types of turf are used to make garden lawns. One is meadow turf cut 3ft/90cm long, 12in/30cm wide, and 1½in/36mm thick; but expect variations. It comes from pasture and is usually the cheapest way to buy turfs.

Cultivated turf is the other type and is sometimes known as seeded turf. It is grown especially for sale, costs more than meadow turf, and is sold in rolls, but before buying it is important to check the exact size because it can vary.

ADVANTAGES OF LAYING TURFS

❀ A usable surface is usually created about four weeks after laying.
❀ Eliminates problems with birds, cats, and dogs.
❀ Ideal for families with young children.
❀ Turfs can be laid from spring to fall, but not when the soil is dry. If it becomes dry, regular watering is essential.

DISADVANTAGES OF LAYING TURFS

❀ More expensive than sowing seeds.
❀ Much heavier work than sowing seeds.
❀ Turfs have to be laid within 24 hours of delivery. If left rolled up, the grass becomes yellow and the edges begin to dry. If laying is delayed, be prepared to unroll the turfs and water them.

HINTS AND TIPS

Always buy a few more turfs than you need. This is important where the sides of a lawn are curved. Also note that because turfs are laid in a staggered pattern there is always some wastage at the ends.

laying turfs

1 Prepare the soil thoroughly and rake in a general fertilizer. Stretch a garden line along one side of the planned lawn and lay a turf alongside it. Lay other turfs, with their ends butted against each other.

2 Put a wide, strong plank on top of the laid turf and stand on it to lay another line, closely abutting the first row and with the end joints staggered. Never stand on the turf because it causes indentations.

3 Improvise a firmer by tapping on a plank of wood with the heel of a hammer, or fashion one from a thick piece of wood 45cm/18in square, with a vertical pole 1.5m /5ft long, fixed at its center.

4 Trickle a mixture of sieved soil and peat into the joints and use a broom or a besom to work it into the cracks. When the lawn is complete, use a sprinkler to soak the lawn area gently but thoroughly.

▲ *A well-maintained lawn creates a sense of space and highlights plants and other ornamental garden features.*

looking after lawns

Lawns are essential garden features creating attractive, restful and permanent foils for ornamental plants. They also unify a garden and provide recreational areas for children and pets. With a little care, lawns can be kept in peak condition and will withstand most household wear and tear.

Repairing lawn edges

After a few years it is inevitable that the edges of lawns become damaged and unsightly, but it is quite easy to repair them. (See opposite page.)

Repairing holes in lawns

Where a lawn is used as a play area for young children and pets, holes soon appear. Make repairs as soon as possible, so that the damage does not become any larger. (See opposite page.)

▲ *Lawns need regular attention the year round to keep them tidy and smart. If a lawn is neglected it becomes an eyesore.*

Leveling bumps and depressions

An uneven lawn with bumps and depressions can easily be leveled if these are less than 5ft/1.5m wide. Stretch a garden line over the center of the depression or bump, and use an edging iron to cut a line about 2½in/6cm deep along it. Then measure 12in/30cm-wide strips at rightangles to the center line and cut along them. Use a garden spade or a turfing iron to cut under the turfs, from the center outward, and roll them back to expose the bump or depression. Then either remove excess soil or fill and firm compost over the area, so that it is level. Replace the turf and firm it. Sprinkle compost between the cracks and water the area thoroughly.

Bare areas

These usually result from excessive wear. Fresh grass can be encouraged to grow by placing wire netting over the bare area and keeping it moist, but if the soil is compacted, more radical treatment will be required. Fork the area to about 6in/15cm deep and add some

horticultural sand. Level, refirm and sprinkle lawn seed over the area at 1½oz per sq yd/50g per sq m. Water the area lightly, allow the surface to dry slightly, then place clear polyethylene sheet over it. Remove the sheet when the grass seedlings are growing strongly.

LAWN ROUTINE

Lawns are often neglected, yet with regular care they can be transformed into areas that enhance the whole garden. Three tips guaranteeing success are:

❀ Mow the grass regularly from early spring to early or mid-fall. Use a grass box to collect the cuttings, except when the weather is hot and dry.

❀ Feed lawns during spring and early summer. Use quick-acting fertilizers and apply them every six to eight weeks except during dry periods. In late summer and early fall use slow-acting fertilizers. Always follow the application rates recommended by the manufacturer.

❀ Aerate lawns in late summer. To do this, push the tines of a garden fork 4in/10cm deep and 3in/7.5cm apart into the lawn surface, or use a proprietary hollow-tine fork. Then rake a top-dressing compost mixture into the soil. Prick the surface of the lawn in spring before adding fertilizers.

repairing the edges of lawn

1 Place a piece of wood, 8–9in/20–23cm wide, 12in/30cm long and ½–¾in/ 12–18mm thick over the damaged area and place one of the narrow ends flush with the lawn's edge.

2 Now use a half-moon edging iron to cut about 2½in/6cm deep into the lawn, not omitting to cut the corners. Remove the piece of wood and use a spade to lift the turf and reverse it.

3 The broken area will now be toward the lawn's center, with the cut part flush with the edge of the lawn. Fill and firm the damaged area with compost, and sow it with lawn seed.

repairing a hole in a lawn

1 Dogs and children often make holes in lawns; but repair is easy. Place a piece of wood 10–12in/25–30cm-square over the hole and then cut round it using a half-moon edging iron.

2 Remove the damaged piece of turf. Use the same wood to cut a healthy piece of turf from an out-of-the-way position. Put it in position and level it to align it with the surface of the surrounding grass.

3 Firm the turf gently to ease it into position and dribble compost carefully between the cracks all the way round. Then water the area thoroughly and repeatedly until the turf starts to grow.

chamomile lawns, thyme paths

These lawns and paths are unusual and colorful features that can be fitted into most gardens, whatever their size. Chamomile lawns have a long history and were popular in Elizabethan England, when bowls were played on their scented surface. The aroma of thyme adds a dimension to a garden walk.

Chamomile lawns

These lawns are planted with *Chamaemelum nobile*, formerly and widely known as *Anthemis nobilis*, a prostrate, mat-forming herbaceous perennial with finely dissected leaves that release a fruity scent when bruised and walked on. The non-flowering variety, 'Treneague' has a scent rather like bananas.

Weeds can be a problem in new chamomile lawns and thorough preparation is necessary. Dig the area 12in/30cm deep in winter and remove all perennial weeds. Leave for 12 months, pulling or digging up weeds as they appear. In the second winter, dig the soil again, and plant in the spring.

Planting a chamomile lawn

Rake the area level and shuffle sideways over the surface to firm it evenly. Then, rake again to remove footprints. If the lawn is dry, water the soil thoroughly and wait until the surface is dry and crumbly before planting.

You can plant the lawn in late spring or early summer. Space the plants 6–8in/15–20cm apart in staggered rows, and use a trowel to make holes that do not constrict the roots of each plant. Check that the crown of each plant is just below the surface, then firm the soil and water the whole lawn lightly but thoroughly. When the plants start to grow into a lawn, trim them with sharp hedging shears.

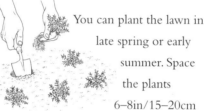

Thyme paths

Use *Thymus serpyllum* (English or wild thyme) to form a colorful, scented path. It is evergreen and carpet-forming, with richly fragrant gray-green leaves, and bears flowers ranging from white to pink to red flowers through much of the summer. When established, this thyme has a 18–24in/45–60cm spread, but for rapid cover set the plants closer together.

Creating a thyme path

During winter, mark the width of the path and dig the area thoroughly to remove perennial weeds. Leave the surface rough so that the weather will break down the surface to a fine tilth. In spring, rake the soil and place stepping stones on the surface (check that the spacing is right for everyone who will use the path). Set the stepping stones into the ground so the surface of each stone is about ½in/12mm above the soil surface. To promote quick covering, set the plants 9–12in/23–30cm apart. Firm the soil around them and water the whole lawn thoroughly. Until the path is established, water it regularly, especially at the edges where the soil tends to dry out.

▲ *Chamomile lawns, formed of finely dissected midgreen leaves with all the fruity fragrance of chamomile, always attract attention.*

▶ *Thyme paths become decorative ribbons of color throughout summer and are ideal for linking one part of a garden with another.*

SCENTED SEATS

These are an original feature in a small garden. They are raised, planted structures about 18in/45cm high, 4–6ft/1.2–1.8m long, and 20–24in/50–60cm deep, planted with chamomile or thyme. Because the bed is raised the soil tends to become dry, especially if the weather is hot and sunny, and so regular and thorough watering is essential. A variation on this type of seat is to intersperse the plants with small paving slabs. As well as providing sitting positions, the slabs help keep the soil moist and cool.

water and rock gardens

Water gardens are becoming increasingly fashionable, and there is little excuse for not having a water feature, whether it be a wildlife pond with frogs and newts, a wall fountain dribbling water onto a shiny group of colored pebbles on the ground, or for the more adventurous, a bog garden with permanently moist soil for growing some special plants. However, rock gardens, with quick-draining soil and exquisitely beautiful small plants may be more your style. All these are quite easily made, with the aid of a few practical tips.

water gardens

Water introduces tranquillity and movement to a garden. Established garden ponds, perhaps nestling in an open, sunny corner of a garden, create a restful atmosphere, especially when covered with waterlilies, and with dragonflies hovering over the surface.

Water features for all gardens

It is quite possible to have a water feature in your garden without digging a pond, and in a garden to be used by young children, an alternative is often welcome. There may be a fountain splashing over pebbles, or water in a shallow trough being recirculated by a pump. Such a feature may be quite small and so there is often room for one on a patio.

A pond can be built to any desired shape or size. The water surface can be level with the surrounding ground or raised by about 18in/45cm. A pond at ground level with an informal outline can be merged with a bog garden or a wildlife area. Several decades ago, ponds were nearly always square or rectangular, and made of concrete. Building one was hard work, and unless it was reinforced it soon cracked. Modern bowl-shaped ponds with gently sloping sides are a popular choice and more durable.

Today, ponds are mainly formed using a flexible liner (also called a pond liner) or come as a rigid liner (called a preformed pond or a molded shell). Flexible liners are used to line holes dug

▲ *Garden ponds introduce tranquillity and peace into a garden. The range of plants is wide, from waterlilies to fragrant marginal plants.*

SELECTING FOUNTAINS

❀ The spray should not fall on waterlilies or marginal plants.
❀ The height of the spray should not be more than half the width of the pond.
❀ In windy areas, use fountains that produce large droplets of water.
❀ Do not allow water droplets to disturb floating plants.

to the desired shape and depth. Their durability depends on the material used to make them. Polyethylene liners are low cost and have a relatively short life, especially when exposed to sunlight. Butyl rubber sheeting is the most durable, lasting for over 20 years, but it is also the most expensive.

Liners must be laid on an underlay to prevent the water pressure from puncturing them on sharp stones. Ready-made rigid liners are sunk into a hole. The cheapest type is made of plastic, which has the shortest lifespan. Glassfiber shells are more costly but will last for 20 years or more.

Choosing waterlilies

These plants need careful selection to insure that vigorous varieties do not dominate and overcrowd small ponds. Waterlilies are usually put into four classifications: dwarf; small; medium; and vigorous. Dwarf types suit ponds with a depth of 4–10in/10–25cm; small lilies need a 6–18in/15–45cm depth; the medium lilies need a depth of 1–2ft/ 30–60cm, and the vigorous type need a water depth of 1½–3ft/45–90cm.

To plant a waterlily (Nymphaea spp), put it in a plastic mesh container with soil and cover it with a layer of clean pea gravel 1in/2.5cm thick. Soak the soil and place the container in the pond. Using bricks as a stand for the container, position it so that the waterlily leaves float on the surface. Remove the bricks progressively as the plant grows, always keeping the leaves on the surface.

Miniponds on patios

Even a patio in the smallest garden can have a water feature. Stout wooden tubs are ideal summer homes for miniature waterlilies and other aquatic plants. They contain only a small volume of water, so unfortunately must be emptied or moved to a greenhouse or a conservatory during winter. First-rate miniature waterlilies include:

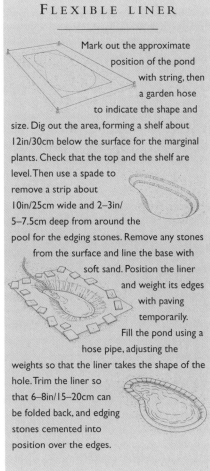

Nymphaea 'Aurora'—pinkish-yellow, then orange and later red.

Nymphaea 'Indiana'— orange, with orange-red stamens.

Nymphaea tetragona— white, with yellow stamens.

Marginal aquatics include:

Carex elata 'Aurea'— narrow, golden leaves.

Scirpus latifolia 'Zebrinus'—quill-like stems banded green and white.

▲ A raised pond creates a distinctive feature on a patio. It needs to be built with materials that harmonize with other garden structures.

FLEXIBLE LINER

Mark out the approximate position of the pond with string, then a garden hose to indicate the shape and size. Dig out the area, forming a shelf about 12in/30cm below the surface for the marginal plants. Check that the top and the shelf are level. Then use a spade to remove a strip about 10in/25cm wide and 2–3in/ 5–7.5cm deep from around the pool for the edging stones. Remove any stones from the surface and line the base with soft sand. Position the liner and weight its edges with paving temporarily. Fill the pond using a hose pipe, adjusting the weights so that the liner takes the shape of the hole. Trim the liner so that 6–8in/15–20cm can be folded back, and edging stones cemented into position over the edges.

bog gardens

Moisture-loving plants may be planted beside an informal garden pond or in naturally occurring wet spots in the garden to make a bog garden. The range of bog garden plants is wide and includes border primulas, moisture-loving ferns, and many colorful herbaceous perennials.

Creating a bog garden

Few gardens have an area where soil naturally remains moist throughout the year. A bog garden built in a dry area is usually better than one planted in naturally wet ground. This is because soil mix in a specially constructed bog garden is constrained within a plastic liner, and this helps to retain moisture throughout the year, whereas soil in what appears to be a naturally moist area usually becomes dry in hot weather. There are a few constructional "musts" and they include keeping the bog garden small enough so that you can reach plants without standing in the soil, which causes unnecessary compaction. To keep the soil mix moist but not waterlogged, the plastic liner should have regular small punctures. When constructing a bog garden, check that the top of the soil is slightly below the surface of water in the adjacent pond. It is important to have a water sprinkler at hand during spring and summer to water the soil during dry weather.

Step-by-step construction

Mark out an area to one side of an informal pond. Use a garden hose so that the shape of the bog garden can be changed several times during its planning stage. Create an attractive outline, perhaps irregular, but still allowing all parts to be reached easily.

Dig out the area, putting the topsoil to one side (ready for refilling), and barrow away the subsoil. A depth of 15–18in/38–45cm is about right. Line the hole with a layer of moist sand 1in/2.5cm thick, and place the liner in the hole. Tuck it under the edge of the pond liner or shell.

Next, puncture the base with holes ½in/12mm wide every 2½–3ft/75–90cm to insure that excess water can escape. Lay clean gravel or pea gravel 2in/5cm thick over the liner, then top up with soil mix consisting of three parts topsoil, three parts peat, and one part clean, lime–

◀ Hostas *thrive in bog gardens and their large leaves can be used to soften the edges of straight-sided ponds in a formal style.*

free grit. Firm the soil gently. Put large stones around the edges of the bog garden to cover the plastic sheeting,

Planting and plants

Spring or early summer is the best time to put in the plants. First, dust the surface with a general fertilizer and fork it lightly into the soil. Then space out the plants on the surface, so that they look attractive. Use a trowel to plant them, from the center of the bed to the edges. Firm the soil around the roots and water over the area gently but thoroughly. Good plants to consider for the bog garden include the following primulas, ferns, and herbaceous perennials.

Primulas

Primula denticulata (drumstick primrose)—dense, globular flowerheads in spring. The color range includes white, blue and mauve.

P. florindae (giant cowslip)—fragrant, bell-shaped flowers in early and midsummer. The color range is light orange to blood red.

P. japonica (Japanese primrose)—flowers borne in whorled tiers on upright stems from late spring to midsummer. The color range includes white, magenta-red, pink, and bright red.

Ferns

Onoclea sensibilis (sensitive fern)—2ft/ 60cm high with pale green fronds.
Osmunda regalis (royal fern)—4–6ft 1.2–1.8m high with pea-green fronds.

Herbaceous perennials

Astilbe × arendsii—lax spikes of red, pink, or white flowers during summer.
Hostas (plantain lilies)—large range, many with single-colored leaves, others variegated.
Iris sibirica (Siberian iris)—blue flowers during early summer.
Lysichiton americanum (skunk cabbage)—bright yellow, arum-like flowers during spring and early summer.
Rodgersia pinnata—large, deep-green leaves, sometimes tinged brown.
Trollius × cultorum (globe flower)—globe-like flowers during late spring and early summer. The range of colors varies from yellow to orange.

Constructing a bog garden

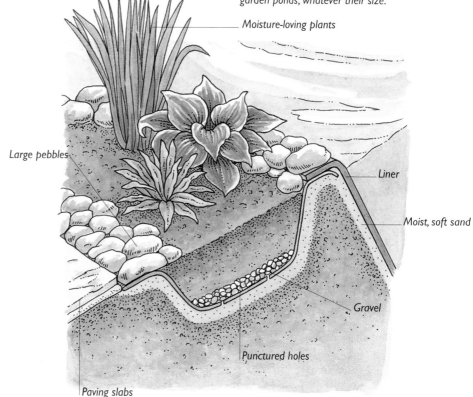

▲ Waterfalls, with cascading water that sparkles in the sunlight, create an extra dimension to garden ponds, whatever their size.

Moisture-loving plants

Large pebbles

Liner

Moist, soft sand

Gravel

Punctured holes

Paving slabs

building a rock garden

Rock gardens make delightful features in small gardens, especially as a large number of small plants can be grown in them. A rock garden can be grown on a gentle slope and on a freestanding mound created from well-drained soil, with stones added in stratified rows.

Rock gardens

If you are fortunate enough to have a garden with a slope toward the south or west, a rock garden is easily created with pieces of natural stone such as limestone or sandstone positioned to resemble stratified rows. For a rock garden with an area of about 15sq yd/4.5sq m you will need between 1–2 tons of stone.

The range of plants for rock gardens is wide and includes alpines and small herbaceous perennials, dwarf bulbs, and miniature and slow-growing conifers. Dwarf shrubs such as *Cotoneaster linearifolius* grow about 12in/30cm high and 20in/50cm wide and give a permanent structure. There are many other shrubs including thyme, the

glorious yellow-flowered *Hypericum olympica*, and *Zauschneria californica* (Californian fuchsia) with red, tubular, fuchsia-like flowers during late summer and early fall.

Freestanding rock gardens

These have natural stone in stratified layers, like a rock garden on a slope. They often provide more space for plants than a rock garden built on a slope because it is possible to plant the front and the two sides. Since the front is usually small, do not dominate it with large, shrub-like plants but use miniature, columnar, and slow-growing conifers to create the impression of height. These include *Juniperus communis* 'Compressa'

STAR PLANTS

Aubrieta deltoidea	*Sedum acre*
Aurinia saxatilis	*Saponaria ocymoides*

◄ *Rock gardens that are harmonized with a gently flowing stream are immediately more interesting than when on their own.*

(18in/45cm high after 10 years) and *Juniperus scopulorum* 'Skyrocket' (6ft/1.8m high after 10 years). Where interest is needed at the base of the rock garden to give the impression of extra width, plant *Juniperus squamata* 'Blue Star' (15in/38cm high and 24in/60cm, wide after 10 years) or *Juniperus × pfitzeriana* 'Gold Coast' (20in/50cm high and 30in/75cm wide after 10 years).

Drystone walls

These walls look wonderful when their sides are covered by colorful flowers. Several rock garden plants can achieve this effect, but perhaps none better than *Aurinia saxatilis*, better known as *Alyssum saxatile*. On a dry-stone wall it spreads 12–18in/30–45cm wide, and trails golden-yellow flowers more than 24in/60cm). There are several attractive varieties. *Aubrieta deltoidea* is an evergreen perennial that bears cross-shaped flowers in shades of rose-lilac to purple in spring and early summer.

Plants may also be grown along the top of the wall so their tumbling foliage softens the wall's sharp outline. Such plants include *Saponaria ocymoides,* with pale pink flowers through most of the summer that trail to about 2ft/60cm, and *Sedum acre* 'Aureum', which has bright yellow flowers and spreads to 2ft/60cm. Raised beds are similar to drystone walls, but with the wall encircling a bed 1½–3ft/45–90cm high up to 5ft/1.5m wide.

Scree beds

Scree beds are often placed around rock gardens. However, in very small gardens they are lovely on their own. Suitable plants range from miniature and slow-growing conifers to dwarf bulbs and perennials such as aethionema, erodium, *Phlox douglasii* and silene.

▲ *Scree beds are ideal for small gardens and can be added to an existing rock garden or constructed as features on their own.*

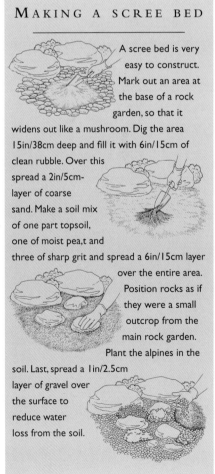

MAKING A SCREE BED

A scree bed is very easy to construct. Mark out an area at the base of a rock garden, so that it widens out like a mushroom. Dig the area 15in/38cm deep and fill it with 6in/15cm of clean rubble. Over this spread a 2in/5cm-layer of coarse sand. Make a soil mix of one part topsoil, one of moist pea,t and three of sharp grit and spread a 6in/15cm layer over the entire area. Position rocks as if they were a small outcrop from the main rock garden. Plant the alpines in the soil. Last, spread a 1in/2.5cm layer of gravel over the surface to reduce water loss from the soil.

wildlife ponds

These ponds create havens for wildlife including aquatic insects, small mammals, amphibians, and birds. Fish such as goldfish and shubunkins, which normally enrich ornamental ponds with color and vitality, should not be put in a wildlife pond because they soon become meals for birds.

Creating a wildlife pond

Wildlife ponds are sometimes thought suitable only for rural gardens, but they are also extremely important in towns where they provide feeding, bathing, and watering places for birds.

A flexible liner, most often butyl rubber sheeting, is usually used. Dig out to a varying depth of 2–2½ft/60–75cm.

This is essential to give pond life a chance of survival when the surface water freezes. Create an irregular outline, with space at one side to form a bog garden (pages 374–375) filled with moisture-loving plants. The pond should also include a gentle slope so that any wildlife can get in and out. Lay moist sand 2in/5cm thick and place the

flexible liner on top. If a path is to be built, allow an overlap of 9in/23cm so that paving slabs can be laid on top. Add another layer of sand to cover the liner, and top with a layer of heavy soil 2–3in/5–7.5cm thick.

Place large pebbles or another material along the edge of the liner to cover it. Fill the pond carefully by standing a bucket on the soil with the end of a hosepipe in it. Allow water to trickle gently over the sides of the bucket into the pond. Oxygenating plants can be planted directly into soil at the bottom of the pond, but waterlilies and marginal plants are best planted in plastic-mesh containers.

Looking after a wildlife pond

Your pond should reflect nature left to its own devices and appear as natural as possible. However, it will need some maintenance, and excess blanketweed,

◀ *Wildlife ponds create restful places in gardens. They attract and create homes for birds, amphibians, and small mammals.*

Constructing a wildlife pond

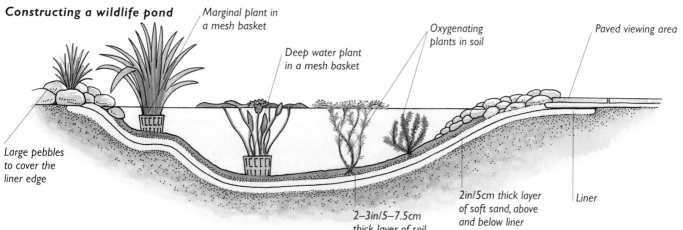

Marginal plant in a mesh basket

Deep water plant in a mesh basket

Oxygenating plants in soil

Paved viewing area

Large pebbles to cover the liner edge

2–3in/5–7.5cm thick layer of soil

2in/5cm thick layer of soft sand, above and below liner

Liner

duckweed, and fall leaves should be removed along with stems and leaves, if too many appear above the water surface. When the pond is newly filled, introduce aquatic life with a few buckets of water from an established pond.

Protecting wildlife

⊛ Never use pesticides or any garden sprays on plants growing in or near to garden ponds. Frogs, toads, and newts are highly susceptible to garden chemicals.

⊛ Do not use weedkillers on lawns surrounding a pond.

⊛ Put ramps at the pond edge giving easy access to small animals and amphibians.

⊛ Where possible, keep a clear area around a pond to reduce the chance of a cat creeping up on birds.

⊛ Keep the area free from overhanging deciduous trees. If left, fall leaves will decay and produce toxic gases.

⊛ Do not put your pond near trees with poisonous berries or fruits, like laburnum.

▶ Many moisture-loving plants can be planted around a wildlife pond. Ferns are especially attractive and many are suited to moist areas.

propagating plants

Within every gardener there is a desire to produce new plants, whether from seeds, cuttings, division, or by layering low-growing stems on shrubs. Many of these methods are easy and involve little time or expense. However, sowing half-hardy annuals in early spring requires a warm greenhouse; the young seedlings are transferred to seed trays and later planted into borders when all risk of frost has passed. Hardy annuals are sown outdoors in late spring where they are to germinate and grow.

simple propagation

The desire to increase plants is a passion for most gardeners, especially if it can be done easily and cheaply. Some ways are almost instant and include dividing clump-forming plants such as some herbaceous perennials. Other methods, such as layering, take longer before a fresh plant is produced.

Dividing plants

After about five years, herbaceous plants become congested and woody, with bare centers. In fall or spring cut down all stems to ground-level and use a garden fork to dig up the clump. Insert a couple of garden forks, back to back, into the clump and lever their handles together, so that the clump is loosened and can be pulled into several pieces. Select healthy young parts from around the outside, and replant them in a border. Discard the old woody pieces.

Layering shrubs and trees

This is a simple way to increase plants, although it may take more than a year before roots form and the new plant can be severed from its parent. It suits woody plants with low-growing branches that can be lowered to soil level. Layering can be done at any time, but spring and late summer to early fall are the best times of year.

Hardwood cuttings

This is an easy way to increase many shrubs and soft fruit bushes. All that is needed is a nursery bed, a spade and horticultural sand. Once taken and inserted in the ground they require little attention. These cuttings are taken in early or mid-fall, and consist of the current year's growth. Shrubs increased in this way include berberis, deutzia, forsythia, *Ilex* (holly), *Ligustrum* (privet), philadelphus, spiraea, and weigela.

To increase blackcurrants (*Ribes rigrum*), in mid-fall cut a shoot 8–10in/ 20–25cm long slightly above and below a bud, and insert it in a straight-sided trench, so that two buds are above the soil. Space them 3–4in/7.5–10cm apart and position them on a layer of horticultural sand. Firm the soil around them. Take gooseberry cuttings in mid-fall by cutting a shoot 12in/30cm long slightly above and below a bud. Remove all but the top four buds and insert the cutting about 6in/15cm deep in a straight-sided trench. Space the gooseberry cuttings 3–4in/7.5–10cm apart and place them on a layer of sharp sand. Firm the soil around them. Whitecurrants and redcurrants are increased in the same way.

SHRUBS AND TREES THAT CAN BE LAYERED

Amelanchier	Euonymus
Azalea	Forsythia
Calluna (heather)	Hamamelis
Camellia	Jasminum nudiflorum
Chaenomeles	Magnolia
Chimonanthus	Pieris
Cornus (dogwood)	Rhododendron
Cotinus	Rhus (sumac)
Cotoneaster	Vaccinium
Erica (heath)	Viburnum

HERBACEOUS PLANTS TO DIVIDE

Achillea	Geranium
Alchemilla mollis	Helenium
Anaphalis	Leucanthemum
Aruncus	x superbum
Astilbe	Lysimachia punctata
Campanula	Monarda
Coreopsis	Perennial asters
Echinacea	Rudbeckia (coneflower)
Erigeron (sea holly)	Solidago (goldenrod)
Filipendula	Tiarella (foamflower)

dividing herbaceous perennials

Hardwood cuttings (privet)

Select a mature, healthy shoot 10–12in/ 23–30cm long, and trim beneath a leaf joint.

Remove all the other leaves except the top six to eight.

1 To divide the roots of a large clump, insert two forks into the clump, and lever the handles together to force the roots apart. Remove the forks and discard the older, central part of the roots.

2 Pull and tease the young parts carefully from around the outside of the clump, making several pieces. Do not separate off tiny pieces which will take a long time to grow into plants that give a good display.

Make a trench 6–8in/15–20cm deep, with one straight side. Sprinkle sharp sand in the base, stand the cutting on it, and firm the soil around it.

layering shrubs

1 Select a long, low-growing, vigorous stem, up to two years old. Make a trench 3–6in/ 7.5–15cm deep, 9–18in/ 23–45cm from the tip of the stem.

2 Lower the stem into the trench and bend it upright, 9in/23cm from its end. At the bend, cut halfway through it or make a tongued cut.

3 Use a wooden or metal peg to secure the stem in the soil and insert a cane, without damaging the stem. Carefully firm the soil around the stem.

4 Tie the stem to the cane, but do not constrict it. When the shoot develops new growth, remove the soil, sever the stem, and transfer to a nursery bed.

383

sowing hardy annuals

Hardy annuals have a relatively short life; they are sown in flower beds in the spring and grow, flower, and die by the onset of cold weather in the fall. Although short lived they create spectacular displays, either in borders specially devoted to them or as fillers in flower beds.

Preparing hardy annual borders

In late fall or early winter, single-dig the soil (to the depth of a spade) and mix in decayed manure or compost, bury annual weeds, and burn perennial weeds. Leave the surface rough but even enough to allow the winter weather to break it down to a friable tilth. In mid- to late spring, shuffle sideways over the soil to consolidate it and rake it level.

▲ *Hardy annuals are often used to fill bare patches in herbaceous or mixed borders during their early years before plants are established.*

Sowing hardy annuals

Hardy annuals are not sown before mid- to late spring, when the soil has warmed up, because the seeds will not germinate in cold, wet soil. Use a trickle of sharp sand to mark areas of different sizes and shapes into which different species and varieties are to be sown. Those at the front of a border should be shallower and smaller than those at the back.

Some gardeners sow annuals by scattering seed on the surface, but this is wasteful. Instead, use a pointed stick to dig straight drills /¼–½in/6–12mm deep and 9in/23cm apart. Make the direction of the rows in each sowing area different from its neighbors. Sow the seeds thinly and evenly, and use the back of a metal rake to push and draw friable soil gently over them. Then firm the soil by using the head of a metal rake. When sowing is complete, use small sticks to mark the ends of each row. This later makes weeding much easier as the rows of annuals can be seen easily. Label each group of seeds with the name and date of sowing. Keep the soil moist.

Birds are often a problem, but they can be deterred by stretching black thread over the area. After germination, when the seedlings are large enough to handle, they must be thinned. The exact spacing depends on the species and variety (check the packet). Thin the seedlings in two stages, first to half the recommended distance, and then to the full spacing.

RAISING BIENNIALS

These are plants that produce flowers during their second season of growth. In late spring or early summer sow biennial seeds in a nursery bed in drills ½in/12mm deep and 9in/23cm apart. Sow the seeds evenly and thinly. After germination, when the seedlings are large enough to handle, thin them or transplant them to another nursery bed. Thinning is better than transplanting if the seeds were sown thinly. For example, thin small biennials such as daisies to 3–4in 7.5–10cm apart, and wallflowers and other tall flowers to 5–6in/13–15cm apart. Where seeds were sown thickly, fork up the clumps and select the strongest seedlings. Replant them 6–8in/15–20cm apart in rows 12in/30cm apart. In late summer or early fall, transplant the established plants into beds or containers.

sowing hardy annuals

1 Dig the soil in winter and in spring rake the surface level. Firm the surface by shuffling sideways to cover the whole area. Rake the surface level and use horticultural sand to mark the sowing areas.

2 Use a straight-edged piece of wood to mark the positions of the drills and a pointed stick to make drills ¼–½in/6–12mm deep and about 9in/23cm apart. Align the drills at a different angle for each sowing area.

3 Sow seeds evenly and thinly in each drill. Do not sow the seeds in clusters because this will result in overcrowding and poor growth. Take care not to waste seeds that fall between the drills

4 When each group of seeds has been sown, use the back of an iron rake to draw and push friable soil over the seeds. Firm the soil over the drill of seeds by pressing downward with the head of the rake.

▲ Hardy annuals are easy to grow and produce a wealth of blooms in many colors and shapes throughout summer. They die down in the fall.

sowing half-hardy annuals

Half-hardy annuals, sometimes called summer-flowering bedding plants, produce bright, summer-long displays in borders, window boxes, wall baskets, hanging baskets, and tubs. These plants are tender nature, which means that they are easily damaged by frost.

Sowing half-hardy annuals

Because these plants are slightly tender they need to be sown in gentle warmth in greenhouses or conservatories in late winter or early spring. Sowing them is not complicated, and the first stage is to fill a seed tray with seed starting mix and to firm it gently, especially around the edges. Mix that is left loose soon becomes dry.

Add more mix to the seed tray and use a straight-edged piece of wood to tap the surface level. Firm the surface by using a soil presser; this is a piece of wood, 5–6in/13–15cm square and ¾in/18mm thick with a handle on one side. Firm the mix to about ½in/ 12mm below the rim of the seed tray. To sow seed, tip a few seeds into piece of stiff card folded into a V-shape, hold it over the mix and tap its end lightly so

sowing half hardy annuals

1 Fill a plastic seed tray with seed-starting mix. Using a soil presser, level and firm it to about 12mm/½in below the top of the tray.

2 Tip a few seeds into a piece of paper folded into a V-shape and tap its end to sow seeds evenly and thinly over the surface, but not near the sides.

3 The thickness of mix covering the seeds varies between species. Check the seed packet instructions and use a sieve to cover them evenly.

4 Water the mix by standing the seed tray in a bowl of water until moisture seeps to the surface. Remove and allow excess to drain away.

that the seed falls evenly over the surface. Do not sow seed within ½in/ 12mm of the tray's edge. Cover the sown seed with mix shaken through a horticultural or domestic sieve to give a fine, even covering. The thickness varies with the species (check the seed packet) but it is usually ⅛–¼in/3–6mm. Water the seed by standing the seed tray in a bowl filled with 1in/2.5cm of clean water. When moisture seeps to the soil surface, remove the seed tray.

Gentle warmth (61–70°F/16–21°C) is needed to encourage germination. This varies for different species, so check on the seed packet. Cover the seed tray with a plastic lid or a sheet of glass, then with a sheet of newspaper, because most seeds need darkness to germinate, although a few do require light.

Check the mix regularly to keep it moist, and wipe the glass to remove any condensation that forms on the underside. Depending on the species, germination takes between 7 and 21 days. As soon as the seeds germinate, remove the newspaper and lift off the glass or plastic cover for longer periods each day. Also, slowly reduce the temperature so that the seedlings adjust to normal weather conditions.

HINTS AND TIPS

Use only clean starting mix when sowing seeds or pricking off seedlings. Soil directly from a garden contains pests and diseases that soon damage seedlings. Also, it may be badly drained and result in root rot.

pricking off seedlings

1 After germination, seedlings grow rapidly and if left, become congested and damaged. As soon as they are large enough to handle, transfer them to wider spacings.

2 Use a small dibble to make holes in the growing mix, 1–1½in/25–36mm deep and 1½in/36mm apart, leaving a margin around the container ½in/12mm from the edge.

3 Use a spatula or an old kitchen fork to loosen a cluster of seedlings. Place them on a piece of moist newspaper so that their roots do not become dry.

4 Hold each seedling gently by one of its leaves, not by its stem, and lower the roots into a hole, so that the roots are at about the same depth as before.

5 Use a dibble to firm the mix gently around the roots, taking care not to squash them. Then level the surface of the compost carefully.

6 Stand the seed tray on a level, well-drained surface. Water the seedlings with a fine rose to settle the mix around the roots.

increasing plants from cuttings

Taking cuttings is a popular way to increase plants and because it is a vegetative process each new plant is identical to its parent. Hardwood cuttings are easy to root and no special equipment or artificial warmth is needed. Softwood and semihardwood cuttings are raised differently.

Softwood cuttings

The tips of fresh growth are used to propagate many houseplants and herbaceous perennials, and they are called softwood or sometimes soft-stemmed cuttings.

Softwood cuttings can be taken from soft-stemmed greenhouse plants through the year, although spring and early summer are the best times. Softwood cuttings from herbaceous perennials are taken in early and midsummer. However, there are exceptions. To encourage the development of soft chrysanthemum shoots early in the year, dormant roots are boxed up in compost during early winter, and kept warm and moist. They produce soft shoots which can be used as cuttings. During late winter or spring; trim them to 2–3in/5–7.5cm long and insert three or four cuttings about 1in/2.5cm deep in pots of equal parts moist peat and horticultural sand. Firm the mix around the cuttings, water them, and keep the pots at 55°F/13°C. Hormone rooting powders also encourage rapid rooting.

Semihardwood cuttings

These firmer cuttings are also called half-ripe and semimature cuttings and are more mature than softwood cuttings. The method is shown opposite.

Hardwood cuttings

Many hardy shrubs and soft fruits can be increased with cuttings from the mature shoots of the current season's growth. In fall to early spring when plants are dormant, cut a firm shoot 9–15in/ 23-38cm long, depending on the shrub. Trim just above a bud at the top of the shoot and just below a bud at the other end. Take a spade and make a trench with one side vertical in a nursery bed, and plant each cutting two-thirds of its length deep and about 4in/10cm apart. Firm soil around them. Hardwood cuttings take about a year to form roots. When rooted, transfer them individually to wider spacing in a nursery bed.

◄ *The hardy deciduous shrub* Chaenomeles *(flowering quince) can be increased from heel-cuttings during mid- and late summer.*

softwood cuttings

Semihardwood cuttings

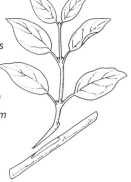

Take half-ripe cuttings during midsummer to the early part of late summer. Select a shoot 4–5in/10–13cm long, with a heel at its base.

Use a sharp knife to trim off the lower leaves and to remove whisker-like growths from the heel.

1 Spring and early summer are the best times to take softwood cuttings. Fill a pot with equal parts moist peat and horticultural sand, and firm it, especially around the edges.

2 A plantpot about 3in/7.5cm wide will hold three or four cuttings comfortably. Use a dibble to make holes approximately ½in/12mm from the sides of the pot and about 1½in/36mm deep.

Insert the cuttings 1½–2in/36–50cm deep in equal parts moist peat and horticultural sand. Firm the mix around them and water gently.

3 Use a sharp knife to trim the base of each cutting, just below a leaf-joint. Also, cut off the lower leaves. Insert one cutting into each hole, then firm the soil around it and water the cuttings gently.

4 To encourage rapid rooting, insert three to five thin stakes, 6–8in/15–20cm into the soil and draw a clear plastic bag over them. Seal around the pot securely with a rubber band.

RAISING SHRUBS FROM SEMIHARDWOOD CUTTINGS

Abelia

Camellia

Ceanothus (Californian lilac)

Chaenomeles (flowering quince)

Chimonanthus (wintersweet)

Cistus (rock rose)

Cotoneaster

Escallonia

Potentilla

Viburnum

care of trees, shrubs, and climbers

Careful planting is essential for all garden plants and especially for long-lived trees, shrubs, and climbers; constricted roots or poor soil will restrict the establishment and subsequent growth of plants. Hedges, evergreen and deciduous, also need careful attention. Pruning is important for ornamental shrubs, trees, and climbers and for fruiting bushes and trees. Roses need yearly pruning with different techniques for hybrid tea, floribunda, climbers, and ramblers.

planting trees and shrubs

Since they form a permanent framework in a garden, always buy strong and healthy trees and shrubs from a reputable nursery or garden center. Inferior plants are never satisfactory and will be a continuing disappointment, whereas healthy plants will give pleasure for many years.

Planting container-grown shrubs

Plant these at any time when the soil is neither frozen nor waterlogged. However, spring is best because it gives the plant all summer to become established before the onset of winter.

Prepare the soil a week before planting by forking a dressing of fertilizer lightly into the surface. The day before planting, stand the plant—still in its container—on a well-drained surface and water the soil. The next day, dig a hole to accommodate the roots, make a shallow mound at the bottom of the hole, and firm the soil around it. Stand the plant on the mound, with its most attractive side facing toward the front of the bed. Adjust its height so that the top of the rootball is slightly lower than the surrounding soil. This can be checked by placing a straight piece of wood across the hole. Draw soil around the rootball and firm it down in layers. Continue to fill the hole, firming the soil with the heel of your boot. When planting is completed, rake or lightly fork the soil to remove foot marks, and water the plant.

Planting bare-rooted trees

Deciduous, bare-rooted trees can be bought from garden centers, nurseries, and through mail-order companies. They are sold leafless during winter and will have been dug up from nursery beds during their dormant period. They too can be planted whenever the soil is neither frozen nor waterlogged.

The first stage in planting begins immediately you get the plant home. Remove all packaging and stand the roots in a bucket of water for about one day. Then plant it or, if the soil is not suitable, heel it into a trench about 12in/30cm deep. Place the roots in the trench, and cover with soil. Before planting, trim long, thin or damaged roots, and any misplaced or damaged branches. Dig a hole large enough to accommodate the roots and follow the steps illustrated on page 135, making sure the friable soil is between the roots.

When supporting a tree by using a vertical stake, knock this into the soil on the windward side before planting the tree, but check that its top will be slightly below the lowest branch. Secure the stake to the tree. Other ways to support trees are described on page 355.

ADVANTAGES OF CONTAINER-GROWN SHRUBS AND TREES

Since the introduction of garden centers in the early 1960s, plants have been increasingly sold in containers. They have many advantages.
◉ Plants receive little check when planted.
◉ They can be inspected before they are bought.
◉ They make an instant garden.

ADVANTAGES OF BARE-ROOTED TREES

◉ They are often cheaper to buy than container-grown plants.
◉ Their roots are usually less constricted than those of container-grown plants.
◉ Unusual species of trees and shrub are not always sold as container-grown plants, but may be available only as bare-rooted specimens from specialist nurseries.

planting a container-grown shrub

1 About a week before planting the shrub, fork a light dressing of a general fertilizer into the soil. Work the fertilizer evenly into the area that is to be planted.

2 The day before planting, thoroughly water the soil in the pot. Dig a hole to accommodate the roots. Make a mound of soil at the bottom and firm it.

3 Lower the rootball into the hole. Use a straight-edged piece of wood to check that the rootball is positioned slightly lower than the level of the surrounding soil.

4 Draw soil around and over the rootball and use the heel of your boot to firm it. Rake the surface level and water the plant and the soil around it thoroughly.

planting a bare-rooted tree or shrub

1 Before planting, thoroughly soak the roots in water. Dig a hole and check that the old soil mark on the stem will be slightly deeper than before.

2 Some shrubs have a "face" side, one that is more attractive than others. Insure that this is positioned to face toward the front of the bed.

3 Spread friable soil over and around the roots and firm it in layers. When planting is complete, rake the soil level to remove all foot marks.

4 When the planting is completed, water the soil and spread a 2–3in/5–7.5cm-thick mulch of garden compost over the soil.

hedges and windbreaks

Hedges have many uses, from creating boundaries and windbreaks to separating and making sheltered gardens for tender plants. Creating privacy and diminishing noise are other roles for hedges, which can be formed of both evergreen and deciduous trees and shrubs.

Multipurpose hedges

Hedges fulfill many roles, some functional, others decorative. Keeping out unwanted animals is important, in country and in urban areas. Several shrubs and trees which make good hedges also have spines or prickly leaves and will keep out most intruders. They include holly, pyracantha and berberis, and all can be encouraged to form low dense growth.

Marking a boundary has always been important, using plants such as beech, privet, and yew, but internal hedges are equally useful for edging paths and separating parts of a garden. Good candidates include lavender and *Buxus sempervirens* 'Suffruticosa' (dwarf box).

Forming a windbreak is important in exposed areas, and the benefits can be felt up to a distance of 30 times the height of the hedge, although most of the protection is in the first third (see page 326). Protecting plants in coastal areas from strong, salt-laden wind is also important. Hedging plants that survive these conditions include tamarisk, and *Hippophae* and *Escallonia* varieties.

Privacy from neighbors is increasingly important. Conifers and privet will provide year-round screens. Reducing road and neighbor noise is also important, and conifers and evergreen shrubs do the job well. When noise is a real nuisance, plant a staggered, double row of hedging plants. Finally, use hedges to make an attractive background for other plants. Yew, for instance, makes a superb backdrop for herbaceous borders, and white flowers stand out well against the dark green leaves.

Planting bare-rooted, deciduous plants

These are planted during their dormant period, from late fall to early spring. Encourage bushiness by cutting back each plant by one-third to a half immediately after planting.

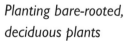
◀ *The slightly tender evergreen shrub* Choisya ternata *(Mexican orange blossom) has flowers and leaves fragrant with the scent of oranges.*

planting a conifer hedge

1 Dig a trench 1ft/30cm deep and 1½ft/30–45cm wide. Water the plants in their pots and place them in the trench. Use a straight edge to check that the top of each rootball is slightly lower than the soil level.

2 Remove the pot and spread friable soil between and around the rootballs. Firm the soil in layers and check that each plant remains upright. Using the heel of your boot firm the soil around the plants.

3 Use bamboo canes to support the conifers, tying one to each plant. Tie a piece of string to the cane, then around the conifer, without restricting the stem. During the first year regularly check the ties.

4 Water the soil thoroughly to settle it around the roots. Add a 3–4in/7.5–10cm thick mulch around the plants and along the sides of the row. Water the plants regularly through the first summer.

SIX POPULAR HEDGES

Buxus sempervirens 'Suffruticosa' (dwarf box)
Hedge height: 8–15in/20–38cm
Hedge width: 6–9in/15–23cm
Plant: 6–8in/15–20cm apart
Dwarf, evergreen shrub, ideal for forming a miniature hedge as part of a knot or herb garden. Bears small, shiny, deep-green leaves.

Cupressus macrocarpa (Monterey cypress)
Hedge height: 6–10ft/1.8–3m
Hedge width: 3½–4ft/1–1.2m
Plant: 18–24in/45–60cm apart
Evergreen conifer with densely packed, bright green foliage. Young plants are sometimes damaged in very cold areas and may need some protection until they are mature.

Escallonia 'Donard Seedling'
Hedge height: 5–6ft/1.5–1.8m
Hedge width: 4–5ft/1.2–1.5m
Plant: 15–18in/38–45cm apart
Slightly tender evergreen shrub with a lax nature, and apple-blossom pink flowers in early and midsummer.

Fagus sylvatica (beech)
Hedge height: 8–12ft/2.4–3.6m
Hedge width: 3½–5ft/1–1.5m
Plant: 18–24in/45–60cm apart
Deciduous, with bright-green leaves when young, then mid-green and yellow and russet tints in the fall.

Lavandula angustifolia 'Hidcote' (lavender)
Hedge height: 1–2ft/30–60cm
Hedge width: 1½–2ft/45–60cm
Plant: 9–12in/23–30cm apart
Evergreen shrub, often short-lived as a hedge, with silvery gray leaves and deep purple-blue flowers from mid- to late summer. Ideal as an internal hedge.

Ligustrum ovalifolium (California privet)
Hedge height: 4–6ft/1.2–1.8m
Hedge width: 2–2½ft/60–75cm
Plant: 12–18in/30–45cm apart
Bushy shrub, usually evergreen but partially evergreen in cold areas, with oval leaves. 'Aureum' is a yellow-leaved form.

pruning ornamental shrubs

Few gardening tasks are cloaked in as much mystery as pruning. Its aims, however, are quite simple, and with ornamental shrubs include better flowers and an attractive shape. Pruning also insures good health by removing any congested and diseased shoots.

When to prune?

The timing of pruning often causes confusion. In temperate areas it is influenced by the cold winter weather and if gardeners did not have to concern themselves with this period, the optimum pruning time for flowering plants would be immediately after their flowers fade. However, as pruning encourages the development of young, tender shoots these would be damaged if late summer-flowering shrubs were pruned immediately their flowers faded.

Deciduous flowering shrubs

These shrubs can be put into three groups according to the time of year they flower—winter, spring, early to midsummer, and late summer. Good choices include:

Winter flowering—*Hamamelis mollis* (Chinese witch hazel), *Cornus mas* (cornelian cherry) and winter-flowering viburnums. They need little pruning, other than cutting back damaged shoots to healthy buds in the spring. Also cut out thin, twiggy shoots and those that grow towards the plant's center.

Spring and early to midsummer flowering—they flower on shoots that were produced during the previous year and include forsythia, philadelphus and weigela. They are pruned immediately their flowers fade.

Late-summer flowering—these plants flower on shoots that develop during the current year and include *Buddleja davidii* (butterfly bush), *Caryopteris × clandonensis* and *Spiraea japonica*. In spring, as soon as all risk of frost has passed, cut out the previous year's flowering shoots to encourage strong new shoots.

◀ Buddleja davidii *(butterfly bush) develops large, tapering spires of flowers from midsummer to fall. Prune them in early spring.*

COLORED STEMS

Shrubs such as *Cornus alba* (redtwig dogwood), *C. a.* 'Sibirica' and *C. stolonifera* 'Flaviramea' (red osier dogwood) produce a mass of young, colored stems if cut down to near soil level in the spring. This gives them a complete growing season in which to develop shoots. These will be attractive in the fall and right through winter.

▶ *Weigela florida 'Foliis Purpureis' reveals a wealth of pink flowers amid purple-flushed leaves. It is an ideal shrub for small gardens.*

Pruning shrubs

Winter-flowering shrubs, such as Hamamelis mollis, need little pruning, other than cutting out dead, twiggy shoots.

Cut out crossing and dead shoots that congest the shrub's center.

Buddleja davidii (butterfly bush), a deciduous shrub with flowers from midsummer to fall, is pruned in early spring.

Evergreen shrubs

These are in leaf all year and require little pruning. In spring, or early summer in cold areas, cut out weak, diseased and misplaced shoots. If the shrub flowers in spring, delay pruning until these fade.

Conifers

Most conifers are evergreen but a few are deciduous and include *Ginkgo biloba* (maidenhair tree) and *Larix* (larch).

Conifers bleed profusely when pruned in spring and summer, and are therefore best cut in late fall or early winter, when there is not an active flow of sap.

Pruning ericas (heath) and callunas (heather)

These evergreen shrubs are kept neat by trimming them with hedging shears. The time to prune depends on when they flower. Remove all the clippings.

❀ *Callunas* and summer-flowering ericas—trim in spring, before growth begins. Cut off dead flowers to form a neat and undulating outline. Plants pruned in this way include *Erica cinerea* (bell heather), *E. vagans* (Cornish heath),

E. terminalis (Corsican heath), *E. tetralix* (cross-leaved heather) and *Calluna vulgaris* (Scottish heather, ling).

❀ Winter and spring-flowering types—they are trimmed as soon as their flowers fade to create a neat outline. They include *Erica × darleyensis* (Darley Dale heath), *E. erigena* better known as *E. mediterranea* (Mediterranean heath), and *E. carnea* (spring heath or winter heath). *Daboecias*—trim off old flower heads and lax shoots in late fall, after flowering has finished. In cold areas leave this task until early spring.

Tree heathers—they need little pruning but in late spring, after their flowers fade, remove straggly shoots.

pruning climbers

Many climbing plants need regular pruning to restrain growth or to encourage the regular development of flowers. Deciduous climbers grown for their attractive foliage require little pruning, other than restricting their size, whereas those with attractive flowers need annual attention.

Pruning climbers and wall shrubs

These plants are so varied in their nature, flowering time, and size that pruning is best described individually.

❀ *Actinidia deliciosa*, still known as *A. chinensis* (Chinese gooseberry)—

▲ *Leafy climbers create privacy and are ideal for separating parts of a garden. This enables cloistered areas to lead directly on to lawns.*

deciduous climber. In late winter, use pruners to thin out and restrict growth.

❀ *Actinidia kolomikta* (variegated kiwi vine)—deciduous climber. If space is restricted, cut back shoots in late winter.

❀ *Akebia*—evergreen climber in mild winters, but usually semievergreen. Thin out and shorten straggly shoots in late winter or spring.

❀ *Berberidopsis corallina* (coral plant)—slightly tender evergreen shrub. Use pruners to thin out overcrowded plants in late winter or early spring.

❀ *Carpenteria californica*—slightly tender evergreen shrub. No regular pruning is needed, other than cutting out straggly shoots after the flowers fade.

❀ *Ceanothus* (California lilac)—many evergreen species can be grown against a wall. Little pruning is needed, but reduce the previous year's growth in spring.

❀ *Clematis macropetala*—deciduous climber. Cut out dead and thin shoots in early spring.

❀ *Clematis montana*—deciduous climber. Little pruning is needed, especially if it is given plenty of space. However, when

pruning is needed to restrain growth, cut back as soon as the flowers fade.

❀ *Clematis flammula*—deciduous climber. From late winter to early spring, cut out weak and dead shoots. Also, cut back to healthy buds any shoots that flowered during the previous year.

❀ *Clematis orientalis* 'Orange peel'—deciduous climber. This is pruned as for *C. flammula*.

❀ *Clematis tangutica*—deciduous climber. Prune as for *C. flammula*.

❀ *Eccremocarpus scaber* (Chilean glory flower)—evergreen sub-shrubby climber. Use pruners to cut out frost-damaged shoots in late spring. If it is severely damaged, the best course of action that you can take is to cut all shoots back to their bases in spring.

❀ *Fallopia baldschuanica* (Russian vine)—deciduous climber. Cut back rampant plants in spring.

❀ *Hedera* (ivy)—evergreen climber. Wide range, from small-leaved types to those with leaves 6in/15cm wide or more. As necessary, cut back rampant plants in spring.

pruning winter-flowering jasmine

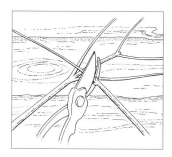 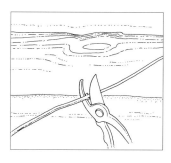 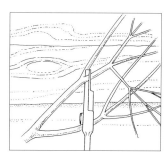 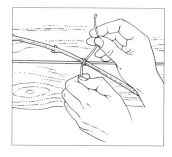

1 Use sharp pruners to cut out crossing shoots; cut each one back to a strong bud.

2 Cut back sideshoots to strong buds to encourage the development of new growth.

3 Where shoots are congested, cut them back to a strong shoot or bud.

4 The last task is to tie all sideshoots to the supporting wires. Use soft string.

❀ *Humulus lupulus* 'Aureus' (yellow-leaved hop)—herbaceous climber. Cut down to ground level all shoots in fall or late winter.

❀ *Hydrangea anomala petiolaris* (Japanese climbing hydrangea)—deciduous climber. No regular pruning is needed, other than trimming to shape and cutting out dead shoots in spring.

❀ *Jasminum nudiflorum* (winter-flowering jasmine)—deciduous shrub. After flowering, cut out weak and old shoots. Also, cut back flowered shoots to 2–3in/5–7.5cm of their bases.

❀ *Jasminum officinale* (common white jasmine)—deciduous climber. After the flowers fade, thin out flowering shoots to their bases.

❀ *Lonicera* (honeysuckle)—deciduous, semievergreen or evergreen climber. No regular pruning is required, other than thinning out congested shoots after the flowers fade.

❀ *Parthenocissus*—deciduous climber. No regular pruning is required, other than

cutting out overcrowded and dead shoots in spring.

❀ *Passiflora caerulea* (passion flower)—slightly tender evergreen climber. In late winter, cut out any tangled shoots to their bases or to soil level. Also, cut back side-shoots to about 6in/15cm of the main stems.

❀ *Vitis coignetiae* (crimson glory vine)—deciduous climber. No regular pruning is needed, but where necessary to prevent the plant from becoming invasive, trim excessive growth in spring.

❀ *Wisteria*—deciduous climber. Prune established plants in winter and summer. In late winter, cut back all shoots to within two or three buds of the point where they started growing during the previous season. In the latter part of midsummer, cut the current season's young shoots back to within five or six buds of the base.

▶ *The dramatically colored* Humulus lupulus 'Aureus' *(yellow-leaved hop) is a herbaceous climber and each year produces fresh leaves.*

pruning fruit bushes and trees

Bush, cane, and tree fruits differ in the way they produce fruits. Some develop fruit on young, newly produced shoots, others on an existing framework. Therefore, pruning must encourage the development of suitable shoots, as well as allow light and air to reach the plants.

Bush fruits

These popular fruits for small gardens need little space and produce fruit within a few years of being planted.

❀ Blackcurrants—on planting, cut all stems to one or two buds above the soil. During the following year, stems develop, which are left to grow and bear fruit. Between late fall and early spring the following year, and thereafter, prune by cutting to ground level all shoots that produced fruits. Also, cut out thin, weak and diseased shoots to allow light and air to enter the bush.

❀ Gooseberries—established bushes have a permanent framework upon which short, fruit-bearing spurs develop. Newly planted gooseberry bushes without a framework of branches should be pruned in winter by cutting back all shoots by half. Prune established bushes in winter; cut out diseased, damaged, and overcrowded shoots. Also, cut back by half all shoots produced during the previous season, and reduce side-shoots to about 2in/5cm long.

❀ Redcurrants and white currants— they have a permanent framework and are pruned like gooseberries.

Cane fruits

Being upright these will fit into narrow positions, perhaps alongside a path.

❀ Summer-fruiting raspberries—they fruit on upright canes produced the previous year. Prune established plants in the fall by cutting out all canes that produced fruit in the summer. Leave the young canes tied to the supporting wires to fruit the following year.

❀ Fall-fruiting raspberries—they fruit on canes produced earlier the same year. Prune established plants in late winter and cut all canes to ground level. In spring, as the canes grow, cut out weak

▲ *Cane fruits, such as raspberries, need yearly pruning to encourage the growth of young canes that will bear fruit during the following year.*

ones at the base and tie the remaining ones to the supporting wires.

✹ Blackberries and hybrid berries—they fruit on canes produced the previous year. Immediately after picking the berries, cut down to the base all canes that produced fruit. Then spread out the remaining young canes and tie them to the supporting wires.

Tree fruits

It usually takes several years before a framework of branches and fruiting spurs is formed. Where space is limited, plant cordon, espalier and fan-trained forms against a wall, or secure them to a framework of tiered wires.

✹ Apples and pears—during the first four years it is essential to develop healthy, well-positioned branches. Once they are established, pruning creates a balance between maintaining and renewing the framework and retaining a proportion of the existing fruiting wood and spurs, while developing others. Creating and maintaining this framework is a task best tackled in winter. However, when apples and pears are grown as cordons and espaliers, pruning will also be needed during the summer to retain the shape and inhibit the growth of unnecessary shoots. Do not be in a hurry for the tree to bear fruit.

✹ Cherries—never prune cherry trees in winter when they are not growing strongly and are unable to prevent the entry of bacterial canker through cut surfaces. They are ideal for growing as a fan against a wall.

▶ *Apple trees need regular pruning to encourage the development of fresh fruiting spurs to replace old ones. Old wood can also be removed.*

✹ Plums—these are usually grown as bushes or fans. When creating a framework of branches in a young tree, prune in mid-spring, just as the sap is rising. Try to create three to five strong branches. Later, prune in early summer, removing dead and diseased wood to keep the tree healthy and not congested. With fan-trained trees, prune in spring to create short side-shoots that grow from the framework.

✹ Figs—these are often inherited in old, town gardens and are easy to cultivate when their growth is limited by restricting their roots. Prune established plants in early summer. Pinch back all young shoots leaving only five leaves to encourage the development of new, fruiting shoots. In early fall, thin out the young fruits (about the size of a pea). These will develop into fruits that can be picked during the following year.

Pruning gooseberries

Pruning raspberries

Summer fruiting | Fall fruiting

pruning bush and species roses

There are many strongly held opinions about the best way to prune roses involving the timing, method, and severity. Here we give the basic philosophy, but you might have to amend your approach according to the rose variety, soil type, and weather.

Large-flowered bush (hybrid tea) and cluster-flowered bush (floribunda) roses

These need regular pruning to keep them healthy and flower-bearing, but there is some disagreement about how and when to prune. Although pruning can be done at any time during a rose's dormant period, in cold areas it is best left until early spring. The optimum time is when growth is beginning and the uppermost buds are starting to swell, but before leaves appear. Rose bushes planted in late fall and during winter are also best pruned in spring. Because leaving pruning until early spring puts bushes at risk from winter wind damage, when their roots might be loosened in the soil, it is best to cut back long shoots in late fall or early winter.

Bush roses respond in distinct ways to the severity in which they are pruned. If they are hard pruned (sometimes called low pruning), with stems cut back to three or four buds, they produce vigorous shoots during the following season. This suits newly planted bushes and weak-growing varieties. Also, it is a technique often used when growing exhibition blooms. Where large-flowered bush roses are grown close together in beds, hard pruning is the best method. It results in a mass of strong stems.

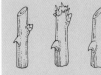

◀ *Most rose bushes need yearly pruning to create glorious displays of flowers and to keep the plant healthy and not congested with shoots.*

If moderately pruned (sometimes called medium pruning), with stems cut back by about one half, growth develops. This suits most bush roses.

When bush roses are lightly pruned (sometimes called long or high pruning), cutting back stems by about one third, only a little growth develops. This suits vigorous varieties and roses growing in light, sandy, and impoverished soils. When light pruning is carried out over

WHEN MAKING CUTS

Take care to make pruning cuts in the right position. A cut too high above a bud encourages a shoot to die back, but if the cut is too close it will damage the bud. Make a sloping cut about ⅓in/6mm above an outward-facing bud. Use sharp pruners with a good action. Ragged cuts with blunt blades make it easier for infections and diseases to enter the stem, and cause it to die back.

several years, it often results in spindly bushes that bear inferior flowers. Encourage better growth by feeding, mulching, and watering plants.

Shrub and species roses

These need very little pruning and none at all during the first two years after being planted. During this period allow the shrub to build up growth. Thereafter, each spring, cut out dead, weak, thin, and diseased shoots. If, after several years of growth, the shrub becomes congested, remove older shoots to enable young ones to grow.

'New English Roses'

These are repeat-flowering shrubs. The aim is to build up an attractively shaped shrub and to encourage the regular development of young shoots. These shrubs vary in size so beware of pruning too severely. When you buy a 'New English Rose' it will probably have been pruned so no more will be needed during the first year. Each spring cut out weak, thin, twiggy and diseased growth. After a few years, also cut out congested growth so that young shoots can grow strongly. Cut the remaining shoots to half their size, but take care not to spoil the shape of the shrub. Some 'New English Roses' can be treated as bushes or climbers.

Pruning hybrid tea and floribunda roses

Hard pruning
Cut back all stems to three or four buds from their base.

Moderate pruning
Cut back strong, healthy stems by half. Cut weak ones back further.

Light pruning
Cut back stems by about one third. Also, cut back sideshoots.

▶ *Roses are equally attractive whether planted in borders with a rich medley of other flowers or on their own in separate beds and borders.*

pruning climbers and ramblers

These roses may appear to be similar, but they have different natures. Climbers have a permanent framework and large flowers borne singly or in small trusses during the latter part of early summer and into midsummer. Ramblers produce small flowers in huge trusses, in midsummer.

Pruning climbers

There are two main ways to prune climbers, and these are influenced by the variety. Pruning takes place in early spring, when growth is just beginning.

Method one—little pruning is needed except for cutting out dead, diseased and old, exhausted wood. Cut back to 3in/7.5cm long all side-shoots that flowered the previous year. Varieties

needing this treatment include 'Casino', 'Climbing Ena Harkness', 'Climbing Étoile de Hollande', 'Madame Grégoire Staechelin', and 'Mermaid'.

Method two—little pruning is needed except for cutting out dead, diseased, and old, exhausted wood. Also cut off withered shoot tips. Varieties suitable for this treatment include 'Compassion', 'Golden Showers', 'Joseph's Coat', 'Parade', 'Madame Alfred Carrière', 'Maigold', 'Meg', 'Pink Perpetue', and 'Zéphirine Drouhin'.

Pruning ramblers

There are three main ways to prune ramblers and, as with climbers, the appropriate method is influenced by the variety. Pruning is in late summer or fall, as soon as flowering has finished. Cut stems of newly planted ramblers to soil level. The following information applies

◀ *Climbing Rose 'Mermaid' has large, single, sulfur yellow flowers and amber-colored stamens. This rose is superb when seen in bright sunlight growing against a wall.*

to established ramblers that will have young shoots bearing flowers the following year, and to shoots that produced flowers in the current year.

Method one—having removed all stems that produced flowers during the current year, tie the young shoots to a supporting framework. However, if insufficient new shoots were produced, leave a few old stems and trim back their lateral shoots to 3in/7.5cm long. Varieties suitable for this treatment include 'American Pillar', 'Crimson Shower', 'Dorothy Perkins', 'Sander's White Rambler', and 'Seagull'.

Method two—cut back all flowered stems to new growth, and cut back one or two old stems to about 12in/30cm above soil level. Where plants are congested and it is impossible to take down stems, cut back lateral shoots to 3in/7.5cm long. Varieties suitable for this treatment include 'Albéric Barbier',

'Albertine', 'Paul's Himalayan Climber' and 'Veilchenblau'.

Method three—pruning is very simple because all you need do is cut out dead and old wood, and cut back the tips of lateral shoots that have flowered. Varieties that have proved suitable for this pruning method include 'Emily Gray', *Rosa filipes* 'Kiftsgate', and 'Wedding Day'.

▲ *Climbing Rose 'Madame Grégoire Staechelin', has long, shapely buds that open to reveal semi-double, glowing pink flowers.*

PRUNING TOOLS

Pruners are ideal for cutting sideshoots on climbers and ramblers, but when severing stouter stems, stronger equipment is essential. Long-handled loppers—with an anvil or bypass cutting action—will cut stout stems from a distance, reducing scratching. A Grecian pruning saw with a curved blade that cuts on the pull stroke is also useful when dealing with neglected ramblers. Wear thick gloves to protect your hands. Place all the pruned stems in a wheelbarrow, or collect them on a large piece of hessian on the ground.

gardening under glass

A greenhouse extends the range of things you can do in your garden. For example, instead of buying half-hardy annuals as bedding plants, you can grow them from seed. Many useful devices make greenhouse gardening easy. They include automatic ventilators, extractor fans, and heated propagation frames. The following pages explain the technicalities of greenhouse gardening. They also show you how to utilize cloches, cold frames, and poly-tunnels, all alternatives to the greenhouse, and especially useful in the vegetable garden.

greenhouse gardening

Greenhouses add a dimension to gardening in a temperate climate, enabling a wider range of plants to be grown. Summer-flowering bedding plants can be sown in gentle warmth in late winter and early spring for later planting in borders and containers when all risk of frost has passed.

Range of greenhouses

Greenhouses range in shape, structure, and size, giving a very wide choice. Where possible, choose the largest greenhouse you can afford that will fit into your garden. Growing plants in greenhouses often becomes a passion demanding ever more space.

❀ Even-span—also called full-span greenhouses, have a traditional outline with a ridged sloping glass roof. Traditionally made of wood, they have a low brick or wood-paneled base, and glass above. Wooden designs are available but aluminum types are popular; these have glass from the ground to the apex.

Even-span greenhouses about 8ft/2.4m wide have a central path, and 3ft/90cm-wide areas on both sides that can be used for staging or growing plants such as tomatoes at ground level. Where a greenhouse is 6ft/1.8m or 7ft/2.1m wide, the spaces will be smaller but still thoroughly practical.

❀ Lean-to greenhouses—these are designed in width and length to suit the wall they are constructed against. Most lean-to greenhouses are glazed from soil level to the top, but with a brick surround to about 2½ft/75cm high they begin to look like a conservatory, especially where there is direct entry into the house.

❀ Hexagonal greenhouses—these have a more modern design and are becoming increasingly popular. They are usually constructed of aluminum with glass. Staging can be bought to fit.

❀ Mini greenhouses—these are for gardens with only enough room for a

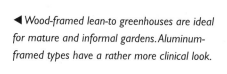

◄ *Wood-framed lean-to greenhouses are ideal for mature and informal gardens. Aluminum-framed types have a rather more clinical look.*

tiny lean-to structure, which can be positioned against a garden wall, a stout fence, or the house. Proprietary staging is available and young plants can be raised in them in spring. However, because the volume of air inside is small, dramatic fluctuations in temperature can occur when the front is closed.

Wood or metal?

Greenhouses were traditionally built with a wooden frame, but increasingly aluminum is now used.

⊛ Timber—the type of wood used markedly influences its longevity. Baltic red wood, also known as yellow deal, is used but needs regular painting. Western red cedar is more durable and, instead of being painted, is regularly coated in linseed oil. The Victorians used long-lasting oak and teak, but nowadays their high cost usually makes them prohibitively expensive.

⊛ Aluminum—this is widely used and, when glass is added, creates a strong structure. The extruded aluminum is designed so that both shelving and insulation brackets can be attached. Because the glazing bars are narrower than those of wood, much more light enters the greenhouse.

▶ *Aluminum-framed greenhouses are available in many interesting shapes, including a wigwam (right) and a hexagonal shape.*

▼ *The all-glass, aluminum-framed greenhouse enables the maximum amount of light to enter the structure.*

POSITIONING A GREENHOUSE

Choosing the right position in a garden for a greenhouse can reduce fuel bills. Try to:

⊛ Position full-span greenhouses so that the span runs east to west. Position lean-to types, against a south- or west-facing wall.

Where possible, position doors on the side away from the prevailing wind. If the door is hinged insure that it does not open directly into the wind; similarly, if it slides, check that it first opens on the side away from the prevailing wind.

⊛ Avoid positions under overhanging trees which block out light. A snapping branch could also cause damage.

⊛ Because strong winds in late winter and early spring soon cool a greenhouse, plant an evergreen hedge several yards away on the north or windward side.

equipment for greenhouses

Successful greenhouse gardening needs a few pieces of equipment. Shading is essential during summer, while heating is needed to germinate seeds and root cuttings. Although tomatoes in growing bags can be placed directly on soil at ground level, staging is needed for seed trays and pots.

Ventilators

Good circulation of fresh air is essential to maintain healthy plants within a greenhouse, especially during summer when the temperature can rapidly rise. A ventilator is really needed on both sides of the roof. In small greenhouses only one ventilator is usually fitted, and this should be on the south side. In large greenhouses, side-ventilators are definitely an advantage.

Ventilators are usually operated by hand, but automatic ones can be fitted. An extractor fan can also be fitted into the gable end of a greenhouse.

Shading

Strong sunlight dramatically increases the temperature and can damage some plants. There are several ways to provide shading and the cheapest and easiest method is to coat the outside in a proprietary whitener. Paint only the central two-thirds of each pane of glass. During summer it wears off and cracks. Wash it off in the fall and reapply the following early summer. Roller blinds fitted to the inside of a greenhouse are expensive, but they can be rolled up during cloudy periods.

Benches and shelving

If you want to sow seeds in spring and early summer, permanent or temporary staging is essential along at least one side of a greenhouse. It also enables plants to be displayed throughout the year. A wide choice of staging is available.
❀ Wooden staging—this is usually fitted in wood greenhouses and has a supporting framework with a surface formed of slatted wood, with 1in/2.5cm gaps between. This allows the free circulation of air around the plants, and free drainage from them.

◄ *Electric-powered heaters and propagation units make raising and growing plants in a greenhouse easy and trouble-free.*

◉ Metal staging—aluminum-framed greenhouses, with glazing bars made of extruded metal, are inevitably fitted with metal benching. The bench can usually be folded down to enable crops to be grown in soil at ground level. The staging is made of aluminum and thick, plastic-coated wire, which allows air to circulate around pots and plants.

◉ Solid staging—this is rarely seen now. It traditionally consisted of a solid base covered with a layer of pea gravel. It is ideal in summer because humidity can be encouraged around the plants by keeping the gravel moist.

◉ Temporary staging—in spring, when seeds are sown and seedlings pricked out, extra space can be created by using strong wire to suspend planks of wood, from wooden glazed bars. These can be used to support seed trays. When watering plants on temporary shelves, insure water does not drip onto plants underneath, because it can damage fragile seedlings. Aluminum greenhouses have proprietary fittings.

Insulating a greenhouse

Preventing warm air escaping is essential, especially in late winter and spring. Check that ventilators and doors fit well, and secure bubble-wrap insulation to the inside of the greenhouse. In wooden structures it can be stapled or pinned to the glazing bars. Aluminum greenhouses have proprietary fittings. Remove the bubble-wrap in late spring.

▶ *Slatted, wooden staging is a traditional way to display plants in a wooden greenhouse. It allows drainage yet keeps the soil relatively warm.*

▼ *In spring a greenhouse enables a wide range of half-hardy annuals to be raised from seed, until they are ready to be planted out.*

SEASONAL CLEANING

◉ In late fall or winter, thoroughly clean the inside and outside of a greenhouse. Clean glass is essential to enable light to enter, while dirty glazed bars may harbor pests and diseases. Always:
◉ Replace cracked panes of glass.
◉ Remove all plants and scrub surfaces with hot water and a disinfectant. Leave the door and ventilators open until the inside is dry.
◉ Check electrical fittings and equipment, ready for next spring.

heating greenhouses

In temperate climates, heating is needed in greenhouses during late winter and spring if summer-flowering bedding plants are to be grown from seeds. Tomato plants can be planted in growing bags or large pots in early spring in a heated greenhouse.

Methods of heating

There are two main ways to heat a small greenhouse, by kerosene or electricity.

✺ Kerosene heaters—these are popular and relatively inexpensive to buy and operate, although it is necessary to have space in a lockable shed away from your house for cans of fuel. The heaters can be moved from one greenhouse to another, and removed in early summer, cleaned and stored. The amount of heat they produce depends on the size of the heater and the length of wick allowed to burn. If the length of the wick is excessive, it will result in black smoke. Single- and double-burner heaters are available, in a range of sizes.

When a heater is being used, check it each evening to make sure that there is sufficient kerosene to burn through the night. Use a small dip stick to check the kerosene level and never tip the heater on its side, especially when it is alight. Kerosene, when it is burnt, produces an equal volume of water vapor, consumes oxygen and also gives off gases, so it is essential to leave a ventilator slightly open at all times.

▲ *Electrical and kerosene propagating units are available and both types are suited for use in a small greenhouse.*

HEATED PROPAGATION CASES

These provide the right conditions for seeds to germinate and cuttings to root without having to heat the whole greenhouse. They are heated by electricity or kerosene, and are available in several sizes. At the end of each season, clean and store the propagation case in a dry shed. Check all electrical cables and connections.

❊ Electricity is a clean, efficient way to heat a greenhouse, but the cables and sockets must be installed and maintained by a professional electrician. Electricity and water are a dangerous duo, so do not take any risks.

A thermostat controls the heater, and there are two main types to consider. Tubular heaters are usually secured to a wall, about 10in/25cm above the ground. They create a gentle flow of rising warm air. If installed under a solid-surface bench, insure that a 4–6in/10–15cm gap is left at the back to let warm air escape and circulate.

Fan heaters also create a good circulation of warm air, which helps to prevent the onset of diseases encouraged by damp, static air. Check that hot blasts of air do not blow directly on plants. Finally, do not use domestic fan heaters in a greenhouse because they are unsafe in a humid atmosphere, and especially where water may be inadvertently splashed on them.

Conserving heat

Since heating a greenhouse is expensive, whether by kerosene or electricity, you must conserve heat. Site a greenhouse so that the maximum amount of sunlight enters, especially in late winter and spring. A hedge positioned on the cold windward side also reduces the heat loss.

The cost of heating does not actually rise in direct proportion to the desired temperature but increases dramatically with each extra degree of heat that is generated. Therefore, assess the optimum temperature required for all the plants and set the thermostat accordingly.

In the fall, check that doors and ventilators fit their frames, and replace any broken panes of glass. Fit draft excluders around doors, and make sure that they cannot be blown open. Also, install bubble-glazing. In exceptionally cold areas, place a large sheet of clear polyethylene over the cold, windward side of a greenhouse. It will need to be securely pegged down to withstand winter weather. Lastly, always check for broken panes of glass after a storm.

▼ *Kerosene heaters are relatively cheap to buy and easy to install in a greenhouse. Both single– and double–burners (below) are available.*

cloches, frames, and tunnels

Cloches and poly-tunnels are frequently used in vegetable gardens to enable early crops and extend their growing or ripening periods into the fall. Cold frames are mainly used to harden off summer-flowering bedding plants. Low-growing vegetables can also be grown in them.

Cloches

The range of cloches is now wide. Once they were all made of glass, but flat and corrugated PVC kinds are extremely popular now for reasons of cost and safety. Note that cloches must not be airtight; a gentle flow of air is essential.

✹ Glass cloches—these allow more light to reach plants than those made of plastic, and they conserve more warmth.

▲ *Bell-jars have a traditional and cottage garden-like aspect that makes them features of interest as well as a way to protect plants.*

There are several types and sizes to suit most crops. The barn cloche is a good choice, formed of four sheets of glass clipped together: two sheets form the sides, with the other two creating a tent above them. Barn cloches are ideal for covering plants up to 12in/30cm high. The other main type is the tent cloche, with a simpler construction and two sheets of glass in a tent-like shape. They are lower than barn cloches and are ideal for young plants and small salad crops such as lettuces and radishes. Less frequently seen are tall, frame-like structures about 2ft/60cm high and 4–5ft/1.2–1.5m wide. They allow a good circulation of air over plants. Instead of glass, some are covered in rigid, clear plastic.

✹ Corrugated PVC cloches—these are extremely strong and resilient and, although they do not transmit as much light as glass, they are less likely to break and are safer to use. Metal hoops hold the corrugated plastic in a half-circle, in close contact with the soil, and prevent it being blown away. PVC is also used to construct barn-type cloches. Clear PVC is used for the top, with opaque PVC often employed along the sides of the cloche and at the ends.

✹ Bell-jars—traditionally made of glass, but modern versions are made from transparent PVC. Alternatively, large, clear plastic bottles with the base cut off can be placed over individual plants or seedlings. Glass jelly-jars are also useful, especially for covering marrow seedlings.

Cloches, tunnels, and bell-jars

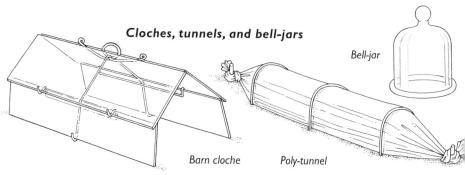

Bell-jar

Barn cloche   *Poly-tunnel*

Poly-tunnels

These have a simple construction, with metal hoops inserted into the ground and polyethylene sheeting drawn over to form a tunnel. Plants underneath require ventilation and therefore it is a daily task to open the front. Unfortunately, polyethylene sheeting has a life-span of only two or three years. Sunlight soon causes deterioration, but it is a cheap way to protect low-growing plants.

Cold frames

English pit lights are now part of garden history, but are still occasionally seen. They were heavy to move and needed a permanent framework on which they could be rested. Later, Dutch lights became popular, as they are much lighter and easier to handle. They consist of a single piece of glass in a frame about 4ft/1.2m long and 2ft/60cm wide. They rest on a wood or brick framework,

12–18in/30–45cm high at the back and 6–12in/15–30cm high at the front. Make sure that the front side faces south or southwest so that plants receive the maximum amount of light. Cold frames are mainly used to acclimatize plants raised in gentle warmth in late winter or spring, to outdoor conditions. Alternatively, they are very useful for growing tender salad vegetables that need a slightly sheltered environment.

▲ Cold frames are useful in spring, when they protect plants while the weather is cold and before they can be planted into a garden.

growing your own food

One of the joys of gardening is to eat food fresh from your own garden. Even in small gardens this is possible by growing salad crops such as lettuces, scallions, radishes, and tomatoes. Fresh herbs, grown in cartwheel herb gardens or pots on a patio or a terrace, are also welcome. Large fruit trees are not practical in small gardens but espalier and cordon apples and pears, and fan-trained peaches and nectarines, are possible. Dwarf apple trees can be grown in large pots in small paved areas and will bear a large crop of fruit.

apples and pears

Apples are among the easiest tree fruit to grow in temperate climates. Pears are also popular, but they are a little harder to grow. Dessert varieties need a sunnier and more wind-sheltered position than apples. In small gardens, grow apples as cordons or espaliers.

Planting and growing apples

In the past, apple trees often grew 20ft/6m high or more, and were difficult to prune and harvest. Today, a dwarf bush apple on an M27 rootstock is ideal for a small garden, where it grows about 6ft/1.8m high and produces 12–16lb/5.4–7.2kg of fruit each year. Cordons, when grown on a similar rootstock and planted 18in/45cm apart, produce 5–7lb/2.2–3.1kg of fruit. Espaliers planted about 14ft/4.2m apart bear 20–30lb/9–13kg of fruit. Bushes demand less pruning than cordons, while espaliers need more attention.

Choose a frost-free site in full sun with shelter from strong wind. Sun is essential to ripen highly colored dessert varieties. Apples usually flower in the early part of late spring; in areas where frosts repeatedly occur at that time, select a late-flowering variety.

Well-drained moisture-retentive soil is essential, especially for dessert varieties. Cooking apple trees grow well on heavier soil. Bare-rooted trees are planted during their dormant period in winter. When planting out, mix in plenty of well-decayed garden compost or manure.

Container-grown trees are planted whenever the soil and weather allow; planting them is fully described on pages 392–393. Support cordons and espaliers with galvanized wires tensioned between strong posts 8–12ft/2.4–3.6m apart; space the wires 15–18in/38–45cm apart to about 7ft/2.1m high. Check the posts every spring for wind damage.

◀ *Apple trees can be grown in tubs or large pots, but plant only those growing on dwarf rootstocks.*

APPLE TREES IN TUBS

An apple tree in a container on a patio is the best way to grow fruit in a small garden. Dwarf rootstocks such as M27 (trees in containers grow to about 5ft/1.5m high) and M9 (up to 8ft/2.4m) make this possible, using 15in/38cm-wide wooden tubs or pots.

Well-drained, moisture-retentive compost is essential and in summer regular watering is needed, sometimes every day. During winter it may be necessary to wrap straw around the tub to prevent the roots freezing and getting damaged. A plastic sheet can also be used to prevent the soil from becoming too wet. Repotting every other late winter is essential, as well as feeding during summer. Large crops are not possible but good varieties to seek include 'Gravenstein', 'Fiesta', 'Liberty', and 'Sunrise'.

Planting and growing pears

The range of rootstocks for pears is limited so that it is not possible to grow pears on trees as small as dwarf apples. Few gardens can accommodate pear trees up to 20ft/6m high, and therefore in small areas it is best to grow pears as cordons or espaliers. Cordon pears planted 18in/75cm apart each produce 4–6lb/1.8–2.7kg of fruit a year, while an espalier yields 15–25lb/6.8–11.3kg.

The same methods are used for planting and supporting pears as for apples, but pears are more susceptible to drought than apples, so be prepared to water the soil copiously during dry periods. It is probably better to select a dessert variety than a cooker, but it will need a compatible pollinator that will flower at the same time. For example, 'Conference' is partly self-fertile and needs other varieties, such as 'Seckel' or 'Harrow Delight'. Alternatively, if you have a warm garden plant the superb 'Comice', also 'Highland' (this has the bonus of keeping the fruits from late fall to early winter).

Cordon

Single, inclined stem

Espalier

Tiered branches

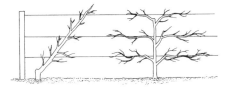

Espalier supports

Straining bolt

Tensioned wire

Supporting posts

▶ *Pears grown as cordons or espaliers are best for planting in a small garden. The fruits are easily picked without using stepladders.*

peaches, nectarines, and plums

Peaches and nectarines need a warm climate. They are closely related; nectarines are smooth-skinned sports (mutations) of peaches, which have fuzzy skins. Nectarines are less hardy than peaches and have smaller yields. Plums are easily grown stone fruits.

Growing peaches and nectarines

In temperate climates, with the likelihood of frost in early and mid-spring and a general lack of pollinating insects at that time, it is often difficult to grow peaches and nectarines successfully.

Where conditions are least favorable, choose a peach rather than a nectarine, and always grow it as a fan trained on galvanized wires against a warm, sunny, south or southwest facing wall rather than as a bush.

Choose a reliable variety such as 'Harbrite' or 'Reliance'. Fortunately, peaches and nectarines are self-fertile.

Construct tiers of galvanized wires before planting a peach or nectarine. Position the lowest wire 1ft/30cm above the ground, with others 8in/20cm apart to a height of about 6ft/1.8m. Secure the wires 4in/10cm from the wall. Because peaches and nectarines are best grown against a wall it is essential to thoroughly prepare the soil by adding plenty of moisture-retentive, well-decayed garden compost or manure. Prepare an area 18in/45cm deep and 3½ft/1m square and position the main stem about 9in/23cm from the wall. Plant bare-rooted specimens in late fall or early winter, and container-grown plants at any time when the soil and weather allow. Choose a two- or three-year-old plant with eight or more branches.

Rather than tie stems directly to the wires, secure them to bamboo canes, and then to the wires. The two main arms should be at an upward 45° angle, with other stems spaced out.

▲ *Plant a fan-trained peach tree against a warm, sunny wall. To maintain the shape, secure the branches to tiers of galvanized wires.*

Always prune peaches and nectarines in late winter or early spring, when growth begins, but never tackle this task in winter. Initially, the purpose of pruning is to encourage the development of a fan. Pruning a two- or three-year-old plant is much easier than creating a fan from a rooted shoot with no side-shoots. On an established plant, cut back each arm of the fan by about one third, making cuts slightly above a downward pointing bud. In the following summer, shoots develop on each arm; allow three to form and tie each of them to a cane. Also, use a thumb to rub out buds growing toward the wall. During late summer, when each of these shoots is 18in/45cm long, nip out their growing points. Picking and storing peaches and nectarines is described on pages 426–427.

Growing plums

These are popular fruits. Because they flower early in the year and are vulnerable to frost, plant them in a mild, frost-free area. Dessert plums especially need a warm, sunny position to encourage good flavor. Plums can be grown in several forms, including standards, half-standards, bushes, and

pyramids, but in small gardens a fan-trained form is better.

Prepare the soil in the same way as for peaches and nectarines, and with a similar arrangement of tiered wires against a wall. Also, plant and prune fan-trained plants in the same way.

See pages 426–427 for information on picking and storing plums.

▼ *Plum trees flower early in the season and therefore need a warm, sheltered position against a wall. This is an ideal form for small gardens.*

Fan trained

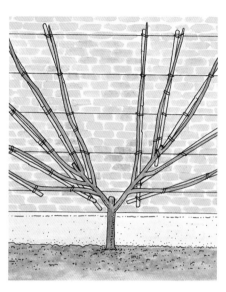

HAND POLLINATING

Peaches and nectarines flower early in the year when pollinating insects are scarce. Therefore, use a soft brush or loose ball of cotton wool to gently dab each flower every other day from the time the buds open until the petals fall.

growing soft fruits

It is surprising how many different types of soft fruits can be grown in a small garden. Raspberries grow vertically, while blackcurrant bushes take up only a little space. Strawberries may be grown alongside paths to be easily accessible, but if space is restricted they can be grown in a barrel.

Strawberries

There are several forms of these popular, easily grown fruits, including perpetual and alpine, but the summer-fruiting varietes are most widely grown. Once planted, they are usually left for three or four years before being discarded, with fresh beds prepared for new plants. It is

possible to grow summer-fruiting types as an annual crop producing high quality fruit, but they will not grow as prolifically as well-established two- or three-year-old plants. Plant bare-rooted, summer-fruiting varieties between midsummer and early fall, and container-grown plants at any time when the soil is workable. In practice, however, they are best planted at the same time as bare-rooted plants.

Prepare strawberry beds by digging the soil in late spring or early summer, and adding well-decomposed garden compost or manure. Remove and burn perennial weeds. Just before planting, dust the surface with a general fertilizer. When planting bare-rooted plants, spread out the roots over a small mound of soil at the bottom of the hole, and check that the crown of the plant is level with the surrounding ground. Firm the soil around the roots. With container-grown plants do not bury the crown but keep it level with the soil surface. After planting, water the soil thoroughly and pull up weeds regularly.

During the following spring, sprinkle a general fertilizer around the plants, water the soil and add a mulch of straw to keep fruit off the soil. When the fruits are red all over, pick them with the calyx attached early in the morning.

Raspberries

There are two types of raspberry: summer- and fall-fruiting. Established summer-fruiting varieties produce most fruit. Pruning the canes is described on pages 400–401, and picking and storing on pages 428–429.

A tiered framework of wires is essential, using strong posts (up to 12ft/3.6m apart) with galvanized wires strained between them at a height of 3ft/75cm, 3½ft/1m and 5¼ft/1.6m above ground. Plant bare-rooted canes during late fall and early winter, or in early spring, spacing them 18in/45cm apart. Immediately after planting, cut all canes to 9–12in/23–30cm high just above a healthy bud.

During the first year, young canes develop and will fruit the following year.

▲ *Blackberry 'Oregon Thornless' has medium-sized fruits in late summer and early fall and can be planted against a trellis or an arch.*

Blackcurrants

These are borne on deciduous bushes for picking during the latter part of midsummer and late summer. Position each plant slightly deeper than usual to allow for soil settlement, and encourage the development of shoots from below. Space plants 5ft/1.5m apart, and cut all stems to about 1in/2.5cm above the surface. Plant young, container-grown bushes at any time of the year when the soil and weather allow. If you plant in summer, wait until the fall and cut out all the old shoots to soil level. Prune fall to spring planting immediately.

STRAWBERRIES IN BARRELS

For more than 100 years strawberries have been grown in wooden barrels with holes cut in their sides. Good drainage is essential. Drill drainage holes in the bottom of the barrel, add clean rubble, and place a 4–6in/10–15cm-wide wire-netting tube filled with drainage material in the center. Fill the barrel with well-drained soil mix, and put a plant into each hole.

▲ Growing strawberries in pots is popular in small gardens. It is a good way to prevent slugs and snails damaging the fruits.

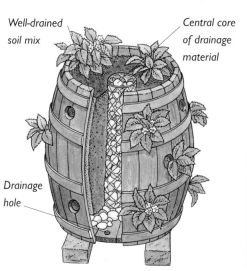

Well-drained soil mix

Central core of drainage material

Drainage hole

Planting blackcurrants

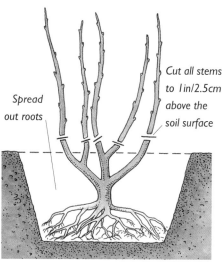

Spread out roots

Cut all stems to 1in/2.5cm above the soil surface

Planting strawberries

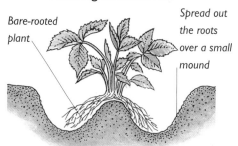

Bare-rooted plant

Spread out the roots over a small mound

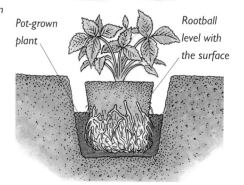

Pot-grown plant

Rootball level with the surface

vegetables for small gardens

Some vegetables, such as asparagus and globe artichokes, are perennials, and once established continue producing crops for several years. Others are sown each year and are rotated around a vegetable plot to insure that they produce the best possible crops.

Salad crops

These are popular and easily grown; there are many interesting and colorful varieties to choose from.

❀ Outdoor cucumbers—also known as ridge cucumbers, are easily grown in fertile, moisture-retentive soil. They are best grown in a warm, sunny position sheltered from cold wind.

In mid-spring dig a hole 12in/30cm deep and wide. Fill it with a mixture of equal parts of topsoil and well-decayed garden compost or manure, and make a mound of soil on the surface. In late spring or early summer, sow three seeds ¾in/18mm deep and 2in/5cm apart. Water and cover them with a large jelly-jar. Water regularly and after germination remove the cover. Later, pull up the two weakest seedlings. When sideshoots have five or six leaves, pinch out their tips to just beyond a leaf joint. Water plants regularly, and feed them when the first fruits start to swell.

❀ Lettuces—these are popular, with a wide range of types. They include Butterheads (cabbage-type, with large, soft, smooth-edged leaves); Crispheads (another cabbage-type, with rounded heads and curled and crisp leaves; Romaine lettuces (upright growth and oblong heads); Loose-leaf lettuces (masses of loose, wavy-edged leaves that are picked individually).

◀ *Vegetables can be grown in even the smallest garden and often close together. Where possible, choose moderately vigorous varieties.*

By sowing seeds at various times, lettuces can be harvested throughout most of the year, though summer-sown lettuces are the easiest to grow. From mid-spring to the early part of late summer, sow seeds thinly and evenly in ½in/12mm-deep drills 10in/25cm apart. Keep the area moist. When seedlings are about 1in/2.5cm high, thin them first to 4in/10cm apart and later to 12in/30cm. Thin small varieties to 10in/25cm apart. From the latter part of early summer to fall harvest the lettuces.

❀ Radishes—from mid-spring to late summer, sow seeds evenly and thinly every two weeks. Form drills ½in/12mm deep and 6in/15cm apart. Germination takes five to seven days and when the seedlings are large enough to handle, thin them to 1in/2.5cm apart. Re-firm the soil around them and water it. Harvest the radishes when they are young. If left, they become woody.

❀ Scallions—in addition to bulbing types, there are scallions, also known as salad onions and bunching onions, which are delicious in salads.

TOMATOES ON A PATIO

To grow tomatoes successfully choose a sheltered, sunny position, preferably in front of a south-facing wall. On a patio tomatoes can be grown in large pots or in a growing bag. When they are grown in pots the tall stems will need to be supported with bamboo canes, but for plants in a growing bag, a proprietary supporting framework is better. Plant two tomato plants in a standard-size bag. There are two types of tomato plant: cordon and bush. Cordon types produce sideshoots which must be snapped off when the plants are young, while bush tomatoes do not require this treatment. When cordon tomatoes have produced four trusses of fruits, pinch out the shoot at two leaves above the top truss. Water and feed plants regularly throughout the summer and pick the fruit as it ripens.

Growing bag

Keep the soil moist

Water the rootball before planting

▲ Varieties with globular roots are quick and easy to grow. Sow seeds evenly and thinly.

▼ Vegetable gardens can be decorative and with plenty of eye appeal. Vegetables can also be grown alongside flowers in cottage gardens.

picking and storing tree fruits

The range of tree fruits is wide and includes apples, pears, nectarines, peaches, and plums. They all have a different nature, both with their picking and storage qualities. The times when they are picked are also variable.

Tree fruits

Careful picking is essential. Fruit that has been roughly handled becomes bruised and damaged, and does not last long when stored. It might start to decay and, worse, make others rot.

⦿ Apples—these vary in their picking time from midsummer to mid-fall. Their storage period is also variable, with some varieties needing to be eaten a few weeks after being picked while others last into next spring.

⦿ Pick apples when the stalk readily parts from the tree. Test each fruit by cupping it in the palm of your hand and gently raising and turning it. If the stalk parts from the tree it is ready for picking.

HARVESTING SWEET CHERRIES

These are left on the tree until they are ripe. Regularly test the fruits to check their sweetness. However, if their skins start to crack, pick them immediately. The stalks should be left attached to the fruits. Cherries are best eaten as soon as they are picked.

Store the apples by placing them slightly apart in slatted trays in a cool, airy, vermin- and frost-proof shed. If the air is dry, wrap them in oiled paper and place the folded side down. Also, regularly check the apples to make sure they are not starting to decay.

Another way to store apples is to place 4lb/1.8kg of the same variety in a polyethylene bag punctured with holes. Fold over the top and place it upside down in a similar shed.

⦿ Pears—these have a shorter storage life than apples and the picking time is more difficult to judge. Some varieties are ready in late summer, others in mid-fall. Judging when a fruit is ready to be picked is the same as for apples. Because early varieties, if left on a tree, become mealy and soft, pick them before they are completely ready by using scissors to sever the stalks. Store in a cool, dry, airy, dark, vermin-proof shed. Place pears individually in slatted trays, leaving space between them. Alternatively, you can wrap them but this prevents the onset of decay being seen.

⦿ Peaches and nectarines—pick the fruit when the skin reveals a reddish flush and the flesh around the stalk softens. This happens from the latter part of midsummer to early fall.

Pick by holding a fruit in the palm of your hand and gently lifting and twisting; it is ready when the stalk separates easily. The fruit is best eaten fresh, but can be stored in a cool place and unwrapped for about a week.

⦿ Plums—pick fruit from the latter part of midsummer to late fall, when it parts readily from the tree leaving the stalk behind. The exact time depends on the variety, but those used for preserving and cooking can be picked before they are ripe, whereas dessert types need to ripen on the tree. Store plums in slatted boxes lined with tissue paper. Check them daily for decay. When gages and damsons are picked the stalk also remains attached to the tree.

▶ *Do not squeeze apples or they will bruise. Cup the fruit in the palm of your hand and twist. If it comes away easily it is ready.*

storing pears

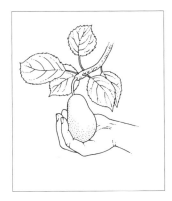
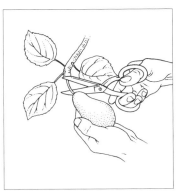
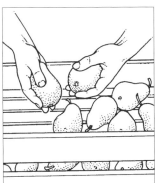
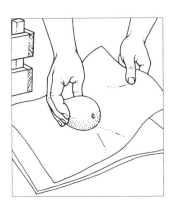

1 Supporting the pear in your palm, lift and twist the fruit very gently. If the stalk readily parts from the tree, the fruit is ready to be picked.

2 Early varieties can be picked before they are completely ready by using scissors. If left too long on the tree they become soft and mealy.

3 Store pears on slatted trays. Space the fruit apart, so that they do not touch. This reduces the risk of decaying fruit contaminating others.

4 Usually, pears can be left unwrapped, but in a dry atmosphere wrap them individually. However, this does cloak the early signs of decay.

harvesting soft fruits

These summer fruits are popular and best eaten as soon as possible after they are picked. Care is needed when picking them to prevent damage that will limit their life. Always put them into wide-based containers so that they cannot be knocked over.

Bush fruits

Blackcurrants—pick these from mid- to late summer. The fruit is ready for picking about one week after turning blue-black. Berries can be picked individually but they keep better when the entire cluster is removed. Place them in a cool, airy place. They can be stored in a refrigerator for about one week. Because not all the fruit will be ready for picking at the same time it is necessary to check it regularly.

Redcurrants and white currants—pick the fruit during midsummer when shiny and colored, picking entire clusters to avoid damage to individual berries. It is necessary to pick over the bush several times, on each occasion picking those

▲ *Gooseberries are a popular soft fruit with a distinctive flavor. Pick them individually when they are fully ripe and evenly colored.*

SAFETY FIRST

⊛ Apart from the risk of other people eating the fruit before you can get them safely into your house, care is needed when picking them. Systematically work down rows or around bushes, so that you do not miss ripe fruit. If you do, it will quickly be eaten by wasps.

⊛ Place berries in small, wide-based flat containers that will not be knocked over. When half-full, transfer into a larger firm-based container. Do not put them where children or dogs can knock them over.

⊛ Where several varieties are being picked, put them into separate containers so that their flavors can later be compared.

⊛ As soon as possible, move the fruit into a cool room where they can quickly loose their "field" heat. And do not put them near strongly scented vegetables or herbs.

⊛ Where freezing is appropriate, do this as soon as possible.

that are ripe. Currants are best eaten immediately, but can be stored in a refrigerator for about one week.

Gooseberries—pick the fruit from the end of early summer, through midsummer to the early part of late summer, depending on the variety. When fully ripe the berries are soft and fully colored. They can be stored in a refrigerator for a couple of weeks.

Strawberries—check the crop daily and pick fruit when it has reddened all over. Pull the fruit from the plant by holding the stalk, so that it remains attached to the fruit. They are best eaten within a few days.

Cane fruits

Raspberries—pick summer-fruiting varieties from the early part of midsummer to the latter weeks of late summer, and fall-fruiting types from late summer to mid-fall. The berries can be picked when fully colored yet still firm. Hold the fruit gently and pull, leaving the stalk and plug attached to the plant. The fruit is best eaten immediately, but can be frozen. To do this, choose firm fruit and put it in the base of a shallow, plastic tray, keeping all the raspberries apart. Place the tray in a freezer and when frozen put the fruit into freezer bags or boxes.

Blackberries and hybrid berries—these are picked when soft and fully ripe. This is best done when the fruit is dry. Wet fruit, especially if slightly bruised, soon decays and becomes moldy. When picking, hold each fruit and pull gently. The plug usually comes away with the fruit. Best when eaten immediately, but can be frozen.

▲ *Redcurrants are an excellent culinary fruit. An established bush will provide about 10lb/4.5kg each year, in mid- or late summer.*

picking and freezing raspberries

picking gooseberries

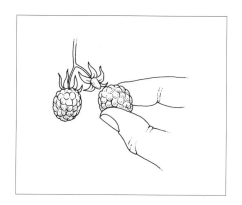

1 Pick the fruits individually, when fully colored yet still firm. The plug (the small stalk) should remain on the plant. It is necessary to pick over the plants several times. If left, the fruits soon decay.

2 Freeze raspberries as soon as possible after picking. Select small, under-ripe fruits and space them apart in a flat-based plastic container. Place in the freezer until frozen and then transfer to freezer bags.

Pick the fruits individually, when ripe and fully colored. This varies between varieties and some are early while others are late maturing and ripening. It is necessary to pick over each bush several times.

growing herbs in small gardens

Several herbs, such as the biennial angelica, are large and dominant—and best planted in herbaceous or large herb borders. Most herbs though, are suitable for small gardens, while prostrate types can be planted between paving slabs arranged in a chessboard pattern.

MAKING A HERB CARTWHEEL

Dig the soil, removing perennial weeds and, if necessary, mix in well-decayed garden compost to assist water retention. Firm the soil evenly, then rake level. Tie the ends of a 3ft/90cm-long piece of string to two canes and insert one in the center of the bed. Use the other end to describe a circle 6ft/1.8m in diameter. Place small pebbles in a 10–12in/25–30cm-wide circle in the center, and larger pebbles around the perimeter. Mark the positions of the spokes with more pebbles, creating triangles about 15in/38cm wide at the base. Water the plants in their containers the day before planting, then arrange them in their pots in the cartwheel in an attractive design. Plant them out, water the soil and, for more intense color, cover the soil with colored gravels.

Cartwheel herb gardens

These are ornamental and functional features that can be tailored to fit areas only 6ft/1.8m square. If possible, use an old cartwheel, but a simulated design is easily created by using large pebbles to mark out the circumference and spokes.

Checkerboard designs

This is a novel way to grow low-growing herbs. Select an area, perhaps 7½ft/2.28m square, and prepare the soil as for a cartwheel garden. Then lay 18in/45cm-square paving slabs in a checkerboard arrangement leaving alternate squares uncovered. Plant the uncovered squares with a selection of low-growing herbs. Where herbs do not completely cover the soil, spread pea gravel or stone chippings over the soil. This will look attractive and has the added advantage of reducing moisture loss.

▼ *Herb wheels, closely planted with segments of contrasting thymes, create an attractive feature that is easy to manage.*

Nine popular herbs

Caraway—biennial with fern-like leaves and umbrella-like heads of green flowers.

Chives—bulbous, with tubular leaves and rose-pink flowers.

Dill—hardy annual with feathery green leaves and umbrella-like heads of yellow flowers.

Fennel—herbaceous perennial with blue-green leaves and golden-yellow flowers in large, umbrella-like heads.

Lemon balm—herbaceous perennial with lemon-scented green leaves.

Mint—herbaceous perennial with invasive roots. Wide range, from spearmint to apple mint.

Parsley—biennial, with crinkled or flat (more strongly flavored) green leaves.

Sage—short-lived shrub, with gray-green leaves and spires of violet-blue flowers in early summer. There are forms with more ornamental leaves (purple, and some variegated) but they are mainly used to create color in borders.

Thyme—low-growing, shrubby perennial. Garden thyme is a superb culinary herb, but there are varieties with colored leaves that may be used to add color to checkerboard designs.

▼ Enhance herb gardens by positioning small and low-growing herbs in spaces left when paving slabs are laid in a checkerboard pattern.

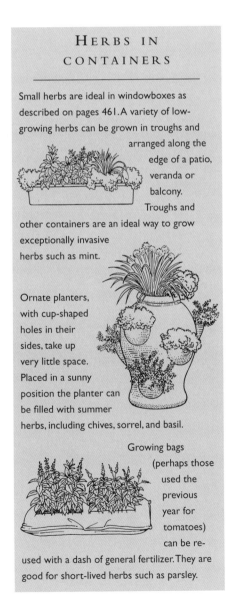

HERBS IN CONTAINERS

Small herbs are ideal in windowboxes as described on pages 461. A variety of low-growing herbs can be grown in troughs and arranged along the edge of a patio, veranda or balcony.

Troughs and other containers are an ideal way to grow exceptionally invasive herbs such as mint.

Ornate planters, with cup-shaped holes in their sides, take up very little space. Placed in a sunny position the planter can be filled with summer herbs, including chives, sorrel, and basil.

Growing bags (perhaps those used the previous year for tomatoes) can be re-used with a dash of general fertilizer. They are good for short-lived herbs such as parsley.

using plants in
small gardens

colorful borders
and beds

Borders bursting with color throughout summer are one of the goals of gardeners. In addition to rich and vibrant displays in a wide range of colors, it is possible to create borders with a distinctive single color theme, such as pink and red, blue and mauve, yellow and gold, and white and silver. Plants with variegated leaves also make attractive borders. They include evergreen and deciduous shrubs and herbaceous perennials.

pink and red garden schemes

Red is a dramatic, fiery, dominant color in a garden, especially when used en masse in full sun, while pink is a desaturated red with a warmer feel. The perception of red changes through the day. In strong light it is bright, but as evening approaches it assumes darker shades until it turns almost black.

Flower borders

There is a wide choice of red and pink flowers for herbaceous borders and flowering bedding displays that will carry the color scheme through from early spring into fall. In herbaceous borders the plants range from tuberous-rooted alstroemerias, through the red and pink forms of the late-flowering *Aster novi-belgii* (Michaelmass daisy) and *Aster novae-angliae* (New England aster), to the dramatic red flowers of *Schizostylis coccinea* 'Major', which is aptly called the crimson flag. Many dahlias, from the smaller ball varieties to giant decoratives with flowers 10in/25cm wide, have lovely red flowers and will provide strong accents of color in late summer.

Spring flowering displays using bulbs and biennials, planted in late summer or early fall, add plenty of color. For a red and blue display, perhaps at the top of a drystone wall, you could plant a blue-flowered form of *Aubrieta deltoidea* adding colorful 'Madame Lefeber' tulips below. Summer displays, mainly of seed-raised plants, also add red and pink flowers, but none so arresting as *Begonia semperflorens* 'Cocktail Series' and *Salvia splendens* (scarlet sage).

BACKGROUND HARMONIES AND CONTRASTS

Many plants, from wall shrubs to ephemeral types in windowboxes, wall baskets, and hanging baskets, look even better against the right background.

Red and scarlet flowers are dramatically highlighted against white walls, while red and pink flowers harmonize with a gray stone wall.

◀ *Pink and red are romantic colors that give warm tones to a border. Pink flowers remain visible in the diminishing light of evening.*

Trees and shrubs

These produce massed displays and distinctive individual flowers. The spring-flowering deciduous azaleas, often in demure shades of red and pink, are a sure sign that gardens are bursting into life. A wild garden, with a high and light canopy of leaves, provides the right setting. Many have the bonus of richly colored leaves in the fall.

Other shrubs with pink or red flowers include the magnificient *Hibiscus syriacus* and *Kolkwitzia amabilis*, aptly known as the beauty bush for its pink, foxglove-like flowers with yellow throats. More dramatic and distinctive are the flowers of the deciduous, spring and early summer flowering *Magnolia liliiflora* 'Nigra'. Its flowers are upright, 3in/7.5cm long and deep reddish-purple. Offering a totally different style, the deciduous shrub *Leycesteria formosa* (Himalayan honeysuckle) has pendulous flowers formed of small, white flowers surrounded by highly conspicuous dark-claret bracts. It has the bonus of purplish-red berries in the fall.

Climbers and wall shrubs

This excellent range includes climbing and rambling roses, clematis and the rhizomatous-rooted *Tropaeolum speciosum* (Scottish flame flower) which dies down to soil level in the fall. From midsummer to fall it produces scarlet, trumpet-like flowers on long stems and loves to clamber through shrubs. Several large-flowered clematis have red or pink flowers including the popular 'Nelly Moser' in which each pale mauve-pink petal has a soft crimson stripe. 'Ville de Lyon' is bright carmine-red and 'Ernest Markham' is vivid magenta with a velvet sheen.

▲ *Many quite different plants create attractive combinations. Here a rose and a variety of slow-growing conifers form a pleasing group.*

▼ *Low beds, perhaps at the edge of a rock garden and mainly planted with pink and red plants, create a feature that radiates warmth.*

Key to planting

1. *Myosotis* (forget-me-not)
2. *Primula* 'Wanda'
3. *Candelabra primulas*
4. *Anemone* × *fulgens*
5. *Magnolia liliiflora*
6. Rhododendrons
7. Azaleas
8. Aubrieta *deltoidea* (*aubretia*)

blue and purple borders

Blue is a calm color and when used in a garden will provide an atmosphere of tranquillity. Blue color schemes are thought to reduce blood pressure and slow up respiration and pulse rates. Enhance the color by adding patches of dull white and pale-lemon flowers, but not strong yellows.

Flower borders

Blue-flowered herbaceous borders usually come to life at the start of summer, when suddenly they abound in color. Perhaps no herbaceous perennial is more noticeable than *Delphinium elatum*.

▲ *Blue flowers create a contemplative and restful garden, while purple is more dramatic and looks best used in smaller groups.*

The large-flowered or elatum types have stiffly erect stems tightly packed with florets during early and midsummer, while the Belladonna forms are smaller, gracefully branched, and superb in cottage gardens. Within each type there is a wide range of colors.

Several perennial asters are blue, including *Aster amellus* (Italian aster) with large, daisy-like flowers with yellow centers. 'King George' is especially attractive, with soft blue-violet flowers. *Aster × frikartii* 'Mönch' is slightly less dramatic, with lavender-blue flowers. Again, the flowers have golden centers. Other blue-flowered herbaceous plants include *Echinacea purpurea* (purple coneflower) with purple-crimson, daisy-like flowers and distinctive large central cones, *Physostegia virginiana* (obedient plant) with spires of pink-mauve flowers, and *Tradescantia × andersoniana* 'Isis' which bears three-petaled, purple-blue flowers.

Several spring-flowering bulbs have blue flowers and include *Hyacinthus orientalis* (common hyacinth) and *Muscari armeniacum* (grape hyacinth), which is an ideal companion for polyanthus. *Myosotis alpestris* (forget-me-not) is a hardy perennial invariably grown as a biennial for its small and fragrant, azure-blue flowers borne in large clusters. There are many varieties and most will happily increase by self-seeding.

Summer-flowering bedding plants include blue-flowered forms of *Ageratum houstonianum*, such as 'Blue Danube' with masses of lavender-blue flowers, and *Lobelia erinus* with varieties such as 'Blue Moon' and 'Cambridge Blue'. There are also several trailing forms that are ideal for planting in windowboxes and in hanging baskets.

BACKGROUND HARMONIES AND CONTRASTS

Blue is a restful color that is at risk from being dominated by strong colors, but here are a few good combinations to try. Position plants with deep-blue or deep-purple flowers against gray stone walls. Soft blue flowers in large clusters harmonize with red brick walls.

Key to planting

1. *Aster amellus*
2. *Delphiniums*
3. *Corylus maxima 'Purpurea'* (purple-leaved filbert)
4. *Cotinus coggygria 'Notcutt's Variety'*
5. *Hydrangea macrophylla* (common hydrangea)
6. *Echinacea purpurea* (purple coneflower)
7. *Physostegia virginiana* (obedient plant)
8. *Ageratum houstonianum* (flossflower)

Trees and shrubs

There are few blue-flowered trees and shrubs but close together they make a magnificient display. *Cercis siliquastrum* (Judas tree) has clusters of rich, rose-purple flowers on bare branches in early summer. Markedly different is *Ceanothus × delileanus* 'Gloire de Versailles', with long spires of fragrant, powder-blue flowers from midsummer to early fall. And most popular of all are the blue-flowered forms of *Hydrangea macrophylla* (common hydrangea).

Several shrubs and trees have richly colored leaves, including *Corylus maxima* 'Purpurea' (purple-leaved filbert), *Cotinus coggygria* 'Notcutt's Variety' with deep-purple leaves, and *Berberis thunbergii* 'Atropurpurea' which bears small, rich purple-red leaves.

Climbers and wall shrubs

These provide superb displays and none more so than California lilacs. Look for *Ceanothus impressus* with clusters of deep

▲ *This partly cloistered water garden creates an oasis of peace and tranquillity.*

blue flowers in spring, and *C. thrysiflorus repens* with light-blue flowers. Clematis need support and few surpass *Clematis macropetala*, with double, light- and dark-blue flowers in late spring and early summer. Other blue-flowering climbers include *Solanum crispum* (Chilean potato vine), *Wisteria floribunda* 'Macrobotrys' and *Abutilon vitifolium* (flowering maple).

▶ *Pale-lemon and dull-white flowers will make the border more conspicuous in twilight.*

yellow and gold gardens

These are bright and dominant, especially when in strong sunlight. Plants with these radiant colors are readily seen in the gloom of early morning and in the diminishing light of evening. Yellow is therefore useful as an edging for summer-flowering bedding displays.

Flower borders

Herbaceous borders are sometimes themed as a single color, such as yellow, but this does not mean that the border only has one color. For example, in yellow and gold borders, yellow and green variegated shrubs can be added to create permanency, height, and contrasting color. Good yellow herbaceous perennials include *Achillea filipendulina* 'Gold Plate' (fern-leaf yarrow) with large, plate-like heads packed with deep-yellow flowers from mid- to late-summer. *Alchemilla mollis* (lady's mantle) is another superb plant, ideal for the edge of a border where it cloaks sharp, unsightly outlines.

The list of herbaceous plants for yellow borders is lengthy and includes *Coreopsis vertillata*, with bright yellow star-like flowers, dahlias, *Phlomis fruticosa* and *Verbascum bombyciferum* (mullein)—with tall flower stems and silver-haired oval leaves. Two others are *Rudbeckia fulgida* (coneflower); this has large, yellow flowers with purple-brown centers. It is superb with *Aster amellus* 'King George'. *Solidago* 'Goldenmosa' (goldenrod) bears fluffy heads of yellow flowers.

◀ *Plants with narrow, yellow-variegated leaves create a dramatic shape and color contrast in a garden. Grow tender plants in pots.*

Trees and shrubs

Yellow-flowering winter and spring trees and shrubs include *Hamamelis* (witch-hazel), chimonanthus and mahonias in winter, and the glorious forsythias, *Berberis darwinii* and double-flowered gorse in spring. Many continue their display into summer, and later. Add accents of color by grouping plants in attractive duos. Around the spreading branches of *Hamamelis mollis* (Chinese witch-hazel) plant the winter-flowering *Rhododendron mucronulatum* with funnel-shaped, rose-purple flowers. For a summer leaf-color contrast, plant the deciduous shrub *Cotinus coggygria* 'Royal Purple', with dark plum-colored leaves.

BACKGROUND HARMONIES AND CONTRASTS

Yellow is a dramatic color, especially when highlighted by a contrasting background. Yellow flowers look good against a white background, while lemon-colored flowers are better suited to a red brick wall.

Climbers and wall shrubs

These range from annuals to shrubs and include the popular *Thunbergia alata*, (black-eyed Susan), a half-hardy annual raised in gentle warmth in spring before being planted in a border or against a trellis when all risk of frost has passed. Alternatively, it will scale a tripod of canes or poles. For winter color against a wall, plant *Jasminum nudiflorum*, the winter-flowering jasmine which produces bright yellow flowers on bare stems throughout winter.

Several slightly tender shrubs benefit from being planted on the sunny side of a wall and include *Cytisus battandieri*, (Pineapple broom). In midsummer it has pineapple-scented, cone-shaped, golden-yellow heads of flowers amid large, grayleaves like the laburnum. *Piptanthus nepalensis*, still better known as *Piptanthus laburnifolius* (evergreen laburnum), is also slightly tender and bears pea-shaped, bright yellow flowers like those of the laburnum

in late spring and early summer. The deciduous and vigorous *Lonicera tragophylla* (Chinese woodbine) is ideal for covering archways, pergolas, and walls. It produces bright golden-yellow flowers from early to midsummer.

▶ *Yellow and gold borders introduce vitality into a garden, with plants ranging from yellow-leaved border plants to glorious sunflowers.*

Key to planting

❶ *Rudbeckia fulgida* (coneflower)

❷ *Euonymus fortunei* 'Emerald 'n' Gold'

❸ *Helianthus annuus* (sunflower)

❹ *Thunbergia alata* (black-eyed Susan)

❺ *Verbascum bombyciferum* (mullein)

❻ *Achillea filipenndulina* 'Gold Plate' (fern-leaf yarrow)

❼ *Solidago* 'Goldenmosa' (golden rod)

❽ *Tagetes erecta* (African marigolds)

▲ *Gardens packed with yellow flowers and foliage are full of vitality. Hoop-like arches add interest and help to create height in a garden.*

white and silver schemes

With their brightness and purity, white flowers have a dramatic impact in strong sunlight. Silver is less dominant and is often described as grayish-white. It is less apparent because silver reflects light at many angles, whereas smooth-surfaced white petals are better reflectors of light.

Flower borders

There are many plants for gray, silver, and white herbaceous borders. Those with gray and silver foliage include *Anaphalis triplinervis* (pearly everlasting) with narrow, silver-gray, lance-shaped leaves that reveal white, wooly undersides. It also bears bunched heads of white flowers during late summer. Its near relative, *Anaphalis margaritacea yedoensis,*

◀ *Borders with white flowers and silver foliage sparkle in even the smallest amount of light, bringing unexpected vibrancy to a garden.*

has gray leaves and heads of white flowers from midsummer to fall.

Many artemisias have silver-colored leaves and none better than *Artemisia absinthium* 'Lambrook Silver', with its silvery gray, finely divided leaves and small, round, yellow flowers during mid- and late-summer. *Artemisia ludoviciana,* the white sage, has upright stems, deeply divided, wooly white leaves, and silver-white flowers during late summer and early fall. *Onopordum acanthium* (Scotch thistle) produces broad, jagged silver-gray leaves.

The range of silver-leaved plants continues with *Stachys byzantina* (lamb's ears), with oval leaves densely covered in white, silvery hairs that create a wooly appearance. The half-hardy perennial *Senecio cineraria*, usually grown as a half-hardy annual, clothes borders with deeply lobed leaves covered in white, wooly hairs. Herbaceous plants with

white flowers include the popular *Leucanthemum maximum*, still better known as *Chrysanthemum maximum* (Shasta daisy), with masses of large, white, daisy-like flowers with yellow centers from mid- to late-summer. *Gypsophila paniculata* (baby's breath) creates clouds of white flowers amid gray-green leaves. With fewer but larger white flowers, *Romneya coulteri* (California tree poppy) blooms from midsummer to fall.

The half-hardy annual *Lobularia maritima*, better known as *Alyssum maritimum* (sweet alyssum), is ideal as an edging to summer-flowering bedding arrangements.

BACKGROUND HARMONIES AND CONTRASTS

Backgrounds suitable for white flowers are limited, and they usually look their best against a red brick wall. This color also suits silver-colored foliage.

Key to planting

1. *Onopordum acanthium* (Scotch thistle)
2. *Anaphalis margaritacea yedoensis*
3. *Artemisia ludoviciana* (white sage)
4. *Carpenteria californica*
5. *Wisteria sinensis* 'Alba' (white Chinese wisteria)
6. *Romneya coulteri* (California tree poppy)
7. *Leucanthemum maximum* (Shasta daisy)
8. *Stachys byzantina* (lamb's ears)

Trees and shrubs

The excellent range includes *Amelanchier lamarckii* (Juneberry) with a mass of white flowers in spring, while *Eucryphia × nymansensis* produces 2¾in/6.5cm-wide, white or cream flowers in late summer and early fall. Other fine shrubs to consider are *Hydrangea arborescens* 'Grandiflora' with pure white flowers in slightly rounded heads from midsummer to early fall. Its relative *H. paniculata* 'Grandiflora' develops large, pyramidal, terminal heads of white flowers during late summer and fall.

Few small-garden shrubs with white flowers are as attractive as *Magnolia stellata* (star magnolia), with 4in/10cm-wide flowers during spring. The narrow, silver-gray, willow-like leaves of *Pyrus salicifolia* 'Pendula' are also attractive, and during spring, pure white flowers appear in terminal clusters. It is best set off by blue spring-flowering bulbs. *Spiraea × * 'Arguta' (bridal wreath) and *Viburnum opulus* 'Sterile', sometimes known as *V. o.* 'Roseum', are other superb shrubs for planting in white borders.

▲ A garden seat creates an ideal pivot for this white and silver garden, and is an ideal theme for a small garden where vibrancy is desired.

▲ Plants in pots, placed on a well-drained surface, create an attractive feature and are ideal as a focal point in small gardens.

variegated foliage

Foliage with several colors never fails to attract attention, and these qualities are found in a wide range of plants from herbaceous perennials to trees, shrubs, and climbers. Many have subdued colors, while others are bright and make a garden look vibrant.

Flower borders

There are more variegated herbaceous perennials than might, at first thought, be considered possible. Well-known variegated hostas include *Hosta* 'Fortunei Albopicta', *H.* 'Crispula' and *H.* 'Gold Standard'. There are many other hostas but perhaps one of the most unlikely variegated plants is *Aegopodium podagraria* 'Variegatum' (variegated goutweed or bishopsweed). It is not highly invasive, invasive, but is best grown in large tubs where it brightens patios with light-green leaves edged with white. The perennial grass *Hakonechloa macra* 'Aureola' is also superb in a large tub or at the corner of a raised bed. Its arching, ribbon-like leaves are variegated buff and gold, with touches of bronze.

Also ideal for borders with their vertical growth are *Iris pallida*, with sword-like, green and yellow striped leaves, and *I. p.* 'Argentea Variegata', with white stripes. The variegated phloxes 'Norah Leigh' and 'Harlequin' are both excellent in herbaceous borders, while *Yucca filamentosa* 'Variegata', with its sword-like leaves, always attracts attention. Give it a prominent position.

Trees and shrubs

These often create dominant displays, especially *Euonymus fortunei* 'Emerald 'n' Gold', a dense, bushy evergreen with variegated bright gold leaves; in winter they are tinged bronze-pink. 'Emerald Gaiety' and 'Silver Queen' also have variegated leaves. *Aucuba japonica* 'Variegata' is also an old garden favorite with its yellow spotted green leaves creating a dominant display. It looks good in spring when surrounded by daffodils. *Elaeagnus pungens* 'Maculata' is another evergreen favorite, with stiff, leathery green leaves splashed gold.

Salvia officinalis 'Icterina' grows about 12in/30cm high and is ideal for planting beside a path, where it cloaks unsightly edges. With its green and gold leaves it

◄ *This small, decorative, rail-type fence harmonizes with ornamental grasses and low-growing plants to create an attractive feature.*

makes an eye-catching feature. An equally striking variety is 'Tricolor', with gray-green leaves splashed creamy white, suffused with pink.

The deciduous *Cornus alba* 'Spaethii' (dogwood) has light-green leaves with irregular gold-splashed edges, with the bonus of bright red stems in winter. A near relative, *C. alternifolia* 'Argentea', is a small tree or a large shrub with horizontally spreading branches bearing small green leaves with creamy white edges. Do not hide its attractive shape.

Variegated hollies have a permanent role in gardens, adding brightness throughout the year. *Ilex* × *altaclarensis* 'Lawsoniana' has green leaves, usually spineless, each with a central yellow splash. It bears orange-red berries in winter. *Ilex aquifolium* has many varieties with variegated, spine-edged leaves, notably 'Golden Queen' with cream-streaked green stems and large leaves broadly edged with gold.

Climbers and wall shrubs

Perhaps the best-known variegated climbers are ivies. They range from the small-leaved *Hedera helix* 'Goldheart', now known as 'Oro di Bogliasco', with dark green leaves splashed yellow, to large-leaved types. They include the variegated *H. canariensis* 'Gloire de Marengo' (Canary Island ivy), with deep green leaves and silver-gray and white variegations. There are several variegated forms of the Persian ivy; *H. colchica* 'Dentata Variegata' has leaves conspicuously edged creamy yellow, and 'Sulphur Heart' has irregular yellow splashes. *Actinidia kolomikta*, a deciduous climber, has green leaves that develop pink-flushed white areas toward the tips.

▶ *Trailing and spreading plants help to clothe the edges of decking. Regular trimming may be necessary to prevent them becoming intrusive.*

▼ *Variegated plants soften this flight of steps and complement the distinctive tiered branches of Cornus controversa 'Variegata'.*

Key to planting

1. *Hakonechloa macra* 'Aureola'
2. *Phlox* 'Norah Leigh'
3. *Yucca fillamentosa* 'Variegata'
4. *Cornus controversa* 'Variegata'
5. *Variegated phormium*
6. *Iris pallida* 'Argentea Variegata'
7. *Hosta sieboldiana* 'Frances Williams'
8. *Hosta fortunei albopicta*

mixed colors

There are two ways to consider "mixed" colors: one is a medley of colors within seed-raised plants such as summer-flowering bedding plants for beds and containers. The other is planning the arrangement of individual colors and this is most dramatically achieved in the larger theater of a garden.

Using mixed colors

Windowboxes, wall baskets, and hanging baskets look wonderful when planted with a single species or variety in a range of colors. For example, trailing lobelia comes in white, blue, lilac, crimson, and red varieties, and all are sold together as mixed seed. A practical advantage of devoting a hanging basket to one variety in a mix of colors is that all the plants will be equally vigorous, and none will grow to dominate its neighbor.

Mixing colors

Mixing colors in a garden is as much a matter of personal preference as one of science. It is useful to use a color wheel formed of three main colors—yellow, blue, and red—and three secondaries—orange, green, and violet—to reveal those that complement or harmonize.

Complementary colors are those with no common pigments, while those that harmonize share some pigments. Yellow and violet, blue and orange, and red and green are complementary, while yellow harmonizes with green and orange, blue with green and violet, and red with orange and violet.

▲ *Plants with variegated leaves create color throughout summer and, if evergreen, the entire year. Many can be grown in pots and tubs.*

SHINY AND MATT SURFACES

The surface of a leaf influences the way it reflects light. A smooth surface reflects light at the same angle at which it is struck by it, and makes the light appear bright. If the surface is matt, light is reflected at different angles and creates a dull surface. In nature, however, few plant surfaces are as smooth as glass, and the scattering of light occurs from most of them.

Mixing and matching

Color planning a garden need not involve vast areas or be expensive. Consider planting a corner of a shrub border, or an area of a wall to start with.

Yellow and gold—many yellow-leaved trees and shrubs form ideal backdrops for purple-leaved plants. If the ratio of yellow to purple is about three to one they appear well-balanced. Plant the dark-leaved *Berberis thunbergii atropurpurea* with yellow-leaved shrubs like *Sambucus racemosa* 'Plumosa Aurea' (European red elder).

Key to planting

1 *Calendula officinalis* (pot marigold)

2 *Coreopsis verticillata*

3 *Cotinus coggygria* 'Notcutt's Variety'

4 *Philadelphus coronarius* 'Aureus'

5 Lupins—in mixed colors

6 *Berberis thunbergii atropurpurea*

7 *Papaver orientale* (oriental poppy)

8 *Geranium* 'Johnson's Blue'

Blue and purple—to create a blue background display, plant *Ceanothus* 'Cascade' against a sheltered sunny wall. It grows about 10ft/3m high and wide, and bears small, rich blue flowers in late spring and early summer. For added interest, plant the slightly tender, evergreen shrub *Choisya ternata* (Mexican orange blossom) in front of it.

Red and pink—take care when using red because it is dominant, and can be overpowering. Against a mid-green background, bright-red flowers such as the hardy annual *Papaver rhoeas* (field poppy) have a three-dimensional effect. However, most red flowers are not totally color saturated and appear more as shades. Pink is a desaturated red and is easier to blend into a garden.

▲ Multicolored hanging baskets always capture attention and often suit more backgrounds than those of a single color.

▼ Packed borders with mixed colors are ideal features in small gardens. Remove dead flowers to encourage repeat flowering.

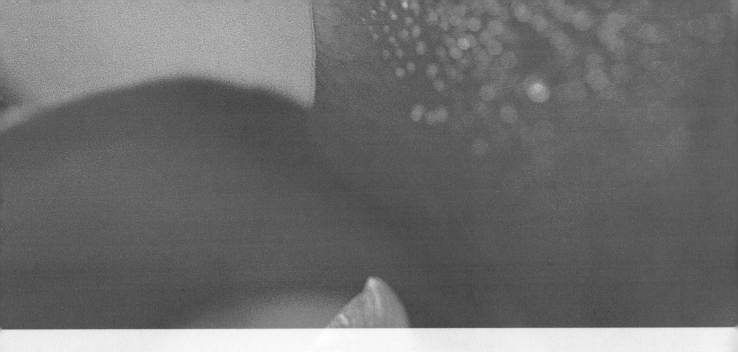

seasonal displays

Colorful displays of flowers and leaves are possible throughout the year. Summer is, of course, the main time when plants flower, and flowering plants range from hardy annuals to herbaceous perennials, shrubs, and trees. Fall is also colorful and is especially known for deciduous shrubs, trees, and climbers with leaves that turn rich colors before falling. Several trees flower during winter, and, in addition, small bulbs can be naturalized in short grass or around shrubs. Spring is eagerly anticipated for its glorious daffodils, flowering trees, and shrubs.

planting for spring color

Bulbs are often thought to signal the start of spring, and several can be used in exciting combinations with shrubs. Spring is also the time of year when many ornamental cherry trees burst into flower and they may also be complemented when underplanted with bulbs, especially daffodils.

Spring-flowering shrubs

One of the most eye-catching shows of yellow is from the bell-shaped flowers of *Forsythia* 'Lynwood'. Like many other spring-flowering shrubs, the flowers appear on naked stems, but the leaves arrive soon after.

Ulex europaeus (gorse), is a yellow-flowered evergreen shrub. It is covered with masses of honey-scented, pea-shaped flowers during spring and early summer, and often continues bearing flowers sporadically until the following early spring.

Amelanchier lamarckii (Juneberry) is deciduous, with masses of pure-white, star-shaped flowers during midspring that never fail to attract attention. *Magnolia stellata* (star magnolia) is smaller, and another white-flowered deciduous shrub. Its individual, 4in/10cm-wide flowers are more dramatic if fewer in number. And *Kerria japonica* 'Pleniflora' is deciduous, with a lax habit and double, orange-yellow flowers about 2in/5cm wide on slender stems during late spring and early summer. Other spring-flowering shrubs include *Chaenomeles* × *superba* (flowering quince), *Cytisus* × *praecox* 'Warminster' (Warminster broom), *Berberis* × *stenophylla*, *Ribes sanguineum* (flowering currant), and *Viburnum* × *burkwoodii*.

TREES FOR SPRING

Prunus padus (bird cherry)—long tassels of almond-scented white flowers in late spring. 'Watereri' has longer tassels.

Prunus subhirtella 'Pendula Rosea'—spreading and weeping tree with pinkish-white flowers.

Prunus 'Accolade'—graceful and open tree with bluish-pink, semidouble flowers during early and midspring.

◀ *Colorful spring displays are essential for shedding winter gloom. Prepare for this by planting spring-flowering bulbs in early fall.*

Spring-flowering bulbs

Some bulbs, such as *Crocus chrysanthus,* which often begin flowering in late winter, can be naturalized in large drifts in short grass, but a more reserved way is to plant groups of spring-flowering bulbs in rock gardens.

Some late winter-flowering bulbs continue their display into early spring and include the pale blue *Chionodoxa luciliae* (glory of the snow), yellow *Eranthis hyemalis* (winter aconite) and white *Galanthus nivalis* (common snowdrop). Others concentrate their flowering in spring and range from *Ipheion uniflorum* (spring starflower), with white to violet-blue, star-shaped flowers, to *Scilla siberica* (spring squill) with deep blue or white flowers. Two species of tulips for spring include *Tulipa tarda*, with clusters of white flowers that reveal large, bright yellow centers, and *Tulipa kaufmanniana* (waterlily tulip), which produces star-shaped white flowers flushed red and yellow on the outside.

STAR PLANTS

Amelanchier lamarckii

Clematis montana

Crocus chrysanthus

Eranthis hyemalis

Kerria japonica 'Pleniflora'

Magnolia stellata

Muscari armeniacum

▶ Kerria japonica *'Pleniflora' makes a lovely display of orange-yellow flowers in late spring and early summer.*

Mixing and matching

As spring progresses there is increasing opportunity to arrange attractive combinations of plants in borders and against walls. For example, two flowers which pair well are *Rosa banksiae* 'Lutea', with double yellow flowers in spring, planted alongside the scented *Clematis montana* 'Elizabeth', a variety of the mountain clematis. The rose has fern-like leaves and lightly scented, clear yellow single flowers during late spring, while the clematis bears an abundance of pale pink flowers at the same time.

Viburnum opulus 'Roseum' (snowball bush), is a deciduous shrub with large, globular, creamy white flowerheads during late spring and early summer. The branches often bow under the weight of the magnificent flowers. For contrast, plant the herbaceous *Hosta sieboldiana* around its edges.

planting for summer color

The intensity of color in a summer garden is almost overwhelming. Herbaceous perennials, hardy and half-hardy annuals, and bulbs fill beds and borders, and climbers and wall shrubs cover walls, trellises, and pergolas. Variegated and colored foliage is a key ingredient.

▲ *Bright-faced lilies, with their distinctive shapes, are beacons of brightness in informal borders, and are at home in cottage gardens.*

Summer-flowering shrubs

A wide and varied choice includes early summer-flowering shrubs such as *Cistus × cyprius*, with 3in/7.5cm-wide white flowers blotched crimson, and *Cistus × purpureus* which has rose to purple flowers blotched dark maroon. *Potentilla fruticosa*, a deciduous shrub with many varieties in colors from yellow to bright vermilion, continues its display into late summer. The glorious philadelphus shrubs never fail to enrich gardens in early and midsummer. Many are richly scented, and there are varieties to suit small gardens.

With the onset of midsummer many hydrangeas burst into flower. *Hydrangea macrophylla* forms a rounded shrub with

STAR PLANTS
Hydrangea macrophylla
Hypericum 'Hidcote'
Laburnum × watereri 'Vossii'
Philadelphus coronarius 'Aureus'
Potentilla fruticosa
Senecio brachyglottis 'Sunshine'

flowerheads up to 8in/20cm wide. These shrubs have the bonus of flowers into early fall. Late summer sees other hydrangeas bursting into color, none more spectacular than *Hydrangea paniculata* 'Grandiflora', with plume-like heads up to 18in/45cm long, packed with white flowers into early fall.

Mixing and matching

Opportunities abound during summer to mix plants in colorful combinations. For an extra bright display, plant *Genista cinerea*, a large deciduous shrub with yellow, sweetly scented flowers during early and midsummer, with the evergreen shrub *Brachyglottis* 'Sunshine', still better known as *Senecio* 'Sunshine'. It has gray, white-felted leaves and yellow daisy-like flowers.

The deciduous tree *Laburnum × watereri* 'Vossii' (golden chain tree) is known for its long, pendulous clusters of yellow flowers and forms a background color contrast with purple lilac.

In wild gardens, the late spring and early summer flowering deciduous shrub *Rhododendron luteum* has sweet, honey-scented yellow flowers. It may be planted alongside a stream, with a dense planting of red variety of *Primula japonica* in front of it. Both plants thrive under a light canopy of deciduous trees. The evergreen shrub *Rosmarinus officinalis* (rosemary) has gray-green leaves and flowers that appear mainly in spring, and then sporadically through to the fall. It looks striking beside the yellow-leaved *Philadelphus coronarius* 'Aureus'.

Lilies for summer color

Lilies are popular and are especially attractive when grouped with other plants. Look for *Lilium candidum* (madonna lily) with white, trumpet-shaped flowers during early and midsummer. Their centers have golden pollen. They are superb when highlighted against a background of the deciduous shrub *Cotinus coggygria* 'Royal Purple', with dark plum-purple leaves. For a less dramatic display, plant the lilies in combination with foxgloves (*Digitalis purpurea*) and a background of blue delphiniums. *Lilium regale* also has white flowers, with their exteriors shaded rose-purple. It creates a rustic and subtle combination with silver birches and ferns such as *Dryopteris filix–mas*.

▲ *Plants with all-green or variegated leaves add interest throughout summer, and they help to suppress the growth of weeds.*

COLORFUL LEAVES

Aucuba japonica 'Variegata'—evergreen shrub with green leaves spotted yellow.

Cotinus coggygria 'Royal Purple'—deciduous shrub with dark plum-purple leaves.

Elaeagnus pungens 'Maculata'—evergreen shrub with green leaves splashed gold.

Humulus lupulus 'Aureus'—yellow-leaved hop, a herbaceous climber with rich yellow leaves.

Philadelphus coronarius 'Aureus'—deciduous shrub with yellow leaves.

Prunus cerasifera 'Pissardii'—deciduous tree with dark red young leaves that turn deep purple as they mature.

Robinia pseudoacacia 'Frisia'—deciduous tree with yellow leaves.

planting for fall color

Fall is thought to be a dull period in the garden, but it is full of colorful flowers, and leaves that turn yellow, orange, gold, and red before falling. And even where the flowers of herbaceous plants have turned brown, they look attractive when laced with dew-drenched spiders' webs.

Fall flowering shrubs and trees

Several shrubs that flower in late summer continue their display into the fall. They include the magnificient *Buddleja davidii* (butterfly bush) with long, tapering spires of lilac-purple, honey, and musk-scented flowers from midsummer to midfall. There are several varieties in white, deep violet, and lavender-blue. *Caryopteris* × *clandonensis* 'Kew blue' has aromatic gray-green leaves and dark blue flowers from late summer, while *Hibiscus syriacus* bears trumpet-shaped flowers from midsummer to early fall, in colors including violet-blue and rose-pink.

The popular *Hydrangea macrophylla* (common hydrangea) is bushy with large, mainly blue flowerheads that continue into fall. Another magnificent summer and fall-flowering shrub is *Lavatera* 'Rosea', (tree mallow), also known as *Lavatera olbia* 'Rosea'. The branching stems bear masses of rose-colored flowers.

Glorious corms

Many people think that corms and bulbs are the same, but instead of having an onion-like structure, the stem bases of corms are greatly swollen. *Crocus longiflorus* has goblet-shaped, lilac and deep bluish-mauve flowers with prominent orange stigmas and orange feathering in the throat during mid- and late fall. And *C. sativus* (saffron crocus), has red-purple flowers, large red stigmas and orange stamens during midfall. A more popular and hardier corm is *Cyclamen hederifolium*, with flowers in a range of colors from white, through pale pink to mauve, from late summer to late fall.

Lilies for fall color

Several summer-flowering lilies continue their display into fall and are welcome for the stately appearance of their

▲ *The leaves of the deciduous shrub* Rhus typhina *(staghorn sumac) turn brilliant shades of orange–red, yellow, and purple.*

flowers, but they need a sunny and wind-sheltered position. *Lilium auratum* (golden-rayed lily) has sweetly scented, funnel-shaped, brilliant white flowers during late summer and early fall. Each flower has a golden-yellow ray or band. *L. henryi* also has sweetly scented flowers, but they are pale apricot-yellow with red spots. They appear during late summer and early fall. A more popular variety is *L. speciosum*, a lily with white, partly crimson-shaded pendent flowers.

STAR PLANTS

Buddleja davidii	*Hydrangea macrophylla*
Hibiscus syriacus	*Lavatera* 'Rosea'

Mixing and matching

You can plant a late summer display that will, in part, continue to midfall or later by planting the 3ft/90cm-high, rose 'Ophelia' with blush-pink flowers among the sky blue, trumpet-like flowers of the early to late fall-flowering *Gentiana sino-ornata*. It grows about 6in/15cm high with a 12–15in/30–38cm spread. The rose continues flowering into early fall, especially in mild areas. For a richer color scheme plant a row of *Sedum* 'Autumn Joy', now known as *Sedum* 'Herbstfreude'. This colorful plant bears slightly domed heads packed with salmon-pink flowers that slowly change through orange-red to orange-brown in mid- and late fall.

▲ *Massed hydrangeas create dominant features from midsummer to early fall. The old flowerheads look very attractive when they are covered in frost.*

SHRUBS AND TREES WITH FALL COLOR

Hamamelis mollis (Chinese witch-hazel)—sharp yellow

Liquidambar styraciflua (sweetgum)—rich orange and scarlet shades

Koelreuteria paniculata (golden-rain tree)—rich yellow

Malus tschonoskii—rich red and yellow

Parrotia persica—crimson, gold and amber tints

Rhus typhina (staghorn sumac)—rich orange-red, purple and yellow tints

planting for winter interest

Corners of gardens devoted to winter-flowering plants create oases of interest when the garden might otherwise be lacking color. Apart from winter flowers, many shrubs and trees have wonderfully colored stems or bark. Some make excellent focal points.

Winter-flowering shrubs and trees

These create a permanent framework around which other plants can be positioned. Many have scented flowers and they include *Hamamelis mollis* (Chinese witch-hazel) and *Hamamelis japonica* (Japanese witch-hazel), both with spider-like flowers borne on naked branches. *Viburnum × bodnantense* 'Dawn' has sweetly scented white flowers, flushed red, from early to late winter, and *V. farreri* bears white flowers over a similar period. Richly colored mahonias are also evident in winter, and few compare with the evergreen *Mahonia × media* 'Charity'. It has tapering spires of sweetly scented, yellow flowers from late fall to late winter.

Glorious bulbs

Some winter-flowering bulbs are slightly variable in the exact time they flower, often blooming on the cusp of late winter and early spring, depending on the weather. The rich golden-yellow, goblet-like flowers of *Crocus chrysanthus* always get plenty of attention. They flower during late winter into early spring, and are superb in a rock garden or when naturalized around a silver birch. The slightly earlier flowering *Iris reticulata* creates a feast of violet-scented, deep blue-purple flowers each with an orange blaze during mid- and late winter. Its diminutive stature, about 4in/10cm high, makes it ideal for a rock

garden or the edge of a path. *I. histrioides* 'Major' bears rich blue flowers at about the same time and looks good in a medley of golden crocuses and especially white *Galanthus nivalis* (snowdrops) which are an essential part of the winter garden. During mid- and late winter it bears white nodding flowers, some slightly scented.

▲ *The diminutive and bulbous-rooted* Iris reticulata *produces a wealth of flowers. It is ideal for planting in a rock garden.*

Mixing and matching

Here are a couple of plants that pair well, with the added benefit of scented flowers. First, try *Helleborus niger* (Christmas rose) around the early to late winter-flowering shrub *Chimonanthus praecox* 'Grandiflorus' (wintersweet). The hellebore has saucer-shaped white flowers, while the wintersweet reveals spicily scented, claw-like flowers formed of yellow outer petals and red centers. The second plant association is *Hamamelis mollis* (Chinese witch hazel), with rich golden-yellow, spider-like flowers in midwinter, and an underplanting of the yellow-green evergreen shrub *Euonymus fortunei* (wintercreeper). A few plants of the low-growing evergreen shrub *Sarcococca confusa* (Christmas box), with white, sweetly scented flowers, add further color contrasts.

▶ *Shrubs with colored stems in winter always attract attention. Here is the thicket-forming Cornus alba 'Sibirica", with bright crimson stems. It is ideal for planting alongside streams.*

◀ *The hardy, evergreen shrub* Mahonia × media *'Charity' never fails to give a dominant display of yellow flowers in winter.*

457

ornamental features

Opportunities to create decorative features are wide in small gardens. These range from hanging baskets and windowboxes, to tubs and pots on a patio or a terrace, bamboo walks, and collections of ornamental grasses. Roses are popular; climbing and rambling roses are useful for draping trellises and pillars with color, while some can be encouraged to clamber up large trees. Scented flowers are always popular and drench gardens in fragrances from almond to vanilla.

windowbox color

By using a combination of spring, summer, and winter displays it is possible to have a colorful garden throughout the year. Spring displays are mainly formed of bulbs and biennials, while summer arrangements rely on bedding plants. Winter displays usually depend on foliage plants.

Creating a year-round display

An attractive windowbox may be positioned on a window ledge or on brackets attached to the wall, about 8in/20cm below the ledge of a casement window. Fit three smaller boxes inside the box, and plant them with seasonal displays. In this way, the windowbox can be given new plantings three times a year.

▲ *Decorative, plaque-like plant containers create distinctive features when mounted on a wall. Eventually they become drenched in color.*

❀ Spring displays—plant these in the fall using spring-flowering bulbs such as hyacinths, tulips and *Narcissus* (daffodils), and biennials like *Erysimum* (wallflowers), *Myosotis* (forget-me-not) and double daisies. When planted, put the container in a cool, well-drained sheltered part of the garden. In spring, when the bulbs are breaking into bud and the biennials are starting to flower, remove the winter display and replace with the spring arrangement.

❀ Summer displays—plant in late spring and initially keep them in a sheltered, frost-free position outdoors or in a well-ventilated conservatory. In early summer, when the spring display is fading, replace with the summer display.

❀ Winter displays—in fall, as soon as the summer display has been dulled by frost, remove it and replace it with the winter arrangement. This should be mainly formed of hardy foliage plants, such as small pots of *Aucuba japonica* 'Variegata', small-leaved *Hedera* (ivy), miniature and slow-growing conifers, winter-flowering *Erica* (heath), and *Calluna* (heather),

variegated forms of *Euonymus japonicus*, and *Hebe* × *andersoniana* 'Variegata'.

Wall baskets and mangers

These resemble hanging baskets cut in half and secured to a wall, but they are large and able to hold plenty of soil. They look good in any position and are especially useful for securing to walls abutting pavements or around patio interiors. Wall basket and manger displays are more limited than windowboxes and can have only spring and summer arrangements. Spring displays are planted directly into the container in fall and left until they flower in spring. When over, all the plants are removed, fresh soil put in its place, and a summer display planted. This lasts until fall, when the spring display is planted.

STAR PLANTS

Aucuba japonica 'Variegata'

Lobularia maritima

Muscari armeniacum

Three seasonal medleys

The range of possible plants is wide but the following suggestions are a fail-safe, attractive design for each season.

❀ Spring—this can be a combination of plants, using biennials such as *Erysimum* (wallflower), double daisies and *Myosotis* (forget-me-not), and bulbs like *Muscari armeniacum* (grape hyacinth), *Tulipa greigii* and *T. fosteriana*.

❀ Summer—For a colorful display plant a combination of trailing lobelia, zonal pelargoniums, *Lobularia maritima* (sweet alyssum), tuberous-rooted begonias and summer-flowering *Viola* (pansy). Position trailing plants at one end or along the front, with the begonia in the center. Container-grown plants will need some feeding and regular thorough watering throughout any dry weather.

▶ *Use upright and bushy plants to achieve a display at the top of a windowbox, and trailing foliage plants to drape the front in color.*

▼ *Instead of planting summer-flowering plants directly into soil in a windowbox, they can be left in their pots and replaced as they fade.*

❀ Winter—this can be a grouping of foliage plants such as small-leaved *Hedera helix* 'Glacier' (ivy), variegated *Euonymus japonicus* and dwarf varieties of the conifer *Chamaecyparis lawsoniana* will look attractive. The winter-flowering *Erica* (heath) adds color.

> ### HERBS IN WINDOWBOXES
>
> A windowbox outside a kitchen window may be planted with a wide range of readily available herbs. Choose a medley of low-growing plants, such as mint, thyme, chives, parsley, marjoram, and French tarragon. The range of mints is wide and includes spearmint and apple mint. Leave individual plants in their pots and place them on a layer of gravel in the windowbox, so that their rims are slightly below the top. Pack moist peat around the pots to keep the soil moist and cool.

hanging baskets

Hanging baskets can bring summer color and winter greenery to featureless spots. They can enliven dull walls with decorative flowers and foliage, and brighten windows, doorways, and porches. They also look eyecatching in small paved areas, such as patios and courtyards.

Displaying hanging baskets

A planted basket should be hung in an eye-catching position—perhaps on either side of a window, about 15in/38cm from the frame. The edge of a balcony or a veranda may be decorated by hanging planted baskets along it to introduce

◀ *Brick columns are a useful site for fixing a hanging basket from a bracket. Position the basket where it cannot be knocked.*

round and cascading shapes to an area that is dominated by vertical and horizontal lines.

A featureless wall or a carport may be enlivened by hanging planted baskets along it, but do not hang them near corners or where they might be knocked. To prevent people knocking baskets hanging from a wall, range planted tubs along the base of the wall, but do not stand them directly below the baskets where water will drip onto them. A few white or pale-colored flowers in the baskets will make them noticeable in twilight. If you hang baskets in a lobby or a porch, they will need to have inbuilt drip trays, or water will spill onto the floor below.

Choosing plants

A hanging basket will be successful only if it is well planted. That means resisting the temptation to cram it with plants.

Once the plants are established, weed out weak ones. A few large, healthy blooms look better than many stunted plants fighting for survival. One rule for achieving an eye-catching display is not to plant too many species. Mixed displays can look good, but four or five well-chosen plants look better than a dozen species in a basket.

Choose plants with contrasting growing habits for a mixed basket—trailing, bushy, and upright. Set a showy plant, such as a fuchsia or an upright geranium, in the center and put trailing plants around the edges and cascading from the sides of the basket. If you buy plants from a nursery or a garden center, your choice of varieties may be limited. Instead, try growing your own, choosing compact plants recommended for hanging baskets. Mix summer-flowering plants with hardy perennials and foliage plants, such as variegated small-leaved *Hedera* (ivy) and small forms of *Euonymus fortunei* with attractive leaves. If you do not want to spray your hanging baskets regularly with insecticides, avoid plants that are prone to pests, such as nasturtiums, which attract blackflies.

Strawberries and tomatoes

Some varieties of these fruiting plants look attractive in hanging baskets. *Fragaria vesca*, the alpine strawberry or *fraise du bois*, is a decorative perennial. 'Alexander' bears small fruits used to decorate pastries. 'Temptation' bears aromatic sweet fruits from midsummer to the fall frosts. A bushy tomato such as 'Tumbler', which produces small, sweet fruits, will look decorative cascading from a basket.

▶ *To create a spectacular hanging basket, use a combination of upright, cascading, and trailing plants. Additionally, daily watering is vital.*

SINGLE-SUBJECT HANGING BASKETS

The following produce eyecatching displays:

Calceolaria integrifolia 'Sunshine'—creates a dominant display packed with yellow, pouch-like flowers.

Fuchsias—use bushy and trailing types. Plants are sometimes slow to create a display, so insure that they are well developed.

Impatiens (busy lizzie)—bright colors.

Solenopsis axillaris —a mass of five-petalled, 1in/2.5cm-wide flowers in a range of colors including blue, white, and pink.

Lobelia (in mixed colors)—trailing plants make a dazzling display.

Petunia grandiflora supercascade series—very free-flowering over a long period, producing large flower heads in a wide variety of colors.

pots and tubs

These popular, versatile containers can accommodate plants of many sizes and types. The agapanthus, with tall stems bearing umbrella-like flower heads, looks good in square, Versailles-type planters, while rounded, evergreen shrubs look better in large, round tubs.

Displaying pots and tubs

There are plants to suit every container, and pots to suit any position in the garden. A small paved area, such as a courtyard, needs at least one dominant plant in an impressive container, around which other planted pots may be grouped. *Fatsia japonica* (false castor oil plant) planted in a very large clay pot is one suggestion. It needs a sheltered position in sun or shade. This evergreen shrub grows well in a container, and in gardens that are located in urban areas.

The top of a flight of steps looks better with several planted pots clustered on it. In a formal garden the stairs look best with just one plant on either side, while a group of small planted pots is better in an informal setting. On a patio, a large trough makes a focal point if placed beneath a window, with attractive planted pots either side.

Make containers for rural gardens from three or four tires stacked and wired together. Wedge a plastic bucket in the top and plant it with spring flowers, such as polyanthus. Paint the tires white to blend them in. In town gardens, small tubs planted with clipped, half–standard *Laurus nobilis* (bay trees) may stand either side of a front door. An ornate urn on a high pedestal makes a magnificent focal point at the junction of wide gravel paths in a large garden. Range planted troughs, available in plastic, glass–fiber,

◀ *Position pots alongside paths as well as on patios. Half-burying pots keeps the soil cool and reduces the need to water them.*

reconstituted stone, and other materials, along the top of a plain wall, the sides of a patio, or the edges of a veranda. Where there is vertical space to fill, choose upright plants like daffodils, but summer–flowering trailing plants look spectacular cascading down a wall or from a balcony.

Foliage plants for tubs and pots

Plants with decorative leaves lend permanency to a patio or a terrace, and unify groupings of flowers, especially

annuals. There is a wide range of these. Evergreen shrubs with variegated leaves include *Aucuba japonica* 'Variegata' with green leaves splashed with yellow, *Hebe* × *franciscana* 'Variegata' with glossy green leaves edged with cream, *Hebe* × *andersonii* 'Variegata' with cream and green leaves, *Choisya ternata* 'Sundance' with radiant golden leaves, and *Yucca filamentosa* 'Variegata' , which has dramatic sword–shaped leaves edged with a creamy stripe.

▶ *Brighten walls by attaching brackets that support pots of many sizes. These can be used in combination with hanging baskets.*

▼ *Clean lines, formed by square containers planted with narrow-leaved, spiky plants, are right for a modern setting.*

CLIMBERS IN CONTAINERS

Several climbers can be grown in containers, but regular watering is needed to make certain that the soil does not dry out. Some are perennials, others are annuals raised from seed each year.

Large-flowered clematis—choose a tub or a large pot. Flowers from early to late summer, depending on the variety, with a range of colors. Ornate metal railings look attractive when covered by the flowers.

Clematis macropetala—choose a large terracotta or wooden tub, fill its base with clean rubble, then add well-drained soil. Put several plants with light and dark blue flowers around the top to encourage cascading.

Humulus lupulus 'Aureus' (yellow-leaved hop)—select a large tub for this herbaceous climber and form a wigwam of 5–6ft/1.5–1.8m-long canes. They become smothered in yellow leaves.

Ipomoea purpurea (morning glory—grown as a half-hardy annual, with large, bell-like flowers in several colors.

Tropaeolum majus (nasturtium)—grown as a half-hardy annual, with flowers in several colors throughout summer.

stone sinks on patios

Where there is no space for a rock garden or even a scree bed, a stone sink on a patio or a terrace is an ideal home for small rock garden plants, dwarf bulbs, and miniature conifers. By selecting the combination of plants you can have an attractive feature throughout the year.

▲ *A stone sink is a perfect place for a miniature rock garden. Standing the sink on bricks helps to reduce the ravages of snails and slugs.*

Selecting and preparing a sink

Ideally, an old stone sink is best for planting. However, a deep, white-glazed sink can easily be modified to give an attractive, well-worn appearance. This is done by scratching the surface, coating it with PVA, and covering with a slightly moist mixture of equal parts of cement powder, horticultural sand, and peat.

Place the sink on four strong bricks; it should have a slight slope toward the drainage hole. Place a piece of fine-mesh wire net over the drainage hole so it cannot get blocked, then a layer of broken clay pots or pebbles over the entire base to facilitate drainage.

POSITIONING A SINK GARDEN

Sink gardens need full sun or partial shade, and a position where they cannot be tripped over. Therefore, unless the patio or terrace is large with a rarely used corner, position a couple of columnar conifers in pots close to the sink to mark it out clearly. Light-colored conifers are better than dark green ones, because they are easily visible in the twilight.

Spread a 1in/2.5cm-thick layer of horticultural sand over the bottom of the sink and half-fill it with a mixture of equal parts of potting soil, moist peat, and grit. If the sink is deep, increase the amount of drainage material. The soil must not contain chalk if lime-hating plants are being used.

At this stage, a few large rocks can be pushed into the soil, inclined at a shallow angle. Add more soil to within 1in/2.5cm of the rim. Position the plants, then add a ½in/12mm-thick layer of rock chippings or pea gravel. The soil will settle, so be prepared to add more surface material later.

Plants for stone sinks

The range of plants is wide and while some, such as dwarf conifers, create height, other rock garden plants are small. Spring-flowering dwarf bulbs create bright, diminutive, dainty features.

▲ *A miniature hedge makes an attractive background for a patio, especially when combined with flowering plants.*

▲ *A stone sink makes a home for hardy, succulent plants such as houseleeks. By leaving plants in their pots the display can be quickly and easily changed.*

Spring-flowering bulbs—include *Crocus chrysanthus* with golden-yellow, goblet-shaped flowers in late winter and early spring, also available in white, blue and purple; *Cyclamen coum* with pink and carmine flowers from midwinter to early spring; *Eranthis hyemalis* with lemon-yellow flowers backed by light green ruffs during late winter and spring; *Iris danfordiae* with honey-scented, lemon-yellow flowers during mid- and late winter; *Iris reticulata* with bluish-purple flowers with orange blazes in late winter and early spring; *Narcissus bulbocodium* with yellow, hoop-like flowers during late winter and early spring; and *Narcissus cyclamineus* with yellow, narrow trumpets with swept-back petals in late winter and early spring.

Rock garden perennials—*Antennaria rosea* has deep pink flowers during spring and early summer; *Campanula cochleariifolia* has blue bells from midsummer to fall; *Edraianthus pumilio*

has lavender-blue flowers from late spring to midsummer; *Erinus alpinus* has bright pink flowers from early spring to late summer; *Lewisia cotyledon* has pink flowers with white veins during late spring and early summer; and *Saxifraga burseriana* has white flowers during late winter and early spring.

Miniature and slow-growing conifers—plant these while they are still small and be prepared to remove them when they grow too large. Position tall ones at one end of the sink, and sprawling types at the other, because they help to create height and shape.

STAR PLANTS

Crocus chrysanthus   *Eranthis hyemalis*

scented gardens

Scented flowers and aromatic leaves can enrich the air with many different fragrances. The range of scents is amazingly wide, and even in temperate regions there is a choice of over a hundred fragrances. They include scents from chocolate and pineapple to banana and lemon.

Siting fragrant plants

The perfect site for a perfumed garden is sheltered from strong winds, which disperse scents, free from frosts, which limit the growing period of tender plants, and slopes gently toward the sun, to capture the warmth that encourages plants to emit their fragrances. Few gardens have all these qualities, but garden areas suitable for perfumed plants can be made by planting hedges, erecting freestanding trellis, and introducing tender plants in frost-free areas.

Flower borders

Many herbaceous perennials emit delicious scents, notably the short-lived, hardy *Hesperis matronalis* (sweet rocket). Its white, mauve, or purple flowers appear in early to midsummer to drench borders with their sweet fragrance, especially in the evening. *Saponaria officinalis* (soapwort) also emits a sweet scent from its single, pink, salver-shaped flowers which appear in mid- to late summer. *Phlox paniculata* has strongly perfumed flowers from mid- to late summer, and is perhaps better known. There are many varieties in colors from white to pink and red.

Establish summer color with rich fragrance in your garden quickly by planting a mix of *Matthiola bicornis* (night-scented stock), which bears pink to mauve flowers during mid- and late summer, and *Malcolmia maritima* (Virginia stock). Sow the seeds in friable soil beneath windows, and in successive sowings from spring to midsummer.

Once a favorite of the French Empress Josephine Bonaparte, *Reseda odorata* (mignonette) is a cottage-garden hardy annual with clusters of small, white and yellow richly scented flowers through the summer. It can be grown in windowboxes and in pots on balconies. It

◀ *This pairing of English lavender (*Lavandula angustifolia*) and rue (*Ruta graveolens*) brings scent and color to small gardens.*

AROMATIC-LEAVED SHRUBS

Caryopteris × *clandonensis*—pungent

Choisya ternata (Mexican orange blossom)—orange

Lavandula angustifolia (lavender)—lavender

Rosmarinus officinalis (rosemary)—rosemary

Ruta graveolens (rue)—pungent and acrid

is said that success and good fortune will attend a lover who rolls in a bed of mignonette.

There are several diminutive bulbs which will bring color and perfume to a rock garden and along the edges of paths. *Galanthus nivalis* (common snowdrop) and *Iris reticulata* both have violet-scented flowers during late winter and early spring.

Trees and shrubs

Many trees and shrubs are sweetly perfumed, and some have an unexpected fragrance. *Prunus padus* 'Watereri' (bird cherry) is a deciduous tree with a spreading habit. It bears drooping tassels

of white flowers which are almond-scented in early summer. *Prunus* × *yedoensis* (Potomac cherry) is also almond-scented. For a cowslip fragrance plant the deciduous shrub *Corylopsis pauciflora*, with pale primrose yellow flowers in mid- and late spring. *Helichrysum serotinum* is known as the

---

STAR PLANTS

Galanthus nivalis

Helichrysum serotinum

Hesperis matronalis

Phlox paniculata

Ulex europaeus 'Flore Pleno'

---

curry plant because it is redolent of curry spices.

For honey fragrance, plant the informal *Ulex europaeus* 'Flore Pleno' (double-flowered gorse). The deciduous philadelphus shrubs have flowers with an orange-blossom aroma that will pervade the garden in midsummer. *Cytisus battandieri* (pineapple broom) bears pineapple-scented, golden-yellow flowers if planted against a south-facing wall, and the deciduous tree *Malus* 'Brandywine' has abundant pink flowers.

▼ *Few scented cottage garden plants are as attractive as* Hesperis matronalis *(sweet rocket), with a rich scent in the evening.*

the flower arranger's garden

Even a small garden can produce enough attractive flowers and foliage for cutting and displaying indoors. They are usually provided by herbaceous perennials and hardy and half-hardy annuals, although the leaves of many evergreen shrubs and climbers can also be added to arrangements.

Herbaceous perennials

These are ideal for providing flowers and leaves for summer arrangements, when they are fresh and bright. Most flowers and leaves are taken from plants growing in borders, but where space allows, grow a few blooms in a spare corner.

Never cut flowers from wilting plants because they soon fade. Water the plants the day before and cut them early in the morning. Place them in a bucket of water and keep the bucket in a cool room for 24 hours. Cut each stem at a 45° angle and remove the lower leaves.

Among the many herbaceous plants you can grow are *Achillea filipendulina* (fern-leaf yarrow), *Alstroemeria* (Peruvian lily), *Aster amellus*, *A. novae-angliae*, *Aster novi-belgii*, *Catananche caerulea* (cupid's dart), *Coreopsis verticillata*, *Leucanthemum × superbum*, *Limonium latifolium*, *Lysimachia vulgaris* (yellow loosestrife), *Phlox paniculata*, *Rudbeckia laciniata*, *Solidago* (goldenrod) and *Tanacetum* (pyrethrum).

Hardy and half-hardy annuals

These enable flower-arranging enthusiasts to have a different range of fresh, bright-faced flowers each year and

▲ *A border packed with a medley of plants creates a reservoir of colorful flowers and differently shaped leaves for cutting.*

STAR PLANTS

Alchemilla mollis

Achillea filipendulina

Calendula officinalis

Coreopsis verticillata

Elaeagnus pungens 'Maculata'

Leucanthemum × superbum

Lysimachia vulgaris

Phlox paniculata

they are cut and prepared for display just like herbaceous perennials. They include *Calendula officinalis* (pot marigold), *Cosmos bipinnatus* (cosmea), *consolida ajacis* (larkspur), *Gaillardia* (blanket flower), *Gypsophila elegans* (baby's breath), *Iberis umbellata* (globe candytuft), *Lathyrus odoratus* (sweet pea), *Nigella damascena* (love-in-a-mist), and *Reseda odorata* (mignonette).

Besides providing fresh flowers, a few hardy and half-hardy annuals can be grown to provide flowers for drying. They include *Celosia* (cockscomb), helichrysum, *Limonium sinuatum* and *Moluccella laevis* (bells of Ireland). Cut them with long stems, just as the flowers are opening. Tie them into small bunches and hang them upside-down in a dry, well-ventilated room.

Attractive foliage

Many types of plants, including herbaceous perennials and evergreen shrubs and climbers, have foliage that can be added to flower arrangements. Those from herbaceous perennials include hostas with variegated and single-colored leaves. The large, leathery, rounded leaves of bergenias are ideal as a background display. Those of *Alchemilla mollis* (lady's mantle) are daintier and their lime-green color is not so dramatic.

Evergreen shrubs such as *Elaeagnus pungens* 'Maculata' are dramatic, with shiny green leaves splashed gold, while those of *Elaeagnus × ebbingei* are leathery and silver-gray. During early summer the stems of the *Lonicera nitida* 'Baggeson's

Gold' (boxleaf honeysuckle) look good, while the leaves of *Brachyglottis* 'Sunshine', better known as *Senecio* 'Sunshine', add a soft gray quality. Some displays have stems of evergreen shrubs meandering at the edges. They include variegated vincas and small and large-leaved *Hedera* (ivy).

▲ *Sweet peas introduce a feast of color to gardens, as well as providing flowers in many colors for decoration indoors.*

SEED HEADS FOR DRYING

Dried seed heads taken from herbaceous perennials are especially useful for winter flower arrangements. There are many plants to choose from, including:

Acanthus mollis (bear's breeches)

Dictamnus albus (burning bush)

Echinops ritro (globe thistle)

Iris foetidissima (stinking iris)

Limonium platyphyllum (sea lavender)

Onopordum acanthium (Scotch thistle)

Physalis alkekengi (Chinese lantern)

▲ *The stiffly erect flower heads of* Acanthus mollis *(bear's breeches) look dramatic in gardens and in flower displays.*

cottage gardens

Few gardening styles have such a relaxed and informal atmosphere as a cottage garden. It is rich in nostalgia, and packed with flowers, fruits, vegetables, and herbs. Such informality can easily be created in small gardens, with arbors and trellises providing secluded areas.

Screening plants

Few climbers compare with the scrambling *Clematis vitalba* (old man's beard), widely seen in English hedgerows. It is usually remembered for its glistening, silky seed heads in fall,

▲ *The large, brilliantly colored flowers of Papaver orientale (oriental poppy) make a dramatic display during early summer.*

which often continue into winter. Elizabethans praised it for covering hedges, but in a small cottage garden it is too vigorous and there are other clematis with more attractive and delicate flowers. They include *Clematis macropetala*, *C. flammula*, and *C. orientalis*. *C. montana* is also attractive but often too rampant for small areas. Honeysuckle is also an excellent cottage garden climber, best given rustic supports. And as well as being grown for food, pole beans can be used as screening plants; try them clambering up a 6ft/1.8m-high tripod.

Cordon and espalier apples also make useful screens. Where possible, plant some of the older varieties with superb flavors and textures. Try 'Rome', a cooking apple, and for eating, 'Esopus Spuitzenberg', 'Gravenstein', 'Arkansas Black' and 'Northern spy' to bring back flavors that were common in the past.

Flower borders

Aim for a medley of shrubs, trees, herbaceous perennials, bulbs, and annuals planted or sown in attractive groups, each

plant complementing its neighbors. From spring to fall memorable plant associations can be created.

✤ Spring—tulips offer a wide range of colors. For a mixture of yellow, orange-red, and blue try a deep-blue forget-me-not and a combination of orange-red and yellow tulips. If you prefer a medley of blue, scarlet, and gold flowers, plant pale blue forget-me-nots and the scarlet and gold single early tulip 'Keizerskroon'. Alternatively, for a white and blue display, plant a carpet of the biennial *Bellis perennis* (common daisy) with violet-blue Parrot tulips. These arrangements are ideal for beds and under windows. For a larger spring display in a prominent border plant the yellow-flowered deciduous shrub *Forsythia* 'Lynwood' with small groups of red-flowered Kaufmanniana tulips.

STAR PLANTS	
Clematis montana	*Hydrangea macrophylla*
Geranium endressii	*Sedum* 'Herbstfreude'

✿ Summer—*Lilium candidum* (madonna lily) has pure white flowers, and is a suitable companion for foxgloves, which have tall stems bearing bell-shaped flowers in a color range from purple, to pink to red. Plant the scrambling *Clematis flammula*, with small, sweetly-scented flowers, and *Aconitum napellus* (monkshood) with its deep blue, helmet-shaped flowers, for an unusual combination of climbers with perennials.

Roses are also superb in summer displays. 'Buff Beauty' bears warm, apricot-yellow flowers that form a pleasing partnership with the lavender-blue *Nepeta* × *faassenii* (catmint) and *Papaver orientale* 'Perry's White' (oriental poppy). Another good combination involves the damask rose 'Mme Hardy', with white flowers, and pink varieties of *Geranium endressii*. The bourbon rose 'Mme Isaac Pereire' is bushy and shrubby, with crimson flowers that harmonize with tulips, lilies, peonies, and lilacs.

✿ Fall—for a large display, plant blue varieties of the hardy, deciduous dome-shaped shrub *Hydrangea macrophylla* in front of the evergreen shrubby *Eucryphia* × *nymansensis*, with cream flowers.

Another attractive duo for the fall is the evergreen border plant *Sedum* 'Herbstfreude' and the bulbous *Colchicum* 'Waterlily'. The *Sedum* is well known for the display created by its richly colored fall flowers, which eventually become orange-brown.

▲ *A combination of tulips and fragrant forget-me-nots (myosotis) never fails to capture attention in spring and early summer.*

▼ *Border geraniums produce magnificent displays throughout summer. There are many varieties and colors.*

ground-cover plants

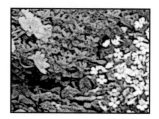

Plants that smother soil with foliage prevent the growth of weeds and are welcome in any garden. The choice is wide and includes herbaceous perennials, shrubs, and a few climbers such as large-leaved ivies like Hedera colchica 'Sulphur Heart'.

Border perennials

Most border perennials are herbaceous but some do retain their foliage through winter. Most prefer full sun or light shade, but others will grow out of the sun.

❀ Sun or shade—although some plants can grow in either light or shade, do not expect the same display in both. Most plants when given plenty of light and moisture will flower better than those in shade with little moisture. The range of plants you need includes *Alchemilla mollis* (lady's mantle) with lime-green, hairy leaves and yellow-green, star-shaped flowers. Bergenias, with their large, elephant-like leaves, also flower in spring. Epimediums are daintier and cover the ground with heart-shaped leaves that assume attractive tints in the fall and through much of winter. *Geranium grandiflorum* is herbaceous, with a spreading habit and blue-purple flowers in early and midsummer. And *Hemerocallis* (daylily) forms large clumps, with arching, strap-like leaves and lily-like flowers. Avoid heavy shade because this reduces its ability to flower.

Persicaria affinis forms mats of lance-shaped leaves and poker-like flower heads during mid- and late summer. *Saxifraga urbium* (London pride) has a more diminutive nature, with rosettes of leaves that carpet the soil and masses of pink, star-shaped flowers during late spring and early summer. *Lamium galeobdolon* 'Florentinum' (better known as *Lamium galeobdolon* 'Variegatum') is vigorous and spreading, with silver-flushed evergreen leaves that display bronze tints in winter. These plants will not thrive in dark shade.

◄ *Smothering the ground with plants looks attractive as well as making gardening easier by eliminating the need to pull up weeds.*

Lysimachia nummularia (creeping jenny) has sprawling stems of rounded leaves and bright yellow, cup-shaped flowers during early and midsummer.

❋ Partial shade—the popular *Ajuga reptans* 'Multicolor' (bugleweed) has purple leaves, while *Brunnera macrophylla* has heart-shaped foliage and sprays of blue flowers in late spring and early summer; it dislikes dry soil. The range of hostas is wide and, with their often large leaves, they soon cloak the soil. *Pulmonaria angustifolia* (with the evocative name blue cowslip) has lance-shaped leaves and funnel-shaped, blue flowers in spring. *Pulmonaria saccharata* has leaves spotted silver-white. *Symphytum ibericum* spreads rapidly, with tubular, white flowers during spring, while *Tiarella cordifolia* (foam flower) is less dominant, with maple-like, light green leaves.

❋ Full sun—in strong sun, plant *Nepeta* × *faassenii* (catmint). It covers the soil with gray-green leaves and lavender-blue flowers from spring to fall. The wooly leaved *Stachys byzantina* (lamb's ears) never fails to attract attention.

Ground-covering shrubs

Many evergreen shrubs with a sprawling or bushy habit are ideal for covering soil with leaves and, sometimes, flowers.

STAR PLANTS

Alchemilla mollis

Hedera colchica 'Sulphur Heart'

Stachys byzantina

Hypericum calycinum (rose of Sharon) is a robust, ground-smothering plant that establishes itself quickly and even covers large banks. Throughout summer it bears golden-yellow flowers. Vincas also smother soil, but are best kept out of mixed lower beds because they are invasive. However, variegated forms are less invasive than all-green types. *Calluna* (heather) and *Erica* (heath) soon cover the ground with attractive leaves and flowers. Like *Gaultheria procumbens* (checkerberry), heathers and ericas need an acid soil. There are many others, including *Pachysandra terminalis*, with deep green leaves.

▼ *Where a large, flat area is planted with ground-covering plants, position large stepping stones to make access and maintenance easier.*

grasses and bamboos

Grasses and bamboos can be used in all kinds of ways, from edging borders to creating screens. And some are ideal for adding to fresh flower arrangements and for drying for winter displays. There are both annual and perennial grasses, while bamboos are long-lived perennials.

▲ *The ornamental grass* Miscanthus sinensis *has strap-shaped, arching stems. Do not constrict it or its natural shape will be spoiled.*

Perennial grasses

Taller perennial grasses look spectacular when planted to fill entire beds, and smaller ones may be planted with annual grasses to make ornamental grass borders. Some are small enough to plant along the edge of a border. These include *Festuca glauca*, about 9in/23cm high with blue-gray leaves, and the dramatic *Melica altissima* 'Atropurpurea', which reaches

---

BAMBOOS FOR CONTAINERS

A few bamboo varieties can be planted in large pots, tubs or wooden boxes, although eventually they will need to be planted in the garden or taken out and divided; this is best done in early summer. Because the roots of bamboos in containers can easily be damaged in cold winters, choose only the hardiest types such as:

Fargesia murieliae (umbrella bamboo)—6–8ft/1.8–2.4m high.

Pleioblastus auricomis (golden-haired bamboo)—3–4ft/90cm–1.2m high.

Pseudosasa japonica (arrow bamboo)—8–12ft/2.4–3.6m high.

about 5ft/1.5m high, with deep mauve spikelets that sweep downward. It is used fresh and dried in flower arrangements.

Perennial grasses come in a wide range of heights, colors, and decorative forms. *Stipa tenuissima* rises to about 2½ft/75cm and bears soft, wispy pony tails. *Miscanthus sacchariflorus* (silver banner grass) is probably the most dramatic of all perennial grasses. It grows rapidly each year to about 10ft/3m high, so it makes a useful screening plant. Space the plants about 18in/45cm apart. During the first year, as it becomes established, it may grow to only 6ft/1.8m. *Miscanthus sinensis purpurascens*, with purple-tinged stems, reaches a height of 5ft/1.5m.

Annual grasses

These grasses can be sown where they are to flower. They are useful for filling gaps in herbaceous and mixed borders, and for achieving a different display in successive years. Many can be cut and dried for use in winter decorations. These include *Briza maxima* (big quaking grass), with graceful, pendent, nodding flowers, and *Hordeum jubatum* (squirrel-tail grass). *Lagurus ovatus* (hare's-tail) develops soft, silky flowerheads with a furry texture.

Bamboos for all gardens

Most of these woody grasses are hardy. Their widely varying foliage and stems may be used to add color and interest to a garden. A few are semievergreen in cold winters, and some are deciduous. They are useful for masking unsightly features, and they make a pleasant rustling sound. A few bamboos, such as *Pleloblastus auricomis* (golden-haired bamboo), are about 5ft/1.5m high and can be grown in a 10in/25cm-wide pot on a patio, while others grow rapidly to 10ft/3m or more.

Three popular bamboos are *Fargesia murieliae*, with graceful, arching, bright-green canes, *Fargesia nitida* with purple stems and narrow, bright-green leaves, and *Pseudosasa japonica* with lance-shaped, dark-green leaves. Some are more distinctive, such as the black-stemmed *Phyllostachys nigra*.

▲ *Where slugs and snails are a problem, spread stone chippings or gravel over the area and stand pots of ornamental grasses and bamboos on it.*

◀ Pleioblastus auricomus *(golden-haired bamboo) is a dwarf variety, with golden variegated leaves, ideal for borders or containers.*

ornamental hedges

Creating hedges is more than just forming a boundary or screen. They can be gloriously rich in scents, have colorful berries, color contrasts within the same hedge, and harmonize or constrast with nearby plants. Even the ubiquitous privet can be attractive.

Hedge duos

To grow an unusual privet hedge, set two plants of *Ligustrum ovalifolium* 'Aureum' to one of *L. ovalifolium* along a row. This ratio produces a decorative, rather formal hedge, and will not allow the more vigorous all-green hedging to smother the yellow. The hedge should be clipped regularly in order to keep it in shape. Plant variegated holly and yew to produce an attractive evergreen hedge which will grow very slowly. Set the plants in the ground alternately, about 4ft/1.2m apart.

Fragrant hedging

There is an astonishing range of hedging plants with fragrant flowers or leaves. The scents they emit include apple and raspberry. Several conifers used for hedging give off an unusual fragrance when their leaves are bruised.

For an apple-like scent plant *Thuja occidentalis* 'Smaragd'. Its dark-green foliage makes a dramatic backdrop for other plants. If a lemon fragrance delights you, choose *Cupressus macrocarpa* 'Goldcrest'. It has soft yellow foliage which, with age, becomes light green. The pineapple-scented *Thuja plicata* (western red cedar) has scaly, shiny, rich green foliage with white marks underneath. It is best reserved for a large boundary hedge. A fusion of resin and parsley is the smell given by *Chamaecyparis lawsoniana* 'Allumii', with soft blue-gray foliage, and *Chamaecyparis lawsoniana* 'Fletcheri' with feathery, blue-green leaves.

◄ *The evergreen shrub* Berberis darwinii *has masses of rich orange flowers in spring, followed by blue berries.*

Roses used for hedging offer more unusual scents, none better than 'Zephirine Drouhin' with raspberry-scented, vivid pink flowers. 'Penelope' has musk-scented, pale pink, semidouble flowers that fade slightly as they age. Several roses used for hedging have a sweet fragrance, including *Rosa rugosa* 'Roseraie de l'Hay' with crimson-purple flowers, 'Felicia' with salmon-pink flowers, and 'Prosperity' with creamy white blooms.

Two evergreen shrubs with memorable scents include *Lavandula angustifolia* 'Hidcote', with deep purple flowers 2in/5cm long and silver-green leaves. *Rosmarinus officinalis* (rosemary) also makes a lovely informal hedge.

Harmonies and contrasts

Color-themed herbaceous borders were traditionally backed by hedges that harmonized or contrasted with them. For example, the dark green leaves of yew highlight white, orange, blue, and green borders, while golden-variegated holly harmonizes with golden borders. Tamarisk (*tamarix*) was frequently used as a backcloth for a gray border.

The deciduous *Fagus sylvatica* (beech), with young leaves that darken from bright green in spring to mid-green in summer, can be a striking backdrop for herbaceous plants. In the fall the hedge has the bonus of leaves that take on yellow and russet tints, competing for attention with end of season flower colors and seed heads.

▼ *Many roses can be used to form floriferous screens. They bring the atmosphere of a cottage garden to an urban plot.*

bush and shrub roses

The range of large-flowered bush roses (hybrid teas) and cluster-flowered bush roses (floribundas) is wide, and each year more are introduced. The many species roses with a dramatic and subtle range of colors extend the range, and the more recent New English Roses make the choice still harder.

Using roses

It was once thought that the only way to grow bush roses was in formal beds flanked by paths or lawns. Today, they are used in many other situations. Prostrate roses cover the soil, patio roses in pots decorate patios, species roses adorn shrub borders, and weeping standards rise from beds and lawns. Small rose bushes can be planted in rock gardens and also in windowboxes. These include 'Baby Masquerade' (yellow to pink and red), 'Cinderella' (white, tinged with pink), 'Darling Flame' (orange-red, with yellow anthers), 'Black Jade' (deep red, almost black) and 'Popcorn' (white, honey-scented).

Weeping standards are well known for their beautiful, cascading outlines. They are produced by nurserymen budding a variety on a rootstock about 51in/130cm high. When mature, the head is 5–6ft/1.5–1.8m high, with stems cascading from the top. Rambler varieties are mainly used and include 'Albéric Barbier' (cream), 'Crimson Shower' (red), 'François Juranville' (salmon-pink), and 'Goldfinch' (yellow, fading to white).

Companion planting bush roses

Bush roses can be attractively grouped with other plants. Plant the buttercup-yellow floribunda 'Chinatown' in front of *Clematis* 'Countess of Lovelace', a large-flowered variety that will flourish sprawling over a fence or a garden wall. The clematis flowers through summer into the fall (double-flowered forms bloom during summer, and single forms in late summer and fall). Its deep lavender flowers look handsome beside those of the yellow rose. Underplant white-flowering bush roses with the evergreen perennial *Tiarella cordifolia* (foam flower), which has a low mound of maple-shaped leaves and creamy white flowers in late spring and early summer.

▲ Rosa gallica officinalis *(apothecary's rose or red rose of Lancaster) bears large, loosely-formed, semidouble, rose-crimson flowers.*

The popular floribunda 'Queen Elizabeth' has cyclamen-pink flowers that look superb highlighted against yew. Plant the large-flowered yellow 'Grandpa Dickson' against the dark purple leaves of the deciduous shrub *Berberis thunbergii* 'Atropurpurea'. And, for additional color, plant the half-hardy annual *Nicotiana* 'Lime Green' in front of them.

Companion planting shrub roses

The range of shrub roses is wide and many are old roses. They range from Albas to Moss roses, and form attractive combinations with other plants. The Alba 'Königin von Danemark' has deep pink flowers that look striking against the silvery leaved, weeping tree *Pyrus salicifolia* 'Pendula'. A splendid

collaboration is the modern shrub rose 'Nevada' with creamy white flowers, and blue delphiniums and campanulas. The 'New' English Rose 'Constance Spry' has pink flowers best highlighted by a cluster of silver-leaved plants.

PATIO ROSES

This is a relatively new group of roses, coming between miniature roses and small floribundas. They are sometimes called dwarf cluster-flowered bush roses and are ideal on a patio. Even when you are sitting down they do not obstruct the view. Most are between 1½ft/45cm and 2ft/60cm high, and include 'Anna Ford' (vivid orange-red), 'Living Easy' (apricot-orange blend), 'Betty Boop' (yellow ivory, edged red) 'Robin Redbreast' (red, with a pale center) and 'Top Marks' (bright, vivid orange-vermilion).

▲ *Roses make distinctive backgrounds for low border plants and often enrich the air around garden benches with rich fragrance.*

▼ *Many shrub roses have an informal habit and can be allowed to cascade and spread across paths and over lawn edges.*

climbing and rambler roses

Climbers and ramblers look dramatic in any garden and are still more spectacular when the color complements its background. A white wall makes a perfect backcloth for roses with yellow or scarlet flowers, whereas a gray stone wall is better for those with pink or red flowers.

Climber or rambler?

As mentioned on pages 404–405, climbing and rambling roses produce attractive flowers, but each is distinctive in several ways. Climbers have a more permanent framework than ramblers and their flowers, when compared with those of ramblers, are larger and borne singly or in small clusters. Rambling roses have long, flexible stems that sometimes grow 3–3.6m/10–12ft in length in one season and bear flowers in large trusses, usually only once a year.

Covering trees

Old, perhaps slightly unsightly trees can be transformed by training climbers to scramble up through their branches. Plant them several feet to one side of the trunk, and replace the soil with a mixture of topsoil and well-rotted garden compost or manure. Firm the soil, plant the rose, water the soil, and use a stout stake to guide the stems to the tree trunk.

Suitable varieties range in vigor, and can be selected to suit the tree that needs brightening. Roses to consider include 'Rambling Rector' (9ft/2.7m, rambler,

 Pergolas and free-standing trellis provide support for many roses. They can be positioned alongside paths and the edges of lawns.

creamy white), 'Emily Gray' (15ft/4.5m, rambler, butter-yellow); 'Mme Grégoire Staechelin' (climber, 20ft/6m, rosy carmine-pink), 'Paul's Himalayan Musk' (rambler, 30ft/9m, blush-pink), 'Sympathie' (climber, 15ft/4.5m, blood-red) and 'Wedding Day' (rambler, 25ft/7.5m, creamy white to blush).

Pillar roses

These contribute interest in small gardens. All you need is a rustic pole 8–10ft/2.4–3m high or a tripod made of rough-cut lumber. In quite a small area, several pillars can be inexpensively

---

GROUND-COVER ROSES

Ground-smothering roses do not form a weed-suppressing blanket of stems, leaves and flowers, but a low mass of color. Choices include 'Baby Blanket' (pink), 'Nozomi' (pearly-pink to white), 'Pheasant' (pink), 'Rosy Cushion' (pink), and 'Snow Carpet' (white). The County Series includes 'Avon' (pearly white), 'Essex' (rich reddish-pink), 'Hertfordshire' (carmine-pink), and 'Wiltshire' (pink).

constructed. Climbers with moderate vigor are best for clothing such structures and include 'Bantry Bay' (semidouble, deep pink), 'Compassion' (salmon-pink, tinted apricot-orange), 'Handel' (creamy, edged pink-red), 'Pink Perpetue' (bright rose-pink), and 'Reine Victoria' (shell-pink).

Climbers for cold walls

A cold wall is not the best place for roses, but a few sturdy ramblers and climbers survive such conditions and produce acceptable displays. Hardy and vigorous varieties to consider include 'Albéric Barbier' (rambler, cream), 'Félicité et Perpétue' (rambler, white), 'Morning Jewel' (climber, bright pink), 'New Dawn' (climber, pink blush), and 'Zéphirine Drouhin' (climber, deep pink).

Companion planting climbers and ramblers

In the same way that bush roses can be planted in attractive arrangements with other plants, so can climbers and ramblers. For example, the rambler 'Bobbie James', which is often grown over pergolas and clambering up trees, has large clusters of semidouble, creamy white flowers that look attractive combined with the lavender-blue flowers of *Nepeta × faassenii* (catmint), a bushy perennial growing about 18in/45cm high. It flowers throughout summer. Another good combination is the modern climber 'New Dawn', with semidouble, blush-pink flowers with the vigorous hybrid *Clematis* 'Perle d'Azure' with light pink flowers. It flowers from early to late summer.

▼ *Rose 'Helen Knight', a distinctive climber, creates a mass of small, buttercup-yellow flowers in late spring and early summer.*

ornamental plants

annuals and biennials

A

Agrostemma githago 'Milas'
CORN COCKLE

Hardy annual with slender, light green leaves and masses of lilac-pink flowers at the tops of upright stems from midsummer to fall.
Height: 3–4ft/90cm–1.2m
Spread: 15–18in/38–45cm
Soil and position: Well–drained but moisture-retentive soil and full sun. Grows well in poor soil.

Amaranthus caudatus
LOVE-LIES-BLEEDING/TASSEL FLOWER

Hardy annual with light-green leaves

and drooping tassels up to 18in/45cm long, packed with crimson flowers during mid- to late summer. 'Viridus' has pale green flowers.
Height: 3–4ft/90cm–1.2m
Spread: 15–18in/38–45cm
Soil and position: Deeply prepared, fertile, well-drained but moisture-retentive soil in full sun.

B

Begonia semperflorens
FIBROUS BEGONIA/WAX BEGONIA

Tender perennial invariably grown as a half-hardy annual for planting into beds and containers in early summer. The glossy green or purple leaves are surmounted from early to late summer by red, pink, or white flowers.
Height: 6–9in/15–23cm/

Spread: 20–25cm/8–10in
Soil and position: Fertile, moisture-retentive but well-drained soil, and a position in full sun or partial shade.

Bellis perennis
ENGLISH DAISY

Hardy perennial, invariably grown as a biennial, for flowering from early spring to fall although it is mainly used in spring and early summer displays. The flowers are daisy-like, bright-faced and white tinged pink, with a central yellow disc. There are several varieties in colors including white, carmine, pink, salmon, and cherry red.
Height: 1–4in/2.5–10cm
Spread: 3–4in/7.5–10cm
Soil and position: Moderately fertile, moisture-retentive but well-drained soil in full sun or light shade.

C

Calendula officinalis
ENGLISH MARIGOLD/POT MARIGOLD

Hardy annual with light green leaves and bright-faced, daisy-like, yellow or orange flowers about 2in/5cm wide from early summer to fall. There are several varieties, some double and a few dwarf.
Height: 1½–2ft/45–60cm
Spread: 10–12in/25–30cm
Soil and position: Well drained, even grows in poor soil and full sun.

Campanula medium
CANTERBURY BELL

Hardy biennial with tall, upright stems that bear blue, white, purple, or pink, bell-shaped flowers up to 1½in/36mm long from late spring to midsummer. The 15in/38cm-high variety 'Bells of Holland' is ideal for small gardens.
Height: 15–36in/38–90cm
Spread: 9–12in/23–30cm
Soil and position: Moderately fertile, well drained soil and full sun. Support plants with small, twiggy sticks.

Cleome spinosa
SPIDER FLOWER

Half-hardy tall annual with lax, rounded heads, up to 4in/10cm wide, of white, pink-flushed flowers

from midsummer to late fall. 'Color Fountain Mixed' has flowers in pink, rose, lilac, purple, and white; 'Rose Queen' is rose-pink and 'Helen Campbell' is white.
Height: 3–3½ft/90cm–1m
Spread: 18–20in/45–50cm
Soil and position: Fertile, well-drained but moisture-retentive soil and full sun.

Consolida ajacis
LARKSPUR

Hardy annual with finely cut leaves and sparsely branched, upright stems bearing spires of blue, purple, red, pink, or white flowers from early to late summer. There are several varieties and strains.
Height: 3–4ft/90cm–1.2m
Spread: 12–15in/30–38cm
Soil and position: Fertile, well-drained but moisture-retentive soil in full sun or light shade. Support plants with twiggy sticks.

D

Dianthus barbatus
SWEET WILLIAM

Short-lived perennial invariably grown as a biennial for flowering during early and midsummer. Some varieties are better grown as hardy annuals. It develops flattened heads 3–6in/7.5–15cm wide, densely packed with sweetly scented, single or double flowers in a wide color range including crimson, scarlet, salmon-pink, and cerise-pink.
Height: 12–24in/30–60cm—range
Spread: 8–15in/20–38cm—range
Soil and position: Well–drained soil and full sun.

Digitalis purpurea
COMMON FOXGLOVE

Hardy biennial with upright stems bearing bell-shaped flowers during early and midsummer. The flower color is wide, ranging from purple, through pink, to red.
Height: 3–5ft/90cm–1.5m
Spread: 1½–2ft/45–60cm
Soil and position: Moderately fertile, moisture-retentive but well-drained soil, and partial shade.

E

Erysimum × allionii
SIBERIAN WALLFLOWER

Hardy, bushy perennial invariably grown as a biennial for flowering from midspring to early summer. It produces a mass of scented, orange

◀ Digitalis purpurea *(common foxglove) is traditional in cottage gardens. With its tall habit it is an attractive background plant.*

flowers in terminal clusters.
Height: 12–15in/30–38cm
Spread: 10–12in/25–30cm
Soil and position: Fertile, slightly
alkaline, well-drained soil, full sun.

Eschscholzia californica
CALIFORNIA POPPY
Hardy annual with delicate, finely
dissected, blue-green leaves and
masses of saucer-shaped, bright
orange-yellow flowers up to
3in/7.5cm wide from early to late
summer. These are followed by blue-
green seed pods. Varieties in scarlet,
crimson, rose, orange, yellow,
white, and red.
Height: 12–15in/30–38cm
Spread: 6–9in/15–23cm
Soil and position: Light, poor, well-
drained soil and a position in full
sun. Fertile soil and a position in
shade reduces the color intensity
of flowers radically.

Helianthus annuus
SUNFLOWER
Hardy annual with large, daisy-like
flower heads up to 12in/30cm wide
during mid- and late summer. There
is a wide range of varieties, some
dwarf, in colors from pale primrose
to copper-bronze. The central discs
are purple or brown.
Height: 3–10ft/90cm–3m
Spread: 1–1½ft/30–45cm
Soil and position: Fertile, well-
drained but moisture-retentive soil
in a sunny, sheltered position.

Heliotropium arborescens
CHERRY PIE/HELIOTROPE
Half-hardy perennial, grown as a
half-hardy annual, with wrinkled,
dark green leaves and fragrant,
flowers like the forget-me-not in
slightly domed heads 3–4in/
7.5–10cm wide from early summer
to fall. Color range from dark violet
through lavender, to white.
Height: 15–18in/38–45cm
Spread: 12–15in/30–38cm
Soil and position: Fertile, well-
drained but moisture-retentive soil
and full sun.

Hesperis matronalis
SWEET ROCKET
Hardy but short-lived perennial
invariably grown as a biennial.
Vertical growth and long spires of
fragrant, cross-shaped, white, mauve,
or purple flowers in early summer.
Height: 2–3ft/60–90cm
Spread: 15–18in/38–45cm

Soil and position: Light, moisture-
retentive but well-drained soil, and
full sun or light shade.

Lavatera trimestris
ANNUAL MALLOW/MALLOW
Hardy annual with an erect but
bushy nature and flat-faced, trumpet-
shaped flowers up to 4in/10cm wide
from mid- to late summer. There are
several varieties, including 'Silver
Cup', 2ft/60cm high.
Height: 2–3ft/60–90cm
Spread: 15–20in/38–50cm
Soil and position: Moderately fertile,
well-drained but moisture-retentive
soil and full sun or dappled light.
Avoid excessively rich soil, which
encourages leaf growth at the
expense of flowers.

Limnanthes douglasii
MEADOW FOAM/POACHED-EGG FLOWER
Low-growing and ground-
smothering hardy annual with
deeply cut leaves and masses of
scented, funnel-shaped yellow
flowers with white edges from
early to late summer.
Height: 6in/15cm
Spread: 6–9in/15–23cm
Soil and position: Well-drained soil
and full sun. Produces self-sown
seedlings the following year.

Limonium sinuatum
STATICE/SEA LAVENDER
Hardy perennial, invariably grown as
a half-hardy annual, with 3in/7.5cm-
long clusters of blue and cream
flowers from midsummer to fall.
There are several varieties, extending
the colors to orange-yellow, salmon,
rose-pink, red, carmine, and lavender.
Height: 15–18in/38–45cm
Spread: 10–12in/25–30cm
Soil and position: Well-drained but
moisture-retentive soil and an open,
sunny position.

Lobelia erinus
EDGING LOBELIA/TRAILING LOBELIA
Half-hardy perennial invariably
grown as a half-hardy annual. Masses
of blue, white, or red flowers from
late spring to fall. There are bushy
and compact varieties, often used
along the edges of borders, and
trailing types for planting in hanging
baskets.
Height: 4–9in/10–23cm
Spread: 4–6in/10–15cm
Soil and position: Moderately fertile,
moisture-retentive but well-drained
soil, and light shade.

▲ *The sunflower (*Helianthus
annuus*), a hardy annual, bears a
mass of large, daisy-like flowers up
to 12in/30cm wide.*

487

Lobularia maritima
(formerly and still better known
as ALYSSUM MARITIMUM)
SWEET ALYSSUM
A popular hardy annual usually
grown as a half-hardy annual.
Densely branched stems bear
rounded clusters of white, violet-
purple, rose-carmine, or deep
purple flowers from early to late
summer. Ideal for forming an
edging to a border.
Height: 3–6in/7.5–15cm
Spread: 8–12in/20–30cm
Soil and position: Moderately fertile,
well-drained soil, and full sun.

Myosotis sylvatica
FORGET-ME-NOT
Hardy biennial or short-lived
perennial with fragrant, pale blue
flowers in lax sprays during late
spring and early summer. There are
several varieties in mixed and single
colors.
Height: 8–12in/20–30cm
Spread: 6–8in/15–20cm
Soil and position: Moderately fertile,
moisture retentive but well-drained
soil and partial shade. Avoid heavy,
waterlogged soil because it
encourages the plants to die
during winter.

Nicotiana × sanderae
TOBACCO PLANT
Half-hardy annual with erect stems
bearing loose clusters of heavily
scented, white, tubular flowers,
7.5cm/3in-long, from early to late
summer. There are many varieties,
in a color range including white,
cream, pink, crimson, yellow, and
lime-green. Some varieties are night-
scented.
Height: 15–24in/38–60cm
Spread: 10–12in/25–30cm
Soil and position: Fertile moisture-
retentive but well-drained soil in
full sun or light shade.

Nigella damascena
LOVE-IN-A-MIST
Hardy annual with bright-green,
fern-like leaves and cornflower-
like blue or white flowers from
early to midsummer. Some varieties
have pale yellow flowers. There are
many varieties, with double and
semidouble flowers. Self-seeding
in full sun.
Height: 1½–2ft/45–60cm
Spread: 6–9in/15–23cm
Soil and position: Light, well-drained
moisture-retentive soil and best in
full sun.

▲ *Flowering tobacco plants*
(Nicotiana) fill the garden with a
sweet fragrance through summer,
especially at nightfall.

Papaver rhoeas
FIELD POPPY/SHIRLEY POPPY
Hardy annual with deeply lobed
green leaves and upright stems
bearing 3in/7.5cm-wide red flowers
with black centers during early to
midsummer. Varieties extend the
color range to pink, rose, salmon, and
crimson.
Height: 1½–2ft/45–60cm
Spread: 10–12in/25–30cm
Soil and position: Ordinary, poor to
moderately fertile, well-drained soil
and full sun.

Papaver somniferum
OPIUM POPPY
Hardy annual with deeply lobed,
gray-green leaves and white, pink,
scarlet or purple flowers up to
4in/10cm wide during early and
midsummer. Some flowers are
double.
Height: 2½–3ft/75–90cm
Spread: 12–15in/30–38cm
Soil and position: Well-drained soil
and full sun.

Petunia × hybrida
PETUNIA
Half-hardy perennial usually grown
as a half-hardy annual, with trumpet-
shaped flowers, 2–4in/5–10cm wide,
from early summer to the fall frosts.
Color range includes white, cream,
pink, red, mauve, and blue, and
bicolored forms.
Height: 6–12in/15–30cm
Spread: 6–12in/15–30cm
Soil and position: Moderately fertile
soil and full sun. Dislikes cold, wet
and shady positions.

Rudbeckia hirta
BLACK-EYED SUSAN
Short-lived perennial invariably
grown as a hardy annual, with
bright-faced, daisy-like flowers,
3in/7.5cm-wide, with golden-
yellow petals and brown-purple
cones at their centers from
midsummer to early fall. Wide
range of varieties.
Height: 1½–2ft/45–60cm
Spread: 1–1½ft/30–45cm
Soil and position: Fertile, moisture-
retentive but well-drained soil and
full sun.

Salvia splendens
SCARLET SAGE
Half-hardy perennial invariably
grown as a half-hardy annual with
upright spires of scarlet flowers from
midsummer to fall. There are several
superb varieties, in single colors and
mixed colors, including rose, pink,
salmon, purple, and white.
Height: 12–15in/30–38cm
Spread: 8–10in/20–25cm
Soil and position: Fertile, moisture-
retentive but well-drained soil and
full sun.

Scabiosa atropurpurea
PINCUSHION FLOWER/SCABIOUS
Erect, branching, wiry-stemmed
annual with mid-green leaves and
single flowers, 2in/5cm wide during
mid- to late summer. There are many
varieties in the color range, from
white through blue to purple.
Height: 1½–2ft/45–60cm
Spread: 6–9in/15–23cm
Soil and position: Moderately fertile,
well-drained neutral to slightly
alkaline soil in full sun.

Tagetes patula
FRENCH MARIGOLD
Half-hardy annual with a bushy habit
and dark-green, deeply divided leaves
and yellow or mahogany red flowers,
up to 2in/5cm wide, from early
summer to fall. Wide range of
varieties, with both single and
double-flowered types. Some are
dwarf. Widely grown in summer
bedding displays, where it always
creates a feast of color.
Height: 12in/30cm
Spread: 10–12in/25–30cm
Soil and position: Moderately fertile
soil and full sun.

Zinnia elegans
Half-hardy annual with upright
stems bearing bright purple flowers,
up to 2½in/6cm wide, from mid- to
late summer. There are many
varieties, in colors including white,
purple, yellow, orange, red, pink, and
even pale green. Some varieties
have double flowers.
Height: 6–30in/15–75cm
Spread: 6–15in/15–38cm
Soil and position: Fertile, well-
drained but moisture-retentive soil
and full sun.

Height: 2–2½ft/60–75cm
Spread: 15–20in/38–50cm
Soil and position: Fertile, moisture-retentive soil and full sun or light shade.

C

Camassia quamash
QUAMASH
Slightly tender, bulbous, herbaceous perennial with broad, spire-like clusters of star-shaped flowers during early and midsummer. Flower colors range from white to blue and purple.
Height: 1½–2½ft/45–75cm
Spread: 12–15in/30–38cm
Soil and position: Fertile, moisture-retentive soil and full sun or light shade. Grows well in moderately heavy soil.

Campanula lactiflora
BELLFLOWER
Hardy herbaceous perennial with a wealth of bell-shaped, light lavender-blue flowers during early and midsummer. There are several varieties, extending the color range to soft pink and deep lavender-blue.
Height: 3–5ft/90cm–1.5m
Spread: 18–20in/45–50cm
Soil and position: Light, fertile, moisture-retentive but well-drained soil and full sun or partial shade.

Coreopsis verticillata
TICKSEED
Hardy herbaceous perennial with finely divided, fern-like leaves and masses of clear yellow flowers from early summer to fall. For a small garden there are compact and dwarf varieties.
Height: 1½–2ft/45–60cm
Spread: 1–1½ft/30–45cm
Soil and position: Moderately fertile, well-drained but moisture-retentive soil and full sun.

D

Delphinium elatum
There are two distinct forms of this popular, hardy, herbaceous perennial. Elatum types have stiffly erect spires, tightly packed with large florets,

herbaceous perennials and other border plants

A

Acanthus spinosus
BEAR'S BREECHES
Hardy herbaceous perennial with distinctive, deeply cut spiny leaves and tall, upright spires of white and purple flowers during mid- and late summer.
Height: 3–3½ft/90cm–1m
Spread: 2–2½ft/60–75cm
Soil and position: Moderately fertile, light, well-drained but moisture-retentive soil, and full sun or light shade.

Achillea filipendulina
FERN-LEAF YARROW
Hardy herbaceous perennial with deeply dissected fern-like leaves and plate-like heads, 4–6in/10–15cm wide packed with lemon-yellow flowers from midsummer to fall. Many excellent varieties.
Height: 3–4ft/90cm–1.2m
Spread: 3ft/90cm
Soil and position: Fertile, moisture-retentive but well-drained soil and full sun.

Agapanthus praecox
AFRICAN LILY/LILY OF THE NILE
Half-hardy evergreen perennial with fleshy roots and large, umbrella-like heads of bright to pale blue flowers from mid- to late summer. There is also a white-flowered form.
Height: 2–2½ft/60–75cm
Spread: 18in/45cm
Soil and position: Fertile, well-drained soil and shelter from cold wind, in full sun.

Alchemilla mollis
LADY'S MANTLE
Hardy herbaceous perennial with hairy, light-green leaves with rounded lobes and serrated edges. From early summer to fall it bears masses of tiny, sulfur-yellow flowers in sprays above the leaves.
Height: 1–1½ft/30–45cm
Spread: 15–20in/38–50cm
Soil and position: Moderately fertile, moisture-retentive but well-drained soil, and full sun or light shade.

Allium moly
GOLDEN GARLIC/LILY LEEK
Bulbous plant with gray-green, strap-like leaves and bright yellow, star-shaped flowers borne in umbrella-like heads during early and midsummer.
Height: 10–12in/25–30cm
Spread: 8–10in/20–25cm
Soil and position: Light, well-drained soil and full sun. Eventually forms a large, spreading clump.

Aster sedifolius
RHONE ASTER
Hardy herbaceous perennial with masses of clear lavender-blue flowers with golden centers during late summer into fall. 'Nanus' is shorter, at 30cm/1ft high.
Height: 2–2½ft/60–75cm
Spread: 15–18in/38–45cm
Soil and position: Fertile, moisture-retentive but well-drained soil and full sun.

Astilbe × arendsii
Hardy herbaceous perennial with fern-like, deep-green leaves and masses of feather-like flowers borne in lax, pyramidal heads from early to late summer. There are many varieties in colors including lilac-rose, pink, rose-red, dark-red, and white.

mainly in shades of blue but also in lavender, mauve, and white. Wide range of varieties and heights. Belladonna forms have branching spikes of cupped florets.
Height: 3–5ft/90cm–1.5m
Spread: 1½–2ft/45–60cm
Soil and position: Fertile, deeply prepared, moisture-retentive soil and full sun.

Dictamnus albus
BURNING BUSH/DITTANY/GAS PLANT
Hardy herbaceous perennial with spire-like heads of fragrant, white, spider-like flowers during early and midsummer. 'Purpureus' has pink flowers with red stripes.
Height: 1½–2ft/45–60cm
Spread: 15–18in/38–45cm
Soil and position: Slightly alkaline, deeply prepared, well-drained soil and full sun.

Echinacea purpurea
PURPLE CONEFLOWER
Hardy herbaceous perennial with 4in/10cm-wide purple-crimson

flowers from midsummer to fall. Each flower has a distinctive cone-shaped orange center. Varieties in white and purple-rose.
Height: 3–4ft/90cm–1.2m
Spread: 1½–2ft/45–60cm
Soil and position: Fertile, moisture-retentive but well-drained, deeply prepared soil, and full sun.

Erigeron speciosus
FLEABANE
Hardy herbaceous perennial with masses of daisy-like, purple flowers from early to late summer. There are several superb varieties, in light pink, lavender-blue, violet-blue, and lavender-violet.
Height: 18–24in/45–60cm
Spread: 12–15in/30–38cm
Soil and position: Fertile, moisture-retentive yet well-drained soil and full sun or light shade.

Filipendula purpurea
JAPANESE MEADOWSWEET
Hardy herbaceous perennial with deeply cut leaves and large, fluffy

heads of carmine to pink flowers during midsummer. There are white and rosy red varieties.
Height: 3–3½ft/90cm–1m
Spread: 15–18in/38–45cm
Soil and position: Slightly alkaline, well-drained but moisture-retentive soil, and full sun or light shade.

Geranium endressii
CRANESBILL
Hardy, herbaceous, ground-covering perennial with deeply lobed leaves and pale-pink flowers, lightly veined in red, from early summer to fall. There are several varieties.
Height: 12–18in/30–45cm
Spread: 12–18in/38–45cm
Soil and position: Well-drained soil in full sun or light shade.

Gypsophila paniculata
BABY'S BREATH
Hardy herbaceous perennial with finely divided stems bearing a mass of small, usually white flowers from early to late summer. There are several varieties, including double or single forms, in white or pink. Also, compact varieties.
Height: 2–3ft/60–90cm
Spread: 2–2½ft/60–75cm
Soil and position: Deeply prepared, slightly alkaline, well-drained but moisture-retentive soil in full sun.

Helenium autumnale
SNEEZEWEED
Hardy herbaceous perennial with a mass of daisy-like flowers, 1–1½in/25–36mm wide, from midsummer to early fall. There are many varieties, in yellow, orange, copper, bronze-red, and crimson-mahogany.
Height: 4–6ft/1.2–1.8m
Spread: 15–18in/38–45cm
Soil and position: Well-drained but moisture-retentive soil and full sun.

Hemerocallis thunbergii
DAYLILY
Hardy herbaceous perennial with large, trumpet-shaped, sulfur-apricot flowers at the tops of stems during

early and midsummer. There are many hybrids, in colors from golden-yellow to pink, orange, and brick-red. Most hybrids have flowers 5–7in/13–18cm wide.
Height: 2½–3ft/75–90cm
Spread: 2–2½ft/60–75cm
Soil and position: Fertile, moisture-retentive but well-drained soil in full sun or light shade.

Kniphofia
RED HOT POKER
Hardy herbaceous perennial, with many species and hybrids. All develop distinctive, poker-like flowerheads from early summer to early fall, in a color range from cream and yellow to fiery red.
Height: 3–5ft/60cm–1.5m
Spread: 15–24in/38–60cm
Soil and position: Deeply prepared, moderately fertile, well-drained but moisture-retentive soil and full sun. Avoid soils that are cold and wet.

Leucanthemum superbum
SHASTA DAISY
Hardy herbaceous perennial with wide, bright-faced, daisy-like white flowers, 3in wide, with large, golden centers from early to late summer.
Height: 2½–3ft/75–90cm
Spread: 1–1½ft/30–45cm
Soil and position: Fertile, well-drained but moisture-retentive, slightly alkaline soil and full sun.

Lychnis chalcedonica
JERUSALEM CROSS/MALTESE CROSS
Hardy herbaceous perennial with small, bright scarlet flowers borne in flattened heads about 5in/13cm wide during mid- and late summer
Height: 2½–3ft/75–90cm
Spread: 15–18in/38–45cm
Soil and position: Well-drained but moisture-retentive soil in full sun or light shade.

Lysimachia punctata
WHORLED LOOSESTRIFE
Hardy, long-lived, vigorous herbaceous perennial with a spectacular display of bright yellow, cup-shaped flowers in whorls up to 8in/20cm long from early to late summer.
Height: 2–3ft/60–90cm
Spread: 15–18in/38–45cm
Soil and position: Fertile, moisture-retentive but well-drained soil, and

◄ Achillea *is popular in herbaceous borders, where it creates distinctive flower heads from midsummer to early fall.*

full sun or partial shade. It grows well in a heavy soil.

Monarda didyma
BEE BALM/OSWEGO TEA/
SWEET BERGAMOT
Hardy herbaceous perennial with dense heads, up to 3in/7.5cm wide, of bright scarlet flowers from early to late summer. Range of varieties, in pink, lavender, violet-purple, and white.
Height: 2–3ft/60–90cm
Spread: 15–18in/38–45cm
Soil and position: Moisture-retentive but well-drained soil in full sun or partial shade.

P

Perovskia atriplicifolia
RUSSIAN SAGE
A hardy, deciduous, shrubby perennial usually grown in a herbaceous or mixed border. Finely dissected, aromatic leaves and upright, branching stems with violet-blue flowers during late summer and early fall. 'Blue Spire' is a variety with lavender-blue flowers.
Height: 3–5ft/90cm–1.5m
Spread: 1½–2ft/45–60cm

Soil and position: Deeply prepared, fertile, well-drained soil and full sun or light shade.

Phlox paniculata
GARDEN PHLOX
Hardy herbaceous perennial with terminal clusters of purple flowers from midsummer to fall. There are many varieties, in colors including pink, violet-purple, mauve, white, bright purple, claret-red and scarlet.
Height: 1½–3½ft/45cm–1m
Spread: 18–24in/45–60cm
Soil and position: Fertile, moisture-retentive but well-drained soil and full sun or partial shade.

R

Rudbeckia fulgida
CONEFLOWER
Hardy, herbaceous perennial with large, yellow to orange flowers about 2½in/6cm wide from midsummer to the fall. Each flower has a dominant, purple-brown, cone-like center. Numerous varieties, including the spectacular 'Goldsturm' with flowers up to 13cm/5in wide.
Height: 2–3ft/60–90cm
Spread: 1½–2ft/45–60cm
Soil and position: Moderately fertile, well-drained but moisture-retentive soil and full sun.

S

Sedum 'Herbstfreude'
(also known as 'AUTUMN JOY')
Herbaceous perennial with pale green, fleshy leaves. In late summer it develops large, slightly domed heads packed with salmon-pink flowers which change slowly from orange-red to orange-brown during mid- to late fall.
Height: 1½–2ft/45–60cm
Spread: 18–20in/45–50cm
Soil and position: Light, well-drained but moisture-retentive soil and full sun.

Solidago hybrids
GOLDENROD
A group of hardy herbaceous perennials with distinctive, plume-like, slightly arching heads of tiny yellow or golden flowers from midsummer to fall. There are many varieties in a range of heights.
Height: 3–5ft/30cm–1.5m
Spread: 10–24in/25–60cm
Soil and position: Moderately fertile, deeply prepared, well-drained soil and full sun or light shade.

Stachys byzantina
(still better known as
STACHYS LANATA)
LAMB'S EARS
Half-hardy herbaceous perennial that smothers the ground with leaves

 Stachys byzantina (lamb's ears) fills a bed with a sea of leaves with a wooly and silvery appearance.

densely covered in silvery hairs which create a wooly appearance. During midsummer it develops spikes of purple flowers. 'Silver Carpet' is a nonflowering form and creates a large net of leaves.
Height: 12–18in/30–45cm
Spread: 12–15in/30–38cm
Soil and position: Well-drained soil and full sun or light shade.

T

Tradescantia × andersoniana 'Isis'
SPIDERWORT
Hardy herbaceous perennial with distinctive, royal-purple, three-petaled flowers up to 1½in/36mm wide from early to late summer. Wide range of other varieties, in colors including white and rich purple.
Height: 1½–2ft/45–60cm
Spread: 18–20in/45–50cm
Soil and position: Well-drained but moisture-retentive soil in full sun or light shade.

bulbs, corms and tubers

Chionodoxa sardensis
GLORY OF THE SNOW

Hardy, bulbous plant with two strap-like leaves and stems bearing nodding, star-shaped, sky-blue flowers, ¾in/18mm wide. with white centers from early to late spring.
Height: 4–5in/10–15cm
Spread: 2–4in/5–10cm
Soil and position: Light, well-drained soil and full sun. Avoid heavy, constantly moist soil. Ideal for planting in rock gardens and along the fronts of informal borders.

Crocus chrysanthus

Hardy cormous plant with cup-shaped, honey-scented, bright-yellow flowers during late winter and early spring. Mainly hybrids available in a color range including golden-yellow, mauve-blue, purple-blue, and dark bronze.

Daffodils—Trumpet types

Hardy, clump-forming bulbous plants with yellow flowers bearing large trumpets during late winter and early spring. The range of varieties is wide and some are bicolored (white and yellow), others all white.
Height: 13–18in/32–45cm
Spread: 3–4in/7.5–10cm
Soil and position: Well-drained but moisture-retentive soil and full sun or light, dappled shade. Ideal for planting in large drifts, under deciduous trees or in the open.

Eranthis hyemalis
WINTER ACONITE

Hardy, tuberous-rooted perennial with lemon-yellow, buttercup-like flowers backed by a distinctive ruff of

deeply cut, green leaves. They sometimes appear during midwinter, but usually late winter and early spring.
Height: 4in/10cm
Spread: 3in/7.5cm
Soil and position: Well-drained but moisture-retentive soil and full sun or partial shade. Grows well in heavy loam.

Galanthus nivalis
COMMON SNOWDROP

Hardy, bulbous, clump-formed plant with flat, strap-like leaves and white flowers from midwinter to early spring. Each flower has six petals, three long outer ones and three short inner ones. 'Flore Pleno' has double flowers.
Height: 3–7in/7.5–18cm
Spread: 3–5in/7.5–13cm
Soil and position: Fertile, moisture-retentive but well-drained soil and light shade. Ideal for naturalizing in woodland gardens.

Hyacinthoides hispanica
BLUEBELL/SPANISH BLUEBELL

Hardy bulbous plant with strap-shaped, glossy green leaves and purple-blue, bell-shaped flowers during late spring and early summer. There is also a beautiful white-flowered form.
Height: 10–12in/25–30cm
Spread: 4–6in/10–15cm
Soil and position: Fertile, moisture-retentive but well-drained soil and light shade. Ideal for naturalizing in woodland gardens.

Ipheion uniflorum
SPRING STARFLOWER

Hardy, bulbous, clump-forming plant with pale-green, grass-like leaves and scented, white to violet-blue, six-petaled, star-shaped flowers during late spring.
Height: 6–8in/15–20cm
Spread: 2–3in/5–7.5cm
Soil and position: Moisture-retentive but well-drained soil and a sheltered position in full sun or light shade.

◀ Tulips are among the most popular garden plants. They are resilient, and will swamp the borders with color each year.

Leucojum vernum
SPRING SNOWFLAKE

Hardy, bulbous, clump-forming plant with strap-like, shiny green leaves and six-petaled, bell-like, white flowers during late winter and early spring. The petals are tipped in green.
Height: 8in/20cm
Spread: 4in/10cm
Soil and position: Moisture-retentive but well-drained soil and light shade or dappled sunlight.

Muscari armeniacum
GRAPE HYACINTH

Hardy, bulbous, clump-forming plant with narrow leaves and upright stems crowded at the top with scented, bright-blue flowers, each with a white rim, during spring and early summer. Several varieties, including the double 'Blue Spike'.
Height: 8–10in/20–25cm
Spread: 3–4in/7.5–10cm
Soil and position: Well-drained soil and full sun. Once established it spreads and can become invasive.

Narcissus cyclamineus

Hardy, miniature bulbous plant with narrow, bright-green leaves and small, deep-yellow trumpets up to 2in/5cm long and petals that are swept back in late winter and early spring. Parent of many hybrids, including 'February Gold', with larger flowers.
Height: 5–8in/15–20cm
Spread: 3–4in/7.5–10cm
Soil and position: Well-drained but moisture-retentive soil and full sun or light shade.

Tulipa

A range of hardy, bulbous plants with globular-like flower-heads at the tops of upright stems during mid- and late spring. The range of flowers and colors is wide; some single-flowers, others double. They are often planted with hardy perennials in spring-flowering bedding displays.
Height: 6in–2½ft/15–75cm
Spread: 6–8in/15–20cm/
Soil and position: Fertile, well-drained but moisture-retentive soil and full sun.

rock garden plants

A

Aethionema 'Warley Rose'
Hardy herbaceous perennial with loosely branched stems and gray-green leaves. Domed heads smothered with deep rose-colored flowers appear during mid- and late spring.
Height: 4–6in/10–15cm
Spread: 12–15in/30–38cm
Soil and position: Light, well-drained soil, and full sun.

Arabis caucasica
ROCK CRESS
Hardy, spreading perennial with gray-green leaves; usually evergreen except in cold wet winters. From late winter to early summer it bears white, cross-shaped flowers; also a double-flowered form.
Height: 9in/23cm
Spread: 18–24in/45–60cm
Soil and position: Well-drained soil

and full sun or light shade. Can be too invasive for a small rock garden and is best grown on a dry stone wall or a bank where it can trail freely.

Armeria maritima
THRIFT/SEA PINK
Hardy evergreen hummock–forming perennial and grass-like leaves. From late spring to midsummer it displays 1in/2.5cm-wide heads of pink flowers. Also white, and rose-red varieties.
Height: 6–10in/15–25cm
Spread: 10–12in/25–30cm
Soil and position: Well-drained soil and full sun.

Aubrieta deltoidea
AUBRETIA
Hardy, low-growing, spreading and, sometimes, trailing evergreen perennial with small, hoary green leaves and masses of rose-lilac to purple flowers from early spring to early summer. Many varieties, including a variegated form.
Height: 3–4in/7.5–10cm
Spread: 18–24in/45–60cm
Soil and position: Well-drained, preferably chalky, soil and a position in full sun.

▲ Phlox subulata 'Temiskaming' is a popular rock garden plant, with brilliant magenta-red flowers during mid- and late spring.

Aurinia saxatilis
(still better known as ALYSSUM SAXATILE)
Hardy, shrubby perennial with gray-green leaves and masses of golden-yellow flowers clustered on branching stems from midspring to early summer. Several varieties including 'Citrina' (bright lemon-gold, 'Compacta' (golden-yellow and 6in/15cm high), and 'Dudley Nevill' (biscuit yellow).
Height: 9–12in/23–30cm
Spread: 12–18in/30–45cm
Soil and position: Well-drained soil and full sun. Ideal for planting in a dry-stone wall.

C

Campanula carpatica
BELLFLOWER
Clump-forming, hardy perennial with tooth-edged leaves and masses of cup-shaped flowers, 1–1½in/25–36mm wide flowers in varying shades of blue to purple, and white, during mid- and late summer.
Height: 9–12in/23–30cm
Spread: 12–15in/30–38cm
Soil and position: Moderately fertile, well-drained soil and full sun or partial shade.

Corydalis lutea
YELLOW FUMITORY
Hardy, bushy, evergreen perennial with fern-like leaves and tubular, spurred yellow flowers from mid- or late spring to late fall.
Height: 15–20cm/6–8in

▲ Saxifraga 'Southside Seedling' bears masses of white flowers, each speckled with red spots, in long, arching sprays.

Spread: 10–12in/25–30cm
Soil and position: Well-drained soil and full sun or partial shade. Thrives on old walls but can become invasive through self-sown seedlings.

G

Gentiana acaulis
TRUMPET GENTIAN
Hardy, herbaceous perennial which forms mats of glossy, oval leaves and masses of trumpet-shaped, upright, stemless, brilliant blue flowers, about 3in/7.5cm long, during late spring and early summer.
Height: 3in/7.5cm
Spread: 15–18in/38–45cm
Soil and position: Well-drained but moisture-retentive soil, and full sun or light shade.

H

Helianthemum nummularium
ROCK ROSE/SUN ROSE
Hardy, low-growing, evergreen shrub with small, glossy green leaves and masses of saucer-shaped flowers during early and midsummer. Many varieties, in a color range including yellow, rose-pink, and red, as well as bicolored forms.
Height: 4–6in/10–15cm
Spread: 18–24in/45–60cm
Soil and position: Light, well-drained soil and full sun. Grows well in poor soil.

I

Iberis sempervirens
PERENNIAL CANDYTUFT

Hardy, evergreen, spreading bushy perennial with narrow, dark-green leaves and masses of white flower-heads during late spring and early summer. The form 'Little Gem' is shorter at 4in/10cm high, and spreading to 9in/23cm.
Height: 9in/23cm
Spread: 18–24in/45–60cm
Soil and position: Well-drained soil and full sun. Thrives in poor soil.

P

Phlox subulata
MOSS PHLOX

Hardy, spreading, and tufted sub-shrubby perennial that forms mats of purple or pink flowers during mid- and late spring. Many varieties, in colors including salmon-pink, pale-pink, lavender-blue, scarlet, bright red, and magenta-red.
Height: 2–4in/5–10cm
Spread: 12–18in/30–45cm
Soil and position: Moderately fertile, light, well-drained but moisture-retentive soil, and full sun or light shade.

S

Saxifraga 'Southside Seedling'
Hardy perennial with a mat-forming habit, dark-green leaves and long, arching sprays of white flowers peppered with red spots during early and midsummer.
Height: 12in/30cm
Spread: 12–15in/30–38cm
Soil and position: Well-drained, gritty, slightly chalky soil, shelter from cold wind and semishaded area. Avoid direct sunlight. It is ideal for planting in crevices between rocks.

Sedum acre
GOLDEN CARPET

Hardy, mat-forming and somewhat invasive, evergreen perennial with yellow-green overlapping leaves and yellow flowers borne in flattened heads during early and midsummer. The variety "Aureum" (formerly known as 'Variegatum') has bright yellow shoot tips from early spring to early summer.
Height: 2in/5cm
Spread: 18–24in/45–60cm—or more
Soil and position: Well-drained but moderately moisture-retentive soil and full sun.

garden shrubs and trees

A

Amelanchier lamarckii
JUNEBERRY/SHADBUSH/SNOWY MESPILUS

Hardy, deciduous, large shrub with mid-green leaves that assume tints in the fall. Clouds of pure white, star-shaped flowers in midspring.
Height: 4.5–7.5m/15–25ft
Spread: 3.6–6m/12–20ft
Soil and position: Moisture-retentive but well-drained, lime-free soil, and full sun or light shade.

Aucuba japonica 'Variegata'
GOLD-DUST TREE/SPOTTED LAUREL

Hardy, evergreen shrub with a rounded outline and oval, shiny, dark green-leaves spotted and splashed yellow.
Height: 1.8–3m/6–10ft
Spread: 1.8–2.4m/6–8ft
Soil and position: Well-drained but moisture-retentive soil and full sun or light shade.

B

Berberis darwinii
BARBERRY

Hardy, evergreen shrub with small, holly-like, glossy green leaves and masses of deep-yellow flowers in late spring followed by blue berries.
Height: 1.8–2.4m/6–8ft
Spread: 1.8–2.4m/6–8ft
Soil and position: Moderately fertile, well-drained soil, and full sun.

Brachyglottis 'Sunshine'
(still better known as SENECIO 'Sunshine')

Hardy, mound-forming, evergreen shrub with silvery gray leaves, white-felted underneath. During early and midsummer it bears bright yellow, daisy-like flowers.
Height: 2–4ft/60cm–1.2m
Spread: 3–5ft/90cm–1.5m

▶ Ceanothus 'Concha', a Californian lilac, looks spectacular in shrub borders and in mixed borders.

Soil and position: Deeply prepared, moisture-retentive but well-drained soil and full sun.

Buddleja alternifolia
Hardy, deciduous shrub with narrow, pale green leaves and sweetly scented, lavender-blue flowers borne along cascading stems during early and midsummer. Usually a shrub, but it can be grown as a standard tree.
Height: 10–15ft/3–4.5m
Spread: 10–15ft/3–4.5m
Soil and position: Deeply prepared, friable, moisture-retentive but well-drained soil and full sun.

Buddleja davidii
BUTTERFLY BUSH/SUMMER LILAC

Hardy, deciduous shrub famed for its long, arching stems and plume-like heads of fragrant, lilac-purple flowers during mid- and late summer, and often into the fall. There are many varieties, in colors including white, dark violet-purple, lilac, and rich red-purple.
Height: 6–8ft/1.8–2.4m
Spread: 6–8ft/1.8–2.4m
Soil and position: Fertile, moisture-retentive but well-drained soil, and full sun.

C

Calluna vulgaris
HEATHER/LING

Hardy, low-growing, bushy evergreen shrub with scale-like leaves throughout the year ranging from green to shades of orange and red.

From midsummer to early winter plants bear spires of single or double flowers, in colors including white, pink, and purple. Wide range of heights and spreads.
Height: 3–24in/7.5–60cm
Spread: 5–24in/13–60cm
Soil and position: Acid, peaty, moisture-retentive soil, and an open sunny position.

Caryopteris × *clandonensis*
Hardy, bushy, deciduous shrub with aromatic gray-green leaves and clusters of blue flowers during late summer into the fall. Several superb varieties including 'Arthur Simmonds' (bright blue), 'Heavenly Blue' (deep blue), and 'Kew Blue' (rich blue).
Height: 2–4ft/60cm–1.2m
Spread: 2–3ft/60–90cm
Soil and position: Friable, well-drained soil, and full sun.

Ceanothus × *delileanus* **'Gloire de Versailles'**
CALIFORNIA LILAC
Hardy, deciduous shrub with an open habit and large heads, 6–8in/15–20cm long, clustered with fragrant, soft powder-blue flowers at the ends of long stems from midsummer to fall.
Height: 6–8ft/1.8–2.4m
Spread: 6–8ft/1.8–2.4m
Soil and position: Fertile, deeply prepared, moisture-retentive but well-drained soil; shelter from cold wind and full sun or light shade.

Ceratostigma willmottianum
CHINESE PLUMBAGO
Half-hardy, twiggy, deciduous shrub with diamond-shaped, dark-green leaves that assume rich tints in the fall. Rich blue flowers are borne in terminal clusters up to 2in/5cm wide during mid- and late summer.
Height: 2–3ft/60–90cm
Spread: 2–3ft/60–90cm
Soil and position: Light, well-drained soil and full sun.

Chimonanthus praecox
WINTERSWEET
Hardy, bushy, deciduous shrub, often grown as a wall shrub, with cup-shaped, scented flowers with pale-yellow petals and purple centers from mid- to late winter. 'Grandiflorus' has larger flowers, with red centers.
Height: 6–10ft/1.8–3m
Spread: 8–10ft/2.4–3m
Soil and position: Well-drained but moisture-retentive soil. Often grown

against a warm, south- or west-facing wall.

Choisya ternata
MEXICAN ORANGE BLOSSOM
Slightly tender evergreen shrub with glossy green leaves that emit the fragrance of oranges when bruised. During mid- and late spring and often intermittently through to late summer, the plant bears clusters of sweetly scented, orange-blossom-like white flowers. 'Sundance' has golden-yellow leaves throughout the year.
Height: 5–6ft/1.5–1.8m
Spread: 5–7ft/1.5–2.1m
Soil and position: Deeply prepared, fertile, well-drained soil and shelter from cold wind.

Cornus mas
CORNELIAN CHERRY
Hardy, deciduous, somewhat twiggy shrub with small clusters of golden-yellow flowers on bare branches from midwinter to spring. Sometimes bears red, semitranslucent berries. Leaves assume rich reddish-purple shades in the fall.
Height: 8–12ft/2.4–3.6m
Spread: 6–10ft/1.8–3m
Soil and position: Moisture-retentive but well-drained soil and full sun or light shade.

Cytisus × *praecox* **'Warminster'**
WARMINSTER BROOM
Hardy, bushy, deciduous shrub with arching stems bearing creamy white, pea-shaped flowers during spring and early summer. 'Allgold' has sulfur-yellow flowers.

▲ Berberis x darwinii (*Darwin's berberis*) is a hardy evergreen shrub with yellow flowers in spring.

Height: 5–6ft/1.5–1.8m
Spread: 5–6ft/1.5–1.8m
Soil and position: Well-drained soil and full sun. Avoid excessively fertile soil.

E

Elaeagnus pungens **'Maculata'**
THORNY ELAEAGNUS
Hardy, evergreen, rounded shrub with leathery, oval, glossy green leaves splashed in gold. Silver-white, fragrant flowers in the fall.

495

Height: 6–12ft/1.8–3.6m
Spread: 6–12ft/1.8–3m
Soil and position: Fertile, deeply prepared soil and full sun or light shade. Tolerant of salt spray in coastal areas.

Erica carnea
ERICA/HEATHER
Hardy, prostrate or low-growing evergreen shrub with terminal clusters of flowers in white, pink, red or purple from late fall to late spring.
Height: 2–12in/5–30cm
Spread: 6–24in/15–60cm
Soil and position: Peaty, acid, moisture-retentive soil, and full sun.

Euonymus fortunei 'Emerald 'n' Gold'
Hardy, bushy, evergreen, densely leaved shrub with bright golden-variegated leaves which turn bronze-pink in winter. Many other attractive varieties, including 'Emerald Gaiety' (creamy white and green) and 'Golden Prince' (young leaves tipped bright gold).
Height: 12–18in/30–45cm
Spread: 18–24in/45–60cm
Soil and position: Ordinary soil and full sun.

Forsythia × intermedia
Hardy, deciduous shrub which in early and midspring creates a wealth of golden-yellow, bell-like flowers. There are several superb forms, including 'Lynwood' (large, yellow flowers) and 'Spectabilis' (yellow).
Height: 6–8ft/1.8–2.4m
Spread: 5–7ft/1.5–2.1m
Soil and position: Deeply prepared, fertile, moisture-retentive soil in full sun or light shade.

Fuchsia magellanica
Slightly tender, deciduous and bushy shrub with a spreading habit and pendent, crimson and purple flowers up to 2in/5cm long from midsummer to fall.
Height: 4–5ft/1.2–1.5m/
Spread: 2–4ft/60cm–1.2m
Soil and position: Fertile, moisture-retentive, light soil and full sun. Provides shelter from cold wind. Ideal for coastal areas.

Genista aetnensis
MOUNT ETNA BROOM
Hardy, deciduous shrub with a lax nature and rush-like branches that bear terminal clusters of golden-yellow flowers during mid- and late summer.
Height: 15–20ft/4.5–6m

Spread: 15–18ft/4.5–5.4m
Soil and position: Light, well-drained, rather poor soil and full sun.

Hamamelis mollis
CHINESE WITCH HAZEL
Hardy, deciduous shrub or small tree with sweetly scented, rich golden-yellow, spider-like flowers borne in clusters along naked branches during early and midwinter. Leaves assume rich shades in the fall.
Height: 6–10ft/1.8–3m
Spread: 7–10ft/2.1–3m
Soil and position: Neutral or slightly acid, moisture-retentive but well-drained soil, and full sun or slight shade.

Helichrysum serotinum
CURRY PLANT
Slightly tender, deciduous shrub with needle-like leaves that when bruised emit a curry-like scent. During early and midsummer it bears clustered heads of mustard-yellow flowers.
Height: 12–15in/30–38cm
Spread: 15–24in/38–50cm
Soil and position: Light, moderately poor, well-drained soil, and full sun. Avoid soils that are cold, heavy, and poorly drained.

Hibiscus syriacus
Hardy, deciduous shrub with a bushy habit and trumpet-shaped flowers, 3in/7.5cm across, in a wide color range from midsummer to early fall. Varieties include violet-blue, white with red centers, and rose-pink.
Height: 6–10ft/1.8–3m
Spread: 4–6ft/1.2–1.8m
Soil and position: Fertile, moisture-retentive but well-drained soil, and full sun or light shade.

Hydrangea arborescens
HILLS OF SNOW
Hardy, deciduous shrub with dull white flowers borne in flat heads up to 6in/15cm wide during mid and late summer. In mild areas they continue into early fall. 'Grandiflora' has larger flower-heads.
Height: 4–6ft/1.2–1.8m
Spread: 4–6ft/1.2–1.8m
Soil and position: Fertile, moisture-

◀ *Ornamental flowering cherry trees never fail to attract attention in spring. Golden daffodils may be planted at the base.*

▶ *Forsythia bursts into flower in spring and is an ideal companion to large-trumpeted daffodils. It is one of the easiest shrubs to grow.*

retentive soil, and full sun or light shade.

Hydrangea macrophylla
BIGLEAF HYDRANGEA/FLORISTS HYDRANGEA
Hardy, deciduous shrub with a rounded shape. There are two forms, Lacecaps have flat heads, 4–6in/ 10–15cm wide, while Hortensias have mop-like flower-heads 5–8in/13–20cm wide. Both flower from midsummer to early fall.
Height: 4–6ft/1.2–1.8m
Spread: 4–6ft/1.2–1.8m
Soil and position: Fertile, slightly acid, moisture-retentive soil, and dappled light. Acid soil insures that blue varieties remain blue. Aluminum sulfate reduces the influence of alkaline soils.

Hypericum 'Hidcote'
ROSE OF SHARON/ST. JOHN'S WORT
Hardy, evergreen or semievergreen, bushy shrub with dark-green leaves and saucer-shaped, waxy, golden-yellow flowers up to 3in/7.5cm wide from midsummer to the fall.
Height: 3–5ft/90cm–1.5m
Spread: 5–7ft/1.5–2.1m
Soil and position: Fertile, well-drained but moisture-retentive soil and full sun. Avoid dry soil in total shade.

Kerria japonica 'Pleniflora'
Hardy, popular, deciduous shrub with long, slender stems and tooth-edged, bright-green leaves and double, orange-yellow flowers, 2in/5cm wide during late spring and early summer.
Height: 6–8ft/1.8–2.4m
Spread: 6–7ft/1.8–2.1m
Soil and position: Moderately fertile, friable, moisture-retentive but well-drained soil and full sun or partial shade.

Kolkwitzia amabilis
BEAUTYBUSH
Hardy, somewhat twiggy deciduous shrub with arching branches bearing pink, foxglove-like flowers with yellow throats during early summer.

The variety 'Pink Cloud' has bright, deep pink flowers.
Height: 6–10ft/1.8–3m
Spread: 5–8ft/1.5–2.4m
Soil and position: Well-drained but moisture-retentive soil and full sun or light shade.

Laburnum × watereri 'Vossii'
GOLDEN CHAIN TREE/GOLDEN RAIN TREE
Hardy, deciduous tree with fragrant, golden-yellow flowers borne in slender, pendulous clusters up to 2ft/60cm long during early summer.
Height: 10–15ft/3–4.5m
Spread: 10–12ft/3–3.6m
Soil and position: Moisture-retentive but well-drained soil and full sun or light shade.

Lavatera 'Rosea'
TREE MALLOW
Hardy, vigorous, soft-stemmed and branching shrub with lobed, gray-green leaves and masses of rose-colored flowers to about 3in/8cm wide from midsummer to the fall.
Height: 5–7ft/1.5–2.1m
Spread: 6–8ft/1.8–2.4m
Soil and position: Light, well-drained but moisture-retentive soil in full sun. Thrives in warm, sheltered position.

Magnolia stellata
STAR MAGNOLIA
Hardy, slow-growing, deciduous shrub with lance-shaped leaves and white, fragrant, star-shaped flowers up to 4in/10cm wide during early and midspring. 'Rosea' has pink flowers.
Height: 8–10ft/2.4–3m
Spread: 8–10ft/2.4–3m
Soil and position: Deeply prepared, moderately fertile, moisture-retentive but well-drained soil, full sun, and shelter from cold wind.

Mahonia × media 'Charity'
Hardy, distinctive, evergreen shrub with leathery, spine-edged leaves and long, upright spires of fragrant, deep lemon-yellow flowers from early to late winter.
Height: 6–8ft/1.8–2.4m
Spread: 5–7ft/1.5–2.1m
Soil and position: Peaty, slightly acid and moisture-retentive but well-drained soil and light shade.

Philadelphus hybrids
MOCK ORANGE
A large range of hardy, deciduous shrubs with a lax habit and single or double, sweetly fragrant flowers during early and midsummer. Hybrids include 'Avalanche' and 'Virginal'.
Height: 3–10ft/90cm–3m
Spread: 3–12ft/90cm–3.6m
Soil and position: Deeply prepared, moderately fertile, moisture-retentive but well-drained soil, and full sun or light shade.

Potentilla fruticosa
SHRUBBY CINQUEFOIL
Hardy, deciduous, bushy but compact shrub with masses of buttercup-yellow flowers, each about 1in/2.5cm wide, from early to late summer and sometimes into the fall. There are several superb hybrids, including 'Red Ace' (glowing red), 'Elizabeth' (soft yellow), 'Sunset' (orange to brick-red), and 'Tangerine' (tangerine-red).
Height: 3½–4ft/1–1.2m
Spread: 3½–4ft/1–1.2m
Soil and position: Light, well-drained but moisture-retentive soil and full sun.

◄ Weigela *is ideal for small gardens, where it creates a wealth of flowers in late spring and early summer. There are many hybrids.*

Height: 5–7ft/1.5–2.1m
Spread: 5–7ft/1.5–2.1m
Soil and position: Poor, well-drained soil, and full sun.

V

Viburnum opulus 'Sterile'
SNOWBALL BUSH
Hardy, deciduous, bushy shrub with white flowers borne in large, round heads during early summer.
Height: 8–12ft/2.4–3.6m
Spread: 8–12ft/2.4–3.6m
Soil and position: Fertile, deeply prepared, moisture-retentive but well-drained soil and full sun.

Viburnum tinus
LAURUSTINUS
Hardy, densely leaved evergreen shrub with dark-green leaves and white flowers, pink in bud, borne in 4in/10cm-wide clusters from early winter to late spring. Several superb varieties, including 'Eve Price' with carmine buds and pink-tinged white flowers.
Height: 7–9ft/2.1–2.7m
Spread: 5–7ft/1.5–2.1m
Soil and position: Fertile, deeply prepared, moisture-retentive but well-drained soil and full sun.

Prunus 'Accolade'
Hardy, deciduous, ornamental cherry with an open spreading shape and masses of blush-pink, semidouble, deep rosy pink flowers in pendulous clusters during early and midspring.
Height: 15–20ft/4.5–6m
Spread: 15–25ft/4.5–7.5m
Soil and position: Slightly chalky, well-drained but moisture-retentive soil and full sun.

Prunus subhirtella 'Pendula'
WEEPING SPRING CHERRY
Hardy, deciduous, spreading and weeping tree with branches packed with pinkish-white flowers during spring. Looks superb when yellow, large-cupped daffodils are planted around it.
Height: 12–15ft/3.6–3.5m
Spread: 10–20ft/3.6–6m
Soil and position: Slightly chalky, well-drained but moisture-retentive soil and full sun.

R

Rhododendron luteum
Hardy, deciduous, stiff-stemmed shrub with fragrant, rich-yellow flowers borne in rounded trusses on naked branches during mid- and late spring. The leaves assume rich shades of purple, crimson, and yellow in the fall.
Height: 6–10ft/1.8–3m
Spread: 5–7ft/1.5–2.1m
Soil and position: Fertile, slightly acid, moisture-retentive light soil and dappled light.

S

Salvia officinalis 'Icterina'
GOLDEN VARIEGATED SAGE
Slightly tender and relatively short-lived evergreen shrub with gold and green leaves. In cold areas it often becomes semievergreen. There are several other superb varieties, including 'Purpurascens' (suffused purple} and 'Tricolor' (leaves suffused purple and pink, and splashed creamy white).

Height: 18–24in/45–60cm
Spread: 18in/45cm
Soil and position: Well-drained soil, warm and sheltered position and full sun.

Spiraea × arguta
BRIDAL WREATH/FOAM OF MAY
Hardy, deciduous, twiggy shrub with masses of pure-white flowers borne in clusters during mid- and late spring. The green leaves create an attractive foil for the flowers.
Height: 6–8ft/1.8–2.4m
Spread: 5–7ft/1.5–2.1m
Soil and position: Deeply prepared, fertile, moisture-retentive but well-drained soil and full sun.

U

Ulex europaeus 'Flore Pleno'
DOUBLE-FLOWERED GORSE
Hardy, spiny, evergreen shrub with honey-scented, golden-yellow, pea-shaped flowers during spring into early summer. Often flowers sporadically until the following spring.

W

Weigela hybrids
Hardy, deciduous shrub with arching branches bearing masses of flowers 2.5cm/1in long in late spring and early summer. Hybrids include 'Abel Carrière' (soft rose) 'Bristol Ruby' (ruby red), and 'Newport Red' (bright red).
Height: 5–6ft/1.5–1.8m
Spread: 5–8ft/1.5–2.4m
Soil and position: Fertile, well-drained but moisture-retentive soil in full sun or light shade.

climbers and wall shrubs

Ceanothus thrysiflorus repens
BLUEBLOSSOM/CALIFORNIA LILAC
Hardy, evergreen shrub, with masses of small, light-blue flowers in clusters 3in/7.5cm long clusters during late spring and early summer. One of the hardiest California lilacs.
Height: 4–5ft/1.2–1.5m
Spread: 5–6ft/1.5–1.8m
Soil and position: Neutral or slightly acid, well-drained, light soil, shelter from cold wind and a position in full sun. Suitable for growing under a window.

Clematis montana
Hardy, vigorous, deciduous climber with pure-white flowers, 2in/5cm wide during late spring and early summer. Several superb varieties, including 'Elizabeth' (soft pink and slightly fragrant), 'Alexander' (creamy white and fragrant), and 'Rubens' (slightly fragrant, rose-pink flowers and bronze-purple leaves).
Height: 18–25ft/5.4–7.5m—or more
Spread: 18–25ft/5.4–7.5m—or more
Soil and position: Fertile, neutral to slightly alkaline, moisture-retentive but well-drained soil, and full sun. Requires a supporting framework; also climbs into trees.

Clematis, large-flowered hybrids
Hardy climbers with characteristic large flowers, usually 5–6in/13–15cm wide. Flowers during summer, the flowering period varying with the variety, with a wide range of colors.
Height: 4–15ft/1.2–4.5m
Spread: 5–8ft/1.5–2.4m
Soil and position: Fertile, neutral to slightly alkaline, moisture-retentive but well-drained soil and full sun. Not self-supporting and needs wires or a trellis.

Fremontodendron californicum
FLANNEL BUSH
Slightly tender, deciduous or semi-deciduous wall shrub with three-lobed, dull-green and downy leaves. Golden-yellow, cup-shaped flowers, 2in/5cm wide, appear through summer into early fall. 'California Glory' is a free-flowering form.
Height: 6–10ft/1.8–3m
Spread: 6–10ft/1.8–3m
Soil and position: Light, well-drained but moisture-retentive soil, a warm and sheltered position and full sun. Is not self-supporting and needs a trellis or supporting wires.

Hedera colchica 'Dentata Variegata'
VARIEGATED PERSIAN IVY
Hardy, vigorous, evergreen climber with thick, leathery, bright-green leaves edged and blotched creamy white and pale green. Leaves are up to 8in/20cm long.
Height: 20–25ft/6–7.5m
Spread: 20–25ft/6–7.5m
Soil and position: Well-drained but moisture-retentive soil and full sun or dappled light. Has a self-clinging habit.

Hedera colchica 'Sulphur Heart'
Hardy, vigorous, evergreen climber with thick, leathery, deep-green leaves splashed and irregularly streaked bright yellow. As leaves age, they broaden and the yellowing becomes less pronounced.
Height: 18–20ft/5.4–6m
Spread: 18–20ft/5.4–6m
Soil and position: Well-drained but moisture-retentive soil and full sun or dappled light. It has a self-clinging nature.

Hedera helix 'Goldheart'
Hardy, evergreen climber with small, shiny green leaves conspicuously splashed with yellow.
Height: 12–20ft/3.6–5m
Spread: 12–20ft/3.6–5m
Soil and position: Well-drained but moisture-retentive soil and full sun or dappled light. Has a self-clinging habit.

Humulus lupulus 'Aureus'
GOLDEN–LEAVED HOP/ YELLOW-LEAVED HOP
Hardy, fast-growing herbaceous climber with a scrambling habit and stems smothered with three- or five-lobed, coarsely tooth-edged, bright-yellow leaves. In the fall, the plant dies down to soil level and produces new shoots in spring.
Height: 6–10ft/1.8–3m
Spread: 6–8ft/1.8–2.4m
Soil and position: Fertile, moisture-retentive but well-drained soil and full sun. Needs a structure up which to clamber.

Jasminum nudiflorum
WINTER-FLOWERING JASMINE
Hardy, deciduous, rather lax wall shrub with pliable stems that bear bright yellow flowers, about 1in/2.5cm wide, from late fall to late spring.
Height: 4–6ft/1.2–1.8m
Spread: 6–8ft/1.8–2.4m
Soil and position: Light, well-drained soil and a position against a north-facing wall. Requires a framework to which the stems can be secured loosely.

Lonicera periclymenum
HONEYSUCKLE/WOODBINE
Hardy, widely grown, deciduous climber with a twining habit and tangled mass of stems. There are two main forms; 'Belgica' (early Dutch honeysuckle) bears purple-red and yellow flowers in early summer, while 'Serotina' (late Dutch honeysuckle) has red-purple and creamy white flowers in late summer and early fall.
Height: 15–18ft/4.5–5.4m
Spread: 15–18ft/4.5–5.4m
Soil and position: Moderately fertile, light, moisture-retentive but well-drained soil. Requires a support.

Wisteria floribunda
JAPANESE WISTERIA
Hardy, vigorous, deciduous climber with leaves formed of 12–19 leaflets. During late spring and early summer it bears large, pendulous clusters of fragrant, violet-blue flowers. There is also a white form.
Height: 25–30ft/7.5–9m
Spread: 20–25ft/6–7.5m
Soil and position: Fertile, moisture-retentive but well-drained soil and full sun. May be planted to cover a large pergola or arbor.

▲ Lonicera periclymenun 'Serotina' (late Dutch honeysuckle) is an informal climber with a relaxed nature and wealth of flowers.

pests and diseases

Soft and tender plants in gardens and greenhouses provide succulent meals for pests and are ideal places for diseases to get established. This applies especially to soft-leaved plants such as hardy and tender annuals and herbaceous perennials. Groups of similar vegetables, such as cabbages and beans, are also at risk. Insects have limited aspirations and their main aims are eating and reproduction, which they do with great zeal in the right conditions.

Why kill insects?

If you do not, plants become unsightly and yields of vegetables and fruits soon decrease. Sucking insects such as aphids cause mottling on leaves and flowers. They also inject plants with saliva that may spread viruses from plant to plant. Even worse, aphids excrete a sticky

COUNTRY TIP

⊛ Small pieces of chopped *Ulex europaeus* gorse when placed in drills of newly sown garden peas help prevent mice eating the seeds.

⊛ Moles cause a problem by making mole hills and by eating worms, but do not kill them because they eat soil pests such as wireworms, leatherjackets, and millipedes. Pushing pieces of slate across their tunnels and inserting a child's windmill into a mole hill helps to deter them. Moles also dislike certain plants. Insert sprigs of elder into mole hills, or plant *Helleborus foetidus* (stinking hellebore), garlic or *Euphorbia lathyris* (caper spurge) nearby.

substance known as honeydew that attracts ants and sooty mold. Chewing pests like caterpillars eat leaves and then excrete on them.

Pests can be eradicated and further infestations prevented in several ways. Spraying with chemicals is an easy option and some chemicals, such as those classified as systemic, make a plant toxic to insects for a specified period; this is influenced by the specific crop and time of year. However, many gardeners prefer to use nonchemical methods.

Garden-friendly ways to control insects and diseases

• Slugs and snails can be lured by a mixture of beer and sugar in shallow saucers. Remove and destroy them the following morning.

• Trap earwigs in inverted pots filled with straw and placed on top of a garden stake. Remove the earwigs each morning.

• Removing dead flowers decreases the risk of diseases spreading.

• Nipping out the young tips of broad beans protects against blackfly infestation.

• Hoe weeds growing between plants. If left to grow, they encourage the presence of pests and diseases. Weeds in neglected corners should also be eradicated. However, if you wish to entice butterflies and moths into your garden it is best to leave them because they provide food and homes for many insects.

• Dig bare soil thoroughly early in the winter and leave the surface rough. Frost and birds will kill grubs and many other soil pests.

• Feeding plants with a balanced diet keeps them healthy and able to resist diseases. Excessive nitrogen makes plants soft and susceptible to diseases.

• Thinning young seedlings when they are large enough to be handled reduces the spread of diseases. Place all thinnings on a compost pile.

• Use bands of burlap or corrugated card in the spring to trap codling moth and gypsy moth caterpillars as they travel down the trunks of fruit trees. Hand pluck and destroy caterpillars periodically.

• Use varieties of vegetables with a degree of resistance to diseases.

• Several insects which feed on pests should be encouraged into gardens. Ladybugs (adults and grubs) eat aphids, scale insects, mealybugs, and thrips voraciously. Lacewing larvae also feed on aphids. Ground beetles live in the soil and eat grubs and the eggs of pests, while rove beetles, which also live in the soil, eat cabbage worms.

Safety first with chemicals

All garden chemicals must be treated carefully and with respect. If carelessly used they can cause harm to the user, to children, and to pets and wildlife. Here are a few ways to insure their safe use:

• Before using a chemical, read the label carefully and check that it is suitable.

• Do not use chemicals from bottles or containers that have lost their labels. Instead, dispose of them safely (see right). Never move chemicals from their original container into a different one.

• Read and follow the instructions on the container. Using excessively high concentrations of chemicals may damage plants. Weak solutions may be ineffective.

• Store garden chemicals in a locked cabinet away from children.

• Check that the chemical will not harm your plants. Ferns, palms, and cacti are easily damaged by some chemicals.

• Before spraying vegetables, check the recommended time between application and harvesting.

• Do not use chemical sprays indoors when caged birds, fish, and other pets are present.

• Do not allow pets to chew or lick sprayed plants. Many chemicals have a residual effect for several weeks.

• Do not use the same equipment for spraying pesticides and weedkillers.

• Clean all spraying equipment very thoroughly after use.

• Wash your hands after using chemicals and, when recommended, use protective clothing such as gloves and a face mask.

• If you have an accident with a garden chemical and have to visit a doctor or a hospital, take along the chemical so that it can be identified.

Keeping pets and wildlife safe

Take all possible precautions when using chemicals in a garden to prevent pets and wildlife from being harmed. Always bear in mind that some chemicals have long-lasting effects.

• When chemicals are being mixed or used, keep pets indoors.

• Use sprays late in the day when few beneficial insects are flying and bees are inactive. Avoid spraying open flowers because they attract beneficial insects.

• Do not spray during windy weather.

DISPOSING OF UNWANTED GARDEN CHEMICALS

Eventually, everyone has a shelf in a garden shed full of unwanted garden chemicals. They need to be disposed of in a safe way. Do not pour them down a drain, bury them in the garden or give to a refuse collector, perhaps camouflaged in an outer wrapping. Instead, consult your local waste disposal authority for advice, especially when the packaging indicates the chemical is either harmful, oxidizing, or an irritant. If the packaging has been lost, assume that it is one of these three.

• Do not allow plant-eating animals such as rabbits and guinea pigs to chew recently sprayed plants.

• Do not use chemicals near garden ponds, bird baths, streams, or ditches.

• Do not spray near wildlife ponds where you may poison frogs, toads, newts, etc.

• When using slug bait, place the bait under tiles where it will be inaccessible to other wildlife.

---

picture parade of pests and diseases

ANTHRACNOSE can affect all beans, causing black, sunken spots on pods, leaves, and stems. Apply a fungicide spray and do not touch wet leaves.

ANTS are encouraged by aphids and sometimes become a pest in rock gardens, loosening soil around roots. Dust the soil with an ant killer.

APHIDS are widely seen on plants in summer. They suck sap, causing mottling and distortion of leaves, flowers, and stems. Use a proprietary insecticide regularly.

ASPARAGUS BEETLES (square orange marks on a black body) chew asparagus leaves. Spray with insecticide as soon as they are seen, and pick off and destroy the beetles.

BIRDS scratch up and eat newly sown seeds and peck flowers. Place

twigs along newly sown rows or stretch black thread over the surface.

BLACK LEG is a disease of cuttings, especially those of pelargoniums. Bases of stems become black and soggy. It is encouraged by cold, wet, compacted, and airless soil.

BLACK SPOT is a fungal disease that affects roses, causing black spots on their leaves. Spray with a fungicide several times. Also, remove and burn fallen infected leaves.

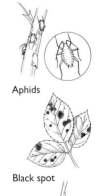

Aphids

Black spot

Botrytis

Cabbage maggots

Carrot fly

Carrot weevils

Clubroot

Japanese beetle grub

Cutworm

Flea beetle

Mealybug

BOTRYTIS (gray mold) is a gray, fluffy mold on flowers, stems, and leaves. It thrives in cool, damp, airless conditions. Reduce congestion among plantings, and spray.

BRISTLY ROSESLUGS disfigure leaves by eating soft tissue between veins. These hairy, slimy larvae usually feed at night, chewing on the undersides of leaves. Spray with an insecticide.

CABBAGE MAGGOTS tunnel into the roots and stems of newly transplanted brassicas, causing yellowing and stunted growth. Protect seedlings with floating row covers.

CARROT FLIES have small, cream-colored maggots that devastate carrots, parsnips, and celery. Rake an insecticide into the soil before sowing seeds.

CARROT WEEVIL larvae defoliate carrot and celery tops before tunneling into the crop. As soon as the symptoms are seen, spray with an insecticide. Pull off infested leaves.

CATERPILLARS are the larvae of moths and butterflies. Pick off and destroy, use insecticides and pull up and burn seriously infested plants.

CATS often scratch light, well-drained soil, disturbing newly sown seeds as well as established plants. Dust soil with pepper. A pea gravel mulch protects rock garden plants.

CLUBROOT attacks cabbages and related plants. Roots distort and plants die. When planting young plants, treat them with fungicide. Acid soil encourages this disease.

CUCUMBER BEETLES can spread disease rapidly through a vegetable garden. Cover seedlings with floating row covers to prevent beetles from feeding on young plants.

CUTWORMS, larvae of certain moths, live in the topsoil. They chew the bases of plant stems, causing them to collapse. Dust soil with an insecticide and remove weeds. Dig the soil in winter.

DAMPING OFF causes seedlings in greenhouses to collapse and die. It results from over-high temperatures, overcrowding, and excessively moist compost. Correct these conditions.

DIEBACK is a disease that causes shoots to die back and downward. Several causes include canker, frost, and waterlogging. Cut out and burn infected parts.

EARWIGS chew flowers, soft stems, and leaves, especially at night. Pick off and destroy, or trap in pots of straw inverted on garden stakes. Dust with an insecticide.

FLEA BEETLES eat holes in leaves of brassicas and related plants, and may kill young plants. They are generally worse in dry seasons. Keep plants watered, and dust with insecticide.

JAPANESE BEETLE GRUBS live in soil and graze upon roots. Later, they pupate and beetles appear. Pick up and destroy these grubs. Also, dig soil deeply in winter.

LEAFHOPPERS cause pale, mottled areas on leaves. They become distorted and may fall off if the

attack is severe. Spray plants with a systemic insecticide.

LEAFROLLERS cause leaves to roll lengthwise, enclosing a grayish-green grub. Pick off and burn small infestations, or prevent damage with an insecticide.

MEALYBUGS appear on stems, leaves, and branches in white, cottony masses. They suck sap and cause distortion. Wipe off small infestations with cotton swabs dipped in isopropryl alcohol.

MICE often dig down to bulbs in winter when searching for food. Cover bulbs with wire netting anchored to the soil. Mice may also infest stores of bulbs in summer.

MINT RUST attacks mint. Orange pustules appear on the undersides of leaves. It is difficult to eradicate. Spray plants regularly if it becomes a problem.

MOLES can be a problem, especially in rock gardens where plants cannot be moved out of the way of their tunnels, and on lawns when they make molehills. Use rocks to block tunnels. Do not use metal traps.

ONION FLIES have small, white maggots that burrow into bulbs. Leaves become yellow and wilt. Pull up and burn seriously infected bulbs. Use insecticides before sowing.

POTATO SCAB produces raised, scabby, distorted areas on skins of potatoes. Only the skin is affected and tubers can still be cooked and eaten. Do not add lime to the soil.

POWDERY MILDEW forms a white, powdery covering on leaves, flowers, and stems. It is encouraged by lack of air circulating around plants, and by dry soil. Keep soil moist and leaves dry, and use a fungicide.

RED SPIDER MITES suck leaves, causing mottling and spin webs. They are mainly a greenhouse pest. Spray plants with an insecticidal soap.

ROOT APHIDS are pests in warm areas where they graze on roots, causing discoloration and wilting. Drench the soil with insecticide.

ROOT ROTS are encouraged by cold, wet soils. Rock garden plants, which require well-drained soil, are especially susceptible. Mix in some builder's sand.

ROSE SCALE, usually seen on old and neglected rose bushes, promotes clusters of scales. Wipe off colonies with isopropryl alcohol and use a systemic insecticide.

RUST is especially a problem with Althaea (hollyhock). Rusts are difficult to control and the best preventive measure is to pull up and burn severely infected plants.

SCALE INSECTS form waxy brown discs under which young insects are born. They suck sap, causing speckling. Destroy seriously infected plants, or use a systemic insecticide.

SLUGS are a particular problem during warm, wet weather. They chew all parts of plants, usually feeding at night. Use slug bait.

SNAILS, like slugs, thrive in warm, wet weather, when they chew plants and rapidly cause damage. Look out for them and pick them off plants, and use snail bait.

SOOTY MOULD is a fungus that grows on honeydew excreted by aphids. It blackens leaves and stems. Spray plants regularly to kill aphids.

TENT CATERPILLARS build silken webs in branches of fruit and ornamental trees where they rest during the day, eating leaves voraciously at night. Although unsightly, they do little permanent damage. Remove the tents by hand, spray, or trap larvae with a sticky substance applied to tree trunks.

THRIPS are tiny flies that fly or jump from leaf to leaf, causing silvery streaks. Flowers become distorted. They are worse in dry conditions. Spray with an insecticide.

VINE WEEVILS are small white grubs that chew roots, so that plants wilt and die. Check the soil if a pot plant wilts unexpectedly. Treat with an insecticide.

VIRUSES attack many plants, causing reduced vigor and mottling of leaves and stems. They seldom kill plants. They are transmitted by sap-sucking insects.

WEEVILS are rather like beetles, often with long or divided snouts. They have legless larvae and, with the adults, chew the roots, stems, and leaves of fruit bushes and trees. Dust or spray with an insecticide.

WHITEFLIES are small insects rather like moths, which infest plants in greenhouses and conservatories. They suck sap, yellowing leaves and flowers. Use an insecticide.

WIREWORMS are the larvae of click beetles which inhabit soil. They chew roots and cause plants to die. Wireworms are especially troublesome in newly dug grassland. Use an insecticide.

Onion Fly

Potato Scab

Rose Scale

Rust

Scale Insects

Thrip

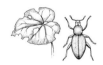

Vine Weevil

Whiteflies

Wireworms

Stinging Nettle

Chickweed

Pigweed

Groundsel

Shepherd's Purse

Lesser Celandine

Bindweed

Coltsfoot

preventing and eradicating weeds

The prevention and eradication of weeds are inevitable garden tasks. There are few gardens without weeds in flower beds, vegetable plots, or at the base of a hedge. As well as being unsightly, they compete with garden plants for moisture, food, light, and space. They also encourage the presence of pests and diseases. Thistles are hosts for leafhoppers and weevils, while cutworms and other pests rely on weeds for winter protection.

Lawns do not escape weeds, and although a peppering of bright-faced daisies is acceptable, yarrow and plantains do not have the same appeal. Weeds in lawns soon cause unsightly patches of compacted soil.

Controlling weeds

If weeds are not to become a problem you must regularly:
• Hand weed in the traditional way to remove weeds. This also enables plants to be closely examined, and pests and diseases to be seen at an early stage. Always place weeds in a box and put annual types on a compost pile; perennial weeds, especially ground elder and couch grass, are best destroyed.
• Hoe the surfaces of flower-beds and vegetables to chop off weeds at surface level. This is ideal for annual

weeds, but does not remove the perennial types. Use a Dutch or grubbing hoe to sever weeds. In seed beds and around small vegetables, a narrow grubbing hoe is useful. In vegetable gardens the yearly rotation of crops helps to discourage the growth of weeds.
• Mulch by spreading a layer of well-rotted manure, leafmold, shredded hardwood mulch or garden compost 3in/7.5cm deep over the soil. As well as depressing weeds, it reduces the loss of moisture from the soil, improves the soil's structure, and adds to its fertility. As an alternative to organic mulches, a layer of black plastic prevents the growth of weeds. A layer of pea gravel over soil in rock gardens also eliminates weed growth, while preventing heavy rain from washing away soil. Incidentally, the ancient Romans used stone mulches around vines and apricot trees.
• Use herbicides (chemical weedkillers) but not recklessly because pets and the environment may be at risk. There are three main types of these chemicals:
1. Pre-emergence weedkillers. These are sprayed on bare ground to kill weed seedlings as they emerge.
2. Total weedkillers. These destroy all plants. Some have long-lasting effects and are ideal for killing weeds on paths and driveways, while others are short-lived for use in beds.
3. Selective weedkillers. These kill weeds without harming the crop.

Annual weeds

These grow each year from seed, then flower, and die. There are often several generations seeded each year. Most grow abundantly and need regular control.

***ANNUAL STINGING NETTLE*—** Upright, nettle-like leaves and small green flowers through summer but does not have a creeping rootstock. Grows in light, cultivated soil and on waste land.

***CHICKWEED*—**Low, sprawling, bushy plant with masses of small white flowers in lax clusters from early spring to late summer. It grows mainly in moist, cultivated, fertile soil.

***GROUNDSEL*—**Upright, with weak and floppy stems, lobed leaves and clusters of small yellow flowers mainly during summer. Grows in waste and also on cultivated soil, especially where it is disturbed regularly.

***PIGWEED*—**Also called goosefoot and lamb's quarters. Upright with diamond- to lance-shaped leaves and green or white flowers through summer into fall. Grows in waste areas, and on cultivated land.

***SHEPHERD'S PURSE*—**An annual with a long, tapering root and upright stems bearing loose clusters of white flowers, mainly in summer. Grows on waste areas and also on cultivated ground.

Perennial weeds

These weeds are long lived and with a strong root system. They are more difficult to eradicate than annual weeds, and soon grow again if any root is left in the ground.

BINDWEED—Pernicious, scrambling climbing perennial with roots that often penetrate the soil to 6ft/1.8m deep. Pink or white flowers appear from early summer to early fall. Widely seen except in woodland.

COLTSFOOT—Distinctive perennial with large, rounded but slightly heart-shaped basal leaves and upright stems bearing yellow, daisy-like flowers from late winter to mid-spring. Widely seen in slightly chalky, moist soils in gardens, and on waste areas.

COMMON SORREL—Also known as sheep's sorrel. Pear-shaped, stem-clasping leaves and reddish-green flowers during early and midsummer. Widely seen in gardens, fields, and on heathland, especially where the soil is acid.

CREEPING BUTTERCUP—Spreading plant with a creeping rootstock that frequently sends up shoots that bear toothed and lobed leaves. Stems bear yellow, buttercup-like flowers from late spring to late summer. Found on wasteland and in cultivated soil.

DANDELION—Also known as the common dandelion. Well-known plant with thick, penetrating roots long, deeply incised leaves, and stems bearing golden-yellow, daisy-like flowers through the year, especially during summer. Widely seen in most areas.

FIREWEED—Also known as hairy willow herb. Tall and patch-forming with upright stems that bear bright purple flowers from midsummer to early fall. Widely found on wasteland roadsides, and meadows.

GOUTWEED—Also known as bishopsweed. A pernicious perennial with a creeping rootstock of slender white roots. Bears small white flowers in terminal clusters from early to late summer. Common in gardens and on waste land.

HORSETAIL—A pernicious perennial with creeping roots that send up shoots. Widely seen in cultivated land, in fields, and on dunes.

LESSER CELANDINE—Also known as pilewort. Has creeping roots and stems and rather fleshy, heart-shaped leaves. Bright, golden-yellow flowers, fading to white, appear in spring. Widely seen on bare ground, in woodland, and alongside hedges.

PLANTAIN—Also known as the common plantain. Has a short, thick rootstock and broad, oval leaves. Spikes of insignificant flowers appear through summer into early fall. Widely seen in waste areas, lawns, and grassland.

QUACKGRASS—Pernicious, rampant plant with spreading, rhizomatous roots that frequently send up shoots. Found in waste places and also on cultivated soils.

RAGWORT—A biennial or perennial with a short, thick rootstock, upright, with much-divided stems and dense, flat-topped clusters of yellow, daisy-like flowers from early summer to fall. Widely found in wet meadows and swamps, and in moist woodlands.

SOW THISTLE—Also known as field sow thistle and common sow thistle. An upright, vigorous perennial with a creeping rootstock and stems bearing loose clusters of yellow, thistle-like flowers from midsummer to late fall. Found on cultivated land, on waste areas, an alongside roads.

STINGING NETTLE—Has creeping roots that send up vertical stems packed with nettlelike leaves and narrow, catkinlike flowers from midsummer to early fall. Widely found on wasteland and at roadsides.

YARROW—Also known as milfoil. Creeping roots develop erect stems with finely divided leaves and flat, umbrella-like heads of white or pink flowers through summer. Widely seen in waste areas, cultivated soil, meadows, and sometimes on lawns.

Creeping Buttercup

Dandelion

Plantain

Goutweed

Horsetail

Ragwort

Sow Thistle

Yarrow

505

gardening
through the year

introduction

One of the beauties of a garden is the way it subtly alters from season to season, so slowly that sometimes you hardly notice the changes taking place. And yet the contrast between the warm and drowsy days of midsummer, with plants in full, luxuriant bloom and leaf, and the frosty midwinter, when the bare branches are rimed with ice and all plant

▼ *The pleasures of the summer garden are intensified by the gentle sound of splashing water from a garden pool.*

life seems to have frozen to a halt, could hardly be more marked. Every season in the garden has its compensations, whether it is the lusty resurgence of life in spring, the brimming bounty of summer, the brilliant colors of fall or the ethereal, sculptural beauty of plants in winter. And every season has its tasks to be performed. But while some times are far busier than others, gardening is definitely a year-round occupation if the garden is going to look good 12 months a year.

Perhaps one of the reasons gardeners find their hobby so relaxing is that plants won't be hurried—they need their time to grow. Although television has made the "instant garden" seem within everyone's grasp, the reality is not quite like that. A large part of gardening's attraction stems from watching a seed or tiny cutting slowly develop into a healthy, mature plant, or watching the small, container-grown specimen you planted years ago grow into a stately, spreading tree. While it may sometimes

◄ *Freesia corms must be planted in late summer if you are to enjoy their scented blooms during the winter months.*

▼ *With a little forward planning, containers can provide color and interest for the patio virtually the whole year round.*

be tempting to dream of a team of garden makers sweeping in to transform your plot overnight, how much more satisfying it is to be able to look around with pride and say "all my own work."

People who tend gardens are usually an optimistic, forward planning bunch— they have to be. Gardening means constantly thinking ahead. There's no point waiting until pole beans are in season before deciding it would be nice to have some of your own to pick; the seeds need sowing weeks before, in spring. And everyone knows that hyacinths make beautiful, scented houseplants for the cold days of winter, but if you want to plant your own, you have to plant them in the earliest days of the fall. The problem is, of course, that because most people lead such busy lives it is all too easy to forget such things, and that is where *Gardening Through The Year* comes to your aid—as an indispensable

memory jogger to what needs doing and when.

The gardening year divides into the four seasons of spring, summer, fall and winter, and if these are each subdivided into early, mid and late season, we have a convenient dozen "mini seasons" to equate (roughly) with the 12 months of the year. Exactly when these fall depends not on the calendar but on the climate in your area, and local climate patterns. And that is why we use these terms rather than specific dates.

The term "ornamental garden" simply refers to the decorative, nonfunctional aspects of the garden— attractive flowers, trees, and shrubs.

I hope that this section of *The Ultimate Book of Gardening* will remind you of all the things you want and need to do, and also encourage and inspire you to try out some new ideas, while reminding you of all that is best in the

garden in the various seasons. But most of all I hope that these pages will help you to enjoy every aspect of your garden and your gardening to the full, whatever the time of year.

spring

Spring is a wonderful season for gardeners. Day by day we can see the garden coming to life, pushing out strong young shoots, unfolding fresh green foliage, laying down a colorful tapestry of flowers. It's also time for us to get to work because this is surely the busiest, as well as the most pleasurable, season of the year.

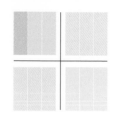

early spring

Ever-lengthening days give us more time to spend in the garden and we need it because there is plenty to be done. Although the days are still chilly, with overnight frost an ever-present danger, there will gradually be more sunshine to cheer things up, and a distinctly milder feel to the air.

Better weather, spring sunshine, and the obvious signs of growth and flowering around the garden make everyone feel optimistic and enthusiastic, but it pays to be cautious for a little while yet. In many places reliably warm weather is still some weeks away.

Most gardeners will be hoping for several days of dry, sunny weather, preferably accompanied by a good strong breeze: ideal conditions for drying out the soil ready for seedbed preparation. The lighter the soil, the earlier this task can be done. It just involves raking the surface until the

soil is reduced to an even texture of fine crumbs, but it's essential to wait until the soil is no longer clinging and sticky.

Although the spring may seem slow to get going, it soon moves up a gear and suddenly gardeners are hard pushed to keep up. There are spring bulbs to support and deadhead, border plants to stake before they start to flop over, containers to get ready for the summer display, and sowings to make both outdoors and inside. There's also planting and pruning to be done, and dozens of seedlings jostling for space in the greenhouse. In fact sometimes it's so busy that there hardly seems time to enjoy the garden itself. So whatever else you do, make time to appreciate that delicious freshness of growth the garden offers now, for there's no other season quite like it.

◄ *As the days gradually become brighter and warmer, eagerly awaited spring flowers surge into growth.*

EARLY SPRING TASKS

General

- Prepare the soil for sowing when the weather allows
- Remove weeds and apply a moisture-retaining mulch

Ornamental garden

- Plant container-grown trees and shrubs, and plant and divide herbaceous perennials
- Support border plants as soon as the shoots start to lengthen

- Sow hardy annuals and Lathyrus odoratus (sweet peas) outdoors
- Prune roses and shrubs such as buddleja, hydrangeas, and Cornus alba (dogwood)
- Remove winter protection from tender plants

- Fertilize spring-flowering bulbs, perennials, and shrubs if not already done
- Mulch round alpine plants with fresh gravel
- Trim back winter-flowering Calluna (heathers)

▼ A fresh dressing of gravel around alpine plants helps to show the developing flowers off to perfection.

Lawns

- Begin mowing regularly; continue to carry out repairs to turf

Kitchen garden

- Dig up the last of the overwintered crops and sow early crops in their place
- Plant early potatoes, rhubarb, and shallots.

- Continue harvesting rhubarb and kale
- Stake fall or early spring-sown beans and peas

- Protect early blossom on fruit trees
- Plant soft fruit bushes
- Check raspberry supports

Greenhouse

- Keep the glass clean for good light transmission
- Sow half-hardy annuals, herbs, and eggplant, cucumbers, sweet peppers, and tomatoes; prick off seedlings sown earlier
- Start chrysanthemums and dahlias into growth to produce cuttings if not already done.
- Take softwood cuttings of overwintered plants started into growth earlier

- Ventilate the greenhouse with care; if possible fit an automatic ventilator to allow a quick response to sudden temperature changes
- Plant tuberous begonias
- Check plants regularly for pests and diseases
- Buy growing bags for tomatoes and other greenhouse crops, and allow them to warm up in the greenhouse

- Store left-over seeds in a cool, dry place
- Repot greenhouse and houseplants as necessary
- Plant out forced bulbs in the garden when they have finished flowering

▼ The greenhouse will soon be filling with softwood cuttings from a range of overwintered plants.

ornamental garden: *general tasks*

Increasing numbers of spring bulbs are opening their flowers every day, making a wonderful display. A little care and attention now will keep them looking good and help to build them up for next year's show. Containers will need to be planted up for summer soon, so start preparing now.

Fertilize spring-flowering bulbs

Bulbs which stay in the ground from year to year often respond well to an application of fertilizer. It does not have any effect on the current season's flowers, but it will help to build up the bulbs and make sure of good flowering for the following year. Regular feeding is particularly important for bulbs that are growing in the restricted conditions of containers.

The time to feed is from the beginning of flowering until the leaves start to die down. It is recommended that you use a high-potash fertilizer, preferably in liquid form which is taken up readily by the plants. Follow the directions on the container regarding frequency of application.

Bulbs which are naturalized in grass are not fed very often because this tends to encourage the grass to grow strongly instead of the bulbs. A feed can be applied every few years, however, especially if the performance of the bulbs is starting to deteriorate.

◀ *An application of fertilizer while spring bulbs are flowering will help to make sure of a good performance for the following year.*

Mulch alpines with gravel

Most alpine plants grow well in poor, rocky, free-draining soil in cold but dry conditions. In gardens they are often killed by excessive moisture which rots the roots, and if it gathers

---

DEADHEAD BULBS

As soon as bulb flowers fade, it pays to remove them by snapping off the stalks just below the flower head. This prevents the flowers from forming seeds, and directs the bulb's energy into next year's display. However, some flower stems do not snap cleanly, and the whole stem tends to pull out of the center of the bulb instead. When this happens use secateurs to cut off the heads. Note that deadheading can only be carried out where practical, and if there are very large numbers of bulbs it becomes too time-consuming.

PREPARE CONTAINERS FOR SUMMER FLOWERS

Pots, tubs, window boxes, and hanging baskets have quite likely been stored away since the end of last summer. Now's the time to get them out and check them over, cleaning them thoroughly and repairing any damage or replacing them where necessary.

Garden centers offer the best choice of new containers at this time of year because later in the spring so many people are buying them that they quickly sell out.

Containers are available in plastic, glass fiber, stone, cement, wood, ceramic, and terracotta, in a wide range of styles and prices.

If you are tempted by a particularly large or heavy container, remember to allow for the extra weight of soil and plants it will hold—some containers are almost impossible to move once they are planted up.

round the neck of the plants it can rot them at ground level.

Remove all weeds from around the plants and prick over the soil lightly with a hand fork. Then top-dress the plants with gravel or stone chippings, tucking them well under the rosettes of foliage and around the necks of the plants. This improves the drainage and makes the bed look much more attractive, showing off the alpines to advantage.

Alpines do not have to be grown in rock gardens. A small raised bed or a shallow trough like an old stone sink can contain an attractive arrangement of plants and provide them with good growing conditions.

Where space is really tight, shallow pans will hold individual plants or small groups, or plants can be tucked into crevices in stone walls.

▶ *Suitable stone chippings for mulching around alpine plants can be obtained ready bagged from most garden centers.*

ornamental garden: *sowing*

Annual plants are among the easiest to grow, but a mixed annual border needs to be properly planned for the best results. Lathyrus odoratus (sweet pea), appreciated as much for its scent as its beauty, can be sown outside now, and herbaceous border plants will benefit from early staking.

Sow sweet peas outdoors

Sweet peas are often grown in rows in the vegetable garden to provide cut flowers, but they also make an attractive feature in the flower border

Dig the soil well where the sweet peas are to grow, and incorporate a dressing of general fertilizer. Tread the soil to firm it, then put the supports in place before sowing the seeds. Special stake clips are available to fix together the tops of bamboo stakes making a wigwam or an A-frame, that is then covered with plastic mesh netting to give the plants something to cling onto.

Use a sharp knife to chip the seedcoat carefully to speed germination, but be careful not to damage the lighter colored eye where the seedling will emerge. Instead of chipping, seeds can be soaked overnight in water to soften the seedcoat if preferred. Sow them about 1 in/2.5 cm deep and some 3 in/7.5 cm apart, or at the base of each cane support.

sow an annual bed

Annuals are among the easiest of flowering plants to grow, and provide many weeks of bright color through the summer. Sowing outdoors can start now, as long as you take care to choose hardy varieties. *Alyssum, Calendula* (marigold), *Clarkia, Centaurea cyanus* (cornflower), *Limnanthes* (poached egg plant), *Nemophila* and *Nigella* are some favorites suitable for early sowing.

Hardy annuals are sown directly where they are to grow, in well-prepared, finely-raked soil. Work out a sowing plan for the bed—put the tallest varieties to the back and aim for a good combination of colors and textures.

1 Mark out the sowing area for each variety by drawing a series of interlocking arcs on the bed, using a pointed stick or a trickle of sand (**right**). Sprinkling packets of mixed seed over the soil rarely produces a good effect.

2 Draw a series of short, parallel drills in the first patch, and sprinkle the seed thinly along the drills (**left**). Rake the soil over lightly and firm it with the head of the rake. Continue sowing the rest of the patches, running the drills in different directions to avoid a regimented appearance.

3 Weed seedlings will germinate freely along with the annuals, but the annuals will be easy to recognize as they will appear in straight rows. Remove the weeds regularly, and thin out the annual seedlings to their appropriate spacings when they are large enough.

SUPPORT BORDER PLANTS

Supports for border plants must be put in place early, well before the plants need them. In this way the stems can be trained up through the supports as they grow, eventually completely hiding them. There are several different types of proprietary supports, ranging from wire mesh rings on legs to hooked stakes which link together. You can also use rings of stakes encircled by garden twine, or twiggy sticks cut from the hedgerow. Whichever method is chosen, aim for a natural effect—unsympathetic staking, where whole plants are tightly trussed, each to a single stake, can ruin the whole effect of the herbaceous border.

◀ *A row of sweet peas will provide dozens of wonderfully fragrant cut flowers for the home through the summer months.*

▶ *Colorful annuals such as nasturtiums, easily raised from seed, will always find a place among groups of mixed summer flowers.*

ornamental garden: *planting*

Container-grown trees and shrubs can be planted all year, whenever the weather is suitable. Those planted now will give an almost instant effect because they are already bursting into leaf. Herbaceous perennials are also emerging once again, having spent the winter underground.

Plant trees and shrubs

Trees and shrubs are particularly valuable in the garden, providing height as well as a permanent, year-round framework. There are so many different types of trees and shrubs to choose from that there is something for every garden, even the smallest plot. Shrubs can provide a range of shapes and sizes, and can be grown for their foliage, flowers, shape, or all three. Evergreens provide year-round interest, while deciduous varieties offer the pleasure of watching the leaves change with the season—unfolding in the spring, reaching their lush pinnacle in the summer and perhaps turning to glowing shades before falling.

Flowers, too, can be had virtually all-year round, even in the depths of winter when they are especially welcome in the garden.

The choice of tree needs great care in a small garden because fast-growing varieties can cause problems with subsidence and damage to drains. However, there are many small and slow-growing trees suitable for small spaces including varieties of *Betula* (birch), conifer, *Malus* (crab apple), *Prunus* (flowering cherry) and *Acer* (maple).

◀ *Evergreens provide color and interest all year. They can be planted whenever the weather is right, but now is a particularly good time.*

plant trees and shrubs

Depending on the weather, it may still be possible to plant bare-root trees and shrubs, but not for much longer. Once the dormant season is over and plants have started into growth, only container-grown specimens can be planted.

PLANT HERBACEOUS BORDER PLANTS

Herbaceous perennials can be planted in the fall or spring, but remember that those planted now may need watering during the late spring and early summer. This is also a suitable time to divide existing perennials that are growing too large for their position—if you didn't manage to finish all the lifting and dividing last fall it can safely be completed now.

Check containerized plants sold at garden centers carefully at this time of year. Some may not be container grown, but the bare-root kind planted up at the end of the dormant season. The root-ball must lift intact from the pot without the soil falling away.

A good quality container-grown plant has a firm root-ball with strong, healthy roots. It can be transplanted with little check to growth at almost any time of year. Recently potted up plants, however, will be slower to establish and may not be worth the higher cost.

Container-grown plants can be planted all-year round, but spring and fall are better than midsummer when high temperatures and lack of water may put extra stress on the plant. Trees and shrubs planted now usually establish rapidly and grow away strongly.

▼ *A well-chosen selection of trees and shrubs add an air of maturity and an important dimension of height to any garden.*

1 Water the plant/tree well the evening before it is planted. Dig a hole deep enough for the top of the root-ball to be just covered, and break up the soil at the base of the hole (**above**).

2 Remove the plant from its pot by tapping carefully around the edge and stand the root-ball in the planting hole (**above**).

3 Fill in around the plant with soil, firming well (**above**). It is vital to keep the soil moist in the spring and summer.

ornamental garden: *pruning*

Pruning is one of those tasks that make many gardeners feel apprehensive because they know that it needs to be done, but they are not sure why or how. The main reasons for pruning are to keep the plant shapely, promote good flowering and fruiting, and encourage strong, healthy growth.

Prune roses

The first step with all types of rose is to remove all dead, dying and diseased wood. Species and old-fashioned roses (such as gallicas, bourbons, and damasks) need very little further pruning; every other year, cut two or three of the oldest stems to ground level to encourage the production of young shoots.

With large-flowered (hybrid tea) roses, all shoots should be cut back by between two-thirds and one half of their length (less vigorous varieties should be pruned hardest). Cluster-flowered (floribunda) varieties are pruned more lightly, cutting the shoots back by about one-third of their length. On both cluster-flowered and large-flowered roses, a quarter to one-third of the total stems can be cut back to the base if desired, to promote the growth of young replacement branches.

PRUNE TREES AS NECESSARY

Ornamental trees do not need regular pruning, but, as with all plants, any dead, diseased or dying branches should be removed as soon as they are seen; large branches could be a danger if left to fall naturally. Remove branches by first undercutting them with the saw, and then cutting from the top to sever them (undercutting prevents the branch from tearing). It is not necessary to seal the cut with pruning paint.

◀ *When pruning roses of any type, use well-sharpened pruners to make a clean cut just above a healthy bud.*

prune shrubs

The correct time and technique for pruning flowering shrubs depends mainly upon the time of year that they flower. Those that flower in late summer usually flower on new wood that has been produced that season; pruning these shrubs hard now, just as they start into growth, will promote plenty of strong new shoots and provide extra flowers.

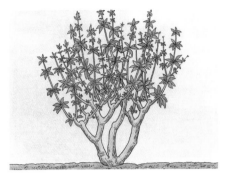

1 Shrubs such as *Buddleja davidii* benefit from being cut back severely now. Branches can be pruned to within 6–12 in/15–30 cm of soil level; long-arm pruners or loppers may be necessary to cut through some of the older stems.

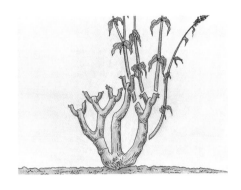

2 Although such pruning may initially look very severe, strong new growth will be made almost straight away. Plants which are not pruned hard tend to become untidy and top heavy, with weak, straggly shoots.

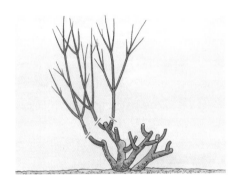

3 *Cornus alba* 'Sibirica' is grown for its brightly colored winter stems, and cutting all stems back to within 3in/7.5cm of the base insures that a good thicket of strong, bright new stems will be produced in time for next season.

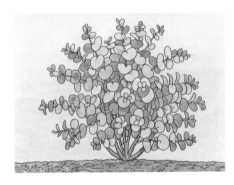

4 Pruning eucalyptus back hard each spring will maintain a bushy shape and the rounded, intensely colored juvenile foliage. Cut all the previous season's stems back to within 3in/7.5cm of the main framework of branches.

5 Some shrubs that flower on older wood should not be cut down entirely in the spring, but should have about one-third of their oldest stems removed each year. This makes sure that they retain a proportion of older wood to carry the flowers while new stems are produced to replace those that are past their best. *Cotinus coggygria* (the smoke bush), *Escallonia*, *Potentilla* and *Sambucus* (elder) are among those shrubs that benefit.

◄ *Climbing plants such as clematis need regular pruning in order to promote the production of strong flowering shoots.*

balcony and roof gardens

Where houses have limited space for a garden, it is tempting to use a balcony or flat roof for growing plants. This can be an excellent idea, but it does need some careful planning. The most important point to assess is the load-bearing capacity of the structure. The combined weight of plants, soil, and water is considerable, and many structures, particularly on older buildings, are not strong enough for the job. It is well worth employing a structural engineer to give you specific advice because the result of overloading could be disastrous.

Once you have received the go-ahead, there are other considerations to tackle. Most importantly, check that the surface is waterproof and has an efficient drainage system to channel away excess water safely. If you live on an upper floor of a block, residents below will tire of streams of water cascading off your balcony onto theirs whenever you water your plants, and damp penetrating into the fabric of a house from a roof garden could be very damaging to the structure.

Access to the garden is another important consideration. Many balconies are very small, and there may not be room to step onto the balcony itself; access

▲ *Plants are best put in containers that are filled with soilless mix because it is much lighter than soil-based mix.*

WEATHER PROTECTION

Roof and balcony gardens in an exposed position will be made much more pleasant for both plants and people if some form of windbreak can be established on the weather side. Trelliswork clothed with climbing plants is often ideal, though if you wish to preserve a view, it may be worth having toughened glass panels professionally installed.

may be through full length doors or only through a window. And with limited access it might make watering, repotting and tidying up, etc., quite difficult. Roofs can also have limited access, often involving awkward stairs or ladders that are fine when you are unencumbered but not much fun when you are trying to maneuver pots, watering cans, or sacks of soil mix up there. Finally, because plants will be grown in containers, remember that watering will be a daily chore in summer. Ask yourself whether it is possible to get a hosepipe to the garden, to fill a watering can nearby, or even to install an outside faucet.

Getting down to business

Once all the questions have been resolved and you are ready to create your garden, you will need to choose furnishings and equipment. Reducing the total weight is usually the primary consideration.

If it is a roof or large balcony that you can walk around, some form of floor covering will probably be necessary. Conventional paving slabs are usually too heavy, but lighter options include timber decking, a thin layer of gravel, shredded or chipped bark, and rubber tiles or artificial turf. Plants are best grown in containers and, again, lightweight plastic or fiberglass pots and troughs are more suitable than containers of clay, pottery, or stone. Large containers can be placed on wooden pallets that will help to distribute the load more evenly. Try to position the heaviest items where the load-bearing supports are—the structural engineer will advise you.

When filling the containers, use soilless mix, based on peat or peat substitutes such as coconut fiber, because it is much lighter than soil-based mix, but it will need more frequent watering and additional feeding.

Providing protection

By their nature, roof and balcony gardens are high up, and more exposed to the wind, which can be very damaging to plants. Because pots and soil mix are necessarily lightweight, they are also easily blown over.

A windbreak in the form of fine-mesh netting or trellis work covered with climbing plants will be a great help, but plants and their containers must be firmly secured to prevent damage in breezy conditions.

SAFETY FIRST

Don't take risks with your balcony or roof garden. Make sure that:
- A professional confirms that the balcony or roof has adequate load-bearing properties
- It is properly surrounded by adequate railings or walls that are regularly checked and kept in good condition
- Plants, containers, and ornaments are completely secure, and there is no risk of them falling over the edge
- Water or debris does not cause a nuisance to people or their property below
- You are adequately covered by insurance

ornamental garden: *plants in season*

Day by day, more fresh young leaves and flowers fill the garden, bringing it alive after its long dormant period. Bulbs are among the most prominent plants, but there are many shrubs, trees, and perennials now putting on a tremendous performance.

▼ *The luscious purple flowers of* Aubrieta *will brighten up any garden at this time of year.*

▲ 'Dark Secret', an early-flowering tulip, is a new cultivar with luscious deep colors that will bring warmth to any garden.

▶ The cheerful pink and white flowers of Anemone blanda are happy in light shade as well as full sun. Blue forms are also available.

kitchen garden: *general tasks*

Now's the time to use up some of those crops that have stayed all winter in the vegetable plot, and start preparing for the new season's harvest. With a little careful planning, it's possible to enjoy fresh produce from the kitchen garden at almost any time of the year.

▲ *Rhubarb is easy to grow in the vegetable garden, but it is the early, tender, forced stems that have the best flavor.*

Harvest rhubarb and kale

Rhubarb is not always considered a gourmet treat but the tender forced stems are a real delicacy at this time of year, far removed from the tough, acid, stringy stalks at the end of the season.

Kale is rich in vitamins A and C, and deserves to be more widely grown. It is usually winter-hardy, grown from seeds planted in early spring and again in late summer. For an earlier crop, start seed in a tray and transplant the seedlings.

The earliest crops of rhubarb are obtained by boxing up roots and forcing them into growth in a greenhouse, but plants can also be forced outdoors, covering the crowns in situ with purpose-made forcing pots or black plastic garbage cans to exclude all light.

Those covered up in early or midwinter will probably have shoots ready for harvesting now, depending on how mild the weather has been in the preceding weeks.

Protect blossom on early-flowering fruit trees

Frosts are still a distinct possibility in early spring, and will kill the blossoms on some of the early-flowering fruit trees such as apricots

USE UP OVERWINTERED CROPS
—

Parsnips will have remained in the vegetable garden all winter, ready for digging up and using as required. Now that spring has arrived, the roots will soon start into growth again, signaled by small green tufts emerging from the tops of the plants. As growth continues, the roots will become soft and flabby and not worth eating, and should be harvested now. Leeks will also start into growth again, producing flower buds that develop in their second year. This results in a solid, rather tough flower stem in the center of the leek that spoils the taste and quality. Any leeks and parsnips remaining should be lifted now and moved to a spare piece of ground until they are used up.

► *A purpose-built framework to support the horticultural blanket will make it easier to protect the early blossoms of fruit trees from frost.*

and peaches, often ruining the chance of a good crop. Protect trees from night frosts by draping them with lightweight horticultural blanket or, if the trees are growing against a wall or fence, attach a roll-down screen of fine-mesh netting. Make sure that the blanket or netting does not damage the blossom as it is being lowered or removed.

When fruit trees flower early in the year, while the weather is still cold, it is worth pollinating the blossom yourself in case no pollinating insects are on the wing. Use a small, soft brush to transfer pollen gently among the flowers. A cosmetic brush is easier to use than the paintbrush that is usually recommended for the job.

STAKE PEAS AND BEANS

The peas and beans that were sown in the fall or early spring should be provided with supports as they grow. For peas this can be plastic netting, supported by stakes at regular intervals; the plants will twine their tendrils around the netting as they grow. Alternatively a forest of twiggy brushwood sticks provides excellent support if you have a ready supply. Beans will also be happy with twiggy sticks, or you can provide them with a series of stakes along each side of the row, with string running around them to prevent the plants from flopping outward.

kitchen garden: *planting and sowing*

It is time for most gardeners to start sowing in earnest at last, although gardeners with heavy soils or gardens in particularly cold, exposed positions may be better advised to hang on just a little while longer. Always garden according to the prevailing conditions rather than calendar dates.

Prepare the soil for sowing

Soil in a seedbed should be broken down to fine, even crumbs, usually known as "a fine tilth." If the soil is left in large clods it is very difficult to get a level seedbed, and seeds will end up being buried either too deeply or too shallowly to achieve good germination.

If the vegetable garden has been left roughly dug over the winter, frosts will have got at the clods of soil, breaking them up by the action of repeated freezing and thawing.

As soon as some dry, breezy weather has dried out the soil surface sufficiently, these clods can be reduced to fine crumbs by raking. Any particularly large clods can be broken down by a smart blow with the back of the rake.

BEGIN SOWING VEGETABLE CROPS

Some time during this month, depending on the weather, a wide range of vegetables can be sown, including beans, carrots, leeks, lettuces, parsnips, summer and fall cabbages, early summer cauliflowers, spinach, and Swiss chard. Draw straight drills using a garden line and a hoe, and sow the seeds thinly along the drill. Rake the soil carefully over the seeds, tamp it down lightly and label the row clearly.

It is too early for the more tender crops such as zucchini, marrows, and bush and pole beans to be sown outside, but they can be raised in pots in a greenhouse for planting out after the last frost.

▲ *A light touch with the rake is necessary in order to produce a fine, even surface to a seedbed. Large stones should be removed.*

plant potatoes

If growing space is limited, plant early potatoes rather than main crops, choosing some of the more uncommon varieties that are impossible to buy from the store. The earliest crops of new potatoes have an incomparable flavor when they are freshly lifted. The foliage of potatoes is sensitive to frost, so take care about the planting time. It generally takes two or three weeks before the shoots show through the soil after planting.

1 As an alternative to immediate planting, seed potatoes can be set on a cool, light windowsill to produce shoots (**below**). The eyes that produce the shoots are clustered together at one end of the tuber (the "rose" end), and tubers should be set in egg cartons with this end uppermost.

3 Draw wide drills using a draw hoe, or use a trowel to make individual planting holes. Plant the potatoes around 5in/13cm deep. Chitted tubers should be dropped carefully into the holes with the shoots at the top; these shoots are very fragile and are easily broken. Unsprouted tubers should be planted with the rose end facing up.

4 Check the rows of potatoes regularly to see when the first shoots appear; they are dark bluish-green (**right**). Be on your guard against frost. If an unexpected frost kills the first shoots all is not lost—new shoots should replace them.

◄ *Most gardens have room for some soft fruit. Early spring is a good time to plant container-grown bushes and canes.*

2 Potatoes should be planted in well-prepared soil, in rows 18in/45cm apart, and spaced 12–18in/30–45cm apart within the row (**below**). Sprouted (or "chitted") tubers will appear through the soil more quickly after planting, but they need to be handled carefully in order to avoid knocking the shoots off.

colorful ornamental vegetables

Many vegetables are now grown as much for their appearance as their table qualities, and several are more than worthy of a place amongst the ornamental plants in the flower borders. The vegetables themselves have become more exciting too, with a whole range of vibrant colors and interesting shapes and textures to liven up the kitchen. Herbs have certainly managed to bridge the gap between the ornamental and useful, with plants like variegated thyme and purple-leaved sage happily providing color in the flower and shrub borders while still offering sprigs for use in the kitchen.

There are several vegetables that would fulfill a similar role if allowed to do so: stately globe artichokes with their dramatic spiky flower heads and divided leaves; carrots with fountains of bright green, finely divided foliage; and florence fennel, its neatly symmetrical, creamy white stem bases topped by clouds of lacy, feathery leaves. The more unusual vegetables include the asparagus pea, a rounded, spreading plant with dainty, light green leaflets, sprinkled with crimson flowers, and the deep purple, round pod bean 'Purple Queen' and 'Sequoia.' The brightly colored fruits of cherry tomatoes are also striking, particularly on varieties developed for growing in pots and hanging baskets: sweet bell peppers can be similarly attractive if prolific, small-fruiting types such as 'Jingle Bells' or 'Ace', which turns from green to red in 65–70 days, are chosen.

Kaleidoscopic choice

A glance at any seed catalog will show what a wide range of exciting and colorful varieties of old favorites are now available. Pole snap beans have always had attractive flowers, and 'Goldmania', as its name suggests, has yellow pods and these can grow to a length of 8in/20cm. The elegant 'Trionfo' has deep plum-purple pods and looks most impressive growing on a trellis.

Bush beans also have a neat, compact habit of growth, and there are several varieties with deep purple beans. Purple-podded beans turn green when cooked, but the varieties 'Goldkist', 'Brittle Wax', and 'Gold Mine' keep their rich yellow color.

▲ *There are many decorative varieties of lettuce available. The contrast of frilly-edged against plain-leaved varieties is always effective.*

Eggplant can be grown in the greenhouse or outside in warm, sheltered gardens. Among the most colourful varieties are 'Purple Rain', and 'Zebra', maroon streaked with white, and deep pink 'Neon'.

Lettuces are available in all varieties of colors and types. There is the red oakleaf 'Red Salad Bowl', 'Red Sails', and 'Cocarde'/'Santa Fe', 'Sweet Red' and 'Sierra' and 'Burgundy Ice' with heavily blushed burgundy outer leaves and light green inner leaves. Some varieties are extravagantly frilly edged, like 'Loma' and 'Lollo Rosso'.

You could liven up your salads even more by adding red salad onion 'Giant Red Hamburger', new Japanese cucumber 'Tasty Jade', rich brown sweet pepper 'Sweet Chocolate', pink and white beet 'Chioggia' and tomatoes such as 'Celebrity', 'Green Zebra', yellow 'Taxi', and 'Sungold' and the 'Striped German'.

In the marrow family, look out for the zucchini 'Gold Rush' and the patty pan squash 'Sunburst' that has scalloped edges to its deep yellow fruit. Swiss chard 'Bright Lights' adds some of the brightest splashes of color to the garden, with pink, orange, red, or white stems, while the kale 'Red Russian' has deep crimson-veined foliage through the winter.

Carrot 'Sweet Sunshine', as its name implies, is a strong, clear yellow, while asparagus 'Purple Passion' has very striking blue-black spears. There are several purple cauliflowers, including 'Purple Head', and 'Violet Queen', and the green Romanesco type 'Tower'.

Sweet corn cobs are available in white ('Silver Queen'), mixed white and yellow ('Double Standard'), yellow and brown ('Indian Summer'), and the extraordinary multicolor 'Indian Corn' for decoration purposes, 'Fiesta'.

▲ *Swiss chard 'Bright Lights' lives up to its name with brilliantly colorful leaf stems. Both stems and foliage are also excellent to eat.*

greenhouse: *planting and sowing*

Increasingly, the greenhouse will be filling up with boxes and trays of cuttings, seedlings, and young plants: make sure that they all have sufficient space to develop, and keep the glass clean for good light transmission. Many houseplants will appreciate being repotted at this time of year.

Continue sowing

The busy sowing season in the greenhouse continues. Adjust the sowing time of greenhouse crops such as cucumbers and tomatoes to the amount of heat you can provide. There is no point in making very early sowings if you cannot supply sufficient, steady warmth to raise young plants. Crops such as bush and pole beans can also be sown indoors for planting out after the risk of frosts, but it may be a little too early for them in many places, and mid-spring is often better.

Sow some herbs now for planting out later in the spring. While many herbs are raised from cuttings, quite a number can be grown successfully from seed, including basil, coriander, dill, fennel, marjoram, parsley, rocket, and summer savory. Sow small pinches of herbs in a pot, because only a few plants will be needed.

SOW HALF-HARDY ANNUALS

While hardy annuals can be sown outside, half-hardy varieties must be kept under cover until the risk of frost is over. They can be sown in the greenhouse now; most need temperatures of 55–70°F/13–21°C for germination.

Suitable species to sow include *Ageratum, Alyssum, Antirrhinum* (snapdragon), *Begonia, Brachycome, Clarkia, Lobelia, Nemesia, Petunia, Salvia, Impatiens* (busy lizzie), *Matthiola* (stock), *Nicotiana* (tobacco plant), *Tagetes* and *Zinnia*. Insure the trays have sufficient ventilation once the majority of the seeds have germinated, and prick the seedlings out as soon as they are large enough to handle.

◄ *Cucumbers sown now will need constant, steady warmth if they are to develop into healthy plants bearing a good crop.*

repot houseplants

Spring is a good time to give
established houseplants a new lease of
life by repotting them in fresh soil mix.
Some will benefit by a move up to the
next size, while others can be repotted
in the same size container if that is
more practical.

1 Water the plants thoroughly the day before
repotting them. Turn the plant upside down
with your hand spread across the top of the pot
and the plant's stem between your fingers (**right**).
Tap the rim of the pot downward sharply on the
edge of the bench or table to loosen the root-ball.

2 Slide the pot off the plant's roots (**left**).
Crumble a little of the old soil away from
around the top, base, and sides of the root-ball,
being careful not to damage the roots.

3 Plants that have filled their pot with roots
are ready for a move up to the next size.
Fill the base of the new pot with fresh mix and sit
the root-ball on it, adjusting the depth of soil until
the top of the root-ball is just below the top
of the pot.

4 Fill in round the sides of the root-ball with
more mix, using your fingers or a stick to
firm and push it right down to the base of the pot
so that there are no air pockets (**left**). Cover the
top of the root-ball with another layer of mix, and
water well.

5 If a plant is already in the largest pot size
that is practical, it can be returned to the
same pot after step 2, with just a little fresh mix
to replace that which has been crumbled away.
Very large plants can be top-dressed instead of
repotted; simply scrape away some of the surface
soil and replace it with fresh, mixed with a little
slow-release fertilizer.

◀ *Houseplants nearly always thrive best
when they are displayed in groups in the home,
rather than as single specimens.*

greenhouse: *pricking off and cuttings*

Seedlings from seeds sown earlier will need to be pricked off to pots or trays, spacing them out to give them adequate space to grow and develop. Cuttings can be taken now from overwintered roots of chrysanthemums and dahlias; these are usually quick and easy to root successfully.

Prick off seedlings

Seedlings are moved on to give them more room once they are large enough to be handled comfortably. It is important to handle them by their seed leaves only, and never by their stems which are extremely delicate; crushing the stem results in the death of the seedling. Water the seedlings a few hours before pricking off, and lever them carefully out of the soil using a dibble to prise them up from underneath.

Make a hole with the dibble in a tray of firmed and leveled soil mix, and then lower the seedling into it, making sure the roots reach the base of the hole. Firm in lightly. Space the seedlings so that their seed leaves are not touching. Water the pricked out seedlings so that the soil is evenly moist, then put them in a lightly shaded place for a day or two to recover.

POT UP TOMATO SEEDLINGS

Tomato seedlings are usually pricked off from the seedtray straight into individual pots. They should be handled, like any other seedling, by their seed leaves only. Tomato seedlings need to be buried more deeply than most seedlings to encourage adventitious roots on the stem that help produce a strong plant. Lower the seedling into the hole so that the seed leaves are just resting on the soil surface, then firm and water the plants.

▶ *Never tug seedlings out of the soil or the young roots will be severely damaged. Use a dibble to prise them out gently.*

take softwood cuttings

Plants that have spent the winter in the greenhouse are now producing strong new growth. The young shoots make ideal cuttings that root quickly to provide a plentiful supply of sturdy young plants. Most softwood cuttings are quick and easy to root in the greenhouse. Plants such as dahlias, chrysanthemums, fuchsias, and pelargoniums can be increased quite easily by this method, providing strong specimens for planting out later on.

1 It is important to use only healthy, vigorous shoots. You can either snap them off the parent plant or cut them off with a very sharp knife or single-edged razor blade (**below**). Since softwood cuttings tend to wilt easily, this job is best done in the morning while the plants are fresh.

3 Insert the cuttings into flats or pots of special seed and cuttings soil mix topped with a layer of sharp sand (**left**). The sand insures good drainage around the base of the stem and improves rooting. Firm the cuttings in with your fingers and water them well, using a fine rose on the can.

2 Cut off the shoots cleanly, immediately below a node (leaf joint), and remove the lower leaves (**below**). The prepared cutting should be about 2–3in/5–7.5cm long with around two fully opened leaves. Leaving excess foliage on the cutting means too much water will evaporate from it.

4 Place a plastic propagator top over the pot or flat, and then shade it from strong sun for a day or two with an upturned flat or piece of newspaper. This flat or newspaper can be removed once the cuttings have recovered and are not found to be wilting.

◀ *Early spring is the time to start dahlias into growth for cuttings. You will need to divide the tubers before planting in late spring.*

mid-spring

The garden really is looking good now, with the trees clothed in fresh young leaves, lawns becoming a richer green and spring flowers at their peak. A little warm, sunny weather brings out a real enthusiasm for gardening and there's certainly plenty to keep the keenest gardener occupied.

▲ *Tulips and forget-me-nots make a classic combination in the spring garden. Next year's spring bedding will need to be sown soon.*

Gardeners are not the only ones who are enjoying the spring weather, and pests and weeds are now thriving. Weeding is a job that needs to be done for a large proportion of the year, but weeds are probably growing most rapidly in mid-spring. It's especially important to keep them under control while garden plants are small because they can easily be smothered by weed growth.

Pests, too, are on the increase, attracted by the tender young growth the plants are making. Slugs and snails are often a particular problem, and aphids (greenfly) can be found clustered on shoot tips, especially on greenhouse plants. Early action helps to prevent an outbreak turning into an epidemic.

There may be some slightly tender plants that appear to have been killed by the winter cold, but don't consign them to the compost pile. It is sometimes well into the summer before they show signs of recovery and start to put out buds. Check by gently scraping a little patch of bark from the main stem—if the wood underneath is green and moist, the plant is still alive.

Spring bulbs continue to make a stunning show; wherever possible they should be deadheaded as they fade, before they have a chance to set seed. Spring bedding plants are also putting on a good performance; make a note to obtain more seeds of plants such as *Erysimum* (wallflowers), *Bellis perennis*, (daisies), *Myosotis*, (forget-me-nots) and so on, so they are not overlooked when they need to be sown in early summer. Buy them when you buy summer bedding plants from the garden center.

There's plenty to do in the kitchen garden, too, with weeding, sowing, and planting out, plus thinning out of crops that have been sown earlier. In the greenhouse shading becomes necessary soon, and ventilation and watering should be increased as the weather grows warmer and sunnier.

MID-SPRING TASKS

General

:: Control weeds, slugs, snails and other pests as they appear
:: Check plants that appear to have been killed by frosts

Ornamental garden

:: Plant summer-flowering bulbs and deadhead spring bulbs. Buy bedding plants from garden centers
:: Continue to sow hardy annuals
:: Take cuttings of border plants

:: Plant Galanthus (snowdrops) "in the green" (while in leaf)
:: Check for reverted shoots on variegated shrubs
:: Check for rose diseases and treat as necessary
:: Plant alpines and evergreens

:: Prune spring-flowering shrubs such as forsythia after flowering

▼ Neatly trimmed edges set off a freshly mown lawn.

Lawns

:: Apply a "weed and feed" combined herbicide and fertilizer
:: Mow and edge lawns as necessary
:: Deal with worm casts and moss
:: Make new lawns from seed

Water garden

:: Begin excavation work for a new pond

Kitchen garden

:: Continue sowing successional crops. Prepare the trench for pole beans
:: Sow winter brassicas outdoors
:: Hoe off weeds regularly
:: Plant out leeks and onion sets

:: Earth up potatoes and plant second early and maincrop varieties
:: Spray fruit with fungicide if mildew has been a problem in previous years

:: Avoid spraying fruit trees with insecticides while pollinating insects are active
:: Prune plums

▼ Seedlings and young plants continue to need potting up and pricking off in the greenhouse.

Greenhouse

:: Apply shading and increase ventilation and watering
:: Check heaters are still working
:: Begin hardening off bedding plants
:: Continue pricking off and potting up as necessary

:: Plant out tomatoes in the greenhouse border
:: Sow pole and bush beans, and melons

ornamental garden: *planting and sowing*

Alpines establish rapidly in mid-spring. If possible, grow them in a raised area so that their small but often exquisite flowers can be appreciated more easily. Galanthus (snowdrops) are best planted now before the leaves die down, and there are many summer-flowering bulbs to plant, too.

Plant snowdrops

Unlike many other bulbs, snowdrops are best planted while they are still in leafy growth; the dormant bulbs do not establish so well and can be disappointing. Many mail-order nurseries specializing in small bulbs advertise snowdrops "in the green," and this is the best way of obtaining some of the more unusual and expensive species and varieties.

If you already have clumps of snowdrops in the garden which you would like to increase, this is a good time to split them up and replant them in new positions. Lift the clumps carefully with a hand fork and tease them apart gently into two or three smaller groups. Replant them straight away, so that they do not dry out. Do not set the small bulbs too deep—aim for 3in/7.5cm. Heavy soils should have a little sharp sand or grit, and well-rotted compost worked in before planting.

PLANT ALPINES

Alpine plants come into their own next month, and this is a good time to plant new specimens. Container-grown plants from garden centers can be bought and planted when they are coming into flower, making choosing attractive varieties easier.

Prepare the soil well, remembering that alpines need free-draining conditions. Plant with a trowel and firm in well. Dress around the plants with a little grit to insure good drainage round the necks and help avoid the risk of rotting.

▶ *The double snowdrop Galanthus 'Flore Plento' is a popular variety, with delicate blooms like frilly petticoats.*

plant summer-flowering bulbs

Although spring is the first season that comes to mind when anybody mentions flowering bulbs, there are lots of species and varieties that make a great show in the summer. They are not difficult to grow, and it's well worth planting some now.

1 Most summer-flowering bulbs like a warm, sheltered position in full sun. The soil must be free-draining to avoid the bulbs rotting; on soils that tend to be heavy, add coarse sand or grit to the planting site and fork it in well (**below**).

3 Dig a planting hole with a trowel, sprinkle a little sand in the base and put in the bulb (**left**). The ideal planting depth will vary from species to species and depends on the size of the bulb. In general plant the bulb at a depth twice that of its height.

2 Bulbs should be planted as soon as they are available from garden centers. Always choose those which are large, firm and unblemished (**below**); avoid small and shriveled bulbs because they will not give good results.

4 Cover the bulb with soil and firm it in position lightly. Once planting is completed, it is a good idea to label the planting areas clearly. This should help you to avoid accidentally disturbing the bulbs before they start to show through the soil.

◀ *Sunny yellow lilies are perfect for brightening up the flower borders in summer and can be planted now.*

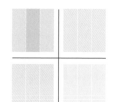

ornamental garden: *planting and protection*

Every garden should have its full complement of evergreen plants. For many species this is a good time to plant, and there is a fine selection of flowering and foliage shrubs and trees to choose from. Apart from their ornamental value, they are excellent for providing shelter in a garden.

Make the most of evergreens

Evergreens are important plants in any garden, giving it form and structure which persists throughout the year. They are especially valuable in winter when other plants are bare and leafless, but they also have a rôle to play in the spring and summer, forming a perfect backdrop for brightly colored flowers.

Many evergreens such as *Escallonia*, *Choisya* (Mexican orange blossom), *Osmanthus* and *Ceanothus* are a little on the tender side and are generally prone to damage from cold and wind, making mid-spring a better time for planting than the dormant season. Choose a free-draining soil and a reasonably sheltered site.

▲ *Evergreen hedges are both decorative and functional, especially when neatly and attractively trimmed.*

▶ *A mixed planting of evergreen and deciduous subjects will make sure the garden retains structure and interest throughout the year.*

plant evergreens

Bare-root deciduous shrubs should be planted in the dormant season, but mid-spring is the best time to plant evergreens. As the weather is often dry at this time of year, special care must be taken not to let the plants dry out in the weeks following planting.

1 Prepare the planting site by digging it over deeply and adding some well-rotted organic matter such as garden compost or manure, or working in a proprietary planting mix.

2 Dig the planting hole, making sure it is deep enough for the top of the root-ball to be just level with the soil surface. Break up the soil at the base of the planting hole.

3 Evergreens are sometimes supplied as root-balled specimens, with the roots wrapped in netting or burlap. Place the complete root-ball in the planting hole before untying and removing the wrapping material, then fill in with soil and firm in the plant as usual (**left**).

4 Evergreens are particularly prone to wind damage because they have their full complement of leaves at planting time. Wind strips moisture from the leaves, leading to scorching and leaf drop. Protect plants in exposed conditions by erecting a temporary windbreak (**above**).

5 Water the newly-planted shrub thoroughly (**above**). Further watering will be necessary throughout the spring and summer after planting unless the weather is particularly wet; it is important that the soil does not dry out before the plant has a chance to get properly established.

ornamental garden: *plant protection*

Much of a gardener's time is spent protecting plants from various pests and diseases, particularly in spring. Slugs are a major problem, but there are various environmentally friendly methods to deal with them. Roses need regular treatment against diseases, and the battle against weeds goes on.

Take safe action against slugs

Slugs and snails are voracious feeders on plant growth, and can do an enormous amount of damage. The chemicals in proprietary slug pellets are an effective but indiscriminate poison that is also toxic to wild animals and household pets. Conseqently, many gardeners have reservations about using them.

One alternative is trapping. Set shallow dishes containing beer or another bait into the soil to attract and drown slugs (though the rims must be high enough to prevent beneficial beetles from suffering the same fate), or place empty grapefruit or orange halves cut-side down on the soil to attract slugs that must be disposed of the following morning. Aluminum sulfate is also sometimes effective.

Biological control is a relatively new technique that is very promising; it uses a nematode with the tongue-twisting name of *Phasmarhabditis hermaphrodita*. The soil must be reasonably warm for it to work, but it can be used from now on through the summer.

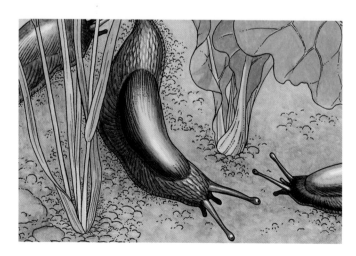

◄ *Slugs usually feed under cover of darkness, and can reduce lush foliage to a skeleton of veins overnight, especially in damp weather.*

CHECK ROSES FOR DISEASE

Roses are subject to a common trio of diseases—blackspot, mildew, and rust. Blackspot is easily recognized because black spots or blotches with an irregular outline cover the foliage, which falls early. Mildew leaves a white powder on young leaves, stunting growth, distorting flowers and spoiling the plant's appearance. Rust is not so obvious at first; small, orange, spore-filled pustules form on the undersides of the leaves, with a pale yellow patch on the top surface. Leaves fall prematurely and the disease can severely weaken the plant.

Check the leaves regularly, including the undersides, for signs of disease. At the first sign, or even before if you have had disease problems previously, begin a regular spraying program. Several appropriate fungicides are on the market, and their use should be alternated for the best results.

keep weeds under control

At this time of year everything in the garden is growing strongly, especially the weeds. Controlling them is important, not only because they make the garden look untidy but because weeds deprive cultivated plants of moisture, nutrients, and light.

1 Weeds are best dealt with while they are still small, when hoeing is very effective (**left**). Choose a dry, blowy day so that the weeds wilt and die quickly. Run the well-sharpened blade of the hoe flat along the soil surface, slicing the seedling weeds off from their roots rather than digging them up.

2 Hoeing is not practical where weeds are growing close to or among cultivated plants because there is too much risk of damage. Hand weeding is often the only option, using a hand fork to remove deep-rooted weeds.

3 Chemical weedkillers are often very effective (**left**). Contact herbicides (such as paraquat) kill the top-growth onto which they are sprayed, but not the roots. They are suitable for young annual weeds but are not so effective on deep-rooted weeds that will regrow.

4 Translocated herbicides (such as glyphosate) are carried to all parts of the plant including the roots, and are best for difficult weeds such as bindweed and couch grass. Great care must be taken to keep accidental splashes of these weedkillers off cultivated plants.

5 Once the soil surface is clear, apply a thick mulch of shredded bark or a similar material (**above.**). This helps keep the ground weed free by preventing the germination of any weed seeds present in the top layer of soil. Any weeds that do appear in the mulch are easy to pull out of the loose material.

◄ *A hand fork is useful to help prise deep rooted weeds out of the soil. Regrowth often occurs from portions of root left behind.*

ornamental garden: *plants in season*

Many shrubs and trees join the throng of flowering plants this month, and increasing numbers of border plants are producing their blooms now, too. The earliest of the spring bulbs are over, but there are still plenty providing a good show of color.

▼ Most Euphorbias *brighten spring with their lime-green flowerheads, but the steely blue leaves often persist right through the winter, too.*

TREES AND SHRUBS

Acer pseudoplatanus 'Brilliantissimum'
(sycamore), *A. rubrum* (red maple)

Amelanchier lamarckii (juneberry)

Berberis darwinii, B. stenophylla (barberry)

Ceanothus (California lilac)

Clematis alpina, C. armandii

Cytisus praecox (broom)

Daphne burkwoodii, D. cneorum

Forsythia

Kerria japonica

Magnolia soulangiana, M. stellata (star
   magnolia)

Malus (apple, crab apple)

Osmanthus burkwoodii, O. delavayii

Pieris

Prunus in variety (ornamental cherry)

Rhododendron

Ribes sanguineum (flowering currant)

Rosmarinus officinalis (rosemary)

Spiraea arguta (bridal wreath)

Ulex europaeus (furze)

Vinca major (greater periwinkle), *V. minor*
   (lesser periwinkle)

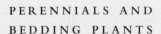

▲ *The stately chalices of* Magnolia ×
soulangiana *blooms are often spoiled
by late frosts in exposed positions.*

▼ *The flowering currant,* Ribes sanguineum, *is
an easily pleased shrub with attractive rosy
flowers and a pungent aroma to the foliage.*

PERENNIALS AND
BEDDING PLANTS

Aurinia saxatilis

Aubrieta

Bellis perennis (common daisy)

Bergenia

Erysimum cheirii (wallflower)

Doronicum (leopard's bane)

Epimedium (barrenwort)

Euphorbia characias, E. polychroma

Helleborus orientalis (lenten rose)

Iberis sempervirens (candytuft)

Myosotis (forget-me-not)

Primula (primrose)

BULBS

Anemone

Bulbocodium vernum

Chionodoxa (glory of the snow)

Convallaria majalis (lily-of-the-valley)

Eythronium revolutum (Western trout lily)

Fritillaria imperialis (crown imperials),
   F. meleagris (snake's head fritillary)

Leucojum vernum (spring snowflake)

Muscari (grape hyacinth)

Narcissus (daffodil)

Tulipa (tulip)

lawns

The lawn is an integral part of the garden, providing a restful green backdrop against which to admire the vibrant colors of the flowers. Lawns that may have looked tired and thin after the stress of the winter should now be growing more strongly, and it's time to help them reach perfection.

Apply lawn fertilizer

In spring, a fertilizer containing high levels of nitrogen will boost growth and help the grass to develop a rich green colour. The phosphates and potash also included in lawn fertilizers stimulate root growth and improve resistance to disease and adverse weather conditions.

▼ *Mid-spring is an ideal time to make a new lawn from seed. Sow in soil that has been carefully prepared to create a fine tilth.*

Fertilizers are available as powders, granules, or liquids. Liquid fertilizers can be applied with a hose-end dilutor; they are fast acting and give a rapid response, but they can be expensive for large lawns. Dry fertilizers can be applied by hand but it is very difficult to achieve an even distribution, and the result can be patchy. The best method is to use a fertilizer distributor, a small hopper on wheels that applies the fertilizer at a given rate when pushed up and

down the lawn. Take care to cover all the grass evenly, and do not overlap strips or leave a gap between them because this will show up as differently colored growth later on.

CONTROL LAWN WEEDS

Where there are only a few, isolated weeds in the lawn they can be treated individually, either by digging them out with a narrow-bladed trowel or special lawn-weeding tool, or by giving them individual doses of weedkiller. "Spot" weedkillers come in the form of wax sticks, impregnated sponges, aerosols, and ready-to-use sprays.

If weeds are more widespread over the lawn surface, an overall application of selective weedkiller is necessary. This should be applied shortly after fertilizing, or you can use a proprietary "weed and feed" product that applies the two together. Be very careful not to allow lawn weedkillers to drift on to cultivated plants or neighboring gardens. Tiny amounts carried on the breeze are enough to do a great deal of damage to other plants.

▶ *Grass seed should germinate rapidly in warm, moist spring weather. This is a good time to repair worn patches by oversowing them.*

mow and edge lawns

A perfect, velvet-textured, emerald-green lawn is the envy of all who see it, but many gardeners seem to find it impossible to achieve. Understanding and employing the correct mowing technique is one simple way to greatly improve the quality of the turf.

1 Now the grass has started to grow rapidly it will need cutting more frequently—once a week at least, and twice a week as spring moves into summer. Before mowing, clear stones, fir cones, sticks, and other debris from the lawn. If you can, wait until the dew has dried.

2 Set the blades at the right height (**right**); scalping is a very common mistake. At this time of year the grass should be left between ¾in/18mm and 1¼in/30mm high, reducing to a minimum of ½in/12mm high in summer (¾in/18mm is better for most lawns).

3 Mow the grass in parallel strips up and down the lawn (**above**). If the mower has a rear roller it will produce the light and dark stripes favored by many people; in this case it is important to keep the mowing strips as straight and even as possible for the best effect.

4 Next time the lawn is mown, work at right angles to the last direction of cut—across the lawn rather than up and down. Alternating the direction at each cut makes sure that the surface of the lawn remains even, and helps control lawn weeds and weed grasses.

5 Once the mowing is finished, trim the edges to give the lawn a neat appearance (**above**). Use long-handled edging shears or, to save time, a powered edger. If the edges are ragged after the winter, recut them in spring with a half-moon edging iron, using a plank as a straight edge.

kitchen garden: *planting and sowing*

Time vegetable sowings so that you have a steady harvest through the summer, without a glut of crops maturing simultaneously. Be particularly careful with vegetables that have a short period of use before they spoil, such as lettuces, which run to seed, and peas, which become tough.

Continue sowing vegetables

As the weather becomes warmer, more and more vegetable crops can be sown. Among those that can be sown outdoors directly where they are to grow are beets, Swiss chard, various beans, carrot, kohlrabi, lettuce, pea, radish, scallion, salsify, scorzonera, spinach, and turnip. When you sow the crops, spacings can be varied according to the size of plant that is required.

Some vegetables are sown now in a seedbed and transplanted to their cropping positions later. They include broccoli, Brussels sprouts, calabrese, cauliflowers, summer, fall, and winter cabbages, kale, and leeks.

SOW CROPS FOR SUCCESSION

"Little and often" is a good idea when it comes to sowing many vegetables for home use. This insures that crops can be picked and used when they are young and tender, and there will be a further supply following from a later sowing. Crops that can be grown in succession include beets, cabbage, carrot, cauliflower, lettuce, pea, radish, spinach, and turnip.

Sow short rows of the crops in question at two to four week intervals, or select a range of different varieties to mature at different times throughout the season.

◄ *Try to keep the vegetable garden weed-free. Supply supports to plants that need them at an early stage of growth for the best results.*

plant onion sets

Onions are easy to grow from sets (small, immature bulbs). It is best to buy heat-treated sets because they are less likely to run to flower prematurely than those that are untreated.

1 Onions need an open position in fertile, well-worked soil which has been broken down to fine crumbs (**right**). Work a little general fertilizer into the soil immediately before planting.

2 The sets can be planted in drills made deep enough for the tops of the bulbs to be just showing above soil level when planted. Space them 2–4in/5–10cm apart in rows 10in/25cm apart: the wider spacing will produce larger bulbs.

3 In fine, very light soil, drills are not necessary—the sets can simply be pushed into the ground at the correct spacing (**left**). On heavier soil, however, this compresses the soil at the base of the set, making it difficult for the roots to penetrate; the onion sets then push themselves out of the ground as the roots start to grow.

4 Birds are often a nuisance, tugging the freshly-planted sets out of the ground. One way to avoid this is to trim away the dead, brown leaves at the tip of the set with scissors or secateurs before planting (**below**): these dead leaves form a convenient "handle" by which birds can tweak the sets out of the soil.

5 Water the sets shortly after planting if the weather turns dry, and keep them free of competition from weeds. Heat-treated sets are often a little slower than untreated sets to start into growth, but they soon catch up.

◀ *It is possible to obtain a satisfying crop of perfect, golden-skinned onions from sets planted in the vegetable garden in mid-spring.*

pollination

Plants reproduce sexually by means of seed. The seed needs to be dispersed as widely as possible, but the plant is at a disadvantage because it is in one spot. Animals and birds, however, can move about freely; one of the main ways plants disperse seed is by encouraging an animal or bird to carry it away. Embedding the seed within a sweet, juicy, edible fruit will certainly attract a range of creatures to help distribute the seed far and wide.

The process of bearing fruit is therefore usually inextricably linked with sexual reproduction and the formation of seed. In order to form seed, pollen grains from the male part of a flower must be transferred to the stigma that is attached to the ovary, the female part of a flower, a process known as pollination.

Pollination is followed by fertilization when the male and female cells fuse to produce an embryo, or seed, which swells to form a fruit. If pollination and fertilization do not occur, the fruit generally (though not always) fails to form. When we grow fruit trees and bushes in our gardens, therefore, we need to make sure that pollination and fertilization of the flowers can take place.

Cross-pollination and self-pollination

Many flowers achieve pollination very easily, without the need for any outside help. Although there can be separate male and female flowers (sometimes on the same plant or sometimes on separate plants), the majority of species bear flowers containing both male and female sexual organs. Sometimes pollen can fertilize the female cells of the same flower (self-pollination), but often the flowers are "self-incompatible." This means that the pollen needs to come from a different flower, or different plant or variety of the same species (cross-pollination).

Many tree fruits such as apples and pears need to be cross-pollinated to bear a good crop of fruit. Some varieties are partially self-fertile so that a small crop will be carried even if no other fruit trees are nearby, but the crop will be greatly increased by cross-pollination. As insects are responsible for pollination, trees must be within insect-flying distance of suitable partners.

▲ *Apple blossom must be pollinated before a crop can be carried. It is usually necessary to grow at least two compatible varieties.*

Pollinating partners

The two varieties of tree grown as partners must be compatible, and must flower at the same time. There are a few incompatible varieties; for example, 'Cox's Orange Pippin' will not pollinate, or be pollinated by, 'Kidd's Orange Red' or 'Jupiter'. Fruit catalogs give details and also have information on flowering times, dividing them into early, mid-season and late, usually indicating this by numbers 1, 2 and 3. Choose two varieties from the same pollinating group—for instance, 'William's Pride' and 'Cheholis', or 'Golden Sentinal' and 'North Pole'. Varieties from adjoining groups usually have sufficient overlap to be successful, but a variety from Group 1 will not pollinate a variety from Group 3.

Some varieties of apple and pear have an extra set of chromosomes and are known as triploids: they will not pollinate other varieties and need to be pollinated by two varieties themselves. 'Jonagold', 'Crispin' and

▼ *Pear blossom: pear trees need to be cross-pollinated in order to produce a decent-sized crop of fruit.*

HAND POLLINATION

In some cases, fruit tree blossoms need to be pollinated by hand. This is normally either because they are in flower very early in the year when there are few flying insects about, or because they are being grown in a greenhouse or conservatory where insect access is difficult. Peaches, apricots, and nectarines are the usual candidates: they are self-fertile, and can be pollinated by blossom from the same tree. Wait until several flowers are open and the pollen can be seen on the anthers. Use a small, soft brush such as a makeup brush to lightly dust each flower, transferring the pollen from one flower to the other.

'Bramley's Seedling' are triploid apples, while 'Merton Pride' and 'Jargonelle' are triploid pears.

Looking after insect pollinators

Bees and other insects are very efficient pollinators of tree fruit. Make sure that you never spray the trees with insecticides during fruit-flowering time.

greenhouse: *general tasks*

Before greenhouse-raised plants can be set outside when the risk of frost is over, they must be hardened off so that the move to cooler conditions is not too much of a shock. Some young plants will be ready for a move to larger pots. With increasing sunlight, greenhouse shading becomes necessary.

Harden off young plants

The move from the warm, sheltered conditions of a greenhouse to the rougher, colder world outdoors can result in a serious check to plant growth. Plants that are moved straight from the greenhouse to their growing positions in the garden frequently seem to "stand still" for a while until they adjust, often losing almost all the advantage they had gained from an early start indoors.

Plants should be gradually accustomed to outdoor conditions over a week or two, a process known as hardening off. A cold frame is ideal for this. Transfer plants from the heated greenhouse to an unheated frame, at first with the roof closed, then gradually increasing the ventilation until the roof is left off altogether. If a frame is not available, plants to be hardened off can be moved from the greenhouse to a sheltered position outside during the warmest part of the day, moving them back inside when conditions get cooler. Gradually increase the length of time they are outdoors before moving them to their permanent planting positions.

◄ *Make sure bedding plants are thoroughly hardened off before moving them to their permanent positions in the open garden.*

CHECK GREENHOUSE TEMPERATURES

Although the weather is now warmer, it is still too early to turn off greenhouse heaters at night. Continue to check the maximum/minimum thermometer regularly to insure that frost-free conditions are maintained. As long as an efficient thermostat is fitted there is no need to worry about wasting fuel; the heater will not start up unless triggered by low temperatures. On sunny days excessively high temperatures will be a problem though, unless the greenhouse is well ventilated. By now the weather should be reasonably mild, so if you are going to be away during the day, open the vents before you leave (unless you have automatic vent openers to do the job for you).

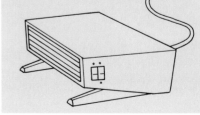

pot up seedlings and young plants

Warmer weather and longer daylight hours mean plants in the greenhouse are growing fast. Move developing seedlings and young plants into larger pots as soon as they are ready—delaying the move will mean a check to their growth. Take care to disturb the roots as little as possible during the transplanting process.

APPLY GREENHOUSE SHADING

Direct sun through the greenhouse glass is sufficiently strong to scorch the foliage of many plants, and shading of at least part of the greenhouse is usually necessary now. Start by shading the roof, then add shading down the side of the greenhouse if necessary as the season progresses. There are various forms of shading, including external or internal blinds, rolls of netting, and paint-on preparations. The paint-on shading usually becomes translucent when wet, automatically allowing extra light to penetrate on dull, rainy days.

1 The size of pot required depends on the size of the plants, but 3½in/8cm pots are usually the most practical first pot. Plants already in individual pots can be moved up to the next size container; do not be tempted to move them to a larger pot than this.

2 Seedlings should be handled by their seed leaves; the young stems are easily damaged. Fill a pot loosely with potting mix and make a hole in the soil with a dibble (**above**). Lower the seedling into it, making sure the roots are at the base of the hole. Firm the soil very gently.

3 Plants are ready for potting on when their roots become visible through the drainage holes of the pot (**above**). Water them well a few hours beforehand, then turn the pot upside down and tap the rim on the edge of the staging to remove the plant.

4 Place a little soil mix in the base of the larger pot and stand the root-ball on it. Fill in round the sides with fresh mix and firm it down; water well. Place newly-potted plants in a partially shaded place for a few days to recover from the disturbance of transplanting.

greenhouse: *planting and sowing*

The season is now sufficiently advanced to start sowing those more tender crops, such as melons and pole beans. Pole beans are planted out in the vegetable garden once the risk of frost is over, but in many areas melons will give the best crop if grown to maturity in the greenhouse.

Sow melons

Although they like warm conditions, melons are not difficult to grow in a greenhouse, and several varieties are suitable for growing in a cold frame or outdoors even in relatively cool climates. The fruits are sweet and aromatic, making a very enjoyable summer crop. Sow two seeds per 3½in/8cm pot of soilless potting mix. The seeds are smaller than those of cucumber, but should be sown on their sides in the same way to reduce the risk of rotting. A temperature of 64–75°F/18–24°C is suitable for germination. The plants are grown on in much the same way as greenhouse cucumbers, but the flowers will need pollinating to make sure good fruit is set. 'Sweet Granite' is one of the hardiest varieties, and 'Ambrosia Hybrid', 'Crème de la Crème Hybrid',

'Honey Pearl', and 'Supersun Hybrid' are also good for outdoor culture (under cloches or in a frame in cold regions). Seek advice from your local garden center which melons really need greenhouse cultivation.

> ### SOW BUSH AND POLE BEANS IN POTS
>
> Although both bush and pole beans can be sown directly where they are to grow once the weather is suitable, raising the plants indoors will enable you to pick much earlier crops. Bush beans have small seeds and can be sown in a seed tray, spacing the seeds to give about 18 plants per tray. Pole beans do best when sown individually in 3½in/8cm pots. Fill the tray or pots with sowing mix, firm it down, and sow the seeds by pushing them below the surface. Cover with clear plastic propagator tops.

◄ *Sow melons now for a very welcome crop later on in the summer. Select varieties suitable for the conditions you can provide.*

► *Tomatoes can be planted in the greenhouse in mid-spring. Pests and diseases must be dealt with to guarantee a good crop.*

plant tomatoes in the greenhouse border

Tomatoes are the most popular food crop for growing in the greenhouse, and can give high yields of fruit in the summer. Young plants are ready for setting out in their cropping positions once the first flower buds start to appear.

1 The greenhouse border is a good place to grow tomatoes because they will be less likely to suffer water shortages than if they are grown in containers. Good quality soil is necessary, preferably enriched with plenty of well-rotted compost or manure.

2 Turn the plants out of their pots by tapping the base of the upturned pot sharply. Dig a hole in the border with a trowel and plant the tomatoes, firming them in well (**right**). Water thoroughly after planting.

3 Greenhouse tomatoes are usually grown as single-stem cordons that need to be supported to enable the crop to develop properly. One method of support is to provide each plant with a tall bamboo cane, tying the stem to the cane at intervals as it grows (**left**). Take care not to damage the stem by tying it too tightly.

4 Another popular method is to train the plants up twine (**below**). Anchor a length of garden twine in the soil near the plant with a hook, or tie it loosely around the tomato stem below the bottom leaf. Take the other end of the twine up to a wire running level with the eaves. Twist the plant's stem round the twine as it grows.

5 Growing bags are a popular alternative to planting in the greenhouse border. Set two or three tomato plants per bag, cutting a cross in the plastic and folding it back to make a planting hole. Frequent watering is essential.

late spring

The weather is mild and there's often a good deal of sunshine. Spring blossom mingles with the early blooms of summer, and foliage still has a wonderful freshness. Gardeners should enjoy the last weeks of spring while they prepare for summer in what is always one of the year's busiest times.

In most areas the risk of damaging night frosts will be over toward the end of the month but in the early days, and in colder regions, you will need to remain on your guard. If your garden happens to be in a frost pocket, you may need to be much more cautious than neighbors only a short distance away who are in a more favored position.

This is a good time to plant up hanging baskets, window boxes, and tubs which are very valuable for injecting concentrated splashes of color in the garden and around the house. They are increasingly popular, with a wide range of new and unusual "patio plants" available at garden centers. Keep them under cover or in a sheltered position for a few days after planting in the early part of the month. Spring bedding plants are past their best now, and

need to be cleared out to make way for the summer bedding—but don't forget to sow spring-bedding plants for next year's display.

Plants are growing strongly now but need to be regularly fed and weeded; pests must be controlled promptly. In the vegetable garden, tender crops such as pole beans, bush beans, and zucchini can be sown safely out of doors.

Finally, a pond is a great addition to any garden, adding a special sort of tranquillity with its shimmering water and colorful plants.

The gentle splash of a fountain or waterfall is an extra delight. This is the best time of year to build a garden pool, and you can rest assured that you are creating a feature that is bound to be enjoyed for many years to come.

▶ *Well-planted containers are particularly useful for adding color to the patio. Wait until frosts are over before putting them outside.*

LATE SPRING TASKS

General

- Check for pests on plants and treat promptly
- Feed strong growing plants
- Treat perennial weeds with herbicide

Ornamental garden

- Plant up hanging baskets, window boxes, and tubs
- Continue staking border plants
- Weed annual seedlings and thin them as necessary
- Remove spring-bedding plants; plant out summer bedding
- Plant dahlias
- Deadhead Narcissus (daffodils). Leave the foliage in place until six weeks after the last flowers fade
- Sow winter-flowering Viola (pansies), and biennials such as Erysimum (wallflowers), Dianthus barbatus (sweet williams) and Myosotis (forget-me-nots)
- Water recently-planted trees and shrubs if the weather is dry
- Trim evergreen hedges as necessary

▲ *Plant up containers with a range of summer bedding plants for a pleasing display.*

Lawns

- Lower the height of the mower blades to give a closer cut. Tackle weeds with a spot weedkiller

Water garden

- Construct and plant up new ponds. Introduce fish once the plants are established
- In existing ponds, divide deep-water aquatics and plant new varieties
- Feed fish, but be careful not to overfeed
- Watch for aphids on water lily leaves, and submerge affected leaves to allow fish to eat them

▼ *Strawing around strawberry plants helps protect the fruit from slug damage and soil splashes.*

Kitchen garden

- Water as necessary, timing the watering carefully for maximum crops
- Continue to make successional sowings for continuity of supply
- Plant out hardened-off pole and bush beans once the risk of frost is over. Sow pole beans and bush beans outdoors
- Thin out seedlings in the rows. Thin carrots late in the evening to avoid attracting carrot root fly. Stake peas
- Plant vegetables in pots and growing bags
- Check plums for silver leaf disease
- Reduce codling moth damage with pheromone traps
- Straw around strawberries and net the plants against birds

Greenhouse

- Ventilate the greenhouse more freely, and water more frequently as the weather gets warmer
- Train and support cucumbers, melons, and tomatoes
- Continue pricking out seedlings and potting up rooted cuttings as necessary
- "Stop" pelargoniums and fuchsias by pinching out the growing points to make them bushier

ornamental garden: *general tasks*

Hardy annuals sown earlier will now be making good headway, and perennial border plants need some attention to keep them in good shape. If you want to propagate garden shrubs, layering is often successful where other methods fail. Pests continue to increase in numbers this month.

Check plants for pests

Garden pests of all sorts continue to thrive in the warmer weather, and plants need to be checked regularly and pest infestations treated

promptly. One of the most troublesome pests is vine weevil. Greenhouse plants are most at risk, but the adult weevils spread outside as the weather becomes warmer. Outdoor weevil activity starts now, and peaks between early summer and mid-fall. You may see leaves that have had characteristic notches bitten out of their margins by the adult weevils

◀ *Grubs of the vine weevil eat away at a plant's root system until it can no longer support the top growth and the whole plant collapses.*

but it is the damage done by the grubs that is more serious: they feed on the roots and can completely destroy the root system.

Suspect vine weevil grubs where plants suddenly wilt and die for no apparent reason, especially plants in containers.

A biological control containing nematodes can be applied now, provided there is a reasonably warm spell of weather. This will be effective against larvae that emerged from eggs laid last fall.

STAKING BORDER PLANTS

Continue to provide supports for border plants from an early stage (see page 513). As the shoots grow, train them gently to the support; tie in where necessary with soft twine, plastic-covered twist ties or raffia. Where twiggy sticks are used, the border plants should be making sufficient growth to cover them almost completely.

Do not allow stems to flop before putting supports in, or they will stay kinked.

This type of support can be raised as the plant grows, but great care is necessary to avoid snapping the stems.

Stakes that link together can be arranged in patterns to provide support for almost any size and shape of plant.

Taller plants such as Delphiniums are likely to need individual stakes for the flowering stems.

increase shrubs by layering

This is a simple way of propagating shrubs with low branches. Many shrubs are suitable for propagation by layering, including magnolias and rhododendrons, that are otherwise difficult to increase. Select a suitable low-growing branch that can be bent down to soil level. It should be a healthy, strong-growing shoot of the previous season's growth.

1 Bend the shoot down to the ground and mark the position where the stem touches the soil, about 9–12in/23–30cm behind the tip of the shoot (**right**). Dig this area over well with a trowel, then dig a hole about 4in/10cm deep with a straight, flat side furthest from the plant.

2 Bend the shoot down again to check the position of the hole. When the stem is lying at the base of the hole, the top 9in/23cm of the shoot should stick out of the ground, held upright by the straight side. Strip the leaves and leaf stalks from the length of stem to be buried.

3 Where the stem must be bent to pull it down into the hole, make a small cut on its underside with a sharp knife (**left**). This injury to the plant will encourage growth.

4 Peg the stem into the hole with a piece of bent wire (**below**), return the soil to bury the stem completely. Tread the soil gently but firmly to firm it back down.

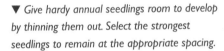

▼ *Give hardy annual seedlings room to develop by thinning them out. Select the strongest seedlings to remain at the appropriate spacing.*

5 Tie the protruding tip of the shoot to a stake in order to keep it upright and then water the soil regularly to keep it moist. Roots will form on the buried portion of stem over the summer, and once the layer is well rooted it can be dug up and separated from the parent.

5 5 9

alpine gardens

Alpine plants contain some of the loveliest species there are. Their growth is neat and compact, and in late spring the plants are often smothered with masses of flowers in brilliant, jewel-bright shades. They need special conditions in which to grow but these are not hard to provide, and alpine plants should be included in every garden. Alpines, as their name suggests, originate from

mountainous regions. True alpines come from areas above the tree line, but the term is often more loosely applied to include plants from lower altitudes that should more correctly be called rock garden plants.

Alpines have a range of features that help them cope with the inhospitable conditions in which they have to grow. They have adapted to low temperatures in strong, direct sun, chilling winds, and poor or almost non-existent soil. Their growth is low, often ground hugging to avoid being battered by the wind; their low, spreading habit also helps them withstand the weight of heavy winter snow without being crushed. Since wind causes high moisture loss from the leaves as the constantly moving air whips it away, alpine plants often have leaves that cut water loss to a minimum—they may be very narrow, or have a waxy or hairy coating that also protects them from the intense, remorseless sunshine of high altitudes. Soil on the high mountainsides is poor and shallow, and plants often grow tucked into the crevices of rocks where they receive some shelter. They need to manage on very little water because the rainfall is low, and water soon drains away in the rocky ground.

Such plants might seem to be ideal for gardens—able to cope with almost any adverse conditions. Of course, this is not really the case. While they are perfectly adapted to life on the mountain tops, they may not adjust so well to some of the features of life at lower altitudes. The main problem is excess rainfall, particularly in the winter. Alpine plants must have free-draining conditions, otherwise they will rot away.

◀ *Alpine rock gardens contain plants that can deal with a range of unfriendly climatic conditions and are extremely tough.*

Rock gardens

To grow well, most alpines need an area to themselves
where they can be provided with the correct conditions.
This often takes the form of a rock garden—a sloping
site studded with rocks to simulate the mountainside.
Care should be taken with the construction in order to
make a rock garden an attractive feature; the rocks
should be laid as natural-looking outcrops, not dotted
randomly over the surface. Since about one-third of each
rock will be covered by soil, fairly large pieces are
necessary to make an impact, and they can be expensive.

▲ *True alpine plants are found in mountainous*
regions above the tree line, but the term is often
used to describe plants from lower altitudes.

In order to insure free-draining conditions, place
a layer of rubble at the base of the site chosen for the
rock garden, then top it with good quality, light topsoil.
Set the rocks in position with care, making sure that the
horizontal strata lines are running in the same direction.
Plant the alpines in appropriate positions, using special
alpine plant soil mix to fill in around them. When the
whole rock garden is completed, finish it off by
topdressing the surface with gravel or stone chippings,
tucking it around the necks of the plants.

Raised beds

A raised bed for alpines is an option where there is
insufficient room for a full-scale rock garden, and has the
advantage of bringing the plants nearer eye-level where
their miniature charms can be appreciated more easily.
Place rubble in the base, and fill the bed with gritty
topsoil; a number of attractive, carefully positioned
rocks on the soil surface will improve the bed's
appearance. Plant the alpines as before, finishing off
with a top-dressing of gravel.

ALPINES IN WALLS

Dry stone walls provide an ideal place to set a few alpine plants. They
can be planted in the top of the wall if there is a suitable gap that can be
filled with some gritty topsoil, and they can also be tucked into the
crevices on the face of the wall. Use a very
narrow trowel or a spoon handle to push a little
soil mix into the crevice and then
carefully insert the roots of the plant,
firming it in with more soil. *Lewisias,*
Campanulas, Gentians, Dianthus, Sedums,
Saxifrages and many others will thrive in
these conditions, and enhance the wall
with their flowers and foliage.

ornamental garden: *planting and sowing*

Most gardeners aim for a good display of flowers for as many months as possible, and now that spring bedding is past its best it's time to set out the summer-flowering plants and containers for the patio. Think a little further ahead to providing color for the fall and winter, too.

Replace spring plants with summer bedding

In most areas spring-bedding plants will have passed their best. Toward the end of the month the weather should be warm enough to plant out summer bedding to replace them, but make sure the plants have been hardened off sufficiently.

Fork over the soil, removing weeds along with the old plants, and work a sprinkling of general fertilizer into the surface. Turn the new plants out of their flats and disentangle the roots: bedding plants grown in individual cells establish more quickly because the amount of root damage is reduced. Plant with a trowel, firming in well, and water in the plants as each section of the bed is completed.

PLANNING AHEAD

Dahlias provide wonderfully colorful blooms in late summer and early fall, and now is the time to plant the overwintered tubers, or cuttings rooted from them earlier in the spring. Since cuttings should be hardened off properly, and must not be planted out until all risk of frost is over, in some particularly cold areas it will be necessary to wait a little while longer.

Flowers are at a premium in the winter and early spring, but winter-flowering viola (pansies) can be relied upon to put up a good show. Sow them now, preferably in a cold frame, for planting out in the fall. Flowers will be produced in mild spells throughout the winter, with a bigger flush in early spring.

▲ *The cheerful yellow glow of marigolds will add life and color to your display of summer bedding plants.*

▶ *Once the display of spring flowers is past its best, containers can be planted up with subjects to provide summer interest.*

plant up containers

Colorful tubs, windowboxes, and hanging baskets are immensely popular, and make very striking, long-lasting displays. Now that the risk of frosts is virtually over it should be safe to plant them and set them outside.

1 Garden centers usually have a good selection of suitable plants at this time of year. Select a variety of upright and trailing subjects, in a range of complementary colors; don't forget to include foliage plants as well as flowering ones.

2 Make sure that your containers have sufficient drainage holes, and enlarge them if necessary. Cover the drainage holes with a layer of coarse material such as large stones or crocks from broken clay pots which makes sure that excess water can freely drain away (**right**).

3 Two-thirds fill the container with potting mix, and mix in some slow-release fertilizer and water-retaining granules (**left**). These absorb moisture and "hold" it in the mix; they considerably cut down the frequency of watering.

4 Arrange the plants, still in their pots, on the surface of the soil until the design is to your liking. Aim to balance tall, upright plants with trailing ones, and to achieve a harmonious combination of colors and foliage textures.

5 Use a trowel to plant up the container, filling in with more soil mix as necessary. Firm the plants well (**above**) and water them well. If possible, leave the planted containers in a sheltered, partially shaded place for a day or two before moving them to their final positions.

texture and color

Most people like a bright and cheerful scene, but color needs to be used with care if it is not to lose its effect. An unplanned "riot of colour" can be very effective in a small area—a hanging basket or tub, for example—but if repeated over the whole garden it has a restless, unsatisfying effect, making the onlooker tired and uneasy.

The color wheel is often used by garden planners as a useful reference tool. A simple color wheel takes colors in the order that they appear in the rainbow—red, orange, yellow, green, blue, and violet—and arranges them in a circle, with each color occupying an equal-sized segment. Colors that are adjacent in the circle

▼ *A cool, relaxing retreat on a hot summer's day: a garden carefully planned in shades of blue, white, and green.*

harmonize, while those that are opposite contrast. More complex color wheels use a much wider range of shades and hues, but the principle is the same.

Different colors have different effects on the onlooker. The hot colors—red, orange, and strong yellow—are vibrant and exciting, while the cool colors—blue, green and white—are restful and relaxing. Color can therefore be used to create the right sort of atmosphere in different parts of the garden.

Intense colors are more effective if they are given a contrasting background; brilliant scarlet flowers will stand out better against a plain green hedge, for example, than they would in a bed filled with other brightly-colored flowers. Use the color wheel to find the greatest contrast to a particular shade (it will appear directly opposite it).

▶ *Yellow flowers are given emphasis when in the vicinity of violet flowers, as the two colors are opposite each other on the color wheel.*

Pastel shades, where the pure hues have been mixed with white, are good for toning down strong colors and helping them integrate more successfully into the garden. Pink, salmon, pale yellow, and cream, for instance, have a cooling, calming effect on intense red, orange and yellow, while pale blue, pale green, and gray help to lighten an otherwise rather dark selection of hues.

When planning a color layout, it is usually better to place the strongest, brightest colors to the front, with paler shades (particularly misty greens, blues, and grays) farthest away. This also helps to make a small area appear larger. You may prefer to use brightly-colored plants as accents, drawing the eye to certain features, perhaps foreshortening a long, narrow border. Whatever the effect you wish to create, the result will be far more successful if it is planned rather than planted at random.

Textures

Careful use of textures can give a whole new dimension to plant associations, both visually and to the touch.

Many different textures are exhibited by flowers and foliage: bold, spiky, lacy, dainty, hazy, feathery, soft, furry, rough, sculptured, and veined, for instance. Groups of plants with contrasting textures can be very effective. Large, bold leaves of a hosta or bergenia make a perfect foil for the feathery flowers of gypsophila or astilbe, for example. Remember that plants can be stroked, as well as seen; the soft velvet of *Stachys byzantina* (lamb's ears) or *Verbascum* (mullein) is intensely tactile.

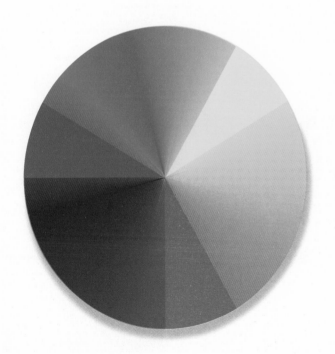

◀ *The color wheel: primary colors, red, yellow, and blue are opposite the secondary colors, green, violet, and orange.*

CHOOSING COLORS

Many more plants in seed catalogs are now available in single colors as well as mixtures, which always used to be more popular. This makes it much easier to plan beds and borders effectively. In fact, mail-order catalogs are more likely to carry single colors than garden centers or shops, and it is sometimes necessary to go to the larger seed merchants for the best selection of varieties.

plants in season

Alpine and rock garden plants will be producing a bright display at this time of year. Wisteria and laburnum are draped with long racemes of colorful flowers, but rhododendrons and azaleas are perhaps the most striking plants this month.

▼ *The fragrant flowers of wisteria are often among the most spectacular blooms in the garden in the late spring.*

▲ The glossy, aromatic leaves of Choisya ternata *(Mexican orange blossom) are a bright lime-green in the variety 'Sundance'.*

▼ Ceanothus *'Concha' : dense clusters of brilliant, sky-blue flowers make this a popular plant for a sheltered spot.*

PERENNIALS AND BEDDING PLANTS

Ajuga reptans
Aurinia saxatilis (Alyssum saxatile)
   (gold dust)
Aquilegia (columbine)
Armeria (sea pink)
Aubrieta
Dicentra spectabilis (bleeding heart)
Euphorbia (spurge)
Geranium
Helianthemum (rock rose)
Iberis (candytuft)
Lithodora diffusa
Primula (primrose)
Saxifraga umbrosa

TREES AND SHRUBS

Aesculus hippocastanum (horse chestnut)
Berberis (barberry)
Buddleja globosa
Ceanothus (California lilac)
Cercis siliquastrum (Judas tree)
Choisya ternata (Mexican orange blossom)
Clematis montana and large-flowered hybrids
Crataegus (hawthorn)
Crinodendron hookerianum (lantern tree)
Davidia involucrata (handkerchief tree)
Deutzia gracilis, D. rosea
Genista hispanica (Spanish gorse)
Kerria japonica
Kolkwitzia amabilis (beauty bush)
Laburnum
Magnolia soulangiana
Malus (apple, crab apple)
Paeonia (peony)
Pieris
Potentilla fruticosa (cinquefoil)
Prunus (ornamental cherry)
Rhododendron (including azaleas)
Robinia hispida, R. margaretta
Rosmarinus officinalis (rosemary)
Sambucus racemosa plumosa 'Aurea'
   (red-berried elder)
Sorbus aria (whitebeam), S. aucuparia
   (mountain ash)
Spiraea arguta (bridal wreath)
Syringa (lilac)
Viburnum opulus (guelder rose),
   V. plicatum (Japanese snowball bush)
Weigela
Wisteria

BULBS

Allium
Anemone (windflower)
Hyacinthoides non-scripta (English bluebell)
Convallaria majalis (lily-of-the-valley)
Fritillaria imperialis (crown imperial)
Hyacinthus (hyacinth)
Leucojum aestivum (summer snowflake)
Tulipa (tulip)

567

water garden: *ponds*

There is a water feature to suit every garden, no matter how small, and it is well worth taking the trouble to build one. Apart from the enjoyment you will gain from the sparkling water, the fish, and the colorful pond plants, all sorts of beneficial wildlife will be attracted to your garden pool, as well.

Add moving water to ponds

A garden pool is always attractive, even when the reflective surface of the water is completely still—but it is even more enjoyable when the water moves. It sparkles and throws off light, making a pleasant splashing sound and helping to keep oxygen levels high for healthy fish and plants.

Movement can be provided by fountains or waterfalls, and large pools can incorporate both. A submersible pump is the easiest way to power them. Fountain kits with a variety of heads for different effects are extremely easy to install once a power supply is made available (use a professional electrician for this). Waterfalls require a little more work. Natural-looking cascades can be tricky to build; avoid preformed fiberglass waterfall sections, and construct a water course lined with butyl, concealed by flat slabs of natural stone to provide the drops.

▼ *The splash of moving water, whether from a waterfall or a fountain, helps to bring a garden pool to life.*

WILDLIFE AND THE POND

A surprising variety of wildlife will find its way to your garden once a pool is established, and much of it will be helpful in your fight against garden pests. Frogs, toads, and newts eat large numbers of insects, and their feeding area extends much farther than the immediate environs of the pond. Birds, who are also valuable pest controllers, will visit the pond in order to drink and bathe, and slug-munching predators will quench their thirst here, too. The spectacular dragonflies that can be seen darting over the surface are not only colorful and attractive but fearsome insect predators. A small "beach" and shallow area of the pond fringed by marginal plants will encourage a range of creatures to visit, and insure that mammals can reach the water safely.

how to make a garden pond

Late spring is the perfect time of year to construct and stock a garden pool. It's an easier process than many people think, and a pond enhances any style of garden. Always site a pool in an open, sunny position, away from overhanging trees.

1 Select the type of pond base you require. Molded fiberglass ponds are popular (**below**), but there is a restricted choice of shapes and sizes. A flexible liner can be used for any shape of pool and is easy to transport home. Butyl rubber has the longest life, but laminated PVC is cheaper.

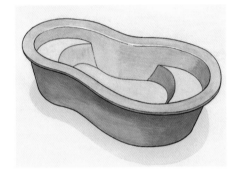

2 Mark out the shape of the pool with rope or a trickle of sand (**below**); simple, flowing shapes are best. Excavate the soil to the correct depth, sloping the sides slightly and creating a shelf for marginal plants some 10in/25cm wide and 8in/20cm below water level. Check that the top of the pond is absolutely level.

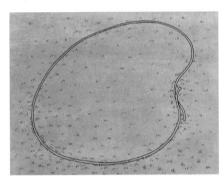

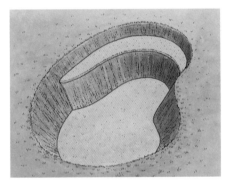

3 You should then remove sharp stones or any other objects that may puncture the liner and cover the base and shelves of the excavation with a smooth layer of sand (**left**). Stretch the liner across the hole; however, it is important not to try to drape the liner into it. You should then weight down the liner edges with bricks.

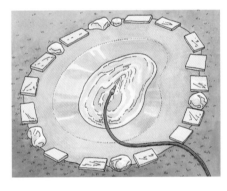

4 Lay a hose in the center of the liner and turn the water on (**above**). The weight of water will gradually stretch the liner and pull it into the hole, moulding it to fit the excavation perfectly. Once the pond is full, trim away surplus liner to leave a 6in/15cm margin all around that can be concealed with a stone edging to the pool.

◄ *Ponds will look after themselves as long as you get the right balance between plants, the wildlife, and water. Make a pool as large as you can, with a minimum depth of 2ft/60cm: very small ponds are the most difficult to keep in good condition.*

water garden: *ponds*

Fish are not essential in a garden pond, but they add a great deal of interest to it and will prevent mosquitoes becoming a problem. Aquatic plants such as Nymphaea (water lilies) are often the crowning glories of a pool; this is the perfect time to plant them, or to divide existing plants.

Introduce fish to garden pools

Any area of still water is likely to be visited by mosquitoes for the purpose of laying eggs, and once the eggs hatch swarms of insects can make life in the garden very unpleasant. Adding fish to the pond provides the perfect answer; they will eat the larvae as soon as they hatch and prevent them reaching adulthood. They are also very attractive, and add life and movement to the water.

Goldfish are the most common type of fish for ponds. They are cheap and easy to buy, and usually problem free. Golden Orfe are also popular with their long, slender shapes and attractive, light gold color.

Shubunkins are a type of goldfish which have mottled shades of silver, blue, red, brown, and black, while Fantails have attractive double tails.

The recommended stocking rate for fish to keep their environment healthy is three to five fish per square yard/meter of surface area of water.

▲ *When stocking fish ponds, it is important to bear in mind the recommended stocking rate of three to five fish per square yard/meter.*

DIVIDE DEEP-WATER AQUATICS

Aquatic plants such as *Nymphaea* (water lilies) and *Aponogeton distachyos* (water hawthorn) eventually grow too large for their planting baskets, and this has a detrimental effect on their growth and flowering. They can be divided at this time of year, giving you extra plants while improving the existing ones.

Lift the basket out of the water (it may take two people) and remove the plant; very overgrown plants may need to have the basket cut away. Divide the plant into smaller sections, each with a healthy growing point. You may need a sharp spade or knife to cut the rootstock. Replant the sections in new baskets of good loam topped with grit. Return them to the pool.

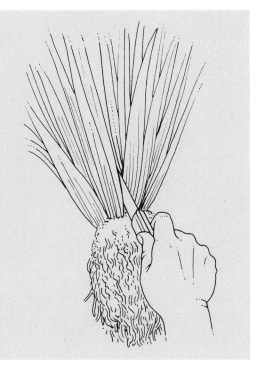

plant aquatics in ponds

The right mix of plants is vital to keep water gardens healthy. Oxygenating plants such as *Elodea canadensis* (Canadian pondweed) are essential to keep the water clear, but aquatics with floating leaves, such as water lilies and water hawthorn, also have an important part to play.

1 Line a perforated plastic planting basket with a piece of ordinary sacking (**below**) and then fill it with good quality, fertile, loamy soil.

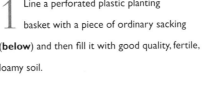

2 Plant the aquatic in the soil, firm in, and water thoroughly. Cover the exposed surface soil with gravel or pebbles to prevent it from being washed out of the basket (**below**).

3 Gently lower the basket into the pool until it is resting on the bottom or marginal shelf, as appropriate (**left**). Using planting baskets is better than planting direct into a layer of soil at the base of the pool as you can remove and trim plants more easily to control their growth.

4 Oxygenating plants are often sold as bunches of unrooted stems, and attaching a small piece of lead weight helps prevent them from floating to the surface. They root quickly though if the bases of the bunches are firmed into wet soil in the planting baskets (**right**).

5 Varieties of *Nymphaea* (water lily) vary in the optimum depth of water they require. Those that require shallow conditions can be planted in deeper areas by setting the planting basket on bricks or blocks to raise its height.

◀ *Feed pond fish with specially formulated food through spring and summer, but remove any food that remains uneaten after 10 minutes.*

kitchen garden: *planting and sowing*

Crops in the kitchen garden are growing apace. If the weather is dry, some are likely to need watering to keep them growing strongly, but it's important to know when to water. It should now be safe to sow pole beans in the open: by the time the seedlings appear, frosts should be a thing of the past.

Sow pole and bush beans outdoors

The soil should now be warm enough for bean seeds to germinate quickly, and by the end of the month, the seedlings should be safe from frosts.

Bush beans are sown in single rows, spaced some 3in/7.5cm apart. Climbing beans and pole beans need supports, and they are generally put in place before sowing; a double row of bamboo stakes, crossing at the top, works well. High yields have also been obtained from rows of stakes spaced 2ft/60cm apart, with stakes 12in/30cm apart in the row, sowing two seeds at the base of each stake.

There are many varieties of bush and pole beans available. With dwarf bush beans, look for varieties that hold their pods well clear of the ground because this avoids beans being eaten by slugs or spoiled by soil splashes. Purple- or gold-podded varieties are easy to pick because the beans are more visible. Stringless varieties of pole bean are popular because the pods are usually more tender, and they stay in good condition longer.

◄ *Flowers on climbing bean plants sometimes fall without setting pods. This is generally due to dry soil conditions; watering will cure the problem.*

WATER VEGETABLES AS REQUIRED

A dry spell at this time of year can result in a check to the growth of young plants, and watering may be necessary. Leafy vegetables such as cabbage and spinach respond well, giving an increased yield at harvest time if they have received a steady water supply throughout the growing season. All transplanted vegetables should be watered after planting until they are well established. Other vegetables, however, should not be watered too soon because watering stimulates leafy growth that may be at the expense of flowering and crop production. Beans and peas should not normally be watered until they have started to flower (unless the plants are actually wilting), but once flowering begins, regular watering will help the flowers to set and promote the formation of a good supply of tender beans.

plant vegetables in containers

Not everyone has room for a vegetable plot, but almost every garden has sufficient space for a few vegetables in pots and growing bags on the patio. If the right varieties are chosen, the harvest can be surprisingly good. When using pots and tubs, insure they have sufficient drainage holes and place a layer of crocks or other coarse drainage material at the base before filling with compost.

1 Prepare tubs and large pots in the normal way. Make sure there are sufficient drainage holes and place a layer of crocks or other coarse drainage material over the base before adding soil mix (**below**). The mix can be soilless or loam-based, as you prefer.

3 Growing bags can also be used for vegetables other than tomatoes (**below**). A bush-type zucchini plant (one plant per bag—it will grow quite large) will give a good crop, and try climbing beans in growing bags placed at the base of fences or walls for the plants to climb up. Both crops need frequent watering.

2 Tomatoes, eggplants (**below**), and sweet bell peppers are among the most commonly grown vegetables in tubs, and young plants that have been hardened off can be planted out now. Add water-retaining granules to the soil mix to cut down the amount of watering required.

4 Other vegetables that can be tried in tubs or growing bags include potatoes, beets, kohlrabi, carrots, bush beans (**below**), lettuce, and radish. Choose fast-maturing, compact-growing varieties—there are several that have been bred specifically for growing in containers on patios or balconies.

▼ *Zucchini make excellent subjects for a growing bag, but they will need frequent and careful watering.*

573

kitchen garden: *pests and diseases*

Birds are normally welcome garden visitors, helping to keep a wide variety of insect pests under control. Unfortunately, they also have less social habits, and can be a real nuisance in the kitchen garden when they start eating the crops. Particularly susceptible crops should be protected now.

Protect crops from birds

Much as we like to see wild birds visiting the garden, they become distinctly unpopular when they start wreaking havoc among developing food crops. The soft fruit season will soon be at its peak, and many birds—particularly blue jays—are just as fond of the juicy fruits as we are, demolishing raspberries and strawberries with amazing speed. Peas are also at risk: colorful, noisy jays are often also the main culprits in eating these.

Where possible, protect susceptible crops with netting, ideally in the form of a fruit cage to allow easy access. Strawberries can be protected with low polyethylene or netting tunnels. Where these are not practical, bird scarers can be tried, as shown on page 693.

PROTECT FRUIT FROM MAGGOTS

Most people will have had the experience of biting into an apparently perfect apple only to find extensive maggot damage. The usual culprit is the larva of the codling moth, and the adults are on the wing any time now. Chemical control of the moth is difficult, but damage reduction can usually be achieved biologically with pheromone traps. They are hung in the trees and lure the male moths to the trap by the use of female pheromones; sticky paper inside the trap insures that the males cannot escape and breed. Such traps were originally used by commercial growers to indicate the best times to use insecticide sprays, but in the garden they can be used as an effective control.

▲ *The soft fruit season is probably the favorite for birds. You will need to protect your garden to prevent them feasting on your crops.*

protect strawberries

Strawberries are a favourite delicacy for many gardeners but without some timely precautions birds, slugs, or disease are likely to devour them before we get the chance. Now is the time to take action to protect the crop, well before the fruits start to ripen.

1 Strawberries are carried very close to the ground, making them vulnerable to damp conditions, soil splashes, and attack by a range of soil-based pests such as slugs and woodlice. This is a good time to surround the plants with clean straw (**right**), tucking it well under the crowns to keep the developing fruit dry and clear of the soil.

2 Where straw is not easy to obtain, fiber or polyethylene mulching mats or sheets can be used instead (**below, left**). They prevent soil splashes and suppress weed growth, but are not so good at keeping slugs and other pests at bay.

3 Many garden birds are extremely partial to strawberries and will be drawn like a magnet when the fruit starts to redden. The only reliable way to protect the plants is by netting (**left**), but as strawberries are so low growing this is not too difficult or expensive.

4 There is no point in simply throwing netting over the plants because the fruit will still be accessible to birds. Strawberry cages are available, or you can make a framework of stakes or plastic poles to support the netting over the plants. Arrange the netting so that it will be quick and easy to remove and replace at picking time.

5 Where birds cause a lot of damage it might be worth investing in a walk-in fruit cage in which all kinds of soft fruit, such as currants, strawberries, raspberries, and blueberries, can be grown safely. Initially expensive, but such a cage is definitely worth it for large crops.

◀ *Silver leaf is a common disease of plums. Badly affected branches should be pruned back until they no longer show a brown stain in the wood.*

greenhouse: *general tasks*

As temperatures and the amount and intensity of sunlight increase, more and more attention will need to be paid to watering and ventilating the greenhouse. This can be difficult if you are usually out during the day, but automatic systems can do the job for you.

Automatic systems

Greenhouses often have to be left unattended during the working day, and this can cause real problems. The weather can be very changeable at this time of year, making it very difficult to judge the amount of ventilation or watering that will be needed while you are out. Automated watering and ventilation systems help to overcome these problems. Automatic ventilators are temperature controlled, and when fitted to at least one roof vent (preferably more) will help to prevent overheating. Watering systems can be bought in kit form. Trickle systems are most popular for small greenhouses; overhead sprinklers can also be used but are more expensive. Other options are timed watering, using a computer fitted to the supply faucet, or capillary matting.

▼ *Trickle watering systems deliver water from a reservoir or the mains through a series of small bore tubes to individual pots or plants.*

CONTINUE PRICKING OUT SEEDLINGS

It is important to prick out seedlings before they become overcrowded in the flats. If they are left for too long, the roots become entangled, leading to root damage when they are eventually separated. Overcrowded seedlings are also more prone to fungus diseases, and water and nutrient shortages. When sowing flats of plants, try to sow the seeds as thinly and evenly as possible. This means the seedlings can be left that much longer in their flats without coming to harm, and will take some of the pressure off you during the busy spring period.

pot up rooted cuttings

Softwood cuttings taken in early spring are usually quick to root, and should be potted up individually as soon as they have developed a good root system.

1 It is not too difficult to tell when cuttings have rooted successfully. The growing tips take on a fresh, green, lively appearance and the whole cutting looks strong and vigorous (**right**). New growth will begin, and it is sometimes possible to see root tips through the drainage holes at the base of the pot.

2 Once the cuttings have reached this stage it is time to pot them up. Gently use a dibble or pencil to prise up a cutting at the edge of the tray, levering it carefully from below to avoid tearing off any delicate new roots (**left**). If the root development is not as advanced as expected, leave the cuttings undisturbed for a while longer.

3 If there is plenty of fresh root growth, move the cuttings to individual 3½ in/8cm pots (**right**). Unnecessary delay means the roots will become increasingly entangled, leading to unavoidable damage when the cuttings eventually have to be separated for potting up.

PINCH OUT YOUNG PLANTS

Plants such as fuchsias and pelargoniums that have been raised from seed or softwood cuttings need to be encouraged to branch out to produce bushy specimens. This is done by "stopping" them—pinching out the growing tip when the plants are around 4 in/10cm high. This will result in strong young growths being produced from the leaf axils down the stem.

fruit and vegetables

The greenhouse provides the opportunity to grow crops that just wouldn't thrive in our climate outdoors. Tomatoes must be the best known of all greenhouse crops, but there are several others that are worth growing.

Tomatoes

Most greenhouse tomatoes are grown as a single stem (cordon) because bush varieties require too much space. They can be supported by stakes, but it is more usual to grow them up twine that is secured to the greenhouse roof, twisting the stems carefully around the twine as they grow. Side-shoots should be removed from the leaf joints as soon as they are visible; it is easier to do this in the morning when the plants are full of moisture. Pinch out the growing tip once it reaches the greenhouse roof.

Plants may need watering several times a day; mix water-retaining granules in the soil in pots and growing bags. Supplying sufficient water is particularly important once flowering and fruit-setting starts, as one incidence of wilting now can cause blossom end rot on a whole batch of fruits. Once the first flowers appear, give plants a fine spray of water every day to help the fruit to set, and begin feeding with a high-potash liquid fertilizer.

Sweet Bell Peppers

Sweet bell peppers do not require side-shooting—they are grown as a bush and are generally provided with a stake as support. Tie the plant's main stem to the stake as it develops. Requirements for watering, feeding, and misting are the same as for tomatoes.

For high yields, pick sweet peppers while they are still green because allowing them to ripen on the plants reduces the total number of peppers produced. If picked as soon as they start to show a tinge of color they will usually continue to ripen over the next few days.

Eggplant

They prefer slightly higher temperatures than tomatoes and peppers, but are otherwise grown in the same way. Like peppers, they are bushy plants, usually supported by a stake. Normally only four or five fruits are obtained from a plant. They should be cut when they are fully colored—normally deep purple, though different colored

◀ *Eggplants like to be in warmer conditions than some other greenhouse crops such as sweet bell peppers and tomatoes.*

▲ *Tomatoes, the most common greenhouse crop, may need to be watered several times a day.*

◀ *Melons: flowers will generally need to be pollinated by hand—you can use a small brush to achieve this.*

varieties are also available. Eggplants are prone to the usual greenhouse pests, but whitefly are often especially troublesome.

Cucumbers

These climbing plants like warmth and high humidity. They are best trained up twine in the same way as tomatoes. All side-shoots produced should have their growing points pinched out at two leaves beyond the flower. Male flowers must be removed because pollinated fruits are misshapen and bitter; the male and female flowers can be distinguished by the miniature cucumber which is present right from the start on the females. Even "all-female" varieties do occasionally produce the odd male flower, so check them regularly.

Water the plants frequently and feed with a high-potash liquid fertilizer. Harvest cucumbers as soon as they are large enough; they are best cut in the morning, when they are firmest.

Melons

Train the stems up twine and pinch out the tip when it reaches the top. Side-shoots should have their growing points pinched out when they have made five leaves. The sublaterals that develop will bear the fruit, and should be pinched out at two leaves beyond the flower.

Pollinate the flowers by hand. Keep the plants well watered and regularly fed with high-potash liquid fertilizer. Harvest the fruit as soon as they are ripe.

BIOLOGICAL CONTROL

Greenhouse crops are particularly prone to two major pests, red spider mite and whitefly. Biological controls have proved an effective way of minimizing damage from them. Red spider mite is controlled by a predatory mite, *Phytosieulius persimilis*, while whitefly is parasitized by a small wasp, *Encarsia formosa*. Controls are available by mail order and from most garden centers. They are not intended to wipe out the pest infestation but to keep it to an acceptable level.

summer

Summer seems like the culmination of the gardener's year—the season that bears the fruit of all our efforts. The days are long, the weather is warm and sunny, and what better place to be than in the garden, enjoying the color and fragrance of the flowers, and the rewarding harvest of home-grown fruit and vegetables?

early summer

The garden retains the freshness of spring while the floral bounty of summer starts to unfold. While there's still plenty to do, the hectic spring rush is calming down, and we can enjoy the garden at a more leisurely pace, especially as the daylight hours stretch out into the evening now.

The weather and watering

While everyone longs for a good spell of settled, warm sunny weather, we also need enough rain to keep the plants growing strongly but droughts do seem to be becoming more common every year. Early summer is often a time of mixed weather with heavy storms depositing gallons of water on the garden within a few minutes, but gardeners need to be prepared to get out the hose or watering can if the weather remains dry for more than a few days. It pays to conserve water by adding organic matter to the soil to increase its water-holding capacity, and by mulching to prevent evaporation from the soil surface.

Plants and produce

At least, though, it's safe to stop worrying about damaging night frosts, and all those tender plants can now go outside, but do take care to harden them off properly first. Conditions should be near perfect for plant growth, and fast-growing plants now need regular care to keep them tied into their supports.

◄ *Flower borders are bursting with color in early summer. Opposites on the color wheel, yellow and purple provide a striking contrast.*

The early spring-flowering shrubs such as forsythia have had their moment of glory, and once the flowers are over it's time to think about pruning the plants. Roses will soon be in full bloom, but all too often the display is spoiled by pests and diseases. The latter can be prevented by regular fungicide sprays, and plants must be checked regularly for pests and treated with the appropriate controls as soon as any are spotted.

The perfect foil for burgeoning flower borders is an emerald-green lawn. Keep the lawn watered, fed, and regularly mown (not too short) for the best results. And note that the vegetable garden should now be producing an increasing number of crops to harvest; this is the time of year when they really taste their best. Toward the end of the summer the strawberries will be ready for picking, with the promise of raspberries and the rest of the soft fruit crop soon to follow.

EARLY SUMMER TASKS

Ornamental garden

- Plant out tender bedding and sow biennials and perennials
- Prune spring-flowering shrubs and trim hedges
- Trim alpines after flowering
- Tie climbers to their supports; increase them by layering
- Tie-in border plants and apply a liquid feed; deadhead as appropriate
- Cut down euphorbias that are past their best
- Treat pests as they appear
- Divide and replant flag irises and Primulas (primroses) after flowering
- Take cuttings of Dianthus (pinks)
- Feed and water plants in containers
- Spray roses against pests and diseases as necessary. Remove suckers
- Lift and divide Narcissus (daffodils)
- Mulch borders to keep down weeds

▲ It's now safe to set even the more tender bedding plants outdoors.

Lawns

- Continue regular mowing and watering, weeding, and feeding lawns as necessary
- Mow areas of naturalized bulbs
- Deal with moles as molehills appear

Kitchen garden

- Continue weeding and watering as necessary
- Earth-up potatoes and lift early varieties
- Sow late crops such as radishes, summer spinach, lettuces, and turnips
- Continue planting out beans, leeks, and winter brassicas
- Pinch out beans and harvest early peas
- Plant out outdoor tomatoes and peppers
- Check vegetables for caterpillars
- Remove runners from strawberries
- Thin young tree fruits
- Summer prune red and white currants, gooseberries

▲ Sweet bell peppers will grow well outdoors in mild areas.

Greenhouse

- Damp down and ventilate regularly
- Feed developing food crops (tomatoes, cucumbers, sweet bell peppers, eggplant)
- Remove male flowers from cucumbers and side-shoots from tomatoes
- Control pests such as whitefly and red spider mite
- Sow cinerarias
- Move pot plants such as azaleas and winter cherry outside for the summer

useful insects

There is a tendency to regard all insect life in the garden as potentially harmful to plants but not all insects are bad news—some are real allies in the fight against pests. It's important to be able to recognize who are your friends, because most insecticides are not so discriminating, and spraying and killing any natural predators will make the problem worse.

Beetles

Although some beetles are pests, there are many useful species. These include ground beetles, which live on the soil surface, hunting out insects, slugs, and worms during the hours of darkness; rove beetles such as the scorpion-like devil's coach horse; and the familiar ladybugs (see opposite).

Capsids

Yes, some capsids are well-known pests but there are other species which are definitely helpful to gardeners. The best known is the predatory black-kneed capsid that helps control aphids and red spider mites on fruit trees. Similar in appearance to capsids are anthocorid bugs, another useful ally, especially on fruit.

Centipedes

Golden brown centipedes scurry over the soil in search of prey—insects, their eggs and larvae, along with small slugs and worms. They are often confused with millipedes (a pest) but millipedes are darker, have more legs that form a thick fringe down the sides, and roll up into a ball rather than running for cover when disturbed.

▲ *Slugs and worms may be dealt with by some useful kinds of beetles, although others are themselves garden pests.*

◀ *Hoverflies like to eat aphids and other soft-bodied insect pests and so are very helpful to the gardener.*

◀ *The familiar ladybug has a voracious*
appetite, consuming huge numbers of aphids
and other pests in its lifetime.

Both adults and, more particularly, larvae feed on large numbers of insect pests, especially aphids. A single larva can consume up to 500 aphids in its three-week life. Before emerging as an adult ladybugs the larva pupates, and the yellow pupa may be mistaken for a Colorado beetle, which it superficially resembles. Ladybugs are most commonly red with either two or seven black spots, but they may also be black with red spots, yellow with black spots and black with yellow spots.

Wasps

Wasps, as everyone knows, sting, and at the end of the summer they are a real nuisance, feasting on ripe fruit, and ruining picnics and outdoor meals. Leaving aside this antisocial behavior, for the rest of the year they are a definite asset to gardeners because they collect all manner of soft-bodied grubs and insects to feed to the young wasp larvae in the nest. Other, less highly visible wasps are also extremely useful—several species are parasitic, laying eggs in the bodies of insect pests that hatch out and slowly consume their hosts. Ichneumon wasps are some of the best known, though rarely recognized in the garden. They have long, slender bodies and are not brightly coloured like the common wasp.

Hoverflies

Hoverflies could easily be mistaken for bees at first glance, though their method of flight is quite different—they hover almost stationary in the air, then make short, sharp darts forward. When they are at rest it's evident that they only have one pair of wings, unlike bees and wasps that have two. The larvae of the various species of hoverfly are very small, but most are efficient predators of aphids and other soft-bodied insect pests.

Lacewings

Lacewings are very delicate insects with pale green, almost translucent bodies, large, lacy wings and very long, constantly moving antennae. Both the adult lacewings and their larvae eat aphids; the larvae are rather insignificant, long-bodied creatures that are pale brown. Lacewings are found all round the garden, and are often attracted by lighting into houses at night.

Ladybugs

Nearly everyone can recognize ladybugs, but perhaps not so many could identify their larvae. While the adults are almost universally regarded as harmless, their small, armadillo-like, blue and orange larvae are likely to be treated with more suspicion, and are often destroyed "to be on the safe side."

ENCOURAGING BENEFICIAL INSECTS

One of the best ways to help beneficial insects is to avoid using insecticide sprays if you possibly can, or to use only those that are specific to pest species and harmless to other insects. Leaving a rough area of the garden with piles of dead leaves and logs, and the hollow stems of dead plants, will also encourage a wide variety of insects. Specific crops can also be grown for them—hoverflies, for instance, will be attracted from far and wide by a patch of buckwheat in flower.

ornamental garden: *general tasks*

Herbaceous flower borders reach their peak later this month and into midsummer, but there is work to be done now to make sure they look their best. Stake or tie-in those plants that need it, and keep weeds in the borders under control. Climbing plants also need care and attention.

▲ *Garden pinks (Dianthus) can be propagated easily from cuttings known as "pipings," which are inserted in a sandy, free-draining soil mix.*

Take cuttings from pinks

Pinks are very popular garden plants. They make neat, low cushions of growth with attractive silver-gray leaves; the flowers are freely produced in a wide range of red, pink, and cream shades, and many varieties are strongly fragrant. The plants are ideal for the front of the border, pots and containers, and rock gardens.

Pinks are also very easy to propagate. They are increased from cuttings that are known as "pipings." The stem has a swollen joint where each pair of leaves clasp it; if the stem is held just below one of these joints and the top part of the stem is tugged gently, it will pull out cleanly at the leaf joint to form a ready-made cutting. Make the pipings 3–4in/7.5–10 cm long; they need no more trimming and can be inserted straight into pots of moist seed and cuttings mix, and firmed in well. The ideal place to root them is in a lightly shaded cold frame where they can remain over the winter.

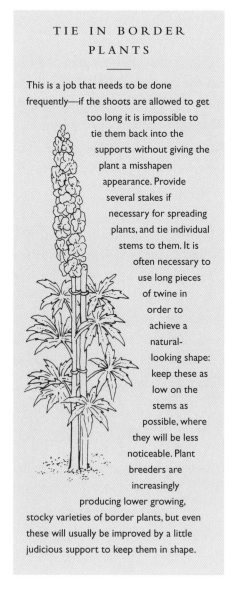

TIE IN BORDER PLANTS

This is a job that needs to be done frequently—if the shoots are allowed to get too long it is impossible to tie them back into the supports without giving the plant a misshapen appearance. Provide several stakes if necessary for spreading plants, and tie individual stems to them. It is often necessary to use long pieces of twine in order to achieve a natural-looking shape: keep these as low on the stems as possible, where they will be less noticeable. Plant breeders are increasingly producing lower growing, stocky varieties of border plants, but even these will usually be improved by a little judicious support to keep them in shape.

train and support climbers

Climbing plants add an extra dimension to a garden. They make use of vertical surfaces such as walls and fences, making them more attractive features; the surfaces also increase the overall amount of growing space, particularly valuable in small gardens. Proper support and training are essential.

MULCH BORDERS

Clear all weed growth from borders and insure the soil is thoroughly moist before applying a thick mulch of bark, cocoa shell, or mushroom compost, etc to prevent further weed growth and retain soil moisture through the summer.

1 A wooden trellis is a popular choice for supporting a climber on a wall; it should be treated with a plant-safe wood preservative. Attach wooden battens to the wall and then screw the trellis panel onto the battens (**below**), or attach it with hooks and eyes. This enables the trellis and climber to be removed carefully when wall maintenance is necessary.

3 Train the shoots of the plant as they grow, aiming to cover the support evenly. Tie the shoots in place with raffia, soft garden twine or plastic-coated metal ties, taking care not to tie them too tightly— make a figure-of-eight loop with the tie to avoid damaging stems (**right**).

4 Several climbers are particularly attractive when allowed to scramble through the branches of trees and shrubs, but avoid very vigorous varieties which will smother their host. A classic combination is *Tropaeolum speciosum* (flame nasturtium) growing through a dark conifer.

2 An alternative support is horizontal, plastic-covered wires stretched taut between screw eyes screwed into the vertical surface. Space the screw eyes every 6ft/1.8m along the wall in rows 18in/45cm above each other and screw them in firmly. Loop the wire through the eyes, twisting it at each end to secure it. Tension the wire by turning the vine eye with pliers (**below**).

ornamental garden: *dividing and planting*

As some of the earlier-flowering garden plants reach the end of their season, it is time to give them a new lease of life by dividing them. And now that the risk of frosts is over, tender bedding plants can safely be set outside in their flowering positions to provide lush colors.

Divide and replant irises

Flag irises make a large, spreading clump once they have been established for several seasons, and the center of the clump can become bare and woody. Once they have finished flowering, plants can be lifted and divided, improving their performance for the following year. Dig up the clump of rhizomes carefully. Identify sections of rhizome around the edge of the clump that have strong young shoots and plenty of fibrous roots, and cut these out using a sharp knife. Discard the old, woody portions. Trim the leaves back to a fan shape about 9in/23cm long and then replant the sections of rhizome in groups of three or five, spacing them some 6in/15cm apart. The top half of the rhizome should remain above ground when planted.

▲ *Once the blooms of flag irises have faded, established clumps of plants can be lifted and replanted to improve next year's performance.*

LIFT AND DIVIDE NARCISSUS (DAFFODILS)

Daffodil bulbs are usually left in the ground from year to year, but those that have been growing undisturbed for several years may start to deteriorate, sometimes becoming "blind" when they produce foliage but no flowers. When this happens it's often because they have become overcrowded, in which case you should lift and replant the bulbs.

Once the foliage has died down, lift the bulbs carefully with a garden fork and shake off the soil. Many will have formed offsets—smaller bulbs around the edge of the main bulb that eventually separate. When the offsets are large enough they will come away easily from the main bulb and can be removed. Replant all the bulbs at the correct spacing, having dug over the planting site first and added a little slow-release fertilizer to the soil.

plant out tender bedding

Many favorite bedding plants are frost tender, and they can't be planted outside until all risk of frosts is over. They are often on sale in garden centers much too early.

Tender bedding plants need to be hardened off (i.e. gradually acclimatized to outdoor conditions) before they are planted out in their flowering positions.

Keep them in a greenhouse, conservatory or other frost-free place at night, moving them outdoors during the day, until it is safe to plant them out.

1 Before planting, prepare the beds and borders where the plants are to grow by forking the soil over thoroughly, removing any weeds. Add an application of general fertilizer and work it into the top layer of soil.

2 Water the bedding plants well the evening before you intend to plant them. When planting, remove the plants from their pots or trays by giving the container a sharp knock on a firm surface to loosen the root-ball; tease the plants apart carefully if necessary (**right**).

3 Plant with a trowel immediately they have been removed from the container (**below**)—do not leave the roots exposed to the air because they will dry out quickly and this will delay re-establishment. Firm the plants into position thoroughly, using your knuckles.

4 Once the bed is planted, water the plants well using a fine rose on the end of the hose or watering can (**below**). Since the weather is often dry and warm at this time of year frequent watering may be necessary, especially in the days immediately after planting.

◄ *Nasturtiums and marigolds provide an attractive mixture of colors, especially highlighted when planted close together.*

ornamental garden: *pruning and trimming*

Several shrubs whose flowers are now finished will benefit from pruning. Other plants will also be bearing faded flowers, and deadheading is an important job from now on to keep the garden looking good. It's also time to give hedges a trim to keep them neat and tidy.

Prune early-flowering shrubs

There are several shrubs which flower in late spring and early summer whose season is now over. They include plants such as ceanothus, *Cytisus* (broom), deutzia, kerria, *Philadelphus* (mock orange), *Spiraea*, *Syringa* (lilac), *Viburnum opulus* and *Weigela*.

These shrubs do not need annual pruning, but if they are becoming overgrown and untidy, now is a good time to tackle them.

Start as always by removing dead and diseased stems, then prune out remaining stems which are old, weak or badly placed. Use pruners or a pruning saw to cut them off at ground level. Up to one-third of the stems can be removed to thin out the growth, and allow light and air into the center of the shrub.

DEADHEAD PLANTS AS NECESSARY

The aims of deadheading are threefold—to prevent the garden from looking untidy, to conserve the strength of the plant by preventing it setting seed unnecessarily, and to encourage the production of more flowers. Plants grown for their fruit, berries, or seedheads should obviously not be deadheaded.

Most plants should have the dead flower heads snapped off or cut with pruners just above a leaf joint; one exception is rhododendrons (including azaleas). They form new buds immediately behind the old flowers, so the dead flowers must be removed very carefully by hand.

◄ *Spring-flowering shrubs such as lilac should have old and weak stems removed to allow light and air into the center of the plant.*

▶ *Suckers from rose rootstocks can be identified by the larger number of leaflets. Dig right down to the root to pull the sucker off.*

trim hedges

Hedge clipping is not the most popular garden chore, but it gives a very satisfying result when it is done properly, and it is worth taking a little time and trouble to get it right. Most hedges need trimming only twice a year, now and in late summer.

1 Clearing up will usually be quicker and easier if a tarpaulin or strong plastic sheet is laid beneath the hedge to catch the clippings (**right**). Where the hedge adjoins a flowerbed or border, a strip of paving slabs running directly alongside the base of the hedge is far easier to work from than the soil of the flowerbed, and, in addition, will help when it comes to clearing up.

2 For a formal hedge, stretch a piece of level twine tautly along the top of the hedge to make sure it is cut to a straight line (**above**). The top of the hedge can be left flat, but cutting it to a pointed shape (like a rooftop) is also attractive, and helps prevent damage from snow in areas that have severe winters.

3 Hand shears are satisfactory for small hedges, but powered hedge trimmers make the job quicker and easier (**above**). Electric trimmers are popular, but great care must be taken to insure that the power cable is kept safely out of the way of the blades, and that a ground-fault interrupter (GFI)—or circuit breaker—is fitted.

4 Begin cutting the hedge from the base, working upward. The sides should slope slightly toward the top, making a wedge shape (**above**). When trimming tall hedges, use a sturdy pair of steps set parallel to the hedge to reach the top. Avoid leaning ladders or steps against the hedge because they will ruin its shape.

ornamental garden: *plants in season*

The season of plenty is beginning now, with more and more plants coming into flower by the day. Roses are among the top favorites in bloom this month, but there are many other flowering shrubs. Border plants are also looking particularly good.

▼ Papaver 'Patty's Plum': individual poppy flowers tend to be short-lived, but there is usually a long succession of blooms.

▲ *Cranesbills, or perennial geraniums, make soft mounds of attractively cut leaves topped by piercing purple-blue flowers.*

▼ *Elegant spires of flowers make the delphinium a classic border plant, perfect for a "cottage garden" effect.*

PERENNIALS AND BEDDING PLANTS

Achillea filipendulina 'Gold Plate' (yarrow)
Ageratum (floss flower)
Althaea
Aquilegia vulgaris (granny's bonnet)
Astrantia major (Hattie's pincushion)
Campanula (bellflower)
Coreopsis (tickseed)
Delphinium elatum hybrids
Dianthus (carnation, pink)
Dictamnus albas (burning bush)
Digitalis purpurea (common foxglove)
Fuchsia (bedding varieties)
Geranium
Heuchera (coral flower)
Iris
Lobelia erinus
Lupinus (lupin)
Nepeta x faassenii (catmint)
Paeonia (peony)
Papaver orientale (oriental poppy)
Pelargonium

BULBS

Allium
Camassia leichtlinii, C. quamash (quamash)
Iris
Lilium (lily)—pictured below

TREES AND SHRUBS

Abelia x grandiflora
Buddleja globosa
Buddleja alternifolia
Ceanothus (California lilac)
Cistus purpureus (rock rose)
Deutzia gracilis
Escallonia
Lonicera periclymenum (common honeysuckle)
Philadelphus (mock orange)
Potentilla (cinquefoil)
Pyracantha (firethorn)
Rhododendron
Rosa (rose)
Spiraea douglasii
Syringa (lilac)
Viburnum plicatum (Japanese snowball bush)
Weigela
Wisteria sinensis (Chinese wisteria)

lawns and water gardens: *general tasks*

A well-kept lawn sets off the entire garden, so it is even more important to keep the grass up to scratch now that the rest of the garden is reaching its peak. The weather may be one thing that is working against you in your efforts to keep the grass lush and green; moles are another problem.

Water lawns as necessary

Grass is rarely killed by drought, but a parched, brown lawn ruins the look of the garden and often becomes overrun by weeds. With care, you can keep a beautiful green lawn without wasting water—an important consideration in these days of increasingly frequent water shortages.

Increase the turf's drought resistance by applying a bulky topdressing in the fall and by never cutting the grass too closely. Raise the height of the mower blades in dry weather. In dry spells, examine the grass closely. If it remains crushed where you walk instead of springing back up ("footprinting"), and the color of the grass is dull, it is time to water. Use an efficient sprinkler to apply a minimum of ½in/12mm of water at a time and water late in the evening to avoid loss by evaporation.

▼ *Watering a lawn too lightly will do more harm than good by encouraging roots to form in the upper, more drought-prone layers of the soil.*

DEAL WITH MOLE DAMAGE

Moles are one of the most frustrating garden pests. They can do terrible damage, particularly to lawns, and are almost impossible to control. Mole scarers are rarely effective, and mole traps kill just one mole whereupon others move in to the vacant territory. The best thing to do is to grit your teeth until the mole has finished constructing his gallery of runs because tunneling then usually ceases. Sweep the molehills evenly over the lawn as soon as they appear—the soil makes a good top-dressing.

Treat anthills in the same way. They are less disfiguring but if they are squashed flat by the mower, patches of grass will be killed and weeds will colonize the area. Ant colonies can be treated with insecticide if really necessary.

make a water feature

Water, especially moving water, is a great addition to any garden. A cobble or millstone water feature takes up little space, and is safe where there are young children. It also provides the sparkle and splash that makes water so entrancing. A competent electrician should provide the power supply to run the pump.

WATER WITHOUT A POND

It is not always practical to have a pond in the garden, particularly if there are young children in the family or as frequent visitors—unsupervised toddlers can drown in seconds, even in shallow water. However, this does not mean that a gardener needs to be deprived of the pleasure of water entirely. Any water feature that does not include standing water should be safe, and many wall fountains are available as kits, though with a little imagination it is easy to make your own. Larger garden centers or water garden specialists can provide you with all you need, including practical advice.

1 Excavate a hole to provide the water reservoir, making it at least 16in/40cm deep with a diameter some 24in/60cm wider than the millstone, incorporating a shallow lip all round the edge. Line the excavation with butyl rubber. A rigid fiberglass mold or plastic tank could be used instead.

2 Set a submersible pump at the base of the reservoir. Build two or three columns of bricks or concrete blocks in the center of the reservoir to take the weight of the millstone, and lay a rust-proof steel mesh over the top of them (**right**). The edges of the mesh are supported by the lip at the top of the reservoir.

3 Run a flexible pipe from the pump up the center of the millstone, with a rigid pipe to deliver the water at the top. This pipe should be set below the surface of the stone to obtain a bubbling spout rather than a jet of water. Arrange cobblestones on the mesh around the edge of the stone (**left**).

4 Fill the reservoir with water and switch on the pump, adjusting the flow to achieve the right effect. Water will bubble out of the center of the millstone and flow over the pebbles back into the reservoir, but it will need frequent topping up to make up for evaporation. Switching the pump off and allowing the stone to dry out regularly will help prevent the formation of algae on the stone.

▶ *Water plays an important rôle in Japanese gardens. This bamboo water feature adds an effective Far Eastern note.*

kitchen garden: *general tasks*

A range of pests and diseases can ruin the appearance of home-grown vegetables and fruit, but if you act promptly it is possible to protect plants against some of them. If you do not want to use chemical pesticides there are usually more environmentally friendly alternatives available.

Protect fruit against pests and diseases

Codling moth is probably the most troublesome apple pest prevalent at this time of year. The small adult

▼ *The dense brown felt that forms on mildewed gooseberry fruits can be rubbed off before cooking, but it is a time-consuming job.*

moths fly at night and lay eggs on developing fruit and nearby leaves. When the larvae hatch, they make their way into the fruit and eat their way through it. Pheromone traps (see page 574) give some degree of control, but if you prefer a chemical remedy, an insecticide such as permethrin can be used in the

middle of this month and again at the beginning of midsummer.

Also look out for gooseberry mildew that starts as a furry white coating on the shoot tips and young fruits, and soon develops into a dense brown felt on the fruits. A range of fungicides can be used to protect plants against the disease.

CATERPILLARS AND BRASSICA CROPS

Most gardeners like to see butterflies in the garden but few of them would welcome the cabbage white. It lays eggs on the leaves of any type of brassica, and they hatch out into ravenous caterpillars that can strip a plant bare in a few days. Hand picking and destroying the caterpillars is possible, but not very practical. A better bet is a biological control that is generally very successful. It combines spores and toxins from a natural bacteria, *Bacillus thuringiensis*. Once infected, the caterpillars die within a few days, but they stop feeding and damaging the plants immediately they have ingested the spray.

earth up potatoes

When the young shoots of potato plants first appear above ground, drawing soil over them gives protection against a late frost. As the plants grow, continuing to earth up prevents bitter green patches forming on the tubers.

1 In cold regions a late frost can still occur in early summer. If potato shoots are just appearing through the soil and frost is forecast, draw soil up to cover the shoots completely. Alternatively, cover the shoots with sheets of newspaper or row covers held in place with soil or stones, but remove this the following day.

2 As the top-growth develops, continue to draw soil up the sides of the stems at regular intervals to form a ridge (**right**). This prevents tubers near the soil surface from being exposed to light that will turn them green; green tubers are inedible as they contain poisonous solanine, which causes severe stomach upsets.

HARVESTING PEAS

Early sowings of peas should now be ready for picking. They are best harvested as soon as the peas reach a useable size—don't leave them to become too big or they get tough and starchy. Wait until the shapes of the peas are just visible through the pod.

3 As an alternative to the process of earthing-up, potatoes can be grown under black poly mulch. Seed potatoes are planted in cultivated soil and black plastic sheeting is laid over the surface; as the shoots develop, slits are cut in the sheeting in the appropriate positions to allow the top-growth through.

4 The earliest potatoes are usually ready to harvest when the plants begin to flower. Scrape away a little soil to expose the tubers—they are ready to lift when they are the size of an egg (**above**). Yields are only small at this stage, but these early crops are particularly delicious.

kitchen garden: *sowing and planting*

The sowing season for vegetables is not yet over. In fact there are several types that can be sown now to extend the season and provide crops in late summer. It's also time to think even farther ahead and plant out some of the vegetables that will see you through the winter days.

Sow successional crops

Although the main sowing season is over, there are several vegetables that can be sown successfully over the next few weeks for picking in late summer or early fall. They include radishes, carrots, beets, corn salad, lettuces, kohlrabi, arugula, radicchio, turnips, rutabaga, and spinach. Care should be taken with the choice of varieties as the summer wears on because some are more suitable for late-season sowing than others, being resistant to bolting, or diseases such as mildew.

Lettuce often fails to germinate when sown in summer because it is subject to high temperature dormancy. This means lettuce should be sown with extra care in hot spells. Water the drills well immediately before sowing to reduce the soil temperature, and sow in the cool of evening for the best results.

PLANT OUT WINTER CROPS

Winter crops such as Brussels sprouts, cabbages, kale, and leeks can be planted out now. All brassicas (members of the cabbage family) need to be planted very firmly because loose planting leads to loosely formed heads without a dense heart, and "blown" sprouts. In all but very heavy soils, firm newly-planted brassicas very thoroughly with the sole of your boot; firm again after watering. If you gently tug a leaf of the plant, the leaf should tear before the plant's roots move in the soil.

◀ *Fast-maturing radish can be sown at intervals all through the summer to provide a succession of young, tender roots.*

plant bell peppers outdoors

Once the risk of frost is over, tender crops such as sweet bell peppers and tomatoes can be planted safely out of doors. Make sure the young plants are thoroughly hardened off before setting them in their final positions.

1 Sturdy young plants that are filling an 3½in8cm pot with roots are the best size for planting out. Select vigorous, healthy plants with deep green leaves; white root tips should be just visible through the drainage holes at the base of the pot.

2 Remove the plant from its pot by placing two fingers either side of the plant's stem, inverting the pot and knocking the rim against a hard surface, eg. the edge of a table. The whole root-ball should slide out of the pot (**left**).

3 Dig a hole with a trowel in well-prepared soil in the vegetable garden and set the plant in it (**left**), covering the top of the root-ball with soil and firming in well with your knuckles. Water well immediately after planting.

4 If the weather should turn cool or windy after planting, young plants can be protected by covering them with a cloche. As the plants grow taller, two cloches can be turned on end to still provide some shelter.

5 Peppers and other tender vegetable crops also grow well when planted in growing bags on a patio (**above**), often a warmer, more sheltered position. Set two plants per bag for the best results. Cut a cross in the plastic and tuck the flaps under to make the planting hole. Plants in growing bags need regular watering and liquid feeding, particularly in dry or windy weather.

◄ *Green bell peppers are simply fruits picked when immature. If allowed, they will ripen to red, orange, or yellow, according to variety.*

greenhouse: *general tasks*

The greenhouse provides ideal conditions for pests, and they've got to be tackled promptly to stop them from multiplying out of control. Greenhouse food crops are developing well, but in order to continue they need to be given the correct fertilizers, especially if they are in pots or growing bags.

Feed greenhouse food crops

Greenhouse crops are likely to be growing either in a small area of border soil that is often depleted of plant food by continued cropping, or in restricted volumes of soil mix in pots or growing bags that cannot hope to supply all the nutrients required throughout the growing season. This means that greenhouse crops need regular applications of fertilizer. The usual crops grown—eggplant, bell peppers, cucumbers, and tomatoes—are fruiting types. They are not normally given fertilizer until they start flowering to avoid the production of leafy growth at the expense of flowers and fruit. Once flowering starts they can be given a compound fertilizer containing some nitrogen and phosphorus, with high levels of potash. Liquid tomato fertilizers are ideal for all fruiting crops.

▲ *Boost greenhouse crops by regular feeding. Liquid fertilizers are fast acting and rapidly absorbed by the plants.*

KEEP PESTS UNDER CONTROL

The warm, protected conditions of the greenhouse encourage rapid, soft growth of plants and provide a paradise for many pests. They can often multiply so rapidly at this time of year that heavy, damaging infestations build up in a matter of days. It is necessary to be constantly vigilant, examining plants carefully for the first signs of a problem. Check the tender young shoot tips where aphids often cluster, and the undersides of leaves where whitefly and red spider mite hide themselves.

Use either biological controls or one of the many insecticides suitable for greenhouse pest control. When using pesticides, read the directions carefully and follow them to the letter. And be sure to allow the necessary harvest intervals to elapse where food crops are being grown.

SOW CINERARIAS

Cinerarias, with their bright, daisy-like flowers, make cheerful winter- and spring-flowering pot plants for the home. Sow seed now in a pot of seed and cuttings mix, scattering the fine seed as thinly as possible. Cover lightly with more mix or a thin layer of silver sand, fit a propagator top and germinate in the greenhouse or a cold frame. Seeds should germinate in 10–14 days, and plants sown now should flower in five or six months' time. Flowers are available in a good range of colors, including red, pink, purple, blue, and white, and there are often a good number of bicolors in seed mixtures.

train cucumbers and tomatoes

These popular greenhouse salad crops should be growing strongly by now. Frequent, regular attention will keep their growth under control and make sure of good crops later on.

1 Greenhouse tomatoes are usually grown as single-stem cordons, trained up stakes or twine. If left to themselves they will form a bush of dense leafy growth; this takes up too much space in the greenhouse and makes the plants difficult to care for.

3 Greenhouse cucumbers produce the best fruits from unfertilized flowers; fertilization gives swollen, misshapen, bitter-tasting cucumbers. To prevent fertilization, male flowers should be removed from the plants as soon as they are seen.

4 Male and female flowers are easy to distinguish; females have a miniature fruit at the base of the flower right from the start (**left**). Even so-called "all-female" varieties produce the odd rogue male flower, which must be removed.

2 Side-shoots are removed as soon as they are large enough to snap off easily (**below**). Check each plant every few days; if the side-shoots become too large they are difficult to remove without damaging the plant. Early morning is the best time to snap them off cleanly.

midsummer

Flowers are at their peak in most gardens now, and deadheading, watering, staking, and harvesting will keep gardeners busy. Make the most of the good weather to enjoy the garden, and on warm nights also make sure you stroll around after dusk to appreciate the night-scented flowers.

Lawns

Lawn grasses are among the first plants to show distress in dry spells. Continue mowing the grass frequently to keep it looking good, but raise the height of the mower blades a little to give the lawn more drought resistance. As long as the clippings are very short, they can be left on the lawn in dry spells to help conserve moisture.

Plants

Rock garden plants and some early-flowering perennials will look better for being tidied up now, so once flowering has finished, cut them back hard. Continue to prune deciduous, flowering shrubs after flowering, too, to keep them to the required size. Many shrubs can also be propagated from semiripe cuttings this month and next.

▶ *Keep the flower borders looking their best by regular deadheading, feeding, and supporting throughout the summer.*

Harvesting

In the kitchen garden there should be plenty to harvest, but successional sowings continue to extend the season. Keep fruiting plants such as beans, marrows, and peas well watered while flowering to insure a good crop. Watering throughout the garden is likely to take up a considerable amount of time in midsummer. Outdoor plants in containers, particularly, can start

suffering from water shortage within hours on hot, cloudless summer days.

Pest and diseases

Fungus diseases can be a particular problem in warmer weather, and a routine of preventive fungicide sprays is a good idea for susceptible plants. Pests should be treated as soon as they are seen—preventive spraying is not generally applicable as far as insecticides are concerned.

MIDSUMMER TASKS

General

■ Check plants for pests and diseases and treat them early
■ Continue watering without wasting water
■ Install garden lighting

Ornamental garden

■ Prune shrubs that have finished flowering as necessary; prune wisteria
■ Continue trimming hedges
■ Prick out perennials and biennials sown earlier
■ Deadhead flowers and cut back rock plants that are becoming untidy
■ Start to take semiripe cuttings of shrubs

■ Look out for fall-flowering bulbs and Madonna Lilium candidum (lilies) and plant as early as possible
■ Cut back early-flowering border plants to encourage a second flush
■ Deadhead, prune, and water plants in containers
■ Cut flowers for use indoors
■ Stake and tie dahlias;

disbud them if large blooms are required
■ Check Aster novi-belgii (Michaelmas daisies) for mildew, and treat if necessary
■ Order spring bulbs from mail-order catalogs

▲ Garden lighting will add atmosphere and enable you to continue to enjoy the garden after dusk.

Lawns

■ Leave clippings on the grass occasionally
■ Increase mowing height in times of drought

Water garden

■ Top up ponds with fresh water as necessary
■ Continue to feed fish to help build them up for winter

Kitchen garden

■ Harvest vegetables regularly as soon as they are ready
■ Check potatoes for potato blight
■ Pick herbs for drying, freezing and use in pot pourri
■ Thin seedlings
■ Plant cold stored potatoes for a fall crop

■ Continue planting winter vegetables
■ Water beans when flowering
■ Remove straw on strawberry beds after fruiting, and cut the foliage from strawberries not required for propagation. Root strawberry runners

■ Cut off foliage affected by silver leaf on plums and other stone fruit
■ Start summer-pruning of trained apples and pears
■ Cut down summer-fruiting raspberry canes after fruiting

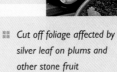

▲ Sow herbs such as coriander ready for potting up for use over the winter months.

Greenhouse

■ Continue training food crops
■ Renew shading as necessary; continue watering, ventilating, and damping down

■ Use fan heaters to circulate cool air
■ Prick off cineraria seedlings
■ Pot up rooted cuttings
■ Sow herbs for winter use

■ Avoid blossom end rot on tomatoes by watering regularly to prevent plants flagging. Feed cucumbers, peppers and tomatoes etc with high-potash fertilizer and pick fruits regularly as they ripen

603

general tasks

Watering is often vital during dry spells, but when incorrectly carried out it can do more harm than good. Most gardeners like to spend as much time as possible in their gardens now, and an outdoor lighting system enables gardens to be appreciated for that much longer each day.

◀ *A seep hose is a very efficient and virtually labor-free way of applying water to the soil; hardly any water is lost by evaporation.*

Water garden plants with care

When watering any plants, it is important to make sure that the soil or compost is moistened right down to the main root area. If just a small amount of water is given it often penetrates only a shallow, top layer of soil; this encourages roots to form in this upper area, making the plant more prone to drought in the future. Water thoroughly or not at all!

Water can be applied in a number of different ways—with a watering can, through a hose pipe, by sprinkler or by seep hose. A seep hose is often one of the most efficient ways of watering because very little water is lost by evaporation. It is simply a length of tubing which is blocked at one end with holes at regular intervals along its length. It is laid on the soil alongside the plants and attached to a hose; water seeps out of the holes on to the soil. If there is a ban on garden sprinklers, remember that the ban includes seep hoses, too!

STAKE BORDER PLANTS FIRMLY

At this time of year heavy storms are not uncommon, and rain and hail can flatten plants in minutes. Even if the flowering stems are not broken, insufficiently supported plants are unlikely to recover their shape fully after such a downpour. As long as border plants have been firmly staked and regularly tied in to their supports, they are more likely to survive without serious damage. Wet weather can cause buds to rot instead of opening fully; this is often seen on roses (particularly the full-flowered, old-fashioned varieties) and is known as "balling." Unfortunately there is little you can do to prevent it; cut off affected buds to encourage a second flush to form.

prepare for vacations

The summer vacation season comes at just the wrong time for the garden, just when everything is growing lushly and needs regular attention to keep it looking good. However, it is worth spending a little time in preparation before you leave to prevent you from being confronted by a depressing jungle on your return.

2 Mow the lawn just before you go, but do not be tempted to cut it more closely than normal because this will damage the turf and make it more prone to drought. If it is overlong on your return, reduce the height gradually over several cuts (**right**).

3 Weed flowerbeds and the vegetable plot thoroughly, hoeing to remove all seedling weeds. Applying a mulch to the soil will help prevent new weed growth and also keep the soil moist.

1 Gather all planted containers, including hanging baskets, together in one spot (**below**). Place them in a sheltered, partially shaded position. Add water-retaining granules to the soil mix if this has not already been done. Give them a thorough soaking before you go, but if you're away for more than a long weekend, ask a neighbor to water them every couple of days.

4 In the vegetable garden, pick all fruiting crops such as zucchini, peas, and beans. Any left to mature on the plants will reduce future production, so arrange for a friend or neighbor to continue the harvest in your absence. Normally they are only to happy to oblige in return for the opportunity of a supply of fresh, home-grown produce!

USE GARDEN LIGHTING TO ADVANTAGE

The garden can be a dramatic place at night with the imaginative use of lights. Spotlights can highlight particular plants or ornaments of interest or form interesting shadows or silhouettes, while underwater lights can make a garden pond a magical feature. Lighting on the patio enables meals to be enjoyed out of doors after dark, and well-placed lighting can be an important safety feature on potential hazards such as paths and steps. Garden lighting kits are generally easy to install (see page 606), but if you have any doubts, employ a qualified electrician to do the job.

ornamental garden: *general tasks*

Dahlias, one of the mainstays of late summer and fall, need attention now to produce prize-winning blooms. Another eye-catcher is the Madonna lily—look out for bulbs which will be on sale soon. And why not extend the amount of enjoyment you get from the garden by installing lighting?

◄ *Low voltage garden lighting kits contain all you need to transform your garden to a magical place during the hours of darkness.*

Install garden lighting

Low-voltage outdoor lighting systems are safe to use and easy to install. Complete kits are available containing everything you will need, including lamps, cables, and a transformer.

First, draw out a sketch of your lighting plan to estimate the amount of cable you will need, and to insure you have enough. Find a suitable position for the transformer (see the maker's instructions for precise details). Lay the lamps in their appropriate positions, then run the cable between them, leaving a long loop at each lamp. Attach the cable to the lamps as instructed, then assemble the rest of the lighting fitting and push the lamps firmly into the ground. When all the lamps are attached, test the system to insure it is working properly. If everything is in

order, the cable running between the lamps can be buried under the soil, making sure it is not likely to be disturbed by future digging.

STAKE AND DISBUD DAHLIAS

Dahlias are important plants for providing color and form in the late summer and fall garden. If large, eye-catching flowers are required, they can be obtained by disbudding the stems. Leave just the terminal bud on each stem, and remove all the buds from the leaf axils below it by snapping them off or rubbing them out. This will need to be repeated several times. Each flowering stem will need to be provided with a sturdy stake, and must be tied in regularly. Earwigs can be a problem, chewing at the petals and spoiling the flower shape. They can be caught in traps consisting of a small pot filled with straw, inverted on the top of the stake. Inspect the traps each morning, and shake out and destroy any earwigs sheltering there.

take semiripe cuttings

Now is a good time to take semiripe cuttings from many shrubs. They are less delicate than softwood cuttings, and need no special treatment. Most will be well rooted by the fall, but can be left in their pots in a sheltered place until the following spring.

1 Choose the current season's shoots which are still pliable, and just beginning to harden and become woody at the base. Cut the shoots with pruners or, if it is small enough, tear them off the stem with a small sliver of bark attached.

2 Remove the lower leaves and, if necessary, trim the stem to just below a node with a knife (**right**). The size of cutting varies from shrub to shrub, but is usually around 4in/10cm long.

3 Dip the base of the cutting in hormone rooting powder, tapping it once or twice to leave just a thin film on the stem (**left**).

4 Insert cuttings into prepared pots of cuttings soil mix topped with a layer of sharp sand (**right**). Place the pots in a cold frame if possible, or a well-ventilated greenhouse, or a sheltered position outdoors. Keep them lightly shaded for the first few days.

PLANT FALL-FLOWERING BULBS

Bulbs such as amaryllis and colchicum, that flower in the fall, can be planted now. Most fall-flowering bulbs prefer a sunny spot in a sheltered situation. The Madonna lily (*Lilium candidum*) should also be planted soon: this is actually summer flowering, but needs to be planted as early as possible for flowers next year. It is a particularly striking lily with large, pure white, heavily scented, trumpet-shaped blooms. Look out for the bulbs appearing in garden centers from now on. Unlike most other lilies the Madonna lily requires very shallow planting, with just 2in/5cm of soil above the tip of the bulb.

ornamental garden: *pruning and deadheading*

Plants are working hard to produce magnificent displays of flowers at the moment, and can easily wear themselves out after a short time. With the correct care, however, it is possible to extend the season so that you can continue to enjoy a garden full of color for as long as possible.

Care for containers

Tubs, window boxes, and hanging baskets have become an indispensable feature of most gardens in summer, spilling over with plants to provide a feast of color.

Because the plants are crowded together in small volumes of soil mix, however, they soon begin to suffer from the effects of competition.

Containers need regular watering, feeding, and deadheading in order to keep the plants flowering for the longest possible period.

The amount of water they need depends on the type of mix in which they are growing and whether they are in a sheltered or exposed position, but it is often necessary to water small containers two or three times a day in hot, sunny weather. Add a dilute liquid feed to the water at every watering, or if you prefer you can incorporate some season-long, slow-release fertilizer granules into the soil. Deadheading (where practical) will help to encourage further flushes of bloom.

▼ *A number of border plants that flower in late spring and early summer will produce a second flush of blooms if cut back after flowering.*

CUT BACK ROCK GARDEN PLANTS AFTER FLOWERING

Many of the rockery plants that were proving such a colorful spectacle a few weeks ago are looking rather bedraggled now that nearly all the flowers are over. Trim back species such as aubrieta, aurinia (alyssum), iberis and cerastium with pruners or a pair of well-sharpened shears, cutting the shoots to about half their length. This encourages fresh new growth and keeps the plants neat and compact. It can sometimes result in another flush of flowers to brighten up the rock garden later in the season, but should certainly improve the flowering of the plants next spring.

prune wisteria

The glorious scented flowers of wisteria are over, but careful pruning now will help to insure a spectacular display next year. Wisteria can be a difficult climber to grow well, sometimes seeming reluctant to flower profusely, but the correct pruning will greatly improve its performance. Remember that further pruning will be necessary in winter.

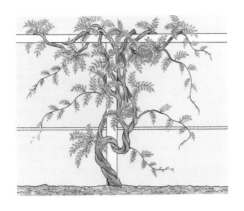

1 Wisteria flowers early, when the leaves are only just starting to open. By midsummer, however, the attractive pinnate foliage has made vigorous growth, and the leafy shoots may be getting out of hand (**above**).

2 Over the next few weeks, cut back nearly all the long shoots to about 6–10in/15–25cm from the main stem (**above**). Any stems needed to fill in the main framework can be pruned more lightly or left unpruned.

3 Climbing plants, including wisteria, always flower better when the flow of sap is slowed down by training the stems horizontally instead of letting them grow straight up. Pull wisteria stems gently into a near horizontal position and tie them to their support (**left**).

4 Summer pruning is only half the story; the shoots you have just cut back will need pruning again in winter, reducing them to three buds from their base. This will help promote the production of flowering spurs.

5 Once summer pruning is completed, make sure the soil around the roots is moist and apply a mulch around the base of the plant (**right**). Wisteria prefers moderately rich, moisture-retentive, loamy soil. In dry soils, the flower buds may drop from the plant before they open fully.

◀ *A second flush of flowers from plants such as perennial geraniums will be especially welcome in a few weeks.*

plants for scent

A garden should not just be a visual delight but should give pleasure to the other senses as well. One of the senses that is most easily pleased is that of smell, and there are all sorts of garden plants with the most wonderful and intriguing scents.

Our sense of smell is actually very complex. Different fragrances can affect us in very different ways; they can also act strongly on our memories, with just one whiff of a particular smell being able to transport us instantly back to an event we had entirely forgotten. Certain scents can be very strong to one person but non-existent to another; similarly one person may find a fragrance wonderful while another finds it offensive.

When we talk of plant fragrance, it is flowers that spring to mind, and there are indeed many blooms that are strongly perfumed. Don't forget, though, that leaves can also be scented, and foliage often has a sharp, invigorating fragrance, never as sweet and heavy as that of flowers. The reason flowers are scented is to attract pollinating insects, particularly moths and butterflies, who use fragrance to locate the blooms—the sweet scent promises nectar. Other flowers are pollinated by flies, and give off a smell of rotting meat to attract them—*Sauromatum guttatum* (the voodoo lily) is well known for its foul scent. The purpose of fragrance in leaves is less clear, but presumably prevents animals from eating the foliage because strongly aromatic substances usually have an off-putting taste.

The way flowers and foliage give off fragrance varies. Some scents travel on the air for long distances, while some flowers need to be sniffed close up before their scent can be detected. Some fragrances are only released after light rain, and many flowers do not give off any scent until the cool of night in order to attract night-flying moths. Some fragrances, like that of violets, are tantalizing, disappearing after a few seconds no matter how hard we sniff the flowers. Most foliage scents are released only when the leaves are rubbed or brushed against.

Fragrance in the garden

It is always pleasant to walk around the garden and enjoy the mingling of pleasant scents, but many gardeners like to concentrate fragrant plants in one area where they

▲ *The Sir Edward Elgar rose not only looks beautiful, it also brings a particularly strong and pleasant scent to the garden.*

can most easily be appreciated—perhaps near the patio, around an arbor containing a seat or under a living room window. The spot should be sheltered so that the fragrance is not dispersed too rapidly on the wind, and be accessible after dark when many plants smell their strongest. Raised beds or tall containers help to bring smaller fragrant flowers to nose level.

Plants needing to be touched to release their scent should be placed where they are likely to be trodden on or brushed past, for example in cracks in paving or by a doorway. Leaves which are within easy reach will encourage passersby to pinch them as they walk past.

Don't try to cram too many strongly scented plants into a small area though, because the different fragrances may compete and lose their impact.

▲ *Hyacinths are among the most strongly scented spring-flowering bulbs, and are especially popular as house plants.*

▲ *There are several varieties of the familiar, sweet-scented honeysuckle, including the richly colored 'Dropmore Scarlet'.*

PLANTS WITH SCENTED FLOWERS

Brugmansia (angel's trumpet)
Buddleja
Chimonanthus praecox *
  (wintersweet)
Clerodendrum trichotomum
Clethra alnifolia (sweet pepper
  bush)
Convallaria majalis (lily-of-the-
  valley)
Cosmos atrosanguineus
Cytisus battandieri (pineapple
  broom)
Daphne odora *
Dianthus (carnation, pink)
Hamamelis mollis * (Chinese
  witch hazel)
Heliotropum (helliotrope)
Hyacinthus (hyacinth)
Iris unguicularis *
Jasminum (jasmine)
Lathyrus odorata (sweet pea)
Lavandula (lavender)
Lilium (lily)
Lonicera (honeysuckle)
Magnolia sieboldii

Mahonia japonica *
Matthiola incana
Narcissus poeticus (poet's
  narcissus) and Tazetta hybrids
Nicotiana (tobacco plant)
Osmanthus burkwoodii
Paeonia (peony)
Petunia
Philadelphus (mock orange)
Phlox paniculata (perennial phlox)
Polianthes tuberosa (tuberose)
Primula (primrose)
Reseda odorata (common
  mignonette)
Ribes odoratum (buffalo currant)
Romneya coulteri (tree poppy)
Rosa (rose)
Sarcococca * (Christmas box)
Syringa (lilac)
Viburnum x bodnantense,
  V. fragrans, V. farreri *
Viola odorata * (English violet)

*winter flowering

plants in season

Annuals are in full flower this month. Easy to grow, they make most effective, colorful garden plants. Summer bedding plants are also in their prime. Trees are looking majestic in full leaf, and there are plenty of flowering shrubs to brighten the garden.

▼ *Lavender not only brings a splash of color to the garden, it also contributes to the marvelous aromas found at this time of year.*

Achillea
Alstroemeria (Peruvian lily)
Althaea
Astilbe
Astrantia major
  (Hattie's pincushion)
Begonia semperflorens
Campanula (bellflower)
Chrysanthemum maximum
Coreopsis (tickseed)
Delphinium elatum hybrids
Dianthus (carnation, pink)
Digitalis purpurea
  (common foxglove)
Echinops ritro (globe thistle)
Erigeron (fleabane)
Fuchsia
Gaillardia x *grandiflora*
Geranium
Geum (avens)
Gypsophila paniculata
Helenium
Hemerocallis (day lily)
Heuchera (coral flower)
Kniphofia (red hot poker)
Lathyrus (everlasting pea)
Lupinus (lupin)
Nepeta x *faassenii* (catmint)
Nicotiana alata (tobacco plant)
Oenothera (evening primrose)
Pelargonium
Penstemon
Phlox paniculata (perennial phlox)
Romneya coulteri (tree poppy)
Scabiosa caucasica
  (pincushion flower)
Solidago (Aaron's rod)

BULBS

Cardiocrinum giganteum
Crocosmia x *crocosmiiflora*
Eucomis bicolor (pineapple flower)
Gladiolus
Lilium (lily)

TREES AND SHRUBS

Abelia floribunda, A. x *grandiflora*
Catalpa bignonioides (Indian bean tree)
Ceanothus (California lilac)
Cistus (rock rose)
Clethra alnifolia (sweet pepperbush)
Cytisus battandieri (pineapple bloom)
Escallonia
Eucryphia
Fuchsia magellanica
Genista (broom)
Helianthemum (rock rose)
Hydrangea macrophylla
Hypericum calycinum (Aaron's beard)
Lavandula (lavender)
Lonicera periclymenum (common
  honeysuckle)
Olearia x *haastii* (daisy bush)
Philadelphus (mock orange)
Rosa (rose)
Vinca major (greater periwinkle), V. *minor*
  (lesser periwinkle)

▲ *Lupins are particularly prone to damage by heavy rain if they are not adequately staked. This variety is 'Gallery Pink'.*

▼ *Free-flowering pelargoniums are a popular choice for hanging baskets and other containers. Deadheading will extend the flowering season.*

kitchen garden: *general tasks*

There are not too many plant diseases that have a really devastating effect on crops, but potato blight is one of them. Take action as soon as you see the first signs of this disease. Also, tidy up strawberry beds now that the crop is over, and propagate the plants by rooting runners.

Potato blight

This disease is common in wet summers, and is remarkable for the speed with which it develops. The first signs are brown blotches on the foliage, sometimes with a white mold on the underside. Symptoms spread rapidly, and within a few days the entire top-growth of the plants may have yellowed and collapsed.

Blight also affects the tubers, causing a dark brown rot. Spores infect the tubers when rain washes them off the top-growth into the soil. If the tubers are of a useable size, as soon as blight is identified on the foliage the top-growth should immediately be cut down and burned, removing all trace of it from the soil surface. Tubers may then escape infection. In damp summers, especially if blight has occurred the previous year, it is worth giving potatoes a protective fungicide spray from midsummer onward.

▼ *Keep a sharp look out for the first signs of potato blight on the foliage. If action is taken straight away, the crop can usually be saved.*

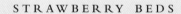

STRAWBERRY BEDS

When strawberry plants have finished cropping it is time to give the bed some radical treatment. At one time it was common practice to set light to the straw as it lay around the plants; the ensuing blaze burned up the leaves and frazzled any lurking pests and disease spores. Risk of the flames getting out of hand is too great for this to be a popular method any longer, however. Instead, the leaves are cut from the plants, using either a pair of shears or a nylon line trimmer: be careful not to damage the new growth in the center of the crowns. Rake up the cut foliage together with the straw, and remove it for burning in a safe place.

root strawberry runners

As long as established strawberry plants are healthy and vigorous, it is easy to produce new plants to extend the bed or to replace old, worn-out plants. Strawberry plants naturally produce a profusion of runners which root quickly and easily.

1 Strawberry runners are freely produced. Long, creeping stolons extend from the plants, bearing two or three plantlets along their length. If not required for propagation, runners are normally removed regularly to prevent a mass of tangled growth (**left**).

2 Select four or five of the strongest, most vigorous runners for propagation and remove the rest. Spread the runners evenly around the plant.

3 The plantlet nearest the parent is always the strongest on the runner, and the ones beyond it should be nipped off and discarded. Plantlets can be rooted direct into the soil around the plant—simply weigh down the runner with a stone or peg into the soil with a loop of wire to prevent it from being blown about (**left**).

4 Alternatively, the plantlets can be rooted into pots filled with either good quality garden soil or soil mix. Rooting the runners into pots makes the plants quicker to establish on transplanting as there is less root disturbance when the young plants are lifted. Either clay or plastic pots are suitable.

TRAIN OUTDOOR TOMATOES

For a good crop of outdoor tomatoes it is essential to choose varieties specifically recommended for outdoor culture. They may be grown as cordons like greenhouse tomatoes, or as bushes, depending on the variety selected. Cordon varieties need regular side-shooting and tying in to their support, but bush varieties generally do not. Some bush varieties are specially bred for growing in patio pots or even hanging baskets, where the stems cascade over the sides. They need no training, but frequent watering and regular feeding are necessary, as for all container-grown plants.

Between mid and late summer, the tops of cordon-grown plants should be pinched out to encourage the fruits to ripen.

Bush varieties form a sprawling mound and do not usually need staking or side-shooting. They carry fruit trusses at the ends of the stems.

5 Half-bury the pots in the soil around the parent plant and peg the runners down into the mix (**above**). When pots are being used, it is important to make sure that the soil mix in them is not allowed to dry out.

kitchen garden: *planting and harvesting*

Herbs are valuable in the garden for their appearance and fragrance, and indispensable in the kitchen. While nothing beats the flavor of fresh herbs, there are several easy ways in which they can be preserved. Midsummer, while they are at their peak, is the time to pick them for storing.

Harvesting herbs

The best time to pick herbs is in the morning of a dry day, waiting until the dew has dried off the foliage. Pick young stems, and do not wash them unless it is absolutely essential.

The age-old method of preservation is drying; it is simple to do and gives good results. Tie the herbs in small, loose bunches—if they are too large, they will go moldy in the center. Hang them upside down in a warm, dry, airy place. The atmosphere in the kitchen is usually too moist and an airing cupboard (with the door ajar), spare bedroom, or garden shed may be more suitable. Once the stems and foliage are completely dry, the herbs can be crumbled and stored in tightly lidded jars.

For faster results, herbs can be laid on racks in a very cool oven overnight. They can also be dried in batches in a microwave, though it is often difficult to get the timing right with this method.

▲ *Select fresh, young shoots of herbs for preserving, picking them early in the morning, once the dew has dried off the leaves.*

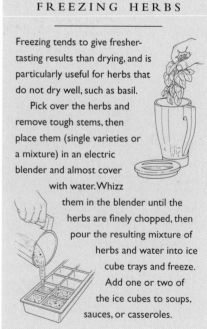

FREEZING HERBS

Freezing tends to give fresher-tasting results than drying, and is particularly useful for herbs that do not dry well, such as basil.

Pick over the herbs and remove tough stems, then place them (single varieties or a mixture) in an electric blender and almost cover with water. Whizz them in the blender until the herbs are finely chopped, then pour the resulting mixture of herbs and water into ice cube trays and freeze. Add one or two of the ice cubes to soups, sauces, or casseroles.

plant out leeks

Leeks are an invaluable winter vegetable, withstanding almost any amount of cold weather. Seedlings from sowings made in trays or a seedbed in spring will now be ready for transplanting to their final positions.

1 Prepare the ground for leeks thoroughly, because they need to be planted deeply in order to develop the maximum length of tender white stems. The crop will benefit from some well-rotted compost or manure worked into the soil before planting.

2 Knock the underside of the seedflat smartly to loosen the roots, and tease the young plants apart carefully. Gather up a handful of seedlings with the bases of the plants in line, and trim the long, straggly roots and leaf tips with a pair of sharp scissors to make the plants easier to handle (**right**).

3 Make planting holes with a wooden dibble some 6in/15cm deep and the same distance apart. A leek seedling is simply dropped into each hole, leaving the holes open (**left**). Make sure the leek drops right to the base of the hole: that's why it's best to trim back the roots.

4 Once planting is complete, water the plants gently; this washes enough soil over the roots to anchor them in place. Each planting hole is filled with water and then left to drain (**right**).

5 If the weather is very dry shortly after planting the seedlings may need to be watered again once or twice, but otherwise they usually need no further attention. They will be ready for harvesting in fall and winter.

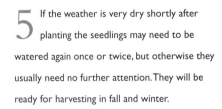

◄ *Continue to keep the vegetable garden free of weeds as far as possible. Increasing numbers of crops are approaching maturity now.*

617

greenhouse

Greenhouse food plants need regular feeding and watering, and there are still seedlings to prick off, rooted cuttings to pot up, and seeds to be sown. If you like the idea of an extra-early strawberry crop next year, now's the time to pot up a few strawberry plants for growing on in a warm greenhouse.

Feed and water food crops regularly

Greenhouse plants such as eggplant, cucumbers, melons, bell peppers, and tomatoes must be given adequate levels of water and plant food in order to keep producing heavy crops. All fruiting plants need high levels of potassium, and a high–potash liquid

fertilizer is a convenient way to supply it. Follow the directions on the pack as regards frequency of feeding.

A common problem with tomatoes at this time of year is the appearance of a dark brown or black, dry, sunken area at the base of the fruit, known as blossom end rot. This is usually caused by the plants running short of water at flowering time, so that sufficient calcium

cannot be transported to the developing fruit. It is too late to do anything for affected fruits, but guard against it happening again by keeping the soil adequately moist at all times. A handful of garden lime can be added to the can of water occasionally as an extra precaution.

▼ *To avoid blossom end rot on the fruits, make sure that container-grown tomatoes never run short of water at any time.*

STRAWBERRY PLANTS

A heated greenhouse lets you pick ripe strawberries weeks before the outdoor crop is ready. Runners that you rooted earlier will provide plants for forcing if they are potted up now. Choose the strongest growers and set them in individual 6in/15cm pots using a soil-based potting mix.

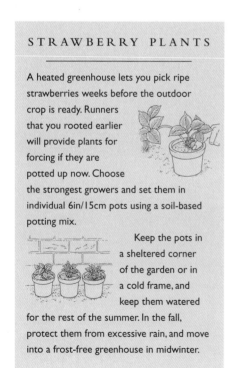

Keep the pots in a sheltered corner of the garden or in a cold frame, and keep them watered for the rest of the summer. In the fall, protect them from excessive rain, and move into a frost-free greenhouse in midwinter.

PRICK OFF CINERARIAS

Cineraria seedlings sown earlier should be pricked off into individual 3½in/8cm pots as soon as they can be handled easily. As with all seedlings, handle them by their seed leaves and not by their stems. Since cinerarias like relatively cool, airy conditions, free ventilation is essential; once established in their individual pots they can be placed in a cold frame. They like bright conditions but should be shaded from strong, direct sunlight which can scorch the large, soft leaves. Further batches of cineraria seeds can be sown now and in a few weeks time to give a succession of plants flowering through the early spring.

herbs for winter

The aromatic flavor of fresh herbs is one of the great pleasures of summer. It is possible to continue to enjoy this through the winter, too, by sowing seeds now for growing in pots indoors.

1 Not all herbs will grow satisfactorily in pots, but basil, coriander, chervil, chives, dill, marjoram, and parsley are well worth trying. Sow enough for several pots in stages, to give a succession of young plants that can be brought from the greenhouse into the kitchen as they are needed.

2 Fill half-trays with moist sowing and cuttings mix and firm it well. Sow the seed thinly and cover it with a thin layer of more soil mix or sharp sand (**below**). Cover the completed tray with a plastic propagator top and set it in a slightly shady, evenly warm place until the seeds begin to germinate.

3 Once most of the seeds have germinated, remove the propagator top and bring the tray into full light. Grow the plants on in cool, airy conditions, pricking them out as necessary to give them more room to develop. When the seedlings are large enough, pot them up at two or three plants to an 3½ in/8cm pot (**left**).

4 Some hardy herbs are evergreen or partially evergreen, and can continue to be used sparingly through the winter. Grow them in tubs and pots outside, but later in the fall move them near the kitchen door to make harvesting easier. Bay, rosemary, sage, thyme, and winter savory are good candidates.

late summer

The garden is at its best now, but despite the profusion of summer flowers and foliage, the first hints of fall soon make themselves felt. Dusk begins to come earlier, and in the mornings there is a hint of mistiness and heavy dew. It's time to start to prepare for the fall and winter ahead.

In dry seasons, watering will be a priority in both the flower and kitchen gardens. Weeds may not be in such profusion as in early summer but must still be dealt with promptly if they are not to get out of hand.

Herbaceous and mixed borders can look splendid this month, but weeding, mulching, staking, and tying-in plants must continue. Staking is particularly important now because late summer storms can bring heavy rain and strong winds to wreck the display. Some of the border plants that were at their best earlier may now need to be trimmed in order to allow later-flowering subjects to be seen. Also take steps to control various pests and diseases before they have a chance to inflict too much damage—mildew on plants such as *Aster novi-belgii* (Michaelmas daisies) is very bad in

some years, but can be kept at bay by regular fungicide spraying of susceptible subjects.

In the kitchen garden there is often a glut as all the crops come to fruition at once. Picking must continue regularly because if pods or fruits of crops such as beans, peas, zucchini and squash are allowed to mature, the plants will stop producing further crops. Surplus

produce should be stored away for the winter and next spring, and now is the time for freezing, canning, and jelly and pickle making.

This is also the time of year when many gardeners take a couple of week's holiday, leaving the garden to fend for itself. This need not mean facing disaster on the return home; a little work put in before the holiday will be more than repaid afterward.

▶ *There should still be plenty of color from the flower borders for some weeks to come. Deadheading prolongs the flowering period.*

LATE SUMMER TASKS

Ornamental garden

- Remove dead flowers from lavender and thyme, and clip plants
- Take cuttings of tender and dubiously hardy perennials to overwinter
- Continue to spray Michaelmas daisies against mildew
- Weed borders and tidy up the plants
- Feed late-flowering border plants

- Check dahlias and chrysanthemums for earwig damage
- Pot up mint for winter use
- Trim back border plants to allow late-flowering varieties to be seen
- Order bare-root shrubs and trees for fall planting
- Plant container-grown shrubs and border plants, keeping them well watered

- Clear out faded window boxes and hanging baskets, and replant them for winter interest; continue to feed and water others
- Trim evergreen hedges for the last time
- Remove annuals that have finished flowering
- Plant Lilium candidum (Madonna lily) bulbs
- Continue to take semiripe cuttings of shrubs

Lawns

- Prepare the site for sowing grass shortly

◀ *Firm strawberries well when planting, and make sure the soil remains moist.*

Water garden

- Aerate ponds in sultry weather

Kitchen garden

- Make a herb garden and take cuttings of shrubby herbs
- Plant strawberries
- Summer prune trained fruit
- Pick early apples as they ripen
- Continue to harvest vegetables and soft fruit, freezing or storing gluts for later use

- Feed outdoor tomatoes with high-potash fertilizer; remove yellowed lower leaves
- Blanch leeks by drawing up soil around the stems
- Sow prickly seeded spinach or spinach beet for a spring crop
- Sow spring cabbages in a seedbed

- Sow Japanese onions
- Thin out new summer-fruiting raspberry canes, tying-in the rest to supports
- Pick fall-fruiting raspberries as they ripen
- Provide squash and pumpkins with straw to keep fruits off wet soil
- Ripen onions by bending their necks

▼ *Early apples are ready for picking when the fruit separates easily from the spur.*

Greenhouse

- Pick melons as they ripen. Continue to pick tomatoes and other food crops
- Regulate watering of food crops carefully
- Watch weather forecasts and close down vents on cooler nights

- Sow cyclamen seed for houseplants; start old cyclamen tubers into growth
- Take cuttings of pelargoniums
- Pot up freesia corms for scented winter flowers

- Check greenhouse heaters are in good working order

summer- and fall-flowering bulbs

Flowering bulbs

Spring is the season that instantly comes to mind whenever flowering bulbs are mentioned, but there are plenty of bulbs that carry magnificent flowers in late summer, and often on into the fall, making a spectacular show right at the end of the season.

Many of these bulbs like a warm, sunny position, and a nicely sheltered site—against the base of a warm wall, for example—is ideal. In areas with cold winters, some need to be lifted once they have finished flowering and stored under cover for the winter. Other types are quite hardy, and can be left in the garden all year round.

Agapanthus campanulatus and *Agapanthus* hybrids (African lily)

Striking, round heads of bright blue, funnel-shaped flowers held above clumps of strap-shaped leaves. Likes a sheltered spot; may need moving indoors for winter in particularly cold gardens.

Canna hybrids (Indian shot)

Bold, exotic-looking plants with large, paddle-shaped leaves, sometimes in bronzy shades, and spikes of brilliantly colored flowers often streaked and speckled. Lift rhizomes in the fall and store under cover.

Colchicum autumnale (fall crocus) Not a crocus at all, but with similar looks. Pink, lilac, or white goblet-shaped flowers in late summer and fall on fragile-looking, translucent stems. Fully hardy.

Crinum x *powelli* (swamp lily)

Sturdy stems carry clusters of large, fragrant, funnel-shaped pink blooms (white in the variety 'Album'). Rather tender; protect the planting area with a mulch of dry leaves or peat, but in very cold areas overwinter plants in pots under cover.

Cyclamen purpurascens

Magenta flowers with typical upswept petals and a delicate fragrance. Leaves are rounded and attractively marbled with silver. Fully hardy.

◄ *Agapanthus, with its striking, round heads of bright blue flowers, gives height and color to summer displays.*

▲ *These magnificent deep red canna lilies bring a richness to the color scheme in the garden.*

Eucomis bicolor (pineapple flower)

Densely packed spikes of flowers are pale green edged with purple; stems are topped off by a pineapple-like tuft of leaves. Frost hardy, but appreciates a winter mulch of dry leaves or similar in cold, exposed sites.

Galtonia candicans (summer hyacinth)

Tall stems with widely spaced, pendulous white bells rising above long, strap-shaped leaves. Frost hardy.

Gladiolus callianthus (acidanthera)

Lopsided, star-shaped white blooms with deep purple markings at the center. Sweetly scented. Lift corms in the fall and store in dry mix over winter.

Schizostylis coccinea (kaffir lily)

Open, star-shaped flowers with satin-textured petals; usually bright scarlet, though pink varieties are available.

Usually a flush of flowers in late summer, followed by the main flowering in mid- to late fall. Frost hardy.

Tigridia pavonia (peacock flower)

A long succession of short-lived flowers composed of three large and three small petals, usually strikingly marked with contrasting bright colors and patterns. Lift the bulbs in the fall and store in dry mix under cover over winter.

▶ *Indian shot (canna) makes a splendid specimen plant with its striking colors and boldly shaped foliage.*

ornamental garden: *general tasks*

Walls and fences often mark the boundary of a garden, but they also have several other purposes. They provide protection from cold winds, keep out stray animals and trespassers, give privacy from neighbors and passersby, and camouflage eyesores that detract from the pleasure of the garden.

Choosing the barrier

The type of screen that is most appropriate depends on the main purpose for which it is required. For protection against strong winds a solid barrier is not a good choice—the air rips over the top of the barrier and comes down the other side in gusts and eddies, often making the problem worse rather than curing it. A permeable barrier such as trelliswork with a light covering of plants, screen block walling or a post and rail fence is better in this situation, because it filters the wind and slows its speed.

For privacy, a solid barrier may be a better choice, though this depends on exactly how the garden is overlooked and by whom—a light, permeable screen may be sufficient to obscure the view from outside. The same applies to views that you wish to obscure from within the garden. Careful positioning of a screen is therefore very important. Moving the screen backward or forward between the object to be disguised and the viewpoint will make a substantial difference to the height or width the screen needs to be.

▼ *A light wooden garden screen may be all that you need to provide some privacy in a garden that could be overlooked.*

FENCES

Fences may be made of wood, plastic, or wire, and prefabricated wooden panels are one of the most popular options. They are made from thin woven slats, or feather-edged boards arranged horizontally or vertically. The panels are fixed to timber or concrete uprights but being solid they are not the best option as windbreaks. Picket fences consist of vertical pieces of timber spaced along horizontal rails; they have an attractive appearance, being formal yet cottagey. Post and rail fences use two or three horizontal rails between uprights; they are relatively inexpensive but are useful only as boundary markers.

Wire fences are not very attractive but are good at keeping out animals and trespassers. When clothed with climbing plants they also give a degree of wind protection and privacy.

overwintering non-hardy perennials

Many popular garden plants are not frost hardy or not reliably so. They are often described as "slightly tender" or "dubiously hardy," and will die in a hard winter. Take some cuttings now and you will have young plants to act as an insurance policy against winter losses.

Plants that may be severely damaged by frost include pelargonium, many varieties of fuchsia, argyranthemum (marguerite), lantana, heliotropium (heliotrope) and *Helichrysum petiolare* among others. Cuttings usually root quickly at this time of year to provide plants for overwintering.

1 Select vigorous, healthy, preferably non-flowering shoots and either snap them off or cut them with pruners (**right**). Trim off the lower leaves, and make a cut with a razor blade or sharp knife just below a leaf node.

2 Insert the prepared cuttings into sandy soil mix in a seedflat or around the edge of a pot (**below**). Water them well using a fine spray, and cover with a clear plastic propagator top. Keep them in a warm, lightly-shaded position.

3 The propagator top can be removed or its ventilators opened once the cuttings show signs of rooting. They can remain in a frost-free greenhouse or conservatory, or a cool, bright room in the home, over the winter months.

EARWIG TRAPS

Check chrysanthemum and dahlia flowers for signs of earwig damage. These flowers are particularly prone to attack from earwigs which eat holes in the petals, and distort the flowerheads by damaging the buds as they open. Night is the main feeding time, when most of the damage is done; during the day the earwigs seek a convenient place to hide. Earwig traps can be set up by inverting a flower pot loosely stuffed with straw on the end of a garden stake near the flowers. This provides an irresistably attractive daytime roost for the pests that can be shaken out of the straw and disposed of.

ornamental garden: *planting and potting*

It's time to look ahead and replant exhausted summer-flowering containers for winter interest. Trees and shrubs can be planted now, too, but remember they need special care after planting in hot weather. And if you fancy some fresh mint for winter, this is the time to pot up a few roots.

Container-grown specimens

Both shrubs and border plants can continue to be planted right through the summer if they have been grown in containers, but it is important to remember to water them regularly. Water the plants in their containers several hours or the day before planting. This makes sure that the top-growth is fully charged with moisture and is able to cope with any disturbance with minimum wilting; it also aids the removal of the root ball from the pot without root damage.

In hot, sunny weather, avoid planting during the middle of the day when the planting site is in full sun; it is better to wait until the relative cool of evening. Water the soil thoroughly immediately after planting: another watering a couple of hours later may be necessary to insure the water penetrates right down to the roots.

POT UP MINT FOR WINTER

A few sprigs of fresh young mint are very welcome during the winter months, and potted roots are easy to encourage into growth while outdoor plants are completely dormant.

The spreading roots of mint can be found just below the soil surface: using a trowel, lift a few long sections. They break easily, but even small portions of the roots will grow, and their removal will not harm the parent. Fill a seedflat with potting mix, firm it well, and press the lengths of mint root into the soil mix surface until they are covered. Cover with another layer of soil and water until it is just moist. Keep the flat in a moderately warm place, either in the greenhouse or on a light windowsill in the home. Once the shoots start to appear, give them as bright a position as possible.

▲ *Containers come in many shapes and sizes; these stylish containers are made from old car lights.*

plant a winter window box

By late summer, many containers of plants are starting to look a little jaded and past their best. Once this stage is reached it is a good time to replant some containers to give interest through the winter, when it will be especially welcome.

1 Remove and discard the worn-out bedding plants and soil. Clean out the inside of the window box, replace crocks over the drainage holes and refill the box loosely with fresh soil mix (**right**).

2 Select plants to give color, form, and flowers over the fall and winter. Suitable choices include winter-flowering heathers and viola (pansies), skimmia, dwarf conifers, variegated hedera (ivy), and small bulbs such as galanthus (snowdrops) and early-flowering crocus.

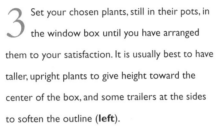

3 Set your chosen plants, still in their pots, in the window box until you have arranged them to your satisfaction. It is usually best to have taller, upright plants to give height toward the center of the box, and some trailers at the sides to soften the outline (**left**).

4 Remove the plants from their pots and set them in the windowbox using a trowel, adding more mix as necessary. Firm in lightly but thoroughly, using your knuckles. Bulbs such as snowdrops can be planted last, pushing them to the correct depth with a dibble (**right**).

5 Water the completed window box and put it in a sheltered place to establish for a few weeks: it can then be moved to its permanent position. Choose a place which will not be exposed to extreme cold or biting winds; plant roots in a container have less protection from cold than when they are buried in the ground (**right**).

◄ *Plant up a hanging basket to cheer up the winter months; this one includes colorful pansies, ivy, and skimmia.*

ornamental garden: *plants in season*

Herbaceous borders are perhaps at their peak this month, being filled with color and flowers. Hanging baskets, windowboxes, and tubs should still be looking good, too, though they may be running out of steam if watering and feeding have not been kept up.

▼ *Among the best of the late-flowering border plants are the aromatic, flat, colorful heads of achillea.*

TREES AND SHRUBS

Buddleja davidii
Campsis radicans (trumpet creeper)
Clerodenrum bungei
Eucryphia
Fuchsia
Hebe
Hibiscus syriacus
Hydrangea macrophylla
Hypericum (St John's Wort)
Lonicera (honeysuckle)
Rosa (rose)

BULBS

Crocosmia x *crocosmiiflora*
Cyclamen purpurascens
Eucomis bicolor (pineapple flower)
Gladiolus hybrids
Lilium (lily)

▼ *The sweet scent of lilies continues to be a major feature of the garden.*

▲ *Many rose varieties have several flushes of bloom to carry them through the summer and into early fall.*

PERENNIALS

Acanthus (bear's breeches)
Achillea (yarrow)
Aconitum (aconite)
Anemone hybrida
Aster
Begonia semperflorens
Chrysanthemum
Gazania
Helenium
Helianthus annuus (sunflower)
Hemerocallis (day lily)
Kniphofia (red hot poker)
Phlox paniculata (perennial phlox)
Romneya coulteri (tree poppy)
Rudbeckia (coneflower)

lawns and water gardens: *general tasks*

As long as the weather has not been too dry, lawns should still be looking good. Next month is the best time to start a new lawn from seed—prepare the ground for it now. Water gardens should also be in good condition, with plenty of color and interest from both floating plants and marginals.

Keeping ponds healthy

Now that floating plants such as *Nymphaea* (water lilies) have spread their leaves to shade much of the water surface from direct sun, any problems with green water due to algae that occurred earlier in the summer should be over. Lilies and similar plants should still have plenty of flowers to add color to the water garden scene, but some of the older leaves will be yellowing and starting to die back. Remove these from the water as soon as you notice them; it is important to keep decaying plant refuse out of the pond as far as possible. Also continue to check the undersides of lily leaves for the transparent blobs of snails' eggs, and remove any found. Water snails can be a serious plant pest, and snails or eggs are often introduced unwittingly when new plants are bought. The ramshorn snail is the only satisfactory species for garden pools.

AERATE POND WATER

Normally, the water in a pond takes in oxygen and releases carbon dioxide at the surface, but in sultry, thundery weather this process becomes very slow or may stop altogether. Fish in the pool can be badly affected, and can sometimes be seen at the surface of the pool gulping in air: if nothing is done they may die. The effect is worst at night, when pond plants are adding to the carbon dioxide content of the water.

The simple remedy is to stir up the water to increase its surface area and allow some of the carbon dioxide to escape. This can be done by leaving fountains or waterfalls running, by stirring the water vigorously with a stick or aiming a forceful jet from a hose into the pool.

▲ *Waterfalls not only look and sound attractive, they can help to keep the water in a pool well aerated—often vital in thundery weather.*

▶ *A well-established, well-kept lawn sets off the whole of the rest of the garden. It will soon be time to start making new lawns.*

prepare sites for sowing grass

Early fall is the best time to sow seed for a new lawn, but now is the time to start preparing the soil. Remember that the grass is going to be a permanent feature for years to come, so it is well worth making sure that the basic preparation is thorough. This is your only chance to get soil conditions right.

1 Clear the site of existing turf, cultivated trees, shrubs and plants and weeds. It is especially important to get rid of perennial weeds because they will be very difficult to control once the lawn is established. Use a weedkiller such as glyphosate where necessary.

2 Once the site is cleared of plant growth, remove any other obstructions there may be, such as large stones, paving slabs and so on (**right**). The cleared site can then be leveled, filling in dips and flattening out bumps.

PREPARING FOR A NEW LAWN

Turf is the quickest way to make a new lawn, giving virtually instant results. Although soil preparation for turf does not need to be quite as painstaking as for seed sowing, it is still worth cultivating the area to be turfed thoroughly well in advance, removing perennial weeds, stones etc. and adding a long-lasting fertilizer to get the grass off to a good start.

3 If the site slopes steeply it may be necessary to reduce the gradient or construct terraces. Where this sort of work is essential, remove the topsoil and stack it nearby, adjusting the levels by moving subsoil. Respread the topsoil evenly once the work is completed.

4 Check the structure and condition of the soil. Add well-rotted organic matter such as garden mix to improve heavy and light soils. Give it a final once-over before sowing (**left**).

kitchen garden: *sowing and planting*

The reward for all your work in the vegetable garden becomes apparent as more and more crops are ready to harvest. It's still time to be thinking ahead, however; there are crops to be sown or planted now for next season, and winter crops to look after for the more immediate future.

Spinach for spring

The tender green leaves of spinach make a very welcome vegetable in the spring, and plants sown now are less likely to run to seed than crops sown in the spring for summer use. Traditionally, prickly-seeded varieties of spinach are the ones to sow in late summer and early fall, using round-seeded types in spring. Many modern hybrids are equally good for both seasons, however.

Sow seeds thinly in drills about 12in/30cm apart; water the soil the day before if conditions are dry. Once the seedlings emerge, thin them to around 9in/23cm. Depending on the weather, there may be leaves to harvest from late fall right through the winter, but the most reliable flush of foliage will be in early spring. Earlier cropping can be obtained if the seedlings are covered with cloches.

JAPANESE ONIONS

Onion varieties such as 'Express Yellow' and 'Senshyu Semi-globe Yellow' are specially bred for sowing in late summer. They are winter hardy, and will give the earliest crop next year in early to midsummer. The timing of sowing is fairly critical, however. Plants  that are sown too soon often run to seed prematurely in the spring, whereas those which are sown too late either give a disappointing crop of small bulbs or die out over winter. Gardeners in cold districts need to sow one or two weeks ahead of those in milder areas.

Sow in rows 9–12in/23–30cm apart, and leave the seedlings until spring; then thin them to 4in/10cm apart. Water the drills before sowing, and damp them down frequently in the days following if the weather is hot, to cool the soil and improve germination.

◀ *Sow plenty of rows of spinach. The leaves shrink so much when they are cooked that you always need more than you think you will.*

plant strawberries

The yield and quality of strawberries usually drops off after three years of cropping, and it is advisable to think about replacing the bed with new plants after this time. Replacing one-third of the plants in the strawberry bed each year means that you will continue to have strawberries to harvest every year.

1 Strawberry plants are prone to a number of virus diseases that reduce their yields, and it is a good idea to buy certified virus-free stock to give them the best possible start.

3 Well-rooted runners in small pots or peat blocks can be bought from garden centers, or by mail order from specialist suppliers. They should be planted as soon as possible after arrival, spacing them around 12–18in/30–45cm apart in rows 3ft/90cm apart (**below**).

2 Prepare the soil well before obtaining the plants, adding well-rotted organic matter and clearing away all traces of weeds, so difficult to control in any well-established strawberry bed.

4 Plant with a trowel (**above**), firming the plants in thoroughly with the sole of your boot. The crown of the plant should be just level with the soil surface. Water after planting, using a medium fine spray on the watering can or hose to avoid disturbing the roots (**below**).

◄ *Crops for harvesting in winter, such as cabbages, should be coming along strongly. Keep them weed free, and water them in dry weather.*

633

kitchen garden: *gathering the harvest*

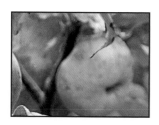

In late summer and early fall crops are ripening daily, and much of the produce may go to waste unless it is picked regularly and stored correctly. Some crops need to be consumed as soon as possible after picking, but others will keep for some time as long as the right storage method is used.

Harvesting and storing produce

The best time for harvesting is early in the day, before crops lose their moisture in the warm weather. Handle the produce carefully so that it is not bruised; any damaged crops should be put to one side for immediate consumption. Once picked, keep fruit or vegetables for short-term storage in a cool, dark place; the salad box of a refrigerator is usually ideal if there is room.

Root vegetables can be left in the ground over the winter, or stored in boxes of almost-dry mix or in paper sacks. Dense-hearted cabbages, ripe squash and pumpkins, and many varieties of apples and pears will keep well in a cool, airy shed; onions and shallots can be plaited into ropes or stored in trays somewhere dry. Don't forget to make jellies and pickles, as these are good, traditional preservation methods for a wide range of fruit and vegetables.

FREEZING

Freezing is probably the most popular method of long-term storage, and is appropriate for soft fruit, or any crop that deteriorates quickly once picked. It preserves the color and flavor of the fruit well, though the texture may suffer in some cases.

Pick over the fruit well; wash it only if essential. It can be open-frozen (ie spread on trays), frozen in containers packed with dry sugar, or frozen in sugar syrup—whichever is most appropriate. Fruit normally cooked (cooking apples and gooseberries, for example) can be cooked before freezing. Remember to label the packs because fruit is difficult to identify once frozen. Most well-prepared fruit will keep in excellent condition for over a year in the freezer.

◄ *Gooseberries for cooking are picked as soon as they are large enough. Dessert varieties, for eating raw, must be left on the bushes to ripen.*

▶ *Pick early-maturing varieties of apple as soon as they separate easily from the tree. Eat them within a few days; they do not store well.*

pruning fruit in summer

Apples and other fruits grown as cordons, fans, or espaliers need pruning in the summer to control their growth. Correct pruning is a vital technique for keeping these forms under control so that the plants remain both attractive and fruitful.

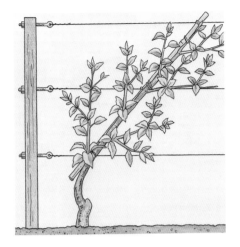

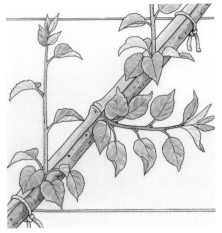

1 Summer pruning should be carried out over a number of weeks as the shoots reach the correct stage. Shoots which are ready for pruning are about pencil thickness, and becoming woody and dark in color at their base (**above**).

2 The first leaves from the base on each shoot are known as the basal cluster and usually consist of three leaves growing in the same place. This basal cluster is ignored when counting the number of leaves on the shoot (**above**).

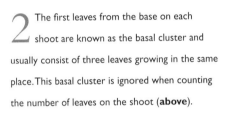

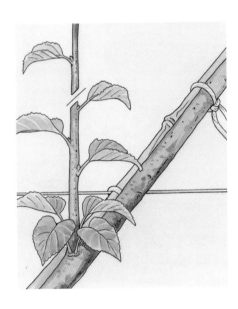

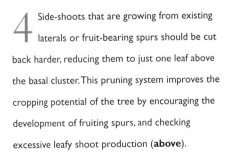

3 The severity of pruning depends on the type of shoot. New lateral shoots which are more than 8in/20cm long, and growing from the main stem, are cut back to three leaves above the basal cluster. Cut just above the bud in the leaf axil, angling the cut slightly so that it slopes away from the bud (**above**).

4 Side-shoots that are growing from existing laterals or fruit-bearing spurs should be cut back harder, reducing them to just one leaf above the basal cluster. This pruning system improves the cropping potential of the tree by encouraging the development of fruiting spurs, and checking excessive leafy shoot production (**above**).

making a herb garden

There's no doubt that fresh herbs make all the difference to home-prepared food, and no keen cook would want to be without them. But herbs are worth growing for many other reasons besides their culinary value, including their wonderful scents, attractive appearance, and their fascinating history.

Because herbs are so special, they are frequently grouped together in a specialist herb garden. Traditional herb gardens are formal, often with very intricate designs. While this is an attractive way of growing them, informal herb beds are also popular and sometimes fit

more naturally into the overall garden design. It's all a matter of personal choice.

Before making a final decision on the style and position of the herb garden, consider the following factors. An open, sunny sheltered position is essential. This encourages the strongest growth from the plants, and makes the herb garden a more attractive place for the gardener to linger, enjoying the fragrances wafting on the still, warm air. If herbs are being grown primarily for cooking, site the herb garden near the kitchen so that it is possible to gather a few herbs quickly even when it is wet or cold. For the same reason, make sure that the main herbs are accessible from a path or firm surface to avoid treading in the mud when gathering them.

Once you have chosen the site, it's time to think about the design. There are many traditional options, from the complicated ribbons and twists of a knot garden to a simple checkerboard of alternate paving slabs and planting spaces. Herbs do seem particularly

◀ *When making a herb garden, include stone slabs to step on in order to make it easier to pick the herbs in wet weather.*

HERB OILS

Pick a handful of strongly aromatic herbs, eg, fennel, marjoram, rosemary, tarragon or thyme, and crush them lightly. Put them in a jar or bottle with a well-fitting lid and pour lightly warmed, good quality oil over them. Olive oil is a favorite, though it does have a strong flavor of its own; grapeseed oil is more neutral, allowing the herb's own flavor to come through. Put the lid on and let the oil stand in a warm place for two or three weeks, shaking frequently. Strain the oil into another jar of fresh herbs and repeat. Use in salads, marinades and rubbed over fish and meat before cooking.

suited to formal arrangements: two intersecting paths dividing a small, square garden into four equal beds is a popular option, especially with a sundial or statue placed at the center to form a focal point.

▲ *Choose healthy, well-established young plants from a garden center or, for more unusual varieties, a specialist herb nursery.*

Selecting the plants

Choose the plants according to your own preferences, but remember to include some evergreens such as bay, rosemary, sage, and winter savory to add interest to the garden in winter. Mix and match plants with variegated, silver or dark foliage, and set plants with broad, bold leaves, such as angelica or lovage, to contrast with the fine, feathery textures of leaves such as fennel and dill.

The majority of herbs prefer light, free-draining soil; their roots may rot in wet soils. They also need soil that is not too rich in nutrients because the best flavors and aromas do not come from soft, lush plants. Dig the site well, as deeply as possible to promote good drainage. If necessary, add some coarse sand or fine grit to the soil to improve drainage around the plants' roots. On poor soils, add a light dressing of bonemeal fertilizer to keep the plants growing steadily through the season.

Buy young, vigorous, container-grown plants from a garden center or specialist nursery. Firm them in thoroughly after planting, and don't forget to label them. Let them become well established before taking too may cuttings, though it will not do any harm to pinch out some of the shoot tips to encourage branching.

▲ *A dressing of gravel around the plants will help to keep the soil surface free-draining as well as finishing off the herb garden attractively.*

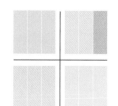

greenhouse: *general tasks*

Increasingly the evenings and nights are becoming cool, providing ideal conditions for diseases such as gray mold unless dead and dying plant material is removed promptly. Now's also the time to check that greenhouse heaters are in working order, ready for when they are needed.

Harvest greenhouse crops

Keep picking eggplants, cucumbers, melons, bell peppers, and tomatoes as they ripen. Take care with the watering of tomatoes; when plants are watered after a dry period the fruits are prone to split. Keep the soil just moist at all times. Remove lower leaves from tomatoes as they yellow; they are of no further use to plants.

Peppers can be harvested while they are still green, or left on the plants to ripen. Pick them just as they begin to turn color, and they will carry on ripening after picking. It is sometimes difficult to judge when melons are ready to harvest, but it is best to rely on your sense of smell.

Ripe melons give off a heady, almost alcoholic aroma from the stem end, and the fruits' skin starts to crack slightly around the base of the stem. Once ready, cut them and eat them as soon as possible because they soon become overripe if left.

▼ *Melons can become very heavy as they mature, and often need to be supported in nets attached to the greenhouse framework.*

TAKE PELARGONIUM CUTTINGS

Pelargonium plants can be cut down in the fall and overwintered in their pots in the greenhouse, but young plants raised from cuttings taken now often do better in the long run. Use vigorous, healthy shoots, preferably non-flowering. If flower buds are present in the growing points of any suitable shoots, just pinch them out as you prepare the cutting. Follow the procedure for softwood cuttings (see page 535), keeping them in a humid atmosphere until they are rooted. If space is at a premium in the greenhouse get rid of the parent plants once you are sure that these cuttings are well rooted.

start new and old cyclamen

Cyclamen, with their graceful, upturned petals on long flower stems, are very popular winter-flowering pot plants. Now is the time to start old tubers into growth after their summer rest, and to sow seeds for new plants.

1 Cyclamen tubers that have been stored in pots of dry soil mix over the summer will probably be producing tiny clusters of leaves on the surface by now. They should be tipped out of their pots and the old mix crumbled away.

2 Very large tubers can be cut into two or more sections, each with a growth bud; dust the cut edges with fungicide powder. Repot into fresh, moist potting mix, so that only the lower half of the tuber is buried.

3 Cyclamen seed is sometimes slow to germinate. Speed up the process by soaking the seed in tepid water for 12 hours, then rinse it under gently running water for 30 minutes to wash away natural germination inhibitors (**above**).

4 Sow the seed in pots of sowing and cuttings mix, pushing it just below the surface (**left**). Seedlings develop with long leaf stalks and a tiny, translucent tuber on the soil surface. Handle carefully when pricking out.

POT UP
FREESIA CORMS

Freesias have wonderfully scented flowers, and corms that are potted up now will give elegant, fragrant plants for the home in the middle of winter. But check when buying them that they are scented varieties, as some of the modern cultivars have unfortunately lost their fragrance.

Plant the corms in gritty mix so that their tips are around 1in/2.5cm below the mix surface, setting six corms to a 5in/13cm pot. Water sufficiently to make the mix just moist. Stand the pots outside in a sheltered place in the garden until frosts are likely, when they should be moved to a garden frame or cool greenhouse.

fall

Enjoy the garden's final, colorful fling of flowers and foliage before the darker days and cool, dull weather of the fall take hold. There's plenty of tidying up to do after the summer, but it's also time to look ahead and start making preparations for the spring to come.

early fall

Many of the early fall tasks involve clearing away the debris of the summer season, but there's also plenty of sowing and planting to do. Warm, sunny days and an abundance of bright flowers, foliage, and fruits make the melancholy job of tidying up after the summer a much more pleasant affair.

Although fall marks the end of the main growing season, it is a busy time in the garden. There are crops to be gathered, leaves to sweep up and tender plants to be protected before the first frost arrives. Misty mornings, heavy dew, and cool weather combine to make ideal conditions for fungus diseases; regular checks and prompt treatment where appropriate are necessary to prevent plant losses.

The dying leaves of deciduous trees and shrubs often make a remarkable display of brilliant color, but all too soon the show is ended by gales which bring the leaves tumbling down. Dead leaves must be removed from garden ponds, lawns, alpine plants, paths, and patios before they can do damage or become a nuisance, and leaf clearing can be a major job in large gardens.

Beds and borders should still be putting on a show with late-blooming plants if varieties have been chosen wisely. Tidy spent border plants and old stems to show off these late-flowering plants to advantage. Weeds continue to thrive and need removing regularly.

Fall is an excellent time for planting both bare-root and container-grown plants. It is also time to plant spring bulbs, always a pleasant task, as we can look forward to their flowers signaling that winter is over in a few months' time.

There are seeds to be sown in early fall, too. Some hardy annuals will brave the winter cold and produce early flowers next summer if sown outdoors now. In the vegetable garden peas and some beans can be tried, and fall is the perfect time to sow a new lawn.

◄ *Border plants such as the architectural, steely-blue* Eryngium *continue to make a bold display well into the fall months.*

EARLY FALL TASKS

General

- Watch out for fungus diseases around the garden
- Deal with fallen leaves
- Clean and put away garden furniture

Ornamental garden

- Plant spring bulbs
- Sow hardy annuals to overwinter
- Take cuttings of evergreens and plant hardy evergreen shrubs
- Move tender plants under cover before the frosts. Provide outdoor protection for slightly hardier ones

- Replace annuals and summer bedding with spring bedding as they fade
- Continue to clear containers and replant with bulbs and spring bedding
- Clear and weed around fall-flowering bulbs and perennials

- Prepare sites for fall planting of bare-root trees and shrubs
- Protect decorative berries from birds
- Take cuttings of old-fashioned and shrub roses
- Check ties and stakes on trees, and adjust if necessary

▲ *Daffodils bulbs should be planted as soon as they become available in the stores.*

Lawns

- Sow new lawns
- Rake and aerate lawns, and give them a fall feed
- Repair bald patches, broken edges, bumps and dips

- Deal with toadstools
- Water garden
- Net ponds against falling leaves

- Remove tender pond plants before the frosts

Kitchen garden

- Plant spring cabbage
- Harvest maincrop potatoes
- Support winter brassicas if necessary
- Lift maincrop carrots and beets
- Thin out seedlings

- Pick outdoor tomatoes and clear away plants
- Harvest pumpkins and squashes before the first frosts
- Sow winter lettuce under a cloche or tunnel

- Plant onion sets for an early crop
- Continue picking apples and pears

▼ *Prick off cyclamen seedlings as soon as they are large enough to handle.*

Greenhouse

- Ventilate the greenhouse and water plants with care
- Bring pot plants such as azaleas and solanums back indoors
- Pick remaining food crops (such as peppers and tomatoes) and discard the plants

- Clean the framework and glass where appropriate
- Plant bulbs in pots and bowls for forcing
- Pot up cineraria and cyclamen seedlings
- Continue to take cuttings of tender outdoor plants as an insurance against winter losses

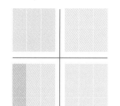

ornamental garden: *general tasks*

Even when late flowers have faded, the fall garden need never be dull. Deciduous foliage can provide some spectacularly brilliant colors; berry-bearing plants continue the show for months, provided birds don't eat the lot. Evergreen plants also start to come into their own in the fall.

Enjoy fall color

Shortening day length triggers off brilliant reds, oranges, and yellows in some deciduous leaves. Plants vary in the intensity of color produced. Acer (maple), berberis (barberry), cercidiphyllum, fothergilla, nyssa (tulepo), parthenocissus (Virginia creeper), hamamelis (witch hazel),

▼ *Fall color from deciduous trees and shrubs can makes a brilliant spectacle. Select varieties specially bred for their colorful foliage.*

and many others provide some reliably colorful species and varieties.

Climate and soil conditions have a major part to play, too. The more marked the contrast between day and night temperatures, the better the leaf color. Wet, mild weather, when the leaves tend to remain green and hang on the trees for longer, can also spoil the show. But other factors are more within our control. Prevent fall leaves from being prematurely blown from trees by planting them in a sheltered

position. Provide fertilizers during the growing season to promote plenty of lush leaf growth to turn color later. For lime-hating plants, acid (rather than neutral) soil greatly intensifies their leaf color.

PROTECT BERRIES FROM BIRDS

Bunches of brightly-colored berries can decorate the garden right through fall and winter, but often the first sharp frost brings flocks of birds to strip the berries from the plants.

Netting (provided it is supported away from the plants to prevent birds pecking through it) protects the berries but usually spoils the appearance of the plants. Bird-deterrent sprays are an alternative; they use a harmless but bitter-tasting compound to make berries unpalatable. Yellow and orange berries are far less likely to be attacked than bright red ones, so try planting varieties such as *Pyracantha* 'Orange Glow' and *Ilex aquifolium* 'Bacciflava'.

TAKE CUTTINGS OF EVERGREENS

Shoots to be used as cuttings should have ripened at the base and be around 6in/15 cm long. Pull them away from the main stem with a small heel of bark at the base; treat them with a rooting hormone combined with a fungicide to prevent rotting, and insert them into trays of sandy sowing and cuttings mix. Overwinter the cuttings in a cold frame or unheated greenhouse; they should have rooted by the following spring.

protect non-hardy plants

A number of garden and patio plants are not reliably hardy in many gardens and need a little help to survive the winter. If you have taken cuttings from these in late summer (see page 625) you will at least have some plants in reserve in case the worst happens.

1 Herbaceous plants die down in the fall and spend the winter below soil as a dormant root-stock. Tender plants may not survive frost and cold penetrating the ground, but an insulating mulch of dry leaves, dead bracken or chipped bark heaped over the root area will help them survive.

2 Small trees and shrubs can be protected from low temperature damage by surrounding them with insulating material such as straw or bracken. The material must be dry to avoid fungus disease, and it must be loosely packed so that air can circulate through it.

3 Surround the shrub with a circle of wire netting supported on stakes, and loosely pack the wire cage with the insulating material. A piece of plastic sheeting over the top will keep the material dry (**below, left**).

4 The roots of plants in containers are particularly prone to cold weather damage. Lag the container with straw or a similar material; bubble wrap sheeting is useful for wrapping around tubs and pots in a double layer (**below**).

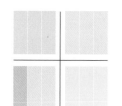
ornamental garden: *planting and sowing*

It's time to prepare for a colorful spring, by replacing summer bedding plants and annuals that are past their best, and by planting spring-flowering bulbs in lawns. New evergreen shrubs can also be planted safely now, as long as they are not likely to be damaged by cold winter weather.

Plant hardy evergreens

Because evergreen plants carry their full complement of leaves at planting time, extra care must be taken to protect them from adverse weather. Strong winds carry moisture away from the leaf surfaces, leading to scorching and leaf fall, and leaf tips and margins can be damaged by hard frosts. Make sure that evergreens planted now are quite hardy; more tender types will do better if they are planted in late spring.

Prepare the soil for evergreens in the normal way, digging deeply and adding some slow-release fertilizer such as bonemeal to the base of the planting hole. Make sure you firm in plants thoroughly; because they have leaves to catch the wind, root rock can be a problem. They should also be firmed back in thoroughly with the ball of your foot after windy or frosty weather. If cold, windy weather strikes after planting evergreens, protect them with a windbreak while they get established (see page 668).

▼ *Evergreen shrubs and trees really come into their own during the fall and winter months, providing color and interesting shapes.*

REPLACE SUMMER BEDDING

Summer bedding and annual flowers will soon be past their best. Over the next few weeks it's time to replace them with spring bedding for some early interest next year.

Put spent plants on the compost pile. Dig the vacant soil over well, removing weeds, and add some slow-release fertilizer; refill containers with fresh potting mix. Plant up beds and containers with spring bedding plants such as *myosotis* (forget-me-not), *viola* (pansies), *primula* (primroses), and *erysimum* (wallflowers), interplanted with spring bulbs such as tulips and hyacinths for an effective display.

naturalizing spring bulbs

Bulbs growing through grass always look particularly attractive during the spring flowering season. Daffodils and crocus are the two subjects most popular for growing like this, but several others are also successful, including *Colchicum* (fall crocus), *Fritillaria meleagris* (snakeshead fritillary), *Muscari* (grape hyacinth) and *Scilla* (squill).

1 Informality is the key to success when naturalizing bulbs. To look as natural as possible, handfuls of the bulbs are scattered randomly over the area, and planted as they fall, with one or two minor adjustments (**above**).

2 Removing plugs of turf and soil to plant the bulbs individually is hard work (**above**). The lawn area should be watered deeply two or three days before planting to soften the turf; a long-handled bulb planter makes the job much easier.

3 Drop a bulb at the base of the hole and replace the soil plug, treading it down lightly with the foot. Make sure the bottom of the bulb is in firm contact with the soil at the base of the hole, not wedged half-way up.

4 When planting small bulbs such as crocus it is often easier to fold back a section of turf and plant direct into the soil below. Cut an H-shape with an edging iron (**left**), undercut and fold back the two flaps of turf. Plant the bulbs randomly into the soil (**below**), water, then fold the flaps back into place and firm thoroughly.

SOW HARDY ANNUALS OUTDOORS

Hardy annuals such as *nigella* (love-in-a-mist), *calendula* (marigolds), *limnanthes* (poached-egg plants) and *helianthus* (sunflowers) can be sown where they are to flower to overwinter outdoors.

5 Before planting bulbs in lawns, remember that the grass cannot be mown in spring until the bulb leaves have died. Choose an informal area of the garden where this will not matter.

6 4 7

bulbs, corms, and tubers

Plants need certain conditions in order to be able to grow—they must have suitable temperatures, sufficient light and an adequate supply of nutrients and water. If some or all of these requirements are not present, the plants must have some strategy for coping with the problem or they will die.

Many plants become dormant in order to survive until conditions become suitable for growth again. The most successful plants do not just become dormant, however,

they also have a store of nutrients and water to help them over the difficult period once they begin to regrow. Bulbs, corms, and tubers are all underground storage organs that hold a reserve of nutrients and water to enable them to start into growth and flower in the appropriate season. Many gardeners think of all these structures as "bulbs," and they are often grouped together and referred to as "bulbous plants" for convenience. However, there are differences between them and the way they grow.

Bulbs are modified leaves with leaf bases attached to a short stem. The leaves are very fleshy and contain food reserves, and the small stem is cone or disk shaped. In the center of the bulb, surrounded by the fleshy leaves, is the flower bud and the immature foliage leaves that will emerge from the bulb when it starts to grow.

On the outside of the bulb there are usually firm, dry scales forming a tunic that helps protect the bulb from moisture loss and damage by pests or diseases. Not all bulbs have these, however; lily and fritillaria bulbs have no papery tunic, and the overlapping leaf scales are very obvious. This makes these bulbs particularly prone to damage and drying out, and they need more careful storage and handling than bulbs with a tunic. The structure of a bulb can easily be examined by slicing an onion in half. The separate, fleshy leaves, cone-shaped basal stem, central embryo flower bud, and protective outer scales are all easy to recognize.

Corms are modified stems. On the outside they are surrounded by the dried remains of the previous year's

◀ *Dahlias have clusters of tuberous roots which carry their growth buds on a short section of the plant's main stem.*

▲ *The daffodil is one of the most familiar true bulbs. Bulbs increase by producing offsets from the base, which eventually separate entirely.*

▲ *Corms are surrounded on the outside by the dried remains of the previous year's leaf bases, so they sometimes look like bulbs.*

leaf bases, making them look superficially like bulbs, and under these leaf bases they have parallel ridges that are the leaf nodes. A new corm is formed on top of the old one every year, and the old one withers away. If a corm is sliced in half, you will see a solid structure, that is not composed of separate leaves like a bulb.

PLANTING THE RIGHT WAY UP

If a bulb, corm, or tuber is planted upside down, this will not stop it growing; however, the stems will have to do a U-turn to grow up to the soil surface, and this bend in the stem will be a weak point that's vulnerable to damage. It is usually fairly easy to tell which is the top of the structure—look for a growth bud or buds at one end and the remains of roots at the other. Some tubers are more difficult because they have a dished surface, but tiny growth buds should be visible. Fritillarias and lilies, without a protective tunic, often have hollow centers where water may collect and cause rotting. It is safer to plant the bulbs on their sides to avoid this happening.

A tuber is another swollen storage organ which may be formed from either the stem or the roots, depending on the plant. The potato is a very familiar stem tuber, while dahlias have clusters of root tubers. On potato tubers, axillary growth buds are found toward one end. These are the "eyes" that grow into shoots from which form roots and eventually, more tubers. The original tuber withers away as its food reserve is used up. Since root tubers usually have their growth buds only on a short section of the plant's stem to which they are attached, each tuberous root must have a small piece of main stem attached to it if it is to grow. Tubers are also solid throughout if sliced through.

The food reserves within bulbs, corms, and tubers exist to help the plant survive its dormant period. This may be in winter when conditions are too cold for growth, or in summer when they are too dry—the timing varies according to species.

ornamental garden: *plants in season*

Early fall may mark the beginning of the end of the growing season, but it is still filled with color and interest. Late-flowering perennials and bulbs, bright fruit and berries abound; and, depending on the weather conditions, the first of the fiery fall leaf tints from deciduous trees and shrubs make themselves evident.

▲ Perovskia atriplicifolia *'Blue Spire'* has attractive, aromatic, gray-green foliage as well as panicles of strikingly blue flowers.

▶ *The butterfly's favorite, Sedum spectabile. The variety 'Iceberg' has pure white flowers instead of the more familiar pink.*

▼ *The dainty flowers of Cyclamen hederifolium are held above attractively marbled leaves that persist right through the winter.*

TREES AND SHRUBS

Caryopteris x *clandonensis*
Ceanothus (California lilac)
Clerodendrum bungei (glory bower),
   C. trichotomum
Erica (heath)
Hebe
Hydrangea macrophylla
Leycesteria formosa
   (Himalayan honeysuckle)
Malus (crab apple)
Perovskia atriplicifolia
Rosa (flowers and hips) (rose)
Vinca major (greater
   periwinkle), *V. minor* (lesser periwinkle)

PERENNIALS AND BEDDING PLANTS

Achillea (yarrow)
Aconitum napellus (aconite)
Anemone hybrida
Aster
Eryngium (sea holly)
Helenium
Hemerocallis (day lily)
Kniphofia (red hot poker)
Rudbeckia (coneflower)
Schizostylis coccinea (kaffir lily)
Sedum spectabile (ice plant)
Solidago (Aaron's rod)

BULBS

Amaryllis belladonna
Colchicum (fall crocus)
Crinum x *powellii*
Crocosmia crocosmiiflora
Crocus (fall-flowering species)
Cyclamen
Nerine bowdenii

◀ *The daisy-like flowers of helenium brighten fall borders with their gloriously rich shades of red, bronze, and yellow.*

lawns and water gardens: *general tasks*

Mild, damp fall weather encourages toadstools—an unwelcome sight in the middle of the lawn—but is ideal for the germination of grass seed. Garden ponds need care now to prevent the water from being polluted with decaying plant matter, and pond fish need help to face the winter ahead.

Remove tender pond plants

Some floating pond plants make an attractive contribution to the pool in the summer, but will not survive a cold winter out of doors. They include the water hyacinth (*Eichhornia crassipes*) and the water lettuce (*Pistia stratiotes*). Remove them from the pond well before the first frosts are due. Overwinter them in a frost-free greenhouse, placed in a washing-up bowl or similar container filled with pond water, with a lining of mud at the bottom. Put them back in the pond in early summer. *Trapa natans* (water chestnut) is also frost tender but is an annual that will not survive the winter anyway. It should also be removed from the pond to prevent the decaying foliage from polluting the water.

NET PONDS AGAINST FALLING LEAVES

It is vital to keep fall leaves out of the pond. Decaying plant material gives off toxic gases which will poison fish and turn the water stagnant. Use fine mesh plastic netting to cover the surface of the pond, insuring that it is pegged down securely all around the edges.

Before putting the net in position, cut down excess growth of oxygenating plants and remove this, together with all dead and dying foliage and flowers from water and marginal plants.

sow a new lawn

Seed is the cheapest way of making a new lawn, and allows most control over which grass varieties are used. Although lawn seed can also be sown successfully in spring, early fall, while the soil is still warm and the conditions moist, is the best time for the job.

1 Give the prepared site a final raking to level it and break down the clods of soil to a fine, even, crumbly texture (**right**). If the soil is loose and puffy, shuffle over the whole site to firm it gently with your feet before raking.

2 Weigh out the correct quantity of seed for the area to be sown (sowing rates should be given on the packs, and are usually about 1–1½ oz per sq yd/35–50 g per sq m). Split the total quantity of seed into two.

3 Sow the first half of the seed mixture over the whole lawn as evenly as possible, working from top to bottom; then sow the second half working from side to side (**left**). This double sowing helps to even out any inconsistencies in the sowing rate.

4 Use a spring-tine rake to scratch the seed lightly into the soil but do not try to bury it (**below**). Using seed treated with a bird repellent will cut down the bird nuisance; if necessary, the lawn area can be protected with plastic netting supported on stakes.

REMOVE TOADSTOOLS FROM LAWNS

Crops of toadstools are common on turf at this time of year, appearing magically overnight. There are many different types of fungi. Most of them grow on organic matter in the soil and are quite harmless. If their appearance spoils the look of the lawn, they can simply be picked off and thrown away—they appear for only a short time each year.

One type that is more serious is *Marasmius oreades* (fairy ring fungus) that can cause obvious, unsightly green rings in the grass. Although various fungicides may be suggested, this fungus is almost impossible to treat successfull; remaking the lawn may be the only answer. The deep green rings may be disguised by treating the lawn with fertilizer to green up the rest of the grass.

◄ *The water hyacinth (*Eichhornia crassipes*) is a serious invasive pest in frost-free areas, but is killed off in the fall in cold climates.*

kitchen garden: *general tasks*

There are sowings and plantings to be made in the kitchen garden, and harvested crops need to be stored away carefully. Make sure winter vegetables are progressing satisfactorily, and give them the protection they need from the bad weather that may be around the corner.

Harvest pumpkins

Pumpkins and winter squashes should be cut and brought under cover before the first frosts. As long as they are fully ripened, they can be stored for many weeks in a cool but frost-free, dry shed. Check the fruit has no signs of damage or rot before storing, particularly where it has been resting on the soil.

Maincrop potatoes should also be lifted now. On a dry, sunny day, fork the potatoes out of the soil and leave them on the surface of the ground for several hours to dry. Store them in burlap or heavy-duty paper sacks, or wooden or sturdy cardboard boxes. Do not use plastic sacks; they retain moisture and cause rotting. Store in a cool, dark place and cover the potatoes to exclude all light.

SUPPORT WINTER BRASSICAS

Winter brassicas such as broccoli, Brussels sprouts, kale, and various cabbages can make quite tall plants. In exposed gardens they run the risk of being blown over because they have relatively shallow root systems. In windy areas, provide each plant with a sturdy wooden stake.

The earliest varieties of Brussels sprouts will now be ready for picking. Start harvesting from the base of the stem, where the largest buttons are, and gradually work upward.

▶ *Winter squashes should store well for weeks, but any that are damaged should be used up straight away as they will only rot in store.*

lift root vegetables

Some root crops will happily stay in the soil right through winter, but others are best lifted at the end of the growing season and stored above ground, especially in areas where the soil is heavy and inclined to remain wet in winter. Wet conditions are likely to cause the roots to rot.

1 Carrots are at their tastiest pulled young (**right**) and eaten straight away, but maincrop varieties make a useful crop for eating throughout the winter. If left in the soil too long they tend to split, which can make them unusable.

2 Fork up the carrots carefully to avoid spearing them, and shake off loose earth. Cut off the foliage (**below**), and layer the carrots in boxes of fine, almost dry soil, sand or peat. Store the boxes in a cool, dark place, eg, shed or garage. Use up any damaged carrots straight away.

3 Beets are often pickled in vinegar, but are also delicious if cooked and eaten like any other fresh root vegetable. The golden variety will not stain pink any other food with which it comes into contact, as the standard red varieties do.

4 Beets are lifted and stored in the same way as carrots, but the leafy tops should be twisted off, not cut with a knife, to avoid bleeding. Lift the roots before they become too big because they are inclined to go woody (**below**).

PROTECT SUMMER-PLANTED POTATOES

If you planted a few cold-stored potatoes in summer to give you new potatoes in the fall and winter, it will soon be time to protect the plants from cold weather, depending on the climate in your area. Use a mulch of straw, dry bracken or similar material along the rows. The first tubers may be ready for harvesting in mid-fall, but in reasonable conditions can be kept in the ground until mid or late winter.

kitchen garden: *planting and sowing*

As well as harvesting the abundance of crops in the kitchen garden now, keep some continuity of cropping going with further plantings and sowings. A little extra protection from the weather can be gained by sowing under cover. Seedlings from earlier sowings need thinning out or transplanting.

Plant onion sets

Onion sets planted in the fall will give an early crop next year, several weeks before maincrop varieties are ready for harvest. Varieties available for fall planting have been chosen for their hardiness and disease resistance, and include 'Early Yellow Globe', 'Yellow Spanish', 'Snow White hybrid', and the red-fleshed 'Red Hamburger'. Prepare the soil thoroughly and mix in some coarse sand or grit to lighten it if necessary, as fall-planted sets need free-draining conditions. Plant the sets in rows 14in/35cm apart, spacing the sets 4–6in/10–15cm apart in the row. Always plant onion sets with a trowel, because simply pushing the sets into the soil can compact the ground immediately beneath them, making it difficult for the roots to penetrate. Fall-planted onions can be ready to harvest as early as late spring, but they can be stored for only a few weeks.

THIN OUT SEEDLINGS

Seedlings from late sown crops, including lettuce, radish, spinach, and turnips, among others, should be thinned out as soon as they are large enough. This thinning is best carried out in progressive stages to allow for plant losses—thin to half the final recommended spacing first, then remove every other plant later on, as necessary.

Where seedlings are very crowded, great care is necessary to avoid disturbing the roots of the plants which are to remain after thinning. If the weather is dry, water the row of seedlings before thinning to make it easier to tease away the unwanted plants.

◀ *Fall-planted onion sets should produce a crop that is ready for harvesting very early the following summer.*

lettuce for winter

It's great to have been able to cut fresh salads straight from the garden through the summer, and it's something that will be sadly missed over the next few months. However, it is possible to have a supply of winter lettuce from the greenhouse—the plants won't be as succulent and full hearted as summer varieties, but they're still worth growing. Sow the seed now; once the seedlings are large enough, they can be transplanted into growing bags, or direct into the greenhouse border.

1 It's important to choose the right variety of lettuce for growing in the greenhouse in winter because only a few are suitable. Check with your local garden center to see what is the best choice.

2 An unheated greenhouse is quite suitable for growing winter lettuce, although heated greenhouses will give a faster-maturing crop. Cold frames and polytunnels can also be used successfully for growing winter salads.

3 Sow the seed thinly on a prepared flat of moist soil mix and cover lightly. Lettuce seed becomes dormant in very hot conditions, so it is important to keep the flat in a well-ventilated, lightly shaded position after sowing.

4 Once the seedlings are showing through, move the flat to full light. Water very carefully to avoid fungus disease. Prick out the seedlings to wider spacings as soon as they are large enough to be handled easily.

▲ *Transplant cabbages to their cropping positions. If preferred, space the young plants closely to obtain "greens" rather than densely hearted cabbages.*

sprayers and spraying

An efficient, easy-to-use sprayer is an essential piece of garden equipment. Pests and diseases are very common, particularly in the kitchen garden, and most gardeners are likely to find themselves needing to spray plants at one time or another. Even organic gardeners need sprayers, for they are used to apply organic remedies and fertilizers.

A sprayer enables a liquid to be applied as a spray of fine droplets, usually by forcing it through a nozzle under pressure. This enables the operator to achieve good, even coverage of the plant being treated. Where just a few plants are involved, a small, inexpensive hand-held sprayer holding about 1 pt/500 ml is sufficient. Although a small hand-held sprayer is useful for houseplants and treating individual plants in the garden, it has its limitations. It is often difficult to mix pesticides in such small quantities, and it is a nuisance to keep refilling the sprayer for larger jobs. Also, operating the trigger action is very tiring during prolonged use.

The next step up is a compression sprayer holding about 1–1¾ gallons/5–8 litres. Typically, this has a hand pump on top, and once the sprayer has been filled and the top screwed on tightly, a few strokes of the pump supply enough pressure to send the liquid through the nozzle in a fine, penetrating spray. This type of sprayer generally has a spray lance attached to plastic tubing to give a long reach. When the pressure of the spray starts to fall, a few more strokes of the pump are required to restore it. This type of sprayer is ideal for most medium to large gardens.

◀ *This type of sprayer is pressurized by a few strokes of the pump every few minutes. A long spray lance is a practical addition.*

▼ *A small hand-held sprayer is fine for occasional use, but is not practical where there are a lot of plants to be treated.*

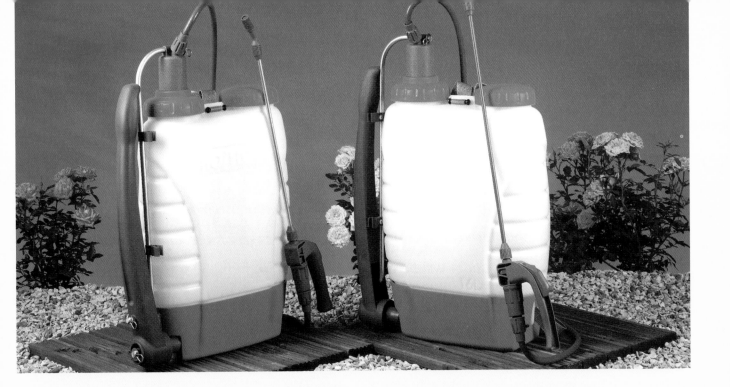

For even larger spraying jobs, a backpack sprayer is useful. This holds 2 gallons/10 litres or more of liquid and comes with straps so that it can be worn like a backpack. A lever on the side is operated with one hand while the lance is held in the other; the lever is pumped up and down gently and continually during spraying. Backpack sprayers are expensive and are only likely to be necessary for very large vegetable gardens or orchards, although they can be useful for lawns or treating large areas of vacant soil with weedkiller. When filled with liquid, a backpack sprayer is very heavy and is unsuitable for those with bad backs.

Sensible spraying
The fine drops from sprayers can travel long distances on the breeze. Never spray on a windy day, when other plants or even neighboring gardens could be unintentionally on the receiving end.

Always follow the instructions for diluting and applying pesticides to the letter, and dispose of any unused solution as advised on the pack. The best times to spray are in the early morning, or in the late afternoon or evening when there is no strong sun to scorch the leaves, and beneficial insects are less likely to be harmed.

▲ *Backpack sprayers are excellent for large-scale spraying jobs, but a smaller, cheaper sprayer is adequate for the majority of gardens.*

If you use a sprayer to apply weedkiller, label it clearly with an indelible marker pen and keep for applying weedkiller only. Never use it to spray cultivated plants with pesticides or fertilizer because traces of the weedkiller may remain, however well it is washed out.

SAFE USE OF GARDEN CHEMICALS

- Store chemicals safely, out of the reach of children and pets, in the original packaging complete with instructions
- Use the most suitable chemical for the job, choosing the least persistent type where there is an option
- Read the application instructions and follow them carefully
- Mix up just enough chemical for the job, avoiding surplus spray solution
- Keep pets and children away while the spray is being mixed, applied, and until it has dried on the treated plants, unless the label advises differently
- Wash out the sprayer thoroughly after use, disposing of the rinsing water on to bare soil or gravel paths
- Use gloves when handling concentrates and solutions, and wash all exposed skin thoroughly when spraying is finished

greenhouse: *general tasks*

Now that the days are shortening, greenhouse plants need all the daylight that they can get, and washing the glass can make an enormous difference. Extra space will be needed for seedlings and tender plants; make room for them by clearing out the remains of summer crops such as tomatoes.

Indoor azaleas

Azaleas should have spent the summer outside in a partially shaded bed, with their pots plunged in soil to prevent them drying out. Their summer holiday is over now so dig them up, clean the pots and bring them back into the greenhouse before the cold weather arrives.

Plants can be repotted if necessary, but don't be in too much of a hurry to move them up a size because they flower best if the roots are slightly cramped. Traditionally azaleas are grown in soil-based potting mix and clay pots, but they also do well in plastic pots and soilless mix as long as you are careful with the watering. The mix should be just moist at all times. Keep the plants in a cool room when they are in flower.

CLEAN THE GREENHOUSE

Even though greenhouse glass may look clean, it will have collected a surprising amount of grime over the summer months, which cuts down the amount of light able to reach the plants inside. Wash the outside of the glass thoroughly with a stiff broom and warm, soapy water, or use a pressure sprayer.

On a mild, dry, preferably sunny day, move the plants outdoors while you clean the inside—scrub down the glass, staging, and framework. This helps to combat overwintering pests and disease spores while making the place look neat and tidy. Don't slosh too much water about inside, and leave the doors and ventilators open to air and dry the greenhouse before moving the plants back in.

pot up flower seedlings

Seedlings of cineraria and cyclamen that were sown earlier should now be ready for potting up. Both are invaluable winter-flowering plants for the home, bringing color and cheer into the house just when it is most needed. Cinerarias that were sown in late spring and early summer will be in flower by early or midwinter; those sown later will flower in spring. Cyclamen usually take around 14 months to reach flowering size.

REMAINING TOMATOES

Greenhouse tomato plants have come to the end of their useful life now, and should be cleared away. Pick any unripe fruit that remains on the plants. Keep the best-developed fruits in a cool, dim place indoors and they will slowly ripen over the next few weeks. Storing a ripe apple or banana with them in an enclosed space, like a drawer or cupboard, will speed up ripening. Small, firm fruits are unlikely to ripen satisfactorily like this, but if there are enough of them they make terrific green tomato chutney.

◀ *Azaleas make attractive winter-flowering pot plants, and are not too difficult to keep successfully from year to year.*

1 Since cyclamen seed germinates over an extended period, not all seedlings from the same sowing will be at the same stage of growth, and not all will be ready for transplanting. Select the largest for moving on, and extricate them carefully from the tray to avoid damaging the rest.

2 Handle the seedlings gently, because they are very delicate. Hold the young plants by the leaves and not by the slender, fragile stems; pot them up so that the tiny developing tuber is sitting on the surface of the compost (**right**). Firm in the roots very lightly.

3 Cineraria seedlings are more robust, and their development should be more even. Depending on their stage of growth, the seedlings can be pricked out into trays, into individual 3½in/cm pots, or moved to larger pots (**below**). Keep the soil mix just moist at all times.

4 Shade newly-transplanted seedlings from direct sun for a few days, using horticultural blanket or a sheet of newspaper to protect them if necessary (**below**). Both cyclamen and cineraria need cool conditions; be prepared to ventilate the greenhouse in sunny weather when necessary.

mid-fall

The tidy-up continues as more and more fall leaves hit the ground and late season flowers fade. As the weather becomes increasingly cold, it's time to protect the more delicate plants. Remain on the alert for frosts, though with luck you may find yourself enjoying a warm and sunny Indian summer.

Tidying up

This is often the time when fall leaf color is at its glorious best, but it won't be long before a windy spell brings the leaves to the ground in drifts. Fallen leaves are not so bad when they are dry and crisp, but once rain turns them to a slimy brown sludge they pose a danger to both plants and people. Remove them from lawns and small, vulnerable plants like alpines before the leaves smother them; also clear them from paths and steps before somebody slips in the decomposing mush and injures themselves.

Cut down spent flowers and dying foliage in herbaceous borders, but don't be too enthusiastic. Some dead, brown stems and leaves have an architectural value, and seed heads can be particularly decorative.

Cold snap

At what time the first frost arrives, and just how bad the weather might be, depends largely on your particular location. Some regions can rely on mild falls and winters, while others can guarantee that freezing conditions will arrive in the near future. Only experience can tell you what to expect, but always be prepared for the worst. Better to prepare your dubiously hardy plants for icy weather that does not arrive, than leave them to be killed by a single unexpected cold snap.

Future plans

As more plants in the kitchen garden finish cropping and are removed, vacant soil begins to appear, ready to be dug over for next spring. The earlier winter digging can start the better, allowing you maximum time to complete a task which can be backbreaking if rushed. If the fall weather is too depressing, cheer yourself up by continuing to plant spring-flowering bulbs and spring bedding to give you something to look forward to at the end of the winter, and start thumbing through new seed catalogs to plan next year's sowing program.

◄ *The deep pink flowers of* **Nerine bowdenii** *stand out in the fall sunshine. The bulb's foliage does not appear until spring.*

MID-FALL TASKS

General

::: Remove fallen leaves from paths, patios, steps and lawns and turn them into leaf mold
::: Clear away all garden debris to avoid pests and diseases
::: Protect vulnerable plants from rain and cold; beware of early frosts

Ornamental garden

::: Tidy herbaceous borders and divide border plants; apply bonemeal to borders and around shrubs and trees
::: Plant tulips and hyacinths; plant lily bulbs as they become available

::: Remove and burn diseased leaves fallen from roses
::: Plant bare-root trees and shrubs
::: Lift and store dahlia roots when the leaves have been blackened by frost

::: Lift and store gladioli and tuberous begonias
::: Finish planting spring bedding
::: Protect newly-planted shrubs from strong winds

▲ This is the ideal time to plant tulips. If planted too early, they start into premature growth.

Lawns

::: Lay turf for new lawns
::: Continue to sweep up leaves and repair damaged areas of grass. Mow as necessary, raising the cutting height of the mower from its summer setting
::: Apply bulky top-dressing

▼ Turf establishes quickly in fall conditions, providing a virtually instant new lawn.

Water garden

::: Remove submersible pumps from ponds; clean and store them under cover
::: Tidy pond plants and marginals, removing dead leaves from the water

Kitchen garden

::: Continue harvesting crops, and store fruit and vegetables. Pick remaining apples and pears. Check fruit and vegetables already in store
::: Remove vegetable plants as they finish cropping; begin digging and adding organic matter to soil. Start a new vegetable plot if required

::: Finish planting spring cabbages
::: Start to fill in seed orders for next year when the catalogs arrive
::: Take hardwood cuttings of soft fruit
::: Plant new rhubarb crowns
::: Prune blackcurrants, blackberries, and hybrid berries

Greenhouse

::: Remove shading and clean the glass if this has not already been done
::: Sow Lathyrus odoratus (sweet peas) for early flowers outdoors next year

::: Take care not to overwater, or splash water about. Remove dead and dying foliage, flowers, and fruit promptly

::: Ventilate whenever possible to maintain an airy atmosphere
::: Heat the greenhouse as necessary to maintain a suitable temperature for the plants

general tasks

Clean up fall leaves and plant remains and transform them into valuable compost and leaf mold for the garden. A number of garden plants need protection from fall and winter weather now. It is not just cold that is the problem; excess rain can have serious effects, too.

Cold protection for plants

Continue to provide protection for plants that may not be reliably hardy in your area (see page 645). It is often difficult to know just how well a particular plant will survive local conditions, but any plant that is described as "rather tender," "dubiously hardy," "half-hardy" or "suitable for favored areas" should be given extra care in regions where there are penetrating frosts. This is particularly important for young plants, or recently planted subjects that have not had a chance to establish properly and become acclimatized to the conditions. Plants such as agapanthus (African blue lily), cordyline (cabbage palm), phygelius, yucca, eucalyptus, passiflora (passion flower), and acacia (wattle) are among many that may need protection.

Remember that many plants that will happily survive overnight frosts where the temperature rises during the day, are likely to be killed by cold spells where freezing conditions persist for several days at a time.

KEEP OFF EXCESS RAIN

It is often excessively wet rather than cold conditions that kills plants during the fall and winter. Plants with furry leaves, such as verbascum, are particularly prone to rotting in wet weather because the fur on the foliage holds on to moisture. Silver-leaved plants are also at risk; they are adapted to dry growing conditions and are often badly affected by a damp atmosphere.

Susceptible plants can usually be protected by covering them with an open-ended cloche, which keeps water off the foliage but still allows air to circulate to help prevent fungus disease from developing.

◀ *It is important to protect susceptible plants against overnight frosts at this time of year. One option is the horticultural blanket.*

how to build a compost pile

Virtually all types of soil benefit from the addition of plenty of rotted organic matter, but the problem is usually finding a handy supply of suitable material. Composting your garden refuse has two benefits — it provides a convenient and valuable supply of the organic matter your soil needs, and is also a means of disposing of awkward, bulky waste.

1 A compost pile is simply somewhere waste material can be gathered together to rot down (**left**). Confining it within a wire, plastic, or wooden bin (it can be either a proprietary composter or a home-made one) keeps it neat, and helps to encourage rapid decomposition by providing the most favorable conditions.

2 Anything organic (i.e. anything that has once lived) can be composted, but avoid animal products and cooked items because these attract vermin. Young weeds, plant refuse, fruit and vegetable peelings are all suitable. Lawn mowings can be added to the heap if they are well mixed with bulkier, more open waste. Add a layer of garden soil to the heap every so often.

SWEEP FALLEN LEAVES FROM PATHS

It is surprising how quickly fallen leaves become slippery when they have been lying around in damp weather. On patios, paths, and particularly on steps they can pose a real danger to pedestrians. Sweep them up regularly; apart from anything else, they are easier to gather up when they are still dry. Pack the leaves into plastic sacks, tie the tops and pierce some holes in the sides of the sack with a garden fork. Leave the sacks in a corner of the garden and eventually the contents will rot down into valuable leaf mold.

3 Once the bin is full, cover the top with a piece of old carpet or cardboard to keep in the heat and keep out excess rain, and allow the contents to decompose to a dark brown, crumbly, sweet-smelling mass (**above**). Occasionally turning the sides of the heap to the middle is hard work, but it does speed up the rotting process.

4 The traditional fall bonfire is a wasteful and polluting affair, but can be used for woody prunings and other material that is too hard to rot down. Diseased plant material and seeding weeds are also best burned rather than composted, as disease spores and weed seeds may not always be killed by the composting process.

665

ornamental garden: *general tasks*

Even though the summer is over, the ornamental garden still contains plenty of interest for the weeks ahead. Some plants need to be lifted now and stored under cover for the winter. Flower borders can be tidied, and many perennials can be given a new lease of life by being divided and replanted.

Decorative seed heads

When clearing up the flower border, it's all too easy to cut down plants that have a valuable role in providing fall and winter interest. Many seed heads are highly decorative, and have strong architectural shapes that are very attractive. Don't be too rigorous about deadheading—leave the final flush of flowers to set seed.

Flowers worth growing for their seed heads include acanthus (bear's breeches), allium, briza (quaking grass), cynara, eryngium (sea holly), festuca (fescue), *Iris foetidissima*, lunaria (honesty), nigella (love-in-a-mist), papaver (poppy), *Physalis alkekengi* (Chinese lantern), scabious (especially 'Paper Moon'), and typha (bullrush). Many border plants also have "everlasting"-type flower heads that are worth preserving when they are dead, including achillea (yarrow), carlina (carline thistle), hydrangea and *Sedum spectabile*. Their russet-brown shades are more subtle than their summer colors, but produce a pleasing effect, especially when lightly iced with frost.

APPLYING BONEMEAL

Bonemeal is a natural slow-release fertilizer that gradually supplies its nutrients to the soil. It provides some nitrogen and a much larger proportion of phosphates, and is useful for applying around perennials, trees, and shrubs during the dormant season.

Always wear protective gloves when applying bonemeal. There is a slight risk of the fertilizer being contaminated with animal diseases, although this risk is extremely small and should not be a concern provided the bonemeal has been properly sterilized. However, if you have any small cuts or abrasions to your skin, bonemeal—and other powdered fertilizers—will make them sting unpleasantly.

divide border plants

Division is an easy way to increase your stock of herbaceous perennials. Not only does it give you a new supply of plants, but it actually improves the performance of plants that have been in place for more than a couple of years. Border plants can also be divided in spring, but mid-fall is generally the best time of year to do the job.

1 Popular border plants such as Campanula (bell flower), hosta, Achillea (yarrow), Echinops (globe thistle) and Papaver (poppies) are all suitable subjects for division. Dig up the whole clump carefully with a garden fork, and place it on a spare piece of weed-free soil or on a plastic sheet on the lawn or path (**right**).

2 Often the center of the clump will be woody and hard, with the strongest shoots growing around the edge. Splitting the clump up will enable you to discard the unproductive center and rejuvenate the plant by replanting the more vigorous sections.

3 Use two forks back to back to prise tough clumps apart (**left**), or cut them with a knife. Smaller plants may be teased apart by hand. As a guide, each portion should be large enough to fit comfortably in the palm of the hand, and must have good roots and strong growth buds,

4 Replant the new portions straight away; the roots will dry out if they are exposed to the air for too long. If replanting in the same place, dig the soil over quickly with a trowel, removing any weeds, and incorporate a little bonemeal or similar slow-release fertilizer.

◄ Sedum spectabile *is one of a number of border plants whose dead flower heads remain attractive through the fall months.*

LIFT AND STORE DAHLIAS

Dahlias in the border need to be protected from cold, wet winter weather in order to survive until spring. As soon as frosts have blackened the foliage, cut down the main stem to about 6in/15cm and lift the tuberous roots. Store them upside down for a few days in order to allow any moisture to drain from the hollow stems, then clean the soil off the tubers and pack them into flats, covering them with almost-dry compost. Store the flats in a cool but frost-free, dry place (such as a garage or shed) over the winter. Gladioli corms and begonia tubers should also be lifted now, and cleaned and stored in boxes of compost in a dry, frost-free place, like the dahlias.

ornamental garden: *planting*

Fall is an excellent time for planting, but in windy areas, it is worth providing a temporary windbreak as protection for newly planted subjects. Bulbs pose no such problems. While many spring-flowering types should have been set out last month, there are one or two that prefer later planting.

Bare-root trees and shrubs

Bare-root plants have been lifted from nursery beds in the open ground, and have to be sold in the dormant season when they are more resilient to the disturbance of transplanting. They are usually cheaper than container-grown plants, and there is often a better choice of varieties available. They are also easier to transport than plants in containers, and can be bought by mail order.

Care should be taken not to let the roots dry out any more than is necessary. Try not to expose them to the air but keep them covered by plastic bags, paper, or burlap sacks during transportation. Ideally bare-root subjects should be planted immediately, but if that is not possible they can be heeled in to a spare piece of ground temporarily, just covering the roots with fine soil. Inspect the roots immediately before planting, and trim back with pruners any that show signs of damage.

▲ *Bare-rooted conifers (here wrapped in burlap for transportation) are best transplanted now during the dormant season.*

PROTECT NEWLY-PLANTED SHRUBS FROM STRONG WINDS

Shrubs that have been planted in exposed positions are at risk of damage from the windy weather that is common at this time of year. Evergreens are most vulnerable because they are still carrying their leaves, but even deciduous plants can be damaged by root rock caused by wind catching the branch framework, or the branches may be snapped off.

Reduce the possibility of damage by erecting a temporary windbreak on the windward side of the shrub. Drive two or three stakes into the ground, and tack windbreak netting, sacking, or even old plastic sacks to the stakes to provide shelter. The windbreak can be removed in late spring next year, provided the plants are sufficiently well established.

▶ *Some of the most attractive tulips are the smaller varieties, such as* Tulipa kaufmanniana *hybrids, with their striking, mottled foliage.*

plant tulips and hyacinths

Spring bulbs such as narcissus (daffodils) and crocuses should have been planted in early fall, but it pays to wait until now, or even until late fall, before planting tulips and hyacinths. If planted too early they make premature growth that may be damaged by cold weather.

1 Tulips and hyacinths make good subjects for the flower border, especially when mixed with spring bedding plants such as wallflowers and forget-me-nots. Dig the soil deeply and add a slow-release fertilizer such as bonemeal.

2 Dig planting holes with a trowel or use a special bulb planter (**right**). Make the holes sufficiently deep for the tops of the bulbs to be covered with twice their own depth of soil. Shallow planting leads to poor flowering.

3 Drop the bulbs into their holes making sure that they are the correct way up, and that the base of the bulb is in contact with the soil at the bottom of the hole. Return the soil to the hole and firm it lightly.

4 Because there will be no sign of the bulbs until next spring, it is easy to forget where they are planted and to damage them by cultivating the ground in winter. Label the area where they are planted to avoid this (**below**).

CONTAINER BULBS

Tulips and hyacinths are also ideal for planting in tubs and windowboxes. The best effects are always obtained by planting only one variety in each container because different varieties flower at different times.

growing variegated plants

The term variegated means marked with two or more colors, usually in an irregular pattern, and as a gardening term it is nearly always applied to leaves. The most common colors on a variegated leaf are green and yellow, or white, though several other colors can be involved, such as pink, red, purple, and orange.

Variegated foliage obviously adds color and pattern to the garden in much the same way as flowers do. It is valuable because it tends to be longer lasting than flowers, and on evergreen plants is present through the fall and winter when flowers are scarce and the garden could easily look dull and uninteresting. Variegated evergreens that merge into the background during the summer stand out splendidly in the dormant season,

seeming to glow with a special brightness. Gold-variegated subjects, particularly, give the appearance of sunshine even on the cloudiest, most miserable days.

Because the green pigment (chlorophyll) in leaves is necessary for efficient photosynthesis (the process by which plants manufacture their own energy), variegated plants, with less green pigment, tend to be at a bit of a disadvantage. This means they are usually slower growing and less vigorous than all-green varieties, and they generally need a position in bright light where they can receive as much sun as possible. If they do not receive sufficient light the variegation may disappear as the plant tries to compensate by producing more green pigment.

Variegated plants should be positioned carefully from a design point of view, too. When planted near each other, they lose their impact and can cause uncomfortable clashes of color and tone. For the best effect, a variegated variety should be surrounded by plain-leaved subjects, preferably of a darker shade, against which the brighter variegation will stand out.

True variegation takes the form of an irregular pattern, but the term is generally used to include more regular markings on leaves, too. There may be a central blotch, often at the base of the leaf near the leaf stem, or a yellow or silver margin of varying widths. Sometimes the leaf is speckled with a contrasting color or is irregularly marbled, while the variegation may have distinct edges or merge into the contrasting shade. Many variegated leaves have just two colors, but others have more and some hedera (ivies) are green, pale green,

◄ Euonymus fortunei *'Emerald 'n' Gold' has
an intense golden variegation that sometimes
becomes flushed with pink in cold weather.*

◀ Ilex aquifolium *'Aurea Marginata', with gold-margined leaves, has the added bonus of being a berry-bearing female cultivar.*

margined), "variegata" (variegated), "maculata" (spotted), and "picturata" (painted).

The following variegated evergreen varieties are attractive and reliable:

• *Aucuba japonica* 'Crotonifolia', 'Picturata', 'Variegata' and others (spotted laurel)
• *Cornus alba* 'Elegantissima', 'Spaethii' (dogwood)
• *Elaeagnus* x *ebbingei* 'Limelight', 'Gilt Edge'
• *E. pungens* 'Maculata', 'Frederici' and others
• *Euonymus fortunei* 'Emerald 'n' Gold', 'Emerald Gaiety', 'Silver Queen' and others
• *Hedera colchica* 'Dentata Variegata', *H. helix* 'Gold Heart Eva', 'Glacier' and others (ivy)
• *Ilex aquifolium* 'Golden Queen', 'Silver Milkmaid' and others (holly)
• *Osmanthus heterophyllus* 'Aureomarginatus'
• *Pieris japonica* 'Variegata'
• *Viburnum tinus* 'Variegatum' (laurustinus)
• *Vinca major* 'Variegata' (greater periwinkle)
• *Vinca minor* 'Argentiovariegata' (lesser periwinkle)

cream, and white, for example, while plants such as *Solenostemon* (coleus) may have four or more colors on the same leaf. Occasionally no green pigment is visible at all—*Berberis* 'Rose Glow', for example, is purple marbled with pink. In these cases, chlorophyll (the green pigment) is still present but is masked by other pigments.

The fact that a species or cultivar is variegated is often reflected in its botanical name. Look for words like "aureomarginata" or "argenteomarginata" (gold or silver

DEALING WITH REVERSION

Variegated varieties have often arisen as mutations or "sports" of a plain-leaved species, and can be unstable—they tend to "revert" to the plain-leaved state. If a plain-leaved branch is produced, it is more vigorous than the variegated shoots because it contains more chlorophyll and will eventually overtake the entire plant. As soon as a plain-leaved shoot is seen, it should be pruned out, cutting it right back to where it joins the main stem. The production of reverted branches sometimes indicates that the plant needs brighter growing conditions.

◀ Aucuba japonica *'Variegata' is an attractive and reliable feature in the garden at any time of year.*

ornamental garden: *plants in season*

In most areas, fall color is now at its peak, but it will not be long before the leaves fall. Seed heads and fruit have an ever-increasing role to play in providing interest, but late-flowering perennials and bulbs are still providing color in many gardens.

▼ *The vigorous climber* Parthenocissus quinquefolia, *commonly known as Virginia creeper, has outstanding fall foliage.*

TREES AND SHRUBS

Acer (maple)
Berberis (deciduous) (barberry)
Cercidiphyllum japonicum
   (katsura tree)
Cotoneaster
Erica (heath)
Euonymus alatus (burning bush),
   E. europaeus and others
Fothergilla major
Hamamelis
Hippophae rhamnoides (sea buckthorn)
Hydrangea quercifolia
Malus (apple, crab apple)
Parthenocissus (Virginia creeper,
   Boston ivy)
Gaultheria mucronata
Pyracantha (firethorn)
Rosa (hips) (rose)
Skimmia
Sorbus
Vitis coignetiae, V. vinifera
   (grape vine)

PERENNIALS

Aconitum napellus (monkshood)
Anemone hybrida
Aster
Gentiana sino-ornata
Liriope muscari (lily turf)
Physalis alkekengi var. franchettii (Chinese
   lantern)
Sedum spectabile (iceplant)

BULBS

Amaryllis belladonna
Colchicum (common crocus)
Crinum x powellii
Cyclamen
Galanthus reginae-olgae (snowdrop)
Nerine bowdenii
Schizostylis coccinea (kaffir lily)

▲ Schizostylis coccinea, *the kaffir lily, is one of the latest flowering border plants. The variety 'Sunrise' has delicate shell-pink flowers*

▶ Purple-leaved Rosa glauca, *usually grown for its purple foliage, has the bonus of bunches of glossy red rose hips through the fall.*

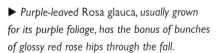

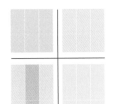

lawns and water gardens: *general tasks*

Ponds still need attention to insure that the water is not being polluted by fallen leaves and other plant debris. If you are planning a new lawn, this is an ideal time to lay turf; if you just want to improve the condition of your existing lawn, a bulky top-dressing applied now will work wonders.

Pond plants and marginals

A water garden can look rather depressing by this time of year with untidy, yellowing foliage and dead and dying flowers of marginals spoiling the pond's appearance.

It is now a good idea to cut the stems right back to just above water level, taking care not to drop any plant material in the water.

If you have not already cut back underwater oxygenators, do so now. These plants produce rampant growth during the spring and summer, and much of it will die back during the fall and winter. It is best to anticipate this by using pruners to reduce the tangle of stems by up to two-thirds. Make sure the cut plant material is removed from the water.

Pond fish may still benefit from feeding, depending on the weather and the number of fish in the pool. If it is still relatively warm, try giving a small amount of food to see how interested they are; continue feeding only if they clear up the food given within 5 or 10 minutes.

▼ *Tidying pond plants and marginals using pruners will cut down on the amount of tangled stems when the plants die back now the summer months have ended.*

REMOVE SUBMERSIBLE POND PUMPS

A submersible pump is the simplest method of powering water garden features such as fountains and waterfalls. If the pump has not already been removed from the water, do so now, cleaning it thoroughly (especially the filter). Store it in a dry place under cover for the winter months.

If it is not convenient to remove the pump—when it is in the centre of a large pond and is not easy to reach, for example—it can be left in place, but it should be switched on and run for a short while every few weeks throughout winter, unless the pond is frozen. Removing the pump in fall will prolong its life, though.

a new lawn from turf

Turf is far more expensive than grass seed but it has one great advantage—it provides an instant effect. It is now easy to obtain special lawn turf made up of fine-leaved grass varieties for high quality, luxury lawns. Meadow turf is cheaper; although the lawn will not be of bowling green quality it will be adequate for most family gardens. Don't underestimate the amount of work involved in laying turf; it is a hard, heavy job, so round up as much help as you can.

BULKY TOP DRESSING

Mix peat (or peat substitute), good quality, sieved loamy soil and medium horticultural sand (but not yellow builders' sand). The proportions of ingredients depend on the underlying soil type—increase the amount of sand on heavy soils, and use more loam and peat on light soils. Spread the top-dressing all over the grass, working it in between the blades with the back of a rake or a stiff broom. It will make the lawn look very messy to start with but will soon disappear, encouraging strong, dense grass growth next spring and summer.

1 Prepare the lawn site in advance, as you would for a new lawn from seed (see page 653). Turf needs to be laid within a day or two of delivery, so make sure you will be able to start laying it straight away.

2 Unfold or unroll the first length of turf and lay it flat on the prepared soil, using a taut line to act as a guide for a straight edge where necessary (**right**). Use the back of a spade or a special turf beetle to firm down the turf and insure good contact with the soil.

3 Lay the next length of turf, butting the short edges closely together, and continue like this until the first row is complete (**right**). Lay the second row tight against the first, staggering the short joints like bricks in a wall. Stand on a plank on the new turf to spread your weight evenly. Continue until the whole area has been covered.

4 Once the turfing is complete, cut the edges of the lawn to shape with a half-moon edging iron, using a taut line (for straight edges) or piece of hosepipe (for curves) as a guide. Trickle a mixture of peat and sand, or some fine soil, into the cracks between the turfs to encourage them to knit together (**left**).

kitchen garden: *general tasks*

Rhubarb is really a vegetable, although it is always thought of as a fruit. In early spring, tender young rhubarb stems are a real delicacy, and this is the ideal time to plant new crowns. Some soft fruit crops are due for pruning, and hardwood cuttings can be taken to increase or replace stock.

Plant new rhubarb crowns

Rhubarb is best grown from certified virus-free crowns (also known as sets). They are available from good garden centers or by mail order, and consist of a clump of fleshy roots topped by a knobbly crown with one or more large, plump buds. Dig plenty of well-rotted garden compost or manure into the planting site. Do not add any lime because rhubarb prefers slightly acidic soil conditions.

Plant the crowns so that the buds are only just covered with soil; if planting more than one crown, set them 3ft/90cm apart. Do not pull too many stems in the spring following planting. 'Cherry Red' and 'Macdonald' are good varieties. Plant the herb sweet cicely nearby, and include a handful of the foliage when cooking the stems. It reduces the acidity, and you won't need to add so much sugar.

▲ *Rhubarb can be planted at this time of year for harvesting in the early spring. Make sure you grow it from certified virus-free crowns.*

WINTER ROOT CROPS

Root crops such as parsnips, salsify, and rutabaga can in most areas be left in the ground overwinter to be pulled as required, but once the foliage has died down there is nothing to show where they are. Mark the rows clearly now. When you start harvesting, begin at one end of the row and move up the marker to show where you finished lifting the crop, so that you know where to dig next time. In very cold weather, when the soil is frozen, it will be impossible to get at the roots, so some should be lifted and stored in boxes of soil in a shed when an icy spell is forecast.

take hardwood cuttings of soft fruit

Soft fruit, such as currants and gooseberries, are easy to propagate by hardwood cuttings. The cuttings can be left in the open garden all winter, and need very little skill to root successfully. The most important point to remember is not to insert the cuttings upside down—it's easier than you might think to make a mistake unless you prepare them carefully.

1 Cuttings are taken in the dormant season, using fully-ripened wood of the current year's growth. Wait until all the leaves have died before cutting the stems with pruners. Use strong, healthy stems of pencil thickness.

2 Each stem can be cut into lengths to give several cuttings; it may be easy to forget which end of the cutting is which. Use sharp pruners to cut stems into 6–10in/15–25cm portions (**right**), making a straight cut at the base of each length and a sloping cut at the top. Treat the bases with rooting hormone.

3 Dig over a suitable piece of moist soil, adding some sharp sand unless it is already free-draining. The cuttings will need to be left in place undisturbed for one year. Make a narrow slit trench with a spade, and insert each cutting so that just the top 2in/5cm is above ground.

4 Firm the soil back against the cuttings with the ball of your foot, and label the row (**left**). Apart from occasional weeding, the cuttings need little further attention. Over winter, corky callus tissue forms over the bases of the cuttings, and new roots should grow from this next spring.

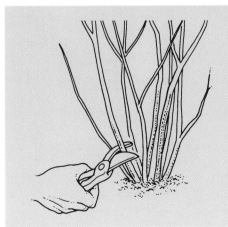

BLACKCURRANTS AND BLACKBERRIES

Blackcurrants carry most of next year's crop on the wood that has been produced this season. Cut to the ground all the branches that carried fruit this year, leaving the strong new growths. The older wood can be recognized because it is gray or black while new wood is pale brown. If you have trouble differentiating between the two, prune at harvest time next year, cutting out the branches carrying fruit as soon as the

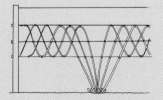

currants are ripe. Blackberries should also be pruned now, again removing the canes that carried fruit but retain the current season's canes. Tie-in the canes which are to be retained to their supports. Damaged, spindly, or weak growths should be removed.

kitchen garden: *harvesting and digging*

Most varieties of apples ripening now are suitable for storing for a few weeks but some will keep until next spring, given the right conditions. In the vegetable garden digging continues as crops are cleared from the ground. If you do not yet have a vegetable plot, this is a good time to get started.

Harvest apples and pears

A few apple and pear varieties may need to be left until late fall, but the majority will have been picked by the end of this month. A number of apple varieties store well, in some instances remaining in good condition until late spring. 'Arkansas Black', 'Golden Delicious', 'Gold Rush', and 'McIntosh' are among the good keepers. Choose unblemished specimens, wrap them individually in sheets of wax paper and store in a single layer in boxes in a cool garage, cellar, or shed.

An alternative method is to place six apples in a strong plastic bag, punch a few holes in the bag with a pencil and tie the top loosely, leaving a small gap. This method is good for varieties that tend to shrivel. Pears do not store for very long though, and need inspecting daily because they must be eaten immediately they are ripe—they spoil within a day or two.

CLEAR VEGETABLE CROPS

—

By now, crops such as runner and French beans, summer cabbages, marrows and so on will be more or less finished, and the plants can be cleared away. Unless the spent crop plants are badly diseased, add them to the compost heap to rot down. Tough, woody stems, like those of some brassicas, are very slow to rot and can either be shredded before being added to the heap, or be burned instead. As rows of crop plants are removed, dig the soil over and add compost or manure as available.

▶ *Apples are ripe and ready for picking once the stalk separates easily from the spur when the fruit is lifted gently.*

▶ *Wrapping apples separately before storing will help to prevent rot spreading if one of them starts to decay. Only unblemished fruits should be stored; damaged apples will not keep.*

start a new vegetable plot

Home-grown vegetables are always welcome, and are very rewarding to grow. While a few vegetables can always be grown in containers on the patio or among the flowers, a dedicated vegetable plot will give you a lot more scope for trying out new, exciting varieties. Make the plot as large as is practical for you to look after.

1 If the vegetable plot is to be made in the lawn, it will be necessary to strip off the turf. This can be done by cutting parallel strips in the grass with a half-moon edging iron, and undercutting the turf with a sharp spade (**left**). Hiring a turf cutter is worthwhile for large areas.

2 If the turf that has been removed is good quality, it can be relaid elsewhere, or perhaps sold. Otherwise, it can be stacked upside down to rot, when it will make an excellent loam for potting or for mixing with growing soil mixes.

3 The newly-exposed soil should be well cultivated, either digging it by hand (**left**) or using a mechanical cultivator. Although the cultivator is quicker and easier, double digging allows deeper cultivation and gives better results in the long run—as long as you have the necessary time and stamina to do it. Spread the job over several weeks if necessary.

4 While digging, incorporate as much rotted garden compost or manure into the soil as possible; this improves fertility and soil structure, allowing heavy soils to drain more freely and light soils to become more moisture retentive. The plot should be left roughly dug over winter to allow frost to break down the clods into finer crumbs.

5 A soil testing kit is a worthwhile investment, giving you an idea of the acidity and nutrient levels in the soil (**above**). Acidity (pH) testing is usually quite accurate and will indicate whether an application of lime is necessary. Nutrient analysis is rather less reliable, but will still give a guide to your soil's fertility.

greenhouse: *general tasks*

Fungus diseases are rife in cool, damp conditions prevalent at this time of year. Poor light levels can be a problem, too; make sure that the maximum amount of light can penetrate the glass. Also, look ahead to spring and summer by sowing sweet peas and planting bowls of bulbs for forcing.

Sow sweet peas for early flowers next year

Fall-sown sweet peas come into flower some four or five weeks earlier than spring-sown ones, and continue blooming for just as long at the other end of the season. The tough coats of the seed can sometimes delay germination, especially in the case of the dark brown or black seeds.

Before sowing it pays to nick the seed coat lightly with a sharp knife, on the side opposite the lighter colored eye where the seedling will emerge.

Sow the seed in pots, or special sweet pea tubes that allow the long roots to develop fully. They do not need warm conditions—59°F/15°C is suitable for germination. Seedlings do well in a cold frame or an unheated greenhouse where they can develop into sturdy plants ready for planting out in their flowering positions in early to mid-spring. Choose paler colored varieties for the best fragrance. 'Unwin's Striped Mix', 'Old Spice Mix', 'Royal Mix', 'Noel Sutton', and 'Quito' are among those recommended for their scent.

▲ *The fragrant flowers of sweet peas (*Lathyrus odoratus*) can be appreciated that bit earlier next year if some seeds are sown now.*

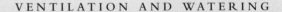

VENTILATION AND WATERING

Fall is a tricky time in the greenhouse. On a chilly, misty morning, it seems obvious to leave the ventilators tightly closed and be very sparing with the watering, but a few hours later fall sunshine can have sent the temperature soaring and leave plants gasping for a drink. If you are away from the house all day, fit an automatic ventilator that will open when the temperature reaches a pre-determined level. Water plants when the surface of the soil feels dry but avoid overwatering because it leads to root and stem rot at this time of year. Also take care not to splash the foliage or crowns of plants, and keep the atmosphere on the dry side to avoid fungus disease such as botrytis.

prepare forced bulbs

Many gardeners find winter a dull and frustrating season, and are impatient for the first signs of spring. It's easy to bring a touch of spring into your home much earlier with bowls of forced bulbs. Plant an assortment of varieties now and you will be enjoying their blooms in the depths of winter, just when you need a fillip.

SHADING

The shading that was essential to prevent foliage being scorched by summer sun is no longer necessary now; greenhouse plants need all the light they can get. Paint-on shading can be removed on a dry day with some elbow grease and a dry cloth, while blinds and netting can be cleaned, rolled up and stored for next year. Clean the greenhouse glass underneath the shading thoroughly.

1 The earliest flowers are obtained from treated or prepared bulbs that have been given special cold treatment to alter their flowering time. Ordinary bulbs can also be forced for early flowering, but they will only be a short time ahead of outdoor ones.

2 Plant the bulbs closely together in bowls or pots of moist, soilless potting mix (**above**)—bulb fiber can be used, but has no special merit over normal mix. The extreme tips of the bulbs should be just visible through the soil when the bowl is filled.

3 The planted bowls now need to be placed somewhere cool and dark for several weeks. The ideal temperature is 35–40°F/2–5°C; a cool garage, basement, shed, or shaded cold frame are suitable. Plunging the bowls in a deep bed of sand or ashes is traditional, and helps keep them evenly cool, moist, and dark. Placing the bowls in an old, still functioning refrigerator in a utility room or garage is a more modern approach, and works well.

4 The bulbs must be left in their cool, dark position for between 10 and 16 weeks, according to variety, to form a good root system. Check them regularly to make sure that the soil does not dry out—water when necessary to keep the compost just moist, never wet (**left**).

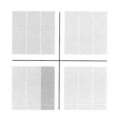

late fall

Tidying up and preparing plants for the colder weather ahead continues, but planning for next season starts in earnest now, with new plantings to be made and seed orders to be filled out. This is also a good time to have the lawn mower overhauled so that it is ready for next spring.

At this time of year we really notice how the days are shortening. For many gardeners, the only time the garden can be seen in daylight is at weekends, and all the tasks that need to be done have to be crammed in to two short days, provided the weather allows. Fortunately there are few really pressing jobs.

It's important though, that you protect the more tender plants before the coldest weather arrives. Night frosts will already have struck in many gardens, but the most damaging, sustained freezing temperatures are usually a feature of the winter. Don't forget to lag outdoor taps and water pipes, too.

Any damage to plants and garden structures caused by fall gales should be repaired quickly. Fences are particularly prone to problems, so check that fence posts and panels are sound. Garden sheds may also be showing signs of wear and tear. Secure roofing felt that has been loosened, and check for leaks inside, carrying out repairs as necessary. It is vital to have dry storage conditions available for many items including tools and machinery, fertilizers and chemicals, as well as produce such as tree fruit and root vegetables.

Weeds seem to keep growing whatever the weather, and weeding should be carried out as necessary. Since many chemical herbicides need weeds to make rapid growth to work most efficiently, hand weeding is generally the best approach in late fall and winter.

◀ *Make the most of late flowers like sedums. A drab time of year is approaching, with fall color finally extinguished by wind and rain.*

LATE FALL TASKS

General
- Note gaps in the borders and make plans to fill them
- Protect outdoor faucets and water pipes from freezing
- Check bonfire piles for hibernating animals before lighting

Ornamental garden
- Continue tidying borders. Leave top-growth for winter protection in cold areas. In exposed gardens, prune roses lightly to prevent root rock
- Continue planting bare-root trees and shrubs
- Take hardwood cuttings from shrubs
- Protect alpines from rain
- Lift chrysanthemums and box roots to provide cuttings in spring
- Finish planting tulips and hyacinths
- Continue to remove weeds
- Tidy alpines and rock gardens

▼ Floating a ball on the water surface can help to delay the pond freezing.

Lawns
- Give a last cut if necessary, then send mower for service and blade sharpening
- Aerate compacted areas
- Continue turfing in mild spells

Water garden
- Protect ponds and fish from cold. Stop feeding fish

Kitchen garden
- Sow beans and hardy peas for overwintering
- Continue digging spare ground
- Begin harvesting parsnips and Brussels sprouts. Lift some root crops for use in case the soil becomes frozen
- Check summer-planted, cold-stored potatoes and lift when ready. Order new seed potatoes from catalogs for the best choice of varieties
- Plant new fruit trees and bushes; begin winter pruning of fruit
- Continue weeding as necessary
- Protect winter brassicas from birds

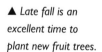

▲ Late fall is an excellent time to plant new fruit trees.

Greenhouse
- Ventilate and water with care; use fungicides where necessary
- Bring bulbs for forcing into the light as they develop. Check that plunged bulbs remain moist
- Insulate greenhouses and frames with bubble wrap
- Pinch out the tips of fall-sown Lathyrus odoratus (sweet pea) seedlings at about 4–6in/10–15cm
- Plant Narcissus 'Paper White'
- Sow sprouting seeds for salads

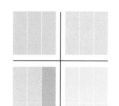

ornamental garden: *general tasks*

If you want to repeat the display of bright, late summer and fall color from chrysanthemums, it's time to lift the roots and box them up for winter, ready to provide cuttings next spring. You don't have to wait until spring to take hardwood cuttings, though; they are easy to root and can be taken now.

Chrysanthemum roots

Some varieties of the so-called florists' chrysanthemum are hardy enough to overwinter in the garden, but the best quality plants are produced from cuttings taken in the spring. As the plants finish flowering now, they can be cut down to around 6in/15cm and the roots lifted carefully with a garden fork. Shake off some of the soil clinging to them, and box up the roots in almost-dry peat or potting mix.

Store the boxes of roots in a frost-free greenhouse or cold frame, garden shed, garage, or similar place. In mid to late winter they will be brought into a heated greenhouse and watered in to start them into growth, but for now they should be kept virtually dry. If you grow a number of named varieties, tie a label around each stem to identify them.

▼ *Chrysanthemums stop flowering at this point in the year; it is time to cut them down and lift their roots with a fork.*

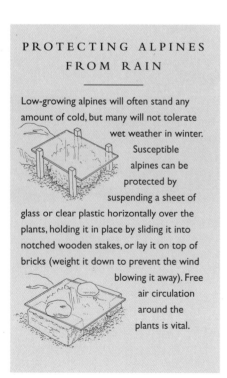

PROTECTING ALPINES FROM RAIN

Low-growing alpines will often stand any amount of cold, but many will not tolerate wet weather in winter. Susceptible alpines can be protected by suspending a sheet of glass or clear plastic horizontally over the plants, holding it in place by sliding it into notched wooden stakes, or lay it on top of bricks (weight it down to prevent the wind blowing it away). Free air circulation around the plants is vital.

take shrub cuttings

Many garden shrubs can be propagated by hardwood cuttings that usually root easily and need very little care. A cold frame is an ideal place to overwinter the cuttings, but a sheltered position in the open garden will do as long as it has some protection from excessive rain. Some cuttings may be rooted by the following spring, but others may take 12 months or more before they are rooted sufficiently to be planted out in their growing positions.

1 Select strong, healthy growth which has been made in the current season. The shoots should be of around pencil thickness; thin, weak stems do not make good cuttings.

2 On deciduous shrubs, most leaves will have fallen, but any remaining can be brushed away (**right**). Cut the stems into 6in/15cm pieces, discarding the thinner tips. Make sure you know which is the top and bottom of each section.

3 With evergreen shrubs, remove the leaves from the lower two-thirds of the stem on each cutting. Dip the bases of the cuttings into hormone rooting powder or liquid (**below**), and insert them into pots of moist, sandy cuttings mix. Then you should place the pots in a cold frame or sheltered spot in the garden.

4 Shrubs that can be increased by this method include aucuba, buddleja, *Buxus* (box), *Cydonia* (quince), forsythia, *Philadelphus* (mock orange), sambucus, spiraea, viburnum and weigela. Climbers such as *Vitis* (grapevine), and trees such as *Salix* (willow) and *Populus* (poplar) also grow well from hardwood cuttings.

TIDY BORDERS

Continue to tidy flower borders, cutting down dead stems and removing dead and dying foliage. If left, they provide handy overwintering sites for a range of garden pests, especially slugs and snails. These can cause an enormous amount of damage in the spring when they feast on the succulent new shoots that start pushing up through the ground.

pleasure from berries

Berry-bearing plants make a brilliant contribution to the fall garden, and their display can last right through the winter too, if you are lucky.

For a plant species to be successful, it needs to reproduce itself freely and colonize as large an area as possible. Each berry contains a seed or number of seeds with the potential for reproduction: some seeds will germinate from berries that ripen and fall to the ground, but this limits the spread of the plant to the immediate area. In order to colonize new ground, the seed must somehow be transported more widely.

In the case of berries, birds and small wild mammals provide the means of transport. They eat the berries, the seed passes unharmed through their digestive system, and is later deposited, often a considerable distance away. The most successful plants are therefore likely to be those that produce the tastiest, most tempting, highly visible berries, which accounts for their showy forms and bright colors—factors also making them desirable decorative garden plants.

Poor show

When a plant has been specially chosen for its berries, it is obviously disappointing when they fail to appear. This event is not all that uncommon, and can be due to a number of reasons. Many species, including *Ilex* (holly) and skimmia, have separate male and female plants. Only the female bears the berries, and only when the flowers

▲ Berberis wilsoniae: *the point of berries is to be eaten by birds, so it is not surprising that beautiful displays may quickly be eaten.*

POISONING BY GARDEN BERRIES

With berries often being brightly colored, highly visible, and similar to edible currants and other soft fruits in the garden, they are very tempting to young children, sometimes with unpleasant or even fatal results. The following plants are grown for their decorative berries, but the berries are poisonous when ingested: lords and ladies (*Arum maculatum*), spindle tree (*Euonymus europaeus*), holly (*Ilex aquifolium*), stinking iris (*Iris foetidissima*), pokeweed (*Phytolacca decandra*), snowberry (*symphoricarpos*), and guelder rose (*Viburnum opulus*). Other plants such as yew (*Taxus baccata*), bird cherry (*Prunus laurocerasus*), privet (*Ligustrum ovalifolium*) also bear poisonous berries, though they are not grown specifically for this feature.

▼ Pyracantha *'Orange Glow' provides a stunning show of rich color in the late fall, making it a desirable decorative plant.*

RELIABLE BERRY-BEARING SHRUBS

* *Aucuba japonica* 'Rozannie', 'Salicifolia' and others (spotted laurel)
Berberis x *carminea* 'Barbarossa', 'Buccaneer' and others (barberry)
Callicarpa bodinieri var. *giraldii* (beauty berry)
Celastrus orbiculatus (oriental bittersweet)
Cotoneaster 'Cornubia', *C.* x *watereri* 'John Waterer'
    and many others
Crataegus x *lavalleei* 'Carrierei' and many others (hawthorn)
Euonymus europaeus (spindle tree)
Gaultheria procumbens (checkerberry)
Gaultheria mucronata
* *Hippophae rhamnoides* (sea buckthorn)
* *Ilex* x *altaclerensis* 'Camelliifolia', *I. aquifolium* 'J. C. Van Tol' and many
    others (holly)
Iris foetidissima
Leycesteria formosa (Himalayan honeysuckle)
Mahonia aquifolium and others
Photinia davidiana, P. glabra
Pyracantha 'Mohave', 'Orange Glow' and many others (firethorn)
* *Ruscus aculeatus* (butcher's broom)
* *Skimmia japonica* 'Nymans', 'Veitchii' and others
Symphoricarpos albus var. *laevigatus* (snowberry), *S.* x *doorenbosii* 'Mother
of Pearl' and others
Viburnum opulus (guelder rose), *V. wrightii* var. *hessei*

* Separate male and female plants are needed

have been pollinated by a male. This means that you need a female variety, and there must be a suitable male variety within insect-flying distance. It usually pays to buy and plant both male and female varieties at the same time to be on the safe side. Take care when choosing varieties though; things are not always what they seem—for example, *Ilex aquifolium* 'Silver Queen' is a male variety, while *I.* x *altaclerensis* 'Golden King' is a female.

A poor show of berries can also be caused by dry soil conditions at flowering time; regular organic mulches will help here. And of course, plants that produce only a few flowers can only bear a few berries. For plants that fail to flower freely, an application of sulfate of potash in the spring and fall can sometimes work wonders.

As far as the plant is concerned, the whole purpose of a berry's existence is to be eaten by a bird, so it is hardly surprising that birds make short work of many attractive displays. There are several ways to protect plants from birds (see page 644). Red berries are the most highly visible against a green background, while species and varieties with yellow, orange, purple, pink, or white fruit tend to be longer lasting.

▲ Berberis × ottawensis *'Superba' (purpurea) offers interestingly shaped berries and leaves to the general garden display.*

ornamental garden: *plants in season*

As flowers and fall foliage fade, evergreens assume an increasingly important role in bringing interest to the garden. Fruits and berries continue to provide color, and there are still flowers on show as long as the right species have been planted.

▶ *The deep blues of* Gentiana sino-ornata *enrich the garden's color scheme.*

▼ *Viburnum tinus 'Eve Price' offers a frothy interest to the fall garden.*

PERENNIALS

Aster

Helianthus (sunflower)

Gentiana sino-ornata

Iris unguicularis

Liriope muscari (lily turf)

BULBS

Colchicum (fall crocus)

Crocus (fall-flowering species)

Cyclamen

Galanthus reginae-olgae (snowdrop)

Nerine bowdenii

Schizostylis coccinea (kaffir lily)

Sternbergia lutea (fall daffodil)

▼ *Sunflowers provide bold, bright splashes of color and dramatic interest.*

TREES AND SHRUBS

Aucuba japonica (spotted laurel)

Berberis (barberry)

Callicarpa (beauty berry)

Clematis orientale, C. tangutica

Cornus alba (red-barked dogwood)

Cotoneaster

Fatsia japonica (Japanese aralia)

Gaultheria mucronata

Jasminum nudiflorum (jasmine)

Leycesteria formosa (Himalayan honeysuckle)

Malus (apple, crab apple)

Prunus x *subhirtella* 'Fallalis' (fall cherry)

Pyracantha (firethorn)

Rosa (hips) (rose)

Salix alba var. *vitellina* 'Britzensis' (white willow)

Skimmia

Sorbus

Symphoricarpos (snowberry)

Vaccinium (bilberry)

Viburnum

lawns and water gardens: *general tasks*

Lawns now start to show signs of wear on heavily used routes as the soil becomes compacted in wet weather. The grass may need a final cut before the mower is sent away for servicing, ready for next spring. Garden ponds should need little attention unless the weather turns particularly cold.

▲ *Aereating compacted areas of lawn is important to help surface water drain away. It is easily achieved with a garden fork.*

Aerating turf

When the soil is moist it is easily compacted. A frequently trodden route across the lawn will soon become muddy now, with its covering of grass gradually thinning and being worn away. Since it is important that air can reach the roots of the grass and that surface water can drain away at all times of the year, action should be taken as soon as worn patches are noticed. If the damage is not corrected, moss is likely to develop in place of the grass.

Try to redirect foot traffic away from the worn places if possible. Use a garden fork to spike the compacted areas, driving the prongs into the turf some 3–4in/7.5–10cm deep. Waggle the fork backward and forward gently to enlarge the holes slightly before removing it. Repeat over the whole area to leave the rows of holes evenly spaced in both directions.

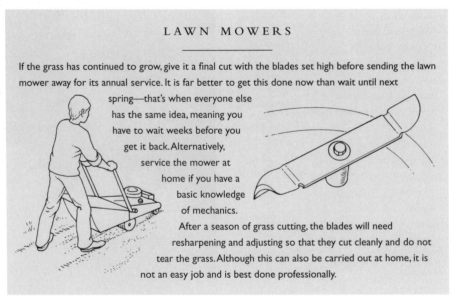

LAWN MOWERS

If the grass has continued to grow, give it a final cut with the blades set high before sending the lawn mower away for its annual service. It is far better to get this done now than wait until next spring—that's when everyone else has the same idea, meaning you have to wait weeks before you get it back. Alternatively, service the mower at home if you have a basic knowledge of mechanics.

After a season of grass cutting, the blades will need resharpening and adjusting so that they cut cleanly and do not tear the grass. Although this can also be carried out at home, it is not an easy job and is best done professionally.

protect ponds from cold weather

If a garden pond freezes over for more than a couple of days, fish may be killed by the toxic gases trapped beneath the ice. The easiest way to prevent this is to install a pond heater.

STOP FEEDING FISH

As the water temperature drops, fish become inactive and will not take food until the water warms up again in the spring. They live off stored body fat through the winter, so it is important to build them up in the early fall. Any food given from now on will sink to the bottom of the pool and rot, polluting the water.

1 At this time of year it is very important to keep the water free of any kind of decaying vegetation, whether this is dead leaves from water plants or fall leaves from nearby trees. Remove dead and dying leaves regularly, and cover the pool with a net if necessary.

2 Remove the pond pump if one is installed, and clean and service it before storing it for the winter (**left**). If the pool is within reach of a power supply, install a pond heater. This keeps only a small area of the pond free of ice, but allows the air in and toxic gases to escape.

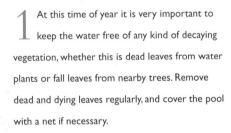

3 If it is not possible to use a pond heater, a ball floating on the surface of the water will delay freezing as it moves about in the wind (**above**). And if the water does freeze, boiling water poured around the edge of the ball enables it to be removed leaving a hole in the ice. Hollow polystyrene packaging material can also be used.

4 Most sunken garden ponds are in no danger of freezing solid, but miniature ponds in half barrels are a different matter—they lack the insulation of the soil around them. In all but mild areas, fish from barrels should be moved under cover. Lagging the barrels with several layers of bubble wrap helps protect water plants.

kitchen garden: *general tasks*

Harvesting the winter vegetable crops usually begins now, once the first few frosts have bitten; protection from hungry wild birds may be necessary, too. Although many gardeners find the whole subject of fruit pruning mystifying, it can be kept quite simple, and will insure maximum crops.

Prune fruit trees

Apple and pear trees that are grown as open-centered bushes or small trees are not difficult to prune. The object is to maintain a well-shaped tree that carries as much fruiting wood as possible, while also bearing young branches to provide replacement fruiting wood in future seasons. Start by pruning out any dead, dying, or diseased branches. Then remove crossing branches, and branches that are growing into the center of the tree. Now cut back strong-growing young laterals (side-shoots) by about half to two-thirds of the current season's growth, depending on how vigorous the growth is (the more vigorous the shoot, the more lightly it should be pruned because winter pruning stimulates growth). The tips of the leaders (main branches) should be pruned more lightly, cutting back the current season's growth by about one-quarter. Finally, remove some of the older branches which have borne fruit to encourage the production of new replacement shoots.

▼ *Long-arm pruners are very useful for reaching high fruit tree branches; you may be able to avoid using a stepladder.*

LIFT ROOT CROPS

Many root crops such as parsnips, rutabaga, maincrop carrots, salsify, and scorzonera are usually hardy enough to stay in the ground all winter, where they will keep in better condition than in store. However, if the weather becomes really cold and the soil freezes, it can be impossible to prise the crops from the icy ground. Lift a small supply now and store them in boxes of soil near the house so that they are easily accessible in cold weather. A few leeks can be stored alongside them because these are also difficult to harvest in freezing weather.

keep birds at bay

A well-planned vegetable plot should contain a variety of vegetables that can be harvested through the winter, but wild creatures will be hungry too, and only too ready to take advantage of a free meal from your garden. Some form of deterrents are often necessary to obtain your share of the harvest.

BRUSSELS SPROUTS AND PARSNIPS

There is a saying that it is not worth harvesting Brussels sprouts and parsnips until they have had a good touch of frost to improve their flavor. Whether frost actually does improve the flavor is open to question, but it is certainly true that they are both hardy enough to withstand severe frosts without damage, allowing the harvest to be extended right through the winter.

1 Brassicas such as cabbages and Brussels sprouts provide invaluable winter fare, but the plants are prone to damage by pigeons. In a cold spell, a crop can be reduced to a skeleton of veins within hours, so choose some protection.

2 Bird scarers can help to deter pigeons though their effect is often disappointing (**right**). Moving, glittery or noisy objects are best. Strips of foil or unwanted CDs can be hung from stakes to shine as they twist in the wind, while children's windmills on sticks provide noise and movement. Tautly stretched tape from old audio or video tapes makes a low hum in the breeze.

3 A physical barrier can be provided by stretching twine between stakes in a criss-cross fashion over the top of the crop, or using horticultural blanket draped over the tops of the plants. This needs to be secured at the edges to prevent it being blown away (**below**).

4 Growing brassicas in a fruit cage is the most reliable answer where pigeons are a real problem. In cold regions, the netting over the top will need to be replaced with large mesh netting for the winter to prevent snow from collecting—its weight would tear the net.

kitchen garden: *planting and sowing*

An out-of-season treat of new potatoes may be available from specially-treated seed potatoes planted in the summer; remember to order potatoes from the catalogs for more conventional planting in spring. Unlikely as it seems, it is also time for sowing some vegetables outdoors for next year.

Sowing beans and peas

As long as you sow the right varieties, both beans and peas will overwinter as seedlings to give early crops next year—you could be picking beans and peas by late spring. Choose a reasonably sheltered site for sowing, on free-draining soil. On heavy soils there is a risk of the seeds rotting, and in this case it is better to sow them in pots or boxes in an unheated greenhouse for planting out in the spring. The crop will not be so early, but it will be more reliable.

Sow beans 4–6in/10–15cm apart in rows 12in/30cm apart; peas are sown rather more closely in the row, at 2–3in/5–7.5cm apart. Depending on your climate zone and prevailing local conditions, your local garden center should be able to advise on the most appropriate varieties to sow in your garden or greenhouse.

▲ *Certain varieties of beans can be sown at this time of year to give a crop late the following spring.*

SUMMER–PLANTED POTATOES

Specially-prepared, cold-stored seed potatoes that were planted in the summer produce a crop some two or three months after planting. Check them now, by scraping away some soil to expose the developing tubers. As long as the majority are large enough to eat they can be lifted when you want to use them. If the weather is mild, the tubers may continue to swell, but most of them will have finished developing by now. Do not lift the entire crop as you would for maincrop potatoes; they keep best if left in the soil up to midwinter, insulated from freezing weather with a mulch of straw or dry bracken.

▶ *Cherry trees grow particularly well if they are trained against a reasonably sheltered wall or fence. Morello types are most popular.*

plant fruit trees and bushes

With the development of dwarfing rootstocks, it is possible for fruit trees such as apples and pears to be grown even in small gardens. Soft fruit bushes such as currants and gooseberries are also easy to grow and provide very welcome crops in the summer.

1 Choose from the wide variety of fruit trees available from specialist nurseries. The plants are often supplied bare root, by mail order, and should be planted as soon as possible after delivery. Most garden centers stock a reduced but reasonable selection, usually container grown.

2 Dig out a planting hole wide enough to take the roots of the tree without cramping, and deep enough for the tree to be planted at the same depth it was growing in the nursery. Fork over the base of the hole and add some well-rotted garden compost or planting mixture.

3 Hammer the stake in position before planting the tree to avoid damaging the tree roots. A short stake is all that is necessary. Check that the size of the hole is correct for the tree, then spread the tree roots out in the base of the planting hole (**above**).

4 Return the excavated soil to the hole, gently jiggling the tree up and down while you do so in order to insure that the soil sifts between the roots. Then you should tread the soil firm with the ball of your foot as you proceed (**above**).

5 When the hole is refilled, attach the tree to the stake with an adjustable tree tie (**above**). Fruit bushes are planted in the same way. If container-grown, remove the root-ball carefully having watered it well a few hours before, put it in the base of the hole and firm the soil around it.

fruit tree rootstocks

It is possible to grow a fruit tree in almost any size garden, no matter how small it might be—apples, pears, and many other tree fruits can even be kept small enough to grow in a tub on a patio.

The method by which the size of the tree is controlled is grafting the fruiting variety onto a separate rootstock that determines the rate of growth. Size is not the only aspect of growth that is governed by the

rootstock; the number of years between planting and fruiting are also affected. Trees on the more dwarfing rootstocks do tend to crop earlier, another benefit for the home gardener.

A great deal of research has been undertaken into dwarfing rootstocks, and still continues, with large numbers of new rootstocks under evaluation. The research is aimed at commercial fruit growers, but new

and improved rootstocks can eventually find their way onto the amateur market.

Small trees are more suitable for gardens where space is limited, and are easier to prune, harvest, and spray. Using ladders and long-handled pruners is awkward and time-consuming; a tree that allows all parts to be reached from the ground is easier to look after.

However, dwarfing rootstocks have some drawbacks. They need staking in their early years, and some need permanent support throughout their lives. Fertile, moisture-retentive soil is also necessary or the crop will be very disappointing .

Really small, dwarfing rootstocks are not necessary for most gardens. A compromise will usually be a better choice, such as the semidwarfing apple rootstock M26 rather than the very dwarfing M27. The trees will still be relatively compact and quick to bear fruit but will put up with poorer soil conditions, be self-supporting after a few years and carry a much bigger crop. The most dwarfing rootstocks are necessary only if you want to grow trees in pots, or train them in very restricted forms such as step-overs.

While, some garden centers have a good choice of rootstocks, it is usually necessary to go to specialist fruit producers to obtain the most recent introductions. Most specialist nurserymen will be happy to discuss your requirements with you, and give you advice on the best rootstock to meet your needs. Some of the newest rootstocks, particularly for cherries, have not yet been grown for long enough to have entirely proved themselves, and some growers have reservations about their hardiness, disease resistance, and compatibility with other fruiting varieties. Rootstocks that do not live up to expectations usually disappear from fruit growers' catalogs within a year or two.

◀ *Fruit trees are a major boon to any garden and the good news that they can be grown in almost any size garden.*

FRUIT TREE ROOTSTOCKS

Rootstock		Approximate size	Years to come into cropping
Apples	M27	under 6ft/18m	2
	M9	6–9ft/1.8–2.7m	2–3
	M26	10–12ft/3–3.6m	2–3
	MM106	12–13ft/3.6–4m	3–4
	MM111	13–15ft/4–4.5m	4–5
Pears	Quince C	12ft/3.6m	3–4
	Quince A	13ft/4m	4–5
Plums	Pixy	6–10ft/1.8–3m	3
	St Julien A	12ft/3.6m	4–5
	Brompton	13ft/4m	4–5
	Myrobalan B	13ft/4m	4–5
	Mariana 4	15t+/4.5m+	4–5
Cherries	Gisela	6–10ft/1.8–3m	3
	Colt	13ft/4m	4–5
	F12/1	16ft+/4.8m+	5–6

GRAFTING ONTO ROOTSTOCKS

Established gardens often contain very large, old fruit trees of unknown origin that can sometimes cause problems. You may want to remove the tree because it is too big, or perhaps need to replace it because it is diseased or reaching the end of its useful life, but you are reluctant to destroy it because it bears crops of attractive, well-flavored fruit that you cannot identify in order to obtain another of the same variety.

In this case it is possible to preserve the stock by grafting stems of the original tree on to a suitable rootstock for replanting. Grafting is a fairly skilled job but if you do not feel confident of being able to do it yourself, one or two specialist nurseries will do it for you for a fee and a supply of suitable dormant stems (scion wood).

greenhouse: *general tasks*

As the weather grows colder, tender plants in the greenhouse are at greater risk of damage. Some plants need only a little protection, and insulating the greenhouse may be sufficient to keep them alive without any artificial heat. Even when heat is required, insulation will help reduce fuel bills.

Insulate greenhouses and frames

Do-it-yourself insulation is a useful way of maintaining temperatures and helping to keep down fuel bills in the greenhouse.

The fact that plants need the maximum amount of light limits the materials that can be used: the favourite is bubble wrap because it is cheap, and easy to obtain as well as work with.

It comes in rolls and can be cut to fit the inside of the greenhouse, keeping each strip as long as possible to minimize the amount of joins. It is usually best to run the strips

horizontally around the greenhouse. Fix the polyethythene in position with pins in a wooden structure, or special clips in an aluminum frame.

Bubble wrap can also be used to insulate the insides of the glass on garden frames.

▼ *Special clips are available to fix an insulating layer of bubble polyethythene to greenhouses that have an aluminium frame.*

FORCED BULBS

Bulbs that are being forced for early flowering should have been kept in total darkness after planting to encourage good root formation. The average dark, cold periods required are 12 weeks for crocus, 12–13 weeks for *Narcissus* (daffodils), 10–12 weeks for *Hyacinthus* (hyacinths) and 15–16 weeks for *Tulipa* (tulips). When the required number of weeks have elapsed and shoots have reached around 1in/2.5cm high, it is time to bring them into full light.

A greenhouse with a temperature of about 50°F/10°C is ideal; relatively cool temperatures are necessary for the leaves and flower buds to develop properly. Wait until the buds are starting to show color before moving the bulbs into a cool position in the home for flowering.

heating the greenhouse

A greenhouse is infinitely more valuable if it can be heated sufficiently to keep it frost free. There are many different types of heaters available to suit a range of different situations and budgets—spend some time over choosing the best type of heater for your particular requirements.

SWEET PEA SEEDLINGS

Sweet peas which were sown earlier in the fall should have germinated and be growing strongly. When the seedlings reach 4–6in/10–15cm tall, pinch out their growing tips. This insures stocky, healthy plants with plenty of side-shoots to bear flowers. Give the seedlings cool, well-ventilated conditions; a cold frame is the best place for them.

1 It is well worth considering running an electricity supply to the greenhouse, but this must be installed by a qualified electrician, using armored cabling and waterproof sockets. If the greenhouse is not too far from the house, it need not be very expensive (**above**).

2 Electric heaters have many advantages. They can be thermostatically controlled, switching on automatically as necessary at any time of the day or night, saving fuel and trouble. Fan heaters provide good air circulation, and a healthy atmosphere for plant growth (**above**).

3 Mains gas can also be installed in the greenhouse where available, but this tends to be unusual (**above**). Greenhouse heaters using bottled propane gas are more common but this is not so convenient because the gas bottles need to be changed regularly. Propane gives off water vapor as it burns, and the moist atmosphere produced can encourage plant diseases.

4 Kerosene heaters are cheap to buy and can be used where mains gas and electricity are unavailable (**above**). They are labor intensive and messy; they need frequent filling with kerosene. Because they are not thermostatically controlled they waste fuel and can be expensive to run. They also give off water vapor and fumes while burning, making greenhouse ventilation essential.

winter

Despite short days and chilly weather, the garden can be a soul-lifting place to be in the winter months. There's evergreen foliage, winter flowers and berries, and the starkly beautiful, architectural shapes of trees and shrubs to enjoy. Add some silver highlights from a sparkling frost and you've a truly magical scene before you.

early winter

The weather is often entirely unpredictable now. Penetrating frosts and icy winds; continuous dull, depressing rain; or mild, calm, sunny days more like early fall: anything is possible. It may not be the best time of year to be working outside, but seize your opportunities when they arise.

A greenhouse is a real boon for a keen gardener now—whatever the weather, you can get on with growing plants in comparative comfort. In contrast to the often bleak scene outdoors, the greenhouse can be full of color from bulbs and pot plants, and given there's enough heat, some seed sowing can begin.

Although the grass has stopped growing and the mower has been put away for the winter, that doesn't mean you can entirely ignore the lawn. This is the time of year when it is most likely to suffer wear and tear, so be prepared to act promptly in order to prevent damage from occurring.

Wild birds can be a nuisance at times, but most gardeners appreciate the life they bring to the garden in winter, and are happy to encourage them. The fall season with its fruit, seeds, berries, and insects is over, and it's time to start putting out food on the bird table. But once you start feeding, you must keep it up because the birds will come to rely on you. Remember to provide water for drinking and bathing, too, particularly in freezing weather.

If the garden is looking dull, cheer it up by planting some containers of hardy winter plants like flowering Viola (pansies) and heathers, and variegated foliage plants. In the kitchen garden there will probably still be winter digging and fruit tree pruning to get on with, and don't forget to send off those seed orders before the spring rush.

◀ *Variegated evergreens like* Hedera colchica *'Sulphur Heart' are particularly valuable for brightening the garden in the winter months.*

EARLY WINTER TASKS

General

- Continue winter digging
- Make paths to avoid wear on lawns
- Cover compost piles to keep out rain

Ornamental garden

- Continue to plant containers for winter and spring interest
- Firm newly-planted trees and shrubs after frosts
- Protect the blooms of Helleborus niger (Christmas rose) with straw on the ground
- Check trees and shrubs for root rock or lifting after frosts, refirming them if necessary
- Order flower seeds from catalogs, especially those needing an early start
- Protect young trees against rabbits with tree guards

Lawns

- Avoid walking over frosted grass. Turfing is still possible in mild spells

▲ *Make a firm path on well-used routes across lawns to avoid regular treading wearing the grass.*

Water gardens

- Thaw holes in frozen ponds

Kitchen garden

- Protect fall-sown bean and pea seedlings
- Order seeds from catalogs
- Prune fruit trees

▼ *Bulbs of Narcissus 'Paper White' planted now should be in flower in about six weeks.*

Greenhouse

- Check the temperature regularly with a maximum/minimum thermometer
- Bring forced bulbs indoors as the flower buds show color
- Sow seeds such as onions and pelargoniums in a heated propagator
- Clean pots and seedtrays ready for the bulk of spring sowing
- Remove faded flowers on cyclamen
- Move cyclamen, primula (primroses) etc., from the home to the greenhouse when they finish flowering. Spray Indian azaleas with plain water regularly
- Plant more Narcissus 'Paper White' (daffodils) for a succession of flowers

plant names

The use of the correct botanical or scientific names for plants is always a contentious subject. Many gardeners find the scientific names unwieldy, impossible to pronounce or spell, and nowhere near as good as the common names they've been using all their life.

Many of these criticisms are true, but there are very good reasons for using scientific names. The first is that common names are not all that common—they vary according to where you live, and often apply to more than one plant. And, of course, different countries using different languages also use different common names.

The scientific names, on the other hand, are controlled by the International Code of Nomenclature to insure that each plant has its own unique name, and that the name denotes its family origins correctly. The names are international, being based mainly on Latin (though Greek and other languages are also used). Once the language of scientific names is understood, the names themselves can convey a great deal of information.

We still use the system of classification of plants developed in the 18th century by Linnaeus, who organized plants into genera and species. The botanical name of a plant is generally in two parts; the first part is the genus (as in *Crocus*) and the second part is the species (as in *chrysanthus*). Included in the name may also be a variety (a naturally occurring, stable variation in the species) or cultivar (a variation which has been selected or bred by man).

For greater clarity, the way the name is written follows set rules. The genus begins with an upper case (capital) letter, the species with a lower case letter, and both are in italics. A naturally occurring variety is also written in italics, with the abbreviation var. in front of it, while a cultivar name is written in Roman type (i.e. non italics), and enclosed in single quotation marks. We therefore have names such as *Ficus benjamina* var. *nuda*, or *Lonicera japonica* 'Aureoreticulata'. A hybrid (cross) between two species or genera is signified by an 'x' before the name, as in x *Cupressocyparis leylandii* (a cross between two genera, *Cupressus* and *Chamaecyparis*) or *Ceanothus* x *veitchianus* (a cross between two species, in this case *C. rigidus* and *C. thyrsiflorus*).

The species names generally provide most

◀ x Cupressocyparis leylandii: *the 'x' denotes that this tree is a cross between two genera; in this case,* Cupressus *and* Chamaecyparis.

▶ Lithospermum diffusum: *improved techniques of plant identification have meant that it is now known as* Lithodora diffusa.

information about a particular plant, often denoting its color, size, growing habit, flowers, or place of origin. Names containing folius describe the leaves, and florus the flowers—as in *albiflorus* (white flowered) or *cordifolius* (having heart-shaped leaves). A few common descriptive species names are given in the box below. (Remember that the spelling will alter according to whether the genus name is masculine or feminine, following the rules of Latin grammar.

One point that many gardeners do find annoying is the way the botanical names of plants are sometimes changed. This is not done on a whim but because new and improved techniques of plant identification have enabled botanists to discover that some plants have been incorrectly classified. *Lithospermum diffusum* has in recent years become *Lithodora diffusa*, for example, and *Coleus* has been reclassified under *Plectranthus* or *Solenostemon*. Irritating as these changes are, they are inevitable as our knowledge of the plant kingdom becomes more accurate and refined.

▲ Coleus *was originally wrongly classified; it has recently been correctly reclassified under* Plectranthus *or* Solenostemon.

DESCRIPTIVE BOTANICAL NAMES

alatus: winged	*maculatus*: spotted
albus: white	*maritimum*: growing near the sea
alpinus: alpine	*meleagris*: speckled
angustifolius: narrow-leaved	*nanus*: dwarf
arachnoides: spider-like or with the appearance of a cobweb	*nummularia*: like coins
baccifera: bearing berries	*nutans*: nodding
candidus: shining, white	*officinalis*: having medicinal use
chinensis: from China	*pictus*: boldly marked, painted
citriodorus: lemon scented	*procumbens*: prostrate
denticulata: toothed	*pumilus*: dwarf or small
dissectus: deeply cut	*repens*: creeping
foetidus: having a fetid smell	*scandens*: climbing or scrambling
fragrans: scented	*sempervirens*: evergreen
glaucus: blue-gray	*spectabilis*: showy
grandifolius: large leaved	*tenax*: tough, strong
hispidus: spiny or bristly	*tortuosus*: twisted
laciniatus: deeply cut into narrow segments	*utilis*: useful
	variegatus: variegated
laevigatus: smooth	*vernalis*: of spring
lanuginosus: wooly	*vulgaris*: common
	xanthocarpus: with yellow fruits

general tasks

Encourage birds into the garden now by providing them with regular, easy meals, and they may stay around to keep down insect pests in the spring and summer. Take care of other animals too—the fish in ponds will be badly affected if the pond stays frozen over for more than a day or two.

Feeding garden birds

As soon as the weather turns cold, birds begin to find it increasingly difficult to obtain sufficient food. Not only are there fewer insects, berries, and fruit in the garden, but there are increasingly fewer daylight hours in which to eat. Supplying food regularly for birds can make all the difference to their survival, especially the smaller species.

Use a bird table placed in the open, and protected as far as possible from cats. A roof over the table helps to keep the food dry. Do not put out more food until the birds have cleared up what is there because excess food falls to the ground and attracts vermin. Suitable foods include peanuts, soaked brown breadcrumbs, apples and other fruit, suet and shortening, oatmeal, fresh (not desiccated) coconut, seeds and so on. Special feeders are available for different foods and species of birds, including models that prevent the food being taken by squirrels.

▲ *Put out a supply of bird food regularly all through the winter months. Once birds start to visit a bird table, they will come to rely on it.*

WINTER DIGGING

Digging is best done a little at a time to avoid back strain, so continue steadily with the job over the next few weeks. Incorporate as much organic matter into the ground as possible while digging, especially on light or heavy soils. Garden compost, stable manure, spent mushroom compost, spent hops and similar materials will all help to improve the texture of the soil, enabling light soils to retain more moisture and heavy soils to drain more freely. If you find digging too hard or time consuming, a mechanical cultivator can be used instead once a whole plot is cleared for cultivation.

protect lawns from wear

Cold, wet conditions increase the likelihood of damage to turf as the soil is easily compacted and the grass is unable to make new recovery growth. A frequently walked route over the lawn—from the house to a garden gate or shed, for instance—will soon become obvious in winter, with the grass becoming thin and eventually bare patches appearing.

Encouraging alternative routes that do not cross the lawn is one solution, but the quickest, most straightforward route is always the one most likely to be used. If this route crosses the lawn it may be best to accept the situation and make a firm path.

An informal stepping-stone path is often an appropriate style; it appears less intrusive than a solid path. A slightly curving route is good, but it should not deviate too much from the more direct, trodden pathway or it will not be used.

1 Insure the stones are placed the correct distance apart to give an easy walking pace. Lay the first slab in place and cut around it with a half-moon edging iron (**below, left**). Undercut the turf with a spade to remove it; excavate the soil and replace with a 1in/25mm layer of sand.

2 Drop the slab into place; its surface should end up just below that of the surrounding grass so that mowing can take place over the top of it. Check the level and settle the slab into place by tapping firmly with the handle of a lump hammer or similar tool (**below, right**).

THAWING HOLES IN FROZEN PONDS

If ponds remain frozen over for more than two days, thaw a hole in the ice to allow toxic gases to escape and prevent them from poisoning fish. Do not break the ice with a heavy object such as a hammer as fish may be harmed by shock waves traveling through the water. Instead, thaw a hole; fill an old tin can or pot with boiling water and standing it on the ice. It may need refilling several times if the ice is thick. If possible, use a pond heater to stop the pool freezing over again.

ornamental garden: *general tasks*

It's a good time to clean up the walls behind deciduous climbers now that the leaves are off the plants; it's surprising how many pests lurk under the tangle of stems. And don't put containers away just because the summer bedding plants have finished—they can be enjoyed through the winter, too.

Containers for winter interest

Many gardeners rely heavily on plants in containers to provide color near the house, on the patio, and around the garden during the summer, but far fewer make full use of them through the winter months.

◄ *Make use of evergreens as well as winter-flowering subjects such as pansies and primulas to give containers winter and spring interest.*

There are lots of plants that will give a good display in winter, even in the coldest weather—try dwarf evergreen shrubs (especially variegated varieties), dwarf conifers, winter-flowering viola (pansies) and heathers, ornamental cabbages, and trailing plants such as hedera (ivy).

Tubs, windowboxes, and even hanging baskets in a sheltered position can be used. In very cold areas, insulate the roots of the plants by lining the inside of the container with bubble wrap before filling with soil mix. Bubble wrap can also be used to lag already-planted containers by being tied around the outside. Be careful with terracotta (clay) containers outdoors in the winter. Porous material absorbs water which expands when frozen, and this can shatter the pot; look for brands which are guaranteed frost proof.

Checking trees for root rock

Recently planted trees (and shrubs) can be disturbed by wind: it catches the branches and rocks the plants backward and forward. This disturbs the roots in the soil and often opens up a hole around the base of the stem; water may channel down and cause rot. Check trees and shrubs regularly; firm them back in the soil with the ball of your foot if necessary.

PROTECTING YOUNG TREES

Newly-planted trees are often attacked by rabbits in gardens near fields or open spaces. Rabbits (and other small mammals) strip off the bark, weakening the tree and making it vulnerable to disease. If they remove a complete strip of bark from around the whole trunk, the tree will die. They can be thwarted, though, by using a rabbit guard in the form of a spiral plastic strip slipped around the trunk. Being spiral, the guard is able to expand as the trunk swells and does not restrict the tree's growth, even if forgotten.

wall maintenance under climbing plants

The appearance of an area of blank wall is greatly improved by growing climbing plants over it, but maintenance work on the wall beneath the plants will be necessary occasionally to keep it in good condition. Now that the climbers are not in active growth, this is a good time of year to carry out such work.

KEEPING HELLEBORE FLOWERS CLEAN

The winter-flowering *Helleborus niger* (Christmas rose) bears its blooms very close to the ground, where they may be spoiled by soil splashes if it rains. When the plants are in bud, tuck some straw or similar material around their base to prevent this.

1 Climbing plants should be grown on a trellis fixed to the wall rather than directly on the wall. It improves the air flow round the plants while making the wall accessible for maintenance. Attach the trellis to battens 2in/5cm thick and fix to the surface of the wall (**right**).

2 Prune back shoots that have outgrown the available space, and thin out the climber's growth if necessary. Unscrew the trellis and carefully lower it, still clothed with the climber's growth, to ground level. Two people are necessary unless the trellis is very small.

3 The wall behind a dense climber is a favorite hiding place for snails, and you will probably find a surprising number clinging to the wall's surface. Remove and dispose of them, and then sweep all the dirt and debris away from the wall with a stiff broom (**right**).

4 Carry out any necessary repairs to brick or plasterwork before reattaching the trellis. If screws are difficult to work with, a hook and screw eye system can be used to attach the trellis instead. Great care is needed to avoid damage to the main stem of the climber while the trellis is being lowered and raised.

◀ *This is the time of year for checking trees and shrubs for root rock; they may well have been disturbed by windy weather.*

709

ornamental garden: *plants in season*

This is the time of year when the bark and branches of both trees and shrubs begin to be appreciated—there are some beautiful and striking shapes, textures, and colors to admire. Plenty of leaves, flowers, such as the beautiful snowdrops, and berries, such as those found in seasonal favorites holly and ivy, can be enjoyed, too.

▲ *Snowdrops are among the earliest flowers of the year. The double flowers of Galanthus nivalis 'Flore Pleno' are especially attractive.*

▶ Hamamelis intermedia *'Westerstede'* (witch hazel) bears its fragrant, ragged-petaled flowers on leafless branches.

▼ *The sweet-scented, pale yellow flowers of Mahonia japonica are carried all through the winter, undeterred by the coldest weather.*

TREES AND SHRUBS

Acer, especially *A. capillipes, A. davidii, A. griseum* (maple)
Arbutus unedo (strawberry tree)
Aucuba japonica 'Crotonifolia' and others (spotted laurel)
Betula, especially *B. ermanii, B. nigra* (black birch), *B. papyrifera* (paper birch), *B. utilis* var. *jacquemontii* (Himalayan Birch)
Chimonanthus praecox (wintersweet)
Cornus alba (red-barked dogwood)
Corylus avellana 'Contorta' (Harry Lauder's walking stick)
Cotoneaster
Elaeagnus x *ebbingei*
Erica carnea (alpine heath)
Euonymus fortunei, E. japonicus (variegated)
Fraxinus excelsior 'Jaspidea' (European ash)
Hamamelis mollis (Chinese witch hazel)
Hedera (ivy)
Ilex (berry-bearing and variegated varieties) (holly)
Jasminum nudiflorum (jasmine)
Lonicera fragrantissima, L. standishii (winter honeysuckle)
Mahonia
Prunus serrula, P. x *subhirtella* 'Autumnalis' (autumn cherry)
Pyracantha (firethorn)
Salix alba, S. babylonica var. *pekinensis* 'Tortuosa' (dragon-claw willow)
Skimmia japonica
Sorbus
Tilia platyphylos 'Rubra' (red-twigged lime)
Viburnum

PERENNIALS

Helleborus niger (Christmas rose)
Iris unguicularis
Schizostylis coccinea (kaffir lily)

BULBS

Crocus imperati
Cyclamen coum
Galanthus (snowdrop)

kitchen garden: *general tasks*

Continue pruning fruit trees during the dormant season, except when the weather is frosty. Winter digging of the vegetable plot should also be proceeding; it is worth digging the ground as deeply as you can, adding plenty of organic matter to improve the soil.

▲ *Protect fall-sown beans and pea seedlings from the worst of the cold weather and wind with mini-polytunnels.*

Protecting beans and peas

Pea and bean seeds sown in the vegetable plot earlier in the fall should have germinated and be showing through the soil by now. Although they are hardy, very cold and windy weather will take its toll of the young plants, so it is worth giving them a little extra protection to see them through the worst spells. Plants can be protected by glass barn cloches placed over the rows that will keep off the worst of the cold weather and wind, and protect the plants from excess rain. The glass acts as a mini-greenhouse, trapping the warmth of any sun there may be. Unfortunately glass cloche are very prone to breakage, and can be dangerous, especially where there are children or pets in the garden. Mini-polytunnels are a safer option, although condensation can be a problem, causing fungal rots to affect the seedlings. One of the easiest materials to use is lightweight horticultural blanket that is draped loosely over the crop. The edges must be pegged down or secured to prevent the blanket from blowing away in windy weather.

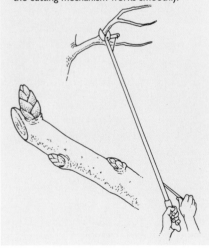

PRUNING LARGE TREES

Most modern fruit trees are grown on dwarfing or semidwarfing rootstocks, but older trees can grow very tall and wide spreading, making pruning difficult. If you use a ladder, have someone hold it steady. Long-arm pruners make reaching high branches easier; make sure the blades are sharp and the cutting mechanism works smoothly.

PRUNING FRUIT TREES

Continue pruning bush trees as described on page 692. Pruning in the dormant season stimulates strong, vigorous growth the following spring, and that is why the major pruning of trees trained as restricted forms takes place in summer. Hard winter pruning of apples and pears grown as cordons or espaliers would result in uncontrolled growth. Winter pruning on trained trees should mainly be restricted to removing dead, dying and diseased wood, and thinning out overcrowded spurs.

Plums should not be pruned in the winter because this invites an invasion by silver leaf disease spores. The disease slowly weakens the trees, and forms bracket fungi on affected branches that release spores mainly during the late fall and winter. The spores enter new wood through fresh wounds. Plums should be pruned in the spring and summer when spores are less likely to be around, and in any case the trees more quickly produce natural resins to seal over pruning cuts. The popular plum variety 'Victoria' is particularly prone to this disease, which also affects almonds, apricots and cherries, although not usually producing such serious effects as it does on plums.

start winter digging

Since digging is satisfying but hard physical work, large plots should be completed in stages to avoid the back problems that trouble so many over-enthusiastic gardeners. Digging is best carried out as early in the winter as possible, leaving the ground rough for the maximum time to allow frosts to break up the clods of soil.

1 Dig a trench one spit (the depth of the spade's blade) deep across the top of the plot (**left**). Throw the soil into a wheelbarrow so that it can be moved to the other end of the plot. Try to keep your spine straight while digging.

2 Fork over or chop the soil at the base of the trench with the spade. Move backward and dig a second trench behind the first (**left, below**). Throw the soil from this to fill the trench in front. Try to turn the soil over as you throw it.

3 Continue in this way until you reach the other end of the plot. If you have any rotted manure or garden compost to incorporate, it should be placed at the base of each trench before it is filled in. Annual weeds can be buried, but perennial weed roots should be removed.

4 Once the last trench has been dug, fill it in with the soil from the first trench that has been barrowed to the end of the plot. Leave the soil surface rough; repeated freezing and thawing of the moisture in the soil over the winter will break down the clods and improve soil structure.

protecting kitchen garden crops

Cloches and polytunnels are useful in almost every season in the kitchen garden, but never more so than when bad weather is threatening to damage crops. They keep off rain, wind, and a degree of frost; they can also protect plants from attack by a range of pests. In late winter and early spring they give early plants that little extra protection that will bring them on well ahead of the rest. Earlier still, they can be used to cover strips of soil required for early sowing. Keeping the rain off the soil will allow it to warm up and become workable much earlier than uncovered areas.

Tunnels and cloches are most suitable for low-growing plants, though with imagination they can also be pressed into service for taller crops. A pair of barn cloches, stood on end and wired together, are perfect around outdoor tomato plants to ripen the last fruits in the fall.

Cloches

Cloches are made from glass or rigid plastic. Glass has the advantage of retaining heat better (like a mini-greenhouse) and being more stable in windy weather, but it is very fragile and dangerous when broken, especially in gardens where children play. It is also expensive, and makes cloches heavy and awkward to move about. Plastic cloches are cheap and lightweight,

▲ *The earliest cloches were used for individual plants. Bell-type cloches are still available, but open-ended styles are now more popular.*

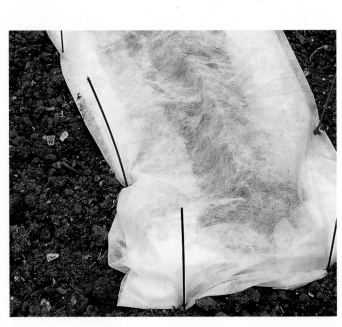

▲ *A lightweight polypropylene blanket provides young plants with surprisingly good protection against adverse weather.*

▶ *The polytunnel is very popular with gardeners because it is cheap to buy and easy to use, though it has a relatively short life.*

and not as easily broken as glass; they do not retain so much warmth and need to be thoroughly secured or they will blow away in even slightly windy weather. Cloches may be made from clear plastic, PVC, twin-walled polycarbonate or polypropylene. All plastic should have been treated with an ultraviolet inhibitor.

Early cloches were bell shaped (*cloche* is French for bell) or lantern shaped, and used to cover individual plants. This individual type of cloche is still available but larger cloches, used end-to-end to cover whole rows of plants, are now more popular. They may be made from two pieces of glass (or plastic) fixed together in an inverted "V" to form a tent shape, or from four pieces of glass to form a barn cloche with its slightly sloping sides topped by a wide tent roof. The barn cloche is useful for taller plants, and can usually be ventilated by raising or removing one side of the roof. Barn cloches are generally made from glass held together by a number of wire clips, and are much more difficult to construct than tent cloches. Another popular cloche shape is an arc, made by bending a flexible, semirigid sheet of plastic, usually corrugated, and securing it with hoops.

To prevent rows of cloches from becoming wind tunnels, they should be fitted with end panels, which sometimes have adjustable ventilators. Cloches with built-in sprinklers are also available for easy watering.

Polytunnels

These are made from plastic sheeting that is stretched over wire hoops positioned over the crop. They are usually available as packs of hoops with a separate plastic sheet, but brands that have the plastic ready fitted over the hoops and which are folded up concertina fashion make erecting the tunnels easier. They are cheap, and easy to use and store.

Floating row cover

This is a term applied to lightweight perforated plastic or fiber materials that lie loosely on top of the crop, and are held in place by the edges being buried or staked in the ground. The material is light and flexible enough not to restrict the crop as it grows. Polypropylene fiber blanket is the most popular kind, and insulates the plants against cold and wind while remaining permeable to air and moisture. It tears easily but with care will last for several seasons, especially if it has strengthened edges. It is available cut to measure from a roll, in sheets, or as a "grow tube" 3ft/90cm in diameter that is cut to length and used to fit over individual plants.

greenhouse: *general tasks*

Get a head start on some of the crops that like a long growing season by sowing seeds now, with the aid of a heated propagator to supply the extra warmth they need. Remember to keep a regular check on greenhouse temperatures to insure that heating systems are working efficiently.

Sowing seeds in a heated propagator

A number of seeds like an early start to give them a long growing season—onions and pelargoniums are two that traditionally are sown in early winter. Seeds need more warmth than growing plants to insure good germination, and the extra warmth can quite conveniently be supplied by using a heated propagator.

Electrically-heated propagators have a heating element sealed into the base that supplies a steady warmth to the soil mix. Plastic seedtray covers help to retain the heat. The warmth leads to a build-up of condensation inside the propagator cover, so adjustable ventilators should be fitted to the covers to prevent the humidity becoming too high.

Various sizes of propagator are available, from models that take a single seed tray to those that can accommodate four trays or more. More sophisticated propagator models have an adjustable thermostat that enables you to vary the temperature according to the requirements of the particular seeds you are sowing—usually from 60–75°F/15–24°C. As an alternative to buying a complete propagator, it is possible to make up your own propagating bench to the size you require by buying soil-warming cables and an appropriate thermostat.

GREENHOUSE TEMPERATURES

A maximum/minimum thermometer is invaluable for insuring that greenhouse heating systems are working efficiently, so make a habit of checking and resetting the thermometer every day. It is important that temperatures do not dip too low, but you should also make sure that fuel is not being wasted by maintaining too high a temperature. The best time to check this is on a cold, frosty morning, insuring that the minimum temperature recorded the previous night was not significantly higher than required. If necessary, adjust the heating thermostat up or down, as appropriate, but do be careful to make only small adjustments at a time.

▲ *Heated propagators can supply a constant warmth to flats of seeds sown in soil mix and help to encourage good germination.*

easy, early flowering narcissus (daffodils)

One of the simplest varieties of narcissus for growing in the home during the winter season is the variety 'Paper White.' It needs no special treatment, and quickly produces multi-headed stems of pure white, star-like blooms with a penetrating, sweet fragrance. Planting several batches of bulbs two weeks or so apart will make sure there is a long succession of blooms for the house.

1 'Paper White' bulbs can be grown in bowls or pots of soilless potting mix, or even on pebbles or in a glass jar filled with water. Plant the bulbs in pots or bowls so that their tips are just showing above the soil surface (**right**).

2 Water the mix so that it is just moist. Unlike most forced bulbs, 'Paper White' requires no cold, dark period. Place the planted bulbs on a windowsill in a light but cool position; a frost-free greenhouse is an ideal place.

3 The plants need bright light as the stems grow, and become very tall and spindly if grown in a warm or dull position. Each stem should be supported with a slender split cane, but take care not to spear the bulbs (**below**).

4 The bulbs will usually come into flower six to eight weeks after planting (**below**). Plants growing in the greenhouse should be taken into the home just before the flowers open. Keep them in a cool, bright position for the longest life.

INDIAN AZALEAS

Azaleas make very attractive winter-flowering houseplants, but they do need moist compost and a humid atmosphere. Plants in bud and in flower should be sprayed daily with a fine mist of plain water. When plants are in the home, keep them in a cool position at 50–60°F/10–15°C, away from artificial heat or direct sunlight.

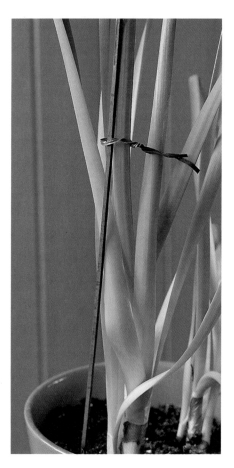

midwinter

This is often the most trying season of the year for gardeners. The weather may be at its most miserable and, although the shortest day is just past, there is no real evidence yet of the daylight hours lengthening. Spring might seem a long way off but in reality there is not too long to wait.

All the dormant-season tasks in the garden continue. Planting bare-root specimens of new trees and shrubs will be possible for some weeks yet; if the weather is freezing or very wet when the plants arrive, heel them in until conditions improve. After heavy frosts, check plantings in case they need firming back into the soil if the frost has lifted them.

The prolonged wet spells show up any badly drained areas. If puddles are still standing on the soil surface hours after the rain has stopped, it is a sign drainage needs to be improved.

This is the most likely time for snow. Snow can make the garden look beautiful, but if you can bring yourself to spoil its unsullied whiteness it's a good idea to take action to prevent it from damaging plants and trees. It's only the physical weight of the snow that does the damage; snow actually helps to insulate plants against the cold.

Some border plants can be increased by root cuttings, and in the vegetable garden the soil can be made ready for early spring sowings. In the greenhouse things are moving ahead rapidly — stock up with the equipment you need for the busy sowing and growing season ahead.

◀ *Midwinter is the most likely time for snow in many regions. It may be beautiful but its weight can cause damage to trees and plants.*

MIDWINTER TASKS

General

▪ *Check and maintain tools before putting them away for the winter*
▪ *Improve drainage where necessary*

Ornamental garden

▪ *Weed and check emerging spring bulbs outdoors*
▪ *Take root cuttings of phlox, Papaver (poppy), Verbascum (mullein) and other border plants*

▪ *Continue planting bare-root and container-grown trees and shrubs, and refirm newly-planted specimens after frost. Heel in bare-root plants when weather is unsuitable for planting*

▪ *Knock snow off evergreens before it breaks their branches*
▪ *Order young plants from seed catalogs for delivery in early to mid-spring*

▲ *Root cuttings are an easy way to propagate many border plants.*

Lawns

▪ *Keep off the grass in frosty or wet weather*
▪ *Watch out for snow mold disease*
▪ *Sweep away leaves and debris*

Kitchen garden

▪ *Continue digging*
▪ *Force outdoor rhubarb for an early crop*
▪ *Sow sprouting seeds for winter salads*
▪ *Order vegetable seeds, seed potatoes, young vegetable plants and onions sets from catalogs as soon as possible*

▪ *Sow beans and peas for an early crop*
▪ *Continue to check fruit and vegetables in store*
▪ *Cover the ground with cloches to dry it out ready for early sowings*

▪ *Continue to plant fruit trees, and soft fruit bushes and canes*
▪ *Complete pruning of fruit trees*
▪ *Deter birds from attacking fruit buds*

Greenhouse

▪ *Remove dead plant material promptly to avoid disease. Ventilate whenever possible to keep the atmosphere dry*
▪ *Buy new seed flats, pots, propagator tops, and labels etc., ready for the main sowing season*

▪ *Continue sowing early seeds in a heated propagator*
▪ *Start overwintering fuchsias and pelargoniums , chrysanthemums and dahlias into growth to provide cuttings*
▪ *Sow Lathyrys ordoratus (sweet peas)*

▪ *Sow some stump-rooted carrots and radishes in a growing bag*

▼ *Grow a quick and early crop of carrots in a growing bag in the greenhouse.*

general garden tasks

Snow hides all the imperfections of the winter garden and covers it in a pristine whiteness, but it can bring problems for the gardener, especially if it persists for more than a few days. Frost is more common than snow in most areas, and brings its own set of difficulties, particularly for lawns.

Preventing snow damage

A moderate fall of snow can pose a real danger to evergreen trees and shrubs. In just a few hours they can be permanently misshapen, or branches can be broken by the weight of snow.

If the snowfall is heavy enough, knock it from the branches of any tree or shrub that looks as though it may be damaged. It is usually easily dislodged with a broom, but you will need to do this shortly after the snow has fallen—don't wait for it to freeze again or it becomes much more difficult.

The thaw brings more problems because a lot of water is released as the snow melts. On lawns, look out for more or less round patches of dying, yellow grass which gradually enlarge and may show signs of a fluffy white mold. This is snow mold, a fungus disease that is common on lawns that have been covered in snow for some time, especially if they have been walked over regularly. Treat the disease with a lawn fungicide.

▲ *Snow may bring a seasonal beauty to the winter garden, but it can also spell problems for some trees and shrubs.*

STORING TOOLS

Garden tools need to be kept in good condition if they are to give good service, and the winter is a good time to give them all a thorough overhaul. Hand tools such as spades and forks should be cleaned thoroughly after use, removing all soil, and the metal parts rubbed with an oily rag. Wooden handles can be smoothed down with sandpaper to prevent splinters.

The moving parts of tools such as shears and pruners should be oiled, and blades of all cutting implements can be sharpened with a carborundum stone. Don't forget to sharpen the blades of tools such as hoes and edging irons as well. Any tools that are not being used over the winter should be stored in a dry place, and tools that have reached the end of their useful life should be replaced before the main growing season starts.

make a cold frame

Cold frames are more useful in the garden than is generally realized. They are invaluable for overwintering slightly tender or young plants, and are ideal for hardening off greenhouse plants destined for outdoors in the spring. While purpose-made aluminum and plastic cold frames can be bought, it is quite easy to make your own, often entirely from waste materials.

1 A typical cold frame has a wooden or brick base about 12–18in/30–45cm high at the back, sloping down toward the front, and is covered with a glass lid called a light. The usual size for a frame is around 4 x 2ft/120 x 60cm but size can be adjusted to suit your needs.

3 If the frame is constructed in a sheltered area it is unnecessary to cement the bricks together. The window frames can be laid on top of the base and held in place by bricks around the edge (**right**). With wooden bases, attach the frames with hinges to make ventilation easier.

2 Demolition yards can often supply glazed window frames very cheaply, and they make excellent lights. Choose those with as large an area of glass as possible because glazing bars cut down the amount of light considerably. Once you have obtained the lights, build the base to fit.

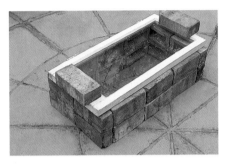

4 On cold days a piece of old carpet or sacking should be laid over the frame for extra protection (**below**); in sunny weather ventilate the frame by removing the light or propping it open with a wooden stay. In windy areas, make sure the open light is secure and cannot be blown away.

◄ *Walking over frosted grass will crush and kill the frozen stems, leaving a pattern of blackened footprints later on. Walking on the lawn in wet weather should also be avoided. Make an extra effort to stick to paths in winter.*

use of fertilizers

Plants make their energy from the sun by photosynthesis, but in order to carry this out, they need certain minerals that they normally absorb from the soil. These minerals are generally referred to as plant nutrients or plant foods. The three main minerals plants require are nitrogen, phosphorus, and potassium, often referred to by their chemical names of N, P, and K. Along with calcium, magnesium and sulfur, they are the minerals required in the largest amounts.

Other minerals are no less important but are needed in only very small quantities. These micronutrients or trace elements include boron, copper, iron, manganese, molybdenum, and zinc. Some other elements, such as cobalt, aluminum, and silicon, are also required by plants, but are thought to be beneficial rather than essential.

In good, fertile soils, enough essential nutrients are available for the plants' needs. In other soils, however, there may be a shortfall of one or more nutrients. This can be due to the physical makeup of the soil, or to repeated heavy cropping that has used up the mineral reserves; it might also be that the minerals are present but not in a form that is available to plants (for example alkaline soils often "lock up" micronutrients such as iron). Where the nutrients are not available in the soil, they can be supplied as supplements in the form of fertilizers.

Fertilizers

Fertilizers can either be straight (supplying one nutrient) or compound (supplying a mixture of nutrients). Details of which nutrients they supply are always given on the pack. The three major nutrients (nitrogen, phosphorus, and potassium—always in this order) are the most popular ingredients of compound fertilizers, and the proportions are often expressed as N:P:K 7:7:7, or just 7:7:7. A fertilizer labeled 5:5:9 is high in potassium, while 30:10:10 is high in nitrogen. Straight fertilizers may be labeled in the same way—for example, sulfate of ammonia 21:0:0, or sulfate of potash 0:0:50.

The three major nutrients are the ones most likely to be in short supply in the soil, but other nutrients can be deficient too. Some fertilizers contain a mixture of both major and micronutrients, while others specialize in providing micronutrients only, and are often called trace element fertilizers. Sometimes the micronutrients are formulated to insure that they will not be altered by the

◀ *Liquid fertilizers are fast acting and give a rapid boost to plants. Some types are formulated for absorption by the leaves.*

soil chemistry and made unavailable to plants; they are known as fritted or chelated compounds, and are ideal for alkaline soils. Other trace element fertilizers are formulated so that they can be taken up by the foliage, a further way of avoiding the soil chemistry problem.

Methods of application

Fertilizers come in the form of powders, granules, and liquids. Always read the application instructions carefully—some powders are applied direct to the soil while others need to be dissolved in water first. The application rate varies according to the product and the type of plant being fed. Wear gloves when handling and applying fertilizers, and keep dry fertilizers off the plants, especially the growth buds because they are likely to be scorched. Liquid fertilizers are less likely to scorch plants and are quick acting; they can be applied through a watering can or a hose-end dilutor for large areas such as lawns. Dry fertilizers can also be obtained as soil sticks or pills for easy application.

Slow-release fertilizers give extended feeding over several weeks. They are normally granules that are gradually broken down to release the fertilizer, and require a combination of moisture and warmth to act.

▲ *Fertilizer granules: it is important to wear gloves when handling and applying any form of fertilizers and keep dry fertilizers off the plants.*

▼ *Fertilizer pills are now available for ease of application to soils where there is a shortfall of important nutrients.*

NUTRIENT DEFICIENCY SYMPTOMS

Nutrient	Symptom of deficiency
Nitrogen	leaves small, pale green or yellow, especially older leaves; growth stunted
Phosphorus	leaves small, tinged with purple; older leaves fall early
Potassium	leaf tips and margins turn yellow or brown, and look scorched; older leaves affected first. Poor flowering and fruiting
Calcium	death of leaf tips and growing points; blossom end rot on tomatoes and peppers, bitter pit on apples
Magnesium	leaves yellow between the veins; older leaves affected first, spreading to young leaves
Sulfur	yellowing of leaves, first on young leaves then spreading to the whole plant. Not a common deficiency
Iron	leaves yellow with dark green veins; young leaves affected first (unlike magnesium deficiency)
Manganese	yellowing and dead patches between the veins on young leaves
Zinc	yellowing between the veins on young leaves; small leaves; browning of buds
Boron	growing points die, leaves deformed with discolored areas
Molybdenum	distinctive strap-shaped, "whip tail" leaves on cauliflowers

ornamental garden: *general tasks*

Even though it is midwinter, there are definite signs of growth from spring-flowering bulbs. Help them on their way by making sure they are not smothered by weeds and debris. Meanwhile, root cuttings are an unusual but easy way of increasing a range of border plants, shrubs, and trees.

Bulbs in store

Many plants that develop specialized storage organs, such as bulbs, corms, and tubers, can be stored over winter in a cool, dry, frost-free place such as a garden shed; if left in cold, wet soil in the garden there is often a real risk

▼ *Boxes of daffodil bulbs can be stored quite safely during the winter months provided their environment is dry and frost-free.*

of them rotting away. However, they are not immune to rotting even when lifted and stored under cover.

There are several fungi and bacteria that are responsible for storage rots. Many of the pathogens are present in the soil while some are airborne, and they usually attack the plants through damaged tissue. Check stored bulbs regularly all through winter, and remove and destroy any

that show signs of rotting. Rots may take the form of red, brown, or black lesions that are often soft but may also be hard and dry; mold growth may also be visible. Dust remaining bulbs with a fungicide powder to try to prevent the spread of the problem.

EMERGING SPRING BULBS
—

The leafy shoots of spring bulbs are already emerging through the soil. Carefully remove weeds, leaves, and other plant debris from around the shoots, and prick over the soil between them with a hand fork if there is room; this helps to aerate the soil and prevents a soil "cap" from forming. Where bulbs are planted under trees, moss may form on the soil surface; this does not harm the bulbs but you may want to scrape away the moss to improve the general appearance. On poor soils, a balanced fertilizer can be sprinkled around the bulbs once the surface has been cleared.

take root cuttings

Most gardeners are familiar with the idea of taking cuttings from shoots and encouraging them to form new roots. Less well known is the technique of growing new plants from sections of root which send out new shoots. This is an easy way to propagate plants, and one of the few methods of propagation which can be carried out in midwinter.

1 A number of shrubs and herbaceous plants can be grown from root cuttings taken in the dormant season; among them are anchusa, *Anemone* x *hybrida*, Papaver (poppy), phlox, Primula (primroses), Romneya (tree poppy), daphne, and *Rhus typhina*.

2 The cuttings can be taken at any time in the dormant season when the soil is not waterlogged or frozen. Herbaceous plants can be lifted carefully, or the plants can be left in situ and the soil scraped away to expose some roots if lifting is not practical.

3 Choose firm, healthy roots, removing two or three from each plant by cutting them cleanly with a knife (**below, left**). Replace the soil around the parent plant and firm it in well. Trim off any whiskery side roots from the cuttings and place them in a plastic bag to prevent drying out.

4 Cut the prepared roots into sections about 2in/5cm long, but make sure you know which is the top and bottom of each piece. Insert into pots of moist, sandy cuttings mix so that their tops are level with the soil surface (**below, right**). Keep in a cold frame over winter.

REFIRM SPECIMENS

A heavy frost can expand the soil and cause it to lift around the roots of newly-planted trees and shrubs, loosening them in the ground. Inspect plants after a frost, and where necessary, firm them back in place by treading around them with the sole of your boot, pushing the soil back against the stems.

ornamental garden: *plants in season*

Evergreen plants continue to give good value, especially the
variegated varieties that light up the garden in dull weather.
Many of the trees and shrubs flowering now have the bonus of
an intense fragrance, and more and more bulbs are blooming.

▼ *Winter-flowering hellebores bring life
to the garden. Although they are frost-hardy,
low-growing varieties need protection.*

TREES AND SHRUBS

Acer (bark effects) (maple)

Aucuba japonica (spotted laurel)

Betula (birch)

Camellia

Chimonanthus praecox (wintersweet)

Cornus alba (red-barked dogwood)

Corylus avellana 'Contorta' (Harry Lauder's
   walking stick)

Cotoneaster

Daphne odora

Erica carnea (alpine heath)

Euonymus fortunei, E. japonicus (variegated
   varieties) (spindle tree)

Garrya elliptica

Hamamelis mollis (witch hazel)

Hedera colchica 'Dentata Variegata' and
   others (ivy)

Hippophae rhamnoides (sea buckthorn)

Ilex (berry-bearing and variegated varieties)
   (holly)

Jasminum nudiflorum (jasmine)

Lonicera fragrantissima, L. standishii
   (winter honeysuckle)

Mahonia

Prunus serrula, P. x subhirtella 'Autumnalis'
   autumnn cherry)

Pyracantha (firethorn)

Salix alba (white willow), S. babylonica
   pekinensis 'Tortuosa'

Skimmia japonica

Sorbus

Viburnum

▲ Pyracantha, *with its startling red berries,
will liven up any garden at this time of year.*

PERENNIALS

Ajuga reptans (bugle)

Bergenia

Helleborus atrorubens, H. foetidus (stinking
hellebore), H. niger (Christmas rose)

Iris unguicularis

Phormium tenax (New Zealand flax)

Viola (winter-flowering pansies)

BULBS

Crocus ancyrensis, C. imperati, C. laevigatus,
   C. tomasinianus

Eranthis (winter aconite)

Galanthus (snowdrop)

Iris danfordiae, I. histrioides, I. reticulata

◀ Camellia x williamsii *'Jury's Yellow'
is a winter-flowering delight.*

kitchen garden: *general tasks*

Plant canes and bushes to extend your range of soft fruits, and take action against birds that destroy fruit buds before they even start into growth. Cloches help to get the soil ready for early sowings, but if you can't wait that long, grow your own salad in a jelly jar in a matter of days.

Protecting fruit buds from birds

Various species of small birds can ruin the potential fruit crop of trees and bushes by pecking at the buds on the dormant branches. Every climate zone and local regions have their particular culprits, even including squirrels. Apples, cherries, gooseberries, plums, pears, and currants can all be affected.

The birds usually eat the tender shoots right in the centers of the buds. It is also believed that sometimes the birds are searching for insects sheltering in and around the buds, and that the damage to the buds is incidental. Either way, the effect is the same: long lengths of branches and shoots are left bare and the fruit crop is reduced. Bitter-tasting bird repellents can be sprayed on the trees but may not be very effective, while bird scarers also give mixed results. The surest way to prevent damage is by providing a physical barrier with netting or horticultural blanket.

▶ *Netting protects a fruit crop from birds, but earlier in the year it can also help to prevent them from destroying the developing buds.*

BUSHES, CANES AND FRUIT TREES

Fruit and vegetables form an important part of a healthy diet, and having plenty of home-grown fruit to harvest will certainly enable you to increase your consumption. Spells of good weather will allow you to plant fruit trees and soft fruit canes and bushes now.

Extend your range of soft fruits by trying some of the new, improved varieties that find their way into the catalogs every year. Particularly popular are the hybrid berries (mainly raspberry/blackberry crosses) such as boysenberry, silvanberry, tayberry, youngberry, sunberry and veitchberry. They should provide a talking point and a good crop of tasty fruit.

sprouting seeds for winter salads

Winter is a difficult time to produce fresh salad crops, but sprouting seeds couldn't be simpler to grow. They are ready in a matter or days, and have a pleasant crunchy texture and a range of interesting flavors. Many varieties are also thought to be beneficial to health, with particularly high concentrations of cancer-preventing compounds. A good range of suitable seeds for sprouting are available from the mail order catalogs of major seedsmen.

1 Sprouting seeds can be grown in a wide-necked glass jar topped with a piece of muslin or fine mesh net secured with an elastic band. A square cut from an old pair of nylon pantyhose makes a good cover.

2 Put a couple of spoonfuls of seeds into the jar and cover them with water; allow them to soak for a few hours or overnight (**right**). Drain the water off through the top of the jar, fill with fresh water, swirl around the jar and immediately drain the water off again.

3 Place the jar of seeds in a moderately warm position. If they are grown in the dark the sprouts will be white; if they are in the light they will be green and have a slightly different flavor. Every day, fill the jar with fresh water, swirl it round and immediately drain it away.

4 After a few days the sprouts are ready to eat (**below**); they will bulk up to almost fill the jar. Among seeds that can be grown are mung beans, alfalfa, and fenugreek; mixtures are also available. Only buy seeds produced for sprouting as many pulses are poisonous if eaten raw.

THE VEGETABLE PLOT

In a sheltered place in the vegetable garden, cover an area of ground with cloches to get it ready for seed sowing a little later. Although the cloches might help to trap what heat there is, this is not why they are useful. Their main purpose is to keep the rain off the soil so that it can dry out, enabling it to be broken down to the fine crumbs necessary to form a seedbed.

greenhouse: *general tasks*

The spring sowing season will soon be upon us, so make sure you have all the necessary equipment. Meanwhile, make a start by sowing sweet peas, and some carrots or radishes for a tasty early crop. Plants that have been overwintering under cover can be started into growth to provide cuttings.

Waking up plants

The roots of plants such as dahlias, chrysanthemums, fuchsias, and pelargoniums have spent the winter in a more or less dormant condition, tucked into almost-dry compost or peat. As long as you can provide a little heat in the greenhouse, it's time to wake them up again, and start them into growth.

Pot up the roots in fresh compost if necessary, and bring them out into the light. Water the compost thoroughly so that it is evenly moist (but not wet) throughout, and maintain a steady temperature of around 45°F/7°C. New shoots will soon be produced, and they can be taken as softwood cuttings to provide sturdy, vigorous new plants for setting out after the risk of frosts is over.

STOCK UP ON EQUIPMENT

When the main sowing season starts, a surprising number of seedtrays and pots will be necessary for all the seeds you want to try. Large volumes of sowing and cuttings mix will disappear quickly, too. Check the state of existing equipment—seedtrays and flats, various sizes of pot, plastic covers, dibbles, presser boards, watering can rose sprays, labels and markers. Discard broken or damaged equipment, and buy replacements. Also buy one or two large bags of compost and leave them unopened in the greenhouse until you need them.

▲ *It is easy to increase your stock of chrysanthemums by taking softwood cuttings over the next few weeks.*

sow some early vegetables

In a frost-free greenhouse it is possible to make a sowing of spring vegetables now, and enjoy some extra early young crops. Both radishes and carrots grow well if sown direct into a growing bag. You won't get a very big crop, but it will be particularly welcome because they will be available so early in the year.

1 Choose the right varieties for a growing bag—they must be short-rooting types. There are lots of suitable round radishes, but carrots need more care. Globe-rooting types such as 'Parmex' are ideal, and stump-rooted varieties like 'Nantes' are also good.

2 Cut out the top of the growing bag, leaving just a border of plastic around the edge. Make short drills in the soil with a cane or dibble, and sow the seeds thinly (**right**). Pull soil back over the top, pat down and water using a fine rose on the watering can.

3 Place the growing bags in the lightest position possible, and keep the soil just moist. When the seedlings emerge, thin them to an appropriate spacing as soon as they are large enough to handle.

4 Keep the soil moist as the plants develop. Start to pull the roots as soon as they are large enough to eat (**below**), taking alternate plants so that the ones that are left have the chance to grow bigger.

SWEET PEAS

If you didn't sow sweet peas in the fall (or if you want another batch of plants), sow some now in exactly the same way. The seeds germinate best at around 50°F/10°C, and can be placed in a heated propagator. They will flower later than the fall-sown sweet peas, but still give excellent results.

lighting for greenhouse and houseplants

Warmth is not the only requirement for plant growth that is missing during the winter months—in addition, light levels are nowhere near the optimum for most plants. Even though the equivalent of summer temperatures can be provided by heating, the plants will not respond as they would in a real summer, simply because they are not receiving sufficient duration or quality of light.

Of course, supplementary lighting is available in almost every home at the flick of a switch. However, the type of artificial light that peope find useful is not that useful to plants.

Light quality
Not all visible light is used by plants for photosynthesis, only light of certain wavelengths. The intensity of light is

▲ *Ordinary fluorescent lighting offers the domestic gardener a useful alternative to the high-power lighting used by commercial growers.*

EFFECTS OF DAY LENGTH
ON FLOWERING

Day length is a very important factor for controlling flowering times in certain plants. In some species flower buds are initiated only when the daylight hours fall below a specific length; they are called "short-day plants" and include chrysanthemums, poinsettias, kalanchoes, and Rieger begonias. "Long-night" plants would be more appropriate because it is actually the number of hours of uninterrupted darkness that is important.) Commercial growers manipulate flowering times very effectively by the use of supplementary or night-break lighting.

When artificial lighting is used by home gardeners, they can unwittingly prevent the flowering of short day plants by decreasing the hours of continuous darkness to which the plants are exposed. A single, short illumination interrupting the hours of darkness may be sufficient to prevent flowers from forming.

▶ *Chrysanthemums are among those flowers known as "short-day" plants because their buds are initiated only when day lengths are short.*

important, too—most forms of artificial lighting have to be placed relatively close to plants for a useful intensity of light to be absorbed.

Most lamps produce heat as a by-product; this heat is sufficiently intense to damage plants when the lamps are placed close to them. This factor alone rules out the use of ordinary household incandescent bulbs as a light source for plants.

Commercial growers use high-pressure sodium and metal halide lamps which have been specifically designed to promote plant growth, but these are expensive, and not particularly attractive in living rooms. A good alternative is ordinary fluorescent lighting; it remains cool in use and provides light of a useful wavelength. Fluorescent tubes give a good spread of light over a relatively large area. Compact fluorescent bulbs have the advantage of being suitable for a normal screw- or bayonet-type light fitting, but they cast their light over a much smaller area.

Using artificial light for plants

Artificial light can be used to boost natural daylight during normal daylight hours, or to extend the length of the day by providing light during the hours of darkness. Extending day length has been found to be the most successful approach. If you are using fluorescent lamps they should normally be positioned 9–24in/23–60cm above the tops of the plants.

In the home, a compact fluorescent bulb in a "rise and fall" light fitting that has been positioned over a group of house plants makes an attractive feature. Alternatively, a plant stand incorporating a fluorescent tube can be constructed.

In a greenhouse, a more utilitarian plant lighting kit can be used; this will incorporate waterproof fittings that are an essential safety feature.

Providing 12–18 hours of total light (including natural daylight) has been shown to give good results for the majority of plants.

late winter

Although the weather can be terrible, there is no longer any doubt that spring is on its way. The days are lengthening; buds on the branches of trees and shrubs begin to swell, and more and more early bulbs are producing their flowers. Get those dormant season tasks finished as soon as you can.

If jobs such as winter digging, planting bare-root trees and shrubs, and pruning fruit trees are not yet finished, this is the time to complete them. In most areas roses can safely be pruned now, too.

A few dry, breezy days will help to get the soil in good condition for sowing to take place outdoors shortly. If you do not know what type of soil you have in the garden, this is a good time to carry out tests.

Flower borders should be tidied, removing weeds and debris that shelter slugs and snails. This is particularly important because the tender young shoots of plants newly emerged through the soil are very vulnerable to these pests. Mulching is equally important because it helps prevent further weed growth, keeps some of the moisture in the soil ready for drier weather, and makes the garden look much tidier and more attractive.

In the greenhouse there are increasing numbers of seeds to be sown and cuttings to be taken. It's vital to insure that the greenhouse heater is properly maintained and adjusted. It will still be needed for some time yet—there will soon be dozens of tender young seedlings that need warmth to develop. Seedlings from earlier sowings need pricking out, and space in the greenhouse will soon be at a premium.

In the kitchen garden, winter crops such as leeks and parsnips need to be used up before they start into growth again, and if you have forced rhubarb and kale for early crops you should harvest them now.

◄ *Now is the time to tidy up your flower borders because any slugs and snails sheltering in weeds and debris will attack young shoots.*

LATE WINTER TASKS

General

- Check tools and equipment, and buy new replacements if needed
- Carry out soil tests on various sites around the garden

Ornamental garden

- Weed and clear borders, and mulch with bark
- Prune roses
- Finish planting bare-root trees and shrubs
- Weed overwintered hardy annuals and provide supports as necessary

- Protect vulnerable plants from slugs
- Sow Lathyrus odoratus (sweet peas) outside
- Continue to plant lily bulbs as available
- Prune winter jasmine after flowering

- Prune summer-flowering clematis hybrids
- Feed flowering shrubs with sulfate of potash

▲ Add moisture-retaining compost to the bottom of the pole bean trench.

Lawns

- Mow the grass lightly if necessary. Carry out repairs to edges and aerate compacted areas
- Choose a new lawn mower if one is needed, before the main mowing season starts

Kitchen garden

- Use up winter vegetables such as leeks and parsnips from the garden before they regrow
- Complete winter digging and apply lime if necessary
- Prepare seed beds if the weather allows
- Use blanket, cloches etc. to protect pea and bean seedlings, and spring greens

- Set seed potatoes to chit (sprout) in a light place as soon as they are purchased
- Plant shallots and Jerusalem artichokes
- Prepare a pole bean trench with moisture-retaining compost
- Harvest forced kale and rhubarb as soon as the shoots are large enough

- Prune fall-fruiting raspberries
- Feed fruit trees and bushes with high-potash fertilizer

Greenhouse

- Clean up the greenhouse to prepare for the new season
- Feed forced bulbs that have finished flowering, ready for planting in the garden later
- Take cuttings from chrysanthemums, dahlias, fuchsias, and pelargoniums

- Begin sowing tomatoes, melons, and cucumbers for greenhouse cropping. Sow half-hardy annuals, and beans in pots for planting out later. Prick out seedlings sown earlier

- Start begonia tubers into growth
- Bring potted strawberries into greenhouse for early crops
- Increase ventilation during the day in suitable weather

▲ Sow bush or fava beans in pots ready for planting outdoors later.

soil testing

There are many different types of soil, varying from county to county and even from one garden to another in the same area. The soil type is of real significance to the way plants grow, and getting to know the soil in your garden is a great aid to successful cultivation.

Soil is derived largely from rock that has been broken down over countless years into tiny particles. The size and type of these particles varies according to the type of rock from which they have been derived, and the way in which they were broken down. The other main ingredient of soil is organic matter. Organic means anything that has once lived—plant or animal remains. These are gradually broken down by a variety of organisms until they form humus, a friable, spongy material whose origins can no longer be identified.

Identifying soil types

Soil types are classified according to their particle size. The smallest particles are clay; slightly larger particles are silt, and largest are sand. The larger the particles, the larger the air spaces between them, and the more easily water can drain away. Sandy soils are free draining, but clay drains very slowly. Sandy soils also tend to be low in plant foods because the soluble nutrients are easily washed away, whereas clay soils are usually richer in nutrients and more fertile. Humus, because of its spongy texture, absorbs moisture and helps to break up tightly-packed soil particles, making it the ideal soil improver for both light sandy soils and badly drained, heavy clays. In general, most soils are a mixture of clay, silt, and sand in varying proportions.

▲ *Simply squeezing a handful of garden soil or rubbing it between the fingers can supply a surprising amount of information about its type.*

▲ *The varying proportions of the main constituents of soil can be seen at a glance if they are allowed to settle out in a jar of water.*

ADDING LIME TO SOIL

Most plants grow best in soil that is just the acid side of neutral, but vegetables may benefit from the addition of lime that reduces the soil acidity. This is largely because clubroot disease, which affects brassicas, is less severe in neutral or alkaline conditions. Lime should not be added unless a pH test has shown that it is necessary; if the pH is 6.5 or above, lime is not needed. It is certainly not necessary to lime the vegetable garden every year as was once a traditional practice.

Carrying out soil tests

Dig up a small handful of soil from just below the surface and moisten it, if necessary, with a little water. Then rub it between your thumb and forefinger; if it feels gritty it is sandy soil, and if it's smooth and slippery or sticky it is silt or clay. Now squeeze the handful of soil tightly then open your hand; sandy soils fall apart while clay soils hold their shape. You can also roll the soil into a ball, then into a long snake, and try to bend the snake into a circle. The more of these steps you can do, the higher the clay content.

Place a further trowel of soil into a clean jelly jar, half-fill the jar with water, put on the lid and shake vigorously. Allow it to settle for several hours. The largest stones and soil particles will settle at the bottom, grading up to the finest clays, while the organic matter will float on the surface of the water. The relative depths of each layer shows the different proportions present in the soil.

Take a number of soil samples from different parts of the garden and use a proprietary soil-testing kit to give a reading (full instructions are on the pack). The most useful test is for soil acidity (pH) because some plants will grow well only in acid soils. Tests for major nutrients (nitrogen, phosphorus, and potassium) can also be carried out, but the results are not always reliable.

▼ *Add lime to the soil only if a pH test shows that it is necessary. It may help to prevent club root disease in the vegetable garden.*

ornamental garden: *general tasks*

The new shoots of herbaceous plants will soon be appearing through the soil in milder regions, and hardy annuals that were sown last fall need to be provided with supports. If you want long-flowering plants especially suitable for containers, it's time to start begonia tubers into growth.

Border plants and slugs

If the weather is mild, some of the early herbaceous border plants will be growing, and their tender, succulent shoots are an irresistible lure to slugs.

Destroy slug habitats by clearing weeds and debris from the border, and the surrounding areas: remember that it is relatively easy and common for them to travel some distance from the shelter of hedge bottoms and similar hideouts.

Protect individual plants by surrounding them with a barrier; crushed egg shells, sharp sand and grit, garden lime, and clinker are traditional deterrents, but strips of plastic are much more effective.

Simply cut strips that are about 3–4in/7.5–10cm wide from empty plastic bottles and push them firmly into the soil around each plant so that 2–3in/5–8cm remains above the ground. At this time of year it's usually a better method than slug pellets.

If you have to use a slug killer, there are a number of organic controls that are less harmful to the wildlife than methiocarb and metaldehyde, including a biological control using a parasitic nematode.

◄ *Slugs spend the day concealed in weedy areas or hedge bottoms, traveling surprising distances to feed during the night.*

MULCHING FLOWER BORDERS

Remove weeds from flower borders and mulch the borders with, say, chipped bark or mushroom compost to deter fresh weed growth and improve the look of the bed. The mulch will also help to retain soil moisture throughout the spring and early summer. Be careful not to apply mulch too closely around emerging plants because it can encourage slugs (see opposite). Leave a clear space immediately around the crowns, described, or mulch up to the plastic strip barriers.

start begonia tubers

Tuberous-rooted begonias make excellent plants for pots and hanging baskets, and are not difficult to keep from year to year. Tubers that have been stored over winter can now be started into growth in a warm greenhouse.

1 Begonias produce rather odd-looking tubers which means it is not always easy to tell which is the top and which is the bottom (**below**). The top is dished, and shows signs of knobbly growth buds; the underside is rounded and whiskery, covered with fibrous roots.

2 Prepare pots of sandy, soilless cuttings mix and press the bases of the tubers into the surface (**below**). The concave side must face upward, and should not be covered with mix. Keep the pots in a light, warm position, ideally about 57°F/14°C.

HARDY ANNUALS

Hardy annuals that were sown last fall should be weeded and the plants thinned out if necessary. Provide them with supports to prevent them from flopping over as they grow. The most inconspicuous supports are twiggy sticks (such as peasticks) that can be cut from hedges or garden shrubs and pushed into the soil among the plants. As the annuals grow, they will hide these supports almost entirely. If your fall sowings did not survive the winter, don't worry—another sowing can be made next month.

3 Keep the soil mix moist, but take care not to splash water into the top of the tuber. If growth buds are slow to appear, lightly mist the tops of the tubers with a fine spray of water once, but otherwise keep the tops dry to avoid rotting.

4 Once strong growth buds appear, the plants can be propagated. Cut the tubers into two or three sections, each with a growth bud, or the buds can be allowed to develop into shoots which are used as softwood cuttings.

739

maintaining paths, patios, and steps

Hard surfaces in the garden will stand a good deal of wear, but they do need regular maintenance to keep them in good condition. This is a convenient time to clean off the winter's accumulated dirt and grime, and spruce up surfaces for the spring; cleaning will also enable you to find and repair any damage that has occurred. The correct maintenance of paths, steps, and patios will not only prolong their lives and improve their appearance, but is a necessary safety precaution. Uneven surfaces can easily cause people to trip, and on steps, this could lead to nasty injuries.

Cleaning

The first step is to brush the whole area with a stiff broom, paying particular attention to corners and under the overhang of steps where litter and soil accumulates. Use a paint scraper or similar tool to loosen compacted dirt in awkward positions, and to scrape out the gaps between paving slabs where weeds often grow. If a pressure washer is available, this is ideal, as it reaches into all the nooks and crannies with a high pressure water jet which has a powerful scouring action. Pressure washers can usually be hired by the day or weekend if you don't want to buy one.

Moss and algae are common where the surface is constantly damp and shady. Remove all traces of their growth; dichlorophen will kill moss and lichens on hard surfaces. Try to correct the conditions that caused their appearance in the first place. As for areas where dirt and soil have lain for a long time, they can appear discolored when first cleaned. These marks can often be removed by a pressure washer or scrubbing. Other stains on paved and concrete areas, such as those caused by oil, can be more difficult to tackle. There are various proprietary products available, or you could try mixing a spirit (such as paint thinner) with sawdust until the sawdust is thoroughly dampened, and apply this in a thick layer over the stain. Sweep it off with a stiff broom and repeat until successful.

Incidentally, concrete will have a longer life if it is coated with a waterproof sealant. Special products are available for applying to old concrete.

◄ *Before any repairs on slabs or concrete are attempted, all loose material must be removed by using a wire brush.*

Repairs

Paving slabs may have settled unevenly to create protruding edges which can trip people up. Where necessary the uneven slabs should be removed, the base leveled and the slabs relaid.

Isolated cracks in concrete or slabs can be repaired. Use a hammer and chisel to chip along each side of the crack to neaten it, then wire brush the crack thoroughly to remove all the loose material. Coat the sides with a proprietary bonding agent before filling the crack with mortar or a patching compound.

Concrete pigments can be mixed with the mortar to help match the surface color, and make the repair less obvious.

▲ *Sometimes it is necessary to use a hammer and chisel along the sides of the crack to open it out before it can be repaired.*

Concrete areas may look unsightly because poor workmanship when they were laid has caused the surface to wear badly, so it is pockmarked with shallow holes. As long as the base is sound, the top can be resurfaced, but the new layer must be at least 2in/5cm thick to prevent it from flaking away. The worn surface must be cleaned thoroughly and coated with a bonding agent before a sand and cement mix is applied. Resurfacing is often only a temporary solution; complete replacement of the concrete may eventually be needed.

◄ *Fill in the prepared crack with mortar or a patching compound, smoothing it out carefully to keep the surface level.*

SAFETY PRECAUTIONS

• Wear eye protection when using a chisel and hammer to work on hard surfaces, or to break up slabs.
• Take care to avoid back strain when trying to prise up or lift slabs—two people make the job much easier than one.
• Wear a mask when working with dry cement to prevent breathing in the dust.
• Protect your skin when handling concrete and mortar; always wear gloves to prevent irritation.

ornamental garden: *plants in season*

The number of flowers blooming in the garden increases rapidly during this time as the winter slowly but surely moves toward spring. Catkins on bare branches elongate and become more prominent, and some of the earliest flowering cherries give a foretaste of the pleasures to come in the months ahead as the days begin to lengthen and the light returns.

▲ Prunus subhirtella *'Pendula Rubra'*
offers a stunning display during late winter.

▲ Hamamelis intermedia *'Westerstede'*, with its delicate yellow blooms, adds color to winter.

▶ Mahonia aquifolium *'Smaragd'* supplies rich shapes and textures to the garden.

TREES AND SHRUBS

Acacia dealbata (acacia)
Camellia
Chaenomeles japonica (Japanese quince)
Chimonanthus praecox (wintersweet)
Cornus alba (red-barked dogwood), *C. mas*
    (cornelian cherry)
Daphne odora, D. mezereum
Erica carnea
Garrya elliptica
Hamamelis (witch hazel)
Hedera colchica 'Dentata Variegata' and others
Jasminum nudiflorum (winter jasmine)
Lonicera fragrantissima, L. standishii
    (winter honeysuckle)
Magnolia campbellii
Mahonia x *media* 'Charity' and others
Prunus incisa 'February Pink' (Fuji cherry),
    P. mume (Japanese apricot) and others
Pyracantha (firethorn)
Salix alba (white willow), *S. babylonica* var.
    pekinensis 'Tortuosa'
Sarcococca hookeriana, S. humilis (Christmas box)
Skimmia
Sorbus
Stachyurus praecox
Viburnum

PERENNIALS

Bergenia
Helleborus niger (Christmas rose), *H. orientalis*
    (Lenten rose)
Phormium tenax (New Zealand flax)
Primula (primrose)
Pulmonaria (lungwort)
Viola odorata (English violet)

BULBS

Anemone blanda
Chionodoxa (glory of the snow)
Crocus
Cyclamen coum
Eranthis hyemalis (winter aconite)
Galanthus (snowdrop)
Iris danfordiae, I. histrioides, I. reticulata
Narcissus (daffodil)

◀ *Daphne mezereum 'Rubra'* is a delight in the garden at this time of year.

kitchen garden: *general tasks*

Dry, breezy days at this time of year will dry out the soil and allow seedbeds to be prepared shortly, but if the weather should turn windy and cold, young crops may need some protection. Jerusalem artichokes are a very easy crop to grow, and the tubers can be planted now.

Protecting seedlings

This is still an unpredictable time of year as far as the weather goes—it can produce some of the coldest conditions of the winter, often after a mild spell has already started plants into growth. The young plants of beans and peas that were sown in the fall can be given a severe set-back by poor weather now, but they can be protected from the worst of it with cloches or lengths of lightweight horticultural blanket.

Spring cabbage plants not planted out in the fall can be set out in their cropping positions when the weather is suitable. Like the pea and bean seedlings, they can be protected with cloches or blanket if conditions deteriorate after planting.

▼ *At this time of year it may be a good idea to use a fleece (or cloche) used to protect pea and bean seedlings against harsh weather.*

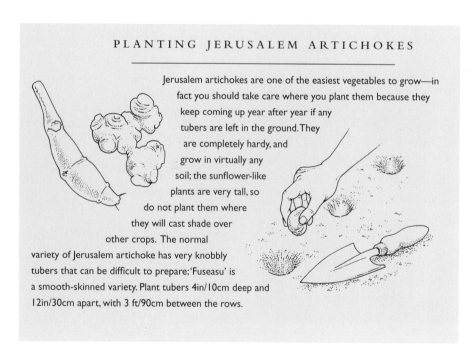

PLANTING JERUSALEM ARTICHOKES

Jerusalem artichokes are one of the easiest vegetables to grow—in fact you should take care where you plant them because they keep coming up year after year if any tubers are left in the ground. They are completely hardy, and grow in virtually any soil; the sunflower-like plants are very tall, so do not plant them where they will cast shade over other crops. The normal variety of Jerusalem artichoke has very knobbly tubers that can be difficult to prepare; 'Fuseasu' is a smooth-skinned variety. Plant tubers 4in/10cm deep and 12in/30cm apart, with 3 ft/90cm between the rows.

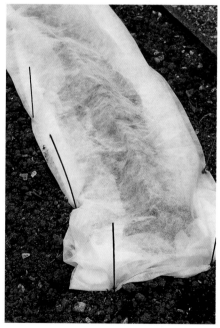

prepare for pole beans

Pole beans are one of the most worthwhile crops for gardeners. They produce a very large crop in relation to the space they occupy, and have an extended season throughout the summer, right up until the first frosts. Although it is a little too early to think about raising the plants yet, it is not too soon to start preparing the soil where they are to grow.

KALE AND RHUBARB

Stems of kale (pictured below) and rhubarb that have been forced into early growth in a frost-free greenhouse should be ready for cutting now. The shoots should have been kept completely dark by covering them with a black bucket or container—this gives the most tender results and prevents kale from becoming bitter. Kale is an unusual luxury vegetable (not to be confused with kale beet, which is quite different). It is often compared to asparagus, but the creamy white stems have a flavor all of their own.

1 Choose a warm, sheltered site for pole beans, preferably moving them to a new position each year to avoid root-rotting fungi building up in the soil. Dig a trench at least one spit deep—more if you can manage it—and 60cm/2ft or so wide. Fork over the soil in the bottom of the trench to break it up (**right**).

2 Beans need fertile, and above all moisture-retentive soil. Adequate levels of soil moisture are necessary to insure reliable setting of the flowers (flowers often drop off unfertilized in dry conditions, leading to poor crops), and rapid development of tender, juicy pods.

3 Add a layer of moisture-retentive material to the base of the trench. Ideally this should be well-rotted manure containing plenty of straw (**below**), but a mix of materials such as grass clippings, spent hops, spent mushroom compost, and even old newspapers can be used.

4 Leave the trench open to the rain until it is time for sowing or planting the beans after the last frosts in the spring. Then make sure the base of the trench is thoroughly soaked, by watering if necessary, before returning the topsoil and treading it thoroughly to firm.

crop rotation

It is not good practice to grow the same crops in the same places in the vegetable garden year after year. There are several reasons for this.

Different crops have slightly different nutrient requirements. Brassicas, for instance, are known as greedy crops (or gross feeders) because they take a high level of nutrients, particularly nitrogen, from the soil. If brassicas are grown on the same piece of ground year in, year out, the nutrients in the soil could soon be exhausted, particularly if no organic matter or fertilizers are added to replace them. Brassicas are also prone to certain specific pests and diseases, such as clubroot; they can persist in the soil, or on crop remains, ready to infect the new crop the following year.

If a different crop is grown in the brassica's plot next year, however, it is likely to take different types of nutrients from the soil. It will also be immune to brassica-specific pests and diseases, so that the cycle of infection can be broken. This practice of insuring that different types of crop are grown in succeeding years on the same piece of ground is known as crop rotation. Deciding exactly which crop should be grown where obviously needs careful planning. There are various crop rotation schemes, but a common one is to divide the types of crops that are grown into three main groups.

Dividing the crops

The first group is the brassicas—cabbages of all types, Brussels sprouts, kale, broccoli, cauliflower, and so on. They have a high nitrogen requirement, and are prone to clubroot disease. The second group is root crops—potatoes, parsnips, carrots, beets, Jerusalem artichokes, salsify, and scorzonera, and so on. They have a slightly lower nitrogen requirement, and are likely to be misshapen if fresh manure has been added to the soil recently. Finally there are peas and beans—these are unusual because they obtain nitrogen from the air rather than the soil, because of nitrogen-fixing bacteria that live

▲ *Cauliflowers fall into the brassicas group of vegetables. This group is known as "greedy crops" because they need a high level of soil nutrients.*

▲ *Peas tend to be placed in a group that includes lettuces and leeks, simply because they are neither root crops nor brassicas.*

▲ *Carrots belong to the root crop group,*
alongside potatoes, parsnips, beets,
and Jerusalem artichokes.

	Bed A	Bed B	Bed C
Year 1	*Brassicas*	*Roots*	*Peas and beans*
Year 2	*Peas and beans*	*Brassicas*	*Roots*
Year 3	*Roots*	*Peas and beans*	*Brassicas*
Year 4	*Brassicas*	*Roots*	*Peas and beans*

SIZE MATTERS

There is one major difficulty with a rotation, and that is the need for each of the three groups to occupy exactly the same amount of space. The imaginative use of miscellaneous crops (such as lettuce, squash, spinach, and so on) can help here because they can be placed in any of the three groups, as necessary, to balance things out. However, the rotation does not have to be followed slavishly—it will have to be adjusted for practical purposes.

on their roots. This means they will actually add to the amount of nitrogen in the soil.

Of course, not all crops fall neatly into one of these three groups. Crops such as rutabaga and turnips are both brassicas and root crops, so which group would they go in? And what about spinach, or squash and zucchini, or onions? Rutabaga, turnips, and kohlrabi are included in the brassica group, mainly because they can be infected by clubroot disease. Since spinach is a hungry crop with a high nitrogen requirement it also fits well into the brassicas. Most other crops such as lettuces, tomatoes, squash, leeks, onions and so on are generally included with the peas and beans, simply because they are neither brassicas nor true root crops. However, there are no hard and fast rules about these miscellaneous crops, and onions are sometimes included with the root crops, while spinach joins the peas and beans, for example.

Establishing the rotation

The vegetable plot is divided into three and each of these three main groups of crops is grown in their own section—for example, brassicas in bed A, root crops in bed B and peas and beans in bed C. Next year, peas and beans move into bed A, brassicas into bed B, and roots into bed C. The following year they all move round one place again, and the year after that they are back where they started.

This means that the bed with roots can be manured at the end of the season ready for the brassicas, and the roots follow the peas and beans that have added nitrogen to the soil to make up for the absence of manure.

Four or five bed rotations are also possible by splitting the groups up further, but they become increasingly complicated. The three-bed scheme is the most practical for the majority of gardens.

greenhouse: *general tasks*

Sowing starts in earnest now, and there should be plenty of material for cuttings from overwintered plants. Don't be in too much of a hurry to forge ahead if you cannot provide reliable heating, though; better to be a little later than take unnecessary risks, because the weather is still cold.

▲ *Take cuttings of plants such as pelargoniums and fuchsias to provide strong young plants for setting out in containers later on.*

Sowing greenhouse crops

Vegetable crops to be grown in the greenhouse through the summer should be sown now, preferably in a heated propagator to keep them at a constant temperature.

Tomatoes, cucumbers, melons, peppers, and eggplant are among those to try; a germination temperature of 65–70°F/18–21°C suits most of them. Don't forget to label each variety individually.

It is easy to sow too many seeds and have to give away dozens of seedlings later on. Most greenhouses have limited space for crops, and no more than six or so plants of each type can usually be fitted in.

Sow the seeds in pots rather than in seedtrays, and save the seeds that are left over for another year. You should be able to store them quite satisfactorily in a dry, screw-top jar for at least one season.

TAKING CUTTINGS

Plants such as dahlias, chrysanthemums, pelargoniums, and fuchsias that have recently been started into growth should be producing shoots suitable for use as softwood cuttings.

Let the shoots grow to 3–4in/7.5–10cm in long before snapping them or cutting them off with a sharp blade. Trim the base to just below a leaf joint and remove the lower leaves; dip the base of the cutting in hormone rooting powder and insert in sandy seed and cuttings mix. Cover trays, flats or pots with a clear plastic propagator cover to maintain humidity while the cuttings root.

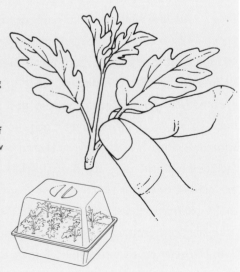

CLEANING UP THE GREENHOUSE

Good hygiene is particularly important when seeds and cuttings are being raised, otherwise plant diseases can lead to excessive losses. Clear out all dead and dying plant material that remains in the greenhouse, and treat any pests and diseases that are seen with an appropriate remedy. Tidy up pots and trays, and sweep down the staging and potting benches. At the same time, check through your stock of garden chemicals and dispose of any that are past their sell-by date, or that have illegible labels or instructions.

beans in pots

If you didn't get round to sowing beans in the vegetable plot last fall, it's still not too late to make sure of an early crop. Sowing seeds in pots in a cool greenhouse or cold frame now should give you pods to pick in early summer. This method is often more successful than fall sowing in areas that have very cold or wet winters.

1 Beans are often one of the first of the new season's crops for picking in the garden. Any variety can be sown successfully in pots now, but for the earliest harvest, choose one of the faster maturing varieties.

2 Fill individual 3½in/8cm pots with sowing mix, and push the bean seeds below the compost surface (**right**). Water with a fine rose until the compost is just moist; label the pots with the variety and date.

3 Beans are very hardy, and do not need high temperatures to germinate. A frost-free or unheated greenhouse or cold frame are good places in which to keep the pots.

4 Once the seeds have germinated, keep the seedlings moist and in a good light to insure sturdy young plants for planting out. Those grown in individual pots will suffer less root disturbance on transplanting, and should produce a slightly earlier crop than those in trays (**left**).

garden
design

introduction

A garden is not only an extension of the house—it is also a blank canvas, or a piece of modeling clay, which you can use to create something that is unique. But with the huge range of plants and materials at our disposal today it can be difficult to know where to begin.

Elements of design

In making a garden you are juggling elements, built and growing, to get a pleasing organization of space, rhythm, perspective, color, shape, and texture. While manipulating all these ingredients you want to produce a harmonious whole—every garden needs to provide a sense of proportion and balance. The smaller the plot the more important it is to create an overall unity. At the same time the way you want to use your plot, the amount of time you have to spend, and also your budget, all come into play.

Golden rules

When thinking about how to design your garden you need first to bear in mind the type of soil you have, the local climate, and the aspect of the plot. There are solutions for every type of soil and for sun and shade, but the first key to success is to go with what you've got rather than making difficulties for yourself by trying to impose shade-loving plants on a sunny garden or vice

▶ *This minimalist garden employs strong hard-landscaping and design features. Perfect for a low-maintenance garden used for entertaining.*

versa. (See pages 970–973 for more information.)

Then you need to ask how you intend to use your garden and what your general situation is. If you have a young family it will be going against the grain to have a rambling cottage garden or an immaculate lawn; if you have little time to spare there is no point in developing the kind of garden that needs constant attention... and so on. If you want to use the space for living, perhaps as an area for entertaining friends, dining, or even practicing sport, rather than gardening, there are lots of ways of doing this too.

If you inherit a ready-made garden don't be in too much of a hurry to dig it up and start from scratch. Instead, live with it for a while to see what it has to offer in each season. And when redesigning, aim to retain any good plants or features and make the most of the garden's advantages. To see what plants thrive in your area observe other people's gardens and to get design ideas visit gardens that are open to the public and note effects that you like and how they are achieved.

▶ *Many different materials can link the garden to the home—reclaimed railroad ties and gravel are a good combination for steps.*

◀ *The geometric lines of this formally planned herb garden are softened as the many different varieties begin to grow and billow out.*

General design principles

Certain general principles apply with almost any garden. The materials you use for paths, hard areas, walls or fences, and screening, and for defining beds where applicable, should be in keeping with

those of the house, and the garden should relate well to the house. It often helps to have a hard surface—from gravel or pebbles, bricks, stone slabs, or even concrete—linking the house with the garden proper. Don't overstep the limitations of the plot and try to cram in more than will happily fit, and do select your plants to suit any constraints imposed by the nature of the soil and the garden's situation.

To make visual adjustments to the plot, use curves to disguise awkward shapes, open areas to make narrow parts of the plot seem wider, and thickly planted areas to narrow down a wide part. If a plot is long and narrow divide it crosswise to make a series of well-shaped areas leading on from each other.

▲ *You can liven up a simple family scheme with wacky furniture such as these sunflower-inspired tables and stools—perfect for young children.*

Safety and convenience of use are important considerations in any garden to be used for leisure, especially by families or older or disabled people. Potential danger spots include changes of level or direction, which should all be gradual if there is any question of special safety needs, and hard surfaces, which should have good grip and not be slippery after rain. Anything that looks as though it could be used needs to be as strong as it looks. This includes posts which a child might climb or an older person lean on to rest, garden seats, which may need to be constructed so that they are easy to get up from by someone elderly, and fences, which may need to be strong enough to be hit by a football or run into by a bicycle. Water is an attraction in any garden but how to use it needs be considered with care as open water can be a danger where children are playing. A well-designed moving water feature, however small, is a delight for everyone who uses the garden for relaxation. Paths and openings should be wide enough, where possible, for two people to walk side by side, and certainly need to be wide enough for one person and a wheelbarrow. If a path leads alongside a border you need to allow extra width for the plants to spill over the edge of the border or the path will be lost in no time. A curving path can look even better if it curves around something such as a beautiful shrub, while a focal point, whether an ornamental tree or shrub, a stone birdbath, a piece of sculpture or a fountain can give the eye something to rest on and give a path something to lead up to.

Using color

Color is an essential element of the garden design, and although it will partly be a question of personal taste there are a few general rules about the effect that colors have—used singly, as a backdrop, or in combination.

Green—There are more shades of green than all other colors put together and it forms an essential buffer and backdrop to colors throughout the garden. Used on its own, it can be clipped and elegant, or lush and jungly, a calm and subtle range of forms, or exotic blend of glossy leaves.

Pink—Pink may be rich and dramatic as in the purple pinks and hot magentas, soft and gentle as in the middle range of rose-pinks, or pale and sugary. It is best set against blues and purples.

Red—Hot reds are exciting and dramatic, but too much will give you the jitters, so tone them down with lots of surrounding, cool green. Exciting contrasts can be made with true blue and scarlet red or bright yellow.

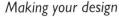
Less can be more. This garden relies on well placed natural materials—rocks, gravel, and grasses—to create a calming impression.

Blue—True sky blue is one of the rarest of nature's colors, but there are numerous other blues ranging from cold, icy pale blue through lavenders to deepest violet. Blues in shade create a somber mood, but look cheery and fresh if combined with yellow in spring. Darker shades suit strong summer light.

Yellow—Yellows, like reds, are warm and inviting, but some are very strong and even brassy, so use these in moderation, with lots of green.

White—This is the most difficult color to use well and white gardens can easily look either insipid or like a pile of dirty washing. But a white garden can also be sophisticated and elegant, especially if lots of architectural, green, large-leaved plants are used to create a lush backdrop. A good rule is to use only warm whites—those with pink or yellow in them, or cool whites—those containing a hint of blue or green. Don't mix them.

Making your design

While you are bound to want to make adjustments as the garden develops, having an overall plan to start with is important, especially where expensive materials and hard construction work will be involved, or when using budget-breaking plants that don't like being dug up and replanted. Start by making a rough plan of your plot, noting any good and bad points, such as shady and sunny, dry or damp areas, good and bad views, good shrubs or trees that you'd like to retain and the direction of the wind.

Use copies of this to map out rough ideas about planning and planting. Then, when you are ready, take the garden's measurements carefully and work out your final plan to scale on squared paper, marking out both position and eventual size of plants you intend to use and the position of all the construction features such as paved areas, steps, and garden divisions. We hope that this book will help by providing some ready-made solutions to a variety of real-life plots whose owners all have very different ideas about what they want from a garden. Seeing how these designs are made up, the plants our designer chose, practical projects for planting or building, and the alternative schemes that can be devised for the same plot should give you lots of ideas to borrow when you are planning your own garden.

If you want a garden full of flowers, give some attention and preplanning to how well the range of colors work together.

water gardens

Water adds an exciting extra dimension to even the tiniest garden. It reflects light, changing clouds, clear blue sky, or nearby plants. A limpid pool creates a feeling of space while flowing water is refreshing to listen to and fascinating to watch, especially when lit at night. Whether still or moving, water attracts a whole range of wildlife—small mammals, frogs and toads, birds, butterflies, dragonflies, and other insects, many of which are beneficial to the garden.

pond and bog garden

If you make a pond the dominant feature in the garden everything else can be designed to acknowledge it. All you will need is somewhere to sit and watch the water and a pathway from which you can observe the life of the pond at close quarters and enjoy all it has to offer.

Guidelines to design

Placing a pond requires some planning. First, a pond needs light and shelter. If the place for sitting and looking at it can be sited with the light falling from behind, it will enhance the pond experience. Once filled, the pond will be kept topped up by the natural rainfall in all but the driest weather, so water supply is not vital. Choose an area not too close to the house and without overhanging trees—fall leaves will decay in the water and make it smelly and shade will cause algae and slime to gather on the water. Full sun is also to be avoided, except for a water lily pond, as this too encourages excessive growth of algae.

The best possible site is a hollow or in a low level of the garden where you'd expect water might collect naturally. Make sure, however, that this is not a frost pocket where plants will fail to thrive, and not a place where the water table will rise higher than the lining of the pond. This will cause the liner to balloon in the middle and you will have an unwanted "hippo" in your pond.

Style and size of pond

When it comes to choosing a garden pond, natural and informal are the key words for all but the grandest or most formal gardens. Make your pond as appropriately large as you can afford. Not only does it look better, but also the bigger the surface

◀ *Moisture-loving plants for a bog or pond garden grow rapidly and are easy to maintain; they soon provide a lush, almost tropical look.*

◄ *Make sure you plant some marginal aquatics in the shallow reaches of the pond to soften the edges where it meets the bank.*

area the less likely it is to suffer from unwanted algae. Keep curves generous and unfussy and avoid a complete circle, which, like squares and rectangles, is suitable only for a formal setting. A kidney shape with a generously proportioned inner curve will look good and allow you to observe pond activity more easily. Modern flexible liners, used with a cushioning layer of underlay, are the best materials for such ponds.

Digging out will create a lot of spoil that you will have to cope with. Rather than disposing of it, you may prefer to landscape the rest of the garden, and use the spoil from the pond to create undulations. Save any fertile topsoil for the planted areas whatever you do.

▶ *This beautiful pond and water feature emulates a mountain stream. The margins are densely filled with bog and pond plants.*

Finishing details

Edge at least half of the pond with a damp garden, or bog area, where moisture-loving plants can grow and soften the outline. They will also provide shelter for wildlife. Include a shelf for marginal plants and a gently sloping shingle beach for small animals to climb in and out of the water. If possible allow for grass to run right to the edge of part of the pond, for a natural look.

If you plan to stock fish, your pond needs to be at least 90cm/3ft deep at the center, in case the surface freezes in winter and so that the fish can hide away from predators. It's a bad idea to introduce ornamental "koi" carp to a natural pond. They need a high quality filtration system and impeccably clean water with plenty of depth. And they also need protection from herons, which, although beautiful birds, will wade in and enjoy delicious takeouts at your expense.

Wood and stone are natural companions to water, and decking in treated timber can extend over the pond so that you can stand above the water. A means of crossing the water, usually best located at the neck of the pond, can be used to add to the sense of flow and link the two sides of the pond visually as well as physically.

designer's pond and bog garden

A constantly damp garden is often the result of badly drained surface water. There may be a heavy clay subsoil preventing drainage, or a hard, compacted surface where the soil has not been cultivated for many years, or the garden may be sited in a hollow which gathers the run-off rainwater from surrounding higher ground.

▲ *A predominantly damp site is ideal for bog plants, most of which are lushly dramatic and will shelter a range of amphibian wildlife.*

GARDEN DATA

location:	New Jersey
climate:	mild
soil type:	wet clay, slighty acid
direction:	east
aspect:	overlooks woodland

Design brief

This is a small garden with a high water table, which makes it difficult to site a pond. In consistently wet weather the pressure from held ground water will cause a pond liner to billow up like a hippo. However, the owners of the garden would like to encourage wildlife and are keen to make the most of their boggy ground. We need to bear in mind that the level of moisture will vary at different times of the year as the water table rises and falls.

Design solution

The answer is to go with the flow! We designed the garden informally, along curvy, natural lines, using timber ties for the decking and bridge, and log rounds to form stepping stones in the grassy path.

The planting is equally informal and concentrates on several big, dramatic feature plants, interspersed with moisture-loving perennials and grasses. The larger plants form natural

–/3.5m x 7m/43ft x 23ft –

barriers so that the whole garden cannot be seen from any one vantage point. The secrecy and intimacy that this kind of planting creates also provides hideaways for small and timid wild creatures.

log stepping stones ①

iris ②

▲ Log rounds used as stepping stones.

▲ Some irises require a wet situation.

plank bridge ③

water butt ④

◄ A simple plank over the pond.

▶ A recycled water tank houses a small lily.

practical projects

▲ Primula vialii *is a hardy perennial.*

A bog—or damp—garden is easily made using flexible lining material and makes a lovely, informal water feature. Bog areas can link a pond to the rest of the garden but they can also form a feature in their own right.

Bogs in nature aren't a feature of open, sunny places, so you need to site this kind of garden thoughtfully. If you haven't made a pond near which a damp garden will be sited, the most natural looking place will be in a hollow (existing or dug out) in a low-lying part of the garden, preferably where there is some shade.

You are aiming to create an area that is constantly moist, yet where there is enough movement of air through the

soil to prevent it from becoming stagnant and provide plant roots with oxygen. When constructed next to a pond the bog garden will absorb some overspill water, but if it is self-contained you will need to top it up in dry weather.

All you do is to make a hollow of a suitable depth and shape and line it with perforated pond liner. A bottom layer of gravel will help drainage, while clean soil and a gravel top-dressing form the planting medium.

▼ *This cross-section shows how a bog garden can be created using simple materials. This will enable damp-loving plants to flourish.*

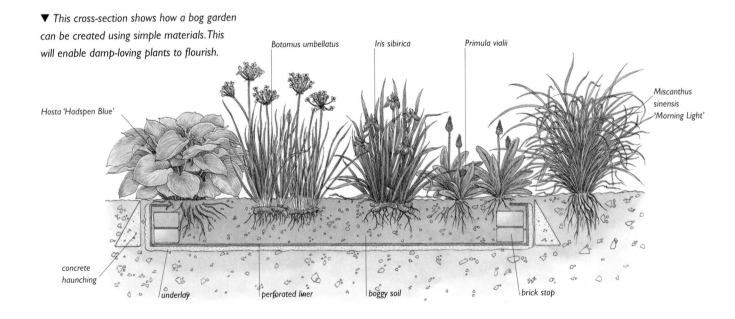

Botomus umbellatus

Iris sibirica

Primula vialii

Hosta 'Hadspen Blue'

Miscanthus sinensis 'Morning Light'

concrete haunching

underlay

perforated liner

boggy soil

brick stop

lining a bog

The aim in making an artificial bog garden is to slow down the rate at which water drains through the soil—easily achieved with a perforated impermeable liner. This will allow you to grow a range of plants that thrive in permanently moist ground. Some added drainage is essential, however, if the soil is not to become stagnant.

DESIGNER'S TIPS

• Make sure the level of the water table will not be higher than the bottom of the new pond or bog garden, especially if you use a flexible liner.

• Don't introduce fish to a pond or plants to a pond or bog garden until at least one week after filling, so that any chemicals in the tap water can disperse.

• Add lots of oxygenating plants—better to have too many and remove some occasionally than too few.

• For moving water features install a pump that is powerful enough to circulate the water effectively. Your supplier will advise you on pump capacities if you supply your pond dimensions.

• Never try to create a bog garden or a pond on high ground. It will look unnatural and it will be hard to maintain adequate moisture levels.

• Don't choose vigorous plants, for example bulrush, for a small garden—they will take over. Some grasses, such as *Phalaris arundinacea* and *Carex pendula* are also very invasive.

1 Dig a hole the shape of the proposed bog garden. Depending on the ultimate size of the plants you wish to grow, this can be up to 1m/3ft in depth. Remove sharp rocks that could pierce the liner and all traces of weeds.

2 Level the base of the hole and line it with a flexible butyl rubber pond liner. Carefully pierce holes in the liner to allow excess water to drain away.

3 Line the base with pebbles or gravel. Avoid limestone chippings if you wish to grow acid-loving plants. Fill with clean garden soil.

4 Flood the area with water prior to planting. You may find it necessary to water the bog generously during prolonged periods of hot, dry weather in summer.

pond and bog plants and planting

Natural-looking planting is best for an informal pond. There may be grasses rustling beside the water, irises wading in the shallows, a few water lilies floating in a still, sunny patch, and streams of trailing plants waving in the water's depths. Water plants have a calming quality and attract wildlife to the pond.

Creating an effect

The plants around the pond form part of the whole scene. Huge leaves of gunnera-like giant rhubarb, ornamental willows, and dogwoods, with their brightly colored winter stems, even small trees such as weeping willow all add mood and atmosphere. Like the aquatic plants within the pond and the marginals at the water's edge they will be mirrored in the water.

Gently sloping banks offer the best hospitality to waterside plants. In a small pond the best way to obtain a slope at the right angle is to make a planting ledge around part of the edge. Do this by digging a wide and shallow step with an almost vertical slope at the back (up to the edge of the pond) and a steep drop down at the front into the pond's depth. The step is then filled with a raked slope of earth, retained by rocks and stones. Of course if the pond is large enough

the sides can slope gently from the edge down to the pond bottom.

Marginal planting area

Allowing the earth of a planting ledge to continue over the liner top, instead of bringing the liner right up and over the edge of the pond, means that the pond is not water-tight and you will have a damp area in which to grow beautiful if unpleasant sounding bog plants (or marginal plants). A piece of perforated liner extending on from the main liner

▶ *The summer-flowering* Primula secundiflora.

can be used to line a shallow hollow dug out next to the pond, extending the pond into a larger bog area. This is then lined with a layer of gravel for drainage and filled with clean soil topped with gravel.

Planting in containers

You can plant directly into soil on your planting ledges, or decide to use burlap-lined planting containers filled with good clean soil and topped with 15mm/⅝in pea gravel. The burlap is then brought up and tied round the top to stop the soil leaking into the pond.

In the pond itself, water lilies are usually planted in special crates that are lowered to the bottom in stages so that their leaves are always floating. If the bottom is too deep, use crates or breeze blocks to make a platform. Submerged plants that oxygenate the water can be dropped

◀ *Pond grass:* Miscanthus sinensis *'Gracillimus'*.

straight in. Their roots will grow downward into the silty pond bed.

Choosing plants

Choose pond plants that are not too vigorous for the size of the pond, with plenty of oxygenating plants to help keep the water free of algae. Better to have too many and have to remove some occasionally than too few. The planting scheme around the pond should not be too hectic. Areas of color should be used against a background of green from foliage plants such as ferns, bamboos, and, grasses. Plants such as water irises give wonderful leaf shape as well as flowers and are naturally at home in, or beside, a pond context. Most suppliers of aquatic plants are knowledgeable and can give good advice on suitable plants.

Profile plants

Miscanthus sinensis
MISCANTHUS

Grasses waving at the water's edge and whispering in the breeze are a key part of the planting in the pond garden. *Miscanthus sinensis* varieties have arching leaves and erect stems with plumes of silky flowerheads in late summer. *M. s.* 'Gracillimus' (maiden grass) has very narrow leaves with white midribs and turns bronze

▶ Iris pseudacorus *is a good bog plant.*

in autumn; *M. s.* 'Morning Light' is similar but with a silvery effect.

ht and sp 1.2m/4ft

Iris species
WATER IRIS

Water irises have a natural affinity with an informal pond. Their fanned, sword-shaped leaves, tall stems, and inimitably graceful flowers are luscious to look at. *Iris pseudacorus* is the yellow flag iris—a true water iris that will grow with its feet in the water; *I. sibirica*, the Siberian iris, is blue or white, and requires rich, moist soil.

ht to 1.2m/4ft or more

sp 90cm/3ft

design alternatives

SKETCHES

Here are some alternative ideas for pond or bog gardens. In both examples the pond is the central feature led to by a path of either stone or decking.

pond

water·butt

grass or bark chip surface

random-laid crazy paving path

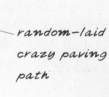

decked patio

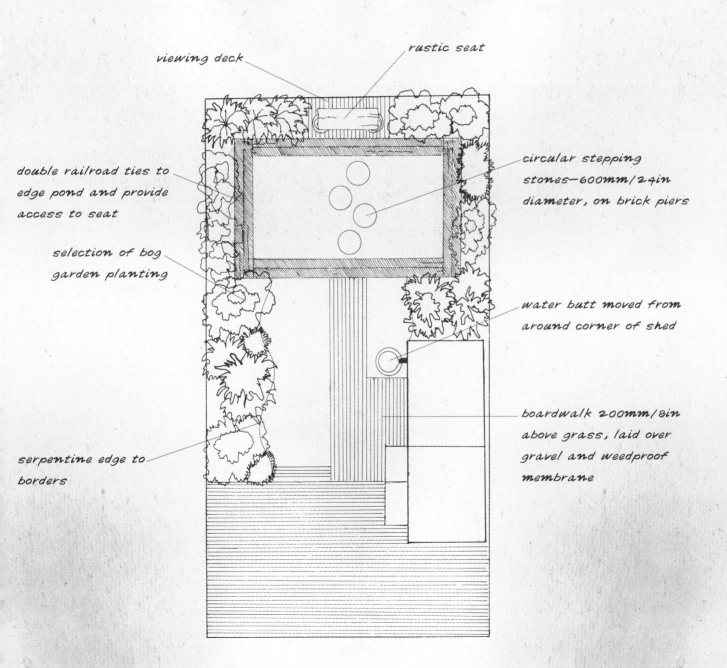

viewing deck

rustic seat

circular stepping
stones—600mm/24in
diameter, on brick piers

double railroad ties to
edge pond and provide
access to seat

selection of bog
garden planting

water butt moved from
around corner of shed

serpentine edge to
borders

boardwalk 200mm/8in
above grass, laid over
gravel and weedproof
membrane

water feature garden

For anyone who hasn't got the space or inclination for a pond there are many delightful ways of introducing water in the garden. "Built-in" features are particularly at home in small-scale surroundings, whether in a small, enclosed garden or in a terraced area or patio close to the house.

◄ *This ornamental metal grid over a formal pond is also a safety feature that prevents children from falling into or playing in the pond.*

Fixed features

The advantage of simple moving-water features is that their installation involves very little work as there is no excavation, and no displaced earth to move. Many can be bought ready-made, though it has to be said that they do not suit everyone's taste. The ingenious can make their own, using a pump kit and a bit of skill. Basically all you need is a sump, a pump, a pipe, and a spout. The sump is the reservoir of water, which is pumped through the pipe to emerge from a spout—or simply from the concealed end of the pipe. The water returns to the reservoir and is continually recycled. The reservoir can be a bowl, basin, or sink, forming part of the feature, or can be hidden away behind or beneath it; the spout can be anything from a huge old bath faucet to an ornamental lion's-head, gargoyle, decorative mask, or a length of bamboo.

Moving-water features are often fixed to a wall, and therefore relatively safe even when there are young children about, but you should always bear safety in mind if you have a young family. If this is not a consideration, and you would rather have a still and silent feature for calm, serene contemplation, it is very easy to produce a miniature water lily pond in a watertight container. If you do this, however, don't even think about adding even the smallest fish (the water could get much too hot in summer, and will freeze in winter). Ground-level features such as fountains or millstones spilling onto

▶ The stone Buddha adds to the mood of contemplation created by the gentle sound of flowing water and simple planting.

pebbles may be safe for children as there is no depth of water, but even the smallest pool and fountain, with any water depth however shallow, would be inadvisable for unattended young children.

Discreet charms

Sometimes discretion is the better part of fixed water features. They are at home in shady positions, where they can gather moss. The sound should be restful not irritating, and not annoying to the neighbors. It becomes more muffled as the depth

of water in the receptacle increases: a depth of 25cm/10in or more creates a restful splash. The rate of flow and the height from which the water falls are also important (the faster and the higher, the noisier). Water falling onto stones creates a soothing splashing sound quite different from the sound of water on water. The wider the delivery pipe, the more restful the gurgle.

Adjusting the flow valve on the pump enables you to vary the rate of water flow. Make sure that the valve is accessible so that you can experiment until you get the visual effect—and sound—exactly to your taste. Art lies in concealment—the pump must not be visible, and preferably should not be audible.

◀ This contemporary water feature comprises a series of stones. The sharp concrete edges are softened by the use of lilies and grasses.

designer's water feature garden

Patios and terraces can often seem devoid of interest. One way of enlivening the space is to add a small, self-contained water feature. This will provide the soft and refreshing sound of water during lazy summer lunches al fresco and a theatrical night-time feature when carefully lit.

▲ *At present, the home and garden do not fully integrate. A water feature on the terrace echoes the stream along the boundary.*

GARDEN DATA

location:	▪▪ *Connecticut*
climate:	▪▪ *cold/windy*
soil type:	▪▪ *light clay*
direction:	▪▪ *west facing*
aspect:	▪▪ *sloping to trees*

Design brief

This imposing 19th-century home has a substantial width of terrace along the two sides of the house facing the garden. The garden slopes down and away from the house and so there is no feeling of the house nestling in its setting. The problem was to find a way of linking the building with the garden below.

Design solution

A stream runs along the far boundary at the bottom of the site and this provided the clue as to how to link house and garden. A water feature integral to the terrace would bring a natural element to the hard landscaping and echo the wilder parts of the garden below. The owners love to entertain and much of the level terrace space is taken up with tables and seating for large parties. An existing old brick wall at one end of the main terrace offered an ideal support for a wall-mounted fountain which would trickle into a reclaimed

– 6m × 3m / 18ft × 10ft –

stone trough. This was set in stone chippings among random sized crazy paving identical in color and texture to the slabs on the existing terrace. By matching colors and textures we were able to move from formal terrace to informal water feature with the minimum of work and cost. The fountain is softened by the planting of large ferns, perennials, hostas and grasses, and aquatic plants.

masque

barrel

ferns

▲ Water spouts out of a mounted lion's head into a reclaimed stone trough.

▲ Waterproofed wooden barrels as containers offer further scope for water plants.

▲ Asplenium ferns appreciate the moist, shady, cool conditions found beside water.

practical projects

Water features look sophisticated but are relatively simple to install. They can be bought complete and ready made or you can buy a submersible pump and devise something of your own imagining, with water from a wall spout or welling from the ground.

▲ *A reproduction antique drinking fountain is an ideal feature for an enclosed courtyard garden, nestling among climbing plants.*

DESIGNER'S TIPS

• If you raise your submersible pump by standing it on bricks you are less likely to suck debris into it.

• Either bring in your pump during the winter, or make sure that you use it for at least an hour once a week to keep it in good order.

• If you have a pump with a filter clean this out regularly.

• **ALWAYS CALL A QUALIFIED ELECTRICIAN TO INSTALL A PUMP.**

Small water features

Water features must be beautiful of course, but for most of us they also need to be simple to install and maintain. The understated is more successful than the overambitious and the design should suit the surroundings in scale and style.

Naturally you need access to an electricity supply, with a length of armored cable and a waterproof connector to connect to the pump. The cable from the supply, protected with armored sleeving, must be safely buried at least 60cm/2ft below the soil surface, and you should always use a Ground-Fault Interrupter (GFI), circuit breaker, fitted to the socket, to cause the circuit to cut out if anything goes wrong. The pump should be completely submerged and connected to the water feature with flexible plastic piping.

A 24-volt pump should be satisfactory for a small feature, with a transformer to adapt the mains supply. This lives inside the house.

▲ *This traditional wall fountain is in a classical style, and would certainly add interest to any terrace or patio.*

▶ *A bubble fountain erupts from the center of an old mill wheel surrounded by cobbles that conceal the reservoir.*

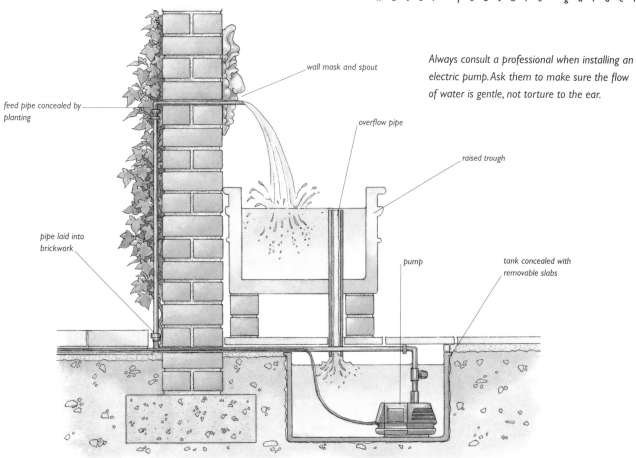

feed pipe concealed by planting

wall mask and spout

overflow pipe

raised trough

pipe laid into brickwork

pump

tank concealed with removable slabs

Always consult a professional when installing an electric pump. Ask them to make sure the flow of water is gentle, not torture to the ear.

water plants and planting

Lush and green are usually the keynotes for planting around a water feature, with ferns and mossy-looking plants enjoying the cool moisture. Exceptions apply to a water bubble, fountain, or rill in a sunny courtyard or on the patio, where pots of spiky and exotic hot-weather plants provide a tropical mood.

Cool schemes

Since few plants like to be disturbed by constantly moving water most planting is done next to the water feature, although leaves and flowers will soften the edges. Shape of foliage and habit of growth are all-important, and you'll be surprised how many shades of green there are for color contrasts. Including a few evergreens such as hellebores, will make sure there is interest throughout the winter months.

◀ Asplenium scolopendrium *'Crispum'*

▼ Helleborus orientalis

WATER PLANTS

Ferns

Ferns make fronds of green, large or small, smooth or crimped, broad or narrow, beside the water. You may be able to grow smaller ones in a crevice in a wall.

Adiantum capillus-veneris (maidenhair fern)—fine, wiry stems with delicate, shell-like leaves; good in shady waterside crevices
ht and sp 15–30cm/6–12in

Asplenium scolopendrium (spleenwort or hart's tongue fern)—tapering, slightly leathery, wavy-edged fronds of bright apple-green (evergreen)
ht and sp 60cm/2ft

A. s. 'Crispum'—densely growing, upright, very frilled, apple-green fronds (evergreen)
ht and sp 60cm/2ft

A.s. Marginatum Group—(various upright and frilly-edged hart's tongue ferns, some with tooth-edged fronds)
ht 35cm/14in
sp 45cm/18in

Dryopteris affinis (golden male fern)—tall stalks have golden brown scales and the unfurling fronds are yellowish green, turning deep green (often evergreen)
ht and sp to 80cm/32in

D. erythrosora—smaller, deciduous variety with reddish coloring
ht 60cm/2ft
sp 38cm/15in

D. filix-mas (male fern)—very tall, clump-forming variety with mid-green foliage
ht and sp to 1.2 m/4ft

Phegopteris connectilis (narrow beech fern)—low-growing, pale-green, bracken-like fern in light yellowish green, for acid soils
ht 20–25cm/8–10in
sp 30cm/12in

Polystichum setiferum (hedge fern)—soft, waving fronds of mid-green for dappled shade (evergreen)
ht 60cm–1.2m/2–4ft
sp 45–90cm/18–36in

Woodsia polystichoides (hollyfern)—small, pale green fern, native of rocky places and ideal for moist, but constantly draining, areas such as in a wall by a

spout (needs shelter/protection from frost)
ht and sp 20cm/8in

Water lilies for a tiny pond

Water lilies (*Nymphaea* cultivars) thrive in still water and a sunny spot. Several are small enough for a miniature pond in a barrel.

N. tetragona 'Helvola'—clear yellow, star-shaped flowers; tiny, maroon-mottled leaves

N. 'Pygmaea Rubra'—rose-pink flowers, deepening to blood red; copper-green leaves

N. 'Sulphurea'—bright yellow flowers raised well above the surface; brown-marked leaves

N. 'Daubeny'—starry blue, yellow-stamened, scented flowers; pointed, olive-green leaves (needs min. 21°C/70°F water temperature summer and 10°C/50°F winter)

Other plants at home beside the water

Arum lily (*Zantedeschia aethiopica*)—white spathes on erect, fleshy stems and broad, smooth, tapering leaves
ht 45–90cm/18–36in
sp to 60cm/2ft

Astilbe (*Astilbe*)—feathery plumes of flowers in red, cream, and pink; good varieties include *Astilbe* 'Bridal Veil' (syn. 'Brautschleier') (creamy white), 'Fanal' (deep crimson), 'Sprite' (shell pink)

▲ Hosta *'Tokudama'*

and *A. chinensis* var. *pumila* (dwarf, reddish pink),
ht and sp 20–90cm/8–36in

Bleeding heart (*Dicentra spectabilis*)—hanging lockets of pink or white, feathery foliage (see page 986)

Candelabra primroses (*Primula* species)—erect stems of tapering or drumhead flowerheads; good varieties include *P. japonica*, *P. pulverulenta*, *P. secundiflora*, *P. vialii*
ht to 45–90cm/18–36in
sp 45–60cm/18–24in

Hellebores (*Helleborus* x *ballardiae* 'December Dawn', and varieties of *H. niger* and *H. orientalis*)—nodding, cup-shaped flowers in plum or white, some pink-stained or with pretty markings
ht and sp to 30cm/12in

Meadowsweet (*Filipendula*)—fuzzy, deeply scented flowers in creamy white, red, and pink; good varieties include *F. rubra* (red stems, peach-pink flowers), *F.r.* 'Venusta' (rose-pink flowers—both these can be very tall), *F. ulmaria* (creamy white—smaller)
ht 60cm–1m/2ft–3ft or more

Hostas (*Hosta* cultivars)—shade-loving plants with broad, attractive leaves and heads of tubular, bell-shaped flowers (see page 861)

design alternatives

SKETCHES

Here are some alternative schemes our designer penciled for our water garden. They follow simple, classical lines using traditional materials such as brick, terracotta, and stone, to complement the central water feature.

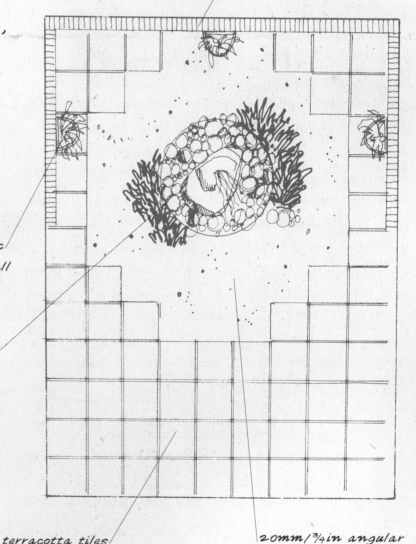

brick wall approx 1.5m/5ft high with brick or tile coping

hanging clay or ceramic planters (purchased), all matching, fixed to wall

pierced boulder water feature (purchased), over pebble base, with planting or irises or grasses to soften edges

terracotta tiles

20mm/¾in angular stone chippings over weedproof membrane

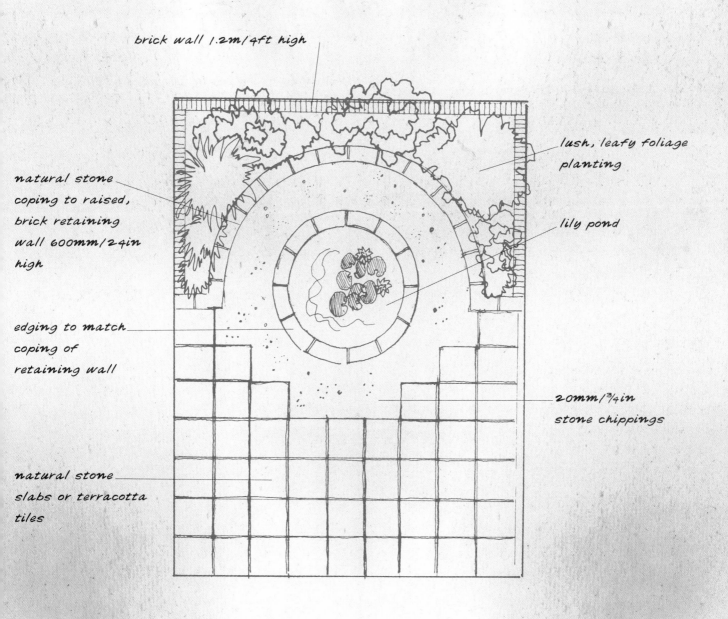

brick wall 1.2m/4ft high

lush, leafy foliage planting

natural stone coping to raised, brick retaining wall 600mm/24in high

lily pond

edging to match coping of retaining wall

20mm/¾in stone chippings

natural stone slabs or terracotta tiles

traditional gardens

The gardens in this section are inspired by some traditional garden classics. They all give the impression of being in harmony with nature or with their built surroundings, and of having an unchanging quality of stillness about them. They are places to sit, places to admire plants and the way they mix and mingle, and also places to enjoy cultivating plants as an occupation.

cottage garden

A cottage garden doesn't have to be in the country, but a small plot with a compact design is a key ingredient. In a cottage garden vegetables, flowers, and fruits are jumbled up together so that the effect is of a haze of myriad colors, textures, and scents with plants allowed to self-seed at random.

▲ *In a cottage garden a wide range of plants— from flowers and herbs to fruits and vegetables—are grown closely together.*

An idyll from the past

The real cottage garden of old was far removed from our romantic visions of today in which flowering plants loll over winding paths attracting bees and butterflies; for the plot around a cottage in the past had to be put to good use. Plants were grown for food, for medicine, and for practical purposes such as dyeing and keeping away fleas and lice or scenting household linen to disguise the smell of mildew. Flowering plants on the whole had a practical function as well as providing visual delight. The crammed appearance of the garden resulted from the need to get as much use as possible out of a small plot.

Modern cottage gardeners can adapt this idea by growing a variety of fruits, herbs, and vegetables among the flowers and by making use of every bit of space, including the vertical. The look is not for those who prefer order. In it plants jostle against their neighbors with not a patch of bare earth in sight. Informality is the key

to this style. The would-be cottage gardener needs to be warned, however, that this look is deceptive. Creating, and even more so maintaining, a successful garden in the cottage style is hard work.

The informality of appearance belies the art and work involved. But if you want to learn to love your plants and have the time, a cottage garden may be the garden for you.

Essentials

It doesn't matter if your house is not a cottage, but ideally the garden should be compact. The surroundings are important. Boundaries in particular need to be in keeping with the style of the garden. True cottagers were gardening gleaners and used what came to hand and so simplicity of materials is best. A wattle or hurdle fence for example is more in keeping than something complicated or metallic, and picket fencing, recycled pallets, or even chestnut paling can lend the right informal tone.

◀ *Filling your borders with traditional plants that suit your soil and situation is the ideal way to create the cottage garden look.*

A good hedge also makes an attractive boundary for this style of garden. For higher hedges a natural look can be achieved using native plants such as hawthorn and blackthorn. Robust shrub roses such as the rugosa roses will make thick flowery hedges with red hips in the fall and winter. Hornbeam or hazel make good deciduous hedges and hazel poles can be used as plant supports. Holly in the hedge makes the garden more interesting in winter, as do low dividing hedges of box, another evergreen. Lavender, rosemary, or roses grown as a low to medium hedge defining areas within the garden will give flowers and scents as well as structure. Climbing plants such as honeysuckle or rambling roses can be used to add flowery confusion to a fence or hedge.

Maintenance

To maintain your cottage garden you will need to be adept with a hoe, for plants and weeds will seed themselves in the spaces. Don't be too ruthless in removing seedlings however, as some self-sown annuals will add their authentic cottage garden charm. It also pays to collect ripe seed from annuals and biennials such as poppies, pot marigolds, and foxgloves so that you can sow them in your chosen places.

Planning and design

Many of the things you grow will need your attention during the summer, and it's as well to allow

▶ *This ancient stone seat makes a perfect resting place in which to appreciate the scents, sights, and sounds of a cottage garden.*

yourself a few stepping places between the apparently closely knit plants so that you can deadhead a rose, pick your currants, goose-berries, or pole beans, adjust the supports and apply the hoe, as well as occasionally, in most summers, water a thirsty phlox or spray a mildewed michaelmas daisy.

In planning your own cottage garden, bear in mind that such gardens, while charming and colorful in spring and summer, can look dull in winter without evergreens to provide interest and color. The essentially unstructured look, with winding paths and informal planting, also needs to include some structural elements if it's not to look a mess.

designer's cottage garden

The cottage garden evolved as a means of growing as many flowers, vegetables, fruits, and herbs as possible in a small space. Everything is jumbled up together, so this style is not for the tidy minded. Cottage gardens are colorful and charming, especially in the spring and summer when they come into their own.

▲ *The established hedges are worth maintaining in this otherwise under-exploited country plot.*

GARDEN DATA

location:	Ohio
climate:	mild
soil type:	chalk/clay
direction:	west facing
aspect:	open downland

The brief

This small, west-facing, country garden has great views of open farmland and often spectacular sunsets. It already has useful, dense, boundary hedges to protect from cold winds and the garden has plenty of sun, but the border beneath the hedge on the south side stays shady and cool until the afternoon. The owners love the idea of a traditional flower garden mixed with a few vegetables. They are young and fit and don't mind the physical work entailed in managing their new plot.

The design solution

We stripped the existing turf, used a nonresidual spray to kill germinating weed seedlings and then dug in loads of ecocompost to enrich the soil. To make life easier we then covered the entire surface of the garden, except for the patio, with a layer of washed pea gravel, allowing for curving paths to connect different areas. The shingle will help to keep weeds

—20m x 9m/65ft x 28ft—

down and they will be easier to remove. No cottage garden should be without at least one fruit tree and for additional structure we included hazel wigwams to support climbing annuals and vegetables. A small wildlife pond is a surprise element in a sunny corner.

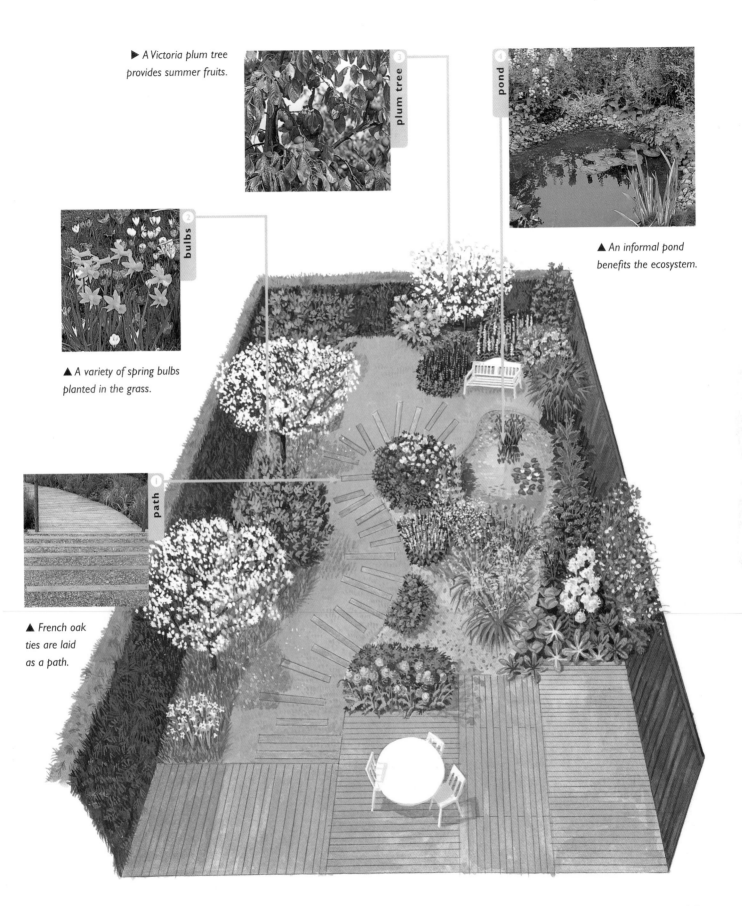

▶ A Victoria plum tree provides summer fruits.

plum tree

pond

▲ An informal pond benefits the ecosystem.

bulbs

▲ A variety of spring bulbs planted in the grass.

path

▲ French oak ties are laid as a path.

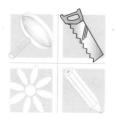

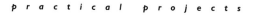

practical projects

True cottagers grew plants mainly for practical purposes, using every inch of space available. Whether or not the plants are to be used, the cottage garden look is still very much in fashion. A multitude of plants of all kinds flourish at close quarters and all you need are plant supports and somewhere to walk.

Minimal skill required

Maintaining a cottage garden will require quite a bit of skill and hard work, but the skills involved in putting it together are not beyond the reach of anyone who can manage a few simple tools. Cottage gardens need frequent titivating, so good access is required, and every available bit of space is used for plants—including the vertical.

A freestanding support for climbing plants is useful if you don't have suitable walls or fences, or have already covered them with plants. It makes a decorative, semipermanent feature to give the garden some structural interest during the winter months when the soil is mostly bare.

The most stable support is wider at its base than at the top and a wigwam shape is ideal as it is unlikely to topple over in strong winds. Straight hazel poles, willow withies, or simple, thick bamboo poles are all equally suitable.

To make a natural looking walkway over the grass, set weather-proofed railroad ties or lengths of pressure-treated timber into the lawn or gravel surface.

◄ *When plants are grown closely together, they support each other to some extent and less staking is therefore needed.*

DESIGNER'S TIPS

• Buy a hoe. You'll need it to remove unwanted seedlings that will spring up everywhere.

• Don't lay fine gravel if you own a cat. It makes a wonderful litter tray!

• Stake tall plants with blue, pink, or red painted bamboo stakes, for protection and added color.

creating a wigwam

Choose a level site for the wigwam, and clear the ground of weeds. Decide how tall you want it to be, then add one half again to determine the length of the individual poles. This is to allow for the slope of the poles and the amount to be buried in the ground for stability.

1 To mark the position of the outer poles, drive a pole into the center of the prepared area and tie a length of string to it. Mark out a circle, approximately 1m/3ft in diameter.

2 Cut a piece of weed-suppressing membrane to the size of the wigwam at the base, make a hole in the center, and slip it over the central pole. Weigh it down with a layer of gravel, or small stones.

3 Drive the poles into the ground around the perimeter of the circle, bending them inwards. Secure them about 30cm/12in from the top with string or wire. Wind rounds of wire or flexible cane at regular intervals up the wigwam.

LAYING A TIMBER PATH

First decide on the position of each timber. Stand on the timber to prevent it moving, and cut along the edge all round with a sharp half-moon edger.

Remove the turf and line the base of the trench with a thin layer of cement. Lay the timber on top.

Tamp down the timber, making sure it is flush with the lawn. When you have finished, check the level with a level.

cottage plants and planting

The cottage garden is at its best in spring and summer, brimming with flowering spring bulbs, summer annuals, and seasonal perennials. Herbs, fruit, and vegetables among the flowers are an essential part of the look. Choose ornamental forms whenever you can. Evergreens give structure, shape, and winter interest.

Cottage garden flowers

An area of rough grass planted with bulbs adds charm to the cottage garden. For a natural look, scatter the bulbs on the ground and plant them where they fall. Choose a spot beneath a deciduous tree or shrub so that the crocuses, daffodils, and other spring bulbs can get the light they need at flowering time.

Herbaceous perennials play a key role in cottage garden planting, with annuals sown or planted out in patches in between. The annuals will self-seed in places where they feel at home and the perennials will quickly form large clumps which can be divided in spring or fall to make more plants. Plants grown close together soon get hungry. Winter gives you the opportunity to mulch the soil with well-rotted farmyard manure or your own garden compost (see pages 826–827), to feed the perennials and keep the soil in good heart.

▶Rosa gallica *is an ancient medicinal plant.*

Small trees and shrubs

A small fruit tree makes an ornamental and useful focal point which will also provide perching places for songbirds. Half-standards (with a clear, short length of stem below the branches) are on the right scale. Attracting wildlife is part of the garden's appeal so use shrubs such as buddleja to draw the butterflies, or plant a pyracantha to feed and shelter the birds, especially in winter.

Profile plants

Aster novi-belgii 'Apple Blossom'
MICHAELMAS DAISY
'APPLE BLOSSOM'

Michaelmas daisies help to extend the life of the garden well into the fall and like all good cottage garden perennials they quickly make generous clumps. 'Apple Blossom' is a soft, old-fashioned pink and is particularly vigorous and hardy. No staking is needed, but the plant may

need to be sprayed to control
powdery mildew.

ht 75cm/30in

sp 45cm/18in

Soil and situation

Very undemanding as to soil. Best in
a light and sunny position but will
flower even in semishade.

Foeniculum vulgare 'Rubra'
RED FENNEL

Tall, feathery-leaved fennel is a
wonderful adornment and a
traditional cottage garden herb.
Red-, bronzed-, or purple-leaved
forms lend a touch of distinction. All
have flattened umbels of yellowish
flowers which add to the plant's
delicate architecture and attract
beneficial hoverflies to the garden.
'Rubra' is a red-leaved form.

ht to 1m/3ft

sp 45cm/18in

Soil and situation

Shaded, well-drained garden soil.

Rosa gallica
FRENCH OR PROVINS ROSE

This is the apothecary's rose of
ancient origin, whose purplish
crimson flowers yield the best rose
oil. It needs little pruning and is small
and compact enough for small-scale
gardens. Use it to add height in
mixed planting.

ht 90cm–1.2m/3–4ft

sp 90cm/3ft

Soil and situation

Fertile, well-drained soil in sun.

▲ *Currant bushes provide vitamin-rich fruits.*

▲ *Fennel has aromatic, feathery leaves.*

SUITABLE PLANTS

Perennials

Centranthus ruber (valerian)
Dianthus (pinks), such as 'Dad's Favourite',
'Gran's Favourite', 'London Delight', 'Mrs
Sinkins', 'Prudence'
Geranium (cranesbill), such as 'Johnson's Blue'
and *G. renardii*
Heuchera (alum root), such as *Heuchera
cylindrica* 'Greenfinch', 'Palace Purple'
Lupinus polyphyllus Russell hybrids (Russell
lupin)
Nepeta (catmint), such as 'Souvenir d'André
Chaudron' (syn. 'Blue Beauty')
Paeonia officinalis (cottage garden peony)
Phlox (phlox), such as *Phlox paniculata*
'Amethyst' (pale lilac), 'White Admiral' (white)
and 'Windsor' (deep carmine pink)
Primula florindae (giant cowslip)
Pulmonaria (lungwort), such as *Pulmonaria
officinalis* 'Mawson's Blue' or *P. o.* 'Sissinghurst
White'
Scabiosa (scabious), such as *Scabiosa caucasica*
'Clive Greaves'
Verbena bonariensis

Annuals and biennials

Alcea rosea (syn. *Althaea rosea*) (hollyhock),
such as 'Chater's Double' or 'Majorette'
Aquilegia (aquilegia, columbine, granny's
bonnets), such as *A. flabellata* (soft blue), *A.
longissima* (pale yellow flowers, very long
spurs), *A. vulgaris* 'Nora Barlow' (extra frilly)
and Mrs Scott Elliott Hybrids (mixed colors)
Calendula (calendula, pot marigold) such as
Calendula officinalis 'Lemon Queen' or *C. o.*
'Orange King'
Centaurea cyanus (cornflower)
Clarkia elegans (clarkia)
Cosmos bipinnatus Sensation Series (cosmea)
Dianthus barbatus (sweet william)
Digitalis purpurea (foxglove)
Erysimum cheiri (wallflower)
Helianthus annuus (sunflower), such as 'Giant
Yellow' and 'Music Box'
Lathyrus odoratus (sweet pea)
Meconopsis cambrica (Welsh poppy)
Nigella damascena (nigella, love-in-a-mist)
Papaver rhoeas Shirley Series (shirley poppy)
Papaver somniferum (opium poppy)

design alternatives

SKETCHES
Two layouts for more formally structured cottage gardens. Design one leads you through the garden, separating different areas with screening while design two leads you through honeysuckle archways to a central, beautiful pear tree.

brick (on edge)

bricked retaining wall raised border

French oak ties retaining raised bed

woven willow or hazel hurdle screen

20mm/³⁄₄in angular stone chippings over weedproof membrane

woven willow or hazel hurdle screen

brick (on edge)

French oak ties retaining raised bed

deck made of French oak ties

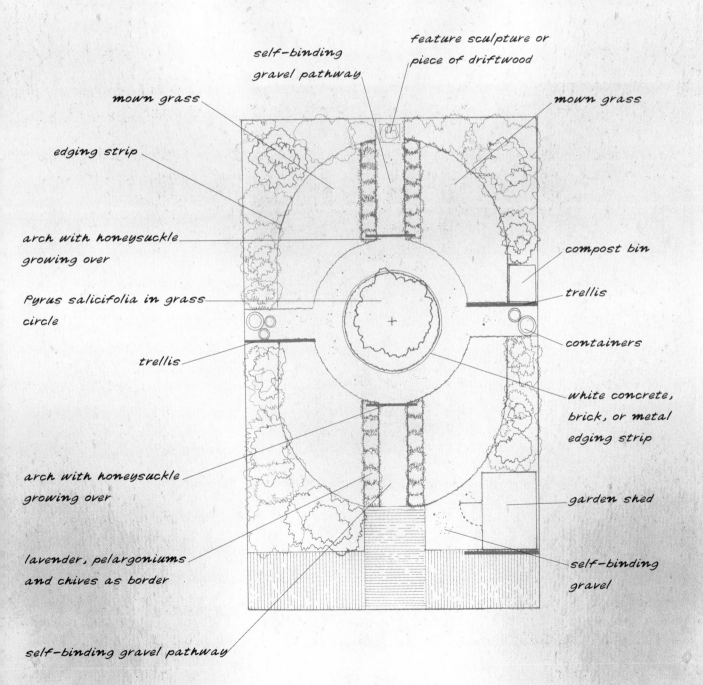

feature sculpture or
piece of driftwood

self-binding
gravel pathway

mown grass

mown grass

edging strip

arch with honeysuckle
growing over

compost bin

trellis

Pyrus salicifolia in grass
circle

containers

trellis

white concrete,
brick, or metal
edging strip

arch with honeysuckle
growing over

garden shed

lavender, pelargoniums
and chives as border

self-binding
gravel

self-binding gravel pathway

rose garden

Roses have been cultivated since ancient times, and gardens to honor these lovely flowers have been devised wherever they will grow. Rose gardens can be heaven on earth—a haven of scent, beauty, and repose. But they do demand good planning and careful maintenance, because roses are not always easy to grow or manage.

◀ *In this rose garden a pathway featuring a series of timber arches provides the opportunities for climbing varieties.*

Design of a rose garden

The classic rose garden or rosarium was usually a garden within a garden. Geometrically designed, it was laid out within a square or oblong, and often quartered. Its regularly shaped beds were grouped symmetrically and separated by straight grass or gravel paths; at its center a perfect circle or oval was set off by a bird bath, sundial, or piece of statuary. Wide arches covered with rambling roses might provide an entrance to the garden and frame its view, while within it other climbing roses would grow up central pillars or be trained along swags of heavy rope suspended between posts. The garden was usually defined by a formal hedge of box, yew, lavender, or rosemary. Well-placed seating allowed enjoyment of the fragrance and beauty of the garden, as well as the structure of the design.

▶ In this classic rose garden, the beds have been edged with aromatic lavender—a traditional choice that complements the roses.

This might seem excessively formal for a smaller garden wholly made over to roses, but there is still much to borrow from the classic rosarium. Treated informally, many of the ingredients can be copied to make a garden with a "time stands still" feel to it. For instance, a sheltering evergreen hedge provides a perfect backdrop; box, rugosa roses, or shrubby herbs make low to medium hedges giving structure and a textural continuity within the garden; instead of sturdy-looking pillars, hazel wigwams can be placed strategically to give inexpensive and natural-looking support to climbing roses and to add high points within the planting. Curving borders and informal planting in deep beds can help to give a relaxed feel to an otherwise formal gardening

approach. Grass, brick, stone, timber, gravel—in fact all the traditional and natural materials—make good surfaces between borders.

Planning the garden

Roses like light, air, shelter, and rich, deep soil, so for a start you need to be sure you have the right sort of plot. Plan carefully, bearing in mind the eventual size of the plants and whether or not they can be kept smaller by pruning, as well as the way each plant grows and its color and scent. It's difficult to get a rose to grow where another one has been established, so after a few years it won't be possible to move the plants around.

Today there are many roses that flower either repeatedly or continuously right up till the fall, so it's possible to choose roses that together will produce flowers over

◀ Roses provide a feast of sumptuous flowers —often deliciously scented—to be enjoyed throughout the warm summer months.

the longest possible season. Roses that have additional attractions, such as red hips or a pleasing shape, add an extra dimension, and a happy choice of companion plants provides contrast.

Companion planting

The spires of plants such as foxgloves or delphiniums, campanula, and tall graceful trumpet lilies look lovely growing among roses, while shade lovers such as violas, geraniums, or heucheras can be used as underplanting. Clematis mingles blissfully with a climbing rose; burgeoning peonies or oriental poppies make a welcome contrast. In open areas lavender, santolina, and sage, or nepeta (catmint) will add an aromatic scent to the roses' sweetness. The idea is not to be too free with companions, but to use fairly bold groups here and there, while underplanting at the roses' feet can thread its way through the whole garden to unite the scheme.

designer's rose garden

Roses evoke the quintessential character of the classic Edwardian, English garden. Their glorious colors and scents and exquisitely shaped, velvety blooms provide universal inspiration for poetry, painting, and music and they are coveted by gardeners all over the world.

▲ *This sheltered garden offers the ideal site for a range of roses. It receives enough sun and has good soil.*

GARDEN DATA

location:	New Jersey
climate:	mild/temperate
soil type:	chalky/clay
direction:	south facing
aspect:	open

The brief

This slightly sloping plot is sunny and sheltered from prevailing winds. The owners have long wanted a rose garden in the romantic style and accept that their garden will be at its most attractive in summer, rather than year-round. There is plenty of support for climbers and ramblers but the garden needs a central focal point and a clearly defined ground pattern, to draw attention away from the square outline shape.

The design solution

The garden is within a modern development and we decided on a contemporary approach rather than traditional, quartered, or otherwise geometrically shaped beds. We made use of the existing boundary fences and wigwams for climbers and ramblers and grouped shrub and ground-cover roses around these schematically by color. We also introduced plants that associate well with roses and some that will provide

—22m x 12m/72ft x 40ft—

structure during the dormant months of winter. We used log roll to edge and retain rose beds. Grass and brick look well with roses and we have used these traditional materials for surfaces and paths, making sure that the beds and borders are accessible for rose-sniffing, cutting, and pruning!

log roll

Log roll is used as edging ▲
for the planting beds.

gazebo

▲ Metal gazebo and statue
provide the central feature.

rose

▶ 'Miss Alice' is a
dramatic rambler.

practical projects

A timber arch for climbing roses is a traditional rose garden feature, and simple arches are useful to give height and a sense of structure in many garden situations. As well as enabling you to grow climbing plants they can also frame a focal point, or allow you to separate your garden into a series of different spaces.

Framing the scene

In every size of plot attention to scale and form brings balance to the scheme. Luckily, what is comfortable for the human figure also generally delights the human eye.

An arch has to be tall and wide enough for practical purposes and ours uses posts that are 3m/10ft long so that they produce a 2m/7ft high opening when driven 60cm/2ft into the ground. This allows the roses to tumble down prettily while still leaving room for the tallest visitor to walk comfortably underneath. The width of the opening is 1.2m/4ft, which is nicely in balance with the height and allows plenty of room for people to walk through without getting entangled with the thorny stems. It also means that there is no problem for two friendly people to walk side by side, and space for pushing a wheelbarrow or lawn mower through the arch.

In our garden a log roll is used to make a border edge. These logs can be set at different heights, allowing you to create a raised border, and they are ideal for a curved bed.

LAYING LOG ROLL

Log roll is one of the most versatile materials for edging beds, borders and pathways, as it is flexible and can be curved in any shape you may

choose. Most has already been treated. Decide how much of the edging you wish to protrude above ground level and dig a trench. Place the

roll in position and, with a mallet, tap it into place, checking the level with a level. Back fill any gaps with garden soil and firm down.

building a rose arch

A timber arch makes a charming support for climbing or rambling roses and is easily made. Use chestnut, birch or thick bamboo poles. When measuring up, you need to allow at least 60cm/2ft of timber below ground for maximum stability. A height of 2.2m/7ft and a width of 1.2 m/4ft will allow most adults to pass through without rose thorns catching on their clothing. For our garden we used four uprights each with three bracers and two 1.8m/6ft poles along the top, again with three bracers. The two uprights were constructed first, followed by the top section.

1 For ease of work, lay the timbers on the ground and mark on the verticals the position of the horizontal cross pieces. Chisel out cross-halving joints at the appropriate points, so that the beams will fit together.

2 Fit the posts together and screw or nail them in place. Depending on the roses' habit of growth, you may need more cross pieces than shown here.

3 Assemble the horizontal top section and fix it in place with long screws.

4 Dig trenches in the ground to the appropriate depth (60cm/2ft is recommended) and insert the finished arch. Use a plumb line to make sure it is vertical. Backfill with soil.

DESIGNER'S TIPS

• Don't have too many fragrant roses in a garden—the mixed scents can be almost overpowering on a still day.

• Add companion plants to soften the woody base of the rose plants and to add variety of texture and form.

• Use bent hazel or willow wands to anchor and contain rose beds—they look gentler than stakes.

rose plants and planting

There is a huge choice of roses, with a few for even the most difficult situations. A rose garden is a long-term creation so it pays to choose carefully. Check before buying that the rose's size and way of growing really are what you want. Visit rose gardens during the summer and consult specialist growers' catalogs.

Making preparations

Roses respond to good care even though they often thrive in polluted city air (its acidity deters mildew and black spot). They like a rich, heavy, but well-drained soil. And as they are going to stay put the ground has to be well prepared for them. At least a month before planting dig the whole garden really well and work in as much manure as you can lay your hands on as deep as possible. This will help to lighten heavy soils and give bulk to sandy soils as well as feeding the roses. It's best to plant in the fall from fresh stock, so prepare beforehand.

Planting bare-root roses

Before planting soak the roots in a bucket while you dig a deep hole wide enough to accommodate the spread-out roots. Mix crumbly soil with bonemeal, and garden compost if you have it, and add to the bottom of the hole. Sit the rose in, with the bulge called the union at the base of the stem just below the surface, fan out the roots and support the rose as you trickle in more soil, tucking it in round the roots as you go. Tread in and water well.

Care and maintenance

Roses need mulching, pruning, spraying, and deadheading. Get hold of farmyard manure if you possibly can, and give each plant a deep mulching in the fall and again in spring. Repeat-flowering roses need an extra feed in mid-summer. (You can use a proprietary rose feed for this.) Pruning is generally done in winter or early spring, and it's best to check on the requirements for each plant. Prevent mildew and black spot by spraying in early spring, and again

◀ R. *'Suffolk' makes excellent ground cover.*

◀ R. 'Wedding Day' is a dramatic rambler.

for a long period and produce bright orange-red hips.

ht 50cm/18in

sp 1.2m/4ft

Rosa 'Wedding Day'

'Wedding Day' is a light and airy rambling rose that will soon ramble over a shed or large arch or cover a pergola. It flowers very prolifically, the apricot buds opening to creamy yellow and quickly turning white. The flowers are single with a boss of bright yellow stamens.

ht and sp to 9m/30ft

Rosa 'Gertrude Jekyll'

This is a strong-growing and disease-resistant English rose (a recently developed breed of shrub roses with all the charm of old roses). Its fragrant, rosette-shaped flowers are a rich pink and it has a "true rose" scent. The shrub can be pruned annually to half its size, which produces the biggest flowers.

ht 1.2m/4ft

sp 1m/3ft 6in

throughout the flowering season depending on how prone the plant is. Look out for aphids (greenfly and blackfly). Spraying with an appropriate insecticide may be necessary but diluted washing-up liquid often does the trick just as well. During the flowering season snip off dead flowers to encourage repeat flowering but remember to leave a final flush of flowers to produce hips in the fall.

Profile plants

Rosa 'Suffolk'

This is a ground-cover rose—a low-growing, dense, and bushy shrub with large sprays of bright scarlet flowers on arching stems, which make it suitable for planters as well. The gold-stemmed flowers are produced

▶ Rosa *'Gertrude Jekyll'* is rich pink.

design alternatives

SKETCHES

Here are two more designs
for rose gardens. Each of
them includes a bench for
sitting, relaxing, and
enjoying the beautiful
results of your labor. Neat
mown grass and fine
gravel complement the
delicate flowers.

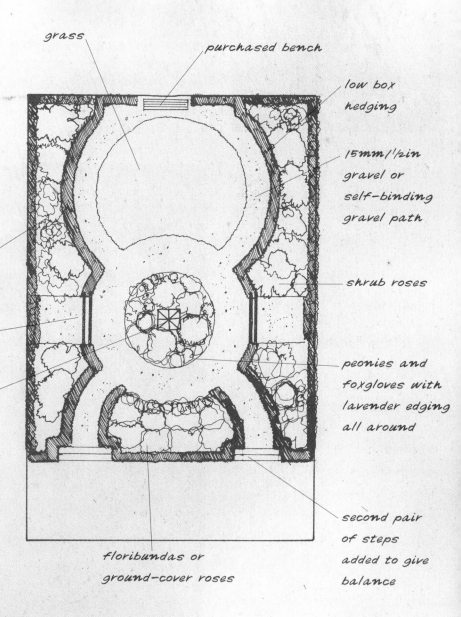

grass

purchased bench

low box
hedging

15mm/½in
gravel or
self-binding
gravel path

shrub roses

shrub roses

timber or metal double
arch to support climbers

central wigwam or
gazebo for climbing roses

peonies and
foxgloves with
lavender edging
all around

second pair
of steps
added to give
balance

floribundas or
ground-cover roses

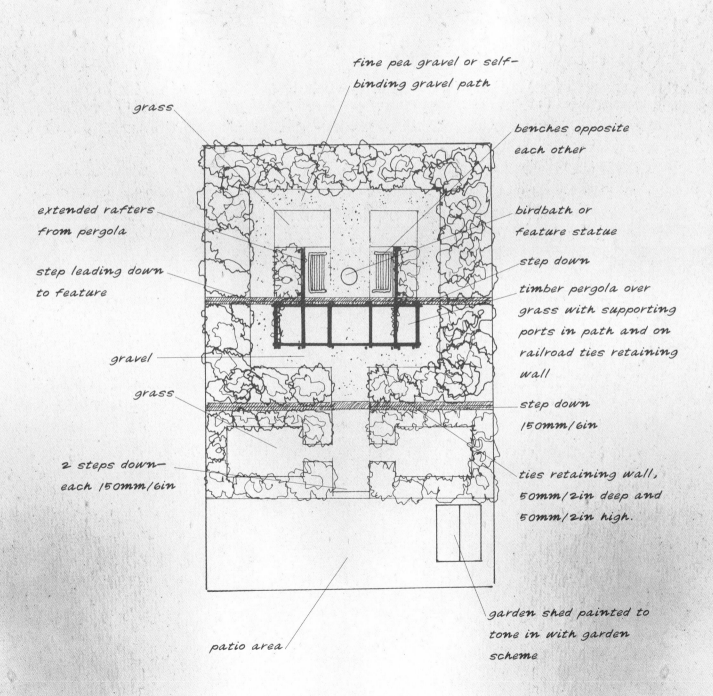

fine pea gravel or self-
binding gravel path

grass

benches opposite
each other

extended rafters
from pergola

birdbath or
feature statue

step down

step leading down
to feature

timber pergola over
grass with supporting
ports in path and on
railroad ties retaining
wall

gravel

grass

step down
150mm/6in

2 steps down—
each 150mm/6in

ties retaining wall,
50mm/2in deep and
50mm/2in high.

garden shed painted to
tone in with garden
scheme

patio area

border garden

The border, with its blend of color and mix of heights and shapes is a true garden classic, even though in fact it is really a 20th-century creation. Just about any garden in any situation can become a border garden—generous paths and deep beds are key ingredients for successful design.

The mixed border

The traditional lush border on a grand scale was at its best in high summer but today's more relaxed planting and the continual introduction of new plants means that the whole garden can be used for borders which have something to offer all year round. While borders in the past consisted of perennials and seasonal bedding plants, today they incorporate climbers, small trees, deciduous and evergreen shrubs, spring- and fall-flowering bulbs, and annuals too.

Perennials still form the mainstay of a border, but the general mix insures there is something of interest from shape and color at almost any time of year. The spring bulbs and early summer annuals bring life and color before the high-summer perennials are at their best. Height is supplied by climbers, and shape, form, and long-term structure are derived from evergreens, trees, and larger shrubs, to make a harmonious whole allowing the color to be seen within a framework.

Most gardens have a sunny and shady aspect and you can take advantage of this to create two borders with very different characters. Hot borders have caught the contemporary imagination.

◄ *A modern mixed border uses shrubs, perennials, and grasses to create continued color, shape, and texture throughout the year.*

► This border relies for much of its effect on the interplay of contrasting leaf shapes and shades of green foliage as a foil to the flowers.

Flowers and foliage with a high intensity of color are the first ingredient, but second is the way they are mixed, in what would once have been considered "clashes," such as deep carmine, orange, and purple with blue. Most of the plants for hot borders are not just stunningly bright colors by accident, they also signal their preference for sun this way. They tend also to offer strong, spiky forms. On the shady side color can be gentle, with white and blue, cream, lilac, or pale pink, and shapes may be softer too. Dark green from evergreens and light green border plants, such as alchemilla, will tie the scheme together.

Essentials

Although the complete effect is important, part of the pleasure of a border garden is the way it leads the eye and allows the foot to follow, so that not all of it is seen at once, and there is always more to discover from a different viewpoint. Curving beds help to create this effect in even the smallest garden. If you can contrive to make the gap between the borders wide at the beginning and narrow at the end this heightens perspective.

Paths and walkways are an essential part of the scheme and you also need somewhere finally to sit and admire the whole thing after inspecting the beds in close-up, if possible at the far end, away from the house. When using curves, try to make them

◄ Pots allow you to plug gaps in borders so you need never see any bare earth. Try a variety of materials such as terracotta and metal.

generously sweeping, not tight and contorted. When two borders face each other in complementary curves with an open area between them they can be enjoyed from many different angles. This helps to give the garden a feeling of greater size too, as you can't take everything in at once and there is more to be revealed round the bend.

Between the beds areas of lawn are traditional, and they are the perfect foil. In a dry garden where grass would need constant attention, gravel or stone can pay a pleasing compliment to the softening effect of flowering plants. The background completes the whole. Of course the ideal traditional border is backed by a yew hedge but this takes space and absorbs nutrients the border plants would be glad to get their roots on. In a small garden, trellis with climbing plants may be better.

designer's border garden

A stunning herbaceous border has long been seen as a pinnacle of gardening achievement. But this traditional form of border was originally designed to be at its best for only a few short weeks when wealthy families visited their country houses for the summer. Today we want interest from our gardens year round.

▲ *This sloping garden offers huge potential for growing both sun- and shade-loving plants, so we schemed the borders accordingly.*

GARDEN DATA

location:	Pennsylvania
climate:	mild/temperate
soil type:	chalky
direction:	east facing
aspect:	open

The brief

This long, east-facing garden slopes steeply downward from the house. A shed and an elderly summerhouse are to be replaced and an old apple tree, awkwardly positioned in the center of the lawn, moved. One long boundary is shady while the other is warm and sunny, so each border will have a very different planting plan, although each will cross-refer to the other by color or form of plant. The view also needs to be restricted at intervals, so that you are keen to discover what lies beyond.

The design solution

The existing layout was reshaped to form two areas of unequal size, to avoid splitting the garden into two exact halves. Within these two areas we repositioned the potting shed and made a feature of the summerhouse. The planting is vibrant and hot on one side and cool and lush on the other, moving from traditional English herbaceous plants near the main house to exotic jungly leaves near the summerhouse. The lawn is unbroken by paths as its steep slope allows good drainage to gullies.

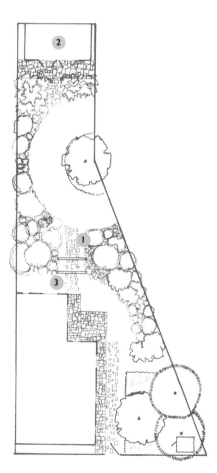

—28m x 15m/90ft x 50ft—

path

▲ *A path set in mown grass leads through the garden.*

summerhouse

arch

▲ *The old summerhouse was replaced.*

▲ *A metal arch was installed for climbers.*

practical projects

Planning the shape and content of the borders is one of the chief projects for this garden, bearing in mind the plants' height, size, shape, and color. Once you have got your designs worked out on paper, trace them in on the ground to see how they will fit and then have fun getting the plants together.

Planting schemes

The aim is to arrange the plants you choose for the border so that there will always be something at its best to take over as other plants fade, to keep it going for the longest possible period. Generous curves can be made on the ground using a length of rope and a peg as a radius. A general principle is to have taller plants at the back and shorter at the front, but not in a regimented way.

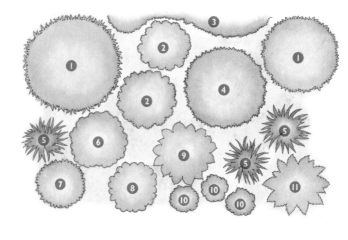

1 Aucuba japonica 'Salicifolia'
2 Thalictrum rochebruneanum
3 Hedera helix 'Glacier'
4 Viburnum tinus
5 Phormium tenax
6 Saxifraga hirsuta
7 Epimedium
8 Trillium grandiflorum
9 Hosta crispula
10 Viola odorata
11 Athyrium filix-femina

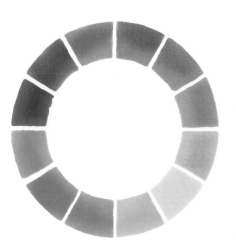

▲ *Color is a key aspect of design. Opposite colors tend to blend well, while neighboring colors work less well together.*

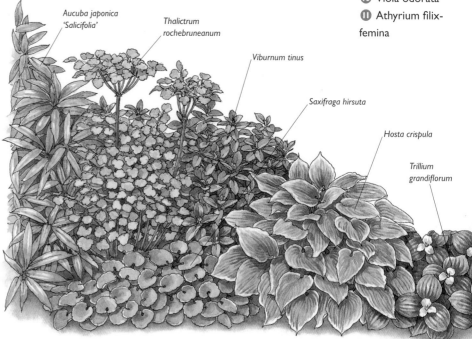

Aucuba japonica 'Salicifolia'

Thalictrum rochebruneanum

Viburnum tinus

Saxifraga hirsuta

Hosta crispula

Trillium grandiflorum

staking plants

Many tall border perennials benefit from staking, particularly those with heavy heads of flowers that can easily flop over, such as peonies or delphiniums. The traditional method is with pea sticks or rods of hazel, and these have the advantage of being unobtrusive once the plants have grown to cover them.

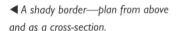
◀ *A shady border—plan from above and as a cross-section.*

1 In early to mid-spring, cut lengths of branching, twiggy hazel (pea sticks) up to 1.2m/4ft long using sharp pruners.

2 Drive the sticks into the soil around the plants, arching them inward, and burying them up to one third of their length.

3 Unless the sticks are very twiggy, it may be necessary to tie the plant stems loosely to them as they grow, with wire, horticultural twine or raffia. Once the plant has reached flowering size, tie in any loose stems.

AN ALTERNATIVE METHOD OF STAKING

Proprietary link stakes are available in garden centers and by mail order and are usually made of metal coated with green plastic. These stakes have the advantage over pea sticks in that they can be used year on year and are more readily available. The fresh growth will soon hide them from view.

At the start of the growing season, insert the uprights in the ground around the plant, pushing them deep into the soil so that the horizontal members support the emerging growth. As the plant grows, gradually raise the stakes until there is enough support against wind damage.

Ring stakes have a circular horizontal disc with a coarse mesh through which the plant stems grow. This type is suitable for plants with tall, thin stems.

border plants and planting

With border planting it's the overall effect that matters, even though of course seeing individual plants at close quarters is part of the pleasure of growing them. Small is beautiful—a limited number of plants well used is much more effective than too many. Foliage makes a foil for flowers and can act as a link between groups.

▲ Hosta *'Whirlwind'* provides strong shapes for a shady border.

Planning and planting

As a general rule repeat planting creates rhythm and harmony and planting in groups (massed planting) is much more effective than planting singly. At the same time, repeating at regular intervals is very dreary— varied repetition is what's called for. Bear in mind when planning the planting what the individual plant's eventual spread will be and don't be tempted to crowd too much in. You will need a few gaps for your feet when tending the plants, and bare patches can be filled with annuals or with plants in pots.

If you are starting from scratch you will need to prepare the border well before you plant, working in plenty of manure or other organic matter in the fall. Although you can improve and control the growing conditions your garden offers to some extent, it's better to concentrate on plants that prefer the conditions you can offer in terms of soil, light, shelter, and exposure than to aim at something difficult to achieve. (See pages 970–973). Most gardens offer at least two aspects, so that there is a range of conditions to exploit, as long as plants with similar needs are grown together.

▶ Viburnum *'Opulus roseum',* suits a sunny border.

Brimming borders

Make the border as deep as you can—1.5–2.5m/5–8ft, or more if you have the space—so that you can grow plants in bold clumps, with plenty of room at the front for smaller plants and space for shrubs, trees and climbing plants behind. As well as grading heights from front to back in this way, plan also for varying heights along the border, with taller groups at intervals. Choosing plants that are hardy will avoid disappointments, and if you select plants that need as little support as possible, or

◄ Calendula *'Pacific Beauty'*.

spring to prevent non-flowering, tangled growth.
ht to 5m/17ft
sp 1.5m/5ft
Soil and situation
Fertile soil, with its head in the sun and its feet in the shade.

plant them so that they can support each other, you will have less work to do. Don't be in too much of a hurry to tidy up when the fall comes. Some plants look wonderful covered with winter frost or topped with a dollop of snow, and many seed heads are attractive, as well as providing food for birds.

Profile plants

Magnolia stellata
STAR MAGNOLIA

A starry-flowered magnolia of modest size and beautifully spreading habit, this is a gift for the border, although it will also stand alone in the lawn. It bears a multitude of fragrant, white, long-petaled flowers before the leaves in early to mid-spring. Spring-flowering bulbs such as scilla and crocus or cyclamen corms can flourish at its feet. It needs shelter from cold wind but is more robust than it looks.
ht to to 3m/10ft
sp to 4m/13ft
Soil and situation
Fertile soil; light but sheltered position.

Heuchera cylindrica 'Greenfinch'
ALUM ROOT

The scalloped, mottled leaves of this heuchera form shiny mounds, above which stand tall, wiry stems carrying spikes of tiny lime-green flowers in stiff, airy panicles. An adaptable plant that's good for hot or cool borders, it flowers in early summer. Similar greenish-flowered heucheras include *H. c.* 'Chartreuse' and *H.* 'Greenfinch'
ht 90cm/3ft
sp 60cm/2ft
Soil and situation
Fertile soil that is well drained but not too dry, in sun or partial shade.

Clematis 'Etoile Violette'
CLEMATIS

This is a viticella clematis with masses of small, nodding violet-colored flowers from early summer right through to fall. Incredibly pretty scrambling through a climbing rose or over a yellow-leaved plant such as *Euphorbia polychroma* or a golden-leaved philadelphus. Another viticella hybrid is 'Abundance' with rose-pink flowers. Cut back each

BORDER MAINTENANCE

Routine work includes:
• mulching round plants with compost or stripped bark in fall/spring to conserve moisture and suppress weeds
• staking in early spring
• watering in dry periods
• hoeing to keep down weeds during summer
• feeding during the flowering season
• controlling pests such as slugs and snails (hostas, dahlias, and delphiniums are particularly at risk)
• removing faded flowers to extend flowering (except where seed heads are wanted, as on Japanese anemone, sedum, and the opium poppies, *Papaver somniferum*)
• dividing over-large plants in the fall

PLANTS FOR THE BORDER

A selection of summer border perennials
• carnations or pinks (*Dianthus* species), delphiniums, echinops (globe thistle), eryngiums (sea holly), geum, hollyhocks, irises, lupins, peonies, phlox
• Border plants for fall
summer hyacinth (*Galtonia*), chrysanthemums, *Clematis vitalba,* dahlias, michaelmas daisies (*Aster* species), montbretia, sedum, see also Plants for cottage gardens, pages 786–787

design alternatives

SKETCHES

These alternatives, hot and shady borders, have been designed according to color. You could create different color planting, e.g. "hot," "cool blue," and "white" as shown in the first variation.

terracotta tiles or crazy paving

garden divided into border areas bounding lawn, by two clipped-box hedges

grass

"cool blue" and spot of yellow e.g: Delphinium, 'Pacific hybrids', lavender and Verbascum 'Gainsborough'

"hot" garden: cannas phormiums, Dahlia ' Bishop of Llandaff', Hemerocallis 'Chicago Apache', Crocosmia 'Lucifer'

terracotta tiles or crazy paving

yellows, e.g. Achillea 'Moonshine', Solidago 'Goldenmosa', Rudbec 'Goldstrum'

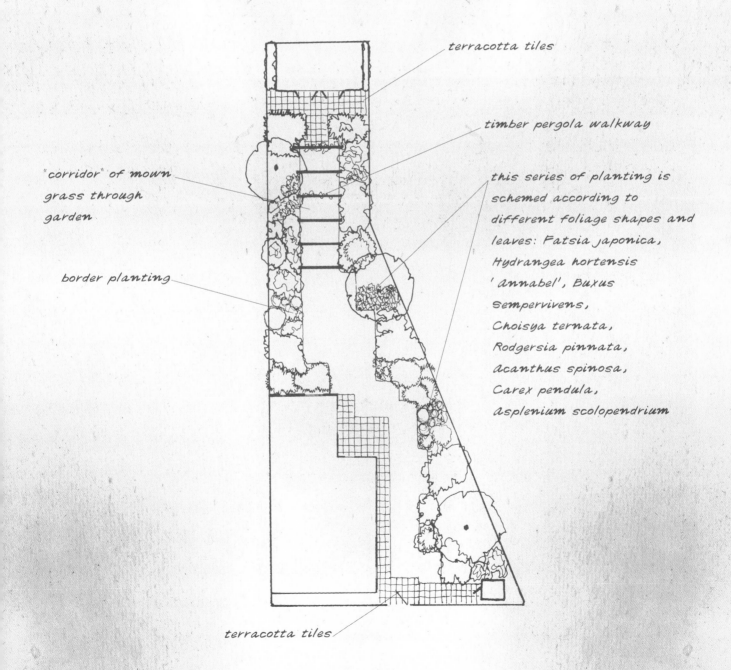

terracotta tiles

timber pergola walkway

"corridor" of mown grass through garden

this series of planting is schemed according to different foliage shapes and leaves: Fatsia japonica, Hydrangea hortensis 'annabel', Buxus Sempervivens, Choisya ternata, Rodgersia pinnata, Acanthus spinosa, Carex pendula, Asplenium scolopendrium

border planting

terracotta tiles

courtyard garden

A courtyard garden can be made from a space which is partially or totally enclosed. It's usually near the house, perhaps linked to it by a patio or terrace, and bounded by walls, fences, or hedges. While some are suntraps, a courtyard at basement level is often cool and shady—a place for intermingled shades of green.

◄ *Black bamboo in galvanized metal containers contributes much to this minimalist courtyard. Stylish dining furniture completes the look.*

An outdoor room

A small enclosed garden at the back of a terraced town house is the ideal candidate for the courtyard treatment. Well-defined by boundaries, it offers a private area generally with no view to worry about losing. Mellow country cottages often have a paved, cobbled, or brick-set area immediately outside the house, with or without a garden beyond, and these areas too make perfect courtyard gardens, although here it may be important not to become too enclosed, as this would risk losing views of the rest of the garden or of the countryside beyond.

Being (generally) next to the house a courtyard becomes another room—a perfect place for dining and entertaining, sun-bathing, dozing, or even to sit and work in. Apart from its "room" quality, the essence of the

In a suntrap courtyard a spiky-leaved plant grown in a classic terracotta container will give a tropical touch.

courtyard is also its hard-landscaping. If you have the stone or brick floor already, be advised to keep it. If not, choose materials that will suit those of your house. Small-sized units are best in a small area.

Again, your courtyard may have natural boundaries already. If not you will need to start by supplying boundaries for enclosure. Be aware that the higher they go the greater your privacy but also the greater the shade. Walls in the same material as the house are unbeatable, with wires or trellis attached firmly to give support to climbing plants. A dense evergreen hedge will offer great privacy but will take several years to grow and will rob the limited amount of soil of its nutrients. Both hedges and walls create dry areas at

the base which are inhospitable to plants. Lightweight fencing can be a very satisfactory alternative, acting as a screen and support for plants, while still letting in light. Screening trellis is right in formal settings while hazel or willow hurdles look good in a more rural country garden.

Structuring the garden

Restraint and some formality are required for courtyard gardens. Decide on your theme and don't try to cram too many ideas into a small space. A lot of the planting will probably be in containers, but it's

◄ Courtyard gardens can be home to many plants, both growing in containers and trained on trellis against the wall.

worth contemplating building raised planting areas filled with earth (with drainage) as these can supply structure and will also need less watering than containers. Again, the materials used should be in sympathy with those of the house and with the enclosure. You may well be looking at the garden from above a lot of the time, for example from a first-floor living room or bedroom, so make sure that the scheme will look as well from this angle as it does when you are actually sitting in it. Because of the shelter it gains from its boundaries a courtyard can be warm and still at night, and is a natural place for fitting subtle lighting for the evening. Good-quality garden furniture can be a key feature.

designer's courtyard garden

A courtyard garden is at its most elegant when it follows clean contemporary lines, with sleek modern furniture. But if you prefer a traditional look you can fill it with pots and containers, and cover the walls with climbers. Paving, tiles, and gravel make the surfaces, and your containerized plants can be changed to suit your mood.

▲ *Contrary to first impressions this dark, overgrown courtyard offers surprising possibilities for a major transformation.*

GARDEN DATA

location:	▪▪ Maryland
climate:	▪▪ mild/temperate
soil type:	▪▪ chalky clay
direction:	▪▪ north facing
aspect:	▪▪ urban enclosed

The brief

This tiny space is dark and shady because of long-neglected boundary plants that have grown out of control. The owner is not a keen gardener but would like some variety of color and interest through the year and would like to use the courtyard as an extra summer room for relaxing and entertaining friends.

Courtyards on the north or east side of the house will be cool and shady whereas ones that face south can be real suntraps. When planning a courtyard garden the first thing to do is to decide how it will be used— somewhere to sit and soak up the sun, a quiet place, or a social area.

The design solution

The area was cleared wall to wall to maximize space and light and the dilapidated fencing was replaced with color-stained screening trellis to allow light to filter through but retain privacy. Small spaces work best if they are not too busy, so we

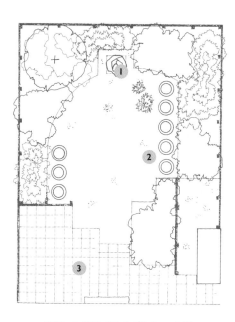

—7m x 9m/22ft x 30ft—

chose unfussy paving to replace the dark, brick patio and combined it with creamy gravel to reflect as much light as possible. Planting is bold and simple, with splashes of color provided by containerized annuals that can be replaced each year. We installed automatic irrigation and one uplight to make a dramatic focal point of the owner's beautiful piece of contemporary sculpture.

sculpture

▲ A large sculpture provides a
dramatic focal point.

pots

▲ Matching containers
always look stylish.

paving

◀ A paved patio provides an unfussy seating area.

practical projects

A courtyard garden is defined by its enclosures. You may be lucky enough to have a ready-made area adjoining the house, but if not, a sturdy, well-supported trellis makes a quick and straightforward enclosure and shelter from winds.

▲ *This wood trellis permits a glimpse through to another part of the garden and allows the garden to have different components to it.*

Making an enclosure

A courtyard garden is a garden on a small scale, where everything is visible at close quarters. It also has a degree of formality that comes from being closely attached to the house, and is an area where you will be sitting and looking around a lot of the time. For all these reasons, good workmanship is important.

Since a large part of the effect will come from plants growing up the enclosure, anything you build needs to be strong enough to take the weight of plants climbing or twining over it, and also sufficiently well finished to make sure that it will wear well.

If you use ready-made trellis panels, choose the strongest available and fix them between strong posts. For easy fixing as well as long life, special metal post holders can be used. Trellis looks good painted to go

with the house or with other features. Dark garden green forms a restful background to plants and French gray is a calming color. If you prefer the look of bare wood, protect with wood seal. Paints, seals, and varnishes are all available in nontoxic, water-based formulas.

◄ *The delicate white and purple flowers of* Clematis sieboldii *complement this trellis. It is an especially good climber.*

DESIGNER'S TIPS

• Choose hard-landscaping materials that complement or match the materials of your house.

• Don't try to create a tropical hotspot if the courtyard is exposed to wind or cold.

• Don't choose a shady and dry area for your courtyard. Unless you use an automatic irrigation system the plants will die and you'll be left with a brown dustbowl. If it's cool it needs to be damp and that may not suit your purpose.

• Decide on a single, main theme for your courtyard: don't have too many ideas crammed into its small space.

• The higher the boundaries, the more shady your courtyard will be.

putting up trellis

Trellis panels are easily erected, but if they are to be a lasting feature in the garden, it is worth taking the trouble to put them up correctly. Good fence posts will carry a guarantee of 15 years or longer. The panels are fixed to timber uprights firmly anchored in the ground. These can either be cemented in or held in place by means of the special posts illustrated here.

Most fencing materials sold today have already been pressure treated to make them weatherproof, but check before you buy.

1 Check the position of the uprights carefully, making sure they are the correct distance from each other and that they are square on to each other.

2 Drive the posts into the ground, using a lump hammer and a wooden block.

3 Knock the uprights into the metal shoes and bolt them in firmly. Use a level to make sure that the post is upright.

4 Screw the panels to the uprights, using rust-proof metal plates.

5 Fix finials to the tops of the posts. Not only are these decorative in their own right, but they will deflect rain that would otherwise collect at the top of the post and cause rotting.

courtyard plants and planting

Small enough to take in at a glance, courtyard gardens offer special opportunities for planting. Planting within the courtyard will usually be in containers or raised beds, while the boundaries can be used to great effect, with hedging plants if you want a "live" boundary or climbing plants to cover walls or trellis.

A courtyard theme

For the best effect stick to a strong scheme, even if you want the effect to be exotic, dramatic, or riotous. Too much going on in a small place will otherwise risk looking muddled. Use containers that are similar in style, whether it's brightly painted buckets, old stone troughs, or Versailles planters. Have a strong theme for plants and don't use too many "highlight" plants—one glorious flowering climber given prominence can be more successful than several in uneasy competition.

Container plants for a sunny courtyard

A sunny courtyard, if also well sheltered, can be host to the most exotic plants. The following can all be grown as striking specimens in large containers in a tropical-style courtyard. All need rich, easy-draining compost.

Agapanthus 'Blue Giant': drumheads of blue flowers on tall stems, broad, strappy leaves
ht 1.2m/4ft
sp 60cm/2ft

Ensete ventricosum (syn. *Musa ensete*): banana-like plant from Ethiopia with enormous leaves in bright olive-green and huge bronze and white flowers
ht to 6m/20ft
sp to 4.5m/15ft

Hakonechloa macra 'Aureola': golden-leaved, mound-forming grass—smaller than most grasses—looks stunning in a container
ht 35cm/14in
sp 40cm/16in

Musa basjoo: a banana plant from Japan with long rippled leaf blades and exotic brown and yellow flowers followed by inedible fruit
ht to 4.5m/15ft
sp to 3.6m/12ft

Phormium tenax (New Zealand flax): clump-forming plant with tall, architectural, strappy leaves and even taller stems of dark red flowers
ht 3m/10ft (leaves), 3.6m/12ft (flowers)
sp 1.8m/6ft

Yucca filamentosa (Adam's needle): rosettes of sharply pointed leathery leaves and upright heads of small cream flowers
ht and sp 90cm/3ft

◀ Yucca filamentosa *in flower.*

◄ *Parrot tulips have striking frilly flowers.*

small. Try some of these varieties:
Hedera colchica, 'Dentata' and *H.c*
'Dentata Variegata': large
green/variegated, tooth-edged leaves,
vigorous growth
Hedera helix 'Gold Heart': small
lobed leaves with yellow centers;
modest growth
Hedera helix 'Maple Leaf': less
vigorous ivy with deeply serrated,
maple-like leaves

Climbers for warm courtyards

These plants will need support from
wires or trellis if grown up a wall.
All grow to 5m/16ft or more.
Clematis armandii: scented, cream-
flowered, early clematis
Clematis montana var. *rubens:* pink-
flowered version of the vigorous
early summer-flowering clematis

Lonicera periclymenum 'Serotina': late-
flowering, very fragrant honeysuckle
Passiflora caerulea (passion flower):
exotic, starry, crown-of-thorns
flowers in creamy white with purple-
blue markings
Rosa 'banksiae': pale yellow or white
clusters of slightly scented flowers in
early spring
Solanum crispum (Chilean potato
vine) 'Glasnevin': vigorous purple-
flowered jasmine-like climbing plant,
but with no scent
Vitis coignetiae grapevine whose leaves
color a rich purple red in the fall
(black grapes are not edible)

Ivies for shady walls

Green ivies are the perfect wall-
climbers for shady courtyards, and
need no support. Ivies with yellow
variegation prefer some sun. Many
leaf forms are available, large and

◄ *Solanum crispum is a vigorous climber.*

TIPS FOR COURTYARD PLANTING

• For a screening hedge the tried and tested
evergreens, box (*Buxus sempervirens*) and
yew (*Taxus baccata*) lend the greatest
distinction, but they are slow to grow. The
wait is worth it, however. *Lonicera nitida* is a
tiny-leaved evergreen superficially similar to
box, that is fairly quick-growing, takes well
to clipping and is easily grown from cuttings.
A golden-leaved version 'Baggesen's Gold' is
also available for sunny situations.

• Raised beds should be built with drainage
unless they are open to the earth. Fill the
base with broken bricks and pebbles, mix a
little gravel in the first layer of earth and
supply weep holes in the walls. Blur the
edges with low-growing bushy or trailing
plants such as lavender or ground-cover
roses in sun, ivies and periwinkle in shade.

• Containers can be used singly, in pairs, or
grouped together. Containers of different
heights and sizes gain unity when grouped
together and enable you to make a
composition of a mixed group of plants.

design alternatives

SKETCHES

These two design alternatives both feature sculptures as their focal point, adopting on the left a contemporary, lush feel, while on the right a more traditional approach.

path lights

Dicksonia antarctica
(New Zealand Tree Fern)

low surround
of ferns or
Aegopodium
podagnia
variegata

box hedging

large flat
pierced stone
with water
trickling over

10mm/½in
gravel

paddle
stones all
round path
(laid over
weedproof
membrane)

tiled patio 300 x 300mm/12 x 12in
quarry tile

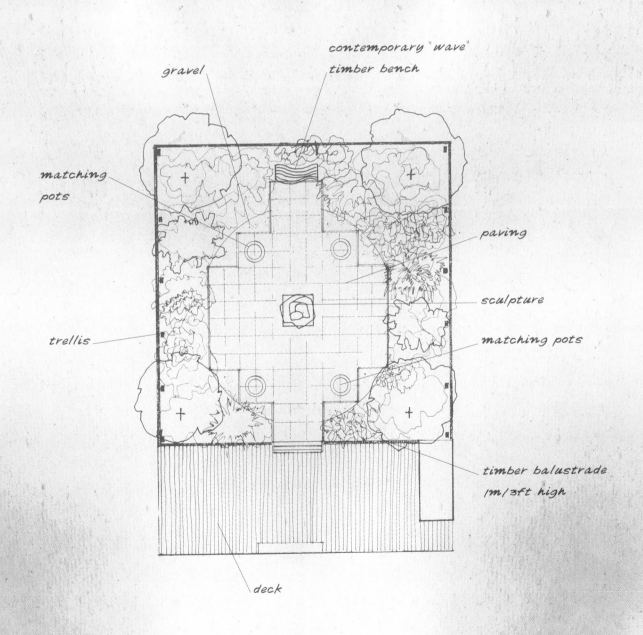

gravel

contemporary "wave"
timber bench

matching
pots

paving

sculpture

matching pots

trellis

timber balustrade
/m/3ft high

deck

useful gardens

Growing vegetables and herbs makes gardening useful as well as enjoyable. But if you have a small garden you probably don't want the whole plot to look too utilitarian. It doesn't need to—kitchen gardens and herb gardens can be designed so that they are a pleasure to look at as well as productive, and they don't have to exclude flowers.

kitchen garden

There's no denying that growing vegetables, herbs, and maybe some fruit for the kitchen takes time and trouble. But this is more than compensated for by the pleasure it gives. This is an orderly way of gardening that many people find not only intensely rewarding, but also very relaxing.

Planning and preparing

To get the best out of the soil you need to grow vegetables in rotation, and you also need plenty of access to tend and harvest the plants. For these reasons separate, rectangular plots divided by narrow paths work well. However, if you prefer a more informal design with curves you can still move your vegetables around from area to area. In this case, make sure that your design allows you easy access to the plants.

For the kitchen garden there are three main types of vegetable crop to be planned for: root vegetables (beets, carrots, turnips, radishes), brassicas (cabbages and kale) and legumes (peas and beans). The onion family can be given a permanent plot or can be moved along with the legumes. Leeks, going in at a different time from most other vegetables, can be put in as and where there is space. They are planted out in summer, and are finished with by the following spring, leaving the ground free for something else. Lettuces can be planted with the roots or legumes and can also go in as "catch crops," to be removed and eaten as their neighbors grow and need the space.

Preparing the plot

Vegetables are greedy feeders, so the soil needs to be well prepared before

◄ *This formally laid-out kitchen garden has raised beds which help to provide good drainage and warm the soil.*

if the crop varies from year to year.

Different types of vegetables also have different requirements, as well as having different effects on the soil. Peas and beans enrich the soil with nitrogen, which is needed by brassicas and leafy vegetables, while root crops help to make the soil comfortable for the legumes. Root crops do best where manure was applied for the previous growing season. Too rich a soil makes them fork under the ground and produce leaf instead of root.

In a big garden, as well as providing beds for three main crop types, you might plan to have a fourth plot for potatoes, which do best on freshly manured soil and which would go around in rotation preceding the root vegetables. Home-grown potatoes are delicious and justify the room—and the work—they take, but not everyone has space to grow and store them in quantity. In our garden we grow a few choice potatoes with the roots and use a fourth area as a permanent site for soft fruits—equally rewarding and worthwhile. You can then pick them at the peak of perfection.

you plant. Ideally you should dig it over well in the fall before you begin and lay a thick layer of manure or garden compost on top (or dig it in); then fork over again in the spring. Finally, rake the beds smooth and level to prepare them for seeds and seedlings.

Reasons for rotating

One reason for moving types of crop from area to area is that it discourages the build-up of pests and diseases. There is something nasty specific to almost anything you may wish to grow, and such diseases and predators are much less likely to get established

◄ *A well-stocked kitchen garden with ornamental herbs and vegetables provides a feast for the eye as well as for the table.*

designer's kitchen garden

Many of us do not have the time and energy needed to grow enough vegetables and fruit to supply the kitchen without ever buying produce from a farmers market or supermarket. So think laterally and mix flowers, fruits, herbs, and vegetables in small quantities, to avoid a glut and satisfy the taste buds.

▲ *A sloping or terraced site is ideal for a kitchen garden. We took advantage of the banks to plant annual flowers and vegetables.*

GARDEN DATA

location:	New York State
climate:	mild
soil type:	chalk
direction:	south facing
aspect:	slopes towards house

The brief

The plot is south facing and open —ideal for early warming of the soil in spring and for growing crops to benefit from even exposure to sunlight. The garden is terraced upward away from the house and these terraces will form the basis for the vegetable beds.

The design solution

Following the linear layout of the garden we used a mini rotivator to level each terrace, to avoid the seeds being washed away by the first rainstorm. The ground was cleared of stones, weeds, and debris and the soil raked to a fine tilth. The brick retaining walls were crumbling so we replaced them with low, but sturdy walls of new, tanalized or reclaimed railroad ties, supported at regular intervals by sawn timber posts. (Reclaimed ties tend to leach messy tar preservative which can contaminate plants.) These also provide a step up from the path and

a place to sit while hand weeding or shelling peas! Paths were laid with bark mulch to intersect the beds and provide a soft but firm surface for wheeling a barrow back and forth. Trellis panels were fixed over sloped banks to help climbers.

▲ *A pot of bright pelargoniums.*

compost

bark path

▲ *Compost bins are hidden from view.*

▲ *Paths are covered with bark chippings.*

─15m x 5m/18ft x 10ft─

practical projects

Compost making is important in any garden, but especially so for vegetables. We used pressure-treated timber to make our own simple compost container, then set diamond trellis over a weedproof membrane as a support for our decorative climbing beans. Other crops can be grown by planting through the membrane.

Feeding your food

Making your own compost is wonderfully satisfying and is also very easy. There are several schools of thought about the finer details of compost making, but everyone agrees that to rot away into beautiful, sweet-smelling plant food, compost in the making requires air and a degree of moisture. If you make your own compost bin (or buy a proprietary bin) and fill it with thick layers of kitchen vegetable waste, grass clippings, annual weeds (not perennials such as dandelions as their roots can grow anywhere), plant clippings, and even the contents of the vacuum cleaner bag, you cannot go far wrong.

HOEING

A practiced hoeing technique is important: keep away from vegetable stems and penetrate not more than 2.5cm/1in below soil surface.

▲ *If you don't have time to build your own compost bin, or your garden is very small, there are excellent, commercially available varieties.*

Layers of soil between vegetable matter speed up the process of beneficial decay, and the faster the bin is filled the more efficiently its contents rot down. Stems and sticky bits and pieces help to admit air, but twigs or branches are too big and won't rot down. Coarser stems are best crushed to give them a good start. You can also put in loosely screwed up paper and card, fall leaves, and waste bits of potting compost from repotting.

building an organic compost bin

The movable compost bin illustrated here is quick to make, and, since it allows excellent air circulation, it will rapidly produce good compost.

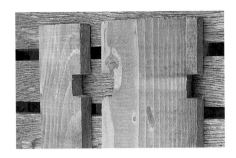

1 Any sort of timber is suitable, provided it is pressure treated. Cut the timber into lengths, ideally of around 1.2m/4ft. (A smaller bin will not make such good compost, as insufficient heat will be generated.) Cut notches toward each end of the timbers so they will fit together.

2 Slot the timbers together. There is no need to screw them in place: in fact, this makes it easier to dismantle the sides once the heap is ready. The bin can then be reassembled elsewhere in the garden.

3 Carry on until the bin is of the desired height. Ideally, make two bins side by side. Once the material in the first bin has rotted down, use it while making a fresh pile in the second bin.

TRELLIS AGAINST A MEMBRANE

Weed-suppressing membrane is the vegetable gardener's answer to prayer and minimizes the amount of back-breaking weeding necessary to keep the vegetables growing strongly. It is designed for use on flat ground, but can also be used against a bank provided you overlay it with trellis panels to hold it in position. Prepare the ground first, then stretch the membrane over it. Cut trellis panels to fit and lay them over the membrane. Nail the trellis in position using long, rustproof nails. Cut holes in the membrane as usual and plant the vegetables through the membrane.

kitchen plants and planting

The most useful kitchen gardens concentrate on produce that can be cropped throughout the season. Flowers for cutting can be grown to jolly the plot along, though many vegetables are ornamental in their own right. Herbs will also give an authentic look and help make full use of your plot.

Mixing in flowers

On the whole it's best to grow flowers separately as they have different growing requirements and get in the way when you are weeding between the vegetables and picking the crop. Many flowers attract beneficial insects such as bees and hoverflies, making them useful as well as pretty, and many have similar requirements to herbs so can be mixed with or grown near them. For the main plan we have grown herbs mostly in containers, but chives or parsley make a neat edging to a bed, where they are easily reached for cutting, and perennial herbs such as rosemary or thyme can be given a permanent home. Little flowers such as *Bellis perennis* (bachelor's button daisies) make a neat edging to herbs or vegetables, and nasturtiums, parsley or chives also look good.

Essentials

Mastering the use of the hoe is essential for those with a kitchen garden as the vegetables you grow must not be placed in competition with weeds for the soil's nutrients. Neatness and orderliness are also an essential part of successful kitchen gardening. Annual weeds can be hoed out without disturbing the crop if attacked while still young. This is best done when the ground is dry so that the weeds won't take root again.

Profile plants

Borago officinalis
BORAGE

With its nodding heads of flower buds and clear blue, five-petaled flowers, borage is a lovely ornament to the kitchen garden. Tiny white

◄ *Borage has attractive blue flowers.*

hairs cover the many-branched plant and catch the light. Borage is easily grown from seed and if it feels at home it will self-seed readily. The leaves have a faint cucumber flavor and are cooling in salads and summer drinks; the flowers are edible too.

ht to 90cm/3ft

sp to 30cm/12in

Soil and situation

Does best in sun and well-drained soil.

Phaseolus vulgaris

POLE BEAN

(climbing varieties)

The rounded, and often stringless, pods of pole snap beans can be more succulent than giant pole beans, and climbing beans make equally attractive plants to grow up trellis or bean poles, or even against a wall. Purple-podded varieties such as

‘Triofono’, and ‘Purple Giant’ look great in a kitchen garden; ‘Purple Giant’ has particularly colorful purple flowers and purple-tinted leaves and stems. The pods turn to green on cooking. A golden-podded climbing variety is ‘Goldmarie’ and this looks well growing with a purple-podded type.

ht to 2.4m/8ft

sp 90cm/3ft

Soil and situation

Needs moist but well-drained soil and full sun.

Beta vulgaris

CHARD

Swiss chard (also known as seakale beet and silver beet) is a type of beet grown for its stems and leaves, similar

▶ *Swiss chard is rich in minerals, especially iron.*

to spinach beet but bigger and with broader midribs. It withstands the winter better as well. The leaves are used as spinach and the white stems and midribs can be cooked separately and eaten dipped in hot melted butter. Ruby chard is a decorative form with ruby red stalks and leaves, but not quite so hardy. Regularly picking a few leaves from each plant insures a constant supply. Perfect for home growing as it needs to be eaten at once.

ht 45cm/18in

sp 90cm/3ft

Soil and situation

Swiss chard likes moist rich soil and doesn't mind some shade.

design alternatives

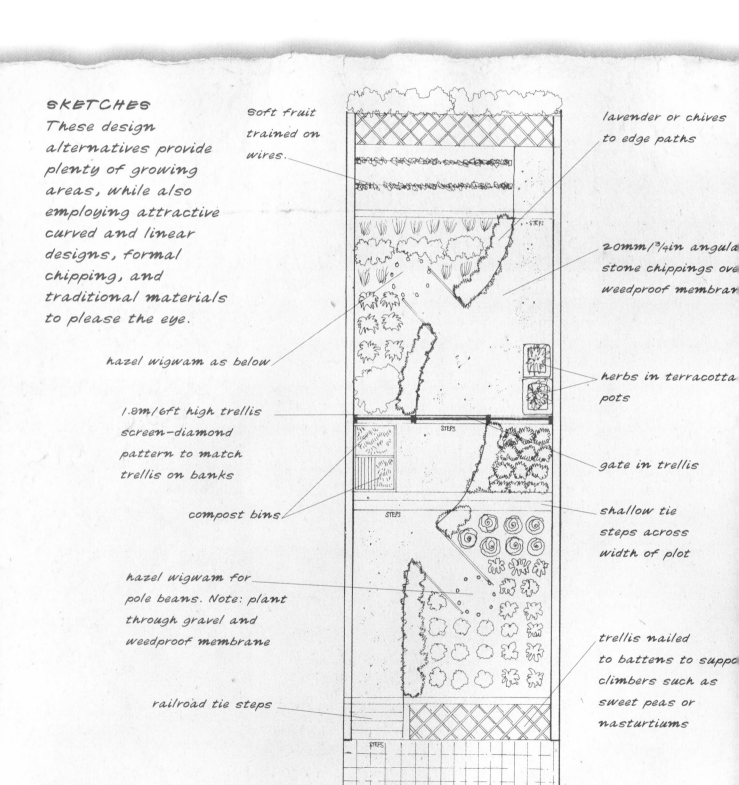

SKETCHES
These design alternatives provide plenty of growing areas, while also employing attractive curved and linear designs, formal chipping, and traditional materials to please the eye.

hazel wigwam as below

1.8m/6ft high trellis screen-diamond pattern to match trellis on banks

compost bins

hazel wigwam for pole beans. Note: plant through gravel and weedproof membrane

railroad tie steps

Soft fruit trained on wires.

lavender or chives to edge paths

20mm/³⁄₄in angula stone chippings ove weedproof membran

herbs in terracotta pots

gate in trellis

shallow tie steps across width of plot

trellis nailed to battens to suppo climbers such as sweet peas or nasturtiums

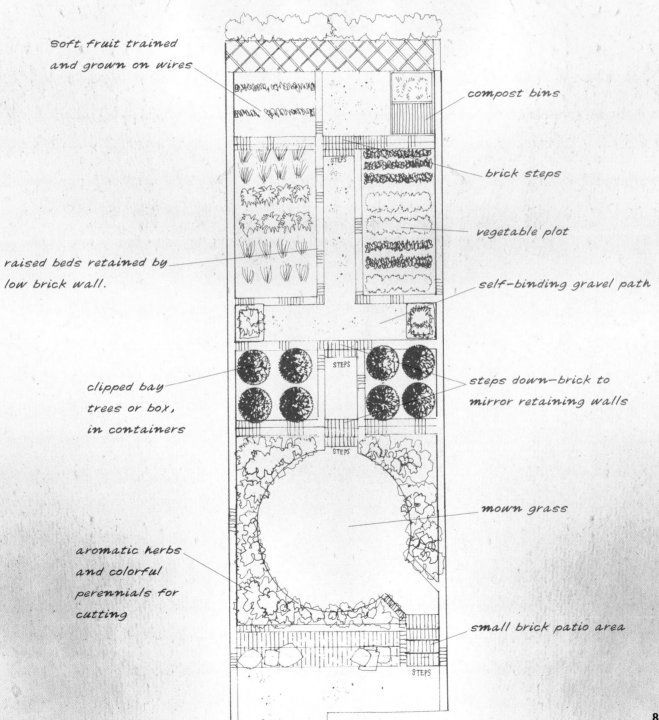

Soft fruit trained
and grown on wires

compost bins

brick steps

vegetable plot

raised beds retained by
low brick wall.

self-binding gravel path

clipped bay
trees or box,
in containers

steps down—brick to
mirror retaining walls

mown grass

aromatic herbs
and colorful
perennials for
cutting

small brick patio area

STEPS

STEPS

STEPS

STEPS

introduction

herb garden

Herbs include annuals such as basil that die at the end of summer and perennials such as lemon balm, fennel, and tarragon that die down over the winter but grow up again each spring. A few shrubby herbs such as bay, rosemary, and thyme flourish during the winter and are available fresh at any time.

Growing herbs together

A well-structured herb garden is a highly ornamental feature in its own right, capable of occupying a defined part of a large garden, or, planned with care, of making an appealing garden in itself. Herbs are used both to flavor food and as medicine, often both at the same time, and they can also be used in a variety of other traditional ways. They offer a rich variety of scents and textures and a herbarium, as the herb garden was once called, is a place to delight the senses. Many herbal plants come from the broad family known as the labiates and the lippy flowers are a magnet to bees so that the garden hums in summer. If you have an interest in history or folklore you may well be lured by the charms of a herb garden and will find yourself making pot pourri and herbal wine as well as using the leaves or flowers in cooking and for herbal teas.

Although there are herbs for a variety of situations and soils many herbs are of Mediterranean origin and need well-drained soil with sun and shelter. Some cultivars with unusual golden or variegated

◄ *The plants in your herb garden can be used for home remedies as well as home cooking, and can be dried for winter.*

▶ *Cobbles set in concrete surrounding a small water feature are a strong design focus of this formally laid-out herb garden.*

coloring, such as gold-leaf forms of sage or lemon balm, thrive if given shade from the summer sun at its strongest. Many aromatics actually prefer soil that is not too fertile.

The garden design

Traditionally, herb gardens have been planned rather in the same way as rose gardens (see pages 790–799) with small plots arranged within a formal, geometric structure, each bed enclosed by a low hedge of clipped box. The geometry and formality are complemented by the use of gravel, brick, or stone paving for paths and the whole is intricately ornamental. Herbs growing in beds without an enclosure can spill out onto the hard surface for a more informal look, and they also take very well to being

planted in containers, which can be used to give more height. Either of these treatments can work well for a patio garden.

While a symmetrical plan based on mirrored beds within a square or rectangle can look over-designed in a smaller garden, the formality of straight-edged planting areas, evergreen edging, and hard surfaces

can be adapted in many ways to produce a garden with a true herbarium appeal but without the over-demanding symmetry. This sort of solution is particularly suitable for an irregularly shaped plot. The materials used for the hard-landscaping of the garden should be in sympathy with the house.

It's worth remembering that a highly formalized herb garden with clipped hedging needs to be kept constantly manicured to look at its best. An informal style can benefit from a slightly negligé look. However you decide to organize your own herb garden, remember that you will need to be able to reach the plants for harvesting, so the depth of bed should not be too great.

◀ *Many herbs lend themselves to a relaxed, informal style of gardening; they look at their best when they are allowed to grow naturally.*

designer's herb garden

Apart from the many culinary herbs, there are hundreds of different herbal plants used in medicine, aromatherapy, cosmetics and perfume, and for dyeing cloth. Some traditional herbs, which self-seed easily, are considered to be little more than weeds by some gardeners, but many more are highly ornamental.

▲ *This dark garden looks unsuitable for herbs, but with some work and careful use of light, it can easily be brightened up.*

GARDEN DATA

location:	▦ Kentucky
climate:	▦ mild/temperate
soil type:	▦ chalk
direction:	▦ west
aspect:	▦ sunny, open to the south

The brief

This small, narrow garden faces west, but is denied a lot of natural light because of its high boundary walls, which are overgrown with ivy and other old, woody climbers. A brick-paved passageway opens to a small sitting area in front of the shed and utility area.

The design solution

We removed all the existing climbing plants. The walls, brick shed, and paving were all jet-hosed to remove dirt and debris, then scrubbed with an antifungicide. All walls were checked for cracks and loose mortar and repointed where necessary.

We painted the walls on either side of the passageway a soft yellow. Trellis panels were color stained sea-blue and battened to the wall along the south boundary. The shed door was painted to match. We replaced the existing rotten wooden arch with a removable, bamboo curtain hung from a simple metal arch, and

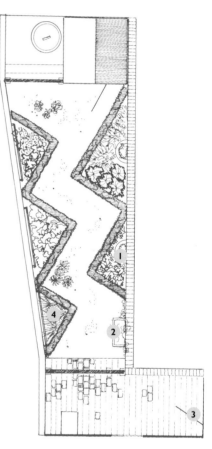

−16m × 6.5m/52ft × 21ft−

positioned another one across the steps to the utility area. Gravel replaced the grass patch and the butler's sink became the basin for the ceramic, "lion" water feature.

fountain

◀ *Masque water feature creates a focal point for the brick walls.*

gate

▲ *A decorative wooden gate creates an old-fashioned look.*

container

▲ *Wall-mounted containers are a perfect accompaniment for a brick wall.*

herb bed

◀ *Strong triangular-shaped beds widen this narrow garden.*

practical projects

Trellis battened to a wall makes a useful framework for many plants. Whatever you intend to grow, make sure that the trellis is fixed just clear of the wall to allow air to flow. In a herb garden it can be used to support nasturtiums (whose leaves, flowers, and fruits are edible), hops, blackberries, and ornamental fruit.

Support and shelter

One of the skills involved in creating a herb garden is to appreciate, and provide, the conditions herbs require. Most herbs (like most vegetables) need warmth and good light, and don't enjoy wind. Providing shelter will be necessary if you have an open position. Bamboo screens can fulfill this function while also being a good-looking way of hiding any unsightly or purely functional parts of the garden. Although temporary, they have a lovely natural look that blends with the simple shapes and planting of the herb garden, and they are cheap and easy to replace.

If you are lucky enough to have a walled garden it will provide maximum shelter. Make optimum use of the wall by growing suitable companion plants up it. Flowering plants such as roses and climbing vegetables such as pole beans, as well as ornamental vines and fruits, can all be grown on trellis and have a natural affinity with herbs.

SCREENS AND CURTAINS

In our client's focus garden (see pages 834–835) we used bamboo curtains to screen off the garbage cans and to separate out different

parts of the garden. These curtains can be put to many different uses—for example in our focus roof garden they are used to

disguise the safety railings (see pages 932–933). Here is a selection of some of the different designs available.

trellis against a wall

In order to grow twining climbers against walls, it is necessary to provide them with some kind of support fixed to the wall. One of the simplest methods uses ready-made trellis panels. If you are using wooden panels, make sure they have been treated with a preservative before proceeding.

1 Cut small wooden battens on which to mount the trellis and drill holes through the length of them. This avoids damage to old walls.

2 Use a masonry bit to drill holes in the wall at the appropriate intervals.

DESIGNER'S TIPS

• Trim clump-forming herbs after flowering, to avoid straggly, woody-stemmed plants.

• If you don't want your herbs to self-seed, trim before they flower. But remember you will have to replace annual herbs with new plants next year.

• Harvest herbs before they flower, in dry, but not hot, conditions.

• Herbs with variegated leaves may be less hardy than those of single-color foliage.

• Chamomile lawns can get untidy and weedy very quickly; be warned.

• Don't experiment with herbal remedies or use them in cooking without reading instructions. Some herbs are very poisonous.

• Beware of rue. It can give you nasty blisters when handled.

• If you have heavy, clay soil, grow your herbs in raised beds.

3 Tap in Rawlplugs to hold the screws. Place the battens in position so that the holes in the battens line up with the holes in the wall.

4 Using long screws, screw the trellis to the wall through the battens. Using battens (rather than fixing the trellis directly to the wall) allows for good air circulation behind the plant.

herb plants and planting

There are dozens of culinary herbs that would grace any garden. And apart from these, herbs in a wider sense include some beautiful and ornamental plants that were once grown for their usefulness, especially in medicine, but which are now known best as garden flowers and shrubs.

Flowers for herb gardens

If you include flowers such as lilies, foxgloves and roses in your herb garden you will be continuing an old apothecary-garden tradition as well as enlivening the garden with spires and mounds of alluring flowers. Selecting widely, you will be able to achieve great variety using only those plants once grown for their use. While it is not advisable to use any of the more powerful plants from the old herbals for self-treatment, growing them to look at is another matter.

As well as the flavoring herbs with which we're still familiar, herbs less widely known, some for kitchen use and some with ancient domestic uses such as keeping away fleas (pennyroyal—a mint) or for making sweetmeats (elecampane), can still be bought from specialist growers. Look out for yellow-headed tansy, blue-leaved rue, red-flowered bergamot and mint-like, blue-flowered hyssop. Add these to the well-known classics such as chamomile, pot marigold, mint, thyme, and lavender.

▶ *Rosemary traditionally accompanies lamb and many Mediterranean dishes.*

Profile plants

Rosmarinus officinalis
ROSEMARY

Rosemary makes a lovely shrub with evergreen piney needles and small light blue flowers which may appear from November until early summer.

ht and sp to 1.5m/5ft but can be cut back

Soil and situation

Well-drained soil that is not too rich and a sheltered position in full sun.

Tropaeolum
NASTURTIUMS

Nasturtiums are well-loved flowers that bring bright color to the herb garden. Bushy and climbing varieties are both easily grown from seed.

ht 30cm/12in (bush) 1–3m/3–10ft (climbing)

sp 45cm/18in (bush) 1.2m/4ft (climbing)

Soil and situation

Well-drained soil that is not too rich in a sunny position.

Salvia officinalis
SAGE

Sage makes lovely purple-blue flowers as well as having attractive, felty gray-green leaves. Golden-leaved and purple-leaved varieties are also available ('Aurea' and 'Purpurascens').

ht 75cm/30in

sp 90cm/3ft

Soil and situation

Fairly fertile soil that is light and well-drained, in a sunny position.

▲ *Nasturtiums have edible flowers.*

▲ *Use home-grown sage for Christmas stuffing.*

SOME COMMON HERBS FOR THE KITCHEN

Annual and short-lived herbs

Basil—*Ocimum basilicum*
spicily aromatic, used in pesto and salads; has an affinity with tomatoes
Dill—*Anethum graveolens*
cool, aromatic flavor blends with fish and potato salad
Garlic—*Allium sativum*
bulbs have strong piquancy for a Mediterranean flavor
Parsley **—*Petroselinum crispum*
indispensable garnishing herb
Rocket **—*Eruca sativa*
brings a pungent, peppery flavor to a mixed-leaf salad

Perennial and shrubby herbs

Bay—*Laurus nobilis*
leathery evergreen leaves for bouquet garni (bay can be grown as topiary)
Chives **—*Allium schoenoprasum*
onion-flavored green leaves for garnish; accompanies cream cheese well
Fennel *—*Foeniculum vulgare*
feathery leaves have a slightly aniseed taste
French tarragon *—*Artemisia dranunculus*
a subtle aniseed flavor for chicken and sauces
Marjoram *—*Origanum vulgare*
a good herb for soups, stews, and bouquet garni; also for pizza
Mint ** *Mentha spicata*
well-known cooling and refreshing herb for

mint sauce, new potatoes, and peas (also known as spearmint), pineapple mint (*M. suaveolens* 'Variegata'), and eau-de-cologne mint (*M.x. piperata* f. *citrata, syn.* M. *citrata*) are some more unusual varieties
Rosemary *—*Rosmarinus officinalis*
aromatic needles go well with lamb; also for pot pourri and cosmetic uses
Sage *—*Salvia officinalis*
for pork dishes and sage and onion stuffing
Salad burnet *—*Poterium sansquisorba*
cucumber-flavored leaves for salads and summer drinks
Thyme *—*Thymus vulgaris*
aromatic herb for bouquet garni and to add to soups and stews

* *needs sunshine and good drainage*
** *needs moisture and semishade*

▲ *Thyme and the annual basil make an aromatic and decorative combination.*

design alternatives

SKETCHES

The first alternative employs rustic secondhand bricks, traditional herbs, and an old-fashioned butler's sink to create a medieval herb garden effect. The second plan is more modern with raised beds, clipped bay trees, and sharper, straighter lines.

secondhand or old stock bricks (must be frostproof) to make irregular-shaped path through garden to shed

10mm/½in pea gravel over weed-proof membrane, herbs planted directly into this

pots of small herbs— thyme, pineapple mint, tarragon, basil

butler's sink with pebbles at bottom, to hold oxygenating water plants such as pontederia cordata lanceolata or seolz watermint

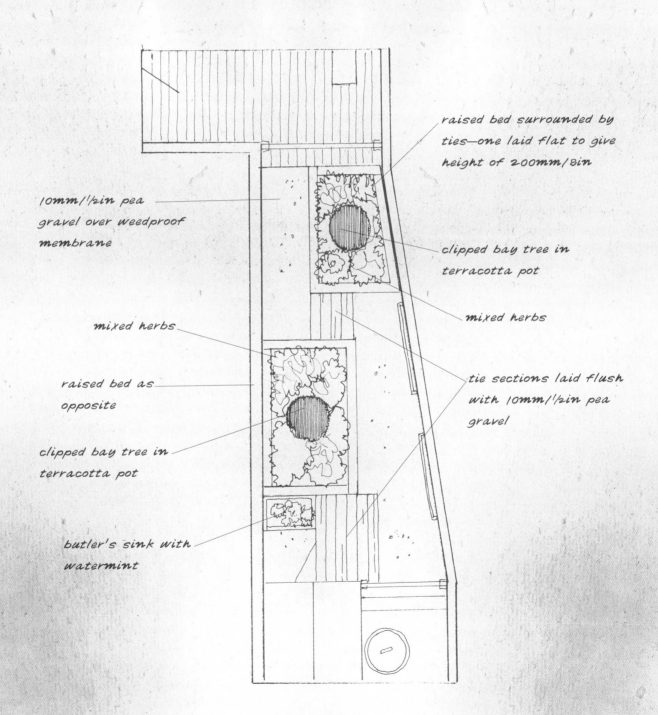

raised bed surrounded by
ties—one laid flat to give
height of 200mm/8in

10mm/½in pea
gravel over weedproof
membrane

clipped bay tree in
terracotta pot

mixed herbs

mixed herbs

raised bed as
opposite

tie sections laid flush
with 10mm/½in pea
gravel

clipped bay tree in
terracotta pot

butler's sink with
watermint

peaceful gardens

The gardens in this section for contemplation and meditation are gardens to sit in, gardens to look at, and gardens in which to find peace. All gardens provide this to some extent but this is the explicit aim of these particular schemes. Of course the peaceful garden may be the result of a lot of preliminary hard work—but the calming results will be worth the effort.

meadow garden

Leave your garden to grow by itself and you'll get a tangle of ineradicable weeds, linked—or partly hidden—by scrambling bindweed and a blackberry thicket. It follows that growing a meadow hazily dotted with wild flowers like an Impressionist painting must be an art and the meadow as a garden must be deceptively contrived.

◀ *Grasses, swaying gently in the slightest summer breeze, are an essential ingredient of every successful meadow garden.*

Wild delights

What a dream of a garden the apparently artless meadow is—and many a plot has room for a little flowering meadow area of its own even when the rest is more conventionally cultivated. A tiny area of meadow in a lawn can be just as effective as a flower bed and can assuage that longing to be at one with nature. An important incidental feature of a wild meadow garden is that it attracts insects to the garden, bringing a peaceful summer hum. With luck, these will include beneficial insects that prey on garden pests, such as hoverflies, ladybirds, lacewings, and bees for pollination.

Many of the plants suitable for a meadow garden are wild native plants, but many more have been borrowed from gardens. Growing in grass and fending for themselves they will be smaller and more subtle. Growing a meadow garden is doing our bit for nature, as native flowers in the wild are a disappearing phenomenon, thanks to the use of herbicides, the ripping up of hedges, the grooming of the countryside and ever-spreading building, as well as the loss of wild areas in towns. But foxgloves, cornflowers, forget-me-nots, scabious, and verbascums were once as common in the wild as poppies on a construction site and ox-eye daisies on a highway bank, and these are typical meadow garden plants for us to grow from seed. Other plants for meadow planting, such as larkspur, tulips, love-in-a mist, and lupins, are wild flowers of another part of the world, and add a slightly foreign charm to the meadow.

Maintenance

The main work in presiding over a meadow garden is in the preparation and planting (see pages 850–851). After that the care needed is much

less than that for a lawn or flower bed. Meadows are self-supporting once they are established and the plants must be allowed to seed themselves. This means that the flowers and grasses must have gone to seed before you do any cutting.

Some cutting is necessary to keep down aggressively competitive weeds and grasses. So, depending on the look you want, cut in the fall for a summer-flowering meadow or at the beginning of summer for spring meadows. The summer meadow can then be kept cut until late in the following spring to keep it at a reasonable height and to continue to discourage unwanted competitors, but it may be left if you prefer. A spring meadow can be mown or scythed during the summer unless it is also planted with summer flowers, in which case after an early summer cut it won't need to be cut again until fall.

Many people prefer to make the first cut a close one. In any case, the mowings must be raked up, not left on the soil to feed it, as the essence of a successful meadow garden is a soil of fairly low fertility. Every so often competing plants may gain the upper hand. Weeding your meadow will help to keep them under control, but sometimes the only answer is to start again.

▶ *Once established, a meadow garden will be self-supporting, but will look slightly different each year as different plants flourish.*

▲ *In meadow planting carefully selected grasses and wild flowering plants mingle and flourish as nature would have chosen.*

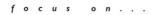

f o c u s   o n . . .

designer's meadow garden

A wildflower meadow humming with insect activity in high summer is a rare and delightful sight. Even in a small garden you can create a minimeadow, either by leaving an area of lawn to grow and produce its own colony of plants or by the deliberate introduction of a mix of wild flowers and grasses suited to the soil type.

▲ *Transforming an area of this large garden into a meadow will attract wildlife whose survival depends on nectar-rich plants.*

GARDEN DATA

location:	▦ Rhode Island
climate:	▦ cold/windy
soil type:	▦ light clay
direction:	▦ west facing
aspect:	▦ sloping towards trees

Design brief

The open space designated for this small patch of meadow planting is part of a large garden which is planted very informally. The soil is thin and chalky—ideal conditions for a dry-meadow planting. The owners want to add a splash of summer color which will be visible from the house and are prepared to learn how to use a scythe in order to "mow" the meadow in late summer. Otherwise, apart from removal of unwanted weeds, it will be left untouched.

Design solution

To avoid unwanted competition from vigorous grasses we stripped the existing turf. We undertook no further soil preparation other than removing surface stones.

There are many possibilities for flower and grass mixtures and even for a minicornfield. Here we chose a selection of plants which can cope with dry conditions and the slightly alkaline soil. Apart from myosotis

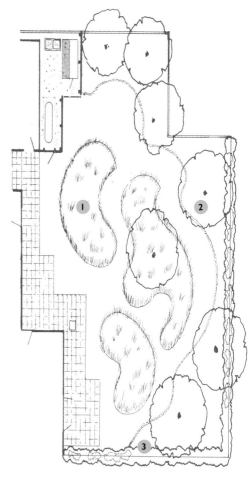

–25m x 13m/80ft x 42ft–

(forget-me-not) the plants are summer-flowering and after two or three years will establish and start to spread more or less vigorously.

flowering cherry

◄ *A flowering cherry is a focal point in the center of our designer's garden.*

ox-eye daisy

traditional hedge

► *A traditional country hedge is a wonderful boundary for a meadow garden.*

◄*Ox-eye daisies were once common in meadows and will grow well in a garden.*

8 4 7

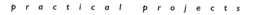

practical projects

To achieve a meadow haze you will need to become adept at raising plants from seed. But most meadow plants are either long-lived perennials or else self-seeding annuals, so once you have done the groundwork your garden should work for you. Seeds are available as named meadow or wild flower varieties and in mixes.

Easy sowing

Most suitable meadow plants can be grown easily from seed, and this is generally the best way to grow plants needed in such large quantities. Some seeds have to be sown directly into the ground as the young plants don't like to be disturbed, while others, such as the meadow cranesbill in our garden, can be started in seed trays and planted out into position as young plants. Seedlings always need light and warmth as well as moisture once they are growing, which means that seeds are generally sown outside only when the earth has warmed up, and the ground needs to be well watered unless it's been raining. Like the grass in our designer's meadow, seeds specifically sold as meadow mixtures are normally sown direct into the ground.

Individual plants

For accent plants, a very good alternative is to buy plug plants, which have been germinated and started off in ideal conditions. These are potted on into larger pots before being planted out in their chosen positions. (See page 973 for more information on buying and transferring plants.)

Grown in this way individual plants benefit from not having their roots disturbed when being moved on. Primrose, harebell, red campion, cowslip, ox-eye daisy, and cornflower are some of the meadow plants frequently available, and of course you can grow your own seedlings in the same way which will give you an even wider choice.

BROADCAST SOWING

For any meadow mixture, prepare the ground as you would for a lawn, except that no fertilizer should be added.

Rake over the surface to make it smooth and level. Scatter the seed by hand. Water in with a fine sprinkler.

sowing meadow seed

If you want more control over the final result than can be achieved by broadcast sowing, as described opposite, sow individual types of seed according to their specific requirements. Remember that germination rates vary depending on the species, and some will self-seed freely, so that the meadow will never look the same two years in succession.

1 Prepare the ground as normal, but add no supplementary fertilizer. For larger seeds, make shallow trenches with a trowel.

2 For smaller seeds, mark rills in the soil with a hoe. Some seed can be surface sown.

3 Sow the seed thinly. For large seed, allow a space of about 1cm/½in between seeds. Fine seed can be mixed with sand. Gently draw the soil over the seeds. Seedlings can be thinned once they have germinated.

4 By summer, the meadow will be a sea of color. The majority of meadow plants will self-seed, and over the course of the years the species best suited to the site will predominate.

meadow plants and planting

The key to a successful meadow garden is to encourage nature to do its best, not try to interfere with it. Having prepared the ground thoroughly, start your meadow by sowing seed in spring. Nature does the rest. Some plants will thrive in a wide range of meadow conditions, but patience is critical to success.

Before you sow

Perennial weeds can be a problem in a meadow garden and eliminating as many as possible before you begin is the aim. Start with a bare plot. Some meadow growers advocate plowing. In a smaller area you might consider rotovating—laying down black plastic for a year to suppress weeds—or even spraying the whole area with a harmless weedkiller (a glyphosphate type). Planting with potatoes for a year (a well-known clearing crop) is also a recommended way of preparing the ground. Those devoted to the task will remove perennial weeds by hand before they begin. Most meadows thrive on soil that is not too fertile so it may be best to remove the top layer of earth in an established garden, especially if the soil is of the fertile, loamy type or has been well cultivated over the years.

To select plants that will be at home in the type of soil and situation you have to offer, spend some time assessing this first, and then browse over the catalogs. The three main types of soil are the more fertile, medium to heavy soils (sometimes called "loamy" or "pasture"), and the poorer chalk, and sandy soils. You also need to assess whether the soil is dry/well-drained (usually in a sunny, open position) or whether it tends to be moist (and often more shaded). Ready-mixed seed such as 'cornfield

◄ Briza media *is a perennial grass.*

▲ Allium sphaerocephalon, *commonly called drumstick allium.*

▲ *Meadow clary will attract bees and insects to your wild garden.*

mix', 'hay meadow mix' (early-flowering), 'flowering lawn mix' (for shorter grass), and 'meadow flowers' (the most wide-ranging) are available. You will also find mixtures on offer for the various soil types, including acid or alkaline soils. Be prepared to spend some time selecting plants that will be at home in your plot. Otherwise of course, you can chance your luck and learn as you go.

Meadow grass

It's important to have suitable grass so that it doesn't dominate the wild flowers but instead acts as a foil for them. The grass itself will produce plumes of beige and buff flower heads which are part of the charm of a meadow garden.

Grass seeds are also available for starting meadows, while some flower mixtures contain a suitable grass seed as well, so check when you buy. If in doubt ask your seed supplier for advice before buying.

MEADOW PLANTING

Meadow in a lawn

You can sow meadow seeds directly onto grass in spring or fall. Cut the grass as low as possible and rake the lawn well to open it up. Broadcast a general "meadow mixture" seed and rake in lightly. (The soil should be moist.) Firm the area with a roller.

Keep the grass fairly closely cut during the first year so that it does not get ahead of the flowers. From year two, cut the grass in early May, then after summer flowering in late August, and again in late October

Moist meadow plants

astilbe	celandine
lady's smock	meadowsweet
mimulus	meadow buttercup
trollius	purple loosestrife

Plants for chalk and limestone

comfrey	cowslip
flax	harebell
hawkbit	knapweed
pinks, Cheddar	toadflax

Shady meadow plants

These plants are also suitable for growing under trees.

betony	bugle
forget-me-not	foxglove
herb robert	purple loosestrife

Bulbs, corms, and tubers for naturalizing

Scatter the bulbs and plant where they land, using a bulb planter. Plant each bulb with twice the amount of soil above it as its own depth. Bulbs are hungrier than true meadow plants and can benefit from an annual dressing of a high-potash fertilizer.

Plants marked (W) are also suitable for woodland conditions and shade.

bluebell (W)
crocus
celandine
daffodil (*Narcissus pseudonarcissus*)
grape hyacinth
lily-of-the-valley (W)
snowdrop (W)
wood anemone (W)
wood tulip (*Tulipa sylvestris*) (W)
wild garlic (*Allium ursinum*) (W)

Plants for thin, dry soils

Also for windswept areas and coastal conditions. Plants marked (S) are for sandy soil.

California poppy (S)	
clover	convolvulus
corncockle (S)	corn marigold (S)
evening primrose (S)	flax
harebell	lupin
mullein	pinks, Cheddar
St John's wort	toadflax
vetch	yarrow

Profile plants

Geranium pratense (meadow cranesbill) is one of the few meadow plants that require rich soil. *Leucanthemum vulgare* (ox-eye daisy) thrives in a multitude of situations. *Briza media* (quaking grass) is a delightful grass for a meadow.

design alternatives

SKETCHES

You can apply these meadow planting ideas to just a small patch of lawn, say 3m x 3m/ 10ft x 10ft—just choose "wet or dry" plantings depending on your soil conditions.

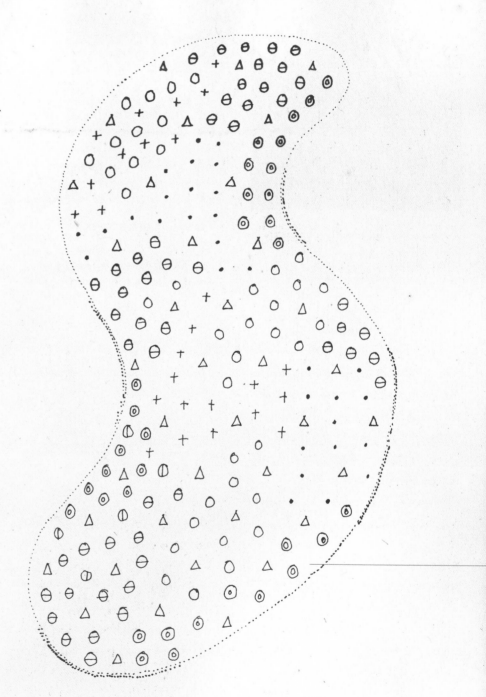

θ   meadow cranesbill

△   ox-eye daisy

①   Tulipa parrotica

◎   Allium sphaerocephalon

○   Nepeta faassenii

✝   Briza media

•   Salvia pratensis

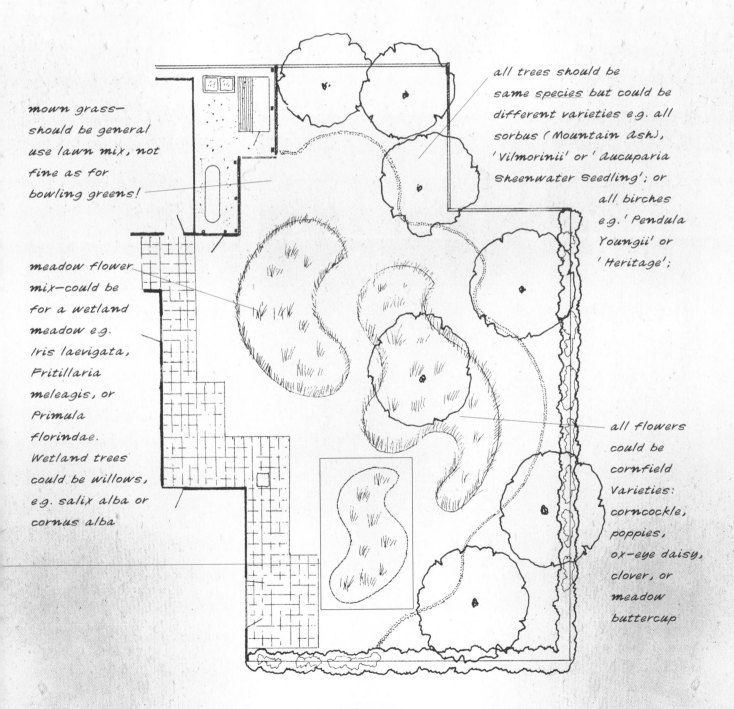

mown grass—should be general use lawn mix, not fine as for bowling greens!

all trees should be same <u>species</u> but could be different varieties e.g. all sorbus (Mountain Ash), 'Vilmorinii' or 'Aucuparia Sheenwater Seedling'; or all birches e.g. 'Pendula Youngii' or 'Heritage';

meadow flower mix—could be for a wetland meadow e.g. Iris laevigata, Fritillaria meleagis, or Primula florindae. Wetland trees could be willows, e.g. salix alba or cornus alba

all flowers could be cornfield varieties: corncockle, poppies, ox-eye daisy, clover, or meadow buttercup

shade garden

If your garden is naturally shady, why not go along with it and turn it into a green and pleasant place? And if you'd like to be out of the sun in a more exposed garden there are plenty of ways of creating a shady spot for an afternoon snooze and for indulging in green thoughts in the shade.

◄ *Hostas, astilbes, lamiums, and lady's mantle are among many plants that positively thrive in the shade and will look wonderful in any garden.*

A shady situation

Sometimes shade in the garden is dictated by the aspect or by neighbors' planting. If you live downhill your garden may well be shady, and if neighbors on the uphill side grow anything in the least bit tall this will exaggerate it. Or it may simply be that the folks on all sides have a taste for trees and this robs your garden of light. If so don't fight them, join them and make your neighborhood into a leafy oasis. Tall buildings, including your own house, can put your garden in shade for much of the time and in this case there is nothing you can do about these shady areas but learn to enjoy and work with them.

Shade is often associated with moisture and there are lots of plants that can be grown in moist, shady situations. If you are unlucky enough to have dry shade, or shade that is wet and water-logged in winter and dry and cracked in summer, your choice will be more limited. Like any peaceful garden, a shaded garden needs to provide you with somewhere to sit. It would even be possible to create a shady bower overhung with green climbing and twining plants in a sunny garden. It is best to locate your shade garden in a spot where it gets a ray of light in the morning or evening if this is possible as these are the times you are least likely to want to flee the sun.

A woodland theme

If your garden is big enough, or if the location is suitable (for example the house is in a wooded area or adjacent gardens already have trees and tall shrubs), a wonderful way to create shade is to grow a woodland garden.

Naturally the trees will take some years to grow, so you need to intend to stay put. There are some lovely plants to grow under deciduous trees, which let through a lot of light in winter and spring before the leaves come out and then cast a magical green dimness. To blend with a woodland theme you'll need a winding path, and open "glades" of grass. Bark chippings and log stepping stones are sympathetic materials for paths. You might also borrow from the meadow garden

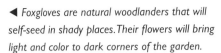

◄ *Foxgloves are natural woodlanders that will self-seed in shady places. Their flowers will bring light and color to dark corners of the garden.*

(pages 844–853) and have some areas of rough grass with woodland- or shade-loving wild flowers.

Bulbs naturalize beautifully under deciduous trees. Scattered and planted naturally, the spring-flowering bulbs look even prettier in newly growing grass and criss-crossed with the shade from branches of trees overhead.

A shade garden with only deciduous trees can look empty in winter. Using evergreens will continue the green theme into the bare season and also help to give a more decisive form to the garden. Many evergreen shrubs grow naturally in forests and supply either brilliant flowers in contrast to their leaves or unexpected scents for winter days or summer evenings.

It will be best to link the woodland area to the house by lower-growing and more formal planting. You don't want to step straight out into a wood, but rather to see it somewhat in the distance. An area of formally planted shrubs and flower companions, perhaps defined by low evergreen hedges, will arrange things beautifully.

◄ *A potted fern brings a touch of sophistication to this shady corner. Ferns suit container planting and can be moved in winter if tender.*

designer's shade garden

A shady site can be turned into a lush and leafy green oasis, or a woodland garden. It need not be without color at most times of the year and can always be planted with a variety of leaf textures and shapes. Dry shade under the canopy of large trees is more difficult, but even here ivy or gaulteria will cope adequately.

▲ *In this garden we decided to screen the summerhouse with trees to create an element of surprise and provide privacy.*

GARDEN DATA

location:	▪▪ *Pennsylvania*
climate:	▪▪ *temperate*
soil type:	▪▪ *neutral—alkaline*
direction:	▪▪ *north facing*
aspect:	▪▪ *overlooks railway bank*

Design brief

The north-facing garden forms a long rectangle, shaded on three sides by neighboring trees and on the fourth side by the house. Some year-round interest is required together with planting to balance the tall surrounding trees. There is a small summerhouse at the far end.

Design solution

We decided to turn the shadiness of the site into a positive feature by creating an informal woodland area round the summerhouse. We planted graceful birches, which will still allow some light through to the woodland floor. We massed different ground-cover plants beneath the trees to flower at different times of the year. A camellia puts on a stunning spring show against the dark green backdrop of the surrounding yew hedge. The planting was surrounded by a deep bark mulch—leaf mold would be even better—and we marked a gently meandering path

—19m x 11m/60ft x 35ft—

with a coarser grade of bark chippings in a lighter color. Nearer the house we contrasted the informality of the woodland with a geometric matrix of slabs set in closely mown grass. Formal box hedges enclose perennials and flowering shrubs and frame the path through the garden to the wood.

▲ Flower beds are edged with clipped box.

▲ Bark chippings are used as
a path to the summerhouse,
and to provide ground cover.

▲ Paving slabs are set in
the mown lawn.

box hedge

bark chips

paving slabs

practical projects

Hedging is a useful feature in many types of garden and a dense evergreen hedge will always add a formal touch and provide structure. A low hedge can be used to divide one part of the garden from another and a high hedge is a perfect way of concealing the "hard work" area of the garden from view.

An evergreen hedge

Box '*Buxus sempervirens*' is *the* plant for a traditional low evergreen hedge. It is ideal for a shady garden as the leaves can lose their strong green color if the light is too strong. We

◄ *There are many types of tools available for trimming box hedge, including shears, pruners, and clippers. Ask your garden center for advice.*

used it to make a neat dwarf hedge to enclose areas of looser planting.

If your budget can run to it, buying young plants is the best way to start, as establishing a hedge is a long-term project without the additional wait for cuttings to take root. However, it is possible to grow a temporary "hedge" using other plants (such as the annual summer cypress, *Kochia scoparia*) while you produce your own box plants, and growing plants from cuttings is very satisfying. So if you know someone whose box hedge needs trimming, step in and volunteer to help.

The best time to take cuttings is late summer, when the new growth is just beginning to ripen and become more woody. When taking cuttings the aim is not to let the plant material dry out. Therefore it's best to do it on a dull, damp day, and

to keep the cuttings in a plastic bag as you cut them. Cut off lengths up to 30cm/12in long, if possible taking them from side shoots. When you have enough, trim the cuttings to the same length, just below a leaf joint, and dip the cut ends into hormone rooting powder. Plant in pots or cutting mix or in a reserved area in the garden. You will need to add horticultural sand to the soil and cover the cuttings with cloches if you strike them in the garden.

DESIGNER'S TIPS

• Don't fight dense, dry shade—just accept that very few plants will thrive there. Try *Dryopteris filix-mas* (male fern), *Euphorbia robbiae* or *Vinca minor*. If there are lots of surface roots, reveal them and put gravel around them to make them a decorative feature in their own right.

• Use yellows and whites to brighten shady corners. *Euonymus japonica, Aureovariegatus* and *Euonymus fortunei* "Silver Queen" are excellent colorful shrubs for shade.

planting a box hedge

An evergreen hedge needs to be very carefully planted and maintained because its success depends on its formal quality. Planting lines should be marked with strings attached to pegs and the plants are normally spaced about 30cm/12in apart for a taller hedge of about 60cm/2ft high, and only 15cm/6in apart for a dwarf hedge. The hedge needs to be trimmed two to three times a year to keep it immaculate.

1 Mark the line of the hedge with a string stretched taut and attached to pegs driven into the ground. Dig a trench along the string.

2 Set the plants in the trench at the appropriate distance from each other and firm them in. Water well, then water daily until the plants are established and growing strongly.

CLIPPING A BOX HEDGE

Box responds well to clipping, which produces a sheer surface of tight, dense growth. Unless you have a very good eye, it can be a good idea to run a horizontal line at the height you wish to trim the hedge.

Box can be trimmed with shears, pruners, or the special clippers shown here. Hold the blades as near flush to the surface as possible. Be sure to trim wayward shoots right back. Trim in spring and mid- to late summer.

shady plants and planting

The garden we designed has shade of its own and needed a selection of plants that would thrive in and enhance it. In other gardens you may wish to grow plants in a light position in order to create shade. Deciduous plants will insure that shade is reduced to a pattern of shadows in winter when you want more light.

Green arbors

Climbing plants grown over an arbor or pergola can create areas of shade in a sunny garden. These structures need to be strongly made—or, if you buy them in kit form, well assembled and installed—as they eventually bear a strong weight and it's disheartening to have to dismantle and rebuild them just as the plants are reaching their peak of glory. Ideally a pergola should lead somewhere or extend all the way along the length of a wall. Plants to grow up trees or large shrubs should be planted some distance from the roots and guided toward their host with canes or strings.

Plants for creating shade

Honeysuckle (*Lonicera periclymenum*) and wisteria (*Wisteria sinensis*) are two lovely scented climbers, along with a few climbing roses. Russian vine (*Fallopia aubertii,* syn. *Polygonum aubertii*) is a terrifically fast climber for creating a green shade, though it will need to be kept severely within bounds—not for nothing is it known as mile-a-minute vine. A true vine, *Vitis coignetiae* provides cooling green leaves that overlap to form a lovely density, followed by a warm red glow in the fall. The hop plant (*Humulus lupulus*) is another leafy climber with flat, overlapping leaves, in green or a sharp greeny yellow (*H. l.* 'Aureus'). All these are deciduous, but shade is not such an objective in the winter, when the twining stems create their own beauty and the extra light will be welcome.

Wall plants in shade

As climbers to provide all-year green in shady places the ivies (*Hedera helix*) are invaluable. Or for a sheltered, shady wall there is *Trachelospermum asiaticum*, with waxy, scented flowers. The climbing hydrangea, *Hydrangea petiolaris* is a vigorous and tolerant wall plant which though deciduous looks good when bare.

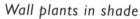
◀ Astilbes are excellent shade plants.

HOSTAS FOR SHADE

Hostas are the perfect plant for moist and shady places, with their generous mounds of overlapping, heart-shaped leaves and stems of small tubular flowers. They love the humus-rich soft earth under deciduous trees, where they get dappled shade. There is now a multitude of hostas, grown mainly for their leaves—often crinkled or rippled and having contrasting margins—in shades of green, golden green, or blue-green. Perhaps the best way to make a selection is to choose what appeals from your local plant center. Some special cultivars are listed here. It's essential to protect hostas from slugs and snails, which are particularly partial to this snack.

Hosta selection
H. 'Blue Wedgwood'
Hosta fortunei var. *aureomarginata*
(syn. *H.* 'Aureomarginata')
H. 'Frances Williams'
H. 'Halcyon'
H. 'Honeybells'
H. 'Sum and Substance'
Hosta sieboldiana var. *elegans*
H. *tokudama*
H. *undulata* var. *albomarginata*
H. *venusta*
H. 'Wide Brim'

▲ *The black birch has beautiful peeling bark.*

Profile plants

Betula nigra 'Heritage'
BLACK BIRCH

This is a tall but graceful birch for a woodland area, its whitish young bark peeling to reveal orange-brown new bark. In early spring it bears long, brown catkins and the brown leaves turn yellow in the fall.

ht 18m/60ft

sp to 12m/40ft

Soil and situation

Fertile, moist soil; shade.

GROUND-COVER PLANTS FOR SHADE

Lamium maculatum (dead nettle), *Tiarella cordifolia* (foam flower), epimedium (barrenwort), and *Vinca major* (periwinkle)

Ajuga reptans
BUGLE

A low-growing, spreading woodland plant with whorls of small, deep blue, or bronze flowers in spikes above the small green leaves.

ht 15m/6in

sp 60cm/2ft

Soil and situation

Moist soil and partial shade.

Astilbe 'Fanal'
ASTILBE

There are many different astilbes for growing in shady conditions, mainly in cream or shades of pink. 'Fanal' is an unusual variety in deep red with very dark foliage.

ht 60m/2ft

sp 45cm/18in

Soil and situation

Dry soil and semishade.

▼ Ajuga reptans *has spikes of deep blue flowers.*

design alternatives

SKETCHES

As a general design principle, when designing a formal, symmetrical garden, always work out the exact dimensions of the hard-landscaping first. This avoids the problem of having to cut the slabs to fit a fixed layout of plantings.

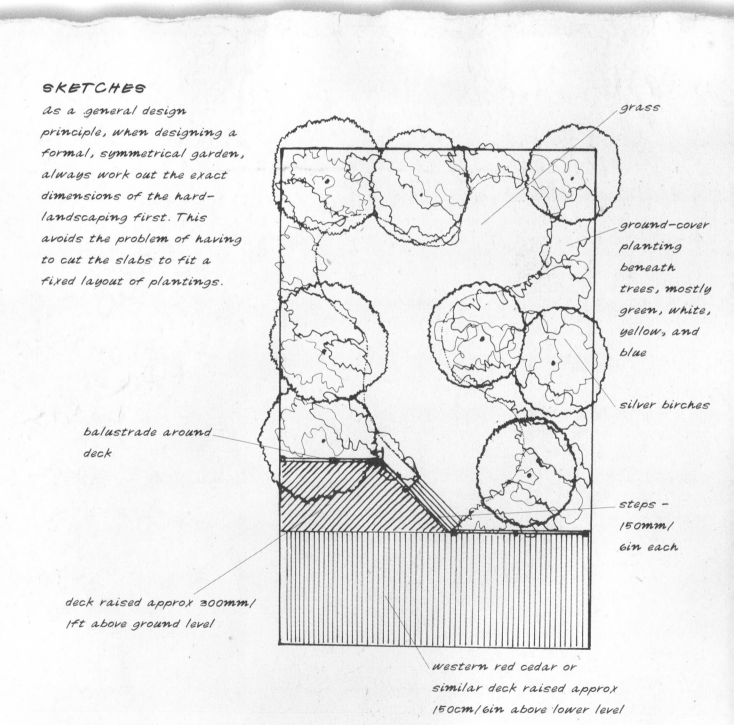

grass

ground-cover planting beneath trees, mostly green, white, yellow, and blue

silver birches

steps – 150mm/ 6in each

balustrade around deck

deck raised approx 300mm/ 1ft above ground level

western red cedar or similar deck raised approx 150cm/6in above lower level

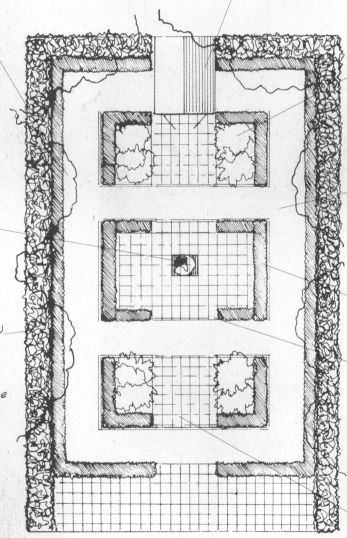

summerhouse 2.4m x 3m/8ft x 10ft,
painted white, or soft yellow

1.5m/5ft hedge of
Thuja plicata
aurea on 3 sides

two matching beds of
white hydrangeas or
Choisya ternata at
either end of garden

sculpture or
statue as main
focal point

creamy white 20mm/¾in
angular stone chippings

clipped buxus (box)
hedge 750cm/30in
high—immediately
next to thuja hedge

clipped box hedges
30in/750cm high

Victorian rope edge tiles
in terracotta or dark
slate blue

cream or white slabs
450cm x 450cm/17in x
17in

nb: This garden is ideal for non-gardeners—
only maintenance is clipping the hedges.

scented garden

Spring and summer are the best times for perfume in the garden, but winter offers its own heady delights—all the more so for being singled out through lack of competition. A scented garden has an added sensuous dimension, but some perfumes can be overpowering on a warm still day, so don't overdo it.

◄ *Roses are among the most richly scented of all plants and no traditional garden would be complete without their distinctive presence.*

The role of scent

Scent is extremely evocative and appeals to a primitive and powerful part of the brain. The compelling power of scent to affect the emotions is intensified by the beauty of many scented plants. At the botanical level scent draws pollinators to a plant. Pale-colored plants often give out their fragrance most strongly at night, when their paleness shows up best, and this is a two-pronged attraction for night pollinators, the moths. Colorful flowers attract day-time pollinators, the bees and butterflies, by their bright color, and therefore in general the more brightly colored flowers tend to offer less scent. Nature is generous, however, and gives us many colorful flowers (such as wallflowers, some roses, and hyacinths) that are also strongly perfumed. Aromatic—as

◄ *Combining a range of scented plants will produce a heady fragrance that hangs in the air and induces a romantic mood.*

pleasures that you will want to linger and breathe in the different parts of the garden. They also seem to go best with a soft approach: curving lawns, which can act as a path unless the garden is large; loose planting, with plants allowed to merge into each other to blend the gentle colors of most scented plants. To coordinate the relaxed and natural theme, willow hurdles form a sympathetic material for plant supports and boundaries. And this is another garden theme that needs seating. A scented seat at the end of the garden will give you somewhere to rest when you're swooning from the mingled scents and pleasures of your plot.

opposed to fragrant—plants have essential oils in their leaves to protect them from heat exposure. The scents of the oils are intensified by heat and give out their best when grown in southern, tropical-type climates. Less sensuous than invigorating, their scent indicates an antiseptic or medicinal value: thought to help protect the surrounding plants and flowers from disease.

Ingredients of the garden

Apart from the main distinction between fragrant and aromatic, it's very difficult to classify scents without referring to other scents— usually those of other flowers. So that roses are described as smelling of violets, lily of the valley, orange blossom, or even lemon, while pinks smell of cloves, and choisya of orange blossom, although buddleja is agreed

to smell of honey. Aromatherapists refer to the "notes" of fragrance, descending from the light and evanescent top notes (for example, associated with lemony scents), to the heavy and lingering base notes, with middle (floral) notes in between. The base notes, found in plants such as the strongly scented lilies, jasmine, night-scented stocks, tobacco plants, and many roses, can be quite overpowering. It's a good idea to mix your plants so that a happy blend is inhaled on the air, with top, middle and base notes all participating. And it makes sense to measure out the more overpowering scents by having areas of quietly scented companions. Scented plants offer so many

▶ *These beds of aromatic plants are surrounded by hedges of tightly clipped box, which has a curious scent of its own.*

designer's scented garden

A scented garden is essentially a romantic and feminine garden and is at its best on a warm summer's evening. The best site, even if it is just one corner of a larger plot, is a sheltered, warm position. Most fragrant plants release their perfumes in warm air and you will enjoy their scent more if it is not being blown clean away.

▲ *The narrowness of this garden will be disguised by the clever use of screens, which also provide shelter from the wind.*

GARDEN DATA

location:	▪▪ Northern California
climate:	▪▪ variable—mild
soil type:	▪▪ slightly acid
direction:	▪▪ south facing
aspect:	▪▪ open

The design solution

This garden is long and narrow and the restricted feeling of a corridor is made worse by the long, straight path which splits the garden into two even narrower slivers.

We designed a more sensuous, but simple ground pattern, employing wide, curving borders with a slim ribbon of grass running between them and screens to shelter each garden room. These both help contain the perfumes of the plants and act as supports for some of the climbing plants. There is a bench from which color, form, and scent can be enjoyed and the garden is lit on summer evenings, to encourage you to linger on with your glass of Chardonnay. We used romantic whites, creams, soft yellows, and blues in this scheme.

The grass path provides a lush, green carpet through the garden that does not distract from the scented air and the hum of bees.

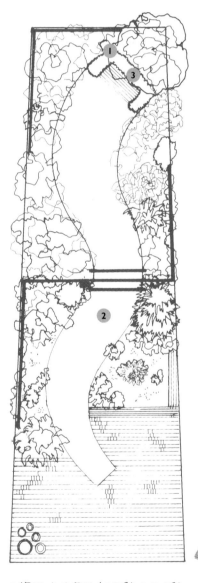

—15m x 6.5m / 48ft x 21ft—

screens

▶ Willow fences provide shelter.

lawn

▲ The lawn curves intriguingly, giving a sense of discovery.

seat

▲ A seat surrounded by scented plants offers an ideal place to unwind

867

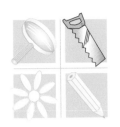

practical projects

To be complete, a scented garden will need a scented seat. This should be located where you will get a view over a large part of the garden, while some of it is still tantalizingly hidden, to give the illusion that there is yet more to be enjoyed.

▲ *There are many types of scented seats; this one has been carefully clipped into shape and surrounded by climbing roses.*

▲ *How better to relax and enjoy the sunshine than on a scented recliner? Simply grow a bed of thyme in the shape required—then lie back!*

A scented seat

The smell of box adds a cool, green note to a scented garden, and clipped box makes a lovely, rather architectural surround for a garden seat. As an alternative, you can create an informal scented seat in a covered arbor, made from a kit—or from your own design if you are sufficiently resourceful. Planted with climbing roses, jasmine, or honey-suckle this will give perfumed shade.

If you have the patience you can make a seat from an earth bank, solidly compacted and planted with thyme or camomile. But such seats, though most romantic, are in truth fragile. Far better is to build a seat into the retaining wall of a raised flower bed and use ordinary cushions for comfort. The scent of the herbs or flowers you use in the bed will still be released as you sit among the plants.

You can also import a stone or wooden seat, make a back for it with box or other clipped shrubs in beds

▲ *For artful simplicity, a rustic wooden seat is placed inside an arbor draped with beautiful scented leaves and flowers.*

or containers and grow beautifully scented plants in boxes at either end. Any ordinary garden bench can be made to look like a more permanent feature and incorporated into the garden by having an alcove made around it in this way.

building a scented seat

Filling a planter with low-growing scented and aromatic plants is a quick and easy way to concentrate perfume in the garden. If you position the planter near a garden seat or bench you can be sure of having fragrance to enjoy whenever you take a break from your labors. Painting the planter to match the seat makes it blend with the scheme.

1 Using a plant-friendly product, paint or stain the planter to match your seat.

2 To make the planter watertight, line with heavy-duty polyethylene. Cut the polyethylene to fit around the top and staple it in position. Punch holes at the bottom for drainage.

BOUNDARIES FOR SCENTED GARDENS

Ideal boundaries are old, warm and mellow brick or stone walls, against which scented climbers can be trained.

Most of us don't enjoy this luxury so use 1.8m/6ft trellis battened to your fence supports.

Grow an aromatic hedge to border your scented garden. *Rosmarinus*, 'Miss Jessup's Upright', or the slow growing *Buxus sempervirens* will make hedges up to 1.2m/4ft high.

3 Plant with your selected plants. Here we used thyme and lavender. A top-dressing of grit looks attractive and improves drainage.

4 Brushing your hand gently over the plants, particularly in hot weather, will release their distinctive aroma.

scented plants and planting

Plants in the scented garden are carefully arranged to make sure that there is something to offer at almost any time of year and at every level of the garden. They cover both fragrant and aromatic plants, including those which flower at nose level and those whose perfume rises up from the ground.

Profile plants

Philadelphus 'Belle Etoile'
MOCK ORANGE

A heavenly scent of orange blossom drifts from the creamy white, four-petaled flowers in early summer. In this species the flowers have a dash of maroon at the center, and the shrub is small enough for any garden. Should be pruned after flowering.

ht and sp 2m/6.5ft

Soil and situation

Well-drained soil; sun or partial shade.

Erysimum × *allionii*
(syn. *Cheiranthus* × *allionii*)
SIBERIAN WALLFLOWER

This is a wallflower with stunning bright orange coloring and a powerful scent to match. A short-lived perennial, it is always grown as a spring and early summer bedding plant.

ht 40cm/16in

sp 30cm/12in

Soil and situation

Fertile, well-drained soil, preferably neutral or alkaline, and a position in full sun.

Viola odorata
ENGLISH VIOLET
OR SWEET VIOLET

A spreading and very fragrant violet, flowering all spring with deep violet-purple flowers, sometimes white or pink. Violets are lovely low-growing

▶ Erysimum *x* allionii, *Siberian wallflower.*

◀ Philadelphus *'Belle Etoile' or mock orange.*

plants for naturalizing in moist, cool places. Various named hybrids are grown (known as florists' violets), including the double violet 'Duchesse de Parme' and the pink-flowered 'Coeur d'Alsace'.

ht 15cm/6in

sp to 40cm/16in

Soil and situation

Fertile, well-drained soil in a semi-shaded position, or in sun as long as the ground is cool.

Shrubs and trees for scent

Choisya ternata
(Mexican orange blossom)
(see pages 944–945)
Daphne mezereum—small, heavily
scented, purple-pink flowers in
winter/spring; must have alkaline soil
ht to 90cm/3ft
Caution: the berries are poisonous
Fothergilla major and *F. gardenii*
(see page 993)
Magnolia grandiflora—magnificent tree
for sheltered areas; summer flowers
with a spicy fragrance
ht 9m/30ft
See also *Magnolia stellata*
(Star Magnolia)
(see pages 807)
Rhododendron luteum
(Ghent azaleas)—rhododendrons and
azaleas are not noted for fragrance,
but these hybrids have a strong, warm
honeysuckle scent and brilliant
yellow flowers in late spring; need
acid soil
ht to 3m/10ft
Sambucus (Garden elder)
(see pages 994–995)
Syringa cultivars (lilacs)—flowers in
purples through to white, with wafts
of the most heady scent toward the
end of spring
ht 1.8–4.5m/6–15ft
(see also pages 890–891)
Viburnum cultivars—all the winter-
and spring-flowering viburnums have
delicious scent
(see page 995)

A SELECTION OF SCENTED PLANTS

Scent in full summer

Heliotropium arborescens (syn. *H. peruvianum*)
heliotrope or cherry pie plant
Lathyrus odoratus sweet pea (see page 977)
Lavandula species lavender (see page 988)
Lilium regale and other lilies (see page 893)
Matthiola bicornis night-scented stock
Matthiola incana Brompton stock
Nicotiana tobacco plants (see page 978)
Pelargonium crispum and *P. x fragrans*
pelargoniums with scented leaves
Petunia hybrids petunias
Phlox paniculata garden phlox (see page 989)

▲ *Midsummer flowering Lilium regale.*

Scent in spring and early summer

Convallaria majalis lily-of-the-valley
Dianthus species pinks and carnations
Erysimum species (syn. *Cheiranthus*) wallflowers
Hesperis matronalis dame's violet or sweet
rocket
Hyacinthus cultivars hyacinth
Narcisssus jonquilla (jonquil) and many other
narcissi
Paeonia 'Sarah Bernhardt'—peony in apple
blossom pink
Primula vulgaris and *P. auricula* primrose and
auricula

Roses for perfume

Almost all roses are perfumed but this is a
selection of favorites
Rosa 'Boule de Neige'—a repeat-flowering
bourbon rose with large flowers like white
camellias
ht 1.5m/5ft
Rosa 'Cardinal de Richelieu'—a gallica rose,
with dusky purple red flowers
ht 1.5m/5ft
Rosa centifolia 'Robert le Diable'—a cabbage
rose, in mauve, pink, violet, and crimson
ht 1.2m/4ft
Rosa damascena—the damask rose has
varieties in white, pink, red
ht to 1.5m/5ft

Rosa gallica officinalis—deep crimson/striped
(see pages 786–787)
Rosa 'Margaret Merril'—small floribunda or
cluster-flowered rose with delicate flowers in
blush white
ht 75cm/30in
Rosa moschata (musk rose)—creamy white
old-fashioned climber
ht to 4m/13ft
Rosa 'Mme Pierre Oger'—a bourbon rose,
globular flowers in silvery pink all summer
ht 1.5m/5ft
Rosa 'Penelope'—a hybrid musk with flowers
in pale salmon pink all summer
ht to 1.2m/4ft
Rosa rugosa 'Blanc Double de Coubert'—
rugosa rose with white flowers all summer; big
red hips
ht 1.8m/6ft
Rosa 'Zéphirine Drouhin'—climber for wall or
trellis with masses of deep rose-pink flowers
all summer (suits a shady wall)
ht 3.6m/12ft
Rosa 'William Lobb'—a repeat-flowering old
moss rose with deep crimson flowers fading
to pale violet
ht 1.8m/6ft

design alternatives

SKETCHES
These plans feature different garden "rooms" which lead one through an adventure of scents, textures, and colors.
The combination of herb, rose and perennial "rooms" insures there is scent throughout the gardening year.

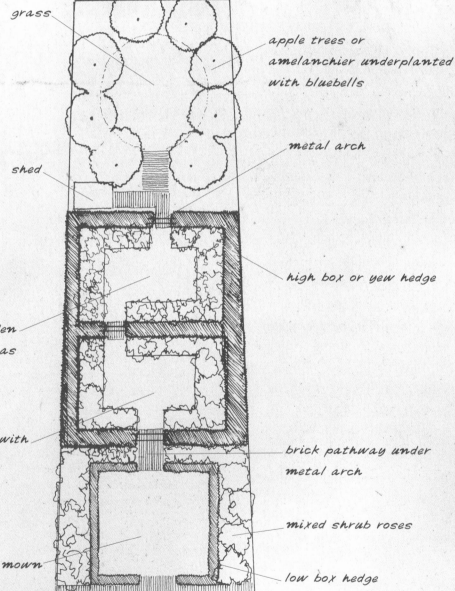

grass

apple trees or amelanchier underplanted with bluebells

metal arch

shed

high box or yew hedge

a perennials garden with mown lawn as center

a herb garden with mown lawn

brick pathway under metal arch

mixed shrub roses

a rose garden with mown lawn

low box hedge

brick patio

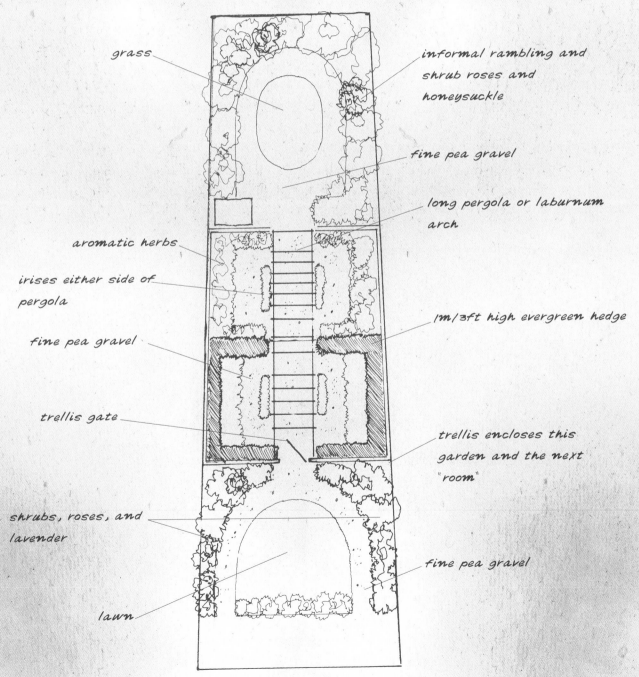

grass

informal rambling and shrub roses and honeysuckle

fine pea gravel

long pergola or laburnum arch

aromatic herbs

irises either side of pergola

1m/3ft high evergreen hedge

fine pea gravel

trellis gate

trellis encloses this garden and the next "room"

shrubs, roses, and lavender

fine pea gravel

lawn

Zen garden

A Japanese Zen garden is understood not in terms of its ingredients but only by looking at its overall meaning—nothing is fortuitous or haphazard. All the elements employed in the garden have a symbolic significance related to a quest for spiritual enlightenment. Restraint and simplicity are the keys.

What are the elements?

Whether or not we understand Zen symbolism, we can borrow ideas from Japanese gardens to make our own peaceful and beautiful retreats that, with care, do not look too much out of place in a Western setting.

When you relax at the end of the garden, perhaps you will think about your spiritual journey through the world. If not, it will still be a nice calm and peaceful place to sit.

While some elements come from Buddhist monastery gardens, the Zen garden of today is largely based on a Japanese invention of early medieval times, and its development responded to the practices of the tea ceremony, which was given mystical and ritual dimensions by the Zen priests and their disciples who took part in it. The participants at a tea ceremony reflected on nature and sought inner stillness by contemplating flowers, pottery, and beautifully illustrated calligraphic scrolls in the confines of a tea house. The Zen garden was the medium through which they passed on their way to the sanctum of contemplation.

A spiritual journey

The garden sought to imitate nature in the wild, and provided a path representing a mountain journey— a metaphor for the spiritual journey in search of the eternal. So the

◄ *Traditionally the clean, simple design of a Zen garden creates a retreat, and the possibility for quiet, tranquil contemplation.*

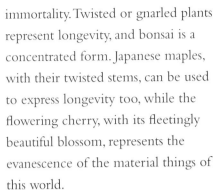

▶ *Boulders and gravel in Zen gardens symbolize mountains and water, associated in Buddhist thought with visions of paradise.*

essence of the Zen garden is that we move through it and lose our baser selves on the way. The ingredients, charged with symbolism, were an entrance (the journey's beginning), a path (the way to knowledge or enlightenment), a seat on which to break the journey and pause in meditation, a gate or threshold, beyond which to move on, leaving behind the social world of the city and entering the world of nature. Finally, there was somewhere to wash the hands, representing a mountain stream and symbolic of purification, and at the journey's end, a tea house as a place of final contemplation.

Symbolism in the garden

Paradise in Buddhist thought was symbolized by mountains surrounded by water, and in a Zen garden water and rocks represent these elements. Much play is made of the contrast between rocks or pebbles and water. When using boulders it's important to lay the stone in accordance with its natural grain. (If you are serious about it, you won't even lay the stone on its side while maneuvering it into position.) Placing the stone in this way makes sense aesthetically, and is spiritually significant. Evergreen plants are used to symbolize

immortality. Twisted or gnarled plants represent longevity, and bonsai is a concentrated form. Japanese maples, with their twisted stems, can be used to express longevity too, while the flowering cherry, with its fleetingly beautiful blossom, represents the evanescence of the material things of this world.

Water itself need not be present. The raked gravel of Buddhist gardens, which has now caught on in the West, is used to represent flowing water. Raking it quietly each morning or evening can be a soothing meditation. Rocks or boulders set within the gravel represent the water-surrounded mountains of paradise. They should be placed at the far end of the garden, as paradise is always distant. Straight lines are to be avoided—the spirit of contemplation follows best a winding path—but they can be broken, and begun again, and this will slow down the rush of energy that is not conducive to contemplation. Overall balance in design is achieved by a measured lack of symmetry.

Colors should be subtle and limited. The natural colors of stone, timber, and bamboo, and the green of bamboo plants and evergreen shrubs form a calm, quiet backdrop.

◀ *This contemporary interpretation of Zen principles features neatly raked gravel and a delicate purple iris planted in bamboo.*

designer's Zen garden

Buddhist monks designed the earliest Zen gardens around 900 years ago. In these gardens austere, abstract arrangements of rocks, water, and plants represent nature in miniature. Western gardeners have returned again and again to this deceptively simple combination of materials to try to recreate this timeless style.

▲ *Recent travels in the Far East inspired the owner of this rectangular plot to design a minimalist Japanese garden.*

GARDEN DATA

location:	▪▪ *Massachusetts*
climate:	▪▪ *temperate*
soil type:	▪▪ *sandy*
direction:	▪▪ *west facing*
aspect:	▪▪ *urban*

The brief

Steve traveled extensively in the Far East before recently acquiring his first house. His rectangular garden is ideally shaped and he would like to use this to advantage to create a minimalist garden with a distinct Japanese influence.

The design solution

For complete privacy and shelter we enclosed the garden on three sides, using screening trellis panels wired to thick bamboo poles. This focuses attention entirely on the garden, ignoring the surrounding landscape and buildings. The basic design flows through three distinct areas in the garden. Inside the boundary a hedge was planted, which will be clipped to form hill shapes as it grows. Large rocks, smaller boulders, pebbles, and paddle stones were carefully chosen to complement each other in size, markings, and color, positioned to create a balanced, asymmetric design. The main surface material is fine stone chippings, raked to suggest the flow of water. Stepping stones lead to a still, calm pool, positioned to reflect the ever-changing sky.

▲ Raked gravel symbolizes flowing
water in Buddhist thought.

▲ A Zen pool is the central feature.

― 31 m x 6m / 100ft x 18ft ―

▲ Boulders set in moss are used as a path.

practical projects

In a Zen garden stone and wood combine with the element of water, and paths and bridges are of symbolic as well as practical importance. All materials must be chosen with care—everything should be natural in an elemental way—and a simple wooden bridge over the water is in complete harmony in this garden.

Zen bridges

We advise you seek professional garden or building advice before building your bridge. There are many designs to inspire, the essential difference is how the timber is laid, lengthways or crossways. Use hardwood or treated softwood in a firm base.

DESIGNER TIPS

• Stone, water, and plants are the three main elements of a Zen garden.

• If possible, choose local stone for all the stones and boulders used in your garden.

• Position large stones and boulders singly, or in groups of three, five, or seven.

• Zen gardens are never symmetrical. Balance is achieved through controlling the asymmetric design.

• Big stones may weigh a ton, or more. Make sure access to your garden is sufficient and be prepared to pay installation costs, which may be much greater than the cost of the stone itself.

• Choose Japanese stone or concrete lanterns and similar ornaments with care—they can look too obviously mock-Japanese.

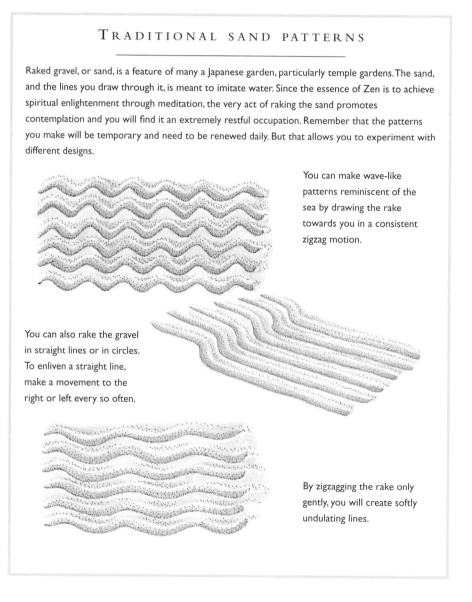

TRADITIONAL SAND PATTERNS

Raked gravel, or sand, is a feature of many a Japanese garden, particularly temple gardens. The sand, and the lines you draw through it, is meant to imitate water. Since the essence of Zen is to achieve spiritual enlightenment through meditation, the very act of raking the sand promotes contemplation and you will find it an extremely restful occupation. Remember that the patterns you make will be temporary and need to be renewed daily. But that allows you to experiment with different designs.

You can make wave-like patterns reminiscent of the sea by drawing the rake towards you in a consistent zigzag motion.

You can also rake the gravel in straight lines or in circles. To enliven a straight line, make a movement to the right or left every so often.

By zigzagging the rake only gently, you will create softly undulating lines.

▼ *This elegant wooden structure is reminiscent of Monet's Japanese Bridge of Giverny, in Northern France. It is a wonderful example of the beauty of simple design.*

▲ *Simplicity is the keynote of any Japanese garden. Rocks, plants, and gravel all play a key part and are each placed with great precision.*

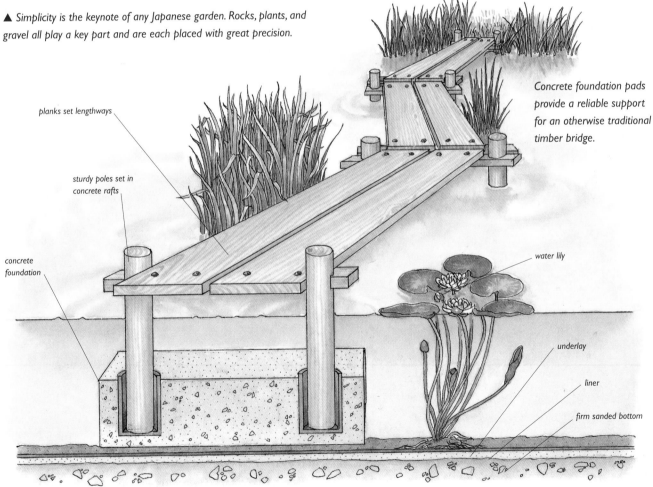

planks set lengthways

Concrete foundation pads provide a reliable support for an otherwise traditional timber bridge.

sturdy poles set in concrete rafts

concrete foundation

water lily

underlay

liner

firm sanded bottom

▲ *This Zen bridge follows a traditional Japanese zigzag course.*

Zen plants and planting

Restraint is the theme in planting a Zen garden. Green is the main color from plants, to contrast with the natural materials used in the garden. A limited amount of blossom—ideally in red—is permitted. The best plants are bamboos; evergreen, glossy-leaved shrubs; and Japanese maple, or a flowering cherry tree.

Bamboos and their care

Closely related to grasses and sedges, bamboos are evergreen, and as well as providing architectural shapes and delightful foliage, they also bring gentle movement and rustling sound to the garden. They grow up to 4m/13ft, in some species even more, and can make island clumps whose spread may sometimes overstep the limits (but see below), as well as lovely hedging and screening plants. Their hollow, woody culms take about three years to mature into canes. The canes are high in silica, which makes them very strong, and they can be cut for use, either as plant supports or for more ambitious projects such as screening. Bamboos are not all fully hardy and are best grown in a sheltered place.

Cultivation

Bamboos appreciate moisture, so when you plant them add plenty of fibrous organic material such as coir or—if you can get hold of it—chopped straw to absorb and retain water. Don't use garden compost, however, as it will be too rich. An occasional feeding with calcium silicate will help them to grow strong culms but otherwise they need no supplementary feeding.

The best time for planting out bamboos is in spring, and it should be just before it rains. The leaves should not be allowed to become dry as they will quickly wither and die,

◀ *Japanese maples suit a Zen garden.*

so look after them until the plants are established by spraying them with water. You can restrict the spread of bamboo by digging around the clump at the desired limits and inserting a rigid, nonperishable plastic collar about 30cm/12in deep or to the depth of the roots.

Profile plants

Acer palmatum var. *heptalobum* 'Rubrum'
JAPANESE MAPLE

More of a shrub than a tree, this form of the Japanese maple has bronze leaves which are red as they first open and which turn a fiery red in the fall. Its spreading and contorted branches give a very authentic Zen appearance.

ht and sp to 6m/20ft

Soil and situation

Fertile, moist but well-drained soil,

◄ Bamboos are essential in any Zen garden.

preferably neutral or acid, and a sheltered position.

Camellia japonica
CAMELLIA

There are literally thousands of Japanese camellias, a most magnificent group of evergreen shrubs with dark green, polished leaves and luscious peony-like winter flowers (also other forms, including single, semidouble and double). The flowers must have shelter from morning sun in areas prone to frost as hastily melted frost makes the petals brown. *A. j.* 'Alexander Hunter' is semidouble, deep red, with yellow stamens; 'Paul's Apollo' (aka 'Apollo') has red, semidouble flowers and suits a temperate climate. 'Dr. H. G. Mealing' is blood red and semidouble; 'Kouron-jura' is dark red and fully double; 'Letitia Schrader' has dark red, large peony flowers.

ht to 8.5m/26ft

sp 7.3m/24ft

◄ A red form of Camellia japonica.

Soil and situation

Must have moist, fertile, well-drained, acid soil and should be mulched with shredded bark. In the northern zones a sheltered north- or west-facing position is ideal.

HARDY BAMBOOS FOR SMALL GARDENS

Chusquea culeou (Chilean bamboo)—delicate, whitish green leaves
ht 4.5m/15ft

Fargesia murieliae (umbrella bamboo)—grayish green culms and apple-green leaves
ht 3.6m/12ft

Phyllostachys nigra var. *henonis* green and very leafy, not completely hardy
ht 9m/30ft

Phyllostachys viridiglaucescens—green and very leafy, not completely hardy
ht to 7.5m/25ft

Pleioblastus auricomus—yellow and green variegated leaves; purple-green culms
ht 1.5m/5ft

Pleioblastus simonii 'Variegatus' (syn. *Arundinaria simonii* 'Variegata')—white-striped leaves
ht to 3m/10ft

Pleioblastus variegatus—cream-striped leaves and pale green culms
ht 75cm/30in

Pseudosana japonica (arrow bamboo)—olive-green culms mature to light beige
ht to 4.5m/15ft

Sasa veitchii—white-edged green leaves and purple culms
ht to 1.8m/6ft

Semiarundinaria fastuosa (Narihira bamboo) thick green culms mature to dark red
ht 6m/20ft

Yushania anceps (anceps bamboo)—shiny, dark green culms, arching when mature
ht 2–3m/6.5–10ft

design alternatives

SKETCHES

These alternative layouts
follow the same *minimalist*
principles, using natural
materials and restrained
planting. Both suit slightly
shaded, rather than fully
open positions, so that
mosses and ferns can
flourish. Use just one
section of these gardens to
make an outdoor Japanese
courtyard or "room."

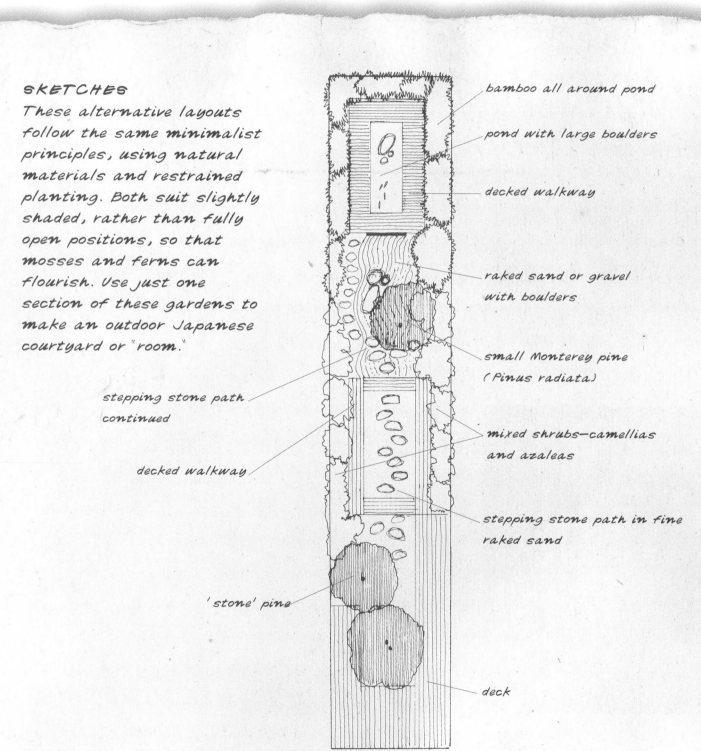

bamboo all around pond

pond with large boulders

decked walkway

raked sand or gravel
with boulders

small Monterey pine
(Pinus radiata)

mixed shrubs—camellias
and azaleas

stepping stone path in fine
raked sand

stepping stone path
continued

decked walkway

'stone' pine

deck

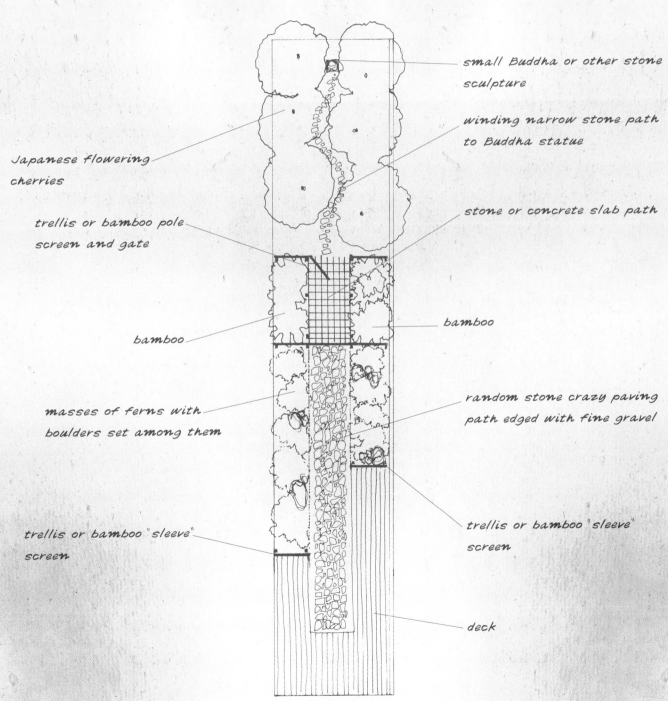

small Buddha or other stone sculpture

winding narrow stone path to Buddha statue

Japanese flowering cherries

trellis or bamboo pole screen and gate

stone or concrete slab path

bamboo

bamboo

masses of ferns with boulders set among them

random stone crazy paving path edged with fine gravel

trellis or bamboo "sleeve" screen

trellis or bamboo "sleeve" screen

deck

883

night garden

Somewhere to eat; ways to walk in safety; the drama of the garden brought out by lighting; nighttime scents—these are the ingredients of a garden to be enjoyed by night. Even if your garden is not intended specifically to be used at night it's a factor to take into account when you're thinking about its design.

◀ *These uplights cast interesting shadows on the rocks, in a minimalist urban garden with strong hard-landscaping.*

Designing for night

Dining outside is always a pleasure, and an area near the house for this is an asset in any garden. In the later summer, dusk begins to come early and it's often at this time of year that hot days leave a lingering warmth behind them. Lighting will be needed, and even by candlelight or by the light of little table lamps, the immediate light has a strange effect on the surrounding darkness, which can make it seem almost threatening. So lighting in the garden comes into play. And it can be used to dramatize the garden and create theatrical features, such as the pale slender stem of a silver birch, a piece of statuary or sculpture, or moving water. (Do remember, however, that your neighbors won't want the light shining on to them, and neither will you want it shining in your eyes.)

▶ *Special submerged lamps are used to illuminate the fountains, while further lighting is used to make a dramatic backdrop.*

Lighting and installation

Lighting for gardens must naturally be safely installed and is not normally a job for the home improver, particularly if you decide you need a mains-voltage system, with a standard 120-volt line for brilliant, intense lighting. For softer lighting a low-voltage (12V) is all you require and to adapt the power supply you need a transformer, which can be plugged into an indoor socket. Low-voltage cable must be safely hidden away so that you can't trip over it or cut into

it in the garden, whereas mains voltage cable must be thoroughly insulated and safely and deeply buried—not to be attempted by an amateur, however capable. Cable-free solar lighting, of course, needs no installation at all, but solar lights can't be expected to provide more than low-level lighting.

Key points

For best results remember less means more. A small amount of well-sited lighting is by far the most dramatic. Lighting should be at different levels, using uplights and downlights set at different heights, and of course the nuts and bolts should not be visible. The basic fittings are flexible spots or broadly rectangular floodlights. Spiked in the ground or fixed at low level these can be used as "uppers" for uplighting, to focus on trees, sculpture, arbors, or large shrubs;

◀ *Carefully positioned lighting will bring a hidden corner of the daytime garden to life after the sun has gone down.*

fixed high up they function as "downers" for downlighting to light paths, patios or trees (in which case called "moonlighting"). Spotlights can also wash light across a wall ("grazing") or give backlight to silhouette plants with architectural shape such as phormiums or with alluring movement such as grasses and bamboo. Shaded lights, such as mushroom types, are good for diffusing light over a low area for paths and steps.

Floodlighting casts a more widely diffused light that's more blurred at the edges than spotlighting. It too can be used either to backlight an area from behind, lighting up the background plants and throwing foreground plants into silhouette, to flood a designated area. Lights are available for wall or post fixing and as spikes. The effect of the light comes partly from the bulb and partly from the way it is housed. Halogen bulbs are generally best for mains or low-voltage use, and must be fully waterproof.

designer's night garden

A garden takes on a magical, mysterious quality at night if it is carefully lit. The key is subtlety and restraint. Good, low voltage lighting extends the use of the garden, enhancing features, while safety lighting is invaluable along a path or beside steps. Portable lamps or candles are best suited for lighting the dining area.

▲ *The owners wanted a garden that would be low-maintenance and allow for evening entertaining or just relaxing.*

GARDEN DATA

location:	▪▪ New Jersey
climate:	▪▪ urban—temperate
soil type:	▪▪ clay
direction	▪▪ west facing
aspect:	▪▪ urban

Design brief

This garden is not used very much in daylight hours as the owners run their own business and often work at weekends. They want a pleasant, low maintenance space in which to enjoy summer evenings with friends and relax after work.

Design solution

The garden is fortunate in containing one of the loveliest of trees—an elegant weeping silver birch. This is a perfect subject for moonlighting, which will show off its delicate, fluttering foliage all summer. In winter the graceful, weeping branches and satiny white bark will provide an attractive focal point through dark evenings. On the other side of the garden we back-lit softly a contemporary stone sculpture. The dark shadowy angles and curves are dramatically heightened at night and while the white sculpture and white birch complement each other they are positioned far enough apart not to fight for attention. Having chosen our subjects we constructed two decks from which to view and enjoy the theatrical effects of the scheme. Four concealed safety lights were added beneath the front edges of the decks to complete this simple scheme and also prevent tripping over the deck.

sculpture

▲ Modern sculpture is a central feature.

up-lit tree

▲ White bark, lit from below, is stunning at night.

candles

◀ Candles elegantly placed on deck.

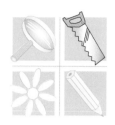

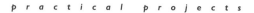

practical projects

Nighttime gardens can be havens of complete peace and tranquility. Forget boom boxes and all-night parties (and anyway these will make you a most unpopular neighbor). Instead concentrate on making a soothing environment where you can relax and find peace after a hard day's work.

Nighttime drama

For most people lighting is a crucial ingredient of a garden at night. Even if you intend to employ an electrician (to be recommended unless you really know what you're

▲ *Lighting need not be subtle or hidden but can be a feature in itself. This dramatic light sculpture takes central place in the garden.*

doing) you will want to know a bit about what is involved and what the options are (opposite).

It's best to think about lighting installation when planning the garden, because installation can cause major disruption. Cable routes need to be worked out with care and it makes sense to install cable for lighting and any water feature at the same time—and certainly before you put in any hard-landscaping.

The main point of outdoor lighting is to accent features of the garden with lighting, generally uplighting, aimed at plants or objects (as described on pages 884–885). This can be done by means of a small spot placed near the object or a more powerful one placed farther away. Spots can be focused on the same object from different places in the garden for high drama and of course you can also have different beams pointing in different directions from the same source. The light should point from where you will sit to

what you will be looking at; think about whether there are various places where you will want to sit and consider the lighting from each.

DESIGNER'S TIPS

• If you plan to have a patio remember to lay the ducting that will carry power cables before you install the paving.

• Make sure that the beam from any light fittings will not shine directly in your eyes as you move through the garden.

• Avoid submerged pond lighting—as often as not it will simply light up algae growth.

• If you are near a street, check that your lighting system will neither be canceled out by streetlights nor dazzle drivers.

BASIC LIGHT FITTINGS

• **Flexible up-lighter**—lights from below: trees, sculptures, pergolas, arbors, or large shrubs can wash light across a wall—called "grazing." Also used to backlight or uplight plants with strong architectural shapes or lots of movement—such as phormiums or grasses.

• **Flexible down-lighter**—lights from above: trees, "moonlighting," paths, or patios.

types of garden lighting

Here are some examples of the many types of lamps, lights, and candles available.

▶ *Accent lighting creates a dramatic effect. Remember that your ground surface may also be highlighted.*

▼ *A simple, lit candle staked securely in the ground is an elegant option for temporary lighting.*

▲ *Low-voltage lighting creates a subtle glow and this small light is hidden in long grasses.*

▲ *A light placed in a border is camouflaged from view, but at night will single out a chosen plant.*

▲ *This lantern holds a night light. It is safely away from children and is removed in daytime.*

▲ *Traditional lanterns attached to the wall are useful for barbecue areas and general lighting.*

night plants and planting

At nighttime a garden will develop hidden depths. As the colors fade in the dusk red takes on a deep, mysterious glow before it too is lost into darkness and just the palest flowers glimmer. Scents of the night arise after a warm day, and calm and tranquillity descend—this is a wonderful time to enjoy your garden.

Plants for nighttime gardens

Romantically minded people will think first of scented plants when planning out a garden for night. From the point of view of dramatic effect shrubs and trees light up well and create an atmosphere, and the foliage of a well-sited evergreen shrub will be welcome near the sitting area to make it feel sheltered and enclosed all year round. For a garden that will be used mainly at night you don't need to worry too much about detail—which will all disappear in the dark. Concentrate on well-shaped trees and shrubs and invest your money in a pleasing piece of sculpture. Incidental scent and pale patches in the dusk will come from annuals and biennials, and from long-lasting plants such as a favorite rose and lovely lilies. For a larger selection of spring- and summer-flowering scented plants see the list on pages 870–871.

Profile plants

Syringa vulgaris, white varieties
WHITE LILAC

Any white lilac is a gift to the night-time garden. Its heady scent marks the transition from spring to summer—the time when we first start to enjoy being out of doors in the evenings—and the pale flowers

◀ Syringa vulgaris, *white lilac.*

ghost beautifully in the dark. 'Mme Lemoine' is a wonderful variety which has heavy heads of double flowers in creamy white. 'Maud Notcutt' has huge, single flowers in white, and the more compact shrub 'Vestale' has long, loose panicles of white flowers.

ht 3.6m/12ft

sp 3m/10ft

Soil and situation

Lilacs flourish best in a rich, fertile, and fairly moist soil, and a sunny situation. They do well on alkaline soils. Prune them every three years to maintain a well-rounded shape.

Dianthus 'Mrs Sinkins'
WHITE GARDEN PINK

Garden pinks and carnations are not difficult to grow as long as they have the conditions they enjoy, and with their sweet, clovey scent they are perfect for sniffing at night. Though long-lived, they generally weaken after a time and need to be replaced

◀ Dianthus *'Mrs Sinkins'*.

about every three to five years. Pinks are generally smaller than carnations; both come in single and double versions and both can be beautifully marked, eyed, ringed, or laced with a contrasting color. The gray foliage is part of their charm. 'Mrs Sinkins' is a lovely old-fashioned white pink—frilly, loose-flowered, and double, and with a longer life than many *Dianthus*. It's well known for its strong scent, making up for the fact that, like most old-fashioned pinks, it does not flower again (until next year) after its first flowering period, in early summer.

ht 38cm/15in

sp 30cm/12in

Soil and situation

Pinks and carnations need neutral, well-drained soil and will flourish on thin, chalky soil. They do best in a sunny position but where the summer is not too hot. A wet winter in cold soil does them no good but otherwise they are conveniently tolerant and hardy.

Matthiola incana 'Giant Excelsior'
BROMPTON STOCKS

Brompton stocks are deliciously scented biennials for late spring or early summer, flowering from seed sown the previous year, and are often bought as young plants ready for

▶ Matthiola incana *'Giant Excelsior'*.

planting out in spring. 'Giant Excelsior' are tall, bushy stocks generally grown as an annual and flowering in early summer. They have the soft, gray-green leaves common to the stocks and the long spikes of heavily scented flowers are in pale pink, deep red, cloudy blue, and creamy white. They may need staking if they grow too tall.

ht 70cm/28in

sp 30cm/12in

Soil and situation

Moist and fertile, well-drained, preferably lime-rich soil, and a position in sun or semishade. At their best in calm, warm weather.

design alternatives

SKETCHES
Two alternative layouts
for this garden offer
different opportunities
for dramatic lighting. a
swimming pool, pergola,
or small water feature
are all suitable
subjects.

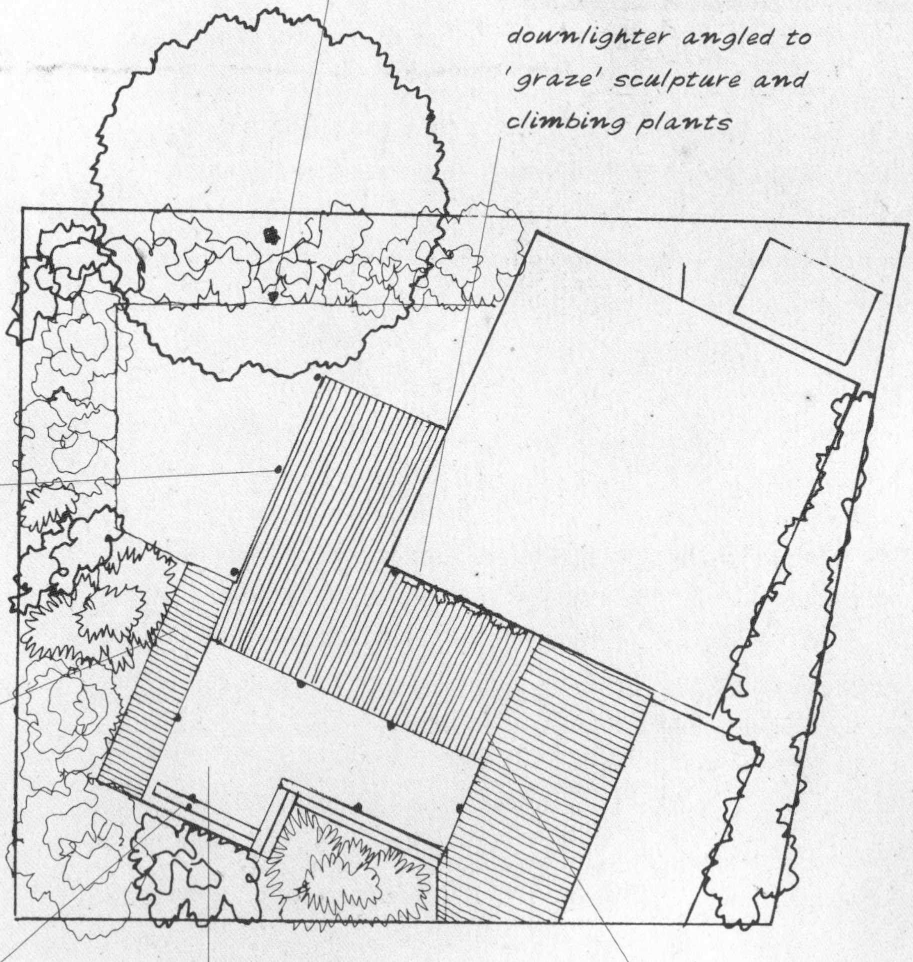

uplighter to light tree

downlighter angled to
'graze' sculpture and
climbing plants

path lights alongside edge
of deck

boardwalk continuation
of deck

Railroad ties walkway for
pond maintenance and
access to plants

formal pond in decking—
could be swimming pool
if preferred

downlighter conceale
just beneath over-
hanging edge of deck

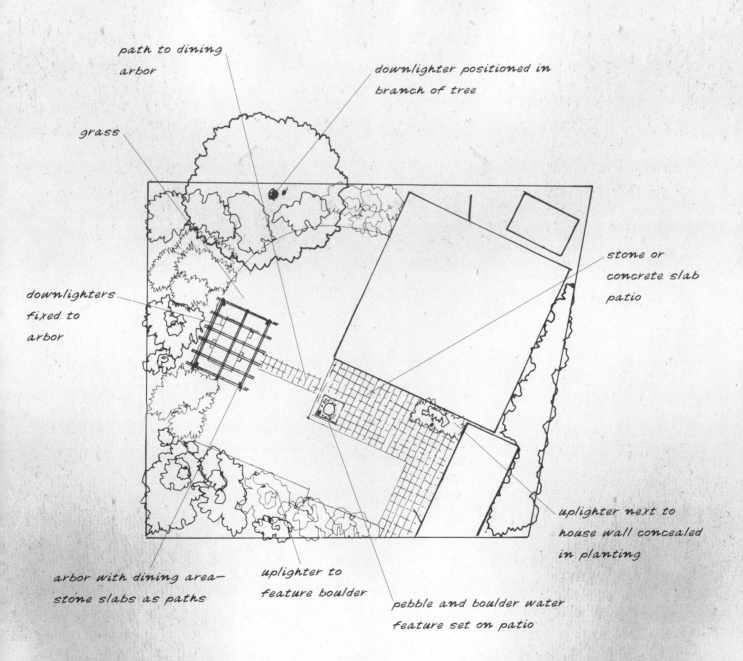

path to dining
arbor

downlighter positioned in
branch of tree

grass

downlighters
fixed to
arbor

stone or
concrete slab
patio

uplighter next to
house wall concealed
in planting

arbor with dining area—
stone slabs as paths

uplighter to
feature boulder

pebble and boulder water
feature set on patio

practical gardens

The gardens in this section answer very practical needs, the first to make a garden that's enjoyable for young children as well as their parents, and the second for people who for one reason or another have restricted movement and who want to be able to garden at elbow height. Gardens like these can offer a great deal to people who are interested in cultivating plants as well as to anyone who simply likes spending time and relaxing in a garden.

children's activity garden

A garden to be used by children should be a happy, fuss-free place. There is no point in cherishing delicate flowers and coddling tall-stemmed beauties here. Even your velvet lawn will have to be put on hold for now, as a much-used play area or mountain bike track is seldom smooth and green.

Blending interests

This doesn't mean that you have to deny yourself the pleasures and attractions of a garden if you have children—in some ways your interests will coincide. Most people want a sitting and eating area close to the house and if this is safely constructed and of ample size, it can double up as a daytime playing area for young children, somewhere they are under your eye or can be seen from the window of a room you frequently use. A small but shady tree makes sure that there won't be too much sun-exposure on sunny days. A safety rail is all that differentiates a play-deck from an adults' barbecue area, and shallow steps down if levels change make good sense for adults who'll be using the area at night.

Rather than having a bald and withered lawn, make over a large area to serious rough and tumble play by using a hard-wearing synthetic play surface. In a bold, curvy shape this area can later become a green lawn, a huge island bed for grasses or herbaceous plants, or even a garden pond when the children get older.

Adventure areas can be created with bought equipment such as chutes or swings or the wooden toadstools in our garden, and fantasy areas can be formed from exciting plants chosen for their toughness as well as their ability to make jungles or savannas.

▶ *A children's garden should be stimulating and colorful; these plastic twists reflect the light and bring color to the garden even in winter.*

People who are good at home improvement can make climbing frames and clambering posts, making sure the timber is smoothly planed and firmly and very deeply set in the ground.

Safe and sound

Especially if your children are young it's a good idea to fence your garden in securely so that you know they're safe. Plastic-coated mesh fencing is fine for this, taking up minimal space and letting through light for the plants, and it can easily be hidden by climbing plants. A sturdy, childproof gate is also a must. A soft ground surface is a good idea for adventure areas and a layer of finely shredded bark laid about 15cm/6in thick over a weedproof membrane is economical for this. Water is such a danger where there are young

▶ *Encourage your children to catch the gardening bug by allowing them a small plot of their own in which to grow plants or vegetables.*

◀ *An old-fashioned swing is tucked in a corner, while lawn space allows room to play.*

children that it is much better not to have a garden pond or permanent paddling pool, however much fun and interest these can offer. Instead use an inflatable paddling pool that is only brought out when someone is on the spot to supervise.

If your garden has a suitably strong tree it will be tempting to install a tree-house despite the cost, and these are increasingly appreciated and used by adults too. At ground level, instead of installing a permanent playhouse (costs money, takes up space), make sure that there is an open area that can be used for making a tent or wigwam,

which will be altogether much better for constructive child development. And if you have a sandbox make sure it's high-sided to keep the sand in— and remember the cat. Even if you have no cat yourself neighboring cats will enjoy this giant litter tray. This is not only unpleasant but also potentially a source of disease, so keep the sandbox covered when it's not in use.

Finally, many children have strong gardening instincts. If this is the case with your child, the thing to do is to select a small area where he or she can make their own garden. Find a position in the sun where many easy annuals and vegetables will grow well, and not too far from the water supply so that watering will not be difficult.

designer's children's garden

It may seem difficult to reconcile the idea of a peaceful green retreat with the exuberant activities of young children, but with careful planning there are many possibilities. Even a tiny garden can offer secret corners in which adults, too, can have their space for entertaining friends and relaxing, while the children have fun.

▲ *Much used as a play area by the children, we designed this garden to be both safe and exciting, keeping parents' interests in mind too.*

GARDEN DATA

location:	▦ *Illinois*
climate:	▦ *temperate*
soil type:	▦ *light clay*
direction:	▦ *south facing*
aspect:	▦ *overlooking woodland*

Design brief

The family comprises two small boys, aged two and four years and their parents. Dad enjoys gardening and both parents feel that plastic play furniture is unsightly and takes up too much space, but want to enjoy the outdoor garden experience and shared play activity with their offspring. Their small garden slopes gently away from the house but there is a drainage ditch at the end of the plot which is potentially hazardous for children.

Design solution

We divided the garden space into hard and soft landscaping, encompassing patio, play deck/ barbecue area, soft play surface with sandbox, mown grass, and planted borders. The decked extension to the patio has safety rails and wide, shallow steps down to the play surface. Inverted, new, timber railroad ties at varying heights, offer climbing and hiding activity and there are grass dens, a woodland toadstool corner, and jungly plants which will withstand some bashing. A 1.2m/4ft high post-and-rail fence with plastic-coated wire mesh panels stapled to it provides a barrier in front of the drainage ditch.

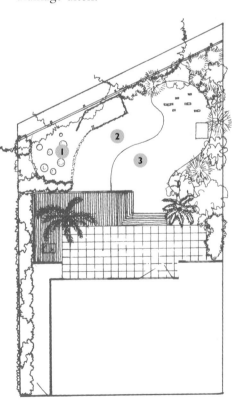

—19m x 12m/60ft x 38ft—

toadstools

▲ *Handmade toadstools give a woodland feel.*

play pen

▲ *Den for the children.*

safety play surface

▶ *Synthetic play surfaces cushion knocks or falls.*

practical projects

Of course there is lots of tempting equipment to buy for a children's activity garden, but there is also a lot that all but the most ham-fisted handyman or handywoman can make on a budget for the adventure play area. Equipping the play area will be fun for everyone.

▲ *This treehouse is simply but sturdily made. A removable canopy is used as roof canvas, and a rope is provided for safety.*

▶ *Adding a chute to this treehouse makes coming down all the more fun. A colorful plastic slide will not splinter or chip.*

Adventure area

No doubt a tree house is the dream of every child, but (a) you need a tree, and (b) they are expensive. If you do have a tree that's strong enough you could provide a rope ladder, a swing, or a tire on a length of rope as an alternative. Hammocks go down well, and will be equally popular with adults.

A very acceptable alternative to a treehouse would be a small garden shed made into a playhouse. (You can often buy secondhand ones from newspaper advertisements.) Paint it up and equip it with curtains and perhaps bean bags to sit on, with a small table, and it will make a wonderful den to escape to. If you have the talent you could consider making a raised decking platform (see page 943) for the shed to stand on, to make it more exciting.

A simple project to please a young child would be to make a proper sandbox, with a removable lid so that the sand will stay clean and dry when not being used. Use planed, pressure-treated softwood and make sure that it's ultrasmooth by sanding all exposed surfaces. Make the pit as big as you can so that other children can be invited to use it too. Be sure to buy proper sandbox sand rather than builder's sand which is not suitable. Special toys—spades and buckets—will add to the fun.

building a sandbox

The important thing to remember when building a sandbox is that it must be child-friendly. Before you begin assembling the box make sure that there are no rough edges and that the timber you use will not splinter easily. The box should be covered when not in use to prevent cats from using it as a litter tray.

▼ *All children love a sandbox, but look out for one with a close-fitting lid to keep out pets.*

1 Fix a block to each corner of the base of the box, either nailing it or screwing it through from the underside.

2 Screw the side pieces to the blocks, making sure they fit snugly.

3 Sand down the box carefully to get rid of any sharp edges. A few coats of an eco-friendly preservative or paint will keep it sufficiently watertight. Fill with sandbox sand.

DESIGNER'S TIPS

• There are lots of approved play surfaces in fun colors.

• Decking makes a warm, friendly surface for year-round play, as long as it is in an open, sunny position and is treated with proprietary nonslip finish.

• Make sure timber for decking, or any wooden surfaces, is planed, not rough sawn, to avoid nasty splinters.

children's plants and planting

You want your children to be able to play happily in the garden, but you don't want your own gardening efforts to be in vain. Your garden needs to be one that the whole family can enjoy, yet where aesthetic standards are met, and where you won't become a nag every time the bike comes out or friends come round to play.

Plant solutions

Probably the best planting solution in a garden where children play is to go bold, unless your garden is big enough for you to have an area away from the house that forms a separate garden room for quiet time only. Grasses are ideal for an adventure area and hardy bamboos can withstand a lot of active wear and tear.

Both cover a lot of ground and need little care once established.

Exciting-looking plants that take up a lot of space and need little attention are also useful: these would include a hardy palm or a foliage plant such as enormous gunnera (*rheum palmatum*) with its huge leaves. More delicate plants are best nurtured away from the play area.

Profile plants

Stipa arundinacea
PHEASANT'S TAIL GRASS

This is a wonderfully wild and wooly grass for a play area. Originating in New Zealand, it has rhizomes by which it spreads to form new tufts of strong green leaves which are tinted burnt orange in the summer, becoming orange-brown in winter. All summer long it whispers and moves in the breeze, with arching waterfalls of feathery flowers in a light purplish greeny brown.

ht 90cm / 3ft overall

sp 1.2m / 4ft

Soil and situation

One of the most tolerant of all the stipa species, pheasant's tail grass will grow in soils from heavy and fertile to light, poor, and dry, and in full sun or partial shade. Dead leaves can be removed in early spring.

◀ *The Japanese aralia has impressive leaves.*

▶ *Red-hot pokers have an instant appeal.*

▶ *Originating in New Zealand pheasant's tail grass is ideal for a children's garden. This playful mound waves gently in the summer breeze.*

Kniphofia 'Bees Sunset'
RED-HOT POKER

Red-hot pokers are fairly tough and resilient and make very striking plants likely to appeal to children. This variety is tall enough to match a small child and throughout the summer it has stiff spikes of flowers in a warm, strong orange, like fireworks rising up from the clumps of strong, grassy leaves. It attracts bees, which might foster an early interest in wildlife, though young children should be warned to take care. For other kniphofias for the garden, see page 988.

ht 90cm/3ft

sp 60cm/2ft

Soil and situation

Needs very well-drained but moist and fertile soil, preferably sandy, and will thrive in sun or partial shade. Although 'Bees Sunset' is hardy, it needs protection from frost.

Fatsia japonica
JAPANESE ARALIA

Strongly architectural, this is an evergreen shrub with large, lobed, leathery leaves on stiff stalks. Small,

spherical cream-colored flowers appear in late summer.

ht and sp 1.8m/6ft and over

Soil and situation

Fairly fertile well-drained soil, with some moisture and dappled shade suit the plant best. It tolerates city air and seashore situations as long as it has shelter from cold wind. The foliage can be damaged by frost but the plant will survive. The leaves may yellow in alkaline soil.

TALL GRASSES FOR THE GARDEN

Tolerate most soils and sun or shade unless otherwise stated.

Cortaderia selloana (pampas grass) tall, white, waving plumes (older children)
ht 2–3m/6½–10ft ('Pumila' is the smallest variety)
needs wind-shelter and a sunny position

Miscanthus sinensis slender leaves and feathery flowers
varieties include 'Gracillimus', 'Klein Fontane', 'Morning Light', 'Silver Feather', 'Zebrinus' (with yellow-banded leaves)
ht 1.5–2m/5–6½ft

Pennisetum alopecuroides (fountain grass) downy caterpillar flower heads
ht 1.2m/4ft

Stipa arundinacea (see profile plants, page 902)

Stipa gigantea (golden oats) blue-gray stems, oat-like flowers
ht 1.8–2.5m/6–8ft
needs a sunny position

Stipa splendens lofty, purple-tinged plumes
ht to 2.5m/8ft

See also Bamboos, pages 880–881

design alternatives

SKETCHES
These two designs
explore alternative
layouts and play
possibilities, including
space for highly active
play such as cycling.
Both use synthetic
play surfaces instead
of lawn.

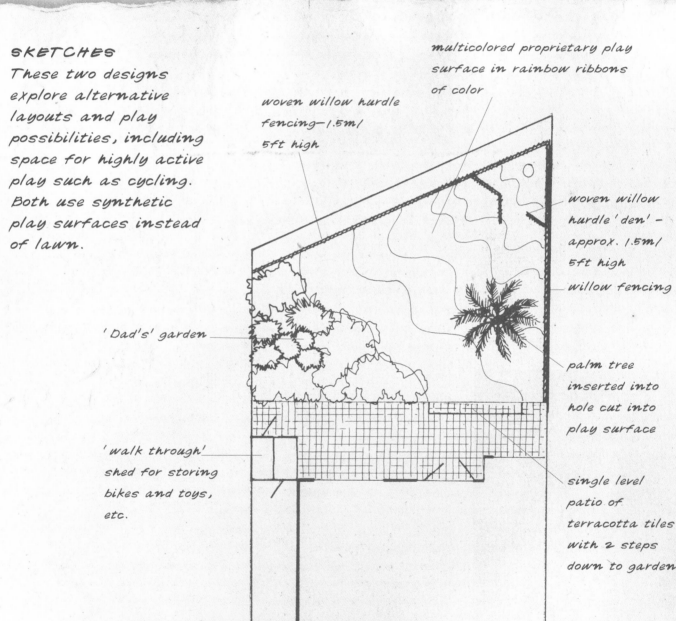

multicolored proprietary play
surface in rainbow ribbons
of color

woven willow hurdle
fencing—1.5m/
5ft high

woven willow
hurdle 'den' –
approx. 1.5m/
5ft high

willow fencing

'Dad's' garden

palm tree
inserted into
hole cut into
play surface

'walk through'
shed for storing
bikes and toys,
etc.

single level
patio of
terracotta tiles
with 2 steps
down to garden

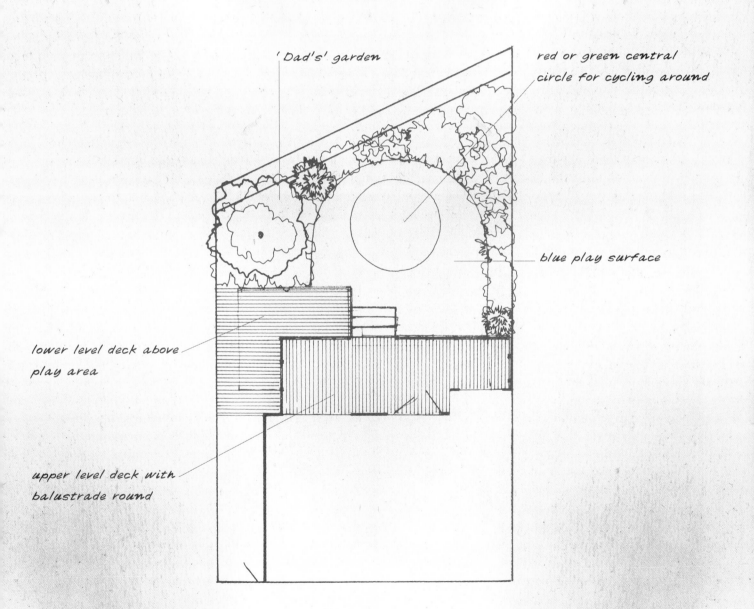

'Dad's' garden

red or green central
circle for cycling around

blue play surface

lower level deck above
play area

upper level deck with
balustrade round

easy-reach garden

In an easy-reach garden the planting areas must be accessible and high enough to be reached without bending—high-sided containers and raised beds offer all sorts of gardening opportunities. Allowing plenty of space and all-round access to the growing areas will make sure that these gardens can be used by everyone.

Key features

Many of the features of a garden that's easy to get at make it simple to maintain, and suitable for weekend gardeners or people who haven't got much time to spend on the garden. The only point to bear in mind is that if you use containers as an alternative to raised beds they will need more watering in dry weather.

A formal design best suits the requirements of gardens in this group as there needs to be a good deal of uncluttered open space. As a lawn for such areas demands too much attention and upkeep the wise solution is to use a hard, nonslip surface. This can be stone or stone substitute paving, brickwork, brick pavers, or rolled gravel, and the choice will depend partly on the style of the house and also on the budget available. It's worth investing in what you really want as this element of the garden is very visible at all times of year and will also have a very long life. Except in a very small garden it's usually more effective to vary the surface material, either as an all-over pattern or by using different materials in different areas, or the effect can be municipal and monotonous.

◄ *Strategically placed planters help add variety in a paved area, and the plants in them are readily accessible.*

Practical considerations

Except where they can be reached from all sides, raised beds or planting containers should be narrow enough for easy access (maximum depth 1.5m/5ft). The sides of a raised bed could also incorporate a seat and if let into the bed this could be used as a place to work on the plants as well as from which to enjoy them. Built features that create maximum effect, such as a rose arch or a long pergola, also provide a visually appealing way of growing plants that require little attention. You might also want to install a formal pool, with wide built-up sides deep enough to provide seating.

For watering, if you can afford the original investment, a built-in irrigation system in the form of a seep hose will be a wonderful aid. If not, the siting of the water supply

◄ *Raised water features are a possibility and ponds make a good choice. Broad edging provides informal seating.*

▲ *Setting seats into the raised beds will allow you somewhere to relax and enjoy the plants.*

needs careful consideration. It might be better to have more than one faucet, connected to short hoses, than to install one long hose.

With so much hard-landscaping it's a good idea to introduce softer material for elements. Instead of being built in brick, raised beds can be framed in timber, which should be pressure-treated to give it the longest possible life, and used in conjunction with heavy-duty plastic sheeting to line the inside of the walls and to retain the soil. A seat with an adjacent bench at the right height to be used as a work top while you are sitting would also be a useful feature for any garden.

designer's easy-reach garden

One of the most labor-saving gardens to maintain is one in which there are raised beds, no steps, and narrow borders. Raised borders are easy on the back, gentle ramps offer ease of movement around sloping sites, and nonslip surfaces can be varied in color and texture to complement the planting.

▲ *At present, the site is not practical for this elderly couple who wish to continue their hobby but have limited mobility.*

GARDEN DATA

location:	▪▪ Virginia
climate:	▪▪ mild temperate
soil type:	▪▪ light clay
direction:	▪▪ south facing
aspect:	▪▪ open, sloping to house

Design brief

Derek and Jean are retired and although they are keen gardeners they find that they no longer have the energy or suppleness for major maintenance work. They would like a garden that allows them to continue to garden well into old age, but that looks attractive as well as being functional. Their garden slopes slightly upward from the house and faces south, so is warm and sunny.

Design solution

We decided upon a simple, fairly formal layout, within which a large variety of plants and vegetables could be contained. A timber-decked ramp was sprayed with fine aggregate to make a nonslip slope up to the main garden. We used a combination of regular-sized, mortared slabs with a slightly gritty surface texture and firmly-rolled, self-binding gravel for the broad pathways. The borders are retained by new, railroad-tie walls, which are wide enough and low

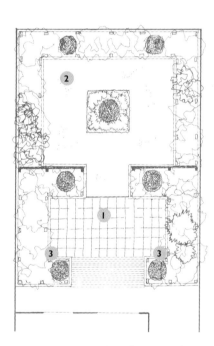

—9m x 14m/30ft x 45ft—

enough to sit on. Brick or stone walls could be used if preferred, but timber makes a warmer seat. The borders are filled with colorful, fragrant and aromatic plants, and flowers for cutting. We added easy salad vegetables and a variety of herbs. All the planting, including the topiary, is low, both for ease of management and to let as much sunlight as possible into the garden.

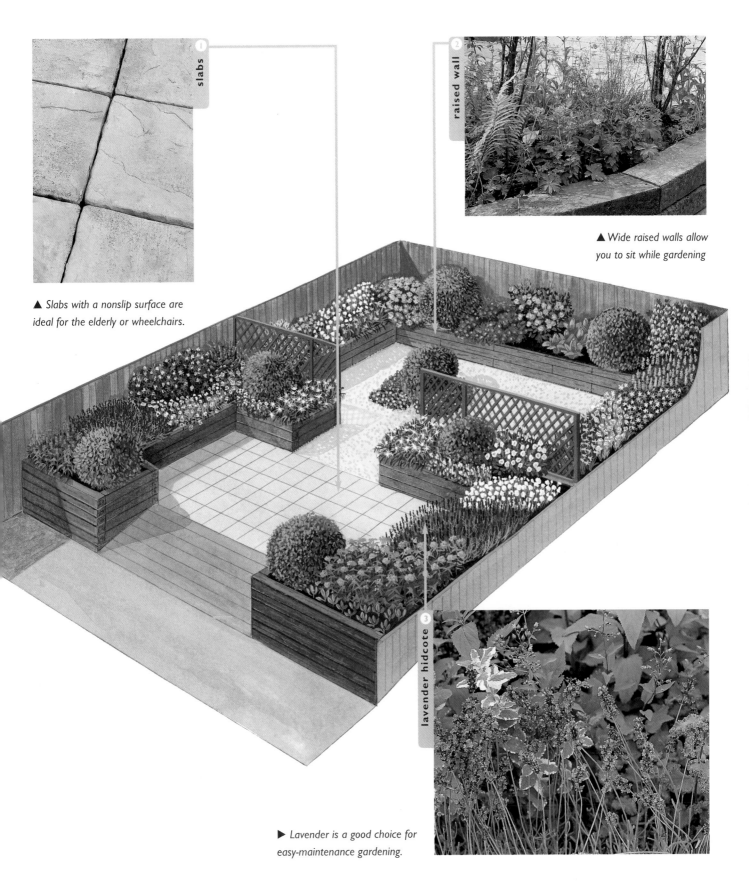

slabs

▲ *Slabs with a nonslip surface are ideal for the elderly or wheelchairs.*

raised wall

▲ *Wide raised walls allow you to sit while gardening*

lavender hidcote

▶ *Lavender is a good choice for easy-maintenance gardening.*

practical projects

Many of the features of an easy-reach garden can be adapted to any garden, and can be borrowed by people who want to make gardening easy for themselves. Nothing in our garden sacrifices the pleasures of a garden to convenience, yet still makes an attractive, low-maintenance space.

Making things easy

Designing for people who for one reason or another have restricted movement and who want to be able to garden at elbow height need not be a problem. Raised beds have many advantages but you would probably need to employ a specialist to build a stone or brick raised planting bed.

However, it is fairly simple to make a long-lasting wooden one, as shown on the opposite page.

You will need to give some thought to paths and changes of level. Many people find it more difficult to handle steep steps or sudden changes of level, so keep all steps broad and shallow and avoid

steep slopes by introducing terracing if necessary, with a series of broad, level areas between short flights of shallow steps. For wheelchair users install a ramp wherever possible. They need to be able to maneuver themselves about freely, so keep paths wide, avoiding sharp corners or awkward changes of direction.

PRACTICAL FEATURES FOR THE GARDEN

A simple rope provides guidance for those with limited vision, or a means of balance for anyone who is no longer confident on their feet.

Raised beds at seat height allow for relaxed gardening. Wheelchair users would also benefit from a low wall they can comfortably reach over.

A gentle curving path with even, smooth slabs and no planting between lawn and path, is an ideal design for wheelchair users as it allows them to maneuver with ease.

building a low retaining wall

You do need not need bricklaying skills to make a raised bed if you opt for reclaimed railroad ties. Check before you buy, however. Some have been treated with tar that can leach into the soil and harm your plants. Look out for new oak ties instead, which will not cause any problems.

1 Pile up the ties to the desired height, interlocking them at the corners. Drive a stake into the ground in the inside corners.

2 Screw the stakes to the ties, using long, rustproof screws.

3 To prevent excess moisture entering the ties from the soil, line the inside of the bed with heavy-duty plastic, nailed in position with rustproof nails. Fill the bed with soil and plant up.

◀ *A low-retaining wall can look wonderful in old brick. The accompanying brick steps are shallow and wide for ease of use.*

easy-reach plants and planting

A large area of an easy-reach garden will consist of hard-surfaced circulation space; raised beds or planters will also comprise harder materials. Planting should aim partly to soften this effect, and full use should be made of plants that will billow and trail over the edges of the planting areas or form soft shapes.

◄ *The fragrant* Trachelospermum jasminoides.

Plants to grow

For people who find tending the plants difficult there are numerous ways of making the job easier, and planting low-maintenance plants and plants that perform well over a long period is perhaps the best start. These include small shrubs such as hebes and potentillas; shrubby herbs and aromatic plants such as lavender, thyme, and sage; perennials with a long flowering period or attractive leaves such as modern pinks, heucheras, and hardy geraniums, and ground-cover plants such as periwinkle (*Vinca major*) and epimedium (see Plant Directory).

For summer color, easy annuals such as California poppy (*Eschscholzia*), nasturtiums (*Tropaeolum*) and candytuft (*Iberis*) can be sown in odd patches where they are to grow. Climbers always add interest to a garden, especially when scented, and many of the best—honeysuckle (*Lonicera*) and jasmine (*Jasminum officinale*) included—need little care. As in any garden the use of evergreen plants, such as box (for low hedging) and formally placed bay trees in pairs, emphasizes structure and acts as punctuation, as well as bringing form to the garden in winter.

CONTAINER PLANTS

Among the plants to make mounds and hide the edges of planters and containers are the smaller roses. Miniature roses only 30cm/12in high include the pink moss rose 'Dresden Doll', 'Lavender Jewel' in pink and lavender, 'Stars'n Stripes' with raspberry pink stripes on white, and the sunny 'Yellow Doll'. The continuously flowering dwarf polyanthas include 'Jean Mermoz' in deep china pink, 'Gloire du Midi' in orange red, 'Marie Pavie' in white, and 'Nathalie Nypels' in pink. All are 60cm/2ft or less in height.

Alpine plants revel in the well-drained conditions offered by a raised bed and can make a lovely tabletop-level display. Most herbs, including annuals and perennials also suit a raised container and are useful as well as scented or aromatic and good to look at.

▶ Lamium maculatum *f.* album *is a white-flowering member of the mint family.*

Profile plants

Lamium maculatum f. *album*
LAMIUM OR DEAD NETTLE

Lamiums—in fact members of the mint family—are excellent and undemanding plants grown mainly for their leaves. They will quickly spread to colonize an area and within the constraints of a container they can't get out of hand. They are perfect for people who don't want to spend too much time fussing over their plants, as they just need clipping after flowering. This is an attractive white-leaved, white-flowered variety.

ht 30cm/12in

sp to 60m/2ft

Soil and situation

Lamiums are tolerant, but this variety does best in well-drained but moist soil and in a shady position.
(See also page 988)

Jasminum officinale
JASMINE

With its heavily perfumed small white flowers and delicate, twining, evergreen foliage this is a lovely climber to plant near a seat. Capable of reaching a great height it can also be kept trimmed. Another *jasmine, J. angulare* is also a sweetly scented form, but with broader leaves, and from a different family there is the jasmine-like *Trachelospermum jasminoides,* which is also fragrant. Less vigorous, both are frost tender and need a very sheltered spot.

◀ *A colorful selection of thymes.*

ht and sp to 11m/36ft

Soil and position

Need moist but well-drained, fertile soil in sun or semishade.

Thymus species
THYME

Though thyme is known as a herb there are numerous species and many named cultivars that make attractive garden plants grown for their colorful flowers as well as their bushy growth and characteristic scent. Liking well-drained soil they are well suited to containers and raised beds and do well in fairly poor, alkaline soil.

ht to 30cm/12in

sp 40cm/16in

Soil and position

Needs very well-drained, gritty soil and full sun.

design alternatives

SKETCHES
These alternative
schemes include the
central concepts of
raised retaining walls,
nonslip surfaces, and
open spaces that can
be maneuvered around
safely and easily.

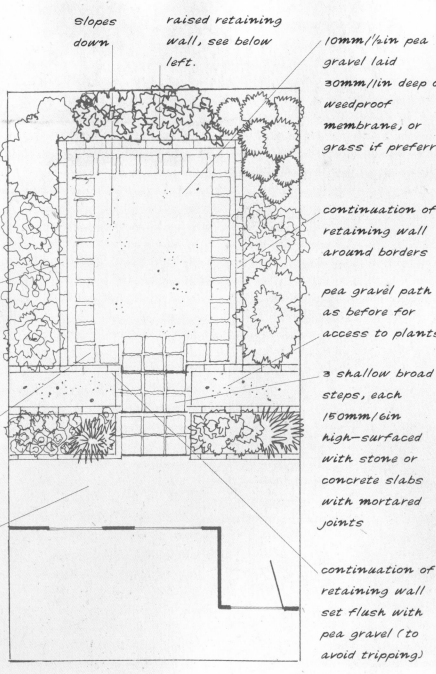

Slopes
down

raised retaining
wall, see below
left.

10mm/½in pea
gravel laid
30mm/1in deep over
weedproof
membrane, or
grass if preferred

continuation of
retaining wall
around borders

pea gravel path
as before for
access to plants

3 shallow broad
steps, each
150mm/6in
high-surfaced
with stone or
concrete slabs
with mortared
joints

raised stone or brick
retaining wall with brick
or stone coping; height of
wall up to 600mm/24in or
as required

stone or concrete slabs
(with mortared joints)
set flush with gravel or
grass

existing patio or
continuation of stone or
concrete slabs

continuation of
retaining wall
set flush with
pea gravel (to
avoid tripping)

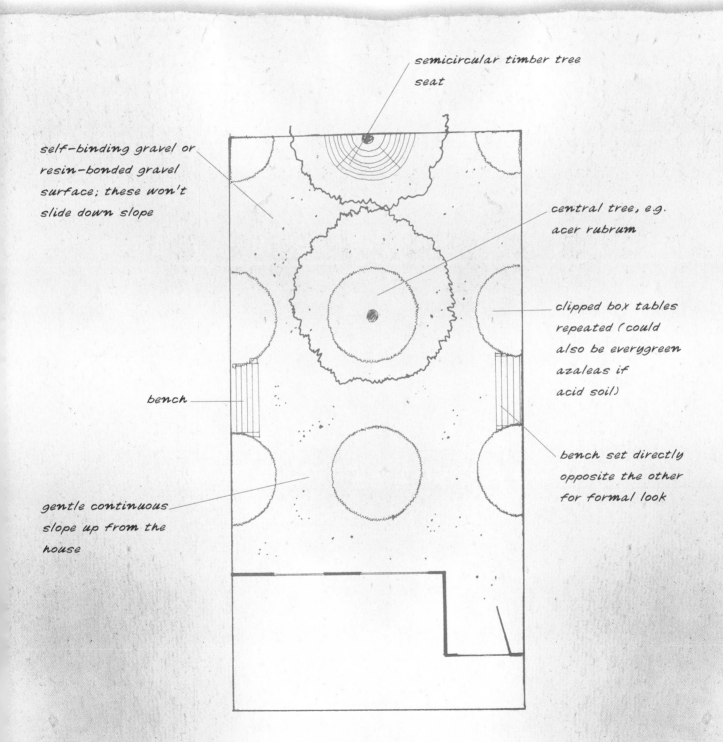

semicircular timber tree seat

self-binding gravel or resin-bonded gravel surface; these won't slide down slope

central tree, e.g. acer rubrum

clipped box tables repeated (could also be everygreen azaleas if acid soil)

bench

bench set directly opposite the other for formal look

gentle continuous slope up from the house

specific location gardens

Every garden is of course unique and its character will be decided as much by the tastes and choices of its owners as by any other factor. Nevertheless, specific situations or contexts do impose certain constraints or offer unusual opportunities in planning and designing. What you can do or can't do in the given circumstances is always a very good place to start.

seashore garden

If you garden right by the sea you can't ignore it. Coastal winds can waft sea salt several miles inland, so even away from the sound of the waves you can be prey to seaside conditions. Coastal gardens offer a challenge and the first problem you need to address is usually that of providing shelter.

Seashore designs

A garden within sight of the sea is crying out for the full seashore treatment, complete with nautical ingredients and ideas from the sea shore: driftwood, sand, gravel and pebbles, shells, anchor chains, and even nets or ropes will all be at home here. A smooth green lawn would be almost impossible to maintain, and would look ill at ease in this setting, whereas hard surfaces are much more appropriate. Likewise the soil will be inhospitable to most plants, and you will need to concentrate on maritime species, and on creating a design through objects and materials as well as plants—although of course you can use containers and bought soil mix for those plants that demand more fertile soil.

Solid timber works well as a material of many uses in a real seashore garden, evocative of old boats and quay-sides, but it's best not to use tarred wood in proximity to plants as tarry poisons continue to seep out for many years—to the plants' distress. If you want to lighten new timber to give it a salt-sea look, the best treatment is to paint it with an opaque white wood stain, which is safe for animals and plants.

Dealing with exposure

One of the things a coastal situation has in common with rooftops (see pages 928–929) is exposure to the wind, and here the winds will be a nuisance not only because of their buffeting, but also because they carry salt with them from the sea. Luckily there are several salt-wind-resistant shrubs and trees that can be used to help to break the force of the wind, planted singly or grouped in key places (see our garden design on

◀ *Decking works perfectly in a seashore garden, especially if the timbers are treated for that salted, worn-away look.*

◄ In a coastal garden, make sure you choose tough plants that can put up with sea spray, strong winds, and heavy rain.

unpleasant view. Panels for fences and trellis screens are also, of course, readily available, and a great deal cheaper than the materials for walls, as well as being much easier to put together yourself.

As an alternative to a built boundary or enclosure a seaside hedge will filter the wind and give shade and shelter while being good to look at in its own right. While the hedge is getting established a temporary netting windbreak can be set up, stretched between posts on the windward side to give protection. See pages 924–925 for suitable shrubs that can be grown as hedging plants for coastal areas.

pages 920–921). A strong screen in the form of a fence or wall that is perforated to let through light and reduce the wind's strength without creating turbulence is sometimes preferable, especially to give privacy in a small area. A fence need not have a straight top and can be painted to enhance the garden scheme rather than left as it is. In the bright coastal light bold colors (other than matt white) work well, while pale ones can look insipid, unless placed in an area of shade, where they look cool.

For total privacy a stone or brick wall will provide complete shelter but a solid barrier does cause wind turbulence. Furthermore, a solid wall has the disadvantage that you can't get a glimpse of the view through it if there's a good one. Despite these disadvantages, if you live in an area where stone is the natural local material, a low stone wall, traditionally built, can be very attractive, particularly where you are creating a courtyard-style garden immediately next to the house. Generally, however, a pierced wall or fence, or heavy-duty trellis is more effective as a windbreak, and works well if you want to hide an

► Natural objects bring a seashore garden to life; this old rowing boat looks as though the sea has carried it straight into the garden.

designer's seashore garden

Gardening by the sea can be a challenging task, but is less so if you create a basic design that does not try to compete with the elemental landscape of sea and sky. There are wonderful pieces of twisted bleached driftwood, shells, and beach cobbles that can all find a place in your seashore landscape.

▲ *This coastal site seems problematic but is easily turned into an attractive, low-maintenance garden.*

GARDEN DATA

location:	▦ Massachusetts
climate:	▦ temperate
soil type:	▦ chalky
direction:	▦ west facing
aspect:	▦ open to seafront

Design brief

The L-shaped garden of this holiday home opens directly on to a stony beach along part of its boundary and is exposed to salt-laden gales. Topsoil is virtually nonexistent and is replaced by shifting shingle and sand. The garden needs a primary shelter belt and must be simply planted for low maintenance, as the owners visit only at weekends.

Design solution

We chose reclaimed oak planking for the deck and for the planked walkway toward the beach. An informal but sturdy "fence" is provided by similar oak planks inserted deeply into the shingle at varying heights. Lengths from old telephone poles would do just as well. The "fence" not only marks the boundary and helps break the force of the wind, but also helps anchor the shingle. We shaped the existing grass sward into a natural wave shape and added some large boulders for variety of texture.

—37m x 10m/112ft x 32ft—

Planting is confined strictly to a few low-maintenance species that can cope with the extreme conditions. These are grouped boldly around and between the boulders to form strong focal points.

◀ *The sitting area is well sheltered from wind.*

deck chair ①

shingle ②

windbreak ③

▲ *A slatted fence makes a good windbreak.*

◀ *Cobbles and shingle mark a natural path to the beach.*

practical projects

The soil is almost always poor in coastal areas, and you are often faced with exposed and windy conditions, even if there is sun. Design to face these challenges by making over a large area to a timber-floored dining and sitting space and building a wooden palisade to act as a windbreak.

A nautical air

In a seaside garden you may enjoy seafood barbecues, do some undisturbed sun worshiping, and take advantage of the local micro-climate to grow something exotic and unusual without having to spend too much time coaxing unwilling plants. Building a palisade fence will help to turn a sunny coastal plot into a more sheltered seaside garden, making it more conducive to planting despite the otherwise exposed situation—the perfect place for growing sun-loving plants and basking in the sun.

This sort of windbreak has a homespun look and there is no need to worry about careful measuring. An uneven top to the fence ties in with the garden's rustic furniture and decking. The decking laid directly into shingle gives a nautical look and the theme is continued throughout. Controlled irregularity is the look you are aiming for and natural, slightly worn, materials are best.

◀ *Seashore dwellers are bound to have lots of visitors, so these gardens benefit from an area for entertaining and feeding that sea appetite.*

DESIGNER'S TIPS

• Remember it may be illegal to remove stones, boulders, pebbles or cobbles from their natural setting, so check first.

• Try to use only native plants and local materials. Anything alien to your seascape will look just that.

• Position driftwood, boulders, and plants to lie directionally along the invisible line of the prevailing wind and weather.

• Gauge the direction of weather fronts from the way that surrounding shrubs and trees grow to lean away from the wind.

building a rustic seashore windbreak

A rustic-looking windbreak is easily made. If you live by the sea, the timbers will soon weather attractively, but if you garden inland but want that distinctive seaside look, try staining them to the appropriate bleached color—a soft whitish gray is best.

1 Dig a trench to a depth of up to a third the length of the longest timber.

2 Line the base of the trench with pebbles or coarse gravel for good drainage around the base of the timbers.

3 Cut the timbers to length. For a really rustic look, make sure the lengths are uneven. Stain the timbers if necessary.

4 Knock the timbers well into the ground using a mallet and a piece of timber held horizontally over the top.

5 Leave a gap between each timber to filter the wind. The uneven topline will break the wind further and look less rigid.

seashore plants and planting

There are many plants for coastal areas. Despite the gales, at least the coastal climate is generally frost-free, and it may even be balmy. Most seashore gardens are exposed to high levels of sunshine and dry conditions from spring to fall, so drought-tolerant, salt-wind-proof sun-lovers are generally required.

SHRUBBY PLANTS FOR COASTAL AREAS

Artemisia absinthium (wormwood)—mound-forming shrub with silvery-gray leaves
ht 90cm/3ft
Cytisus scoparius (common broom)—bright yellow flowers on bright green branches
ht to 2.5m/8ft
Escallonia species—glossy-leaved evergreen for warmer areas; white, pink, or red flowers
ht 1.5–2.5m/5–8ft
Elaeagnus pungens—(see page 992)
Fuschsia magellanica—hardy fuschsia with crimson and purple hanging flowers
ht 1.2–1.8m/4–6ft
Genista hispanica (Spanish gorse)—golden yellow flowers on tough, spiny branches
ht 60cm–1.2m/2–4ft
Olearia x *haastii* and *O. cheesmanii* (daisy bush)—evergreens with white flowers; glossy green leaves have white, felty backs
ht 1.8m/6ft; 3.6m/12ft *(O. cheesmanii)*
Juniperus communis (juniper)—weather-resistant evergreen (dwarf forms available)
ht to 3m/10ft

For plants for sunny, dry areas
see pages 944–945

Plants for the seashore

Plants for hot, dry, sunny places give away their sun-loving, or sun-tolerant nature partly by their leaves, as it's through its leaves that a plant loses moisture. To reduce water loss these plants have small or very narrow leaves, hairy leaves (as in silver- and gray-leaved plants) or waxy leaves. Succulent plants also are adapted to dry conditions, and this includes not only the true succulents (the cacti) but also fleshy-leaved plants such as sedums and houseleeks (*Sempervivum* species). Many flowering plants from bulbs and corms, such as the hardier agapanthus, alliums, and crocosmia can also do well by the sea, given some shelter.

Beating the wind

Wind-resistance is a key feature, as seaside places can suffer gales from fall until late spring and strong winds

▶ *California poppies are bright and adaptable.*

even in summer. The solution is partly to provide shelter, but also to look out for wiry, spiky plants that sift the wind and resist water loss, and low-growing plants whose natural habitat is cliffs and rocks. Even a screen as low as 50cm/20in gives adequate shelter for low-growing plants, and plants themselves can form a screen. Phormiums, elaeagnus, and several olearias (the daisy bush)—see panel opposite—all cope well.

Profile plants

Eschscholzia californica
CALIFORNIA POPPY

These brightly-colored but delicate looking poppy-like annuals are just right for gray pebbles and blue skies. California poppies love the sun and their petals close on cloudy days. They are very easily grown from seed, sown in succession from early spring onward for a continuous display. The characteristic color is orange, but mixtures with flowers in cream and yellow are available.

ht 20–30cm/8–12in

sp 10–15cm/4–6in

Soil and situation

Must have well-drained, poor soil (suitable for sandy and stony soils), and a sunny position.

▶ *Rutus graveolens, common rue.*

◀ *Flowers of the* Cynara cardunculus.

Cynara cardunculus
CARDOON

Related to the globe artichoke cardoon has the same statuesque, thistle-like magnificence and these are very attractive plants with their wooly grayish white stems, spiny gray leaves and purple thistle flowers which attract bees all summer long. Cardoons are best grown from seed. The leaf stalks and midribs can be blanched for eating.

ht 1.5m/5ft

sp 1.2m/4ft

Soil and situation

Well-drained, reasonably fertile soil in full sun, but with shelter from strong winds.

Ruta graveolens
COMMON RUE

Rue is a bushy herb with pretty blue-green leaves and small yellow flowers in summer. It was taken by the Romans to their colonies and is still an ingredient of the fiery Italian grappa. The leaves have a very distinct scent when crushed. It is used more as a decorative plant than as a culinary herb today. **Can cause blisters on sensitive skin.**

ht to 90cm/3ft

sp 75cm/30in

Soil and situation

This species is at its best in hot, dry places, in poor, well-drained or sandy soil and a sunny position.

design alternatives

SKETCHES

Our designer's alternative plans retain the use of organic materials and stong, hardy grasses for planting. They are very simple, low-maintenance designs that make the most of the natural beauty of coastland.

sea buckthorn hedging

standing stones up to 2m/6ft high and down to 1.2m/4ft

seakale and grasses planted in shingle

terracotta tile terrace

"stone" pines

"exposed" area—open to seashore except for fencing

heavy-duty trellis fencing

marram grass

"ties" boardwalk

shingle

trellis screening fencing to divide "inner" garden from "outer" garden

planting around edges to include perovskia, lavender, phormiums

"ties" boardwalk set flush with grass for easy mowing

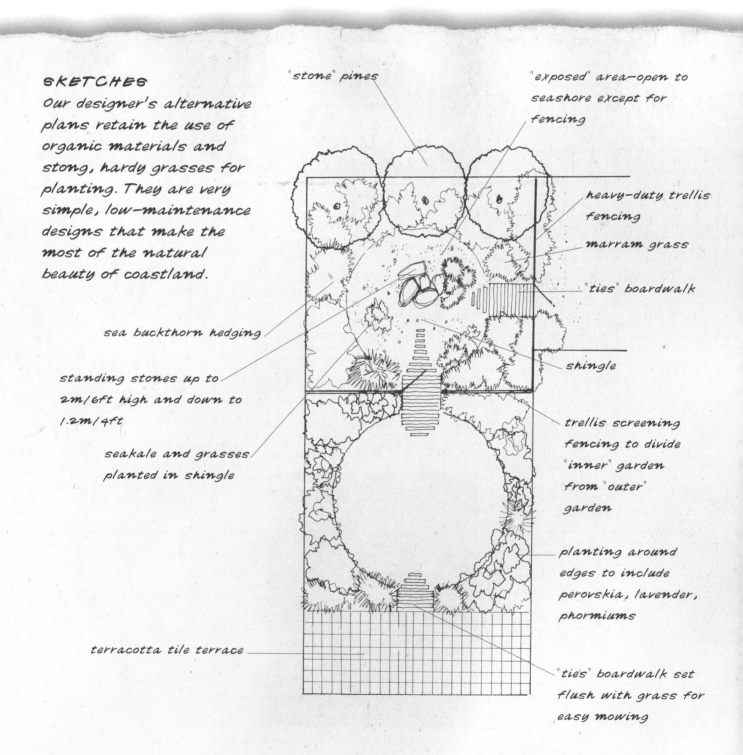

a very exposed garden

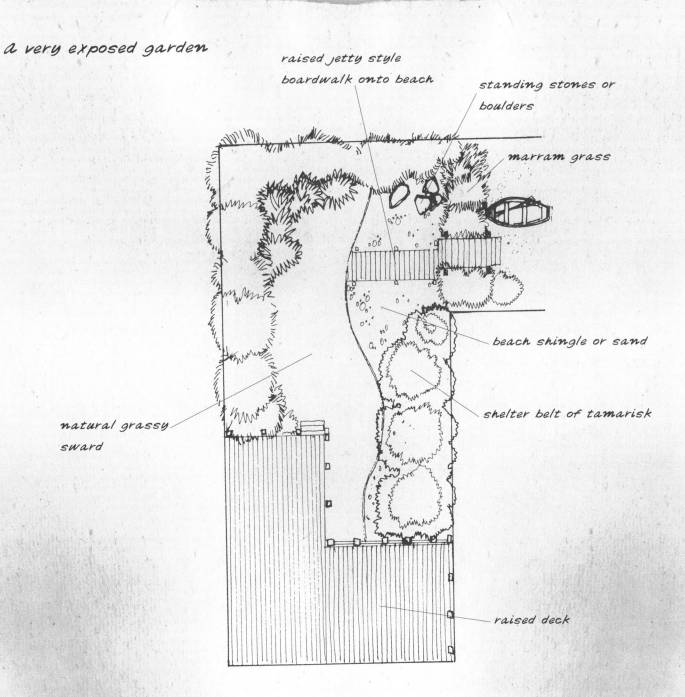

raised jetty style
boardwalk onto beach

standing stones or
boulders

marram grass

beach shingle or sand

shelter belt of tamarisk

natural grassy
sward

raised deck

roof garden

Some of the most exciting modern gardens are those designed for roofs where, with fewer precedents as a starting point, the imagination can take off. And with many problems to face, your ingenuity is called into play to find a multitude of brilliant solutions in terms of plants and overall design.

Problems to be solved

The problems associated with roof gardens are manifold: safety, the challenge to the strength and water-resistance of the roof, and the exposed position being at the top of the list. Before you start there is the question of whether the roof can take the strain and bear the weight of a garden. This is something that must be resolved by a qualified surveyor. Roofs tend to be exposed to the wind, and often also to others' view if there are higher buildings around. Unless you are lucky enough to have a decent parapet to which you can fix a windbreak you will have to take advice about this matter too. Then there is the question of access, which makes bringing plants and materials to the site quite a challenge. The materials used on the roof will almost certainly have to be lightweight and easily portable, partly in order to

◄ *A roof-top garden can be as innovative as you like, as this modernistic design shows.*

convey them there and partly because there will probably be weight restrictions in force. When laying a surface you will have to make sure that rainwater can still run off the roof and drain away as before, and that it will not get trapped and cause damage (for example, it is not a good idea to fix decking bearers crosswise against the "fall" or incline of the roof where they will impede the run-off of rainwater).

Lightweight solutions

Light asbestos slabs (perfectly safe), lightweight decking in pressure-treated timber, gravel or stone chippings are all possible materials for the roof surface in preference to heavy stone or concrete paving. Screening for privacy, enclosure, and shelter should be strongly constructed and heavy-duty to withstand the buffeting of the wind

▶ *Balconies have comparable problems, and solutions, to roofs on a smaller scale.*

and must be securely fixed and bolted to the walls to insure your safety. A built-in store for tools and barbecue equipment will be welcome to save hauling things in and out. A convenient water supply will be necessary as planting soil mix will dry out quickly in this situation—it may be possible to install a rainwater tank on the roof, against a wall to take the weight, but automatic or semiautomatic irrigation will be necessary.

Plant containers can be fiberglass, plastic, or aluminum, as well as timber, and if necessary they can be bracketed to the perimeter wall so that their weight isn't transferred to the roof surface. Because of weight limits lightweight soil mix will be needed for planting.

Enjoying your position

If, as often in older houses, the roof is at second-floor level over a back extension, with the house wall behind it, a patio can be created by building a timber frame bolted to the wall. Plants can be grown over this frame to make a green shady place to sit beneath.

Basking on a roof can make you feel rather smug—a bit like being on horseback and talking down to people on foot. Getting a bird's eye view of the neighborhood is bound to make you feel one-up. So when possible, enjoy this by maintaining a sense of height and keeping the view, if only in part, by using strong, open trellis. And if you place plant containers along the top of a parapet wall they must be securely fixed to the parapet and carefully watered to make sure there is no danger of their falling off and injuring, or dripping onto, anyone below.

◀ *Screened for privacy and shelter, this roof makes good use of lightweight timber for decking and fitted seating.*

designer's roof garden

A roof garden is the perfect get-away-from-it-all solution for city dwellers. Relatively private, it can be a pleasant retreat for weekend breakfasts, summer sunbathing or drinks parties. Or it can be a simple space for a few containers positioned just outside a window where you can reach them for watering.

▲ *This small roof-top needs work and a good safety rail, but its stunning view over the countryside lends the area great potential.*

GARDEN DATA

location:	▦	New Jersey
climate:	▦	mild temperate
soil type:	▦	n/a
direction:	▦	north facing
aspect:	▦	open rooftops

The brief

The offices of a small family-owned company are two floors above ground level in the center of a busy coastal town. Although it's exposed to strong salt-laden winds the staff decided to utilize this small flat roof as a garden space, to be enjoyed from inside the building and to add variety and interest to the views of the town roofscape and country beyond.

The design solution

We chose tough, woven, polyethylene netting to form a perfect lightweight windbreak that allows light through to the plants but protects them from strong winds. A "crazy log" floor makes a perfect decorative surface for this roof and lets air circulate beneath the containers. Galvanized buckets make great planters—we drilled holes for drainage, painted the buckets the steely blues and greens of the nearby sea and grouped them around the roof space. They were then planted

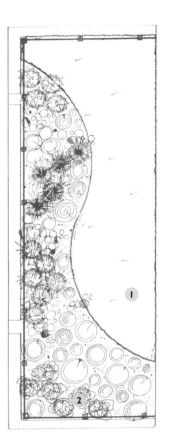

–9m x 4m/30ft x 12ft–

with phormiums, eryngiums, seakale, easy-care grasses to catch the breeze, and sedums. We set the containers among scattered white beach cobbles. For summer flowering we included white pelargoniums and for fun, you could add a windsock or flag.

▲ *Plastic or galvanized buckets make smart and lightweight containers.*

▲ *Artificial turf provides light, hard-wearing flooring.*

practical projects

Most roof gardens are likely to be exposed and windy. They are also by their nature "built" gardens to be used as outdoor rooms—very private spaces that are as much used for living as for gardening. Providing shelter as a windbreak and to give you privacy will be a key priority.

▲ *A bamboo, hazel, or willow screen will help camouflage safety rails as well as providing an effective and attractive windbreak.*

Boundary materials

Your windbreak should be at least 1m/3ft high and firmly fixed with wire or staples to stout posts which must be bolted to the roof parapet. Black or green net creates the least visual impact for neighboring buildings. If you fancy something wacky and the town planners don't mind you can use barrier netting of the type seen on construction sites. Bamboo, hazel, or willow screens make extremely attractive windbreaks, with sufficient support, but need to be replaced every five years or so.

Surfaces

Make sure there is a slight slope away from the building to a drainage gully, which must be kept clear of debris and which should run to a stormwater downpipe. Now use your imagination. Make a grassy roof with artificial turf, or play-surface matting which comes in a range of bright colors. It can be cut to fill the space or to make patterns and glued to the roof. A simple, elegant surface is easily made with modular decking tiles laid amongst pale stone chippings, no more than 5cm/2in in depth. The ultimate roof garden has a

BUYING ADVICE

If you buy plants at the garden center or nursery, there are a number of things to look out for. Check the leaves for signs of pests or disease (left), avoid plants that have moss growing on the container because they have been in it for too long, and if possible check that the roots are healthy (right).

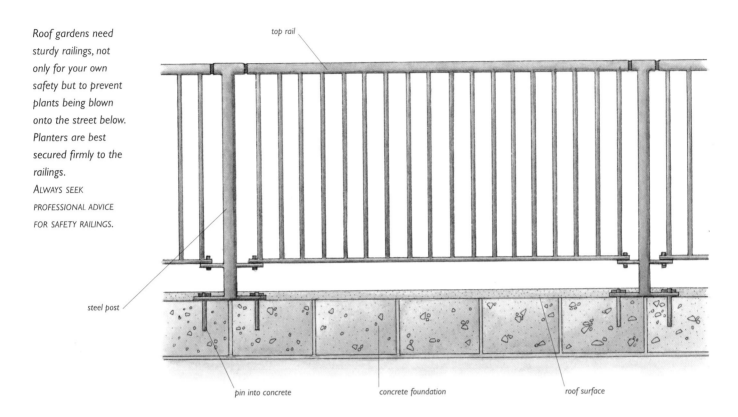

Roof gardens need sturdy railings, not only for your own safety but to prevent plants being blown onto the street below. Planters are best secured firmly to the railings. ALWAYS SEEK PROFESSIONAL ADVICE FOR SAFETY RAILINGS.

top rail

steel post

pin into concrete

concrete foundation

roof surface

real turf surface that grows wild flowers, but this requires professional assessment and installation. You also have to be nifty with a pair of scissors, to keep it shorn.

Now choose your containers. Ideally these should be of plastic or galvanized metal, rather than heavy terracotta or stone which may also be susceptible to cracking in icy weather. Choose plain, simple shapes. Select larger pots than you think each plant will need. This allows room to line the insides of the pots with moss before planting, to help keep the roots cool during hot weather. Add perlite to the soil mix to reduce weight.

DESIGNER'S TIPS

• A good windbreak protects plants over a distance at least five times its height.

• Choose lightweight, but strong materials. Buy a lightweight soil mix specially designed for roof and balcony gardens. Trees are OUT!

• Make sure you can reach your plants to water them. Better still, install automatic irrigation, so no one has to take on the job of plant monitor.

• Light your office roof garden to cheer up dark winter afternoons. One or two uplights are enough for a small space.

◄ *Safety railings are essential for all balconies and roof gardens. This simple metal wire rail fits in perfectly with the balcony's metallic design.*

roof plants and planting

A roof-top site is likely to be exposed to every kind of weather. So, even with a windbreak, a choice of resilient plants will be a priority. And the roof will probably be open to the sun too, so include some sun-lovers and plants such as grasses, which respond beautifully to breezes on sunny days.

Plants for sun and wind

Resourcefulness is required when planting a roof garden. You want to make the most of what is usually a small and inaccessible space and you are likely to want low-maintenance plants so that you can spend more time sitting in the garden than tending plants. Whatever you choose it's as well to accept from the outset that you will probably have to do more replacing of plants here than in any other type of garden.

Many herbs enjoy an open, light and sunny spot. Thymes, lavenders, rosemary in particular thrive in such a position. Plants for dry and well-drained soils, including some grasses, broom or gorse, are also ideal. Plants that are too tall will catch the wind except in a sheltered corner so it's best to choose lower-growing varieties rather than risk top-heavy plants toppling over (light grasses, however, such as *Stipa gigantea* should be safe as the wind is filtered through them). The best way to make variations in height is through planters of different sizes or standing on stepped stands, and these should be placed mainly around the roof edges unless you are sure the structure is sound enough to bear the weight of pots placed centrally.

◀ Eryngium x oliverianum, *sea holly.*

SUITABLE ROOF PLANTS

Allium flavum—low-growing, yellow, summer-flowering allium
ht 30cm/12in
Buddleja davidii varieties (buddleja)
(see page 991)
ht to 3m/10ft
Crambe maritima (seakale) (see page 985)
ht 75cm/30in
Kniphofia (red hot poker) (see page 988)
ht 90cm–1.8m/3–6ft
Santolina chamaecyparissus (cotton lavender)
gray-green mounds with buttony yellow flowers
ht 50cm/20in
Pleioblastus pygmaeus var. *distichus* (pigmy bamboo)—short, very leafy green bamboo
ht to 90cm/3ft
Sedum spectabile (sedum or ice plant)
(see page 990)
ht 45cm/18in
Stipa gigantea (giant feather grass)
(see pages 903)
ht 1.8–2.5m/6–8ft
See also plants for seaside gardens, pages 924–925

▶ Pennisetum alopecuroides *'Hameln'*.

Profile plants

Eryngium × oliverianum
ERYNGIUM

Eryngiums or sea hollies are excellent plants for a roof garden as their architectural, branching stems filter the wind and the spiky bracts which surround their cone-shaped flower heads look good in strong light. *Eryngium × oliverianum* has particularly frosted-looking stems, bracts, leaves, and flowers in silvery blue, sometimes purple-tinted. Flowers during the whole summer.

ht 90cm/3ft

sp 45cm/18in

Soil and situation

Poor, well-drained soil, sunny situation.

Pennisetum alopecuroides varieties
FOUNTAIN GRASS

These grasses have many varieties suitable for roof-tops because of their dense, low, mound-forming growth and undemanding nature. The feathery bottle-brush flowers rustle over narrow arching leaves all summer. In 'Hameln', a compact form, the flowers begin in early summer and the leaves become golden yellow in the fall as the flowers turn from white to a soft grayish brown. 'Bunny' is another variety to look out for.

ht 60cm–1.5m/2–5ft

sp 60cm–1.2m/2–4ft

Soil and situation

Light, well-drained but fairly fertile soil, in a sunny situation.

◀ Phormium tenax, *a hardy, strong plant.*

Phormium species
PHORMIUM

Given a sunny, warm situation phormiums are tough as old boots and there are several good, smaller species of this striking architectural plant. *Phormium cookianum* is the mountain flax, normally with yellowy green coloring, but the hybrid 'Maori Sunrise' has apricot and pink stripes and bronze outer edges to its leaves. The species *P. tenax* itself is something of a giant, but 'Bronze Baby' is a dwarf hybrid with bronze-colored leaves which turn downward at the tips. 'Dazzler' has leaves striped red, orange, and pink.

ht and sp to 2m/6ft;

75cm/30in ('Bronze Baby')

Soil and situation

Well-drained but fairly fertile soil in a sunny situation.

design alternatives

SKETCHES

Roof gardens are ideally suited for strong, innovative designs. Here our designer has employed different surface materials, and foliage-interest plants.

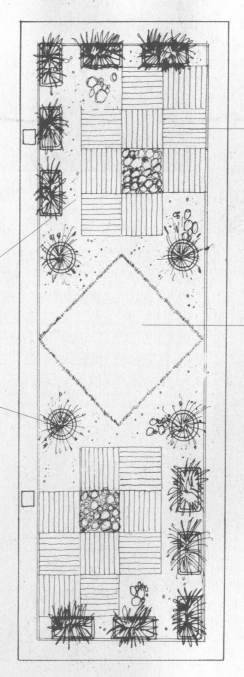

modular decking boards (available from building supply stores)

20mm/³⁄₄in stone chippings with scattered beach cobbles

artificial turf

matching containers planted with a variety of grasses (automatic irrigation needed)

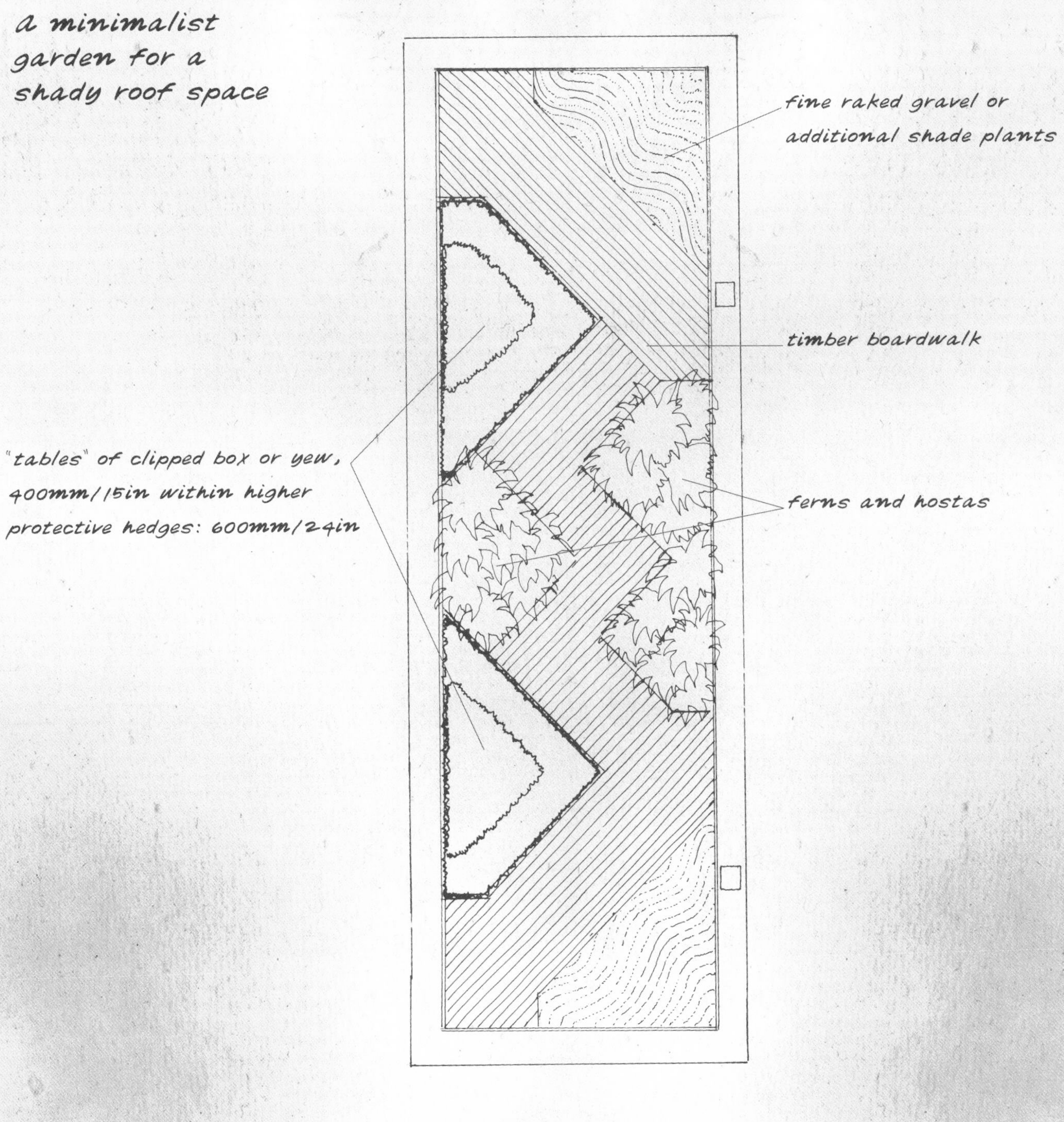

a minimalist
garden for a
shady roof space

fine raked gravel or
additional shade plants

timber boardwalk

"tables" of clipped box or yew,
400mm/15in within higher
protective hedges: 600mm/24in

ferns and hostas

patio garden

A patio is not necessarily an enclosed garden, but is best if sheltered for privacy and protected from drafts. There is no reason for a patio to be at the back of the house. If the front garden is warm and sunny, and you enjoy some privacy from the neighbors, why not make that your outdoor room?

Outdoor living

Ideally the patio garden will be right next to the house, preferably situated so that you can spill out on to it and use it as an extension to a living room or dining room. Because you want to use it for sunbathing and for outdoor eating it will have a great deal in common with a sunny seashore garden and with sheltered courtyard gardens. You don't have to devote your whole garden to a patio, but if the plot is small this may well be an ideal design solution.

A patio garden is perfect for people who are too busy to spend a great deal of time on the garden and who want to use it mainly as living space. The area should have a firm surface, and at least part of this should be suitable for furniture. A pebbled patio is not usually very successful as chairs and tables can't stand on it properly. The best choices are paving, brickwork, or timber decking, which make pleasant surfaces for sunbathing and are less unforgiving when plates and glasses are dropped on them. Whatever you choose, the surface is going to be a major investment in this type of garden, and it's wise to consider carefully which is best for you. In a large area you might like to vary the materials used, and provide planting space between stone slabs or bricks, or in gravel to avoid too hard a look.

◀ *Providing places for plants in the patio will soften the overall effect of this garden which can easily be dominated by the hard patio materials.*

◀ *Established planting at the front of the house provides shelter from wind and prying eyes.*

Equipping your patio

Enjoy planning your barbecue equipment and patio furniture. In the long run it is generally best to make a serious investment and get well-designed tables and chairs that look good and will last well. If you buy hardwood, cast-iron, or good-quality aluminum furniture you can leave it out in all weathers. Wood will need oiling every year and metal furniture may need painting occasionally, but both will enhance your garden and age well. If you buy plastic you will need somewhere to store it during the winter—and it doesn't have the same style. Resin café tables and chairs are a possible alternative and pack away neatly for winter storage.

Cooking outdoors

If you expect to be having frequent meals outdoors, consider building a barbecue into a wall on the patio as part of the design. This may be a job for a qualified builder. However, a free-standing barbecue, in materials that blend with walls or floor surfaces, is within a confident home improver's scope. The essential ingredients are a back and two sides, with a burning rack raised above ground level so that air can feed the fire, and a cooking rack above it. The

rack should be about 90cm/3ft high for comfort, and should be wide enough to have areas at each side that are not directly above the fire, so that cooked food can be pushed to the side to keep warm. The side walls should be wide enough to hold utensils, food supplies, and perhaps plates. A shallow pit below the burning area will help to prevent ashes blowing about the patio. However, a fixed barbecue may be unsightly in winter.

Whatever the design of your barbecue, it should not be placed beneath overhanging trees, or close to shrubs or flowers, which might catch fire. Ideally it will be close to the kitchen so that supplies can be kept refrigerated until they are needed and easily conveyed to the cooking area.

Lighting will enhance the patio at night (see pages 884–885 for more information). And, without spoiling the atmosphere, it's a good idea to make sure that the area around the barbecue and the path to and from the kitchen are well lit for safety. These safety lights can always be turned off for romantic dining by candlelight or lamplight.

◀ *A patio can provide privacy or a romantic retreat. This tucked away corner is an example of a covered patio space.*

designer's patio garden

A front patio makes an instant statement about a house and its owners. It is the setting in which visitors first view the house and welcoming area. It is also usually less private than the back garden and should therefore be simply designed, in harmony with the style and materials of the house, secure and easily maintained.

▲ *This front patio garden leaves much to be desired, especially as there is no back garden to compensate.*

GARDEN DATA

location:	▦ *Connecticut*
climate:	▦ *temperate*
soil type:	▦ *neutral*
direction:	▦ *east facing*
aspect:	▦ *partially shaded*

The brief

This small space, bounded by low brick walls, typifies the size of many front gardens on housing estates. In this instance the developers have used cheap materials and mixed several different colors, shapes, and textures together to make an uninspired and unwelcoming garden, which does not relate at all to the attractive mews-style house it fronts. Although there is not much of it, the existing planting is unharmonious and out of scale with the house. As there is no back garden this tiny area must double for its owners as somewhere to sit and relax.

The design solution

We liked the gray stone setts that are used to pave the private roadway to this small development and decided to echo them by using similar small unit setts to replace the existing concrete slabs. Instead of paving wall to wall we left a generous border for planting and varied the surface

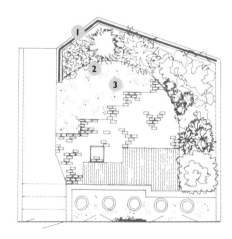

—7m x 6m / 22ft x 19ft—

texture by introducing creamy white stone chippings. These also define the shape of the paved area. Close to the house we laid a timber deck, which provides a small seating area bounded by brightly-colored plants in containers. In colder weather it can be used as a stage for winter-flowering violas and heathers in carefully grouped containers. We erected neat, timber, picket fencing along the front boundary wall, to afford some privacy without casting dense shade. The planting is simple—fragrant, white flowering climbers and lush, leafy, evergreen foliage, with vivid splashes of hot color.

▶ Hostas thrive in a
shady area.

▲ Planting helps create privacy.

▶ Stone chippings
complement the pale paving.

practical projects

Timber decking is a versatile and practical complement to many garden styles. It looks at home in formal and informal situations and can be contemporary or traditional, depending on how it is used. It mixes well with many other materials and is a sympathetic foil to planting.

Types of decking

The simplest decking is made from planks supported by joists, themselves resting on bearers of timber or brick. Ready-to-assemble kits are available, as well as framed squares that can be simply bedded on sand.

Raised decking must be very strongly constructed and is not a construction job for the inexperienced. Built on joists over foundation posts secured to concrete pads it can be attached to the house wall by a timber wall-plate.

Use pressure-treated softwood, which can be painted or stained and varnished. Always use timber which is suitable for your garden design, which comes from renewable sources, and is produced with minimal harm to the environment.

PICKET FENCING

To form a right-angled corner fix the rails so that one side of the corner overlaps those on the other side of the corner. Then drive a long nail through the overlapping rail to the end of the overlapped rail so the join will not part.

To assemble your fence place the arris rails on a flat surface and lay the pales over them. Make sure that the pales are evenly spaced and nail them to the rails. Now nail to the supporting uprights (set about 1.9m/6ft 6in and 2.7m/9ft apart), driving in two nails per arris rail. Use a level to check rails are horizontal.

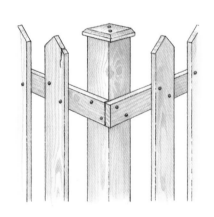

Below are four common styles of pales.

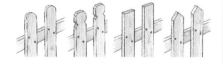

building a deck

A raised deck attached to the house makes a seating area for adults or, with a safety rail around it, a play area for children.

1 The posts which support the deck must be set in concrete. It does not matter if the ground is uneven, as the posts can be cut to different heights to insure that the finished deck is level. Correct spacing is important, however, if the weight is to be spread evenly. Place the concrete pads in position and bolt down the metal plate and socket fixings.

2 If the deck is to be secured to the house, attach a timber wallplate to the wall, bolting it securely to the masonry. The plate should be notched to the correct size at regular intervals to take the ends of the deck joists.

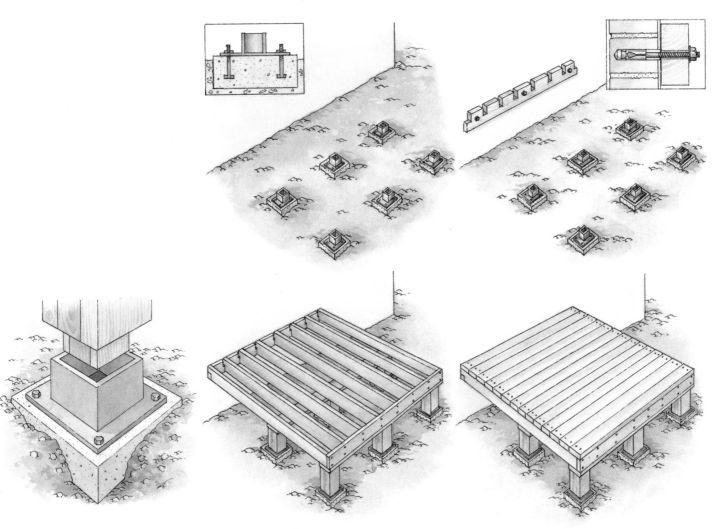

3 Insert the posts into the metal shoes. The base of each post should be cut to fit snugly into the sockets. Shorten the posts to the desired height, if necessary.

4 Attach the outer joists, butt joining them at the corners. Trim the intermediate joists to length and cut notches at one end to fit into the wallplate. Nail or screw them into position.

5 Lay the decking timbers, cut to length, over the joists, with suitable gaps between them of 8–10mm/3–4in to allow excess rainwater to drain through (but not wide enough to cause a hazard). Nail or screw them down using hot-dipped galvanized nails or brass screws. Finish the deck with exterior woodstain.

patio plants and planting

For a good-looking, low-maintenance patio that enhances the house invest in the building and construction, choosing the best materials you can afford, in keeping with the house. Then invest some more in long-lived, evergreen plants that will give shape and interest throughout the entire year.

Plants for form and flowers

Even in a sunny patio, a choice of evergreen shrubs will provide you with shaded areas, and an underplanting of shade-loving plants such as the leafy hostas (see pages 860–861) and ferns (see pp 774–775), and winter- or spring-flowering helle-bores (see page 987) will fit the bill nicely. Foxgloves *(Digitalis purpurea)* will self-seed in semishade, while patches of lady's mantle can spill over on the hard surfacing in sunny areas.

Summer-flowering plants, such as pelargoniums or nasturtiums grown from seed, can be grown in pots near the house for shelter and ease of care, and climbing plants such as clematis and jasmine can be grown on trellis up the walls of the house. Most patios will get plenty of sun (or you wouldn't choose to have them where they are) and there are many plants that thrive in these conditions. Plants for roofs and seashore gardens will be suitable for sunny patios too (see pages 924–925 and 934–935).

Profile plants

Choisya ternata
MEXICAN ORANGE BLOSSOM

This is a very glossy evergreen shrub with beautifully scented small white blossoms. It flowers over a long period in late spring and throughout summer, giving it the appearance and fragrance of an orange tree in blossom. The leaves release a pleasant aromatic scent when crushed. Preferring warmth and shelter, but extremely tolerant and needing little or no pruning, these are excellent plants for providing year-round structure and interest. A golden-leaved cultivar, 'Sundance' is also available.

◀ Choisya ternata, *Mexican orange blossom.*

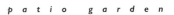

◄ Ilex aquifolium *'J.C. van Tol'*.

Ilex aquifolium 'J.C. van Tol'
HOLLY

When choosing a holly tree for a small garden you need one that is shapely, not too large, and self-fertile so that it will produce berries without a partner. 'J.C. van Tol' is obliging in all these respects and is particularly generous with its bright red berries. It has smooth, beautifully glossy leaves from dark purple stems and a variegated variety, 'Golden van Tol', with yellow-edged leaves is also available. The tree is slim in shape and very hardy, so that it can be used to provide shelter for less robust plants.

ht 3–5.5m/10–18ft

sp 1.8–3m/6–10ft

Soil and situation

Ordinary garden soil, preferably with some moisture, and any position, in sun or shade. The variegated form needs sun for best coloring. Tolerates polluted city air.

ht to 1.8m/6ft

sp to 2.5m/8ft

Soil and situation

Ordinary, well-drained garden soil, and a position in sun or partial shade. In colder areas *Choisya* does best against a sheltering wall. Cutting off any frost-damaged shoots in spring encourages new shoots to grow.

Mahonia × media 'Charity'
MAHONIA

The mahonias are useful low-maintenance plants well suited to a patio garden and rewarding anyone who plants them with lily-of-the-valley-scented flowers in winter or early spring, depending on the variety. 'Charity' flowers all winter, with long racemes of small yellow flowers in plentiful bunches. Glossy, dark-green, rather holly-like leaves make the plant attractive when it's not in flower and blue-black berries follow on from the flowers.

ht to 3m/10ft

sp to 2.5m/8ft

Soil and situation

Although tolerant, mahonia prefers humus-rich, moisture-retaining soil and a position in light shade; the plant will brave some wind and winter exposure.

PLANTS FOR SUNNY PATIOS

These plants all like dry, sunny situations. Those marked * can be grown between paving stones or in gaps in brickwork to soften the hard surface.

Armeria maritima (sea thrift)—tufts of gray-green leaves; bright pink summer flowers ht 20 cm/8 in

Cortaderia 'Gold Band' (syn. *C.* 'Aureolineata')—grass with gold-margined leaves; ht 1.8m/6ft

Euphorbia characias (see page 986)

Lavandula species* (see page 988)

Kniphofia caulescens (see page 988)

Phormium cookianum ssp. *hookeri* 'Cream Delight' and *P. tenax*—tough, sword-like leaves ht to 1.8–3.6m/6–12ft

Santolina species* (cotton lavender) – silver-grey leaves and tiny yellow flowers ht 30–80cm/12–32in

Sedum spectabile (see page 990)

Yucca filamentosa and *Y. gloriosa* (yucca) sword-like leaves ht to 75cm/30in

▶ *Winter-flowering* Mahonia x media *'Charity'*.

design alternatives

SKETCHES
These two alternatives
make use of mixed
shrub and perennial
planting. We chose
materials for the hard-
landscaping and
retaining walls that
complemented the
brickwork and
architectural style of
the house.

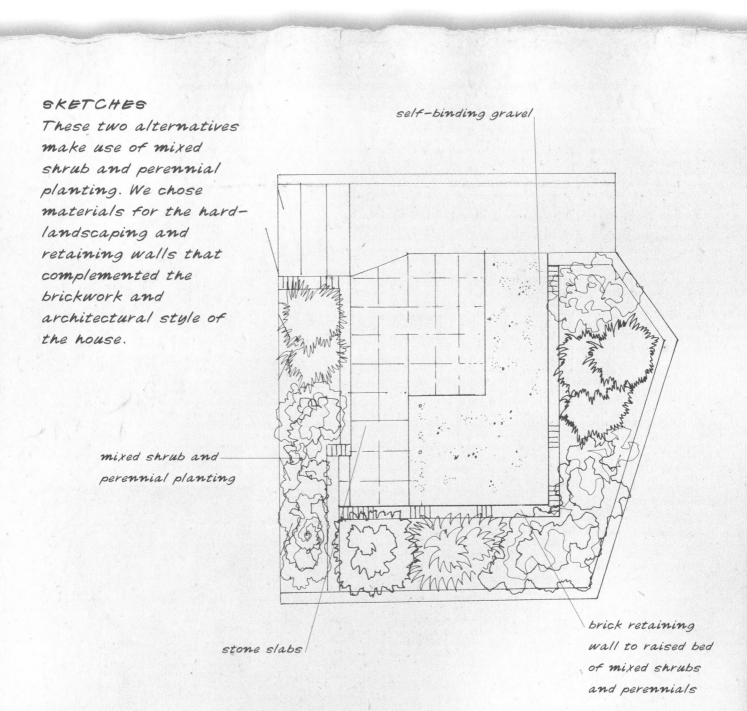

self-binding gravel

mixed shrub and
perennial planting

stone slabs

brick retaining
wall to raised bed
of mixed shrubs
and perennials

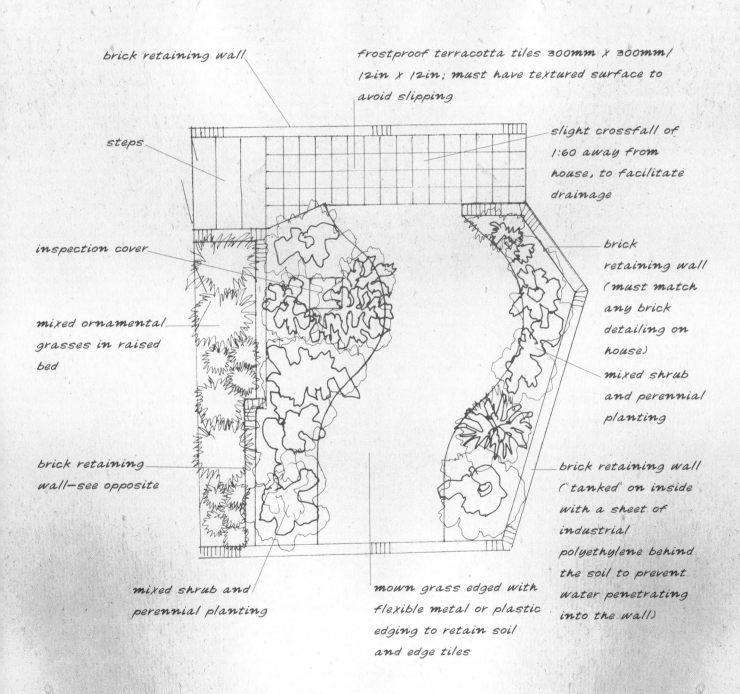

brick retaining wall

frostproof terracotta tiles 300mm x 300mm/ 12in x 12in; must have textured surface to avoid slipping

steps

slight crossfall of 1:60 away from house, to facilitate drainage

inspection cover

brick retaining wall (must match any brick detailing on house)

mixed ornamental grasses in raised bed

mixed shrub and perennial planting

brick retaining wall—see opposite

brick retaining wall ("tanked" on inside with a sheet of industrial polyethylene behind the soil to prevent water penetrating into the wall)

mixed shrub and perennial planting

mown grass edged with flexible metal or plastic edging to retain soil and edge tiles

seasonal gardens

Gardening is partly about enjoying the seasons. And while winter slips mysteriously into spring, spring into summer, and time never stands still completely, there are still marked pauses—in summer and in winter—when for a season we can enjoy a garden that is almost unchanging.

summer garden

Most gardens are at their best in summer, but unless they are well planned their glories can be surprisingly fleeting. And while there is a riot of summer-flowering plants on offer you need to be disciplined in using them if your garden is not to look like a not very exciting patchwork quilt.

◀ *The majority of plants flower in summer, insuring that the garden will be a rainbow of color and scent.*

A garden for summer

There could be many good reasons for choosing to make a summer garden—apart from wintering abroad. When you first move into a house you may want to give the garden you inherit a year to see what it has to offer—in terms of plants and general advantages and disadvantages—before laying in with a spade or weedkiller. You may be on a budget and have very little to spend on perennial plants and shrubs. You may want to lay out the basic structure of the garden bit by bit as you can afford it and fill in with temporary color meanwhile. Or you may simply be a sun-loving person who chooses to hibernate in winter.

If you have a sunny garden your choice may be to concentrate on making it a blaze of color during the summer in "hot border" style. In

◀ *Summer gardens can be full of color. Whatever your taste, there is a huge choice of summer-flowering plants to choose from.*

conditions in a dry garden generally look better surrounded by gravel, chippings, or paving. Pots and containers can stand on such surfaces to give extra interest and contribute solid shapes to the scheme.

At the end of the season you can have a great clear-up, digging or forking over the areas between any permanent plants, putting into store any containers that are not frost-proof and any bulbs that are not hardy. Spread bought or home-made compost or manure on the soil, especially around shrubs; plant out wallflowers and biennials; take in your pelargoniums; plant bulbs

other situations a gentle blur of softer colors may be your aim. In either case, since buying plants can be expensive, consider growing annuals and biennials from seed. Most of the plants we buy as bedding plants can be grown relatively easily at home in a small greenhouse or mini-greenhouse against a house wall. Many traditional favorites can be sown directly into the ground, either in spring as the earth warms up, or in the fall for an earlier display and stronger plants the following year. Biennials, or plants grown as such (such as the aquilegias and verbascums in our summer garden), are usually sown in the summer of the year before they flower, and renewed every year. In a summer garden you will be able to plant them out in the same fall as you tidy up the garden for the end of the season

and the start of winter.

A place to sit
Using your garden mainly in summer may also mean devoting a great deal of it to a patio or sitting area, and this also cuts down on the work of gardening. A patio by the house still has advantages of convenience if you want to use it for cooking and eating, but a sheltered place to sit and read, doze, or dream somewhere farther away will be an asset in summer. A sitting area that gets the morning or evening sun is ideal.

For the sitting area it's best to use hard surfaces, as the lawn soon gets thin and brown if it's over-used. And although a green lawn is a good foil for summer borders, plants that enjoy

▶ *Spires of pale foxgloves in a shadier, patio area will bring a cool note to the color scheme of a summer garden.*

designer's summer garden

A summer garden sacrifices year-round color and structure in order to be at its glorious best for just a few months of the year. Sumptuous flowers and fragrances assail the senses only briefly, but provide memories of long summer days spent lazing in the garden that will sustain you through the dark winter evenings.

▲ *This small garden must exploit its natural attributes, brick walls and a strawberry tree, with the minimum economic requirements.*

GARDEN DATA

location:	East Long Island
climate:	mild/temperate
soil type:	neutral
direction:	east facing
aspect:	open

Design brief

This tiny garden belongs to first-time home owners who are furnishing and decorating their home on a shoestring budget. It is an almost empty plot but has two valuable features: a 1.5m/5ft brick wall which, although neglected, encloses and shelters the garden, and a young *Arbutus unedo*, 'strawberry tree'. This beautiful tree is evergreen, has sensational, coppery, peeling bark, clusters of white, scented flowers and edible fruits. We recommend that in any summer garden you do not abandon evergreen planting altogether, because a large, bare patch of earth can look very dreary unless it is supported by some strong shapes of trees or shrubs.

Design solution

We chose very simple, geometric shapes that would allow the garden to be constructed as economically as possible. Unfussy lines define the broad flower borders without

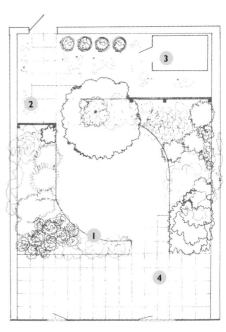

—10m X 7m/32ft X 22ft—

distracting from their show of color. We used basic materials: regular sized, natural colored paving slabs laid to exact measurements, to avoid cutting; tanalized timber trellis, and stone chippings to match the paving. The walls were repointed where necessary and coated with masonry paint in a shade of warm cream. The planting is in rich reds, yellows, orange, creamy whites, and blues, with silver-gray and green foliage.

tomatoes

▲ *This sunny corner is ideal for tomatoes.*

summerhouse

▲ *A summerhouse is a perfect retreat.*

border

▶ *A low-level summer border allows views of the lawn.*

patio

▶ *Patio has room for table and chairs.*

practical projects

Once the paving has been laid, the walls painted, and the screening fixed, our summer garden relies a great deal for its effect on annuals and short-lived plants, grown from seed. Container planting is also a major feature, with summer plants from pelargoniums (geraniums) to tomatoes, flowering shrubs, herbs, and bulbs.

If you enjoy being in the garden on a winter's day, turning the compost pile, and catching up with jobs left over from the fall, including the digging, these are among your projects for a summer garden. You will also be justified in spending evenings in front of the fire, selecting seeds from the catalogs.

When spring comes, it's time to sow annuals as the earth warms up, and then turn your attention to containers. Buy the best you can afford, as cheap terracotta flakes in the frost and needs to be replaced, and cheap plastic looks cheap. A mixture of sizes in a limited range of types usually works better than a jumble or too many pots the same size. You will have to water at least once a day in hot, dry weather—the smaller the container, the more frequently it will need watering. Clay containers lose moisture to the air, while plastic can overheat the roots. Wooden troughs or barrels keep their contents reasonably damp, especially if lined with moss. All containers should have plenty of drainage. Be generous when planting. Three, five, or seven plants of the same kind and color in a medium-sized pot make more impact than the same number of mixed colors.

At the end of the summer remove plants that won't survive the winter and put the potting mix onto the garden or the compost pile. Clean out the container and store for winter. Alternatively, plant with winter-flowering plants or bulbs for spring. Plants which need warmth and shelter can be brought indoors in containers.

▲ *To grow seedlings simply place them in moist soil mix. Cover the tray with glass or clear plastic and leave somewhere light and warm.*

DESIGNER'S TIPS

• Keep the layout simple; showy summer flowers will provide all the interest.

• Include one or two trees to provide height and dappled shade.

• Beautiful foliage is just as valuable as short-lived flowers.

• Make sure at least one-third of your plants have evergreen, bark, or skeletal shape interest for quieter seasons of the year.

• Be prepared to keep on dead-heading flowers as they fade, to help prolong the flowering period.

• Fills gaps with annuals in pots or sown in situ.

• Install automatic irrigation to cope with long, dry spells.

planting a summer container

Planted up in late spring, a container can provide interest throughout the summer if you use long-flowering plants such as pelargoniums, fuchsias, and bedding plants. Be sure to set them off with some reliable foliage plants, such as small-leaved ivies or the trailing *Helichrysum petiolare*.

1 Line the base of the container with crocks, pieces of broken pots, or cobbles. You can further improve the drainage by adding a layer of gravel or horticultural grit.

2 Add the soil mix, to about two thirds of the pot's depth. You can lighten the mix by forking in perlite or vermiculite. To cut down on watering later, add water-retaining crystals.

3 Begin to plant the pot with your choice of plants. For the best effect, cram them in. Fill up around each plant with more soil mix. To allow for watering there should be a gap of around 25mm/1in between the top of the pot and the surface of the compost.

4 Add slow-release fertilizer. This is best applied in pelleted form: the nutrients are released gradually over the summer, making further feeding unnecessary.

5 Water the container well. Water regularly throughout the summer, even if you used water-retaining crystals. Containers look best when grouped together rather than dotted singly around the garden.

summer plants and planting

A large part of a summer garden will be used as an outdoor room. The aim is to make the surrounding areas a riot of color—or a gentler haze, depending on the aspect and on your taste—to please the eye. Some permanent planting using shrubs, small trees, or evergreens will help to give a more composed look.

◀ Crocosmia 'Lucifer' *is a real eye-catcher.*

Using summer color

In full summer there are lots of hot or striking colors for drama and excitement in the garden. Strong reds, oranges, and yellows look good in bright light and have a completely different effect when used together than when dotted lightly about. But the effect, though exciting and exotic, can be almost too strong unless you make contrasts or use shades of green, and plants with silver foliage, to tone it down. For this reason it helps to have a lawn to act as a green foil for a hot border. Green from foliage plants helps both to calm what might otherwise seem too bright and to make the transition between colors that don't look good side by side.

Annuals and bedding plants

Growing your own summer plants instead of buying them in trays from the garden center or supermarket not only saves you money—it also gives you the chance to grow superior plants in colors of your choice instead of the standard mixtures. Petunias, impatiens (busy lizzies), tobacco plants, snapdragons, and

many less familiar bedding plants, including the clarkia and lavatera (see pages 975 and 977), can all be grown quite easily.

Annuals like the lovely opium poppy (*Papaver somniferum*) don't take kindly to being moved, and need to be sown where they are to grow, and others (including calendula or marigolds) are difficult to buy as plants yet incredibly easy to grow. Biennials such as the verbascums and sweet williams (*Dianthus barbatus*) in our garden are also quite easy to raise from seed. Pelargoniums can be tricky and are probably best raised from plugs (available from garden centers and by mail order).

▶ *The strawberry tree has attractive fruit.*

Profile plants

Crocosmia 'Lucifer'
MONTBRETIA OR CROCOSMIA

Crocosmias are summer flowers from corms, with flowers like miniature lilies in vibrant oranges and reds and strappy green leaves, revealing their close cousinship with irises. Originating from South Africa crocosmia cultivars now grow in temperate climates all over the world. 'Lucifer' is a deep, bright, fiery red and will quickly form strong, healthy clumps that can be thinned in the fall if they get too big. Their normal height is at the lower end of the scale.

ht 1–1.5m/39in–5ft

sp 8cm/3in

Soil and situation

Crocosmias do well in any well-drained soil, in a sunny position; they like heat and light but must not dry out completely.

Arbutus unedo
STRAWBERRY TREE

The strawberry tree is a rounded, evergreen shrub or small tree with reddish-brown bark and clusters of cream-colored, waxy, bell-shaped, pendent flowers in the fall. The round, bumpy-surfaced fruits redden as they ripen. This takes a year, with fruits maturing as new flowers appear.

◀ *The long-spurred* Aquilegia longissima.

ht 4.5m/15ft   sp 3m/10ft

Soil and situation

Fertile garden soil preferably and in a warm, sheltered position.

Aquilegia longissima
AQUILEGIA OR COLUMBINE

This elegant version of the country columbine or old maid's bonnets is a lovely pale lemon yellow, and the flowers have unusually long, bright yellow spurs. The flowers are fragrant and the leaves are delicate and ferny. Although it is strictly a perennial it is best grown as a biennial for fresh plants each year.

Aquilegia is fairly easily grown from seed, which should be sown during the fall months.

ht 60–90cm/2–3ft

sp 45cm/18in

Soil and situation

Well-drained soil, including poor soil, and a sunny situation.

9 5 7

design alternatives

SKETCHES

Due to the amount of
time spent outside in
summer, our alternative
schemes make good use
of patio and seating
areas, as well as mown
lawn for relaxing.
Remember these
gardens act as an
additional "room" so do
not let your planting
overtake available space.

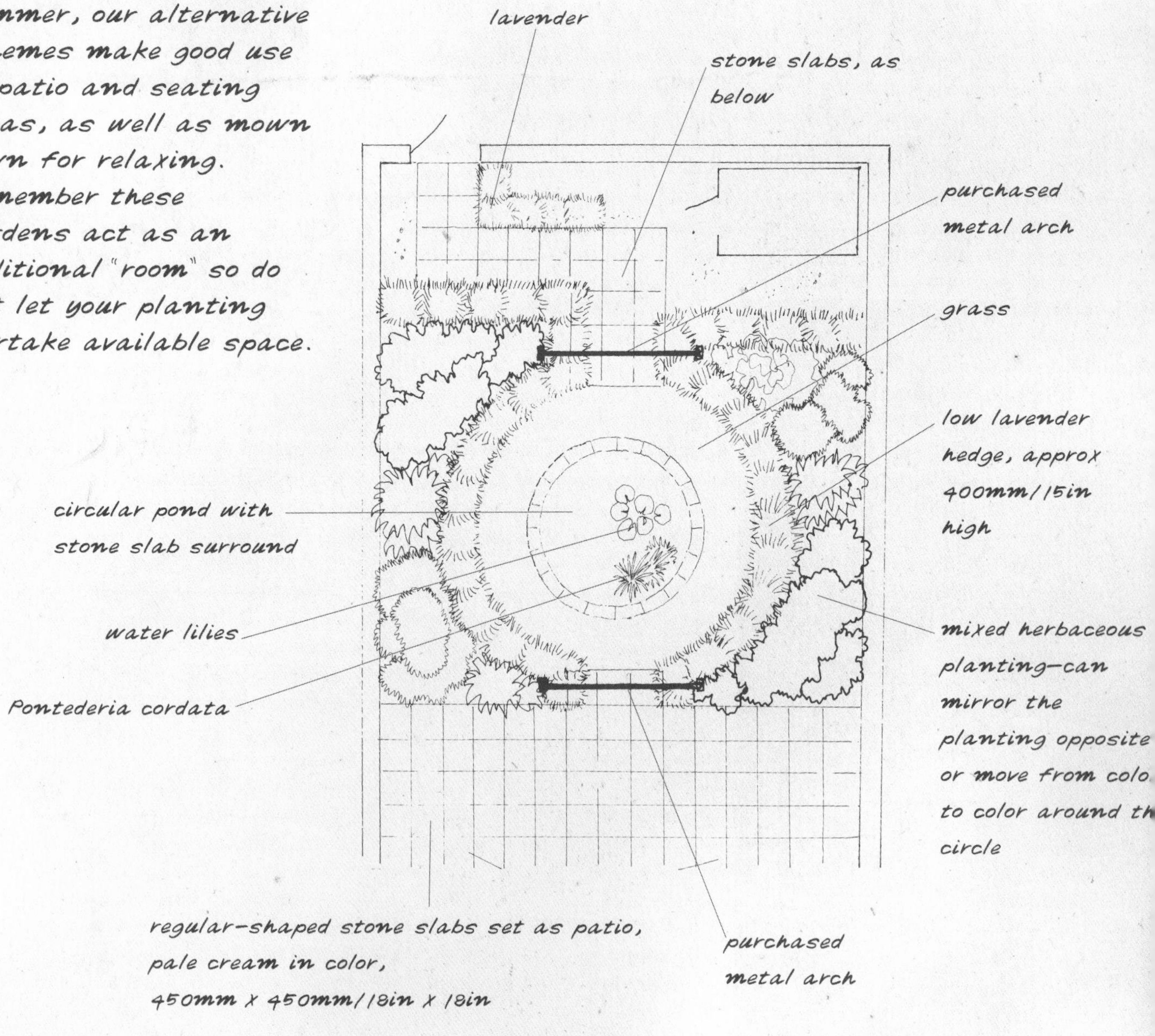

lavender

stone slabs, as
below

purchased
metal arch

grass

low lavender
hedge, approx
400mm/15in
high

circular pond with
stone slab surround

water lilies

Pontederia cordata

mixed herbaceous
planting—can
mirror the
planting opposite
or move from colo[r]
to color around th[e]
circle

regular-shaped stone slabs set as patio,
pale cream in color,
450mm x 450mm/18in x 18in

purchased
metal arch

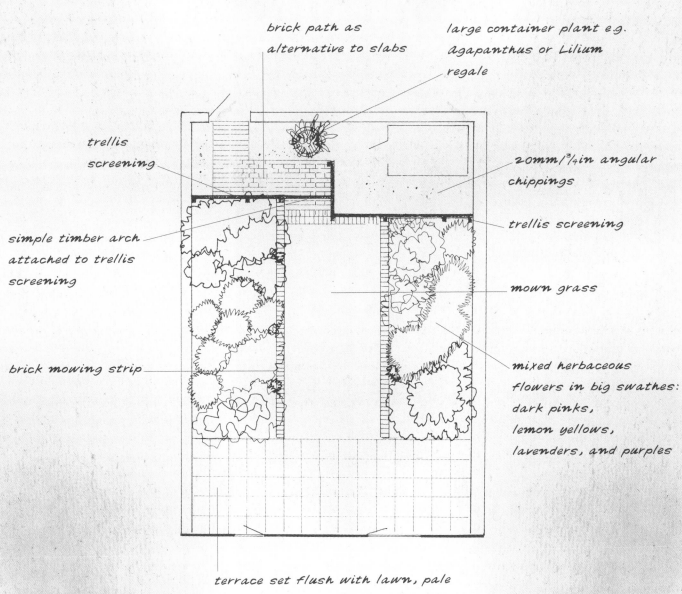

brick path as
alternative to slabs

large container plant e.g.
Agapanthus or Lilium
regale

trellis
screening

20mm/³/₄in angular
chippings

simple timber arch
attached to trellis
screening

trellis screening

mown grass

brick mowing strip

mixed herbaceous
flowers in big swathes:
dark pinks,
lemon yellows,
lavenders, and purples

terrace set flush with lawn, pale
creamy regular slabs, 450cm x
450cm/18 in x 18 in

winter garden

Winter reveals the essence of your garden. With all the growth of spring and summer stripped away and nothing but the bare bones left there can still be much to please—visually, for example, or from scented plants. Creating a garden for winter can be satisfying and rewarding.

◄ *A light covering of snow brings a beautiful change to the garden. Shapes of leaves are highlighted against the cold, blue winter sky.*

Designing for winter

Making a winter garden need not be such a challenge, but it does demand more decisiveness from the start than the summer garden because you will need to form a permanent structure that is pleasing in its own right, while in the summer garden you are distracted by temporary color and camouflaging foliage. You can easily make instant changes in summer by moving plants about or adding pot plants where color is needed, and you can always do something different next year.

A winter garden will rely for its structure partly on the layout of paths and any hard-surfaced areas, and the materials used for these can add color and texture. Warmly colored old bricks, for example, will be welcome in the winter light, echoing the shining reds and gentle browns of bare bark. Evergreens are also a key to expressing structure, and an evergreen hedge forms a contrasting backdrop to border plants at any time of year. The beauty of white-stemmed trees such as silver birch is highlighted by an evergreen background, too, as is the color of winter-flowering heathers.

Formality, because of the importance of structure, is at home in a winter garden. While an ivy-covered trellis or well-clipped yew hedge will mark the outline of the garden, other evergreens can make pleasingly formal patterns within it. Box, tightly clipped, may be used as in grand formal gardens to make low hedges in geometric patterns defining planting areas, and rounded bushes of box or bay, or single-stemmed standardized bay trees form strong exclamation marks to emphasize the overall structure.

▶ *Hard-landscaping, topiary, and sculptures become the dominant features in winter, when much of the garden is bare.*

Enjoying winter sun

Keep in mind the direction of the sun's low rays and plan to make the most of any area that gets the brief midday sun. On sunny winter days a sheltered place to sit can be appreciated to the full, if only for an hour. Try to insure that sunlight will be falling onto features such as colorful dogwood stems and dry winter grasses (and, at the same time, that delicate winter-flowering camellias are not sited where they will be hit by early sun as this can cause damage on frosty mornings). Structural planting and the built ingredients in the scheme must act as a backdrop, rather than preventing the precious winter light from shining on plants that need it for

their effect or, indeed, into the house.

Walls, fences, trellis, gates, and pergolas are on display at this time of the year, unless hidden by ivy or evergreens, so need to be chosen with care. Handsome containers come into their own now, as do well-positioned sundials, garden statues, or sculptures—center-stage is often best for winter gardens, which will be mainly viewed from indoors.

Winter visitors

Don't be in too much of a hurry to tidy the garden before the winter. Grasses, seed heads, and architectural plants look magically transformed when picked out with hoar frost or a thin layer of snow, and many provide food for hungry winter birds too. A birdtable in your garden will allow you to appreciate winter visitors from your warm home.

◀ *The attractive railings that surround this garden become an even stronger feature when summer plants die down.*

designer's winter garden

A winter garden shows off structure, texture, and form perhaps more than any other garden. The shapes of plants take on a mysterious beauty when rimmed with hoar frost and you notice the extraordinary skeletons of seed heads and the delicate tracery of branches across a wintry sky.

▲ *Strong shapes, evergreens, and careful planning will be needed if this garden is to make an impact in winter.*

GARDEN DATA

location:	▦ *Massachusetts*
climate:	▦ *mild*
soil type:	▦ *neutral*
direction:	▦ *east*
aspect:	▦ *open*

The design brief

The owners of this traditional country cottage want their east-facing front garden to be at its best during the long winter months. Their sitting room overlooks the garden and they envisage cosy log-fire days during which they can observe and enjoy the garden from indoors, or wander out to feed the birds. The site is level and roughly triangular.

The design solution

The garden is shaded during the short winter afternoons but benefits from morning sunshine. To add color we used old brick for the paths, although crazy paving or flagstones would be equally appropriate. We chose strong architectural shapes and some warm colors for the planting, which will be backlit by morning sunlight. The design adopts a more formal approach than we would employ for the larger and more private back garden. The layout counterbalances the strongly

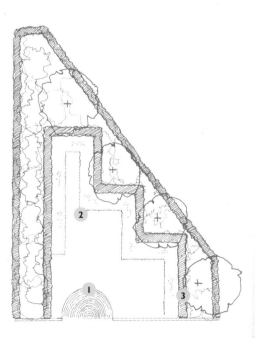

—*18m x 14m/58ft x 46ft*—

triangular shape of the site and incorporates dramatically contrasting planting of tightly clipped evergreens with looser, breezy grasses and perennials. These are selected for their interesting seed heads that are less likely to collapse in a mild and wet winter. We added a bird feeding station, positioned where it can be viewed from indoors.

brick patip

bird table

▲ The birdtable will be a
focus of interest.

▲ Old bricks make a warm
patch of color.

box hedge

► The low box hedge is
tightly clipped.

practical projects

For any of a host of reasons you may want to concentrate your gardening efforts and produce a garden mainly for winter, to be enjoyed as you walk through it on your way in and out of the house, and to be viewed mainly from indoors. If so, aim to make a well-structured garden, with plenty of well-used hard materials.

Hard surfaces

If you have lengthy summer vacations away from home, or spend summer weekends walking, swimming, on sailing, or decorating the house, you won't have too much time left over to admire, or work in, the garden at this time of year. Summer gardening may not be for you, so instead spend a weekend or two in the summer setting up the hard-landscaping for your winter garden.

For paths and other hard surfaces it pays to buy the best materials you can afford. In our garden we used carefully laid bricks to make a feature in its own right. Whatever your design, the surface is always going to be on view so good materials are worth the expense.

As for the work involved, care and attention to detail are important: laying hard surfaces takes time, but no over-demanding skills are required, and what you save by supplying your own labor you can spend on the materials.

PLANTING TREES

Fall to spring is the best time to plant. Start by digging a hole large enough to take the root-ball with space to spare for well-rotted manure and compost.

Using a stick laid across make sure the root-ball is level, then knock in the stake without damaging the roots. Add the soil, firm well with your boot, then water.

Secure the tree trunk to the stake with an adjustable tie so that the tree won't rock in the wind. Remember to check growth regularly and loosen the tie.

laying a brick path or patio

Brick paths are easily laid, but it is important to use the right kind of bricks. House bricks look attractive initially, but are unsuitable, since they tend to flake and crack in freezing weather. Use paviors, sometimes called pavers, that are specially designed for pathways, available from garden centers, home improvement stores, and builders' merchants.

1 Level the ground and tamp down to compact it. Cover with a layer of sharp sand, and tread this down firmly. Check the level. Set the bricks in position, butting them tightly together.

If your design has straight lines make sure they really are straight. If a geometric feature (such as our circle of bricks) is used be sure of your geometry, and if you use curves in an informal scheme make sure the curves are pleasing (try them out using a hosepipe filled with water, doing this on a warm day, when it will be easier to manipulate).

Bricks and crazy paving need to be carefully and neatly laid but neither needs to be set in concrete. They can be laid on a level bed of sharp sand over a layer of firmly compacted, weed-free earth some 10cm/4in deep. Laying a water-permeable membrane between the earth and sand will help prevent weeds from growing through gaps.

2 Brush more sand over the surface of the bricks to fill the gaps and to prevent movement between them.

3 Place a length of strong board over the path and tamp down the bricks with a lump hammer. Brush more sand over the top to fill any remaining gaps.

winter plants and planting

There is plenty of glowing, sun-catching color from bark, stems, and even leaves, for the winter garden, and almost all the winter-flowering shrubs have a wonderful fragrance as well as being surprisingly easy to grow. Most of them also provide excellent material for cutting for the house.

Flowers, bark, and evergreens

Evergreens are a key feature of a successful winter garden. The formal design on pages 962–963 uses the classic box and yew, which clip neatly to shape. For a less formal garden the common laurel (*Prunus laurocerasus*) is excellent, shade-tolerant, and vigorous, and garden birds often nest among its broad, leathery leaves. Various conifers, including gold, blue, and pale green junipers, bring color in winter, as well as contributing

their interesting shapes, and the good old garden privet in green or gold (*Ligustrum ovalifolium* and *L.o.* 'Aureo-marginatum') is a useful standby for garden hedging.

Dogwoods (*Cornus* and *Salix* species) are outstanding for their winter stems, in reds and oranges, lively light browns, yellows, and lime or olive green. Silver birches (*Betula* species) have pale silver-white or orange-red stems and the strawberry tree (*Arbutus unedo*) has bright, peeling, cinnamon-red winter bark. Many maples (*Acer* species), especially those known as the snakebark maples, are also grown for their bright, peeling winter bark. Fragrant flowers are part of winter's bounty, and these include the delicately perfumed snowdrop (*Galanthus nivalis*) and blue and purple-blue short-stemmed winter-flowering iris, *Iris reticulata*. (See the panel on the right for more examples.)

◀ *Erica carnea has excellent winter foliage.*

PLANTS FOR WINTER FRAGRANCE

• *Chimonanthus praecox* (syn. *C. fragrans*) (wintersweet)—bushy shrub with small, fragrant, brownish yellow, purple-centered flowers on bare stems; needs to be in a sheltered position
• *Daphne odora* (daphne)—woody evergreen shrub with small, very fragrant, purplish pink winter flowers
Caution: the berries are poisonous
• *Hamamelis mollis*; *H. x intermedia* 'Pallida' (syn. *H. m.* 'Pallida') (witch hazel)—well-shaped shrub with very fragrant, spidery, yellow flowers on bare branches
• *Lonicera fragrantissima* (honeysuckle)—semievergreen honeysuckle with creamy, scented winter flowers
• *Mahonia x media* 'Charity' (mahonia)—evergreen shrub with very fragrant yellow flowers and glossy green leaves (*Mahonia aquifolium* is similar but with denser heads of flowers)
• *Petasites fragrans* (winter heliotrope)—tall and spreading plant with dense clusters of scented greenish or yellowish flowers in rosettes of light green leaves
• *Viburnum farreri* (formerly *V. fragrans*), *V. grandiflorum* and *V. x bodnantense* 'Dawn' (winter-flowering viburnums)—all have small, pinkish white scented flowers

Profile plants

Buxus sempervirens
BOX

With its small and neat evergreen leaves and dense growth, box is a wonderful hedging plant for a low or medium hedge, as well as being *the* plant for topiary. Young plants 20–30cm/ 9–12in high are used for hedges, planted 30–40cm/12–16in apart, and one third of the growth must be clipped back in the first spring to encourage thick, bushy growth.

ht 3m/10ft unless clipped lower
sp to 1.8m/6ft
Soil and situation
Thrives in any ordinary garden soil in sun or partial shade.

Erica carnea
WINTER HEATH

Ericas are almost indistinguishable from heathers; this species has many named varieties which all make a wonderful display in winter, with masses of pink, purple, red, or white flowers over the springy mounds of needle-like foliage. *Erica carnea* is a particularly useful species in that it will tolerate alkaline—chalky or limy—soils if given good drainage (most heathers sulk if not in peaty or acid soils). Among the many varieties to choose from, 'Aurea' is a gold-leaved form with pink flowers, and 'Vivellii' has bronze leaves and deep magenta flowers.

▶ *Hellebores have exquisite winter flowers.*

▶ *Salix britzensis have colored stems.*

ht 30cm/12in
sp 60cm/24in
Soil and situation
Well-drained garden soil and a light position. Heavy soils can have sand dug in to lighten them.

Prunus serrula
FLOWERING CHERRY

This particular ornamental cherry is especially attractive in winter because of its shining, mahogany- or coppery-colored, peeling bark. In spring it produces slim, willow-like leaves and clusters of small white flowers. The leaves turn yellow in the fall and the tree takes on a pleasing, rounded shape.

ht 8m/26ft
sp 5.5m/18ft
Soil and situation
Ordinary well-drained garden soil, particularly if it is somewhat limy, and a light position. The tree should be staked until it is growing well (see page 964 for more on staking).

design alternatives

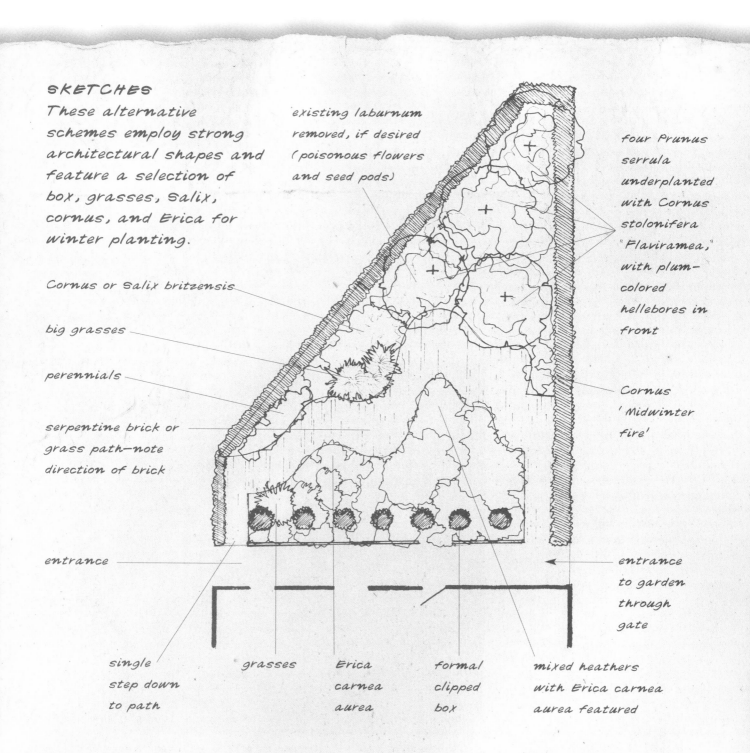

SKETCHES

These alternative schemes employ strong architectural shapes and feature a selection of box, grasses, Salix, cornus, and Erica for winter planting.

Cornus or Salix britzensis

big grasses

perennials

serpentine brick or grass path—note direction of brick

existing laburnum removed, if desired (poisonous flowers and seed pods)

four Prunus serrula underplanted with Cornus stolonifera "Flaviramea," with plum-colored hellebores in front

Cornus 'Midwinter fire'

entrance

entrance to garden through gate

single step down to path

grasses

Erica carnea aurea

formal clipped box

mixed heathers with Erica carnea aurea featured

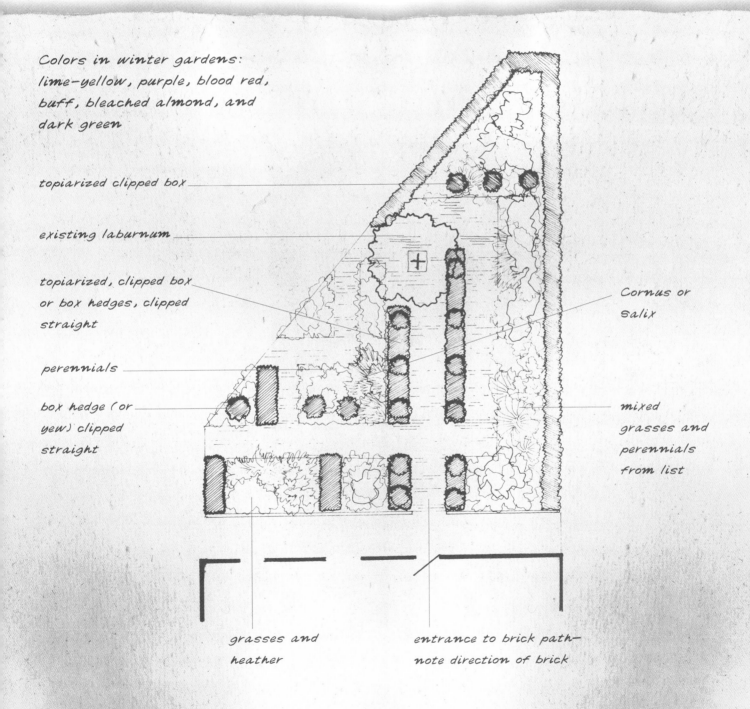

Colors in winter gardens:
lime-yellow, purple, blood red,
buff, bleached almond, and
dark green

topiarized clipped box

existing laburnum

topiarized, clipped box
or box hedges, clipped
straight

perennials

box hedge (or
yew) clipped
straight

Cornus or
Salix

mixed
grasses and
perennials
from list

grasses and
heather

entrance to brick path—
note direction of brick

starting a garden

To get the best from your garden, you need to put in a bit of spade-work as well as thoughtful planning. Understanding your soil and situation helps you to select plants that will thrive. Any time you devote at the beginning to preparing the ground and making a gardening plan will be repaid many times over.

◄ *Rhododendrons are among the plants that are particular as to soil pH. They should be planted in acid soil in order to thrive.*

Heavy soils are also cold so that seeds don't germinate and get off to a good early start. Chalk soil is similar in many ways but also lacks nutrients. This is the poorest of all soils, and it is also highly alkaline.

Acid and alkaline soils

Alkaline soils are found in areas of chalk and limestone. They are usually lighter in color than acid soils. It is often believed that clay soils are always acid, but this is not necessarily the case—these types of soil can be strongly alkaline too.

Acidity and alkalinity are measured in pH, on a scale from 1 to 14. Anything lower than 4 is strongly acid and anything higher than 8 is strongly alkaline. For most plants the absolute ideal is a pH of 6.5—just slightly acid, as pH 7 is neutral—but between 4 and 8 most plants are

Understanding the soil

Essentially you need to know whether your soil is light or heavy, acid or alkaline. When it's wet, pick up a handful and squeeze it. Light, sandy soil will feel gritty and leave your hands fairly clean, while heavy soils feel muddy and slimy, and will cling to your hands and be difficult to clean off.

Light soils are good because they are well drained and quick to warm up in spring. But they need lots of organic material to supply and retain nutrients. Some light soils contain peat, rather than sand, which makes them warm, well-drained, and rich in nutrients already.

Heavy clay soils crack in summer and form a cold, wet mass in winter, preventing air from reaching the plants' roots. Their nutrients are unavailable to the plants unless the texture is improved to aerate the soil.

PLANTS FOR ALKALINE SOIL

buddleja (*Buddleja*)

campanula

Mexican orange blossom (*Choisya ternata*)

clematis

hardy geraniums (*Geranium*)

hellebores

lilac (*Syringa*)

mock orange (*Philadelphus*)

pinks and carnations (*Dianthus* species)

potentilla

red-hot poker (*Kniphofia*)

ACID SOIL

Most plants are happy on acid soil but the following plants demand it:

azaleas and rhododendrons

camellias

heathers, except *Erica carnea*

lilies, with some exceptions (see page 983)

IMPROVING THE SOIL

Improve the drainage of heavy soil in localized areas by digging in grit at the rate of one bucketful per square meter/yard. It is best to avoid limestone chippings if you wish to grow acid-loving plants.

All soils are improved by the application of organic matter, and this will raise the fertility of poor, dry soils. Use garden compost, well-rotted farmyard manure, spent mushroom compost (usually alkaline) or hop waste.

happy as long as the soil's texture and organic content are good. There are many plants that thrive in alkaline soil and a very few that must have acid soil (see box above).

Kits are widely available for testing the acidity or alkalinity of the soil, either giving the actual pH, or using a color chart as an indicator. Follow the instructions carefully and take readings in different parts of the garden. If your soil is alkaline it is best to go with it and choose plants accordingly. The main aim is to improve the structure so that plants can get air, food, and warmth.

Improving the soil

Incorporating manure or organic matter helps any kind of soil. (You

◀ You will need a range of tools to make and maintain a garden. Try to keep them clean.

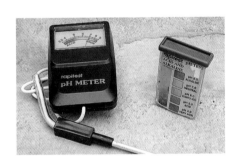

▲ To make the most of your garden's natural advantages, you can test the pH of your soil either with a meter (left) or chemical kit (right).

should not use peat for this because of the devastation it causes to the areas where it's extracted.) Organic material such as home-made compost or leafmold, farm manure, mushroom compost, and wood chippings improve

soil texture, adding moisture-retentive bulk to sandy, gritty, and other well-drained soils and opening up heavy clay soils and making them warmer. It also adds nutrients (the amount and type varies depending on the particular material), and encourages earthworms and other creatures whose activity in the soil helps to break it down and make it more hospitable to plant roots.

Organic material can be incorporated by digging or forking but it can also be used as a mulch, scattered around individual plants while the soil is wet in spring. (Wood chippings are best used this way.) This helps to conserve moisture in the soil while it slowly breaks down

◄ *Foxgloves are natural woodlanders that will thrive in a woody shady garden, though they are also tolerant of some direct sunlight.*

and becomes incorporated. Digging (with a spade) is particularly important to break up heavy soils, and is best done during September through November.

The simplest way is to dig out a trench a spade deep, keeping the spade vertical (putting the soil to one side) then to fork over the lower layer of soil and fork in the organic material. Dig a neighboring trench and throw the top layer of soil over the forked soil in the first trench, leaving it in rough clods to be broken down by the winter weather (the surface will now be higher than originally). Carry on like this over the whole area, finally using the soil from the first trench to top the last one. In the spring you simply need to

fork the whole area over again to break up any large particles.

Understanding the situation

While most garden plants need good light, some positively flourish in shade and others—coming originally from deciduous woodland—need partial or dappled shade. If you are lucky your garden will be able to offer a variety of positions so that you can meet requirements from full sun to full shade. In addition some plants do best in an open position, while others require shelter from the wind. Open positions usually go with exposure to the sun, but shelter does not necessarily mean shade (some plants need sun and shelter).

Many plants will be unhappy exposed to strong winds, and specially tough and resilient plants are needed for such situations, whether there is sun or shade. You

MEASURING UP

To mark out a path or flower bed, drive a stake or tent peg into the ground and attach a length of string to it.

Pull the string taut and tie to a second stake. You can move the stakes at will to alter the angle or placement.

▶ *Taking time over planting pays dividends. Plants will establish more quickly and grow more strongly. Remember to label your plants.*

need to bear all these requirements in mind when selecting plants. The plants listed in the directory on pages 974–995 have been selected as being generally tolerant of a wide range of conditions, even though many have preferences and some have special requirements, which are also listed.

Buying plants

The simplest way to stock your garden is to buy container plants from nurseries or garden centers. This enables you to see the plant at its best, and container plants can be planted at any time of year as long as you're prepared to water them well to get them established if it doesn't rain. Choose a nursery which is thriving and where the plants in

general look strong, healthy, and cared for. If it grows on its own so much the better as the plant will have been well looked after from the start. Some nurseries specialize in certain kinds of plants, which will usually be those that grow well in the locality, and the owners are also often happy to pass on advice.

Look for plants with strong stems, healthy leaves and plenty of buds. Reject plants if roots are coiled round the top of the pot or protruding from the holes at the base—this means they have been too long in the pot and have become pot bound. Also reject any plant with

◀ *Most bulbs are best planted when dormant and should be buried to twice their own depth in suitable soil conditions.*

signs of disease (mildew, for example) or insect infestation. Before planting, water well, ease the plant out of the pot and tease out the roots with your fingers or a small fork. Make sure the planting hole is bigger than the root ball, fork a little compost or general fertilizer into the soil at the bottom of the hole, place the plant in, replace the remaining soil, firm, and water.

Some plants, especially roses and small trees, may also be bought as bare-root plants (often from specialist nurseries or by mail). These are available in the appropriate planting season (whether fall or spring). It's important to keep the roots moist if you are unable to plant at once, either by placing the plants all in one hole and piling earth over the roots or by wrapping them in wet burlap.

plant directory

ANNUALS AND BIENNIALS

Annuals and biennials are short-lived plants usually grown for one season only. After flowering they die down and only rarely survive the winter. Annuals come into flower within 12 months of the seed being sown. Biennials usually flower in the second flowering season of their lives. Both can be raised quite easily from seed and bring color and variety to the garden.

◄ Alcea rosea (syn Althaea rosea) hollyhock.

Alcea rosea
(syn *Althaea rosea*)
HOLLYHOCK

Hollyhocks are lovely old-fashioned flowers with large rosettes or (in the double form) pompons of flowers towering above the leaves in spires, best grown as a biennial although they may last. The flowers come in a range of colors which all blend well together, from deep crimson, maroon, and violet purple to white, pink, and chalky yellow. A real cottage garden plant, hollyhocks grow quite happily against a house wall or through cracks in paving and also look good in a sunny border where their height can be appreciated. They flower from late summer onward, attracting butterflies and bees. *A. r.* 'Chater's Double' (tall) and *A. r.* 'Majorette' (short) are double forms, the latter flowering a little earlier and being particularly good in a mixed grouping.
*ht 1.8m/6ft or more (tall),
60–90cm/2–3ft (short)*
sp 60cm/2ft
Soil and position
For well-drained and even stony, but fertile, soils in a light, sunny position. In all but sheltered places they will need staking.

Bassia scoparia
(syn. *Kochia scoparia*)
SUMMER CYPRESS
OR BURNING BUSH

This green-leaved bedding plant looks like a miniature conifer, adding shape and solidity to a planting scheme. Well used it can be a useful foliage plant, bringing a temporary mound of bright new green into the garden. You can grow it in a pot instead of topiary, or line the plants up to make a summer-long "hedge". In the fall it colors up to a glowing bronze-red before succumbing to harsh weather. A non-reddening variety, 'Evergreen,' is also available.
ht 90cm/3ft
sp 45cm/18in
Soil and position
Almost any, though light soil and open position are best.

Bellis perennis
ENGLISH DAISY

English daisy is a little garden daisy that flowers in late spring in shades of pink, red, and white—some bicolored, and each with a yellow center. Grow these neat little plants as a biennial from seed the previous summer, or buy as small plants. 'Carpet Mixed' and Pomponette Series are a good choice.
ht to 20cm/8in
sp 15cm/6in
Soil and position
Well-drained soil in sun or partial shade.

Brachyscome iberidifolia
SWAN RIVER DAISY

The Swan River daisy produces masses of daisy-like flowers in shades of blue or pinkish purple, sometimes with an inner ring of white. Can be grown easily from seed sown in spring but does best in a sunny spot. In warm, sheltered places it will even seed itself into cracks in stone walls. Good for hanging baskets and containers; flowers from early to late summer.

ht 23–45cm/9–18in
sp 30cm/12in
Soil and position
Very well-drained soil in a sunny, sheltered position.

Calendula
CALENDULA/POT MARIGOLD

Calendula or pot marigold is a good old-fashioned garden flower, easily grown from seed. The bright orange petals of the plant originally grown in plots and gardens, *C. officinalis*, were dried and used in winter stews. There are now many attractive cultivars in shades of bright orange, orange-yellow, and cream, with lance-shaped, pale green leaves. *C. officinalis* Pacific Beauty Series includes a large, warm yellow marigold with the name 'Lemon Queen' as well as many others with unusual and subtle shades.

ht 30–60cm/1–2ft
sp 30–45cm/12–18in

Soil and position
Likes even poor soil, as long as it's well-drained, and seeds itself merrily in a warm, sunny position.

Centaurea cyanus
CORNFLOWER

The familiar cornflower is at home in informal schemes and will flower for a long period as long as you cut off stems as the flowers die. Seeds can be sown in spring but the plants are stronger and earlier to flower if you start them off the previous fall. Mixed shades of pink, white, and purple are available as well as the original blue. Can be grown in pots or containers for a patio display. Need the support of twiggy sticks in less sheltered positions.

ht 20–75cm/8–30in
sp 15cm/6in
Soil and position
Do best in ordinary well-drained soil and good light. Will tolerate some drought.

Clarkia
CLARKIA AND GODETIA

Easy plants to grow from seed, *Clarkia elegans* or clarkia has cheerful, salmon-pink flowers bustling up the stems (also purple and lavender pink shades). *C. amoena* or *godetia* has silky, tissue-papery, more delicate flowers, mainly in shades of pink and white, some with interesting markings. All flower during the main summer months after a spring sowing outdoors. A fall sowing will produce earlier-flowering plants the following year. (*Clarkia elegans* is now properly called *Clarkia unguiculata* but the name is not widely in use.)

ht 30–90cm/1–3ft depending on variety
sp 20–30cm/8–12in
Soil and position
Clarkia need well-drained, slightly acid soil with protection from full sun—often flower best in dry, poor soil.

Consolida ajacis
LARKSPUR

Larkspur, the poor man's delphinium, has flowery spikes of spurred flowers in blue or mixed shades of pink, ruby red, white, and violet, and finely cut leaves. This plant is very much at home in an informal border. The seeds can be sown in the open in early

◀ *The purple flowers of the Swan River daisy, Brachyscome iberidifolia.*

▲ *Centaurea cyanus or cornflower, ideal for informal gardens.*

spring and the plant will usually self-seed. Giant Imperial Series are particularly strong and well-branched.

ht 90cm/3ft (dwarf varieties 30cm/12in)
sp 25cm/10in
Soil and position
Undemanding as to soil, as long as it is well drained.
CAUTION: LARKSPUR SEEDS ARE POISONOUS.

Cosmos bipinnatus
'Sensation Mixed'
COSMOS OR COSMEA

The airy, daisy-like flowers of cosmos have a delicacy that is enhanced by their feathery foliage, and the plants flower from mid- to late summer until the first frosts from seed sown indoors in spring. The common variety 'Sensation Mixed' produces tall flowers in white and lilac-y pinks and purples. Individual shades are available from within the Sensation Series.

ht 90cm/3ft
sp 45cm/18in
Soil and position
Reasonably fertile, moist but well-drained soil and a sunny position.

Dianthus barbatus
SWEET WILLIAM

There are many garden dianthus, including pinks and carnations.

▲ Salvia splendens, *salvia flowers throughout the summer.*

D. barbatus are the fuzzy, bright-colored sweet williams that have an old-fashioned appeal and are best grown as biennials from seed sown early the previous summer and planted out in the fall, or bought as bedding plants in spring. There are many varieties. Most are banded or bicolored with a central eye and have a sweet scent. Cutting the plants back after the first flowering early in the summer will usually encourage a second crop of flowers. Plants can be left to chance their luck over the winter and may develop into good clumps in the right soil conditions.
ht 45cm/18in
sp 25cm/10in
Soil and position
Well-drained, fertile soil, preferably slightly alkaline, and a bright, sunny position.

Digitalis purpurea
FOXGLOVE
Foxgloves need no introduction.

Grouped together in a semi-shady spot they add tranquillity to any garden, and of course are useful for their height as well. As well as the purple shade that gives the plant its name, foxgloves now come in shades of cream, apricot, and pink. Excelsior Hybrids are in shades that blend well together and are tall-growing. *D. g. f. albiflora* is a pure white-flowered form. Because of their height they need staking in all but the most sheltered spots.
ht to 2m/6ft 6in
sp to 60cm/2ft
Soil and position
Tolerate all but extremes but prefer humus-rich soil and dappled shade. They are excellent in light woodland, and will seed themselves where suited.
CAUTION: ALL PARTS OF THE PLANT CAN BE HARMFUL IF EATEN.

Erysimum cheiri
(syn. *Cheiranthus cheiri*)
WALLFLOWER
It would be hard to manage without this beautifully scented bedding plant in late spring. The flowers may be simple and not very large but the velvety petals have wonderfully intense colors, from deep blood red and crimson to bright eggyolk yellow. The single-colored varieties 'Blood Red' and 'Cloth of Gold' speak for themselves, and 'Persian Carpet' gives a good mixture of shades. They can be grown from seed sown the previous spring but are readily available as young plants in late fall. Plant close together for the best effect. *E.* 'Bowles Mauve' is an evergreen perennial, but without the wallflower scent. It flowers throughout the year.
ht to 45cm/18in

▶ Helianthus annuus, *annual sunflower.*

sp to 30cm/12in
Soil and position
Well-drained, fertile, fairly alkaline soil in a bright position.

Euphorbia marginata
GHOST WEED
Also known as 'snow-on-the-mountain', this hardy annual euphorbia adds a touch of class. Although the plant does flower, its white-marked foliage is what appeals. Given the right position it will flourish all summer grown from a spring planting outdoors. It's also a good plant for patio pots or containers.
ht 60–90cm/2–3ft
sp 30cm/12in
Soil and position
Needs a light, well-drained soil and an open, sunny position.
CAUTION: THE SAP CAN CAUSE IRRITATION TO THE SKIN.

Gomphrena globosa
GLOBE AMARANTH
Globe amaranth is unusual and colorful and fairly undemanding. Its robust clover-shaped flowers come in shades of red

and pink; its bushy shape makes it a good border filler. The flowers can be dried for indoor use. Flowers all summer from seeds sown indoors in spring.
ht 30–60cm/1–2ft
sp 40cm/10in
Soil and position
Needs well-drained, fairly fertile soil and a sunny position.

Helianthus annuus
ANNUAL SUNFLOWER
In recent years many new forms of the cottage garden sunflower have been produced, so dwarf plants as well as towering giants are available. Flowers are in shades of yellow and orange and the central disk develops into the heavy seed head which will attract birds when ripened. 'Pacino' is a good reliable, traditional variety; dwarf varieties include 'Music Box' and 'Teddy Bear'.
ht to 5m/15ft (tall); 45cm/18in (dwarf); 70cm/28in ('Music Box'); 90cm/3ft ('Teddy Bear')
sp to 60cm/2ft
Soil and conditions

Well-drained, humus-rich soil, including alkaline soil and soil that is fairly dry. The plants need a warm summer to do well.

Ipomoea
MORNING GLORY

Morning glory is an annual climber with twining stems to be grown from seed sown in late spring. It has heart-shaped leaves and singly borne flowers in flattened trumpet shapes, wide and flaring, usually in a bright, clear blue. Each one lasts only a day, but the plant is covered with flowers all summer. A few plants together will quickly grow up a fence or climb up a wigwam. The variety *Ipomoea purpurea* has flowers in pink, pinkish blue, purple, and white. *I. tricolor* (syn. *I. violacea*) has white-centered, sky-blue flowers.
ht 3m/10ft
sp 30cm/12in
Soil and position
Well-drained, but fertile soil in a sheltered, sunny position.

Lathyrus odoratus
SWEET PEA

Members of the pea family, sharing the wiry tendrils by which pea plants cling to a support, sweet peas have wavy-edged flowers in a very wide range of pastel colors, with some in bright, deep reds, and darkest purple. Not difficult to grow from seed sown outside in the fall or indoors in late winter or early spring, they can also be bought as small plants in pots in late spring and will flower from early summer until the fall. Delicious scent (in most varieties) and luscious colors make them delightful cut flowers as well; the more you cut the more the plants produce. Plant out in groups and provide netting, tall twiggy sticks or other supports. 'Jet Set Mixed' and 'Knee High' are dwarf varieties suitable for patio pots.
ht to 2m/6ft 6in to 2.5m/8ft;
1m/39in ('dwarf' varieties)
sp 15–25cm/6–10in (the plants grow into each other planted at these intervals)
Soil and position
Fertile, deeply dug soil that is moist but well-drained, and a

▶ *Sweet pea,* Lathyrus odoratus.

◀ *The tobacco plant,* Nicotiana, *suits well-drained soil in sun or partial shade.*

light, sunny, but sheltered position.

Lavatera trimestris
ANNUAL GARDEN MALLOW

This annual garden mallow makes a shrubby, flowery plant that belies its ease of growth. One of the commonest varieties is the pink-flowering 'Silver Cup', which is showy and cheerful but a bit too pink for some tastes. Try 'Mont Blanc' for a snowy white. Seeds can be sown directly outside in spring.
ht 75cm/30in
sp 40cm/16in
Soil and position
Light, well-drained, fairly fertile soil and a sunny but sheltered position.

Limnanthes douglasii
POACHED EGG PLANT

Poached egg plant forms a low and spreading mass of eggy yellow-centered flowers that are very attractive to bees and

ladybugs (which devour greenfly). Flowering in mid-summer, they can be sown in early fall or mid- to late spring. Where the plant feels at home it will self-seed for the following year.
ht to 23cm/9in
sp 15cm/6in
Soil and position
Needs a well-drained, but moist soil and open, sunny position.

Lunaria annua
(syn. *Lunaria biennis*)
HONESTY

Also known as 'money plant' because of its round, flat seed heads, *Lunaria annua* most commonly has purple flowers. *L. a.* var. *albiflora* has white flowers, *L. a.* 'Variegata' has white-splashed leaves, and *L.a.* 'Alba Variegata' is blessed with both. The plant usually self-seeds. Mature plants grow from the seedlings of the previous year's spring sowing.
ht to 90cm/3ft
sp 30cm/12in
Soil and position
The plants are undemanding.

Meconopsis cambrica
WELSH POPPY

Not immediately recognizable as a poppy, Welsh poppy is a bright, clear yellow and somewhat shorter than most annual poppies. It shares the silky petals, hairy stems, and nodding flower buds of other poppies and frequently pops up in just the right place. Similar, but even more unusual, is *M. grandis*, the Himalayan poppy, with flowers of a stunning blue.
ht 38cm/15in
sp 20cm/8in
Soil and position
Almost any reasonably well-drained, but not dry, soil in partial shade. Hot dry summers do not suit this plant.

Moluccella laevis
BELLS OF IRELAND

Bells of Ireland has spikes of unusual greenish flowers which can also be dried for winter flower arrangements. What appear to be the flowers are really green calyces that look like elfin caps, almost hiding tiny, slightly scented white flowers. The plant flowers in late summer. Seeds can be sown indoors in early spring or outdoors in late spring, where the plants are to flower.
ht 60–90cm/2–3ft
sp 20cm/8in
Soil and position
Needs fertile, well-drained soil and a sheltered position.

Nemophila menziesii
NEMOPHILA

This is a spreading, low-growing flowering plant for rockeries and border edges. The pretty, light green foliage is almost hidden by the masses of small, pale-blue, white-centered flowers in the best-known variety 'Baby Blue Eyes'. A classy black and white version, 'Penny Black', and the pure white 'Snowstorm' give the gardener plenty of choice. The plants, which flower throughout the summer, can be grown from seed sown outside in late spring.
ht 20cm/8in
sp 30cm/12in
Soil and position
The plants like well-drained, fertile soil but need some moisture, and thrive in part shade as well as full sun.

◀ *Nigella damascena, love-in-a-mist.*

Nicotiana
TOBACCO PLANT

The tobacco plants widely on sale for summer planting are usually Domino Series cultivars and come in various colors from red and deep pink to white, cream, and lime green, mauve and purple. These are very cheerful and have some scent, but if fragrance is what you're after the taller *Nicotiana alata* is worth looking out for. The milky white or lime green flowers are especially well scented at night. A rather different species, the tall *N. sylvestris* has heads of strongly scented, pendent flowers, long, narrow and tubular, from branching stems above broad, tobacco leaves. All are normally grown as biennials and flower from early to late summer.
ht 30cm/12in (Domino Series); 2–3ft (N. alata); 4–5ft (N. sylvestris)
sp 30cm/12in; 60cm/2ft (N. sylvestris)
Soil and position
Fertile, well-drained, moist soil and sun or light shade.
CAUTION: THE FOLIAGE CAN BE A SKIN IRRITANT.

Nigella damascena
LOVE-IN-A-MIST

Love-in-a mist does have a misty look, because of its mass of wispy foliage and misty blue flowers. The inflated seed pods are an extra attraction. This annual is a cottage garden favorite that looks at home in many other situations too. A mixed strain is available in a range of moody blues, pinks, and purples, and white (Persian Jewels Series mixed). Purists, however, like to stick with 'Miss Jekyll', in beautiful blue. The seeds are best sown where they are to grow as doesn't like being transplanted.

ht 40–45cm/16–18in
sp 23cm/9in
Soil and position
Moist, fertile, well-drained soil and a sheltered sunny spot. Does best in fairly cool summers.

Papaver
POPPIES

Every flower garden is enhanced by annual poppies. They have a long flowering season, wave about in the breeze and catch the light beautifully, are tissue-paper fine and fleeting and come in lovely colors. *P. rhoeas* Shirley Series, the Shirley poppy comes in single and double varieties in watercolor shades of pinks, light purple, white, and occasionally orange and red. *P. somniferum*, known as opium poppy, has various shades of sultry pink, purple, and occasionally white or red, and bluish leaves, seed heads and stems.
ht 90cm/3ft (P. rhoeas); to 1.2m/4ft (P. somniferum)
sp 30cm/12in
Soil and position
Reasonably fertile, well-drained soil in good light.
CAUTION: CAUSES POISONING IF EATEN.

Rudbeckia hirta
RUDBECKIA

Rudbeckia hirta, sometimes known as coneflower, are perennials that are grown as annuals, casting a warm glow in the garden in later summer and early fall. The flowers are large, single petaled and daisy-like, in shades of warm yellows, reds and reddish browns, with conical centers of purple-brown, and are borne on sturdy, branching stems with a mass of simple, darkish green leaves. Among the best are 'Rustic Dwarfs' in a good range of dark-zoned and flecked colors; 'Goldilocks' with double or semidouble golden flowers, and 'Marmalade' with large,

bright yellow flowers. 'Becky Mixed' is a dwarf variety in a mix of colors. Cut the stems after flowering to prolong the flowering period.
ht 60cm/2ft; 25cm/10in ('Becky Mixed')
sp 30–45cm/12–18in
Soil and position
Fertile, well-drained soil and a position in full sun.

Salvia splendens
SALVIA

This is a perennial grown as an annual bedding plant, flowering during the whole summer and surviving even the early frosts. With their vibrant flowers they are widely used in park bedding schemes. There's no need to stick to red salvias as the spikes of tubular flowers now come in a range of pinks, purples, and muted orange as well. 'Blaze of Fire' speaks for itself; Cleopatra Series are violet purple; others to choose are S. s. 'Phoenix Mixed', S. s. ' Phoenix Purple', and 'Sizzler Mixed' in the Sizzler Series.
ht 30–40cm/12–16in
sp 25–30cm/10–12in
Soil and position
Needs a soil with good drainage and a light position with plenty of sunlight.

Scabiosa atropurpurea
PINCUSHION FLOWER

Pincushion flower or sweet scabious has lilac blue flowers carried singly on narrow, wiry stems all summer. The loose, wavy petals surround a 'pincushion' center and the flowers attract butterflies and bees. They are best grown in small groups in an informal border. Short-lived perennials, they are usually treated as a biennial (with seed sown the previous spring) or annual. 'Double Mixed' and 'Dwarf Double Mixed' have flowers in shades of white, pink, and purple, as well as blue.
ht 90cm/3ft; 45cm/18in (dwarf types)
sp 20cm/8in
Soil and position
A well-drained, fertile, limy or even chalky soil is best and an open, sunny position.

Tropaeolum
NASTURTIUM

Nasturtiums are easy annuals that are very well worth growing for their bright, velvety, spurred flowers and round, flat, grayish green (and edible) leaves. Most make bushy, low-growing little plants but some are climbers that quickly scramble up a fence or trellis, or over another plant. Many named hybrids are available, in single colors (scarlet, orange, mahogany, yellow, and cream), or with white-splashed leaves. Alaska Series has leaves that are marbled with cream and pink. Look out for blackfly, which tend to gather on the backs of the leaves.
ht 30–60cm/1–2ft; 1–3m/3–10ft (climbers)
sp 45–60cm/18–24in
Soil and position
Flower best when grown in poor but well-drained soil, and in a sunny position.

▼ Meconopsis cambrica, *Welsh poppy, is small with bright yellow flowers.*

◀ Allium christophii, *allium.*

BULBOUS PLANTS

Bulbous plants produce a huge range of flowers, not just in spring but at almost every time of year, and for every situation from well-drained rockeries to moist meadows and pondsides. Allowing the foliage to die down naturally after flowering enables them to build up their resources for the following year, and when they feel at home they thrive. This list includes plants grown from bulbs, corms, and rhizomes—all being food-storage organs which enable the plant to survive the dormant period.

Agapanthus africanus
AGAPANTHUS OR
AFRICAN LILY

In late summer agapanthus has drumheads of bell-shaped or trumpet-like flowers on tall, stately stems, usually in shades of blue although some varieties are white. This striking plant has a mass of long, spear-shaped leaves, and is excellent for containers as well as in garden beds. In all but the most mild and sheltered areas needs protecting with a thick mulch in winter.
ht 60–90cm/2–3ft (a few varieties much taller)
sp 45–60cm/18–24in
Soil and position
Must have a light, well-drained but moist soil or potting soil mix, and needs a very light position.

Allium christophii
ALLIUM

This member of the onion family produces lilac-colored globes of star-shaped flowers on tall stalks, and strappy gray-green leaves, making an architectural plant. There are many different species of allium, producing flowers from spring to fall and in a wide range of heights from dainty to stately. *Allium christophii* flowers in early summer. *A. giganteum* is a giant version with dense round heads of purplish flowers in summer.
ht 60cm/2ft (Allium christophii); 1.5–2m/5–6.5ft (A. giganteum)
sp 15cm/6in (both)
Soil and position
Not fussy as to soil, as long as it is fairly well-drained. Needs a sunny position.
CAUTION: THE JUICE FROM THE BULBS CAN CAUSE SKIN ALLERGIES OR A RASH.

Anemone blanda
WINDFLOWER

Flowering in early spring in shades of heavenly blue, bluish pink, pinky purple, and pure white, this daisy-like anemone, with its deeply cut leaves, is a lovely plant for a semiwild "woodland" area or rock garden, and will soon spread widely if it feels at home.
ht 15cm/6in
sp 10cm/4in
Soil and position
Well-drained soil that is not too dry, in a position in sun or partial shade. Grows well under deciduous trees as it flowers before the leaves open.

Arum italicum
LORDS AND LADIES OR
CUCKOOPINT

Closely related to the wild woodland plant, the garden arum has very glossy leaves in winter and early spring, from the center of which springs up a sturdy spike of minute flowers surrounded by a sail-like spathe in creamy green. In late summer the spike becomes a head of bright red beady berries. The variety *A.i.* 'Marmoratum' (syn. *A. i.* 'Pictum') has marble-patterned, variegated leaves. The less hardy *Arum pictum* has narrow, white-veined leaves.

ht 30cm/12in

sp 15cm/6in

Soil and position
Humus-rich but well-drained soil in any position from full sun to shade.

Chionodoxa
GLORY OF THE SNOW

In early spring chionodoxa produces bright, wide-open, starry flowers amid shapely mid-green leaves. *Chionodoxa forbesii* (sometimes sold as *C. luciliae*) is the species usually grown; its flowers are a clear blue with white centers, or, in the variety 'Pink Giant', a lovely soft pink. Chionodoxa is a good plant to grow in a rockery or under trees, where it will seed itself and spread freely.

ht 10–20cm/4–8in

sp 2.5cm/1in

Soil and position
Well-drained soil with adequate moisture, in sun.

Colchicum
COLCHICUM OR
AUTUMN CROCUS

These delicately colored early fall-flowering crocus-like plants have acquired the name 'naked ladies' from the fact that their broad, most un-crocus-like leaves appear at a completely different time from the "naked" flowers. Some are rare and sought-after (and expensive to buy) but *C. autumnale*, the meadow saffron, and *C. speciosum* are both quite widely available. Both come in several varieties, in white and rosy lilac-pink.

ht 10–15cm/4–6in

sp 8cm/3in

Soil and position
Fertile garden soil and an open, sunny position.

Crinum × Powellii
CRINUM

Crinums are lily-like flowers from South Africa and many of them

▲ Agapanthus africanus *or African lily.*

don't like a cold climate. But *Crinum × Powellii* is surprisingly hardy and bears its hanging pink or white trumpet-shaped flowers well into the fall. Each sturdy stem bears six to eight flowers and the bulbs form clumps, with broad, strap-shaped leaves. Protect with a thick mulch in winter in all but very mild areas.

ht 90cm/3ft

sp 30cm/12in

Soil and position
Well-drained soil, with moisture, and a warm, sheltered spot.
CAUTION: ANY PART OF THE PLANT CAN CAUSE SEVERE STOMACH UPSET; THE JUICES CAN CAUSE SKIN IRRITATION.

Crocus
CROCUS

Spring-flowering crocuses are a must in any garden, planted under trees, in a rockery, or in pots on the patio or corners of

the border. Among the earliest to flower are *C. tommasinianus*, in delicate shades of amethyst blue to lilac, and (in 'Ruby Giant') reddish purple. The bolder *C. vernus* comes in the same color range, including brighter shades, but also in golden yellow ('Dutch Yellow'), and with feathered forms (as in 'Joan of Arc') or stripes ('Winston Churchill'). These usually flower in mid-spring, as does *Crocus angustifolius* or cloth of gold, which has yellow flowers that are bronze-stained on the outside, with a delicate fragrance. The corms soon spread, forming small clumps. Robust forms are good for naturalizing in grass.

ht to 10cm/4in

sp 2.5cm/1in

Soil and position
Well-drained soil and a sunny situation, where they will not be disturbed.

Cyclamen coum
CYCLAMEN

This winter-flowering native of northern Turkey will flourish in the shelter of trees and shrubs. Flared-back flowers come in white and shades of pink and purple, and the flat, heart-shaped leaves are very dark green and usually attractively marbled in silver. Flowers continue until mid-spring. Must be bought from a licensed source to insure that illegally imported, wild corms are not used.

ht 10cm/4in

sp to 15cm/6in

Soil and position
Well-drained, humus-rich soil that does not dry out in summer; sun or partial shade.
CAUTION: ALL PARTS OF THE PLANT CAN CAUSE SEVERE STOMACH UPSET IF EATEN.

◄ Eranthis hyemalis, *winter aconite,* flowers in late winter.

Erythronium dens-canis
DOG'S TOOTH VIOLET

With their backward-flaring petals and marbled leaves these little plants look similar to cyclamen and flower in spring. The leaves are broad and pointed, with purplish brown splodges, and the flowers are in white, pink, or lilac, depending on the variety. 'Lilac Wonder', 'Pink Perfection', 'Snowflake', 'White Splendour', and 'Purple King' all live up to their names. Erythroniums look pretty growing under trees or shrubs, in rockeries, or naturalized in the lawn, and they spread to form small clumps.
ht and sp 10–15cm/4–6in
Soil and position
Well-drained, humus-rich soil that does not dry out in summer, in lightly dappled shade.

Fritillaria imperialis
CROWN IMPERIAL

This is a large and striking member of the fritillary family, flowering in late spring. Whorls of spiky, pale green leaves top the orange, bell-shaped flowers clustered at the tops of strong brown stems. The variety *F. i.* 'Lutea Maxima' has lemon-yellow flowers.
ht to 1.5m/3–5ft
sp to 90cm/12in
Soil and position
Fertile, well-drained soil in sun or partial shade.

Galtonia
SUMMER HYACINTH

True to the family they come from, galtonias look like loose-flowered hyacinths. The closely packed buds toward the tops of the stems open into pendent, bell-like flowers and the plants form clumps with wide, strap-shaped, slightly arching leaves.

Dahlia
DAHLIA

Dahlias jolly up the garden in late summer and last until the first frosts. Apart from the cheerful pompom-headed and multipetaled cactus types there are elegant single flowering dahlias for those who like restraint and dwarf-dahlias that don't need staking (as the others generally do). 'Bishop of Llandaff' is a peony-flowered form with brilliant red flowers and stunning reddish black foliage; 'Easter Sunday' is a white, single form with a 'collerette' of small petals around the central yellow disc; 'Moor Place' is a pompon dahlia in a rich clerical red'; 'Hamari Gold' is a multi-petaled decorative dahlia in a bright, warm golden orange, and 'Princess Marie Jose' is a single-flowered dahlia in soft pink.
ht 60cm–1m/2–3ft
sp 45–60cm/18–24in

Soil and position
Fairly heavy, fertile soil and a sunny position.

Eranthis hyemalis
WINTER ACONITE

Bright yellow, buttercup flowers surrounded by green ruffs open on short stems in late winter, at the same time as the snowdrops, advising us that we'll soon be getting into our gardening boots again. In summer the plants disappear, to put out leaf again the following winter. Over the course of the years, provided they are at home, they will spread to form large clumps.
ht and sp 8–10cm/3–4in
Soil and situation
A well-drained, moist soil that doesn't dry out in summer and a sunny or semishaded position.

▶ Dahlia *'Bishop of Llandaff'* has brilliant red flowers and black foliage.

Galtonia candicans, the fragrant, white-flowered form, is the one most usually grown but there is also a more unusual galtonia with pale green flowers, *G. viridiflora*. They flower in late summer. Mulch the plants for winter protection in all but the mildest areas.

ht 1m/3ft
sp 20cm/8in
Soil and position
Well-drained soil that remains slightly moist in summer and a sunny, fairly sheltered position.

Iris
IRIS

Broadly, irises divide into two types: bulbous (grown from bulbs, and usually quite small) and rhizomatous (grown from rhizomes, and including the larger irises as well as some dwarf ones). Many of the rhizomatous kind are bearded, with rough crests on the three large, dropping outer petals or "falls" characteristic of all irises.

Bulbous irises include Spanish, English, and Dutch. Dutch flower in white, yellow, and blue in early summer, with the English (white, purple, and blue), and Spanish (white, purple, blue, and yellow), flowering later. Another bulbous type is the small and lovely winter-flowering *Iris reticulata* (with flowers in blue or purple).

Beardless, moisture-loving rhizomatous irises include the mid-summer-flowering *I. pseudacorus*, the yellow flag or water iris, a must for streams and pondside, and *I. sibirica* or Siberian flag, with blue or purple early summer flowers.

Bearded rhizomatous irises come in all sizes, from dwarf to tall. Two good, fragrant ones are *I. pallida* 'Variegata' with lilac blue flowers and green and yellow striped leaves, and the lovely winter-flowering *Iris*

▶ *Iris reticulata, a bulbous iris.*

unguicularis, almost hiding its low-growing lavender, blue, and lilac flowers among its leaves. Other favorites include 'Langport Smoke' in a clear, soft blue; 'Langport Song', with ruffled, lemon-yellow petals; 'Black Knight', dark purple; 'Bronze Cloud', copper and lavender blue, and 'Dante', golden bronze and raspberry red.

ht and sp 5–100cm/2–39in
Soil and position
Bulbous irises need well-drained soil and an open, sunny, sheltered position. Rhizomatous irises generally like warm, alkaline soil and a sunny, sheltered position, but the beardless, pondside ones like moist soil and semishade, and yellow flag will grow in water at the pond edge.
CAUTION: CAN CAUSE STOMACH UPSET IF EATEN.

Leucojum aestivum 'Gravetye'
SUMMER SNOWFLAKE OR LODDON LILY

Leucojum plants look like enlarged snowdrops. Small, flaring, bell-like flowers, in white, with green spots on the pointed tepal (a kind of petal) tips, hang prettily from the stem tops, just above the narrow, straplike leaves. *Leucojum aestivum* 'Gravetye' is a reliable variety which flowers in late spring. The lower-growing *L. vernum* flowers in early spring.

ht to 60cm/2ft (Leucojum aestivum); 20cm/8in (L. vernum)
sp 10cm/4in
Soil and position
Moist soil and, dappled shade.

Lilium
LILY

Lilies are a firm gardening favorite. They offer a huge choice, and the following are just a few favorites among lilies that

are undemanding and fairly easy to obtain. *Lilium candidum*, the madonna lily (white, very fragrant, midsummer flowering, and one of the few to need alkaline soil); *L. longiflorum*, the Easter lily (actually flowering in midsummer, very fragrant, lime-tolerant); *L. regale*, the regal lily (fragrant, white, with deep pink streaks on the outside, midsummer flowering); *L. mackliniae* (pink, unscented, midsummer flowering), *L. monadelphum* (fragrant, creamy yellow, purple-spotted inside, flowering early summer, tolerates lime); *L.* 'Enchantment' (rich orange, flowering early summer, not scented). *L.* 'Star Gazer' has beautiful reddish-pink flowers with darker spots; it is midsummer flowering.

ht to 1m/3ft or more; to 60cm/2ft (L. mackliniae)
sp 15–20cm/6–8in

ht 10–15cm/4–8in
sp 5cm/2in
Soil and position
Almost any reasonably well-drained soil in a sunny position.

Narcissus
DAFFODIL AND JONQUIL

There are far too many narcissi to begin to select—from short for rockeries and pots to tall for borders and from early to late flowerers. Among the smaller ones 'Tête a Tête' is a dwarf in cheerful yellow for early spring, 'Minnow' is a pale dwarf for mid-spring, N. cyclamineus is an early-flowering species with backward flaring perianths and long, narrow trumpets, and N. cantabricus is an enchanting white hooped petticoat daffodil with wide funnel-shaped trumpets and tiny pointed perianths. Late in the season N. poeticus, a tall species, produces fragrant white flowers with tiny orange cups instead of trumpets. The many hybrids include: 'Actaea' (white with orange centers); 'Cassata' (soft yellow); 'February Gold' (bright yellow); 'Ice Follies' (one of the best and most beautiful white varieties); 'St Keverne' (sturdy, with bright yellow flowers); 'Minnow' a dainty dwarf, with cream of yellow flowers); 'Suzy' (rich yellow with red cups); and 'Rainbow' (white and pink). Sturdy hybrids are useful for naturalizing in grass.
ht 20–50cm/8–20in, sp16cm/6in (hybrids and N. poeticus);
ht 15–20cm/6–8in,
sp 5–8cm/2–3in (the rest)
Soil and position
Ordinary garden soil and a sunny, light position.

Nerine bowdenii
NERINE

Nerines have wavy, loosely grouped lily-like flowers on tall, narrow stems, and strap-shaped, rather grass-like leaves; they flower from late summer and right through the fall, making them even more appreciated. While most species are not suitable for growing outdoors in a cold climate *Nerine bowdenii*, with its light raspberry pink flowers, is hardy and robust. *N. b.* 'Mark Fenwick' (aka 'Fenwick's Variety') is a stronger and taller variety, with deeper pink flowers, and *N. b.* f. *alba* has white or palest pink flowers.
ht 50cm/20in
sp 8cm/3in
Soil and position
Well-drained soil in a sunny and sheltered position, for example by a house wall.

Tulipa
TULIP

You can buy mixed tulips in unspecified colors and they will flower cheerfully in later spring, but sometimes only a special tulip will do. Among the many stunning varieties are 'Angelique' (double, pale pink); 'Golden Apeldorn' (bright yellow with black base), 'Queen of Night' (very dark, almost black); 'Spring Green' (white flowers with green feathering); 'White Parrot', and 'Black Parrot' (with twisting, fringed petals in white/almost black). Finally the small, early flowering water-lily tulip *T. kaufmanniana* has wide-open, scented flowers in cream or yellow, sometimes with contrasting centers.
ht 30cm/12in ('Angelique');
60cm/2ft ('Golden Apeldorn' and 'Queen of Night');
40cm/16in ('Spring Green');
55cm/22in ('White Parrot', and 'Black Parrot'); 20cm/8in (T. kaufmanniana)
sp 8–15cm/3–6in
Soil and position
Well-drained soil in a sunny, fairly sheltered position.

Soil and situation
Unless otherwise stated lilies require well-drained neutral or acid soil enriched with compost or leaf mold and a position in sun or lightly dappled shade.

Muscari
GRAPE HYACINTH

Grape hyacinths produce blue flowers arranged like miniature grapes on upright stems in spring, surrounded by a mass of somewhat untidy arching, grassy leaves. Unnamed varieties are generally available but it's worth looking out for *Muscari neglectum* (syn. *M. racemosum*), which has white-rimmed flowers in very deep blue, and *M. aucheri*, whose pale blue, almost drumhead flowers are again white rimmed and whose leaves are a pleasant grayish green.

PERENNIALS

Perennials form the mainstay of most garden planting, lasting from year to year and normally flowering annually. We have included in this section not only herbaceous perennials that die back over winter and grow up again in spring, but also some of the smaller shrubs. The plants listed here include some that flower in winter and fall as well as spring and summer.

Alchemilla mollis
LADY'S MANTLE

This is a "must-have" for almost any type of garden, at home in a formal or informal setting. Bundles of tiny, greenish yellow flowers weigh down the light stems for the whole summer and the downy, lobed leaves catch drops of rain or dew at the center. The plant lolls gracefully at the front of a border, forms large clumps, and self-seeds. Grows prettily in gravel or between the paving stones too.
ht 60cm/2ft
sp 75cm/30in
Soil and position
Prefers a fairly moist, rich soil but tolerates dry, fairly poor soils too. Thrives equally well in sun or semishade.
SLUGS AND SNAILS CAN ATTACK YOUNG LEAVES.

Anemone × hybrida
(syn. *A. japonica*)
JAPANESE ANEMONE

A tall and lovely plant for later summer, with flowers of white or shades of moody pink on upright, branching stems. The simple flowers, wide open and with a central boss of orange-yellow stamens are mainly single, as in the white 'Honorine Jobert', but 'Whirlwind' (white) and 'Queen Charlotte' (pink) are semidouble. The deeply toothed leaves cluster beautifully round the stem axils.
ht 1.2m/4ft
sp 60cm/2ft
Soil and position
Needs moist but well-drained, rich soil in sun or semishade.

Aquilegia
AQUILEGIA

Aquilegia, also known as columbine, granny's bonnets and old maid's bonnets, is a well-loved, old-fashioned garden plant and there are many hybrids, named and unnamed. Its flower bonnets with their distinctive spurs nod down from graceful stems which rise up from a mass of lobed leaves, often a grayish green. Flowering in early summer, this is a pretty plant for a cottage garden or meadow garden. Not long-lived, but generally self-seeding it will often colonize an area when it feels at home.

Types to choose include *A. vulgaris* hybrids, including the neatly frilled 'Nora Barlow'; *A.* Mrs Scott Elliott Hybrids, often bicolored with very long spurs; *A. longissima*, pale yellow flowers with very long spurs; *A. flabellata*, soft blue.
ht 90cm/3ft
sp 60cm/2ft
Soil and position
Likes well-drained soil and cool conditions.

Campanula persicifolia,
BELLFLOWER/CAMPANULA

There are many garden campanulas, including low-growing alpine varieties, most having flaring tube- or bell-shaped flowers in shades of blue, with white, some cream, and the occasional pink. *Campanula persicifolia* is tall and spiry, with slender stems sporting delicate-looking, harebell-like flowers of sky blue. *C. p. alba* is a similar white-flowered version. Slightly more uncommon, the smaller

▲ Anemone x hybrida (syn. A. japonica), *Japanese anemone.*

C. alliariifolia has stems of downward-facing, narrow, white flowers and *C.* 'Elizabeth' has extremely narrow, pink-flushed flowers, offset by deep-toothed foliage. All flower from mid- to late summer, especially if the stems are cut after flowering. Beware of tiny slugs and snails, which can ravage the flowers.
ht 90cm/3ft (C. persicifolia);
45cm/18in (C. alliariifolia); to
40cm/16in (C. 'Elizabeth')
sp 30cm/12in (C. persicifolia);
45cm/18in (C. alliariifolia); to
40cm/16in (C. 'Elizabeth')
Soil and position
Like moist but well-drained soil and partial shade.

Crambe cordifolia
COLEWORT

Tall, spreading and airy, this plant from the cabbage family has many-branching stems and a froth of tiny white flowers against enormous veined and crinkled leaves. The flowers are fragrant, and attractive to bees. *Crambe maritima* or sea kale is similar but low-growing and with thick, bluish leaves; it grows well in maritime conditions. Both plants flower in early summer. The stems of sea kale can be blanched in winter for spring eating.
ht 1.8m/6ft (C. cordifolia);
75cm/30in (C. maritima)
sp 1.8m/6ft (C. cordifolia);
60cm/2ft (C. maritima)
Soil and position
Need a sunny position, sheltered from wind, in well-drained, alkaline soil.

Dicentra spectabilis
BLEEDING HEART

In late spring and early summer the fleshy, dark pink stems of graceful *Dicentra spectabilis* (called by country people "ladies in the bath") are bowed with pink lockets hanging along their length. In the form *Dicentra spectabilis* 'Alba' the flowers are white and the stems green and more wiry. The plants form feathery-leaved clumps. *Dicentra formosa* is a similar but much lower growing plant.
ht 75cm/30in (Dicentra spectabilis); to 45cm/18in (Dicentra formosa)
sp 45cm/18in (Dicentra spectabilis); to 45cm/18in (Dicentra formosa)
Soil and position
Moist but well-drained, compost-rich soil in a sheltered, shady spot. Likes alkaline conditions.

Echinops
GLOBE THISTLE

Strong and sturdy, these plants have round drumheads of blue, thistle-like flowers and spiny, down-backed, gray-green leaves. The flowers, produced toward the end of the summer, are very attractive to bees, and dry well for dried flower arrangements.

E. bannaticus 'Blue Globe' and the slightly more compact *E. ritro* 'Veitch's Blue' both have particularly well-colored flowers.
ht to 1m/3ft
sp 45–60cm/18–24in
Soil and position
Although at their best in full sun and poor, fairly dry, well-drained soil, globe thistles will grow in almost any position.

Epimedium
BARRENWORT

Sometimes known as bishop's miter or bishop's hat from the shape of their leaves, these are excellent ground-cover plants, especially for growing under trees and shrubs. There are many types available, and although they are grown mainly for their leaves many have attractive small flowers in yellow, orange, red, or pink. Choice varieties include *E. × rubrum*, with crimson flowers and red and reddish brown leaves that are particularly striking in winter; *E. × versicolor* 'Cupreum', which is very tolerant and has coppery leaves and pink flowers; and *E. × v.* 'Sulphureum', with coppery leaves and yellow flowers. Check other species

◀ Eryngium, *sea holly.*

when you buy, as some are fussy and some die down in winter.
ht to 30cm/12in
sp indefinite
Soil and position
Woodland conditions with semishade to full shade, and moist, humus-rich soil.

Eryngium
SEA HOLLY

The overall effect of these architectural plants, with their holly-like leaves and cone-shaped flowers surrounded by arresting, spiny bracts, is of spiky shapes and gray-blue or metallic blue coloring. *Eryngium × oliverianum* is a good long-lived variety with silvery blue coloring that ages to purple-blue, while *E. × tripartitum*, also long-lived, is slightly taller, lighter in form, and more dainty, with violet-blue coloring. All flower until the fall and are good for cutting and drying.
ht 60cm–1m/2–3ft
sp 50–60cm/20–24in
Soil and position
Needs a sunny position and very well-drained, ordinary soil that does not get waterlogged during the winter months.

Euphorbia
SPURGE, MILKWEED

Great favorites with knowledgeable gardeners, spurges provide a wide choice of bushy plants, generally evergreen, with strong, sappy stems, often a leaning habit, and flowers of yellowish green. *E. nicaeensis*★ has domes of lime-yellow, green-bracted flowers in spring and blue-green, curling leaves growing all the way down the strong stems. *E. characias*★ is tall and erect with densely flowered stems. Its flowers have purple nectar glands, though the subspecies known as *E.c. wulfenii*

has greenish yellow flowers. The much smaller *E. polychroma* is very lime-yellow, starry flowering and mound forming. Other spurges to consider are *E. amygdaloides*★★, *E. cyparissias*★, *E. myrsinites*★, *E. griffithii* 'Dixter'★★ and *E. g.* 'Fireglow'★★.
ht 80cm/32in; sp 45cm/18in (E. nicaeensis)
ht and sp 1.2m/4ft (E. characias)
ht 40cm/16in; sp 60cm/2ft (E. polychroma)
ht 75cm/30in; sp 30cm/12in (E. amygdaloides)
ht 20–40cm/8–16in; sp indefinite (E. cyparissias)
ht 10cm/4in; sp to 30cm/12in (E. myrsinites)
ht 75cm/30in; sp 90cm/3ft (E. griffithii)
Soil and position
Those marked ★ like a sunny spot in well-drained soil; those marked ★★ need light, dappled shade and a moist soil with plenty of humus. *E. polychroma* adapts to sun or partial shade.
CAUTION: THE MILKY WHITE LIQUID IN THE STEMS IS POISONOUS IF INGESTED AND CAUSTIC TO THE TOUCH.

Geranium

CRANESBILL, GERANIUM

You can become addicted to geraniums and their modest charms. These are hardy, and, given conditions they like, very long-lasting plants, with flowers in shades of pale pink to magenta, white, and light sky blue. They have lobed or deeply cut leaves and simple, wide-open flowers, often delicately veined or deeply stained at the center, and they vary from small and compact to large clump-forming. Among the best are the very reliable G. 'Johnson's Blue', with warm blue flowers; G. *sanguineum* 'Album' (white), G. *s.* 'Shepherd's Warning' (deep pink), and G. *s.* var. *striatum* (pale pink, delicately marked with deeper pink). G. *renardii*, which flourishes in poor soil, has velvety leaves and dark-veined pale lavender flowers. The meadow cranesbill, G. *pratense*, is blue, with white varieties, and flourishes in meadow-type conditions with rich, moist soil. The large G. *maderense*, (evergreen leaves, red stems, light magenta flowers) is short-lived in gardens but easily grown annually from seed.

ht to 45cm/18in, sp to 75cm/30in (G. 'Johnson's Blue')
ht 30cm/12in, sp 40cm/16in (G. sanguineum 'Album')
ht and sp 15cm/6in (G. s. 'Shepherd's Warning')
ht and sp 10cm/4in (G. s. var. striatum)
ht and sp 30cm/12in (G. renardii)
ht to 90cm/3ft sp 60cm/2ft (G. pratense)
ht and sp to 1.5m/5ft (G. maderense)
Soil and position
Unless stated above geraniums are happy in ordinary, well-drained garden soil, in sun or partial shade. The smallest species need very good drainage, with added grit or sharp sand.

Helleborus argutifolius
(syn. H. corsicus)
CORSICAN HELLEBORE

This large, shrubby-looking hellebore has bunches of small, pale creamy green flowers for a long period from late winter and interesting, tooth-edged, leathery leaves throughout the year. The shorter *Helleborus foetidus* is very similar, also tough and shrubby looking, but with lime-green flowers, rimmed with crimson and lasting well into spring.

Shorter hellebores, best grown in groups, are the pure white *Helleborus niger* or Christmas rose and *Helleborus orientalis*, the lenten rose. Both have large and tender-looking, cup-like flowers, the first in late winter, the second in early spring. 'Potter's Wheel' is a good variety of the Christmas rose, generous with its pure white flowers. Lenten roses have plum colored flowers and there are many subtly shaded hybrids, named and unnamed.

ht 90cm/3ft, sp to 1.2m/4ft (Helleborus argutifolius)
ht 60cm/2ft, sp 45cm/18in (Helleborus foetidus)
ht and sp 30cm/12in (Helleborus niger)
ht and sp 45cm/18in (Helleborus orientalis)
Soil and position
Fertile, well-drained but moist, limy soil; shade or partial shade.
CAUTION: THE PLANTS ARE POISONOUS IF EATEN AND THE SAP CAN CAUSE IRRITATION.

Hemerocallis
DAY LILY

Members of the lily family, day lilies have sword-shaped leaves and twisting stems. They bear their flowers for only a day, but continue to produce new flowers during the whole of the summer. Many varieties have now been bred and there is a wide choice of colors and flower shapes, from spidery to double and triangular. The plants form large clumps. Among those to choose are 'Berlin Red' and 'Red Precious' (red), 'Cartwheels' (orange), 'Lemon Bells', and Marion Vaughn', (shades of yellow), and 'Pink Damask' (pink). Shorter, so-called dwarf varieties such as 'Golden Chimes' and 'Stella de Oro' (yellow) are also available.

ht to 1.3m/4ft
sp to 90cm/3ft
Soil and position
A sunny position in fertile, moist, rather heavy but well-drained soil. Will also tolerate partial shade.

Heuchera
HEUCHERA OR CORAL FLOWER

A member of the saxifrage family, heuchera can be grown as ground cover in light shade, or in clumps in borders, where the flowers will attract bees. The plants make mounds of foliage out of which spring panicles of tiny flowers on tall stems. Most of the named varieties are red or coral pink but the species H. *cylindrica* offers green-flowered varieties such as 'Greenfinch', which can be used to much more subtle effect. Good red varieties include 'Red Spangles' and 'Coral Cloud'. If you want to use heuchera as a foliage plant try 'Palace Purple' (chocolate), 'Pewter Moon' (gray) or 'Snow Storm' (flecked white).

ht to 90cm/3ft, sp 60cm/2ft ('Greenfinch')
ht 50cm/20in, sp 25cm/10in ('Red Spangles')
ht 75cm/30in, sp 30cm/12in ('Coral Cloud')
ht and sp to 60cm/2ft ('Palace Purple')
ht to 40cm/16in, sp 30cm/12in ('Pewter Moon')
ht and sp 30cm/12in ('Snow Storm')
Soil and position
Moist but well-drained, preferably neutral soil in partial to full shade.

◀ Geranium, *cranesbill or geranium.*

Kniphofia
RED-HOT POKER

Red-hot poker is certainly a striking plant, in height, form and color, and it can be just what's needed to make bright points of color or as a foil for softer plants. Torches of red or orange flowers rise erect from the bundles of strap-like leaves in a show-stopping way in summer, with exact flowering times depending on the cultivar. Among the tall and reds you might choose the brilliant *K.* 'Atlanta' (red and yellow, flowering early summer), or the massive *K.* 'Prince Igor' (pure, brilliant red for the end of the summer). *K. caulescens* is a very hardy red-hot poker with more muted colors (dull purple red topping light yellow), flowering from late summer into the fall; the lower growing variety *K.* 'Bees Sunset' has warm light orange flowers throughout the summer, and for a yellow poker of modest height there is *K.* 'Sunningdale Yellow', which flowers from mid- to late summer.
ht 1.2m/4ft, sp 75cm/30in ('Atlanta')
ht 1.8m/6ft sp 90cm/3ft ('Prince Igor')
ht to 1.2m/4ft, sp 60cm/2ft (K. caulescens)
ht 90cm/3ft, sp 60cm/2ft ('Bees Sunset')
ht 90cm/3ft, sp 45cm/18in ('Sunningdale Yellow')
Soil and position
Fertile, sandy or well-drained soil in a sunny position. Tolerates light shade.

Lamium maculatum
LAMIUM OR DEAD NETTLE

Lamium is a ground-cover plant for shaded places, grown mainly for its tooth-edged white- and silver- mottled leaves. *Lamium maculatum* f. *album* has pure white flowers throughout the spring and early summer, as well as white-patterned leaves; *L. m.* 'Roseum' is its pink-flowered partner. *L. m.* 'White Nancy' has green-edged, silver leaves and white flowers, and *L. m.* 'Aureum' has yellow and white leaves, although (unusually for plants with golden variegation) like the rest, it must have semi-shade. The plants spread quickly and are hardy, keeping their leaves throughout the winter as long as it's not too wet.
ht 23–30cm/9–12in
sp to 60cm/2ft
Soil and position
Thrives in shade and semishade in ordinary soil. *L. m.* 'Aureum' needs more moisture and a more fertile soil than the others.

Lavandula
LAVENDER

Lavender (really a shrub) needs no introduction as a well-loved garden and herb garden plant for warm and well-drained sites. The flowers can be dried and used in pot pourri and for scenting linen. The bushy plants, with their gray-green leaves, look good even when not covered in the fragrant flower spikes. *Lavandula angustifolia* is the old English lavender, also know as *L. officinalis* or *L spica*. The variety 'Hidcote' is a true deep lavender blue; the more compact 'Munstead' is purple blue. 'Hidcote Pink' is (as its name suggests) a pink-flowered form, while 'Nana Alba' is small and neat and white-flowering. A less hardy and more unusual lavender is French lavender, *L. stoechas*, with flaring purple bracts above the flowers.
ht 60cm/2ft, sp 75cm/30in ('Hidcote' and 'Hidcote Pink')
ht 45cm/18in, sp 60cm/2ft ('Munstead')
ht and sp 30cm/12in ('Nana Alba')
ht and sp 60cm/2ft (L. stoechas)

▲ Kniphofia, *red-hot poker.*

Soil and position
Very well-drained soil, and a position in full sun.

Papaver orientale
ORIENTAL POPPY

Gardens need poppies. *Papaver orientale* is the brilliant orange-red poppy commonly seen in established gardens, but there are many hybrids, known by their own names, giving a wide choice of color and patterning. 'Black and White' is a luscious double creamy white poppy with black stamens; 'Bonfire Red' speaks for itself; 'Cedric Morris' has full-blown petals in soft pink, with black blotches at the center; 'Beauty of Livermore' is a clear poppy red, and 'Mrs Perry' is black-blotched salmon pink.
(See also *P. somniferum*, page 978)
ht to 90cm/3ft
sp 60–90cm/2–3ft
Soil and position
Fertile soil, including heavy soil as long as it is well-drained, and a sunny position.

Penstemon cultivars
PENSTEMON

With their profusion of foxglove bells and their tall but bushy growth these are lovely, though not very hardy or long-lived border plants, which flower well into the fall. In recent years more and more hybrids have been developed to widen the range of colors and improve hardiness. Colors vary from strong to pastel, mainly pinks, magenta and purples, but also blue and white. Give frost protection where winters are cold, and protect from slugs and snails, which are partial to this dish. All the following are hardy: 'Alice Hindley' (lilac blue), 'Apple Blossom' (apple blossom pink), 'Blackbird' (deep purple),

'Garnet' (garnet red), 'Hidcote Pink' (pale pink), 'Mother of Pearl' (pearly lilac and pink), 'White Bedder' (white).
ht and sp10–60cm/4–24in
Soil and position
Penstemons need fertile soil with good drainage, especially during winter, and a warm, sheltered position in sun or partial shade.

Perovskia atriplicifolia
RUSSIAN SHADE

More people should grow this tolerant, shrubby plant for its tiny lilac blue flowers and gray-green, sage-scented leaves on wiry stems. The flowers are produced toward the end of the summer but, with its mass of tall and upward-branching grayish stems and narrow, tooth-edged leaves, the plant looks good all summer. *P*. 'Blue Spire' is very generous with its deep violet-

blue flowers. *P*. 'Hybrida' has lavender-blue flowers and is a little less tall.
ht 90cm–1.5m/3–5ft
sp to 90cm/3ft
Soil and position
Needs a sunny position in freely draining soil but will grow in poor, dry, or chalky soil. May not survive winter in cold, damp conditions, but may revive if cut back in spring.

Phlox paniculata
GARDEN PHLOX

With their evocative, slightly woody scent and heads of simple, open flowers, these are good, long-lived herbaceous border plants. They flower in full summer, mostly in the pink, white and dusky purple color range, and often with a contrasting eye. Good specimens include 'Alba Grandiflora'

▶ Penstemon *cultivars*, penstemon.

(white), 'Amethyst' (violet), 'Blue Ice' (blue-tinged white with contrasting eye), 'Eva Callum' (deep pink with contrasting eye), 'Eventide' (lavender blue), 'Prince of Orange' (orange-red), 'Prospero' (pale lilac, edged), and 'White Admiral' (pure white). Plants may need staking in windy spots and frequent watering in dry weather.
ht 80cm–1.2m/32in–4ft
sp 60–90cm/2–3ft
Soil and position
Fertile, heavy, moist but well-drained soil and a position in sun or partial shade.

Potentilla
POTENTILLA

There is a huge range of potentillas for the garden. They are in fact shrubs, but many make nice, well-rounded little bushes, small enough to blend well with perennials and border plants. They have attractive small leaves, sometimes deeply cut or silvery, and are incredibly floriferous, usually covered with small and delicate buttercup-like flowers from early summer until late fall.

Flowers are in white and all shades of yellow, orange, red, or pink. Among the many small garden hybrids are *Potentilla* 'Gibson's Scarlet' (blood-red flowers with dark centers), 'William Rollinson' (semi-double, flowers in red flecked with yellow) and *P. nepalensis* 'Miss Willmott' (raspberry pink with carmine markings). *P. recta* (pale lemon-yellow) and *P. fruticosa* 'Abbotswood' (delicate white flowers) are a little larger.
ht 30–45cm/12–18in, sp 60cm/2ft
('Gibson's Scarlet', 'William Rollinson', 'Miss Willmott')

◀ Lamium maculatum, *Lamium or dead nettle.*

ht 60cm/2ft, sp 45cm/18in
(P. recta)
ht 75cm/30in, sp 1.2m/4ft
(P. fruticosa 'Abbotswood')
Soil and position
Must have very well-drained soil, which need not be too fertile. Flower best in full sun.

Pulmonaria
PULMONARIA OR LUNGWORT

Also known as "soldiers and sailors," this is a lovely low-growing plant for early spring, one of the first to flower, and growing bigger and better as the season continues. When the flowers are over the white-blotched leaves come to the fore, and remain decoratively in the garden all summer and fall. The flowers are a beautiful blue, or in

some varieties varicolored pink and blue. Choice white varieties are also available, and a few are pink or red. Good blue varieties include *Pulmonaria* 'Mawson's Blue' (deep blue), *P. officinalis* 'Royal Blue' and *P. o.* 'Blue Mist'. *P. o.* 'Sissinghurst White' is the white to go for.
ht and sp 30cm/12in
Soil and position
Moist, fertile soil and a position in partial shade. Lungwort grows well beneath deciduous trees and shrubs.

Sedum spectabile
ICE PLANT

There is something cactus-like about this plant, with its fleshy, gray-green stems and leaves, and its densely packed flat flower heads of starry pink flowers attracting butterflies in late

summer. The plant has a rounded, compact shape and dry flower heads are an attraction throughout the winter. *Sedum spectabile* 'Autumn Joy' and *S. s.* 'Brilliant' are good varieties.
ht and sp 45cm/18in
Soil and position
Grows best in well-drained slightly alkaline soil, in full sun.

Stachys byzantina
LAMB'S EARS OR WOOLY BETONY

Soft, silver-gray and felted leaves are the main feature of this plant for dry places, although in summer it also has taller spikes of small purplish pink flowers set in whorls among tiny gray leaves and rising above the lamb's ear leaves. However, the main part of the plant is low-growing and it also spreads well and is

▲ Pulmonaria, *pulmonaria or lungwort.*

evergreen—or evergray— except that a damp winter can end its life.
ht to 45cm/18in
sp 60cm/2ft
Soil and position
Must have very well-drained soil (though will tolerate poor soil), and an open, fairly sunny position.

Verbascum
VERBASCUM OR MULLEIN

An elegant, tall, spiry plant with gray, felted leaves, verbascum is sometimes short-lived but is easily grown from seed. The flower spike ascends from a rosette of leaves in summer and some varieties are very tall. *Verbascum bombyciferum* with its immense height and sulfur-yellow flowers is an accent plant and a half. Many named garden varieties are available for those who want something a little less lofty or more subtly colored. *V.* 'Cotswold Beauty' has purple-centered yellow flowers; the flowers of 'Gainsborough' are

chalky yellow, and 'Pink Domino' has rosy or purple pink flowers. *V. phoeniceum* (purple mullein) hybrids give pink, white, and purple flowers.
ht 1.2m/4ft; to 1.6m/6ft (Verbascum bombyciferum)
sp 30–60cm/1–2ft
Soil and position
Alkaline, well-drained to dry soil, including poor soils. Does best in sun.

Verbena bonariensis
VERBENA

Tall, wiry, branching stems produce many small heads of bright purple flowers throughout the summer and early fall at varying heights. The stems are spruce green and pleasantly rough. Sometimes grown as an annual bedding plant, verbena survives the winter if protected from frost.
ht to 1.2m/4ft
sp 45cm/18in
Soil and position
Well-drained soil and full sun.

◀ Sedum spectabile, *ice plant,* 'Mawson's Blue' *variety.*

TREES AND SPECIMEN SHRUBS

Trees and shrubs give shape and form to the garden and can act as strong focal points. They need to be chosen and positioned with care as they make a permanent feature that can take up a lot of room, and make areas of shade, but they compensate by adding height and substance and helping to bring structure to the plot. The plants selected here are all suitable for smaller gardens and many have something of interest to offer for more than one season.

Acer
MAPLE

There are several ornamental maples whose height keeps to within ordinary garden limits, and they usually have bark appeal as well as leaf appeal and fall color. *Acer griseum* is a paper bark maple with peeling, orange-brown bark and broad, flat, three-lobed leaves which turn orange to red and scarlet in the fall. An advantage is that it can be grown as a single- or multistemmed tree. *Acer henryi* is a smallish, shapely maple which colors bright orange-red in the fall and *Acer rufinerve* (red vein maple) is a taller but less spreading maple with green and white striped bark, and red and orange leaves in fall.
ht and sp 5–10m/16–32ft
Soil and position
Fertile, well-drained (but not dry) soil, in a light position.
(*Acer* 'Rubrum', page 881)

Amelanchier lamarckii
AMELANCHIER
OR SNOWY MESPILUS

Bronze unfolding leaves almost disappear as small white starry flowers smother the branches of the plant in spring. Amelanchier becomes less interesting as the

flowers die and leaves turn green, but in later summer coral pink fruits develop and then the leaves turn bright red. If the birds leave the fruits to ripen they eventually turn black. Can be grown as a single or

▲ Acer palmatum, *Japanese maple 'Dissectum Atropurpureum'.*

multistemmed plant.
ht 3m/10ft
sp to 3m/10ft
Soil and position

Moist, preferably neutral or acid soil in a light position.

Berberis sieboldii
BERBERIS OR BARBERRY

A spiny shrub with shiny reddish stems and clusters of small yellow flowers in late spring. In the fall these develop into red shining berries and the pointed leaves turn a magnificent vivid red in a display that lasts over a long period. The plant can be grown in a wide range of soils.
ht and sp 90–120cm/3–4ft
Soil and position
Likes soils from sandy to almost boggy and a position in full sun.
CAUTION: TAKE CARE WHEN HANDLING BERBERIS BECAUSE OF ITS SPINES. ALL PARTS OF THE PLANT CAN CAUSE STOMACH UPSETS IF EATEN.

Buddleja davidii
BUDDLEJA
OR BUTTERFLY BUSH

Most people know buddleja, with its arching branches of honey-scented flowers that attract butterflies to the garden in late summer. Growing in densely covered plumes, the flowers are normally in shades of purple, from light soft bluish purple to deepest royal purple, though they also come in white. *Buddleja davidii* 'Black Knight' has the darkest flowers, 'Empire Blue' has lavender blue flowers, 'Harlequin' is cerise and has cream-margined leaves, and 'White Profusion' has very long tails of white flowers. The species *B. alternifolia*, with more delicate, clustered flowers and willow-like leaves, is a more unusual alternative that flowers earlier in the year.
ht to 3m/10ft
sp to 4.5m/15ft
Soil and position
Ordinary, well-drained garden soil in full sun.

Ceanothus 'Gloire de Versailles'
CEANOTHUS OR CALIFORNIA LILAC

From ground-level upward, pale blue powderpuffs of flowers enliven this hardy California lilac all summer. Ceanothus makes a lovely plant for a warm, sheltered spot and grows well against a wall; many forms are to be found. 'Gloire de Versailles' is deciduous but in the late-spring-flowering 'Cascade' the little leaves are evergreen and the flowers a brighter blue.
ht and sp 1.5m/5ft or more ('Gloire de Versailles'); up to 3.6m/12ft ('Cascade')
Soil and position

These shrubs need good drainage and like poor, sandy soil. They must have warmth, and shelter from cold winds.

Cornus kousa var. chinensis
KOUSA DOGWOOD

This is a neat, upright shrub or small tree with minute green flowers surrounded by showy white bracts. In hot summers the flowers sometimes develop strawberry-like fruits and the tapered oval leaves are a bright crimson red in the fall.
ht to 7m/23ft
sp 4.5m/15ft
Soil and position
Almost any soil, as long as well-

◀ Buddleja davidii, *buddleja or butterfly bush 'Black Knight'.*

drained, and a position in sun or partial shade.

Cornus officinalis
DOGWOOD

This very hardy multistemmed dogwood is grown for its gray, brown and orange winter bark and purple-red fall leaves. Tolerant of most soils, it is very vigorous. Other dogwoods with colorful stems include *C. stolonifera* (dark red), *C. stolonifera* 'Flaviramea' (yellow-green), and *C. alba* (red). All look good growing near water, or where the winter light can filter through the stems.
ht and sp 3m/10ft (C. alba); ht and sp to 4.5m/15ft (C. officinalis); ht 1.8m/6ft, sp 3.6m/12ft (C. stolonifera)
Soil and position
Ordinary garden soil in an open, sunny position.

Cotinus
SMOKE BUSH

The smoke bush has leaves that color brightly in the fall and flowers that create the impression of plumes of smoke in summer. *Cotinus* 'Grace' has red and orange leaves in the fall; *Cotinus coggygria* 'Royal Purple' has smoky pink plumes of flower and purple foliage which provides a foil for many garden flowers and which colors bright red in the fall.
ht and sp 5m/16ft
Soil and position
Ordinary garden soil and a sunny position to bring out the best foliage color.

Cotoneaster
COTONEASTER

Cotoneasters are a family of very obliging shrubs which produce a wealth of red berries to attract the birds in the fall and generally

keep their leaves throughout the winter. The leaves are dark green and often color up to red during the winter. In late spring plants bear a mass of small white flowers. The handsome, tree-like *Cotoneaster* 'Cornubia' has broad, semievergreen leaves and bright bunches of clear red fruits which weigh down the stems in the fall and often last all winter. *C.* 'Exburiensis' has yellow fruits.
ht and sp 6m/20ft ('Cornubia'); 4.5m/15ft ('Exburiensis')
Soil and position
Ordinary well-drained, or even dry, soil in sun or partial shade.

Elaeagnus pungens
ELAEAGNUS

This is a strong evergreen shrub with glossy green leaves, making it particularly useful in winter. In the variety 'Maculata' the leaves are gold outlined with deep green, and 'Dicksonii' has yellow-edged leaves. Elaeagnus has small but extremely fragrant cream-colored tubular flowers in the fall.
ht and sp to 4m/13ft or more but can be kept trimmed
Soil and position
Puts up with most soils and situations, including by the sea.

Eucalyptus gunnii
EUCALYPTUS OR CIDER GUM

This is a fast-growing Tasmanian tree that flourishes in European climates. The rounded young leaves, like the peeling bark, are a silvery gray, and the plant may produce more than one trunk. The leaves are evergreen and the young leaves are the prettiest, so the stems are best cut back each year in early spring to encourage new growth. The tree produces creamy white flowers in late summer to early fall.
ht 14m/46ft
sp 4.5m/15ft or more
Can be grown as a shrub trimmed to

ht 1.8m/6ft
sp 1.2m/4ft
Soil and position
Fertile, slightly acid, moist soil
and a sunny position with shelter
from cold winds.

Fothergilla major
FOTHERGILLA

Scented, cream-colored fuzzy
flowers in spring before the
leaves appear and radiant yellow
or yellow and scarlet leaves in
the fall make this a shrub for two
seasons. It spreads broadly and is
fairly low-growing. *Fothergilla
gardenii* is similar but smaller and
more compact and with crimson
fall leaves.
ht to 2.5m/8ft, sp to 1.8m/6ft
(Fothergilla major); ht 90cm/3ft, sp
to 1.2m/4ft (F. gardenii)
Soil and position
Needs light, acid soil and will
flourish in any position from full
sun to semishade.

Genista aetnensis
MOUNT ETNA BROOM

Graceful and arching, brooms
make fountains of golden flowers
in the summer months. Mount
Etna broom makes a rounded
small tree, the stems completely
hidden by flowers in full
summer. *G. cineria* is a lower-
growing multistemmed shrub,
billowing with sweetly scented
flowers in early summer.
ht to 6m/20ft, sp to 5.5m/18ft
(Genista aetnensis); ht to 3m/10ft,
sp to 2.5m/8ft (G. cineria)
Soil and position
Light, well-drained soil,
including poor soil, and a warm,
sunny position.

Hamamelis mollis
HAMAMELIS OR CHINESE
WITCH HAZEL

Witch hazel is a must for anyone
who wants winter fragrance. The
wispy yellow flowers on the bare
twigs actually benefit from cold,
which prolongs the flowering

▶ *Cotinus,* smoke bush, requires a
sunny position for best color.

period; the rounded leaves turn a
soft warm yellow in the fall.
H. × intermedia 'Pallida' (syn
H. m. 'Pallida') has red-centered,
pale yellow flowers. Plant
hamamelis near the house or
the front path, so that you can
sniff it when you walk by.
ht and sp to 2.5m/8ft
Soil and position
Needs a fairly rich, moist soil
that is neutral to acid and a
sheltered spot in full sun or
semishade.

Hebe
HEBE

Hebes are staunch plants,
keeping their small, leathery
leaves all year and flowering for
a long period, as well as
forming neat, compact bushes
that generally grow well in
containers. In some varieties
the leaves are variegated, while
the numerous small flowers are
usually in shades of bluish
purple, with some pink- or
white-flowering varieties.
H. 'Autumn Glory' has flowers
in a warm purple blue, while
H. 'Midsummer Beauty' has lilac
colored flowers fading to
white, and both flower from
mid-summer until late fall.
H. speciosa 'Sapphire' is covered
in flowers of a warm, soft blue.
ht to 1.5m/5ft
sp 1.2–1.5m/4–5ft
Soil and position
Almost any soil, including chalk,
as long as it's well-drained, and a
sunny position. Hebes dislike real
cold, but withstand salt-laden
winds well.

Kolkwitzia amabilis
BEAUTY BUSH

A mass of delicate silvery pink
flowers gives rise to the name
beauty bush. The shrub can be
difficult to get started, but it

rewards persistence, producing its
lightly-scented foxglove-like
flowers on arching branches in
late spring and early summer.
ht to 3.6m/12ft
sp to 3m/10ft
Can be pruned to keep it smaller.
Soil and position
Ordinary, well-drained soil in a
sunny position. Flowers best in a
soil that is not too rich.

Lonicera periclymenum
HONEYSUCKLE

Honeysuckle climbs by twining
and can be grown on trellis or
fencing or over a large shrub.
A lovely plant for a scented arbor
or to grow against the house
wall, round the door, or over a
garden shed. All varieties of

Lonicera periclymenum have the
heady honeysuckle scent.
Here are some excellent choices:
L. p. 'Belgica' (purplish red and
yellowish cream) flowers in late
spring and early summer;
L. p. 'Graham Thomas' (white,
becoming yellow) flowers
through from midsummer until
the fall; and *L. p.* 'Serotina'
(creamy white inside, purple-red
outside) flowers from midsummer until late fall.
ht and sp 3.6–6m/12–20ft
Can be trimmed to suit the space.
Soil and situation
Ordinary, well-drained soil with
added compost or manure.
Flourishes in partial shade but
will do well in sun if the roots
are shaded.

◀ Lonicera periclymenum, *honeysuckle.*

Malus
CRAB APPLE

Crab apple trees are grown for their fragrant spring apple blossom and small and ornamental apple-like fruits that generally last from fall and into the next spring. Good and fairly compact specimens include *Malus* 'Crittenden', profusely covered in apple-blossom pink flowers followed by small bunches of bright red berries; *M.* 'Golden Hornet', with white flowers and warm yellow crab apples, and *Malus × arnoldiana*, which has pink flowers opening from pinky red buds and fading to white, followed by red-flushed yellow fruits.
ht 4.5–5.5m/15–18ft
sp to 6m/20ft
Soil and position
Ordinary to rich garden soil which is well-drained, can take sun or partial shade.

Pieris japonica
PIERIS

This is a large and spreading evergreen shrub with cascades of little vase-shaped, waxy flowers in spring and copper red new leaves. The variety 'Debutante' is slow-growing and very hardy, and in mid-spring its leaves are almost hidden by a mass of creamy white flowers. Unlike most other forms of pieris this one is a dwarf, making it ideal for smaller gardens, roof gardens or patios.
ht and sp to 3m/10ft
Soil and position
Must have lime-free, well-drained soil; flowers best in full sun. Provide shelter from cold winds to prevent frost damage.

Potentilla
POTENTILLA

Potentillas come in all sizes and the small ones can be thought of as belonging with perennials. As a larger shrub, *Potentilla fruticosa* var. *arbuscula*) (syn. *P. arbuscula*) comes in many varieties, with flower colors in all shades of yellow and orange, as well as white, pink, and red. The buttercup-like flowers occur over a very long period from late spring onward. All have pretty leaves, some finely dissected.
ht 90cm–1.5m/3–5ft
sp to 1.5m/5ft
Soil and position
Light, or even poor soil, as long as it is well-drained; a light, sunny position for best flowering is required.
(See also page 989)

Prunus
PRUNUS OR
FLOWERING CHERRY

The term 'prunus' covers a huge range of flowering cherries, plums and almond trees, many grown only for their clouds of spring flowers and not bearing fruit. Among these one of the loveliest is *Prunus* 'Shirotae', a Japanese cherry (syn. *P.* 'Mount Fuji'). This is a spreading tree with large, white, fragrant flowers, and stunning orange-red fall foliage.
ht 6m/20ft
sp 7.5m/25ft
Soil and position
Ordinary, fairly well-drained soil, preferably alkaline. May need support in exposed, windy areas.

Rhus typhina
STAGSHORN SUMAC

Stagshorn sumac produces spectacular orange-red leaf color in the fall, and has velvety twigs with smooth bark. It throws up suckers to form a multistemmed tree or bush and takes happily to being pruned to size.
ht 3–4.5m/10–15ft
sp 3–4.5m/10–15ft
Can be cut to the ground each year in spring to produce vigorous new shoots and best foliage.
Soil and position
Will thrive in any soil that is not waterlogged. Best in a sunny position.
CAUTION: THE SAP CAN CAUSE SKIN BLISTERS.

Robinia pseudoacacia 'Frisia'
GOLDEN ACACIA
OR ROBINIA

A most ornamental foliage tree that makes a lovely backcloth for other garden plants, this acacia lookalike has stalks of small, paired leaflets, golden green in color, which ripple in the breeze. Older trees have white pea-flowers which hang down in clusters in early summer. Robinias can be trained to grow against a wall and trimmed to size or grown as free-standing trees. Eventually, it must be admitted, they can grow rather large.
ht 7.3m/24ft and eventually more
sp 3–4.5m/10–15ft
Soil and position
Any soil that does not get waterlogged, including alkaline soils, and full sun to light shade, as long as the tree is not exposed to harsh winds.

Sambucus racemosa 'Sutherland Gold'
GARDEN ELDER

This is an ornamental garden version of the common country elder and has upright, cone-shaped panicles of tiny white-ish cream flowers in early summer, followed in late summer by heads of small, bright red berries. The abundant golden leaves have finely cut edges.
ht and sp 3m/10ft but can be trimmed to size

Soil and position
Almost any soil in dappled shade.

Sorbus aria 'Lutescens'
WHITEBEAM

This is a shapely, smallish
whitebeam with silver-gray
young foliage, later turning gray-
green. The leaves flutter white in
the breeze because of the dense
white felt on their undersides.
In late spring the tree has light
and airy corymbs of small,
creamy white, fuzzy flowers
ht 9m/30ft
sp 7.5m/25ft
Soil and position
Ordinary, well-drained garden
soil in an open, sunny position.

Sorbus commixta
MOUNTAIN ASH

The mountain ash or rowan
makes a good specimen tree
with its pinnate leaves and white
spring flowers which develop
into firm round fruits in late
summer. Most also have good fall
leaf color. 'Embley' has plentiful
flowers followed by bright red
fruits. The glossy, dark green
leaves are particularly well-
shaped and put on a fall
show of red and orange.
ht 10m/32ft
sp 7m/23ft
Soil and position
Well-drained but moist garden
soil and a position in sun or
semishade.
CAUTION: ALTHOUGH THE
FRUITS CAN BE USED FOR JELLY
THEY CAUSE STOMACH UPSETS
IF EATEN RAW.

Spirea 'Arguta'
FOAM OF MAY
OR BRIDAL WREATH

This is a pretty and graceful
shrub; abundant white flowers
clothe the arching stems in late
spring and the stems themselves
have an appealing reddish tint
when bare from fall to early
spring. *S. thunbergii* is rather

similar, and there are many other
spireas to choose, including the
(usually) pink-flowered *S. japonica*
which flowers in summer.
ht and sp to 2.5m/8ft; S. japonica
and S. thunbergii are smaller
Soil and position
Well-drained but reasonably
moist soil in sun or partial shade.

Symphoricarpos albus 'Laevigatus'
SNOWBERRY

Snowberries have to be chosen
carefully as they can colonize an
area, producing scrappy stems
and little fruit. However a good
snowberry is well worth
growing, especially for its effects
in winter. This one, with its large
white winter berries on delicate
stems is a good choice.
ht and sp 1.8m/6ft but can be kept
trimmed
Soil and position
Tolerates any soil except wet,
and any position from full sun to
shade.
CAUTION: THE BERRIES CAUSE
STOMACH UPSET IF EATEN AND
SOME PEOPLE FIND THEIR JUICE
IRRITATING TO THE SKIN.

Viburnum
VIBURNUM

There are so many viburnums
for the garden that this species
deserves several entries.
 Winter-flowering species,
with very fragrant pinkish white
flowers in small clusters on bare,
twiggy stems, are *Viburnum farreri*
(syn. *V. fragrans*), *V. grandiflorum*,
and *V. × bodnantense* 'Dawn', an
offspring of the two.
ht to 3m/10ft, sp to 2.5m/8ft
(Viburnum farreri);
ht and sp 1.8m/6ft
(V. grandiflorum);
ht 3m/10ft, sp 2m/6ft 6in
(V. × bodnantense 'Dawn')
 Viburnum × burkwoodii has
rounded balls of clustered
fragrant, white, tubular flowers
in spring.

ht and sp 2.5m/8ft
 Viburnum tinus is a robust,
evergreen viburnum that bears
white flowers, sometimes almost
continuously, from late fall till
late spring.
ht to 3m/10ft
sp 1.8m/6ft
 Viburnum opulus, the guelder
rose, is a deciduous viburnum
with hydrangea-like heads of
creamy white flowers in late

▲ *Sambucus racemosa 'Sutherland Gold'.*

spring, followed by jelly-red
berries in the fall.
ht to 3m/10ft
Soil and position
Fertile, fairly moist garden soil in
sun or semishade.
CAUTION: THE FRUITS OF
VIBURNUM OPULUS CAN CAUSE
STOMACH UPSETS IF EATEN.

glossary

acid
refers to acid soil; a pH below 7.0 (see pH). Suitable for lime-hating plants

adventitious roots
roots springing directly from the plant stem

alkaline
referring to soil having a pH greater than 7 (see pH), unsuitable for lime-hating plants

alpine
generally, a small plant suitable for a rock garden, alpine house or a stone sink, but correctly one that in its natural habitat grows on mountains, above the level at which trees thrive but below the permanent snow line

annual
a plant that grows from seed, flowers, and dies within the same year. However, many plants that are not strictly annual are treated as such. For instance, *Lobelia erinus* is a half-hardy perennial usually grown as a half-hardy annual, *Mirabilis jalapa* (Marvel of Peru) is a perennial grown as a half-hardy annual, and *Impatiens walleriana* (busy lizzie) is a greenhouse perennial invariably treated as a half-hardy annual

anther
the pollen-bearing male part of a flower. A small stem called a filament supports each anther; anthers are collectively known as stamen

aphid (greenfly)
a well-known and widely seen pest, which breed rapidly and sucks sap. Besides causing leaves, stems, and flowers to pale and pucker, this pest transmits viruses which cause further deterioration

aquatic plant
generally, a plant that grows in garden ponds, partially or totally submerged

axil
the junction between a stem and leaf, from where side-shoots or flowers may develop

B

bare-root
plants that are lifted from the open ground for transplanting in the dormant season

bedding plant
a plant raised and used as a temporary decoration in a bed or a border. Biennials, such as wallflowers, are planted in the fall to create a spring display, and half-hardy annuals that have been raised from seeds, sown in spring in gentle warmth in a greenhouse, are planted into beds as soon as all risk of frost has passed

biennial
a plant that makes its initial growth one year and flowers the next, then dies. Many plants are treated as biennials. For example, *Bellis perennis* (common daisy) is a hardy perennial usually grown as a biennial. *Dianthus barbatus* (sweet William) is perennial frequently grown as a biennial, although some are now grown as annuals

biological control
the deliberate use of a natural organism to control a pest or disease

black spot
a fungal disease that attacks and disfigures roses

blanching
the exclusion of light from the stems of some vegetables to whiten and improve their flavor. Leeks, celery, Belgian endive, and kale are examples of vegetables that are blanched

blind
a shoot with a growing point that has not developed properly

blossom end rot
a disorder where tomatoes and related plants bear fruit with a sunken, dark brown patch at the base. It is caused by lack of calcium in the tissues as the fruit is developing, generally because of water shortage

blown
loosely formed or over-mature, e.g. Brussels sprouts that fail to form dense, tight buttons, or flowers such as roses that have passed their best

bog garden plant
a plant that thrives in perpetually moist conditions. Such positions can be created around a garden pond or in a specially constructed bog garden

bolting
the premature shooting up and flowering of vegetables. Lettuces, beetroot, spinach, and radishes are most susceptible

bonsai
the growing of a mature plant in a miniature form in a small, shallow container. Bonsai began more than 1,000 years ago in China, and spread to Japan. Plants are kept dwarf by regular pruning of roots, leaves, and stems

botrytis
also known as gray mold, a fungal disease chiefly found in badly ventilated and damp greenhouses. Soft tissue plants such as lettuces and delicate flowering plants are particularly susceptible

bract
a modified leaf, usually resembling a petal. The brightly colored flower-like heads on poinsettias, the white petal-like appendages around the flowers on *Davidia involucrata* (handkerchief tree), and the white or pink-flushed petal-like structures on *Cornus florida* (flowering dogwood) are examples.

brassica
a member of the cabbage family, including vegetables such as Brussels sprout, cauliflower, turnip, and so on

budding
a method of increasing plants when a dormant bud of a desired variety is inserted into a T-shaped cut in the stem of a root-stock. Roses and fruit trees are often increased in this way

bulb
a storage organ with a bud-like structure. It is formed of fleshy scales attached at their base to a flattened stem called a basal plate. Onions, tulips, and daffodils are examples. The term is used wrongly to include tubers, rhizomes, and corms, which have a different structure

bulbil
an immature miniature bulb at the base of a mother bulb

C

callus
corky tissue that forms over damaged or cut stems. Before rooting, the cut ends of cuttings produce a callus

capillary
the passage of water upward through soil. The finer the soil, the higher the water rises. The same principle is used in self-watering systems for greenhouse plants in pots

catch crop
a quick crop, usually of salad vegetables, that is sown, grown, and harvested between crops that take longer to develop

chlorophyll
the green coloring materials found in all plants, except a few parasites and fungi. It absorbs energy from the sun and plays an important role in photosynthesis, the conversion of sunlight to energy

chlorosis
a disorder, mainly of leaves, with parts showing as whitish areas. It can be caused by viruses, mutation, or mineral deficiencies

cloche
the French word for bell-glass, meaning any tunnel-like structure made of glass or plastic used to protect early crops, usually vegetables. Also used to extend the growing season of vegetables into the fall. A floating row cover is a lightweight film of perforated plastic or fiber lying loosely on top of the crop

clone
a plant raised vegetatively from another and identical to its parent

cold frame
an unheated, protective structure, usually with solid sides and a removable glass or plastic lid

compaction
the process whereby the air is squeezed from between soil particles by heavy loads on the

surface (such as repeated treading). This destroys the soil structure, impedes drainage and makes the soil unsuitable for root growth

compost
the organic substance produced by rotting down vegetative matter that is used as a soil improver or top-dressing. Can be bought commercially as well as homemade

compost additives
materials such as vermiculite and perlite that are added to compost in hanging baskets to aid the retention of moisture

container grown
a plant raised in a container for subsequent sale and transplanting to its permanent position in a garden, either in the ground or in a container. Such plants, including trees, shrubs, roses, and herbaceous perennials, can be planted at any time of the year when the soil is not too wet, dry, or frozen. Container-grown plants experience little root disturbance and soon become established

containers
pots, tubs, hanging baskets, window boxes etc which are used for growing plants

cordon
a form of trained fruit tree. Cordoning is an ideal way to grow apples and pears in a small garden, or greenhouse tomatoes. Some cordons have a single stem, others two or three. Pruning removes side roots

corm
an underground storage organ formed of a stem base greatly swollen laterally (eg a gladiolus). Young corms (cormlets) form around its base, and can be removed and grown in a nurserybed for several seasons before reaching flowering size

courtyards
originally, open areas surrounded by buildings or walls, perhaps inside a castle. Nowadays, usually paved areas at the rear of a building and surrounded by a wall

crocks
pieces of broken clay pots used to cover drainage holes in

containers. They are placed concave side downward

crown
the part of a plant where a collection of stems is produced. Herbaceous plants have a crown at soil level where the roots and stems join. The crown of a tree is where the head forms on top of the trunk

cultivar
a shortened term for "cultivated variety" and indicating a variety raised in cultivation. Strictly speaking, most modern varieties are cultivars, but the term variety is still widely used because it is familiar to most gardeners

cuttings
a vegetative method of propagation. Portions of plants that are detached and encouraged to grow new roots or shoots (or both) in order to make new plants. Cuttings may be taken from stems, leaves or roots

 D

deadheading
the removal of faded flowers to prevent the formation of seeds and to encourage the development of more flowers

deciduous
a plant that loses its leaves at the beginning of its dormant season, which is usually in the fall or early winter. This usually applies to trees, shrubs, and some conifers, such as Ginkgo biloba (maidenhair tree)

deficiency
a shortage of one of the essential nutritional elements, causing specific symptoms that need to be quickly diagnosed and rectified

disbudding
the removal of buds from around the sides of a main, central bud to encourage its development. Some chrysanthemums and roses are treated in this way

division
a vegetative method of propagation or plant reproduction, by splitting a root clump. Herbaceous perennials with fibrous roots are usually propagated by division

dormant
plants, seeds and so on, that are temporarily not in active growth

drawn
thin and spindly after being in crowded or dark conditions

drill
a narrow depression made in the surface of soil, usually formed with a draw hoe or a pointed stick, in which seeds are sown. Most vegetables are sown in this way, but peas are sometimes sown in flat-bottomed trenches so that three rows can be sown close together

dry-stone wall
a retaining wall of natural stone made without cement. Plants can be set between the stones so the wall becomes draped in plants

dwarfing
rootstocks that control the growth of varieties which are grafted on to them, making them smaller and more compact than they would be if they were growing on their own roots. Semidwarfing rootstocks have a less pronounced dwarfing effect

 E

earthing up
drawing soil up around the stems of plants. This may be blanch them (e.g. leeks and celery), encourage the growth of tubers (e.g. potatoes) or simply to help support them in the ground, especially against strong wind (e.g. tall brassicas)

espalier
a method of training fruit trees in which lateral branches are trained horizontally along tensioned wires spaced 23–30cm/9–12in apart

evergreen shrubs
trees and conifers that stay green through the year without shedding their leaves. In fact they drop some of their leaves all year round, while producing others

 F

F1
the first filial generation, the result of a cross between two

pure-bred parents. F1 hybrids are large and strong plants, but their seeds will not produce replicas of the parents

fan-trained
a method of training fruit trees so their branches radiate outward like the spokes of a fan

fasciation
a freak condition in which stems or flowers are fused and flattened. The affected parts are best cut out

fertilization
the sexual union of the male cell (pollen) and the female cell (ovule). Fertilization may be the result of pollination, when pollen falls upon the stigma. However, not all pollen germinates after falling on a stigma

filament
the slender stalk that supports the anthers of a flower

fillis
a type of soft string, usually green, used for tying up plants

floret
a small flower that is part of an entire flower

floribunda rose
a rose classification now termed cluster-flowered bush rose

floriferous
flowering freely and bearing an abundance of flowers

foam liner
used to help retain moisture in hanging baskets

foliar feed
a fertilizer applied to foliage to encourage growth. Not all fertilizers are suitable

force
to encourage a plant into early growth, usually by providing extra warmth. Light is often also excluded from plants being forced

friable
soil that is crumbly, light, and easily worked. The term applies especially to soil being prepared as a seed bed in the spring

frost
frost occurs when the temperature falls to 32°F/0°C or below. When this occurs only at ground level it is called a ground frost; when the freezing temperatures extend upward it is known as an air frost, which is more damaging to plants

frost pocket
an area where cold air collects—usually at the bottom of a valley, in a hollow in the ground, or against an obstruction such as a solid wall. Temperatures in frost pockets remain lower than in surrounding areas, and plants in such an area are more liable to cold damage

frost tender
plants that are killed or seriously damaged by frost

fungicide
a chemical used to combat fungal diseases, such as black spot and mildew

force
to encourage a plant into early growth, usually by providing extra warmth. Light is often also excluded from plants being forced

friable
soil that is crumbly, light, and easily worked. The term applies especially to soil being prepared as a seed bed in the spring

frost
frost occurs when the temperature falls to 32°F/0°C or below. When this occurs only at ground level it is called a groundfrost; when the freezing temperatures extend upward it is known as an air frost, which is more damaging to plants

frost pocket
an area where cold air collects—usually at the bottom of a valley, in a hollow in the ground, or against an obstruction such as a solid wall. Temperatures in frost pockets remain lower than in surrounding areas, and plants in such an area are more liable to cold damage

frost tender
plants that are killed or seriously damaged by frost

fungicide
a chemical used to combat fungal diseases, such as black spot and mildew

G

garden compost
vegetable waste from kitchens plus soft parts of garden plants, decomposed and subsequently dug into the soil or used to form a mulch around plants

genus
a group of plants with similar botanical characteristics. Some genera contain many species, others just one

germination
the process that occurs within a seed when given adequate moisture, air, and warmth. The coat of the seed ruptures and a seed leaf or leaves grow up toward the light. A root develops at the same time. However, to most gardeners germination is when seed leaves appear through the surface of the compost in pots or seed trays, or through the soil in a garden

glaucous
grayish-green or bluish-green color, usually describing stems, leaves, or fruit of ornamental trees, shrubs, and herbaceous perennials

graft
a method of propagation, when the tissue of a chosen variety is united with a rootstock of known vigor. It is used to increase fruit trees and, sometimes, roses

green manuring
the growing of a crop such as mustard that can be subsequently dug into the soil to improve its physical structure and nutritional value

groundcover
a low, ground-hugging plant that forms a mat of foliage. It is frequently used to discourage the growth of weeds

growing bag
originally introduced to grow tomatoes on disease-infected soil, but now widely used to grow many flowering and food crops

H

half-hardy
a plant that can withstand fairly low temperatures, but needs protection from frost

half-hardy annual
an annual plant that is sown in gentle warmth in a greenhouse in spring. The seedlings are transferred to wider spacings in pots or seed trays and planted into the garden or a container when all risk of frost has passed

half-standard
a tree with a stem (trunk) 75cm-1.2m/2½-4ft long between the ground and the lowest branches which form the head

hardening off
the gradual acclimatization of protected plants to outside conditions. Garden frames are often used for this purpose

hardwood cuttings
a vegetative method of reproducing woody plants, such as trees, shrubs, and soft fruits, by severing pieces of stem when ripe and inserting them in a rooting medium. The cuttings are usually inserted later into a nursery bed in a sheltered part of a garden

hardy
a plant that is able to survive outdoors in winter

haulm
the top growth on some vegetables, such as peas, beans, and potatoes

heel
a hard, corky layer of bark and stem torn off when a side-shoot is pulled away from a main stem to form a cutting. Heel cuttings usually root more rapidly than normal cuttings. There is also less chance of the base of the cutting decaying

heeling-in
the temporary planting of trees, shrubs, and conifers while awaiting transfer to their permanent sites. It is often done because the final planting position has not been prepared, or the soil is too wet or frozen for planting to take place

herbaceous
a plant that dies down to soil level in late summer or fall, after the completion of its growth. The following spring it develops fresh shoots

herbicide
a chemical formulation that kills plants and is commonly known as a weed killer

hermaphrodite
having male and female organs on the same flower

hormone
a growth-regulating substance that occurs naturally in plants and animals. Additional and synthetic amounts are used to induce plants to root rapidly. Others are used to stimulate the growth of weeds so they burn themselves out

humus
the organic remains of rotted-down vegetable matter that improves soil structure

hybrid
a cross between two distinct parents. Crosses are often between plant varieties; they may also be between species (interspecific hybrids) or less often between genera (intergeneric or bigeneric hybrids). F1 hybrids are a first generation cross between two selected, pure-breeding parents and have the advantage of uniformity and, often, of hybrid vigor

hybridization
the crossing of one or more generations to improve a wide range of characteristics, such as flower size, time of flowering, sturdiness, fruit size and quality, and plant size

hybrid tea rose
a rose classification now replaced by large-flowered bush rose

I

inflorescence
the part of a plant which bears the flowers

insecticide a chemical used to kill insects

internode
the part of a stem or shoot between two leaf joints (also called nodes)

John Innes compost
loam-based compost, formulated during the 1930s at the John Innes Horticultural Institute in the UK. Composts for sowing seeds and potting were standardized. They are made up of loam, horticultural sand, and peat, with fertilizers

lateral
a side-shoot growing from a main stem of a tree or a shrub. The term is often used when discussing the fruiting and pruning of fruit trees

layering
a vegetative method of propagation by lowering stems and burying a small part of them in the ground. By twisting, bending or slitting the stem at the point where it is buried, the flow of sap is restricted and roots develop. Rooting takes up to 18 months. Once rooting has taken place, the new plant can be severed from its parent

leaching
the draining of nutrients from the soil. Leaching is most apparent in sandy soil since the fine particles in clay soils tend to retain nutrients

leader
the terminal shoot or branch that will extend the growth of a plant

leaf axil
the area where the leaf stem joins the plant stem, from which growth buds often arise

leafmold
decayed leaves. Leafmold can be spread over the surface of soil as a mulch, or dug into the ground during winter.

lime
an alkaline substance used for countering acidity in the soil and improving clay soil

loam
fertile, well-drained, good-quality top-soil

loam-based compost
compost mainly formed of fertile topsoil with the addition of sand, peat, and general fertilizers

macronutrients
the minerals required by plants in relatively large quantities, including nitrogen, phosphorus, potassium, calcium, magnesium, and sulfur

maiden
the first year of a fruit tree after having been budded or grafted

mangers
containers similar to wire-framed wall baskets, but with a wider metal framework

marginal plants
plants that live in shallow water at the edges of ponds. Some marginals also thrive in boggy soil surrounding a pond

micronutrients
minerals required by plants in very small quantities, such as iron, molybdenum, manganese. Also known as trace elements

mildew a fungus disease that attacks soft-tissued plants. There are two main types of mildew. Downy mildew affects chiefly lettuce and onions, while powdery mildew affects mainly fruit trees, roses, and chrysanthemums

mulch
material applied in a layer to the soil surface. It may be organic (e.g. compost, shredded bark) or non-organic (e.g. gravel, plastic sheeting). Mulch retains soil moisture and inhibits weed growth

mulching the technique of covering the soil around plants with well-decayed organic material such as garden compost, peat or, in the case of rock garden plants, stone chippings or 6mm/¼in gravel

mutation A part of a plant, usually the flower, that differs from the plant's inherited characteristics

neutral
soil that is neither acid nor alkaline (on the pH scale this would be 7.0). Most plants grow in a pH of about 6.5

node
a leaf joint, or the point where another stem branches out from the main one

NPK
a formula for the percentages of nitrogen, phosphate, and potash in a compound fertilizer

'New English Roses'
a group of roses raised by David Austin Roses in the UK, in which modern rose varieties were hybridized with old roses. This created a new group that combines recurrent flowering with the colors and flowers characteristic of old varieties

organic
the cultivation of plants without the use of chemical fertilizers or pesticides

organic
derived from material that has once lived (i.e. plant or animal remains)

oxygenators
submerged pond plants which produce oxygen to keep the water clear and healthy

pan
a compacted and impervious layer in the soil that restricts the flow or water and air

pathogen
disease-causing organism

patio
originally the Spanish word for an inner court, open to the sky and surrounded by a building. The term was introduced into America, where it came to mean any paved area around a dwelling

peat
partly decayed plants. Peat is usually acid

peat-based compost
compost made mainly from peat, with the addition of fertilizers

perennial
the popular term for a herbaceous perennial; also any long-lived plant, including trees, shrubs and, perennial climbers

pesticide
chemical used to control pests including insects, slugs and snails, mites, and so on

pH
a scale used to define the acidity or alkalinity of a soil-water solution. The scale ranges from 0–14, with 7.0 as neutral. Figures above 7.0 indicate increasing alkalinity, and figures below 7.0 indicate increasing acidity. Most plants grow well in a pH of 6.5 and this is usually taken to be the neutral for plants, rather than the chemical and scientific neutral 7.0

photosynthesis
the growth-building process in plants when chlorophyll in leaves and other green parts is activated by sunlight. It reacts with moisture absorbed by the roots and carbon dioxide from the atmosphere to create growth

pinching out
the removal of the tip of a shoot or a terminal bud to encourage the development of side shoots

pleaching
the technique of training and pruning a line of trees planted close together to form an aerial hedge. The base of each tree is free from branches, but from head height upward, their branches are interlaced. They are pruned to form a neat outline

pollen
the male fertilizing agent from the anthers

pollination
the transfer of pollen from the anthers onto the stigma

potting compost
traditionally, a compost formed

of loam, sand, peat, fertilizers, and chalk. The ratio of the ingredients is altered according to whether the compost is used for sowing seeds, potting-up or repotting plants into larger containers. However, the destruction of peat beds to acquire peat is not environmentally friendly and therefore many modern composts are formed of other materials

potting-on
transferring an established plant into a larger pot

potting-up
transferring young plants from a seed tray or a seed box into a pot

pricking off
moving a seedling from the tray or pot in which it germinated to a container where it is given more room to develop

propagation
raising new plants

pruning
the removal with a knife, shears or a pruning saw of parts of woody plants. Fruit trees are pruned to encourage better and more regular fruiting, and to insure that they remain healthy for a long period. Shrubs are pruned mainly to encourage better flowering. Pruning some shrubs also encourages the yearly development of attractive stems

racemes
a flower head containing a number of individual flowers that are carried on an unbranched stem

reconstituted stone
a manufactured stone used to produce a wide range of plant containers and garden ornaments. Its surface mellows to a pleasing color

repotting
moving a container-grown plant to a fresh pot which may or may not be larger than the one in which it is currently growing

reversion
the tendency of a plant to return to its original state, for example, when a variegated-leafed plant that originally occurred as a mutation from a plain-leafed variety begins to produce plain-leaved shoots again. Many mutations are unstable

rhizomatous
an underground or partly buried horizontal stem. Rhizomes can be slender or fleshy. Some irises have thick, fleshy rhizomes, while those of *Convallaria majalis* (lily-of-the-valley) are slender and creeping. They act as storage organs, and perpetuate plants from one season to another

ridging
a method of winter digging that leaves a large surface area of soil exposed to the elements. Long ridges are left on the soil's surface

ring culture
a method of growing tomatoes in bottomless pots on a gravel base

rootstock
a plant used to provide the root system of a plant that is grafted on to it because for some reason the grafted variety is not suitable for growing on its own roots (*see* dwarfing)

rotation
the moving of vegetable crops to different areas of soil each year to prevent the build up of pests and diseases

runner
a shoot that grows along the ground, rooting into the soil at intervals (eg strawberry runners)

scion
a shoot or a bud that is grafted or budded onto a rootstock

scree
a freely drained area of grit, gravel and small stones for growing alpine plants

seed leaf
the first leaf (sometimes two) that appears after germination

self-fertile
a plant with flowers that can be fertilized by its own pollen. This applies chiefly to fruit trees

self-sterile
the opposite of self-fertile (see above)

semiripe
shoots that have just begun to harden at their base but are not completely woody

shrub
a woody perennial with stems growing from soil level and no trunk. Some plants can be grown either as shrubs or trees

sideshoot
a shoot growing out from the side of a main shoot

sink garden
an old stone sink partly filled with drainage material, then with free-draining compost. Sink gardens are planted with miniature conifers, dwarf bulbs, and small rock garden plants. They are usually displayed on terraces and patios

softwood
shoots that are still soft and flexible, and show no signs of woodiness

softwood cutting
a cutting of non-woody growth (ie a green shoot)

soil mix
the medium used for growing plants in containers instead of garden soil. Various mixes are available for seeds, cuttings, and mature plants

soilless mix
growing mix that contains no loam. Most once based on peat, but composts made from peat substitutes such as coir are now common

species
a group of plants that breed together and have the same characteristics

species rose
a term popularly used to describe a wild rose or one of its near relatives

sphagnum moss
a type of moss, once used widely to line wire-framed hanging baskets. It is moisture-retentive and creates an attractive feature. Now, it has been almost entirely replaced by black plastic

spit
the depth of a spade's blade, usually 25-30cm/10-12in. The term is usually given to the depth at which soil is dug

sport
an accidental change in shape, size or color of a flower or a plant

spur
a short branch on a fruit tree, from which fruits are borne

stamen
the male part of a flower, formed of the anthers and filaments

standard
a tree with a stem (trunk) about 6ft/1.8m long between the ground and the lowest branch which forms the head

stigma
the female part of a flower which receives pollen

stock
the root part of a budded or a grafted plant

stomata
a minute hole, usually on the underside of a leaf, that enables the exchange of gases to take place. During respiration plants absorb air, retaining and using oxygen, and giving off carbon dioxide. During photosynthesis plants absorb air, using the carbon dioxide and giving off oxygen

stooling
the process of cutting down a tree or a shrub to or near soil level to encourage the development of young shoots. This may be done when budding or grafting fruit trees. The term is also used to describe the cutting down of some ornamental shrubs (eg dogwoods) to near ground level to produce attractively colored stems

stopping
pinching out a terminal bud to encourage branching of the stem

strain
seed-raised plants from a common ancestor

stratify
a method of helping seeds with hard coats to germinate. The seeds are placed between layers of sand that are kept cold, usually for the duration of one winter

style
part of the female reproductive organs of a flower; linked to the stigma and the ovary

sub-shrub
a small, spreading shrub with a woody base. A sub-shrub differs from a normal shrub in that when grown in a temperate region its upper stems and shoots die back during winter

subsoil
soil that lies below the depth at which soil is normally cultivated

sucker a basal shoot arising from the rootstock of a grafted or budded plant

synonym
a previously used botanical name for a plant. It frequently happens that a plant is better known and sold under a name by which it was formerly known

systemic
chemicals that enter a plant's tissue, so that when an insect sucks the plant's sap, it dies. The length of time systemic chemicals are active within a plant depend on the type of plant and the temperature

tap root
a long, strong, primary root on some plants, going deep down into the soil

tender
vulnerable to damage by cold temperatures, especially frost

tendril
a thread-like growth which enables a climber to cling to a support

terrace
an open, paved area lying immediately outside a house. Terraces on successive levels may be connected by flights of steps

thinning
the removal of seedlings or shoots to allow others to develop more strongly

tilth
friable topsoil in which seeds are sown. It also acts as a mulch on the surface of soil, helping to reduce moisture loss

tine
a prong on a rake or a garden fork

tip-bearing
usually a type of fruit tree which bears its flowers and fruit at the tips of shoots

top-dressing
fertilizer or organic matter applied to the soil surface; also mulches such as gravel around alpine plants

topiary
the clipping and shaping of densely leaved shrubs and hedging plants into patterns and shapes

topsoil
the top layer of soil, often taken to mean the top-spit (q.v.), 10–12in/25–30cm deep. The soil at this level should not contain subsoil (q.v.), which is sticky, heavy, and often composed of clay

transpiration
the loss of moisture from a plant

trace elements
minerals required by plants in very small quantities (*see* micronutrients)

tree
a woody plant with a single, clear stem between the roots and the lowest branches

triploid
having three sets of chromosomes. Triploid need to be pollinated by two other varieties rather than one

truss
a cluster of flowers or fruit. The term is usually used to describe clusters of tomatoes

tuber a swollen, thickened, fleshy stem or root. Some tubers are swollen roots (eg. dahlia), while others are swollen stems (eg. potato). Tubers are storage organs that perpetuate plants from season to season

variegated
having two or more colors. Usually applied to leaves, but can also describe stems and flowers

variety
see cultivar

veranda
a word derived from a Hindi word, meaning a gallery at ground level and on one side of a house (sometimes surrounding it). The sides of a veranda are partly or wholly open on the garden side

versailles planter
a large, square-sided container originally from Versailles, France. Early Versailles planters were made of lead or slate, while modern ones are constructed from fiberglass or wood

watershoot
a sappy, quick-growing shoot that arises from buds on trunks and branches, especially on old, neglected fruit trees

wildlife pond
an informal pond, usually positioned toward the far end of a garden, inhabited by frogs, birds, insects, and small mammals

windbreak
a shrub, tree or conifer used to create a screen to reduce the wind's speed

index

container gardening

Anthony Atha would like to thank his wife, Anthea, for putting up with him while
he was writing this book.

He would also like to thank Fiona Biggs, Michael Whitehead and Sarah Yelling
at Bridgewater Books for all their help during the whole process, and Liz Eddison
for taking and sourcing the lovely pictures that appear throughout the book.
Thanks also to Coral Mula and Ann Winterbotham for the charming illustrations.

Finally, he would also like to thank all gardeners who enjoy growing things.

The publishers would like to thank the following for the use of photographs:
LIZ EDDISON **Garden Designers:** Susanna Brown 26; David Brunn 91; Butler Landscapes 93
(Chelsea 2000), 16–17, 20, 28, 59; Terence Conran 45, 219; Guy Farthing/Marshalls 53b;
Alan Gardner 23; Gavin Landscaping 98bl, 99; Elizabeth Goodwin & Sylvia Whitehouse 52;
Carol Klein 39; Lindsay Knight 21, 94; Landart 92; Wynniett-Husey Clarke 56–57, 63r;
NEIL HOLMES 138, 200, 224bl, bc, 229bl, 233bl, tr, 234bl,br, 235bl, bc, 236br, 237bl, 238bl,
239bl, br, 240bl, 241bl, tr, 243bl, 246br, 248bc, 250bl, 251bl, 252tl, 253bl, 259tr
HARRY SMITH COLLECTION 61, 54l, 104, 105, 132, 133r, 209, 226, 229tr, 230bl, bc,
231bc, br, 232br, 242bl, 244tl, 245br, 253bc, br;
DAVID SQUIRE 114bl, br.

With additional thanks to Roger Benjamin, Georgina Steeds
and Smith's Nurseries, New Denham, Middlesex.

the small garden

With thanks to

Roger Benjamin

Georgina Steeds

Smith's Nurseries, New Denham, Middlesex

LIZ EDDISON **Garden Designers:** Artisan Landscape Company (Tatton Park 2000) 369r;
Susanna Brown (Hampton Court 2000) 465b; David Brum (Hampton Court 2000) 286b, 440b, 464b,
(Chelsea 2000) 265b, 268-69, 309 bl; Julian Dowle 299;
Kevin Dunne (Tatton Park 2000); Alison Evans (Tatton Park 2000) 281t;
Guy Farthing (Hampton Court 2000) 301, (Tatton Park 2000) 333br;
Alan Gardner, Hampton Court 2000 285; Gavin Landscaping 359;
Chris Gregory (Chelsea 1999) 332b; Toby & Stephanie Hickish (Tatton Park 2000) 452b;
HMP Leyhill (Chelsea 2000) 378; Carol Klein 270b, 443b; Lindsay Knight (Chelsea 2000) 287r, 352,
314-315; Land Art (Hampton Court 2000) 278–279, 302–303b, 300b;
Karen Maskell (Hampton Court 2000 – Natural & Oriental Water Garden) 289b, 358b, 370–371, 372,
Room in the Garden 309t; Alan Sargent (Chelsea 1999) 297 t, 303 t (Chelsea 2000) 272, 284 b, 373;
Paul Stone 310b; Jane Sweetser (Hampton Court 1999) 297b;
Michael Upward & Richard Mercer 475; Pamela Woods (Hampton Court 1999) 434–435, 441;

THE GARDEN PICTURE LIBRARY 598 b

NEIL HOLMES 396, 397, 419, 422, 456b, 457t,b, 478b, 489, 493t,b, 495, 498, 499;

PETER MCHOY 357 tl, tr, bl, br

HARRY SMITH COLLECTION 352b, 353, 355, 356, 369l, 394, 400, 401, 402,
404, 405t, 406–407, 408, 409t,b, 410, 411t,b, 420, 421

SPEAR & JACKSON 346, 347

DAVID SQUIRE 341tl,tc,tr,br, 349, 385br, 393bl,bcl,bcr,br, 412, 413, 466, 469, 483, 491

gardening through the year

The publishers would like to thank Roger Benjamin, Georgina Steeds, and Smith's Nurseries, New Denham, Middlesex, UK, for their help with properties, and the following for their help with images:

LIZ EDDISON **Garden Designers:** Aughton Green Landscapes (Tatton Park 2001) 631b; James Basson (Hampton Court 2000) 626bl; David Brun (Hampton Park 2000) 562b; Bill Cartlidge (Tatton Park 2000) 509r & 556; Paul Dyer (Chelsea 2001) 630br; Sarah Eberle (Hampton Court 2001) 522; Guy Farthing (Hampton Court 2000) 508 & 506, 519bl; Sally Fell (Hampton Court 2001) 518b, 646br; David Gibson (Tatton Park 2001) 539b; Carol Klein, 592; Douglas G.Knight (Tatton Park 2001) 560, 561; Colin Luckett (Tatton Park 2001), 624; Angela Mainwaring (Hampton Park 2001) 582; Tom Stuart-Smith (Chelsea 2000) 512b; Ian Taylor (Chelsea 2001) 605br; Geoffrey Whiten (Chelsea 2001) 597bl

NEIL HOLMES 662bl; 673t, b; 686, 687t, b; 689t; 720; 734

HOZELOCK 576bl; 658b,r; 659

PARASENE 699tr, bl

HARRY SMITH COLLECTION 527t; 551; 574; 575bl; 584r; 596b; 632; 638; 644; 653bl; 678br; 692; 693bl; 699tl, br; 704; 705tr; 707b; 721bl; 728; 732; 745bl

garden design

In memory of Godfrey Golzen

Bridgewater Book Co. would like to thank Sue Hook for the
garden schemes and designs.

LIZ EDDISON **Garden Designers:** Butler Landscapes 928; Christopher Costin 910bl, br, 953tr;
Paul Dyer 259b; Sarah Eberle 933; Guy Farthing/Marshalls 813b; Folia Garden Designers 769b;
Professor Masao Fukuhara 875b; Marney Hall 921br; Graham Hardman 879tl;
Susan Harman 857tr; Stephanie Hickish 864; Carol Klein 856bl; Colin Luckett 811tr;
Natural & Oriental Water Gardens 756–757, 769tr, 875t; Angel Mainwaring 811bl, 910bc, 939b;
Jane Rendell & Sarah Tavender 885b, 887b, 889cl, bcr; Alan Sargent 929b, 761bl;
Judith Sharpe 922; Ian Taylor 884, 874, 885t, 888tl; Robin Templar Williams 768;
Geoffrey Whiten 803bl, 867cl; Wynniatt-Husey Clark 810, 813tr, 881b
NEIL HOLMES 761tr, 778–779, 790, 791t, 870tl, 891tl, 945t,b, 957tr, 974, 982, 984, 985, 990tr, bl
HARRY SMITH COLLECTION 774l,r, 775, 783tl,tc, 806br, 807, 842–843, 850bl, 861tl, 870br,
890, 903bl, 913t, 934l, 935t, 956–957b, 967tr, 979